THE NATURE OF THE BOOK

THE
NATURE
OF THE
BOOK

Print and Knowledge in the Making

ADRIAN JOHNS

THE UNIVERSITY OF CHICAGO PRESS

CHICAGO AND LONDON

ADRIAN JOHNS is assistant professor in the Department of Sociology and Science Studies Program at the University of California, San Diego.

The University of Chicago Press, Chicago 60637
The University of Chicago Press, Ltd., London
© 1998 by The University of Chicago
All rights reserved. Published 1998
07 06 05 04 03 02 01 00 99 98   1 2 3 4 5
ISBN: 0-226-40121-9 (cloth)

Library of Congress Cataloging-in-Publication Data

Johns, Adrian.
    The nature of the book : print and knowledge in the making /
Adrian Johns.
        p.   cm.
    Includes bibliographical references (p.   ) and index.
    ISBN: 0-226-40121-9 (alk. paper).
        1. Printing—Social aspects—Europe—History.   2. Printing—Social
aspects—England—History.   3. Books—Europe—History.   4. Books—
England—History.   5. Europe—Intellectual life.   6. England—
Intellectual life.   7. Transmission of texts.   8. Science—Europe—
History.   9. Science—England—History.   10. Science publishing—
Europe—History.   11. Science publishing—England—History.
I. Title.
Z124.J64   1998
686.2'094—dc21   97-47252
                                                                CIP

⊗ The paper used in this publication meets the
minimum requirements of the American National Standard
for Information Sciences—Permanence of Paper for
Printed Library Materials, ANSI Z39.48-1992.

For Alison

TO THE SOURE READER

If thou dislik'st the Piece thou light'st on first;

Thinke that of All, that I have writ, the worst:

But if thou read'st my Booke unto the end,

And still do'st this, and that verse, reprehend:

O Perverse man! If All disgustfull be,

The Extreame Scabbe take thee, and thine, for me.

ROBERT HERRICK, *Hesperides* (London, 1648), 3

CONTENTS

ILLUSTRATIONS

ACKNOWLEDGMENTS

The writer of any book inevitably accrues debts, and when its theme is as interdisciplinary as this one those debts are particularly keenly felt. During the near-decade that it has taken to complete this work, I have received generous help from a wide range of people. I am conscious of the inadequacy of any acknowledgment I can now give in return.

I must first thank Simon Schaffer. Simon supervised my work as a graduate student in the Department of History and Philosophy of Science in Cambridge, Great Britain, and has inspired it then and since. His combination of tolerance, omniscience, and humor has always stimulated and sustained my work. Without him this book would have been less imaginative and less rigorous.

The research on which *The Nature of the Book* is based was begun and largely carried out in Cambridge. During my years in the History and Philosophy of Science community there, I enjoyed the help and company of a large number of colleagues. Among them stand out Henry Atmore, Jim Bennett, Domenico Bertoloni-Meli, Dan Browne, Michael Dettelbach, Marina Frasca-Spada, Jan Golinski, Jeffrey Hughes, Robert Iliffe, Nicholas Jardine, Stephen Johnston, Sachiko Kusukawa, Julian Martin, Sue Morgan, Oliver Morton, Iwan Morus, Cornelius O'Boyle, Stephen Pumfrey, Anne Secord, Jim Secord, Emma Spary, Richard Staley, Jennifer Tucker, Andrew Warwick, and Frances Willmoth. I should like to record my thanks not just to these as individuals, but to the Cambridge History of Science community as a whole, which continues to provide an unrivaled atmosphere in which to share ideas and enthusiasms.

Beyond that community, in conversations ranging across Europe and North America I have received assistance from Mario Biagioli, Ann Blair, Warren Brown, Peter Burke, Justin Champion, Bill Clark, Patrick Collinson, Elizabeth Eisenstein, Robert Frank, Anne Goldgar, Mark Goldie, Michael Hunter, Myles Jackson, Dan Kevles, Paulina Kewes, Ben Marsden, Peter Mathias, David McKitterick, John Morrill, Sheila Munby, Robin Myers, Brian Ogilvie, Adam Perkins, Ted Porter, James Raven, Robert Richards, Martin Rudwick, Sue Sadler, Larry Stewart, and Robert Westman. I should like to single out for thanks Frances Willmoth, who as editor of the correspondence of John Flamsteed has been extraordinarily generous and helpful with material relating to him. I am likewise indebted to Professor Owen Gingerich, who as well as patiently explaining aspects of Flamsteed's astronomy to me has permitted me to reproduce an important document in his possession (see fig. 8.11). Kevin Knox read the manuscript closely at a late stage and suggested a number of last-minute improvements, not all of which I was able to implement as fully as they deserved.

I should like particularly to thank six other individuals. The influence of Don McKenzie and Roger Chartier permeates the pages of this book. I felt fortunate and privileged when they agreed to act as examiners of the original thesis, and they have continued to provide much useful advice and support ever since. Steven Shapin has been inspirational both in person and through his work. He and Anthony Grafton read this book from end to end, and have helped in countless ways to make it accurate, readable, and even interesting. At Downing College Jonathan Scott provided much-needed reassurance, and personified the easily forgotten point that academic historians need not fear to be open-minded, unorthodox, and imaginative. And at the University of Kent, in the face of grievous economic constraints Crosbie Smith kept his head while all about him seemed to be losing theirs.

During my career as a graduate student I was the fortunate recipient of funding from the British Academy and the Royal Society, as well as Corpus Christi College, Cambridge. That support has since been continued by a number of other bodies. In 1990–91 I was Munby Fellow in Bibliography at Cambridge University Library. Between 1991 and 1994 I held a Research Fellowship at Downing College, Cambridge. From 1994 to 1996, I served as Lecturer in the History of Science at the University of Kent at Canterbury. Latterly I enjoyed a position as Senior Research Fellow at the California Institute of Technology, Pasadena, California, before being appointed in early 1998 to an assistant professorship at the University of California, San Diego. I thank each of these bodies for providing the financial and social encouragement without which such a large project could scarcely have been launched, let alone completed. Caltech in particular provided extremely generous help with photographic and other costs.

Several libraries and archives have been most helpful. I should like to mention in particular the following: the Bodleian Library, Oxford; the British Library, London; the British Museum (Department of Prints and Drawings), London; Cambridge University Library (especially the Manuscripts and Rare Books Rooms); the Corporation of London Record Office; the Guildhall Library, London; the Henry E. Huntington Library, San Marino, California; the Inner Temple Library, London; Nottingham University Library; the Public Record Office, London; the Regenstein Library, at the University of Chicago; the Royal Society Library; Southampton Record Office; the archives department of the Worshipful Company of Stationers and Newspaper-Makers (formerly the Stationers' Company), London (where Robin Myers was especially helpful); the Whipple Library, Cambridge; and the William Andrews Clark Library, Los Angeles.

This book has been "through-composed," as it were. It was conceived as a single coherent argument, and its chapters were never intended to stand alone as discrete papers. Nonetheless, earlier versions of passages now presented in chapter 6 have previously been published in James Raven, Helen Small, and Naomi Tadmor, eds., *The Practice and Representation of Reading in England* (Cambridge: Cambridge University Press, 1996), and in Ole Peter Grell and Andrew Cunningham, eds., *Religio Medici: Medicine and Religion in Seventeenth-Century England* (Aldershot, England: Scolar Press, 1996); portions of chapter 7 appear in different form in "Miscellaneous Methods: Authors, Societies, and Journals in Early Modern England," *British Journal for the History of Science* (forthcoming), and are reproduced with the permission of the Council of the British Society for the History of Science. I thank each for permission to reproduce relevant sections. Earlier versions of all the chapters have been presented at a number of seminars and conferences in Britain, Continental Europe, and the United States. Their venues were too many to recount here, but particularly useful symposia were held at: the Universities of Oxford, Cambridge, and London; conferences of the British Society for the History of Science and the History of Science Society; conferences on the Republic of Letters at Paris and Leyden; the Datini Institute, Prato, Italy; UCLA; UCSD; the University of Chicago; Northwestern University; and Cornell University.

Michael Koplow's extraordinary diligence and accuracy as copyeditor saved me countless times from error and oversights. Finally, I must thank Susan Abrams, executive editor at the University of Chicago Press. When future readers review the literature in the history of science produced during the 1980s and 1990s they will rightly laud Susan's important role in shaping the field. I am grateful for her unwavering encouragement, wisdom, and, not least, patience.

This book is dedicated to Alison Winter. More than anyone else, she has made this work possible. She has read the whole text several times over at various stages in its composition, and has transformed it at many key points; it certainly could not have been completed without her input. She has also put up with my glum presence during research and writing, with almost endless sympathy and support. Offering the finished product to her is but a meager and inadequate gesture in response.

A NOTE ON
CONVENTIONS

The Nature of the Book makes extensive use of manuscript and printed sources dating from the sixteenth, seventeenth, and eighteenth centuries. In quotations from such materials, spelling, punctuation, and typography have generally been kept as close as possible to the originals, except that *u, v, w, i,* and *j* have been modernized. Use of the intrusive "*sic*" has been kept to a minimum. I have occasionally capitalized letters in quotations that happened to appear at the start of my sentences.

The City of London was (and is) not quite the same as the city of London. The former refers to the area within the walls, which fell under the traditional jurisdiction of Lord Mayor and Aldermen. The latter signifies the general conurbation as it had developed and spread beyond the bounds of the City itself. Parts of this conurbation therefore lay under different authorities, in particular those of Middlesex, Surrey, and Westminster.

In early modern England the legal year began in late March. England also recognized the Julian calendar (often called "old style"), which was ten days behind the Gregorian calendar ("new style") by this time employed in most of Europe. This can easily result in confusion over dates. In this book, dates are generally given in the old style, and in the form 11 February 1635/6. On the rare occasions when some confusion may arise, the Gregorian date is also given: e.g., 11/21 February 1635/6.

Some delicate issues of terminology arise when one discusses early modern books. Among the most salient are the following:

- The term *publisher* was known and used in early modern England, but it carried different meanings from its modern counterpart. Some of its contemporary connotations are teased out in the text of this book; I have tried to use the word only where those connotations are intended. More commonly I have employed the term *undertaker,* which is less ambiguous and more historically appropriate.

- Strictly speaking, a *stationer* (with a small *s*) was someone who followed the trade of a paper-stationer. A *Stationer* (capital *S*) was someone who was a member of the Stationers' Company—which included not only paper-stationers, but also printers, booksellers, and binders, plus a relatively small number of individuals who did not actually practice any of the skills associated with paper and printing. After the incorporation of the Company in 1557, all of these "faculties" were, as a participant remarked, "constituted in one Body and Society, under one generical and individual term of *Stationer*." [1] I follow suit. Incidentally, I refer to Stationers—both printers and booksellers—as "he or she." This is not simply modern propriety; both men and women worked in the book trade. It has long been maintained that the Stationers' craft was unusually tolerant of, and profuse with, female practitioners operating in their own right—something the legal status of which still remains in need of investigation. [2]

- A still more controversial term is *piracy*. It appears many times in this book. I have used it to mean any attributed violation of copy-ownership (or "propriety"). John Feather has argued for a more restricted usage, claiming that even though contemporaries used it in just such a wide sense, they were wrong to do so. [3] Feather points out that there is a formal legal definition (that is, the printing without his or her permission of a text that was clearly and legally owned by another agent), and claims that to honor actors' categories in this case is to generate unnecessary confusion. It is a point that has been repeated by other authors and is discussed in the course of this book. However, while such precision is probably necessary in matters of technical bibliography, the stipulation seems rather too restrictive for a work such as this, which deals with social, cultural, and intellectual history. Such a book is entitled to recover the broader meanings recognized by contemporaries—indeed, it is its duty to do so. Contemporary usage provides warrant. Someone might call an unauthorized printing of personal letters a piracy, for example, even though their ownership had not been registered beforehand; similarly, an unauthorized reprint produced in another country for sale on the Continent might be accounted a piracy, although it was outside English legal jurisdiction. There are no legal terms for such cases, although individuals certainly felt them to be transgressions of some sort. It would be awkward to have to resort every time to "unauthorized reprint" or some such formula. For the sake of conciseness and dramatic value, then—and not least to capture something of the sheer sense of outrage displayed by the aggrieved—I have chosen to follow what I take to be the emerging usage of the time, and call these activities by the generic label of piracy. This

1. *London Printers Lamentation*, 2. See also Stationers' Company, *Registers 1554–1640*, I, 114; II, 5–6; Blount, *Glossographia*, s.v. "Stationer"; Campbell, *London Tradesman*, 126–7; Blagden, *Stationers' Company*, 19 n. 1; Belanger, "Booksellers' Sales of Copyright," ii–iii.

2. Erickson, *Women and Property*, 30; Earle, *City Full of People*, 107–55.

3. Feather, "English Book Trade and the Law," 64–5; Feather, *Dictionary*, 207–8.

need not preclude finer categorization, of course, and I have taken care to make clear the formal status of specific claims.

- An *author* is taken to be someone acknowledged as responsible for a given printed (or sometimes written) work; that is, *authorship* is taken to be a matter of attribution by others, not of self-election. A *writer* is anyone who composes such a work. A writer therefore may or may not attain authorship. A *text* is the content of any written or printed work, considered apart from its particular material manifestation.

For reasons of economy, the footnoting convention of Shapin's *Social History of Truth* and Eisenstein's *Printing Press as an Agent of Change* has been adopted. Full bibliographical details of all works cited are included in the bibliography.

1

INTRODUCTION

The Book of Nature and the Nature of the Book

Pick up a modern book. This one will do: the one you are looking at right now. What sort of object is this? There are certain features about it of which you can be reasonably confident. Its professed author does indeed exist and did indeed write it. It contains information believed to be accurate, and it professes to impart knowledge to readers like you. It is produced with its author's consent, and it is indeed the edition it claims to be. If the dust jacket announces that it is the product of a given organization—in this case the University of Chicago Press—then this too may be believed. Perhaps you may even say to yourself that that fact vouches for the quality of its content. You may safely assume that the book you now hold will have been printed in many copies, and a copy of the same book bought in Australia, say, will be identical in all relevant respects to one bought in the United States or in Great Britain.

Begin to use this object. It should immediately become clear that there are things about its proper utilization of which a reader like you can be equally confident. This book has not been produced with a specific, individual reader in mind. To some extent, at least, it is a commercial product, designed to appeal to purchasers. Its cost may have limited its readership somewhat, but its distribution will still have been fairly widespread, and it may be available for consultation in a number of libraries. Readers will not have to endure any formal vetting or approval process before being permitted to read this book. You yourself are free to carry it around and to lend it to others. You are not free, however—beyond certain legal limits—to reproduce its contents in your own right for commercial gain. Nor may you now proceed to issue translations, epitomes, or abridgments of those contents. It is improbable (but not impossible) that you will choose to declaim the text of this book aloud in a public place, and it is even more unlikely that you will make it the focus of a collective act of commemoration, worship, or similar ritual. Some books are indeed used in these ways, incidentally, but this is probably not going to be one of them. In short, while in

1

some respects this book's usage is up to you, in others it appears to be quite closely constrained.

That we can assume all these things of such an object—that such an object actually exists—derives from our living in what many people call "print culture." Such phenomena, we say, are due to printing. Or rather, we would say this, but so infallibly reliable are they that we rarely even have to articulate the relation. It is obvious, self-evident, even necessary. The practical consequence is that we do not have to agonize over the reliability of a published book before we can put it to use. We do not need to undertake investigatory work to confirm that its author does exist and that its text is authorized. No literary spy need be hired to ascertain that it was indeed made by its stated publisher and that its contents will be the same as those of another copy of the same book found in any other place. In our world, all these characteristics are inherent in virtually any published book (and the duties of a "literary agent" are comparatively mundane). We take them for granted, every day of our lives. We depend on them, and our reliance is, by and large, justified.

It is this very self-evidence that encourages us to ascribe all these characteristics to a technological order of reality. If called upon, we may assert that printed texts are identical and reliable because that is simply what printing *is*. The identification is as momentous as it is straightforward. It has become the point of departure for all current interpretations of print and its cultural consequences, and is the root from which the very concept of "print culture" has grown.[1] It is thereby also the foundation of a conviction that that culture has rendered possible the establishment of veracious knowledge in modern society. Yet this book argues that it is substantially false. Not only that: *The Nature of the Book* maintains that it is probably the most powerful force resisting the acceptance of a truly historical understanding of print and any cultural consequences it may foster.

This book contends that what we often regard as essential elements and necessary concomitants of print are in fact rather more contingent than generally acknowledged. Veracity in particular is, it argues, extrinsic to the press itself, and has had to be grafted onto it. The same may be said of other cognate attributes associated with printing. In short, *The Nature of the Book* claims that the very identity of print itself has had to be *made*. It came to be as we now experience it only by virtue of hard work, exercised over generations and across nations. That labor has long been overlooked, and is not now evident. But its very obscurity is revealing. It was dedicated to effacing its own traces, and necessarily so: only if such efforts disappeared could

1. For this term, see below, pp. 10–11, and Eisenstein, *Printing Press*, I, 43–159. I am not sure of its genesis; Eisenstein, its prime recent exponent, seems to take it from McLuhan (e.g., *Gutenberg Galaxy*, 146–9).

printing gain the air of intrinsic reliability on which its cultural and commercial success could be built. Recovering it is therefore a difficult task, but one well worth attempting. This book tries accordingly to excavate the complex issues involved in the historical shaping of print—issues that our conventional notion of print culture obscures with all the authority of a categorical definition. *The Nature of the Book* is the first real attempt to portray print culture in the making.

Yet how could print conceivably be anything else? If it were really the result of a significant process of historical construction, then surely we could not now find it so obvious, universal, and undeniable. If it could have developed differently, then surely it would now differ noticeably from place to place, and in any one place it would still bear the traces of its development. We would see the wreckage of failed alternatives all about us. In practical terms, we would indeed have to worry about the specific status of a given printed book in order to use it. Questions of where it had come from, who had made it, and whether or not its putative author acknowledged its content would all need to be posed and answered before we could safely trust any printed book. That they do not constitutes a powerful reason to accept the obvious.

Even a little reflection suggests that there is greater complexity to the subject than this. Any printed book is, as a matter of fact, both the product of one complex set of social and technological processes and also the starting point for another. In the first place, a large number of people, machines, and materials must converge and act together for it to come into existence at all. How exactly they do so will inevitably affect its finished character in a number of ways. In that sense a book is the material embodiment of, if not a consensus, then at least a collective consent. Its identity can be understood accordingly, in terms of these intricate processes. But the story of a book evidently does not end with its creation. How it is then put to use, by whom, in what circumstances, and to what effect are all equally complex issues. Each is worthy of attention in its own right. So a printed book can be seen as a nexus conjoining a wide range of worlds of work. Look closely and you are likely to find simplicity and inevitability in neither the manufacture of an object like this nor its subsequent construal. The processes leading to the deployment of a book and those consequent upon its use both depend on too many contingencies. That in turn means that print cannot be as straightforward as it seems.

One way to appreciate the implications is to examine more closely places where printing exists, but where its cultural consequences seem very different from those familiar to us. There are two such places, separated from us by space and by time. The first may be found in certain regions of the world where, to international publishers' disgust, so-called "piracy" has become a prevalent commercial practice. You could not be so sure of all those "self-evident" facts about this book if you had bought your copy in such a place. It might indeed prove reliable. But it might also have been produced by an anonymous manufacturer, and have different contents. Its purported author might have no idea of the claims it contained. Some such companies produce not just unauthorized reprints of existing books, but wholly new texts claiming to be written by best-selling authors. Their products threaten to compromise both the economic production of authorized works and, by generating correspondingly divergent readings, their reception. The potential effects are suggested by the most notorious of all recent controversies to arise from publishing. The author Salman Rushdie was complaining of piracy of his works in Pakistan and India long before the appearance of his *Satanic Verses*. When it did appear, the book was properly published in neither country; the protests that occurred in Lahore and elsewhere, and that first set in train the events leading eventually to Khomeini's fatwa, centered on the public reading of unauthorized copies and photocopied extracts. A Penguin representative even noted that piracy would permit readers to circumvent the Indian government's subsequent ban on the book.[2]

Rushdie's is admittedly an extreme case. But for good or ill, countless authors and publishers have encountered to some degree the loss of control induced by piracy. It means that the experiences associated with print are indeed different from those familiar to most Western readers. And any suggestion that the intrinsic cultural consequences of technology have simply been inadequately realized in such settings would be difficult to endorse. The evidence of recent international trade disputes indicates that modern technology, far from eliminating such practices, may even be facilitating them. The arguments currently raging over such matters are intense and important. Few claim to know how they will end.[3]

The alternative is to look not to other places in our own time, but to other times in our own place. It is possible to argue not only that print may differ from place to place, but also that its nature has changed over time even in our own society. If this is so, the implications are again substantial, but in rather different ways. Such an argument compels us to reappraise where our own concept of print culture comes from, how it developed, when it took hold, and why its sway continues to seem secure. These are

2. *The Times*, 24 November 1984; Appignanesi and Maitland, *Rushdie File*, 42; Pipes, *Rushdie Affair*, 24, 85, 113, 201–2.

3. These disputes extend far beyond "copyright" as conventionally understood, and include conventions now being forged to cover the "inventions" and "texts" produced in areas such as biotechnology and genome research. The economic, cultural, and moral implications at stake in these, as in the battles raging over computer and music software, are truly massive. For confrontations between the USA and China over the latter, see Faison, "Copyright Pirates."

some of the questions addressed in the following chapters. Tactically forgetting that we ourselves "know" what printing is, *The Nature of the Book* begins by asking the question of what printing *was*. It addresses how the people of the sixteenth, seventeenth, and eighteenth centuries constructed and construed the craft, in their own setting and for their own ends. This entails comprehending the complex social processes by which books came to be made and used in their society—the society in which printing first really thrived, and in which any consequences it might have were first fully manifested. The result is that what began as a tactical decision to forget our own knowledge is soon vindicated as rather more. As chapter 2 will show in detail, early modern printing was not joined by any obvious or necessary bond to enhanced fidelity, reliability, and truth. That bond had to be forged.

If an early modern reader picked up a printed book—*De Natura Libri,* perhaps—then he or she could not be immediately certain that it was what it claimed to be, and its proper use might not be so self-evident. Piracy was again one reason: illicit uses of the press threatened the credibility of all printed products. More broadly, ideas about the correct ways to make and use books varied markedly from place to place and time to time. But whatever the cause, it is not easy for us to imagine such a realm, in which printed records were not necessarily authorized or faithful. What could one know in such a realm, and how could one know it? We ourselves routinely rely on stable communications in our making and maintenance of knowledge, whether of the people around us or of the world in which we live. That stability helps to underpin the confidence we feel in our impressions and beliefs. Even the brisk skepticism we may express about certain printed materials—tabloid newspapers, say—rests on it, inasmuch as we feel confident that we can readily and consistently identify what it is that we are scorning. Instability in records would equally rapidly translate into uncertainty of judgment. The most immediate implication, then, would be epistemic.

In a sense, the point is a well-entrenched one. It has been made at least since the sixteenth century, when printers and others took to lauding their craft for its power to preserve. The contrast they drew was with previous scribal forms of reproduction, which they delineated as intrinsically corruptive. It now seems almost indisputable. We should recognize, however, that the first identification of that contrast was partly a product of interest. Printers stood to gain from what was originally a contentious argument, not a straightforward observation. If, on the other hand, it is not printing per se that possesses preservative power, but printing put to use in particular ways, then we ourselves may usefully draw some rather different distinctions. We may look not just for differences between print and manuscript reproduction, but for different ways in which the press itself and its products have been (and continue to be) employed. The roots of textual stability may be sought as much in these practices as in the press itself. And knowledge, such as it is, has come to depend on that stability. Here, then, is one way in which a social history of print can prove not just interesting, but consequential. A reappraisal of print in the making can contribute to our historical understanding of the conditions of knowledge itself.

TYCHO BRAHE, GALILEO GALILEI, AND THE PROBLEMS OF "PRINT CULTURE"

The central concern of this book is the relation between print and knowledge. As its title suggests, to pursue this theme it focuses in particular on *natural* knowledge—knowledge of Creation and of humanity's place within it. To that extent, *The Nature of the Book* may be regarded as contributing to the discipline known, rather anachronistically, as the history of science.[4] It proposes a new account of how early modern Europeans put printing to use to create and maintain knowledge about the natural world.

The focus on the history of science is not, however, an exclusive one. The ambit of *The Nature of the Book* is not exhausted by scientific knowledge, and none of its conclusions should be regarded as restricted to science alone. Science is treated here as just one among a range of activities characterized by the creation and use of knowledge. The historical problems identified in the course of this book were so general that they applied to all of them, from scriptural exegesis, through astronomy, experiment, and alchemy, to the formation of political ideologies and representations of gender. All make their appearances in the following chapters. Nonetheless, the widely accepted status of modern science as the most objective, valuable, and robust kind of knowledge currently available makes it a peculiarly appealing subject for the historian of printing.[5] This high status means that any conclusions demonstrable for science stand a chance of being accredited a fortiori for other activities now held in lower repute. Furthermore, the history of science offers an unusually clear opportunity to discuss the assumptions and implications of the historiography of print. For it is in the history of science that one finds the figure who, more than any other, personifies print culture as conventionally understood. That figure is the Danish nobleman and astronomer Tycho Brahe (fig. 1.1).

4. As explained further below, I share other historians' doubts about using the terms "science" and "scientist" in reference to periods before they became recognized by contemporaries, and will therefore employ them sparingly in this book. For the issues involved, see Jardine, "Writing Off the Scientific Revolution"; Copenhaver, "Did Science Have a Renaissance?"; Pickstone, "Past and Present Knowledges"; and the polemical argument in Cunningham and Williams, "De-centring the 'Big Picture.'"

5. I should stress the attributive and pragmatic character of such a representation; claims that scientific knowledge actually *is* objective are, of course, extremely controversial, and the image of science as such has been questioned many times.

FIG. 1.1. Tycho Brahe: different representations for different readers. (*top left*) Hand-copied portrait. Reproduced from Tycho Brahe, *Opera Omnia*, I. (By permission of the Syndics of Cambridge University Library.) (*top right*) Printed portrait from the work in which Tycho attacked Ursus. Tycho Brahe, *Epistolarum Astronomicarum Libri*. (By permission of the Syndics of Cambridge University Library.) (*above left*) Tycho with his mural quadrant, as portrayed in a presentation impression of the *Astronomiae Instauratae Mechanica* (1598). (By permission of the British Library, C45.h.3.) (*above right*) Michael Sparke's English version of Tycho's mural quadrant portrait, published with his astrological prophecy in 1632 as *Learned Tico Brahae his Astronomicall Conjectur*. (By permission of the Syndics of Cambridge University Library.)

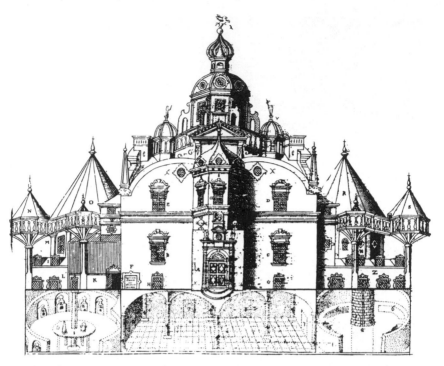

FIG. 1.2. Changing representations of Uraniborg. (*above*) Elevation, as shown in Tycho's
own publication. Tycho Brahe, *Astronomiae Instauratae Mechanica* (1598). (By permission
of the British Library, C45.h.3.) (*opposite*) Elevation, as printed after Tycho's death. Curtius
[L. Barrettus, pseud.], *Historia Cœlestis*. (By permission of the Syndics of Cambridge
University Library.)

In 1576 the king of Denmark granted Tycho feudal powers over a small
island named Hven, lying in the sound just north of Copenhagen. Here
Tycho erected a remarkable castle-observatory, in which he lived and
worked for the next two decades. His work at this palatial observatory,
which he called Uraniborg (fig. 1.2), resulted in an unequaled series of observations and interpretations of the heavens. They secured for him a reputation as the greatest of all astronomers. Almost immediately, Tycho himself
became an icon of the very enterprise of astronomy. Mathematical practitioners in succeeding generations came to see in him an unimpugnable
model of the harmony of nobility and "mechanic" skill. In the hands of
modern historians, moreover, Tycho has again proved a powerful emblem,
in two important and revealingly paradoxical respects. First, Uraniborg has
become the outstanding Renaissance exemplar of the importance of locale
in the making of knowledge.[6] This is an important issue, to be addressed

6. Hannaway, "Laboratory Design." Shackelford has responded to Hannaway, with more
heat than really necessary, in "Tycho Brahe."

later in this chapter. At the same time, however, Tycho has come to per-
sonify the role of print in transcending place and rendering natural knowledge universal. He has thus become emblematic of the transformation of
local craft into global science. This latter apotheosis has been due above all
to Elizabeth Eisenstein's *The Printing Press as an Agent of Change*. Published
in 1979, this is still probably the most influential anglophonic interpretation
of the cultural effects of printing. Yet *The Nature of the Book* pursues for the
most part a quite different approach from hers. A consideration of Tycho
Brahe provides the ideal opportunity to specify how and why it does so.[7]

The unifying concept of Eisenstein's argument is that of "print culture."
This "culture" is characterized primarily in terms of certain traits that print
is taken to endow on texts. Specifically, those produced in such an environment are subject to conditions of *standardization, dissemination,* and *fixity*.
The last of these is perhaps the most important. According to Eisenstein,
printing meant the mass reproduction of precisely the same text, repeatable
on subsequent occasions and in different locations. No longer need any
work suffer the increasing corruption that Eisenstein assumes to be endemic
to any "script culture." She focuses on this attribute of fixity as the most
important corollary of the press, seeing it as central to most of the effects of
print culture.[8] For example, in conditions of fixity the simple practice of
juxtaposing texts became immensely significant. Newly available printed
representations of opposing astronomical, anatomical, or other knowledge
could be placed side by side, and their viewer could now be confident that
conclusions drawn from comparing such reliable texts would be worthwhile.
Correspondents on the other side of Europe could do the same, with representations that could be supposed identical.[9] Such scholars no longer
needed to concern themselves primarily with the fidelity of their representations, and were freed from spending their lives eradicating scribal mistakes. It was fixity that liberated them from such labor and thus made possible the progressive improvement of knowledge. This is the basis on which

7. Eisenstein, *Printing Press*, abridged as *Printing Revolution*. For examples of Eisenstein's
influence in a range of fields, see Tribble, *Margins and Marginality*, 3–4; Neuschel, *Word of
Honor*, chap. 6; Olson, *World on Paper*, 37 and passim; Rose, *Authors and Owners*, 3–4;
Sommerville, *Secularization*, 48, 70, 79, 178, 180, 219 n. 1; Anderson, *Imagined Communities*,
30–49; Eamon, *Science and the Secrets of Nature*, 6–9, 94–6; Lowood and Rider, "Literary
Technology and Typographic Culture" (where "typographic culture" and "print culture" are
indistinguishable). Many more could be cited. It is difficult to be sure, but I would estimate
that Tycho Brahe is referred to at least as frequently in *Printing Press* as any other Renaissance
figure.

8. Eisenstein, *Printing Press*, 71–88, 113–26.

9. Eisenstein, *Printing Press*, 74–5, 597; *Printing Revolution*, 42–88. It is worth pointing
out that these phenomena are similar to those attributed by anthropologists to the invention
of writing, e.g., in Goody, *Logic of Writing*, 134–8, 174.

Eisenstein can claim that the Renaissance and Reformation were rendered permanent by the very permanence of their canonical texts, that nationalism developed thanks to the stabilization of laws and languages, and that science itself became possible on the basis of phenomena and theories reliably recorded.[10] With this new foundation of certainty at their disposal, "scientists" (as Eisenstein insists on calling them) could begin to develop new doubts about their previous authority, namely antiquity. The "Scientific Revolution" was thus inconceivable without a preceding printing revolution.[11] And for Eisenstein Tycho Brahe personifies both.

Eisenstein's Tycho was an autodidact. This in itself was remarkable: before the printing revolution, not enough faithful editions could have been amassed in one place to enable him to teach himself. But while he was doing this, Tycho was able to place authoritative printed representations of the Copernican and Ptolemaic systems of the heavens side by side before his eyes. By this simple process of juxtaposition, he could immediately see that there were serious discrepancies. Later, working on Hven, he instigated a program to rectify the data and theories on which astronomy was based. He and his assistants labored for years to produce a systematic corpus of recorded observations of the heavenly bodies, using not only Tycho's own careful observations but those sent to him by astronomers across central Europe. When ready, Tycho could then supervise the correct printing of this vital material in his own printing house, using paper made in his own paper mill (figs. 1.3 and 1.4). As a result, one nova—"Tycho's star," as it came to be called—became "fixed" to the extent that it continued to be shown on celestial globes long after it had disappeared from the sky.[12]

In this guise has Eisenstein's Tycho entered a current debate over science itself. Bruno Latour has built an account of the making and power of science on her representation of a print culture, first in his concept of "immutable mobiles"[13] and more recently in that of "mediators."[14] Latour identifies the collection and deployment of durable paper entities as the foundation

10. Eisenstein, *Printing Press*, 80, 117, 180–2, 200–10, 212, 646. The argument about nationalism has since been developed more thoroughly by Anderson in *Imagined Communities*, esp. 41–9.

11. Eisenstein, *Printing Press*, 107, 186, 193–4, 197, 640; Hunter, "Impact of Print"; Leed, "Elizabeth Eisenstein's *The Printing Press as an Agent of Change.*"

12. Eisenstein, *Printing Press*, 577, 583–4, 593, 596–603, 623–5, 629–30, 640, 699.

13. Latour, *Science in Action*, 52, 132–44, 226; Latour, "On the Powers of Association"; Latour, "Visualization and Cognition." Compare also Latour, "Give Me a Laboratory"; Latour and Woolgar, *Laboratory Life*, 45–53, 69–88; and Callon, Law, and Rip, *Mapping the Dynamics of Science and Technology*, 7–14, 35–99.

14. Latour, *We Have Never Been Modern*, 77–82, 128–9, 138; Latour, "Technology Is Society Made Durable," 104–6, 127; Latour, "Where Are the Missing Masses?" 237.

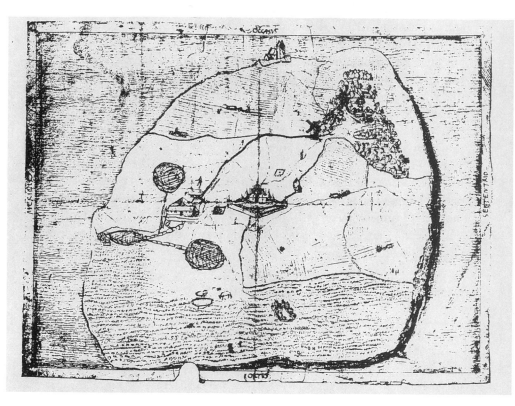

FIG. 1.4. The island of Hven. (*above*) Map from Tycho Brahe's manuscripts, showing the paper mill in relation to Uraniborg. Tycho Brahe, *Opera Omnia,* IV. (By permission of the Syndics of Cambridge University Library.) (*opposite*) The printed map issued by Tycho in his *Astronomiae Instauratae Mechanica* (1598). (By permission of the Syndics of Cambridge University Library.)

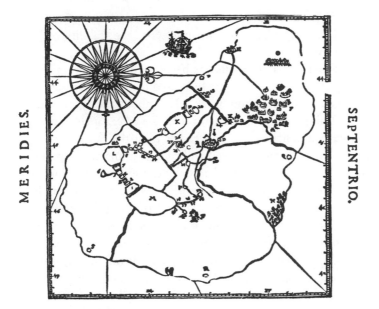

of science's success. The creation and circulation of such objects, Latour maintains, enabled Tycho to master natural and social entities that were otherwise beyond reach. He could use print both to capture heavenly bodies, as Eisenstein claimed, and, furthermore, effectively to turn every observatory in Europe into an extension of Uraniborg. This he achieved by distributing printed forms on which astronomers could enter their observations before returning them to the central site of Hven.[15] In doing so, he pioneered a practice central to the development of modern science. For this, Latour thinks, is essentially how the modern laboratory sustains its authority too. The Latourian laboratory is an inscription engine, dedicated to the construction, collation, dispersal, and accommodation of such materials. It is a compelling and enormously influential argument. And it is consonant not only with Eisenstein herself, but more extensively still with her inspiration and bête noire, Marshall McLuhan.[16] Latour's vision of science in

15. Latour, *Science in Action*, 52, 132–44, 226–7; Latour, "Drawing Things Together"; Latour, "Visualization and Cognition," 11–14; Latour, "Politics of Explanation," 159; Callon, Law, and Rip, "Putting Texts in Their Place," 223, 228–9.

16. A plausible summary of McLuhan's views in relation to Latour's might run as follows. Like Latour, McLuhan urged the importance of what he called the "network" as a category of analysis, important in deciding ways of perceiving the world. He too identified a railway system as the representative network par excellence (compare Latour, *We Have Never Been Modern*, 117; and Latour, *Aramis*). What McLuhan's networks achieve—what lends them their power—is their ability to produce changes in scale. They permit individuals and organizations to localize and universalize by allowing them to magnify and reduce traces of the

action depends on Eisenstein's "print culture"—and thereby implicitly on McLuhan's "Gutenberg Galaxy"—to underwrite the stability of both knowledge and society.[17]

The Tycho of Eisenstein and Latour has become the incarnation of textual, social, and epistemic order. But just how credible is this Tycho? There is something altogether too neat, too immaculate, about the figure and his achievements. As Philip Marlowe put it in *The Big Sleep,* such testimony displays "the austere simplicity of fiction rather than the tangled woof of fact."[18] Maybe the Tycho so far portrayed will change somewhat if we investigate more closely how his "mediators" actually came into being and were put to use. For Tycho does indeed represent perhaps the purest example of a particular kind of printing, and a particular way of using the products of the press. Like Regiomontanus before him, and Hevelius after, he controlled his own printing operation. His was a singular printing house, however. It was as geographically isolated on the island of Hven as it was socially isolated from the companies of the European book trade. It was even physically embedded in the five-meter high, five-meter thick wall that enclosed his entire estate. Such isolation meant, at least in principle, that Tycho could produce books when, for whom, and in whatever form he liked.[19] Works like his *Astronomiae Instauratae Mechanica,* which described Uraniborg in all its glory, were scarcely intended to be *published* at all, but were to be distributed as gifts to patrons at courts and universities (fig. 1.5). The more prestigious were not just printed books, but hybrids—hand-colored, individualized tributes, presented to their intended recipients on specific dates.[20] Tycho meant to bypass the structures of the international book trade altogether.

---

things on which they wish to operate to roughly the same size without destroying them. The "message" of his networks is that they permit such control; and what is perceived as reality is in fact the current state of competing networks in dynamic interaction. The boundary between natural and social must therefore be forgotten when considering them. In such a world of natural/social hybrids, power comes from "translation." This is the agency by which we "enlarge the scope of [our] action" and affect sites distant from ourselves. See McLuhan, *Understanding Media,* 3–21, 56–61, 89–105, 338–45, 346–59; compare Latour, *Science in Action,* 108–21, 223–32, 247–57, and *We Have Never Been Modern,* 10–12, 49–142. A reassessment of McLuhan is, I think, overdue, though attention to his work is currently reviving. Eisenstein herself roundly denied following him, but with an insistence and a perseverance that almost amounted to protesting too much: e.g., *Printing Press,* ix–xi, xvii, 40–1, 88, 129, 171.

17. Compare Shapin, "Following Scientists Around," 541, 545–6.

18. Chandler, *Chandler Collection,* I, 143.

19. Thoren, *Lord of Uraniborg,* 144.

20. Brahe, *Astronomiae Instauratae Mechanica* (1598); Brahe, *Opera Omnia,* V, 317–8. A list of known copies with their recipients is in Norlind, *Tycho Brahe,* 286–93.

FIG. I.5. The presentation of an astronomical volume to an absolute monarch: Hevelius offering his *Cometographia* to Louis XIV of France. The vignette portrays Hevelius's dedication of the book to Louis; it does not represent a real scene. Hevelius, *Cometographia*. (By permission of the Syndics of Cambridge University Library.)

The recipient of a book like Tycho's *Astronomiae Instauratae Mechanica* was thus likely to be found in a distinctive place: a royal court or a university. Here a book took its place and gained its meaning only amid a vast arsenal of other objects directed to similar ends. It would be encountered alongside natural curiosities, thaumaturgical wonders, mathematical devices, paintings, musical compositions, alchemical medallions, magical machines, and other books (fig. 1.6). In such surroundings, every aspect of appearance and handling mattered for creating an impact. The reader of such a work, in such a place, would be consciously engaging in a distinctive system of practices and ideas—in Tycho's case, feudal ones. The giving and receiving of such gifts was an important part of court culture, enmeshed in conventions of status recognition, reciprocation, and reward. This could not fail to affect the way in which that reader regarded the book. It was invested with enhanced credit, being untainted by "mechanick" influence, and it was accorded the privileged reception due to such a noble gesture.[21] The veracity of its contents warranted respect. They could not be dismissed without cost. Yet at the same time such a gesture all but commanded creative responses—including challenges—from suitably prestigious interlocutors. Tycho's book would now fall subject to the conventions surrounding philosophical and mathematical disputes in these settings. The variables that determined both whether a "scientific" debate would even take place, and, once battle had been joined, how it would proceed, were local ones: to whom one pre-

21. Westman, "Astronomer's Role." See also Hannaway, "Laboratory Design"; and compare Eamon, "Court, Academy and Printing House," 41.

FIG. 1.6. The place of books in the cabinet of curiosities. In places like this—a museum of curiosities in Naples—books, along with crocodiles, fossils, and a panoply of natural and artificial marvels, served to facilitate conversation (see Findlen, "Courting Nature," 68-9). Imperato, *Historia Naturale*. (By permission of the Syndics of Cambridge University Library.)

sented the book, through which channels it was distributed, with which patron it was identified. Disputes like this were affairs of honor, conducted through appropriate intermediaries and champions. Printed books were their vehicles. That was what they were *for*.[22]

When, therefore, Tycho found himself attacked by Nicolai Reymers Baer (or Ursus), a recognized mathematician but a man of low birth whom he himself had accused of plagiarism, a scientific debate was not the principal outcome. Rather unusually, Tycho did in fact deign to reply himself. But

22. In addition to the works of Biagioli and Hannaway cited here, see Findlen, "Economy of Exchange"; Findlen, "Courting Nature," esp. 61; Moran, *Alchemical World*, esp. 9, 93–4, 97, 110–2; Smith, *Business of Alchemy*, 49–50; Daston, "Factual Sensibility"; and Davis, "Beyond the Market." Compare also the difficulties experienced by Becher in translating commercial documents for courtly readers: Smith, *Business of Alchemy*, 139.

he did so with a series of elaborately indignant letters to his fellows across Europe, which he had printed on his press at Uraniborg and circulated in 1596. In this correspondence he recited the tale of Ursus's alleged theft and argued that, whatever the date of Ursus's publication, Tycho had *printed* the cosmology first. Ever willing to recall his opponent's low birth, he even seems to have suggested that Ursus be executed for his presumption. But the more philosophical side of the dispute he delegated to a second, the relatively humble Kepler. The result was Kepler's "Defense of Tycho against Ursus," a remarkably sophisticated historical argument for the status of astronomical hypotheses and their creators. It was never printed.[23]

Much even of this story could be taken as reinforcing Eisenstein's image. However, two elements make it less confirmatory. The first is that Tycho was extremely atypical in his successful use of print. Other writers regarded him not as representative of their own situation, but as a model that they sought, with widely varying degrees of success, to emulate. Like most icons, he stood for an ideal that was unrealizable. The second is that, as his argument against Ursus implies, even Tycho himself found the ideal impossible to achieve. That was why he built his own printing house and paper mill: he discovered that he could not otherwise obtain acceptable materials and workmanship.[24] Even with these in place, moreover, most of his work remained unprinted until after his death.[25] Latour's preprinted forms, for example, seem to be mythical; Tycho did correspond extensively, but left no trace of having used such objects.[26] And while he began producing the images and descriptions for the *Astronomiae Instauratae Mechanica* as early as

23. Brahe, *Epistolarum Astronomicarum Libri*, 33–4, 148–51; Brahe, *Opera Omnia*, VI, 61–2, 179; Jardine, *Birth of History and Philosophy of Science*, 9–28 and passim (15 for Ursus's peasant background); Dreyer, *Tycho Brahe*, 183; Rosen, *Three Imperial Mathematicians*. Tycho's decision to strike at Ursus personally (which Kepler, for one, found surprising) may well be related to the fact that, as Hannaway points out, his status was feudal in origin; Tycho was not a courtier. See Hannaway, "Laboratory Design," 589 n. 11. For Tycho's conflicts see also Gingerich and Westman, *Wittich Connection* (which contrasts Tycho's treatment of Ursus to his response to the relatively well-born Wittich), and Thoren, *Lord of Uraniborg*. I am grateful to Robert Westman for conversations about this affair, which remains one of the more controversial among scholars of early modern astronomy.

24. Brahe, *Opera*, VI, 224, 365 n; VII, 214, 274; IX, 175; X, 302. Even with the mill in working order, he remained reliant on the cooperation of nearby parishioners to provide raw materials, as they were exhorted to do in regular "rag sermons."

25. In particular, the star catalogue (circulated only in manuscript until years after Tycho's death, and then inaccurately printed) and the *Astronomiae Instauratae Progymnasmata* (begun at Uraniborg, but completed only under the aegis of his heirs in 1602).

26. I have found no trace of these preprinted forms in Tycho's *Opera Omnia*, nor in any relevant secondary authority. I am also unable to find Latour's source for this central claim; it may well derive from an imaginative reading of certain passages in Eisenstein's *Printing Press*, e.g., 626–7.

1585, soon after building his printing house, the volume was not completed until thirteen years later. By that time he was in exile in Hamburg—the only place he could find with printers capable of finishing the book, even though he had brought his own press with him from Hven. Taken by his son to the Holy Roman Emperor, the book now became an instrument in Tycho's attempt to secure imperial patronage.[27] This proved successful, and he removed to Prague. But he soon discovered that even here, in the center of the empire, no printer able to undertake his prized star catalogue could be found. He was reduced to circulating hand-copied versions, and the catalogue remained unprinted on his death (fig. 1.7).[28]

At that point his works began to fall out of court circles altogether. They descended into the hands of the book trade. Even the *Astronomiae Instauratae Mechanica* was reprinted commercially. Such books were likely to be produced to different standards. They stood at risk of piracy and imitation, despite Rudolf II's stern commands forbidding such "printers' frauds." They were also likely to be read in different ways, by different people, in different places and for different reasons. Their accreditation became far more insecure. So, for example, the English astronomer royal, John Flamsteed—who, as we shall see, identified himself profoundly with Tycho—dismissed the posthumous printing of his star tables as, quite simply, a "fraud."[29] Tycho's inscriptions appear to have become distinctly mutable once they fell out of his control and left the courtly matrix (fig. 1.8).

If even Tycho Brahe found it so difficult to maintain his printed materials as mobile and immutable, what hope is there of explaining the achievements of less powerful figures in Eisenstein's terms? Attempting to do so would mean attributing to printed books themselves attributes of credibility and persuasion that actually took much work to maintain. It would thereby draw our attention away from important problems that any individual, even Tycho, had to overcome.[30] Talk of "print culture" is strangely ethereal when compared to Tycho's struggles. It stands oddly disconnected from the professed experiences of real historical figures. For example, who actually

27. Brahe, *Opera*, V, 317–8; VIII, 166, 177, 388.

28. Thoren, *Lord of Uraniborg*, 150, 185–7, 367, 381–97, 414–5, 421, 478. Tycho had planned to present the catalogue to Rudolf II on New Year's Day, apparently a customary occasion for gift-giving: Kaufmann, *Mastery of Nature*, 106. For Rudolf II's undertaking to provide a "new Uraniborg," see Brahe, *Opera*, VIII, 178, 188. It is also likely, of course, that Tycho's circulation of the catalogue in manuscript was intended to enhance its status as a collectible object.

29. Brahe, *Astronomiae Instauratae Mechanica* (1602); Curtius, *Historia Cœlestis*; Flamsteed, *Preface to John Flamsteed's "Historia Cœlestis Britannica,"* 99–100. For Rudolf's condemnation of "Typographorum fraudem," see Brahe, *Opera*, II, 9.

30. Compare Schaffer, "Eighteenth Brumaire," 178–92, on the concept of the "ideal reader."

printed (and reprinted) Tycho's pages? It is a question worth asking, since Tycho himself spent many frustrating years seeking suitable printers—and the astronomer Christoph Rothmann, at least, believed that Ursus had been able to plagiarize his world system because he had been employed in Tycho's printing house.[31] And how were those pages employed by their recipients? Of what use were they *to them*? How did Tycho ensure that such distant readers took them as authoritative, especially when, as was often the case in early modern testimony about celestial observations, they conflicted with figures produced locally? Eisenstein and Latour begin by decreeing such issues peripheral. *The Nature of the Book* does the opposite. If we are to understand how and why printed texts became trustworthy, it argues, we need to appreciate all of them, in something approaching their full "woof."

The disconnected air exhibited by Eisenstein's account is not accidental. In her work, printing itself stands outside history. The press is something *"sui generis,"* we are told, lying beyond the reach of conventional historical analysis. Its "culture" is correspondingly placeless and timeless. It is deemed to exist inasmuch as printed texts *possess* some key characteristic, fixity being the best candidate, and carry it with them as they are transported from place to place. The origins of this property are not analyzed. In fact, the accusations of technological determinism sometimes leveled against Eisenstein may even be wide of the mark, since she consistently declines to specify *any* position on the question of how print culture might emerge from print.[32] But the example of Tycho does suggest that the focus of her approach is *in practice* highly selective. The portrait it generates identifies as significant only the clearest instances of fixity. It regards instances when fixity was not manifested as exceptional failures, and even in the successful cases it neglects the labors through which success was achieved. It identifies the results of those labors instead as powers intrinsic to texts. Readers consequently suffer the fate of obliteration: their intelligence and skill is reattributed to the printed page. Tycho's labors deserve better. To put it brutally, what those labors really tell us is that Eisenstein's print culture does not exist.

There is an alternative. We may consider fixity not as an *inherent* quality, but as a *transitive* one. That is, it may be more useful to reverse our commonsense assumption. We may adopt the principle that fixity exists only inasmuch as it is recognized and acted upon by people—and not otherwise. The consequence of this change in perspective is that print culture itself is

31. Dreyer, *Tycho Brahe*, 184 n. 1.

32. Eisenstein, *Printing Press*, e.g., 159, 166–8, 609 n, 89–90, 702–3. See also Grafton, "Importance of Being Printed." The fact that Eisenstein is simultaneously too provincial (thus missing the contingent elements of print culture by her lack of a comparative perspective) and not local enough (thus missing the work needed to make print culture at all) may be inferred from Cohen's discussion in *Scientific Revolution*, 357–67.

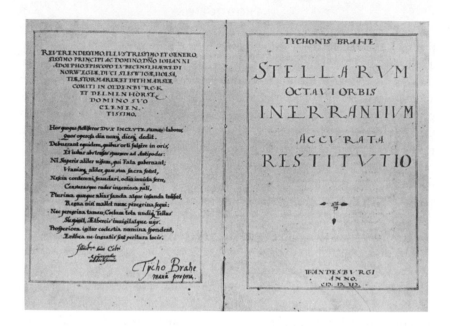

FIG. 1.7. Tycho Brahe's star catalogue, distributed in manuscript to princes and patrons. Note the careful imitation of a printed page. Reproduced from Norlind, *Tycho Brahe*, 297. (By permission of the Syndics of Cambridge University Library.)

immediately laid open to analysis. It becomes a *result* of manifold representations, practices and conflicts, rather than just the monolithic *cause* with which we are often presented.[33] In contrast to talk of a "print logic" imposed on humanity,[34] this approach allows us to recover the construction of different print cultures in particular historical circumstances. It recognizes that texts, printed or not, cannot compel readers to react in specific ways, but that they must be interpreted in cultural spaces the character of which helps to decide what counts as a proper reading. In short, this recasting has the advantage of positioning the cultural and the social where they should be: at the center of our attention.

If Tycho Brahe has hitherto been made the personification of print culture, then the experiences of his near-contemporary, Galileo Galilei, may in turn stand for this new approach. In 1610, Galileo produced the first of a series of dramatically successful books, called the *Sidereus Nuncius*. In vivid illustrations, he showed mountains and valleys on the surface of the Moon,

33. Compare the discussions of power in Latour, "On the Powers of Association," and Latour, "Technology Is Society Made Durable." This suggestion has obvious resonances with certain works in critical theory, such as Fish, *Is There a Text in This Class?* Since my aim is primarily historical I shall not be making many explicit links with such material, though the parallel deserves to be noted. Compare also McKenzie, *Bibliography and the Sociology of Texts*.

34. E.g., Kernan, *Printing Technology, Letters and Samuel Johnson*, 48 ff.

FIG. I.8. Iconic representation of the preservation and publication of Tycho Brahe's manuscripts. The four Holy Roman Emperors shown are Rudolf II, Ferdinand II, Ferdinand III, and Leopold I. These respectively sponsored Tycho's writings (*paravit*), preserved and digested them into tables (*usurpavit*—which could also mean "usurped"), recovered them from Kepler's family and saved them from damage during the Thirty Years' War (*recepit*), and published them (*publicavit*). The motto dedicates the book to the emperors as rulers of the two realms represented by the globes—exerting dominion over the terrestrial world politically, and over the celestial by possession of these manuscripts. The imperial message is reinforced by Ferdinand II's gesture towards Hercules, always a symbol of Hapsburg aspirations. Ironically, the double meaning of the term *usurpavit* could well be apt: Curtius's manuscripts were actually very corrupt copies, which did Tycho's reputation no favors in the eyes of astronomers such as John Flamsteed. (Evans, *Making of the Habsburg Monarchy*, 332–4; McDonald, "Maximilian I"; Ashworth, "Habsburg Circle"; Dreyer, *Tycho Brahe*, 371–4.) Curtius [L. Barrettus, pseud.], *Historia Cœlestis*. (By permission of the Syndics of Cambridge University Library.)

and the discovery of new stars in Orion and the Pleiades (fig. 1.9). These and other "nebulous" regions—the Milky Way in particular—could now be resolved into stars. Above all, however, Galileo revealed four previously unknown satellites revolving about Jupiter, providing a vivid model of Copernican cosmology. This discovery, embodied in a small book, would soon establish him as the foremost philosopher on the Italian peninsula. Yet it

FIG. 1.9. Illustrations of the lunar surface, from the first and three subsequent editions of Galileo Galilei's *Sidereus Nuncius*.

These are perhaps the most famous of all early modern scientific illustrations. They were the first images to show the lunar surface, revealing it to be rough and cratered, and constituted an important element in the campaign to establish the imperfection of this heavenly body. It is especially striking, then, to note the transformations wrought on Galileo's images through their reproduction. Here, the first row (*across*) of pictures is Galileo's own, printed in his Venice edition of the *Sidereus Nuncius* (1610). The second comes from an unauthorized impression issued almost immediately in Frankfurt. Note that the sequence of the first two pictures has been reversed. Moreover, the exigencies of such unauthorized printing dictated speed and economy, and as a result changed the images themselves. As well as showing degradation in each picture, the first and fourth images of this impression were in fact printed from the same woodcut, rotated through 180°. The third

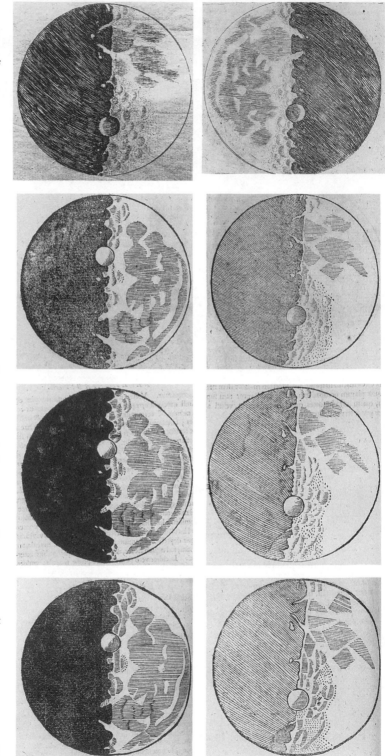

version reproduced here was issued in London in 1653. It reused the same blocks as the Frankfurt edition, again duplicating the first and fourth images. It also reiterated the sequence of the unauthorized version. So did the fourth version, printed in 1683. By this time the painstakingly crafted verisimilitude of Galileo's original drawings had been significantly eroded—a degradation in which the practices of piratical reproduction had played a large part.

(*top row*) Galileo Galilei, *Sidereus Nuncius* (Venice, 1610). (*second row*) Galileo Galilei, *Sidereus, Nuncius* [*sic*] (Frankfurt, 1610). (*third row*) Galileo Galilei, *Sidereus Nuncius* (London, 2d ed., 1653). (*bottom row*) Galileo Galilei, *Sidereus Nuncius* (London, 3d ed., 1683). (By permission of the Archives, California Institute of Technology.)

was not just for the intrinsic value of these observations that the *Sidereus Nuncius* had such an impact. In fact, Galileo and his allies deployed the book brilliantly to make its success.[35] He was angling to enter the court of an absolute prince, Cosimo II de' Medici, whose family had long been linked iconographically to Jupiter. Paying for the printing himself, Galileo named his new Jovian satellites accordingly. As the "Medicean stars" they formed the centerpiece of the book he now presented to the grand duke. It was not easy. Galileo actually had to change the name in mid-printing, after Medici officials told him that his original choice of "Cosmian" would not meet with approval; the new name was glued over the old on the pages already printed. He then went in person to make the presentation, ensuring that Cosimo would successfully see the new phenomena through his telescope. When Galileo distributed additional copies to princes and cardinals across Europe, along with spyglasses to support his claims, he did so under the carapace of Cosimo himself via the Medici diplomatic service. In promulgating the announcement, Galileo had presented Cosimo with heroic and noble homage, for which the conventions of patronage suggested an appropriate response. When that response came, Galileo declared that his whole "being" had been transformed. Perhaps for the first time, a mathematical practitioner underwent the transfiguration into court philosopher.[36]

Galileo was trying to create a new kind of authority on, and for, natural knowledge. The construction of this persona and the elaboration of his work in cosmology and mechanics thus took place together, and both rested on the skillful exploitation of patronage dynamics at an absolutist court. The point is a rather subtle one. Patronage was not simply something that could be used as a tool to achieve aims defined by other, perhaps scientific, criteria. It helped constitute at once what were reasonable aims to adopt, what were good claims to make in pursuit of those aims, how they could best be made, and to which audiences. Evidence came into being and was accredited by means of the civil culture of the court. There was no "Galileo, scientist" standing outside this cultural realm and manipulating its mechanisms in order to achieve objective ends. It is important to appreciate this, since at each crucial moment of transition—from Venetian patronage to Florentine, and thence to papal—books were central to Galileo's advance. From the *Sidereus Nuncius,* so effective in raising him to Cosimo's court, to the

35. Galilei, *Sidereus Nuncius* (1989), 1–24, 87–113; Biagioli, "Galileo's System of Patronage"; Westfall, "Science and Patronage."

36. Galilei, *Sidereus Nuncius*, 19, 90–1; Galilei, *Opere*, X, 353; Biagioli, *Galileo, Courtier*, chap. 2. John Dee did request the title of Philosopher and Mathematician to Emperor Rudolf II before Galileo achieved his own elevation in Florence, but without success: Clulee, *John Dee's Natural Philosophy*, 224. Westman, "Astronomer's Role," is essential for understanding the significance of this transfiguration.

Dialogo, which triggered his downfall at the hands of Pope Urban VIII's Inquisition, books were key elements in any strategy to take advantage of patronage opportunities.[37]

At court, what appear to modern eyes to be scientific disputes were seen by participant and spectator alike in these different terms. They would be triggered and structured by Galileo's patron for purposes of diversion and the expression of status. He was expected to produce entertaining and involving debates, and to challenge other court philosophers of sufficient rank.[38] While it was important not to lose such a dispute, it was also important to conduct it properly; and, as Tycho Brahe had known, regular challenges by qualified individuals were imperative to show that one's status was being recognized. So, for example, when the Medici ambassador presented a copy of the *Sidereus Nuncius* to imperial mathematician Johannes Kepler, he responded correctly with a printed reply dedicated not to Galileo, but to the ambassador. In a sense, Galileo was engaging with Kepler; but Cosimo was also communicating with the Holy Roman Emperor.[39] Unlike Tycho, however, Galileo had no private press. His book fell immediately into the hands of commercial printers. By late 1610 an unauthorized impression had appeared in Frankfurt, his fine illustrations marred by hasty reproduction. For the rest of the century these adulterated images would be reproduced repeatedly. Countless readers saw them—far more, in all likelihood, than ever came upon the authorized originals of what are probably the most momentous astronomical images of their era.[40]

Even exempting such piratical enterprises, the social dynamics of challenges were modified by the unavoidable involvement of new personnel and places. The case of Galileo's 1623 work, *Il Saggiatore,* is instructive in this respect. It was printed in April and May in a few hundred copies. In October the work was ritually presented to the pope and important cardinals. This was the courtly aspect of its production. But Galileo's allies also used the

37. For this portrayal I am indebted to Biagioli, *Galileo, Courtier,* esp. chaps. 1, 2, 6. See also Eamon, "Court, Academy and Printing House"; Biagioli, "Galileo's System of Patronage." Some aspects of Biagioli's work—particularly his claim regarding the association between Cosimo and Jupiter—have been strenuously challenged by Shank, with results that remain inconclusive at the time of writing. The particular thrust of Shank's attack means that it does not directly impinge on my own argument. See especially Biagioli, "Playing with the Evidence," and Shank, "How Shall We Practice History?"

38. Biagioli, *Galileo, Courtier,* 163; Biagioli, "Galileo's System of Patronage," 30; Castiglione, *Book of the Courtier,* esp. 68 ff.

39. Drake, *Galileo Studies,* 131–8.

40. Galilei, *Sidereus Nuncius* (Venice, 1610); Galilei, *Sidereus, Nuncius* [*sic*] (Frankfurt, 1610). It is perhaps worth adding the rider that the latter edition was unauthorized as far as anyone then or now has known; Galileo (like Isaac Newton later in the century) was quite capable of perpetrating his own "unauthorized" publications. The point remains that he was unable to oversee the production of the work, and in particular that of its illustrations.

book in what looks much more like a process of publication. They did so in order to expose the tactics of a Jesuit antagonist lurking behind the pseudonym of "Lotario Sarsi." They ensured that one of the licenser's copies was delivered early to the Sun bookshop. This was a well-known center for libertine literature, which the Jesuit would surely be monitoring for such works. Its proprietor had agreed to cooperate in the plan. Sure enough, "Sarsi" arrived and seized upon that very copy. He "changed color" on the spot, attacked the bookseller himself as personally responsible for the text, and left declaring loudly that he would take up the challenge and produce a rebuttal within three months. In so doing, he revealed himself as Orazio Grassi, lecturer in mathematics at the Collegio Romano and the Jesuits' most prestigious architect. The bookseller immediately told Galileo's allies of his outburst. Two of them wrote excitedly to their friend to tell him the news, whereupon Galileo came to Rome and successfully preempted Grassi's rebuttal.[41] Access to the bookshop, and the character of both the premises and its proprietor, had transformed the dispute.

Here was something quite alien to Tycho's Uraniborg. For Galileo too, however, despite this success it was ultimately to prove an inauspicious development. In the events of his notorious fall not only the printers and booksellers, but the entire licensing and publication mechanism, would be implicated. The *Saggiatore* incident led directly to this far more significant affair. It began in 1623 with the election of Galileo's ally, Maffeo Barberini, as Pope Urban VIII. This was the spur for Galileo, becalmed in Florence, to seek a position of favor in Rome itself. He did so by using two tools: *Il Saggiatore* itself, which he redirected at the last moment and presented to Urban, and his long-projected Copernican work on the tides. The first of these was a great success. After the incident at the Sun bookshop, Urban had it read to him at table, and seems to have relished its wit and rhetorical dexterity. He began to accord Galileo audiences, in which his favor seemed clear. So clear, in fact, that Galileo probably understood himself released from a private instruction issued some years earlier not to engage in public support for Copernicanism. He returned to Florence and began writing his greater work, which became the momentous *Dialogo . . . sopra i due Massimi Sistemi del Mondo*.

The *Dialogo* was not immediately or obviously scandalous. In fact, it successfully underwent an extensive licensing procedure, such that the

41. Galilei, *Opere*, XIII, 145–8; Galilei, *Sidereus Nuncius*, 94, 102; Redondi, *Galileo: Heretic*, 28–67, 179–83; Drake, *Galileo at Work*, 268–77, 279, 284–5, 287–8. It is perhaps worth stressing that those involved in this plan probably knew "Sarsi's" actual identity throughout; the objective was to get an open declaration from Grassi of the fact, and of his future intentions.

printed edition could boast as many as five imprimaturs.[42] Initially planned to appear in Rome in 1630, it was finally published only in 1632 in Florence. The book was in the event duly licensed in both cities, but nonetheless it caused a stir. Another of Galileo's Jesuit opponents, Christoph Scheiner, immediately repeated Grassi's error by revealing his outrage in front of the bookseller, who dutifully reported it back to his friends.[43] Murmurs soon spread that Galileo had violated Bellarmine's confidential instruction, which was rumored to ban him from even discussing the issue of Copernicanism, let alone supporting it. Events then moved very quickly. In April, Galileo's ally and patronage broker in Rome, Ciampoli, fell from grace, just as Urban came under stringent attack from Spanish interests for insufficient zeal in pursuing the Thirty Years' War and the struggle against heresy. This was a crucial development. Ciampoli was just the kind of intermediary needed by such a book to smooth its progress in courtly circles; he it was who had read *Il Saggiatore* to Urban at table. Without such mediation the *Dialogo* would soon prove vulnerable, especially as the pope now associated its publication with Ciampoli's newly established impropriety. In these circumstances, what might otherwise have been appreciated as witty dialogic sallies came to be read very differently. Papal sensibilities took its barbs as personal affronts. That summer Urban called in the book, appointing a commission to investigate the circumstances of its appearance. In the autumn he transferred the case to the Inquisition. In February Galileo was summoned to Rome. From April until June negotiations continued in secret. The pope urged the Inquisition on, however, and Galileo was finally resolved to be "vehemently suspected of heresy"—one of the most serious offenses in the Inquisition's ambit. He was forced to abjure, and sentenced to permanent house arrest.[44]

Sudden and irrevocable, Galileo's fall has remained one of the most resonant incidents in history, let alone in the history of science. Here, as throughout Galileo's life, the uses of a book had proved crucial to the transformation. This was no Tychonic success story. It would be difficult to identify fixity or immutability as important to the role of the *Dialogo* at any stage of its story. Galileo's fate was decided by different criteria. His fortunes, and in Mario Biagioli's terms perhaps even his identity, rested on the way in which his book would be read. As scholars working in the last two decades

42. Its five licenses are reproduced in Galilei, *Dialogue*, [2]. For problems over printing and licensing, see Drake, *Galileo at Work*, 311–14, 319–20, 332–44, and Westfall, "Patronage and the Publication of Galileo's *Dialogue*," esp. 386–7, 393.

43. Galilei, *Opere*, XIV, 359–60.

44. Finocchiaro, *Galileo Affair*, 32–9; Drake, *Galileo at Work*, 344–52. After this chapter was written, Paula Findlen and Tara Nummedal kindly showed me their "Scientific Books in the Seventeenth Century," which includes an excellent discussion of Tycho, Galileo, and Kepler.

have revealed, Galileo was a fine mathematician, a profound philosopher, a superb rhetorician, a devious antagonist, and an agile courtier; but even he could not control such readers.[45]

FROM FIXITY TO CREDIT

A new historical understanding of print is needed. What will it look like? One immediately evident feature will be its regard for the labors of those actually involved in printing, publishing, and reading. Another will be its respect for their own representations of printing, embracing both its prospects and its dangers. The dangers in particular will loom larger and more substantial than they have hitherto. Historians tend to disregard such perils as accidental; early modern readers and writers knew otherwise. They had good cause to fear that in the realm of print seemingly in prospect, authorial control over such efforts as Galileo's would be undermined. More than that, some of them thought that it was *already* undermined. Increasingly they articulated responses by which the culture of the learned gentleman could be saved from this "mechanick art." Perhaps we should remind ourselves of the extent to which those responses appeared to fail— of the extent to which the print culture of the eighteenth century could be perceived by contemporaries, not as a realization of the rationalizing effects now so often ascribed to the press, but as destabilizing and threatening to civility. Such a stance, artificial though it would be, might help us to distance ourselves from the apparent stability of our own print culture, with its uniform editions, mass reproduction, and typographical fixity. Early modern fears would then begin to appear not as incidental lapses, defined a priori as marginal, but as credible statements of experience. They would finally be recognized as no less substantial than the phenomenon of fixity itself.

The Nature of the Book tries to treat all sides of the world of print with equal historiographical respect. In so doing, it inherits and attempts to develop initiatives central to the current state of cultural history. In particular, it reflects the important French field of *histoire du livre*. This field, at first associated with the *Annales* movement, has since the 1950s developed into an academic industry in its own right.[46] At the same time, its approaches

45. Biagioli, *Galileo, Courtier*, 2–3, 87. For the different aspects of Galileo cited here, see also Drake, *Galileo at Work*; Feyerabend, *Against Method*; Moss, *Novelties in the Heavens*; Wallace, *Galileo's Logic of Discovery and Proof*.

46. Its origin is conventionally dated to the appearance in 1958 of Febvre and Martin's *L'Apparition du Livre* (which has appeared in English translation as *The Coming of the Book*). Perhaps its most ambitious recent product has been Martin, *History and Power of Writing*. I have surveyed the field and its implications at greater length in Johns, "Science and the Book."

have changed substantially. Its original practitioners dedicated themselves to accounting for the effects of printing in terms of quantitative measures of manufacture and distribution. They divided up the realm of print by subject matter and by the social character of purchasers, hoping to arrive at objective indices of cultural change. In fact, fewer useful figures emerged than had been hoped for. But the approach, so representative of *Annales* historiography, nonetheless had—and still has—substantial advantages. Above all, it suited commonsense perceptions of what it is that most properly characterizes print: the large-scale reproduction and distribution of precisely the same objects. Eisenstein's representation of print culture effectively embodies those same perceptions, albeit without the quantification. However, as illustrated by the examples of Galileo and Tycho, there were also costs to such a strategy. One was that it was effectively "indifferent to the objects themselves." It assumed that successive editions of a work were essentially the same, whatever their variations in text, format, or appearance. It would have accounted the Venice edition of Galileo's *Sidereus Nuncius* the same as the unauthorized Frankfurt impression.[47] Another, equally serious, disadvantage was that it remained silent about how the objects being counted were employed by readers such that they could have divergent cultural consequences. It could not have explained the different receptions accorded Galileo's *Dialogo,* because it ignored what Roger Chartier calls the "intellectual 'labor'" required to put a book or paper to use.[48]

Chartier himself has been central to efforts to address these costs. He has worked to recover the different modes of labor surrounding printed materials, revealing how readers in local settings could "appropriate" in different ways the books they read. From this perspective, ways of reading are recognized as "social and cultural practices." Like other such practices, they have a history, and one that can be reconstructed. The practical implications prove substantial. Sensitivity to the historical character of these practices often shows that an apparently authoritative text, however "fixed," could not compel uniformity in the cultures of its reception. In practice, rather the reverse seems to have happened. Local cultures created their own meanings with and for such objects. For example, during the Counter-Reformation, printed images issued in large numbers in an attempt to standardize religious practice instead frequently served as vehicles for continued differentiation. The elements of a printed book—its format, layout, and typography— acted as no more than elements in an instrument, the book itself, that was useful for constructing knowledge. They were the tools, among others, with

47. Chartier, "Postface," 624–5. Contrast Eisenstein, *Printing Revolution*, 21–2; Eisenstein, *Printing Press*, 80–90, 103–4.

48. Chartier, *Cultural History*, 33–4.

which users forged readings. In general, we may conclude that print entailed not one but many cultures, and that these cultures of the book were themselves local in character.[49]

As the opening pages of this chapter implied, there was one concern in particular that possessed early modern readers, and that may be used as a key to the rest. Could a printed book be trusted to be what it claimed? Perhaps a reader would be prudent to reserve judgment. On the most obvious level, whether a *Sidereus Nuncius* printed in Frankfurt was really Galileo's text, or an *Astronomiae Instauratae Mechanica* produced in Nuremburg was really Tycho's, could justifiably be doubted. More broadly, the very apprehension that printed books might not be self-evidently creditable was enough to rule out any possibility of their bearing the power attributed to them by most modern historians. And that apprehension was widespread. Piracy and plagiarism occupied readers' minds just as prominently as fixity and enlightenment. Unauthorized translations, epitomes, imitations, and other varieties of "impropriety" were, they believed, routine hazards. Very few noteworthy publications seemed to escape altogether from such practices, and none at all could safely be regarded as immune a priori. It was regarded as extremely unusual for a book professing knowledge—from lowly almanacs to costly folios—to be published in the relatively unproblematic manner we now assume. Contemporaries had good reason to be wary. Their editions of Shakespeare, Donne, and Sir Thomas Browne were liable to be dubious. So were those of Robert Boyle, not to mention the first "scientific" journal, the *Philosophical Transactions.* Even Isaac Newton's *Principia* suffered from unauthorized reprinting. From Galileo and Tycho to Newton and John Flamsteed, no significant learned author seemed to escape the kinds of practices soon colloquially subsumed under the label of piracy. This meant that even when a book was not so treated, the possibility that it might be still permeated the negotiations, practices, and conventions by which it was made, distributed, exchanged, and used. If piracy was as widespread as commonly feared, then trusting any printed report without knowl-

49. These and similar points have been made in many contexts: Chartier, *Order of Books*, 16–17; Chartier, "Culture as Appropriation"; Chartier, "Publishing Strategies," 155–60; Chartier, "Practical Impact of Writing," 122–6; Chartier, *Culture of Print*, 1–5; Chartier, "Du Livre au Lire"; Chartier, *Cultural Uses of Print*, 3–12, 70; Chartier, *Lectures et Lecteurs*; Chartier, "Texts, Printings, Readings"; Chartier, *Passions of the Renaissance*, 1–11, 110–59, 326–61, 362–95; Bourdieu and Chartier, "La Lecture"; Martin, "Pour une Histoire de la Lecture"; de Certeau, "Reading as Poaching"; Darnton, "History of Reading"; McKenzie, "Typography and Meaning"; McKenzie, *Bibliography and the Sociology of Texts*; Martin and Vezin, *Mise en Page*. On the specific theme of *mise en page* see also Laufer, "L'Espace Visuel du Livre Ancien"; Laufer, "Espaces du Livre"; Pastoureau, "L'Illustration du Livre." Compare also the fascinating discussion of "kitsch" in Clark, "Scientific Revolution in the German Nations," 97–8.

edge of those processes could be rash. Profound problems of credit thus attended printed materials of all kinds. Without solutions there could be few meaningful uses for books—and perhaps no durable reasoning from them.

It should not be surprising, then, that contemporaries did not always identify fixity as a central characteristic of print. Surveying the books available to aid ocean navigators, Edmond Halley, for one, noted that "the first Editions have generally been the best; frequent Copying most commonly vitiating the Originals."[50] Even when people did refer to enhanced reliability, it was often in the face of direct evidence to the contrary. Textual corruption of even such closely monitored texts as the Bible actually increased with the advent of print, due to various combinations of piracy and careless printing.[51] The first book reputed to have been printed without any errors appeared only in 1760. Before then, variety was the rule, even within single editions. Martin Luther's German translation of Scripture was actually beaten into print by its first piracy, and in succeeding years the proportion of unauthorized to authorized texts was roughly ninety to one; these included Luther's own translation, newly ascribed to others (including Catholics), and others' work reattributed to him. A century later, the first folio of Shakespeare boasted some six hundred different typefaces, along with nonuniform spelling and punctuation, erratic divisions and arrangement, mispaging, and irregular proofing. No two copies were identical. It is impossible to decide even that any one is "typical."[52] In such a world, questions of credit took the place of assumptions of fixity.

In attending to this issue, *The Nature of the Book* builds on Steven Shapin's identification of trust as a key element in the making of knowledge.[53] Where Shapin concentrates particularly on intersubjective trust, asking fundamental questions about *whom* one should believe, why, and in what circumstances, *The Nature of the Book* identifies a similar issue in the trust accorded to printed materials. It asks how readers decided *what* to believe. A central element in the reading of a printed work was likely to be a critical appraisal of its identity and its credit. Readers were not without resources for such an assessment. When they approached a given book, with them came knowledge about the purposes, status, and reliability of printed materials in general—knowledge they used to determine the appropriate kind and degree of faith to vest in this unfamiliar object. Yet here too they also brought to bear knowledge about kinds of people. Their worries about

50. *Atlas Maritimus & Commercialis*, i–iii.

51. Black, "Printed Bible." Eisenstein dismisses Black's argument out of hand: *Printing Press*, 80.

52. Newman, "Word Made Print," 106–7 and passim; de Grazia, *Shakespeare Verbatim*, 15–19, 42; Kernan, *Printing Technology*, 48.

53. Shapin, *Social History of Truth*; Schaffer, "Social History of Plausibility," 129.

literary credit were often resolved, as a matter of everyday practice, into
assessments of the people involved in the making, distribution, and reception of books. Readers worried about who decided what got into print, and
about who controlled it once it was there. The twin problems of whom and
what to credit were in practice often combined into one.

When early modern readers determined a book not to be worthy of
credit, they could do so on a number of grounds. It was in the attribution
of "piracy," however, that the issues of credibility and print particularly converged. The term seems to have been coined by John Fell, bishop of Oxford,
to describe the rapacious practices of London printers and booksellers. It
had a technical meaning: a pirate was someone who indulged in the unauthorized reprinting of a title recognized to belong to someone else by the
formal conventions of the printing and bookselling community. But it soon
came to stand for a wide range of perceived transgressions of civility emanating from print's practitioners. As such, almost any book could, in principle, find itself accounted a piracy, whatever its actual circumstances of
production and distribution. Historians of printing have therefore miscon-
strued instances of alleged piracy in at least two senses. First, they have seen
piracy, like fixity, as inherent in the object, and not as a contestable attribution. Second, furthermore, they have assumed cases of piracy to be exceptions, accidental (in the philosophical sense of the word) to the essentially
stabilizing character of print. Contemporaries were not so sure of this. Incidents that have been retrospectively dismissed as isolated and exceptional
often seemed to them commonplace and representative. They might even
be seen as attempts to undermine, and thereby to reform, the whole structure of the book trade. Even when conducted in more humdrum circumstances, moreover, and with less ambitious ends in sight, piracy still had
powerful implications. Its apparent prevalence affected the economic and
cultural conditions of all printed and written communication. It conditioned the accreditation of printed materials of all sorts, from the humblest
ABC to the most elaborate encyclopedia.[54]

54. An inspiration for this treatment, as for other aspects of this book, has come from
medieval history. Medievalists have devoted much attention to activities of "forgery" and
"plagiarism." They have constructed a sophisticated historiography addressing the diversity
of acts since subsumed under such labels, immersing the subject in a detailed and authoritative treatment of the cultural uses of writing and reading in general. Medieval "forgery" is
appropriately seen as a form of truth-creation, justified (and perhaps even determined) by
contemporary ideas about the nature and purposes of writing. It was also extraordinarily
common. Perhaps half the documents known from Merovingian times are by our lights fake,
and two-thirds of the documents known to have been issued to ecclesiastics before 1100 would
now be reckoned forgeries. See Grafton, *Forgers and Critics*, 24–5, 30–32; Clanchy, *From
Memory to Written Record*, 118–20, 231–57; Stock, *Implications of Literacy*, 59–87; Constable,
"Forgery and Plagiarism." For a robust contrasting view, see Brown, *"Falsitas pia sive Repre-*

For the learned, and for natural philosophers in particular, this had peculiarly important consequences. In the agonistic field of early modern natural knowledge, allegations of piracy readily shaded into charges of plagiarism. Such allegations therefore extended to the reputation of authors. That
is, unauthorized printing threatened to "unauthorize" authors themselves.
Even more important, it threatened the credibility to be attributed to their
ideas. Like print itself, piracy therefore had *epistemic* as well as *economic*
implications: it affected the structure and content of knowledge. For an enterprise like experimental philosophy, in particular, which depended implicitly on the trust accorded to the printed reports issued by its protagonists,
the consequences threatened to be nothing short of devastating.

The Nature of the Book provides the first extensive taxonomy of practices
labeled piratical—from piracy itself, through abridgment, epitomizing, and
translation, to plagiarism and libel. It not only traces the people, places, and
practices through which books came into existence and were circulated. It
also shows how allegations of impropriety in general, and of piracy in particular, emerged from the practices of the printing house and bookshop. It
thus explains how and why such allegations gained their apparent ubiquity.
Moreover, it then proceeds to ask how these changes could possibly be
comprehended in terms of the polite civility supposed to guide intellectual
conduct, and how claims that such practices had been pursued affected the
reception of the works concerned. In short, it addresses precisely the epistemic significance of piracy.

Printers and booksellers were manufacturers of credit. They had to be.
The skills of those producing and trading in books, and the perceptions
of those using them in learned work, might not intersect harmoniously.
Whether or not they did at the moment of publication, moreover, accounts
of printers' and booksellers' actions might still be drawn upon later by critics
and rivals to challenge the value of any particular book, for example by
alleging piracy. When they did succeed in remaining in the background—a
rarer achievement than we might suppose—it was likely to be the result of
hard and continuing work carried out "behind the scenes." A principal aim
of *The Nature of the Book* is to recover this work and display its importance.
While it mentions many instances in which publishing enterprises failed to
proceed smoothly, then, its intent is not just to attest to the frequency of
such failure. It instead substantiates Marc Bloch's dictum that "a good cataclysm suits our business." The historian, Bloch pointed out, often depends
on "calamities" for the preservation and revelation of information, and this

---

hensibilis." For these medievalists' perspectives on print—which deserve more attention than
they have received—see Clanchy, "Looking Back," and Rouse and Rouse, *Authentic Witnesses,* 449–66.

is no exception.[55] Problems and disputes were often the occasion for the creation of records documenting practices that remained unrecorded in cases of more successful publication. This volume is accordingly concerned to use such testimony to display the commonplace and unremarkable quite as much as the disastrous and spectacular; and especially to use the latter to reveal the former. The indispensable agency of printers and booksellers might remain unnoticed, for example, since the credit of their products depended on its being so. They themselves developed sophisticated ways of ensuring that they stayed just sufficiently in the background to avoid suspicion of either subterfuge or authorship. But in disputes the character of a bookseller or printer mattered. For readers attuned to its significance, anonymity itself might then become a source of suspicion.[56] Historians can put the resulting allegations to use as evidence. They need no longer be complicit in the cabal by their own silence.

The ways in which such agents thought of and represented themselves were therefore of central importance to the received credit of printed knowledge. The point is not a simple one. What it was for a printer or bookseller to act "properly" could be determined in any number of ways. The principles of such propriety were consequently liable to vary. Yet it is impossible to understand impropriety without at the same time comprehending these, the conventions of propriety that were allegedly being violated. The two came into being in tandem. Chapter 3 thus addresses the ways in which printers and booksellers themselves fought to create a trustworthy realm of printed knowledge by articulating such conventions. The civility they adopted was complex, but it was also highly consequential. On its central concept of "propriety" rested the authorship of every writer who aspired to profess knowledge in print. Its maxims, reconstructed below, were important not just because of their use in resolving individual cases of piracy or unlicensed printing, but because they became central to the trade's representation of itself as a respectable craft. How printing should properly be practiced, in what ways it should properly be regulated—in effect, what printing itself *was*—would all be defined by reference to them. The epistemic significance of piracy therefore extended, reflexively, to printing itself: the very nature of print remained unresolved throughout the early modern period, and piracy was central to its resolution. From the practical régime described in chapter 3 emerged print culture itself.

Chapters 4 and 5 trace how this happened. Chapter 4 tells the story of John Streater, a printer with a remarkably sophisticated republican philoso-

---

55. Bloch, *Historian's Craft*, 74–5.
56. For example, in his attacks on Ursus, Tycho Brahe was given to remarking upon his antagonist's book's having been published without a printer's name, as was customary for "notorious libels": Jardine, *Birth of History and Philosophy of Science*, 16.

phy. Streater's actions threatened to transform the nature of print and society simultaneously. His activities and interests ranged widely, from soldiering and arms dealing to natural magic and law reform. In particular, though, Streater tried to redefine the grounds of proper action for printers and book-sellers by doing *historical* work of an extraordinarily ambitious sort. He rewrote the history of printing in an attempt to reconfigure its governing political culture and thereby redefine its current and future identity. The initiative was then inherited from Streater himself by others who pursued cognate goals through the eighteenth century. Chapter 5 examines their ri-valries. It explains the new historical identities they forged for both print and its propriety.

In fact, the use of historiographical work to create new identities and proprieties is an idée fixe of this book. It has become well known that schol-arly figures attempted this kind of enterprise fairly frequently. So, however, did craftsmen and hacks. Joseph Moxon placed the press and the printer in a tradition of the mathematical sciences going back, through Tycho Brahe, to Vitruvius; chapter 2 describes his work. Streater and his ally, the em-bittered ex-Cavalier Richard Atkyns, told the history of printing as one of proto–industrial espionage. Sir Thomas Browne constructed a history of plagiarism, and Joseph Glanvill articulated a double-usurpation theory of ancient philosophy in order to criticize Aristotle and make room for the experimentalists of the Royal Society. These characters appear in chapter 7. Astronomer Royal John Flamsteed, the subject of chapter 8, went further still, and constructed three parallel histories: that of his own feud with New-ton; that of Tycho's with Ursus (of which he thought the former was a re-capitulation); and a full history of astronomy from biblical times to the pres-ent, designed to culminate in its own appearance at the head of Flamsteed's great *Historia Cœlestis Britannica.* Through these he tried to guide posterity to an understanding of his own proper identity. Each of these historio-graphical projects plays its part in the narrative that follows. I take such historical self-representation to be of central importance in constituting the identities agents felt themselves to possess, and hence in influencing their notions of proper action for their contemporaries too. The historiographical efforts recounted in chapter 5, in particular, led directly to the assumptions of reliability and credibility from which the print culture of the modern age arose. And the present work is of course no exception to this rule. The transformed history presented in *The Nature of the Book* is intended to en-courage new thinking about the character of print in our own age.

The sources of print culture are therefore to be sought in civility as much as in technology, and in historical labors as much as in immediate cause and effect. The "printing revolution," if there was one, consisted of changes in the conventions of handling and investing credit in textual materials, as much as in transformations in their manufacture. The point deserves to be stressed explicitly. I do not question that print enabled the stabilization of texts, to some extent; although fixity was far rarer and harder to discern in early modern Europe than most modern historians assume. I do, however, question the character of the link between the two. Printed texts were not intrinsically trustworthy. When they were in fact trusted, it was only as a result of hard work. Fixity was in the eye of the beholder, and its recognition could not be maintained without continuing effort. At no point could it be counted on to reside irremissibly in the object itself, and it was always liable to contradiction. Those faced with using the press to create and sustain knowledge thus found themselves confronting a culture characterized by nothing so much as indeterminacy. If printing held no necessary bond to truth, neither did it show a necessary bond to falsity or corruption. Each link remained vulnerable to dispute. It is this epistemic indeterminacy that lends the history of the book its powerful impact on cultural history. Understanding how it could be overcome to make knowledge and hence cultural change is what the history of the book is for.

There did exist strategies that could be adopted in order to secure as much credibility for printed objects as readers needed. Chapters 6 and 7 describe such strategies, as pursued by gentlemen and philosophers in a number of different settings. They argue that their pursuit was vital for the establishment of both new philosophies of nature and new practices of knowledge-making. A central tactic in most cases was that of attributing trust to a book on the basis of an evaluation of a person. Look closely at attributions of credit to printed materials, and, as already noted, there will generally be an attribution of credit to an individual involved. "It must be only by the Marks and Properties of an *Imposture,* that we can know an *Imposture* from that which is a real Truth, when attested unto us," counseled Humphrey Prideaux in a much-read analysis of the credibility of alleged scriptural writings. But in identifying such "marks" of imposture, attention should center on consideration of its maker and his conduct. If the producer seemed a wicked man, using "craft" and "fraud" to propagate a claim for his own interest, then that claim could justifiably be accounted a falsehood.[57] Prideaux's recommendation was conventional enough. Similar exhortations appeared in many works of his era. In action, these skills were therefore intriguingly recursive. Readers assigned credit to printed materials

---

57. Prideaux, *True Nature of Imposture*, "A Discourse for the Vindicating of Christianity from the Charge of Imposture," 6–8. For a fascinating and extremely suggestive treatment of early strategies of credit adopted in an effort to circumvent piracy, see Newman, "Word Made Print." For bible printing and reading see also Cole, "Dynamics of Printing," and Tribble, *Margins and Marginality*, 11–56.

on the grounds of knowledge about their makers, which was in turn assessed partly in terms of printed sources already accredited. In such ways might knowledge become more secure.

But this was only one of many possible strategies. From the printing house and bookshop, through the craft center of Stationers' Hall, to the learned sites of the Royal Society of London and the Royal Observatory at Greenwich, *The Nature of the Book* identifies the techniques developed in each location by which books could be appraised and accredited. The use of print for making knowledge depended on these local practices of printing, exchange, and reading. The bookshop and printing house were regularly identified as places of promise and achievement. But they were also centers of conflict, plotting, and betrayal, where the proprietor could exhibit a notable fluidity of social identity. In anachronistic terms, he or she—the book trades were remarkable for the participation of both men and women—merged the roles of socialite, friend, ally, entrepreneur, and even spy. His or her responsibility for the contents of a book seemed almost infinitely negotiable: however tactically unwise, outbursts such as those by Grassi and Scheiner against the bookseller were not intrinsically unreasonable. Hence the merging of trust in people with trust in things. Concerns over the effect of printing were readily expressed in terms of such practitioners. Bookshops represented points of attraction for potential Brunos and Patrizis, it was said, in part because those who ran them were so inclined. They were also frighteningly good at their work. To flirt with anachronism once more, besides being manufacturers of credit, seventeenth-century booksellers were the best sociologists of literature of their day.

The autonomy and creativity of Continental scholar-printers in these respects are well known. Eisenstein conjured an image of what she called "print-shops" as "'polyglot' households"—nodal points for the transfer of people, writings, and knowledge. The European "print-shop," she suggested, was where the "scholar" and the "craftsman" really met.[58] In some respects, and under certain circumstances, the smaller printing house or bookshop of London, Paris, or Rome could become a similar social site. Indeed, the household unit typically found here was perhaps rather more appropriate for such sociability than the relatively large operation of an Elzevir or a Plantin. But it also had to operate under more evident regulatory constraints. Eisenstein's view was that printers and booksellers were "natural" enemies to outside regulation of any kind. In fact, this was far from the case. In cities like London and Paris, the vast majority supported licensing

---

58. Eisenstein, *Printing Press*, 139, 399–400, 443–7, 520–2, 581–603, 653–4. Compare Zilsel, "Genesis of the Concept of Scientific Progress."

and similar régimes. They had good reason to do so. Those systems were deemed necessary to guarantee trust, order, and propriety in their craft.[59] Livelihoods therefore depended on them. A new understanding of these measures is needed. It must acknowledge their use to suppress texts of which the state disapproved—a use that was certainly real, but that included publications discreditable for reasons of piracy as well as of sedition or obscenity. But it must also appreciate the obverse of this function: the central role contemporaries ascribed to such systems in the maintenance of any trust at all in the realm of print. Printers were "mechanicks," as much in need of "licensing" as preachers (especially "mechanick" preachers) and medical practitioners (the analogue here being "empiricks"). For similar reasons, the book trades themselves participated in their own regulation.

Some went further still. They proposed ways to change the very nature of the printing enterprise and to transform the character of its practitioners.

59. Eisenstein, *Printing Press*, 442. It is also significant that early modern images of the press showed a greater diversity than recognized by Eisenstein. Eisenstein shows only the complimentary iconography of Prosper Marchand ("The press descending from the heavens"); we need also to remember the devils chasing each other through the printing house portrayed in Huss's *La Grante Danse Macabre*, and broadsheets mocking those who believed anything produced by the press. Something of this iconographic range is reproduced in chapter 5 below. For an example of the importance of Catholic censorship in astronomy, see Gingerich, "Censorship of Copernicus."

FIG. I.IO. Hevelius's "Civic Stellaeburg" in Danzig (now Gdansk). Hevelius's city building housed every device needed for an astronomer, from telescopes and lens-making equipment to a printing house. He sought to guarantee the credibility of his printed representations by doing all the corresponding activities, from observing to engraving, himself. His success was mixed. Still he needed imperial privileges to forbid other printers' "frauds"; and astronomers like John Flamsteed felt able to cast doubt on his accounts of these processes. Hevelius, *Machina Cœlestis*. (By permission of the Syndics of Cambridge University Library.)

There were ambitious attempts to establish a non-"mechanical" printing house for learned work, for example. In England the most notable such effort was Archbishop William Laud's at Oxford. Inherited by John Fell at the Restoration, Laud's initiative was eventually secured as Oxford University Press.[60] The appointment of quasi-genteel "patentees" was, as chapters 3 and 4 show, an even more ambitious strategy to change the very nature of printing so as to eliminate problems of discredit. Patentees were wealthy printers or booksellers—or even gentlemen from outside the trade altogether—to whom the crown granted exclusive rights to key titles, or indeed to whole classes of publication. One patentee held the right to all law books, for example; another held that to all bibles. It was reckoned that they and their books would be securely trustworthy by virtue of their gentility and their dependence on royal favor. In the eyes of some, they could become a model for a future realm of print guaranteed by a decreed civility. Perhaps an urban equivalent to Tycho's civil press—or at least, to Hevelius's at Stellaeburg—could be constructed (fig. 1.10).

60. Ward, *Oxford University Statutes*, I, 205–6, declaring that an *architypographus* must be appointed so that "sordid and vulgar artizans may not pervert the indulgence of that most clement prince [Charles I] to their own private lucre . . . experience has shown [that] these mechanical artizans . . . pay the least possible attention to calligraphy, or the beauty or elegance of the work, but thrust into publication any works, however rude and incorrect."

To the early modern world, then, the character of the printing house and the civil order in which printed books could be accorded trust were interdependent. Bookshops too were places encouraging novel interactions, as indeed were institutions such as the Royal Society. Throughout this book close attention is therefore accorded to the details of such locations. Readers will be led down the darkest alleys of London, and guided through homes and workplaces to reveal their characters with an intimacy few early modern gentlemen can have shared. But here, it may be thought, crouches a paradox. Does the importance of print not lie precisely in its ability to transcend such local contexts and enable communication across wide distances? Surely such a close focus on individual locations risks obscuring this, the most consequential issue of all. It is a real question, with implications beyond the understanding of print alone. The next section addresses this apparent paradox, and from a correspondingly broad perspective. For a central theme of *The Nature of the Book* is to see this power to transcend place as something itself in need of explanation.

PLACE, PRACTICE, AND KNOWLEDGE

> Books are a load of crap.
> PHILIP LARKIN, "A Study of Reading Habits," *Collected Poems*, 131

The Nature of the Book concentrates for the most part on one country, England, and in particular on its capital city, London.[61] The focus is by no means exclusive, and in fact discussion does extend across Europe as appropriate. Nevertheless, the question must arise: why? The choice may appear arbitrary. More to the point, it may seem perverse to address questions of the identity and consequences of print by examining *any* one location, when the very essence of print, supposedly, is that it enables human beings to transcend their immediate circumstances and communicate reliably with others in different times and places. These are important questions. One plausible answer to the first derives from the extensive attention that historians have directed at the emergence of polite commerce in Augustan England.[62] As part of this, England became one of the earliest nations to de-

61. Strictly speaking, from the early eighteenth century Britain succeeded England as the political entity in question. Since my discussion covers a long period before union, and in any case concentrates on the region around London, I have generally referred to England here. The issue of national identity was a charged one, however, as has been brought to the fore in such recent studies as Colley, *Britons*; Russell, *Fall of the British Monarchies*; and Morrill, *Nature of the English Revolution*, 91–117.

62. The most recent and comprehensive survey is the massive three-volume series formed by Brewer and Porter, *Consumption and the World of Goods*; Bermingham and Brewer, *Consumption of Culture*; and Brewer and Staves, *Early Modern Conceptions of Property*.

velop a sophisticated commercial culture of printing and publishing, and its concepts of authorship, liberty of the press, and intellectual property have been of influence across the world. It warrants attention for that reason alone. But a further justification may also be advanced—one that addresses the more fundamental question of why it is appropriate to focus on any one location at all.

This book concentrates on the implications of printing for knowledge, and for knowledge of nature in particular, for reasons already outlined. It does so at what was undeniably a time of extraordinary creativity in the history of science. Early modern England witnessed not only the invention of experimental philosophy and the advent of the Royal Society, but the achievements of such figures as Francis Bacon, William Harvey, Robert Boyle, and Isaac Newton. *The Nature of the Book* aspires to address some of our founding assumptions about how such successes were attained. To do so, it concurs with much current work in the history of science in relating knowledge to its particular social and cultural settings. The universality of science, such work suggests, is an achievement realized only through much hard work. That work is necessarily specific to its particular sites, be they medieval universities, Renaissance courts, or Victorian laboratories.[63] Such are the places that have harbored the kind of skilled practices through which knowledge has been created and sustained. From this perspective, museums, laboratories, and royal palaces are seen as not just architectural structures, but distinct social spaces generating different practices fertile of new knowledge.[64] The knowledge fashioned in such places answers the needs of the moment, addresses the questions of the time, and satisfies the standards of the local culture.

For the historian, print and science share a rather intimidating characteristic. Both appear to transcend place. Scientific knowledge, it has been asserted, is by its very nature true wherever one may find oneself. That is what constitutes its claim to objectivity.[65] Print seems blessed by a similar

---

63. See especially: Shapin, "House of Experiment"; Biagioli, *Galileo, Courtier*; Hannaway, "Laboratory Design"; Westman, "Astronomer's Role"; Ophir, Shapin, and Schaffer, *Place of Knowledge*; Outram, "New Spaces in Natural History"; Moran, *Alchemical World of the German Court*; Smith and Agar, *Making Space for Science*. For the importance of localization in the history of the "scientific revolution," see also Porter and Teich, *Scientific Revolution in National Context*, and Schuster, "Scientific Revolution," 223–4. Jardine's *Scenes of Inquiry* lucidly explains the philosophical issues at stake.

64. De Certeau, *Practice of Everyday Life*, 117. Elias's treatment of the royal court, for instance, illustrates how it merged family and government in a coherent figuration: Elias, *Court Society*, 1, 41–65; Foucault, "Space, Knowledge, and Power."

65. Ophir and Shapin, "Place of Knowledge," 3–4; Porter, *Trust in Numbers*, 217–9 (which notes the widely cited certificate of science's universality, that "the same textbooks can be used all over the world"); Johns, "Ideal of Scientific Collaboration."

transcendence: in many historians' hands, it appears to hint at something floating apart from specific, compromised, adulterated actuality. Just as appreciations of science have too often eschewed attention to the detailed intricacy of knowledge in the making, so cultural historians' appreciation of print has too frequently stopped short at the doors of the printing house.[66] But if the universal character of science can be appraised as an achievement, warranted and maintained by situated labors, may the same not be true of print? The suggestion is at the core of this book's approach. Searching for print culture in the making, we actually zero in not just on London, but on particular streets, buildings, floors, and rooms. We shall try to recover the identities, representations, and practices of the people who lived and worked in those rooms. And we shall see how hard they worked to create the realm of print, in a complex and unforgiving web of such domains. The close attention paid by *The Nature of the Book* to the intricate details of individuals' practices, characters, and motivations, far from being peripheral, is thus essential. Such a focus must be adopted in order to show how print, like scientific truth, attains the level of universality—by the hard, continuous work of real people in real places.

This makes the conjunction of the history of print with that of science especially intriguing. The juxtaposition becomes only more curious when one recalls the enormous—perhaps even defining—role that historians have almost unconsciously ascribed to print in the history of science. That history is routinely represented in terms of a chronological skeleton, the joints of which are dates such as 1543, 1632, 1687, 1789, 1859, and 1905.[67] These years are etched in the memory of every historian of science with a permanence no others can match. They seem ineluctable. Novel historiographical approaches leave them unscathed. And all, of course, are publication dates, ranging from Copernicus's *De Revolutionibus* (and Vesalius's *De Humani Corporis Fabrica*) to Einstein's revolutionary paper introducing special relativity. To that extent, the history of print and that of science are tacitly acknowledged to coincide. Yet, strangely, recent historiography has implicitly directed attention away from the conjunction. The reason for this apparent paradox is subtle, and even rather profound.

There is a sense in which the history of early modern science no longer exists. Historians now employ all the resources of cultural and social histo-

66. This could not be said of bibliographers, but then these have often been too modest in their historiographical objectives. Historians of the book such as Henri-Jean Martin are a more consequential exception, for which see above, pp. 28–30.

67. The dates of Copernicus's *De Revolutionibus*, Galileo's *Dialogo*, Newton's *Principia*, Lavoisier's *Traité Élémentaire de Chimie*, Darwin's *Origin of Species*, and Einstein's "Zur Elektrodynamik bewegter Körper" respectively.

riography in an attempt to explain why people made certain claims in certain circumstances, and why they were or were not believed; whether or not such claims are, to modern eyes, "scientific" has ceased to seem so important. Indeed, although the early modern world recognized something it called "science" (or, more likely, the Latin *scientia*)—namely, the kind of demonstrative knowledge produced by geometers or infallible logicians—it did not acknowledge anything like the modern enterprise. And it certainly did not harbor any scient*ists*.[68] The consequences of accepting this prove substantial. The extent of acceptable topics has widened enormously. Movements previously assumed peripheral—Jesuit philosophy, for example, or, perhaps most spectacularly, hermeticism—have been reassessed as powerful and authoritative in their particular settings. More canonical subjects have also been transformed. Experimental philosophy and Newtonianism, in particular, are no longer seen as gaining straightforward victories over self-evidently inferior opposition. On the contrary, they are seen as struggling for credibility in a cultural bazaar filled with more different candidates for natural knowledge than had ever existed before, offering greater potential rewards. Their proponents' strategies must accordingly be understood as developing in response to these formidable and effective opponents. As they did so, they themselves diverged; it is difficult now to identify any one thing to call "Newtonianism." An appreciation of the viability of alternatives has thus had enriching implications for our understanding of the canonical successes of the "scientific revolution" too.[69]

But this appreciation of a far wider range of places and practices has also had its costs. If natural knowledge was such a localized thing, then the processes by which it came to be transferred from place to place become rather mysterious. Talk of diffusion or dissemination will not now pass muster. The evocation of an all-powerful central source from which influence spreads across an inert terrain is no longer tenable, because sites of reception previously supposed passive are now recognized to have been vital, dynamic, and appropriative. Notions of "popularization" become equally problematic, since they too generally posit audiences as passive receptacles of influence rather than positive agents of appropriation.[70] With respect to

68. For the origins of the latter term see [Whewell], review of Sommerville's *On the Connexion of the Physical Sciences*, 58–60, and Ross, "*Scientist*," 71–5.

69. Dear, "Jesuit Mathematical Science"; Henry and Hutton, *New Perspectives*; Hannaway, *Chemists and the Word*; Webster, *From Paracelsus to Newton*; Schaffer, "Newtonianism." For other rehabilitations see Feingold, *Mathematician's Apprenticeship*; Gascoigne, "Universities and the Scientific Revolution"; Gascoigne, "Reappraisal of the Role of the Universities"; Feldhay, "Knowledge and Salvation"; Feldhay and Elkana, *After Merton*.

70. An excellent alternative is presented by Secord, "Science in the Pub." See also Latour, *Science in Action*, 132–44.

knowledge based in experiments the problem is especially evident. The transfer of this particular species of practical, performative knowledge to different sites could never be straightforward, if only because the replication of the localized skills in which such knowledge was based proved riddled with difficulties. Early modern experimentalists knew this all too well; it has only recently been rediscovered by historians. But what was most flagrantly true for experimental knowledge was also true, if less obviously, for other claims to epistemic authority.

Here lies another reason to focus on England. In London, the Royal Society (chartered in 1662) pioneered solutions to these intractable problems. In part it did so by aggressive intervention in the realm of print. A long-term consequence was a transformation in both print and natural knowledge. Indeed, one of the most interesting and unusual aspects of Restoration experimental philosophy was that it explicitly confronted this situation. Robert Boyle and his colleagues at the Society recognized it remarkably early, and advanced notably cogent solutions. One aspect of their responses is well known, and has been extensively analyzed of late. For all its difficulty of achievement, experimental philosophers appealed to replicability as testament to the truth of the knowledge they professed. In one sense, that very difficulty was an asset: it helped make successful repetition in different cultural settings a robust criterion of truth. The result was a claim about replication that has become central to the authority of modern science. But the character of the obstacle to replication also deserves note. As has become well known, successful repetition of an experiment elsewhere often required the transfer of more than just written or printed materials alone. Extensive social contact between practitioners was needed in order to reproduce cultural skills and settings in a new site. A skilled practitioner might even have to travel in person between the two locations in order for the attempted replication to succeed—or, for that matter, for it definitively to fail. It thus seems that nobody in 1660s Europe built an air-pump successfully by relying solely on Boyle's textual description of the engine. Some, we know, tried; all, we think, failed.[71]

A key assertion of the sociology of knowledge has been that this is true not just in practice, but in something approaching principle. Experimental knowledge of the kind sought by Restoration natural philosophers must necessarily be founded in skills, the character and application of which can never be stipulated exhaustively by written rules. Replication requires the re-creation of a performative and interpretative culture in which candidate attempts can be conducted. Building new air-pumps could indeed be done

71. Shapin and Schaffer, *Leviathan and the Air-Pump*, 229–30, 235.

from recipe-like textual instructions, but only if interpreted in a shared recipe-reading culture. That is one reason why such knowledge seems to be inescapably social: it depends on the face-to-face interactions that help constitute such a culture.[72] It is also why some historians of science have directed their attention away from what they think of as "texts." These are not, they suppose, the prime building blocks of either society or knowledge.

Yet there must be more to say about the importance for the construction of natural knowledge of the construction of print. Early modern natural philosophers did make and use a variety of written, printed, and engraved objects. They labored over books, periodicals, letters, "schemes," and any number of similar textual and pictorial materials. They expended very large amounts of time and money doing so—larger, as chapter 7 will show, even than those expended on experimental instruments like the air-pump. Even the most basic historicist sensibility is likely to rebel at the thought that all this activity was intrinsically futile. In fact, it is possible to argue that it was central to enterprises dedicated to making knowledge—even experimental ones.

Several historians have already noted that experiments often did not, in fact, need to be replicated at all. Rhetoric helped.[73] Boyle and his interlocutors developed sophisticated and prolix ways of writing reports of their experimental trials. By stating explicitly every circumstance of the experimental scene, a report sufficiently crammed with detail could aspire to persuade distant readers that they had as good as been there themselves. In that event, they effectively became "virtual witnesses" to the experiment itself. Such virtual witnessing could thereby render the actual practice of replication largely otiose. The skills of an experimenter may indeed have demanded complex cultural modes of transfer and appropriation, then, in which texts were not omnipotent (fig. 1.11). But if "texts" were ineffective for transmitting manual skills, more tangible objects could be put to use to mediate the creation of consensus by means of recruiting readers. Books, periodicals, papers, letters, maps, graphs, and diagrams did move back and forth between sites, proving extremely useful tools for the making and maintenance of knowledge. Rhetoric, however persuasive, came into being and achieved its effects only when incarnated in such objects. Historians of science need

72. Collins, *Changing Order*, 55–7, 70–73, 77; Gooding, Pinch, and Schaffer, *Uses of Experiment*, 10–13; Lynch, *Scientific Practice and Ordinary Action*, 211–4. Compare Lawrence, "Incommunicable Knowledge," for tacit knowledge in the history of medicine. Eamon, *Science and the Secrets of Nature*, is the most recent work to concentrate on recipe-like texts: see esp. 130–33.

73. Dear, "*Totius in Verba*"; Dear, *Literary Structure*; Gross, "Rhetorical Invention"; Bazerman, *Shaping Written Knowledge*; Moss, *Novelties*. For "virtual witnessing," see Shapin, "Pump and Circumstance," and Shapin and Schaffer, *Leviathan and the Air-Pump*, 22–79.

FIG. 1.11. Reading skills juxtaposed with experimental dexterity. David Ryckaert III, *The Alchemist* (1648). (By permission of the Syndics of Cambridge University Library.)

to begin considering in detail their processes of manufacture, distribution, and use.[74]

Use in particular is important here. It raises rather a subtle issue, hinted at in general above but now requiring explicit attention. Almost all historians put themselves in the place of early modern readers and assume that their own act of reading replicates that of their historical counterparts. But this substitution may not be entirely innocuous.[75] A rather different approach is suggested if one identifies reading itself as a skill, just as historically specific as the more obvious dexterity involved in experimentation. If reading has a history, then assuming that modern readers' responses to a printed page accurately reproduce those of seventeenth-century men and women becomes problematic. Attendance to the conventions constraining the appropriation of printed objects in particular historical settings seems much more pertinent. Agreement across cultural spaces arose out of the exercise of such reading skills. Rhetoric, however expert, depended on them. The ques-

74. There are exceptions. Golinski, *Science as Public Culture*, and Stewart, *Rise of Public Science*, largely escape this charge by paying close attention to contexts of use.
75. Chartier, *Pratiques de la Lecture*, 7; Chartier, *Cultural History*, 40.

tions addressed in *The Nature of the Book* are of a correspondingly specific order: of how an experimental paper was actually composed by *this* writer, made by *these* workmen, distributed by *these* merchants and diplomats, and discussed in *these* ways, by *these* people, *here,* in *these* circumstances, with *these* results. This very minuteness of focus enables it to trace a grand process: the elaboration of a print culture and a culture of natural knowledge in tandem.[76]

Chapter 6 pursues this specificity to its most intimate level. It examines how early modern people represented reading itself, in terms of their very minds and bodies.[77] Directing attention to the human frame, it asks how readers sought to understand their experiences in terms of its "passions." The implications of their quest extended very widely indeed: from the fortunes of Protestantism to the transmutation of metals, and from the education of gentlemen to the development of women's authorship. It also impinged directly upon their responses to Creation. Investigating the "book of nature" was thus a profoundly reflexive process: early modern people arrived at natural knowledge through reading, a skill that they in turn understood in terms of the natural knowledge so gained.[78]

Recognition of the ineffable character of skill thus need not imply that print is a peripheral subject for the historian of science. On the contrary, in the future we shall need to marry the two. The history of reading suggests one way to do so. The salience of printed books and papers cannot now simply be exorcised by alleging the inability of texts to determine their readers' conclusions; that they were unable to force concurrence does not

76. Gingerich and Westman are among the few historians of Renaissance science to have consistently attended to the entire history of books, from writing to reading: e.g., Gingerich, "Copernicus's *De Revolutionibus*"; Gingerich, "Censorship of Copernicus"; Westman, "Proof, Poetics, and Patronage"; Westman, "Reception of Galileo's *Dialogue*"; Gingerich and Westman, *Wittich Connection.* William Eamon, although his work centers on books, does not generally venture into such details: see especially his *Science and the Secrets of Nature,* and also his "Books of Secrets"; "Arcana Disclosed"; "From the Secrets of Nature to Public Knowledge"; "Court, Academy and Printing House." Rostenberg's *Library of Robert Hooke* is another recent exception to the rule, but one riddled with errors.

77. See also Johns, "Physiology of Reading in Restoration England" and "Physiology of Reading and the Anatomy of Enthusiasm."

78. Shapin, *Social History of Truth,* xviii–xix. For the image of the Book of Nature, see Eisenstein, *Printing Revolution,* 455–6, 471–8; Brooke, *Science and Religion,* 75–81; Blumenberg, *Lesbarkeit der Welt*; Findlen, *Possessing Nature,* 55–63 (much the most interesting recent set of remarks on the subject in English); Dingley, *Vox Cœli,* sigs. [A5^r]–[A6^r]. For shifts in the modern significance of the metaphor, see also Traweek, *Beamtimes and Lifetimes,* 160–1. Nehemiah Grew referred to John Wilkins holding the Bible in one hand and Grew's own book—some pages from the book of nature—in the other, as a commentary on the first, "by which, in part God reads the World his own Definition, and their Duty to him": Grew, *Anatomy of Vegetables Begun,* sigs. A4^r–[A7^r].

mean that such objects were not interpreted at all. The reading of a book is no less skillful, and no less local, than the conducting of an experiment.[79] To understand the transformation of science into an apparently universal culture, then, we need to create a history of the reading practices surrounding scientific books as detailed and intricate as the appreciation we already have of the experimental practices surrounding scientific instruments. *The Nature of the Book* marks the beginning of that enterprise.

NATURAL KNOWLEDGE IN ENGLAND: WISDOM IN THE CONCOURSE

> Wisdom crieth without; she uttereth her voice in the streets: She crieth in the chief place of concourse, in the openings of the gates: in the city she uttereth her words, saying, How long, ye simple ones, will ye love simplicity? and the scorners delight in their scorning, and fools hate knowledge? Turn you at my reproof . . . But ye have set at nought all my counsel, and would none of my reproof: I also will laugh at your calamity . . . For the turning away of the simple shall slay them, and the prosperity of fools shall destroy them.
>
> PROVERBS I : 20 – 32

Translating the experiences of Galileo and Tycho into the rather different situation of late Renaissance England is not a straightforward task. The courts of Elizabeth, James I, and Charles I never attained the culture of absolutism surrounding those of Rudolf or Cosimo—much though they may have tried—and there was no official court philosopher here.[80] Yet in some ways English natural philosophy disputes were modeled on such Continental forms. Books and manuscripts played just as central a role in English courtly life, and percipient historians have noted the extent to which those presented at court might be assumed to bear the patron's authorship.[81] Nor did this courtly role end with the Civil War. As we shall see in chapter 8, as late as 1712 not one of the four hundred copies printed of John Flamsteed's

79. See especially Chartier, "Culture as Appropriation"; Chartier, *Pratiques de la Lecture*; Chartier, *Lectures et Lecteurs*; Chartier, "Texts, Printings, Readings"; Chartier, *Passions of the Renaissance*, 1–11, 110–59, 326–61, 362–95; Martin, "Pour une Histoire de la Lecture"; de Certeau, *Practice of Everyday Life*, 165–76; Cressy, *Literacy and the Social Order*, 1–18; Darnton, "History of Reading."

80. The nearest equivalent was John Dee, as attested in the possibly sarcastic remarks of real courtiers: Sherman, *John Dee*, 7–8; Roberts and Watson, *John Dee's Library Catalogue*. See also above, note 36. Compare Harriot, who made similar observations to Galileo's but was unable to make them count: Jacquot, "Thomas Harriot's Reputation"; Henry, "Thomas Harriot and Atomism"; Cormack, "Twisting the Lion's Tail."

81. Goldberg, *James I and the Politics of Literature*, e.g., 1–9. James I had visited Uraniborg itself: Thoren, *Lord of Uraniborg*, 334–5; Brahe, *Opera*, II, 11–12.

Historia Cœlestis—the greatest work of observational astronomy then in existence—seems actually to have been sold, but volumes were distributed through diplomatic channels across Europe and as far as Muscovy. Flamsteed, like Tycho in Prague, held the title of royal astronomer, and chapter 8 will show the extent to which he modeled every aspect of his conduct on Tycho's. But the difference between English and imperial natural knowledge may be measured by his failure. Although his observatory on Greenwich Hill more than matched his predecessor's Uraniborg for the accuracy of its instruments, Flamsteed had no private printing house. For him, the consequences were to prove calamitous.

In England, there was no noble Tycho Brahe able to boast his own autonomous printing operation. There was no way in which the production of learned books could be taken out of commercial hands. Philosophers could not hope to emulate Tycho's success—partial and compromised though even that success was—because they had to live and work in an environment of city and court in juxtaposition. They had to reconcile civility with commerce. They had to utter their wisdom in the streets of London, where its reception would be far from secure. The first thing to appreciate about the articulation and reception of natural knowledge in early modern England is its insecurity. The achievements of the Royal Society were consequently but one element in a continuing history of attempts to discipline print and render it a sound platform for building a godly nation. That history included the development of vital and lasting new concepts of authorship, publication, and reading.

A series of proposals for the reform of knowledge and its circulation grappled with this situation. Most influential were the ambitious schemes put forward by James I's lord chancellor, Sir Francis Bacon. Bacon's identification of a trinity of transforming inventions—compass, gunpowder, and press—is, of course, famous. It is often assumed from this proclamation that Bacon recommended the open printing and publication of knowledge to aid in its advancement. Yet this is a misapprehension. Bacon in fact represented the printing press as a prime example of how inventions should *not* be sought. He believed that there was "nothing in the art of printing which is not plain and obvious." Speaking to Queen Elizabeth through the personified figure of Natural Philosophy, he called the press "a gross invention," which had been not so much invented as "stumbled upon and lighted on by chaunce."[82] And he certainly did not recommend unrestricted publication of knowledge, urging rather its retention within a tiny community of

---

82. Martin, "'Knowledge Is Power,'" 97–103; Martin, *Francis Bacon*, 64–8; Bacon, *Works*, IV, 100, 113–5. However, in the *New Atlantis* the (anonymous) inventor of printing did merit a statue in the gallery of inventors: ibid., III, 165–6.

royal licentiates. Both opinions derived from his view of the purpose and organization of knowledge. Bacon aimed to make natural philosophy a sector of the state. Regarding himself primarily as a statesman and royal counselor, he wished to establish an administrative mechanism for generating natural knowledge that would best serve the advancement of the crown. The best natural philosopher, in this vision, would be the best state official. His greatest targets in proposing this scheme were thus what he called "voluntaries": individuals who claimed a right to profess knowledge independent of the state's bureaucracy.[83] In order to eradicate such dangerous knowledge-peddlers, it would be necessary to "purge the floors of men's understandings," and to replace their independent notions with rigid, unified rules of operation. "The business," he decreed, "must be done as if by machinery." The press was the exception that proved this rather daunting rule. It was a device discovered by chance, and by disorganized artisans. Yet it had prospered, and the commonwealth had profited by its success.

Or had it? True, there were many new books to be read; but this did not mean that they conveyed any more genuine knowledge. Bacon urged that his bureaucracy create new editions of classic authors, "with more correct impressions, more faithful translations, more profitable glosses, more diligent annotations," the implication being that the creations of the press were at present profoundly *un*satisfactory. Besides, open printing encouraged dangerous ambitions. Bacon therefore insisted that his own proposals be known only to "some fit and selected minds," and that the knowledge produced by his state machinery be similarly guarded. In the *New Atlantis,* his grand vision of a political state founded on natural knowledge, the personnel of Solomon's House were required to take an oath of secrecy. Only three selected individuals were allowed to be "Interpreters of Nature." The governors would authorize only approved conclusions to be made public on their periodic "circuits." And the deep knowledge on which their useful promulgations were based would never be revealed at all.[84]

A problem of authorship thus coincided with that of knowledge. In Bacon's era, ambitious treatises of natural knowledge were being written by an unprecedented multiplicity of writers: not only royal counselors, but lawyers (like Bacon himself, and later Sir Matthew Hale), mathematical practitioners (like Robert Recorde, Sir Henry Billingsley, Robert Norman, and Thomas Digges), university scholars (like Nathaniel Carpenter and John Wallis), churchmen (like John Wilkins and Seth Ward), and physicians (like William Harvey, William Gilbert, and Robert Fludd). Soon women like Margaret Cavendish would be added to their number. What was their claim

---

83. Martin, *Francis Bacon,* 56–63, 121–6, 150, 163, 173.

84. Bacon, *Works,* III, 165–6, 323–5; Martin, *Francis Bacon,* 149–51, 163–4. Contrast the portrayal in Elsky, *Authorizing Words,* 200–4.

to legitimacy in so acting? How were their arguments properly to be resolved? Ironically, all claimed to offer unity and an end to the discord inspired by the very proliferation of voluntaries in which they themselves participated. Even natural magicians, conventionally identified as the worst of voluntaries, tried to establish their credentials as bringers of order by waxing indignant at the "cavilling, brabling" and seditious scholastics.[85] Whether expressed as ridicule or hostility, opposition to illegitimate authorship became a pervasive feature of English writing on the natural world.

Bacon's was a forthright statement of one ideal for the determination of disputes in natural knowledge. It effectively envisaged an English social equivalent of Uraniborg. All practitioners must be licensed by court officers, resolution of arguments must be centralized and decisive, word of the debates must be restricted to the central legislators, and there must be no publication to the populace without central approval. Printing, dispersal, and reading of books were to be monitored by a privileged élite according to its civil conventions. For a Jacobean counselor it was a tempting prospect. And it would be repeated in various forms by successive systematizers later in the century. Gabriel Plattes's proposed state "Laboratory," for example, would admit only someone prepared to stay inside "till he be brought forth to go to the Church to be buried." Even this seemed mild compared to Macaria, where anyone dispersing unlicensed opinion would, quite simply, be executed.[86]

But although Tychonic isolation was tempting, it was not achievable. Courtly aspirations notwithstanding, in England there would always be other printers, booksellers, writers, and readers at work. The fact was that book dispersal did not operate entirely through diplomatic and courtly channels. There was a national and international book trade, and before long even books directed at restricted audiences—including, as already observed, both Tycho's and Galileo's—participated in it. Courts were continuously being reminded of the unpredictability (and worse) that could result, and again England's was no exception. If the propriety of disputes was that of the court—or, for that matter, the university—then the very involvement of the book trade introduced an important new element. It was not necessarily disastrous; Galileo, after all, embraced this realm for a while with

85. For a particularly insistent example see Fludd, *Mosaicall Philosophy*. Fludd raised the denial of controversy into an ontological principle, insisting that all apparent contrariety in the natural world must be referred to the undivided action of God; the quarrels of scholastics, he thought, corresponded to their idolatrous respect for natural oppositions such as antipathies.

86. Plattes, "Caveat for Alchymists," 87; [Plattes], *Description of the famous Kingdome of Macaria*, sig. B2ʳ (contrast the misleading impression given in Eisenstein, *Printing Press*, 305, which is often repeated by historians). Winstanley made preaching for hire one of the few capital offenses in an ideal society: Hill, *Turbulent, Seditious and Factious People*, 338.

creativity and skill. But it was definitely threatening. Printing and bookselling were concentrated almost exclusively in the vast social morass of London, a city represented by most courtiers and scholars as incipiently rebellious and fascinatingly venal. As would-be authors complained, Wisdom might find as heedless an audience in these streets as in those of Old Testament times.[87] Philosophers would be forced to see the problem with particularly stark clarity.

We cannot say how Galileo would have fared had he been an Englishman. The nearest equivalent to his struggles in Rome and Florence, however, was a controversy over Copernicanism and related issues that occurred in 1634–46 between Alexander Ross and John Wilkins. Wilkins indeed took the *Sidereus Nuncius* as his model, reproducing one of its images of the Moon.[88] But the differences between the two cases are as revealing as the similarities. There was scant trace in this dispute of Tycho's sterilized way of printing and distributing texts, and of Galileo's recourse to court conventions. Wilkins's initial tract was anonymous, and was displayed in the shop of the most incendiary Puritan bookseller in London, Michael Sparke, who had earlier introduced Tycho himself to the London public in the guise of a Protestant millenarian prophet (fig. 1.12).[89] Sparke's was the most prominent name on the title page. His notoriety, like that of Galileo's bookseller in Rome, fueled the conflict. Ross did attempt to use the issue for preferment in the church, but with minimal success. He ended up a bookseller's hack, churning out pedantic diatribes against every original thinker of the time. Neither writer managed to gain an audience at court, if that was their aim. In a sense, neither achieved authorship at all.

The *aspiration* to authorship, however, stood at the center of the Wilkins-Ross dispute, just as it had of Bacon's concerns. It was expressed as a mutual repudiation of the illegitimate "singularity" displayed by those who boasted, not reasoned knowledge, but passionate "fancy." Reconciling aspiration with credit was clearly difficult. To assert originality while avoiding the taint of singularity became a central problem for writers in all fields.

87. Abiezer Coppe, for one, put himself in the place of Wisdom: Mack, *Visionary Women*, 105. For later uses of the text, see Vincent, *Literacy and Popular Culture*, 174–5.

88. [Wilkins], *Discovery*; [Wilkins], *Discourse*; Ross, *Commentum de Terrae Motu*; Ross, *New Planet no Planet*. The standard treatment remains McColley, "Ross-Wilkins Controversy," but see also Johns, "Prudence and Pedantry." Ross seems to have been an early example of the professional author, paid by booksellers like Richard Royston to produce tracts for popular sale. See Glenn, *Critical Edition of Alexander Ross's 1647 "Mystagogus Poeticus,"* 625. His role should be compared to that of the Dominican Tommaso Caccini in Galileo's struggles: Finocchiaro, *Galileo Affair*, 28–9, 136–41, 282; Blackwell, *Galileo, Bellarmine*, 112–6.

89. Brahe, *Learned Tico Brahae his Astronomicall Conjectur.*

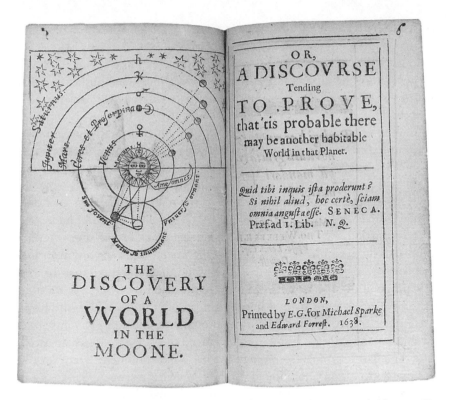

THE
DISCOVERY
OF A
WORLD
IN THE
MOONE.

OR,
A DISCOVRSE
Tending
TO .PROVE,
that 'tis probable there
may be another habitable
World in that Planet.

*Quid tibi inquis ista proderunt ?
Si nihil aliud, hoc certè, sciam
omnia angusta esse.* SENECA.
Præf. ad 1. Lib. N. 2.

LONDON,
Printed by *E.G.* for *Michael Sparke*
and *Edward Forrest*. 1638.

FIG. 1.12. [Wilkins], *The Discovery of a World in the Moone*. Frontispiece and title page. (By permission of the Syndics of Cambridge University Library.)

Some simply listened to the advice of their peers, and kept silent. Others relied on a flourishing and successful manuscript distribution system to evade the charge.[90] Still others, like Wilkins himself, chose to insist upon a "Philosophical Liberty" to suggest (but not to insist upon) ideas at variance with those espoused by received authorities. Geographer Nathaniel Carpenter actually funded his own printing and publication.[91] Wilkins took a further step, and ingeniously appropriated the conventions of modesty to avoid the charge of singularity. A writer must display hesitancy and probability, not a stentorian insistence on the certainty of his ideas, in order to reconcile credit with authorship. Doing so, one could avoid the trap of "boldness" into which singular authors invariably fell. Modesty could hold the commonweal together. Wilkins thus argued that Ross's "singularity" encapsulated at once his "conceit" for his own ideas, his "servile and superstitious" attitude to authority, and his slavery to "sense" rather than "discourse and

90. Love, *Scribal Publication*; Woudhuysen, *Sir Philip Sidney and the Circulation of Manuscripts*, 27–203, 224–41.

91. Davis, "Religion and the Struggle for Freedom," 514–5; Shapiro, *John Wilkins*, 55; Feingold, "Mathematical Sciences," 388–400.

reason." Wilkins's opponent was the archetypal "captious" man.[92] In contrast, Wilkins himself had begun to articulate principles of authorship that historians of science will recognize as characteristic of early experimental philosophy.

Wilkins's espousal of modesty and a liberty of philosophizing immediately reminds the modern reader of Boyle. But a significant difference exists. Wilkins's argument extended to questions normally the preserve of the mathematical sciences, not just natural philosophy and natural history. This division—between disciplines devoted to the mathematical representation of phenomena and those characterized by their collection and philosophical investigation—was ancient and persevering. Wilkins was one of several important figures to advocate a novel realignment. But such a transformation was as yet far from complete. One should therefore recall that the specific program of experimental philosophy proposed by Boyle was far from the only candidate for natural knowledge on offer. Even within the Royal Society itself, there were noteworthy alternatives, including various plans for natural and artificial histories, and indeed the "Physico-Mathematicall-Experimentall Learning" recommended by Wilkins himself. Isaac Newton was one contributor who pointed up the differences between Wilkins's and Boyle's conventions.[93] All, however, from mathematicians to alchemists and from experimentalists to physico-mathematicians, found themselves facing the problems of authorship and reception cast up by contemporary printing. The Royal Society helped all to address those problems, and it did so partly under the aegis of Boylean principles. It is in this context, then, and not just in that of Boylean experimental philosophy itself, that the Society's experiences of print proved consequential. It is not just that the virtuosi—as the Society's fellows were widely known—pioneered ways of dealing with print; those ways became central to the fortunes of natural knowledge of diverse traditions.

The Society's own success has always been signaled by its publishing enterprises—which included the first "scientific" periodical, the *Philosophical Transactions,* and Isaac Newton's masterpiece, the *Philosophiae Naturalis Principia Mathematica.* But an account of the role of the book and other printed materials in the Society should end with these, not begin with them. One must first reconstruct the efforts to enact conventions of reading within

92. [Wilkins], *Discovery*, 3; Wilkins, *Discourse*, 136–8, 144, 146–8, 226; Wilkins, *Of the Principles and Duties of Natural Religion*, 138–9, 203–4; Shapiro, *John Wilkins*, 239. Gassendi and Boulliaud also found Ross unimpressive: Mersenne, *Correspondance*, IV, 324–6, 348.

93. Kuhn, "Mathematical versus Experimental Traditions," 35–52; Dear, *Discipline and Experience*, 2–3, 8–9, 227–43, 245–9; Westman, "Astronomer's Role," 116–33; Whitaker, "Culture of Curiosity," 82–5.

the Society itself, by which incoming books and papers could be handled and, perhaps, published in conditions of civil trust. In its interactions with the book trade, too, the Society worked hard to establish mastery, so that its productions would not be reprinted, translated, or even pirated without its consent. The maintenance of faith in its reports—and therefore in important natural and technical conclusions—depended on its success. Without these conventions it could not have built up and maintained renown as a location in which personal authorship would be safe. Indeed, upon them rested the very possibility of reconciling personal probity with the aspiration to philosophical authorship. Without them even a respected virtuoso might fall victim to a printer's conduct. "All ye Stationers" had to be "reduced to better Termes of Reason & honesty," warned John Beale, an active fellow of the Society. But the Society had to start with its own Printer, who generated "ye loudest outcrye" of all. "I wish he had subscrib'd his own name, & not mine," Beale complained after seeing the printed version of one of his papers, for readers would otherwise ascribe its "Phantastical, Imprudent, or Distracted" character to the authorship of Beale himself. "Wee should have more prudence, than to expose our reputations to the humour of such a sordid man."[94]

Surely, it may be objected, printing may have affected the communication of knowledge, but scarcely its creation. Chapters 6 and 7 challenge this assumption by looking in close detail at the practices of knowledge-making in the Royal Society, and at the notions of reading and representation that underlay them. Chapter 7 in particular addresses the fortunes of natural philosophy. Chapter 8 then extends the scope of this analysis. It proceeds to examine one of the major mathematical sciences, namely astronomy. It demonstrates that not even apparently "raw" empirical observations and rigorously quantitative calculations could escape the implications. To do so it traces in detail the course of an astronomical dispute of central importance to the history of science.

From 1675 Astronomer Royal John Flamsteed worked to construct a catalogue of the positions of the fixed stars. It promised to be the greatest work of observational astronomy ever produced. But by the end of 1712 Isaac Newton, Edmond Halley, and John Arbuthnot had printed and dispersed a text of his work, against Flamsteed's vehement opposition. The unauthorized volumes presented a radically different view of the role of the astronomer from his own—one implying that he had been sorely deficient as a public servant. Even its apparently objective positional figures had been changed in the course of Halley's extensive "correction" of the press. The

94. Beale to Oldenburg, 15 March 1669/70: Oldenburg, *Correspondence*, VI, 560–1.

chapter shows in detail how booksellers, printers, and natural philosophers combined in alliance to achieve their aims. If they failed, even elementary statements of observation would prove vulnerable. Together chapters 7
and 8 therefore demonstrate the centrality of the issues raised by earlier sections of the book for both philosophical and mathematical approaches to
Creation.

One reason Flamsteed suffered was that his observatory stood on Greenwich Hill, several miles distant from the clamor and grime of London. The
character of the metropolis itself represents a final reason to focus on England. The unprecedented expansion of London created a unique urban
environment with powerful and assertive craft communities. Here, as the
Restoration virtuosi always stressed, the creation of natural knowledge must
be a collaborative enterprise. It must draw together not just gentlemen, but
printers and booksellers too—not to mention the critical readership thronging the coffeehouses. The labor would be long, and it would be hazardous to the good names of all involved. Philosophical writers would have to
negotiate all the obstacles facing every other kind of would-be author, including regulatory régimes, piracy, skeptical booksellers, and unruly readers.
Printers and booksellers, for their part, would suffer frustration, ridicule,
debt, prison, and death. The story of natural knowledge in this period
should embrace all their efforts. This book thus proceeds in a trajectory
from the printing house and bookshop to the Royal Society and the Royal
Observatory: from Joseph Moxon and Francis Kirkman to Isaac Newton
and John Flamsteed. It is a valuable realignment. Emphatically, intellectual
history cannot be just the history of intellectuals.[95]

Scientific debate as such was unknown in the early modern world. We
would be unjustified in artificially selecting what seems to us the "scientific"
content of disputes such as that between Newton and Flamsteed in order to
explain the successes of some theories, artifacts, and individuals over others.
It is scarcely a novel proposition. A vast amount of work has been done to
reveal the historical and cultural specificity of such strategies. What is more
original is the suggestion that we need to appreciate just how important
conventions of propriety in books' manufacture, dispersal, and use really
were in the practice of natural philosophy. Adding this appreciation may
result not just in an extension of our knowledge, but in a change to the very
essence of our historical perceptions. Early modern London, where the cultural construction of print coincided with the fashioning of experimental
philosophy, offers unusually intriguing possibilities for such an approach. So
intriguing, perhaps, that it is possible to suggest a still greater implication.

95. Contra Krieger, *Ideas and Events*, 53.

"Do books make revolutions?" asks Chartier, and answers that books them-selves do not, but the ways they are made, used, and read just might.[96] We can rephrase his query to ask, "Do books make *scientific* revolutions?" But the answer may well stay the same.

96. Chartier, *Cultural Origins of the French Revolution*, 85–7.

LITERARY LIFE

The Culture and Credibility of the Printed Book

in Early Modern London

INTRODUCTION

"Behold now this vast City," commanded John Milton in 1644. Wandering through the streets and alleys of wartime London, by turns sordid and splendid, dank and magnificent, Milton unearthed in their teeming garrets a providential "City of refuge." There Londoners were hard at work, zealously seeking out wisdom. They were "reading," he proclaimed, "trying all things, assenting to the force of reason and convincement." What more, he demanded, could be asked of a nation "prone to seek after Knowledge"? What more need be done to create "a Nation of Prophets"?[1]

That the London citizenry could spend the Civil War "trying all things" in this way depended on a profound acquaintance with the products of printing. If ever an early modern society qualified for the term "print culture," this one did. How, though, should one characterize that culture? Milton himself advanced one important cautionary principle. As he testified, participants did not invest their faith indiscriminately in all printed materials. They "tried" the works they met with, appraising them critically both against each other and against their own prior knowledge. The conclusions they drew, and the actions they undertook as a consequence, rested as much upon this active process of adjudication as upon the textual contents of the books themselves. The specific subject of reading will be dealt with in chapter 6. Here it is sufficient merely to note the implication that the distinctive cultural realm that came into being around print could not be straightforwardly deducible from its texts alone. On the contrary, its character depended upon a vast array of representations, practices, and skills, which extended from the printing house, through the bookshop and marketplace, to the coffeehouse, study, salon, and home—and thence back to

1. Milton, *Areopagitica*, 30.

the printing house again. Each of these sites played its part in determining how exactly it was that printing came to be so important in Milton's world.

It may therefore be appropriate for us to heed Milton's example, and start by approaching print in terms of a large number of distinct cultural settings. Without intending anything particularly profound by the coinage, I shall call these settings *domains*. Domains—examples of which include the printing house and bookshop, but also the city square, courtroom, and coffeehouse—were dynamic localities defined by physical environment, work, and sociability. Discrete but interlocking, they both exhibited and were constituted by particular clusters of representations, practices, and skills. In them men and women (and children too) could labor to establish or contest issues of all kinds, including those relating to print and its products.[2] They therefore deserve to be addressed in close detail. In principle, the number of domains in Milton's London was, of course, infinite. But for current purposes some are evidently more germane than others, and a critical survey need not be infeasible. An excellent way to approach the domains of print, this chapter argues, is to begin by interrogating the people and places making them possible: the agents and abodes of the book trade.

First, the agents. Who were they? The question is not as simple as it may at first seem. Formally, all of the men and women concerned in the book trade were supposed to be subsumed under the one title of "Stationer." That is, they were all supposed to be members of the Company of Stationers, the legally recognized body that had been chartered by Queen Mary in 1557 to oversee the "art and mystery" of printing. Much more will be said of this Company in this and following chapters. But it is worth noting at the outset that the term "Stationer" denoted far more than a simple institutional affiliation. It in fact predated the introduction of printing, and even in the seventeenth century it signaled a persevering notion of craft competence that did not always explicitly recognize new distinctions of labor and skill being created around the press. To be a Stationer thus meant adopting a distinctive cultural identity, and one by no means reducible to the "logic" of the press itself. The characteristics of that identity conditioned how every individual Stationer perceived his or her knowledge, conduct, and action. By comparison, categorization into "bookseller," "printer" or "wholesaler"—let alone "publisher" or "editor"—was relatively unfamiliar. Although they did exist,

2. A comparison is appropriate with Becker's notion of "art worlds." Such a "world" is "a network of cooperating people, all of whose work is essential to the final outcome." It validates its own knowledge and skill, and appreciation of its products as aesthetic is coextensive with recognition of its social figuration. Interestingly, given chapter 5 below, art worlds also create their own histories. Becker, *Art Worlds*, 24–5, 36, 39, 346, and passim. The term *domain* is nonetheless preferred here since it combines associations of place, power, and property. Compare also the discussion in Poovey, *Making a Social Body*, 5–8, which I came across only after writing the above.

and, for reasons explored below, were being articulated with increasing frequency and consistency, such terms possessed nothing like the resonance of
"Stationer."[3] Printers and booksellers acted first and foremost as Stationers,
and it was as Stationers that they and their actions were judged.

This had considerable consequences. The making and communication
of knowledge of all kinds depended increasingly on print, and it was
through the agency of Stationers that printed materials both came into being
and reached their users. The decisions structuring print culture were overwhelmingly Stationers' decisions, arrived at by reference to Stationers' perspectives. Their interests and practices therefore had direct implications for
virtually all learned activities. Knowledge itself, inasmuch as it could be embodied, preserved, and communicated in printed materials, depended on
Stationers' labors. That is why we need to examine closely how their community articulated and understood its different activities and ideals. What
follows is thus an attempt to capture something of the Stationers' world,
and to demonstrate its salience to the conduct and structure of intellectual
life in early modern England.

The Stationer is one focus of this chapter's attention. As it will make
clear, however, Stationers' virtues were conventionally appraised in terms of
the qualities of the locations in which they lived and worked—in particular,
bookshops and printing houses. In assessing their community and its significance, there is consequently an important question of social space to be
considered. Like the Rembrandt conjured by historian of art Svetlana Alpers, printers and booksellers adopted practical conventions peculiar to their
workplaces, and those conventions both effected and affected what they produced. Making books, like making paintings, was a craft. It was bound up
in craft customs of considerable complexity, exercised in particular locations.
Only by the pursuit of those customs could print be sustained as a viable
enterprise. Only if all those customs cohered harmoniously could Stationers'
activities retreat into invisibility for readers and writers, and later for historians too.

This chapter thus attends to how Stationers and others both constructed
and construed the behavior appropriate to two vital places: the printing
house and the bookshop.[4] In doing so, it argues, they created distinctive

---

3. For the origin of such divisions see Lowry, *World of Aldus Manutius*, 16–17. The intent
here is similar to Mario Biagioli's in his nuanced treatment of "socioprofessional identity"
(*Galileo, Courtier*, 2–5, 11–101), although Biagioli's term itself is rather ungainly and has for
that reason not been adopted here.

4. Alpers, *Rembrandt's Enterprise*; Goffman, *Presentation of Self*. The best treatment of an
English printing house remains McKenzie, *Cambridge University Press 1696–1712*, I, passim.
Although he treats the Cambridge operation, McKenzie notes that his findings are relevant
to London houses too: I, 93.

cultural domains, in which books were embedded throughout their manufacture and initial assessment. However, the walls of the printing house and bookshop were manifestly anything but hermetic. The community dealing in printed materials as its staple trade did not exist in isolation, either socially or physically. On the contrary, it inhabited and depended upon a thriving capital city that by 1700 had become one of the main urban centers of the world. London formed a distinctive domain in its own right. Printers and booksellers of the period would typically use the compound term "Citizen and Stationer of London" to describe themselves, and we need to understand the importance of both its elements. Our analysis must accordingly proceed beyond the portals of the printing house and venture into the streets of England's capital city.

The development of London affected all aspects of British life. Indeed, the political history of seventeenth-century England, it has been said, was the story of "one of Europe's weakest crowns defied, broken, and replaced by its greatest city."[5] The significance of the bookshops and printing houses of this unruly metropolis lay as much in the interactions they fostered between Stationers and other citizens as in practices internal to the premises themselves. The question of access is an obvious example: who among the citizenry could enter a printing house, and under what conditions—and what could they do once they were inside? To realize the importance of the metropolitan setting is also to broach a much broader topic. Stationers instigated and conditioned effects that extended far beyond their printing houses and bookshops, and into the coffeehouses, tenements, townhouses, inns of court, garrets, and taverns spread across the city. In addition to examining the internal arrangements of the printing house and bookshop, we must therefore attempt also to embrace these domains. In short, we need a topography of the places of printed material in early modern London.[6]

Obeying Milton's terse command, the argument of this chapter begins by proposing such a map. Inasmuch as this means simply identifying the areas of the city in which printed books could be found, the discussion will draw upon valuable work already done by bibliographers and historians of the book trade. But by bringing together their conclusions with those of social historians and historians of science, and by directing their findings to

5. Scott, "Restoration Process," 624. Until the end of the seventeenth century English printing was permitted only in London, Oxford, Cambridge, and York. Provincial printers began to operate on any discernible scale only in the eighteenth century: Feather, *Provincial Book Trade*; Belanger, "Publishers and Writers," 5–6; Alston, "British Book Trade." The only exception worth noting here is William Bentley's printing house in Finsbury, authorized by Parliament in 1644 to produce bibles.

6. Compare Martin, "Prééminence de la Librairie Parisienne"; Martin, "Espaces de la Vente"; Kirsop, "Mécanismes Éditoriaux," 19 ff.

the specific end of understanding how books could be put to use to create and sustain knowledge, it is possible to go far beyond the concerns of such investigators. We can begin to suggest how the "social geography" of the printing house and bookshop meshed with that of the wider urban environment, and how together they conditioned the knowledge that could be produced and encountered in early modern London.[7]

It was in this wider environment that printed materials were located, "tried," and put to use. The chapter proceeds to show that representations of the conduct proper to a printing house and bookshop could be highly germane to those activities. Such representations could be deployed by critical readers to construct or undermine the worth of particular works. When faced with a given printed book, an important initial step for such urban readers was to appraise the probity of the people and places involved in its fashioning. This was a real and common undertaking. Contemporary readers and Stationers alike used the knowledge outlined in the early parts of this chapter—knowledge about where printing was properly to be exercised, how it was properly to be practiced, and by whom it was properly to be managed—to discriminate qualitatively between the printed books they actually encountered in their daily lives. Cultural and intellectual history depended on the outcome.

THE TOPOGRAPHY OF THE METROPOLITAN BOOK TRADE

Stuart historiographer James Howell likened the London he knew to a book. If Tacitus had called the city a "Mart" fifteen hundred years earlier, he asked, what name would it merit now, since "being compared to what she was then, [the city] may be said, in point of magnitude, to be as a large Volume in Folio, to a book *in Decimo Sexto*"? Howell's comparison, implying as it does an acknowledgment of the centrality of the printed book to early modern metropolitan life, may stand as an epigraph to the discussion presented in the following pages. For by Howell's time, Londoners were strikingly conversant with the printed word. The city enjoyed a relatively large literate population, and their everyday experience of newspapers and pamphlets being read aloud in coffeehouses and taverns meant that even illiterate citizens had become acutely aware of the importance of print in creating the social world in which they lived.[8]

7. Raven, "Mapping the London Book Trade." For the concept of "social geography," see Heal, *Hospitality in Early Modern England*, 29.

8. Howell, *Londinopolis*, "To the Renowned City of London." For the extent and effects of literacy see Cressy, *Literacy and the Social Order*, and Spufford, *Small Books and Pleasant Histories*. For coffeehouse uses of print embracing the illiterate, and the political concerns

Where were printed objects made, encountered, and put to use? The question is an important one. Large though it was—and expanding at an unprecedented rate—to its inhabitants London was hardly an undifferentiated entity (fig 2.1). From Nashe and Taylor to Pope and Swift, the poets and wits who exploited its topography so effectively were capitalizing on a significant cultural truth. Life in London tended to be remarkably localized.[9] The Scottish visitor who found the metropolis to be "a great vast wilderness" to its residents, most of whom had no more idea of the city beyond their immediate environs than they had of Paris or Moscow, was discovering an aspect of the city that was widely remarked upon. Adjacent quarters might be only yards apart, yet in social terms they were apparently different worlds.[10] The very highest echelons of society perhaps excepted, this distinctness was not generally one of rank, nor of what contemporaries called "quality." Both rich and poor, upstanding and dissolute, genteel and down-at-heel lived in close proximity. Rather, citizens identified themselves in terms of their localities, in ways that cut across such "vertical" divisions but instead honored ties of neighborhood. For them, community was delimited by street, ward, and parish—and also, importantly, by trade (which is one theme of the following chapter). They tended to live for much of their lives in and around one precinct, and such local structures seem to have developed a primacy similar to that found in rural villages of the period. This was reflected in the practices of law and administration, both of which operated largely through the extensive participation of local householders.[11] Transgressive practices too were often locally conditioned. Defamation provides one example, which saw printed materials adapted to traditional forms of abuse such as the libel posted to an enemy's doorpost as a potent and public

---

arising therefrom, see Harris, *London Crowds*, 27–31, 98–103; Pincus, "'Coffee Politicians Does Create.'"

9. Boulton, *Neighbourhood and Society*, 60–1, 97–8, 166 ff., 187, 294; Alexander, "Economic Structure," 59; Power, "Social Topography." For literary representations of London's topography see Rogers, *Grub Street*, and Manley, *Literature and Culture*, 212–93. See also Boulton, "Residential Mobility," Glass, "Socio-economic Status," and De Krey, *Fractured Society*, 1–8, 171 ff., which discusses the local character of city politics.

10. For London's expansion, see: Porter, *London*, 131; Finlay and Shearer, "Population Growth"; Boulton, *Neighbourhood and Society*, 1–5; Fisher, *London and the English Economy*, 173–83; Rappaport, *Worlds within Worlds*, 61 ff.; Earle, *Making of the English Middle Class*, 17; Earle, *City Full of People*, 7–16; Liu, *Puritan London*, 43–5.

11. Archer, *Pursuit of Stability*, e.g., 126; Watt, *Rise of the Novel*, 201–2; Earle, *Making of the English Middle Class*, 205; Boulton, *Neighbourhood and Society*, 207; Levine and Wrightson, *Making of an Industrial Society*, 279–80; Earle, *City Full of People*, 171–8. But Seaver, *Wallington's World*, 192, describes a Puritan artisan who conceived of politics on a Europe-wide, providentialist scale. For the classification of early modern ranks see Wrightson, "'Sorts of People.'"

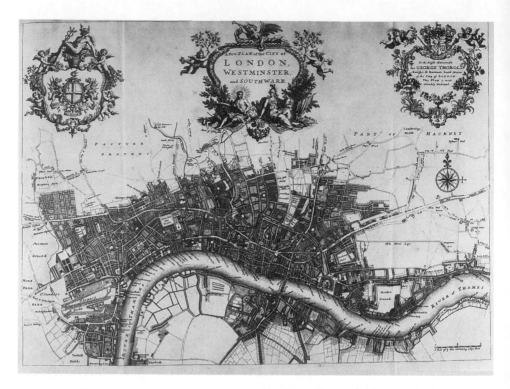

FIG. 2.1. London in the late seventeenth and early eighteenth centuries. Strype, *Survey of London*. (By permission of the Syndics of Cambridge University Library.)

form of challenge. But locality was also defined in terms of more fundamental characteristics: ways of life and thought, personal habits, dialects, and even passions. Famously, Joseph Addison found the city "an aggregate of several nations." "The inhabitants of St. James's," he concluded, "notwithstanding they live under the same laws, and speak the same language, are a distinct people from those of the Temple on one side, and those of Smithfield on the other, by several climates and degrees, in their ways of thinking and conversing together." [12]

In general, then, different metropolitan areas possessed identifiable characters. Perceiving themselves pressed on all sides by a seething wilderness of unfamiliar faces, gossip, and wheeler-dealing, citizens found such characters all the more useful in assessing their surroundings. The location of an ac-

---

12. *Spectator* 403 (12 June 1712); Burke, *Historical Anthropology of Early Modern Italy*, 95–109, esp. 107–8; Cressy, "Books as Totems"; Archer, *Pursuit of Stability*, 78. For an impressive example see Fludd, *Doctor Fludds Answer unto M. Foster*, sig. A3ᵛ: Fludd was compelled to respond to William Foster "by [his] setting up in the night time two of the frontispices or Titles of his booke, as a Challenge, one each post of my doore." Fox, "Aspects of Oral Culture," 13 cites a parallel example from Lancashire.

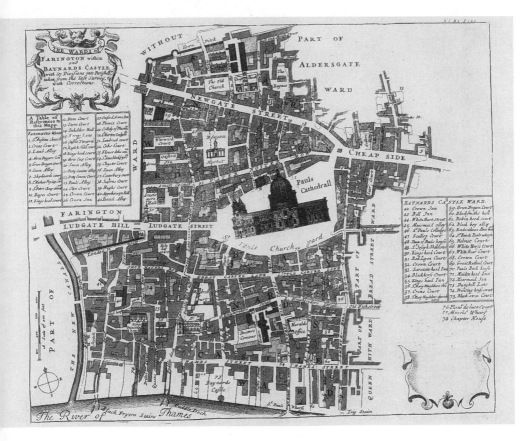

FIG. 2.2. Saint Paul's Churchyard and Barnard's Castle, showing Stationers' Hall and the King's Printing House. Booksellers thronged the precincts of Paternoster Row and Ave Mary Lane, whose buildings, owned by the Stationers' Company (and indicated here as "Stationers Rents") were surveyed by Leybourn in 1674. The trade publisher Randall Taylor occupied one of these premises. Printers also congregated further to the south of the cathedral, in the maze of alleys leading down to the Thames. Strype, *Survey of London*. (By permission of the Syndics of Cambridge University Library.)

tivity within the City (or outside its jurisdiction, in one of the festering suburbs) was perceived to be highly pertinent to its recognition or otherwise as a worthy element in the commonwealth. Confirming the analogy with village life, Defoe remarked that for someone whose trade was concentrated elsewhere in London to set up shop in Saint Paul's Churchyard, the center of the book trade (fig. 2.2), would be "the same thing as for a country shop-keeper not to set up in or near the market-place."[13]

As this implies, the book trade itself could not but be subject to such perceptions. In size alone it was striking. Among modern historians, Michael

13. Power, "Social Topography," 215–22; Sennett, *Fall of Public Man*, 54–63; Defoe, *Complete English Tradesman*, 98–100.

Treadwell estimates that there were over 150 bookshops in London by 1695, and Margaret Plant that there were some 188 by 1700. Contemporary assessments varied, but some put it much higher.[14] They were quite possibly right to do so, given the number of temporary and highly mobile stalls being erected. These did not appear on official records, except occasionally as the subject of complaints from more established Stationers. Visitors, especially, noticed what to the citizens themselves had become unremarkable. Jan Amos Comenius was one such, declaring just before the Civil War that "there are truly not more bookstalls at Frankfurt at the time of the fair than there are here every day." But the shops and stalls that so impressed travelers like Comenius were far from uniformly distributed. "They have their particular Quarters," noticed Samuel de Sorbière, "such as St. *Paul's Church-Yard*, and *Little-Britain*, where there is twice as many as in the *Rue Saint Jacque* in *Paris*." Discussion in terms of these areas is both useful and warranted, not least because the trade itself divided its practitioners according to topography. In 1697, for example, the Stationers' Company classified its constituents in terms of six districts: Fleet Street, Westminster, Holborn, Saint Paul's Churchyard, Little Britain, and Cornhill.[15] Contemporaries knew well the differences and similarities between such zones.

For prosperous booksellers, in particular, the best-known center was the precinct around Amen Corner, Saint Paul's Churchyard, and Ave Maria Lane. The identification of this area with the craft of the Stationers was an old one: Stow recorded that text writers had kept shops there since well before the invention of printing. By the middle of the seventeenth century, if not before, it was known for its "good houses, inhabited by noted Tradesmen," and had become a popular rendezvous for people of quality. The trade's concentration here persisted to the extent that in 1700 there were some thirty bookshops in Saint Paul's Churchyard itself, and the trade was fast expanding into neighboring Paternoster Row. Here lived the Whig grandee Awnsham Churchill, for example, who will play a major role in chapter 8. It seems that the status of the area declined somewhat after the fire of 1666, when many of the more prosperous citizens decamped to the west, to new and fashionable squares like Covent Garden. But the booksellers stayed, finding it "well situated for learned and studious Mens access,"

14. Treadwell, "English Book Trade," 360; Plant, *English Book Trade*, 64. For a contemporary (and hostile) estimate see Atkyns, *Original and Growth of Printing* (1664), sig. D4ᵛ: "There are at least 600 Booksellers that keep Shops in and about *London*, and Two or three Thousand free of the Company of *Stationers*." Pollard and Redgrave, *Short-Title Catalogue 1475–1640*, III, 232–59 contains an authoritative survey of the London trade in the earlier part of the period.

15. Glass, "Socio-economic Status," 231–2 n. 11; McKenzie, "London Book Trade," 10; Alexander, "Economic Structure," 58; Sorbière, *Voyage into England*, 16; SCB F, fol. 260ʳ⁻ᵛ.

and John Strype remembered Paternoster Row being "so resorted unto by the Nobility and Gentry, in their Coaches, that oft times the Street was so stop'd up, that there was no passage for Foot Passengers." The Old Bailey, just beyond Ludgate, proved a ready source of select customers, as, indeed, did the cathedral itself. But less acceptable forms of publishing were also entertained. At the notorious Star Chamber trial of William Prynne for his *Histriomastix*, two of the judges wanted their grisly sentence (the public severing of Prynne's ears) to be carried out in Saint Paul's Churchyard, as a message to all prepared to deal in such material. Their wish was denied only when Archbishop Laud objected that the site was sacred ground.[16]

As Thomas Nashe put it, Saint Paul's Churchyard had become the "Exchange of all Authors."[17] Anyone wanting to write, translate, edit, or otherwise produce a text was well advised to come here to do business. Places for the use of books as well as for their production also proliferated, so that by the 1680s the Churchyard seemed the ideal site for a religious library aimed at young gentlemen tempted to dally too long in coffeehouses. Commerce and sociability converged in a series of such sites, which multiplied inexorably throughout the seventeenth and eighteenth centuries. The first of the City clubs began to meet at the Castle Tavern, Paternoster Row, in 1695, and continued there for a hundred years, with booksellers among its most prominent members. The Castle was also perhaps the key meeting point for authors, booksellers, and printers intent on making deals for the production and distribution of books.[18] Up to 1755, sales of "copies" were held at the Queen's Head, another tavern nearby. The Chapter coffeehouse, also in Paternoster Row, had by then become yet another center, where authors such as Oliver Goldsmith and William Buchan could hobnob with the booksellers who made their names famous. In Saint Paul's Churchyard itself, Child's, another coffeehouse, became the favored haunt of physicians and fellows of the Royal Society—and we shall see Edmond Halley making good use of it in chapter 8.[19] The disposal of entire libraries took place by auction at

16. Stow, *Survay*, 129, 648–9; Treadwell, "English Book Trade," 360; Porter, *London*, 70–1, 95–116; Strype, *Survey*, I, 195; CUL Ms. Dd.6.23, pp. 30, 32, 33, 39. For descriptions of the area in the sixteenth century, see Blayney, *Bookshops in Paul's Cross Churchyard*; and for a map of it in the Restoration, see Pollard and Redgrave, *Short-Title Catalogue 1475–1640*, III, between 246 and 247.

17. Nashe, *Works*, I, 278; Nicholl, *Cup of News*, 42–3. Earle was more explicit: Saint Paul's was "the great Exchange of all discourse . . . the general Mint of all famous lies": Agnew, *Worlds Apart*, 86–7. Men "all turne Merchants there," he continued.

18. Evelyn, *Diary*, IV, 367–8; Rogers, "Clubs and Politics," 51–2. Flamsteed and Newton held meetings at the Castle with bookseller Awnsham Churchill: Baily, *Flamsteed*, 235, and below, pp. 582, 594.

19. Belanger, "Booksellers' Sales," 49, 158–9; Lillywhite, *London Coffee Houses*, 151–2, 156–8; Lawler, *Book Auctions*, 73–5, 109–11, 126–8, 130–7, 175–7.

coffeehouses across the area. Virtually every building in the precinct—taverns, coffeehouses, printing houses, bookshops, and even simple residences—had a role to play in the making and moving of words. In this area the topography of print should be measured on a small scale, in feet and yards.

At its center was the cathedral itself. By the early seventeenth century Saint Paul's was in a decidedly decrepit state. It had become the city's main thoroughfare for gossips and peddlers. Stalls threatened to smother the building, and, in poignant defiance of Scripture, commercial deals were routinely struck in the nave. ("The *Buyers* and *Sellers* have drov'n out the *Temple*," lamented Richard Flecknoe.) The Stationers' church, Saint Faith's, was to be found in the very crypt of the cathedral, and the booksellers rented warehouse space elsewhere under the building. In the Great Fire of 1666 they consequently suffered more than perhaps any other community. Not only were their shops and houses burnt to the ground, but this sanctuary too was utterly destroyed. Thousands of books were vaporized. Their ashes were carried by the wind as far as Windsor.[20]

North of Saint Paul's, another major center for the trade was to be found in Duck Lane and Little Britain (fig. 2.3). This was a less exclusive area. Its heyday was in the later seventeenth century, when international book dealer Robert Scott stood out in its trade community. Here also lived the only printer whom John Collins would trust with mathematical texts, the "very worthy honest person" William Godbid, and the enterprising Moses Pitt, who was something of a Stationer-virtuoso until struck down by bankruptcy. But although secondhand booksellers and newspapermen continued to live and work there well into the eighteenth century, its cachet had by then declined. Jonathan Swift would soon draw upon the area's low repute in telling printer John Barber that he wished a "pox on the modern phrase *Great Britain*, which is only to distinguish it from Little Britain, where old cloaths and books are to be bought and sold." Even so, writers might still need to come here to pursue their projects. It could be a grim life for those who did. Edmund Bohun, Tory squire, political apologist, and future licenser, was forced to live in "dark, stinking, and inconvenient" lodgings when his bookseller maintained him in Little Britain in 1685. His wife fell ill immediately, and two other family members contracted smallpox.[21]

Yet Little Britain never attained the notoriety of zones like Smithfield,

20. Evelyn, *Diary*, III, 454–60 (compare Conway, *Letters*, 277, for similar fallout in Kensington); Flecknoe, *Miscellania*, 140.

21. Rigaud, *Correspondence of Scientific Men*, I, 200; II, 15, 468; Bohun, *Diary and Autobiography*, 66, 71; Rogers, *Grub Street*, 256–7. For Pitt's disaster see Harris, "Moses Pitt and Insolvency."

Grub Street, and Moorfields, outside the City and north of Bedlam, where the hacks pilloried in Pope's *Dunciad* came to live (fig. 2.4). Moorfields in particular had always been an area of dubious reputation. It was one of London's main bawdy-house districts, and suffered violent rioting in 1668 when mobs of apprentices and others—amounting, according to one report, to some forty thousand people—attacked its brothels. Fashionable gentry came here in search of entertainments both licit and illicit. Robert Hooke, too, regularly wandered through the bookstalls. Hooke, who scrupulously named in his diary all his contacts of any status, hardly ever recorded the identity of Moorfields book dealers, though he did those of Saint Paul's Churchyard and Little Britain.[22] As this implied, Moorfields was where the lowest ranks of the trade gathered: those unrecognized by the Stationers' Company, and the "private" printers of Quaker and other illicit books.[23] Yet still their efforts were not restricted to such disreputable literature. Shortly after the death of his patron, Robert Boyle, Hooke was shocked to discover "neer 100 of Mr Boyles high Dutch Chymicall books ly[ing] exposed in Moorfeilds on the railes." Local dealers could clearly get their hands on learned and substantial texts, as well as on pamphlets and ephemera. Hooke's dismay merely confirms that this was scarcely considered a suitable venue for his erstwhile master's library. In fact, it was not unknown for titles to follow in their successive impressions a clear social and topographical trajectory. Exhibited in folio in Saint Paul's Churchyard, an impression of the same work took on very different connotations when located in Moorfields, Smithfield, or Bartholomew Square.[24]

These were not the only places in which bookshops could be found. Throughout the city, they tended to congregate beside major thoroughfares and around focal points like bridges, city gates, and public buildings.[25] Perhaps twenty stood along the main city concourse extending from Cheapside to Cornhill. From 1668 the richest of all Stationers, Thomas Guy MP, lived here, at the junction of Cornhill and Lombard Street. Others could be

22. Harris, *London Crowds*, 82 (and 192–3 for further serious rioting by weavers in 1675); Harris, "Bawdy House Riots"; Rostenberg, *Library of Robert Hooke*, 49–65. Compare Shapin, "Who Was Robert Hooke?" 262–3.

23. E.g., SCB E, fols. 47ᵛ–48ʳ.

24. Hooke, "Diary," 223. A complex example is Robert Recorde's *Ground of Arts*, one of the key documents of the mathematical sciences. This was reprinted many times after 1543, beginning in Saint Paul's Churchyard, moving through Knightrider Street, Barnard's Castle, Fleet Street, Cornhill, and Little Britain, and arriving in 1640 at Smithfield.

25. Compare Martin, "Espaces de la Vente," 90–1, 103–4. Unlike those in Paris, London bookshops did not congregate along the banks of the river, perhaps because imports had to go through the one entry point of the Customs House, but also because there was no riverside promenade. Robert Hooke planned one. The porosity of London's bounds is demonstrated in Porter, *London*, 132–3, 138–40.

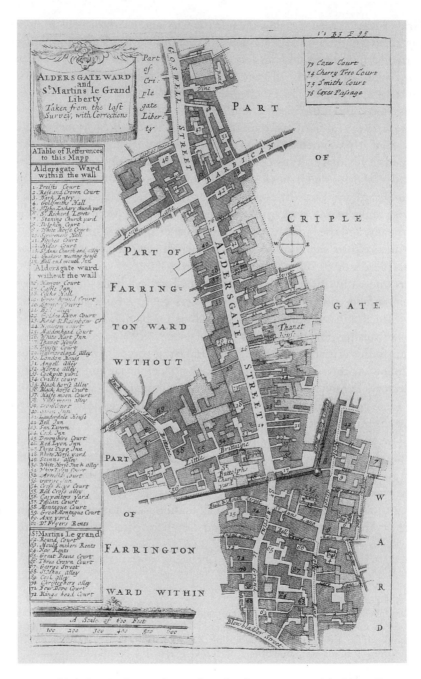

FIG. 2.3. Little Britain. Strype, *Survey of London*. (By permission of the Henry E. Huntington Library, San Marino, California, RB 143032.)

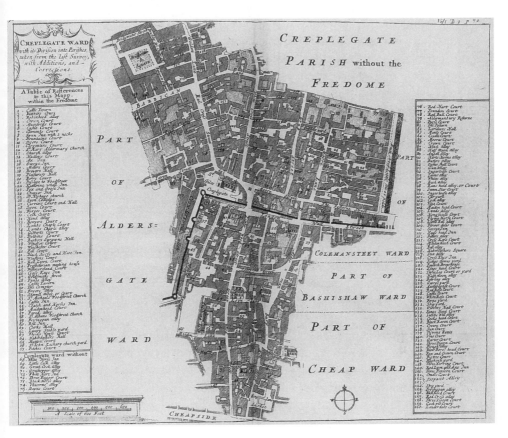

FIG. 2.4. Grub Street and the approaches to Moorfields. Strype, *Survey of London*. (By permission of the Syndics of Cambridge University Library.)

found in Westminster, and along Fleet Street—where there were around twenty-five booksellers' shops by the 1690s, including that of Jacob Tonson (which also housed Tonson's lodger, William Congreve). London Bridge, the only fixed route across the Thames, also supported a few bookshops. Still more could be found where local communities generated specialized markets. At the Royal Exchange, for instance, Robert Horne was "the principal person that prints mercantile affairs." Other booksellers dwelt around the Tower, to meet the needs of mariners, and next to the inns of court, to serve the wealthy and demanding students of what was often spoken of as a de facto university.[26]

26. Treadwell, "English Book Trade," 360–1; Howell, *Londinopolis*, 31; Rigaud, *Correspondence of Scientific Men*, I, 176–9, esp. 177; Taylor, *Mathematical Practitioners*, e.g., 55–7, 86, 99, 193. John Beale reported that Captain Samuel Sturmy's *Mariner's Magazine* (1669)

It would thus be too simplistic to suggest that book dealers could be found only in the major areas of trade concentration. Nonetheless, for the most part someone searching for learned works would not need to look much further than the vicinities of Saint Paul's, Little Britain, the Fleet Street and Cornhill thoroughfare, and perhaps Moorfields. Anyone wanting to *produce* such a work would similarly go first to one of these few precincts. In particular, it was to these districts, and especially to Saint Paul's Churchyard, that the men of the Royal Society went when they wanted to purchase, borrow, read, and respond to the books of their Continental counterparts. And it was here that they went when they wanted to spread the word of their new experimental philosophy.[27]

Printing houses were of rather more immediate concern to the authorities than bookshops, largely because they seemed to offer greater opportunities for regulation. Their numbers were therefore relatively closely monitored, and as a result can now be stated with greater confidence. Repeated attempts were made to limit the number of printing houses to twenty, besides the King's Printers and those for Oxford and Cambridge Universities. These efforts were especially intense in the early years of the Restoration, when those keen to display their loyalty to the crown chose to blame the "miserable confusions and Calamities" of the previous two decades on printers' "monstrous excess and exorbitant disorder." Samuel Parker, for one, praised the 1662 Press Act for suppressing "the very engine of rebellion."[28] But, as was so often the case with early modern governance, such attempts met with only partial and qualified success. There were at least 53 houses in 1661–2, as the Restoration's printing régime was being constructed and put into effect. Some 40 were still operating by the time of the Fire, and a list made in 1675 mentioned 23. This was the lowest point. By 1705, ten years after the end of the Press Act, numbers had risen again, and there were about 62, not including the royal printers. Two decades later Samuel Negus could count a dozen more still, and by this time a provincial trade was also thriving.[29]

---

was being printed for four Stationers: "1st Mr Thomas at ye Adam & Eve in litle-Brittaine. 2ly Mr Thomson in Smith-Field. 3 Fisher on Tower-hill. 4 Hurlock at London-Bridge." The sequence of names, and the declining use of titles, suggests something of the standard topographical hierarchy. Oldenburg, *Correspondence*, IV, 424–7, esp. 426.

27. E.g., Gunther, *Early Science in Oxford*, XII, 398.

28. *London Printers Lamentation*, 2–3; Parker, *Bishop Parker's History of his Own Time*, 22–3; 14 Car. II, c. 33, § 10. The Restoration régime also tried to delimit even more closely the number of typefounders to just four masters, since this offered a still more auspicious opportunity for restriction. It was also hoped that with few sources of type available, the producers of illicit books could be identified by comparing their typography to specimen sheets stored centrally.

29. Hetet, "Literary Underground," 37–8, 104–5, 244, 257; SCB D, fol. 82ʳ (mentioning 59 masters in 1663); Maslen and Lancaster, *Bowyer Ledgers*, xxiii.

Reduction to the levels envisaged in 1662 had by this time long been virtually unthinkable. Even at its most effective, regulation had never succeeded
in reconstructing the world of printing in the image of the law.

It is worth stressing that none of the surveys on which these figures are
based was exhaustive—especially if they are taken as indicating numbers of
presses, rather than of printing houses per se. They included neither clandestine operations nor abortive courtly enterprises like the press apparently
projected by Sir Samuel Morland, Charles II's Master of Mechanicks. Nor,
indeed, did they encompass presses operated by enterprising individuals like
the Peter de Peene who purportedly made one the size of an hourglass to
carry around the country and display at fairs.[30] Nonetheless, they do provide
useful evidence for the general extent and topographical disposition of the
trade, and for its changing fortunes over time. What they show about its
disposition is that, like bookshops, printing houses clustered around Saint
Paul's. Printers clearly stood to benefit from being close to the social center
of the book world. But since they did not rely to the same extent on retailing, and were relatively free to dispense with opportunities for unplanned
face-to-face contact with passersby, printers could also afford to live farther
to the south, in the less expensive area between the cathedral, Barnard's
Castle, and the river. The biggest operation of all, the royal printing house,
could be found in a decaying building in Blackfriars, slightly west of this
zone. When the trade itself listed printers according to their location, it thus
identified centers both here and to the north, around Smithfield, Bartholomew Close, and Aldersgate Street. These were all areas of dubious character.
Here lurked nonconformist conventicles, currency counterfeiters, republican plotters, and illicit printers alike, secure in the uncharted crannies of
Dunghill Lane, Dark Lane, and Town's End Lane.[31]

These were the zones into which one had to venture in order to participate in the production of printed materials. We shall see that the social characteristics attributed to such areas affected the perceived epistemic status of
those materials. In fact, they could hardly fail to have some such influence.
Books trumpeted their provenance on their title pages, thereby associating
themselves for disparate audiences with their precise points of origin. Ironic
title pages capitalized on this consciousness of place, creating fantastic spatial universes for themselves. "EUROPE," declared one: "Printed by *MARTIN
CLAW CLERGIE*, Printer to the *Reverend Assembly of Divines*, and are to be
should [*sic*] at his Shop in *Toleration Street*, at the *Signe* of the *Subjects Liberty*, right opposite to *Persecuting Court*." A joke, of course, but one with a

30. Dickinson, *Sir Samuel Morland*, 44–5; Leybourn, *Pleasure with Profit*, Tract III, 29.
31. Treadwell, "London Printers and Printing Houses"; Hetet, "Literary Underground," 17.

point; and like all good jokes, it reflected a real truth about the culture in which it seemed funny enough to be worth telling.[32]

PRINTERS AND PRINTING HOUSES

When the Great Fire swept through Saint Paul's Churchyard, it destroyed the cathedral and obliterated the livelihoods of a host of citizens. Thomas Sprat, hard at work on his apologetic defense of the Royal Society, was profoundly impressed by the sufferers' fortitude in the face of this catastrophe. He declared himself convinced by their stoicism that "not only the best *Natural*, but the best *Moral* Philosophy too, may be learn'd from the shops of *Mechanicks*." The opinion was not in itself new. Indeed, it was already something of a European commonplace—in Italy, too, contemporary writers were prone to remark that philosophical knowledge "lives in the shops and in the countryside, as well as in books and academies."[33] But the "mechanicks" around Saint Paul's who suffered most in the Fire were the Stationers, whose work had been reduced to the ashes now softly descending on the south of England. So if Sprat's sentiment was justified, one of the most important "shops" in which natural philosophy could be found was that of the Stationer.

This section examines one kind of Stationer's premises in particular: the printing house. Passage through such an establishment was fast becoming obligatory for writers wanting to sustain claims to knowledge. Moreover, the printing house proved especially central to the kind of Restoration natural philosophy lauded by Sprat, both because the virtuosi made a point of stressing the epistemological value of workshop practices and because they consciously adopted novel forms of printed communication in order to promote their new experimental philosophy.[34] These are themes that recur later in this book. Having asked where printing houses could be found, however, and having appreciated in general terms that their locations could have cultural consequences, we now need to ask a more specific set of questions about them. To begin with, what did a printing house look like? More important, how did its occupants and visitors view it, and how did its social character affect its products? It is telling that when the printing house first appeared, contemporaries did not know what to call this strange hybrid of

32. [Overton], *Arraignement of Mr. Persecution*, title page. For the usefulness of such jokes, see comments in Collinson, *Birthpangs of Protestant England*, 5, and Darnton, *Great Cat Massacre*, 77–8. Real shop signs expressed meaning, too, as remarked below.

33. Pallavicino, *Del Bene*, 248, 168, 346–7, cited in Ginzburg, "High and Low," 37; Sprat, *History of the Royal Society*, 120–1.

34. Sprat, *History of the Royal Society*, e.g., 80, 121 (but compare 66–7, 130, 341–2, 378).

library, scriptorium, study, home, and workshop. Far from exerting a determining logic on their conduct, it was itself a blank slate ready to be inscribed
with their aims, predilections, and prejudices. So what cultural resources did
they in fact draw upon to describe it, and how did they labor to create for it
a proper role in their society? Was it to be a private space, inaccessible to
authors and gentlemen, or a physical embodiment of the republic of letters,
free, apparently, of all such boundaries?[35] These were pressing questions in
early modern Europe, and should be addressed with corresponding seriousness by the modern historian.

One may reasonably doubt whether there was such a thing as a "typical"
printing house in early modern London. Nonetheless, we can articulate
some elements that were probably common to many of the workshops and
other premises used by Stationers—and which were certainly common to
their representation. Again, it is useful to start by considering where presses
were normally used. In both Oxford and Cambridge, by a strange coincidence, early presses were set up in buildings called theaters. After the Cambridge press departed, its building actually became an anatomy theater. In
London, likewise, isolated presses were set up in special locations for specific
work: at the Customs House, for example, and at Parish Clerks' Hall.[36] But
these were exceptional cases. In general, printing houses were just that:
printing *houses*. They were established in buildings that were originally
dwelling places, and that remained so. Above the workshop itself, such a
building would often house the master printer and his or her family, and
not uncommonly the apprentices and journeymen too. Even John Field's
relatively large premises in Cambridge, which had six presses on the first
floor and a drying room on the second, was connected via the upper story
to Field's family home.

This juxtaposition of domestic and vocational quarters was common
throughout Western Europe. In Paris, too, printers often worked in buildings that were not only dwellings but retail sites, with a press on the second
floor above a bookshop on the first.[37] However, while Henry Hills, printer

35. Shaw, "'Ars Formularia.'" See also Binns, *Intellectual Culture*, 399–435, esp. 400–1,
416 ff. A nineteenth-century translator rendered the 1636 Oxonian term for printing house,
opificium, as "laboratory": Ward, *Oxford University Statutes*, I, 205; Oxford, *Statutes of the
University of Oxford*, 187–8. Goldgar's *Impolite Learning* is the most sustained analysis of the
civility underpinning the republic of letters.

36. McKenzie, *Cambridge University Press*, I, 16; Johnson and Gibson, *Print and Privilege*,
42; Hetet, "Literary Underground," 244; SCB C, fol. 286ᵛ; SCA, Suppl. Doc. I.A, Env. 11,
xiii (list of printers). The Customs House press was presumably for printing bills of lading
and similar material.

37. Earle, *Making of the English Middle Class*, 26–7; McKenzie, *Cambridge University
Press*, I, 30–2; Martin, "Espaces de la Vente," 91; McKitterick, *Cambridge University Press*,
275–7.

to King James II, did sell the Catholic almanacs and tracts he printed "next door to his House in Black-fryers," most London printing houses were smaller operations, less capable of combining the offices of production and exchange. They would contain two or at most three presses, worth the relatively small sum of about £5 each. A substantial proportion had only one. The number of workmen varied similarly, ranging from eighteen in the king's house down to just one in some of the smallest. This is admittedly an underestimate, since it excludes such personnel as proofreaders, "devils," and "flies," and it is likely that numbers grew somewhat over the years. By the mid-1720s, when Benjamin Franklin worked there, John Watts's printing house was employing about fifty people. Nonetheless, such figures show that London printing was principally a small-scale enterprise. The Stationers' Company was encouraged to "restraine" the size of printing houses, and in this at least it could point to some success.[38]

Within the building, workplace and living area were generally kept fairly discrete. Indeed, the consequences of not doing so could be serious, as we shall see. But their proximity nonetheless affected both the character of the printing house and the practices believed appropriate within it. For example, it encouraged new associations based on the structures and language of the family. Booksellers addressed each other as "brother," and the oldest workman in a printing house would be called its "father." Again, this was by no means unique to England; in France, too, the *compagnonnages* into which journeymen coalesced would commonly be led by a "mother." It has been suggested that the elaborate paraphernalia of Freemasonry may have derived partly from such usages. The first recognized lodge in England certainly met in Saint Paul's Churchyard, with Stationers prominent among its members, and the interplay between commerce and arcana that this suggests makes for an attractive theme.[39] However, I am here more interested in the mundane than the exotic, and shall concentrate more on other, more everyday consequences.

Domesticity was not simply figurative. In fact, the entire trade was profoundly dependent on ties of kinship and marriage. Evidence for this is easy

38. *Catholick Almanack*, 1687; Stationers' Company, *Registers 1554–1640*, I, 248; IV, 532–3; McKenzie, "Printers of the Mind," 54; Hetet, "Literary Underground," 104–5, 245–53; Foxon, *Pope*, 15–17; George, *London Life*, 282.

39. Chartier, *Passions of the Renaissance*, 470 ff.; Belanger, "Booksellers' Sales," 15–18; McKenzie, "Economies of Print"; [Kirkman], *English Rogue Continued*, 194; Moxon, *Mechanick Exercises on the Whole Art of Printing*, 323; Songhurst, *Minutes of the Grand Lodge of Freemasons*, viii, 3–4 and passim. For connections between commerce and magic see Smith, *Business of Alchemy*. Among many treatments of Continental houses, see Rychner, "Travail de l'Atelier," Materné, "Social Emancipation," and Darnton, *Business of Enlightenment*, 177–245. I have relied rather on studies of English houses, which were similar in many respects but generally smaller and dedicated to more local markets.

to find. Livewell Chapman was apprenticed to Benjamin Allen; he later married his master's widow and took over their bookshop, becoming one of the leading producers of radical literature in the Interregnum.[40] At the other political extreme, Henry Clements, an episcopalian Tory bookseller, was the son of the apprentice and maid to bookseller Richard Davis. Richard Banks's printing house descended through brother, apprentice, son, and wife, staying in the same dynasty for almost a century. Henry Faithorne was not only apprentice but nephew to John Martyn, Printer to the Royal Society, and consequently benefited from Martyn's contacts among the virtuosi.[41] As such examples suggest, it would be artificial in the extreme to draw a categorical distinction between family and business in the world of the Stationers. Whig bookseller John Dunton was even urged to marry one Sarah Doolittle, daughter of a writer the publication of whose writings had established Dunton in his trade, since "then you'll have her *Fathers Copies* for nothing"—and it may be that this sort of calculus was not so very rare.[42]

If the representation of domesticity was a commonplace, then, this was largely because familial links permeated a printer's workplace. Refusal to correspond to such a strongly based representation carried consequences. It left a Stationer vulnerable to challenge. Archbishop Laud's Oxford printers, for example, were mandated to print in their own homes. When the Stationers' Company wanted to attack them as constituting a threat to its members' interests, it did so by alleging that they were not in fact resident in the building housing their presses. Their argument was significant, as it encapsulated a fundamental moral principle consonant with domesticity. The Company held that absentee masters, like absentee fathers, would permit lax conduct, leading to a number of notorious evils. Three in particular were to be feared: inferior workmanship, seditious printing, and piracy.

One of the costs of failing to conform to the domestic ideal could therefore be a questioning not just of the printer, but of the texts he or she produced. Repeated allegations of sexual impropriety leveled at both Whig and Tory Stationers in the Restoration drew upon such preconceptions to just this effect. Francis Smith, Henry Hills, and Benjamin Harris were all attacked in this way, with pamphleteers impugning the worth of their publications by questioning their Stationers' domestic morality. So, most persistently of all, was the régime's surveyor of the press, Sir Roger L'Estrange. As

40. Greaves and Zaller, *Biographical Dictionary*, s.v. "Chapman, Livewell." One of William Larner's two servants was actually his brother, John Larner: [Larner], *True Relation*, title page, 16.

41. Hodgson and Blagden, *Notebook of Thomas Bennet and Henry Clements*, 6; McKenzie, *Stationers' Apprentices 1641–1700*, 108; Avis, *Sixteenth Century Long Shop*. Faithorne served with Martyn in 1672–9, then was active as a bookseller until 1688. Like Martyn, he became Printer to the Royal Society.

42. Dunton, *Life and Errors* (1705), 72, 74; Ward, *Oxford University Statutes*, I, 205–6.

overseer of the book trades for the Restoration court, L'Estrange should have exemplified propriety; yet he was regularly accused of prosecuting liaisons with Joanna Brome, widow of his printer ally, Henry Brome, and printer in her own right of L'Estrange's partisan *Observator*.[43] Such charges depended for their efficacy largely on the acknowledged juxtaposition of home and workplace in the Stationer's premises. As is discussed at greater length shortly, family members other than the patriarch might well work in the printing house. Dunton's actual wife, Elizabeth, for example, became his "*Bookseller,* [and] *Cash-Keeper,*" and his pronouncement that she "manag'd all my Affairs for me" was not just shallow gallantry. In these circumstances, tales of cuckoldry and license added piquancy to disquiet about female authority.

Such disquiet was always likely to manifest itself when the conventional office of the housewife seemed at risk of elision with what for contemporaries was a less consoling image of the woman in charge. In the domains of printing and bookselling this was often a possibility, even allowing for the extensive range of activities then recognized as "housewifery." Not only did women like Elizabeth Dunton and Elizabeth Calvert (and, later, Dorcas Lackington) assist their husbands in ways demanding commercial initiative and skill. Others ran printing houses themselves. Most who did so were probably widows, like Brome, and later Calvert herself (and for that matter Susan Streater in chapter 4); but that was far from invariably the case, and there were women who learned the craft by apprenticeship. This exacerbated tensions already generated between representations of patriarchy, on the one hand, and on the other actual domains where the practical relations between the sexes were far less confined and straightforward. Women were supposed to be simultaneously creative, cooperative, and subordinate. It proved a difficult balance to maintain, fostering both resentment and opportunities. Hence, in part, the strenuous assertions of the patriarchal household in the printing house and bookshop—and the rituals of fraternity to be found in them and in the Stationers' Company as a whole. As well as resting on familial representations, Stationers' conventions sometimes chafed at them when they implied seemingly contradictory duties. It was but one sense in which the domains of print were riven by representations of gender.[44] A profusion of conduct books provided ample resources for

43. Harris, *London Crowds,* 133, 147–8; Keeble, *Literary Culture of Nonconformity,* 108. For a few of the many attacks on L'Estrange, see Toryrorydammeeplotshammee Younkercrape [pseud.], *Sermon Prepared to be Preach'd,* 17, sig. E1ʳ⁻ᵛ; N. N., *Hue and Cry,* 6, 8, 10–16; Theophilus Rationalis [pseud.], *New News from Bedlam,* 3, 25, 61–70.

44. Roberts, "'Words They Are Women, and Deeds They Are Men,'" 140–1; Hunt, *Middling Sort,* 46–72; Hill, *Women, Work, and Sexual Politics,* 153, 243; Clark, *Struggle for the Breeches,* 34, 63–4; Amussen, *Ordered Society,* 34–66.

identifying and characterizing associated misdemeanors. But in all such arguments, the point being made was really a simple one: that the home, as the archetypal site of morality and patriarchal authority, should guarantee standards of reliability and sobriety in the exercise of the Stationer's craft.[45] A ready way to cast doubt on the latter was therefore to question the former.

Such was the primacy of the bond between domestic and occupational propriety that it suggests itself as a principle in terms of which the complex practices of the early modern printer may be understood. Before proceeding to examine the cultural effects of printing, we need to address these practices. Fortunately, in assessing these aspects of the printing house we have the benefit of a remarkable piece of contemporary testimony. This is Joseph Moxon's *Mechanick Exercises . . . Applied to the Art of Printing*—a work of almost four hundred pages, issued in parts in the course of 1683–4. This was by some decades the first detailed account of the London printing house. Moreover, it was the creation of a participant. Moxon, the son of a separatist printer based in Holland, exercised the craft himself (fig. 2.5). He was familiar with printing practices both in London and in the Low Countries, and his account was based on his own intimate knowledge of what actually happened in printing houses. Moxon's work provides valuable material for reconstructing the domain of printing, especially when correlated with evidence from other sources. Yet it was not innocent of partiality. It also betrays an intense awareness of how different representations of that domain, including Moxon's own, could serve not just to mirror reality, but to create it.[46]

Joseph Moxon was principally a practitioner of what Stephen Johnston calls "the mathematicalls." In particular, he was an expert globe maker. But he had begun printing with his father as early as 1647. Since then he had worked with a number of printers and booksellers, including such radicals as William Larner, and he was to continue either printing or publishing works on the mathematical sciences until 1686. In 1662 he successfully petitioned for the title of hydrographer royal in order to produce "yᵉ most exact and perfect Waggoner in the English Tongue" under royal protection. After the Fire, in which he lost his premises, he also began to cut letters. Yet Moxon never became a member of the Stationers' Company, and despite his royal title the Company targeted him for suppression at least twice.[47]

45. Dunton, *Life and Errors* (1705), 100; Madan, "Oxford Press," 116; SCA, Suppl. Doc. I.A, Env. 5, xiv (see also SCB D, fol. 2ʳ for a similar complaint about Cambridge); Erickson, *Women and Property*, 11. Barnaby Bernard Lintot translated *Galateo* in 1703: Woodhouse, "Tradition of Della Casa's *Galateo*," 20–21.

46. A related point is treated by Chartier, *Cultural History*, 1–16 and 95–111.

47. Moxon, *Mechanick Exercises on the Whole Art of Printing*, xxxiii–xxxiv, 409–41, 481; Jagger, "Joseph Moxon," 195; SCB D, fols. 87ʳ, 101ᵛ, 212ʳ. Apparently a member of the Weav-

FIG. 2.5. Joseph Moxon. Moxon, *Tutor to Astronomy and Geography*, 4th ed., 1686. (By permission of the Syndics of Cambridge University Library.)

It was typical of Moxon that he tried to make his cutting of letters into a "philosophical" enterprise, insisting that characters must henceforth be constructed only according to Vitruvian principles. He had already learned to cultivate gentlemen virtuosi. Soon after beginning to make type, then, he was providing letter for both John Wilkins's universal character and Robert Boyle's Irish bible project. He further developed links with several other fellows of the Royal Society, among them Halley, Pepys, Brouncker, and Hooke (whose Gresham lectures he attended).[48] In 1677–8 he therefore de-

ers' Company, Moxon could nevertheless approach the Stationers' court to stop another printer comprinting his copies: SCB D, fol. 241ᵛ. He probably regarded his patent as hydrographer royal, which authorized him to make "Globes, Maps, and Sea-Platts," as the legitimation for his printing activities. By "Waggoner," Moxon and his contemporaries meant a book of nautical maps, after one issued by Dutchman Lucas Janssen Waghenaer in 1584.

48. Moxon, *Regulae*, 3–4 and passim (his instructions here being directed principally to workmen engaged in carving inscriptions for buildings); Moxon, *Mechanick Exercises on the Whole Art of Printing*, xxxv, xxxviii, 357 ff.; Hooke, *Diary*, 14. Moxon borrowed the Society's telescope, and he was chosen to supply a globe for Wren's "telescopical moon": Birch, *History*, I, 403, 469; II, 156. He dedicated his *Tutor to Astronomy & Geography* (1665) to Brouncker, albeit speculatively.

cided to approach Hooke and John Evelyn to license his *Mechanick Exercises*
through the Society's privilege. The tracts themselves began to appear
shortly thereafter, in January 1678. Five hundred copies were printed of each
issue, retailing at sixpence each. They led to Moxon's being proposed for
fellowship. There was opposition to his candidacy, but he was nonetheless
elected the following November, on the same day as Edmond Halley.[49]
Meanwhile, Moxon made use of president of the Society Sir Joseph Williamson's position as overseer of the *London Gazette* to publicize the *Exercises*
in the government's periodical. Even so, sales proved sluggish. Copies would
still be on sale as late as 1686. The first volume was successfully completed
in 1680, however, just in time for Moxon to attempt unsuccessfully to replace John Martyn as Printer to the Society. The project was then discontinued amid the furor of the Restoration crisis of 1679–83. It resumed only in
1683, when Moxon endeavored to provide security for his periodical in the
form of subscriptions. He promised to continue publication provided he
could woo sufficient subscribers to guarantee breaking even on the project.
Apparently he was successful, since the volume on printing did begin to
appear. It was finally finished in the summer of 1684 (fig. 2.6).[50]

The key to Moxon's representation of printing was the one figure in
whom the entire craft was apparently encapsulated: the master printer.
Moxon's master was far more than a simple craftsman. This figure was certainly no mere printer "as he is Vulgarly accounted." In his influential
"Mathematicall Praeface" to Euclid, the Elizabethan polymath John Dee
had made a point of distinguishing a true architect from "a *Carpenter* or
Mason." Moxon followed suit, modeling his master printer explicitly on this
ideal of the architect. His inspiration, like Dee's, was Vitruvius—an authority to whom we have already seen Moxon appealing in his letter-cutting
project, and whose significance will be discussed further below. The master
must be adept at the art, then, but he must also be much more. By "a
Typographer" Moxon meant "such a one, who by his own Judgement, from
solid reasoning with himself, can either perform, or direct others to perform

49. Moxon, *Mechanick Exercises on the Whole Art of Printing*, xlv, 14; Birch, *History*, III,
441–2; Hooke, *Diary*, 337–8. It is important to realize that the Society's own periodical, the
Philosophical Transactions, was at this moment facing an uncertain future following the death
of its founder, Henry Oldenburg. The *Mechanick Exercises* should be seen as one of a number
of candidates to replace it: see below, pp. 531–40. Moxon presented a globe to the Society a
year later, but then failed to pay his dues, and was excluded from lists of fellows from 1682:
Birch, *History*, III, 519; IV, 159–60. Jagger ("Joseph Moxon," 202) credibly suggests that
Moxon allowed his fellowship to lapse in pursuit of the position of Printer to the Society.

50. Moxon, *Tutor to Astronomy & Geography* (1686), [272]; Moxon, *Mechanick Exercises
on the Whole Art of Printing*, xlv–xlix; Hooke, *Diary*, 448; Birch, *History*, IV, 26; *Collection of
Letters for the Improvement of Husbandry and Trade* I, 14 (13 March 1682/3), 168; II, 2 (c.
October 1683), 48. Subscriptions for the resumed publication cost 2d. per sheet, plus 2d. for
every plate.

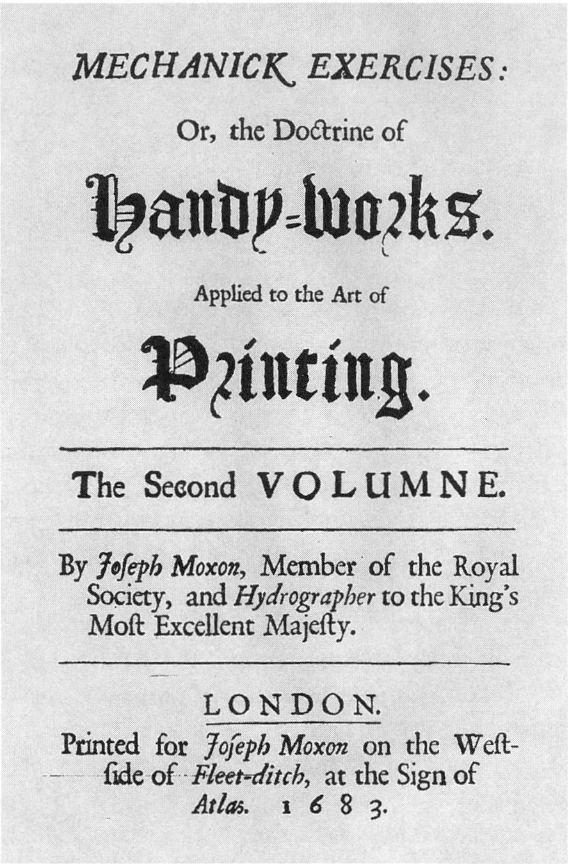

MECHANICK EXERCISES:

Or, the Doctrine of

Handy-works.

Applied to the Art of

Printing.

The Second VOLUMNE.

By *Joseph Moxon*, Member of the Royal Society, and *Hydrographer* to the King's Most Excellent Majesty.

LONDON.

Printed for *Joseph Moxon* on the West-side of *Fleet-ditch*, at the Sign of *Atlas*. 1 6 8 3.

FIG. 2.6. Title page to Joseph Moxon's *Mechanick Exercises*. (By permission of the Syndics of Cambridge University Library.)

from the beginning to the end, all the Handy-works and Physical Operations relating to *Typographie*." That is, he was the "Soul" of the enterprise. The lesser workmen were as "members of the Body" governed by his natural authority.[51]

The master's main function was to provide something called a "*Printing-House*." This "strange" expression meant not just the physical "House, or Room or Rooms" in which presses were placed; again, that was merely its "Vulgar" meaning. In the "more peculiar" sense familiar to printers themselves, it referred to the apparatus of the trade maintained in its proper arrangement. Thus "they say, Such a One has set up a *Printing-House*, when

---

51. Moxon, *Mechanick Exercises on the Whole Art of Printing*, 10–12; Dee, "John Dee his Mathematicall Praeface," sigs. a3ʳ⁻ᵛ (for an "Arte"), d3ʳ–d4ᵛ: the architect "is neither Smith, nor Builder: nor, separately, any Artificer: but the Hed, the Provost, the Director, and Judge of all Artificiall workes, and all Artificers." For Vitruvius on the figure of the architect, see *De Architectura*, I, 1–17 (pp. 22–36).

thereby they only mean he has remov'd the Tools us'd in his former House." The master must provide almost all these tools, and he must ensure their correct assemblage. The only exceptions to this rule were the compositor's composing stick, which was traditionally an object of some personal sanctity, and the ink itself, the making of which was liable to be dangerous.[52]

These exceptions notwithstanding, at the outset the master must "Philosophize with himself" to determine that the room in which the printing house was to be erected bore a "rational proportion" to the work done in it. This philosophizing, like that of the virtuosi Moxon so revered, involved considerations of number, weight, and measure: of space, matter, light, and heat.[53] The floor must be solid and horizontal, the walls must be firm, and, most important of all, the ceiling must be strong enough that the presses could be braced to it by the stout beams depicted in contemporary engravings. The room must be of "convenient capacity" for the machinery, each press needing about seven feet by seven feet of floor space. A nearby window must extend high enough up the wall to cast light on the workers, and each press must be carefully placed so that the light from this window fell directly onto its forme and tympan. But the windows must not be too large either, lest the "violence of *Winter*" freeze the paper and type, thus causing the whole printing operation to seize up. Since printers customarily used paper panes in their windows, and winters in the late seventeenth century were very cold, this was a distinct possibility.[54] Other extremes of temperature must also be taken into account. The press should be sited in the northern part of the room, so that "the *Press-men*, when at their hard labour in *Summer* time, may be the less incommoded with the heat of the *Sun*." Finally, if kept in the same room, every frame of cases holding type required an additional four and a half by five and a half feet, extra space being allowed for easy passage. However, Moxon remarked that in English houses these cases were generally erected in another chamber, with its own careful arrangement (fig. 2.7).[55]

52. Moxon, *Mechanick Exercises on the Whole Art of Printing*, 15–16, 40–1, 82–4. Ink was made by a process that could lead to violent explosions.

53. Moxon, *Mechanick Exercises on the Whole Art of Printing*, 17; BL Ms. Add. 4386, fol. 70^r. Compare John Dunton's statement that a good master "deserves the Title of a *Virtuoso*, and to be numbered among the Philosophers": Dunton, *Religio Bibliopolae*, 40. For this problematic text see Parks, *John Dunton*, 47–9, and Dunton, *Life and Errors* (1818), I, xxv.

54. Moxon, *Mechanick Exercises on the Whole Art of Printing*, 17; BL Ms. Add. 4386, fol. 70^r. This happened, suitably enough, to Robert Boyle's *New Experiments and Observations Touching Cold* (1683): Boyle, *Works*, II, 467. Compare also Peter Heylyn's complaint that one of his polemics had suffered because "the extreme cold weather overtaking the Printers . . . hath benummed the fingers of the *Compositors*, and dulled the eyes of the *Correctors*": [Heylyn], *Observations*, sig. [A4^{r-v}].

55. According to McKenzie, *Cambridge University Press*, I, 18, this use of separate rooms

TYPOGRAPHIA HARLEMI PRIMVM INVENTA
Circà Annum 1440.

Currat penna licet, tantum vix scribitur anno,
Quantum uno reddunt præla Batava die:
Addidit inventis aliquid Germania tantis:
Hollandus cæpit. Theuto peregit opus?

Saenredam invent.   veldr̃ sculp.
                                          P. Scriverius?

FIG. 2.7. The interior of a printing house. This engraving after Saenredam is generally taken to be the most accurate image available. Although it portrays a Dutch house, its characteristic elements were probably present in English houses too. The image itself, ostensibly portraying the first printing house of all, that of Laurens Coster, was in fact of the Haarlem operation of Adriaen Roman. But it was intended to display the essence of a printing house rather than the accidental characteristics of any particular one. Ampsing, *Beschryvinge ende lof der Stad Haerlem in Holland* (1628). (By permission of the Bodleian Library, University of Oxford, Douce A.219.)

Occupying center stage, the press itself should be a carefully designed artifact. Moxon recommended a new design, which he attributed to globe maker and cartographer Willem Jansen Blaeu of Amsterdam—"a Man as well famous for good and great *Printing*, as for his many *Astronomical* and *Geographical* exhibitions to the World." This attribution was highly significant, and seems to have been unique to Moxon. He had probably learned about Blaeu during the early 1650s, when he had resided in Holland. Moxon had immediately appreciated the virtues of his fellow mathematical practitioner; his own first book was a translation of Blaeu's treatise on the use of globes. Blaeu had worked with Tycho Brahe in Uraniborg and, Moxon confided, according to "the general report of many of his personal acquaintance" had himself made "all or most of the *Syderal Observations* set forth in

---

was the main difference between English and Continental layouts. For the latter see Clair, *Christopher Plantin*, facing 97.

Tycho's name."[56] Tycho had rewarded him by letting him take manuscript copies of these unpublished observations to Amsterdam, where he had incorporated them into his famous globes. Eventually Blaeu had set up his own printing house there, in which he had erected nine of his new presses in a row, naming them after the Muses.

To associate the new press with Tycho Brahe's instruments and observations—and even to claim that Blaeu had created both—was to link printing to the most powerful modern icon of the mathematical sciences. Moxon himself was under no illusions about the status of this icon: he had elsewhere called Tycho "*Hercules the Second*." And his own regard for Blaeu was sufficient for him not only to translate the latter's work, but actually to write a book of his own and issue it under the same title.[57]

This press was therefore no product of artisan trial and error. It was rather "a Machine invented upon mature consideration of Mechanick Powers, deducted from Geometrick Principles." As its pedigree warranted, Blaeu's press was distinguished by the "Matter, Form and Position" of its parts. In place of older machines' "make-shift slovenly contrivance," here at last was one "proper for its intended purpose." It was a notable claim, not least because it seems to have been rather unrealistic. The material difference between Blaeu's press and the one Moxon so castigated is to modern eyes slight, and there is little evidence that the supposedly better press was much used in England at all (although James Watson did testify to its employment in Scotland) (figs. 2.8 and 2.9). On the contrary, working presses were generally of the older type, and were constructed by workaday joiners and smiths who developed the necessary skills in the course of their routine duties. Real presses often broke down, and required repeated attention if they were to keep working. Real presses were artisanal through and through. Nonetheless, Moxon's eulogy remains remarkable for its argument that mechanical knowledge, and even philosophy, underlay the proper frame and operation of a true printing press.[58]

Just as the pressroom must be well chosen, so the compositors' room must similarly be arranged with a view to questions of light and passage. The distributing frame must be in the center, for illumination and ease of access

---

56. Moxon, *Mechanick Exercises on the Whole Art of Printing*, 1962 ed., xxii, 45–8, Appendix IV, 395; Blaeu, *Tutor to Astronomy and Geography*; Thoren, *Lord of Uraniborg*, 200.

57. Moxon, *Mechanick Exercises on the Whole Art of Printing*, 373–4; Moxon, *Tutor to Astronomie and Geographie* (1659), sig. *3ʳ.

58. Moxon, *Mechanick Exercises on the Whole Art of Printing*, 45–9, 373–4; McKenzie, *Cambridge University Press*, I, 39–47, 85, 132–3, 137; Minard, "Agitation in the Work Force," 114–5; [Watson], *History of the Art of Printing*, 22. Most surviving Continental presses are, however, of Blaeu's design: Gaskell, "Census."

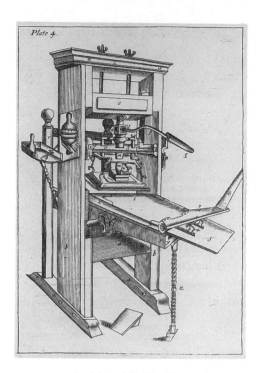

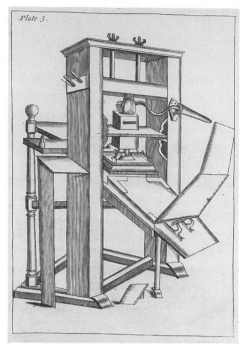

FIG. 2.8. (*above left*) The Blaeu printing press. The differences between this and the older press (fig. 2.9) are to modern eyes slight: the Blaeu press uses an iron hose, not a wooden one (g), there are changes to the catch for the bar (p, q), and the height of the gallows (4) is adjustable. That Moxon made so much of these differences (plus a few others too small to be seen in this image) reflects his regard for the harmony of printers' movements around the press, which such nuances noticeably affected. (Moxon, *Mechanick Exercises*, 273-4, 373-4.) Moxon, *Mechanick Exercises*. (By permission of the Syndics of Cambridge University Library.)

FIG. 2.9. (*above right*) The "Old-fashion'd" press. The sparseness of the image conveys Moxon's dislike of this press. Moxon, *Mechanick Exercises*. (By permission of the Syndics of Cambridge University Library.)

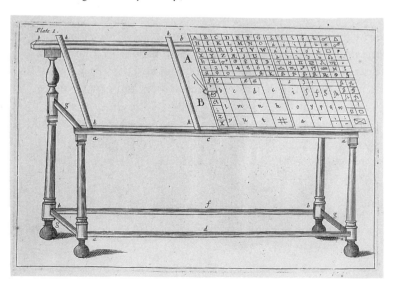

FIG. 2.10. The compositor's cases. Moxon, *Mechanick Exercises*. (By permission of the Syndics of Cambridge University Library.)

to the forme being constructed; unused cases should be kept in the "least frequented" part of the chamber. Each case of type should be positioned with ample space around it. A fire must be kept burning so that the compositors could leave type in front of it to dry in another carefully contrived case.

Here the compositor or compositors worked to arrange type for printing. Metal types were disposed in two cases composed of rectangular divisions of various sizes, each dedicated to one character (fig. 2.10). These cases sloped toward the worker, who would stand before them with the written copy propped up before him. He would compose by putting letters plucked from the appropriate case into an iron composing stick grasped in his left hand, which held about eight or nine lines. When full, he emptied the stick into a wooden frame called a galley. Once a page of letters had been inserted, the galley was complete. The compositor would then "tie it up" and go on to the next. On completing a sheet's pages in this way, he would put the galleys into an iron frame called a chase, and fix them in position with wedges. The resulting "forme" could then be carried to the pressroom.[59]

Although it can be described in outline in such simple terms, in practice composition was a highly developed skill. A compositor would be expected to produce some one thousand to twelve hundred characters—about an octavo page—an hour, and the imperative to work quickly was strong. This required the rapid and coordinated use of manual dexterity, memory, and aesthetic judgment. Moxon himself insisted that the compositor must be something of a "Scholler." We know relatively little about the education and abilities of actual compositors, not least because their skill was never communicated in writing. But although Ralph Thoresby found one he considered "ingenious," and in Philadelphia Franklin worked beside another who had run away from Oxford, it seems plausible that many did not live up to Moxon's exhortation. Even Franklin's Oxonian was apparently "idle, thoughtless and imprudent." Indeed, Moxon's call was rehearsed with telling consistency by later writers, who held that a compositor must boast "a tolerable Genius for Letters," a good memory for learning languages, a perfect knowledge of grammar, and fluency in Latin and Greek. Foreign compositors often possessed these capabilities, it seemed, which was why they could produce correct editions. British workers did not.[60]

Here we start to see how the skills exercised in the printing house could have immediate implications for the pages being printed. For a compositor did not just slavishly copy a writer's manuscript. On the contrary, he enjoyed

59. Moxon, *Mechanick Exercises on the Whole Art of Printing*, 16, 18, 27–33, 202–3; compare Campbell, *London Tradesman*, 121–2.

60. McKenzie, *Cambridge University Press*, I, 85, 132–4, 137–8; Minard, "Agitation in the Work Force," 114–5; Hunter, *Diary of Ralph Thoresby*, II, 97; Franklin, *Autobiography*, 42–3; Campbell, *London Tradesman*, 123.

substantial freedom in his settings.[61] This interpretative responsibility derived in part from the special caliber of the compositor's skills; but it also resulted from the central place those skills occupied in maintaining the reputation of the master. "It is necessary [that] the *Compositers* Judgment should know where the Author has been deficient," Moxon cautioned, so that "his care may not suffer such Work to go out of his Hands as may bring Scandal upon himself, and Scandal and prejudice upon the *Master Printer.*" While the copy provided by the author should ideally be the compositor's sole "Rule and Authority," this consideration meant that that ideal could never be attained. Because of the "carelessness" of some authors and the "ignorance" of others—in short, because writers did not possess printers' skills—manuscript copy could never simply be reproduced in print. A good compositor must therefore actively "discern and amend" his "*Copy.*" He must take care not to reproduce letters mechanically, but to "read" his copy "with consideration." By this Moxon meant that he must "get himself into the meaning of the *Author,*" and then use typography to make that meaning clearer than any author could. Moreover, in order to do this the compositor must not only reconstruct authorial meaning, but also anticipate readership. In arranging his different fonts and sizes of characters, he aimed to make the finished sheets "the better sympathize with the *Authors* Genius, and also with the capacity of the Reader." As if this were not enough, he must all the time remember to render the finished page "graceful to the Eye, and pleasant in Reading."[62]

As such instructions confirm, the appearance and even the content of printed pages could be closely affected by the skills and conceptions of the printers producing them. In the final appearance of the page were implicated the compositor's knowledge, dexterity, interpretation of authorial meaning, and anticipation of readers' competences. This extended even to the very letters themselves. In establishing a printing house, type was likely to be the most expensive single element. But Moxon insisted that the characters to be reproduced in a printing house were properly the concern of the master printer, and decreed that his philosophical master have complete sets of some eight to ten different typefaces. He must also possess characters for music, Greek, Hebrew, Syriac, "Astronomical Signs, *Planets, Aspects, Alge-*

61. All the compositors in Cambridge could set Latin, most English, and some Greek: McKenzie, *Cambridge University Press*, I, 110.

62. Moxon, *Mechanick Exercises on the Whole Art of Printing*, 192–219; Dunton, *Life and Errors* (1705), 88–9. Moxon tried to give authors rules for the use of italics: 250–1. Compare Richardson's comments, cited in McKenzie, *Cambridge University Press*, I, 67, and BL Ms. Add. 4386, fols. 37^r, 45^r, for comment on the inadequate composition of arithmetical works, "either for want of knowledge or application." An informed discussion of compositors' autonomy is in Burton, *Anatomy of Melancholy*, I, xlviii–liv.

FIG. 2.11. Moxon's proposal for producing letters by applied geometry. Moxon, *Regulae Trium Ordinum Literarum Typographicarum.* (By permission of the Syndics of Cambridge University Library.)

braical Characters, Physical and Chimical Characters, &c." Here Moxon departed significantly from prevailing practice, which might involve the repeated use of worn type decades old. His ideal master, on the contrary, would carefully consider the shapes of his letters and their generation from "Mathematical Regular Figures." Typography itself must become a mathematical science, moreover, openly taught and subject to geometrical rules (fig. 2.11). Only by applying this principle could a master hope to approach the letters of the Ancients, which, Moxon affirmed, had been constructed strictly from "Circles, Arches of Circles, and Straight Lines." He recommended employing the microscopes of his virtuoso friends to examine and construct such letters, and the use of mathematical instruments to measure and perfect their proportions. He himself produced separate instructions for the construction of ideal characters based on these maxims. He publicized them in the first specimen sheet of characters ever printed in England.[63]

63. Moxon, *Mechanick Exercises on the Whole Art of Printing*, 19–21, 21–4, 25, 87, 97, 87–120; Moxon, *Proves.*

With such a range of resources, Moxon's master printer would be well
equipped to produce any learned book. Yet capital costs were not the only
ones involved. Charges and rates of pay must also be fixed. These were typically determined according to the difficulty of the composing, exotic languages and difficult formats (those involving a variety of type sizes as well as
those posing lexical problems) fetching a higher rate than English prose. If
the material to be printed were complex enough to slow the composition
appreciably, then the presses might even have to halt work altogether to
await the compositors, and that added further to the expense. Mathematical
works were among the most problematic in this respect. Early in 1683, just
as Moxon was printing the *Exercises*, the printer of the *Philosophical Transactions* was complaining of inadequate remuneration at eighteen shillings
per sheet, since a tide table alone took five days to compose. Similarly,
printer Moses Pitt had told John Pell in 1666 that mathematical tables were
especially slow and expensive work: he actually had to "cast severall new
figures & Brass Rules" for them, he pointed out, "which makes the worke
so Chargible that we can only worke of[f] Halfe A sheet At A Time." In
this case not only the pressmen but the compositor had to "stand still," since
Pitt could not afford enough special type to set even one sheet at a time.
Furthermore, good correction was essential for such complex material, and
this added to his difficulties. Lord Brouncker, who was inspecting the sheets,
had fallen ill. Pitt was reduced to begging Pell for different material for the
compositor to work with while proofs awaited Brouncker's recovery.[64]

Pitt's experience reminds us that the compositor was not the only worker
entitled and entrusted to make changes. The permanent office of corrector
was not well established by this time. Nevertheless, wanting the attentions
of a figure like Brouncker, most houses would employ some form of reader
on a case-by-case basis to help remove "errors."[65] This individual became
part of the printing house domain, and, like the compositor, had to act with
the master printer's reputation in mind. The skills Moxon stipulated for
such a reader were therefore again daunting. Of languages he must know at
least English, Latin, Greek, Hebrew, Syriac, Chaldaic, French, Spanish, Italian, High and Low Dutch, Saxon, and Welsh. He must also be familiar with
general principles of etymology, and be well-acquainted with all the skills of
a compositor.

This prodigious individual occupied a "little Closet" adjoining the compositors' room. There someone "well skill'd in true and quick Reading"

64. Gunther, *Early Science in Oxford*, XII, 13–14; BL Ms. Add. 4279, 201.
65. Moxon, *Mechanick Exercises on the Whole Art of Printing*, 382; McKenzie, *Cambridge
University Press*, I, 84–5. For correctors in the King's Printing House in the 1630s see Stationers' Company, *Registers 1554–1640*, IV, 20.

would be appointed by the master to read the copy aloud to him as he checked it against the proofs.[66] The process would be repeated once, or at most twice. After that, any further errors to come to light were reckoned the corrector's responsibility, and he could be held liable to pay a compensatory fine for them. For this reason, a "revise"—a copy printed off before beginning the impression itself—might be provided to reassure the corrector that suggested changes had indeed been implemented. But paper was too expensive to throw away so casually; indeed, the undertaker (and in many cases the author) was generally expected to pay for it. All sheets of such valuable material had to be accounted for.[67] Instead of a revise, the first sheets of a print run would therefore often be checked as the rest were being printed off. In such a case, books would inevitably be made up of sheets in different states of correction. The consequence was that no two final copies out of a given edition would necessarily be the same. Indeed, in its modern sense the very concept of an "edition" is entirely anachronistic. For books such as the first folio of Shakespeare, not only is there no pair of identical copies in existence, but there is no straightforward way of positing a "typical" printed copy against which "variants" might be calibrated. There were, it has been estimated, some twenty-four thousand variations in the text of the King James bible between its first printing and the 1830s. The myth of the standardized impression did not survive the reality of the printing house.[68]

Once carried to the press, the forme was in the hands of the pressmen. These almost always worked in pairs, although it was not unknown for just one worker to operate a press. Their work was fast, physical, and highly coordinated. It was performed "with various Set and Formal Postures and Gestures of the Body." Moxon described these physical motions in detail; a

66. Moxon, *Mechanick Exercises on the Whole Art of Printing*, 246–7. The issue of proofing in the seventeenth century is complex and difficult, and has attracted an extensive historiographical literature. See, for example, Simpson, *Proof-Reading*; McKenzie, *Cambridge University Press*, I, 67–9, 85; McKenzie, "Printers of the Mind," 44 ff.; Blayney, *Texts of "King Lear,"* 188–218; McKitterick, *Cambridge University Press*, 236–41, 243–8. William Dugard was freed in 1648 as "helpfull in the Correction of the Companies Schoole bookes," which may indicate a systematic approach: SCB C, fol. 251ʳ. SCB D, fol. 200ʳ is less ambiguous in implying such an approach.

67. Moxon, *Mechanick Exercises on the Whole Art of Printing*, 239; Maslen and Lancaster, *Bowyer Ledgers*, xxviii, xxxii; McKitterick, *Cambridge University Press*, 285–8.

68. De Grazia, *Shakespeare Verbatim*, 15–19; Black, "Printed Bible," 411–4, 459; Orgel, "Authentic Shakespeare," 11. Papermaking only really started in England at the end of the sixteenth century. Even after that most printing paper continued to be imported, generally via Amsterdam: Coleman, *British Paper Industry*, 4–88. The main cost of producing a prestigious book might well be paper: McKenzie, *Cambridge University Press*, I, 141, 144; Materné, "Social Emancipation," 212. By Campbell's time the proof was read by the master printer if there were no corrector, and the revise was sent to the author for his or her corrections: Campbell, *London Tradesman*, 122–3.

much simpler account will have to suffice here. The pressmen would fix the forme onto a stone that could be rolled out from under the press. On the side of the press was a vessel holding ink. Two leather balls stuffed with wool would be used to spread ink from this vessel on the forme. A sheet of paper would then be taken from the dampened heap, laid out on a frame called the tympan, and secured by the frisket. This assemblage was turned down onto the forme. The carriage—stone, forme, and paper—was then rolled under the main body of the press, to lie beneath the platen. Then "two Pulls of the Handle perform[ed] the Business." (Two pulls were needed because the platen covered only half of the forme, which would therefore need to be repositioned after the first pull.) The carriage was immediately rolled out again, and the paper taken off and laid out on a table. The process would then be repeated for the next sheet. After one side of all the sheets had been printed, another forme would be inserted for the other side. If other colors than black were to be printed, the operation would have to be repeated again for each ink.

Throughout this process, the two pressmen would work together. One laid on the sheets, put down the tympans and frisket, ran the carriage in and out, and removed the printed sheets; the other distributed the ink. "Both the *Press-mans* Hands at the same time [would be] ingaged in different Operations," Moxon remarked, in a continuous activity of great precision and skill.[69] Such precision was made possible only by a workman's long acquaintance with the "constant and methodical posture and gesture" needed at the press, "which in a train of Work becomes habitual to him, and eases his Body." This union of knowledge and the body deserves emphasis, since the result was visible in the regularity of printed sheets. The habituation of gesture, posture, and labor was what made those sheets as uniform as they could be, since "a *Pull* of the same strength upon the same *Form*, with the same *Beating*, and with the same *Blankets*, &c. will give the same Colour and Impression." Without the bodily "habit" of presswork, printed sheets would have lacked that quality of sameness.

Wooden presses were heavy and troublesome to work. The men who labored with them, exercising such intense physical discipline for long hours in order to reproduce Moxon's Vitruvian characters with harmonious regularity, had to be burly as well as skillful. They were known as "horses" (or, in France, "bears") because of "the hard Labour they go through all day long." Accounts written by near-contemporaries referred to pressmen who would "perspire in face and mouth and hand" as they worked, "sweating

---

69. Moxon, *Mechanick Exercises on the Whole Art of Printing*, 252–311, esp. 292–9; Campbell, *London Tradesman*, 121–2.

out their innermost bodily fluid."[70] Working for up to fourteen hours a day, a pair of such workers might be expected to produce some twelve to fifteen hundred sheets in that time—that is, to make about 250 impressions an hour. They were paid according to how much work there was to do, and perhaps for how much they themselves would contract for. Like the master printer, however, Moxon's pressman was no mere laborer. He not only reaped "great satisfaction" from "the contemplation of the harmonious design and Make of a *Press*," but could immediately see the cause of any breakdown. Since the press was built "by the Rules of Architecture," the pressman must know those rules himself in order to operate and maintain it correctly. In short, he was endowed with "a competency of the Inventers Genius."[71]

Pressmen, compositors, correctors: it is difficult enough to track down these workers. We can say little about their attitudes, practices, and lives. But there were still other inhabitants of the printing house who remain even more elusive. Among them were the "devils," "spirits," "boys," and "flies" whom we rarely encounter in contemporary descriptions, but who seem to have been essential to the smooth running of any printing operation. They included young boys employed mainly to take sheets off the press after each impression, but also to act as general dogsbodies. Young girls might also be employed as readers, declaiming aloud before correctors. Such subordinates—and the printing house at Cambridge also paid a cluster of other workers, including street sweepers—were vital if work were to continue unimpeded. But their presence was scarcely ever remarked upon unless they could be blamed for something having gone wrong. Only then did they warrant notice.[72]

70. Binns, "Four Latin Poems on Printing," 41; Gaskell, *New Introduction*, 124–33; Moxon, *Mechanick Exercises on the Whole Art of Printing*, 303, 329. For "bears"—and other interesting details—see Balzac's description of an Angoulême printing house, in *Lost Illusions*, 3–20.

71. Some pressmen did other jobs too. See McKenzie, *Cambridge University Press*, I, 91; Febvre and Martin, *Coming of the Book*, 131–2; Moxon, *Mechanick Exercises on the Whole Art of Printing*, 327; SCB D, fol. 27ᵛ. McKitterick, *Cambridge University Press*, 268 records that the Cambridge workers in the mid–seventeenth century would work at least a twelve-hour day, beginning at six in the morning, and were expected to make 2,500 impressions (i.e., 1,250 sheets) in that period. Piecework as such was established only in the eighteenth century. In the seventeenth, it was more common for employees to be paid a standard weekly wage for as long as a job lasted, thus giving rise to concern if they were kept waiting: McKenzie, *Cambridge University Press*, I, 78–93, 138. As well as from records in the history of printing, information on working hours can be inferred from other social-historical sources. For example, during the Commonwealth residents of the Stationers' district around Saint Paul's Churchyard complained of soldiers "playing at nine pinnes at unseasonable times." It was determined that "resonable times" were between six in the morning and nine at night: BL Thomason Tract 669f16(5).

72. Moxon, *Mechanick Exercises on the Whole Art of Printing*, 338; *Grub Street Journal* 147 (26 October 1732), 148 (30 October 1732); *Gentleman's Magazine* 2 (1732), 1020; McKenzie,

Together, all of these workers maintained their own rules and practices. These printing-house conventions might be kept deliberately obscure. They are therefore now hard to recover, but they seem to have conditioned both life and work to a considerable extent. By a custom that in Moxon's era had already existed since "Time out of Mind," the collective working in a printing house was known as a "chapel." Its oldest workman would be known as the chapel's father, and, continuing the domestic theme, any journeyman marrying or becoming a parent was expected to signal the fact before the chapel by some ceremony. To enter, newcomers and apprentices alike had to pay a fine of a half-crown, which Moxon called a "*Benvenue.*" They were then expected to honor a cluster of "Customs and By-laws" enforced in each chapel, the breach of which was punishable by a further penance, called a "Solace." Offenses included excessive inebriation (a problem encountered by Isaac Newton in his dealings with printers), fighting, abusiveness, and the inappropriate use of equipment (in particular, the handling of a compositor's prized composing stick). Recalcitrant offenders might well find themselves beaten.

Such chapel conventions unified the workplace, rendering it a community. They established common maxims of civility among insiders and constituted a body of knowledge possessed only by the privileged few. In the same way, they served to mark outsiders for exclusion. Solacing could thus be incurred for what seem to us trivial breaches of politeness, and was extended to unfortunate strangers entering the house and acting in such a way as to constitute "affronts" or "indignities" to its members. It was an offense to go into the royal printing house and ask for a ballad, for example, since such work was reckoned to be beneath so exalted a workshop.[73] And the solace system also reinforced in certain respects the ordering of the printing environment favored by the Stationers' Company. An important example is that of "copy-money." Seventeenth-century printers routinely received this copy-money, a payment introduced early in the 1620s to replace the previous custom of granting free copies of a book to its printers. The earlier custom had resulted in the wide circulation of unauthorized copies, and the manufacture of piracies based on them. Copy-money would, it was hoped, assist

---

Cambridge University Press, I, 71–2. For invisible "laborants" becoming noticeable after accidents, compare Shapin, *Social History of Truth*, 362–3.

73. Moxon, *Mechanick Exercises on the Whole Art of Printing*, 323–9. Newton's experience was of a compositor called Lightbody, whom Richard Bentley had proposed as a suitable workman for the second edition of the *Principia*. "I proposed to our Master Printer to have Lightbody come down & compose," Bentley told Newton, "which at first he agreed to; but the next day he had a character of his being a mere sot, & having plaid such pranks yᵗ no body will take him into any Printhouse in London or Oxford; & so he fears he'll debauch all his Men. So we must let Him alone": Newton, *Correspondence*, V, 7.

attempts to eliminate these. It continued to be paid throughout the first half of the eighteenth century. Chapel rules reinforced the practice. They decreed it an offense for a workman to take sheets from the printing house if copy-money were being paid, and otherwise for him to take any before the whole book had been printed.[74]

The chapel thus created and enforced a collective morality in the printing house, and one that need not be opposed to the master's interests. So much so, in fact, that the master even sponsored some of its activities. The best known of these was the "*Waygoose*" (later "wayzgoose") feast. This was held "at his own House" every year, when the paper windows in the workrooms were replaced. It signaled the beginning of working by candlelight. The Waygoose feast also coincided with the autumn fairs, particularly Saint Bartholomew's in London and Stourbridge in Cambridge, and all the festivities accompanying them. As with copy-money, so in this case it is possible that the feast's popularity was a principal cause of printers' retention of paper windows well into the eighteenth century, by which time they were architectural anachronisms.[75]

A chapel made the moral content of its conventions manifest when an apprentice first graduated to full membership. It seems that he or she would generally be subjected to an elaborate celebratory ritual before elevation. Versions of what was called the *Depositio Cornuti Typographici*, an elaborate morality play performed at such occasions, appeared in print in Germany several times before the apparent decline of the custom in the mid–eighteenth century, and it is almost certain that London apprentices underwent similar, if less Teutonically formal, rituals. The central theme of the *Depositio* was redemption, or death and resurrection. The apprentice was ridiculed, mocked, and even ceremonially anatomized, before being revived, baptized, and welcomed as a new colleague. The accompanying festivities included speeches in praise of the art and mystery of printing, and declarations by the chapel workers that "by customs old we've stayed." Such occasions also drew prominently upon stories of the providential invention of printing, the larger significance of which is discussed in chapter 5. German rites thus lauded the town of Mainz and its hero, Johann Gutenberg, and scoffed at rival claims on behalf of Haarlem and Laurence Coster.[76]

All these elements reinforced the central message of the *Depositio*, which was to invest in new printers the civilities of the craft. "Beware of lies and

74. McKenzie, "Printers' Perks"; McKenzie, *Cambridge University Press*, I, 73, 75; Johnson, "Printers' 'Copy Books'"; Gaskell, *New Introduction*, 48, 173.

75. Moxon, *Mechanick Exercises on the Whole Art of Printing*, 327–8; McKenzie, "Printers' Perks."

76. Blades, *Account of the German Morality-Play*, 24–7. I thank John Bidwell for drawing this book to my attention. It merits comparison with Contat, *Anecdotes Typographiques*.

slander," they would be warned. They were cautioned against romance, quarreling, and spreading rumors—just the kind of conduct liable to foster discord in a tight social community—and urged to remain steadfast in their labors. As what amounted to a visitor in the master's home, a novice would be advised to "Be modest at the table/As an invited guest." Homilies also included advice to work according to the seasons, to go to church regularly, to dress properly, to keep promises, and never to borrow money. In sum, the newcomer was told that "If you'd gain approbation,/Still keep in mind your station." This dictum marked the climax of the ceremony. In English printing houses, at least, rude songs would then be sung. These were handed down for generations and were apparently still known at the start of the nineteenth century, when investigators found that aged Stationers could still recall very similar rituals to the German *Depositio* being practiced in the London trade. But by then one change at least had occurred. Their specifically fraternal character, although always present, had grown more prominent. The rituals increasingly manifested the exclusion of women from craft communities perceiving themselves under threat. Charles Manby Smith thus found his chapel holding a riotous mock-wedding when he got married, and in around 1800 an apprentice would talk of "burying his wife"— that is, of ending his apprenticeship—with a ribald bacchanal.[77]

It would thus be wrong to imply that the conventions imbued by such ceremonies were fixed and uniform across all sizes and types of printing operation. Doubtless local distinguishing differences were part of their appeal. Nonetheless, journeymen could move between printing houses doing temporary work, and seem to have encountered few problems doing so. This practice was known as "smouting." A friend of Benjamin Franklin even suggested that they travel across Europe together as journeymen printers, financing their tour in this way. Practices cannot have differed too radically between houses, or such a suggestion could scarcely have been made.[78] And Franklin's own experience in London, famous as it is, is worth recalling here for its hints relating to the world of solacing. Working in Watts's unusually large printing house in Lincoln's Inn Fields in the mid-1720s, Franklin became known as the "water American" because of his reluctance to drink beer. His account of life there is daunting. "We had an alehouse boy who attended always in the house to supply the workmen," he later recalled. "My companion at the press drank every day a pint before breakfast, a pint at breakfast with his bread and cheese, a pint between breakfast and dinner, a

77. Black, *Guilds and Civil Society*, 123, 125–6; Blades, *Account of the German Morality-Play*, 36 n, 50–52, 91–7; Clark, *Struggle for the Breeches*, 4–6, 13–4, 34.
78. McKenzie, *Cambridge University Press*, I, 136; Moxon, *Mechanick Exercises on the Whole Art of Printing*, 351–2; Hetet, "Literary Underground," 167.

FIG. 2.12. Benjamin Franklin in the printing house. A nineteenth-century reconstruction that represents graphically, if imaginatively and with heavy moralistic overtones, the contrast between Franklin's rationality and the rowdy conduct of the printers in a traditional chapel. *The Leisure Hour* 367 (6 January 1859), 8-10, after a painting by Eyre Crowe. (By permission of the Syndics of Cambridge University Library.)

pint in the afternoon about six o'clock, and another when he had done his day's work." Franklin found all this drinking "detestable," and recommended his fellows to eat bread instead. He was transferred for his pains to the separate compositors' room, where the occupants demanded five shillings for liquor as an initiation fee. Franklin refused, until driven to pay up by "little pieces of private mischief" (fig. 2.12).[79]

Resolutions such as this took effect behind the paper windows of the printing house. The outside world could discern them only through their results: the glistening sheets of paper produced by such premises in their thousands. But first those sheets had to be dried and collated. The time needed for this varied according to season—Alexander Pope's translation of Homer, for example, was "retarded by the great rains that have fallen of

79. Van Doren, *Benjamin Franklin*, 51–3; George, *London Life*, 282. Compare an earlier writer's advice to "tak[e] out a coin, and [buy] more liquor for the thirsty workers," quoted in Binns, "Four Latin Poems," 41.

late, which causes the sheets to be long a-drying." Contemporary images show sheets hanging up in the printing house itself, around the press. Once dried, they were taken down and transferred to a separate chamber called the "warehouse." It might be a bookseller's, rather than the printer's: with cavalier exaggeration, Sorbière guessed that every book dealer in London had "Two or Three Ware-houses" to fill. In any case, the boundary between bookselling and printing had been reached, and it proved negotiable. Both printers and booksellers stored printed pages, and in practice so-called "warehouses" could be made out of almost any room. The use of Saint Paul's vaults for this purpose has already been mentioned. The Stationers' Company itself employed both its kitchen and à series of chambers above its hall, although here weight presented a problem. In many cases, a warehouse keeper would be hired to guard the sheets. This was clearly a responsible post, demanding a trustworthy occupant. At the Oxford press, the warehouse keeper was actually the senior employee. But he was usually subordinate to the master printer or bookseller. Indeed, the Stationers' Company eventually decided that the Treasurer of its "English Stock"—that is, the man entrusted with keeping accounts for a vastly profitable patent vested in the Company, of which more in chapter 3—was, in fact, really a warehouse keeper, and must be labeled as such in order to underline his status as a "hyred Serv[an]t."[80]

As well as guarding them, the warehouse keeper would also direct the sheets' collation, packaging, and distribution. Ideally, he should keep a complete record of books so distributed, detailing the sums paid and to whom they had been sent. He should also detail all those not actually sold, but lent out by authority of the master—a considerable number, perhaps, if heavy borrowers like Robert Hooke were in any way representative.[81] The mechanisms of such distribution depended on how particular publications had been undertaken. When bookseller Henry Rhodes had a new title to sell, for example, he would send a bookbinder around the shops of retailers

80. Hodges, *William Congreve*, 225; Sorbière, *Voyage into England*, 16; Myers, "Financial Records," 6; SCB C, fol. 230ᵛ; SCB D, fols. 16ʳ, 130ʳ; SCB E, fols. 79ʳ–80ᵛ; SCB F, fols. 72ᵛ– 76ᵛ. These passages contain a useful codification of the proper practices of a warehouse keeper/treasurer. See also the legal opinion presented in "Mr Attorney Generalls opinion upon a Case relating to Mr Tooke," Guildhall Library Ms. 11,985, fols. 1ʳ–2ʳ. This concerned Benjamin Tooke, who was accused of embezzling English Stock books while stockkeeper. As well as its warehouse space, the Company also maintained a room where seized books were stored, sometimes for a remarkably long time: SCB C, fols. 278ʳ, 281ʳ; SCB D, fol. 63ᵛ.

81. Moxon, *Mechanick Exercises on the Whole Art of Printing*, 311 and n, 317–8, 322. The documentation kept by master printers is unclear, though the Scottish printing house run by the Stationers' Company seems to have kept at least a wages book, a receipts book, and a debt book: SCB D, fol. 173ᵛ. References to Robert Hooke's everyday practice of borrowing books from Stationers occur throughout his *Diary*.

known to deal in that particular kind of book, clutching a paper outlining subscription terms. He would then collect the required copies from the printer's warehouse and deliver them directly. Others employed such intermediaries as servants, binders, and their own spouses to assemble and disperse tracts. As will become clearer below, this might enable printers or booksellers to maintain a discreet distance from their own productions.[82]

A highly involved domain of work and community thus obtained in the printing house. It was a régime well suited to promoting the trade's priorities of continuous work and steady production. But this discipline not only determined the rate and efficiency of book production; it also affected what books appeared, and in what form. For example, shared and concurrent printing were routine for all printing houses except perhaps the king's. This meant the printing of more than one book at a time on a given press, and the simultaneous working of more than one printing house on a given book. The combination helped ensure steady and continuous work for the printers and compositors, as the inevitable delays in any particular project could be filled by work on another.[83] But it also meant that individual texts took longer to produce. Astronomer Royal John Flamsteed complained bitterly about this aspect of the practice, as we see in chapter 8. But Flamsteed was concerned not just about speed. Concurrent printing also had more subtle implications. Since no one printer encountered the whole text of a book produced in this way, it militated against the illicit production of supernumerary copies by pressmen; secretly making more copies than contracted for had otherwise become the easiest form of piracy. Flamsteed was as concerned about this as he was about simple delays, and concurrent printing did reduce the threat. For a similar reason, it proved invaluable for Stationers engaged in the production of prohibited or unauthorized books, since the workmen, remaining ignorant of the full import of the works they were printing, could tell inquisitive questioners only about their own contributions. Thomas Creek, for instance, who produced part of the speeches of the regicides shortly after the Restoration, declared that he did not know what proportion of the whole he had handled; nor could he know for sure who had printed the rest. His ignorance may have been genuine—and in-

---

82. Blagden, "Memorandum Book of Henry Rhodes," 110–12; Hetet, "Wardens' Accounts," 45; *Exact Narrative*, 60. Bookbinders, who turned dried sheets into finished objects, were reputedly subservient creatures, "Dependant on the Bookseller" for sustenance. They supplemented their faltering incomes by selling pamphlets or stationery: Campbell, *London Tradesman*, 135. For restrictions on the employment of servants, see Stationers' Company, *Registers 1554–1640*, I, 15–16.

83. Blayney, "Prevalence of Shared Printing"; Blayney, *Texts of "King Lear,"* 31–2, 35; McKenzie, *Cambridge University Press*, I, 104–5, 111; Minard, "Agitation in the Work Force," 114; Gaskell, *New Introduction*, 164.

tentional. Creek printed the same sheets in a second impression, some of the type having been left standing. This was apparently normal practice. Andrew Marvell's *Second Part of the Growth of Popery*, similarly, was printed in at least five houses, using untitled manuscript sheets so that the workmen could claim ignorance of its identity, if not of its general character.[84] Many political pamphlets, and indeed whole treatises, were produced in this way. James Harrington's enormously influential work of republicanism, *The Common-Wealth of Oceana*, is another example: its two final sections, produced after a Cromwellian "Spanell questing" had "sprung" it out of its first printing house, were printed at the same time, independently of each other, in separate houses (fig. 2.13). But such practices were not restricted to outlawed books. Works of philosophy and other learning were made this way too—in the same houses, by the same workmen, and even at the same time.[85] Since very few printing houses specialized in learned work—perhaps none at all in London, although one should remember the struggling Oxford press under Fell and later its Cambridge equivalent under Bentley—knowledge remained lodged in the same premises as ephemera and pamphleteering. Learned scholars and gentlemen alike had to commit their tomes to be printed in the midst of almanacs, pamphlets, and (in the case of Newton's *Principia*) pornography.[86]

84. *Exact Narrative*, 37–8, 42–3; McKenzie, "London Book Trade," 20–1; Crist, "Francis Smith," 301–3. See also PRO SP 29/397, nos. 55–6, for John Starkey doing the same. In 1671 the Company resolved that in all cases of distribution among different houses, their names must be given to L'Estrange: SCB D, fol. 189ʳ. For using a false running head in pirate printing, see SCB D, fol. 173ʳ, and compare fol. 222ʳ.

85. Harrington, *Common-Wealth of Oceana*, sig. [a2ᵛ]; Feather, "Publication of James Harrington's *Commonwealth of Oceana*"; McKenzie, *Early Printing House at Work*, 4–10; McKenzie, "Printers of the Mind," 10–11, 18, 54, 64–6. For examples, see also SCB D, fols. 129ʳ, 134ʳ; SCB E, fol. 100ᵛ; SCB F, fols. 2ʳ⁻ᵛ, 20ᵛ. See Cook, "First Edition of *Religio Medici*" and Huntley, "Publication and Immediate Reception of *Religio Medici*" for concurrent printing in an illicit *Religio Medici*; Peters, "Print-World Ideology," discusses the effects of the illicit printing of plays. Gilmont, "Printers by the Rules" suggests that Continental houses made less use of concurrent printing.

86. One project to encourage learned printing is adumbrated in Bray, *Essay towards promoting all Necessary and Useful Knowledge*, 10–11. As related below (p. 320), the *Principia* was printed under Edmond Halley's oversight by Joseph Streater, who had inherited what was one of London's biggest printing houses from his parents, John and Susan Streater. Joseph became an almanac printer of ill repute and was targeted by the Stationers' Company for prosecution as the capital's leading producer of "lewd" books (especially *Sodom, or the Quintessence of Debauchery*, reputedly by Rochester): CLRO, Guildhall Sessions, files SM59, SF356, April–May 1688, and Mayor's Court Interrogatories 140.12, November 1687–January 1687/8; SCB F, fol. 125ʳ; Thomas, *Long Time Burning*, 23–4; Hammond, "King's Two Bodies," 28–9. The importance of access to printing houses in natural philosophical debates (below, chapter 7) lends this a significance beyond the merely prurient, especially given Halley's contemporary reputation for impiety. Halley was also notorious for associating with London lowlife; his alliances with Streater, Senex, Parker, and others, indicated in chapter 8, would repay further study if sufficient evidence for such an investigation could

draught comes to be a work,his speech being faithfully inserted
in this place, may give, or receive correction unto amendment.
For what is written will be weighed but conversation, in these
dayes is a game,at which they are best provided that have light
Gold.

It is like the sport of women that make flowers of straws,
which must be stuck up, but may not be touched: Nor, which
Arist. Rhet. is worse, is this the fault of conversation onely. But to the
Examiner, I say, *if to invent method, and to teach an art, be all one,*
Let him shew that this Method is not truly invented,or this Art
is faithfully taught.

I cannot conclude a Circle, (and such is this Commonwealth) without turning the end into the beginning. The
time of Promulgation being expired, the Surveyors were
sent down, who having in due season made report that their
work was perfect,the *Orators* followed,under the administration
of which officers,&Magistrates theCommonwealth was ratified
and established by the whole body of the people, *Curiatis,Cen-
turiatis,*and *Tributis Comitiis.* And the Orators being by vertue
of their Scroles or lots, members of their respective Tribes,
were elected each first Knight of the third List, or Galaxy:
Wherefore having at their return, assisted the *Archon* in putting the Senate, and the People or Prerogative into motion,
they abdicated the Magistracy both of Orators and Legislators.

THE

The Corollary.

OR the rest (sayes *Plutarch* closing up the
story of *Lycurgus*) when he saw that his
Government had taken root, and was in
the very Plantation strong enough to
stand by it self; he conceived such a delight within him, as G O D is described
by *Plato* to have done, when he had finished the Creation of the World, and saw his owne Orbes
move below him: For in the Art of Man,being the imitation of nature,which is the * Art of G O D, there is nothing   * *Hobb*
so like the first Call of beautifull Order, out of Chaos and
Confusion, as the Architecture of a well order'd Commonwealth. Wherefore *Lycurgus* seeing in effect,that his Orders
were good, fell into deep Contemplation how he might
render them, so far forth as is in humane providence, unal-
terable and immortall. To which end he assembled the People, and remonstrated unto them, that for ought he could
perceive,their Policy was already such, and so well established, as was sufficient to entayle upon them and theirs, that
virtue and felicity whereof humane Life is Capable.

Neverthelesse, there being another thing of greater Con-
cernment then all the rest, whereof he was not yet provided
to give them a perfect accompt, nor could,till he had consulted the Oracle of *Apollo*; he desired that they would observe his Lawes,without any change or alteration whatsoever, till his return from *Delphos*; unto which all the People
chearfully and unanimously engaged themselves by promise, desiring him that he would make as much hast as he
could. But *Lycurgus* before he went, began with the Kings
and the Senators, and thence taking the whole People in
Order, made them all swear unto that which they had promised, and then took his Journey. Being arrived at *Delphos,*
he sacrificed unto *Apollo,* and afterwards enquired if the policy which he had established, were good and sufficient for
a virtuous and an happy Life. (It hath been a Maxime
with Legislators,not to give Checks unto the present Superstition, but to make the best use of it, as that which is al-
wayes the most powerfull with the People ; otherwise
though *Plutarch* being a Priest, was interested in the cause,
there is nothing plainer then *Cicero* in his Book *De Divina-
tione* hath shewed it, that there was never any such thing as
                    P p   an

FIG. 2.13. James Harrington's *Oceana* as an example of concurrent printing. Discontinuities in typography and pagination reveal the point at which the copy was divided between two printing houses. Harrington, *Common-Wealth of Oceana*. (By permission of the Syndics of Cambridge University Library.)

In consequence, gentlemen who wished to see their writings in print had to use no little skill themselves. The exercise of printers' autonomy, so central to the domain of the master printer, was not always appreciated by those outside that domain. Cases where the composition resulted in an apparently different text from that originally submitted were reckoned to be frequent, and, as Moxon's representation implied, they might well be serious enough to "corrupt & pervert the sence." Stationers themselves warned explicitly of the dangers. Michael Sparke, for one, expressed the fear that even his own documents would be mutilated by "a new *poyson*" added to the copy in press, so that "the *truth* of the *story*" would be "quite altered." John Dunton likewise cautioned "every *Bookseller* that concerns himself in Printing" to

---

now be recovered. At present, we know that Halley associated with such people, but very little more.

"peruse the Copy as it goes to Press; in Regard, I have smarted more than once for being too credulous in this Respect."[87]

Dunton's advice was important. It effectively warned that would-be authors keen to exert some restraint over the interpretative autonomy of printers had, as it were, to "play the Stationer" themselves. They must learn something of the printer's skills. Edward Tyson was one natural philosopher well aware that he lacked such capabilities. Tyson beseeched the experienced Robert Plot to oversee his work and identify for him which words should appear in italics or capitals. More effectively, writers tried to enter the printing house and monitor in person the practices affecting their pages. They became acutely conscious that such access to the press was vital if their intended meanings were to survive the printing process intact; otherwise a printer could excuse almost any inconsistency by claiming that the author's "perusal" had been unobtainable. Edmund Gibson, for example, had to move from Oxford to London and lodge with bookseller Awnsham Churchill in order to prevent what he foresaw as the adulteration of an edition of Camden's *Britannia*.[88] Such was the dedication essential for promulgating truths in print.

Obtaining and exercising this access could be tricky. It called for delicate negotiation with both the master printer and the bookseller who would generally be "undertaking" the project—and, given the strength of chapel customs, perhaps even with the journeymen too. Gentleman or not, the would-be author was not necessarily dominant when knocking at the door of the printing house. His status approached that of a guest—or even, as in Gibson's case, a lodger—in the Stationer's home. The latter might feel entitled to make strenuous demands on his time, especially if the press were threatened with lying idle. And he or she could expect those demands to be met. This certainly proved to be the fate of Gibson, who, in ensuring that his book would not prove "a lasting scandal," paid the price in enduring the printers "tread[ing] in my heels." In this sense the way of life of the Stationer temporarily prevailed over that of the gentleman—and not vice versa.[89]

87. Prynne, *Unbishopping of Timothy and Titus*, 176 ff.; [Sparke], *Truth Brought to Light and Discovered by Time*, sigs. a1ʳ–a2ᵛ; Dunton, *Life and Errors* (1705), 88–9.

88. Gunther, *Early Science in Oxford*, XII, 9; Webster, *Displaying of Supposed Witchcraft*, sig. [Yy3ᵛ]; Walters and Emery, "Edward Lhuyd, Edmund Gibson, and the Printing of Camden's *Britannia*," 112–4; Huntington Ms. HA 1424–6. Compare the earlier case of Harington, who saw his late Elizabethan translations through the press himself: Cauchi, "'Setting Foorth' of Harington's Ariosto."

89. McKerrow, *Introduction*, 205–9. Compare Byrom's account of meeting the younger Tonson and Watts, "who have been telling me how I must manage, and so forth": Byrom, *Selections from the Journals and Papers*, 59. The idea that an author's presence could usefully be compared to that of a guest derives from a suggestion made in conversation by D. F. McKenzie. On hospitality in a genteel home, see Heal, *Hospitality in Early Modern England*, 300–51.

Even if they were not physically present at the printing house, moreover, the daily schedule of would-be authors could often fall subject to the printers' régime. "I have forty times more trouble in printing a book then I have in writing one," wailed Henry More as he discovered this for himself. Those engaged in "undertaking" or "editing" learned works complained endlessly of their subjugation to the time of the printers. Roger Cotes thus told Newton that while they labored over emendations for the second edition of his *Principia*, "The Compositor dunn's me every day" for copy. Richard Bentley, too, who was highly conscious of the aesthetics of typography and paper, pointedly mentioned receiving a Newtonian emendation only as the relevant passage was "in the Compositors hand." [90] Such demands on a gentleman's pleasure were uncomfortable, and were duly resented.

Reading played an important part in this local dissolution of cultural authority. True, the autonomy of the master printer stood to be qualified by the convention of submitting proof sheets for approval to some—not necessarily all—writers. There was an element of social status involved in this: Lord Brouncker had proofs sent to him (when he was well enough), but the relatively lowly Robert Hooke went to John Martyn's bookshop himself to collect his. Sometimes a bookseller would be prepared to send proof sheets to a gentleman writer even if he lived far away—in Cambridge, say, like More, or Yorkshire, like Henry Power. But otherwise some more local figure might be agreed upon to oversee them. In the case of Power's *Experimental Philosophy*, James Allestry had sheets approved both by Power in Halifax and, in London itself, by Hooke and John Wilkins. Here—as indeed in any initial appraisal of a manuscript—the authority of the printer might well extend to his or her engagement of a qualified figure like Brouncker, where the assessment of the individual as "qualified" would often rest with the master involved. Serious issues of honor were easily kindled in such circumstances, especially when the local protagonist was himself a gentleman, accustomed to his freedom of action and determined to stand by his word. The implications for authorship could be substantial. Henry Wharton, for example, was engaged by bookseller Richard Chiswell to "View and correct" a historical work by John Strype. Trouble arose when Strype tried to insist that Wharton pass all his corrections to Strype himself, whose decision would determine which were published. Wharton preferred to forward them directly to Chiswell for printing. "Upon the whole I found M[r] Strype unwilling that the publick correction of his errors should proceed from any but himself," Wharton remarked to the bookseller; but "if he expects to have my corrections communicated to him, he must Engage to you, to print them entire and Verbatim, as I shall transmitt them to you, and you must

90. Conway, *Letters*, 396; Cohen, *Introduction to Newton's "Principia,"* 218–22, 234.

assure me that it shall be so done." Only with such an assurance would he
agree to reveal his corrections, and "therein use that Civility towards the
author, which men of letters owe to each other, and which one friend oweth
to an other."[91]

There are many accounts of the sufferings of writers in seeing their works
through the press—so many, in fact, that they have come to seem stereo-
typed. But these considerations of civility help us to see the reality behind
such stories. Gibson's experience was thus eclipsed by Ralph Thoresby's, undergone while overseeing the production of his *Topography of Leeds*. Thoresby found that the Stationers' demands came to affect every aspect of his
life. He was forced to move from Yorkshire to London, and to begin lodging
with the mother of his bookseller. There the need for a constant supply of
copy kept him at work every day from four in the morning, "writing for the
press till almost blind." Thoresby also had to attend daily the three different
printing houses that were working concurrently on his book, where he corrected sheets himself. Soon he was forced to abandon daily prayers because
of the masters' "pressing so hard upon me to keep the four compositers at
work." Even when he resolved to assert his gentility, abandon this schedule,
and leave London, his work was not over. Thoresby now had to spend yet
more early mornings rewriting his manuscript as instructed by the printer,
in order to render it "intelligible" to the workmen in his absence. Back in
Yorkshire, he then enjoyed five months of relative peace before hearing that
one of the three printing houses had burnt to the ground, destroying its
portion of the book. Thoresby returned to London once again, only to find
that his bookseller had fallen victim to bankruptcy and the bottle, and had
disappeared. It took him another three months to negotiate the obscure
procedures of the trade, satisfy the demands of the various printers, and
reach an agreement with the decadent and evasive Stationer.[92]

Given the degree of creativity exercised in a printing house, one needs to
think as carefully as gentlemen like Thoresby did about the status of manuscripts there, and about the relation between manuscripts and the texts they
contained. As should have become clear, when written materials were reproduced in print the process was by no means one of slavish reproduction. On
the other hand, neither were manuscripts subject to unrestrained alteration.
Conventions limited and guided the transformation. The implications are
clearest for stage plays, since historical bibliographers have expended most

91. BL Ms. Sl. 1326, fol. 39^{r-v}; Conway, *Letters*, 371–2; CUL Ms. Add. 4, no. 27. Allegations of incivility could easily affect the credibility of historians like Strype, and such a threat
was being hinted at by Wharton here.

92. Thoresby, *Diary*, II, 97–163, 182, 208–248 (and compare 369 ff.); Thoresby, *Ducatus
Leodiensis*.

of their energy on this kind of literature. With such material, the term *original* seems to have carried the connotation not of a single, unique set of written sheets, but of a particular performance or reading of the work. The written sheets represented a fallible, and perhaps incomplete, record of this event. Compositors could thus make the changes their cultural position demanded, not only because of the prized virtue of the master printer, but also because they held in their hands no sacrosanct text at risk of desecration. The term *copy*, on the other hand, meant two things: the actual manuscript that the compositor followed as he or she set type, and the title or text to which the Stationer could claim to possess some right according to trade customs. These were at first the same thing (when Stationers fought over the "copy" of the King James Bible, for example, there *was* a unique set of sheets to which this term referred), but the senses diverged as time went on. A copy in the second sense could then be represented as properly comprising all that the work in question *should be*, as well as all that a particular manuscript copy *was*. And around this concept could be built a régime capable of protecting the investment of time and money made by a Stationer in transforming the corrupt, singular manuscript into the printed title. It could be made the center of a system of property, and even, later, of copy "rights."[93]

During the seventeenth century, the book trade came increasingly to be structured around the ownership of such copies, at first principally by printers and later overwhelmingly by booksellers. The shift was an important one. By the end of the century the trade was dominated by those booksellers whose "chief Riches and Profit" lay in "the Property of valuable Copies." It was increasingly the copy-owning bookseller rather than the printer who was the motor of publishing. This meant that while master printers might prize their skill and knowledge within the printing house itself, they found the trade community as a whole an increasingly uncongenial environment for preserving and recognizing those qualities. The interests conditioning the world of the printed book seemed no longer to be theirs. This recognition threatened the everyday cooperation of Stationers in every aspect of their lives. It generated rich potential for conflict.

Within the Stationers' Company, too, booksellers came to dominate. In common with other trades, printing and bookselling were witnessing an increase in the scale of businesses and a corresponding move toward higher levels of capital. This was reflected in occupancy of the more elevated ranks

93. Campbell, *London Tradesman*, 128; de Grazia, *Shakespeare Verbatim*, 88–92; Blayney, *Texts of "King Lear,"* 258–91. It may be that contemporaries saw another resonance in the term as it came to exercise this structuring role, for agricultural society was typically ordered around communities of "copy-holders." See, for example, Levine and Wrightson, *Making of an Industrial Society*, 83–151, and Agnew, *Worlds Apart*, 58.

of the Company. L'Estrange noted that "The *Stationers* . . . would Subject the *Printers* to be absolutely *Their Slaves*; which they have Effected in a Large Measure already." In the next century, William Strahan, too, would recall the position his fellow printers had been in as one of "slavery." There were even suggestions that the printers, feeling increasingly disenfranchised, might secede to form their own company.[94] Based on their claim to unique craft knowledge, this plan was supported by several of the most prosperous masters, including John Streater, the subject of chapter 4 of this book. L'Estrange himself revived it in 1679, when the Press Act lapsed. He considered the printers to be the most loyal of Stationers, potentially at least, because their interests coincided with those of the crown in restricting the autonomy and power of booksellers.[95] The separate company was never in fact formed, but that it was seriously proposed underlines the gravity of the situation facing master printers in the later seventeenth century.

The contested supremacy of the master printer brings us back to Moxon. It is essential to appreciate Moxon's objective when producing his *Mechanick Exercises*. At the start of this section I mentioned that Moxon's account needs to be read not just as an accurate portrayal of the printer's domain, but as a representation that, like all constructed representations, served a purpose. We can now see why. At the time of its printing, the status of the master printer, which Moxon so lauded, was under threat. His was therefore a pointed and polemical statement of the master's virtues—all the more so given his own controversial position with respect to the Stationers' Company. In this context it is significant that he dedicated his *Exercises* to the overseers of Oxford University's printing house, who, like Moxon himself, were engaged in a bitter struggle for survival against the Company. He even began with an account of the early history of printing written by the mathematician John Wallis in defense of Oxford's press. As chapter 5 demonstrates, such historical accounts were of central importance in arguing for rival cultures of print. Moxon's historiography directly challenged the legitimacy of the Stationers' Company over Oxford, just as his Vitruvian rhetoric challenged the booksellers' supremacy over the master printers.

---

94. L'Estrange, *Considerations and Proposals*, 27, 26; *London Printers Lamentation*, 2; Blagden, "Stationers' Company in the Civil War Period," 5–7; Blagden, *Stationers' Company*, 148 ff. For the general phenomenon see Earle, *City Full of People*, 67–8.

95. McKenzie, *Cambridge University Press*, I, 9–10; *Brief Discourse*; Hetet, "Literary Underground," 30; Crist, "Government Control of the Press," 51; Atkyns, *Original and Growth of Printing* (1664). Journeymen complained that if they tried to set up a printing house, the booksellers refused to stock their products, the patentee printers pirated them, and agents of both "breake the Petitioners houses, imprison their bodies, seize their goods, and deface their presses." Excluded from the trade by a closed shop of printers and booksellers, they were reduced to appealing to the crown for redress: Stationers' Company, *Registers 1554–1640*, IV, 525–7, 533–4.

Such rhetoric signaled Moxon's elevation of printing to the status of a "Science." What constituted a "Science" he defined by reference to architecture, and in particular the architecture of Vitruvius. Letters must be Vitruvian, presses must be architectural, and masters must be architects. The importance of this strategy lay in Moxon's identity as a practitioner of the mathematical sciences. In his day, those sciences were in the throes of a long period of expansion and redefinition, with men like Blaeu in the forefront. Their proponents were claiming for them a new significance for the creation of natural knowledge and material prosperity alike. Vitruvius had become a central resource for such writers, who valued him not just for his descriptions of practice, but more significantly for his account of the capacities and qualities of a master practitioner.[96] Moxon likewise appropriated from Vitruvius a cultural identity for the master printer that served his purpose.

Moxon's account of the cultural identity of the master printer was thus not just a description, but an argument. His concentration on practice was a key component of this defense of the master. Emulating and extending the programmatic statements of Sprat and Glanvill, the apologists for the Royal Society, Moxon had declared the aim of his *Mechanick Exercises* to be the promulgation of "Experiments," which were to be "described in Workmens Phrases." They were to range over the entirety of each craft considered. However, Moxon entertained no easy illusion that the skills of the artisan could be garnered from the simple act of perusing a printed page. "*Cunning* or *Sleight*, or *Craft* of the Hand," he recognized, "cannot be taught by Words, but is only gain'd by Practice and Exercise." Nobody could become a skilled printer, in particular, by the "bare reading" of his account of printing. Nonetheless, he did maintain that words could convey the "Rules" obeyed by all working printers in their printing houses. The tracts were thus designed to propound a positive account of a certain culture of handicraft labor, so as to encourage gentlemen to become "conversant" in such crafts. The point was that a gentleman could understand the culture of a printing house even though he may remain personally innocent of the manual labor of printing. Booksellers—the routine intermediaries between gentlemen and printers—were notably absent from his representation. And the *Exercises'* publication in periodical form was an important element in achieving

96. Moxon, *Mechanick Exercises on the Whole Art of Printing*, 10. Moxon had actually published his own translation of Giacomo Barozzi da Vignola's architectural work, *Vignola*, proclaiming its utility for "young Artists." Printing was unusual with respect to the other handicrafts treated by Moxon in his insistence that it was a mathematical science, whereas the others were more mechanical: compare Moxon, *Mechanick Exercises: or The Doctrine of Handy-Works*, sigs. A2ʳ–[A4ᵛ], 117. For seventeenth-century Vitruvians see Bennett, *Mathematical Science of Christopher Wren*, 12–13, and Yates, *Theatre of the World*. For "the mathematicalls," see Bennett, "Mechanics' Philosophy"; Bennett, "Challenge of Practical Mathematics"; Johnston, "Mathematical Practitioners and Instruments."

Moxon's purpose. The issuing of a book in regular parts was unusual; it had been pioneered only a generation earlier by John Streater, who had found it helpful in his attempts to evade political opponents. For Moxon, it certainly meant that his argument would reach the right readers at an affordable price. It also suited the Royal Society's ideal of modest authorship. But the "Miscellanious method," as John Houghton called it, also meant that the prudent Stationer need not advance a rash investment on one speculative venture. The *Mechanick Exercises* therefore themselves instantiated the very prudence that their texts described.[97]

BOOKSHOPS AND BOOKSELLERS

We have tracked the creation of a printed book as far as its arrival in the warehouse. We have now reached the threshold of sites devoted to public access and exchange. Pursuing the trail further proves a task of no little complexity, as the processes and practices of distribution, exchange, sale, and use were manifold. Most books, however, had to pass through some sort of retail site. Here was another place replete with issues of skill, knowledge, and culture—another domain where gentlemen and Stationers, by combining conventions of civility, worked to construct and construe printed books.

John Dunton's first recommendation to would-be booksellers was to "*Take a convenient Shop in a Convenient Place.*" As noted above, a house fronting onto a major thoroughfare or within a recognized Stationers' district was ideal for the purpose.[98] Here a bookseller could create a distinctive space associated with his or her individual personality, and identify it as such by a particular sign. Such "decorations" made an impression: Sorbière thought them "as valuable as those of the Stage," and compared their impact to that of the palace of Whitehall, to the latter's disadvantage. The semiotic impresarios who created such an effect included Jacob Tonson, who owned Shakespeare copies and lived at the Shakespeare's Head, and Francis "Elephant" Smith, who was named after his shop at the Elephant and Castle. Rather more macabre were Edmund Curll's choice of the Pope's Head after he had successfully fleeced poet Alexander, and the radical Langley Curtis's choice of "the Sign of Sir *Edmondbury Godfrey*," the exclusionists' Protestant

97. Moxon, *Mechanick Exercises: or The Doctrine of Handy-Works*, sigs. A2ʳ–[A4ᵛ]; *Collection of Letters for the Improvement of Husbandry and Trade* 1 (8 September 1681): 1–4; 14 (13 March 1682/3): 168.

98. Dunton, *Life and Errors* (1705), 70; Boulton, *Neighbourhood and Society*, 167, 189; Moxon, *Mechanick Exercises on the Whole Art of Printing*, 311 ff.; Gaskell, *New Introduction*, 142–5. For mechanisms of distribution see also Blagden, "Memorandum Book of Henry Rhodes," 110–12; Hetet, "Wardens' Accounts," 45; *Exact Narrative*, 60.

martyr. Such signs carried meaning as well as serving a functional purpose. Indeed, in a metropolis without street numbers, they created a veritable theater of mnemonic associations for citizens to register in their memories.[99] But the principal basis for this strong identification of the place with the proprietor was probably more mundane. It was that bookshops, like printing houses, were generally their patrons' homes.

A survey carried out by William Leybourn for the Stationers' Company in the 1670s allows us to describe what the city building housing a bookshop or printing house must have looked like (fig. 2.14). It would have a brick-paved cellar, a shop or workshop on the first floor, a kitchen on the second, bedrooms on the third, and garrets above those.[100] The cellar would contain the house's "vault" or "seat of easement," and also storage space for beer or coal. The first floor then had one large room for the shop, with a fireplace and openings onto the street; there might also be a smaller chamber at the back, and perhaps a yard too. The two stories above that would be divided into smaller rooms, each floor being partitioned in the same way. Larger houses included such features as a dining room with a picture rail, lockable closets and dressers, and a "withdrawing room" with shelving, divided by a passage from the dining room and a kitchen. On the third floor would be sleeping quarters, and perhaps a nursery, or another withdrawing room. Above that were perched the garrets for servants or apprentices, lit by skylights and sometimes incorporating a lead funnel to channel waste directly into the cellar. In such a structure, as Arlette Farge, Daniel Roche, and others have observed, the stratification of society was rendered literal: master, apprentices, and servants inhabited the same building, but on different levels.[101]

99. Geduld, *Prince of Publishers*, 14–15; Crist, "Francis Smith," 7; Straus, *Unspeakable Curll*, 183; *Absalom Senior*, title page; Sorbière, *Voyage into England*, 16–17. Compare Dunton, *Life and Errors* (1705), 286, on Walter Kettilby. For Tonson's sign and the identity of Shakespeare see also de Grazia, *Shakespeare Verbatim*, 79–83. For the concept and practice of memory theaters, see Yates, *Theatre of the World*; Yates, *Art of Memory*; Spence, *Memory Palace of Matteo Ricci*; and Carruthers, *Book of Memory*.

100. SCA, Leybourn, "Survey." There is a remarkable degree of uniformity among the buildings in Leybourn's survey. They were not necessarily let to printers or booksellers, although some certainly were: Randall Taylor, for example, occupied one. Compare Earle, *Making of the English Middle Class*, 207–9, and Weatherill, *Consumer Behaviour*, 6–13, 137–65. For the uses of upper floors see SCB C, fol. 231ʳ, and Hannaway, "Laboratory Design," 602. Note that I use the American convention for numbering floors, not the British.

101. Roche, *People of Paris*, 102–3, 110–5; Farge, "Honor and Secrecy of Families," 575 ff.; Hetet, "Literary Underground," 182. For how such stratification could be viewed as part of the natural order, see Ross, *New Planet no Planet*, 35–6. These rather impressionistic judgments will be supplemented in the near future by more thoroughgoing studies by James Raven and others. For a general account of the origins of such buildings, see Vance, *This Scene of Man*, 152–3, 159–60, 230–40.

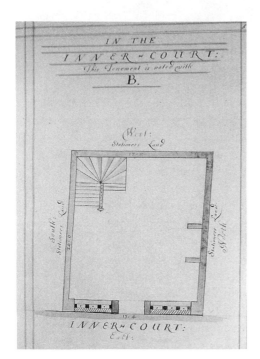

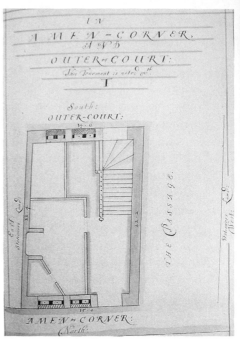

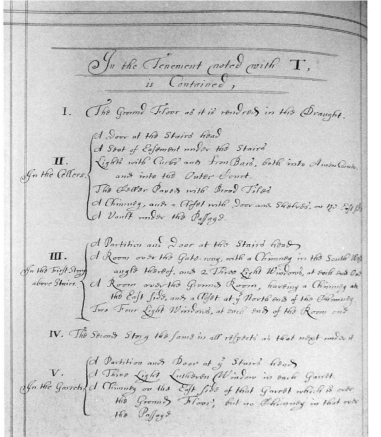

FIG. 2.14. City buildings owned by the Stationers' Company and surveyed by William Leybourn after the Fire of London. Leybourn described many buildings, all of which displayed similar characteristics. All had a basement with "seat of easement," a first-floor space used for retailing or craft, a second (and generally third) story devoted to domestic arrangements and entertaining, and servants' garrets in the roof. This was the kind of building occupied by most London printers and booksellers. (By permission of the Master and Wardens of the Worshipful Company of Stationers and Newspaper-Makers.)

In early modern London the letting of rooms was one of the main sources of income. Homes though they were, most city shops were rented rather than owned freehold. Many of these buildings would therefore also house other dwellers, and perhaps even other trades, as well as a printer or bookseller. Dunton himself said that he had rented only "half a Shop," as well as his warehouse and "a fashionable Chamber." And even if he or she occupied the building alone, an individual retailer would sometimes sell goods of several trades from the one location.[102] The result was a series of juxtapositions resonant with potential implications. One deserving particular note is that of the bookseller with the coffeehouse.

After their introduction in the Interregnum, coffeehouses rapidly prospered (fig. 2.15). They became central to the political culture of the Restoration, and in chapters 7 and 8 we encounter their equal centrality to natural philosophical culture. Like printing houses and bookshops, they were represented as fomenting a heady mixture of the heights of truth and the depths of deception. A coffeehouse was "the Mint of Intelligence, and Forge of Lies." "He that comes often saves *two pence* a week in *Gazettes*," it was said, "and has his News and his Coffee for the same charge." Relations were not always harmonious—in the late 1720s, coffee-men and booksellers fought for ascendancy in the world of gossip and newsmongering. But the fact was that print and coffee suited each other. The most dangerous establishments of all, it was agreed, were "those Coffee houses, which are most frequented by reason of this Paper-Fuel." And they had a disturbing tendency to be found side by side. The second coffeehouse to open in London shared a building with bookseller Daniel Pakeman, one of the Stationers involved in producing Harrington's *Oceana*—or at least, it did until Pakeman sued the proprietor for keeping a fire and so risking conflagration. Bernard Lintot's bookshop, which stood next door to Pakeman's a generation later, itself became a coffeehouse. High Churchman Thomas Bennet owned a coffeehouse as well as a bookshop; so did radical Ben Harris. As we shall see in chapter 4, when Samuel Speed was arrested in 1666 his premises, too, were shared

102. Dunton, *Life and Errors* (1705), 70; Boulton, *Neighbourhood and Society*, 85–6; Earle, *City Full of People*, 167; Earle, *Making of the English Middle Class*, 46; Munby, "Fragment of a Bookseller's Day-Book," 304. An example of the consequences of renting can be seen in the tale of Moses Pitt. Pitt's was a corner shop, rented from a landlord. But the landlord did not own the land immediately in front of the shopfront, and in the late 1670s a neighbor decided to build on it. Pitt woke up to find a wall before his window, leaving the shop "darkened & stopped up & made like a Dungeon." In addition, his landlord had taken advantage of the Fire of 1666 to extend his property a little into the next plot; the neighbor now decided to rectify matters by carefully dismantling the entire wall. The house fell down. The neighbor had also interrupted a water course in the process, so the remains then flooded. Eventually Pitt was forced to leave Saint Paul's Churchyard; he was replaced by his ex-apprentice, Samuel Smith. Harris, "Moses Pitt and Insolvency," 185–6, 191.

Paris Cher Monsⁱ Trolaria   Sold by C.Dicey & Co in Aldermany Church Yar

FIG. 2.15. A coffeehouse at the close of the seventeenth century. Note the papers on the
table in the foreground and the tables in the rear devoted to conversations on different
subjects. (By permission of the Bodleian Library, University of Oxford, Douce Prints
W.1.2[203].)

with a coffeehouse. Edmund Curll provides yet another example, to be discussed below. Throughout central London, it seems, the coffeehouse and
the bookshop were to be found in close proximity.[103]

The well-known importance of coffeehouses for the reading and discussion of printed materials lends a frisson to this juxtaposition. This is
especially true in the case of Pakeman, given Harrington's strenuous espousal of new forms of sociability, which culminated in the coffeehouse
meetings of the Rota. For the coffeehouse was easily the Restoration's most
notorious center for conspiracy and communal reading alike. High Churchmen and nonconformists, gentlemen, retailers and mechanicks—and men
and women, for the notion that coffeehouses excluded women is baseless—
all flocked to this attraction. There, even if it were not actually bought, "Any

103. Ashcraft, *Revolutionary Politics*, 141–2; Knights, *Politics and Public Opinion*, 172–3;
Poor Robin's Almanack, 1687, sig. [C6ᵛ]; *Character of a Coffee-House*, 1; Harris, *London News-
papers in the Age of Walpole*, 30 –31; *Arguments Relating to a Restraint upon the Press*, 25; Ellis,
Penny Universities, 33– 4, 99; Lillywhite, *London Coffee Houses*, 382; Harris, "Moses Pitt and
Insolvency," 183; Dunton, *Letters Written from New-England*, 143. For the interior of a coffee-
house, see also *Knavery in all Trades*, sig. D3ʳ.

new Book especially, or Pamphlet, may be easily borrowed"—even "by him, that hath not Money enough, perhaps, to keep Company." There arose distinct zones within the coffeehouse, devoted to different topics of debate and boasting different tracts to be read. The "Treasonable Table," where opposition pamphlets could be discussed, became a major attraction. *"Harry,"* demanded one caricature Tory of his coffeehouse attendant: "Pray inform me, what it is that the *Whigs* are reading at the next Table, which makes them so merry about the mouth[?]" The materials dispersed and discussed here gained distinctive meanings by virtue of their exposure in such a distinctive setting. But coffeehouse reading, while it was likely to be witty, and was often political, was not necessarily Whig. Sir Roger L'Estrange himself, who thought that such settings made manuscript newsletters at least as dangerous as printed ones, and who wanted a clause added to coffeehouse licenses preventing the exposure of newspapers, proved as much. L'Estrange was well known to be "the Soul of all Coffee houses, and the delight of those that love to dung and read at the same time."[104]

Yet the juxtaposition of bookshop and coffeehouse was just one of many to be noted. Occupying such confined and encompassed premises, surrounded by gossip and conspiracy, a successful bookselling business consequently required the active preservation of delicate systems of trust and honor among people in constant proximity to each other. Booksellers relied implicitly on trust between themselves and any number of interlocutors: not only customers, but writers, printers, chapmen, journeymen, apprentices, family, and, of course, other booksellers. Good "credit" was the key to the maintenance of a bookseller's vocation. It was, Defoe said, "the choicest ware he deals in." And economic credit rested on personal credit. The prosperous Stationer might have to rest deals worth very large amounts of money indeed on little more than his word and his reputation as a citizen of "substance." But, as Sir Richard Steele put it, "Credit is undone in whispers." It was a fragile asset, highly vulnerable to personal antagonisms of a kind that the modern historian may all too easily dismiss as trivial. It was therefore

104. Lillywhite, *London Coffee Houses,* 467; Pincus, "'Coffee Politicians Does Create,'" 814–6; Hetet, "Literary Underground," 29, 114; PRO SP 29/51, no. 10(i); Harris, *London Crowds,* 28–9; Theophilus Rationalis [pseud.], *New News from Bedlam,* 43–4; Hammond, "King's Two Bodies," 23–4; Ellis, *Penny Universities,* 52–3; Hammond, "Censorship," 40–41; Toryrorydammeeplotshammee Younkercrape [pseud.], *Sermon Prepared to be Preach'd,* 12; *Arguments Relating to a Restraint upon the Press,* 14–16, 24. The author of *Arguments Relating* claimed to have seen London workmen habituating the coffeehouses, "poring upon Seditious, Heretical and Treasonable Papers." It was a common complaint, and in late 1675 the government briefly tried to close down all coffeehouses because of it (PRO SP 45/12, nos. 343–5). L'Estrange's favorite coffeehouse was Sam's, the "general Randevouz" of the anti-exclusionists: N. N., *Hue and Cry,* 7–8; Theophilus Rationalis [pseud.], *New News from Bedlam,* 43.

wise to watch what one said—or, in the "canting" slang apparently in everyday use, to "stow your whids and plant 'em." It was prudent to be sparing with one's faith in others, too. Bookseller Francis Kirkman was a notable victim of misplaced reliance. His partner, a printer "in whom I much trusted," died in his debt, thereby setting Kirkman on his own road to piracy and near-ruin. Money regulated the operation of such trust, of course, as well as depending upon it. But it is worth remembering that in an age of currency debasement, money itself was by no means necessarily trustworthy—and in 1696, as the coinage crisis reached its peak, it was reported that "No trade is managed but by trust." [105]

One can thus see the book trade as representative of a society conceiving of itself as an aggregate of patriarchal households, held together by fragile attributions of credit. Descriptions in such terms were commonplace, extending much further than the theorized version found in such works as Filmer's *Patriarcha*. As noted above, their articulation occurred partly because many bookshops were *not* in fact straightforwardly patriarchal. Women did substantial work in perhaps half of them, and ran around ten percent themselves. Patriarchal representations were thus norms to be asserted as much as they were observations of social fact. But in this respect the Stationers' domains mirrored society as a whole. Homes were omnipresent in early modern writers' representations of their own social world. They were widely reckoned the seminaries of church and state, where servants and children were "fitted for the public assemblies" in "a private Commonwealth." [106] Households, not individuals, were the building blocks of society, and the more diverse they seemed, the more contemporaries sought to stipulate their proper characteristics.

With bookshops, as with printing houses, the ideal suggested ways of conceptualizing practical conventions. For example, apprentices were treated as elements in a household, somewhere between sons, pupils, and servants.

---

105. Hoppit, "Use and Abuse of Credit," 68; Earle, *City Full of People*, 172–3; Defoe, *Complete English Tradesman*, 225; Farge, "Honor and Secrecy of Families"; Roche, *People of Paris*, 119; Earle, *Making of the English Middle Class*, 107, 115–18; [Head], *Canting Academy*, 48; K[irkman], *Unlucky Citizen*, sigs. [A7ʳ]–[A8ʳ]; BL Ms. Add. 5540, fols. 64ʳ–65ʳ. Kirkman further testified that booksellers tried to deal with just one wholesaler, so as to build up trust in a relationship mediated by exchange and credit more than by straight monetary transactions: [Kirkman], *English Rogue Continued*, 195–6. Defoe referred to the "terms of art" and "cant" of a trade: Defoe, *Complete English Tradesman*, 36–8.

106. Aristotle, *Politics*, I, xii–xiii; Filmer, *Patriarcha*; Underdown, "Taming of the Scold"; Hill, *Women, Work, and Sexual Politics*, 243; Hill, *Society and Puritanism*, 429–66; Collinson, *Birthpangs of Protestant England*, 60–62; Pollock, "Living on the Stage," 85. For Filmer as representative see Goldie, "John Locke and Anglican Royalism." Compare the French situation described in Dewald, "Ruling Class in the Marketplace," and Darnton, *Great Cat Massacre*, 79–104.

Kirkman himself declared that "I consider the Tye of an Apprentice to be, for the time, as solemn as that of *Matrimony*," and cautioned that masters who took on apprentices "take as great a charge upon them for the time, as if he were their own Child." Dunton agreed, maintaining that the master's paternalistic concern for his apprentice should not cease at freedom but continue throughout his later working life. Even when no actual filiation was involved, apprentices could take over and continue their erstwhile masters' interests. This was certainly true for those concerned with natural philosophy. The example of Henry Faithorne and John Martyn has already been cited; another is that of Samuel Smith, who served his time with the virtuosic Moses Pitt, inherited his master's concern for natural knowledge, and became distributor of Newton's *Principia*.[107] Specialist dynasties grew up around such inheritances.

This common representation delimited proper conduct. We can infer this by registering the sorts of behavior regarded as *un*reasonable for apprentices. Such transgressions were recorded in a number of cases brought before the city courts. One apprentice, Joseph Reekes, resented his master's marriage and tried to run away; another, Thomas Weekes, suffering acute lovesickness, was bought apothecaries' remedies by his master only to repay him by theft and the spreading of sordid tales. Nathaniel Ponder sent his apprentice to writing school, only to find him systematically embezzling books to sell through a confederacy of other boys—which, incidentally, lends important independent corroboration to what might otherwise be thought the least believable of Francis Kirkman's claims cited below, namely the existence of an organized network of apprentices making and selling piracies on a large scale. John Fish complained when he was expected to look after his master's bookshop all winter with no fire in the room. He was forbidden to read while standing there—an expected privilege, apparently, and one seen as a kind of ersatz education well before Michael Faraday's time.[108] There is a domestic ring to such complaints that is more than simply tactical, especially, perhaps, as these were the cases that reached the mayoral court itself and as such must have been particularly intractable. It therefore paid for masters to conform to domestic representations too, since aggrieved

107. K[irkman], *Unlucky Citizen*, 52, 146–8; Dunton, *Life and Errors* (1705), 70, 76; Boulton, *Neighbourhood and Society*, 102, 134, 139–40; BL Ms. Sl. 4279, 202. For the duties and rights of apprenticeship, see Rappaport, *Worlds within Worlds*, 234–7, and Earle, *City Full of People*, 19–66. On the patriarchalism of domestic industry see also: Laslett, *World We Have Lost, Further Explored*, 1–21; Fletcher and Stevenson, *Order and Disorder*, 31–3; Archer, *Pursuit of Stability*, 215–8.

108. CLRO, Mayor's Court Interrogatories 334, 487, 291, 419 (and below, note 175). Compare Dunton, *Life and Errors* (1705), 34. For use of Faraday's alleged experiences as a bookseller's apprentice, see Smiles, *Self-Help*, 43, 143–4.

FIG. 2.16. Impressions of the bookshop. (*above left, top and bottom*) A Dutch bookshop of the mid–seventeenth century. Note the juxtaposition of books with pictures, mathematical instruments, and other commodities, the counter separating customers from books, and the presence of what are probably the bookseller's wife and apprentice. (By permission of Rijksprentenkabinet, Amsterdam, RP-T-1884-A-290.) (*above right*) A bookseller's stall in the Palais, Paris, portrayed by Abraham Bosse. Again, note the counter and the bookseller (or perhaps the bookseller's wife) indicating the virtues of a book to the gentleman customer. (By permission of the Syndics of Cambridge University Library.) (*opposite left*) Two neighboring Amsterdam bookshops, showing similar characteristics. Note the counters facing the street, which would be used to display tempting title pages. Phoonsen, *Les Loix et les Coutumes du Change des Principales Places de l'Europe.* (By permission of the Syndics of Cambridge University Library.) (*opposite right*) Negotiating with a bookseller in the bookshop. Saldenus, *De Libris.* (By permission of the Syndics of Cambridge University Library.)

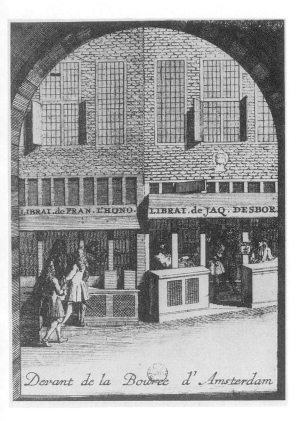

apprentices could generate accusations and revelations of real impact—as when an apprentice named Philip Oliver informed on his master John Bringhurst's illicit printing of seditious pamphlets in a Leadenhall "corner" because it had reduced his role to that of a menial.[109]

Into this domestic setting came customers. What did they encounter when they did so? It is hard to say. For reasons explored in chapter 6, contemporary images of English bookshops are exasperatingly rare (figure 2.16 shows Contintenal establishments of comparable size). Written testimony, however, is slightly less difficult to come by. Thomas Blount, for one, implied that booksellers dealt only in books "ready bound, and trimmed up." But most sold unbound books as well, the title pages of which would be set out as advertisements to attract passersby. Once hooked, people could often stay and read within the premises before choosing whether to buy. Some—

109. CLRO, Mayor's Court Interrogatories 443. Strype mentioned that the lord mayor could summon any citizen on the complaint of another, and determine the controversy. This may have happened quite frequently in an informal way; more often, though, this authority was "refracted" through the Company hierarchies, as detailed in the next chapter: Archer, *Pursuit of Stability*, 54–5.

Hooke is an example previously cited—could even borrow books.[110] We know little about what happened in the shop itself, however. Encounters there were rarely recorded, and we shall see that when they were, gentlemen complained of breaches of confidence. It is thus unclear, for instance, whether one could freely get books oneself for inspection, or whether an assistant was expected to hand them over a counter to customers. It may well have been that the latter was more usual, as seems to have been the case in France. L'Estrange—a hostile yet minute recorder of every aspect of Stationers' practices—certainly claimed that booksellers were able to prevent the sale of his own pamphlets by not showing them to customers. And as the *Weekly Medley* folded in 1720, it likewise complained that "when these papers have been asked for, they have been hid and refused by those persons whose business it was to vend them, and others exposed to sale in their room."[111]

Such complaints drew on a wider awareness of the dominant role of the proprietor. Indeed, Francis Kirkman rejoiced in the "sole Rule and Command of my Shop and Books." Kirkman stressed that the bookseller's advocacy might be markedly interventionist. When a potential customer entered his shop, he testified, a good bookseller "hath such ways of preferring and recommending of it, that they seldom go and not buy." He would "open the book, and if it be Divinity, shew them one place or another, out of which he will preach to them, and tell them, that very saying or discourse is worth all the money in the world." He might even promise a refund if the reader proved unsatisfied—but "you shall hardly ever get your money again."[112]

There is, then, testimony that some booksellers would go out of their way to guide their customers' choices, and that such guidance exploited the layout of the premises. On the other hand, when Company searchers came "into his House" in 1646, they found William Larner with fourteen sheets of a libel by the Leveller John Lilburne displayed "openly" for sale, among the rest of his stock. They were "lying in *Larners* Window before him, as he stood to worke." Some two decades later, eminent Stationer Benjamin Tooke said he had seen "several quires" of a seditious work lying visible in

110. Blount, *Glossographia*, s.v. "Stationer"; Pepys, *Diary*, I, 56–7. See also the extensive record of John Byrom's days in the 1720s spent "reading in a pamphlet shop," "reading at a bookseller's stall," staying at Vaillant's shop "looking over the books a good while," going into Innys's and "read[ing] there all afternoon till after six," and so on: Byrom, *Private Journal and Literary Remains*, I, 94–5, 99, 102, 105, 108, and passim.

111. Martin, "Espaces de la Vente," 94; Crist, "Francis Smith," 221–2; Black, *English Press*, 17–18. See also the sarcastic comment about Prynne's verbose title pages in *Character or Ear-Mark of Mr. William Prinne*, 3.

112. [Kirkman], *English Rogue Continued*, 206; McKeon, *Origins of the English Novel*, 247–8. Compare Gibson, "Bibliography of Francis Kirkman," 62 n.

Benjamin Harris's shop, and could be sure that they were all from the same book because he had been able freely to riffle through the sheets. Such testimony implies a degree of openness. Perhaps, however, freedom of access was restricted to those within the Stationers' community.[113] The question is an important one, not least because the right of its officers to enter members' premises was key to the Stationers' Company's role in maintaining propriety in the trade. Moreover, we shall see that on this issue of access hinged the reception, and even the definition, of many a printed book. Critics might claim that it had been produced and distributed secretly; Stationers like Larner would respond that anything sold so visibly and displayed with such freedom of access must be legitimate, at least in intent.

Decisions as to the propriety of bookselling practices, hinging on issues of visibility and access, thus became germane to the fate of printed books. If it was usual to set title pages out in view of pedestrians, for example, then *not* displaying them could count as evidence of illicit intent, since knowledge of their availability was then entirely dependent on negotiation—and implicitly privy negotiation—between bookseller and customer. A complex and loaded discourse of public and private developed over such points. The following exchange provides a good example. It occurred during the trial of Thomas Brewster in 1664 for *The Speeches and Prayers of some of the late Kings Judges* and *The Phoenix of the Solemn League and Covenant.* Peter Bodvell, Brewster's apprentice, is testifying about the first of these.

JUDGE KELLING: Where was this Book kept? Publickly, as other Books, or in other Roomes?

BODVELL: In the Shop my Lord.

KELLING: Were they Publickly to view as other Books?

BODVELL: Not so Publick as other Books, but publick enough, Mr. *L'Estrange* knows.

CHIEF JUSTICE HYDE: I know you use to let your Titles of a New Book lie open upon your Stalls, did you lay these open?

BODVELL: No my Lord, they did not do so.

HYDE: Who was the cause they did not, did your Master direct the privacy?

BODVELL: I think he did, we had some Direction to that end.

HYDE: Not to lay them open upon the Stall.

BODVELL: *No.*[114]

113. [Larner], *True Relation*, 3, 14; Howell, *State Trials*, VII, "Trial of Benjamin Harris," 926–32. Compare SCB E, fol. 124ᵛ, for advice that selling a book in sheets normally constitutes evidence that the vendor is involved in its printing. Goffman, *Presentation of Self*, 141–3, discusses the preferential access often granted to fellow tradesmen in places of work. See also Agnew, *Worlds Apart*, 48–50, for suspicion of those not involved in the same trade.

114. *Exact Narrative*, 41, 44; see also 54, and 49 for Hyde's comments. It is important to realize that in such trials, it was the judge who determined that a work was seditious or

The Phoenix was likewise sold in Brewster's premises, he continued, but not "publickly, with the Title Page lying open upon the Stall as other books do, when they are newly out." Copies were kept in an upper room—that is, in the home. Some were in a secret hole in the wall, others under the bed. Similarly, one of the elements in the prosecution of Elizabeth Cellier for *Malice defeated* was that she had sold tracts from her own home. Kirkman confirmed all this, adding that it was often a bookseller's apprentice who developed the necessary personal knowledge of customers' interests to sell them pirated, factious, obscene, and unlicensed books "privately." [115]

Such cases exploited widely acknowledged features of bookselling. The prosperous London bookseller had a wide potential customer range, embracing tradesmen, churchmen, lawyers, schoolmasters, Members of Parliament, gentlemen, and aristocrats. Open to passersby and customers, servants and gentlemen, the bookshop constituted something of a cultural frontier between street and home. It could be both pronouncedly open and, when its proprietor so wished, the site of transactions requiring privacy, even secrecy. The transactions conducted across this frontier were correspondingly heterogeneous in character. A bookseller like Henry Rhodes dealt not just with book purchases, but with a wide variety of arrangements resting on mutual trust, such as the buying of lottery tickets and the transmission of mail. Some booksellers' agreements went for a year without repayment; others did not involve money at all. [116] And those which did not were sometimes the most important.

The home and shop of the bookseller doubled as sites for conversation (fig. 2.17). Here, provided he were a skillful host, the bookseller might even take center stage. Moses Pitt was one who could recall lunching with mayors, and discussing Francis Bacon with a company of gentlemen in his own premises. [117] But the foremost example of such an "Amphibeous Mortal" was surely Jacob Tonson. Among aristocrats, Tonson looked like a bookseller; among booksellers, he appeared an aristocrat. His Jekyll-and-Hyde character was widely recognized. "In these Times of Piracy," Ned Ward testified, Tonson was "Chief Merchant to the Muses." Pope and his friends addressed him as "You that are least a bookseller." A skit attributed to Defoe

---

blasphemous; the jury decided upon only the fact of publication. See Keeble, *Literary Culture*, 99–100.

115. *Exact Narrative*, 53; Howell, *State Trials*, VII, "Trial of Elizabeth Cellier," 1183–1218; [Kirkman], *English Rogue Continued*, 213–4.

116. Blagden, "Memorandum Book of Henry Rhodes," 29–31, 103. On liminal spaces, compare Foucault, "Of Other Spaces," and Goffman, *Presentation of Self*, chap. 3.

117. E.g., Pitt, *Account of one Ann Jeffries*, 3–4; Pitt, *Cry of the Oppressed*, sig. a4ᵛ (for gentlemen meeting in a bookseller's house in the 1650s and discussing Bacon); Yarranton, *England's Improvement*, I, 110–1 (for projectors agreeing to meet "at the Booksellers house" to arrange the printing of an innovative windmill design).

FIG. 2.17. The bookseller as host: reconstruction of a scene in John Murray's dining room in the nineteenth century, when many of the foremost authors could be found there. This is a late example of a social setting pioneered by booksellers like Tonson around 1700, if not much earlier. *Harper's Monthly*, 10 (1885), 518. (By permission of the Syndics of Cambridge University Library.)

described Tonson in consummately repulsive glory, holding forth about his power amid the revelry of the Kit Cat Club. It was in such hands that book-shops could become places for meeting and discussion. Their distinctive so-ciability originated long before the salons of the eighteenth century, and per-sisted alongside them. The great Victorian medical and scientific publisher John Churchill was to recall that in around 1800 the bookseller's shop had still been "the daily resort of medical men, who met [there] in friendly inter-course." The bookseller would even provide daily newspapers for them.[118]

The domestic part of the building, as well as the shop itself, was thus important for the Stationer's fortunes. Just as consequential as the two spaces of shop and home, however, was the boundary between them. This can readily be analyzed in the terms pioneered by sociologist Erving Goff-man. The existence of what Goffman called a "backstage" area—here the home, or "upstairs"—could allow the reputable impression sustained by the proprietor in the relatively visible part of the establishment—the book-shop—to be prepared, modified, and retracted in convenient privacy. To

118. [Ward], *Secret History of Clubs*, 360, 370; [Defoe?], *Faction Display'd*, 15 (for Tonson's resulting withdrawal and threat of retaliation, see Ellis, *Penny Universities*, 233–4); Aymard, "Friends and Neighbours," 449; R. D., "Obituary: John Churchill," 198.

that extent its existence was essential to the propriety of the business. Defoe was not the only contemporary to assert that a retailer must dissimulate in the shop. Since he was "alwaies in publique" while standing there, he must "fear . . . himselfe" continuously, taking care to display no passions, no "fire." This required preternatural self-control. The successful ones managed it, but lost no time in relinquishing the mask once they could retreat out of sight. "They would go up stairs from their shop, and fall into frenzies, and a kind of madness, and beat their heads against the wall."[119] The resort to privacy was necessary to the successful maintenance of credit, not to say sanity itself.

The existence of such an "upstairs" was thus crucial for the production and distribution of printed materials.[120] To bring customers and their negotiations upstairs, however, was to run the risk of transforming a routine and necessary withdrawal into something more sinister. It would be hazardous to define too abstractly conceptual a division, but a useful ploy for prosecutors and critics alike was often to draw a moral distinction between practicing trade in a building that also housed a dwelling place, and mixing home and business *within* that building. The former was quite proper—indeed, as we shall see, it was legally obligatory. The latter could readily be made to appear suspicious. This was the point being made in the interrogation of Bodvell. It was also implied in prurient rumormongering about women booksellers, such as that linking Joanna Brome to L'Estrange. Such tactics clearly drew upon representations of the conduct proper to the home and to this singularly political kind of shop, and of the effects of mixing the two.

Tactics of this kind came in especially useful in circumstances arising from the searches and interrogations that were routine to the Stationer's life. Some were carried out by other Stationers as part of the trade's self-regulation, others by government officials such as L'Estrange. This was the clearest context in which the potential for privacy was both convenient and, it might be claimed, dangerous. In his campaign on behalf of Elizabethan printing patentees, for example, Christopher Barker charged the campaigning pirate John Wolfe with just such an elision, alleging that he had "gathered diverse Conventicles in his howse" and thereby "incensed the whole Cittie." For at least the next century, it became standard to portray bookshops as "Rendezvous of the most dangerous malcontents in Town." Both

119. Goffman, *Presentation of Self*, chap. 3; Defoe, *Complete English Tradesman*, 114–5. Throughout this book, Defoe assumed that the family of the tradesman resided "upstairs": e.g., 151–2. Agnew, *Worlds Apart*, 80–2.

120. And it remained so. Almost two centuries after Calvert, Thomas Wakley would meet collaborators upstairs at a printing house in Fleet Street to discuss the production of their new medical journal, *The Lancet*. "The sanctum was seldom violated," recalled one; "the printer's boy was the only person admitted." Clarke, *Autobiographical Recollections*, 12–20.

FIG. 2.18. Edmund Curll in his "Literatory." Curll, portrayed as literally two-faced, is seen masterminding the printing of controversial newspapers and lascivious books. This, the caricature claims, rather than its supposed production of antiquarian and erudite works, was what the literatory was for. *Grub Street Journal*, 147 (26 October 1732). (By permission of the Syndics of Cambridge University Library.)

Thomas Hobbes and Samuel Parker believed the Great Rebellion to have been "chiefly hatched in the shops of tradesmen."[121] The claim was not without warrant. Particular booksellers could indeed use their stewardship of such heterogeneous spaces to further particular ideals and interests. Behind the scenes and up the stairs, an interested London bookseller became a significant actor in cultural events. One example was notorious pirate Edmund Curll's "Literatory" (fig. 2.18). This was a short-lived center for

121. Stationers' Company, *Registers 1554–1640*, II, 17–19; Ashcraft, *Revolutionary Politics*, 72. Jeffreys described Harris's shop as a place where activists gathered to smoke and talk sedition: Howell, *State Trials*, VII, "Trial of Harris," 927. J. C. Davis, who controversially claims that the Ranters of the Interregnum were more a creation of Presbyterian Stationers than a real, coherent sect, has in this respect resurrected a claim about the power and autonomy of the craft's practitioners which was very much current in early modern England itself: Davis, *Fear, Myth and History*, 107 ff.

antiquarianism that Curll established in his own home in Bow Street, Covent Garden, right next door to Will's coffeehouse.[122] Others were more politically pointed. Nonconformists wanting to know about Penn's Quaker colony could get information at Benjamin Clarke's shop; radical writers in the Interregnum could count on a sympathetic reception at Giles Calvert's. Calvert is a particularly striking example, since he seems to have become something of a gatekeeper for radical groups. Both "a Sectary and a Bookseller" himself, it was apparently Calvert who assessed Laurence Clarkson's religious integrity before introducing him to the Ranters.[123]

Yet the bookshop as a site for plotting was not necessarily republican or nonconformist. One should not assume, let alone romanticize, connections between commerce and radicalism. George Thomason was one Presbyterian Stationer to become actively involved in royalist conspiracy after the regicide: he had many secret conversations with a Stuart agent in an "inner roome" of his premises. Coke and Rushworth claimed to have "bene often in that verie roome," where they had "discoursed verie freely." During the crisis of 1659–60, Hyde, too, could count on bookseller Henry Twyford to support an intelligence network; we shall meet Twyford again in chapter 4. Later, Benjamin Tooke was alleged to have supported L'Estrange's efforts by acting as his agent within the trade, with the support of "that true *Romish Elf*" Nat Thompson.[124] Successful printing and bookselling could support royalism as well as a commonwealth.

122. Hetet, "Literary Underground," 126, 145; McKenzie, "London Book Trade," 12; Straus, *Unspeakable Curll*, 140–5; Nichols, *Literary Anecdotes*, I, 454–7. Curll's club provides a suitable title for this chapter, as it epitomizes the ambiguity of private social arrangements facilitated in the book trade, and the resultant problems in interpreting even quite highbrow printed texts. Ian Hunter and David Saunders have independently made it emblematic in a different way in their polemical essay, "Lessons from the 'Literatory.'"

It is worth correcting here an impression that has been maintained over several decades concerning John Innys, Freemason and printer of the third edition of Newton's *Principia*. Nicholas Hans stated in 1951 that Benjamin Worster gave public lectures in Newtonian philosophy at Innys's shop, and this opinion has latterly been repeated by Jacob and Rousseau. In fact, Innys's shop was only used to receive subscriptions for attendance at the lectures, which were held in Little Tower Street. See: Hans, *New Trends*, 141–2; Jacob, *Radical Enlightenment*, 125–6; Rousseau, "Science Books," 208, 246 n. 65; Worster, *Compendious and Methodical Account*, title page and 230–9.

123. McKenzie, "London Book Trade," 12; Hetet, "Literary Underground," 126; Edwards, *Second Part of Gangraena*, 9. See also Edwards, *Third Part of Gangraena*, 62, for a radical preacher lodging at Calvert's house.

124. Spencer, "Politics of George Thomason," 18–9; Ogle et al., *Calendar of Clarendon State Papers*, IV, 225; Theophilus Rationalis [pseud.], *New News from Bedlam*, 2, 12, 28–9, 42–4, [47–8 (incorrectly marked as 39–40)]. For Tooke's Toryism see also Kitchin, *Sir Roger L'Estrange*, 282–3. Compare Roger Norton's testimony that during the Interregnum he too had been ready to "conceale and entertaine at his house, soundry persons of trust and quality" sent by Charles Stuart "upon his most weighty affairs," and that they had "held frequent consultations" there with London agents: Plomer, "King's Printing House," 371. For other royalists see Potter, *Secret Rites*, 7–22.

The role of the Stationer and his or her premises need not end with publication. A printer or bookseller might continue to be cited as evidence for a book's falsity or veracity long after its initial appearance. In such cases the character and credit of Stationers extended to cover the character and credit of the knowledge professed in printed texts, sometimes even to the degree that their personal testimony would be invoked. John Wood's *Practicae Medicinae Liber*, for example, urged that "if anyone has any doubts about the preparation of any remedy described in this book, or about the apparatus needed," he should "go to the printer, who will, for a consideration, demonstrate . . . the method." Michael Sparke's Puritan history of James I similarly referred skeptical readers to "the Stationer that hath been at the charge of Printing," who would show them the relevant documents. This was one way in which the credit of the Stationer channeled directly into the kind of credibility on which knowledge might be founded.

That it could do so rested heavily on representations of place and person. Michael Sparke opined that Saint Paul's Churchyard Stationers were distinguished by keeping good households, in which they entertained clergy, gentry, and travelers. As a result, he said, they had come to be respected as "*men in name and fame of credit.*" It was that name and fame that underwrote the knowledge circulating in print. But the reputation was an unstable one; the reason Sparke recorded it was that he believed it to be profoundly endangered. A Stationer's credit was always being challenged and reconstructed on new foundations of character and position. That the bookshop bordered on the Stationer's home was of prime importance in this dynamic. Kirkman reported that his first master "used to stay still at home, in his Closet, and do his business there, and if sent for to a Tavern or publique house, to send word he was at home, and was there ready to do their business." He always attended church on Sundays. This Kirkman regarded as close to the ideal. His second master, on the other hand, whatever his personal qualities, could never be found at home, but was always in the tavern. "The credit of the one was not so good," he judged, "but the other was as bad." [125]

The production and use of printed materials—in particular books, but also pamphlets, journals, and the ephemera such as tickets and subscription lists without which societies and academies could scarcely have functioned—depended on the bookshop and printing house. The bifurcated representation of the workplace as a home *and* as a business was consequently made central to the production and reception of printed books. All those withdrawing rooms delineated by Leybourn became meeting points for booksellers, writers, and readers: forums for negotiation, skill, and the

---

125. Binns, "STC Latin Books," 354; [Sparke], *Truth Brought to Light and Discovered by Time*, 1; Sparke, *Second Beacon*, 8; K[irkman], *Unlucky Citizen*, 169–70, 172–4.

articulation of arguments. Out of them came recognized authorship and, ultimately, public knowledge.

HOME TRUTHS

Henri-Jean Martin has characterized the social space of a printing house as "internal." He means that the procedures that together made books took place largely out of sight of the street. The obscurity of the craft skills pursued in a printing house made those procedures opaque to most gentlemen. As we have seen, the point must not be oversimplified. Those who succeeded in becoming authors entered printing houses almost routinely, and that out of a necessity perceived to arise from the very culture of the printing craft itself. But the transit across a Stationer's doorway carried consequences. It was certainly the case that seventeenth-century polemicists, lawyers, licensers, and Stationers all identified the place of printing as crucial to the cultural politics of the book trade. It is thus imperative to investigate how they achieved this identification, and to what ends.

If writers entered printing houses almost routinely, readers, too, were not unknown to do so. But this was less usual, and it always carried an attendant risk. Access to the printing house could become important in the course of even learned and arcane disputes, since revealing the processes by which a book had been constructed inevitably cast some doubt on the supremacy in that process of the proclaimed "author." Freedom of action being central to the definition of a gentleman, such doubt threatened to dissolve the most important bulwark of his credibility. William Prynne, perhaps not surprisingly, was a particularly masterful exponent of this kind of strategy. In 1630 Prynne sarcastically claimed that he had "repaired to the *Printing House*" to examine the sheets of Giles Widdowes's *Lawlesse Kneelesse Schismaticall Puritan* as they were being printed. He reported that he had "found the written Copie" there, "so mangled, so interlined and razed by *Mr. Page*, and others who perused it before its approbation, that there was scarce one *page* in all the Coppie, in which there were not severall written Errours, Absurdities and Impertinencies quite expunged." Lumpen puns aside, Prynne implied that Widdowes's text had been riddled with errors, perhaps even heresies, and that his feeble attempt at authorship had been subjected to the correction of mechanics. It was a powerful and damaging insinuation—and, the requisite access being gained, it could be applied to virtually all writers who appeared in print.[126]

126. Prynne, *Lame Giles his Haultings*, 2–3. Locke wanted rigid monitoring of his printer's workshop, to the extent of tracking down every single piece of paper: *Correspondence*, V, 34–6. See also Potter, *Secret Rites*, 1–7, and the informer's testimony in Hetet, "Literary Underground," 114.

The culture of the printing house, which gave printers such substantial interpretative sway, also provided the opportunity for all sides in debates to attribute damaging material to this agency. Many mimicked Prynne's approach. On the other hand, it might be possible to "rectify" a mistake—that is, to identify it as such without impugning the character of its author—by explicating it in terms of printers' conduct and dubbing it a printing error. Reluctant to attribute a factual mistake to "such an accurate Author as F. *Lamy*," for example, Jean Cornand de la Crose resolved to "cast the fault upon the Printer." This sort of displacement could be found in all disciplines, from the empirical to the esoteric. In 1701, Groening published in his *Historia Cycloeidis* a set of "conjectures on typographical slips in Newton's Mathematical Principles of Philosophy." Attributed to Huygens, Gregory noticed that they were in fact Newton's own annotations, which had passed through several hands in manuscript before being "secretly printed" and "malitiously published" in this way "by the contrivance of M. Libnitz." Meric Casaubon also referred to the strategy of displacement when he found that even the exemplary Allacci had made the world a thousand years too old—"which, I am very confident, was not his meaning; though, how to rectifie it, as a fault of the Printers, I know not." And Robert Boyle was said to have been inclined to ignore a "grosse errour" of Thomas Hobbes as the fault of the printer; only Hobbes's determination to defend it caused Boyle to abandon this civility and enter the lists against him. The most notorious instance of all, however, was surely that of the Milton edition produced by Richard Bentley. Bentley adduced an "editor" to account for places where he believed the published text erroneous. Jacob Tonson, whose nephew undertook the edition, was privately scathing. Tonson owned the manuscript of book 1 of *Paradise Lost*, and could retort that "the several places he affirms were altered by ye printer, are exactly true to the coppy." It is revealing that it was the Stationer, not the scholar, who was able to call upon such authoritative evidence. Moreover, Samuel Simmons, the original printer, had by no means been the poor man Bentley depicted. "I remember him," Tonson declared, "And he was look^t upon [as] an able & substantial printer." To someone with such knowledge, Bentley's notes themselves threatened "to ruin the esteem for ye Author."[127]

That books could be "rectified" by reference to the practices of Stationers' domains was an important aspect of their use. In effect, arguments over the circumstances in which a book was made and displayed came to constitute claims of its potential for seditious, blasphemous, or obscene

127. *Memoirs for the Ingenious*, 8 (August 1693), 259–63; Cohen, *Introduction to Newton's "Principia,"* 186–7, 196 n. 8; Hiscock, *David Gregory, Isaac Newton and Their Circle*, 26–7, 32; Casaubon, *Of Credulity and Incredulity*, 300; "Burnet Memorandum," in Hunter, *Robert Boyle by himself and his Friends*, 29; Geduld, *Prince of Publishers*, 128–30, 184–8.

meaning—or, on the other hand, for its positive worth. Whether a book contained safe, reliable knowledge could be questioned by asking whether it had been produced in conditions of propriety, or affirmed by asserting that it had. Hence Prynne's own claim, when he himself stood accused for *Histriomastix*, that the prosecution was unjust because the book was "not printed beyond the seas, nor in corners, nor unlycensed, nor privately dispeirced." [128] His point was that London-printed, socially visible, licensed, and publicly dispersed pages were ipso facto of sound political import. It was a common argument, and its central element was the propriety of the printing house.

A printing house, as already observed, must be represented as both private and public. On the one hand, it could not be open to all and sundry. The craft skills of the workers must remain mysterious, and it must be subject to the proper uninterrupted oversight of the master over his household. On the other, however, it must avoid being labeled "private" in the seventeenth-century sense, meaning illicit, secret, or seditious. Printers engaged in such dubious operations were said to do their printing in "holes," or in "corners." Moxon defined a "hole" as "a place where private Printing is used, *viz*. the Printing of Unlicensed *Books*, or Printing of other Mens *Copies*." That is, privacy immediately generated the two great evils of the trade: sedition and piracy. The notion was accordingly destined to become central to disputes over the status of printed materials. It reappeared countless times throughout the early modern period, from Prynne's indignant denials before Star Chamber to Bunyan's Mr. Hate-Lies, testifying against No-truth that "this was not done by stealth, or in a corner." [129]

According to Moxon, printing in holes was lucrative and fairly common. There is reason to believe him. The Stationer's Company certainly never lacked for spoils when it launched its periodic purges of offenders, and getting hold of presses, at least, seems to have been fairly easy. The renegade George Wood managed to use five in four years. Successive measures passed by both Parliament and the Company attempted to curtail such operations, however, aiming to discover "Printing-houses, and Presses erected in by-

128. Foster, *Notes from the Caroline Underground*, 40; Boulton, *Neighbourhood and Society*, 207. For developments in notions of privacy, see Chartier, *Passions of the Renaissance*, 1–11, 134–40, 257 ff.

129. CUL Ms. Oo.vi.93, no. 6, fols. 39–47; Bunyan, *Holy War*, cited in Hill, *Turbulent, Seditious and Factious People*, 244; Moxon, *Mechanick Exercises on the Whole Art of Printing*, 343; compare the Company's definition in Stationers' Company, *Registers 1554–1640*, I, 15. Compare also Anthony à Wood's cry, in Blount, *Correspondence*, 149–50: Fell and his printers "have, not in the Theater, but at a privat press elsewhere, printed without my consent or knowledge, my preface to my book, leaving out divers things and putting in what they please—horrid roguery and villany!"

places and corners, out of the Eye of Government."[130] Parliament eventually ruled that printers must work only in "their respective Dwelling Houses, and not elsewhere." This was a point also stressed by L'Estrange as crucial for any attempt to regulate the press. In fact, L'Estrange wanted to go further. He urged that the very design of those homes must be regulated: none should be permitted to have a back door or other secure means of exit.[131] The consequence is remarkable. It was not by chance that printing houses were set up in homes; the conjunction was formally obligatory. By corollary, a "private" press was one established *anywhere but* the space that society today considers archetypally private. Truth was made at home; lies emerged from holes.

The main concern of illicit printers, Moxon said, was "to get a *Hole Private.*" That meant first finding "Workmen Trusty and Cunning to conceal the *Hole,* and themselves." Supernumerary apprentices and immigrants (especially Dutchmen) were allegedly employed to do illicit printing "With More Secrecy Privaty And Securaty." The hole itself must then be established in a place that masked the noise of the press. Cellars or isolated sheds were good choices; so might be a noisy weaver's workshop. Some illicit printers abandoned the claustrophobic streets of London altogether and went out into the country.[132] The illicit presses of which we know were hidden in enterprising and unpredictable ways—as they had to be. They included the conventionally private upstairs of a Stationer's London building, one such "Private" press being found in Baptist printer Andrew Sowle's house "in two upper Rooms to which there was no passage but through Trapp-doores." An informer designating himself "H. H."—surely Henry Hills—was able to trace another to one of five houses in Blue Anchor Alley, but among "so many back doors, bye-holes and passages, and sectarians so swarming thereabouts" was unable to track it down any further.[133] Another

---

130. Stationers' Company, *Records of the Court,* xiv–xvi; Stationers' Company, *Registers 1554–1640,* IV, 535; I, xxxi, 23; Firth and Rait, *Acts and Ordinances,* I, 184–7; II, 245–54. The phrase about the gaze of the state was coined for the Company: [Parker], *Humble Remonstrance,* sig. A2ᵛ. For other examples see Crist, "Francis Smith," 274, and SCB F, fol. 207ʳ.

131. Firth and Rait, *Acts and Ordinances,* II, 698; L'Estrange, *Considerations and Proposals,* 4. Compare Stationers' Company, *Registers 1554–1640,* I, 14–15, §§ 25–6. The apparent misfortune of Elizabeth Poole, the landlady mentioned below, was that the room she let to a printer "had accesse, at an out doore wᵗʰout any Ingresse to [her] House at all"; but since she might well be the same Elizabeth Poole who had been a prominent Interregnum prophet, the ingenuousness of this claim could be doubted: PRO SP 29/239, no. 93.

132. Hetet, "Literary Underground," 18, 106; Moxon, *Mechanick Exercises on the Whole Art of Printing,* 343; SCB C, fol. 266ʳ; SCA, Suppl. Doc. I.A, Env. 11, I (a list of seized presses including one found twenty miles outside London).

133. Hetet, "Literary Underground," 144, 169. Hills was a spy for the Tories in 1682, and he was paid out of the Secret Service fund under James II: PRO SP 29/419, no. 162; Akerman, *Moneys Received,* 155, 179.

was seized at a coffeehouse, yet another in a garden shed. Informer "Parliament Joan" found William Dugard's press in Merchant Taylors School, where he was a schoolmaster as well as maintaining an interest in the printing of Salmasius's defense of Charles I. Livewell Chapman kept one in his landlord's house, and Ben Jonson described another working in a hollowed tree trunk by the light of a glowworm. One illicit printer hid counterfeit ABCs in his "Cisterne." The number of hiding places was almost limitless.[134]

The need to search out these holes presented the Stationers' Company with perhaps its biggest headache. A subject's home, as John Locke stressed, was his castle. Stationers like John Streater agreed, strenuously repudiating eavesdroppers and meddling neighbors. To enter this fortress a searcher needed a warrant. Without proper authorization, officers were vulnerable to legal retribution, and quite possibly physical assault.[135] But the Company, like other London craft corporations, claimed the right and the duty regularly to inspect its members' premises, and attempted to exercise this obligation with reasonable frequency. The resulting tension was strongly felt. After more than a century of attention, Stationers were acutely aware of what they regarded as their liberties, and this awareness manifested itself in determined obstruction. Officers found themselves "abused and disturbed" when trying to enter their buildings. In the early 1640s Richard Herne even threatened to kill the Master of the Company himself if he entered his house. One result of the Company's insistence on searching was thus a seemingly endless sequence of encounters at the threshold of printing houses and bookshops, in which even the most banal architectural features of the building became consequential. For example, Joseph Hunscot, who spearheaded much of the Company's enforcement effort in the 1640s, once found himself questioning a woman selling Lilburne's pamphlets in the streets while Lilburne himself was in Newgate jail. She turned out to be the daughter of one

134. SCB D, fols. 79ᵛ; 234ᵛ; SCA, Suppl. Doc. I.A, Env. 3, x, and Env. 5; *Kingdomes Intelligencer*, 29 September–6 October 1662; Hetet, "Literary Underground," 33; Pritchard, "George Wither's Quarrel," citing Jonson's *Time Vindicated*; Greaves, *Deliver Us from Evil*, 218; Green, *Calendar of Proceedings of the Committee for Advance of Money*, III, 517–8; Crist, "Government Control of the Press," 58; Crist, "Francis Smith," 102; Howell, *State Trials*, VII, "Trial of Smith," 950–4. For Dugard see also Strype, *Survey*, I, i, 203. On another occasion the two Company wardens, two messengers, the beadle, and the porter all came to Smith's premises and searched "every room as well as my warehouse." Smith kept this warehouse, Mearne claimed, "in a private place on the Top of the Leads of the Globe Tavern" in Cornhill. Smith retorted that, far from being private, it was actually "in the open street." By 1689 he was estimating his total damages incurred through such actions at over £2,000. He and his family now depended on charity: Smith, "Case of *Francis Smith*."

135. [Streater], *Observations*, 36–7; Blagden, "Accounts of the Wardens," 76–7; *Impartial Protestant Mercury*, 56 (1 November 1681); Blagden, "English Stock," 169; Locke, *Correspondence*, V, 790; SCA, Suppl. Doc. I.A, Env. 4, viii; Env. 5.

Browne; so Hunscot moved to detain him. But Browne escaped, since his house was "in a Garden, and having three or foure severall doores." He then threatened not only to sue Hunscot, but "to knock out [his] braines if he came any more to search his house." Hunscot subsequently petitioned to stop Browne's "printing in Corners," but to little avail. Then again, Lilburne's *England's Birthright* was successfully printed by Larner. The door of Larner's house was subsequently blocked to the Master and wardens of the Company, while the printers escaped down a rope suspended out of a rear window.[136]

In the Restoration such frustrations only multiplied. The 1662 Press Act restated the Company's search rights "for the better discovering of printing in Corners without License," and in addition it enjoined a penalty for any landlord who, like Chapman's, let his property for the use of a printing press. This was sometimes put into effect: Elizabeth Poole of Southwark was one householder actually interned for letting a room to a printer. In any case, it provided the incentive—all-important in an age before professionalized police forces—for searchers to persevere in their efforts, since they stood to benefit from any fines imposed on such landlords.[137] But the issue of entry remained problematic and central to the fate of regulatory efforts, not least because it was not only printers' houses that were being entered. L'Estrange was infuriated by the use even of peers' homes to harbor seditious books (especially, he tactfully claimed, by their servants). An anonymous Tory agreed, claiming that seditious Stationers were "seldom taken, because the Procurers House becomes a Sanctuary, and the great Master of it a Patron."[138] And 129 Stationers later submitted a petition against "the secret Underminings & Intrudings of forreiners into the houses of Noble men and others."

The issue culminated in the Restoration régime's statutory attempt to regulate the press. The greatest difficulty in passing the Press Act itself appears to have been the Lords' objection to its search clause. With such powerful individuals threatened in their own homes, feelings ran high, and the original bill was abandoned altogether. The king himself urged Parliament forward, however, and behind the scenes the Company too agitated for an Act. Eventually it was indeed passed, with a limited provision exempting

---

136. Siebert, *Freedom of the Press*, 174 (and 186 for Herne employing mercuries to distribute pamphlets while he was in prison); Hunscot, *Humble Petition*, 3–7. For the Company's search rights see also PRO SP 29/39, nos. 92–5.

137. 14 Car. II, c. 33, §§ 9, 14; SCB F, fol. 171ᵛ; PRO SP 29/239, no. 93. After the Act expired in 1679, the authorities found that while they could still act once publications were on the street, they could not routinely enter printing houses. Restriction efforts were crippled, and only a few prosecutions were mounted. For Poole, see above, p. 129, n. 131.

138. *Arguments Relating to a Restraint*, 26–7. For nobles' concepts of privacy, see Pollock, "Living on the Stage of the World."

from search not only peers' homes, but those of any commoner not directly involved in the book trade. Even this was too much for Locke. "How the gent much more how the Peers of England came thus to prostitute their houses to the visitation and inspection of any body much lesse a messenger upon pretence of searching for books I cannot imagin," he declared. He found the provision "a mark of Slavery."

L'Estrange, on the other hand, believed the new provisions insufficient. The new "Surveyor of Imprimery" wanted what were known as "general warrants" to be issued, providing a still greater legal validation for his searches. The validity of such general warrants—which authorized entry without reference to a specific cause—was highly contentious. They could certainly be effective: Francis Smith claimed to have been "40 Times a Prisoner" in twenty-four years, eighteen of them under general warrants. But Stationers like Smith, already attuned to their liberties, repeatedly complained that such warrants were illegal. When Messenger of the Press Robert Stephens obtained a general warrant to enter "any Booksellers or Printers Shops or Warehouses, or elsewhere whatsoever," Smith would stand his ground and refuse to honor it, alleging that it contravened Magna Carta. His appeal had a long and tortuous history, both within the Stationers' community and in other London companies.[139] Others were even less compliant. One constable found himself confronting over twenty violently angry printers when he tried to enter John Streater's printing house under such a warrant, in an incident discussed further in chapter 4. Faced with aggressive opposition like this, the Company had to issue a series of declarations enjoining compliance with its right of entry. But even its own bylaws could be questioned. Vowing to obtain damages for violation of Magna Carta, Whig Stationer Richard Janeway actually arrested for trespass the Company searchers who had entered his house and, he claimed, "Ransacked" it while looking for illicit almanacs. "Let the Company see whether their Pretended (though to all men unknown) By-Laws will Indemnifie them," he threatened. Such arguments often lost—but not always. The lord chief justice himself supported Smith's case on one occasion.[140]

Stationers' Company wardens, who organized most searches, were well

139. PRO SP 29/39, no. 92; PRO SP 29/51, nos. 5–10; PRO SP 30/F, no. 45; Smith, "Case of *Francis Smith*, Bookseller"; *Arguments Relating to a Restraint*, 26–7; SCB F, fol. 21ᵛ; SCB D, fol. 77ᵛ; Hetet, "Literary Underground," 16, 27; Kitchin, *L'Estrange*, 105, 128–9; Seaward, *Cavalier Parliament*, 158–9; *Journals of the House of Commons*, VIII, 425b, 429b; 14 Car. II, c. 33, §§ 9, 18; Locke, *Correspondence*, V, 790; Crist, "Government Control of the Press," 53, 58; Crist, "Francis Smith," 274–5; SCA, Suppl. Doc. I.A, Env. 4, viii; Env. 5; Smith, *Account of the Injurious Proceedings of Sir George Jeffreys*, [16 (incorrectly marked as 20)]; [Larner], *True Relation*, 8–9, 14.

140. PRO SP 29/277, nos. 34–5; PRO SP 44/34, fol. 40ᵛ; [Streater?], *Character of a True and False Shepherd*; *Impartial Protestant Mercury* 56 (4 November 1681); Howell, *State Trials*,

acquainted with printing houses. As far as the Privy Council and courts were concerned, however, what went on in such a place was most often recorded in the form of the snapshot glimpses obtained by forced entry. It is therefore worth recalling the skills and procedures employed in these ambushes. L'Estrange's corps of men to invade a printing house typically comprised himself, a printer, a constable, one of the king's messengers, and the crony who would have been watching the building for him. They would try to surround the building. Then they would lie in wait until long into the night, watching for nocturnal printing to begin. Finally, they would pounce. After it was all over, the team would retire to a nearby tavern to celebrate its achievements.[141] The printer was brought along for his special skills: he could provide a quick comparison of the remains of a hastily broken forme with newly printed sheets, and a confirmation that they were indeed the same. He knew where to look for incriminating evidence and could estimate immediately how many copies had been printed. The most important such official was Robert Stephens, who had been trained as a printer before becoming royal messenger of the press. His fellow messengers, who probably lacked his extensive practical experience, rapidly gave up, but Stephens lasted for decades. Starting out as L'Estrange's servant, he was made messenger in 1678 with a salary of £50 from the Secret Service fund, plus expenses and £5 per annum from a grateful Stationers' Company. But his specialist skills soon made Stephens a figure of suspicion even to his own boss, who came to believe that they were being deployed to undermine his own authority. For his part, Stephens concluded L'Estrange to be an ineffective suppresser of popery, and an actively counterproductive one of sectarianism. He called him "the great Publisher of all the Phanatic Books, which are hardly known till they are mention'd in the Observator," and encouraged the publication of licensed pamphlets attacking him. L'Estrange and Stephens became enemies, perpetrating a lasting and angry feud.[142]

After gathering the evidence, L'Estrange had to make a case. The familial structure of early modern commerce now provided rich opportunities for both prosecution and defense. In particular, distinctions between patriarchal

---

VII, "Trial of Francis Smith," 950. In the last case more informal measures were then adopted, the local JP suggesting that L'Estrange get "some unhappy boys" to go through a back window and open the door.

141. Brodowski, "Literary Piracy," 51–2. Janeway reported that the searchers who invaded his own house were so "Flushed" with their meager discovery of a gross of illicit almanacs "that they immediately Repaired to the Three Tun Tavern to Rejoice, where they spent far more than they will get by the Discovery": *Impartial Protestant Mercury* 56 (4 November 1681).

142. *Exact Narrative*, 19–20, 22, 23–4; Crist, "Francis Smith," 78–9, 109–10; Rostenberg, "Robert Stephens," 136, 139; Crist, "Government Control of the Press," 54; PRO SP 29/424, no. 151.

representations and the quotidian practice of gender roles could be exploited. Stationers thus used legal loopholes such as the law of coverture to good effect. Coverture was a common-law doctrine involving the notion that a wife was virtually the property of her husband. She was therefore not considered responsible for her actions, in the same way that a seventeenth-century servant was deemed to be "included in his master." It was a terrifyingly sweeping principle, which could be used to support the total loss of all a woman's goods and possessions in a disenfranchisement that, as Amy Erickson points out, no man ever underwent unless convicted of treason. Yet the practice was more complex than the bald legal theory implied. Stationers and their spouses in particular could turn the principle to their advantage, to claim that the wife had been in charge whenever a dangerous book had been sold. Jane Curtis, for example, testified that she had distributed a seditious tract while her husband Langley was "in the country a hundred miles off." James Astwood likewise claimed to have been "abroad" when his wife received the manuscript for the seditious *Ra-Ree Show*. Smith and Braddyll used the same tactic. It was an effective one: L'Estrange could only observe such testimony with exasperation.[143]

Stationer Samuel Speed juxtaposed "the truth of Wives" with "the Fidelity of Servants." Both required care in their deployment. Because of their subordinate status, the testimony of journeymen—or lesser workers, such as devils—could be either useful or dangerous to a defense. We have already encountered Bodvell's revelations. Such agents held privy knowledge and so could give evidence for a prosecution. But they might then find themselves blacklisted and ruined. If for the defense, such testimony could serve to distance the master from the contents of a work in which he had been involved, especially when combined with concurrent printing and the coverture principle. Even eminently respectable Stationers routinely used intermediaries such as binders and their own spouses to collate and distribute potentially questionable books, hence dissociating themselves from them. In a city where court politics moved at a rapid and inscrutable rate, this was only prudent. One printer's wife thus testified that she had received half a dozen copies of a particular book from Benjamin Harris's shop, "but not of him; for he was either gone out, or not in the way, but she had them of his man." Ralph Smith, called in for printing Zachary Crofton's *Berith Anti-Baal*, claimed it had been printed in his name while he lay ill. Robert Boulter testified that he had not printed a pirated almanac, but that two hundred

---

143. Erickson, *Women and Property*, 3, 5–6, 24–6, 100–1, 224–9; Howell, *State Trials*, VII, "Trial of Jane Curtis," 959–60; Crist, "Francis Smith," 292–7, 306; SCB E, fol. 110ʳ; *Observator* I, 165 (5 July 1682); Hetet, "Literary Underground," 170; Weatherill, *Consumer Behaviour*, 139. For other examples of such exploitation of gender-based legalities, see *State Law*, 18–19, and Bell, "Elizabeth Calvert," 28–38.

copies had been "left at his shop wth his Servant." [144] The heresiographer
Thomas Edwards likewise bemoaned Richard Overton, "an Independent
Book-seller and a member of Master *John Goodwins* Church." "All kind of
unlicenced Books that make any ways for the Sects, and against Presbyterians, are sold at his shop," Edwards claimed, "and tis given out the man sels
them, but not the Master." Even writers could be made use of in such a way.
Penn would dictate his Quaker tracts directly to the compositor, thus allowing the master to claim that he never knew "the poyson therein contained."
Such answers were readily given, L'Estrange complained. "And there's an
end of the Search."

But servants' testimony was not always so useful for a defendant. They
might also be held to reveal damaging matters of fact inadvertently. Like
Brewster, Benjamin Harris suffered for this. Harris had given sixpence to a
printer's man who was working on a book that L'Estrange considered seditious. Even though the man would not affirm that the gift had been meant
as an incentive to hasten the work, Harris was nonetheless convicted because
he did reveal that the transaction had occurred at night. Besides, Hyde reckoned that it was ridiculous "for a man to pretend he did not know, when he
being Master, sends for the proofes by his Servant[; or] for any man to
suppose this is not the Masters Act." It was well understood that servants
were subject to the master's will. "Directing it to be done privately" merely
confirmed the intention. [145]

Full and dramatic use of these conventions was made in the well-known
prosecution of John Twyn. Twyn had been the Stationers' Company's agent
overseeing the old royal printing house in Scotland during the Interregnum, and in 1660 he came back to London to become a radical printer.
In 1663–4 he was arrested and tried for advocating the death of the
king in printing *A Treatise of the Execution of Justice*. Evidence about the
interior of the printing house was central to the progress of his trial. Ser-
jeant Morton thus testified that "this man would have done it with all the
privacy that could be." Twyn had worked by night. He had used two presses
in one room. One had been operated by Twyn himself, the other by his
servants, working "by his Command and in his presence." This pressroom
was situated above his composing room, in the private part of the building.
Twyn had composed part of the text himself, printed sheets, and corrected
proofs, "all in his own house." When L'Estrange burst in, his response had

144. Valerius Maximus, *Romae Antiquae Descriptio*, 290–1; Harris, *London Newspapers*,
144–5; Hetet, "Wardens' Accounts," 45; Howell, *State Trials*, VII, "Trial of Harris," 927;
Greaves, *Deliver Us from Evil*, 211–12; SCB D, fol. 149ᵛ; SCB F, fol. 114ᵛ.

145. Edwards, *Second Part of Gangraena*, 9; Edwards, *Third Part of Gangraena*, 148–52;
PRO SP 29/233, no. 140; PRO SP 29/51, no. 10(i); Howell, *State Trials*, VII, "Trial of Harris,"
928; *Exact Narrative*, 44.

been to break the formes, and to try to spirit away the printed sheets by the somewhat desperate expedient of throwing them out of the window.[146]

Twyn's servant (that is, an apprentice named Joseph Walker) was now called to the stand. He tried to say as little as possible to incriminate his master, but ended up giving damning evidence in spite of himself. Walker testified that they had printed only part of the copy, amounting to three sheets. They had not done a title page, nor a running head, although the manuscript itself had had a title. They seem to have followed standard procedure in the concurrent printing of illicit books. To make sure the proofs were correct, the servant would carry the sheets to Twyn in the kitchen, and Twyn would then return them to the "Workhouse" about an hour later. The corrections were in a hand "not much unlike his," and the servant confirmed that Twyn routinely corrected copy himself. No other corrector was normally employed, but for longer works (he mentioned Hooker's indisputably orthodox *Laws of Ecclesiastical Polity*) one might be brought in.

This testimony was of prime importance, since L'Estrange was principally concerned to prove that Twyn had corrected the copy. He thought it impossible to do so without reading the text and therefore being conscious of its treasonous content. Even if the pressmen had been ignorant, he had told Twyn as they sat in the constable's house after his arrest, "the Corrector must certainly know what it was." Twyn maintained that "I did never read a line of it in my life." But his insistence was futile. The implication that he had composed and corrected the text was indeed decisive. "Is it possible you could Compose, and not read a line of it?" asked Hyde in disbelief. Twyn was convicted of high treason. In a display of Stuart justice at its most demonstrative, he was hanged, drawn, and quartered.[147]

THE CHARACTER OF AN AMPHIBIAN:
THE REALITY AND REPRESENTATION OF STATIONERS

> We know there is nothing impossible with God—and it may be a metaphysical puzzlement, whether there be any thing impossible with a Stationer.
>
> TORYRORYDAMMEEPLOTSHAMMEE YOUNKERCRAPE [pseud.], *A Sermon Prepared to be Preach'd*, sig. A2ᵛ

Truths were produced at home—the home of a Stationer. The character of the Stationer therefore came to be seen as playing a central part in establish-

---

146. *Exact Narrative*, 12–13, 16–17, 22, 24, 28–9. For a detailed analysis of the evidence presented at this trial see McKenzie, "London Book Trade."

147. *Exact Narrative*, 13–16, 18–19, 21, 26–7, 30, 35, 73–8. Twyn was still rejecting the argument from correcting practice as he stood on the scaffold itself. "You understood *English*, or else you could not Correct it," retorted the attendant: "if you understood *English*, or sense, you could not be ignorant that it was a *Horrid* piece of *Treason*, such as no honest man ought to see and conceal one half hour."

ing the status of the works he or she made and sold. In a sense this should hardly be surprising to historians: it is well known that Continental printers and publishers became influential in the development of religious and other knowledge. But these connections between household and workplace, between attributed skills and attributed credit, and between the character of the Stationer and the character of the books he or she produced, have not hitherto been explored in depth. They need to be. The figure of the Stationer dominated representations of print culture in early modern England, and thereby conditioned much else besides.

Like other tradesmen, the bookseller needed to be "capable of making a judgment of things" so that he or she could be "fenced against bubbles and projects." Judgment was essential if one were to avoid ruin at the hands of "delusive schemes"—of which the book trade knew all too many. In the example cited above, as well as using Wharton, Richard Chiswell himself read over Strype's historical work before printing it, and judged its quality. It is true that booksellers were advised not to rely solely on their own judgment when deciding whether or not to undertake a publication. In medicine, for example, "the Work ought to have the Approbation of a Physician, who is a proper Judge of Books." But such advice underlines the fact that it was the bookseller who referred the candidate text to such a judge, and who determined the weight to be accorded that judge's assessment. The Stationer was the judge of judges.[148]

In managing publications, Stationers, and often booksellers in particular, controlled events. The practices and representations of their domains affected every character and every leaf of their products. Isolating a consistent, identifiable, and immutable element attributable to the individual author would be virtually impossible in these circumstances. Attributing authorship was thus intensely problematic for both contemporary and future readers. A priori, virtually any element in a work might or might not be the Stationers' responsibility, in virtually any field of writing. Francis Howgil accused them of having "belied" Quaker books. John Goodwin attacked Presbyterian booksellers for committing "most un-Christian falsification, even that which some would call Forgerie," in their reproduction of his own words. "You talk of *correcting the Press*," Goodwin raged, "but you should do well in the first place to *correct* your selves. For you are the crooked thing that most needs streigtning." Even Thomas Hobbes's works allegedly suffered at

148. Defoe, *Complete English Tradesman*, 44–7; CUL Ms. Add. 4, No. 121; Campbell, *London Tradesman*, 131. See also Curll's stipulation of his prerogative to exclude certain fables from La Fontaine that he judged "too immaterial in their Subjects for an English version": BL Ms. Add. 38728, no. 121. The importance of "character" identified in this section should be compared to the motifs explored in Korshin, *Typologies*.

the insistence of their Stationer, who objected to the philosopher's being presented as "the true [republican] Hobbes speaking his mind" and refused to publish Hollar's engraved portrait. The reading of a book could in consequence be substantially affected by the perceived conduct, and above all the perceived character, of the Stationer or Stationers who had produced it.[149]

In the making of a book, authorship was thus distributed over a number of individuals and groups. Its identification was left to be fought for later. If a printed book did not correspond to the writer's words, asked Robert Burton, "whom do you blame?" The corrector, the printer, or "everyone?"[150] Burton himself licensed the reader to attribute responsibility to everyone. As we shall see, however, the authorities more helpfully formalized this problem in the epistemology of reading by recognizing Stationers themselves as authors. It is thus imperative to understand the cultural identity a Stationer attempted to construct and protect in the course of his or her work, along with the characteristics attributed to them by readers in appraising their power and influence.

What, then, was the character of a Stationer? To answer that question we need to call upon the full range of representations adopted by Stationers: how they saw themselves and their practices, and what part they thought they should properly play in political, popular, and learned culture. In fact, the "character of a Stationer" was the product of a long process of historical construction, and was much discussed by contemporaries. What will be represented here is necessarily simplified, and moreover should be read in conjunction with the account of Stationers' historiography presented in chapter 5. These were only some of the resources available throughout the period to those wishing to analyze the conduct and character of Stationers.

Jacob Tonson, as noted above, was regarded as a social amphibian. In this he was representative: the character of a Stationer was most commonly assessed in terms of the compatibility or otherwise of commerce and civility. The question was a general one, not restricted in its implications to the book trade. London was conventionally pictured as the epitome of successful commerce—to Howell, as to Harrington, the city was simply "Emporium"[151]—and the great trading companies dealt in staggering sums. The

---

149. Howgil[l], *Fiery Darts of the Divel Quenched*, 2, 11; Goodwin, *Fresh Discovery*, 60–61, 72; Nullius Nominis [pseud.], *An Apologie for the Six Book-Sellers*, 4; Rostenberg, *English Publishers in the Graphic Arts*, 38. Compare Elzevir's behavior (Warrender, "Early Latin Versions of Thomas Hobbes's *De Cive*," 44–5) and the fate of Hobbes's *Of Liberty and Necessity* (Mintz, *Hunting of Leviathan*, 110).

150. Burton, *Anatomy of Melancholy*, I, xl, xli–xliv.

151. Howell, *Londinopolis*, title page; Harrington, *Political Works*, 295–8. Compare R. H[ooke?], *New Atlantis . . . Continued*, 35, 84; and see also Earle, *City Full of People*, 3, 5.

nobility, too, were deeply implicated in the world of money by the later seventeenth century. Rhetoric might contrast public life with commerce, but in reality the distinction was by no means consistent, and the commercial world itself was riddled with the paraphernalia of contemporary political culture—with crown appointments, patents, and offices. The privilege of being regarded as honorary gentry was granted relatively freely to great merchants. But it was only very grudgingly accorded to retailers, and hardly ever to craftsmen. Defoe urged that this was an artificial distinction, claiming that "the most noble Descendants of *Adam's* Family, and in whom the Primogeniture remained, were really *Mechanicks*." But even he accounted the genteel shopkeeper an "amphibious creature," traversing basically divergent worlds of honor and venality. Civility was the issue here, not money per se: it was notorious that worldly success made "cits" not polite but ruthless and arrogant. "This thing call'd prosperity makes a man strangely insolent and forgetful," testified Tom Brown. "How contemptibly a cutler looks at a poor grinder of knives, a physician in his coach at a farrier on foot, and a well-grown Paul's church-yard bookseller upon one of the trade that sells second-hand books under the trees in Moorfields." [152]

The conventional image of the bookseller that has descended to us from the eighteenth century reflects something of this allegation. The image is that of the crude and mercenary opportunist. We imagine him—it is always a he—ruthlessly exploiting poets and hack writers, and maintaining them penniless, ailing, and miserable in their Grub Street garrets as they slave over journeyman criticism paid by the line. But this portrait is far from a good likeness. It is scarcely applicable at all to the sixteenth and seventeenth centuries, when commercial society was less developed, and even for the eighteenth it masks both a representation and a reality far more complex. Stationers were not gentlemen as formally defined; but that did not mean that they were the unprincipled, rapacious exploiters of Hogarthian legend, dedicated to accruing capital by any means. It is true that the supposed subservience of tradesmen of all kinds to commercial "interest" was a key component in their received identity, and that the charge had regularly been leveled at Stationers in particular since long before 1600. It was personified in such figures as the papist bookseller who stashed his loot in a handy "*House* of *Office*" before joining the Cavaliers at the battle of Worcester, only to be fatally overcome by the fumes when he returned to sift it out a fortnight later; or the Anabaptist printer who, when questioned how he could "in *conscience*" produce a book that the sternly Presbyterian Michael Sparke

152. Defoe, *Plan of the English Commerce*, 1–5; Dewald, "Ruling Class in the Marketplace," 52; Earle, *Making of the English Middle Class*, 7–8, 11–12.

deemed irreligious, replied that "if the *Devill* himself should give him or bring him a Book that he was sure to get by, he would *print* it." But consistent avarice of this order was scarcely credible, and was always qualified to an important extent by the demands of custom, religion, morality, and civility.[153] Thus Sparke himself, one of the most important Stationers of the Caroline and Civil War periods, thought that his comrades should pray at least three times a day, fast, and give alms; at their deaths, they should bequeath funds to endow hospitals or free schools.[154]

Advice of this sort was available from a variety of sources. While it does not straightforwardly reflect reality, it is less divorced from it than is the image of the greed-driven lout, or even that of the self-interested agent of economic rationality. It provided a repertoire of representations in terms of which contemporaries could understand and respond to the conduct of the Stationers they actually met.[155] In these circumstances, the figure of the avaricious rogue becomes less credible still, even though, perhaps, it may have been useful in certain extreme cases. Defoe made the point—adopted much later by Max Weber—that any tradesman who *were* simply rapacious would soon lose credit, and therefore face ruin. Politeness was not just prudent; it was profitable. Booksellers were particularly wise to observe polite conventions, moreover, since they were especially likely to be exposed to genteel conversation in their premises. Any who might be tempted to brute exploitation would soon conclude that to be a very ineffective way to do business.

The cluster of civilities appropriate to commercial life went by various names. John Wilkins, for one, spoke of *wisdom* as "the art of business"—something of which, unlike their natural knowledge, his contemporaries could be confident and proud. Among the virtues to be displayed were discretion and confidentiality. Others pointed to the many maxims encapsulated in the term *prudence*. Whatever its name, its principles were widely understood. Thomas Sawbridge was one Stationer to put such principles into practice, when, "loth to bring any scandal upon a man of his Coat," he tactfully declined to prosecute the notorious shoplifting vicar of Croydon.[156]

153. As is clear even from these examples, the religious and political connotations of which should be obvious. Sparke, *Second Beacon*, 5–8. Sparke's picturesque charge that the book-buying public "eats brown bread to fill the *sleeping Stationers* belly with Venison and Sacke" should also be noted, in [Sparke], *Scintilla*, 5.

154. Sparke, *Crums of Comfort*, sig. A5ʳ; [Sparke], *Second Part of Crums of Comfort*. The best-known bequest on such lines was, of course, that of Thomas Guy, which provided for the foundation of Guy's Hospital.

155. Shapin, *Social History of Truth*, xx–xxi, provides a thoughtful argument for the use of such materials. The use of such repertoires of civility in commercial as opposed to genteel life is still underinvestigated.

156. Wilkins, *Sermons*, 171, 188–9; *Case of the Inhabitants of the Town and Parish of Croydon*, 2, 8–9. On shoplifting see [Head], *Canting Academy*, 53, 106. Stealing books could have

Evidence that other Stationers were likewise conscious of propriety can be seen in a variety of legal cases, especially those in which booksellers tried to make what was called a "defense of trade." This involved claiming that the publication of an alleged "libel" was simply part of their routine commercial practice, that no particular intent could be inferred, and that they should therefore not be identified personally with its content. A defense of trade thus involved the claim that no deliberate malice had been attendant on one's actions. William Larner's defense concerning those tracts by Lilburne was representative of this strategy. He maintained that, "some of them being brought to the shop," he had bought twenty-five copies. He had done so, he maintained, "after the manner of the Trade of *Book-sellers*, (which is to buy Books, of all sorts, brought to their shops, not examining the Persons that bring them, either names, or Places of abode,) . . . not knowing what they were for matter, or examining the Person, what he was that brought them, or where was his aboad." He had never read the contents.

The point of such an argument was to distinguish between the Stationer and the book. The strategy depended on representations of the character, work, and workplace of the individual being tried. Larner thus told the House of Lords that he had been a volunteer for the parliamentary forces in the Civil War, his parents had been "plundered by the Cavaliers," and he had a pregnant wife at home who begged that he be permitted to follow his "calling" in order to support the family. After the Restoration, similarly, character witnesses would testify before Chief Justice Sir Robert Hyde that Thomas Brewster was "civil" to his neighbors, attended Anglican service regularly, and was a member of the trained bands. In practice, defenses of trade were rarely successful—Brewster should be cashiered forthwith, Hyde snorted, and Larner had stayed in prison too—but the fact that they were frequently resorted to, and the tactics commonly used in them, make them useful resources for the historian.[157]

These gleanings may be supplemented by funeral sermons held for deceased Stationers. On these occasions the preacher would paint a moral portrait of the deceased, typically holding him or her up as an example for others to emulate. The particular qualities chosen for emphasis were, then, those conceived most important for the character of a Christian Stationer. An example was the sermon preached by Francis Atterbury over the body of High Church bookseller Thomas Bennet, but intended, Atterbury insisted, "not so much in the Honour of the Dead, as for the Use of the Living."

---

serious consequences: one William Bond was executed in 1721, having originally been transported for the crime. See Earle, *City Full of People*, 66.

157. [Larner], *True Relation*, 3, 16; *Every Mans Case*; *Exact Narrative*, 54–5, 62–4. For the argument against such claims of trade, see 46–7.

Despite Atterbury's own high-flying predilections, his characterization of the required qualities was probably reliable: certainly, it was endorsed even by the Whig theologian Benjamin Hoadly, during an ensuing argument about "the Nature of *Virtue*" itself.[158] Another such sermon was that preached by an anonymous minister for Bennet's erstwhile partner, Henry Clements, the theme of which was the repudiation of worldly materialism for the life of the soul. This minister too announced that his aim was to "admonish the Living" of "the Shortness and Uncertainty of Life, and the pious Use that may be made of it." They would discover that use by following Clements minutely. "You must transcribe him in your Actions," he insisted, following a strict "Duty of Imitation."

Such discourses drew on standard tropes of Restoration morality to articulate a character in distinctive ways. First, they rested on a proclaimed foundation of familiarity. Atterbury claimed to have known Bennet personally for more than twenty years, and it was on this basis that he extolled the bookseller's conduct as "Exemplary." Clements's eulogist likewise claimed long acquaintance. Each then listed a sequence of essential virtues, embracing religious practices, moral conduct, family life, and vocational civility. A firm Anglican, Bennet had always appeared "compos'd and serious" during services, manifestly "in earnest, and truly affected with what he was doing." In private, too, he had pursued his devotions, and his family had thus been subject to proper "Government." He had been prudent, of good temper (usually), and "a mighty Lover of Regularity and Order." Firmly rooted in his domestic life, these principles had also guided "any Business of Consequence," so that he had managed his affairs with "the utmost Exactness." In public argument, he had voiced his views soberly, if vigorously: his "private Conversation" remained as "soft and easie, as his Principles were stubborn." His example had encouraged his peers to be active and industrious, while Bennet himself had been careful to inculcate the same values into his servants by reading "useful Discourses" to them every Sunday. The key point was that the devotional and moral governance of his household intersected in every respect with that of his Stationer's work.

For his part, the preacher of Clements's funeral sermon affected to stumble over his words when he came to this key point of the conjunction of domestic and civic virtue. Clements had been "a Private, I ought to have said a *Public*, Person," he stammered, "for I am sure in his Station he was a *Public* Good." It was for this reason that he could be used to display the "Qualities and Characters which distinguish and form a Man for a *Publick*

---

158. Atterbury, *Sermon* (1706), 3; [Hoadly], *Letter*, 3–4. This was answered in Atterbury's *Fourteen Sermons*, preface, i–lxix, which was pirated as *Large Vindication*; Hoadly replied again in *Second Letter*, which answered the authorized version.

Good." Indeed, he had been so "adorn'd with good intellectual Endowments" that he "might have been eminently useful in a much higher Station,
if the Providence of God had plac'd him in it." The bookseller had exhibited
"an unblemish'd Strictness of Morals." He showed that it was essential for a
Stationer to be "a Lover of Justice, and true to ones Word, and faithful in
ones Commerce and Dealings with other Men." This conduct was under-
written by his devout Christianity, pursued, after a rational examination of
its doctrines, within the Church of England. He had always used the Anglican liturgy "in his private Family," the minister recalled. At home, he had
been "a dutiful Son, a tender and obliging Husband, an affectionate Father,
a prudent, careful, and kind Master, and a most hearty Friend." In work,
too, Clements had been "eminent for Humility, and Devotion, and an universal Charity," and had always displayed "a true Christian Sweetness and
Benignity of Temper." In fact, his constancy in maintaining friendship even
with those of the church who had fallen on hard times (a translucently veiled
reference to the nonjurors) showed Clements to have possessed nothing less
than "heroic" virtue.

The point is not so much whether Bennet and Clements were *really* devoted, pious, and familial, the perfect masters of their vocation. We have no
way of assessing that. Rather, portraits like these had real effects not only on
their own standing, but on broader perceptions of what an ideal printer or
bookseller should be like.[159] They were therefore also likely to affect the
status of the publishing projects they in fact undertook. In the following
section we shall see a dramatic example of how Bennet's character as a veracious witness could destroy a learned scholar's reputation as an author.
Moreover, if the character of the Christian Stationer was properly assessed
in terms of domestic virtue, personal credit, religious constancy, and moderate temperance, then links were constantly being constructed between
vocation, family life, piety, and soteriology. Such pronouncements make
the modern reader think immediately of Max Weber. In one sense, these
sermons hardly count as unequivocal support for Weber's thesis: that for
Clements reeked of the rhetoric of Sacheverell, and anyone who can make a
Calvinist out of Atterbury deserves admiration. But in another, it surely
comes as no surprise to see an "ethic" of proper conduct articulated in the

159. *Christian's Support*, 20–25; Atterbury, *Sermon* (1706), 13–16. It is ironic, then, that
Atterbury's sermon was pirated by a printer definitely not regarded as such a paragon—
Henry Hills Jr., the most notorious pirate of the years before 1710—and in a form that made
it appear downright uncouth: Atterbury, *Sermon* (1707), 12: "Several of his *Auditory* were,
perhaps, entire Strangers to the Person, whose Death we now lament; and the greater part of
you, who were not, had, for that reason, so just an *esteem* of him, that it will [1706 edition:
"not"] be unwelcome to you, I presume, to be put in mind of those good *Qualities* which
you observed in him."

book trade, since one of Weber's main exempla, Benjamin Franklin, was himself working as a printer when he contracted the condition.[160] The articulation of such an ethic was what figures like Atterbury were doing, too, when they constructed the character of a Stationer.

Other writers went further still, describing not only how an ideal bookseller should act, but what his philosophy should be. Moses Pitt recommended that he publish biographies of Boyle, Bacon, and Hale. John Dunton's ideal education likewise would include natural philosophy. His model bookseller must "prefer *Galileo's Tube* to *Ptolomy's Spectacles*, and the Discoveries of our English *Royal Society*, to the blind Conjectures of the Peripateticks." He would believe the world to be composed of a "*Flux* [of] Particles," and would like to be cremated, so as to be "resolved into the *Elements* of which I was first compounded." He would be enthusiastic about recent astronomical works, being, of course, a Copernican. Dunton himself believed in "*ten Thousand more Worlds* than are already discovered," all of them perhaps inhabited. Christians all, these alien beings were referred to by the Bible as Thrones, Denominations, and Principalities; their true nature could be elaborated either through natural philosophy or through a cabalistic exegesis of the Book of Genesis. In fact, Dunton held that he himself had "*ranged all the boundless Tracts of the Universe*" as a spirit, before being conceived and called down to live an earthly life in the Poultry.

In such hands, Moxon's stipulations about the Vitruvian virtues of the master printer took on a new resonance. Like Moxon, Dunton insisted that "most, if not all, the *manual Trades* in the World" were "but the several *Species* of Practical Philosophy." The "Mechanick" executed the theories expressed in texts by the scholar; "what the one dictates from the *School of Nature*, the other experiments in the *Shop of Art*." So Dunton, again like Moxon, insisted that the Stationer's activity was a philosophic one. "Neither would Men know how to keep themselves in Action, or maintain Commerce, where [*sic*] it not for the Sake of *Philosophy*." Indeed, he maintained, "every *Smith, Carpenter, Mason*, &c that makes an Improvement in his Craft or Mystery, deserves the Title of a *Virtuoso*, and to be numbered among the Philosophers."[161]

Some Stationers did indeed dabble in the practices of the virtuosi—and more than dabble. In the sixteenth century, John Stow had known Reyner Wolfe to be a great collector of antiquities. After the Restoration, Edmond Halley found himself viewing stars with "the Printer" when he visited He-

---

160. Bennett, *Tory Crisis*; Weber, *Protestant Ethic*, chap. 2, esp. 48–50, 65. Nicholas Tyacke has recently been among a number of historians to stress that anti-Calvinist churchmen could be intimately involved in commerce: Tyacke, *Anti-Calvinists*, e.g., 193, 220–2.

161. Pitt, *Letter*, 15, 19–22; Dunton, *Life and Errors* (1705), 26–34; Dunton, *Religio Bibliopolae*, 1–3, 16–7, 40–8, and passim.

velius in Danzig to assess his observational techniques; Moxon observed for himself in London. William Leybourn, as well as practicing as a surveyor in the aftermath of the Fire of London, acted as mathematician, teacher, and inventor, and printed and sold books dealing with all of these subjects. William Cooper, alchemical bookseller, maintained his own doctrine that there were really three books of nature, not two: Creation, Scripture, and the human body. But perhaps the most enterprising of all, apart from Moxon, was Moses Pitt. As early as 1655, Pitt had had conversations in his master's bookshop about Francis Bacon. For decades after that he devoted himself to a series of natural-philosophical, mathematical, and natural-historical projects. He contributed testimony about fairies to Henry More and Joseph Glanvill's project to vindicate the existence of spirits, produced an issue of Robert Hooke's *Philosophical Collections*, and at the same time, like Moxon, developed an alliance with Oxford University to produce bibles against the opposition of the Stationers' Company (and, he insisted, against popery too). His great project for a new *English Atlas* was perhaps the most ambitious of all Restoration publishing enterprises in natural knowledge. Its eventual failure reminds us of the perils as well as the achievements of such activities. Robert Boyle himself ("we have been in conversation together," Pitt remembered proudly) recommended him, and Pitt planned the first biography of Boyle before his own bankruptcy scuppered the project.[162]

The vision of the polite and even virtuosic Stationer had its adherents. But perhaps not too many. In further exemplification of his ideal, Dunton proceeded to recite the "Characters" of all the London Stationers he could remember, mentioning to what extent they reached the proper standard. The themes, again, were conventional enough: civility, "punctuality" in affairs, honesty, religious devotion, and humility. But they combined in only one or two individuals. One was Alexander Bosvile, who lived at the Dial and Bible, Fleet Street. "He is a very genteel person," reported Dunton: "it is in Mr. Bosvile that all qualities meet, that are essential to a good Churchman, or an accomplished Bookseller." Another was Ebenezer Tracy on London Bridge: "His Religion is not confin'd to the Church any more than the Shop—His Behaviour in his Family is Grave and Exemplary—His Devotion constant—His care over his Household is Tender and Impartial—And to his *Servants* he seems a Father rather than a Master."[163] But these were shining exceptions.

Dunton portrayed the domestic and religious virtue of the bookseller as

162. Altick, *Shows of London*, 7; RGO Ms. 1.42, fols. 186^r–187^r; Halley, *Correspondence and Papers*, 42–3; Kenney, "William Leybourn"; C[ooper], *Philosophicall Epitaph*, 1–3; Pitt, *Account of one Ann Jeffries*; Pitt, *Cry of the Oppressed*, sig. A4^v, 113 ff.; Pitt, *Letter*, 15, 19, 21–2. For the *English Atlas* project, see below, pp. 447–9, 451–3.

163. Dunton, *Life and Errors* (1705), 288; Plomer, *Dictionary . . . 1668 to 1725*, 294.

intimately linked to his propriety as a Stationer. His model must display virtue in his relations with authors, retaining their friendship. That meant that in particular he must know "how to value a good copy." He "never abridg'd another Man's Copy, or purchas'd his Author by *out-bidding*." Thus John Salusbury was a notable counterexample to Bosvile and Tracy. Salusbury was a "desperate Hypergorgonick *Welchman*," foppish, silly, and morose, who "wou'd hector the best Man of the Trade." He was also, significantly, a pirate of "STOLN COPIES." Furthermore, good booksellers were, Dunton feared, practically extinct. Most now were men like Salusbury, or Samuel Lee of Lombard Street, who lived a "Thief" and died a "HYPOCRITE":

> Such a Pirate, such a Cormorant, was never before—*Copies, Books, Men, Shops,* all was one, he held no Propriety, Right or Wrong, Good or Bad, till at last he began to be known, and the Booksellers not enduring so ill a Man among 'em, to disgrace 'em, *Spew'd him out*, and off he marcht for *Ireland*, where he acted as *Fellonious*-LEE as he did in *London*. And as LEE liv'd a Thief, so he dyed a HYPOCRITE; for being ask'd on his Death-bed, if he'd forgive Mr. *C——* (that had formerly wrong'd him) Yes, said LEE, *if I dye I forgive him; but if I happen to live, I'm resolv'd to be reveng'd on him.*

Dunton declared himself "really afraid that a *Bookseller* and a *Good Conscience* will shortly grow some *Strange* Thing in the *Earth*": for "he who designes to be the best Christian, must dip himself the least in Business." His own celestial origins notwithstanding, even he had to admit that "*Booksellers* in the Gross are taken for little better than a Pack of *Knaves* and *Atheists*." [164]

The explicit link being made by Dunton was between "copy" and "character." A good Stationer valued copy. A bad one did not, and practiced piracy. This simple equation was extremely important; its effects will permeate the rest of this book. Dunton was not original in identifying the linkage, however, nor was he unique in his pessimistic assessment of the Stationers as a collective. George Wither had given the classic description of the "Meere" Stationer long before. Wither's "honest" Stationer corresponded to Atterbury's portrait, being "both an ornament, & a profitable member in a civill Commonwealth." But his "meere" Stationer was "one of the most pernitious superfluities in a Christian goverment." Wither had labeled this character "the Devills seedman; seeing he is the aptest Instrument to sowe schismes, heresies, scandalls, and seditions through the world." Dis-

---

164. Dunton, *Life and Errors* (1705), 56, 287, 291, 295; Plomer, *Dictionary . . . 1668 to 1725,* 26–7, 186–7; Dunton, *Religio Bibliopolae,* 1. Note that Dunton's priority was scrupulousness toward other booksellers, not toward authors.

honest booksellers were even worse, he thought: they were "needelesse excrements, or rather vermine." Such parasites would not think twice about publishing works in such a form as to "belye [the] Authors intentions," nor about circulating rumors that they were libelous just to increase sales. They used fraudulent titles, forged authors' names, and employed hack writers to create scandalous pamphlets. No Anglicans they: their temple was the tavern. That was in 1624. At the other end of our period, half a century after Dunton, Campbell still believed that a bookseller *should* display "a Genius for Letters, a general Knowledge of Books and Sciences, a clear Head, and a solid discerning Judgment." His education, as befitted a judge of learned works, should be "as liberal as if he were designed for any of the learned Sciences," and he must be as skilled in the ways of men and things as "either the Divine, Lawyer, or Physician." But still the reality failed to match the ideal. "I wish I could say, that the present Generation of Booksellers in general deserved this Character," Campbell sighed; "I am afraid they do not." [165]

The character of "booksellers in general" mattered, because contemporaries were convinced that it prevailed in determining what appeared in print—what could be bought, sold, borrowed, and read. But the character of *particular* booksellers mattered equally. This, however, was appraised by reference to representations of character in general. The name of the Stationer on a book's title page could tell a prospective reader as much about the contents as could that of the author. This was particularly the case with radical tracts, which often appeared anonymously. If the Stationer were an agitator like Henry Hills, Giles Calvert, or John Streater, then a reader's attitude to the work might be prefigured accordingly. Hills in particular was renowned for his papism: his "dreaded" name on the title page was "a fair warning to the reader not to venture any further," wrote a Protestant polemicist. On the other hand, Dunton said of Richard Chiswell that "His NAME at the Bottom of a Title Page, does sufficiently recommend the Book." Such names remained available for recall into the maelstrom of news and city politics for decades. John Trundle, pirate of pamphlets (and of *Hamlet* too), was still being mentioned in ballads almost thirty years after his death, and a loyalist almanac was still disparaging Michael Sparke's testimony before Star Chamber after more than half a century. The names appearing on title pages were thus often recognizable, with known allegiances and interests. Readers' willingness to draw conclusions accordingly encouraged Richard Allestry not to have his anonymous *Whole Duty of Man* printed by his kinsman James Allestry, because of their common surname. Instead he gave

165. Wither, *Schollers Purgatory*, 10, 116, 119, 121–2, 124–5; Campbell, *London Tradesman*, 134.

it to Timothy Garthwait, with whom James was in secret partnership.[166] Some Stationers' names even came to have a totemic value, on the scale of a L'Estrange or a Jeffreys. Catholic printer Nat Thompson, like L'Estrange, was burnt in effigy in Smithfield, but where L'Estrange's house was only besieged, Thompson's was demolished. Such actions climaxed on 11 December 1688, when the mob burnt Henry Hills's home to the ground in a terrible night of rioting directed against the centers of London Catholicism.[167]

As such actions vividly attested, it was in terms of religious and political affiliations that the primacy of the Stationer attracted most comment. The Stationers' was perhaps a politicized community by its very nature. Kirkman, for one, thought that its political and religious divisions were being deliberately cultivated through the preferential placement of apprentices with Stationers of particular political views. In addition, some Stationers became widely known for activities other than bookselling, and in these cases the importance of such feeling to them was at its clearest. Thus Sparke was prominent among witnesses claiming at Laud's trial that the archbishop had manipulated the book trade in favor of popery (fig. 2.19).[168] Arminian Baptist Francis Smith was preaching to crowds of four to five hundred in Goswell Street by 1670, and was a prominent electioneer during the exclusion crisis. Dorman Newman, too, became a preacher, and it is possible that Larner did as well.[169] Kirkman claimed to have met a bookbinder during the Civil War who became a tub-thumping preacher, and who maintained his own peculiar natural and moral philosophy (an ersatz Epicureanism). Another Stationer, although not a tub thumper himself, was reported to have threatened to kill anyone touching the preacher at his conventicle during civic strife in 1670. Under Queen Anne, as befitted a more restrained age, both Awnsham Churchill and Thomas Guy served as MPs. But perhaps the most emphatic declaration of allegiance of all was that made by the Stationers who served as soldiers: men like Henry Hills, William Larner, John

166. Crist, "Francis Smith," ix; Speck, *Reluctant Revolutionaries*, 179; Dunton, *Life and Errors* (1705), 280; Johnson, "John Trundle," 193; *Poor Robin's Almanack* (1687); Elmen, "Richard Allestree," 19–27.

167. Harris, *London Crowds*, 187; *Merlinus Verax* (1687), sig. D4ᵛ; Holt, "A Jesuit School in the City," 157; Beddard, *Revolutions of 1688*, 9–10, 13–15; PRO SP 44/97, p. 15. See also the report of a "*Cavalcade*" through the streets of London, in *Impartial Protestant Mercury* 60 (18 November 1681).

168. K[irkman], *Unlucky Citizen*, 146–8; Prynne, *Canterburies Doome*, 179–86, 243–4. See also Prynne, *Breviate of the Life of William Laud*, for a "poore Printer" who burst into Saint James's in November 1633 and threatened Laud's life.

169. Crist, "Francis Smith," 41, 176–7; Smith [pseud.], *Vox Lachrymae* (a spoof of a sermon by Smith); Dunton, *Life and Errors* (1818), I, 210–11. When Larner refused to testify before the Committee of Examinations, he was told to "speak as if you were a Preaching": *True Relation*, 6.

FIG. 2.19. The Stationer as public agent: Michael Sparke waiting to testify in the trial of Archbishop William Laud (denoted in the image by the letter *A*). Sparke is in the foreground, signified by the letter *S*. Prynne, *Hidden Workes of Darkenes Brought to Publike Light*. (By permission of the Syndics of Cambridge University Library.)

Streater (who employed old comrades in his printing house), John Bellamy (who helped supervise the fortification of London in 1643), Joseph Hunscot, and Luke Fawne, all of whom fought for Parliament against Charles I. Benjamin Alsop later served with Monmouth in his disastrous 1685 invasion. Among royalists the evidence is less clear, but Leonard Lichfield certainly boasted of accompanying Charles I's army with a traveling press on "Dismall *Edg-Hill-day*," while William Sheares took up arms, and Richard Royston even changed his name to signal his allegiance to the crown.[170]

Individual initiatives could be made more effective by collective action. Stationers increasingly formed into groups. Dunton in particular remarked upon the prevailing fashion for collaboration. Collaborative publication was not unknown even by 1600, and by the beginning of the eighteenth century it was commonplace. It was often the most effective way of raising capital for a large project. However, during the Restoration its frequency seems to have increased during political upheavals, perhaps because of the degree of distributed responsibility that it afforded. In collaborative ventures, no one Stationer was unambiguously responsible for the entire text. The most successful opposition booksellers, especially a group whom L'Estrange labeled the "confederates," consistently operated in such consortia. After about 1680, their strategies stabilized into the practice known then as "publishing," and by its modern historians as "trade publishing," in which a proxy Stationer would be paid to put his or her name on the title page in place of that of the party actually responsible. This was one way to avoid the identification of a given title with the Stationer funding its production. There were two main trade publishers' premises, one Whig and the other Tory. The Whig one stood in the Company rents near Stationers' Hall, where it was run successively by Randall Taylor, John Whitlock, Elizabeth Whitlock, and John Nutt, and in the eighteenth century by John and Elizabeth Morphew. The Tory operation, fifty yards away in Warwick Lane, was run by Richard Baldwin and later by his widow, Abigail. This enterprise lasted into the 1760s in the hands of James Roberts. Taylor, Baldwin, and their fellows could hope to escape with defenses of trade. With such decoys in effect, the problem of evidence facing prosecutors became still more thorny. Even when involvement in an illicit publication was well known, "the very fact was so disguised by syncopated or fictitious Names, that [the perpetrators] cannot be prosecuted." An anonymous Tory complained that printers who used such mechanisms were "Highway-men in Masks." L'Estrange and Samuel Parker responded by adopting the Hobbesian argument that the

---

170. K[irkman], *Unlucky Citizen*, 14–19; De Krey, "First Restoration Crisis," 570; [Larner], *True Relation*, 9–10; Simpson, *Proof-reading*, 232; Lindley, *Popular Politics and Religion*, 252; Potter, *Secret Rites and Secret Writing*, 7–19.

authorities should police not internal states of conscience, but overt acts and practices. "Confederacy"—the act of gathering together—was just such a policeable activity. So Parker attacked "trading combinations" as "nests of faction and sedition." In this light, a defense of trade, whatever the character of the Stationers involved, became the very evidence on which a conviction could rest.[171]

Toward the end of the seventeenth century the cooperation of wholesaling groups of Stationers became more systematic. By 1710 a system of wholesaling "congers" was well established, protecting members' copies and sharing large-scale publishing projects; William Innys was the major specialist in science and medicine to be associated. Members of a conger could collaborate to exclude Stationers accused of unsound practices, especially piracy. They also partially dissolved the identities of particular craftsmen and shopkeepers into the collective. The production of newspapers, in particular, by such groups was therefore welcomed because it seemed that they could not dictate content as closely as had individual booksellers. But others maintained that the congers simply generated new opportunities for transgression. Dunton himself resented their aspirations, and decried the main partnership as nothing but a "pyrate-Conger."[172]

Such activities, since they extended beyond simple retailing, qualified the Stationer's character. Good credit rested on domesticity. Dunton associated the Stationer's bad reputation not with the home, then, but with the "downstairs": with the running of a shop. His most fundamental advice was thus not to "keep *open Shop*" at all. Retailing forced the bookseller to "be Dishonest, and tell Lies." Dunton recommended instead "a Convenient *Ware-house*," supplemented by "a good Acquaintance among the Booksellers." The honest bookseller should operate entirely by wholesale and exchange. Publishing one impression would be enough to get started. By exchange with other booksellers, the newcomer would soon fill his premises with "all sorts of Books, saleable at that Time." In his warehouse, the wholesaling Stationer could then maintain a stock of books the contents of which he had himself vetted for quality and decency. A retail shop inevitably

171. Johnson, "Nicholas Ling"; Crist, "Francis Smith," 18; *Exact Narrative*, 52; Treadwell, "London Trade Publishers"; Treadwell, "English Book Trade," 360; Ashcraft, *Revolutionary Politics*, 69–72, 96–7; *Arguments Relating to a Restraint*, 26–7. The identification of press pirates with highwaymen became a commonplace. "I know no Difference between this Practice [of piracy] and Robbing on the Highway," declared Campbell; "only, that the one is punishable, and the other is not." *London Tradesman*, 133–4.

172. Belanger, "Booksellers' Sales of Copyright," 2–8; Sutherland, *Restoration Newspaper*, 213; Treadwell, "London Trade Publishers," 131; Hodgson and Blagden, *Notebook of Thomas Bennet and Henry Clements*, 91 n. 2; see also 76. For Edmund Curll dealing with "The Conger," see, BL Ms. Add. 38730, no. 63.

compromised such thoroughgoing prudence, forcing the bookseller to trade in immoral material. A good wholesale bookseller would not have to employ authors writing irreligious books, and could use his control for good by "perus[ing] the Copy as it goes to Press" to ensure its orthodoxy. Above all, wholesaling from warehouses would reduce piracy, the notorious practice that had meant that "the *whole Trade* has almost ruin'd its Reputation and its Honesty."[173] In short, a return to reliance on the Stationer's character alone would eliminate the dangers of the bookshop.

Dunton's proposal was a practicable one. Such exchange was indeed becoming prevalent, and wholesaling "publishers," like congers, seemed to some to be distinguished by their lack of "that *Pride and Arrogance* that is found in the Carriage of some Publishers." Michael Sparke was among the first to attempt to secure his own credit by professing himself "a *Stationer* and a *wholesaleman*," and by the Restoration it was an everyday part of the Stationer's life.[174] Again, success in exchange depended on personal contacts, reputation, and trust more than on brute cash. Kirkman identified acumen in this process as the most essential prerequisite of all for a successful bookseller:

> he in general is accounted the fittest servant of our Trade, that can out-wit and over-reach his brother bookseller; for it is not so much our keeping Shop, and selling a few books to Scholars, Parsons, Gentlemen, nor sending to Country Chapmen, for in that we use a constant price, and there is not much wit or craft to be used therein; but the craftiest part of our profession consisteth in making an Exchange-note with other booksellers to the best advantage.

The confederates, too, distributed their products by exchange and barter. Enoch Prosser, in a letter intercepted by L'Estrange, remarked incredulously that "I hear it objected that Mr. Larkin and my self cannot Publish the Book as well as others, because we have no Shops; therefore no occasion or motive to exchange with Booksellers." But it was not always the booksellers themselves who negotiated exchange. Kirkman remarked that "in this way of exchanging books for books, we [apprentices] have the most occasion of exercising our wits," for "this matter is commonly left to our management." Crafty apprentices could even cooperate with a printer to make supernumerary copies, which could then be split fifty-fifty and be sold by "Combination, Confederacy, and Correspondency" between apprentices

---

173. Dunton, *Life and Errors* (1705), 72, 87–9. A model bookseller, Awnsham Churchill, was just such a warehouse trader: 280.

174. Treadwell, "London Trade Publishers," 101, 131; Sutherland, *Restoration Newspaper*, 213; Sparke, *Second Beacon*, 5, 8; Hodgson and Blagden, *Notebook of Thomas Bennet and Henry Clements*.

from different bookshops. So developed was this practice, he reported, that the apprentices even maintained their own warehouse, which they ran as a thriving joint stock.[175]

There were other alternatives to retailing. Book auctions began in the Restoration and rapidly attained a remarkable popularity. Held at first in coffeehouses, by the mid-1680s they were taking place even in Gresham College itself. Like booksellers, auctioneers developed and played upon popularly recognized identities, William Cooper, originator of the practice, being particularly known for his alchemical interests. They effectively created a vibrant market in secondhand books and surplus stock. Otherwise, tracts could be bought at stalls in inn yards and at any number of temporary shacks erected in markets.[176] There were also innumerable mechanisms for the borrowing and swapping of "libels," both printed and manuscript, of which the coffeehouse conversation was only the most notorious. But most easily of all, perhaps, printed matter could simply be bought, sold, and exchanged in the open street.

This sort of distributive work depended on a constellation of personnel now all but forgotten. An army of chapmen, "higglers," and others spread books to fairs and markets in London itself and across the country (fig. 2.20). Together they represented a complex system of interests for which Stationers and government alike had to allow. Agents listed by L'Estrange as involved in this enterprise included not only "the *Printers* themselves," but "*Stitchers, Binders, Stationers, Hawkers, Mercury-women, Pedlers, Ballad-singers, Posts, Carryers, Hackney-Coachmen, Boat-men,* and *Mariners.*" They were frequently and loudly repudiated by the propertied Stationers, but the survival of the book trade itself depended on their work. This was forcefully brought home to the Stationers' Company in 1688, when the turmoil of the invasion meant that chapmen were unable to circulate the Company's almanacs, and it lurched £500 into the red as a result.[177]

Many types of distributive and exchange work were relatively contingent, but some acquired more constant and stable identities. Chapmen, for example, circulated around the country on more or less regular routes. Hawkers "cried" books (especially, it was alleged, piracies) on the streets,

175. *Observator in dialogue* II, 198 (10 January 1684/5); [Kirkman], *English Rogue Continued*, 211–13; Belanger, "Publishers and Writers," 11; *English Rogue Continued*, 212–3. For Larkin, see below, note 180, and p. 331.

176. *Catalogus Librorum . . . Matth. Smallwood*; Lawler, *Book Auctions*, 1–45; Chartres, "Capital's Provincial Eyes"; Hunter, *Diary of Ralph Thoresby*, I, 230–2 (for an auction that became so overcrowded that the floor collapsed).

177. L'Estrange, *Considerations and Proposals*, 1; SCB F, fol. 111ᵛ; Myers and Harris, *Spreading the Word*. For the lives of chapmen, see Spufford, *Great Reclothing*.

appealing directly to reading customers (fig. 2.21). They were pervasive, even managing to drop pamphlets in front of the king himself as he walked through a courtyard in Windsor. Poor and self-employed, hawkers were regarded as unseemly, to say the least, and the new squares erected after the Fire were intended to exclude them.

Mercuries were rather different. They were also a rather more novel presence in the city. "*Mercury's?*" asked the ghost of Attorney-General Noy in a pamphlet printed in 1641: "They are a people never before heard of, a Sect which no age ever understood." Strafford's specter explained. They sold books wholesale from the press, carrying them "up and downe" London and distributing them from shop to shop. They congregated at the Exchange, Temple Bar, and Charing Cross. The ghost went on to remark that "there are men *Mercury's*, and women *Mercury's*, and boy *Mercury's*; Mer-

FIG. 2.20. (*below left*) The chapman. Thomas Carr of Lincoln, "the well known Dealer in Almanacks, Fish &c." Engraving, 1804. (By permission of the Syndics of Cambridge University Library.)

FIG. 2.21. (*below right*) The hawker. Reproduced from Taubert, *Bibliopola*, II. (By permission of the Syndics of Cambridge University Library.)

cury's of all sexes, sorts and sizes." Larner, too, testified that it was "*the manner and custome of all our Trade, to buy all manner of Bookes, being carried about to be sold at shops by Men, Women, & Children, and those being brought to my house.*"[178] But most mercuries seem to have been women. They were often the wives or widows of printers, and this, along with their liminality in the world of the book trade and of reading, made them useful informants. Mercuries could take peculiar advantage of their conventional invisibility amid patriarchal domains that in fact depended on them. During the Interregnum, one of them, dubbed "Parliament Joan," was maintained as a particularly effective informer, selling counterfeit royalist papers in an effort to identify the distributors of real ones. Her real name was Elizabeth Alkyn, and she had turned to this trade after her husband had been hanged by the Cavaliers. After the Restoration, the official *London Gazette* came to take advantage of a similar dispersal régime. It relied on a network of "book women" paid a salary of a hundred free copies a month for their efforts; informers got free copies.[179]

It is worth noting that information flowed in more than one direction through the agency of mercuries. "Intelligence," as such information was called, could be of social or economic use as well as political. Toward the end of the century, for example, the *Athenian Mercury* reported that its rival, the *Lacedemonian Mercury*, sold "not enough to pay for Paper, much less for Print, and Copy." "This I am positive in," declared the journal's undertaker, "because I made an enquiry of the MERCURYWOMEN about it." Such examples illustrate the ubiquity and longevity of a culture structured by intrigue, privy knowledge, complex conventions of access and exclusion, and the constant possibility of informers. A slang developed to articulate the attendant hazards. Its terms for the regulators, at least, were distinctly canine. L'Estrange became known as Towzer, perhaps after a dog once lost in London by the duke of York. Informers and searchers were called spaniels, beagles, or, in L'Estrange's case, the "Devills Blouldhound."[180]

178. Knights, *Politics and Public Opinion*, 183; *Description of the Passage of Thomas late Earle of Strafford*, sig. A4ʳ⁻ᵛ; [Larner], *True Relation*, 3, 16; *Every Mans Case*; Sennett, *Fall of Public Man*, 55; Harris, *London Newspapers*, 38–9; McKenzie, "London Book Trade," 24–5; Hetet, "Literary Underground," 116–7.

179. Green, *Calendar of the Proceedings of the Committee for Advance of Money*, I, 517–8; Frank, *Beginnings of the English Newspaper*, 204; Siebert, *Freedom of the Press*, 224; O'Malley, "Religion and the Newspaper Press," 31; *The Moderate*, 47 (5 June 1649), sig. (aaa)ʳ. Alkyn's identity was, however, known to some royalists by mid-1649: *Man in the Moon*, 8 (5 June 1649), 74. It is possible that her husband was the John Alkyn apprenticed as a Stationer in 1612: McKenzie, *Stationers' Company Apprentices 1605–40*, 72. For similar plebeian women's "networks" see Clark, *Struggle for the Breeches*, 34–41.

180. [Gildon], *History of the Athenian Society*, 35; Ashcraft, *Revolutionary Politics*, 9, chap. 8, 423 ff. (but see also Goldie, "John Locke's Circle"); Jose, *Ideas of the Restoration*, 32;

The existence of such a constellation of interests and occupations meant that the book trade in reality was not the stable and secure community of patriarchal households that it represented itself as being. All these agents were problematic, for three connected reasons: they were mobile, many of them were women, and they thrived outside the householder élite entrusted with governing urban life. Both economically and culturally, they therefore made that élite uneasy. It cost perhaps £100 to set up a bookshop, but a stall was much cheaper. As such, stalls represented "a manifest prejudice and disincouragem^t to shopp Keepers," even though the space they occupied could be delimited by local courts.[181] Moreover, hawkers were free to carry their books "into Inns Coffee houses and other places of resort" and sell them there, "to the great detrim^t and abuse, both of Booksellers and the buyers of Bookes." They could even enter gentlemen's homes to do so. Thomas Dekker referred to hawkers carrying sheets to genteel houses in the country, too, where they would add flattering epistles and sell them to the proud occupants. By the Restoration, booksellers were complaining that with hawkers visiting them at home, nobles and gentry did not come out to their shops, "where they usually bought other bookes besides what they intended." And half a century later, in the late 1730s, hawkers of the unstamped press would throw their copies through the open windows of gentlemen whom they knew to be interested customers, and settle up later. "The Creditors of the Government [were being] pillag'd and cheated by the joint Craft of the Publisher and Reader," complained the *Daily Gazeteer* of such tax-dodging tactics.[182] Attempts to regulate the book trade thus stressed the model of the stable, domestic household not only because existing bookshops and printing houses departed from the ideal, but also because hordes of peddlers seemed positively to subvert it.

Conflict thus simmered continuously between shopkeepers, stallholders, and hawkers. With the willing assistance of government, regulation of the places and people involved in bookselling became increasingly rigorous. In 1649 Parliament ruled that all "vagrant persons, of idle conversations" who had "accustomed themselves after the maner of Hawkers, to sell and cry about the streets, and in other places, Pamphlets, and other Books" were to

Zwicker, *Politics and Language*; Sharpe and Zwicker, *Politics of Discourse*, 15–17, 43–4, 235–8, 271–3; C[leveland], *Poems*, 89; PRO SP 29/99, no. 73; *Man in the Moon*, 23 (26 September 1649), 187–8. George Larkin and his wife became major informers for L'Estrange: PRO SP 29/424, no. 151; PRO SP 44/34, fol. 54^r.

181. SCB F, fol. 101^v; Boulton, *Neighbourhood and Society*, 73 ff. Franklin also estimated £100 as the cost of "a little Printing House": Franklin, *Autobiography*, 27.

182. SCB F, fols. 21^v, 68^v; SCA, Suppl. Doc. I.F, Env. 25; Dekker, *Lanthorne and Candle-Light*, sigs. E3^v–F3^v; Judges, *Elizabethan Underworld*, 361; Harris, *London Newspapers*, 29.

be "whipt as common Rogues." The 1662 Press Act enjoined that "no Haberdasher of Small Wares Ironmonger Chandler Shopkeeper or other person or persons whatsoever not being licensed in that behalfe by the Lord Bishop" could deal in books, especially English Stock books and bibles, without a full seven-year apprenticeship. A proclamation decreed that such agents must be prevented from selling books "[on] the Streets, and in other places of Publick resort, and also in Coffee houses, Taverns, and private Families." [183] Nonetheless, legal opinion advised that although selling a book in the street constituted good evidence that a hawker knew its origin, this "mere vendor" could not be held legally responsible for its content, as a domiciled Stationer often could. There were thus repeated exhortations against placeless book traders. Attempts to suppress them alternated with initiatives to force them into accepting the discipline of the Stationers' Company. Propertied booksellers volunteered money to the City to further this end, and sponsored Stationer William Lathom to act as a paid vigilante against such operators. [184]

Such concerns extended beyond the bounds of London itself, following in the tracks of the chapmen trudging the length and breadth of the country. In provincial towns booksellers were just as politically engaged as their London fellows. In Bristol, for example, Thomas Wall and Charles Allen fought their own local battle of Whig against Tory during the 1670s and '80s. For interested citizens of such towns, this raised its own problems, especially if they lived too far from London to visit the metropolis. One must then deal with such an agent, whatever his or her conflicts, in order to maintain credit and communication with a metropolitan Stationer. The networks established for such purposes by Stationers and other book traders traversed the country. They even reached beyond, to Ireland, Europe, and America. They were routinely put at the service of gentlemen clients. It was thus not uncommon for a network of booksellers to serve as the communications channel between two distant gentlemen cooperating on a publication—or on any valued enterprise, which might not have anything to do with books. If

183. Stationers' Company, *Registers 1554–1640*, IV, 531–2; Firth and Rait, *Acts and Ordinances*, I, 1021–3; II, 245–54; 14 Car. II, c. 33, § 7; SCA, Suppl. Doc. I.A, Env. 2, ii. See also Env. 5: a warrant from the Privy Council of 28 April 1686 against "divers Haberdashers of small wares Ironmongers Chandlers Shopkeepers and other persons not being licenced in that behalf by the Lord Bishop" taking books into "Gentlemens Chambers" to sell.

184. SCB E, fol. 124ᵛ. For moves to suppress hawkers and stallholders, see also SCB C, fol. 196ʳ; SCB D, fols. 144ᵛ, 150ᵛ; SCB E, fols. 7ᵛ, 89ᵛ, 90ᵛ; SCB F, fols. 16ᵛ, 40ᵛ, 52ᵛ, 104ᵛ, 119ʳ, 121ᵛ, 143ʳ–144ʳ. For Lathom, see SCA, Suppl. Doc. I.A, Env. 10, i. Compare Boulton, *Neighbourhood and Society*, 76–7; SCB F, fol. 101ᵛ; PRO SP 44/31, fol. 75ᵛ; Crist, "Francis Smith," 110–1.

it were a publication, however, then the interests of the mediators might transform as well as facilitate the result of their mediation. In any case, such facilities provided for learned interaction at a distance, at a time when postal services were less than dependable (and could be monitored by unwelcome readers), and when the thriving newsletters remained little concerned with such material. Not only the availability of printed knowledge in a particular area, but the creative contribution of that area to the natural knowledge published there and elsewhere, could therefore depend on book dealers' characters and contacts. In Norwich, for example, Sir Thomas Browne found that "Mr Oliver the bookeseller," having heard of a written description of a comet, wanted to "write it out that hee might gratifie his freinds & customers." The newsletters had mentioned the comet, he added, "butt to litle or no purpose or any information." [185] Browne had his own London contacts, but local gentlemen friends were, in the immediate instance, dependent on the enterprising Mr. Oliver. In chapter 7 we shall encounter a proposal to exploit this network systematically for the advancement of natural knowledge.

Between the printing house and the reader there was thus a complex set of personnel and interests—interests that could not be circumvented by anyone hoping to become an author, and could equally be drawn upon by antagonists keen to question a writer's work. Again, however, enterprising writers could put this situation to use. Even though they could try to attend at the printing house or houses, it remained all but impossible to monitor them with absolute confidence. Developing a relationship of trust with a knowledgeable bookseller could help. It was "best to deale with some substantiall setled stationer," cautioned the experienced. Only such a figure could hope to have the acquaintances, skills, and knowledge necessary to guide a book through the trade. There were narrow limits to the control any would-be author acting alone could exercise, and adroit enrollment of these aides could be a great asset. Notable "authors" of the period can therefore often fruitfully be resolved into bipartisan writer-Stationer alliances: Isaac Newton and Awnsham Churchill, to cite the example treated in depth in chapter 8, or William Prynne and Michael Sparke, or Robert Boyle and Andrew Crooke. When women started to become authors in appreciable numbers, they too exploited such alliances. Martha Simmonds, one of the most prolific, thus relied on her husband Thomas and brother Giles Calvert. Without these partnerships, the harmonious operation of print culture remained a distant and unachievable prospect. We shall return to these par-

185. Barry, "Politics of Religion," 175–6; Browne, *Works*, IV, 149–50, 175; Cosin's testimony to Gunning, in CUL Ms. Mm.2.23, 166–8.

ticular alliances later. Here, though, we should note that theirs was certainly not a pure mind-body duality. Neither creativity nor drudgery was exercised exclusively by one party.[186]

Official attributions of authorship wisely recognized the Stationers' importance. "Printing alone is not enough," remarked Hyde, carefully distinguishing the punishable component of authorship; "It is the *publishing* of it which is the *Crime*." Lord Chief Justice Sir William Scroggs therefore tried to combat authors by prosecuting their booksellers and printers—for, as he observed urbanely, scribblers, like vermin, were safe only as long as they stayed secret. But the authorities soon went further, and decreed that all books must be "signed with the Printers name." The idea was to establish culpable responsibility in the Stationers who produced and sold them. In 1682 the Stationers' Company formally concurred, ruling that the entrance of a title into its register signified that "the Printer or Publisher there[of] may be knowne to justifie whatsoever shall be therein conteined." "A Printer he is a publick Agent," Hyde now confirmed: "he is to do what he is able to answer." Proposals were made that not only printers, but "Binders, Stitchers, Concealers, Sellers, Publishers, & Dispersers" be legally considered authors, too, unless they confessed the names of the actual writers. So, in extremis, might readers, since (as L'Estrange put it) "ye very reading . . . a Libell to any Man is, in Law, ye Publishing of it." But Stationers, slippery though they could be, were easier to police than the readers thronging London coffeehouses. During the Tory reaction of the 1680s, when these measures reached their apogee, the Stationer's problem was thus, as Francis Smith put it, that "I must find the author, or be deemed author myself."[187]

Deeming the Stationer to be culpable served to crystallize attention on the concept of authorship in both of the two senses identified by modern writers like Michel Foucault, Martha Woodmansee, Carla Hesse, and, most clearly, Roger Chartier. Certainly, this was designed to give the state someone to prosecute: its aim was to create a person in whom responsibility for

186. Crawford, *Women and Religion*, 173–80; Browne, *Works*, IV, 55. Andrew Tooke, professor of geometry at Gresham College, provided much of the evidence concerning Gresham for Strype's *Survey of London* through his bookseller brother, and was able to suppress unfavorable comments from the text: Ward, *Lives of the Professors of Gresham College*, 193–4; CUL Ms. Add. 9, no. 345; Morrison, "Strype's Stow," 48–9.

187. *Exact Narrative*, 48, 70, 72; Howell, *State Trials*, VII, 703; Firth and Rait, *Acts and Ordinances*, I, 184–7; SCB E, fols. 161^v–162^r; SCA, Suppl. Doc. I.A, Env. 2; Hetet, "Literary Underground," 29; Howell, *State Trials*, VII, "Trial of Francis Smith," 957; PRO SP 29/51, no. 10(i). That a disperser or undertaker of papers was "involved in the Guilt, *tho' he knows not the Purport of them, nor ever heard them read*," had been established by Star Chamber under Elizabeth: *State Law*, 12–13, 57. Successive legislation now enjoined that printers annex both their and the author's names and places of residence "at length": e.g., Firth and Rait, *Acts and Ordinances*, II, 249; Stationers' Company, *Registers 1554–1640*, I, 21.

the contents of the work could be said to reside. But it was also hoped that the device would eliminate unauthorized printing—the practice increasingly called "piracy." As time went on, this came to be the more important justification for the strategy. Addison, for example, opposed a law forcing the naming of writers, since "scarce One Part in Ten of the Valuable Books which are Publish'd are with the Author's Names; I mean not only of State Books, of Politicks, but of Religion, Science, and Humanity." But he did want to see the forced naming of Stationers on title pages. This would, he believed, destroy the practices of "*Pyrate* Printers." Defoe too urged that a law declaring the last seller of a work to be the author, and forcing his or her naming on its title page, would give "a Patent to the Author" and thereby prevent piracy.[188] The need to eliminate piracy necessitated naming some proprietorial author, and the leading candidate was obvious. This was the last, explicit consequence of the character of a Stationer.

PRESS-PYRATS AND PAMPHLET-NAPPERS: KNOWLEDGE AND AUTHORSHIP IN THE REALM OF THE STATIONERS

The power of the Stationer fueled a controversy that had flared since the very invention of printing: who, if anyone, controlled printed knowledge? Ever since its invention, allegations had been leveled that the press had fallen into the hands of "unlettered men" who "corrupted almost everything." In the seventeenth and early eighteenth centuries, claims intensified that one bookseller or another was a "Press-Pyrat" or "Pamphlet-Napper." Such claims came to constitute important ammunition in wars not just over editions of books, but over their contents.

They focused on two evils always associated with the trade: sedition and unauthorized printing. Learning—and natural knowledge in particular—was sometimes linked to the first, for example in the cases of such figures as Charles Blount and Henry Stubbe.[189] We shall examine the rather subtler

---

188. Chartier, *Order of Books*, 39–43, 61–88; Chartier, *Forms and Meanings*, 25–42, esp. 36–7; Foucault, "What Is an Author?"; Woodmansee and Jaszi, *Construction of Authorship*; Hesse, *Publishing and Cultural Politics*; [Addison], *Thoughts of a Tory Author*, 2, 6, 30; [Defoe], *Essay*, 16, 21. That having a name on a printed work was the essential thing for which to legislate was endorsed by a variety of writers, among them John Asgill in his *Essay for the Press*, 7. A trade comment written on a draft for a new press act expressed concern at such initiatives, pointing out that a master could not hope to understand all the languages he was expected to print and was thus not to be accounted "a fitt judge of the matter": CUL Ms. Oo.vi.93, no. 6, fols. 39–47.

189. Lowry, *World of Aldus Manutius*, 29, 38; Sutherland, *Restoration Newspaper*, 14; Rochester, *Letters*, 206–13; SCB E, fols. 52ᵛ–53ʳ, 56ʳ; SCA, Suppl. Doc. I.A, Env. 3, i. Blount's offending text was his *Anima Mundi*. A Charles Blount was listed in 1684 as an unlicensed printer, but there is no indication as to whether this was the same man: SCB F, fol. 17ᵛ. For Stubbe see Jacob, *Henry Stubbe*, and Cook, "Physicians and the New Philosophy."

example of John Streater in chapter 4. But contemporaries feared far more consistently its vulnerability to the second. The "pernicious Custom of Piracy," warned Campbell in the 1740s, was alike "the last Discouragement to Learning and the greatest Inconvenience which the honest Bookseller labours under." The cluster of practices subsumed under this dramatic label were, many believed, profoundly distorting credit and knowledge. We therefore need to understand much more about piracy. To begin with, we need a thorough taxonomy of piracy, clarifying what sort of acts could be labeled as piratical.[190] But that must be only the springboard for a series of more important and more difficult questions. How was piracy practiced? How extensive was it? How could a reader detect a piracy? And, perhaps most important, what effects did it have on readers' perceptions of print in general?

Like Russian families, all happy publications are alike, but an unhappy publication is unhappy after its own fashion. The historiography of printing has almost always been directed at articulating happiness, and has been correspondingly concerned with issues of uniformity. Instability, conflict, and piracy have always been relegated to the historiographical periphery, and have been much less studied. The assumption has been that the many individual cases in which such difficulties occurred were just that: individual. They were therefore, in the philosophical sense, accidental. What little historical investigation there has been of piracy has generally foundered on this problem of essentialism. Assuming uniformity as the essential core element of printing, the aim of such investigation has generally been to ascertain whether or not a given accusation of piracy was true by assessing it against that assumption. In practice, that has typically meant appraising such claims—and all too often dismissing them—according to twentieth-century conventions of literary property. By such lights it is frequently concluded that "real" piracy was very uncommon. In the course of a wide-ranging argument, Mark Rose, for example, has recently remarked that "genuinely" unauthorized publication was rare, and that allegations that it had occurred were more often than not simply manifestations of the "stigma of print."[191] On their own terms, such assessments may satisfy. But they have their costs. For one thing, resolving to determine the inherent truth or falsity of a piracy allegation commits the historian to refighting old battles; in most cases accusations of piracy were contentious when they were first made, and they are not going to be any easier to decide now. Moreover, we are not often in a position to determine whether a given publication was "genuinely" unauthorized or not. We cannot enter the minds of long-dead

190. Campbell, *London Tradesman*, 133–4. The closest thing to a taxonomy that is known to me is contained in Brodowski, "Literary Piracy," 30 and passim.
191. Rose, *Authors and Owners*, 21–2.

participants, nor can we recover the unwritten gestures and conversations in which authorization might have been communicated. We *can* track the practical construction and contestation of piracy claims, however. We can see how contemporaries decided their validity—on what grounds, by what evidence, and through what procedures—without presuming to judge the truth of their decisions. And by concentrating on the labor that early moderns undertook, first to publish a book at all, and second to construe it as either pirated or not, we can reach a different sort of understanding.

There remains the option of adopting a strict legal definition of piracy. One could then count as true piracies only those instances in which the law was clearly and conclusively violated. This has the advantage of clarity. Besides, it serves to establish the prevalence of piracy beyond reasonable doubt. Even excluding the great cases it fought against such as Richard Atkyns, the Oxford University printers, and John Seymour, the Stationers' Company alone went to law against alleged pirates at least forty times in the years between 1660 and 1720.[192] And these are merely the cases of which we know: there were almost certainly others. There can thus be no doubt that piracy was a constant phenomenon. This aside, however, the benefits of strict legalism are outweighed by its drawbacks. Most obviously, it tends to assume static definitions of entities—in both the book trade and the law—that in fact were fluid throughout the period, literary property being an evident example. Moreover, any such approach will still radically underestimate the extent of piracy as experienced by contemporaries. The vast majority of incidences that came to light were dealt with not by the legal system, but by the Stationers' own private court, discussed below in chapter 3. Hundreds of allegations were made there. And in fact contemporaries routinely referred even to incidents that never reached *any* tribunal as notorious piracies. Ultimately, no legalistic definition will be satisfactory because the improprieties referred to by contemporaries were *not* simply legal ones. They permeated the domains of print, occupying the far more amorphous territory of civility.[193]

Fluid and contested though it may have been, there was a reality to piracy. To begin to understand it we need to recall the power of the Stationer, and see the practice through a Stationer's eyes. Fortunately, we can turn to a contemporary witness. Bookseller Francis Kirkman, disenchanted after his pirating accomplices had betrayed him to the Company, responded by

192. Brodowski, "Literary Piracy," 54–5. For Seymour's case, see Blagden, *Stationers' Company*, 193–6.

193. John Feather's legalistic approach suffers from all these drawbacks. See in particular his *Dictionary*, s.v. "copyright," "piracy"; and his "English Book Trade and the Law," 64. But see also Cole, *Irish Booksellers and English Writers*, which investigates the specific issue of Irish reprints in detail.

FIG. 2.22. Francis Kirkman. K[irkman], *The Unlucky Citizen Experimentally Described*. (By permission of the British Library, G.17717.)

printing the nearest thing we have to a "pirate's progress" (fig. 2.22).[194] Writing in the early Restoration, he presented a remarkably complete testimonial to the practices and prevalence of piracy.

Kirkman described an alehouse conversation in which a bookseller's apprentice recounted the experiences of his master as he entered the trade in the years immediately prior to the Civil War. At first the newcomer's small stock of books was kept "in his Shop," since he could not maintain a warehouse. He soon noticed that the most successful booksellers in London dealt mainly in "such Books as we call Priviledged ware," namely those printed for the Company as a whole—"Testaments, Psalters, Grammars, [and] Accidences." These they bought wholesale from the Company's stockkeepers, who stored them in the warehouse at Stationers' Hall. Sales and profit margins were small but certain with such stock; "other Books, either of Divinity, History, &c. were not so certain, though more profitable." The newcomer therefore followed suit, and began to deal with a particular

194. [Kirkman], *English Rogue Continued*, sigs. A6ʳ–A7ʳ. For Kirkman's career and piratical activities, see Gibson, "Bibliography of Francis Kirkman."

wholesaling bookseller who could get these and other books for him. Eventually, however, he discovered by chance that the volumes he obtained had not actually originated with the Stationers announced on their title pages. The bookseller had printed them himself, "though they were none of his Copy." This the newcomer found baffling, since "the greatest sort of Booksellers" so frequently inveighed against comprinting as "heinous and unlawful."[195] But he resolved to investigate further.

He discovered that the wholesaling Stationer had received over £5 for five hundred copies of a five-sheet text. Asking a printer how much it cost to print such a work, the novice found that £10 would pay for two thousand copies. So it seemed that some 50 percent of the pirate's price had been profit. But the lucky novice had happened upon the very printer who had produced the work in question. Working "in four or five places for expedition," he revealed, he had secretly printed five thousand copies, not two thousand, the supernumerary surplus being his own "share." So the printer too had profited, by perpetrating a piracy of a piracy. As for the poor copy owner himself, it seemed that he was "but a young man," who had hit upon the copy "by chance"—"and though the Law forbids such doings, as the printing one anothers Copies, yet the great ones commonly devour and eat up the little ones." Perhaps this unfortunate was even in debt to the grandees, and as such unable to complain. "We do such jobbs very frequently," explained the pirate printer, "especially for the Grand ones of the Company." To pirate the grandees' copies, on the other hand, or copies belonging to the Company and under their protection, was "very dangerous." A retributive lawsuit would probably be mounted. Pirating books too large to be printed in a short time was also risky. Such piracy was indeed practiced, but by another method that the printer would not reveal.

The novice now decided to embark on such an enterprise himself. He began with the *ABC*, which, being on one sheet, was relatively quick to print. Finding a trustworthy printer, he bought three hundred legitimate copies to mask the pirated ones. Then he sold or exchanged both batches. He gained more than £5, plus—and this was much more important—good credit. The printer now proposed entering into a more ambitious piracy. Having printed a pirated sermon in a week in two separate houses, the novice and the printer distributed it via mercuries and chapmen (who extended its distribution into the country) at a penny less than the normal price. They profited £25 each.

With his business established on a firm footing, only now did the book-

195. [Kirkman], *English Rogue Continued*, 194–6. For privileged books see below, chapter 3.

seller decide to "play above board" and obtain some copies of his own. He did so, "and glad was he to see his name in print, supposing himself now to be some body." But senior booksellers did not appreciate his ambition. They attempted to "crush" him by exerting their authority in their bookshops to obstruct sales:

> if my Master had printed at that time the best book of Chirurgery, Husbandry, Cookery, or the like in the World, and though the book had been famous enough, so that every one desired it, and asked at any booksellers shop for it, they would have said to their Customers, Truly Sir, there is such a book, but in regard it is a foolish idle thing, and of no weight, I will not trouble my shop with them; but Sir, here is another of the same Subject, that is much better, and in great esteem with ingenious and knowing men.[196]

Thus did the bookseller "disparage other mens books, and prize his own, the buyer being so civil as to believe him." Only if the customer stood his ground and insisted would he declare that this was the first he had heard of the book's quality, and promise to endeavor to get a copy; "and then it may be, for all this Discourse he will shew you one, as if left by chance." According to Kirkman, it was a "general Maxime" that a bookseller never volunteered a book of another's printing to a customer unless he had obtained it at preferential rates. Good works consequently languished unread until the grandees could buy their copies.

Finding that "factious Sermons" sold best in such times of trouble, the novice now learned shorthand, got himself "acquainted with most of the factious Priests about Town," and took to noting their sermons at length. Every so often he would get the preacher to correct a text, and then he would print it. In this way he became "very intimate" with radicals, and at length grew to be their main publisher. Such was the demand he created that he prospered and became rich. Now he could demand any book on credit and he was able to open a warehouse and expand into the provinces. Other grandees ceased to obstruct his business. Authors recognized him as a bookseller to whom to sell their copy, and when they approached him he drove a hard bargain. To one presumptuous poet who requested payment, he replied that "you ought rather to pay me for printing it, and making you famous in print." And he himself moved to create texts. "If he had a desire to have any thing writ in History, Poetry, or any other Science or Faculty, he had his several Authors, who for a glass of Wine, and now and then a meals Meat and half a Crown, were his humble servants." These hacks were

196. [Kirkman], *English Rogue Continued*, 197–201. Compare Blount, *Correspondence*, 151–2.

unpaid, getting at most six or a dozen copies of the finished book as presentation copies.[197]

The bookseller thrived, to the extent that he was eventually elected to the livery of the Company. Although "chargeable at first," the elevation soon paid for itself, as the shares he now obtained in the Company's copies, all of which were perennially popular, never returned less than a 20 percent dividend. Besides, as a partner in those copies he was himself now freed both to join in the printing of supernumerary piracies of Company titles and to resell seized books for profit. Soon he had "a shop very well furnished with all sorts of bound books, and two or three warehouses full of books in quires," as well as property in land and houses, and debts owed to him amounting to some £1,000. Such a sum implied that he must control the credit of a substantial part of the Stationers' community. And the instrument of this man's success had been piracy.

Kirkman reported the Civil War as the time when piracy had blossomed, and this was a widely held view. Yet he did not imply that it or its effects had decreased since.

> In the late times of Liberty, when every one printed what they pleased, if one Bookseller printed a book that sold, another would get it printed in a lesser Character, and so the book being less in bulk, although the same in matter, would sell it for a great deal less in price, and so undersel one another: and of late there hath been hardly a good book but it is epitomized, and for the most part spoiled, only for a little gain: so that few books that are good, are now printed, only Collections and patches out of several books; and Booksellers employing the meaner sort of Authors in spoiling anothers Copies by such Epitomes.[198]

L'Estrange maintained that it was partly poverty, caused by the inequitable structure of the Company, that caused printers to persist in the practice. They were, he said, "forc'd either to play the Knaves in Corners, or to want Bread."[199] Kirkman disagreed. He insisted that piracy was profoundly embedded in the trade, with both prosperous and poor Stationers alike finding it useful. It was as central to their lives as printing itself.

Kirkman testified that pirates were neither necessarily indigents, restricted in their impact to pamphlets and ephemera, nor a distinct category

197. [Kirkman], *English Rogue Continued*, 202–4. An example—one among many—of a sermon the publication of which was justified by the threat of shorthand transcriptions being printed without authorization is Simeon Ash's *Support for the sinking Heart*: see esp. sig. A2ʳ.

198. [Kirkman], *English Rogue Continued*, 201–10.

199. L'Estrange, *Considerations and Proposals*, 2. The Master of the Stationers' Company likewise characterized private printers as "meane people" ready to "hazard any thing to gaine a Livelyhood as they call it": PRO SP 29/244, no. 77.

of Stationers entrenched in opposition to the trade's orthodox hierarchy. There is evidence that he was right. The Royal Society's Printer, John Martyn, was repeatedly convicted of pirating didactic texts, and John Streater scandalously accused Andrew Crooke, who printed for Robert Boyle (and, secretly, for Hobbes), of a grand plot to subvert other booksellers' copies en masse. In the eighteenth century, the Bowyers printed the third edition of Newton's *Principia*, but also an edition of Boerhaave's *Aphorismi* with a false imprint declaring it to have been printed in Leyden.[200] Even someone like John Ogilby—a royal patentee, and a self-proclaimed paragon of copy propriety—was at it, as his assistant revealed: "Mr. Ogilby having the King's License to print all things of his own Composing or Translating, kept a Press in his house, and under the Name of Leyburn or some other Master Printer, did also Print any other Works."[201]

Moreover, conviction for unauthorized printing was no barrier to advancement. One victim even proposed to publish "the whole History of Piracy, wherein the World shall see how the Greater Men of the Trade have rais'd their Estates."[202] And indeed, we know of several Masters of the Company who survived charges of practicing piracy, the most notorious being Henry Hills.

Pirates were therefore not a distinguishable social group. They existed at all ranks of the Stationers' community, and at times were among its most prominent and upstanding members. However, each generation did produce its mythically squalid "pirate king," as it were, whose exploits were spectacularly infamous. To begin no earlier, there was the self-proclaimed Luther of the trade, John Wolfe, who flourished in the 1580s. Wolfe was followed by George Wood in the Jacobean years. After a short lull under the more stringent Caroline policy known as "Thorough," piracy burgeoned, by all accounts, in the 1640s. Fittingly, the Civil War produced a pirates' republic, in which any number of anonymous and pseudonymous corsairs operated with reputed impunity. With the Protectorate and Restoration, Henry Hills and (less egregiously, but no less effectively) John Field succeeded to the throne. Hills subsequently bought the title of king's printer, and under James II rose to be Master of the Stationers' Company. He was

200. SCB C, fols. 263ʳ, 287ᵛ; SCB D, fols. 93ʳ, 105ᵛ, 132ᵛ; Hetet, "Wardens' Accounts," 44 (compare Oldenburg, *Correspondence*, III, 591–4); Maslen and Lancaster, *Bowyer Ledgers*, xxiii–xxiv, 227.

201. Van Eerde, *John Ogilby*, 80–2, 84–5. Aubrey found Ogilby a "cunning Scott" who "must be held fast" in negotiations over printing: Williams, "Edition of the Correspondence of John Aubrey," 149–50.

202. How, *Thoughts on the Present State of Printing and Bookselling*, 23. How was identified as exemplary of "several Booksellers who have taken upon them to set up Printing-Houses, and Use and Exercise the Art of Printing": *Case of the Free Workmen-Printers*; Harris, *London Newspapers*, 82.

forced into exile in 1688, however, and when he died soon after that his disinherited son Henry Jr. took over his crown. He now became the most infamous pirate of the first decade of the eighteenth century. According to Ned Ward, at "*the Club of Broken* SHOPKEEPERS," which met at a tavern near the Exchange called the Tumble-Down Dick, one could meet any number of ruined booksellers "flinging out as many Invectives against *Harry Hills*, and the rest of the Pyrates, as if they had given him cause to think 'em worse Rogues than those that were hang'd last Sessions."[203]

Notorious though he was, Hills was succeeded by an even more infamous pirate. This was Edmund Curll, who thrived through the 1720s and beyond. Curll had started early. As an apprentice, his own master had sued him for conspiracy to defraud. Setting up his own premises as soon as he could, Curll then began to produce pamphlets, and soon larger works. Medicine was a favorite subject. He even enterprisingly claimed that a translated "Treatise of the use of Flogging in Venereal Affairs" for which he had been prosecuted was properly considered a work of physic. Not all his products were piratical, of course, and at the height of his reign he was printing such books as Gregory's *Elements of Catoptrics and Dioptrics* and the complete works of Sir Thomas Browne. Nonetheless, his reputation was that of the implacable enemy whom Alexander Pope spent so much time and energy trying to destroy. Curll in his turn was succeeded by the apparently crazed Jacobite William Rayner, who spent the 1730s manufacturing discredit as pirate, spy, and dispenser of universal remedies from his "Elixir Warehouse" in Southwark. Rayner was still operating at the time of the Jacobite rising in 1745. Each of these pirates, in fact, worked directly either for or against the crown, whether overtly or in secret. A history of these men, their motivations and their effects would be a fascinating document, but it is still a long way from being written.[204]

Perhaps because his own experience was in the printing of plays, however, Kirkman omitted one aspect of piracy that no major London bookseller could ignore. This was the issue of foreign reprints of desirable works, im-

203. Treadwell, "London Printers," 43; Brodowski, "Literary Piracy," 309–16; [Ward], *Secret History of Clubs*, 100.

204. Haig, "'Unspeakable Curll'"; Hancox, *Byrom Collection*, 39; *View of the many Traiterous, Disloyal, and Turn-about Actions of H. H.*; *Life of H. H.*; Straus, *Unspeakable Curll*; Sherburn, *Early Career of Alexander Pope*, 149–85; Harris, *London Newspapers*, 91–98; Iliffe, "Author-Mongering"; Walters, "Booksellers in 1759 and 1774," 290. For Curll's informing see *Gentleman's Magazine*, 68.i (1798), 190–1. Curll's edition of Browne remained unfinished—he denounced a rival's version as "pyratical," advised readers to avoid "Pyratical Counterfeits, who dare not proceed any further," and himself ceased production: Straus, *Unspeakable Curll*, 302–3. BL Mss. Add. 38728 and 38730 contain many documents recording Curll's legitimate dealing in copies, including Gregory's (38728, no. 36) and Browne's (38730, no. 184).

ported and sold at cheaper prices than the English trade could match. French booksellers in London, such as Jean Caillou, Anthony Boudet, and Jean Boileau, who proved extremely useful to the virtuosi for their Continental contacts, were on this account suspect. So were the "Latin booksellers," including John Martyn and James Allestry, Printers to the Royal Society.[205] But the forces conditioning imported reprints were more powerful than could be controlled by monitoring these individuals alone. Whether the Stationers' Company liked it or not, by the time it had come into being in the mid–sixteenth century there had long been a large and thriving international book trade in Europe. Control in any one country had consequently become very difficult.[206] The Channel made the prospect for oversight more promising in England. But the London book trade had itself been established by immigrants, and books had, of course, always been transported to and from the Continent (even in the 1420s, decades before the press had been invented, an Italian visitor had advised a friend transporting trunks of cloth across the Channel to "pretend they are books and all will be well"). By the mid–sixteenth century there was no serious problem getting European books into London bookshops.[207] Every year in the period before the Civil War there arrived "a hundred, or at least eighty great *Dryfats* [i.e., sealed cases] from beyond the *seas* with *Books*." It is impossible to estimate the proportion of this traffic that was illicit, but the persistency of English printers' and booksellers' complaints implies that it was substantial, and the Stationers' Company was usually able to come up with convincingly large hauls of contraband when pressed to show results.

What concerned Whitehall was that political tracts would be found among such seizures. They would be imported under the label of "razors," "scissors," or some other such merchandise, and addressed to an innocent third party for onward delivery to the distributor.[208] What concerned the Company, on the other hand, was the importation itself—and especially

205. Hooke, "Diary," 116, 122, 146; Rostenberg, *Library of Robert Hooke*, 90–1; SCB C, fol. 274ᵛ; SCB D, fols. 150ᵛ, 151ᵛ, 153ʳ; Stationers' Company, *Registers 1554–1640*, IV, 530–1, 536; Firth and Rait, *Acts and Ordinances*, I, 184–7; 14 Car. II, c. 33, § 4. See also SCA, Suppl. Doc. I.A, Env. 3, xiv, and Env. 5, ix–x, about the Company's reasons for searching incoming crates. On the rear is a list of suspect booksellers that includes James Allestry and Robert Scott. The French booksellers are listed for prosecution in SCB F, fol. 23ʳ.

206. For the establishment of these networks, see Braudel, *Civilization and Capitalism, II: Wheels of Commerce*, 72, Febvre and Martin, *Coming of the Book*, 220–6, and Armstrong, "English Purchases of Printed Books."

207. Gordan, *Two Renaissance Book Hunters*, 54; Pettegree, *Foreign Protestant Communities*, 84 ff. (a reference I owe to David McKitterick); Winger, "Regulations," 38. Sir Thomas Browne advised his son, then in Frankfurt, to "Buy no bookes, . . . for by London wee can send for such bookes as those parts afford": Browne, *Works*, IV, 30.

208. Sparke, *Second Beacon*, 8. See Crist, "Francis Smith," 328–31, for importation of opposition tracts.

that of books first printed in London. For fears had arisen that imports posed a serious threat to the indigenous trade. Domestic printing was generally both worse and more expensive than Continental. Many learned writers before the Interregnum, such as Harvey and Fludd, accordingly took their texts abroad to be printed. Some continued to do so long after—in chapter 8 we shall encounter Joseph Crosthwait voyaging to Holland for the purpose in the 1720s. In such circumstances the very survival of a domestic printing trade seemed uncertain. Laud himself defended his Star Chamber restrictions on printing by claiming that English printers had to be protected from Continental competition.[209]

Continental houses were indeed willing to reprint English books, both for further distribution in Germany, France, and beyond, and for reimportation into London. Perhaps the best-known example of the latter enterprise, because so politically sensitive, involved bibles. One of the few Englishmen actually to see such an operation was William Nicolson, future bishop of Carlisle. In 1678 Nicolson found, in Amsterdam, "Widdow Shippers print house":

> there were 18 hard at work printing, and 6 or 7 setting letters. They print here many English Bibles of all sizes; upon the titlepages of which they sett— *London printed by R. Barker and the Assigns of John Bill* etc. And they were (whilst I lookt on) printeing a small English Bible in Octavo, which they sett printed by the aforesaid, A.D. 1609. They showed me also severall books printed here with the title pages as if at Collen, Leipsick, Mentz etc. whence it comes to pass that you may buy books cheaper at Amsterdam, in all languages, than at the places where they are first printed: for here the Copy costs them nothing.[210]

The size alone of the operation is impressive: this printing house was comparable to the largest in England. In an effort to eradicate such imported reprints, the Company required that no packets of imported books be opened "in any Private Ware-house." They must be taken to a special room in Stationers' Hall for the purpose. In 1662 the import of *all* books in English was banned, regardless of whether they had been printed before or not. The problem did not end, however, and in 1739 legislation aimed against

209. *Brief Discourse Concerning Printing and Printers*, 13; Simpson, *Proof-reading*, 231; Howell, *State Trials*, IV, 497; Sharpe, *Personal Rule*, 650. Fludd, *Doctor Fludds Answer*, 21–2, claimed that English printers had demanded £500 to undertake his elaborate works, whereas the De Brys in Frankfurt had sent him a gratuity. His works were reimported to London, where they "did offer themselves" in bookshops to Meric Casaubon: Casaubon, *Letter*, 21. Perhaps this curious phrasing reflects the insistent patter of a remembered bookseller.

210. Stoye, *English Travellers Abroad*, 257. For cross-border infiltration in the Enlightenment, see Darnton, *Literary Underground*, 122–66.

Irish piracies again aspired to bar the import of English-language books from Europe.[211]

These were important commercial concerns. But they were not *only* commercial—and piracy was not necessarily a purely mercenary exercise. It could be a powerful strategy in a number of different genres of struggle. In a system reliant on the regulatory activities of Stationers themselves, for example, "private" printers could target for piracy the profitable copies sustaining the Stationers charged with discovering them. Nor was the Company itself exempt: in the 1640s, campaigners illicitly printed copies of its formal tickets summoning a common hall in order to further their aims, and a later generation of reformers printed its charter in an effort to undermine the Company's hierarchs. It is even likely that the creative practices witnessed by Nicolson were going on in London itself. Presbyterians claimed that thirty thousand popish books had been printed in the capital, displaying "*Paris*, or other places beyond the Sea, prefixed, as if they were printed there." Only a participant's eye could spot the deception. "Yet we, and all the Booksellers and Printers in *London*, that have seen or shall see them, do upon such sight know that they are printed in *London*," they added, thus stressing the indispensable role of the Stationers in both detection and transgression.[212]

With piracy regarded as an omnipresent hazard, no individual was automatically immune from the label of pirate, and no book too grand to be called a piracy. The consequences for both authorship and the reading of printed materials were substantial (fig. 2.23). To modern historians it often appears that the introduction of printing led to an augmentation of certainty, with uniform editions and standardized texts providing the sure fulcrum with which intellectual worlds could be overturned (or protected). To contemporaries, the link between print and knowledge seemed far less secure. If by the mid–seventeenth century "the Kingdome seeme[d] to be all Intelligence," it also seemed to be all uncertainty. In the realm of print, truths became falsehoods with dazzling rapidity, while ridiculous errors were the next day proclaimed as neglected profundities. One London divine was overheard pitying "*this great and famous City*, [in which] *I behold a Collubies, a very rabble of all opinions . . . One week this is a truth, and almost an Article;*

211. SCB D, fol. 153ʳ; Stationers' Company, *Registers 1554–1640*, IV, 530–1, 536; Firth and Rait, *Acts and Ordinances*, I, 184–7; 14 Car. II, c. 33, § 4; Feather, "Commerce of Letters," 410; Cole, *Irish Booksellers and English Writers*, 2. Compare Michael Sparke on chapmen distributing falsely printed bibles introduced from overseas in 1646: *This is to certifie* (Thomason dated this single-page offering to 7 August 1646 and attributed it to Sparke).

212. SCB C, fol. 224ᵛ; *Charter and Grants* (n.d.); *Charter and Grants* (1761): SCA, Suppl. Doc. I.F, Env. 24; Fawne et al., *Beacon set on Fire*, 6–7.

FIG. 2.23. The perils of piracy: an author retreats upstairs in tears as the pirates prepare to
distribute unauthorized copies of his works across the land. "Tim Bobbin's Rap at the
Pirates," in Collier [Bobbin, pseud.], *Human Passions Delineated*. (By permission of the
Syndics of Cambridge University Library.)

the next week it is no such matter, but some other thing is the right." John
Rushworth was moved to collect eight volumes of records, so concerned was
he by reports of Parliamentary speeches that had never been spoken, declarations that had never been passed, battles that had never been fought, and
victories that had never been obtained. To such witnesses, the world of print
was characterized not by the accumulation of knowledge, but by "scattered
reports, dated at such a time, and from such a place; whose mushroom credit
sprouts this evening and dies before that hour next morning." Far from
fixing certainty and truth, print dissolved them. It exacerbated the ephemerality of knowledge—indeed, that was precisely why diurnals insisted so
strongly on their historicity and permanence, promising, as parodied in *Hudibras*, that great deeds would be "register'd by fame eternal,/In Deathless
pages of Diurnal." [213] In the Restoration, the proclamation of "facts" would
take place in an environment of unprecedented epistemic instability.

213. *Kingdomes Weekly Intelligencer* 250 (7 March 1647), 857; [Fisher], *Feast of Feasts*, 2;
Rushworth, *Historical Collections*, I, sigs. b^v–b2^r; *Weekly Medley*, 17 October 1717; Black, *English Press*, 87; [Butler], *Hudibras. The Second Part*, 5; [Butler], *Hudibras. The First Part*, 165.

Print, and piracy in particular, consequently gave rise to fierce concern for the verification of any and all printed materials. Booksellers took to affirming credit for learned texts by all sorts of evidence, including testamentary. William King, making what was a rather mordant joke, suggested using statements of place to secure credibility:

> I am told that, if a Book is any thing useful, the Printers have a way of pirating on one another, and printing other persons copies, which is very barbarous. And then shall I be forced to come out with "The True Art of Cookery is only to be had at Mr. Pindar's, a Pattern-maker's, under St. Dunstan's Church, with the Author's Seal at the Title Page, being Three Saucepans, in a Bend proper, on a Cook's Apron, Argent. Beware of Counterfeits." [214]

As we have seen, this was a parody of a real and frequent response. Others were also tried. All proved less than wholly successful, for the simple reason that they still depended upon printing and its domains. Early in the sixteenth century, for example, Luther and others had developed printers' marks (descended from notarial signets, themselves created to solve a problem of credit in an earlier age) into a way of allowing texts to carry their authentication with them. But rivals counterfeited the marks, too, so the method proved futile.[215] A later victim of supernumerary printing tried to evade it by the extraordinarily expensive technique of using his own custom-made paper, complete with a unique watermark. But even this could be circumvented, since impropriety need not even involve reprinting. Sheets could simply be stolen from the warehouse and resold, as when "laborer" John Watson took sheets from Evan Tyler's "Dwelling House" and transferred them to Benjamin Harris for resale. In such cases even the use of unique paper would prove ineffective. Parliamentary attempts at licensing the publication of its proceedings were likewise to little avail, for a reason analogous to that which had foiled Luther. Printers simply forged the licenses, or appended important speeches to the trivial ones permitted. Parliament conceived this to have potentially catastrophic consequences, since a printer with such power could theoretically produce "Acts" bringing about virtually any situation he or she desired.[216] Certainly, some of the speeches reproduced in the press as given by prominent MPs were false through and

214. King, *Original Works*, III, 64–5; compare Eco, *Faith in Fakes*, 173–9.

215. Black, "Printed Bible," 433–4; Hirsch, *Printing, Selling and Reading*, 25. See also Newman, "Word Made Print." Such devices were used by most printers from Fust onward: Davies, *Devices of the Early Printers*. A survey of English ones is in McKerrow, *Printers' and Publishers' Devices*.

216. Gibson, "Bibliography of Francis Kirkman," 64; SCB D, fol. 182ʳ; Lambert, "Beginning of Printing for the House of Commons"; *Expresse Commands*. See also *London Gazette* 5041, 12 August 1712, for a notice that an edition of the Report to the Commissioners for the

through. More troublingly, the perceived veracity of others oscillated with the political situation. In 1660 Parliament even voted the document decreeing its own dissolution in 1653 to be "a forgery."[217]

As an attributed quality, piracy was a label attached to an object by users, not one residing in the object itself. That attachment was always contestable, and two texts did not have to be identical for one of them to qualify as a piracy. Epitomes, translations, and extracts might be accounted improper, as also might the unauthorized use of maps to make globes. The trade developed sophisticated mechanisms for determining such issues, to which virtually no author was privy. These mechanisms are discussed in chapter 3. For now, it is important to note that there was no way of discerning definitively from content alone whether or not a book was a piracy. Indeed, piracy itself should be seen as one among a repertoire of categories being developed to help contemporaries think about and practically cope with the world of print. Print itself certainly did not guarantee the value of what it produced and reproduced. Rather, those making use of it needed to develop new tactics to construct and maintain their claims to truth. Allegations of piracy were among those tactics.

We see this most clearly in the newest literary forms: the diurnal, the newspaper, and, as will be further evinced later, the experimental journal. These were the sectors of printed literature that most depended on being credited by readers. But they were also the sectors whose credit was most suspect. These were therefore the genres that first developed rhetorical procedures to project authenticity in the domains of print to the highest degree. Travelers' tales were another example; yet another was that of the confessions and last thoughts supposedly uttered by condemned criminals. The ordinary of Newgate developed a thriving trade in these confessions, which were printed so as to appear as soon as possible after an execution—sometimes too soon, so that they faithfully described the deaths of criminals who had in fact been reprieved. They developed an elaborate rhetorical armory in defense of their fragile credit. In one particularly poignant example, the printer even claimed that the hangman himself would "testify on oath that a few minutes before that cap was drawn over Simms' eyes he told him that

---

Act about Public Accounts is "surreptitious, false in the Calculations, and full of the grossest Errors; and printed without the Consent or Knowledge of the Author."

217. Miller, "Shattered *Violl*," 33–4; *Presse Full of Pamphlets*; Pepys, *Diary*, I, 12. Royalty both in England and abroad attempted to secure records of their *res gestae* by stamping medals; as soon as the medals' designs were reproduced in print they were pirated, imitated, and lampooned. See Burke, *Fabrication of Louis XIV*, 3, 131, 135–49; Marin, *Portrait of the King*, 121–37.

he had given the account of his life to no one except J. Nicholson, the Printer in the Old Bailey." Swift and Fielding had no difficulty at all satirizing such rhetoric.[218]

As this rather desperate example implies, Stationers fought to establish the credit of diurnals, journals, speeches, and papers. The concept of news was an important beneficiary. The earliest corantoes—irregular single-sheet collections of reports from the Continent—had been introduced from Amsterdam in the 1620s by Stationers decried as "swindlers and liars." The printer's remained the dominant presence in a newspaper for decades thereafter, the mere writer often being something of a hired hand. Printers would change or add to their copy, and in a number of cases those whom the writer had attempted to dismiss went on producing rival editions of the periodical until reemployed. The result was chronic instability dressed up as unprecedented fidelity. Most newspapers vaunted their permanence and authenticity, but lasted only a few issues. A writer of such a piece had little of the freedom of action a gentleman was supposed to enjoy, and his or her authorship was very dubious. John Cleveland even described a diurnal writer as "one, whom by the same figure that a North-Countrey Pedler is a Merchant-man, you may style an Author."[219] Such a would-be author's credit might rest on the successful projection of the Stationer's conduct and character.

How could a gentleman be an author? In these circumstances, it was far from clear. Henry Peacham was far from unique in advising gentlemen to abjure the vocation of writing altogether. Authors were certainly assigned what might now seem a low status. John Stow, who after a lifetime's literary labor emerged clutching a license to beg, may stand as emblematic. But the real difficulty was subtler than mere status or pecuniary reward. The *Tatler* hit the mark when it complained that the art of writing had become "meerly Mechanick," to be performed by the dogged application of constraining rules. In his profound analysis of the importance of conventions of gentility in early modern England, Steven Shapin reveals why this might be such a problem. Shapin identifies freedom of action as central to the identity of the gentleman. A true gentleman was considered "his own man": he was not dependent on any "interest," and could follow prudence without the

218. Raymond, *Invention of the Newspaper*; Harris, "Trials and Criminal Biographies," 23–4. For travelers' tales see McKeon, *Origins of the English Novel*, 100–7, and Adams, *Travelers and Travel Liars*.

219. Frank, *Beginnings of the English Newspaper*, 12, 25, 150, 201, 233, 269; Sutherland, *Restoration Newspaper*, 29, 78–9, 215–7; Raymond, *Invention of the Newspaper*, 13–54; Harris, "Management of the London Newspaper Press," 95–6; Johnson, "John Trundle," 197; C[leveland], *Character of a Diurnal-Maker*, sig. ¶2ʳ.

distortions necessitated by trade or service. Yet to become an author such a figure had, of necessity, to subject himself to those who *were* tradesmen or servants. The Stationers' possession of essential skills and contacts made this unavoidable. He became their guest or lodger, and they became the "masters" of his time and work. What was regrettable about printing, then, was that it constrained a gentleman's defining freedom. Every aspect of the printing house and bookshop militated against the supremacy of one's "pleasure." The gentleman who entered the world of printing was reducing himself to just one participant in a collective of craft operatives, and not necessarily the controlling one. Authors, as the exasperated Robert Burton testified, were "almost ignored" by Stationers as their books were being printed. In his own printing house, John Twyn would not normally bother to discuss the author of a work with his apprentice, but he would discuss the person—a Stationer—"for whom they were printed."

This much could be said, perhaps, of most craftsmen with whom gentlemen had to interact. But most crafts did not then create objects claiming to instantiate the knowledge, wit, character, and virtue of the gentleman concerned. Gentlemen were thus further "punished," in Burton's words, when their works appeared in bookshops. "On account of their judgment I now sink to the depths, [and] now again I am lifted up onto the stage," wailed Burton; his name was "fastened to gates and door-posts, and to anyone you please I stand exposed as a slave put up for sale." The permanence and exposure accorded a printed book by its being produced in around a thousand copies, qualified and circumscribed though that permanence was, meant that the sign of the gentleman's constraint was visible, and that it endured. This was only reinforced by the convention that authors had no right to their work once published; the "copy" was vested in the Stationer and could be pirated by his or her rivals. A prospective author or artist need not be entirely without power, especially, as is explained in chapter 3, if he or she could recruit allies either at court or in the Stationers' Company; but success demanded hard work, much skill, and many contacts. Gentlemen thus repudiated authorship not out of simple snobbery, nor from affected repugnance at "the stigma of print," but because the character of the Stationer impinged on fundamental elements of the genteel identity. It was partly with this in mind that writers talked of their impotence before the pirates. "It is now-a-days the hard fate of such as pretend to be Authors, that they are not permitted to be masters of their own works," complained one: "for, if such papers (however imperfect) as may be called a *copy* of them, either by a servant or any other means, come to the hands of a Bookseller, he never considers whether it be for the person's reputation to come into the world." The good name of a gentleman should never lie "in the power of a Bookseller." Burton's ultimate complaint—the reason why he lapsed into silence again, fearful of saying anything too pointed—was that "these men here" had become "my masters." [220]

The consequences of these concerns were dramatically demonstrated in one of the best-known intellectual disputes of the time: the clash between Richard Bentley and Charles Boyle that dominated the "battle of the books" from the mid-1690s into the eighteenth century. Bentley, keeper of the royal library at Saint James's, collided with Boyle, the nephew of Robert and champion of the Tory bastion of Christ Church, Oxford, over the latter's edition of the so-called "Epistles of Phalaris." [221] Bentley claimed that the letters were spurious. What sparked off their quarrel, however, was a short passage in Boyle's preface. He had wanted to include a collation of a manuscript housed in the king's library. But Bentley, acting out of what Boyle sarcastically called his "singular humanity and justice," had apparently refused to allow the manuscript to be seen for long enough for the collation to be carried out properly. When Bentley himself came across a gift copy of the volume, printed for distribution among Oxford colleagues before its London publication, he promptly wrote to Boyle denying the charge. Bentley requested that he "put a stop to the publication of his Book, till he had alter'd that Passage, and printed the Page anew." He reckoned Boyle could do this quite simply, by intervening at the printing house. Boyle retorted that, being in Oxford, he could hardly step in so easily. In any case, he had quizzed his bookseller, Thomas Bennet, who had handled all the transactions with Bentley, and Bennet had confirmed his version of events. Bennet insisted not only that Bentley had procrastinated over lending the manuscript, but that he had openly insulted Boyle in his bookshop, which stood at the sign of the Half-Moon in Saint Paul's Churchyard. Eventually Bennet would state this case at length in a published affidavit. [222] The resulting dispute thus came to depend as much on representations of this bookseller and his premises as on rival accounts of scholarship and the classics.

220. Peacham, "Truth of our Times," in Peacham, *Complete Gentleman*, 188–92; Ransom, *First Copyright Statute*, 48; Burke, "Popular Culture," 49–54; Shapin, *Social History of Truth*, 38–41, 43–52, 156–92; Woodmansee, "On the Author Effect"; *Exact Narrative*, 18; Burton, *Anatomy of Melancholy*, I, xl–xliv; King, *Original Works*, III, 43; McKenzie, "Speech-Manuscript-Print." For the flourishing of manuscript communications as a result, see Love, *Scribal Publication*, 35–137, 177–230.

221. Phalaris [pseud.], *Phalaridis Agrigentinorum Tyranni Epistolae*; Monk, *Life of Richard Bentley*, I, 63–6. The most authoritative account of this exchange is Levine, *Battle of the Books*, 47–84.

222. Bentley, *Dissertation*, iii, v–vii, xxviii, xxxiv–xxxvi; Boyle, *Dr. Bentley's Dissertations . . . Examin'd*, 2–5, 9, 18 ff.; *Short Account of Dr. Bentley's Humanity and Justice*, 97–140; [Whately], *Answer to a late Book*, 143.

The developing clash soon made Bentley "the Common Chat of *Coffee-houses* and *Taverns.*" There, many readers apparently believed Boyle to have asked for the manuscript in person, and therefore that Bentley had wantonly insulted a gentleman by his refusal to cooperate. This was the "affront" against Bentley's honor that motivated his response. Was it acceptable, he demanded, for Boyle to "put a public Affront upon me, upon the bare complaint of a Bookseller"? Wits soon began to allege that Bentley also showed other aspects characteristic of the "pedant"—the sour, ungrateful, and tedious figure conventionally reckoned to be antithetical to true authorship. In particular, they charged that he had revealed himself to be a *"Notorious Plagiary"* in his own printed works. The Christ Church party even deposited "the very individual *Manuscript*" of one of Bentley's earlier works at Bennet's bookshop, where interested readers were invited to compare it with the printed text and confirm for themselves his authorial insufficiency. Under these circumstances, Bentley could scarcely refrain from responding.[223]

Bennet himself thus became a key character in the affair. Bentley hardly had to agonize long before rejecting his testimony. "My Credit will go further than this Bookseller's," he insisted. Bennet, he claimed, had been both lazy and negligent, and had tried pass off his own failure as Bentley's. As the battle progressed Bentley's side built on this allegation, repeatedly attributing to Bennet the sort of low threats that a stereotypical pirate would make. He was thus reported as willfully altering the texts he printed, and as vowing that "If they Printed any *Reflections* upon him, he'd be even with them, and have them exposed all the Town over." Such assertions, by undermining Bennet's credit, threatened his version of events at the Half-Moon.[224] For he was a key figure not least because of the importance attached to the insult allegedly uttered against Boyle by Bentley in his premises. Bentley claimed that his comments had been directed only against the epistles, not against Boyle, and that their import had been corrupted by the bookseller's mediation. However, Bennet adduced testimony from the wit and later lampooner of the Royal Society, Dr. William King, who claimed to have overheard the conversation personally. King expressed himself appalled at the "Rude and Scurrilous Language" Bentley had been happy to "throw out at Randome in a *Publick Shop.*" But what was the character of the Half-Moon? *Was* it public, and open to the street, or was it a private home? Could speech overheard there properly be repeated elsewhere, or would that constitute a betrayal of private conversation? Any assessment of Bentley's behavior while he was there depended on such prior characterization. King for one had no doubt. He lambasted Bentley for his conversational conduct. "I thought

223. *Short Account of Dr. Bentley's Humanity and Justice,* 75–6, 26–30, 32–3. For the pedant, see Shapin, "'Scholar and a Gentleman,'" and Johns, "Prudence and Pedantry."
224. Bentley, *Dissertation,* xx–xxi, xxviii, xxxvii; [Whately], *Answer to a late Book,* sig. A4^r.

we were talking of Books in the way of *Scholars,*" he acidly commented, "whereas He Answers me like a Bookseller."[225]

The bookshop had become the most important site of the debate. Bentley insisted that the only occasions he and Bennet had ever talked of the manuscript were in the Half-Moon. King's comment was thus cruelly well judged. Yet there was a more specific edge to the charge. The Half-Moon possessed a particular character, which both contributed to and was reinforced by Bennet's personal repute. Everyone knew that one would find specific kinds of people there: the High Church Tory wits allied with Christ Church and Charles Boyle. How, then, Bentley demanded, could he ever have been so foolish as to insult Boyle, whom he had never met, "in a public place, and before [Boyle's] Friends?" The *"Gentlemen of the Half-Moon"* were constituted by such questions as a distinct coterie—a "Club"—with its own degenerate ideas of sincerity and learning, meeting exclusively in the rooms of the Half-Moon to drink coffee and plan its latest railleries. It shared traits with the most characteristic Restoration concoction of private plotting and public politics, the cabal. If, on top of this, Bennet himself betrayed conversations overheard there, who would ever be safe in the Half-Moon? Nobody, concluded an anonymous contributor.

> Is it not enough to make a man afraid, Mr. *Bennet,* of calling in at the Sign of the *Half-Moon*? and ought not a man to have a care how he moves his Lips there? least his words should be catch'd up as they drop from his Mouth, and afterwards, it may be, *affidavited* against him, put into print, and made part of a Lampoon upon him. These are dangerous Considerations, Mr. *Bennet!*[226]

They turned out to be more dangerous for Bentley than for Bennet. In this engagement, the character of the bookseller and his conversation, added to that of his premises and its public, became central to a scholarly debate. In the long run, the letters of Phalaris would indeed be concluded spurious; to that extent, Bentley emerged victorious. But in terms of the immediate conflict, he was not so fortunate. In his encounter with Bennet and the Half-Moon, Bentley was branded a pedant—and for the rest of his life he was never able to shake off this damning label. His experience exemplified the difficulties attendant upon aspirations to the authorship of knowledge.

Yet if a gentleman found it hard to be an author, authors found it increasingly easy to proclaim themselves gentlemen. Along with the attendance at a bookseller's premises that was virtually essential for success, the

225. Bentley, *Dissertation,* xxxv–xxxvi; *Short Account of Dr. Bentley's Humanity and Justice,* 118–21, 134–8; [Whately], *Answer to a late Book,* 193–5; King, *Original Works,* I, xxviii; see also King's "Dialogues of the Dead, relating to the Present Controversy Concerning the Epistles of Phalaris": ibid., I, 133–86.

226. Bentley, *Dissertation,* xx, xxxiv–xxxv; [Whately], *Answer to a late Book,* sigs. A4ʳ, A6ᵛ, 144, and passim; Harris, "Moses Pitt," 183.

act of announcing authorship circumvented restrictions on the interaction of ranks. At the same time, new cultural identities and distinctions were being elaborated, conditional upon respect for Stationers and their craft. "Editors, Commentators, Interpreters, Scholiasts and Criticks," complained the *Tatler*, maintained "a greater Esteem for *Aldus* and *Elzevir*, than for *Virgil* and *Horace*." But such esteem facilitated the construction of their respective activities and their evaluation by others. It also permitted the establishment of their achievements as knowledge.

Two such personas may be identified as particularly significant. The first was that of the woman author. Women involved in the domains of print exercised creativity in many ways by exploiting divergences between patriarchal representation and practical action, as we have seen. One of the most dramatic was in becoming authors themselves. Conventionally, women were expected to cleave to a trinity of virtues: modesty, chastity, and silence. Aspersions cast on any one of these threw the other two into doubt. Besides, no woman was permitted to attend university, so very few attained the knowledge of Latin necessary for readers to respect their works. Women daring to venture into print were thus taking substantial risks, and not only economic ones (although the latter certainly existed, the really determined, like the radical Mary Pope, financing their own publications). They had to defend their conduct with great care, and appear, even more than gentlemen, to repudiate claims to authorship altogether. So the few women to appear in print in Tudor and Jacobean times generally did so as translators, and often of devotional works. In the mid–seventeenth century this changed with remarkable abruptness. Published works by women began to appear in numbers that were appreciable, if still small compared to those of men. These first women authors often claimed not to be authors at all. As chapter 6 shows, they combined awareness of their lack of formal learning with contemporary representations of the passionate and sensitive female body to proclaim themselves uniquely truthful channels for the Word of God, freed from the ambitious impediment of reason. The most visible female writers were prophets like Pope, Mary Cary, Elizabeth Poole, and— most prolific of all—the remarkable Lady Eleanor Davies; these were followed by Quakers like Martha Simmonds. Most were edited by male apologists, or allied to male Stationers. After anonymity and deity, however, could come authorship, and with it changing concepts of the self. In the Restoration, women like Aphra Behn, Katherine Philips, and Susanna Centlivre could announce themselves playwrights, poets, and the authors of novels. Hannah Wolley and Mary Tillinghast pioneered works on housewifery and medicine for other women. Mary Holden published astrological predictions, and Jane Sharp wrote to defend midwives from male incursions into their trade. And Margaret Cavendish attempted, with less success, to become an author in philosophy. It was an achievement of sorts when, as happened in Charles II's reign, such women's names became authoritative enough to be appropriated by pirate printers for a wide range of spurious and unauthorized books.[227]

The second persona was that of the experimental philosopher. Experimental philosophers were particularly vulnerable to the practices of piracy because of the importance of printing in establishing their knowledge and techniques. In 1719, for example, Jean Theophilus Desaguliers found his *Lectures of Experimental Philosophy* being pirated with an unauthorized preface. He had given Paul Dawson, a pupil introduced to him by Sir Richard Steele, a copy in order to help him follow the lectures. Dawson had then sold it to the booksellers as "approved" by Desaguliers himself. Desaguliers could only produce his own satisfactory edition after the booksellers had "made me Satisfaction, and purchased the Copy of me." Yet even then, significantly, he was unable to get a new impression printed, and his own "edition" produced in response to the unauthorized issue was in fact composed of the original sheets simply reissued with a new preface and a long list of substantial errata. Fifteen years later, when he published his *Course of Experimental Philosophy*, Desaguliers still feared that these same sheets would reappear under the title of his new text and be sold as the genuine article.[228] And he felt the same effects again when he translated 'sGravesande's *Mathematical Elements of Natural Philosophy*. His own version had to be printed at extraordinary speed in order to preempt a rival consortium's inaccurate translation, and was as a result rife with errors in both text and plates; these the publishers effectively attributed to an outraged 'sGravesande himself. In such contexts, Desaguliers made haste to screen *himself* from charges of impropriety. In complaining of the piracy of his lectures, in particular, he admitted that "I might be thought to ascribe to my self what is not my own" if he failed to specify details "copied from some Papers lent me by *William Jones.*" Piracy had immediately made him fear the more dangerous accusation of plagiarism, which would have put at risk his authorship, his knowledge, and his livelihood.[229]

227. Crawford, "Women's Published Writings"; Hobby, *Virtue of Necessity*, 9, 26–53, 165–89; Mack, *Visionary Women*, 10, 15–17, 33, 84–5, 91, 96–7, 106–19; Nussbaum, *Autobiographical Subject*, 127–77. For the situation before the Civil War, see Lewalski, *Writing Women*, and Lamb, "Cooke Sisters." For a discussion in European context, see Hufton, *Prospect before Her*, 424–62. See also below, pp. 413–5, for this subject considered in relation to the histories of reading and the body.

228. Earle, *City Full of People*, 86; Dewald, "Ruling Class in the Marketplace"; *Tatler* 3 (14–16 April 1709); *Tatler* 158 (11–13 April 1710).

229. Desaguliers, *Lectures of Experimental Philosophy*, sig. A3ʳ; Desaguliers, *Course of Experimental Philosophy*, I, sig. C2ᵛ; Desaguliers, *System of Experimental Philosophy* (the unauthorized version; both editions sold for five shillings); Allamand, *Oeuvres Philosophiques et Mathématiques de Mr. G. J. 'sGravesande*, I, xxvii–xxxvi; 'sGravesande, *Mathematical Ele-*

Faced with such problems, natural philosophers and others put all the strategies of accreditation outlined above to use to guarantee the status of themselves and their knowledge. In mathematics, history, law, and philosophy (including natural philosophy) alike, the credit of printed reports depended on the success of these strategies. The end result was richly ironic. To deter pirates, Stationers and writers were told to change the texts of their books as frequently as they could. Stephen Austen, bookseller for the Newtonian lecturer Benjamin Worster, thus explained in the second edition of Worster's *Principles of Natural Philosophy* that "the unskilful Practice of Bookmenders" had forced him to justify a number of changes made since the first printing. Interested readers could see the corrected printer's copy itself, he averred, and witness that there were no alterations which were not approved, to "Page and Line," in "the Author's own hand Writing." Going still further, Desaguliers himself announced that he would "write my Name in each Book with my own Hand" so as to deter piratical translations. These men had discovered the central, overwhelming paradox rending early modern print culture. The only really effective way to guarantee the authenticity of their printed sheets was to abandon the defining element of print itself. Forsaking mechanical uniformity, they returned to inscribing their authorship by hand.[230]

THE STATIONERS' COMMONWEALTH

The Schollers Purgatory [is] discovered in the Stationers Common wealth.
GEORGE WITHER, title of *The Schollers Purgatory*, "Imprinted for the
Honest Stationers," 1624

In early modern England, knowledge had to be made, articulated, communicated, and defended in a Stationers' commonwealth. This chapter has attempted to display some of the salient characteristics of that commonwealth. Several things may now be said concerning the printing and reading of learned books. In the first place, it was conducted in the same spaces as the

---

ments, I, sig. [a4ʳ⁻ᵛ], xvii; II, sigs. A4ʳ–[A5ᵛ] (references I owe to Simon Schaffer). The rival edition of 'sGravesande was undertaken by booksellers William Mears and James Woodward. It was allegedly overseen by Newtonian John Keill, although Allamand denied this: *Oeuvres Philosophiques*, I, xxix.

230. Worster, *Compendious Account*, v–xviii, esp. viii; Desaguliers, *Course of Experimental Philosophy*, I, sig. c4ᵛ; Gold, "Battle of the Shorthand Books," 7–8. See also Black, *English Press*, 18, for attempts to outwit a "Grand pirate printer," and compare *Weekly Intelligencer of the Common-wealth* (7 June 1659), 39, on printers who "counterfeit" the journal "in several Pamphlets, using our form of words": "We therefore the only experimented Authors hereof, desire all to be cautious in buying any other; and in testimony that these and only these were the anciently (and still are) approved ones, we have here-unto subscribed our hands."

production of ephemera and pamphlets, by the same people, and often at the same time. Thus works of knowledge were subject to the complex practices and priorities refined within the book trade—and these were not developed primarily for the benefit of prospective authors. In the printing house, compositors and pressmen used their skills to create and preserve the good name of the master printer, by configuring books according to Stationers' conventions. In the warehouse and bookshop, other Stationers took decisions that substantially affected the reception of the resulting volume. Printers, booksellers, and writers all had to work hard to coordinate a wide variety of processes if a printed book were to appear an inscription of an author's thought.

Authorship and reading both changed radically. It seemed an "Age of Paper-prostitutions," personified in the figure of the professional "scribbler" who subsisted by selling his honor to booksellers by the line. Scroggs even posited these "mercenaries" as a third pole on which the English nation was threatened with impalement, alongside papists and fanatics. Attempts to curb them showed little success. By the early eighteenth century Addison was estimating that two to three hundred families lived by scribbling, and the printers themselves reckoned that two-thirds of their number depended on pamphlets for their survival.[231] The Stationers' commonwealth was a land where scholarship, skills, and scribbling converged. This was the social reality into which natural philosophers had to venture (fig. 2.24).

The Stationers' commonwealth was distinctive not only socially, but epistemically—and even epistemologically. Credit was fragile and ephemeral to an extraordinary degree. The conditions in which knowledge must be constructed, maintained, and defended were riven by private deals, intrigue, and distrust. The concept of piracy was invented as the most vivid representation of this cultural predicament. The phenomenon, never uniquely defined, was regarded as endemic, and it threatened the credibility of every printed sheet. It meant that any given printed book might not be what it claimed to be. The characteristic feature of the Stationers' commonwealth, as a result, was uncertainty.[232]

That uncertainty applied to readers too. One could never guarantee a "fit" readership for any given printed book. Stationers may have been attributed almost divine powers, but not even a Stationer could determine future

231. Suckling, *Fragmenta Aurea*, "To the Reader"; [Addison], *Thoughts of a Tory Author*, 30; McKenzie, "London Book Trade," 25.

232. The theft of books reached an apotheosis of sorts when Prosper Marchand portrayed two thieves stealing the Book of Fate, which Jupiter had sent to Athens for binding, replacing it with a "Counterfeit," and running off to "find some *Bookseller*, that will give us Ten thousand Crowns for the Copy." Stealing a prophetic text had the dubious advantage that the thieves could look in the book itself to discern their future punishment for their deed. Des Perriers, *Cymbalum Mundi*, 35–6, 39, 52.

W. Kent jnv.

P. Fourdrinier. sculp.

FIG. 2.24. The elephant and the bookseller. Gay's updated fable pointed up the virulence of authorial combat in Augustan London, the capacity of booksellers to foment such strife, and the wisdom of declining their invitations to participate. It told of an elephant—a creature, as readers of Pliny well knew, "For science and for sense renown'd"—discovering a volume of natural history in a bookshop. The elephant is inspired to reflect on the eagerness of humans to identify unpleasant characteristics as natural to certain animals while ignoring their far more damaging presence in themselves. What spaniel cannot learn fawning techniques from a courtier? Whereupon the bookseller, thinking that he has discovered a "genius," tries to recruit him as a pamphleteer. "Since you're learn'd in *Greek*," he suggests, "let's see / Something against the Trinity." He is brusquely dismissed. Human hacks are more vicious than "game cocks" spoiling for a fight, and there are enough of them already without the wise elephant joining their ranks. Gay, *Fables*. (By permission of the Syndics of Cambridge University Library.)

appropriations. It was consequently feared that print could be almost preternatural in its effects on the supposedly uncritical "people"—John Webster's "ignorant asses (who visiting Stationers shoppes their use is not to inquire for good bookes but new bookes)." William Gilbert drew attention to the effects on natural knowledge in his hugely influential *De Magnete*. Gilbert remarked upon the "ocean of books" flooding London, whereby "the common herd and fellows without a spark of talent are made intoxicated, crazy, puffed-up." He complained that so many books encouraged the mob to "profess themselves philosophers, physicians, mathematicians, and astrologers, the while contemning men of learning." *De Magnete* itself, it has been argued, was written in an attempt to seize back magnetism, which had been fashioned into one of the major argumentative resources of unlicensed magical practitioners, and return it to the armory of natural philosophers.[233]

How the mob might interpret a work could therefore come to be of greater concern than any supposedly objective reading—and even than the author's own intention. William Prynne's "greatest crime" in publishing *Histriomastix* was thus, as his counsel admitted before Star Chamber in the most momentous of all such examinations, "that he did not bethinke himselfe, w^t interpretation theire might bee made of his writings." "That must not bee allowed him in excuse," replied the normally jovial Lord Cottington: "he should not have written any thinge that would beare construcion, for hee doth not accompany his booke, to make his intencion knowne to all that reades it." Laud agreed, remarking that a writer like Prynne "cannot tell of what disposicions his reder will be." Sir Robert Heath supported this with the contention that "the common people when they reade his booke, they will take him to bee a man of judgement and believe him." The remarkable "interpretation" favored by these judges was that *Histriomastix* was a thousand-page pamphlet: a "Libel in *folio*." They were encouraged to decide this by the character of Prynne's bookseller, Michael Sparke, who was "a greate offender in this kind of printing." A determined Presbyterian, Sparke's *Crums of Comfort*, which he compiled "out of divers mens works," became perhaps the best-selling prayer book of the century, and his name was immediately recognizable to city readers. The appearance and typographic format of the book, too—which were almost certainly Sparke's responsibility—lent weight to their fears. *Histriomastix*, they opined, "justifieth it self by Authors with an high hand, *That is there*, and *that is there*." Its ostentatious annotation made it all the more dangerous. Person, place, compositorial skill, and reading practice: all the resources for assessing printed books had now been deployed, and the court felt secure in sentencing Prynne to lose his ears.[234]

233. Webster, *White Devil*, sig. A2^r; Gilbert, *De Magnete*, sig. *ii^v ("Sed quid ego in tam vasto Librorum Oceano, quibus studiosorum ingenia perturbantur, fatiganturque; quibus ineptioribus, vulgus & homines importunissimi inebriantur, delirant, inflantur, & tumultus faciunt literarios, seque philosophos, medicos, mathematicos, astrologos profitentur, & viros doctos negligunt, contemnuntq[ue]"); Pumfrey, "William Gilbert's Magnetic Philosophy," 14–73, 89.

234. Prynne, *New Discovery of the Prelates Tyranny*, 8–9; Gardiner, *Documents*, 32; Butler, *Theatre and Crisis*, 314 n. 2; CUL Ms. Dd.6.23, 24–6, 30; Foster, *Notes from the Caroline Underground*, 37, 42; Sparke, *Crums of Comfort*. Sparke was also something of a poet: *Dimension of the Hollow Tree* has verses by him. For Cottington, see Sharpe, *Personal Rule*, 150–2. Many writers have commented on the prevalence of this sort of "application" (as Jonson called it) in the reading of printed works: e.g., Wallace, "'Examples are Best Precepts'"; Zwicker, *Politics and Language*, 31–69.

Although the distinctive trait of the Stationers' commonwealth was uncertainty, that uncertainty could still be resisted. The best strategy for a writer was to enter the printing house and attend the press in person. If that failed, he or she must try to form alliances with others, gentlemen or Stationers, who could attend and possessed the knowledge to intervene successfully. Such a capability was widely accepted to be essential for the safe production and distribution of publications. Printers' and booksellers' interests were not necessarily coincident with those of gentlemen writers, and the latter had to prevail. "If the bookseller be thus criminal," L'Estrange cried in one of his characteristic moments of exasperation, "what will become of the author!" What became of the author was that he had to turn Stationer himself.

Further measures became possible if the "author" were not an individual but a group. The Quakers ruled that only Friends be employed in making and binding their books; the Royal Society obtained its own printing privilege and appointed individual booksellers to oversee the press. In this way each could regularize dealings with the trade. The collective could tempt booksellers and printers into properly docile conduct by offering all of its publishing work to the one operator, and it could know whom to blame if things went wrong. The Royal Society, Fell's allies in Oxford, and the Quakers can be seen as exerting analogous efforts to discipline the culture of the book trade to their respective benefits.

But the most authoritative and effective of such disciplining efforts—and the one that the Quakers and the virtuosi in practice imitated—was that mounted by London's printers and booksellers themselves. Their main authority was the Stationers' Company, the orders and bylaws of which were pasted on the wall of every law-abiding printing house and bookshop.[235] In the last analysis Stationers appealed to their Company's customs in order to justify their conduct. They appealed to its representations and mechanisms to protect credit and augment certainty in the realm of print. It was the Stationers' Company that occupied the vanguard in the struggle against piracy and discredit. We therefore need to look closer at its conventions, and at how contemporaries attempted to monitor, mitigate, alter, and even extend them. In the following chapter they are examined in depth, in an analysis reaching into the central space of the book trade. It was a space hardly any author ever entered, but one that Stationers regarded as embodying their vocation: Stationers' Hall.

235. Kitchin, *L'Estrange*, 387; O'Malley, "'Defying the Powers,'" 81–2; SCB D, fol. 60^r; SCB E, fols. 58^v, 61^v, 102^v, 116^r, 157^r.

3

"THE ADVANCEMENT OF

WHOLESOME KNOWLEDGE"

The Politics of Print and the Practices of Propriety

INTRODUCTION

Printers and booksellers were skilled at their vocations. They could—and, given the importance of the master's good name, should—use their prized craftsmanship with creativity as well as dexterity. In determining how best to employ their expertise, these men and women were no mere dupes of avarice. They were strongly influenced by the need to strive for and maintain credit in their local environs, and the best way to do that was by establishing a good character. The previous chapter asked what qualities combined to constitute a good character for a Stationer. This one shows how the entire craft community worked to sustain them for the book trade as a whole.

Foremost among the virtues of a model Stationer was adherence to the principle of "copy." This meant the recognition of another's prior claim to the printing of a work in which he or she had been first to invest time, skill, capital, and credit. Such recognition entailed a principled repudiation of what contemporaries were learning to call "piracy." Universal adherence to copy would, in principle, have eliminated any need to doubt printed materials because of their being printed. Such universal adherence proving unachievable, in the real world those who depended on books expressed serious concern about the practices pervading the domains of print. It seemed to them that the book trade had generated a culture of plagiarism and "counterfeits."[1] The achievement of authorship itself had become volatile and transient. The wits thronging the coffeehouses and taverns of Augustan

---

1. For uses of this term see SCB C, fols. 198ʳ, 291ᵛ, and SCB D, fols. 15ʳ, 28ʳ, 79ᵛ, 119ᵛ, 131ʳ, 138ʳ. For a formal definition see Nelson and Seccombe, *Periodical Publications*, 78–9. Compare *Perfect Diurnall* (21–8 May 1649); and Siebert, *Freedom of the Press*, 217. "Counterfeiting" was also a theatrical or poetic concept, as described in Murray, *Theatrical Legitimation*, chap. 2.

London had powerful strategies at their disposal for challenging the worth of any printed book, the character of any printed author, and the truth of any printed statement.

Yet readers did come to trust and use print. Books were, in fact, produced, sold, read, and put to use. The epistemological problems of reading them were, in practice, superable. And this is the key: such problems were soluble *in practice*. While the typographical certainty that modern historians all too readily attribute to early printing is a chimera, seventeenth-century readers settled for looser, practical criteria of trust—criteria that may have been much less absolute than that technological standard, but were far more realizable. Such readers judged the printed books they met by what they knew of the people, places, and practices implicated in their production, distribution, and use. This was pragmatic, expedient, ad hoc reasoning; but in the main, it worked.

The reason it worked was that the daily conduct of the book trade was not simply disordered. In fact, the Stationers had developed their own concept of civil order, of which "copy" was a manifestation. Their concept was different from any standard recognized by genteel, clerical, or scholarly convention, and it reigned in places beyond the surveillance of virtually any gentleman, minister, or scholar. For that reason, the Stationers' civility has often been mistaken, then and now, for bald rapacity. Far from creating and inhabiting an amoral chaos, however, printers and booksellers used elaborate mechanisms to deal with all the problems of piracy, and they prized these mechanisms for their role in securing their own credit. They thereby created a cultural régime capable of disciplining the domains of print. With this régime in place and functioning, trust in printed books could become a routine possibility.

The "first and greatest end of order in the Presse," the Stationers maintained, was "the advancement of wholesome knowledge." Printing itself was "a great means to advance Learning amongst us"; with that scarcely anyone would have disagreed. But not many would have demurred from their ensuing point, either: that "it is not meere Printing, but well ordered Printing that merits so much favour and respect."[2] The body entrusted with creating such "well ordered Printing" was called the Stationers' Company. As the guarantor of the "good behaviour and civil conversation both in word and deeds" of all its members, this Company underwrote an order of print in the wider realm. It acted continuously to beat back threats to that order. This chapter addresses the Stationers' Company and its practices.

---

2. [Parker], *Humble Remonstrance*, sigs. A1^r–A2^r. For the writing of this tract see Mendle, *Henry Parker*, 15–6, 144–8.

In particular, this chapter identifies conventions of what the Company called "propriety." Propriety, it argues, may be seen as the key to Stationers' Company civility. It is often said that modern notions of literary property—and, in legal terms, copyright—originated in this propriety, and many historians have described it in correspondingly teleological terms. But the concept was not simply copyright manqué; nor was it just a matter of legal definition and mundane administration. As Paul Langford has put it, property is "a way of looking at the world, as well as a means of sharing it out." In the Stationers' Company, conventions of propriety thus came to occupy a central place in the representation of the trade both to itself and to the country at large. In their articulation, the very identity of print was at stake.[3]

Whatever morality the Stationers adopted would necessarily be of political import. Inasmuch as this chapter deals with the regulation of printing, it therefore touches on the concerns of an extensive and controversial literature discussing "censorship" in the period.[4] In the sixteenth century, almost from the first introduction of printing, Tudor administrations had instituted measures designed to temper any ill effects the new craft might have, and channel it toward approved ends. The Stationers' Company itself was one product. From then on, state regulation and craft morality developed in concert, this imperative only sharpening under the Stuarts.[5] As is now widely accepted, a pervasive belief emerged that some kind of regulation of printing was essential. Not even Milton's ringing proclamation of a republic freed from licensers was entirely innocent of qualification, and at the Restoration Roger L'Estrange was largely justified in assuming that "no man denyes the *Necessity* . . . of *Regulating* the *Press.*"[6] Such statements should not be interpreted as voicing admiration for simple repression. The early modern state had neither the ideology, nor the finances, nor the mechanisms, nor the police and personnel to construct a régime of censorship recognizable as such to late twentieth-century eyes. On the contrary, the reality of seventeenth-century law and administration was that it operated through the participation of householders involved in the particular activity

---

3. Stationers' Company, *Registers 1554–1640*, I, 13; Langford, *Public Life and the Propertied Englishman*, 4–5. The most recent teleological history tracing the development of copyright is Feather, *Publishing, Piracy and Politics.*

4. See especially: Patterson, *Censorship and Interpretation*; Hill, "Censorship and English Literature"; Worden, "Literature and Political Censorship"; Lambert, "Printers and the Government"; Lambert, "Richard Montagu"; Smith, *Literature and Censorship.*

5. For Tudor efforts at positive use of the press, see Elton, *Policy and Police*, chap. 4. For restrictions see Loades, "Theory and Practice of Censorship."

6. L'Estrange, *Considerations and Proposals*, 1; [Asgill], *An Essay for the Press*, 2; Worden, "Literature and Political Censorship"; Soman, "Press, Pulpit and Censorship," 442. *Areopagitica* has been the subject of much fruitful discussion recently: e.g., Miller, "Shattered *Violl*"; Blum, "Author's Authority"; Dunn, "Milton among the Monopolists."

under constraint, and printing was no exception.[7] Any regulation, whether statutory or not, would depend upon the skills, knowledge, and personal dedication of Stationers themselves. Politics and propriety were necessarily inseparable. But this also meant that under no conceivable early modern régime could the Stationers hope to construct their own order, isolating the commerce of communication from considerations of state. Or could they? Once voiced, the very possibility raised terrors: so much so that it stimulated profound reflections on print and politics alike.

Licensing and propriety were thus both represented as integral not only to the concerns of the Stationers, but to those of the state. They constituted the conditions of existence for printed knowledge itself. As Samuel Parker warned, the necessary consequence of an unregulated printing trade would be "the great liberty of lying." Few indeed yearned for such a dystopia. So press regulation, by the state and by the Stationers' Company in tandem, found support not just for its suppression of heresy and sedition, but as a positive bulwark for Protestantism and property. If Foxe's nation were to fulfill its providential destiny, its people had to be instructed in "wholesome knowledge." Printing—but "well ordered" printing—seemed a good way to encourage the process.[8]

THE STATIONERS' CASTLE

The Stationers' Company had—and still has—a central location. It maintained its headquarters in what had been a large medieval house, once owned by the earls of Pembroke. This was Stationers' Hall, and it was the focus of the London book trade (fig. 3.1).[9] If one wished to enter the Stationers' commonwealth, this was where its front door was to be found.

By the first decade of the seventeenth century, when the Company took possession of this building, Stationers' Hall had become an enormously important place—a point of passage, rendezvous, and negotiation for all members of the book trade. If writers were compelled to go to bookshops and

7. McLynn, *Crime and Punishment*, 17–35; Wrightson, "Two Concepts of Order"; Fletcher and Stevenson, *Order and Disorder*, 15–26; Brewer and Styles, *An Ungovernable People*, 18–20.

8. Parker, *Bishop Parker's History of his Own Time*, 22–3. For licensing as positive recommendation see *Arguments Relating to a Restraint upon the Press*, 16. For Foxe see Haller, *Foxe's "Book of Martyrs" and the Elect Nation*. Foxe's *Acts and Monuments* was a copy owned by the Stationers' Company itself, and it was the preferred choice for presentation as a gift both to worthy patrons and to prisoners in need of moral examples: SCB C, fols. 214ᵛ, 232ᵛ, 248ᵛ; SCB D, fol. 55ᵛ.

9. Stow, *Survay*, 649; Blagden, *Stationers' Company*, 206–8, 212 ff. Blagden's account will undoubtedly be superseded by Blayney's forthcoming study, announced in Blayney, *Bookshops in Paul's Cross Churchyard*.

Stationers Hall, near Paternoster Row.

FIG. 3.1. Stationers' Hall in the eighteenth century. (In the possession of the author.)

printing houses to pursue their projects, the people who ran those establishments had in turn to go to the hall to regulate and maintain theirs. Indeed, for important occasions the Company's entire membership could be
summoned to meet at the hall.[10] The announcements they heard there included declarations of new state regulatory measures, proclaimed by word
of mouth. The building also served as a center for Company celebrations,
for which dinner could be provided from an adjoining kitchen. And the hall
was a center not only for the personnel of the trade, but for its distinctive
products. Even those dealing in books from Continental Europe found it
an obligatory passage point, since by law all such importers had to bring
their cases of books straight from the Customs House to the hall to be
opened there before Company witnesses. Closer to home, it housed a considerable bulk of the printed materials on which virtually the entire domestic
trade depended for its continued economic viability. Here, above and below
the main chambers, could be found warehouses in which were kept the
books published by the so-called "English Stock." The credit of almanacs,
in particular, came to be trumpeted as depending on their originating at

10. E.g., SCB C, fols. 178^{r-v}, 205^r, 211^{r-v}, 218^r, 259^r; SCB E, fols. 161^v–162^r; SCB F, fols.
12^v–13^r, 205^r.

Stationers' Hall. Hence Poor Robin's advice, repeated year in, year out until at least the end of the eighteenth century: "Let him who despises all counterfeits call/For the Almanacks publish'd at Stationers' Hall." [11]

Use of the hall's main chamber was not restricted to Company meetings. Provided the Company agreed, other events could also be held there, such as aldermen's wardmotes and, in the 1690s, evenings when the Society for the Gentlemen Lovers of Musick would gather to listen to Purcell. The first meeting of the Union Fire Office occurred there in 1714. Desaguliers's Freemasons likewise met in the hall in 1728, and there is even evidence of a quack medical practitioner delivering his lectures there, the better to "satisfie the Publick at once in the Truth of this discovery by Evident Demonstration." [12] The hall complex could, then, be entered by a wide range of people. But there was a gatekeeper present to regulate any such access. And visitors were not normally permitted to pass beyond the main chamber, into the far more restricted rooms behind it.

The institution that created this powerful resource of credit was the most important and regular to convene in the hall: the Stationers' court. Every month, the "assistants" of the Company—its oligarchic grandees—convened as a tribunal possessed of wide disciplinary and political powers over the trade. Normally the court met on the first Monday of the month, beginning at ten in the morning. [13] It is useful to consider its conventions in terms of the physical structure of the hall itself. Recent work has stressed the importance of architecture in early modern governance, and Stationers' Hall provides a peculiarly good example of this. Unfortunately, no historian has found a contemporary image of the hall as it was before the fire. However, the survey undertaken by William Leybourn after the conflagration displays very clearly the setting and layout of the restoration completed by 1674 (fig. 3.2). What Leybourn's survey reveals is that Stationers' Hall was not just a hall. It was a castle. [14]

Castles were built according to routine practices and plans, and their

11. E.g., SCB D, fols. 15ᵛ, 153ʳ; *Old Poor Robin* (1791), title page. Compare *Ladies Diary* (1716), sig. [A1ᵛ]: anyone sending "New *Aenigma's, Questions* or *Answers*" should do so to the "Author" at Stationers' Hall.

12. SCB D, fol. 167ʳ; *London Gazette* 3340, 3343, 3346 (November 1697); Lillywhite, *London Coffee Houses*, 81–2, 534; Songhurst, *Minutes of the Grand Lodge of Freemasons*, 93. Examples could be multiplied: for example, a lottery called the "Mathematical Adventure" was drawn at the hall in 1699, after tickets had been sold at coffeehouses: Lillywhite, *London Coffee Houses*, 488.

13. Stationers' Company, *Registers 1554–1640*, I, 5, § 1. For numbers attending see SCB C, fol. 181ʳ; SCB D, fol. 52ʳ; SCB E, fols. 18ᵛ–19ʳ; SCB F, fols. 12ʳ, 13ᵛ. After the Fire, courts met on Tuesdays until 1669.

14. Robert Hooke attended some of Leybourn's work on the hall and surrounding properties: Hooke, *Diary*, 330, 331–2.

structures served to facilitate a recognized way of life (fig. 3.3). In its medieval heyday the castle had been the center of most local governance. Built to oversee a defined space of land, it was the source of law, authority, and defense for that area.[15] In particular, one can identify certain common features of the *urban* castle, a fabric designed not so much for sieges as for administrative tasks. Such a castle was typically built against the city wall. Its main gate would lie opposite the wall, facing into the town, while a postern elsewhere would allow unobserved access and retreat. The structures of governance facilitated by this material structure would likewise be standardized. The castle provided its own court to deal with discipline in a defined area known as its *fee*, in which the town had no jurisdiction. These castle courts were private, with their own rituals and procedures. Visitors were barred at the gate while they were in session, and participants were expected to keep secret what happened there. Some fees survived into the nineteenth century as privileged trading areas, where businessmen could operate without obtaining city freedom. By that time the castle form had been adopted as symbolic of authority by many other administrative bodies. Monasteries, schools, Oxbridge colleges, physics laboratories, and hospitals all ended up looking like fortresses. So did the company hall.

Stationers' Hall, like most early modern halls, had been adapted from a medieval fabric.[16] Even in its rebuilt form, it was laid out as a typical urban castle—which was precisely what its building had once been. Built against the city wall, the hall's outer gate faced into the city. The courtroom was then the innermost chamber in a complex of yards and buildings. To get to it one had to pass first of all through a line of Company-owned shops and houses fronting onto Ave Maria Lane, into an outer courtyard that might be identified as the outer bailey. A gap through another row of Company buildings then led into a second yard, recognizable as the inner bailey. From there a stone staircase led into the Common Hall, where the whole Company could meet—a large ceremonial space, comparable to the great hall of a castle. Beyond that was a small lobby. Here the beadle would sit on court days, waiting to be summoned by a bell set into the wall. Only when it rang could he lead the visitor into the room beyond, where the Company grandees sat behind a table in strict order of seniority. This was the equivalent of the lord's private chamber, or solar. Here sat the Stationers' court.

This was obviously a special place, and it became more so as the century progressed. Entering the "baileys" of the complex before about 1630, one

15. Pounds, *Medieval Castle*, 184–96, 207–15, 265–72, 297, and passim.
16. Tittler, *Architecture and Power*, 25–6, 47–8. Compare Heal's treatment of the "social geography" of the great house, in *Hospitality in Early Modern England*, 29–48; see also Hillier and Hanson, *Social Logic of Space*, ix–22, 157.

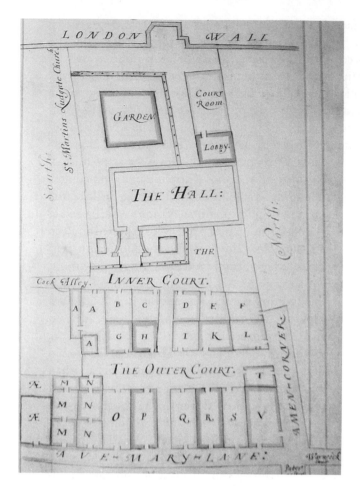

FIG. 3.2. William Leybourn's plan of Stationers' Hall, drawn in 1674. Note the extensive structural similarities to the designs shown in figure 3.3. (By permission of the Master and Wardens of the Worshipful Company of Stationers and Newspaper-Makers.)

would have found poultry and pigeons in the hall and yards, men playing bowls in the garden, clothes hanging out to dry, boys running to and fro throwing stones at each other (and, it seems, at the hall itself), and, above it all, the fumes produced by the kitchen. The doors of the hall would be open, allowing people to pass through into the building. Little by little, all this was changed on the order of the assistants. The kitchen was converted into a warehouse, the poultry and pigeons driven out, the children kept away by means of "an oaken peece of Timber wth iron Spikes."[17] And the hall itself was locked up and kept private, especially on court days. Any member caught revealing the "secrets, conferences or consultations" negotiated there

17. SCB C, fols. 247^v, 266^r, 278^r; SCB D, fols. 13^v, 22^r; SCB E, fols. 30^v, 112^r, 153^v; SCB F, fols. 129^r, 146^v, 158^r, 161^v; SCB G, fol. 39^r.

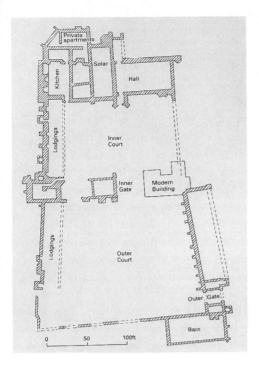

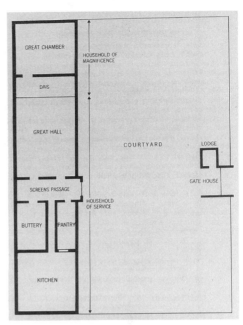

FIG. 3.3. (*left*) The medieval castle. Pounds, *The Medieval Castle in England and Wales*. (By permission of Cambridge University Press and the Syndics of Cambridge University Library.) (*right*) The division between the household of service and the household of magnificence in an early modern great house. Heal, *Hospitality in Early Modern England*. (By permission of Oxford University Press and the Syndics of Cambridge University Library.) Stationers' Hall inherited the characteristics of such buildings, and the Company put them to use in creating an orderly craft community.

could be fined, and even expelled.[18] There is evidence that the secrecy was effective: when a restoration of monarchy became inevitable in 1660, the haggard and bearded figure of Sir Richard Browne emerged from a seven-month concealment in Stationers' Hall that had begun immediately after his implication in the failed Booth uprising against the republic. Browne had survived repeated attempts to discover his hiding place. He became lord mayor the following autumn.[19]

Other London companies possessed remarkably similar buildings. De-laune called them "stately and sumptuous *Palaces.*" It is not necessary to

18. Stationers' Company, *Registers 1554–1640*, I, 14. Compare the 1641 complaint that petitioners to Parliament had revealed "all yᵉ Secretts & misteries of this profession": SCB C, fol. 178ʳ; Blagden, "Stationers' Company in the Civil War Period," 8. For courts' increasing exclusion of the festive world from the later sixteenth century, see Tittler, *Architecture and Power*, 27, 146–50.

19. Pepys, *Diary*, I, 64 (but the evidence for this assertion about Browne is unclear); PRO IND 1/8909, fol. 5ʳ; PRO SP 25/79, pp. 435–6; PRO SP 77/32, fol. 306ʳ⁻ᵛ; PRO SP 25/115, p. 3.

claim uniqueness in order to find the parallel between Stationers' Hall and a castle interesting, just as it is not essential to insist on an absolute identity between castle and company hall in order to find their similarities suggestive. The "fee" for such a hall was now not a real space of land, however, but the "virtual" territory represented by the company's trade, and in the case of the Stationers that meant printing and bookselling. Practitioners of these crafts brought disputes of all kinds to this court, and it was expert in dealing confidentially with all the dubious aspects of what was becoming, thanks to its decisions, a print culture of some consistency. The influence of those decisions was pervasive; only a few extraordinary cases ever proceeded beyond the castle walls into the realm of the national legal system, and all trade disputes had first to be presented here before a protagonist could go to law.[20]

Not all sections of society routinely used this court. All Stationers did, but virtually nobody else. Authors, in particular, hardly ever went there. It is true that a few did come to the hall, mainly either to demand that a particular title be accorded the Company's protection or to declare that they would not tolerate piracy of a given work. But even this was very rare, and their attendance at the court itself was all but unknown.[21] Government officers like L'Estrange sometimes came, but more often they expressed themselves in letters. More senior officials, such as the secretaries of state or the lord mayor, never appeared in person; they too used correspondence. Lawyers did sometimes arrive to report on other courts, but that was likewise rare.[22] At the other end of the social scale, the unpropertied of the trade— hawkers, "higglers," mercury-women, peddlers, chapmen, and the like— exerted something of a negative presence, inasmuch as the court regarded them as an evil to be controlled, if not eradicated, and to that end spent much of its time discussing their habits and whereabouts; but they too seldom actually put in an appearance. Servants, on the other hand, entered almost every month, if only to carry all these pieces of paper back and forth. However, theirs was a silent presence. Very rarely did they warrant a mention in the minutes, and then only because they had contravened some unwritten article of protocol.[23]

20. Delaune, *Angliae Metropolis*, 307–8; Stationers' Company, *Registers 1554–1640*, I, 14. See also Kirschbaum, *Shakespeare and the Stationers*, 28, for Sidney's *Arcadia*.

21. I know of only a handful of instances in the period 1600–1720 when authors appeared in the court. See, for example, SCB D, fols. 60ᵛ, 86ᵛ (John Fuller), and 131ʳ (John Ogilby— who was a printer, however, as well as an author). Even when writers did attend, they would have to withdraw during discussions: SCB D, fol. 5ᵛ (a Leicestershire minister); compare fol. 62ᵛ (an author refusing to accept a Stationer's suggestion that the court mediate their dispute).

22. E.g., Marchamont Nedham: SCB C, fol. 292ʳ.

23. E.g., SCB E, fol. 36ʳ, referring to two messengers sent from Shaftesbury in early 1677

The overwhelming bulk of those appearing and making an impression at the Stationers' court were propertied members of the Company. That is, the court was the forum for the householding Stationers whose practices and concerns were the core subject of the previous chapter. Printers, binders, and booksellers decided issues of the proper conduct of the book trade themselves here, sealed away from the street, where writers and readers experienced the consequences. One result of this conventional isolation was that writers stood a much greater chance of surviving the processes of publication—of becoming authors—if they had an "insider" as an ally. Chapter 2 argued that successful authors may often be resolved into writer-Stationer partnerships, largely because of the conventions of the bookshop and printing house. To that argument can now be added the fact that Stationers alone had ready access to their castle, Stationers' Hall. As will soon become clear, such access could be of prime importance for the safe production and reception of printed knowledge. These champions were vital allies for writers determined to fight for the credit of their knowledge in printed form. Not only were writers themselves ineffectual gladiators: they could not even get into the arena.

The court observed complex codes of dress and conduct. These conventions were rarely enunciated, but were certainly important nonetheless. They constituted an outward and visual guarantee of the moral propriety of proceedings. For the whole trade was assumed to be represented here, and in particular in the person of the Master. All debates had to be addressed to him. Speeches must be "serious," with nothing to give offense. "Decent apparel" had to be worn, and contributors must speak bareheaded. Only one person was permitted to speak at a time. The sum effect was to produce a space redolent of commercial probity, in which disputes of trade—which, in this very special trade, meant disputes of knowledge and authorship—could be resolved, or at least channeled and contained so as to avoid violent upheaval. Contraventions were thus regarded seriously. When a member "fell into a very great distemper & rage," and "gave o^r Master, ye Wardens & others of the Assistants p'sent very evill & opprobrious Language," he "so disturbed ye Co^rt y^at no proceedings of the Co^rt could goe forward." It had to be dissolved, and he was suspended from his assistantship. To act "uncivilly" was sufficient to interrupt the court altogether.[24]

If there was one figure who was vital to the smooth functioning of the

demanding that the Company suppress the *Pacquet of Advice*. L'Estrange had warned the court to steer clear of the tract, and it refused to give the messengers a copy of his warning.

24. Stationers' Company, *Registers 1554–1640*, I, 5–6; SCB F, fol. 56^r–v; SCB C, fol. 232^v. For other breaches of etiquette see also SCB C, fols. 238^r, 243^r. For the importance of dress and conduct in general in hall settings, see Tittler, *Architecture and Power*, 100–28.

court, it was the Stationers' clerk. The clerk was no mere amanuensis. In his office at the hall, he was a conventionally invisible agent who in fact wielded much influence.[25] He was expected to be a trained attorney, and the protocols regarding his duties were so complex that, although the clerk was in principle elected, the number of plausible candidates was always limited.[26] He it was who drew up and oversaw the Company's legal documents and transactions (including important bylaws concerning the regulation of copy), acted as mediator with the Oxford press and the Court of Aldermen, and safely guarded most of the Company's papers.[27] He might also be entrusted with handling the prosecution of private printers. In addition, it was the clerk who kept the keys to the hall and could let it out to suitable applicants.[28] There was a clerical assistant to help, but still it was hard work.

The clerk possessed an unequaled knowledge of the intricacies of Company affairs and practices. He was the only individual involved in all the decisions of every court and committee. As such, he could be called upon in person to testify as to their intentions long after the event, especially if the textual record (itself constructed by the clerk of the time) seemed unclear or was challenged. His record attested that the court's decisions were reached openly by competent individuals, and could be decisive in future debates.[29] Exceptionally, meetings to resolve such debates might even be held in his own house—where, apparently, he kept crucial Company documents in a wooden box. Much of what we now know about the Company's operation in fact derives from the archive created by successive clerks for their and the court's use.[30] The importance of his dependability became evident when one incumbent lapsed and recorded court minutes incorrectly: the Master and wardens had to oversee their reconstruction in person, and such was the

25. For his office (apparently an old cellar warehouse) see SCB C, fols. 30ᵛ, 273ʳ⁻ᵛ, and SCB F, fol. 256ᵛ. His role should be compared to that of Henry Oldenburg at the Royal Society: below, pp. 497–9.

26. Stationers' Company, *Registers 1554–1640*, I, 12, 18–19; SCB D, fol. 223ʳ; SCB F, fols. 205ʳ–206ʳ, 257ʳ ff. In midcentury the Company found itself in trouble after having granted reversions to the clerk's post years earlier. The complainant went as far as the king himself: SCB D, fols. 22ʳ, 59ᵛ, 69ᵛ–70ʳ, 74ʳ. Clerk John Lilly became a lawyer on his resignation (e.g., SCB F, fols. 69ʳ, 121ᵛ).

27. SCB C, fols. 272ʳ; SCB D, fols. 15ʳ, 47ʳ; SCB F, fol. 95ʳ ff. The clerk could also enter a caveat with the lord keeper against patents that might threaten Company copies: SCB E, fol. 14ʳ.

28. SCB C, fol. 272ʳ; SCB D, fols. 47ʳ, 80ʳ, 132ᵛ, 230ʳ; SCB E, fols. 7ᵛ, 13ʳ, 29ᵛ, 36ʳ, 60ʳ, 108ᵛ–109ʳ; SCB F, fols. 91ʳ, 44ᵛ, 97ᵛ.

29. Compare Nussdorfer, "Writing and the Power of Speech," 110.

30. SCB D, fol. 169ʳ; SCB E, fol. 150ᵛ. The only other houses in which meetings might be held were those of the wardens or the Master. The clerk seems particularly to have been responsible for the salvation of the Stationers' archive during the Fire of London, which consumed the hall and all its contents.

complexity of the task that it took fully eight months for the record to be repaired.[31] He was at the same time enjoined to keep proceedings strictly secret from outsiders—one clerk refused even the royal messenger of the press access to the Company register. By the 1690s the clerk was expected to give bond for the impressively massive sum of £1,000 for correct fulfillment of his duties (by comparison, an unlicensed printer might expect the authorities to impose on him a bond of some £300).[32] Large though it was, this was not an unrealistic amount, since the Company's well-being, and hence the good order of the London book trade, depended on the veracity, reliability, and knowledge of its clerk.

The clerk aside, the beadle was the most important of the court's lesser agents. Normally a member of the trade himself, he acted as general messenger, searcher, and attendant to the Table of Assistants, and on occasion almost as a personal servant to the Master and wardens. He was provided with a house close to the hall to facilitate his performance of these duties. This was necessary because the beadle was expected to serve the assistants on a daily basis, and to attend at every court. He was also supposed to collect copies of all books published and forward them to the royal and two university libraries, and to pay the Company's traditional charity to the parish.[33] Above all, he played a central role in the practice of regulation, especially in communicating between the court and Stationers risking its retribution; for example, in 1679 he was ordered to inspect all printing houses at least once a week in company with the messenger of the press.[34] So that he could act as a legal witness for the Company in such contentious affairs, he was formally removed from its ranks, as was his deputy, the underbeadle or porter.[35] Finally, the beadle occupied an important place in Company ceremonies, and it was requisite that he behave accordingly. Randall Taylor, appointed in 1674 in the first annual election to the post, emphatically did not, and

31. SCB F, fols. 244ᵛ, 256ʳ; see also SCB F, fols. 182ʳ–183ᵛ. In addition, see the statement acknowledging one clerk's irreplaceable skills, in SCB C, fol. 267ʳ.

32. SCB F, fols. 192ʳ, 205ᵛ. Only the Table of Assistants had free access to the register: SCB F, fol. 259ᵛ. For bonds on opposition printers, see PRO SP 29/77, no. 49; PRO SP 29/80, nos. 63, 108; PRO SP 29/83, nos. 95–6; PRO SP 29/98, no. 37; PRO SP 29/155, nos. 70–1; 14 Car. II, c. 33, § 10. The amount of £300 was derived from Parliament's 1649 measure (Firth and Rait, *Acts and Ordinances*, II, 249).

33. SCB D, fols. 29ᵛ, 91ʳ, 147ʳ, 155ʳ, 226ᵛ; SCB F, fol. 94ʳ. The Bodleian Library at Oxford had received copies since 1611, by private agreement. The legal deposit requirement dates from the 1662 Press Act. See Partridge, *History of the Legal Deposit of Books*, 17, 23–5. The clerk later took over this task.

34. E.g., SCB D, fols. 9ʳ, 160ʳ, 179ᵛ, 209ʳ, 215ᵛ, 236ʳ; SCB E, fol. 78ᵛ; SCB F, fol. 234ᵛ. Stationers' Company, *Registers 1554–1640*, I, 12–13, 19. Like the wardens, the beadle had to be indemnified: SCB C, fol. 214ʳ.

35. SCB E, fol. 114ʳ; SCB F, fols. 10ᵛ, 150ʳ; SCB G, fols. 87ᵛ–88ʳ, 211ᵛ. The post of underbeadle was discontinued in 1692: SCB F, fol. 168ᵛ.

was dismissed after repeatedly acting "sausily" to the Master.[36] As a result, the Table of Assistants drew up a list of explicit "Orders about the Beadle," outlining a string of conventions of proper conduct that had hitherto remained tacit. He must remove his hat when in the presence of the Master or wardens, never enter the court during a sitting unless summoned, not presume to dine at the same table as the assistants (nor with the livery at any "publique meeting"), and regularly attend the Master and wardens at their homes.[37] Such rules again underline the importance of civility in the Stationers' court.

The Stationers' court needed few material tools. One, however, was of prime importance. On the table before the assistants on court days lay an alphabetical list of titles that the clerk had compiled. Another such list hung on the wall. These were the names of the copies owned by the Company itself: those titles and categories of books that it alone could legally publish. They were kept at hand, the clerk recorded, "to the end the court may the better observe whether any [of] the members of this Company comprint upon them."[38] These titles represented a substantial part of the Company's assets. Some had been assigned to it by royal letters patent. The right to all schoolbooks was one example; another was that to all almanacs and prognostications. Perennially popular, these were reliable annual sources of both substantial profits and work, the latter to be shared among printers for whose otherwise idle hands the devil might find a use. Others had become the Company's by virtue of entrance in its own "register." These two systems—royal patents and the Stationers' Register—were the two mechanisms by which the producer of a printed book could associate him- or herself with that book and hope to provide some security against comprinters. They were to prove instrumental in fomenting a great debate destined to reconstitute and reshape the realm of print itself.

COMPANY ORDERS

Before tracing the course of this great conflict, it is necessary to describe the character of the communal culture that found its focus in Stationers' Hall. It was this that lent the court its practical authority. When printers and booksellers brought their disputes to their Company court, they were displaying their recognition of this community.

36. SCB D, fol. 236[r]; Stationers' Company, *Registers 1554–1640*, I, 13, 19. SCB F, fols. 46[r], 168[r]. Taylor had been involved in "counterfeit" primers before his appointment: SCB D, fol. 180[v]. For another example of the importance attached to the beadle's behavior, see SCB C, fol. 295[r].

37. SCB E, fol. 153[v].

38. SCB F, fols. 55[r], 142[r]. The laws of the Company were hung on the wall of the Common Hall: SCB E, fol. 140[r].

Queen Mary had incorporated the Stationers' Company in 1557. Although some form of guild for text writers and illuminators had existed for at least two hundred years before that, the newly chartered Company was different. It was expected to encompass the regulation of all practitioners of the book trade in the capital, from the meanest bookbinder to the king's printers. The Company was intended to oversee that trade, preventing seditious publishing and putting a stop to unauthorized printing.[39] However, the Stationers' Company was never simply repressive in character. Like the other London companies, the Stationers' was to constitute and exemplify proper practice for its trade at the same time as eliminating improper conduct. This it did, and as time went on its activities widened in scope. By the late sixteenth century, the Company had become central to the creation of a culture. By virtue of decisions reached in its court, the Company now established and protected its members' property rights in books, rented tenements and taverns to members (and to nonmembers too), lent money to hard-up Stationers, and when they were too old to work helped to maintain them as pensioners.[40] It was a success, and it would retain its powers longer than most other metropolitan companies.

Similar corporate bodies were being established in many other European cities, but the structure of the London Company was distinctive. In German guilds, for example, master printers, booksellers, and journeymen were generally admitted with equal status, while in France and Holland master printers alone participated. Journeymen and booksellers did sometimes try to form their own collectives in these countries, but the masters forbade them (with occasionally violent results). In London, neither of these situations obtained. The Stationers' Company did admit all involved in the trade, including journeymen, master printers, binders, booksellers, and paper-stationers—in the 1550s, such a comprehensive and stable division of vocations in any case hardly existed.[41] But in doing so it established a strict hierarchy of status. This hierarchy pervaded the culture of the book trade. So prevalent was it that despite their inclusion, the journeymen could cite France, Holland, Italy, and even Spain as countries in which their fellows received more favorable recognition.[42] And the Company of course excluded

39. For the Company's history see Blagden's fine *Stationers' Company*. See also Pollard, "English Market," 19.

40. These too could become instruments of regulation. In 1678 any member found printing an unauthorized book was banned from ever receiving a pension: Stationers' Company, *Registers 1554–1640*, I, 16; SCB C, fol. 234^r; SCB F, fol. 22^r.

41. Kellett, "Breakdown of Gild and Corporation Control," 394; Voet, "Printers' Chapel"; "Note of the State of the Company of Printers, Bookesellers, and Bookebynders comprehended under the name of Stacioners," in Stationers' Company, *Registers 1554–1640*, I, 114–6 and 144, esp. 114.

42. *Brief Discourse Concerning Printing and Printers*, 23.

Ranks	Offices	Support
ASSISTANTS	Master Upper Warden Under Warden	} COURT
	Clerk	
LIVERY	Renter Warden Renter Warden	
COMMONALTY		
	Beadle Porter, or Underbeadle Cook Whifflers, etc.	

FIG. 3.4. The social and administrative structure of the Stationers' Company.

women from all but the lowest ranks. Successful as they might be in printing and bookselling, women could not become grandees as Stationers.

The Stationers' Company, like other London companies, adopted a hierarchy composed of the three ranks of freeman, liveryman, and assistant (fig. 3.4).[43] The lowest of these was freeman, or yeoman. This was the status that one obtained after completing an apprenticeship, normally of seven years, to an existing member of the Company (freemen could bind one apprentice each, liverymen two).[44] In certain circumstances one might also be allowed to "translate" from another company into the Stationers', in which case it was likely, but not inevitable, that one would enter at the rank of freeman. Either way, before being accepted one had to swear an oath to keep the Stationers' customs and consultations secret, and to obey a bylaw

43. On the oligarchic structures of London companies in general, see also Archer, *Pursuit of Stability*, 18 ff., 56–7, 102–11; Rappaport, *Worlds within Worlds*, 215 ff.

44. In one exceptional case a disabled man was allowed out of charity to be bound as an additional apprentice to a freeman. SCB F, fol. 207[r–v]; SCB D, fol. 89[r]; Stationers' Company, *Registers 1554–1640*, I, 166. Attaining freedom after the period of apprenticeship was normally routine, but in exceptional cases the Court of Assistants could refuse it: e.g., SCB C, fol. 270[v]. Sons of Stationers could also be freed by patrimony, but this was a relatively rare occurrence.

against the printing of unlicensed books. Although ritualistic, such an oath was by no means merely a formula. It provided, as David Sabean has put it, "a means of putting a person's eternal life at stake in order to control external behavior," and it was regarded with consonant seriousness. As late as 1690 a Quaker who refused to swear was denied the freedom.[45]

Once past this point, a new freeman entered the main body—or "commonalty"—of the trade.[46] Freemen could now exercise all the crafts of a Stationer, and could also extend the exercise of those crafts into the future by taking apprentices. They enjoyed only limited influence in the Company, however. They were not accorded a voice at its annual assembly, or Common Hall, and being mainly wage-earning journeymen and small booksellers they tended to be acutely vulnerable to the interests of more senior members. They could soon find themselves out of work during lean times, or if a master printer or bookseller decided to risk employing workmen not of the Company. The latter contravened Company rules, but was sometimes done nonetheless. This was the position of the newcomer in Francis Kirkman's story retailed in chapter 2, before he discovered the liberating powers of piracy.

Liverymen, occupying the next rank in the hierarchy, carried far more influence than freemen in the institutions of the Company and the City alike. Under James II there were therefore calls for their loyalty to be ensured by imposing a separate oath on those elected. Elevation was a rare and rather expensive privilege. It cost £20, which could be a substantial barrier, and moreover the choice of individuals to be nominated lay with the existing court of the Company. Under these circumstances, not many Stationers became liverymen. The livery numbered some twenty to thirty at a time in the sixteenth century, and not many more later. Those who were nominated, however, committed an offense if they tried to refuse. They could be fined for their disrespect, and even sued at law if particularly stubborn.[47] The main practical reason for this was that liverymen were liable to be called up for a

45. Stationers' Company, *Registers 1554–1640*, I, 17–19; SCB F, fol. 146ʳ. Seven years later, however, a Quaker was allowed to serve as renter despite his refusal to swear an oath: SCB F, fol. 265ᵛ. For the cultural importance of oaths see, for example, Sabean, *Power in the Blood*, 44; Hill, "From Oaths to Interest"; Langford, *Public Life and the Propertied Englishman*, 102 ff.; and (for their importance in the history of science) Hunter, "Alchemy, Magic and Moralism."

46. Blagden, "Stationers' Company in the Civil War Period," 3; Blagden, *Stationers' Company*, 162, 278; Stationers' Company, *Registers 1554–1640*, I, xli–xliii. This was the highest rank reached by women. Widows of freemen routinely became freewomen, and from the mid-1660s there are also cases of women being admitted by patrimony and apprenticeship. Only in 1937 did women gain equal status in the livery.

47. SCB F, fols. 34ᵛ–35ʳ, 68ᵛ; Stationers' Company, *Registers 1554–1640*, I, xliii, 3–19 (esp. 10), 24; SCB D, fol. 90ᵛ. See also Blagden, "Stationers' Company in the Civil War Period," 3–4.

number of important and onerous duties within the Company. These will
be discussed below.

Freemen and livery alike were under the oversight of the Table of Assistants. This was the court and governing council of the Company: the select
and (usually) honored body entrusted with so many important decisions.
To be elected an assistant was accordingly an honor bestowed upon only a
few approved liverymen.[48] Assistants had to pay a charge for their election,
and supply the court with a suitably formal celebratory dinner. In return,
they attained a position in which it was their privilege to elect almost all
future Company officials, resolve almost all trade disputes, and determine
almost all Company policy. The assistants took virtually all of the decisions
affecting the Stationers as a community, from the appointment of even
minor servants (such as the cook, the underbeadle, and the "Whiflers or
Ushers" needed for ceremonial occasions) to the resolution of piracy allegations. Their number grew as time went on, from about ten in the 1550s
to twenty-eight in 1645; by 1684 there were twenty-six, and a year later a
list of twenty-seven was suggested. But active attendance was almost always
smaller still, and could fall as low as nine.[49] This caused some concern.
As the Company's membership extended beyond active practitioners of the
book trades, it came to be feared that other trades might gain a powerful
voice among the assistants. In 1688 the Table therefore ordered that only
practicing printers, booksellers, or binders could be elected.[50] This reflected
not only the administrative importance of the body, but also its role as a
representation of the craft as a whole.

Perhaps the assistants' most obviously consequential decisions were their
elections for the most senior posts of the Company. They appointed a number of important officers annually, from the ranks of the livery and the assistants themselves. The first such post was that of renter warden, or "renter."
Every year, the assistants selected two renters out of the livery; the junior
renter would normally be promoted to the senior post the following year.
They had to supply a dinner for the assistants and livery on Lord Mayor's
Day, but more than that renters performed a wide range of duties for the
Company. In particular, it was their job to collect both rents owed by its
tenants and "quarterage" owed by its members, this latter being a regular
payment supplying the staple income of the Company. Until 1691 they also

48. Stationers' Company, *Registers 1554–1640*, I, xliv, 7–9, 19. All new assistants were
expected to have served or fined as renter: SCB D, fol. 13[r].

49. SCB D, fol. 13[r]; Stationers' Company, *Registers 1554–1640*, I, 13; SCB D, fol. 223[r].
Elections could be close, as when a beadle was chosen by eight votes to seven in 1660: SCB
D, fol. 56[r–v]. In 1660 the court's quorum was set at nine, in 1676 thirteen: SCB D, fol. 52[r];
SCB E, fols. 18[v]–19[r]; SCB F, fols. 12[r], 13[v]. In 1642 a reformist Master suggested a court of 30,
32, or 34, but no number was agreed on: SCB C, fol. 181[r].

50. SCB F, fol. 98[r].

disbursed payments to the Company's employees.[51] Service in this as in higher offices was in principle obligatory, but it tended to be time consuming and could even prove expensive. There were consequently repeated calls to spread the load by appointing more than two officials. These meeting with no response, many liverymen chose to pay a fine imposed by the court rather than take the trouble of serving. This signaled a courtesy by the court and its recognition by the payer. Common as it became, however, fining was never a right, and the Table could always force recalcitrant members to serve.[52] One reason it might have to do so was that the renter, like other specialist officers, needed a fairly subtle practical knowledge of the workings of the Company and the practices of its members. The lack of such knowledge would be "a great Obstruccon to the Service" a renter could do, and he might even prove worse than useless in what was an important, if unsung, post.[53]

The most important elections the assistants held, however, were those for the Master and wardens, who were chosen from their own ranks. These were elected at the end of June every year—an event celebrated by a venison feast provided by the renters. Usually the election was by balloting box, but if an obvious candidate existed the box might be set aside and the election held by "Generall Vote," as when Sir Thomas Davies was elected during his stint as lord mayor. In 1691, in a move the details of which it would be interesting to know, it was even suggested that the box be burned.[54] The wardens elected by this procedure occupied an extremely important position, celebrated by the lavish election dinner they held annually for the assistants and livery. Second only to the Master, they enjoyed substantial effective autonomy in deciding the construction and effects of court decisions. Wardens were also entrusted with the Company's fortunes in dealing with such vital interlocutors as the printers at Oxford and York, London's Court of Aldermen, and the archbishop of Canterbury. And they were instrumental in exchanges with dangerous litigants such as Richard Atkyns, whom we shall meet again later. Most of all, they oversaw regulatory activities such as searches. Since they could end up in jail as a direct result, they had to be indemnified against legal retribution.[55]

The wardens' practical power was extensive and double-edged in a way

---

51. Stationers' Company, *Registers 1554–1640*, I, 6, 11–12, 21–2; SCB F, fol. 154ʳ. Sometimes a renter would come from the Table, and it was reckoned that by virtue of their additional authority assistants got better rates of collection: SCB C, fol. 254ᵛ.

52. SCB D, fols. 18ᵛ, 24ᵛ, 34ʳ ff.; SCB F, fol. 132ʳ⁻ᵛ. It was also ruled that requests to fine must be made before the actual voting took place: SCB D, fol. 44ᵛ.

53. SCB D, fol. 32ʳ.

54. Stationers' Company, *Registers 1554–1640*, I, 7–8, 18; SCB D, fol. 142ʳ; SCB F, fols. 58ᵛ–59ʳ, 149ʳ; Rivington, "Sir Thomas Davies."

55. SCB C, fol. 246ᵛ; SCB D, fols. 132ᵛ, 219ᵛ.

that was representative of early modern policing practices. A warden had the opportunity to determine the thoroughness with which search orders were executed, and to compile evidence brought before the Stationers' court. He was often the most important figure in regulatory activity of all sorts. Yet that also meant that he could warp seizure processes to his own benefit, for example by conspiring to resell seized stock. There were several accusations of such malpractice, most notoriously those leveled by the radical Francis Smith against Samuel Mearne, a Tory intrudee. In the Civil War, too, Samuel Man had already set "an evill example in regard of trust in the Company" by dealing in the "Counterfeit" books he should have been suppressing. Richard Royston, again, was alleged to have warned Stationers like Andrew Crooke before their premises were searched, and to have resold books that he had seized—even those the sheets of which had been sentenced to become waste paper in the royal kitchens.[56] Their practical independence in such matters as the Atkyns case or the conflict with Oxford again led to claims that they were putting their own interests before those of the Stationers' community.[57] In all, as was widely the case in early modern policing, the effects of the wardenship largely depended on the individual incumbent. Men like Mearne pursued active, not to say adventurous, policies. Royston, on the other hand, was subjected to complaints not only that he was corrupt, but that he was idle too.[58]

For a conscientious warden, service was inevitably time-consuming. It was also likely to prove costly. As with the renter's position, it was sometimes possible to fine rather than serve. But in this case only service could make one eligible to serve as Master. It therefore might well be worth the trouble. The Master was the most honored and powerful individual in the Company. He held the casting vote in the court of assistants, and, less formally, the Table routinely endorsed his suggestions.[59] Under James II both he and the wardens had to take the oaths of Allegiance and Supremacy, such was their practical influence over the conduct of the trade.[60] Within the Company,

56. For Mearne, see Crist, "Francis Smith," 78–88. For other cases see SCB C, fols. 206ʳ, 207ᵛ (Samuel Man, who was elected Master soon after), 236ʳ–237ᵛ (Henry Seile); SCB D, fol. 127ʳ (Octavian Pulleyn and son). Francis Kirkman had made the same claim: above, p. 166.

57. For example, Streater's allegations, in SCB D, fols. 136ʳ ff., 206ʳ, 207ᵛ, 209ᵛ; see also SCB F, fol. 141ᵛ (for Henry Hills's conduct as Master).

58. Hetet, "Wardens' Accounts," 41–3.

59. SCB D, fol. 74ᵛ; Stationers' Company, *Registers 1554–1640*, I, xxx; SCB E, fol. 74ᵛ.

60. There are many examples, e.g., SCB C, fol. 296ʳ, and SCB D, fols. 13ᵛ, 15ʳ. See also below, pp. 317 note 146, 318, for Roper's role in fanning the Atkyns dispute. For oaths, see SCB F, fol. 39ʳ⁻ᵛ. The Master and wardens also had to renounce the Solemn League and Covenant as void and illegal: SCA, Suppl. Documents, Box F, envelope 11. In 1660, too, the court took the oaths: SCB D, fols. 56ᵛ, 59ʳ–61ʳ. The oaths were dispensed with during James II's attempt at toleration: SCB F, fol. 95ʳ.

the few days between the casting of votes for a new Master and the opening of the ballot box were even labeled an "Interregnum"; during this time, some felt, no legitimate court could meet. However, the Master's personal autonomy, like that of the wardens, meant that he was occasionally liable to allegations of corruption. In 1698, for example, Richard Chiswell complained that the Master and bookseller Samuel Smith were pirating his copy of Horace. Earlier, Luke Fawne had objected to the Master's issuing insulting remarks against him (a complaint that sounds trivial, but was less so given the credit and prestige attached to the Master as the personification of the Company: such remarks severely threatened Fawne's all-important good name). And after his deposition and death, it emerged that Henry Hills had been in the habit of excusing, in exchange for a hefty fee and £5 for a dinner, importers whose stock was seized.[61] My impression is that such allegations were rarer than those against the wardens, however, partly because it was generally the latter who actually executed Company policies, and partly because, as mentioned above, the Master was reckoned to represent the entire community of Stationers in his person, so that any attack on his credit was of far graver consequence. Such an attack could indeed be mounted, but to do so was to raise the stakes to a dangerously high level.

Elections to all these positions were not generally determined by candidates' personal qualities. Rather, elevation was normally decided on the basis of precedence. Whoever was "next in course" would routinely fill the position.[62] Precedence was thus an extremely important principle at every level of the Company, not least for the ambitious among the commonalty. Only in elections for wardens and Master was it qualified with any frequency, principally by a concern for political acceptability. Nevertheless, although contests did occur for such positions, precedence meant that the choice was still conventionally limited to a few viable candidates. The combination could therefore lead to some strange-looking decisions, such as the election to the mastership of Henry Hills, a recently condemned producer of illicit Catholic books, or of Richard Royston, who was concurrently being forced to relinquish copies felt to infringe Company rights.[63]

Yet the principle of precedence should not be seen as the sole key to understanding such appointments, since precedence itself remained a contestable concept. Should it be calculated from the date of one's freedom, or

---

61. SCB D, fols. 27ʳ, 75ʳ, 83ʳ; SCB F, fol. 141ᵛ; SCB G, fol. 6ᵛ.

62. SCB C, fol. 289ʳ; SCB D, fols. 2ʳ, 3ᵛ.

63. For Royston, see SCB D, fols. 219ʳ, 220ʳ, 221ʳ, and SCB F, fols. 56ᵛ–57ʳ. Henry Hills was elected shortly after being convicted of producing Catholic almanacs with the queen's approval: SCB F, fols. 65ᵛ, 69ʳ⁻ᵛ, 90ᵛ. His election was evidently seen as politically prudent. One printer of unlicensed books was elected Master five times at the start of the century, however: Kirschbaum, *Shakespeare and the Stationers*, 31.

from that of one's elevation to the livery—and should fining instead of serving in a particular office have any implication for precedence?[64] If a member
had translated from another company, should his seniority in that company
still be valid? So often did individuals press such issues that by the later
seventeenth century they had had a substantial effect on the composition of
the Company's ruling ranks. In practice the existing court decided their outcomes.[65] Precedence itself thus could not determine all issues, as, within
certain conventional limits, the court could redefine precedence to suit its
own ends. For example, if there were not enough candidates of sufficient
vintage for a senior office, the court might render lesser members eligible by
allowing them to fine for several years' service in an inferior position at one
go.[66] Nonetheless, such was the perceived importance of the principle that
the court's verdicts were always finally couched in the language of preserving
precedence.[67] The very insistence on its constancy, it may be inferred, served
to legitimate the court's practical autonomy in determining the Company's
governance.

The court's influence on the hierarchical order of the Company was thus
profound. The assistants alone voted on elections, and liverymen and assistants could not be created without court approval. It is true that there was
opposition to this custom of self-selection: by 1641 Michael Sparke found
strong support for his complaint that "six or 8 of the Eldest Combining,
carry all to their own mark," and the commonalty protested that they too
should participate in the annual elections. But such opposition was neither
consistent nor, more important, successful.[68] Perhaps more consequential
were a number of individual disputes centering on precedence. If a candidate
who felt himself to be entitled to a post on the basis of seniority were overlooked, he might react with explosive anger. In 1653, for example, Samuel
Man complained about his "injury" in not being chosen Master. The assistants in turn resented the "injury" done to them by his angry comments,

64. E.g., SCB D, fols. 23ʳ, 91ᵛ. The Company decided that service took precedence over
fining, basing its decision on the custom of the Court of Aldermen. For the controversy
surrounding John Streater's election, see SCB D, fols. 33ᵛ, 43ᵛ, 45ʳ.

65. SCB E, fol. 71ʳ. However, in practice measurements of precedence were controversial,
and it was the court that decided on competing claims: Stationers' Company, *Registers 1554–
1640*, I, 6, 9–10, 24; SCB D, fols. 23ʳ, 91ᵛ. Compare SCB F, fols. 155ʳ–156ʳ, 174ᵛ ff. for the
case of Giles Sussex.

66. E.g., for upper warden: SCB C, fol. 225ʳ⁻ᵛ.

67. For cases showing the importance of seniority and its dependence on the conventions
of the court, see, for example, SCB C, fol. 241ᵛ; SCB D, fols. 23ʳ, 33ᵛ, 43ᵛ, 71ᵛ, 91ʳ, 95ʳ; SCB
E, fols. 115ʳ ff., 130ʳ.

68. SCB D, fol. 141ᵛ; SCB E, fol. 130ᵛ; SCB F, fols. 95ʳ, 117ʳ, 127ᵛ; Blagden, "Stationers'
Company in the Civil War Period," 8; SCB C, fols. 203ᵛ–204ʳ. On electorates and electoral
procedure in London companies, see Archer, *Pursuit of Stability*, 102–11. For reformers' use
of piracy, see above, p. 171.

and he soon withdrew his "hasty & unadvised language."[69] A series of such conflicts raged in the Restoration, following attempts by the crown to "intrude" into assistantships a number of Stationers whose politics were approved and who, it was hoped, would be active in using Company procedures to quell opposition publishing.[70] In such arguments precedence and royal prerogative clashed ominously.

As such conflicts implied, the implications of this ladder of hierarchy and precedence extended far beyond the Company itself. The Stationers were acutely conscious of their place in a larger, City-wide, order—and, through that, of their place in the universal social ranking of Stuart England. This position was regularly displayed in ceremonial and ritual performances. Official processions, church ceremonies, and feasts commemorated the Stationers' Company in its urban and national location.[71] And like those of the other London corporations, the Company's charter formally linked its structure to those of both civic and monarchical power.[72] This meant that there were two possible routes of access to higher authority, leading to the lord mayor and to the king. These routes were open in both directions. In the event of irreconcilable discord within the Company itself, Stationers could appeal upward to these superior powers; and they in turn could decide for themselves to intervene in Company activities. Each was rare, but neither was unknown. Disputes over precedence, in particular, were taken very seriously by the first of these powers, the City authorities. The lord mayor took a dim view of violations of seniority, since they undermined the hierarchical order that in theory unified his City. The mayor was the highest civic authority to which parties aggrieved in this respect could generally appeal.[73] Provided they enjoyed the right contacts, though, members could also apply in extremis to the crown itself—the other power to which the Company was linked. In the 1680s, for example, a precedence dispute went as far as

69. SCB C, fol. 283ʳ. Man was rewarded with election in 1654 and 1658.

70. *Impartial Protestant Mercury* 60 (18 November 1681); Harris, *London Crowds*, 154.

71. SCB C, fols. 287ʳ, 290ᵛ; SCB D, fols. 54ᵛ, 70ʳ, 78ʳ; SCB E, fols. 31ᵛ, 70ᵛ, 72ʳ. For London's constitution see Pearl, *London*, 49–68; de Krey, "London Radicals." For a sermon preached to the Company see Whitfield, *Sermon on the death of the late Lord Bishop of London*. The Company was particularly concerned for the position of its pew in Saint Paul's: SCB D, fol. 109ʳ. The importance of this issue is strikingly demonstrated by Gough, *History of Myddle*, 77–84, in which a floor plan of the pews in the local church becomes in effect both a social map of the local community and a table of contents for the book itself; see also Underdown, *Revel, Riot, and Rebellion*, 29–33.

72. Stationers' Company, *Registers 1554–1640*, I, 3–19; Feather, *History of British Publishing*, 31 ff.; Soman, "Press, Pulpit and Censorship," 442. For the legal status of charters see Levin, *Charter Controversy*.

73. For various complaints, see SCB C, fols. 224ʳ⁻ᵛ, 251ʳ, 290ᵛ; SCB D, fols. 18ᵛ, 24ᵛ, 34ʳ, 118ᵛ, 206ʳ; SCB E, fol. 9ʳ; SCB F, fols. 134ᵛ, 136ʳ, 140ʳ, 150ʳ. See also Archer, *Pursuit of Stability*, 54–7.

the Privy Council. To pursue this course was obviously to play a very powerful card indeed.[74] But while appeals flowed one way, power flowed the other. As superior elements in a single political fabric, both the mayor and the king could intervene in Company affairs, for example by intruding members into assistantships—and both tried to do so. The court might resent such interference as infringing on the craft's customary order, but could not ultimately prevent it. When, for example, the lord mayor tried to intrude one Giles Sussex, the court at first indignantly refused to accept his order. They were "under a publique trust for the weale of the Company," the assistants protested, and such an intervention put at risk their sworn duties to the trade; they could never accept it, either "as Christians, as English men, as free Citizens, or as Station[rs]." The Master and wardens were interned in Newgate for daring to voice such insubordination.[75]

The relation between the Stationers' internal hierarchy and civic and national authority was not simply linear, however. There was also an intended *parallel* between Company government and such grander political structures. So, for example, the king presided over the Privy Council, or over the House of Lords and House of Commons, as the mayor over the Courts of Aldermen and Common Council, and as the Master over the assistants and commonalty. Thus Thomas Delaune percipiently remarked that the administration of the London companies by master, wardens, and assistants should "exactly correspond with the general Government of the City, by a Lord *Mayor, Aldermen,* and *Common-Councel . . .* so excellent a *harmony* there is in this Government." An anonymous writer likewise observed that Common Council was "as the *Parliament* of our *City,* and our *Mayor* as the *King* thereof, and our *Aldermen,* as the Peers, the *Commonalty* the *Commons* thereof." This meant that the practices and procedures of one form of government were, ideally, to be mirrored in others. Arguments drawn from the customs of one court could consequently prove effective in guiding the determinations of another, lower one, even when no actual jurisdiction was being imposed by the former on the latter.[76] To deploy arguments over precedence was in effect to adduce this entire wider culture of governance.

As just observed, the Stationers displayed their place in this network of power in an endless round of ceremonies. In early modern Europe, spurning ritual amounted to declaring oneself outside society—it therefore, on Aristotelian grounds, made one less than human. This was certainly true of Stationers. Ceremonies played a vital part in the Company's calendar, both

---

74. Crist, "Francis Smith," 236–43; SCB D, fols. 7[v] (for an appeal to Cromwell), 215[r].

75. SCB C, fols. 251[r], 254[v], 265[r-v]; SCB E, fols. 63[r]–69[v], 113[r] ff., 142[v]; SCB F, fols. 9[v], 175[v]–176[r] (see also fols. 155[r]–156[r], 174[r]–175[v]); Blagden, *Stationers' Company,* 158.

76. Delaune, *Angliae Metropolis,* 308; *London's Lamentation*; SCB D, fol. 23[r]. Compare also the use of the seal: SCB D, fols. 21[v]–22[r], 136[v].

FIG. 3.5. The Stationers' Company barge. (By permission of the Master and Wardens of the Worshipful Company of Stationers and Newspaper-Makers.)

celebrating and helping to constitute its proud communal identity. Funerals provided one occasion for such rituals. When King's Printer Thomas Newcomb died, for example, his body lay in Stationers' Hall overnight. His funeral cortège was accompanied out of the hall the following morning by a ceremonial hearse bearing his arms and pulled by a team of six in full regalia, "Eight or Ten Divines," six high-ranking pallbearers, at least forty relations, the assistants "in their Formalities," and about two hundred "Gentlemen," including both Stationers and others. The statement of substance was unmistakable.[77] Royal and mayoral processions called for even greater displays of pageantry, sometimes involving the Company's barge (fig. 3.5).[78] Feasts, too, such as the one provided every May Day at Stationers' Hall, served to increase "love and good Neighbourhood" in the trade. They were apparently taken seriously as embodying and reinforcing harmonious coexistence.[79] In addition, senior Stationers, especially the Master and wardens,

77. Sabean, *Power in the Blood,* 38–40; *Impartial Protestant Mercury* 73 (30 December 1681–3 January 1681/2).

78. The Company's first recorded use of a barge was in 1662 for a royal procession (SCB D, fol. 76ʳ). This was a hired vessel; only in 1679 did the Company obtain its own. Blagden, *Stationers' Company,* 261. On London processions as spectacles of power, see also Backscheider, *Spectacular Politics,* 4–29, 37–56.

79. Moxon, *Mechanick Exercises on the Whole Art of Printing,* 329–30; Howell, *Londinopolis,* 46; Archer, *Pursuit of Stability,* 54, 74, 84, 116–9.

were expected to donate plate to the Company. Such donations likewise served "to encourage & keep up ye Governm^t. of the Company," and their bequest was encouraged. Throughout, great importance was attached to propriety of comportment and sobriety of conduct. Since the whole craft and its community were assumed to be represented on such occasions, assistants knew that gowns must be worn "for the better Goverment of this Company," and rudeness was severely deprecated. In particular, to use "rude & saucy Language" to the Master was to insult the art and mystery of printing itself.[80]

In addition to the formal hierarchy of commonalty, livery, and assistants, a marked ordering of labor and livelihoods was also developing within the Stationers' community. As remarked in chapter 2, it was similar to distinctions that were appearing at much the same time in several other London corporations. Compared to journeymen and printers, "privileged" master printers (that is, those possessed of royal grants conveying particular printing rights) enjoyed a pronounced enhancement in wealth and status from the mid–sixteenth century. More significant, from soon after this time the booksellers began to achieve an ascendancy that would last until at least the mid–eighteenth century. Theirs was the prosperity produced by printing, and they increasingly dominated the upper ranks of the Stationers' Company. Complaints of the booksellers' disproportionate influence thus arose from as early as the 1580s, and intensified for at least the next hundred years.[81] At length, it became difficult even for successful master printers to rise to the pinnacle of the Company's hierarchy. As a result, it was increasingly the bookselling interest that presided over the regulation and representation of Stationers during this pivotal period. By 1663, journeymen complained, booksellers had grown so "bulkie and numerous" that "there is hardly one Printer to ten others that have a share in the Government of the Company." The transformation threatened to prove radical. A Company that had been chartered "in favor of Printers, and for their encouragement and security" was now in the hands of an entirely different group, and one pursuing a potentially antagonistic "interest." With booksellers in charge, it was said, even those printers who did reach the rank of assistant "either dare not stand for the Interest of Printing, for fear of losing a Work-Master; or will not, because they have an interest among them." The new hierarchy further destabilized the printers by hiring "forreiner[s]" and granting them

---

80. SCB D, fol. 18^v; SCB F, fols. 2^r, 46^r, 56^{r-v}; Stationers' Company, *Registers 1554–1640*, I, 5–6, 13–14. Something of the Company's ritual is described in Moxon, *Mechanick Exercises on the Whole Art of Printing*, 329 ff. For breaches of etiquette see SCB C, fols. 232^v, 238^r, 243^r.

81. Stationers' Company, *Registers 1554–1640*, I, 114–6; Blagden, "Stationers' Company in the Civil War Period," 6–7.

the freedom to "usurp the exercise of the Printers calling." They had even erected a printing house themselves, "by a joynt stock of their own, and call it, *The Companies House*." To compound this, unlike other City companies, the Stationers maintained no yeomanry organization. There was thus no regular forum in which lesser members could voice views different from those of what was fast coming to seem a de facto élite superimposing itself on the Company's de jure oligarchy.[82]

This brief analysis of the Company's structure and ambiance shows why its members so willingly took their problems to Stationers' Hall. It suggests why they sought and respected the court's arbitration, and also, paradoxically, why that same court's decisions were increasingly likely to cause controversy. On the one hand, every element of Company structure and ceremony served to reinforce the impression that the court of assistants, and in particular the Master, represented the entire craft community. Declining its mediation therefore implied placing oneself outside the civil polity of the trade—making oneself an outlaw, as it were. On the other, concerns about precedence and oligarchy vitiated this representation, and hence reduced the respect accorded some court pronouncements. Furthermore, given the interlocking character of the practices and representations prevalent in the Company, what disputes did arise were always open to construal as attacks on its fundamental culture—and thereby on a far wider polity. Conflicts that originated within the Stationers' community could readily extend to implicate the very security of the city and the nation. In one respect this prospect became reality.

THE STATIONERS' REGISTER AND THE MAXIMS OF "PROPRIETY"

Central to the Stationers' civility was the Register Book of Copies—or, by association with its distinctive location, the "Hall Book" (fig. 3.6). This was a handwritten volume, held by the clerk and producible by him before the court.[83] By Company custom, what Stationers called a "copy" belonged to the member concerned once he or she had "entered" it in this volume. Entrance provided a perpetual tenure based in Company convention. The register was thus an archive of such conventional freeholds, extending back to the very foundation of the Company. Its authority depended on the power of Company custom.

82. *Brief Discourse Concerning Printing and Printers*, 3, 4, 5–6, 12; *London Printers Lamentation*, 2. Blagden, "Stationers' Company in the Civil War Period," 5–7, includes comparative figures on the numbers of booksellers and printers occupying senior posts throughout the period.

83. From 1693 he was expected to bring it to every meeting: SCB F, fol. 192ᵛ.

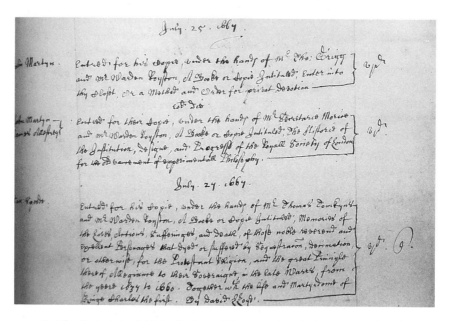

FIG. 3.6. The Register Book of the Stationers' Company. A typical entry, recording the title to Thomas Sprat's *History of the Royal Society*. (By permission of the Master and Wardens of the Worshipful Company of Stationers and Newspaper-Makers.)

Once entered, a copy could be "assigned" to other members in a variety of ways. It could be sold, exchanged, mortgaged, or even subdivided into shares.[84] But the entry itself remained on record as the authoritative documentation of customary right. The system meant that securing the status of a given title could involve considerable research. L'Estrange's translation of Josephus, for instance, was almost consigned to oblivion by a partnership of rival booksellers tracing their ownership to an entrance made nearly a century earlier.[85] And the register continued to be referred to as authoritative even after its formal regulatory function had declined. In 1729 Jacob Tonson still believed that he could discover the time of printing of Congreve's *Old Bachelor* by searching for its entry in "the Hall Book." Although not all published titles were entered in the register, then, those that were gained a powerful genealogy of recorded legitimacy. This authority had consequences, however, for their texts. After the Fire in 1666, Evelyn told Clarendon regretfully that "our Book-sellers follow their owne judgment in

84. For good examples of assignments, see SCB F, fols. 87ʳ (L'Estrange's translations) and 196ʳ⁻ᵛ (Sare's *Turkish Spy*).

85. Kirschbaum, *Shakespeare and the Stationers*, 56. Compare the case of Daniel's *Historie*: SCB F, fols. 44ʳ–47ᵛ, 71ʳ⁻ᵛ, 77ᵛ.

printing the antient Authors according to such Text as they found extant when first they entred their Copy." This meant not only that the better texts recovered by scholars remained unpublished, but that "Errors repeate & multiply in every Edition."[86] Here was a paradox typical of the Stationers' commonwealth: that a régime depending on the absolute constancy of a written manuscript resulted in unreliable inconstancy in its printed products.

There is a sense in which modern historians have not forgotten the register. Several studies of the conventions surrounding entrance and publication appeared after Edward Arber published his edition of the major registers in 1875–94, particularly in the first decades of the twentieth century. However, such studies concentrated exclusively on determining whether certain canonical literary (and especially dramatic) works were "really" piracies. They attempted to establish or reject the authorship of such books, being inspired to follow this method primarily by the first folio's condemnation of preceding Shakespeare editions as "stolne, and surreptitious copies, maimed, and deformed by the frauds and stealthes of injurious imposters, that expos'd them." "Perhaps no line of Shakespeare's has been more carefully scrutinized" than this of his booksellers, remarks Margreta de Grazia, so that "nothing less than the status of the Shakespearean texts has depended on whether Heminge and Condell's claim has been regarded as factually true or false."[87] The aim of such studies, then, was to produce a verdict on the worth of a small clutch of texts. Important though this aim was, it meant that they fell foul of the criticisms advanced in chapter 2 against treatments of piracy that begin from the assumption that there is a constant definition of the concept. They did not appreciate the dynamic, constructive role of the practices and processes by which seventeenth-century parties themselves worked to establish or dispute the credit of printed books. Those early twentieth-century studies can still be valuable, provided they are read with their purpose in mind. However, there has until now been nothing resembling a detailed analysis of the strategies of accreditation practiced in the seventeenth-century Stationers' world, and nothing at all on their development between around 1620 and the first so-called Copyright Act of 1710.[88]

86. Hodges, *William Congreve*, 149–50; Peters, *Congreve, the Drama, and the Printed Word*, 11–12; Evelyn, *Memoirs*, II, 225.

87. Shakespeare, *Complete Works*, xliii; De Grazia, *Shakespeare Verbatim*, 43.

88. See especially: Pollard, *Shakespeare's Fight with the Pirates*; Greg, *Shakespeare First Folio*; Greg, "Entrance, Licence and Publication"; Greg, *Some Aspects and Problems*, 63–81, 89–102; Simpson, "Literary Piracy"; Greg, "*Ad Imprimendum Solum*"; Kirschbaum, *Shakespeare and the Stationers*; Sisson, "Laws of Elizabethan Copyright." Ransom, *First Copyright Statute*, was more general in scope. For effects on textual content, see also Orgel, "Authentic Shakespeare"; Loewenstein, "Script in the Marketplace"; Williams, *Craft of Printing*. See also Feather, *Publishing, Piracy and Politics*, 17–20, 24–28, 32.

The precise format of an entrance in the register varied slightly, but in
essentials it remained much the same over the period. The owner—usually
a Stationer, but in rare instances the writer or even another figure altogether—had to come to the hall in person, with notification by a licenser
and a warden that the text was acceptable. He or she then paid the clerk
sixpence for the entrance. To choose an example at something less than
random, this entrance appeared in 1667:

Mr John Martyn	Entred for their Copie, under the hands	
Mr James	of Mr Secretarie Morice and Mr Warden	vi d.
Allestrey	Royston, A Booke or Copie Intituled, The	
	Historie of the Institution, Designe, and	
	Progresse of the Royall Society of London	
	for the Advancement of experimentall	
	Philosophy.[89]	

Here Thomas Sprat's *History of the Royal Society* was entered to the Printers
to the Royal Society, John Martyn and James Allestry, under a license by
Secretary of State William Morrice and with Company approval granted by
the warden, Richard Royston. The fee of sixpence (vi d.) was recorded. The
writer's name was not mentioned, and the title recorded for the book, although quoted *in extenso*, was not exact—implying perhaps that the title
page, at least, had not yet been printed.

Once made, an entry like this became the documentary foundation of
a vast range of potential future acts. It might simply lapse into unread
oblivion. On the other hand, it could become the guarantee on which a
valuable property could be built, or a legal testament to the responsibility of
the Stationer for the work, or even evidence in a piracy complaint. Given
such possibilities, and especially if a work were likely to be subjected to
reprinting, it paid to choose the wording of the entry wisely. One list of
entries made in 1669 thus included such details as whether or not an edition
contained notes, how many sheets it comprised, and which specific translation was referred to. All these elements were thereby included in the definition of their respective copies. Yet specificity of this order could itself be
double-edged, since it could be taken to imply that only literal copies would
be illegitimate; it was sometimes better to be vague in wording an entry, and
rely on subsequent negotiations in the Stationers' court to establish the es-

---

89. SCA, Register Book F: Entries of Copies 1656/7–1682/3, p. 335; Stationers' Company,
Registers 1640–1708, II, 379. It is at first sight puzzling that Sprat's work should have been
entered, since Martyn and Allestry had the Royal Society's privilege. That they had to protect
their copy illustrates well the relative authority of Company custom and Royal Society
prerogative.

sential identity between rival publications.[90] Only two other variable features merit notice here. The first is what came to be called a *salvo*. This was a Latin clause—"*Salvo iure cuiuscunque*" (everyone's right being preserved)—qualifying an entrance as inferior to any earlier title that might later be rediscovered.[91] Toward the end of the century it became customary to add this clause to all entrances in an attempt to mitigate conflicts. The other change worthy of remark occurred after 1695, when the Press Act lapsed for the last time. Licenses were thenceforth not required, and only the warden's approval was generally subjoined.

The clerk's part in the process of entrance was central. He was an unavoidable gatekeeper guarding access to the register, and thus to what passed for property in the Stationers' commonwealth. In 1676 the Company even ruled that no book could be publicized in any catalogue unless licensed and entered under the clerk's signature.[92] Yet he was scarcely ever referred to publicly. One of the very few authors who did mention him was Samuel Butler, who described the "Modern Critic" as one who "fancies himself Clerk of *Stationers-Hall*, and nothing must pass Current, that is not entered by him." It was an apt comparison, juxtaposing as it did criticism with clerkship. For Butler knew that it was the clerk, as the official on the scene, who in practice decided whether a proposed entry would be permitted. He was certainly entitled to refuse entrance if he were suspicious, and there is evidence that the possible grounds for suspicion included textual content. Parliament effectively recognized as much in 1643, when it vested in the clerk the impressive duty of licensing all small pamphlets.[93] Moreover, his importance did not end with the moment of entrance. The Company and individuals alike relied on the clerk's intimate knowledge of the register whenever disputes over entries arose. This was the case both before every entry was made, when his role was routine and unrecorded, and whenever rights to a copy were disputed in the Stationers' court. Nobody else possessed such knowledge, partly because the clerk alone had uninterrupted casual access to the register, and partly because its many thousands of entries remained both unindexed and without cross-references.

There is ample evidence of the clerk's exercising such powers. Nathaniel Ponder threatened to sue him over one instance, when he refused to enter

90. SCB D, fol. 151ʳ. Individual Stationers could divide copies by private agreements, but these were liable to fuel disputes: SCB D, fol. 27ʳ⁻ᵛ.

91. SCB D, fol. 37ʳ; SCB F, fol. 218ᵛ. For an example in English, see Stationers' Company, *Registers 1640–1708*, II, 408.

92. SCB E, fol. 34ᵛ. In 1664 the clerk, George Tokefield, had actually printed his *Catalogue of such Books as have been Entered in the Register of the Company of Stationers*, which he promised to continue annually.

93. Butler, *Characters*, 182; Firth and Rait, *Acts and Ordinances*, I, 186.

Marvell's *Rehearsall Transpros'd*. His refusal was presumably based on the clerk's assessment of the text's political references, and the Company indemnified him for his decision.[94] He also refused to allow a dictionary because it might jeopardize not only other editions of the same dictionary, but different dictionaries too.[95] And the clerk denied Stationer Thomas Vere a view of the register when he arrived late one night claiming that he wished to check an entry to the Company's "English Stock." Alerted by this, he forthwith sued Vere for selling "counterfeit" almanacs. In addition, the clerk was also entitled to refuse what were called *assignments*—that is, transfers of the rights recorded in entries to other individuals or partnerships. He exercised this prerogative when Michael Sparke tried to reassign a medical work in 1653. Sparke provided substantial written evidence, but the clerk denied his assignment on the grounds that it should have been a "public" transaction, vetted by the assistants.[96]

On the other hand, the clerk's powers also extended to the positive acceptance of entrances for projected books for which no text yet existed. Booksellers could thus insure themselves against rivals long before a proposed publication. By entering a generalized title, they could prevent the subsequent entrance of competing books on a given subject. This has since become known as a *blocking* entrance. A similar tactic was to print the text of a small part of an author's work, but enter it under a grandiose title anticipating the appearance of later texts; the Stationer would then own those texts before they had even been written. Or, less formally, the clerk could simply agree with a Stationer not to allow a rival to register a title on a given topic. Such an agreement was known as a *caveat*; it constituted an unwritten compact between the clerk and the favored Stationer. Some caveats were recognized, even ordered, by the Stationers' court. The notorious Peter Cole made full use of these strategies: a generic entrance he made in 1646 of Jeremiah Burroughs's sermons, he then "having not any of the Sermons," blocked a real edition from being produced thirteen years later. At the Restoration, Cole claimed to have spent upwards of £5,000 in entering and preparing for the press medical books that rivals alleged to be equally spurious. His requested exemption from the licensing provisions of the Press Act was not forthcoming, and he later committed suicide as a bankrupt.[97]

94. SCB D, fol. 210ᵛ. For Ponder see Hill, *Turbulent, Seditious and Factious People*, 289–90.

95. SCB D, fol. 51ᵛ. The court agreed with the clerk in his decision.

96. SCB C, fols. 275ᵛ, 297ʳ; SCB F, fols. 44ᵛ, 71ʳ⁻ᵛ; Sisson, "Laws of Elizabethan Copyright." In 1677 the court effectively delegated much of its active oversight of assignments to the clerk by ruling that he alone must compose and submit all such documents for its approval: SCB D, fol. 238ʳ; SCB E, fol. 47ʳ, repeated in SCB E, fol. 95ʳ.

97. SCB D, fols. 46ʳ–50ᵛ; Greg, *Some Aspects and Problems*, 112–22. For Cole's adventures see also SCB C, fols. 197ʳ, 230ʳ, 269ᵛ, 271ʳ⁻ᵛ; Blagden, "'Company' of Printers," esp. 6–7,

On such a scale, strategies of entrance thus had serious repercussions. Heresiographer Thomas Edwards reported sectarian bookseller Richard Overton using a similar tactic for slightly different purposes, when Overton tried to intimidate Edwards by telling him that a reply to his *Gangraena* had been entered and must therefore be about to appear. In fact it was never published. "I never knew before now, that books were entred into the Hall-Book, but just when they were going to the presse," Edwards commented. The clerk could make it so.[98]

The register was a textual record of great authority. Yet its practical use depended on unwritten, individual knowledge and face-to-face conversations. In those skills lay the potential both to establish and to destroy what later historians would come to call literary property.[99] Only under James II, when the campaign against poorly regulated printing was at its height, did the Table move to restrain this situation. It tried to make the clerk keep a waste book of candidate entrances, which would be vetted by the court before being transferred to the authoritative register. The mechanism would have secured the register within the court's purview. But it was both cumbersome and legally dubious, and it seems to have been short-lived. In 1698 the court tried again. By this time the register system was anyway beginning to lose its efficacy, but the court moved to lessen reliance on the clerk's unique knowledge by ordering all new assignments to be cross-referenced to relevant previous entries. Again the attempt was unsuccessful. The clerk maintained his unique position—one that, when he finally retired, had to be filled by a committee of no less than seventeen senior Stationers.[100]

The authority of the register originated in Company convention, and not directly in the law of the land. Successive legal measures did enjoin the entrance of copies,[101] but these were generally measures to fix the enterer's responsibility for content so as to give the state someone to prosecute, not attempts to establish literary property per se.[102] This, in all probability, was

---

17; Poynter, "Nicholas Culpeper." Cole had provided unlicensed books and information on religious radicals to Thomas Edwards: Edwards, *Gangraena*, 82–3, 111–2. His suicide is recorded in PRO SP 44/22, p. 328.

98. SCB D, fol. 50ᵛ; Edwards, *Second Part of Gangraena*, 110. The convention Edwards referred to was what permitted—and still permits—the use of ancient register entrances as rough guides to the timing of long-past publications. For examples of caveats, and arguments against them, see SCB D, fols. 29ᵛ, 51ᵛ, and SCB G, fols. 25ʳ, 27ʳ⁻ᵛ. For blocking entrances see also Kirschbaum, *Shakespeare and the Stationers*, 10, 14, 46–7, and Ransom, *First Copyright Statute*, 40–1 (involving Wolfe).

99. E.g., SCB C, fol. 297ʳ; SCB F, fols. 44ᵛ, 71ʳ⁻ᵛ.

100. SCB F, fols. 81ᵛ–82ʳ, 157ʳ, 184ᵛ; SCB G, fol. 6ᵛ.

101. Stationers' Company, *Registers 1554–1640*, IV, 530; Firth and Rait, *Acts and Ordinances*, I, 185, II, 249, 251; 14 Car. II, c. 33, § 2; Greg, *Shakespeare First Folio*, 31.

102. For this crucial distinction, see Chartier, *Order of Books*, chap. 2, and Foucault, "What Is an Author?" 108–11. Although disputes had to be heard at the Stationers' court

also Sir Roger L'Estrange's real reason for insisting upon entries' being made: he wanted to be able to identify immediately the Stationer responsible for any questionable book by addressing himself to one central location. There is little evidence that L'Estrange devoted himself to the pursuit of Stationers solely for their omitting to enter copies, although when he sought them for other reasons a failure to have made an entrance did provide convenient evidence, and perhaps grounds for arrest.

Even within the Company itself the register did not enjoy unambiguous recognition. The decision to enter a title was in effect an act of civility by the Stationer to his or her community, signaling acknowledgment of its mores. It testified to willingness to abide by the Company's conventions. Not until 1682 did the court itself stipulate compulsory entrance, and then only at L'Estrange's prompting. Violation of an entrance had become formally punishable slightly earlier.[103] Before that time, and in practice thereafter, not all books that were printed were also registered. Far from it: estimates vary widely, but it seems that perhaps a third of printed titles were never entered.[104] Such unentered books, once published, could still sometimes be defended against piracy, since the Stationers' court might take well-attested first publication as implying a practical moral right. But there was no guarantee of this. A printer or bookseller who declined to enter a title was therefore taking a risk. One case in which that risk might be worthwhile would be that of a very small pamphlet addressing a local and immediate issue. Such a title might not be reckoned worth the fee for entrance: its viable lifetime would be very short in any case, and the risk of a pirate venturing to reproduce it in that lifetime correspondingly small. Nonetheless, unentered titles *might* be counterfeited, and the counterfeits *might well* flourish unhindered. Civility aside, piracy was one of the greatest incentives for entrance.

It was in the event of a dispute that entrance proved invaluable, since it set the terms for investigation and adjudication. That is, while it could not guarantee impunity from piracy, it could promise a recognized protocol for reaching a peaceful and proper conclusion when piracy was alleged to have

---

before they could become legal cases, the Company did maintain standing counsel for such events, and on the rare occasions when members refused to acknowledge the court's authority was prepared to use it: e.g., SCB D, fol. 58ᵛ. Such counsel included the recorder of London (SCB D, fol. 4ʳ), and from 1696 the attorney general and solicitor general were retained to help in the struggle against pirates: SCB F, fol. 243ᵛ; SCB G, fol. 70ᵛ. Whig publisher Richard Janeway was one of the few to deny the Stationers' court's authority, but even he soon conformed: SCB E, fol. 146ʳ, 150ʳ.

103. Stationers' Company, *Registers 1554–1640*, I, 22–4, 26. Symmons asked that the entrance to him of Charles I's works be deleted less than a month before the battle of Worcester; he was presumably anxious to avoid allegations of responsibility for the text: SCB C, fol. 265ᵛ. Dunton could still claim ignorance in 1690: SCB F, fol. 148ᵛ.

104. Gaskell, *New Introduction*, 183–5; Greg, "Entrance, Licence and Publication."

occurred. Without entrance, on the other hand, printers and booksellers might find themselves plunged into combat with swarming competitors, and committed to enduring ruinous legal costs in tortuous attempts to protect their investments. The likely result, bankruptcy, had harrowing consequences. We know of several Stationers who died penniless, their personal and financial credit fatally impaired after an encounter with piracy. Even in debtors' prison they could not escape moralism, moreover, with bankrupt Stationers like Samuel Speed continuing to produce their wholesome homilectics from within the jail itself. On the whole, it seemed better to stay solvent, and to place one's faith in the morality of the register.[105]

The recognized protocol signaled by entrance was that of the Stationers' court. All complaints had to pass through this tribunal before they could be referred to the wider legal system. In such matters the Stationers' court thus operated as a largely autonomous body. Over the course of more than a century, it developed its own principles of argument and its own archive of precedents.[106] No other body even approached the expertise of this court in dealing with every element of print culture. This had several important implications, not least because the Stationers' court had a different purpose from a court of law. In incidents not involving the Company's own assets, at least, it tried to reach compromises, even on rather Solomonic terms. Principal courts of law, on the other hand, often labored to establish hard distinctions, separating culprit from victim once and for all. The Stationers' court's procedures were those of a commercial and civil conversation, the primary imperative being to pacify antagonists by consent rather than to distinguish a felon and execute a punishment. Only when the Company itself was plaintiff did this cease to be the case. The moral and commercial order of printing and printed books was consequently constructed in terms appropriate to this domain, and not, say, in the language of natural rights to which eighteenth-century polemics would later resort.

All printed books were subject to this régime. Like an institutional Francis Bacon, it took all knowledge to be its province. In practice, records report the Stationers' court's engaging in debate over works as diverse as Walton's *Compleat Angler*, bills of lading from the Port of London, innumerable almanacs, the works of Cato, Latin grammars, a *Clavis Americae*, the Bible, books of palmistry, and Spenser's *Shepheards Calendar*.[107] Many more could be listed. No type of printed material, of whatever size, shape, or cost, was in principle beyond the jurisdiction of the court. Indeed, parties who

105. Speed, *Prison-Pietie*; Streater, Cole, Pitt, and Francis Smith were among those falling to bankruptcy.

106. E.g., SCB F, fols. 194[v]–196[r].

107. SCB C, fols. 279[r], 283[r], 281[r], 282[v], 285[r], 287[r], 287[v], 292[v].

refused its arbitration on such grounds would be construed as admitting misdemeanor thereby, since they would be placing *themselves* outside the morality of print. In one particularly delicate case concerning biblical annotations the court did try to refer a complainant to Parliament, but even then the speaker simply returned the case straight back to the Master and wardens.[108]

In the court, ownership of a publication was routinely called "propriety." In the seventeenth century the words *propriety* and *property* were virtual synonyms, of course, and they share an etymology from the Latin *proprius*. Nonetheless, the usage reminds us that in the Stationers' community offenses against the property enshrined by convention in the register were seen simultaneously as offenses against proper conduct. That is, they were genuinely, necessarily, and unavoidably contraventions of propriety, undermining the intricate web of conventions and credit by which a craft was sustained.[109] More even than the court itself, the register thus came to epitomize the Stationers' representation that theirs was a respectable, even moral, art. And this representation was rooted in everyday practice, since disputes over "propriety" were among the court's most common business.

Typically, a Stationer would arrive claiming that some other bookseller or printer was comprinting a title he or she had already entered in the register. This may have taken courage: "the Complainant shall be sure to have his Copy re-Printed out of spite," warned Henry Parker, so that "the ruine of himself and family, is made the reward of his zeal and forwardnesse."[110] The allegation having been made, however, the beadle, the clerk, or, in serious cases, a warden would be dispatched to the alleged offender's printing house to stop any more work from being done on the piece in question, and he or she would be summoned to reply to the complaint. If the printer or bookseller thus summoned denied the charge, then the issue would generally be delegated to a small group of supposedly neutral "umpires" or "referees." These would be expected to investigate and report, and if possible to resolve the conflict quietly. The members of this group would be selected either by the court (in which case a warden would generally be included) or else by the consent of both sides in the argument, each side nominating half of the referees. Both parties had to agree over its composition before the group could begin to act.[111] The referees would then interview all involved,

---

108. SCB D, fols. 9ʳ, 47ʳ⁻ᵛ.

109. Compare comments in Rose, *Authors and Owners*, 17–19. In fact, the word *propriety* attained its fully moral connotation only in the mid–eighteenth century.

110. [Parker], *Humble Remonstrance*, sig. A3ʳ.

111. The same procedure was also used for resolving other disputes, even those of permanent significance for the future of the Company: SCB C, fols. 198ʳ, 211ᵛ, 218ᵛ, 222ᵛ; SCB D, fols. 5ʳ, 7ʳ (art. 4), 131ᵛ, 168ʳ.

and ask the clerk to inform them of any relevant previous entrance in the register. This done, they would attempt to find a solution acceptable, if no more than that, to all sides. If unable to broker such a settlement, they would then report back to the Table. In such cases the complainant might be given permission to go to law. More commonly, however, the Table would impose its own idea of a resolution, determined by the Master and wardens. In the pursuit of peace, its solutions in such cases tended to satisfy no party immediately involved. It is an indication of the social authority of the court that they were never rejected.

The mere existence of a previous entry would not necessarily be conclusive in this context. An entry could rarely be so clear that an accusation could not in principle be mounted against a given book, since whether the later publication repeated *essential* material from that referred to in the entry could always be disputed. At the same time, it was rare for even a generalized entry to be so broad in scope that an alleged piracy could not be defended as falling outside its definition. In many controversies, then, the issue could not be decided simply by establishing an identity or difference between titles. The alleged interlopers might have used a different title for what was claimed to be essentially the same work—in which case the determination of what was often called the "substance" of the two would be at issue. Or the complaint might be that the particular book in question fell within a *type* that happened to be restricted to certain Stationers—an almanac, say, or a prayer book. It was then the generic identity of the work, rather than its actual textual content, that was at issue. Or else the complainant might be making a case based on a *similarity* between texts, rather than an outright identity—this may have been the kind of principle on which the clerk was acting when he disallowed the dictionary referred to above. In all these cases and more, the parties involved had to make an assessment not just of whether a previous entrance existed, but of the actual contents of competing works, and sometimes even their meanings. To put it in deliberately anachronistic terms, Stationers needed to become at once skilled literary critics, adept sociologists, and dedicated historians.

By such decisions was the identity of a text established, its stability guaranteed, and its authorship fixed. Bookseller Michael Sparke's battle over Comenius's *Janua Linguarum* provides one example, illustrating the complexities into which such charges could propel the umpires (table 3.1). The relevant phase of the struggle began in late 1643, when one of the parties complained to the court. Sparke and his antagonist, Thomas Slater, agreed to refer the dispute to a committee of four "referrees." So complex was their investigation that by the time they reported almost a year had passed. During that time the referees had met all the parties and "heard what allegations they would respectively make for themselves." They had also "viewed their

TABLE 3.1 Editions of *Janua Linguarum* and *Porta Linguarum* in England, 1615–85

Year	Author(s)	Title	Undertaker(s)	Format	STC
1615	[W. Bathe, W. Welde]	*Janua Linguarum*	H. L[ownes], for M. Lownes	4°	14466
1616	[W. Bathe, W. Welde]	*Janua Linguarum.* 2d ed.	H. L[ownes], for M. Lownes	4°	14466.5
1617	[W. Bathe, W. Welde]	*Janua Linguarum.* Another ed.	R. F[ield], for M. Lownes	4° in 8s	14467
1617	[W. Bathe, W. Welde]	*Janua Linguarum.* Another issue	R. F[ield], for M. Lownes	4° in 8s	14467.5
1619	[W. Bathe, W. Welde]	*Janua Linguarum.* [3d ed. of 14466?]	[H. Lownes, for M. Lownes?]	4°	14467.7
1621	[W. Bathe, W. Welde]	*Janua Linguarum.* 4d ed. of 14466	H. L[ownes], for M. Lownes	4°	14468
1623	[W. Bathe, W. Welde]	*Janua Linguarum.* 5th ed.	H. L[ownes], for M. Lownes	4°	14468.5
1626	[W. Bathe, W. Welde]	*Janua Linguarum.* Another ed.	H. Lownes	4°	14469
1627	[W. Bathe, W. Welde]	*Janua Linguarum.* Another issue	H. Lownes	4°	14470
1631	[W. Bathe, W. Welde]	*Janua Linguarum.* 7th ed.	R. Young; sold by G. Lathum	4°	14471
1631	J. A. Comenius, J. Anchoran	*Porta Linguarum*	G. Miller, for M. Sparke and T. Slater	8°	15078
1631	J. A. Comenius, J. Anchoran	*Porta Linguarum*	G. Miller, for the author	8°	15078a
1631	J. A. Comenius, J. Anchoran	*Porta Linguarum*	G. Miller, for M. Sparke	8°	15078.5
1633	J. A. Comenius, J. Anchoran	*Porta Linguarum.* 2d ed.	T. Cotes, for M. Sparke	8°	15079
1633	J. A. Comenius, J. Anchoran	*Porta Linguarum.* Another issue	T. Cotes, for T. Slater	8°	15079.5
1634	T. Horne, T. Poole	*Janua Linguarum.* 8th ed.	R. Young; sold by G. Lathum	8°	14472
1636	J. A. Comenius, T. Horne	*Janua Linguarum Reserata.* 3d ed.	R. Young; sold by T. Slater	8°	15077.3
1637	J. A. Comenius, J. Anchoran	*Porta Linguarum.* 3d ed.	A. Griffin, for M. Sparke	8°	15080
1638	J. A. Comenius, T. Horne	*Janua Linguarum Reserata.* 4th ed.	R. Young; sold by T. Slater	8°	15077.5
1639	J. A. Comenius, J. Anchoran	*Porta Linguarum.* 4th ed.	A. Griffin, for M. Sparke	8°	15081
1640	J. A. Comenius, J. Anchoran	*Porta Linguarum.* Variant	A. Griffin, for M. Sparke	8°	15081.5
1640	J. A. Comenius, J. Anchoran	*Porta Linguarum.* Variant	A. Griffin, for M. Sparke	8°	15081.7
1640	J. A. Comenius, T. Horne, J. Robotham	*Janua Linguarum Reserata.* 5th ed.	R. Young	8°	15077.7

1641	J. A. Comenius	*Janua Linguarum Reserata.* 5th ed.	R. Young; sold by T. Slater	8°	C5511
1643	J. A. Comenius	*Janua Linguarum Reserata.* 6th ed.	J. Young; sold by T. Slater	8°	C5512
1645	J. A. Comenius	*Janua Linguarum Reserata.* Another ed.	J. Young; sold by T. Slater	8°	C5512A
1647	J. A. Comenius	*Janua Linguarum Reserata.* Another ed.	J. Young, for T. Slater	8°	C5513
1650	J. A. Comenius	*Janua Linguarum Reserata.* Another ed.	W. Du-gard, for T. Slater	8°	C5514
1652	J. A. Comenius	*Janua Linguarum Reserata.* Another ed.	E. Griffin and W. Hunt for T. Slater	8°	C5515
1656	J. A. Comenius	*Latinae Linguae Janua Reserata*	W. Du-Gard; sold by J. Clark	8°	C5521
1659	J. A. Comenius	*Janua Linguarum Reserata.* Another ed.	E. Cotes, for the Company of Stationers	8°	C5516
1662	J. A. Comenius	*Janua Linguarum Trilinguis*	R. Daniels	8°	C5518
1665	J. A. Comenius	*Janua Linguarum cum Versione Anglicana*	R. Daniels	8°	C5508A
1667	J. A. Comenius	*Janua Linguarum Reserata.* Another ed.	E. Cotes, for the Company of Stationers	8°	C5516A
1670	J. A. Comenius	*Janua Linguarum Trilinguis*	J. Redmayne	8°	C5519
1670	J. A. Comenius	*Janua Linguarum cum Versione Anglicana*	J. Redmayne	8°	C5509
1670	J. A. Comenius	*Janua Linguarum Trilinguis*	J. Redmayne; sold by J. Williams for J. Baker	8°	C5519A
1673	J. A. Comenius	*Janua Linguarum Reserata.* Another ed.	for J. Baker	8°	C5517
1673	J. A. Comenius	*Janua Linguarum Reserata.* Another ed.	T. R. and N. T., for the Company of Stationers	8°	C5517A
1674	J. A. Comenius	*Janua Linguarum Novissime.* 4th ed.	J. Baker	8°	C5510
1685	J. A. Comenius	*Janua Linguarum Trilinguis*	E. Redmayne	8°	C5520

Unless otherwise stated, the first name in the Undertaker(s) column is that of the printer. 4° = quarto; 8° = octavo; 4° in 8s = quarto in eights. *Sources:* Pollard and Redgrave, *Short-Title Catalogue* (before 1641); Wing, *Short-Title Catalogue* (1641–1700). STC numbers refer to entries in these catalogues.

sev'all Entries in the hall Booke," and "p[er]used the sev'all impressions of the said books." The court now heard all the arguments all over again, "to ye end that noe matter on either part might passe untaken notice of," and both sides agreed that they would abide by the resultant decision. That decision was complex. *Janua Linguarum* had originally been printed in four languages. In 1634 it had been reprinted by Robert Young in two, with corrections and emendations by Thomas Horne. The Table ruled that all previous entries of this text be "vacated," and that the eighth edition in both four *and* two languages be reentered to Young's heir, James Young. But meanwhile Comenius's *Porta Linguarum* had been translated by one John Anchoran and printed for Sparke. Young had reprinted this for Slater in 1643, without Sparke's authorization, along with additions by Horne and John Robotham, under the title *Janua Linguarum Reserata*. This had been a genuine offense, the court decided, "the substance thereof being wholy the said *Porta*." The outcome was a typical compromise, aimed at generating peace rather than retribution: the later text—the *Porta Linguarum*—would in future belong equally to Sparke and to Slater. It was to be entered anew in the register under both their names. After a year's deliberation and negotiation, the definitions of two texts had been fixed, their relative originality resolved, the "Coppie" identified, and its ownership assigned, all for the sake of stability in the Stationers' commonwealth. The very possibility of either text being openly published had been determined. And all of this had been achieved without the slightest involvement of the writer, Comenius.[112]

The court developed an elaborate practical taxonomy of similarities and differences between texts. Aggrieved Stationers could argue their claims by reference to this taxonomy. A book might be judged to offend if it constituted an "epitome," an "abridgment," a "translation," or even a "paraphrase" of another.[113] Pictures or engravings might also be accounted irregular on similar grounds.[114] During the construction of such decisions, Stationers' Company personnel had to make fine judgments not only on the financial and social circumstances of texts, but on their contents too. Indeed, in this process any division between content and context should be

---

112. SCB C, fols. 195^{r-v}, 207^{r-v}, 209^{r-v}, 212^{r-v}, 238^r. Comenius himself had left England some two years earlier, disillusioned at Parliament's failure to back his pansophic projects: Webster, *Great Instauration*, 51, 108–9.

113. For examples, see: SCB C, fols. 238^r (an epitome), 240^v–241^r (printing copy in the course of another book), 250^r (annotations), 266^v–268^r (a martyrology "part whereof is Collected out of the booke of Martyrs"—see also Woodward, "Thomas Fuller"); SCB D, fols. 8^r (comprinting part of a copy), 28^r (a translation of the copy appearing in two other books), 47^{r-v} (annotations), 50^r (a translation of the *Assemblies Catechism*); SCB F, fols. 154^{r-v} ("paraphrases"), 198^v (an abridgment of annotations).

114. SCB D, fol. 11^{r-v}. For the subsequent period see Hunter, "Copyright Protection."

seen as an *outcome* of negotiation rather than its determinant. And what gave any resulting attribution its authority was less its inherent rightness than the customary respect owed by Stationers to their Company and court. Only very occasionally would a Stationer continue to question whether a violation had really been perpetrated after the Table reached a decision.[115] In a particularly important instance, to be encountered again in chapter 4, Thomas Roycroft declined to accept the Company's categorization of one of his productions as a law book. Yet even Roycroft agreed to halt printing. Such was a Stationer's respect for the court and for the civil order it embodied.[116]

It is an indication of the primacy of such protocols that they could even be initiated before entrance itself. Indeed, in an informal and unrecorded sense such an assay was carried out by the clerk whenever an entrance was requested, since it had to pass the test of his knowledge of the register. But either the Company itself or its more powerful individual members could also request a more formal investigation, particularly for suspected violation of a generic patent (such as those for almanacs or law books). Roger Norton, for one, was permitted to inspect an accidence before its entrance to another individual, since he claimed a generic patent on Latin didactic titles.[117] In such controversial cases, entrance might be refused if a new book were decided to be simply a *development* of an old one. This happened for the *Confession of Faith* resolved upon at the Savoy in 1658. Despite threats from the Council of State, the Company decided that "that pretended new Confession" was simply an embellished version of the old one authorized by the Assembly of Divines, which it already owned. For specialist works, a suitably qualified reader—what we would now call an expert—might prove necessary to resolve such subtleties. The mathematical practitioner, surveyor, and Stationer William Leybourn, for instance, was called upon to vet an astronomical text by Vincent Wing, presumably for possible infringement of the Company's almanac patent.[118]

Particularly difficult in this respect were texts that were self-confessedly based on existing works: translations, for example, or scriptural exegeses, or abridgments such as those of Foxe's *Acts and Monuments*. In the case of translations, during several long disputes it was ruled that they should be entered only when the actual translated text to be published was in being, and that entrance should be granted to the first individual able to show the

115. SCB E, fols. 169ᵛ–170ᵛ.
116. His partner, John Streater, entertained no such respect and refused to desist. SCB D, fol. 75ᵛ; below, p. 305.
117. SCB D, fol. 128ᵛ. Samuel Speed's printer refused to bring in sheets to compare their contents with copy owned by Anne Moseley: SCB D, fols. 139ᵛ–140ʳ.
118. SCB D, fols. 37ʳ, 128ᵛ, 133ᵛ.

clerk such a complete text. Stationers had been making blocking entrances to prevent rivals producing *any* translation of a given work.[119] But the issue was never really resolved, and continued to be debated well into the eighteenth century as the regulation of publishing moved into the legal realm. A crucial case then was that between George Burnet and William Chetwood in 1720 over Thomas Burnet's *Archaeologia Philosophica*, which had originally been published in Latin in the Low Countries in 1692. Excerpts featuring a rather injudicious imaginary conversation between Eve and the serpent had been published by the notorious atheist Charles Blount in an unauthorized English translation, which gave the title a certain notoriety, and when Burnet died Chetwood led a group of booksellers in a project to publish a full English text. George Burnet, Thomas's executor, sued in Chancery. Chetwood defended himself by arguing that a translation, "which in some respects may be called a different book, and the translator may be said to be the author," was not constrained by the 1710 Act. The court sympathized with this argument. Yet it eventually ruled against Chetwood because the book contained "strange notions" better kept concealed from "the vulgar."[120]

This conveys some idea of the extensive range of available conventions according to which books could be categorized. Such conventions had consequences in the making and destruction of authorial reputations. Peter Cole, for example, may or may not have spent the £5,000 he claimed entering medical titles, but he certainly played a key part in creating the reputation as an author of one of the best known of all medical writers, Nicholas Culpeper. Such was the impact of Cole's notoriety upon the authorial credit of this figure that Culpeper's widow herself had to venture into print several times to vindicate the authenticity of his posthumous works, once calling forth as many as nine witnesses. Even today, it remains unclear how much of Culpeper's oeuvre was actually written by him.[121] As this implies, in this cultural setting there was no widespread conviction that the author of a text had a uniquely privileged right to decide its fate. Indeed, publication without express authorial consent seems to have been an acknowledged reality. Highbrow bookseller Humphrey Moseley, who almost single-handedly maintained a canon of poetic and dramatic publications through the Civil War and Interregnum years, righteously defended the practice, alleging that it preserved works that otherwise would be lost. "I have not the Author's *Approbation* to the *Fact*," he admitted, "but I have *Law* on my *Side*." Mose-

119. SCB D, fol. 50ᵛ.
120. Burnet vs. Chetwood, 2 Mer. 441; Rose, *Authors and Owners*, 49–51.
121. Thulesius, *Nicholas Culpeper*, 147–78.

ley reckoned that it was "no man's *Praerogative* to *fire* his *own House.*" [122] Even on the rare occasions when an author's will was invoked in Stationers' negotiations, it was generally as a tactic to secure victory in a particular affray, not as a result of any general moral principle. For example, when John Martyn, later Printer to the Royal Society, asked that a proposed English translation of Sanderson's *Cases of Conscience* (of which he held the Latin copy) be disallowed, he remarked that the author "intended to publish it in English by his owne Copie." Martyn claimed that the proposed version had been translated "without the Drs consent & by such a p'son too as may mistake the Drs sence & meaning & so blemish his reputacon." [123] The court did decide to consult Sanderson, as a matter of civility. But still nobody suggested that he himself be regarded, let alone registered, as owner of the work.

Nonetheless, some writers did use the register themselves, although this was very rare. [124] One who did was Astronomer Royal John Flamsteed, who, as we shall see in chapter 8, had his own strong reasons for suspicion of Stationers. Another was Frenchman Denis Papin, who entered his "continuacon of ye new digester of bones" to himself in 1687. [125] His licenser was John Hoskyns, at the Council of the Royal Society. Papin was perhaps attempting to ensure security for his name as inventor of the device, as well as for his printed piece. As an outsider—he repeatedly attempted to establish himself at the Society, with fragile success—Papin perhaps felt that he needed to protect himself without intermediaries. Or, more straightforwardly, it is possible that no Stationer would undertake his work. In any case, he understood that a writer need not be entirely impotent. This principle extended beyond the moment of entrance itself. Since the Stationers'

122. "Thou seest how *Saucie* I am *grown*," he continued: Vaughan, *Olor Iscanus*, sig. [A6^r–v]; Kirschbaum, *Shakespeare and the Stationers*, 106–7 (see also 97 for an instance involving Hartlib). I am grateful to Paulina Kewes for discussions concerning Moseley.

123. SCB D, fol. 55^r; Sanderson, *De Obligatione*. The rival translation was Sanderson, *Several Cases of Conscience*. Compare the last-ditch resort to the author's executors in SCB D, fols. 17^v, 28^r–30^r.

124. The suggestion sometimes made that only Stationers could possess copies before 1710 is false, although stipulations to that effect were occasionally declared. In practice non-Stationers could make entries, although it was not common for them to do so. Compare Rose, *Authors and Owners*, 4; Feather, *Publishing, Piracy and Politics*, 24–6.

125. Stationers' Company, *Registers 1640–1708*, III, 315. Papin was introduced to the Society by Huygens in 1675: Oldenburg, *Correspondence*, XI, 378–81. He tried for years to gain a place in the London experimental community by virtue of his "digester," and was always concerned for the protection of his status as its inventor. See, for example, Browne, *Works*, IV, 120–2, 126, for his trials with the device, and 186 for its publication. In 1687 he had been concerned to fight off foreign competitors; he was about to depart for a professorship in Marburg. See Pumfrey, "Who Did the Work," 141–2. The Company still maintains a register for inventions, operating as a kind of alternative patent. Few inventors now use it.

court was not *quite* autonomous, authors of rank or influence could sometimes intervene in its decisions. Licensers, privy councilors, and archbishops
provided useful channels for those eager to do so, as might a figure like
Sir Roger L'Estrange. In 1646, for example, when he wanted Peter Cole's
entrance of his sermon on the Book of Revelation crossed out, preacher
Thomas Goodwin not only sent word himself, but also had the licenser
supply his own order.[126] Needless to say, though, this was a response beyond
the means of many. In practice even someone as well connected as Francis
Bacon found it "troublesome," and for most writers it was all but impossible. Even if it could be achieved, moreover, the offending Stationer, while
prevented from actually printing the work, would probably retain its propriety. Nobody else could then legitimately publish it. So the end result
could well be that one's book was preserved inviolate from unauthorized
emendations only at the price of remaining forever unprinted.[127]

LICENSING: PROPRIETY AND POLITICS

What linked the Company's procedures immediately to wider mechanisms
of political governance was the licensing system. This was the régime under
which Stationers had to submit any text they wished to publish to be read and
approved beforehand by one of a small number of authorized officials. Any
non-Stationer responsible for a publication was likewise supposed to obey
its protocols. Modern historians have debated the role of the licensing régime as a system of censorship with extraordinary intensity. This section
takes a different, perhaps more historically sensitive, approach, examining
licensing as a practice. It asks who typically became a licenser, and how a
licenser properly conducted himself. It thereby displays the intimate links
between licensing and the propriety of the Stationers.

Licensing was based on a series of laws and decrees dating back to at least
1530 (table 3.2).[128] Its principal foundation, however, was a Star Chamber
decree of 1586. The subsequent legal history of the practice is straightfor-

126. SCB C, fol. 230ʳ; Stationers' Company, *Registers 1640–1708*, I, 215. The mention in
court of the subject of the sermon, and the nature of that subject—the seven vials of God's
wrath poured out on the earth, and the mark and number of the Beast, both of which readers commonly interpreted in ways leading them to propose radical political and even military interventions—make it likely that Goodwin feared his sermon would be construed as
dangerous.

127. Kirschbaum, *Shakespeare and the Stationers*, 126–36; Greg, *Shakespeare First Folio*,
45–6. The disputes over Bacon's *Essays* were exemplary of the processes outlined here: Stationers' Company, *Records*, 178, 204, 326–8, 335; Greg, *Some Aspects and Problems*, 56–8.

128. The early history of trade regulation is rehearsed in Hirsch, *Printing, Selling and
Reading*.

wardly rehearsed. The original decree was reinforced by Sir John Lambe's of 1637, inspired by the Caroline policy of rigorous governance known as "Thorough."[129] Then, when Star Chamber collapsed in July 1641, the authority of this prerogative régime collapsed with it. Parliament no more relished the prospect of unregulated printing than had Charles I's Privy Council, however, and forthwith attempted to oversee the book trade through a cluster of committees. With the Lords and Commons frequently at loggerheads, this attempt soon dissolved into a maelstrom of contradictions. The chairman of the Commons Committee for Printing even found himself under arrest for publishing his own works. The result was an explosion of discredit in the realm of print. Finally, in 1643, a new licensing ordinance was issued.[130] But enforcement remained practically impossible, the trade oligarchy and the parliamentary committees continuing to act for divergent interests. In 1647 a further ordinance therefore followed, establishing a new locus of control in the London Committee for the Militia. After the execution of Charles and amid the furor over the Ranters, yet another bill was passed, reinforcing this measure. This lapsed in September 1651. Disputes between radicals and Presbyterians in the Stationers' Company led the Company to press for a further bill, and in January 1653 the Act was restored. Under Cromwell's Protectorate, control of the press was tightened yet further.[131] But with the chaos of 1659 the licensing régime again became ineffective, and once more the number of pamphlets being produced soared.

When Charles Stuart was restored in 1660, he immediately moved to reimpose order on the book trade. At first he employed royal prerogative to enact regulations by proclamation. But in 1662, at his express request, Parliament passed the most comprehensive licensing bill of all. It became known as the Press Act.[132] This Act was renewed periodically until 1679. In that turbulent year the Commons declined to make time to renew it yet again, and it thus lapsed. Once again pamphlet wars erupted. Royal prerogative struggled in vain to control opposition printers, hindered by the *ignoramus* decisions of Whig juries. Meanwhile the Stationers' Company, galvanized by both court influence and the threat to its members' proprieties, lobbied for the reintroduction of the Act. Even after the Restoration crisis had subsided, however, the state continued to rely on prerogative (now, after scandalous shrieval elections in the City of London, imposed by

129. Stationers' Company, *Registers 1554–1640*, II, 807–12; IV, 528–36.
130. Siebert, *Freedom of the Press*, 46, 165–81; Fletcher, *Outbreak of the English Civil War*, 70–80; Firth and Rait, *Acts and Ordinances*, I, 184–7.
131. Siebert, *Freedom of the Press*, 188–90, 230–1; Firth and Rait, *Acts and Ordinances*, I, 1021–3; II, 245–54, 696–9.
132. 14 Car. II, c. 33.

TABLE 3.2 Measures Regulating the Press, 1586–1710

Date	Measure	Licensers	Offenses and Punishments
1586	Star Chamber Decree	Archbishop of Canterbury; bishop of London; lord chief justice; lord chief baron	Illicit press: 1 year; printing or causing to be printed an un-licensed book: 6 mths; selling/binding one: 3 mths. Printing permitted only in London, Oxford, Cambridge; restricts number of workers
1637	Star Chamber Decree (lapsed 1641)	As above, plus: earl marshall (heraldry); chancellors of Oxford and Cambridge	Illicit press: whipping; other offenses: decided by Star Chamber. No English-language books to be imported; licenses needed for reprinting old titles; restricts printing to 20 named masters; restricts typefounding to 4 named founders
1643	Parliamentary Ordinance	12 divines (divinity); 4 lawyers (law); heralds, kings of arms (heraldry); Sir Nathaniel Brent, master of Paul's School, Mr. Farnaby (philosophy); Stationers' clerk (pamphlets); John Booker, readers at Gresham College (mathematics, almanacs)	Destruction of presses and materials; additional as court decides

1647	Parliamentary Ordinance	As above, plus parliamentary appointees (news)	Destruction of presses and materials. Writer: 40sh/40 days; printer: 20sh/20 days; seller: 10sh/10 days; hawker: whipping
1649	Act of Parliament (lapsed 1651; revived 1653; lapsed 1659)	As above; army licensers	Destruction of presses and materials. Writer: £10/40 days; printer: £5/20 days; seller: £2/10 days; buyer: £1 per book
1662	Press Act (lapsed 1679; revived 1685; lapsed 1695)	Archbishop of Canterbury; bishop of London; lord chancellor, etc. (law); secretaries of state (history, etc.); earl marshall (heraldry); chancellors of Oxford and Cambridge. [As delegate of the secretary of state: the Surveyor of the Press. By prerogative: the Royal Society (and later the Royal College of Physicians)]	Forfeiture, plus punishment at court's discretion; excludes John Streater
1710	Copyright Act	No licensing	

Sources: Stationers' Company, *Registers 1554–1640*, II, 807–12; IV, 528–36; Firth and Rait, *Acts and Ordinances of the Interregnum*, I, 184–7, 1021–3; II, 245–54; 14 Car. II, c. 33; 8 Ann., c. 21.

Tory juries) to maintain control. But when James II succeeded in 1685, he reimposed the Act, which would now operate in conjunction with a Stationers' Company newly subjugated to royal control (by means to be addressed in chapter 4). It then remained in force through the Revolution of 1688, only to lapse again in 1695. Despite the strenuous appeals of the Company, extended over many years, it was never again restored.[133] What has retrospectively been labeled the "Copyright Act" of 1710 was in effect a qualified response to the Stationers' pleas for the protection hitherto provided under the licensing régime. And as that implies, the angelic renown of the former is perhaps as exaggerated as the demonic reputation of the latter.

This brief survey of the legal bases of licensing reveals only its barest outlines, ignoring entirely its practice and wider cultural meanings. One learns nothing from such a survey of the extent and severity of enforcement, tactics of evasion, or degrees of support for the procedure. Evasion, at least, was extensive: just as a large proportion of published books were never entered, so a large proportion lacked licenses. L'Estrange even claimed that Stationers removed imprimaturs from books that *had* been licensed, in an attempt to generate uncertainty and (presumably) a lucrative frisson of risk. Most of all, such a survey masks any epistemic consequences that the licensing system may have had—that is, any implications for the making and communication of knowledge. Nevertheless, it is still worth noting that in the period 1586–1695 some form of licensing was in force for all but nine years, and that whenever it lapsed pamphlets and piracies seemed to flourish. This conjunction of pamphleteering with piracy indicates the real strength and significance of licensing. It combined the political interest of the royal court with the proprietorial interest of the Stationers' court.[134]

The practices of licensing and registration were closely intertwined. Indeed, after the former had lapsed Daniel Defoe would describe the resulting piracy as an even worse evil, and propose the reintroduction of a licensing régime to combat it.[135] The Company's mechanisms of search and seizure were the same for piracies and unlicensed books alike, although the court felt itself free to return seized materials in the former case but not in the

133. Crist, "Government Control of the Press"; Harris, *London Crowds*, 130–1, 154–5; Feather, *History of British Publishing*, 54–5; Feather, "Book Trade in Politics"; Astbury, "Renewal of the Licensing Act." In fact, government control of the press continued, especially through the use of the law of libel: see Kropf, "Libel and Satire."

134. A controversial argument to this effect is presented by Lambert, "Printers and the Government," and Lambert, "Richard Montagu." Eisenstein, on the other hand, represents printers as enthusiasts for deregulation: e.g., *Printing Press*, 419, 442. For L'Estrange's comments, see PRO SP 29/39, no. 92. Booksellers themselves urged that unlicensed books be prosecuted at common law, with the proceeds from any fines going to whichever private individual brought the prosecution: Fawne et al., *Second Beacon*, 11.

135. [Defoe], *Essay on the Regulation of the Press*, 19 ff. See also Defoe's anonymous *Attempt towards a Coalition* and *Letter to a Member of Parliament*.

latter without higher authorization.[136] Within the Company itself, too, procedures of registration and licensing coalesced. They had originated together
in the sixteenth century, and, as remarked above, it was at the urging of
L'Estrange that the court made entrance in the register compulsory. At the
moment of registration all entries were supposed to be accompanied by evidence of a license.[137] In 1677 the Privy Council extended this, ordering that
entries be made not only with a license, but also with security that that
license would be printed truthfully at the beginning of the published book.
L'Estrange also maintained that the licenser's name must be included in any
entry, and in 1685 this too was enforced by royal command.[138] In such times
of political stress the Company's registration procedures could indeed become potential tools of suppression, the Company itself declaring that it
would refuse to enter texts that the state regarded as subversive. But this
exposed state will to the individual interests of the Stationers appointed to
the posts of Master, warden, clerk, and beadle. L'Estrange was particularly
furious to find Henry Hills prepared to use his warden's authority to enter
books attacking L'Estrange himself.[139]

Stipulations about licensing were put into action at the moment of registration. Once made, entries tended to become sacrosanct simply because
of the primacy of Stationers' convention. The court was reluctant to delete
one even if the work in question were deemed illegal, since to do so risked
undermining the principle of archival permanence on which the entire system depended. Even in such a politically prominent case as Prynne's *Histriomastix*, the entry of which to Michael Sparke had been ordered expunged, the court resolved that "the same is to be entred to him againe in
case it shall be allowed to be sold." Besides, the court conceived that its legal
power to cancel duly entered titles was limited.[140] So, for example, the entry
in 1698 of an anonymous *Life of John Milton* that was later found to contain
matter "of ill consequence" was allowed to stand, even though the warden
who had approved it was reprimanded.[141]

136. E.g., SCB D, fol. 41ᵛ. The principle was that "the same Authority was necessary to
bee obtayned for the release of the said bookes [as that] whereby they were seised": SCB C,
fol. 234ᵛ; see also fols. 275ʳ⁻ᵛ, 279ʳ–280ᵛ.

137. This was even applied to the works of Robert Filmer: SCB E, fols. 93ʳ, 53ʳ; SCB F,
fol. 29ᵛ; *At a Court held at Stationers-Hall* (broadside, SCA, suppl. docs., series I, Box A,
env. 2, iii).

138. SCB E, fol. 53ʳ; SCB F, fol. 29ᵛ; *At a Court held at Stationers-Hall.*

139. PRO SP 29/424, no. 151.

140. SCB C, fol. 130ʳ; SCB F, fol. 26ʳ; Stationers' Company, *Registers 1640–1708*, IV,
241. The court pointed out to L'Estrange that an entrance constituted evidence of responsibility, and thus facilitated the prosecution of perpetrators of entered libels but not of unentered ones.

141. SCB G, fol. 18ʳ. This was John Toland's *Life*, published in 1699: Stationers' Company,
Registers 1640–1708, III, 485.

This tension between craft conventions and governmental wishes meant that the Stationers' court became perhaps the main site at which the practices of licensers were revealed and discussed. This in turn meant that the revelation was before a very restricted audience, and the discussion was constrained by the customs of the court. Such incidents were most likely to materialize in the course of debates over propriety. The example of James Cranford is a case in point. A Presbyterian minister of decided opinions, Cranford was appointed a licenser by the parliamentary ordinance of 1643. Like Thomas Edwards, whose *Gangraena* he not only licensed but wrote a eulogistic preface for, Cranford represented the growth of sectarianism in the church as a gangrene. He told the lord mayor that heretical writings must be "condemned to the fire" and their harborers put to death.[142] Yet in practice it was the Stationers' court and not the mayor which decided such matters, and there Cranford's practice was found to be less harshly effective than his rhetoric. Within weeks of giving this advice he was found to have licensed a piracy.[143] Moreover, he had already been implicated in an argument that is highly instructive of the negotiations entailed by the combined licensing and entering processes. The argument concerned the work of Catholic philosopher Sir Kenelm Digby.

Digby was in exile. After being interned by Parliament at the outbreak of the Civil War, he spent the years 1643–9 as an attendant to Queen Henrietta Maria, trudging between Rome and Paris in search of funds for the royalist war effort. During this time he wrote a lengthy work that was published in Paris in late 1644 as *Two Treatises, in the One of which, the Nature of Bodies; in the Other, the Nature of Mans Soule, is looked into: in way of discovery, of the Immortality of Reasonable Soules*. At least two English editions followed rapidly. One was produced by George Thomason and Octavian Pulleyn, the other by Francis Egglesfield, Edward Blackmore, and John Williams. Their consequent confrontation helped to define the identity of the work.

Digby had constructed his *Two Treatises* both as a defense of the immortality of the soul, and as a reconciliation of that doctrine with a thorough-going mechanical philosophy.[144] Like most such texts, his book could not be categorized simply and incontestably as either philosophy or divinity, especially when its authorship by a papist renegade was taken into account.

142. Cranford, *Haereseo-machia*, 4–5, 42, 50; Haller, *Liberty and Reformation*, 140; Liu, *Puritan London*, 79; Edwards, *Gangraena*, sig. πᵛ; Edwards, *Second Part of Gangraena*, sig. πᵛ; Edwards, *Third Part of Gangraena*, sig. πᵛ. Cranford was able to cite *Gangraena* while it was still unpublished. He was to be dismissed in 1649 for reputedly writing anonymous royalist works: *The Moderate*, 36 (20 March 1648/9), 369.

143. PRO SP 16/513, nos. 30, 39.

144. His correspondence with Catholic clerics reveals the arguments Digby felt himself to be treating: BL Ms. Sloane 2781, fols. 78ʳ–83ᵛ; BL Ms. Add. 41846, fols. 1ʳ–91ᵛ. See also Henry, "Atomism and Eschatology."

The two rival partnerships took advantage of this. Thomason and Pulleyn took their copy to Sir Nathaniel Brent, licenser for philosophy. Egglesfield, Blackmore, and Williams took theirs to Cranford, licenser for divinity. Both approved their copies. At this point, however, the *Two Treatises* lurched into a bitter internal struggle in the trade. Thomason was involved in a fierce fight over the culture permeating the Company, his party being led by Michael Sparke and composed of a Presbyterian group of Stationers opposed to what they perceived to be the excessive power of a few patentees.[145] Egglesfield, on the other hand, a patentee and staunch episcopalian, opposed Sparke's reforms. The conflict reached its climax in January 1645. A meeting of the whole Company at Stationers' Hall dissolved into chaos when one of Thomason's allies interrupted to tell the assembled assistants bluntly that "they were not fitt to sitt at that Table." It was only ten days later that Thomason and Pulleyn complained to the same court of their competitors for Digby's text. The process of referees was immediately instituted. Fortunately for us, Cranford was "hindred by my lamenes" from attending, and as a result a written copy of his testimony has survived.[146]

Cranford reported that he had granted Egglesfield a provisional license on the basis of seeing the manuscript's title, and without reading the text. That provisional license had been intended to give the Stationer permission to plan its printing, but not actually to begin work until Cranford had "perused" the text itself. Now he had done so. "The truth is," he explained, "veiwing onely the Title, The imortallity of the Soule (for what he speakes of bodies is in order to the soule) I thought I had reason to Conceive that it did belong to a divine." But when the rival booksellers' arguments had come to light he had looked again. He now found that the writer "handles the point onely philosophically as a Naturalist in the first pte, & in the second as a Metaphysitian." Therefore, Cranford now admitted, "I see that by the Ordinance of Parliam^t it is w^thout my Limitt." He therefore consented that his license be revoked. Moreover, Cranford went on, he could now see "some things upon reading the booke, wch if they may passe in the Schoole of Nature (as they may if such as are authorized doe allow) yet will scarse hold in the Schooles of Divinity." This opinion was seconded by a letter from Brent requesting entrance to Thomason and Pulleyn. Egglesfield himself could not be found to testify, and his cause was defeated.

Thomason's success, then, lay in persuading the court, through the licenser, that Digby's book should be recognized as philosophy and not as divinity. This was a potentially contestable categorization, especially since

145. Blagden, "Stationers' Company in the Civil War Period"; Rostenberg, *Literary, Political,* 161–202; Spencer, "Professional and Literary Connexions"; Spencer, "Politics of George Thomason."

146. SCB C, fols. 211^r–v, 213^r–v.

even a licenser as attuned to the presence of popery as Cranford had confused the two.[147] In fact, the licenser had actually read the text only at the Stationers' urging. But the Digby case did not rest there. On 24 April, almost three months after their first complaint, Thomason and Pulleyn returned to the court. In the midst of another stormy meeting over Company politics, the Digby affair resurfaced. Egglesfield and his partners had been reprinting copies of their own edition, despite the earlier ruling. Cranford was called forth, as was Egglesfield's group. There was an angry exchange of allegations before the court decided to restate and enforce its earlier decision. The defeated partners' book was now defined as *both* unlicensed *and* a counterfeit. They were to bring all copies to the hall to be disposed of, failing which Thomason and Pulleyn would be permitted to go to law. Egglesfield's defeat coincided with the eclipse of his party in the Company: four days later, all the assistants resigned.[148]

There are several interesting messages to be gleaned from this struggle. One is the paramount importance of the Stationers' court, and of the propriety of copies within that court. The licensing system impinged on the issue only after it was invoked by Thomason and Pulleyn, and then by the court, to suppress what they saw as a counterfeit. The licenser did not even peruse the text until the Stationers required it. The court then became the arena for determining which publication would become Sir Kenelm Digby's *Two Treatises*—in the absence of Digby and both licensers. Egglesfield's partnership quite possibly saw Thomason's version as a counterfeit too, but, being absent from the court, was unable to establish this account as authoritative. Negotiations such as these must have occurred in many cases when a book was decided to be worthy of suppression, but they usually took place in person, face to face. That is why insufficient records remain to reproduce them.

The example of the *Two Treatises* also indicates a strategy by which one could obtain a license for a questionable book. A bookseller could submit a manuscript to a licenser ignorant of the issues in a given field. As Cranford admitted, licensers knowledgeable in different areas necessarily used different criteria to reach their decisions. This was a useful insight for anyone planning to exploit the customs of the book trade for his or her own purposes. A similar technique was to be used by Robert Hooke later, as is re-

147. SCB C, fol. 219^{r-v}.
148. SCB C, fols. 218^v–219^v. Yet it is possible that the pirates eventually won. It is telling of the potency of such practices that the only editions of Digby's work to survive seem to be those by Williams of the Egglesfield group, not those by Thomason. Indeed, Williams was still reprinting the text twenty-five years later. For the internal struggles of the Company, see *To All Printers, Booke-sellers, Booke-binders.*

counted in chapter 7; and Lord Brouncker, president of the Royal Society, employed a variant against Henry Stubbe. The likelihood of such a strategy's succeeding was increased by the heavy workload imposed on licensers. They were often unable to read the full text of a submission, especially in the case of long, dense works like Digby's. One licenser complained of being forced to read "six or eight hours in a day" just to keep up.[149] But if licensers were thus forced to read selectively, on what grounds did they decide how to spend their licensing time?

There was no such "art," "trade," or "mystery" as licensing. It was not conducted by Stationers, nor by a distinct company. So who were the licensers? How did they learn what it was to read in the manner of a licenser? In theory, they had at first been ecclesiastical officers appointed by the church. Before the Civil War, however, a remarkable variety of individuals, clerical and lay, felt authorized to sign imprimaturs. Parliament's 1643 ordinance changed this, establishing new categories of expertise. The ordinance named twelve licensers for divinity, eight for law, five for "Physick and Chyrurgery," three for heraldry, three for "Philosophy, History, Poetry, Morality, and Arts," Parliament itself for parliamentary printing, the Stationers' clerk for pamphlets (an extraordinarily important responsibility), and two more individuals for "Mathematicks, Almanacks, and Prognostications." Cranford's difficulty over Digby's *Two Treatises* derived from this categorization, since the main licenser for philosophy was Sir Nathaniel Brent. For mathematics, Parliament chose the readers at Gresham College (Samuel Foster and John Greaves) and the partisan astrologer John Booker.[150] In the 1662 Act these categories were blurred again, as the licensing of philosophy was once more entrusted to the appointees of the archbishop of Canterbury and the bishop of London. But the notion of the licenser as a figure of credit in a particular province remained. And there was also one major change. The secretaries of state delegated their own licensing duties for a wide range of works to Sir Roger L'Estrange, who became Surveyor of the Press. L'Estrange wanted to charge a shilling per license, supplementing this income with the proceeds of a patent on all printed "Intelligence." Meanwhile the Royal Society gained for itself the right to license its own works and printers; more is said about this in chapter 7. From 1687 it was joined by the College of Physicians.

Licensers were expected to be knowledgeable in the fields over which

149. Bohun, *Diary and Autobiography*, 110.

150. For Foster and Greaves, see Ward, *Lives of the Professors of Gresham College*, e.g., 85–6, 137–8; Parker, *Familiar to All*, 131–2. For the range of individuals involved in licensing before the Civil War, see Greg, *Some Aspects and Problems*, 41–62, and Greg, *Licensers for the Press*, 107–9.

they were to hold jurisdiction. Those for divinity, for instance, were often
Lambeth Palace chaplains, intent on rising in the ecclesiastical hierarchy.
Among the names to appear on imprimaturs were several later to belong to
prominent bishops, such as Samuel Parker. Under the 1662 Act such chaplains were supposed to license some political tracts too, which meant that
they had also to be astute politicians. Charles Blount, aping Milton, resented
the junior status of such officers. He found it "the greatest Affront and Discouragement" imaginable for a gentleman to be forced to offer his work "to
the hasty view of an *Unleasured Licenser*, perhaps much his Younger, perhaps
much his Inferior in Judgment, perhaps one who never knew the Labour of
Book-writing." In this the licenser reinforced the denial of a gentleman's
freedom of action that was exercised by the Stationers and described above
in chapter 2. Moreover, the licensers were not neutral men. Parker himself,
author of the uncompromising *Discourse of Ecclesiastical Polity*, was anything
but a disinterested reader. The most famous licenser of all, Sir Roger
L'Estrange, stands out in this respect; L'Estrange was probably the most
impressive polemicist of court and conformity in the Restoration.[151]

What was it to act "properly" as a licenser? Again, the question is complex and intractable. The conventions of the post seem to have been entirely
unwritten, and, significantly, licensers themselves were often unsure how to
act. Certainly, the licenser did not in practice enjoy a position of unqualified
power over the booksellers, printers, informers, writers, and readers with
whom he had to deal. On the contrary, to be a successful licenser involved
creating and maintaining a fragile cooperative alliance with all these parties.
Many failed. It was not uncommon for a licenser to fall foul of opponents
in the city, at court, or in Parliament—or, perhaps most commonly, to
become a victim of the very Stationers he was trying to restrain. Licensers
who tried to impose inflexible orthodoxies were especially liable to find
themselves ridiculed, if not actually ousted. John Bachelor was one such,
condemned by Thomas Edwards as "Licenser-Generall of the Sectaries
Books." Bachelor was a radical; but even the most loyal were vulnerable in
the ephemeral world of printed politics. In 1633, for example, William
Buckner, a chaplain to Archbishop Laud, found himself arrested after licensing Prynne's *Histriomastix*. Twelve years later, the licenser of Nedham's
Hue and Cry after Charles I was likewise imprisoned—until it was pointed
out that he had in fact failed to read the tract, at which he was set free. As
late as 1693, Tory licenser Edmund Bohun was ousted from office after approving a tract entitled *King William and Queen Mary Conquerors*, which

151. PRO SP 29/39, no. 94; [Blount], *Just Vindication of Learning*, 6; Ashcraft, *Revolutionary Politics*, 22 ff., 44, 239 ff.; Kitchin, *Sir Roger L'Estrange*.

contradicted Whig ideology. The lapse of licensing two years later was brought about partly by Whig antagonism to Bohun.[152]

Such an incident—the downfall of a licenser—affords a unique insight into the conventions such an agent was expected to observe. Not least, written justifications might be preserved of the event, justifying the discharge or resignation by reference to conventions of proper conduct that, therefore, had to be articulated explicitly. Three important examples may be cited. The first, and simplest, is the principled stand made by Gilbert Mabbott. Mabbott was appointed by Fairfax as the army's licenser in September 1647. In May 1649 he resigned his post. He had come to sympathize with the Levellers, and had already called for an overhaul of licensing. In justification for his resignation, though, Mabbott cited four specific factors. First, he claimed that "many thousand" pamphlets had been published with false licenses in his name, "on purpose (as he conceives) to prejudice him in his reputation amongst the honest party of this Nation": a telling indication of the vulnerability of a licenser's credit in the pirates' realm. Second, he felt the whole system to be papist and illegal, serving to keep the people in ignorance in times of episcopal tyranny. Third, it represented a monopoly, "In that all mens judgements, reasons, &c. are to be bound up in the Licensers." All authors must be sure to work only within the limits of the licenser's understanding. And fourth, it was, he conceived, lawful in any case to print any book as long as the author and printer appended their names to the work, "so they may be lyable to answer the contents thereof." This was an early instance of the move to advance authorship as a regulatory principle in place of licensing that Chartier and others have identified elsewhere.[153]

The second example is more consequential. Perhaps the most detailed surviving testimony to the character of licensing was recorded by George Abbot, archbishop of Canterbury from 1611. Charles I's sequestration of Abbot from his office in 1627 followed immediately upon his refusal to license for publication a sermon by Robert Sibthorpe in favor of the forced

152. Pride et al., *Beacons Quenched*, 6; Edwards, *Third Part of Gangraena*, 102–5; Gardiner, *Documents Relating to the Proceedings against William Prynne*; Raymond, *Invention of the Newspaper*, 42–8; Bohun, *Diary and Autobiography*; Goldie, "Edmund Bohun"; *King William and Queen Mary Conquerors*, esp. 16–25 for the repeated citation of Bohun himself. For Bohun see also Johns, "Natural History as Print Culture." CUL Sel.3.238 contains what I take to be Bohun's collection of printed and manuscript records relating to this period, including letters congratulating him on his appointment as licenser, taking him to task on licensing conduct, and commiserating with his fall, as well as his own defenses of both himself and the licensing system in general (see esp. nos. 334, 359).

153. *The Moderate*, 46 (29 May 1649), 519; *Perfect Diurnall*, 304 (28 May 1649), 2530–31; Siebert, *Freedom of the Press*, 213–7; Raymond, *Invention of the Newspaper*, 57, 65–71; Chartier, *Order of Books*, 48–51. See also Freist, *Governed by Opinion*, 27–75 for licensers in the 1640s.

loan. Abbot had at first objected that the "occupation" of licensing was a matter for his chaplains, not the archbishop himself; but Charles's messengers insisted that he deal with the work personally. Incensed by his treatment, Abbot then wrote down in dialogue form the exchanges that had taken place between himself and the king's agent, William Murray, over the manuscript of Sibthorpe's work, which had traveled back and forth to court several times. He detailed exactly the passages at which he had balked, why, and what the royal response had been. At first content to have Murray report his objections for him at court, when they became matters of theology Abbot had found himself engaged in a written debate with the then bishop of Bath and Wells, William Laud. Murray then arrived with orders not to permit Abbot even to handle Laud's paper, but to read it aloud to him and await his written response. Abbot's objection that he was unused to reading such materials with "one sitting by me," and that such treatment was "neither Manly nor Schollar-like," was futile. His chief objection at this point became the implication that he must approve the sermon based only on "the credit of the Writer," since he could not check the sources either of the sermon itself or of Laud's endorsement. Under these circumstances, he refused to extend his own credit to such a suspicious document. It was finally approved by the bishop of London, and Abbot was banished to Kent. He was a victim, he believed, of Buckingham's courtly ambition. The licensing demand had been conceived by Buckingham in order to force Abbot's hand, so that "either by my Credit his undertakings might be strengthned, or at least I might be contemned and derided, as an unworthy fellow." This was the impossible choice eventually faced by all political licensers; Abbot was the highest of all to suffer its consequences.[154]

A third good example arises in the case of Henry Oldenburg. Oldenburg was the secretary of the Royal Society in the Restoration, half a century after Abbot's conflict with Buckingham. As such, he was a vital participant in the invention of experimental natural philosophy. Historians have recently come to see his creation of correspondence networks and of the first "scientific" journal—the *Philosophical Transactions*—as among the most important single achievements of the revolution in natural knowledge then occurring. Oldenburg stands in current historiography as a beacon of the free exchange of knowledge through writing and print.[155] Yet he was also a licenser. He became one in February 1676, when Secretary of State (and future president of the Society) Sir Joseph Williamson appointed him to certify political books. As a Royal Society officer, he had already played an important part in the machinery of what was itself a corporate licenser. But

154. Rushworth, *Historical Collections*, I, 440–8.

155. Hall, "Oldenburg and the Art of Scientific Communication"; Henry, "Origins of Modern Science"; Hunter, "Promoting the New Science."

this was to be a different matter. The false licenses complained of by Mabbott were again the cause of his appointment: the sheer number of such forgeries had made Williamson's action necessary. Immediately Oldenburg ran into problems. The bookseller Richard Bentley approached him to license a tract named *Hattige*, a thinly disguised satire on the conduct of Charles II and his latest mistress. Oldenburg hesitated. He was reluctant to refuse it outright, lest he "made men shy of me by seising and keeping yᵉ books they brought to me." In such an event the "Mercenary men" selling it would clandestinely "spread yᵐ much further, than me thinks they can doe, when they bring yᵐ to the Licenser." In other words, by strictly enforcing suppression Oldenburg felt that he ran the risk of ruining his cooperation with the Stationers, and thereby of producing the paradoxical effect of spreading *more* illicit books to a *wider* audience. He wrote anxiously to Williamson to ask advice.

An anonymous informer had in fact already betrayed Bentley to the secretary of state. Immediately, Williamson had issued a warrant to L'Estrange to search for the Stationers involved. Meanwhile Williamson himself read the tract and took careful notes. Bentley was apprehended and examined two days later. He alleged that *Hattige* had been brought to him by one Sebastian Brémont about a month before, and that he had been promised a second part in about a week. It was presumably this second part that Oldenburg had seen. But eleven days after his first worried query, and five weeks after Bentley's examination, he abruptly resigned his commission. He had been a licenser for barely three months. He had come to suspect unnamed parties of uttering "sinister suggestions" to "raise Jealousies" against him. Oldenburg feared that they had tried to excite "disquieting suspicions concerning my affection to yᵉ Government." For a German Emigré who was once imprisoned in the Tower of London on suspicion of spying, this was hardly a baseless fear. He was particularly concerned that Brémont, who was well known at court, had not been arrested, and that no attempt had been made to disown the book's dedication to the lord chamberlain. Such inaction might well indicate that some intrigue was at hand, of which the licenser might all too easily become a victim. Oldenburg therefore relinquished the appointment. He had found the time taken by the post excessive, he continued, and claimed that this alone would in any case have led to his resignation before long. He preferred his private work, and the mediation of the correspondence of the Royal Society, to "so very nice [i.e., precise] and laborious a taske, wherein 'tis very difficult to please universally." Finally, Oldenburg declared himself satisfied that he had fulfilled the requirements of a good licenser. That is, he had "rejected a farr greater number of Books and Papers than I have licensed, being sensible of their perniciousness to yᵉ Publick." Even those that he had indeed licensed had usually

been approved by Williamson himself beforehand. It seems that Williamson
had insisted on this for a trial period of some six weeks, after which Oldenburg would be free to license what titles he felt fit. Beyond this trial period
to inculcate the necessary skills, no "rules" had ever been provided for him
to follow.[156]

Oldenburg's case epitomizes some of the acute problems experienced by
licensers. With a minimum of advice, they were expected to exercise their
judgment in highly delicate court or political matters with which few could
hope to have adequate familiarity. It was all too easy for a licenser to fall
victim to court intrigue, and Oldenburg felt it wiser to abandon the post
than to risk humiliation. They were often subject to suspicions of criminal-
ity or sedition. And they depended on the cooperation of the Stationers—
which meant, as Oldenburg realized, that attempts to impose a suppression
risked being entirely counterproductive.

Although licensers were not all-powerful, they remained authoritative allies in conflicts over the credit of books and their contents. In assessing their
authority here we have to delve into the realm of rumor and hearsay, for the
important reason that the negotiation needed to get a work licensed was
pursued largely in conversation and not in writing. For example, Henry
More had to submit his work for approval to Samuel Parker. When More
stayed in Cambridge, Parker insisted on changes so substantial that they
implied a dismantling of the text. The next time he published, however,
More went to Lambeth himself and had dinner with the archbishop. This
time Parker passed the book "at the first sight, seeing from the very title
whither it tended."[157] This was exactly what Cranford had done, but without the personal interaction with the author and a patron to safeguard his
decision.

Such conversations were important because the inability to find a compliant licenser could undoubtedly prove a severe disadvantage, even if the
book in question were not actually suppressed. This was particularly clear
in the case of Henry Stubbe. Stubbe complained to Robert Boyle of the
difficulty of getting his attacks on the Royal Society published. He claimed
to have been told that Lord Brouncker, the president of the Society, had
"bragged" that "he would license it, if I would send it unto him." This
Stubbe had done, but Brouncker had then refused to allow the text. As a

156. Oldenburg, *Correspondence*, XII, 254–5, 263–5. The warrant appointing Oldenburg
as licenser is reproduced there; another copy, sent by the secretary of state's office to the
Stationers' Company to inform the bookselling community of the appointment, is in SCB
E, fol. 17ʳ. See also PRO SP 44/43, p. 72; PRO SP 30/F73; PRO SP 29/380, nos. 206, 208;
PRO SP 29/381, no. 1; PRO SP 44/334, p. 164. Alan Marshall attributes Oldenburg's fall to
Williamson in his *Intelligence and Espionage*, 55–60.

157. Conway, *Letters*, 232–4, 293–5, 302–5 (esp. 303); Shapin and Schaffer, *Leviathan and
the Air-Pump*, 292.

result Stubbe had had to rely on a poorly printed unlicensed edition and, being absent from London, had been unable to supervise its printing or distribution. "I durst not come up to see it done," he told Boyle, "for fear of some mechanical philosophers and their stratagems." His ally, Robert Crosse, suffered similarly. He complained that his attacks on the Royal Society were passed on by a licenser to the Society's propagandist, Glanvill, who then had them privately printed to humiliate him. Crosse apparently wrote an angry piece attacking Bishop John Fell, too, after being denied a license.[158] For such actors, licensers were not just constraints in the communication of knowledge; they were participants.

Stubbe claimed to fear "imprisonment, perhaps death" as a consequence of his unlicensed writings. The former, at least, never came to pass, and, conspiracy theories aside, his drowning in 1676 is more likely to have been due to ale than assassins. But Stubbe also suspected collusion between the Society and the chaplains at Lambeth Palace in expunging elements of his text, and, given the conversational character of licensing, this was a more realistic concern. It is also worth noting his claim that others had been able to plagiarize his work with impunity as a result. Here the issue of literary propriety seen in cases such as that of Digby's *Two Treatises* resurfaced—and, as in the cases cited in chapter 2, a philosophical context lent the issue of propriety overtones of personal plagiarism. But by June 1670 Stubbe's tone had changed. He now wrote an optimistic letter to Boyle asserting that his campaign against the Royal Society was on the verge of success. He had come to enjoy the licensing protection of the College of Physicians and the bishop of London, while Peter Gunning, the licenser at Cambridge, had tried to block a set of heroic verses dedicated to the Society by Peter du Moulin.[159] Stubbe's assessment still proved wrong, but that does not mean that in gauging its chances by his relations to licensers he was entirely unjustified.

The role of the Stationers in this face-to-face negotiating of the licensing process could be decisive. With Digby exiled in Paris, the fate of his book depended on rival factions within the Stationers' Company. Stationer Michael Sparke's experience of manipulating officials likewise allowed him to fool the hapless chaplain William Buckner in the *Histriomastix* case. When Henry More was in Cambridge, he entrusted his licensing affairs to the prominent Stationer patentee Miles Flesher, or to his own Stationer landlord Walter Kettilby. Brouncker's Royal Society, as we shall see, had its own domesticated Stationers as well as its right to license their productions.

158. Wood, *Athenae Oxoniensis*, IV, 122–4.
159. Boyle, *Works*, I, xc–xciv, xcvii; VI, 579; RS Ms. Boyle L. 2, fol. 143ʳ; Hunter, *Science and Society*, 137–8; Jacob, *Henry Stubbe*, 137–8. Du Moulin had succeeded in getting a license in Gunning's absence.

Stubbe, on the other hand, was forced to rely on an illicit printer, and he paid the price.

By the mid–seventeenth century, then, the state and the Stationers in concert had evolved a complex set of procedures for the establishment and regulation of propriety. Their focus was the register. Titles entered in this book were maintained to their enterers by the customs and ordinances of a Company that, in theory, embraced all their competitors under its regulatory régime. In the course of the consequent disputes over propriety, Stationers decided among themselves issues of identity and difference between texts. During a century and a half of animated discussion they developed a sophisticated and flexible social machinery for determining such issues. Its very confidentiality was in a sense exemplary. Discord must remain beneath the surface, leaving only an impression of seamless harmony. Amid a print culture characterized by ephemerality, transience, and discredit, *here*, Stationers indicated, could be found the embodiment of printing as a reliably self-regulating craft. Were their régime to fail, they implied, the result would be a fatal anarchy of discredit. No reader would be able to rely on printed books containing "wholesome knowledge."

But the register was not explicitly enshrined in law. "Literary property" is consequently an anachronistic and misleading term for the propriety it supported. When Stationers talked of "copy," they meant one out of a cluster of customs internal to their particular community, maintained by virtue of communal representations and habitual civilities.[160] Nonetheless, thanks to the culture of licensing, that propriety extended its range into the world of authorial rights and responsibilities. Authorial civility was inextricably entangled with Stationers' civility. For the modern figure of the individualized author to be constructed, this had to change. It was only with the lapse of the Press Act, then, when licensing disappeared and with it statutory protection for entries in the register, that the case for a *natural* property right in textual works began to be made on any discernible scale. After 1695 — and especially after 1710 — the site for the construction and maintenance of propriety rapidly departed from Stationers' Hall to the courts of the common law. As early as the mid-1720s, the Stationers' court had virtually forgotten how to handle piracy cases at all.[161] The shift was decisive. Different strategies became increasingly appropriate.

By this time more than two-thirds of London booksellers could lay claim to some copies; at least forty derived their main income from such copy

160. Loewenstein, "Script in the Marketplace," 269.
161. See the cases of abridgments of ecclesiastical and civil history brought in 1722: SCB H, pp. 115–6, 124–8. Note that the spokesman for the pirates here was Francis Fayram, who was to be the unauthorized printer of Newton's *System of the World* (below, p. 512).

ownership.[162] There was thus a substantial constituency for attempts to pre-serve Stationers' conventions. For the rest of the eighteenth century, copy-holding Stationers accordingly tried to prosecute at law alleged pirates of titles either entered in the register or, increasingly, established by first pub-lication. New concepts of authorship were constructed in the course of their attempts. In law courts, it became far more appropriate to argue at the level of principle. Lawyers, Stationers, and writers alike thus appropriated the latest Lockean notions of the entitlement lent by labor, applying them to intellectual work as Locke himself had applied them to physical. "Invention and labour are the marks of property," or so the argument ran, and these marks could be discerned in literary works as much as in inventions.[163] Tech-nology and natural philosophy also became crucial resources for these efforts. They supplied protagonists with both powerful arguments and important exemplary authors. Aristotle, Gassendi, Descartes, and Newton were the key authorial archetypes for at least one combatant, while rivals to bookseller John Dunton's *Athenian Mercury* suggested that a possessive Stationer like Dunton was essentially akin to the "Inventor of any small Mechanical In-strument."[164] By the 1760s, after two generations of such arguments, judges were building verdicts on the three pillars of the Lockean philosophy of property, works of natural philosophy such as Wollaston's High Church *Re-ligion of Nature Delineated*, and the precedent of Harrison's chronometer: it should be the same, remarked one, "whether the Case be *mechanical*, or *Literary*; whether it be an *Epic Poem*, or an *Orrery*."[165]

That was one side of the argument. Alternatively, true knowledge might be regarded as something founded in Creation. In that case, as one judge put it, "Invention and labour, be they ever so great, cannot change the na-ture of things, or establish a right, where no private right can possibly ex-ist." Truth could not be parceled out. "The Inventor of the Air-Pump had certainly a Property in the *Machine* which He formed," the same judge splendidly opined, "but did He thereby gain a Property in the *Air*"?[166] Lockean philosophy could thus be used to bolster claims to an inviolable,

---

162. Treadwell, "English Book Trade," 360.

163. Sir Joseph Yates, in *Speeches or Arguments*, 49; Yates was expressing at most qualified support for this notion.

164. *Letter to the Society of Booksellers*, 27. Compare Smith, *Lectures on Jurisprudence*, 399; Buckley, *Short State of the Publick Encouragement given to Printing*, 3; [Defoe], *Vindication of the Press*, 11; Locke, *Two Treatises of Government*, 327–44; [Gildon], *History of the Athenian Society*, 7, 14, 33–5.

165. *Speeches or Arguments*, 30; Burrow, *Question Concerning Literary Property*, 42–4, 70, 101. For the connection with patents for invention, see MacLeod, "Accident or Design?"; MacLeod, *Inventing the Industrial Revolution*, 196 ff.

166. *Speeches or Arguments*, 50; see also Rose, *Authors and Owners*, 87, for a similar senti-ment with respect to Newton.

perpetual property in authorial works, and patents for invention suggested protection for a limited time; but, as Condorcet and Diderot were debating in France at the same time, Enlightenment principles could also lead one to question whether literary property were conceivable at all. And all the while, practical efforts to defend the Stationers' customary propriety were becoming increasingly ineffective.[167] Adam Smith would eventually define the first purpose of government as being "to prevent the members of a society from incroaching on one anothers property," and name copyright as one of the only two kinds of monopolies to be justifiable in this context. But he could do so largely because it remained so fragile—both in fact and in theory.[168]

The propriety of print, based in the register and licensing mechanisms, had always rested on a pragmatic quadruple alliance between Stationers, writers, readers, and the state. It is perhaps not surprising that some contemporaries yearned for an alternative. For some gentlemen, even the Stationers' register seemed insufficient protection. Others resented and feared the power it left in the Stationers' hands. For each, an alternative did indeed exist. The writer or Stationer involved could go to Whitehall and appeal to the crown itself for protection to be granted under letters patent. A book thus "patented" was defended from comprinting by royal power. It was freed from the realm of the register—and simultaneously, as we shall see, from that of the licenser. In the seventeenth and early eighteenth centuries, patents became an increasingly attractive proposition. But they also became increasingly controversial. As the following section and chapters 4 and 5 explain, they gave rise to a struggle that threatened to transform print culture itself.

PRIVILEGES

A royal "privilege" was a personal favor from the monarch. It sprang, in theory, directly from the royal will. Put simply, the sovereign issued an "open letter" under the Great Seal, which enjoined all subjects to obey the conditions it stipulated. The recipient of that letter was in the proud position of receiving a royal gift.[169] Such "letters patents" were issued for a wide

167. Campbell, *London Tradesman*, 136. For the French debates, see the excellent discussion in Hesse, *Publishing and Cultural Politics*, esp. 104. For German arguments of similar scope, see Woodmansee, *Author, Art, and the Market*, 35–86. Campbell's book itself carried the stern warning: "By Authority. Whoever Pirates this Book will be Prosecuted": sig. π^v.

168. Smith, *Lectures on Jurisprudence*, 5, 11, 399–401, 472; Smith, *Wealth of Nations*, II, 733, 754.

169. Armstrong, *Before Copyright*, 26. A brief summary is in Davenport, *United Kingdom Patent System*, 14–20. In this respect the legal concept of the patent was a transcription of anthropological reality: see Davis, "Beyond the Market"; Findlen, "Economy of Exchange"; Findlen, "Courting Nature"; Johns, "Natural History as Print Culture."

range of purposes, to which the protection of books was a late and minor addition. In particular, they had long been used to intervene in commerce. Medieval kings had employed the device to suspend by royal prerogative the regulations of civic guilds in order to allow foreign workmen to operate. In the mid–sixteenth century it had again been put to commercial use, this time as a key element in the Elizabethan drive to encourage trade and manufactures.[170] Later still, Elizabeth and the Stuarts found patents to be a good way of both raising income and providing rewards to their courtiers, granting them enormously profitable monopoly rights in everyday products such as (most notoriously) soap. It was in this context that the use of royal prerogative to regulate trades and crafts became increasingly contentious. Londoners began to object strenuously to what they represented as crown interference, claiming that by ancient custom they enjoyed a right to exercise their trades freely within the City.[171] A complex struggle ensued, replete with allegations of court corruption and city aggrandizement. Eventually Parliament passed the so-called Monopolies Act of 1624, which attempted severely to delimit the scope of such privileges. Yet Charles I persisted in granting patents after his accession, and with the decay of his finances in the late 1630s the rate at which they were issued actually accelerated.[172] This use of patents for "projects" should be seen as intimately linked to the issue of printing privileges. The two kinds of gift were obtained in essentially the same manner and had essentially the same force. And in both cases antagonism to "monopolists" peaked at the outbreak of Civil War.

The issuing of patents granting the sole right to print or sell specific titles was an early consequence of the desire to regulate the new craft of printing. Across Europe, early applications were based on claims to have been the first to exercise the craft in a particular legislation; in England, the king's printer was awarded the first by Henry VIII. Later, however, the principle was extended, giving certain individuals rights, not just to specific works, but to whole classes of titles.[173] For example, there were patents in all law books,

170. Thirsk, *Economic Policy and Projects*, 51 ff.; MacLeod, *Inventing the Industrial Revolution*, 10–19.

171. The "Case of Monopolies," Darcy vs. Allein, 1602, was argued on this basis: 11 Co. Rep. 84b. See also Tailors etc. of Ipswich, 11 Co. Rep. 53a, and the Case of the City of London, 8 Co. Rep. 121b. In this context it is worth pointing out that the lord mayor occasionally demonstrated that he felt he had the right to allocate literary proprieties too: SCB E, fol. 45ᵛ.

172. "An Act concerning Monopolies and Dispensations with penall Lawes and the Forfeyture thereof": 21 Jac. I, c. 3; Asch, "Revival of Monopolies"; Sommerville, *Politics and Ideology*, 155, 102–3; Wormuth, *Royal Prerogative*, 12–19; Weston and Greenberg, *Subjects and Sovereigns*, 29 ff. In London such views coalesced in the idol of Magna Carta: Holt, *Magna Carta*, 316–37, 321; Thompson, *Magna Carta*, 100–20.

173. Armstrong, *Before Copyright*, 1–11; Feather, *Publishing, Piracy and Politics*, 11–14; Blagden, *Stationers' Company*, 32; Winger, "Regulations Relating to the Book Trade," 52;

and in all Latin schoolbooks.[174] Before long, patented books included an extremely wide range of titles, from primers and Psalters, through a large number of legal works, to Cunningham's *Cosmographicall Glasse* and classical authors such as Cicero. They began to prove highly profitable. But their purpose was not simply financial. It was hoped that by extending protection in this way, a new grade of tradesman would be created, wealthy and powerful within the book trade but directly dependent on crown favor. Patents thus promised to replace the power of the Stationers' community with that of the monarch. By the seventeenth century, moreover, such a caste had indeed come into being. The role and status of this caste—the patentees— were to prove bitterly controversial.[175]

The establishment of patents was swiftly followed by their first infringement. In the competitive environment of a rapidly expanding book trade, such comprinting soon became notoriously common. Given that patented books included some of the most elaborate being published, the monetary sums involved could be immense. For example, a nine-volume *Critici Sacri* produced by Cornelius Bee and others in the early Restoration cost about £1,000 in manuscripts and for preparing and "*methodizing*" the copy, even before paper and printing for the six-year project had been accounted for. The newly restored Charles II granted Bee a fourteen-year patent forbidding others from printing "any *part* or *parcell*" of the work, and Bee also took the precaution of entering it in the Stationers' Register at a cost of about £7. But when one Matthew Poole undertook a rival "*Synopsis of the Critical and Other Commentators upon the Bible*," incorporating several of the same writers in "*Epitome*," this one rival alone threatened Bee with utter ruin.[176]

The financial and personal stakes involved in patent contests were thus high. But their foundation in royal prerogative lent the violation of patents an additional significance that did not attach to the piracy of titles entered in the Stationers' register. Privileges, unlike entrances, were immediately actionable at law. When infringements occurred, their holders could take the matter to court rather than to Stationers' Hall. A different set of justificatory arguments therefore grew up around them, appropriate to this different setting. In particular, it was easy to present defiance of a patent as something

---

Febvre and Martin, *Coming of the Book*, 241–2. The same action was being taken at the same time in other countries; the first patents of all probably appeared in Venice at the end of the fifteenth century.

174. These are listed in Pollard and Redgrave, *Short-Title Catalogue*, 200–2.

175. Stationers' Company, *Registers 1554–1640*, II, 60–1, 61–2, 746–7; Blagden, "Stationers' Company in the Civil War Period."

176. Winger, "Regulations Relating to the Book Trade," 81; Simpson, "Literary Piracy"; [Bee], *Case of Cornelius Bee*.

approaching very close to sedition, since privileged books could be regarded as bearing the authority—and even the authorship—not just of the writer but of the crown itself.[177] This was clearly a representation bearing extraordinary implications. To perceive the full extent of those implications, however, it is necessary to say something about the nature of crown authority in Stuart England.

Royal prerogative was the crown's right to exercise power, both through the normal mechanisms of the law and also, in exceptional circumstances, above and beyond those mechanisms. It seemed the "essence" of crown authority: to challenge the prerogative was to attack kingship itself. What historians call the political nation was therefore virtually united in recognizing its legitimacy, at least before the 1640s.[178] Some prerogative powers were largely redundant—it was still technically possible to exempt subjects from paying Danegeld, for example. Others were far more consequential, but still largely uncontested. Such powers, which included the regulation of the coinage, certain customs revenues, and weights and measures, were considered part of what was called "ordinary prerogative." They were largely beyond argument, and were in any case generally regulated by normal mechanisms of the law. More controversially, however, the king could deploy "absolute prerogative." This meant overruling the routine implementation of the law. The monarch could "dispense" with the execution of laws in particular cases, and even (by extension) "suspend" the relevant statutory clauses altogether.[179] He could also enact positive measures, by issuing direct proclamations. Bacon and Donne had these powers in mind when they likened prerogative actions in the world political to miracles in the world natural: both were divinely willed events superseding normal laws.[180] But if the exercise of prerogative was a miracle, in this context it was an enduring one. Press regulation was based on this power both before the Civil War, when the prerogative court of Star Chamber was its overseer, and in the years 1679–85, when the Press Act was in abeyance.[181]

Everyone accepted that the king should normally rule according to law. To do otherwise would constitute "arbitrary" government, opposition to

177. Goldberg, *James I and the Politics of Literature*, 1–3, 59; Kernan, *Printing Technology, Letters and Samuel Johnson*, 27–35.

178. Ashton, *English Civil War*, 3–15; Burns, "Idea of Absolutism."

179. Hale, *Prerogatives of the King*, xlviii–liv, 257; Weston and Greenberg, *Subjects and Sovereigns*, 10–15.

180. Donne, *Essays in Divinity*, 81 ("*Nature* is the *Common Law* by which God governs us, and *Miracle* is his *Prerogative*"); Martin, *Francis Bacon*, 129–34; Martin, "'Knowledge Is Power,'" 199–204; Weston and Greenberg, *Subjects and Sovereigns*, 10–12.

181. Western, *Monarchy and Revolution*, 61–2; Siebert, *Freedom of the Press*, 27 ff.; Crist, "Government Control of the Press."

which was one of the great shibboleths of early modern England.[182] But disputes arose over what circumstances justified suspending that principle, and over how far the king could then go in exercising his absolute prerogative. Well before Hobbes, absolutists were insisting that the king must be reckoned to hold the sole sovereignty in the realm. He was therefore, they inferred, the sole author of all laws. Parliament was simply a counseling body, not a source of authority. It followed that the king could freely overturn not only ordinary statutes, but even clauses that might be inserted specifically stating that they were not to be overturned. It was then the subject's duty actively to obey the monarch in everything except direct contradictions of divine law, and even then to offer no more than passive submission. No mere human could justifiably act against the prince; only God, whose vicegerent he was, could properly presume to punish him.[183] As Bacon and Donne implied, then, the subjugation of the polity to the will of the monarch was part of a comprehensive system of Creation that could be suspended only by God himself.[184] King James I gave a characteristically bracing evocation. Even God called kings gods, he pointed out, and with reason.

> Kings are justly called Gods, for that they exercise a manner or resemblance of Divine power upon earth: For if you wil consider the Attributes to God, you shall see how they agree in the person of a King . . . they make and unmake their subjects: they have power of raising, and casting downe: of life, and of death: Judges over all their subjects, and in all causes, and yet accomptable to none but God onely.

However, such a forthright representation was not unanimously endorsed. Important common-lawyers—especially James's own chief justice, Sir Edward Coke—tried to qualify the notion of prerogative by asserting that it had historically been bound by the common law. Furthermore, they claimed that it still was.[185] The implication was rather subtle. Common-

---

182. Daly, "Idea of Absolute Monarchy," 241–5; Daly, *Sir Robert Filmer*, 53–5. For the distinction between "absolute" and "arbitrary" government, see also Bossuet, *Politics*, 81, 263–4.

183. Hale, *Prerogatives of the King*, l–li, 10–11; Sommerville, *Politics and Ideology*, 36–9, 101.

184. Knafla, *Law and Politics*, 197–201; Wormuth, *Royal Prerogative*, 40–46, 88–98; Weston and Greenberg, *Subjects and Sovereigns*, 1 ff.; Sharpe, *Politics and Ideas*, 7–23, 53; Figgis, *Divine Right of Kings*, chap. 7. Filmer did not stress the naturalistic argument: Daly, *Sir Robert Filmer*, 32–6, 97 ff., 154.

185. James I, *Political Works*, 307–8; Pocock, *Ancient Constitution and the Feudal Law*, 31–2, 35–55; Hill, *Intellectual Origins of the English Revolution*, chap. 5; Lockyer, *Early Stuarts*, 51–67; Davies, *Early Stuarts*, 19–20. Contrast Burgess, *Politics of the Ancient Constitution*, 5–6.

lawyers like Coke were not revolutionaries. They did not endorse action against the king himself, even in the event of apparent illegality. Although he himself could not be prosecuted for illegal actions, however, the king's *agents* executing those actions were vulnerable to legal retribution. In effect, it was taken as axiomatic that kings could not command illegality. If an action were illegal—as, given Coke's qualified view of prerogative, it might be—then the monarch could not have commanded it in the first place. So whenever a king issued a command, declared Sir Dudley Digges, "though by Letters Patent," if the command were illegal, then "those Letters Patent are void, and whatsoever ill event succeeds[,] the executioner of such commands must ever answer for them." In the Restoration, president of the Royal Society Sir Joseph Williamson was said to have found his position as secretary of state dangerous for just this reason.[186]

It was, then, the *use* of the prerogative that made it the subject of such intense debate. The controversy over royal prerogative was not driven by philosophy, but by practice. And it was practical implications that forced people to take sides. In particular, foremost in the minds of common-law writers was the threat they felt prerogative in action posed to a subject's property. If the king could exercise absolute prerogative freely, it was feared, then nobody could be secure in any possession. These fears escalated before the outbreak of the Civil War, and revived (in some) at Cromwell's ascendancy; they emerged forcefully again after the Restoration, when "arbitrary" government was identified with the insecurity of property associated with legally untrammeled (and recognizably French) sovereignty.[187] Charles II and his brother, James II, used prerogative powers to suspend execution of the Acts against Catholics and dissenters, much to the dismay of many in Parliament and the church. When James seemed ready to strip Oxbridge dons of their fellowships, since such posts were held as freeholds it was interpreted not only as an ominous gesture toward popery, but as an attack on the fundamentals of property too. Some even thought him likely to attempt a restoration of the monastic lands appropriated at the Reformation.[188]

As we have seen, however, individuals and collectives could see "propriety" not only in the ownership of goods and land, but also in customary practices. Some maintained that custom, defined as "common usage" exercised "time out of mind" (that is, for long enough to have no known moment of origin), could be appropriated by particular individuals or trade bodies, and then could not legitimately be alienated without their

186. Sommerville, *Politics and Ideology*, 101; Hale, *Prerogatives of the King*, 15; Browne, *Works*, IV, 92–3.

187. Sommerville, *Politics and Ideology*, 154; Miller, "Potential for 'Absolutism,'" 188.

188. Goldie, "Danby, the Bishops and the Whigs"; Speck, *Reluctant Revolutionaries*, 42–3, 144; Ogg, *England in the Reigns of James II and William III*, 196–200.

consent.[189] In 1624 parliamentary debates over monopolies focused on this aspect of prerogative, resolving that patents granted over a particular enterprise unlawfully displaced any preexisting freedom to work in the field.[190] It was in this context that trade and commerce became a key battleground between defenders of absolute prerogative and those of the common law.

It might be supposed that the London companies would be the natural allies of the common-lawyers in this debate. Yet a complicating factor compromised their position. This was the fact that the very charters by which those companies were incorporated were themselves products of royal prerogative.[191] The monarch granted their charters by letters patent, and any ordinances made by a chartered company had first to be vetted by the lord chancellor and lords chief justice for possible interference with royal wishes.[192] In the event of a company's becoming too impertinent, the crown could redeploy the same power and create new corporations to reconfigure the trade in question. Charles I actually did this, in a sustained attempt to circumvent the Monopolies Act. When the Press Act lapsed in 1679, his son seriously considered using this same power to incorporate a new Company of Printers to oversee the press.[193] In extreme circumstances, companies were even vulnerable to dissolution by the same power as had created them. "As a corporation thus made hath its original from the king," warned Hale, "so in some respects it hath its preservation." Common-lawyers and the members of the corporations themselves might see them as autonomous—something Hobbes characteristically likened to "many lesser Common-wealths in the bowels of a greater, like wormes in the entrayles of a naturall man"— but the crown believed otherwise.[194]

This was not merely an abstract idea. There did exist a recognized mechanism for the dissolution of a charter. The crown could issue a writ of quo warranto, alleging that the charter's present holders failed in practice to ful-

189. Pocock, *Ancient Constitution and the Feudal Law*, 32–8; Thompson, *Customs in Common*, 97–8. Toward the end of the seventeenth century the date of 1189 began to be taken as marking the beginning of "legal memory," and "time out of mind" to apply to any custom that seemed to have been immemorial at that date: Burgess, *Politics of the Ancient Constitution*, 256 n. 60.

190. Sommerville, *Politics and Ideology*, 155, 102–3; compare Wormuth, *Royal Prerogative*, 12–19, and Weston and Greenberg, *Subjects and Sovereigns*, 29 ff.

191. Hale, *Prerogatives of the King*, 240–5; Morgan, "Whose Prerogative"; *London's Lamentation*.

192. Stationers' Company, *Registers 1554–1640*, I, 4. This was also an issue for the Royal Society: Birch, *History*, I, 253. For a legal account of the status of charters, see Levin, *Charter Controversy*. Finch, Scroggs, and North used this rule to issue a public statement endorsing the Stationers' Company's new ordinance decreeing the printing of names on all publications in 1679: *To all men to whom these Presents shall come*.

193. Asch, "Revival of Monopolies," 365; Crist, "Government Control of the Press," 50–1.

194. Hale, *Prerogatives of the King*, 243; Hobbes, *Leviathan*, 230. Compare Samuel Parker in Ashcraft, *Revolutionary Politics*, 72. See also Morgan, "Whose Prerogative," 48, 51–5.

fill the conditions according to which it had originally been granted. An action of this sort was all but impossible to fight, since no charter's set of articles could possibly include all the further "meta-articles," as it were, necessary fully to determine the manner of its own future application. That impossibility meant that the crown was rarely going to lose a quo warranto case. The king would then regain possession of the charter in question, and could issue a new one incorporating whatever new conditions he might find expedient. Under Charles II and James II this procedure came into its own as a technique for remodeling boroughs and companies alike, so as to place trustworthy men in positions of practical authority and provide the right electoral prospects for Parliament.[195] In two bursts of activity concentrated in 1661–4 and 1682–5, the crown extensively revised the charters structuring much of England's trade and polity alike.

In this cause, as in others, retrospective verdicts have tended not to side with the defenders of high prerogative. But their arguments were neither facile nor based solely in self-interest. In fact, they saw royal supremacy as essential for the defense of individual property, arguing that the king must be free and powerful to defend his subjects' possessions fairly and successfully.[196] In part their arguments concentrated on landed property, but the prerogative right to customs revenues, at least, meant that the crown also had an interest in encouraging mercantile and trade endeavor, if only to help evade the need for parliamentary financing. This was a fact well known and worrying to the Restoration Whigs. Moreover, Tories were able to point out that trade itself was not free from arbitrary power. They observed that artisans increasingly found themselves subjected to tradesmen, quite without warrant. Printers, for example, endured an increasing and essentially arbitrary subjugation to booksellers. L'Estrange, for one, was keen to exploit this latter division. Moreover, booksellers' "arbitrary power," as Lord Chief Justice Sir William Scroggs explicitly called it, extended thence to the authors they effectively controlled. From this perspective, the existing chartered companies simply rendered such arbitrary domination durable. There was a substantive and important point here, and one particularly relevant to the domains of print.[197]

195. Miller, "Crown and the Borough Charters"; Sacret, "Restoration Government and Municipal Corporations"; Jones, *Revolution of 1688*, 43 ff. The reference to "meta-articles" is not merely theoretical: L'Estrange did in fact propose that the Stationers pass "a By-Law to oblige yᵉ Company to see their own By-Laws put in Execucon": PRO SP 29/39, no. 2. For quo warranto proceedings during the Middle Ages, and the forms of proof resorted to, see Clanchy, *From Memory to Written Record*, 21 ff.

196. Sommerville, *Politics and Ideology*, 134. Compare: Ashcraft, *Revolutionary Politics*, 252; Daly, *Sir Robert Filmer*, 53–4; Harris, "'Lives, Liberties and Estates.'"

197. Ashcraft, *Revolutionary Politics*, 14, 18–19, 232–3; Howell, *State Trials*, VII, 703; Harris, "Tories and the Rule of Law." George Jeffreys made a similar case in prosecuting Francis Smith: Howell, *State Trials*, VII, 934.

With trade organization so intimately bound up with notions of correct government, dissatisfaction over printing patents was readily represented as political action. Indeed, their first prominent opponent, Elizabethan printer John Wolfe, was portrayed in exactly this way. Wolfe had originally been an apprentice to the patentee John Day. After returning from a journey to Italy, he had applied for a large patent. It had been refused.[198] Wolfe then turned into a radical critic of the entire notion of prerogative copies. Proclaiming himself the trade's equivalent to Luther, he and a band of colleagues began systematically to comprint patented books. In response the patentees portrayed him as a potential insurgent, gathering "conventicles" in his home and "pretending suche skill in lawe, as to Discourse what the Prince by her highnes kingly Office may Doe." Wolfe, they alleged, had rejected his "Dutie toward god, toward [his] prince and [his] neighbor." Patentee William Seres thus claimed that in opposing printing patents as "agaynst the lawe," his followers "derogate[d] the princes awthoritye" over not just printing but all trades. They were, he warned, "disordered perverse and daungerous persons," who "oppose[d] themselves agaynst the quenes majesties prerogatyve."[199] The patentees deliberately contrasted themselves to this portrait, stressing that as royal clients they were genteel, and hence, as gentlemen, reliable.[200] And the richer ones, like Day, did indeed inhabit the fringes of the gentry. Thus while opponents of prerogative copies were claimed to destabilize not just the polity of printing but the polity at large, patentees could be trusted to produce safe books embodying safe knowledge—ridding almanacs, for example, of "fantasticall and fond prophecienges."[201] Faced by such antagonism, at length Wolfe's campaign grew violent. His old master, Day, found that he needed to deploy royal power to open a shop in Saint Paul's Churchyard, against the opposition of what his friend the archbishop of Canterbury called "sum enviouse bookesellers"; Day and his family narrowly escaped being murdered shortly afterward by an apprentice involved in pirating patented books.[202]

198. This was perhaps the patent opposed in Stationers' Company, *Registers 1554–1640*, I, 468. See also Strype, *Survey*, I, 222.

199. Stationers' Company, *Registers 1554–1640*, I, 144; II, 771–3, 776, 778–82. Barker accused Wolfe of "Machevillian devices," a pointed charge since Wolfe was in fact responsible for introducing Machiavelli's works to English readers. See Huffman, *Elizabethan Impressions*, 3; Donaldson, *Machiavelli and Mystery of State*, 86–110.

200. Stationers' Company, *Registers 1554–1640*, I, 114–5, 144. See also 751–3, 784–5, 807–12.

201. Stationers' Company, *Registers 1554–1640*, II, 753–69, 817–9. For the patentees' using what looks like piracy in defense of their interests, see: Pritchard, "George Wither's Quarrel," 27–33; Carlson, "Wither and the Stationers"; Stationers' Company, *Records of the Court*, xiv–xvi. For the political importance of prophecy see McKeon, *Politics and Poetry*, and Curry, *Prophecy and Power*.

202. Stationers' Company, *Registers 1554–1640*, I, 454, 466; II, 18–19, 753–69.

In this affair originated three of the most distinctive features of the seventeenth-century Stationers' commonwealth. First, the Privy Council's response to Wolfe included the germs of what later became the Star Chamber proclamations for regulating the trade, principally through the institution of licensers. From this date until the abolition of Star Chamber and the outbreak of the Civil War, press regulation would be the province of the prerogative courts as well as of the Company. Second, the patentees were sufficiently concerned to donate some of their copies to the Company to be held for the benefit of its poorer members—a donation that later became the foundation of the so-called English Stock, of which more below.[203] Finally, the treatment of the offenders set a precedent. Their description as seditious and sectarian stuck. A generation later, George Wither, another frustrated patentee turned pirate, would be described as having "bene woed by Sectaries." The association of patent piracy with sedition formed one of the most important elements of the fundamental conflicts traced in chapters 4 and 5.

Yet Wolfe was not, in fact, punished as a traitor. Far from being hanged, drawn, and quartered, he was bought off by being granted the (patented) position of Printer to the City of London, and was appointed a Company searcher. This strategy stuck, too. So although patent infringement was represented as a political act long before the time of the Stuarts, and continued to be so portrayed throughout the seventeenth century, culprits were more often brought into the fold than outlawed altogether. Moreover, not only did poachers become gamekeepers; the patentees themselves began to use what looked very much like piracy to defend their interests. Finding himself on the wrong side of the Stationers' Company grandees, George Wither, for example, complained that he was almost bankrupted by their publishing of his works "contrived, altered and mangled at their owne pleasures, without consent of the writers."[204]

It is possible to trace a tradition of vociferous discontent about printing patents extending from Wolfe in the sixteenth century until beyond the end of the seventeenth. The context of such conflicts, as hinted above, was that of the wider concern about monopolies.[205] Printing privileges were specifically excluded from the Monopolies Act, and James I and Charles I together made another forty-three individual grants.[206] But the relation between printing and other patents remained a matter of controversy. Might it be possible to envisage a printing patent of wide enough ambit that despite the

203. Stationers' Company, *Registers 1554–1640*, II, 751–3, 784–5, 786–9, 807–12.
204. Pritchard, "George Wither's Quarrel," 33, 41; Stationers' Company, *Records of the Court*, xiv–xvi.
205. An early example, ca. 1577, is in Stationers' Company, *Registers 1554–1640*, I, 111.
206. 21 Jac. I, c. 3, esp. § 10; Altick, *English Common Reader*, 19–20.

craft's exclusion it would still count as a monopoly, and as such be illegal? If so, had that point been reached? Moreover, both advocates and critics were adamant that the practices associated with privileges had broad consequences for the reputation of the craft and the credit of its products. Opponents of patents asserted that patentees produced books of bad quality and charged exorbitant prices for them. The privilege for legal texts, for example—perhaps the most consequential of all patents—meant that its holder could "Print the Books with bad Impressions, and yet make the Subject pay as dear for them, as for the best." In which case, how could the laws themselves be trusted? Such charges were made repeatedly. "*Why are Printers said to be the most lawless men in a Kingdom?*" demanded Richard Head a generation later; "Because they commit Faults *cum Privilegio*." And in 1713 the Scottish printer James Watson, observing that printers had descended in status until they were "scarcely class'd or esteem'd above the lower Forms of Mechanicks," blamed squabbling patentees for the degeneration. Many bible patentees no longer employed correctors, he alleged, and the pressmen they exploited were forced to work up to eighteen hours a day.[207]

Supporters of the patents régime, on the other hand, retorted that the security associated with privileges enabled the production of worthwhile texts that would never appear at all in other circumstances. They had a point. The making of elaborate folio volumes demanded substantial investment, which without due protection would only be ventured by the extremely foolhardy. But they further averred that gentlemen patentees, soaring above the commercial fray, could produce works of higher quality and fidelity than would be possible in an environment of ruthless competition between mercenary Stationers. They explicitly and consistently identified virtuous *people* with veracious *printing*. Thus John Wallis—licenser and keeper of Oxford University archives, as well as skilled mathematician and cryptographer—claimed that the abolition of privileges would prevent the production of a "fair edition" of any work of knowledge. Instead, he wrote, "every obscure Printer may presently Print the same in a small Letter and on worse Paper, and thereby ruin those at whose charges such Books were prepared for the press."[208]

Such arguments displayed the complex interactions of piracy, propriety, power, and knowledge. In the conflict over patents three subjects were central: the relation between print and political power; the very different consequences of a print culture governed by Stationers from one overseen by crown-appointed gentlemen; and the explicit identification of substantial

---

207. [Head], *Canting Academy*, 161; *Case of the Booksellers and Printers Stated*, 1; [Sparke], *Scintilla*; [Watson], *History of the Art of Printing*, 3, 11–22.

208. Astbury, "Renewal of the Licensing Act," 322. Compare Price, *Patrons and Musicians*, 178–87, for the effects of patentees' views on the availability of printed music.

works of knowledge as seriously affected by the issue. The patents conflict held the potential for a fundamental reconsideration of the nature, order, and consequences of printing in early modern society—a potential that chapter 4 sees realized.

One category of patents ought, perhaps, to have remained apart from this battle. In addition to those granted to individuals, privileges were also awarded to the Stationers' Company itself. In particular, from 1603 a clutch of titles and categories of books became the property of the Company, to be administered for the benefit of its poorest members.[209] This was a hugely profitable catch: the kinds of books concerned were those that always sold in the highest quantities, and some, especially almanacs, needed to be reprinted regularly. It became known as the English Stock. Its purpose was to prevent any recurrence of John Wolfe's insurgency by eliminating its constituency of discontented printers.[210] The incentive to conform was sharpened by withholding English Stock work from those guilty of unlicensed printing. And, to an extent, it was indeed above the fray. In 1641, Sparke's campaign against monopolies largely spared the Stock because of its avowedly philanthropic purpose.[211]

The Stock was divided into 105 "parts," which were allocated among the three ranks of the Company and administered as a joint stock. Fifteen, worth a third of the total, were assigned to the assistants. Thirty more, worth another third, went to approved liverymen. The remaining third were sold to between sixty and eighty of the commonalty; Sparke recorded that in practice these parts were often unofficially subdivided among members.[212] These partners provided capital for the Stock and benefited from its dividends. Newcomers had to swear an oath not to comprint any of the Stock's copies, and provide a dinner for the Table (Robert Scott, the printer of mathematics, refused his stock because the cost of this feast threatened to

209. This decree caused a new category of illicit practice to arise: printers would claim on the title page of a book that it had been produced abroad, so as to avoid the limit on copies. All Giordano Bruno's books were actually printed by John Charlewood in London, although they claimed to derive from Venice or Paris. Bruno wrote that this was "in order to sell them more easily and also to be able to issue them in more copies." See Woodfield, *Surreptitious Printing*, 20–1, 62–8. A list of English Stock titles in 1620 is provided in Pollard and Redgrave, *Short-Title Catalogue*, 200–2.

210. Blagden, "English Stock"; Feather, *History of British Publishing*, 37–8; Stationers' Company, *Registers 1554–1640*, III, 42–4. Standing formes were kept for some of the regularly printed titles, which were distributed to named printing houses every year. See SCB E, fol. 100ᵛ, for a list of these formes and the printing houses to which they were to be sent in 1680, and SCB C, fol. 190ᵛ, and SCB E, fol. 153ʳ for examples involving almanacs.

211. Stationers' Company, *Registers 1554–1640*, I, 17; IV, 525–6; Blagden, "English Stock."

212. Blagden, *Stationers' Company*, 94 n, 131; Blagden, "Stationers' Company in the Civil War Period," 5–6; Feather, *History of British Publishing*, 36–8; Stationers' Company, *Records of the Court*, viii–xi (see also xi–xiii for the smaller Latin and Irish Stocks); SCB E, fols. 118ʳ–121ʳ.

prove greater than several years' combined dividends).[213] The allocation of parts in the Stock was determined according to conventions of precedence similar to those operating in the Company more generally. Nevertheless, with the approval of the court of assistants, they could be bought and sold (to other Stationers), inherited, or mortgaged for ready cash. In particular, widows of freemen routinely kept their husbands' shares, to the extent that by 1644 over 25 percent were held by women.[214] Approval was not automatic, however; Roman Catholicism seems to have debarred a Stationer from holding stock, for instance, and in 1689 a serious dispute arose over whether those who were not practicing printers or booksellers should be allowed to hold shares.[215]

The English Stock soon became an extremely important element in the London book trade. The economic implications of the almanac privilege alone were huge. By the later seventeenth century the printers lucky enough to be engaged by the Company were regularly producing 500,000 copies in the last two months of every year, and perhaps fifty million were printed in the succeeding century. It is probably no exaggeration to say that the Company and its customs depended on the safe preservation of this one corporatized patent. That was why Company officers so doggedly pursued an endless stream of piratical competitors springing up not only in London, but in such towns as York, Chester, Exeter, Bath, and Leeds. Moreover, probably the most consequential adoption of the proprietorial concept of epitomes was developed in this context.[216] The Company justified its patent by defining an almanac as, in "substance," the annual calendar. The calendar was then itself represented as an epitome of the Book of Common Prayer, to which it was always affixed—and printing of which was restricted to the Company for safety's sake. Astronomer Royal John Flamsteed's attempt at a learned annual ephemeris, discussed further in chapter 8, may well have been one victim of the Company's efforts to maintain this privilege.[217]

213. SCB D, fol. 158ᵛ; SCB F, fols. 194ᵛ–196ʳ.

214. E.g., SCB C, fol. 288ᵛ; SCB D, fol. 107ᵛ; SCB E, fol. 74ᵛ. The same disputes arose over precedence as we have seen in the Company as a whole: e.g., SCB D, fol. 161ʳ.

215. SCB C, fol. 208ᵛ; SCB F, fols. 122ᵛ–123ʳ, 150ʳ, 216ᵛ–217ʳ; Blagden, *Stationers' Company*, 95–7.

216. Blagden, "Thomas Carnan"; Blagden, "Distribution of Almanacks." James Cotterell was fined £4 in 1664 for printing one thousand copies of a three-sheet almanac, and a month later the court decided that no almanacs whatsoever could be printed without its express approval: SCB D, fols. 88ᵛ, 90ʳ. It was fairly routine for the court to make such pronouncements; see, for example, SCB, fol. 43ʳ.

217. SCB D, fol. 193ᵛ; Hunter, "Science and Astrology"; Company of Stationers vs. Seymour, 1 Mod. 257, 3 Keble 792 (the latter being perhaps a curious decision, since the astrologer in question was John Gadbury, a Catholic who was about to be arrested for the papist orientation of his almanacs: Curry, *Prophecy and Power*, 72–6). Compare Company of Sta-

As well as requiring such inventive measures for its own defense, the Stock inspired, not to say funded, much of the rest of the Company's policing activities.[218] The assistants could adopt almost any measure they considered necessary to preserve its viability. That included comprinting against the comprinters: Company searchers could seize offending books and reprint them to "their owne proper use benefitt and behoofe." But despite its ostensible purpose, the Stock never quite managed to remain beyond controversy. Critics complained that it was hijacked by a few oligarchs, who kept supernumerary apprentices in an attempt to depress wages. Their ability to allocate Stock work as they pleased made journeymen their "perpetuall bondsmen."[219] Some Stockkeepers (as the six Stationers elected annually by the court to run the Stock were called) seem even to have pirated Stock titles themselves. The combination of Company and patent, promising as it had seemed, thus never really succeeded in overcoming the fundamental problems of the book trade.

Like the register and license system, patents were integral to proposals for regulating the press. While the former promised the restriction of individual seditious titles and the punishment of transgressing Stationers, the latter held out the more radical prospect of a reformed, gentlemanly community that would lack the motivation to produce such material altogether. Patentees might not have to submit their texts to a separate licenser, with the controversial consequences described in the next chapter. The relation between licensing and patents was also signaled by the Company's habit of referring to books as having its "license" to be printed. The usage was common for privileged titles belonging to the Company—printers would pay well for the Company's "Lycense" to print Stock books such as the works of Cicero. One way to obtain such a "license" was to persuade a prominent gentleman, such as an MP, to write to the court requesting permission to print a work falling under its patent; civility decreed that it would usually consent. Conversely, to print "w^th^out any lycence of this Comp^y^," as the Oxford printers did, was reckoned a serious matter.[220] Indeed, although

tioners vs. Lee, 2 Chan. Cas. 66 and 2 Show. K.B. 258, and Company of Stationers vs. Partridge, 10 Mod. 105. For an advertisement showing alleged links between piracy and the corruption of astrological data, see *Currant Intelligence* 55 (29 October–1 November 1681).

218. Stationers' Company, *Registers 1554–1640*, II, 786–9; III, 42–4, 679–82; Blagden, "Stationers' Company in the Civil War Period," 5–6; Feather, *History of British Publishing*, 36–8; Stationers' Company, *Records of the Court*, viii–xi; SCB C, fol. 256^r^; SCB E, fols. 118^r^–121^r^; SCB F, fols. 194^v^–196^r^.

219. Stationers' Company, *Registers 1554–1640*, III, 42–4, 679–82; IV, 525–6.

220. SCB E, fol. 47^v^; SCB F, fols. 25^r^, 66^v^, 132^r–v^, 162^r^, 195^r–v^, 263^r^; SCB G, fol. 80^r^. For threats see SCB E, fols. 64^r^ (for Mearne's "friends" paying £25 for a "licence" to print Cicero, and persuading the Company to warn Elzevir against importing copies), 151^r^, and 153^r^ (for

licensing is thought to have ended in 1695, there is evidence that in this sense it remained surprisingly intact. The Company held the rights by its English Stock patent to all almanacs, but the privilege stated that they first had to be licensed. It continued to use this article well into the eighteenth century to assert its right. Reiterating the nature of the patent to one would-be violator as much as thirty years later, the Company's clerk thus told him that even Stock almanacs "cannot be Printed without the Allowance of the Arch-bishop of Canterbury & Bishop of London." "And they have Actually Re-fused to lycense your Almanack," he added, "so that it is not in the Com-panys power to Print it if they would."[221]

CONCLUSION

The previous chapter outlined a Stationers' commonwealth in which the credit of printed materials was profoundly compromised. This chapter has described the interlocking social mechanisms devised by Stationers and po-litical governors in an attempt to reduce that commonwealth to order. It addressed the mechanisms available for generating and protecting credit in printed books. Those mechanisms were effective only insofar as they were put to use by particular agents and in particular places. The Stationers were their unavoidable participants. The discussion has thus focused on the col-lective civility of the Stationers, as created by their Company. It has de-scribed the formation and structure of this Company, displaying its connec-tions to civic and national political structures. The links were such that the Company represented a hierarchy autonomous enough that internal prece-dence could propel politically suspect Stationers to positions of practical responsibility, and yet integrated enough that violations of its own hier-archy implicated those of the city and nation. On the one hand, the king and lord mayor could intrude favored Stationers into senior positions; on the other, the assistants could indignantly denounce those intrusions. At a time when profound changes in the trade were occurring—in particular, when publishing booksellers were confirming their dominance over retailers and printers—such issues generated serious and far-reaching conflict. How-ever, the Company's hierarchy was confirmed and celebrated in an annual round of ceremonies, processions, sermons, and feasts. The civility affirmed on such occasions was not recognizable from classical maxims, and bore little resemblance to that of Castiglione or Cicero, but it was nonetheless real, complex, and consequential.

Acts and Monuments). For infringement see SCB F, fols. 177ᵛ–178ʳ (Samuel Smith vs. Thomas Dring, again over Cicero). The Company's 1694 ordinance stipulated that no text be printed without the "Licence or consent" of its owner: SCB F, fols. 205ʳ–206ʳ.

221. N. Cole to W. S——, 1 October 1724: GL Ms. 18760, I, fol. [19ʳ].

The principal site at which print credit was safeguarded was Stationers' Hall. In this castle met a Stationers' court that developed practical procedures for resolving peacefully all of the most violent arguments disfiguring the world of print. Authors and readers almost never entered this court, and could have little idea of its procedures; but their faith in print and its products depended on it. The discussion in this chapter breaches the walls of this institution to reconstruct for the first time the arguments and procedures through which the genuine was distinguished from the "counterfeit," the authorial from the unauthorized, and the printable from the unprintable.

The mechanisms of order fell into three principal categories: the Stationers' register, licensing, and royal privileges. Each was considered here in practice. The register was a book recording propriety in copies for the Stationers themselves; it was put to use almost exclusively in the Stationers' own court, and came to represent the Stationers' view of themselves as safe and orderly. This was propriety imposed on writers and readers by the Stationers' community. Privileges were almost the very opposite: granted at the request of individuals, they represented propriety imposed on printers and booksellers by royal fiat. Whereas violation of entrances in the register warranted an investigation by the Stationers' Company, violation of a patent could well be construed as near-sedition. The search and investigation machinery of the Stationers' Company tended to be common to both, however, with corresponding dependence on the skills and interests of particular Stationers. And both threatened the credit of a publication, in that a "counterfeit" undermined both the textual authority and the economic viability of its archetype. The amounts of each involved in such cases could be huge: with a multivolume edition of biblical writers such as Cornelius Bee's, thousands of pounds and the pristinity of Protestantism were at stake.

Licensing was another, connected response to a print culture characterized by endemic distrust. It was a machinery for producing credit. Books bearing a license, defenders of the practice often claimed, were "distinguish'd like Money, by a Royal Stamp." Would-be readers would know before purchasing it that a licensed book was no counterfeit and, moreover, "that there is no Poison in the Composition." Licensing thus acted as a public demarcation of knowledge from error. "All that are truly Learned" must therefore approve the practice. Recall that Samuel Parker reckoned that the Restoration's Press Act had been passed principally against "the great liberty of lying." Defenders accordingly maintained that the point of licensing was not simply to suppress works. It also guaranteed the epistemic and commercial probity of the very printed sheets to which an imprimatur *was* affixed. As Parker implied, a license was a badge of distinction. With licensing abandoned, every pamphlet's credit was placed on an equally insecure footing. That was why Defoe could allege that "an unrestrained *Press* gives a kind of *Imprimatur* to every thing that comes from it," bestowing on every ephemeral pamphlet a "publick *Note* of *Distinction*."[222]

As the discussion in this chapter has underlined, the practice of licensing necessitated the maintenance of fragile alliances within and beyond the Stationers' community. It could not possibly be a "censorship" system recognizable to modern eyes. Licensers had to create for themselves reading practices that would permit them to negotiate the labyrinthine protocols of the Stationers, while still retaining the power to restrict messages they might deem harmful. Henry Oldenburg discovered the disquieting truth that in this realm an attempt at brute suppression actually had the effect of spreading the dangerous message more effectively. Being a licenser was thus a very difficult task, made only more so by the fact that the credit signaled by the imprimatur was often taken to be the licenser's own. It was thus one at which many failed. Oldenburg was one such. In chapter 7, however, we shall see how Oldenburg's Royal Society was altogether more successful at fashioning for itself an identity as a *corporate* licenser.

Yet works that otherwise would have been published *were* denied licenses. As Oldenburg insisted in the course of resigning, he himself had rejected far more titles than he had passed. It may not have been repressive by twentieth-century standards, but the Stuart licensing régime did have consequences that caused serious concern to those subjected to its practices. Both Milton and the early deists, especially Charles Blount, argued that it raised the possibility of authors' works being permanently corrupted, if not lost altogether. If a licenser could erase and amend within a text, then how creditable was a licensed book as a reproduction of its writer's words? They chose their examples, significantly enough, from natural philosophy. After his appearance in *Areopagitica*, Galileo in particular became a totemic figure for campaigners such as Blount, Locke, and Tindal. Now was the moment of his construction as a Protestant hero of free thought.[223] And James II's appropriation of licensing by royal prerogative for Catholicism raised the prospect of Locke's friend, the private heresiarch Isaac Newton, becoming the English Galileo. The recondite character of his knowledge would not save it. "If there be found in the Book any one Opinion that thwarts the *Licenser's* Humour, whether it be of a Vacuum, Motion, Air, or never so inconsiderable a Subject," Locke warned, "the sense of that great man shall to all Pos-

---

222. *Arguments Relating to a Restraint upon the Press*, 16; [Defoe], *Letter to a Member of Parliament*, 41–2; *Man in the Moon*, 17 (15 August 1649), 142–3. For books themselves as marks of distinction, compare Chartier, "Publishing Strategies," 180–2.

223. Milton, *Areopagitica*, 23; [Blount], *Just Vindication of Learning*, sig. A3ʳ, 6–8, 11. Milton, of course, claimed to have met Galileo in Italy: French, *Life Records*, II, 413.

terity be lost." Defoe, too, declared after licensing had lapsed that any revival would cause "Dissertations and Transactions in all Sciences" to "fall to the Ground." Tindal agreed, echoing (almost certainly unconsciously) the experience of Sir Kenelm Digby. "We could not then hope for an impartial account even in natural things," he insisted, "since an evident Truth in Philosophy has been thought a Monstrous Error in Divinity."[224] With the licensing system in place, Locke demanded, "who knows but if the motion of the Earth may be found to be heretical as the asserting Antipodes once was?"

This ringing declamation appeared only in the 1690s, when England had apparently been secured for Protestantism, and King James was safely self-flagellating in Saint Germain. Licensing ended in 1695. Fittingly, the second edition of Locke's own *Essay Concerning Human Understanding* was one of the last books to appear with such an imprimatur; Tindal suggested that had licensing still been strongly enforced, it could not have appeared at all.[225] For Locke, experience and reasoning lay at the core of the very definition of a human being. Whoever attempted to hinder the communication of experiential knowledge therefore invaded "the natural Rights of Mankind." In succeeding years this kind of argument would begin to come to the fore. It is explored further in chapter 6, in an analysis of the crucial question of what Locke and his contemporaries believed the practice of reading to be. Still, however, the claim was not that printing per se was beneficial. It had indeed enabled readers to "furnish themselves with Notions and Discourses sutable to rational Creatures," as an anonymous writer conceded as early as 1663 — but only when properly exercised.[226] So while the representation of the press as a providential force for truth had become common, it remained contestable. Even the Stationers' own representations tempered praise for their art with warnings about the need for it to be subject to "order." The provision of that all-important order was what their Company was for. The next chapter explains how the practices it pioneered came to generate an urgent need for radical new accounts of printing—of its definition, its culture, its history, and its future.

224. [Defoe], *Essay on the Regulation of the Press*, 5; [Tindal], *Letter*, 29–30; [Tindal], *Reasons against Restraining the Press*, 9.

225. Locke, *Correspondence*, V, 785; see also IV, 614–6; Astbury, "Renewal of the Licensing Act"; Stationers' Company, *Registers 1554–1640*, III, 462; [Tindal], *Letter to a Member of Parliament*, 29–30; [Tindal], *Reasons against Restraining the Press*, 9–10 (his other example was Thomas Burnet's work on the history of the earth). Compare Meli, "Leibniz on the Censorship of the Copernican System," and for a contrasting view see Gregory, *Modest Plea for the Due Regulation of the Press*. On attempts to control the press after 1695 see Hanson, *Government and the Press*.

226. [Tindal], *Letter*, 7, 27; Ashcraft, *Revolutionary Politics*, 50–64; *Brief Discourse Concerning Printing and Printers*, 22–3.

4

JOHN STREATER AND THE

KNIGHTS OF THE GALAXY

Republicanism, Natural Knowledge, and the Politics of Printing

THE COMMONWEALTH OF BEES

Stationers' practices were political practices, in at least two senses: they incarnated social relations within the craft community itself, and they had extensive consequences for the wider social order. Their civility impinged upon the mores available to the reading audiences of their time. The previous chapter described the construction of this Stationers' civility, and outlined attempts to regulate it through patents and licensing. The very nature of printing, as represented and recognized by contemporaries, was forged by these practices. This chapter extends the argument further. It shows how the nature of print could be transformed. Its subject is the work of a man unusually active in refashioning knowledge, political order, and print culture alike: a soldier, pamphleteer, and printer named John Streater.

The chapter begins, as is appropriate for a discussion of seventeenth-century politics, with a beehive. It is March 1650. Charles I has been dead for over a year; England is a republic, a commonwealth, ruled over by a purged parliament. General Oliver Cromwell is in Ireland, fighting the bloody battles that are to result in the greatest displacement of population in that island's history. On the way to join him from London is an artillery train comprising some forty horsemen. The squadron is proceeding to Milford Haven for embarkation, heading for the siege of Clonmel.[1] Crossing from Gloucestershire into Wales a day or so before they are due to reach the coast, the soldiers find themselves billeted at a small town called Eastington. There the officer in command is entertained by the local parson. Finding him unexpectedly interested in issues of husbandry and natural philosophy,

1. PRO SP 25/64, p. 107.

the minister decides to show this young officer a new invention of which he is very proud. That evening, as the Sun sets, he leads him into his garden and reveals with a flourish a "stately square Pillar" standing in its center. The four sides of the pillar are fitted with iron doors. Opening them, the minister reveals glass panels set into the sides of the pillar. As the rays of the Sun strike the western face of the pillar, the officer, peering in at the opposite side, can see that within is illuminated an entire living "City." The edifice is an apiary.

His beehive, the minister declares, is "an Hyeroglyphick." It was originally topped by a statue emblematic of industry, making the whole "an Hyeroglyphick of labour." But the wind has brought this statue down, and by now it has been replaced by a cluster of dials and weatherglasses, a clepsydra, and a weathercock built by the techniques of mathematical magic such that it will "speak the Winds seat at Mid-night." The whole is surmounted by Latin inscriptions lauding the virtue of the bees' industry and community, and it is this in particular that the fabric now represents. It is "obvious to my Phantasie," explains the minister, that in its "Grandeiur" the pillar has become a "Hyeroglyphick of their Hyerarchy."

Remarkable though the apiary's architecture is, however, its most striking attribute is its use of glass panels. Thanks to these windows, the fascinated soldier is able clearly to observe the bees' "society." For the first time, he can survey directly the "stately City of the Bees." He can watch "their discharging of many severall and various Offices," including funeral processions (complete with somber music) and rituals of waiting on their "Commander or King." And he can see that the bees live under nothing less than "a perfect and exact Government." It is a memory that will remain with him.

The name of this minister was William Mewe. A pastoral cleric, and long an acquaintance of Sir Henry Vane, in the 1640s Mewe had been associated with the Assembly of Divines. At one point he had considered becoming a polemical author, but the prospect of confronting as formidable an opponent as John Milton had made him think again. Since retreating from the ideological fray in London, in his Gloucestershire haven he had remained receptive to curious visitors. "I like them well that veiw *Magnalia Dei in Minimis*," he averred. With his transparent apiary revealing the bees' every policy and practice, Mewe could entertain such interested guests in the evenings with "a diary of their Negotiations." He could even "shew my Friends the Queens Cells, and sometimes her person, with her Retinue." Moreover, he was proud of his creation not just because its transparent panels permitted the observation of bees' society, but because their transparency, he reckoned, "suits with the nature of that Creature." Inspired by the light shafting through their chamber, the bees were "much taken with their [own]

Grandeiur, and double[d] their taskes with delight." They produced more honey in his apiary than in any other hitherto built.[2]

Mewe's hospitality helped word to spread of his invention. Before long, the Etonian Nathaniel Ingelo had written to him on behalf of Samuel Hartlib to inquire about the device. Mewe suggested that Hartlib visit Eastington in person to see the apiary; instead, Hartlib sent some books of husbandry, and in exchange asked for a "full description of the transparente hyve." He also requested that Mewe send any spare hive he might possess to London, for perusal by the Committee for Trade and Foreign Affairs. The state itself might be interested in Mewe's invention.

Bees became the subject of special interest in the 1640s and 1650s. They came to occupy a prime place in the wide-ranging programs of reform in husbandry and manufactures that have been charted definitively in Charles Webster's *The Great Instauration*. For one thing, they promised substantial economic rewards. Mewe's hive, he guessed, might "be woorthe this nation 300 000li a yeere" if erected in every parish in the land, and Hartlib was keenly interested in this calculation. As Timothy Raylor has pointed out, high-quality honey was an extremely profitable luxury commodity in early modern Europe, and such estimates were by no means necessarily absurd. But bees also held out the prospect of superior, political benefits. "When I saw God make good his Threat, and break the Reines of Government," Mewe himself testified, "I observed, that this pretty Bird [the bee] was true to that Government, wherein God and Nature had set it to serve." This, more than any merely economic spur, was what had moved him to construct his apian city-state.[3] It promised a solution to England's problem of social and political order. With a hive like Mewe's, one could observe "perfect and exact government" at a time when England herself enjoyed neither.

2. Hartlib, *Reformed Common-Wealth*, 41–9; [Streater], *Observations Historical, Political, and Philosophical*, no. 8, 57–8; Baxter, *Holy Commonwealth*, xvii–xviii; Smith, *Literature and Revolution*, 302. The account given here is an imaginative reconstruction of a meeting that almost certainly took place. That Streater saw Mewe's hive in its Gloucestershire location is evident from his testimony in *Observations*; and he certainly did embark for Ireland from Milford Haven in March 1650, on the road to which Eastington stands. It is not absolutely certain, however, that this was the occasion for his seeing the hive. In summer 1997 I visited Eastington myself. The church still stands, as does its vicarage; and there are beehives next to the churchyard.

3. Hartlib Papers, 26/29/49A (notes for queries to be addressed to Mewe, in the hand of Sir Cheney Culpeper); Hartlib, *Reformed Common-Wealth*, 46–7; Webster, *Great Instauration*, 162–3; Raylor, "Samuel Hartlib." The literature exploring the various political and moral lessons to be learned from bees was very extensive indeed. See, for example, Butler, *Feminine Monarchie*, sigs. B2ᵛ, D3ᵛ (and K3ʳ–L3ʳ for transcriptions of bee music); Levett, *Ordering of Bees*, 65–9; Purchas, *Theatre of Politicall Flying-Insects*; Rusden, *Further Discovery of Bees*, sig. [A6ʳ⁻ᵛ], 9–11. For an overview, see Thomas, *Man and the Natural World*, 62–3, 70. For a Continental example, see Findlen, *Possessing Nature*, 214–6.

Bees thus had what were referred to as "uses moral," as well as uses economic. Their husbandry was spiritual husbandry, useful as much for the soul of the beekeeper as for monetary profit. There was a "Morality and Theologie or Divinity of Bees," just waiting to be discovered and applied. As Raylor rightly says, bees were commonly recognized to be sound economists and good husbandmen; they were clean, chaste, pious, and impeccably ethical. They were also excellent geometers and exemplary architects—as witness the form of a honeycomb. Not only that; to what else could one attribute the performance of the adept bee than to an animal alchemy, "so naturally doth the Bee transmute what it sucks into Honey . . . inriched with a rare Quintessence"?[4] This, Mewe revealed to a correspondent, was what he was really after: he wanted to observe *both* "their work and government." Little wonder then that Hartlib also wanted Mewe to reveal any "experiences" he might have to offer. He was eager for any insights that might aid "the advancement of theire commonwealthe amonge us."[5]

For all these reasons, Hartlib had long been concerned to collect information about bees and their keeping. Mewe's transparent hive now became central to his efforts. Soon, other such apiaries were being built. John Wilkins, parliamentary intrudee at Wadham College, Oxford, constructed one of the most impressive in the gardens of the college. Henry Oldenburg spoke of seeing "here in Dr. Wilkins' garden two very fine glashives wch I am much taken w^th, both for ye entertainment, this invention giveth to ye mind, about the curious workmanship of this creature, and then, the mercy wch thereby the same may receave for its busy pains."[6] Visiting in 1654, John Evelyn was proudly shown a set of such apiaries, "built like *Castles* & *Palaces* [and] adorned with a variety of dials, little statues, [and] vanes." Much taken with them, Evelyn carefully drew one, and later visited Hartlib himself to see his own version. Wilkins gave an empty hive to Evelyn for his own garden at Sayes Court. Much later, King Charles II would make a special trip to see it, and by 1678 he would have one of his own.[7]

Hartlib began collecting material on beekeeping in earnest in about 1650–1. His efforts bore fruit in a publication appearing in 1655, entitled *The Reformed Common-Wealth of Bees*. Its centerpiece was a dramatic illustration of Mewe's hive, created by a "prodigious young scholar" whom Wilkins had introduced to Evelyn on his visit: his name was Christopher Wren (fig. 4.1).

4. "Bees out of the falling dew, by a perculiar fermenting virtue, doe really transmute what they suck into Honey": Hartlib, *Reformed Common-Wealth*, 27, 29–30; Raylor, "Samuel Hartlib," 105–6.

5. Hartlib, *Reformed Common-Wealth*, 41; Hartlib Papers, 26/29/49B.

6. Oldenburg, *Correspondence*, I, 101–3.

7. Evelyn, *Memoirs*, I, 271; Parry, "John Evelyn as Hortulan Saint," 130–1; Raylor, "Samuel Hartlib," 105; Rusden, *Further Discovery of Bees*, 29.

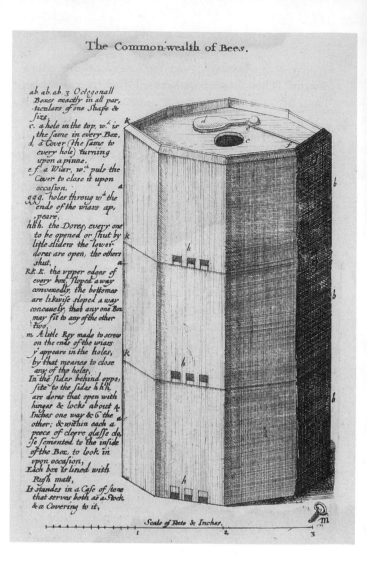

The Common-wealth of Bees.

ab. ab. ab. 3 Octagonall
Boxes exactly in all par,
ticulars of one Shape &
Sise;
c. a hole in the top, w.^ is
the same in every Box,
d, a Cover (the same to
every hole) turning
upon a pinne.
e.f. a Wiar, w.^ puls the
Cover to close it upon
occasion.
g.g.g. holes throug w.^ the
ends of the wiars ap,
peare,
h.h.h. the Dores, every one
to be opened or shut by
litle sliders the lower
dores are open, the others
shut,
R.R.R. the vpper edges of
every box, sloped away
convexedly, the bottomes
are likewise sloped away
concauely, that any one Box
may fit to any of the other
two,
m. A litle Key made to screw
on the ends of the wiars
y appeare in the holes,
by that meanes to close
any of the holes,
In the sides behind oppo,
site to the sides h.h.h.
are dores that open with
hinges & locks about 4
Inches one way & 6 the
other; & within each a
peece of cleere glasse cla,
se cemented to the inside
of the Box. to look in
vpon occasion,
Each box is lined with
Rush matt,
It standes in a Case of stone
that serves both as a Stock
& a Covering to it,

Scale of Feete & Inches.

FIG. 4.1. The apiary encountered by John Streater in Gloucestershire, as drawn by the young Christopher Wren. Hartlib, *Reformed Common-Wealth of Bees*. (By permission of the Syndics of Cambridge University Library.)

The Oxford construction had not worked well, mainly as a result of its having been built three apian stories high. Introduced at the base of this structure, the bees declined to ascend far within it. Nonetheless, and despite demanding skilled cabinetry, Wren's design—his first published architectural image—was to produce practical imitators in estates across the country. And no wonder: Hartlib had prepared the book in order to present it, along with such a hive, to the most important beekeeper in the land—Oliver Cromwell.[8]

The Reformed Common-Wealth of Bees also represented a reunion for Mewe and the soldier he had entertained so hospitably. That soldier had

8. Hartlib, *Reformed Common-Wealth*, 50–52; Raylor, "Samuel Hartlib," 91–2, 104–5.

gone on to serve three years in Ireland, before returning to London to embark on a notable series of political activities. His name was John Streater,
and in his guise as printer he had produced the book for Hartlib and the
notorious radical bookseller Giles Calvert.[9]

In this chapter I want to make Streater stand, like Mewe's apiary, as
a hieroglyphic. His encounter with Mewe's beehive was representative of
a consistent interest that he displayed in matters of natural and political
knowledge—two spheres he believed inseparable. Streater thought such
knowledge—its creation, distribution, and control—was the key to creating a stable and lasting commonwealth. And as a printer himself, he was in
a special position to make and deploy artifacts embodying the forms of such
knowledge of which he approved. In doing so he constructed an important
and influential articulation of republicanism. One of the aims of this chapter
is to reconstruct for the first time Streater's account of the politics of knowledge and action. Its framework is thus in a sense biographical, and it tells a
story that deserves to be told in its own right.[10] But the chapter also addresses a number of more general issues. It suggests that the history of political or scientific thought is also the history of political or scientific books,
their makers, and their readers; and at the same time, it is the history of the
skills through which books have been made, distributed, and put to constructive use. Those skills have changed over time. By concentrating on a
figure who made books both as a writer and as a printer, we also further
the questioning of authorship advanced in preceding sections of this book.
Authorship and authority alike are better seen as *attributions to* a book (by
Stationers, readers, legal inquisitors, and others) than as *attributes of* a book.
They were matters of cultural practice and negotiation. Since they were not
intrinsic, they could be challenged. Almost paradoxically, by adopting a biographical focus this chapter questions the assumed historiographical primacy
of the philosophical author.

If Streater is to be a hieroglyphic, then like Mewe's invention he is perhaps most suitably a hieroglyphic of labor. His story is an emblem of the

9. Streater's name does not appear on the title page of Hartlib, *Reformed Common-Wealth*
itself but is displayed on that of *Reformed Virginian Silk-worm*, with which it was issued as a
single tract.

10. Existing biographical sources on Streater include the *Dictionary of National Biography*,
and Greaves and Zaller, *Biographical Dictionary*, III, 211–2. Neither is entirely trustworthy.
The most extensive contemporary account is Streater's own, in *Secret Reasons of State*. He also
appears in passing in many modern accounts of the political history and thought of his time,
especially those involving appraisals of James Harrington. Yet he has not generally been recognized as an original and intelligent writer. Pocock's rather grudging acknowledgment that
he was not "illiterate" is representative: Pocock, "James Harrington and the Good Old
Cause," 34; Harrington, *Political Works*, 6–14, 38. The only author to attempt a reappraisal is
Nigel Smith: see his *Literature and Revolution*, 196–9, and "Popular Republicanism in the
1650s."

cultural work by which books were made and put to use. This is work that intellectual history too often contrives to forget. But Streater is also emblematic of the work needed on a more general level to construct a usable representation of printing and its effects. The chapter demonstrates the salience of natural knowledge for the decisions he took to just this effect, over a period of some three decades. His labors can be seen as culminating in an audacious plan to refashion print itself. They also helped to generate the greatest single text of natural philosophy ever produced in England, and perhaps the world: Isaac Newton's *Principia*.

REPUBLICANISM IN THE INTERREGNUM:
LAW, MAGIC, AND CREATION

John Streater was born in Lewes, Sussex. It was a godly town, and Streater's was a godly family. His brother Aaron, for example, combined sectarianism with illicit medical practice and a keen interest in explosives. He left Lewes and ended up a radical preacher in London. When he died, John promised Hartlib that he would pass on Aaron's papers on the cultivating of saltpeter, the central ingredient of gunpowder and therefore a substance of no little political importance.[11] Like his brother, by this time John Streater had left the country and taken the road to London. He began an apprenticeship to Stationer Robert Hoskins there in 1635. But at the outbreak of civil war he interrupted his service in order to join the parliamentary army. He served at Newbury, and was wounded at Edgehill.[12] By now his twin vocations had been established. Trade and soldiering would vie for his commitment henceforth.

When he was eventually freed, in June 1644, Streater almost immediately hastened to establish his own enterprise as a Stationer. It was an exciting moment to become a printer or bookseller. The war, along with the collapse of Caroline licensing and privileges, had witnessed a dramatic increase in printing and pamphleteering. The result was an explosion of uncertainty. Printers, booksellers, and readers alike reeled from an environment of "counterfeiting," and the citizenry dissolved into a "rabble of all opinions." Knowledge appeared and disappeared daily, with alarming tran-

---

11. McKenzie, *Stationers' Company Apprentices 1605–1640*, 85; McKenzie, *Stationers' Company Apprentices 1641–1700*, 83, 160. For Aaron Streater see his *Letter sent to my Lord Maior*, in which, describing himself as a "Divine, and licensed Physitian" (p.6), he defends Brownists as peaceable; Cook, *Decline of the Old Medical Régime*, 82. For Streater's promise see Hartlib Papers, 39/1/22A. There was another brother, Thomas, who was apprenticed to John almost immediately after the latter was freed as a Stationer in 1644; nothing further is known of him. For saltpeter see Webster, *Great Instauration*, 377–80. For Lewes's Puritanism, see Thomas-Stanford, *Sussex*, 16, 22, 29, 31, 94, and Fletcher, *County Community*, 62, 70–72, 124.

12. [Streater?], *Clavis ad Aperiendum Carceris Ostia*, 26.

sience. Indeed, as attested in chapter 2, this was why printed reports insisted so strongly on their historicity and permanence. It is hardly surprising, then, that when Streater set up as a bookseller and printer himself he immediately encountered opposition. The Stationers' Company was facing both internal turmoil and extraordinarily fragile trading conditions. It was unsympathetic to new printing houses and immediately moved to suppress Streater's as one devoted to counterfeiting the Company's titles. Streater countered by suing its wardens.[13] It was the beginning of a conflict which would last three bitter decades.

Rebuffed by the Stationers, Streater returned to the army. He probably fought in the New Model in the second civil war, before being summoned to Ireland. There he remained for three years, acting as a fortifications engineer and reaching the rank of quartermaster-general of the infantry. But his service came to an abrupt end in 1653. Streater had obtained leave from his commander, Fleetwood, and returned to London. He arrived there in early April, just in time to participate in the crisis surrounding the fall of the Rump Parliament. His experiences in those fraught days horrified him. Streater found himself an eyewitness to the tense scenes in Cromwell's headquarters in the Cockpit, adjacent to Parliament itself, during the days leading up to his decisive action against the Rump. There he listened dismayed to Cromwell's speeches to the officers immediately before and after the expulsion of the MPs.[14]

Streater had believed that the Rump was about to dissolve itself in favor of successive periodic assemblies. Hearing the general speak, he concluded immediately that Cromwell had in truth intervened to preempt this action on behalf of a corrupt army interest, and to preserve his own threatened command. The implications "astonish[ed] and amaze[d]" him. Cromwell must intend "nothing lesse then making himself absolute Lord of his Country." Even as he listened to the general's speech to the officers, Streater scribbled down ten points questioning his justification of the expulsion. He then distributed them, before Cromwell's own eyes, among the officers in the Cockpit.[15] His action, they declared, was "next door to Monarchy," and

13. SCB C, fols. 239[v], 242[v], 248[v]. Given that later antagonists would claim that Streater learned his trade by printing during his service in the New Model Army, it is interesting to speculate on whether he might have been involved in the clandestine printing for army radicals between 1646 and 1650, and even before the advent of the Levellers, which Austin Woolrych has discerned: Woolrych, *Soldiers and Statesmen*, 34–5, 44.

14. Streater, *Secret Reasons of State*, 2–6; Gentles, *New Model Army*, 424–39.

15. Thus, at least, according to Streater himself: Streater, *Secret Reasons of State*, 2–6, where the queries are reprinted; "Ten Queries"; Worden, *Rump Parliament*, 368–9; Cromwell, *Writings and Speeches*, II, 634; Howell, *State Trials*, V, 370; Woolrych, *Commonwealth to Protectorate*, 69–70, 76, 130–131.

nothing less than "a preparation to Absoluteness and Tyranny." Streater's queries suggested instead a new six-month Parliament, to be elected by the citizens "according to their undeniable Rights." But it was a futile gesture, albeit a brazen one. Streater's prompt skepticism notwithstanding, anger at the end of the Commonwealth hardly proved overwhelming. Even his own reaction was laced with mordant irony. When Oliver's major supporter, the Fifth Monarchist Thomas Harrison, informed him blandly that Cromwell "sought not himself, but that King Jesus might take the sceptre," Streater replied that "Christ must come before Christmas" or else "he would find his place occupied."

Among troops back in Ireland, however, discontent was more vociferous. Several officers began to express unease at the coup, and Cromwell himself grew concerned at the soldiers' "evill intentions." Indeed, it is virtually certain that before setting foot back in England, Streater himself had already been involved in radical political discussions in the army in Ireland. He claimed that he had composed a political tract there, which on arriving in London he had entrusted to the supreme radical bookseller, Giles Calvert. Under Calvert's stewardship it appeared in print at the end of March, some three weeks before the Rump's expulsion, as *A Glympse of that Jewel, Judicial, Just, Preserving Libertie*. Here Streater had described his favored form of society, in retrospect making explicit the grounds for his opposition to Cromwell's action. The central attribute of that society was the "duty" it enjoined on all citizens actively and continuously to watch to their freedoms. Every reader must "Indeavour to understand thy Liberty," and in particular to know "the Power of thy Judges, thy right, the Lawes." Such knowledge was the foundation of a free commonwealth. Ignorance alone permitted "the assumed Lording of Usurpers." So that all might acquire knowledge of "Affaires," Streater therefore exhorted his readers to "converse often with knowing men: and let knowing men endeavour to inform the lesse knowing." Streater was urging citizens to raise themselves into critical commonwealthsmen by active conversation and vigilant reading.[16]

In making this case, Streater deployed a respectable degree of learned classicism. He referred to the histories of such ancient figures as Caesar, Lycurgus, and Alexander to support this central argument for knowledge. But he was also making a point about practice. It was a frequent commonwealth theme: that "liberty," the self-rule made possible by understanding, could be possessed only by those who both were knowledgeable and put their knowledge to good use. This meant that the people must exercise their

16. Streater, *Glympse*, sigs. A2ᵛ–A4ʳ. A comparison is appropriate with Milton's representation of a critical reading citizenry in *Areopagitica*, published almost a decade earlier and in a very different polity: Smith, "Popular Republicanism."

knowledge in a sustained and active practice of *judgment*. Thus the era when Rome had been at its greatest, Streater insisted, had been when "every member of that Common-wealth perfectly understood the mysteries of State, and were competent Judges in all matters and causes arising in the Commonwealth." In such a state "every one was an able defendant of their Libertie and Countrie." Not only was a republic of this character possessed of liberty; it would also be strong, because its constituent "interests" would be harmonized. The prowess of republican Rome at this time was therefore comprehensible, since "it is hard to oppose such a composed Body, by such a Body or Power as is acted or supported by the Counsels or Interests of few." But Rome's power had declined, he continued, when the "secret reasons of State" were monopolized by "few, or one person." The application to his own commonwealth was clear, since the English republic had in three short years emphatically reversed a reputation for military impotence confirmed during two generations of Stuart rule. In Streater's own time, too, it would be "the policy of him that would invade the liberty of a people, to keep them ignorant." This would be a formula for weakness as well as tyranny.[17]

This led immediately to a recommendation for action. Streater urged that "the Lawes of the Commonwealth should be explained and abbreviated, fit for the understanding of every one of capacity."[18] This would facilitate the construction of his knowledgeable commonwealth. However, unlike an ancient city-state, England was too large for its people to meet together "in a Market-place, or in a Theater" to judge "matters of State" in a vast collective conversation. So a Parliament must be elected as a "Representative" of the people to fulfill this function, and its laws must be printed. In such a system, government would still remain "essentially" in the people, since all citizens would be "equally interested" in the assembly's deliberations and decisions. The way to avoid this régime's being overturned by a single person would then be to ensure annual reappointments to positions of power, both military and civil, with previous holders barred for five years. Judges, too, should be elected annually, "out of the Learned of the Law."

Streater proposed an extra reason for this: a reason based in physiology. "Continuance in any one action or undertaking whatsoever, burdeneth the

17. Streater, *Glympse*, 1–2, 5. For the importance of the republic's military successes in bolstering republicans, compare Scott, *Algernon Sidney and the English Republic*, 20–1, and Scott, "English Republican Imagination," 42.

18. Streater, *Glympse*, 5. That the law should be printed in English had long been a central tenet of the Levellers: see, for example, *The Moderate*, 32 (20 February 1648/9), 315; 33 (27 January 1648/9), 322–2; 39 (10 April 1649), 397. Contrast this to Hobbes's view that "it belongeth to the essence of all other Lawes [than the law of nature] to be made known, to every man that shall be obliged to obey them, either by word, or writing, or some other act": *Leviathan*, 187–9. In Hobbes's version the aim is to generate obedience and peace on the part of the people; in Streater's, it is to ward off the threat of tyranny in the powerful.

spirits," he maintained; "for the spirits that give life to all action, most usually spend vigorously upon noveltie; but being spent, are no other then as
tired jades, that leave one half of their work undone." He was referring to
the animal spirits that, in contemporary physiology, spurred the human
body into motion. These spirits circulated ceaselessly in a living body, being
channeled through the blood vessels and nervous system to vivify, transmit
sensations, and coordinate actions. As will be explained further in chapter 6,
the passions modulated by these spirits were of extraordinary significance
for the everyday lives of early modern men and women. All their experiences, and all their reasoning too, depended on them. Here, then, was a
compellingly general reason, inscribed in Creation itself, why offices should
be held only for "one year, not more, rather less." It lay at the core of Streater's entire polity. His paramount aim was to unify the dynamics of diverse
administrative and political mechanisms—corporations, companies, and
courts. He believed he could do so by constructing an intricate, yet perpetual, network of circulations, modeled on the natural order. The channels
for these motions—the equivalent of nerves, or blood vessels—would be
laws, for "there is nothing preserveth Nature more then Law." [19]

The army's reaction to all this was unsympathetic. Streater was court-
martialed and discharged.[20] But this was not enough to silence him. Six
weeks later, he was arrested for producing what was probably the first issue
of a periodical, *The Grand Politick Informer*, the purpose of which was again
"the setting forth the danger of Trusting the Arms of a *Common-Wealth* in
the hands of a single Person." No copies of this are known to have survived,
although a hostile response has that quotes extensively from its target's attacks on military rule.[21] Streater was now interrogated, before being imprisoned on the authority of Barebone's Parliament for "publishing of Seditious
Pamphlets against the State." [22] But such was his anxiety "to unmask and
unrobe the state of things," and "discover the reasons of state" underlying
present affairs, that he managed to produce an issue of his *Informer* even
from within the jail itself. He now alleged that trial by jury was about to be
abolished—a claim immediately taken up by other radicals—and warned

19. Streater, *Glympse*, 2–3, 7, 9. In 1656 William Sheppard's *Epitome of all the Common
and Statute Laws of this Nation now in force* was published, the first vernacular translation in
one volume. See Matthews, *William Sheppard*, 125–6.

20. He claimed to have resigned ([Streater?], *Clavis*, 26), but his choice in the matter was
probably limited. Colonel Matthew Alured, another officer serving in Ireland, was by now
also in London and had produced his own petition against Cromwell. Alured's immediate
prospects looked even worse than Streater's: he escaped execution only after pleas of mitigation from Fleetwood. Birch, *Collection of the State Papers of John Thurloe*, II, 285, 286, 294–
5, 313–4, 709, 719, 728, 733.

21. Streater, *Secret Reasons of State*, 6. The response is *A Stop to the mad Multitude*; Stationers' Company, *Registers 1640–1708*, I, 428, 430.

22. PRO SP 25/70, pp. 283, 284, 363, 366.

that this was merely the prelude to a sinister plan "that the Records of the Nation should be burned." This would ease the new régime's acquisition of power by making all property reliant on its whim, and by preventing opponents from pleading on the basis of such documents as Magna Carta or the Petition of Right. Reason of state would be rendered irrevocably secret. It was the rank antithesis to Streater's ideal of public knowledge through printed laws. Under such a dispensation, he pronounced, "the people may account it a favour to live."[23]

Streater repeatedly appealed for his release by means of habeas corpus. The authorities fought hard to keep him interned. On 14 November, the keeper of the Gatehouse received orders that he was a special prisoner of the Council of State, too dangerous to be released. A week later Parliament voted that he be detained indefinitely. Apart from his own defiance, as Streater almost certainly knew, there was an ulterior reason for this assiduity. Also keen to secure his freedom was the Leveller leader John Lilburne, then interned in the Tower. A release for Streater might well establish a precedent for a parallel action on Lilburne's part.[24] Streater himself thus took care to have the exchanges in his several hearings "taken in short hand." He later ensured that they were published, along with arguments that he had prepared for the court but never actually voiced. The ostensible reason was to demonstrate that nothing must stand against law and reason—not even Parliamentary orders.

Most of his previously philosophical themes here reappeared as legal arguments. Streater especially appealed to what he called "Record," and to Magna Carta in particular. He maintained a case about the status of such legal documentation in general, as the subject's only shield against slavery. Law was "written by the finger of God," he declared. Just as in the natural world God bound even himself by laws, so the national law was "as well binding to the Law-giver, as to those that are to give obedience unto it." "If he create a World, and willeth it to continue," God himself must undertake to "support it in its beauty and strength, and by his providence support the several beings in it." Here Aristotle could be called into the lists. He provided an authoritative voice for Streater's opinion that *"Where just Law ruleth, there God may be said to rule."* Aristotle was also the source for the

23. [Streater], *Further Continuance of the Grand Politick Informer*, 39, 42; Woolrych, *Commonwealth to Protectorate*, 294–5. A journal of early 1654 called *The Politique Informer* was not evidently connected to Streater's. Contrast Wren's preference for monarchy because its "Debates are clearest, the Results of them most secret, and the Execution sudden": [Wren], *Considerations*, 67–8.

24. [Streater?], *Clavis*, 2–3 and passim; [Streater], *Further Continuance*, 42; Howell, *State Trials*, V, 366–406; PRO SP 25/70, p. 286; PRO SP 25/72, pp. 55, 89; *Journals of the House of Commons*, VII, 353; Woolrych, *Commonwealth to Protectorate*, 205; Streater, *Secret Reasons of State*, 6–8; Gregg, *Free-Born John*, 334.

dictum that "it is better to govern by good Laws, then good men." But law stood for nought if it could not be exercised. Practice counted for everything.[25] Here, Streater observed that the return against him named neither the supposedly seditious pamphlet for which he was held, nor in what way it was seditious, nor any time or place of a suggested crime. "Generals" were "nothing in Law," he maintained—they could not be recognized as a cause for imprisonment. What was left was the likelihood that the Council of State had interned him for "secret reasons of State." The legality of causes of this sort, Streater argued, had been exploded by Coke's insistence that *"the Law admitteth not of matters of Pleasure."* Since Parliament had always set great store by its rhetoric of legality, it must release him. "A Parliament, as they command Law, may be called the Wisdom and Reason of the Nation," and "It is not to be supposed that a Parliament will act contrary to their wisdom and policie, which is the Law."[26]

Thanks largely to a number of rather transparent delaying maneuvers, in the short term these painstakingly constructed arguments proved futile. Streater's imprisonment stretched into the new year. However, in February 1654 he was finally released. Barebone's Parliament had disintegrated, and the court deigned to regard its restraining order as lapsing with it. Immediately Streater returned to printing. After issuing his own account of the case, he resumed the production of periodicals. In each of them he aimed to provide "Politicall Rules" for undermining a military "Tyrant."[27] He rapidly became a master at this enterprise, varying titles and publication intervals in order to evade pursuers, but maintaining a coherent text throughout that could be collected and bound up to form a political treatise. Produced by a renegade under clandestine and hazardous conditions, these arguments mattered hugely to their creator. The most significant of them was the eleven-issue *Observations . . . Upon Aristotle's First Book of Political Government.* Sold by Richard Moon, an old apprentice of Giles Calvert's and himself a religious radical of note,[28] Streater prepared this work because in it, he be-

25. Streater, *Secret Reasons of State,* 7–8, 14; [Streater?], *Clavis,* 7–9, 12, 16–17, 34, 42, postscript; Exodus 31:18; compare [Streater], *Observations,* 43.

26. [Streater?], *Clavis,* sig. A2ᵛ, 10–13, 16–19.

27. *Mercurius Aulicus* (three issues) and *The Loyal Messenger* (one) are hesitantly attributed to Streater by Nelson and Seccombe, *British Newspapers and Periodicals 1641–1700.* The attribution is uncertain, so I have not made anything of these pamphlets—although *Loyal Messenger,* 32, does advertise *Clavis,* and the sarcastic treatments of both the Cromwellian court and the Protectorate's press licensers that are displayed throughout *Mercurius Aulicus* are plausibly Streater's.

28. Moon had been trained by Calvert in the 1640s. A native of Bristol, he returned there on the Restoration and became a prominent local Quaker, often arrested by the authorities for suspected sedition. See McKenzie, *Stationers' Company Apprentices 1641–1700,* 26; Barry, "Press and the Politics of Culture"; PRO SP 29/81, nos. 73–73(iv).

lieved, "the Excellency of a free State was maintained, and the Inconveniences of a Tyranny, or Single Person, were fully demonstrated."[29] It is therefore worth pausing over this, Streater's most extended political work.

Streater affirmed that government was an "*Art.*" It was not just a practice for which "Rules" could be identified, but one that must be taught and communicated, "as other Arts and Sciences are." Once again, then, issues of knowledge and its communication—or circulation—were to be central to this account of politics. Streater maintained that it was essential for a stable commonwealth that its citizens seek after "perfection and excellency" not just in political practice, but in all skilled endeavors—"in Government, in the arts and sciences[,] in building, in the professions of all Artificers, in husbandry and all things else." It is worth noting that these were Streater's own fields of knowledge: he was a fortifications engineer (and therefore a practitioner of the then-flourishing mathematical sciences), a printer, a pamphleteer, and, at least potentially, an apiarist. Even if the ultimate goal of perfection could not be obtained in such enterprises, the mere effort might still produce "singular advantage," just as alchemists' pursuit of the philosopher's stone had generated "many rare chimical experiments." So, again, the communication of skilled knowledge expedited a free state. It was for this reason that when "unjust persons" attained power, they invariably found it their "interest" to "suppress" public knowledge, and not only that of governance per se. "Some may say these things are not fit to be published to common view," Streater thus acknowledged of his own work. "Truly, they may as well say, that the Bible ought not to be published"—or, for that matter, Machiavelli, Suetonius, Tacitus, Polybius, Plutarch, and Bodin.[30]

Such knowledge was obviously political; but it also concerned the natural order. As Hermes Trismegistus affirmed, the reason humans had been granted an understanding sufficient to comprehend "the order of the Celestial bodies" was in order to "rule and govern the Terrestrial." Streater's commonwealth would thus be "according to Nature." Creation provided invaluable material for its formation. Moreover, Streater felt that "every man, according to nature, should have a share" in that enterprise, since each

29. Streater, *Secret Reasons of State*, 18. Streater's work on Aristotle demands comparison with Hobbes's discussion in *Leviathan*, and (not least because of its title) with Sir Robert Filmer's *Observations upon Aristotles Politiques*, which is reprinted in Filmer, *Patriarcha*, 235–86. There is no evidence that Streater was in deliberate engagement with Filmer, however.

30. [Streater], *Observations*, 1, 38. On the republican notion that governance was an "art," see Scott, "English Republican Imagination," 47. For the importance of the mathematical sciences (which included fortifications and gunnery) at this time, see: Bennett, "Challenge of Practical Mathematics," 188–9; Bennett, "Mechanics' Philosophy"; Willmoth, *Sir Jonas Moore*; Johnston, "Mathematical Practitioners." For the problems of credit and civility associated with these practices, see Shapin, "Robert Boyle and Mathematics"; Shapin, *Social History of Truth*, chap. 7.

individual was a microcosm, embracing the entire world: "fire, air, water, and the earth, tempered and mingled together, are really and substantially in his compounded body."[31] As each human body participated in the macrocosm, so each individual must participate in the commonwealth. States were components in an order of nature.

Streater's view of nature accordingly extended to his account of the historical origins of communities. All "Society" had originated, he believed, in his own craft of fortification. Walled and governed communities alike had been produced by this "*Art*," from a natural need for self-defense. At length, these ancient fortified towns had developed into monarchies, and then further into commonwealths ruled by laws. Even now, it was evident that tyrants feared the power and cohesion of great cities. But such states, being natural bodies, were necessarily dynamic. A "Stationary condition" could only be a temporary one. States must either increase or decrease, could never continue for long in stasis, and tended to corrupt if not reinvigorated. The way to counter such corruption was "to do as Nature doth in mans body," and expel corrupting humors. Otherwise, just as a putrefying body changed into other, verminous, kinds of life, so a putrefying state would change. Monarchy would degenerate into tyranny, aristocracy into oligarchy, and a commonwealth into popular anarchy.[32]

Streater found convincing evidence for this in the society of bees. Bees provided a model for the creation of cities, by the expansion of families into precincts and streets, and thence for the development of stable polities.[33] It was now that Streater recalled meeting Mewe and being shown his apiary. There he had seen, he remembered, "a perfect and exact Government." He had observed bees cleaning the streets, conducting night watches, providing storehouses, celebrating funerals in full mourning regalia, laboring, and performing all the other "Offices" appropriate to a "stately City." Recalling Pliny, he remarked that bees elected a "Commander or King" who ruled "with great industry," fulfilling his function of "directing and incouraging the work of the Common-wealth." Here, then, was an excellent model for a Streaterian state.

This became particularly clear when the swarm established a new colony. First, spies were dispatched to find a place free from "stinke." Then "Master Bees" trumpeted the warning to all to prepare their belongings for removal. When they arrived at their new site, the bees began to build their city by laying out regular, sanitary streets. They provided for the community before individuals, establishing stores under guard for the common use. Bees that

31. [Streater], *Observations*, 74, 3–4.
32. [Streater], *Observations*, 5, 49.
33. [Streater], *Observations*, 18, 37–8.

had lost their stings fighting for the commonwealth were among the first provided for out of such funds.[34] The exact "Forms and Orders of Government" pursued in such matters differed slightly in different "Hives or Common-wealths," their precise manner of operation being effectively determined by the "Art" of the builders. Nonetheless, their cities invariably prospered on the basis of this "common stock," which was used sparingly, with no individual being permitted to destroy or devour the common provision, nor, above all, to make himself master over the collective. All bees obeyed their governors, because their commands were issued "for the good of the Commonwealth."[35]

A city or commonwealth was the final cause of a bee; it was what a bee was *for*. So it was of a human being. This too Streater derived from what he called "*Natural Philosophy*." Just as in Creation God had conceived of "the form of the whole universe" before its "parts"—and had continued creating ever since, in the shape of new insects, plants, and people—so in politics the whole was prior to its parts, and the public to the private. If private "Interest" were ever deemed prior to public, that was a symptom of political and cultural degeneration. An army was just such a private interest. As such, it could produce only governance that was not merely unnatural, but counternatural. It must therefore prove transient, unstable, and corrupt.[36]

To preserve the public interest, Streater again drew on physiology. It was "a maxime in Philosophy," he maintained, that "in the body of a Commonwealth, the ministers of State and the Magistrates may be likened to the veins and Sinews in the body of a man." In the human frame, veins served to channel blood and spirits, while sinews "actuat[ed]" the body. So, in a direct parallel, "ministers of State, and Magistrates are to convey justice and vertue to every part of the body, and be as staies and helps to the motion of the Commonwealth." But just as the body could decay, so ministers could sink into corruption, at which point the commonwealth must expel its humors. The best way to preserve human life was "by renewing of blood and flesh; the which must be done with great judgement, by the taking away of part of the old." Similarly, "the renewing of Officers in a Commonwealth . . . doth renew the age thereof: it doth prevent corruption." Streater proposed that this renewal could be achieved through annual elections to all positions of power.[37]

This was much more than an analogy. Galen had testified that over long

---

34. It is overwhelmingly tempting to read this as a reference to Streater's own plight as a wounded officer. He was also repeatedly sued for employing ex-soldiers in his printing house, taking advantage of a 1654 ordinance in favor of former troopers: PRO SP 25/77, p. 495.

35. [Streater], *Observations*, 57–8.

36. [Streater], *Observations*, 1, 35, 66–7.

37. [Streater], *Observations*, 9–16, 22, 51.

periods, custom could become "ingrafted" into nature. Streater accordingly felt that to make "slaves" of citizens was simultaneously to impair their na-tures—that is, to occlude powers that were of the essence of a human being. To make "slaves" of animals had similar effects. The horse provided clear evidence for this. In Old Testament times, horses had been fearless and valiant creatures. An ancient horse had been a proper "Theater" on which "heroick men should act the part of their valour." The modern breed was very different, thanks to centuries of subordination and misuse. There had been "a perfect degeneration in their kind." This was true of all creatures compelled to spend their lives in improper work. The importance of labor was thus critical. Horses had degenerated not because of being worked, but because they had been worked in the wrong ways. Similarly, the diverse kinds of "industry" practiced in a commonwealth, which crucially included the exercise of critical judgment, were perhaps the major cement of socia-bility, and they needed to be devised to accord with nature. This was true of bees as much as of humans: Mewe's hive had originally been consecrated to industry, and Streater renewed that dedication. The frame of the natural order was thus being corrupted as the history of corrupt statecraft unfolded. So it was now "requisite," Streater advised, "that every thing should be im-ployed in that which is most sutable to its nature." To restore both humans and horses to their Old Testament stature, and to procure a secure polity, it would be essential to take extensive measures to remedy natural knowledge. To this end Streater proposed a grand program of "experiments" on crea-tures, to be funded by the state.[38]

These experiments would be devoted to revealing the *uses* of creatures. Streater was explicit about how they could be pursued. "Nature," he reck-oned, "hath appointed every thing for a several end and purpose." To that end all creatures were "marked" in various ways, "the better to describe and distinguish their several natures, qualities, and dispositions." By investigat-ing these markings, humans could "upon the first view of them" detect a creature's "intrinse nature." Streater's natural knowledge was thus a knowl-edge of *signatures*. Such knowledge led to practical benefits. This was be-cause the world was alive, operating continuously by secret agencies of attraction and repulsion. A seed, for instance, was of "an attractive nature." When planted, "it draweth unto it the strength of the earth, to assist it in perfecting its work of production of increase." The earth was the "mother"

---

38. [Streater], *Observations*, 33–5. It is worth noting that Streater was writing some years before the wide recognition of something called "experimental philosophy." His usage is intriguing in the context of his connection with the Hartlib circle, members of which were at the time of his writing involved in constructing such a philosophy. In using the word, of course, Streater certainly did not mean anything closely resembling the twentieth-century laboratory experiment.

of all such production, and thus the source of all human benefit.[39] This was no longer the philosophy of Aristotle. This was the language of natural magic.

An exploration of this language brings us back to the politics of circulated knowledge. In Eastington, Streater had listened with fascination to the different sounds made by bees while executing their different offices. This had encouraged him to reflect on connections between what he called "voice" and the different kinds and qualities of labor. But only humans had the peculiar kind of "voice" called speech. Among humans, speech served to distinguish "profitable" labor from "unprofitable," and just conduct from unjust. Knowledge of these proprieties, distributed in speech and words, was what distinguished humans from bees. It was thus speech that revealed tyranny. So tyrants attempted to limit it, and to deny "that noble priviledge of Liberty of speech."[40] But just as true knowledge, truly communicated, was essential to a stable commonwealth, so there were iniquitous forms of knowledge and communication too. Primary in both camps were what Streater called "the Magicks."

There was, Streater acknowledged, a "natural Magick" that was essential to a free and strong commonwealth. This was the true "knowledge of nature." Proper medical magic, for example, was "onely a knowledge of Spetial cures Physically." But there were other magics which could be used for harm. This could be confirmed by an examination of ancient history, and in particular of Old Testament Egypt. So effective had some ancients' knowledge of "herbs, drugs, minerals and excrements" become that at length Egypt had begun to consider "them onely fit for government that were experienced in the Magicks"—and especially in astrology, "supposing that those are not fit for government that cannot discern the future, as well as the present condition of a Kingdome." By these means magicians had gained a reputation as proximate to the divine, and had been able to prescribe forms of worship for political ends. Those magicians who, like Moses, worshipped the true God, had ordained the proper worship of him. Those who followed other deities, on the other hand, ordained the idolatrous worship of their own false gods. The Egyptian sorcerers had practiced such illicit knowledge with particular skill, maintaining their false government and false religion, "the which they did not by charms as some suppose, but by the working and operating by some secret cause."[41]

The implications were not limited to ancient Egypt. In recent years, the

39. [Streater], *Observations*, 34–5.
40. [Streater], *Observations*, 58–9.
41. Hobbes portrayed Egyptian priests as being liars as well as enchanters: Hobbes, *Last sayings*.

papacy had rediscovered this practice. It had adopted its own "Magicks," able to "turn the stoutest Prince out of his Throne." Like the ancients', such magics relied on the attribution of supernatural causes to natural effects. "Reliques of Saints" were in fact simply "artificial compounds, fit for some certain cures." Similarly, when the water appearing in some spring had passed through minerals in the earth such that it acquired a curative property, the papists quickly appropriated the spring and dedicated it to a saint.[42] "By this means people are so fastened to a superstitious belief of a vertue in dedication," Streater pronounced, "that the Pope sitteth much surer in his Chair, then otherwise he would." And Catholic magic worked: "though slow in motion, yet it is sure." In all these instances, it operated by identifying and manipulating "Contrarieties." Revealingly, this was of a piece with Catholicism itself. The church displayed diverse facets to appeal to all humors and passions. Knowledge was offered to the contemplative, order to the austere, jollity to the jovial, and miracles to the credulous. This was a religion based essentially on division, on contrariety, because it rested on these appeals to the passions.

Streater felt this insight to be supremely important; so much so that it warranted rehearsal even years later. At the peak of the crisis of 1659, he would issue a new tract urging that the introduction of "Consistence in Government" by union of diverse "Interests" was imperative in the struggle against popery, and that governance by the self-proclaimed saints had now to yield to this more urgent necessity. Fascinatingly, Streater here gave details of how the Jesuits put their "Natural Magick" into practice, using "Engine-work" to construct fake miracles. For example, they could devise machinery to make the eyes move in a statue of the virgin and child. But such magic was not restricted to mechanical ingenuity; it was a complete repertoire of techniques for making and exercising power over others. He even described witnessing himself the effectiveness of Jesuit magic.

Streater's memory of this magic was fresh when he was printing the *Observations*. His experience concerned a professed prophet named Paul Hunt, who had been imprisoned with him in the Gatehouse in January 1653/4. Hunt had prophesied a Stuart restoration, and believed that he had been sent by God to instruct Cromwell to resign the Protectorate. At this time the Gatehouse also held three imprisoned Jesuits, led by the remarkable Thomas Ramsey (also known as Thomas Horsley, or Joseph Ben Israel, he had landed near Newcastle and successfully infiltrated a Baptist congregation before being discovered). This trio used Hunt to mount a demonstration of their powers, apparently for Streater's benefit. They forged a proph-

---

42. In 1658 it was perhaps Streater who singled out its treatment of such springs and minerals as a key reason for translating Olaus Magnus's *Compendious History of the Goths*: see "J.S."'s preface.

ecy in Hebraic-angelic script, and, after hiding it in his cell, told Hunt that they had heard mysterious singing in the night. He found the sheet, and at length they persuaded him that he had been the recipient of a divine revelation in the jail itself. They had the decency to intercept his desperate letters to Cromwell after the message—letters that would have led to Hunt's immediate hanging had they been received—but, constructing fake replies to them, managed to keep the pretense going at will. This was powerful magic indeed, worthy of "the admiration of many worthy Gentlemen, (State-Prisoners there at that time), who saw in part what might be effected in things of that nature." [43]

Catholicism and Catholic magic alike thus exploited contrariety to powerful effect. They prospered by appealing to the humors and interests of a divided, passionate polity. The result was clear from history and experience. Eventually, in Old Testament times, division had become endemic, to the extent that "almost every one had a God." This seemed to be becoming true of 1650s England too, when there was more pretense at religion than ever before, but less religious unity. Such divisions, Streater believed, had been "wheels to the Chariot of design" driven forward by Cromwell. To press home the point, he displayed an extended parallel between the rise of the Protector and that of Nero. [44] His point was that to be above the law, as Nero became, was to be outside it. It was "unsociableness." Such an individual, by violating Aristotle's definition of humanity as a social animal, became a mere beast. A tyrant therefore could—and should—be slain. Streater repeated the message in another periodical, his *Politick Commentary Upon the Life of Caius Julius Caesar*. There could be no mistaking whom Caesar was intended to represent. Given what had befallen him, it seemed clear that Streater was calling for no less than the assassination of Cromwell. [45]

The speed of Cromwell's reaction shows that Streater was taken seriously. His message had been proclaimed at a particularly tense moment, not least because it followed closely on the discovery of an assassination plot against the Protector. Just six weeks after his release, Streater thus awoke to find his house surrounded by a troop of Thurloe's musketeers. But he had been forewarned by "one of the Protector's Councel," and escaped. For four months he now stayed in hiding, continuing to produce his works on Aristotle and

---

43. S[treater], *Jesuite Discovered*, passim, esp. 9–10. This pamphlet is an expanded version of [Streater], *Observations*, 43–8. For Ramsey, see Katz, *Sabbath and Sectarianism*, 25–33 (Streater's incident being mentioned on p.32; I am grateful to Nigel Smith for the reference). Streater's concern to specify the magic used by papists should be seen as part of an emerging campaign against "priestcraft," a term coined by Harrington: see Champion, *Pillars of Priestcraft Shaken*, and Goldie, "Civil Religion of James Harrington."

44. [Streater], *Observations*, 43–4, 57–64, 76–7.

45. [Streater], *Observations*, 53–4; Streater, *Glympse*, 1–2, 10; [Streater], *Politick Commentary*; *Perfect and Impartial Intelligence*, [2] (26 May 1654), 16.

Caesar from secret corners across London. Streater even spirited a message to Cromwell himself from his refuge, demanding to know "what was the reason of his so violent prosecuting of him." Cromwell did not reply. It was only by employing a London minister trusted by them both that Streater could ascertain the Protector's determination to capture him "dead or alive"; his only alternative to imprisonment would be to volunteer for the imminent (and ill-fated) West Indies expedition then being projected. Prudently, he refused to come forward.

However, so little public anger had been displayed against Cromwell that before long further struggle began to seem futile. Streater therefore now approached John Desborough, Cromwell's brother-in-law and an old comrade from the Irish campaign, to intercede for him. Under Desborough's urging, Cromwell consented to let Streater live "quietly and undisturbed" if he would agree to stop printing against him. Streater acceded, and signed an engagement to that effect on 18 October 1654.[46] On that very day, however, three more of his Irish army colleagues intervened to destroy the treaty. A petition against the Protectorate appeared on the streets of London, signed by Colonels Thomas Saunders, John Okey, and Matthew Alured. Their petition rehearsed many of Streater's themes, urging that by fostering private interests both in himself and in a standing army, Cromwell threatened "the Publike Interest of the Commonwealth" in "*constant successive Parliaments*." Engagement or no engagement, the advent of this new challenge meant that Streater was too dangerous to leave at liberty.

Less than a month after the truce, Streater found himself cornered by a squadron of cavalry in a 1 A.M. raid. At dawn, he managed to send word of his arrest to Desborough, whose honor was implicated in the apparent betrayal. Desborough forthwith demanded to speak to Cromwell. He challenged him personally about the arrest. Cromwell justified it by alleging that Streater had been overheard "discoursing" with "Parliament-men" about "matters of dangerous Consequence," and Desborough reported this back to Streater. It was true, Streater acknowledged. He had been maintaining by casuistry and civil law that the engagement presented for signing by MPs in the new Protectorate Parliament was vacuous. It declared their allegiance to "*the lawfull power of the Protector*," and as far as Streater was concerned Cromwell had none. He had advised signing it anyway, however, since otherwise good men would be excluded from the House. This had then led on

---

46. Streater, *Secret Reasons of State*, 18–19; Hobman, *Cromwell's Master Spy*, 40. Streater's engagement, witnessed by Desborough and Charles Worsley, is in Birch, *Collection of the State Papers of John Thurloe*, II, 680. As is often the case with him, we do not know the identities of crucial intermediaries at this juncture. It is tempting to guess that Desborough was the informant in the case of Thurloe's raid.

to a discussion of the causes of changes in government, along Streaterian lines, and then, via a consideration of oaths, to the different political uses of religion in monarchies, aristocracies, and democracies. Streater wrote out the exchange in full for Desborough, who not only managed to procure his release but ventured to defend him again in future.[47]

This narrow escape did not deter Streater from working. He himself perhaps authored a mordant *Picture of a New Courtier*, sarcastically demolishing those supposed commonwealthsmen who had thrown in their lot with the Protectorate.[48] In printing others' works, though, he concentrated mainly on mysticism, and on natural philosophy of a Paracelsian or Hartlibian bent.[49] These had been interests ever since he began printing, and they had become central to his vision of a commonwealth.[50] Now, Streater and Giles Calvert embarked on an ambitious project to translate and print the complete works of Jakob Böhme. They situated the importance of these works in terms of current debates over "the Light within"—the very debates over

47. Saunders, Okey, and Alured, *To his Highness*; Streater, *Secret Reasons of State*, 19–20. On the political expediency of professing religion, see also [Streater], *Observations*, 43. Again, we do not know the identity of the "Parliament-men" involved in this conversation—nor, indeed, whether they were Rumpers or members of the new Protectorate Parliament, the pledge for which was the subject of discussion.

48. It also attacked Desborough. Streater's authorship of I.S., *Picture of a New Courtier* is nevertheless plausible for a number of reasons, none of them conclusive. First and foremost, Streater was consistently antagonistic to what he called "flatterers," since their testimony was inherently untrustworthy; in fact, the flatterer came to constitute a villainous type to be contrasted to Streater's heroic commonwealthsman. Beyond that, both participants in this dialogue have been parliamentary soldiers; they were at Saint Albans for the New Model's *Remonstrance* of 1647, as, feasibly, was Streater (*Observations*, 50). Cromwell's worst offense is described as the "imprisoning of men contrary to law, at his own will and pleasure; yea, many of the Common-wealths best friends," and the Protector maintains "a great herd" of spies, "to ensnare the plain-hearted." (For Streater's hatred of spies and prying neighbors, see [Streater?], *Clavis*, sig. [B4ᵛ].) The author thus shares key concerns with Streater. He also claims privy information from the Stationers' community, albeit to the perhaps unlikely effect that Cromwell has been reading the works of the late earl of Strafford.

J.S., Συλλογολογια, has also been associated with Streater, but is less likely to be his. However, since the preface, signed "*J.S.*," implies that the original author was already dead, it may be that Streater was indeed responsible for the publication, but that he was bringing to view a manuscript written by someone else.

Streater's antagonism to "flatterers" perhaps had a personal target. This was Henry Hills, once a comrade in the New Model Army and now the Stationer most notorious for informing and betrayals. Hills remained a client of the army, and of Cromwell, in whose funeral cortège he participated. They were long-term antagonists, and in 1656 Streater was instrumental in a campaign against a privilege on Bible printing granted by Cromwell to Hills: Birch, *Collection of the State Papers of John Thurloe*, IV, 584; PRO SP 25/76, p. 572; PRO SP 25/77, p. 17; PRO SP 18/126, no. 92.

49. E.g., Naudé's *History of Magick*, Lemnius's *Secret Miracles of Nature*, and Bromhall's *History of Apparitions*.

50. His earliest known publication was Nicholas of Cusa's Ὀφθαλμος ἁπλους. For such works, see Smith, *Perfection Proclaimed*, esp. 120, 136–42, 185–214.

the proper status of the person in creating knowledge that are addressed below in chapter 6.[51] A related issue was at stake in his work on vernacular medicine, something central to fierce debates over unlicensed medical practitioners, and, moreover, a clear instance of the use of printing to further commonwealth ideals of collective knowledge: John Smith's *Compleat Practise of Physick*, for example, based itself on a rhetoric of common good. Together Streater and his allies created an outpouring of vernacular Paracelsian and lay medical books never matched before or since.[52] The "public interest" impetus behind these efforts was well expressed by Hartlib, who pointed out the "affection to the publick" they displayed, in contrast to "Muck-worms" who concealed knowledge "for private ends." And, he continued, "it were to be wished, that every one to whom God (from whom comes every good & perfect gift) doth impart any rare and profitable Secret of Industry, would open himselfe towards his Brethren." Were this to happen, "then would all hands be set a work, and every one would become instrumentall to serve himselfe and his Neighbours." This would befit "Members of the same Christian, and Human, and Nationall Society." In furthering this project, Streater was thus proving that he understood "what it is to be a good Commonwealths-man in the State."[53]

Becoming a good commonwealthsman by the making and ready distribution of knowledge: it was in this context of work, endorsed publicly by Robert Boyle, that Streater printed Hartlib's *Reformed Common-Wealth of Bees*. Its centerpiece was Mewe's apiary. Hartlib himself drew the appropriate moral. When God set Adam to keep the Garden of Eden, he had meant for him to exercise "Industry," both in "discovery of the fruitfulnesse of perfect nature" and in rendering the garden "answerable to the perfection of his own imagination." For although nature was perfect before the Fall, yet in some respects its perfection lay dormant in "the seminal properties of the Earth"; what "Marriages and Combinations" between "proper Agents and Patients" would produce was left to Adam to investigate. Although sin meant that we were far inferior to Adam in knowledge, we could still, by becoming "faithful and laborious Servants" to nature, "find out the Seat of Gods Vertue in her," and "trace the Way of his Operation." This, he announced, was the message of "your Apiary in the Country." Revealing "the Wisdome of the Creator" in the apiary, and thence through this printed representation,

51. Böhme, *Concerning the election of Grace*, sigs. A1ᵛ–A2ʳ; Böhme, *Aurora*, sigs. A1ᵛ–A2ʳ. Given Streater's contemporary—and contentious—printing of bibles, it is significant that the translator had access to the polyglot bible before it was published.

52. Smith, *Compleat Practise of Physick*; Dobbs, *Foundations of Newton's Alchemy*, 49–53, 62–80.

53. Hartlib, *Reformed Virginian Silk-Worm*, sig. A2ᵛ; compare [Boyle], "Epistolical Discourse." For Hartlibian calls for openness in the context of the Stationers, and a possible connection to Milton, see Dunn, "Milton among the Monopolists."

Hartlib affirmed that "such things should not be concealed, because they are reall Demonstrations of his Power." In the mid-1650s, Streater, Hartlib, Calvert, and Mewe were laboring to mitigate the Fall. They did so by producing new and powerful knowledge of nature, and by exemplifying in the distribution of that knowledge a new politics of circulation.

Streater's major labor of this time, however, was undoubtedly the production of James Harrington's classic of republican literature, *The Common-Wealth of Oceana*. Streater printed this in mid- to late-1656, in clandestine collaboration with a few fellow workers. Given their probable publication dates, it is not unlikely that he was printing his favored works of natural knowledge as he did so, producing them concurrently, sheet by sheet. *Oceana* itself was certainly printed on several presses working simultaneously. It had to be. Agents of the Protectorate—agents almost certainly pursuing Streater, not Harrington—chased the manuscript through the printing houses of London. They forced Streater to divide the copy and disperse it to three separate houses, where it could be printed beyond the surveillance even of Harrington himself. In the collated result, Harrington's name did not appear on any of the three title pages forced on the book; Streater's did. The implications of Streater's complicity are thus considerable, and begin with the mere fact of the book's being published at all. But they are also significant for considering its content, not least because recent work on Harrington has returned to something clearly recognized by his first editor, John Toland: the importance for him of natural philosophy.[54]

Toland alleged that Harrington had convinced himself that "no Government is of so accidental or arbitrary an Institution as people are wont to imagin, there being in Societys natural causes producing their necessary effects, as well as in the Earth or the Air."[55] This, it has been suggested, was what made *Oceana* original, and what persuaded Harrington of the possibility of an immortal commonwealth. *Oceana* was to be Harvey's circulation of the blood writ large, or the circulation of the planets writ small. Perhaps more exactly, it was to recapitulate in the body politic a circulation of the animal spirits in the human frame. In this it was close to work being done at the same time by Harvey's immediate disciple, Thomas Willis.[56] Physicians like Willis—as well as Streater—thought that the nervous system and the functions of the mind operated through extremely fine material spirits

54. Hartlib, *Reformed Common-Wealth of Bees*, 43–6; Feather, "Publication of James Harrington's *Commonwealth of Oceana*"; Scott, "Rapture of Motion"; Scott, "English Republican Imagination," 47–51; Diamond, "Natural Philosophy"; Cohen, "Harrington and Harvey."
55. Harrington (ed. Toland), *Oceana*, xvii.
56. Willis, "Anatomy of the Brain." For the circumstances surrounding this work see Willis, *Thomas Willis's Oxford Lectures*, 37–49, 52 ff.; Frank, "Thomas Willis and His Circle"; Bynum, "Anatomical Method." The main source for anatomical work in the period is Frank, *Harvey and the Oxford Physiologists*. See also below, pp. 392–7.

distilled from the blood. They could track these spirits' paths by detailed anatomical dissection. Willis was even able to show how, in moments of stress, they could escape the body altogether and form specters. Perhaps this is what Harrington himself believed was happening when, in the Restoration, he insisted that his own animal spirits could form images in the air around him—images, to be specific, of bees. Toland certainly thought so, and he linked Harrington's *Mechanics of Nature* to the work of such physician–natural philosophers as Archibald Pitcairne.[57]

The congruences between Harrington's and Streater's (earlier) republicanisms are compelling. Both maintained that governance in an imperfect world was an art, the essence of which lay in the imitation of nature. Both thus placed great faith in the centrality of current natural philosophy to that art, putting hermetic and materialist knowledge to immediate political use. In so doing, both aspired to stipulate the channels through which the material spirits of a commonwealth—its people—could flow, in complex and eternal circuits. Both believed that those channels were fixed above all by laws, or even that they *were* laws: Harrington repeated, as had Streater, the dictum that proper government was that of laws, not men. Both felt that that constituted government by reason, rather than by passion. The liberty of the body politic therefore consisted in the empire of laws; its alternative was tyranny, represented as enslavement to the passions. Physicians knew that the physiological distinction between the two must be sought in the routes taken by the animal spirits in the body. Similarly, maintained both Harrington and Streater, reason in a commonwealth was distinguished by the regularized flow of its animal spirits. In both natural and political bodies, the end of such circulation led to corruption. Rule of law was as close as possible to the rule of God.[58]

These congruences raise clear questions of authorship. For Harrington, this was always problematic. Toland himself found that his originality was still in need of defense in 1700, half a century after *Oceana*.[59] Certainly, Harrington shared virtually all his concerns, to a detailed degree, with Streater, the printer who labored to produce his words. He may even have cited Streater—and he did not cite many authors—in arguing for the representation of "the lower sort of the people" in an assembly.[60] But ultimately Harrington's republicanism should not simply be reascribed lock, stock, and barrel to Streater. To do that would amount merely to reinstating an anach-

57. Harrington (ed. Toland), *Oceana*, xxxviii.

58. Harrington, *Political Works*, 169–70; compare another republican, Algernon Sidney, in Scott, *Algernon Sidney and the English Republic*, 35–7. On the passions see [Streater], *Observations*, 59–60, [62 (incorrectly marked as 58)].

59. Harrington (ed. Toland), *Oceana*, xviii.

60. Harrington, *Political Works*, 193, citing Συλλογολογια.

ronistic notion of authorship about a new individual. Streater's political philosophy *does* imply that a reappraisal of Harrington and what is called "Harringtonianism" is needed, but its aim should not be simply to redescribe "Harringtonians" as "Streaterians." There were no such heroes living under the Protectorate, as Streater himself recognized. Rather, the conclusion ought to be that authorship itself was a collective enterprise. Its attribution to any one individual was retrospective, contingent, and contestable. For seventeenth-century readers, as for modern historians, apportioning creativity was rarely straightforward.

Yet in one respect a distinctive contribution by Streater may be suggested, however hesitantly. It is possible that the title of Harrington's work, which has always remained rather mysterious, owed something to him. "Care ought to be had," Streater had explained in the days of Cromwell's coup against the Rump, "to unite all bodies in a Commonwealth, so as to depend one upon another, for the good of the whole." By this means the unified body would become "powerful," he had maintained, in the same way that "a drop of water," flowing into the sea, "becometh part of that infinite body." Streater's circulating commonwealth was just such a unified body of free-flowing spirits, infinite not in extent but in the circulating motions of its component particles. It was, in short, an "Ocean." [61]

THE KNIGHTS OF THE GALAXY

From 1656 until the Restoration—years in which Streater remained a committed commonwealthsman—Harrington's schemes received much attention. Hostility focused on an aspect of *Oceana* that more sympathetic readers tended to ignore. Whereas Henry Oldenburg, for example, took notes only from the "Preliminaries"—blandly ignoring the entire mythological apparatus of the main text, and silently translating its nomenclature term for term back into historical names, dates, and places—antagonistic pamphleteers concentrated on the fanciful style of what Harrington himself had defended to Cromwell as a "Political Romance." [62] In particular, they ridiculed its cosmology. Perhaps they too had a point. Matthew Wren is now

61. Streater, *Glympse*, 7. See also the discussion of the word *Oceana* in Harrington, *James Harrington's Oceana*, 227–30. *Oceana* has never been a recognized Latin word, of course, let alone one that means "ocean"; my speculation is that it may be a feminized derivation from *oceanus*—a classical term that in Harrington's lifetime was used to refer to a hypothetical sea extending indefinitely across the globe, and therefore capable of eternal circulation. This would correspond to etymological conventions by which a place was named after its personified, generally female, "genius" (as, for example, *Roma* and *Europa*). I am grateful to Warren Brown for conversations on this point.
62. Oldenburg's notes are in Royal Society, Ms. 1, fols. 90ʳ–96ʳ. For Harrington's comment see Harrington (ed. Toland), *Oceana*, xix.

the best-known respondent to concentrate on Harrington's "mechanicks," but in this respect he was not unique. It was claimed that Copernicanism had been established by Act of Parliament, and that this was appropriate for a commonwealth ruled by Harringtonian rotation. Royalists demanded of the commonwealthsmen "whether it be not expedient to ship them all for *Oceana*," and suggested that "Mr. *Harrington* our famous modern *Columbus* discoverer of that floting *Terra incognita*, be desired to be the Pilot to conduct them hither, who for his paynes deserves to be made Knight of the Sunne." Noticing the cosmology had here also meant, typically, noticing the cosmological names given to the various offices in Harrington's state.[63] So Harringtonian supporters were, like the Archon's Orators at the end of *Oceana* itself, rewarded by the title of "Knights of the Galaxy"[64]—but the accolade came from mocking opponents.

Streater—the equivalent, thanks to his printing skills, of an Orator— became an important knight, especially with the collapse of the Protectorate in 1659. He took full part in the dramatic upheavals of that and the following year. Apart from producing justifications of his own conduct, he devoted himself to defending his commonwealth. First, though, he returned to the army. On 6 May, Fleetwood and the army's general council decreed that the Rump Parliament be restored. Like other officers decommissioned at the expulsion, including Alured, Streater was now restored to his rank, being appointed commander of the artillery train. Parliament even pondered sending him back to Ireland.[65] Meanwhile calls for a return to the "fundamentals of our *Good Old Cause*" multiplied, and he again devoted himself to writing and printing tracts in defense of the Rump.[66] He was probably responsible for the augmented republication of Sexby's *Killing Noe Murder*, which had called for the assassination of the "Pest," Cromwell,[67] and certainly printed almanacs attacking the Protectorate lawyers who had kept him in prison.[68]

---

63. *Democritus turned States-man*, 3–4; [Wren], *Considerations*, 67. Compare also *Bibliotheca Militum*, 4–5; *Mercurius Politicus* 352 (12 March 1657), 7641–4.

64. Harrington, *Political Works*, 227.

65. *Declaration of the Officers*; Hutton, *Restoration*, 39–40, 109; PRO IND I/8909, fols. 46ᵛ, 49ʳ; *Journals of the House of Commons*, VII, 714.

66. *Humble Petition and Addresse of the Officers of the Army*; S[treater], *Continuation of this Session of Parliament*, 3, 6, 8, 12.

67. Sexby [Allen, pseud.], *Killing Noe Murder* (1657), sig. [B3ʳ]; Sexby [Allen, pseud.], *Killing, No Murder* (1659), 14. There is evidence that Streater's responsibility may have been genuine: the 1659 edition cites his *Continuation . . . Justified* (on p. 3), in which (p. 8) Streater had restated that a ruler who ignored the rule of law became "unto the *People* no other but as a *Wilde Beast*; which Nature hath instituted to be destroyed." In a new appendix, the 1659 editor stressed precedents among the Roman emperors, and the importance of publicly known laws in preventing tyranny. It is also possible that (Streater's?) hostile biography of Cromwell was the source of the notion: I.S., *Perfect Politician*, 349 (usually attributed to Henry Fletcher).

68. Capp, *Astrology and the Popular Press*, 109, 409.

When a royalist declared that Streater's own habeas corpus case had proved that the Parliament had been "dissolved" and could therefore claim no further legitimacy, Streater responded with a particularly thorough polemical demolition, significant for its explicit defense of *Oceana*, which was necessitated by his antagonist having called him one of Harrington's "disciples." "That a *Commonwealth* may be Governed as Mr. Harrington describeth, is certain," he roundly declared: "nay, *England* it self." To bring about this transformation, Streater hoped that Fleetwood might become the Olphaus Megaletor Cromwell had declined to be.[69]

What this new Archon might produce Streater made clear with his own description of the matter, form, and power of a commonwealth. It was based on the city-state of Ragusa (modern Dubrovnik). This was the epitome of the state he had long advocated, with annual elections, the army remaining under the firm control of a council, and those entrusted with high office expecting soon to return to a private capacity. By such "often changing of Officers," the state of Ragusa preserved itself. This, Streater declared, was "the true Embleme of a Free-State." But there was an important qualification to be made, because Streater knew full well that, given the chance, England would vote for such a representative body as would "deprive them of the blessed Government of a Free-State." So Streater would have elections only "with such Qualifications, as may preserve the Interest of the Commonwealth." This was permissible because of the definition of liberty enshrined in the idea of a free state, which recognized not license but adherence to reason. "Liberty consisteth not in every ones doing what he listeth," Streater observed; "this Liberty would not consist with Society." Rather, "true Liberty" lay in "a convenient and necessary Bondage."[70]

Printing and authorship were not the end of his activities. On 13 October, Lambert and Fleetwood expelled the Rump again in a new coup. Along with both Presbyterians and Rumpers, Streater recoiled at the action. He joined with Vice Admiral John Lawson, Colonels Saunders and Alured, and some four hundred others in protesting.[71] In Scotland, General Monck declared his opposition and began to move his forces south. Lambert marched to intercept him. Back in the capital, with the outcome of Lambert's action impossible to predict, Streater resolved on desperate action. He decided to seize the Tower of London.

One Lieutenant Fitch, a Rump appointee in command of the Tower, was

---

69. *Word to Purpose*; S[treater], *Shield against the Parthian Dart*, 17.

70. S[treater], *Government Described*, esp. 8. This notion of liberty as an instrumental subjection to fixed laws was central to the concerns of republican writers: see Davis, "Religion and the Struggle for Freedom."

71. BL Ms. Add. 4165, fols. 38ᵛ–39ʳ; Underdown, *Royalist Conspiracy*, 292–3; Rugg, *Diurnal*, 11–2.

also aghast at the change. He, Streater, and others now plotted to take the Tower and declare for Parliament. It would be a crucial victory, since the fortress housed virtually the entire state arsenal. Fitch was to open the gates on 12 December and admit Streater, Okey, and Scot with four loyal companies.[72] Robert Whitley, a royalist agent in London, described what happened in a dispatch to his superiors across the Channel. The city's "youth and rabble" were "desperate," he reported. Apprentices and "anabaptists" had been holding armed meetings at dead of night, and the army's guards were perilously fatigued. Things had seemed ripe for a plot.

> On Monday yᵉ Tower should have bin put into yᵉ hands of Okey, Scot, Streater and some other of yᵉ late Parlements frinds, but discoverd by Miller (Lᵗ Collonel to Baxter) and prevented by Desborow, Huson and some others, who went thither in yᵉ night, ceased upon Fits (yᵉ present Governor) and secured it for yᵉ army. Fits and 2 Captaines are in hold, and Miller commands yᵉ place; they say Scot is fled and Okey imprison'd.[73]

The design had failed. Fleetwood had heard of the plan just a day before it was to have taken place, and arrested Fitch. Desborough was put in charge of the Tower.[74] Okey, Streater, and Scot escaped.

They fled east, to a rendezvous with the navy. There Lawson, another who owed his military career to the Rump, had a long history of ambivalence at best toward the Protectorate and the politicking of the army. He had met with fellow commonwealthsmen as early as September 1654, while Streater was in hiding, and had raised discontent in the fleet at that time in the hope of fomenting opposition to Cromwell. In his private conspirings, Sexby had continued to claim to royalists that Lawson would provide ships for a putative invasion. In 1656 he had resigned, and in spring and summer exerted himself to ally Fifth Monarchists and commonwealthsmen (including Okey, and at least colleagues of Streater) against the Protector.[75] Recalled to the navy by the Rump in 1659, he did not intend now to see a resumption of military rule.

Lawson's fleet weighed anchor and set sail up the Thames for London, taking on board Streater and Okey as it did so.[76] It paused at Gravesend while Lawson's manifestoes to the City were printed under Streater's man-

72. Firth and Davies, *Regimental History*, I, 343.

73. Nicholas, *Nicholas Papers*, IV, 190–3.

74. Firth and Davies, *Regimental History*, I, 344.

75. Capp, *Cromwell's Navy*, 56, 122–4, 128, 134–47, 376–7, 382–3, 396; compare Davies, *Gentlemen and Tarpaulins*, 120–126.

76. Davies, *Restoration*, 183. In May, Henry Neville had portrayed Streater and Lawson leaving in a huff a card game involving Cromwell, Pride, and Harrison: [Neville], *Shufling, Cutting and Dealing*, 6.

agement. Encouraged by this gesture, Royalist and Presbyterian support began to emerge. Portsmouth came out in revolt against Fleetwood. Anthony Ashley Cooper, Thomas Scot, and others wrote from there declaring for the Rump, supporting the abortive design on the Tower, and asserting that Monck would now ensure the safety of "the interest of this Commonwealth." [77] Streater also printed his own *Letter* to Fleetwood, warning that his current actions threatened eventually to allow the state to "fall into the hands of *Charls Stuart*." He declared that Fleetwood's proposal for new elections was, among all the "Models of Government" currently on offer, "one of the worst, and most Inconsistent that can be imagined." Being founded in the "particular Interest" of the army, it could produce only new changes, and ultimately a restored monarchy. Only Monck could now guarantee "the Interest of the Publick." [78]

After a period of turmoil and uncertainty, Fleetwood and the Council of Officers admitted defeat and relinquished power. Monck marched into London unopposed. The Rump returned on the evening of 26 December, guarded by Okey and Alured from any attempt by the secluded members to enter. [79] The next day Streater was reinstated as its printer. [80] As an added reward, he was also restored to military command, taking charge of the regiment hitherto led by perhaps the most notorious of all army figures, John Hewson, who only two weeks earlier had helped foil his designs on the Tower. [81] However, even as the direction of political change became clearer, Streater was not yet ready to acquiesce in a Restoration. He was soon implicated with Okey in another plot to preserve parliamentary rule—a project that merited only a blistering reprimand from Monck. [82] More significant was his action in the short but critical few days between the readmission of the secluded members and the final dissolution of the Parliament. On 12 March, in the first unambiguous move away from a republic, the House passed a bill putting control of the militia in the hands of officers overtly opposed to a commonwealth. Streater declined to print it—a decision rapidly recognized as offering a vital opportunity for army opposition. Monck hesitated, as officers demanded of him that he prevent the Act's enforcement. He yielded and appealed to the House to forbear. Only William

77. Birch, *Collection of the State Papers of John Thurloe*, VII, 797–8 (16 December 1659); Lawson, *Two Letters*; Underdown, *Royalist Conspiracy*, 294–5.

78. Streater, *Letter sent to His Excellency the Lord Fleetwood*, 2–4.

79. Davies, *Restoration*, 184–9; *Six Important Quaeres*.

80. With John Maycock.

81. Firth and Davies, *Regimental History*, II, 415; *Journals of the House of Commons*, VII, 810.

82. Nicholas, *Nicholas Papers*, IV, 193–204 (referring to "Sectaryes and [the] Rump Party" in alliance); Ogle et al., *Calendar of the Clarendon State Papers*, IV, 593.

Prynne held fast: rushing to Streater's house, he succeeded in forcing through the printing operation.[83] The next day the Rump dissolved for the last time.

One more action would occur to set the seal on the commonwealth. Three weeks later, John Lambert, the last and most formidable of the committed republican commanders, escaped from the Tower. Intelligence implied that he was heading for the Midlands and planning an uprising to save the republic. Monck reacted by stationing Streater at Coventry, where rumor suggested Lambert intended to hold his rendezvous. Even in the mood of depressed resignation that by this time had gripped most republicans, Lambert's reputation gained him a force of soldiers. They rode to him from at least six regiments, and a search party sent out to find him defected as soon as it did so. John Okey, recently Streater's co-conspirator, joined the band. Before long Lambert's force had its first success, as Monck's commander was thrown out of Warwick Castle. Agitators reappeared in the army, and civilian rebellions materialized in seven counties.

Monck's intelligence was good. Lambert had arranged a rendezvous twenty miles south of Coventry, at the resonant old battlefield of Edgehill. No sooner had he got there than Streater and his fellow commander, Ingoldsby, attacked him and the few soldiers who had arrived on time. Streater's five hundred men were the only ones to fire in the engagement; Lambert's soldiers turned their weapons to the ground and soon fled. Lambert himself was captured, and gleeful London news-sheets retailed the story of his horse's struggling to extricate itself from the mud of a plowed field. The uprising had depended on his authority; with Lambert taken, it collapsed. Thus ended the only armed opposition to Restoration. After this, and with the unmistakable results of the elections to the Convention Parliament, Streater reconciled himself to the inevitability of monarchy.[84]

It was a notable moment: Streater, hitherto the most steadfast of commonwealthsmen, accepting rule by a single person. Less than a month before, he and Okey had cooperated to obstruct the militia bill, and, rumor suggested, had even considered assassinating Monck. Now they found themselves on opposite sides across a muddy battlefield. Ludlow, bitterly disappointed, waxed fittingly providential about Streater's betrayal, reckon-

---

83. *Journals of the House of Commons*, VII, 878–9 (15 March 1659/60); Hutton, *Restoration*, 102–3; *Perfect Diurnall or the Daily Proceedings* (no printed date. Thomason: 19 march, 1659/60), 2.

84. Hutton, *Restoration*, 98–9, 107, 109, 114–6; Firth and Davies, *Regimental History*, I, 78–9, 158–61; Historical Manuscripts Commission, *Report on the Manuscripts of F. W. Leybourne-Popham*, 176–8; Davies, *Restoration*, 336. Ingoldsby and Streater had met in Ireland: Gilbert, *Contemporary History*, III, 296–9.

ing that God must be using him as an instrument "to point at our sin." But Streater, however symbolic, was scarcely alone:

> as there had bin a consenting (instead of building the howse, and doing the worke of God, when there was an opportunity) to build a Babell, and to prosecute a personall interest before the publique, therefore are they given up to the confusion of language, and to be divided one against another. . . . Thus our enemyes, even those of our owne howse (and none of Charles Steward's party) were instruments, yea rods in the Lord's hand, to scourge us, that so his displeasure might the more appeare therein.[85]

JOHN STREATER AND THE RESTORATION: A NEW POLITICS OF PRINTING

The restored monarchy achieved a surprisingly easy disarmament. In July Streater was demoted to major; by October his regiment had been disbanded altogether. His military vocation terminated, he returned to printing. Here too he would face obstacles. With Charles returned the authority of licensers and Company alike. But during the next two decades, in perhaps the most remarkable phase of a remarkable life, Streater would play a central part in mounting an unprecedented challenge to the very foundations on which the culture of print in his era rested. That challenge would be based in his two paramount concerns: public knowledge and the law.[86]

A commonwealthsman with Streater's past was never likely to remain above suspicion in Restoration London. As early as 1661 he was among a number of ex-officers arrested for plotting, and he would be detained several more times over the next two decades. Samuel Parker soon singled him out as a dangerous republican.[87] Even after his own death, his widow, Susan, would be cited in an accusation against the notorious Whig Slingsby Bethel for calling the king and duke of York bastards.[88] However, to extrapolate a consistent history of republican opposition from such episodes would be rather too simplistic.[89] In the streets and alleys of London, every passerby

85. Ludlow, *A Voyce from the Watch Tower*, 88, 114–6; Underdown, *Royalist Conspiracy*, 255, 277.

86. For the extent to which this conflict grew to involve virtually the entire book trade community, see Brodowski, "Literary Piracy," 202–55. There are extensive records among the Chancery papers at the PRO documenting the progress and diversification of the conflict: see especially C7/588/1, C8/303/125, C9/31/126 and C10/178/3.

87. Greaves, *Deliver us from Evil*, 71, 219; Parker, *Bishop Parker's History of his Own Time*, 17.

88. [Streater], *Observations*, 36; Firth and Davies, *Regimental History*, II, 417; PRO SP 29/404, no. 237.

89. The possibilities and drawbacks of such an approach are amply illustrated in Jacob's *Henry Stubbe*.

was a potential spy, informer, plotter, or renegade—or perhaps a conforming royalist. In such a place, a householder lay at the mercy of a group whom
Streater himself consistently despised: gossiping neighbors. Streater was a
natural candidate for their conspiracy stories. He railed against these "Informers or Tale-bearers," who ruined many families by their insinuations.
"Nothing can tend more to the detriment of the people in general," he
insisted, "then the countenancing of Informers, or such as make suggestions
against any one." They were "plagues of a Nation." He even recommended
that "Eves-droppers" found loitering near a household should be arrested as
a matter of policy.

This opinion combined with a strong view of the household as a civil
and productive space. Streater had long avowed that a house was properly
its proprietor's "Castle," which "ought not to be entred" unless "by order
and due course of Law." It should even provide protection against royal prerogative. Yet since Cromwell's day he had discerned a trend for searches to
be undertaken upon the mere "suspicion" aroused by neighbors' reports. It
is in this intense and claustrophobic world of rumor and strong feelings that
his occasional arrests need to be placed. So when searchers arrived at his
printing house in 1670 with a general warrant granted after his pamphleteering against the Conventicle Act, for example, he and his workers did not
go quietly. The deputy surveyor of the press went to grab a manuscript sheet
lying on the case of letters in front of the compositor, William Thomas,
who quickly snatched it and stuffed it in his pocket. The accompanying
constable forthwith tried to arrest Thomas. But the latter refused to "come
along wth Him," and a riot ensued, in one of the very few printing houses
in Britain large enough to mount one. "The whole Company almost (to y^e
Number of nere Twenty Persons) fell into an Uproar," reported the officer,
"some Crying out they were free-born subjects, & not to be medled with
by such a Warrant."[90] The constable's invocation of the king's name proved
counterproductive, as the chapel "on ye Contrary" mounted "a Generall
Clamour" and secured the safe escape of the compositor.

There was another, more orthodox, side to Streater's activities. Soon after
the restoration of the monarchy, he had been confident enough to petition
the king for reimbursement for the printing he had undertaken in 1659–60
for Parliament—work done, he now claimed, "to the king's service."[91] His
request was heard. In 1662 Streater, uniquely, was exempted from the measures of the Restoration régime's new Press Act. This Act was seen as ex-

---

90. [Streater?], *Character of a True and False Shepherd*; [Streater], *Observations*, 36–7;
[Streater?], *Clavis*, sig. B4^v; PRO SP 29/277, nos. 34–5; PRO SP 44/34, fol. 40^v; Firth and
Davies, *Regimental History*, II, 417.
91. PRO SP 25/108, p. 39; PRO SP 44/5, p. 38; PRO SP 44/13, p. 14.

tremely important by the authorities, since "the exorbitant Liberty of the Press [had] been a great Occasion of the late Rebellion in the Kingdom."[92] Yet Streater was permitted to "print what he pleases, as if the Act had never been made." This extraordinary freedom allowed him to develop a printing operation of almost unrivaled size. By 1668 he had the second largest private printing house in London, with five presses. His success was resented, which may also help explain his antagonism to informers—they continued to allege that he was "no wayes quallified for regular Printing."[93] But success it was.

Streater needed such a large establishment to pursue his major enterprise of these years, which was the printing and distribution of law books. It was this enterprise that led him to propose his radical reconstruction of the order of print. The origins of the proposal, however, lay in the nascent conflict between patents and the Stationers' register which was introduced in chapter 3. There it was explained that, as the book trade grew in size and complexity, so the two mechanisms of civility represented by patents and the register came increasingly into conflict. But as that conflict intensified, so the issue came to crystallize around one patent in particular: that covering books of the common law. This was one of the oldest and most important privileges. By a satisfying coincidence, in fact, it was exactly the same age as the Stationers' Company. In 1557, as the Company received its charter, Richard Tottel had been granted a patent to common law books. Tottel had held it until his death, when it had fallen to a clerk of the signet named Charles Yetsweirt. He and his widow maintained the privilege until 1597, when a further grant was made to Bonham Norton and Thomas Wight. When this latter patent expired in 1629 a reversion was issued to one John More. It was with More that the real controversy began.

More immediately farmed the privilege out to three Stationers, in return for a lump sum plus annual payments.[94] Chief among this triumvirate was the ambitious Miles Flesher. In succeeding years Flesher worked steadily to accrue to himself not only this but several other large privileges, aggressively comprinting the books of other Stationers trying to register legal titles to themselves at Stationers' Hall. By 1641 he was already being singled out as the most notorious monopolist in the trade.[95] He persevered in these tactics

92. 14 Car. II, c. 33; *Journals of the House of Commons*, VIII, 425b. Charles maintained the pressure for the bill to be passed with a personally written note to the House: *Journals of the House of Commons*, VIII, 429b.

93. *Journals of the House of Lords*, XV, 546b; Hetet, "Literary Underground," 19–21.

94. McKitterick, *Cambridge University Press*, 131–2; Stationers' Company, *Records of the Court*, ix; Stationers' Company, *Registers 1554–1640*, V, lvii–lviii. There is a survey of early law printing in Pantzer, "Printing the English Statutes."

95. Pollard and Redgrave, *Short-Title Catalogue 1475–1640*, III, 200; SCB C, fol. 227ᵛ; Sparke, *Scintilla*, 4–6 (where the Huntington copy, classmark 482490, has the contempo-

through the Civil War and Interregnum, when, along with Roger Norton and Richard Royston, Flesher was one of a coterie of actively royalist booksellers.[96] The old royal patents themselves became unenforceable during these years, but such determined individuals could still attempt to protect their titles, either by entering them in the Stationers' Register, by comprinting, or by making use of the Company's search and seizure provisions. Flesher did all three. He had long been something of an irritant to the Stationers' Company, attacked for printing not only law books but such valuable Company copies as the Psalms and Foxe's *Acts and Monuments*. But from 1642 he became an assistant, lent the Company substantial sums, and began to attend court meetings with remarkable regularity. The strategy worked. Flesher succeeded in becoming warden in 1649–51, and attained the mastership itself in 1652–4. From this position of strength he could use all the Company's protocols to fight very effectively for his titles. Indeed, under such leadership the Company itself became something of a patentee, taking over the Bible privilege and the office of king's printer.[97] Its attempts to persevere with searches and seizures in order to protect such rights led one radical to condemn the Company for becoming "as mischievous as any *Pattentees* in *England*."[98] For himself, Flesher particularly defended his law titles, however strenuously other Stationers such as Richard Hodgkinson and Henry Twyford might assert their own claims to them.[99]

We can see something of the complex strategies called for in the face of these vicious struggles thanks to a documented case involving the reports of the eminent judge Sir George Croke.[100] The Stationer involved was Richard Hodgkinson, who had been assessed as a delinquent in 1649 but was now a

---

rary note, "Observe this abuse"); Blagden, *Stationers' Company*, 138 ff. Flesher and Sparke were present when the Company decided to combat the comprinting of law books: SCB C, fol. 197ʳ.

96. Williams, "First Edition of *Holy Living*," 102.

97. Blagden, *Stationers' Company*, 140–1. Sparke was prominent on the committee handling the Bible appropriation, the story of which is complex. But the Protectorate regarded itself as entitled to assign literary properties by fiat, and under Cromwell the Bible was granted to Henry Hills and John Field over the ignored protests of the Company and others. See SCB C, fol. 289ᵛ, for another example, when the Company protested that such orders would "destroy" members' property. See also Nash, "English Licences to Print," for copy ownership and licensing in the 1640s.

98. *Every Mans Case.*

99. For Interregnum struggles over legal texts see: SCB C, fols. 274ʳ, 281ʳ; SCB D, fols. 14ᵛ, 16ʳ, 17ᵛ, 23ᵛ, 25ʳ⁻ᵛ, 28ʳ–30ʳ, 35ʳ–36ᵛ, 39ᵛ–41ᵛ, 46ᵛ, 60ᵛ. Richard Hodgkinson had been in trouble over Cowell's *Interpreter* even before the war: Plomer, *Dictionary . . . 1641 to 1667*, 99. For an example of the printing of legal texts during Flesher's supremacy, see Matthews, *William Sheppard*, 120 ff., 211–2. For Flesher's tactics see Blagden, *Stationers' Company*, 138–45.

100. See the fragment headed *About the 7th of March 1655*, which is discussed in Spencer, "Printing of Sir George Croke's Reports."

fierce competitor with Flesher for legal printing.[101] Around 12 September 1656, two lawyers, John Whiting and Clement Spelman, approached the warden of the Stationers' Company asking that Croke's *Reports* be entered to Hodgkinson, and requesting him "to take a care that none else should meddle with the printing of them." Three days later they took Hodgkinson with them to ask the clerk for an entrance. The clerk refused, citing a prior entrance to one Warren. Whiting and Spelman, unusually for non-Stationers, forthwith appealed to the Stationers' court. There they reaffirmed their agreement with Hodgkinson and "disclaimed the Entrance of *Warren*, as surreptitious." Still no entrance was permitted. A month later Hodgkinson and two supporters again went to the hall, where they displayed "the Copy"—that is, the manuscript they were printing—in a further attempt to gain an entrance. It was again refused. They now elevated the process into the legal system. Upper Bench heard Whiting's case, along with responses from both the Company and Warren, before ordering that "the former pretended Entry to *Warren*, so surreptitiously obtein'd, should be *obliterate*." Yet again Spelman, Whiting, and Hodgkinson went to the Stationers' court to demand execution of this order; yet again the issue was "put off." As the Company grandees saw it, it had been "the matter of right in the Copie" which had "begot all the Controversie," and the claimants' relation to Croke's executor, Sir Harbottle Grimstone, remained unclear. In March Spelman and Whiting returned with Grimstone's written consent. But now the Master was too ill to attend, and in his absence nothing could be done (fig. 4.2).

On 20 October 1657, printing finally began on the part of the *Reports* covering Charles I's reign. Standing in the middle of the pressroom, Whiting would repeatedly declare to the journeymen—"and to sundry other Persons (before them in the Work-house) which he hath brought hither to see that work, and Printing"—that he had agreed with Hodgkinson for all the *Reports*, and that those covering Charles's reign constituted only about a third of the total. He would rage at Hodgkinson in front of the workers for continuing to undertake other work in the midst of this great project—which was, of course, a standard and necessary printer's practice. Claiming that he had ensured him employment for seven years, Whiting would even "drive . . . Customers from his the said *Hodg.* house that have come to him about work." The reason for his incivility became clear when two booksellers came to the printing house and begged Hodgkinson to print for them part of a rival set of reports. Whiting, standing in the same room, refused. He "would not for 100*l.*" that this competitor should appear before his own edition.

---

101. Green, *Calendar of the Proceedings of the Committee for Advance of Money*, II, 1167.

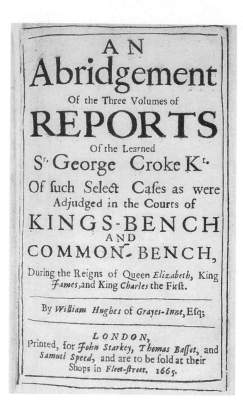

AN
Abridgement
Of the Three Volumes of
REPORTS
Of the Learned
Sᵣ George Croke Kᵗ·
Of fuch Select Cafes as were
Adjudged in the Courts of
KINGS-BENCH
AND
COMMON-BENCH,
During the Reigns of Queen *Elizabeth*, King
James, and King *Charles* the Firft.

By *William Hughes* of *Grayes-Inne*, Efq;

LONDON,
Printed, for *John Starkey*, *Thomas Baffet*, and
Samuel Speed, and are to be fold at their
Shops in *Fleet-ftreet*, 1665.

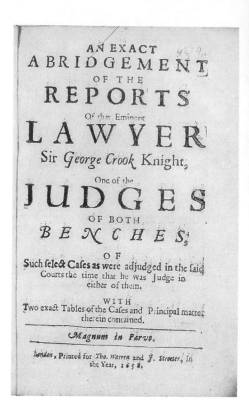

AN EXACT
ABRIDGEMENT
OF THE
REPORTS
Of that Eminent
LAWYER
Sir *George Crook* Knight,
One of the
JUDGES
OF BOTH
BENCHES;
OF
Such felect Cafes as were adjudged in the faid
Courts the time that he was Judge in
either of them.
WITH
Two exact Tables of the Cafes and Principal matter
therein contained.

Magnum in Parvo.

London, Printed for *Tho. Warren* and *J. Streeter*, in
the Year, 1658.

Shortly after this, Hodgkinson was able to tell Whiting that the material for Charles's reign was all but complete. He now needed the copy for James's. Without it the presses would stand idle, which would be "very chargeable." But Whiting now became curiously evasive. He did show Hodgkinson the manuscript so that the printer could estimate the number of printed sheets it would call for, but immediately took it back again, claiming that it was to be checked by Justice Matthew Hale and that it would not be ready for two weeks. That delay grew longer every time Hodgkinson asked. Eventually Whiting retreated into the country when Hodgkinson's queries grew pressing. Only then did his problem become apparent.

Almost a year after the last involvement of the Stationers' court, printer William Godbid suddenly appeared there bearing a letter from Grimstone asking that Croke's Jacobean *Reports* be entered to him. Hodgkinson was present. Having "formerly left a Caveat against the same," he urged that entrance be refused. Moreover, he continued, Whiting had "fraudulently" recovered the manuscript from the printing house. In response, Godbid brought a letter from Grimstone demanding entrance and "affirming the right in him only." Hodgkinson, the letter maintained, had only been employed to print part of the reports, "which (if it had been Entred) he was to have given Bond for the Copie." Hodgkinson responded by asserting that

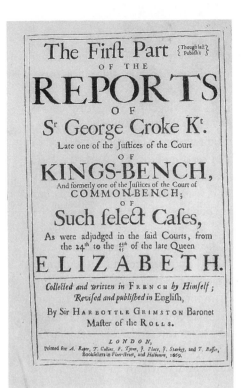

The Firſt Part {Though laſt Publiſh't}
OF THE
REPORTS
OF
Sʳ George Croke Kᵗ.
Late one of the Juſtices of the Court
OF
KINGS-BENCH,
And formerly one of the Juſtices of the Court of
COMMON-BENCH;
OF
Such ſeleƈt Caſes,
As were adjudged in the ſaid Courts, from
the 24ᵗʰ to the ⁴⁴ᵗʰ of the late Queen
ELIZABETH.
Colleƈted and written in FRENCH *by Himſelf ;*
Reviſed and publiſhed in Engliſh,
By Sir HARBOTTLE GRIMSTON Baronet
Maſter of the ROLLS.

LONDON,
Printed for *A. Roper, T. Collins, F. Tyton, J. Place, J. Starkey,* and *T. Baſſet,*
Bookſellers in *Fleet-Street,* and *Holbourn,* 1669.

FIG. 4.2. Title pages of rival printings of Croke's *Reports* and their *Abridgement*, by John Streater and others. Note the multiplicity of Stationers involved in antagonistic versions. (By permission of the Henry E. Huntington Library, San Marino, California, RB 329103, RB 432047, RB 433540.)

Grimstone himself had once conceded his own right to the whole *Reports*. Grimstone, informed by the clerk, denied all knowledge of this. He had assigned to Whiting an interest only in the Caroline *Reports*, and no more. If "that idle fellow"—"such were Sʳ Harbottle's words," noted the clerk fastidiously—had made a misleading agreement with Hodgkinson, he had had no authority from Grimstone to do so. Any promise made by Whiting could not, then, divest him of his property. He suggested that the printer sue Whiting rather than maintain an illegitimate property claim. In the meantime, he had sold to Godbid his "prop'tie & interest" in the copy. Parliament itself now stepped in on Grimstone's side. After long debate, the Company complied. Grimstone's edition could proceed.[102] The printed result, then, was a series of different books calling themselves Croke's *Reports*. One of them, produced by "J.S." (probably Streater), was much more hastily printed, some 150 pages shorter, and, "for the good of the People of these Nations," half the price of the others. Hodgkinson too carried on printing Croke's text "contrary to order." Large profits and a huge future market were at stake, and, parliamentary fiat notwithstanding, it was hard for readers to

102. SCB D, fols. 17ᵛ, 28ʳ–30ʳ. For Harbottle Grimston on unauthorized law printing, see Saunders, *Authorship and Copyright*, 37.

know which version was authentic. The problem was, as Grimstone himself put it, that the producers of such editions "care not how they blot mens Credits." [103]

Streater had thus been involved in battles over legal printing long before the Restoration—and the bookseller for *Oceana*, Daniel Pakeman, was also chiefly known for producing law books. Such struggles clearly manifested in action his advocacy of a commonwealth of reading citizens. With the Restoration, however, the situation once again changed radically. Privileges once more promised to become enforceable, and with a new dispensation looming the profits to be made from a new generation of law books would be huge. However, Flesher had omitted to pay his annual charge back in 1640. More's daughter, Lady Martha Acheson, now seized the opportunity and sued him for the patent. After all the divisions, subcontracting, and farming out to which the patent had been subject over the preceding decades, not least the unresolved Croke affair, other claimants also came forward. In particular, both the king's printers and the English Stock—which had bought into an earlier version of the patent by 1605—mounted claims. [104] A chaotic and lengthy struggle was about to ensue. The Company reached agreement with most rivals, and itself took control of Flesher's right; but More's heir was to prove far more recalcitrant. [105]

More's daughter had married Richard Atkyns, a veteran Cavalier and the son of an eminent judge. [106] Like most old-guard royalists, Atkyns saw no reason why individuals associated with the Interregnum régime should retain benefits now in the gift of the crown. He moved to reassert the original patent, citing his services for Charles I. He soon achieved some success. By November 1660 the restored king had granted a privilege to his brother Edward Atkyns on his behalf, carrying the sole printing of law books for forty years after the expiration of the More patent in 1668. [107] The Company immediately struck back. It seized sheets from the houses of Atkyns's printers, hoping to obstruct his capacity to exploit the privilege for long enough to construct a legal challenge.

One of the printers thus interrupted was John Streater. As late as 1661, Streater had still been printing legal texts for the English Stock. [108] But now

103. Croke, *Reports* (1657), sigs. A2ᵛ–A3ʳ, [A6ᵛ]; Croke, *Second Part of the Reports* (1658), sigs. A1ᵛ–[A2ʳ]; Croke, *First Part* (1659), sigs. A1ʳ–[A4ᵛ]; PRO SP 18/124, no. 106(xvi); PRO SP 18/126, no. 3(vii); PRO SP 18/126, no. 8(i).

104. Blagden, *Stationers' Company*, 93, 144.

105. SCB D, fol. 69ʳ⁻ᵛ.

106. For Atkyns's previous history, see *Biographia Britannica*, I, 255–6; for their uneasy marriage, see Atkyns, *Vindication*.

107. PRO SP 38/19, p. 58.

108. SCB D, fol. 65ʳ.

he departed decisively from the Company and forged an alliance with Atkyns. Streater and two allies—Henry Twyford, an Interregnum law printer
and one-time royalist agent, and James Flesher, son of Miles—agreed to pay
Atkyns £100 a year each to print the books covered by the privilege.[109] Others might comply with the Company; from now on, Streater would not. He
declined to acknowledge the court's authority over him, and refused to stop
printing on its command. For their own part, he and Atkyns now moved to
assert their own right. Not yet wishing to challenge the Company head-on,
they instead moved to arrest Samuel Speed, who was presuming to print law
books in defiance of both patent and Company (fig. 4.3). A vicious commercial battle was in the offing, at the very time when the new régime would
most need authoritative legal texts. Facing chaos, the government issued an
injunction against the printing of all law books whatsoever until the dispute
was resolved.[110]

Prevented from producing law books, Streater now turned his printing
house once more to the manufacture of political arguments. In a series of
tracts, he and Atkyns mounted a sophisticated case not just for their own
patent, but for royal privileges in general. As the title of Atkyns's most important work indicated, they composed a history of such grants extending
right back to *The Original and Growth of Printing* itself (fig. 4.4). Asserting
that the first introduction of the press into England had occurred at the
personal instigation of the king, they sought to legitimate the crown's continued retention of powers over printing by characterizing it as royal and
personal *property*. In that case, they maintained, the preservation of patents
was essential for two reasons. First, they were clearly a central manifestation
of royal prerogative. If they were to be declared void, crown prerogative
would necessarily fall, and the disorder of the 1640s would inevitably return.
Second, moreover, the very Company officers now offering to police the
trade on behalf of the restored king had previously served the Protectorate
and the regicides, demonstrating at best their lack of principle and at worst
a continuing and disingenuous republicanism. Atkyns claimed that such unprincipled conduct would always prevail in the current culture of printing,
because it was in a company's nature to act according to "interest." For the
crown to ask it to restrain its own members and suppress its own products
was clearly unrealistic.

109. *Case of the Booksellers and Printers Stated*, col. 2; Blagden, *Stationers' Company*, 144;
SCB D, fols. 101ᵛ, 102ᵛ. Twyford had been one of the strongest challengers to Miles Flesher
in the 1650s.
110. SCB D, fols. 75ʳ⁻ᵛ, 78ᵛ, 85ʳ. Streater and Atkyns got another injunction in 1667–8:
fol. 134ʳ; PRO SP 44/25, fol. 65ʳ⁻ᵛ. Speed shared premises with the Rainbow coffeehouse:
Lillywhite, *London Coffee Houses*, 467.

What here thou Viewest, is the Gravers Art
A shape of man, only the outward part
Peruse the booke, therein more plainly read
Vera Effigies Samuels Speed.

F. H. Van Hove fec:

FIG. 4.3. Samuel Speed: Stationer, unfortunate victim of Streater and Atkyns, and prison moralist. Speed, *Prison Pietie*. (By permission of the Syndics of Cambridge University Library.)

FIG. 4.4. (*below*) Frontispiece and title page to Atkyns, *Original and Growth of Printing* (1664). Charles II is shown flanked by Archbishop Sheldon and the earl of Clarendon (holding the great seal), and above his effective restorer, Monck (now duke of Albemarle). Note the motto held by Sheldon and Clarendon: "Scripture and the laws are the pillars of the crown." Monck's quotation from Cicero—a call for arms to yield to political authority—derives from *De Officiis*, I.xxii.77, and *In L. Calpurniam Pisonem Oratio*, 72. (By permission of the Henry E. Huntington Library, San Marino, California, RB 64671.)

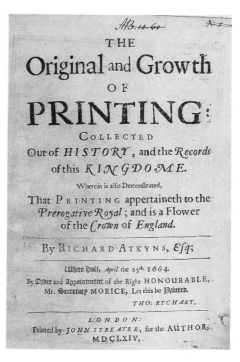

THE

Original and Growth

OF

PRINTING:

COLLECTED

Out of *HISTORY*, and the *Records* of this *KINGDOME*.

Wherein is also Demonstrated,

That PRINTING appertaineth to the *Prerogative Royal*; and is a Flower of the *Crown* of *England*.

By RICHARD ATKYNS, *Esq*;

White-Hall, *April* the 25th. 1664.

By Order and Appointment of the Right HONOURABLE, Mr. Secretary MORICE, Let this be Printed.

THO: RYCHAUT.

LONDON:

Printed by *JOHN STREATER*, for the AUTHOR, MDCLXIV.

The solution, Atkyns insisted, was to reappoint patentees, and to elevate their power above that of the Company. As crown servants, subject to the direct sanction of the king, patentees could hardly fail to be loyal.[111] Moreover, they would not be tradesmen, but conforming men of independent means. In short, they would be gentlemen. As such they would incline to be trustworthy, and could resist the mercenary mentality leading to seditious publishing.[112] With this proper gentlemanly oligarchy to oversee it, printing could return to the pure state it had enjoyed before its incorporation. That incorporation, in other words, had reduced its status from that of an "Art," properly owned and regulated, into a "Mechanick Trade," dictated by the mercenary interests of mechanicks.[113]

Atkyns and Streater claimed that the embodiment of this degradation was the Stationers' register.[114] Entrances in the register represented the Company's self-confident assertion of political autonomy, since they implicitly defied royal prerogative. In the case of law books the results threatened to be especially grave, moreover, since their owners gained the power effectively to alter the laws of the land. The Company had deliberately confused the claims respecting these contested copies, in order to prevent the issue coming to a final decision; it had twice recently elected Miles Flesher Master (in 1662 and 1663) to further its claim, and was devoting all available funds to the cause.[115] Atkyns now announced that had the Company not been prevented by the injunction against printing, it would have "altered the Ancient Law-Books, and cast them into a new Modell of their own Invention." If permitted to continue, the Company's actions would mean that "by degrees the state and truth of the good Old Lawes by which Men hold their Lives and Estates, should utterly be lost and forgotten, and new Laws fram'd to fit the Humours of a new Invented *Government*."[116]

The new legal basis for press regulation, the Press Act of 1662, therefore did not reach to the core of the matter. It gave statutory force to royal patents, yet at the same time endorsed the rights recorded in the Stationers' register.[117] This was an irreconcilable contradiction. Directing his argument

111. Atkyns, *Original and Growth of Printing* (1664), sig. E1ʳ.

112. Prynne himself had *complained* of this: Inn. Temp. Ms. Petyt 511, vol. 23, fol. 18ʳ.

113. Atkyns, *Original and Growth of Printing* (item A4134 in Wing, *Short-Title Catalogue*): a broadsheet of about 1660, later expanded into Atkyns, *Original and Growth of Printing* (1664), a pamphlet of thirty-two pages. Unless otherwise stated, all references below are to the 1664 pamphlet. The same argument is repeated with significant embellishments in [Atkyns and/or Streater], *Kings Grant of Privilege* (1669). Brief reference to Atkyns's argument is made in Weber, *Paper Bullets*, 147–51.

114. For an example see SCB D, fol. 194ᵛ. Atkyns had complained to the Privy Council that by entries in the register "a private propertie is pretended to be gained"; Charles ordered that no entry be made against previously granted patents, since that endangered prerogative.

115. Atkyns, *Original and Growth of Printing*, sigs. [D3ᵛ]–[D4ʳ].

116. Atkyns, *Original and Growth of Printing*, sig. [D4ʳ].

0117. 14 Car. II, c. 33, §§ 2, 5.

to Parliament as it considered renewing the Act, Atkyns therefore called straightforwardly for its repeal. He wanted it to be replaced by a new bill, designed to "Establish Propriety" around a system of patents. Such a bill must unambiguously elevate privileges over the register. It must also take enforcement out of the hands of the Stationers themselves, "who onely can offend, and whose Interest it is to do so," and reinstate the principle that ultimate control of the press lay in the king rather than Parliament or the Company.[118] In effect his point was a Hobbesian one, although Hobbes was the one absolutist whom Atkyns could not be seen to cite. Like Hobbes, Atkyns knew that if the "Power which is intire and inherent in Your Majesties Person, and inseparable from Your Crown, should be divided," it must be "of dangerous Consequence."[119] He had begun his argument by asserting that "the least loss of Power in a Magistrate, is a great Detriment to his Government," and by asserting that printing belonged to the king both as supreme magistrate and as personal proprietor. It was as a result of just such a division and delegation of royal power that the Civil War had occurred.[120] The Company's charter made it nothing less than a "Petit *State*," Atkyns remarked, and therefore "inconsistent with *Monarchy*."[121]

This identification of the register with aspirations to autonomy from royal supremacy was not in itself new. As early as 1636, the crown had complained that the register represented a threat to "as absolute a right of his Ma^{ts} p^{r}rogative as that of Coyning."[122] But the expression of this principle presented by Atkyns and Streater was both more consistent and more influential than anything that had gone before. Their case was therefore of much greater general significance than might at first seem. They were effectively arguing that corporations such as the Stationers' Company represented interests irreconcilable with monarchy. They therefore advocated the destruction of the Company and with it the extensive practical civility it embodied.

118. Atkyns, *Original and Growth of Printing*, sigs. B2^r–[B4^r], [E3^v]–[E4^r].

119. Atkyns, *Original and Growth of Printing*, sig. B1^v. For how Hobbes's antipathy to any division of power led to the detailed prescription of practice, see Shapin and Schaffer, *Leviathan and the Air-Pump*, 92–109, 110–154. Hobbes was himself planning to write a detailed defense of the prerogative: Williams, "Edition of the Correspondence of John Aubrey," 126–7. See also Hobbes, *Behemoth*, 126, and Hobbes, *Leviathan*, 224–5, for how the pretense to personal "propriety" tended to the dissolution of a commonwealth.

120. Atkyns, *Original and Growth of Printing*, sigs. B1^r–B2^v. The claim that printing belonged to the king as personal proprietor should be noted; its significance is explored in the following chapter.

121. Atkyns, *Original and Growth of Printing*, sig. E2^r. Compare Hickeringill's statement a generation later that the Stationers' Company had become "a *Body-Politick*" with its own laws: *Speech Without-Doors*, 32–4. An earlier argument on similar grounds was advanced by William Ball in *Stationars and Printers*.

122. Greg, *Companion to Arber*, 339–40. Compare Prynne in Inn. Temp. Ms. Petyt 511, vol. 23, fol. 18^r.

They should be replaced by a comprehensive new system of press control based directly on crown prerogative.[123] A titular corporation of some sort might still exist in such a régime, but it would be subject to frequent, routine, and minute intervention by crown officers in all its practices. The source of trade identity would no longer be the collective of Stationers, but the king.

At the center of Atkyns's moral critique of the Stationers lay his claim that they had reduced printing to a "Mechanick Trade." Like Moxon, the great defender of the printers (and another outsider), he therefore had to reflect on "the signification of the Word *Mechanick*." Its Latin root signified a handicraftsman, he conceded, and the term therefore referred unproblematically to printers, binders, and founders. But Atkyns alleged that it embraced all tradesmen whatsoever, since a more distant etymology from Greek betrayed its older, wider reference to "a *Cunning Contrivance* of the Head, as well as Hand."[124] A mechanick was thus someone who, through cunning and craft, "pervert[ed]" a God-given art by exercising it for lucre, thereby creating a trade. An example might be a common fiddler who, playing tunes for money, perverted the art of music properly practiced by gentlemen. Atkyns thus held that it was not its practical nature alone that made a craft mechanick, but its subjection to avaricious interests. A gentleman might, in principle, possess knowledge of the practical intricacies of printing. Such knowledge merely "tend[ed] different wayes" according to the cultural identity of its possessor.

This argument had much in common with contemporary representations of commerce and gentility in general. Yet Atkyns was emphatic about the particular status of Stationers. The implications of a brewers' company, say, would be negligible in comparison. Atkyns insisted that there was as much difference between a brewer and a Stationer "as between a Pyrate that robs a Ship or two, and *Alexander* that robs the whole World."[125] The special power of print to define entire cultures made its mechanick manifestation especially dangerous. Stationers, in short, were pirate kings. Or rather, the real pirate kings were the powerful oligarchy controlling the Stationers' Company: the booksellers. Booksellers represented avarice unleavened by craft honor. They had usurped both power from the printers and propriety from the king.

Atkyns's major and immediate targets, then, were the booksellers. His

123. Atkyns, *Original and Growth of Printing*, sigs. E2ʳ and [E4ʳ] (Proposal III). See also his points in PRO SP 29/88, no 132. *A Brief Discourse Concerning Printing and Printers* is filed next to these arguments by Atkyns.

124. Atkyns, *Original and Growth of Printing*, sig. [C4ʳ⁻ᵛ].

125. Atkyns, *Original and Growth of Printing*, sig. [E4ᵛ].

proposed alternative of patentees would effectively eliminate the power of this caste by constructing a new and stable alliance between gentility and craftsmanship. Atkyns insisted that although patentees *could* become skilled in the practices of the printing house, they did not *have* to do so. A patentee would generally strike a deal with a particular printer, enjoining that he or she work to certain standards. The patentee would then examine the sheets, and could refuse payment if they fell short of those standards. The printer's "Interest" would then be to print the text "perfect and fair." The management of a bookseller became superfluous when the operation was arranged in this fashion. Thanks to the network of mercuries available in the capital, Atkyns observed, a bookseller would not even be needed for distribution. Retailers could always be supplied "out of the She-Shopkeepers in *Westminster-Hall*." [126]

This was therefore an extraordinarily radical proposal. Atkyns wanted to transform not only administration and regulation systems, but every aspect of the authorship and printing of books. The figure he wished to eliminate—the bookseller operating as "undertaker" for a publication—was the keystone of an entire culture of production, circulation, and accreditation. In chapter 8, we shall see such an undertaker playing a crucial role in the construction and destruction of astronomical knowledge, when the first astronomer royal, John Flamsteed, fought against Isaac Newton's appointment of Awnsham Churchill to the post. Flamsteed, like Atkyns, came to believe that the very existence of an undertaker compromised genteel authorship. Atkyns wished to replace this régime with one explicitly reliant not only on royal power, but on the mainly female community of mercuries that the formal hierarchy of the Stationers' Company so resolutely excluded.

Atkyns's call for a curb on the booksellers tapped a rich vein of resentment among certain members of the Stationers' Company itself. Those members were the printers. Since the beginning of the century they had been complaining of their eclipse in the Company. A group of printers now revived their call for the Company to be divided, and a new company of printers created with powers to regulate the trade. [127] Atkyns favored this call insofar as its advocates denied the claim of the bookseller-controlled Stationers' Company to be a loyal agent of the crown. [128] Roger L'Estrange, himself angling to be appointed "Surveyor of Imprimery," usefully concurred. "The

126. Atkyns, *Original and Growth of Printing*, sigs. D1ᵛ–D2ᵛ.

127. *Brief Discourse Concerning Printing and Printers*. The printers claimed that booksellers refused to enter their copies, and counterfeited them. Their call dated back to at least 1651, and was very probably heard before the Civil War: Blagden, "'Company' of Printers," 4–6, 11.

128. *London Printers Lamentation*; *Brief Discourse Concerning Printing and Printers*; Atkyns, *Original and Growth of Printing*, sig. D2ᵛ; Blagden, "'Company' of Printers."

Question is now, By whom, *the Government and Oversight of the Press is to be* undertaken," L'Estrange declared, "and the Contest lyes at present betwixt the *Booksellers* and *Printers*, which although Concorporate by an Ancient Grant, are in this point become Competitors." Yet both L'Estrange and Atkyns were ultimately unenthusiastic in their support for a separate printers' company. They believed that since it would after all still be a *company*, its creation would in the end only replicate the existing problem. Such a body would cleave to the public good only so far as suited "the *Particular Good* of the *Company*." L'Estrange proposed instead a board of six crown-appointed "Surveighers" to oversee the trade; Atkyns favored patentees. Both wished to redefine the book trade around royal power.[129]

It might be assumed that Atkyns's campaign was doomed to failure.[130] Yet such an assumption would be entirely wrong. Almost immediately his strategy found success. Secretary of State Sir Edward Nicholas advised the Stationers' Company to get a new charter as early as 1661, and in the beginning of 1664 the crown started legal proceedings against the existing document.[131] Faced with this extreme threat, the booksellers repudiated Atkyns's attack with equal force. They utterly denied themselves to be the "mechanicks" he had portrayed. Moreover, they argued vehemently that such royal grants as the law patent were illegal, since they violated Stationers' customary conventions of propriety. The Stationers' representation of these conventions now took on an interesting new guise. "The Author of every *Manuscript* or *Copy*," they now insisted, possessed "(in all reason) as good right thereunto, as any Man hath to the Estate wherein he has the most absolute property." Taking either from the proprietor without consent must be illegal. Consequently, any Stationer purchasing such "Copies" from an author would gain "the Authors right." The title recorded by due license and entrance in the register therefore became a perpetual freehold. Forced by Atkyns to articulate the foundations of their propriety, the booksellers had enunciated what would soon become the fundamental principle of a century of conflicts over copyright: an alliance between author and Stationer forged in perpetual, authorial property. The author was being recognized as never before, in the service of Stationers' power.[132]

Streater himself responded directly, declaring that the state had instituted law patents to prevent "Errors and Seditions" from being printed and disseminated. Patents, he held, prevented "Innovations, or false construction

---

129. L'Estrange, *Considerations and Proposals*, 24, 26, and passim. For a related proposal to vest oversight of the press in twelve printers, compare PRO SP 29/139, no. 95.

130. Especially since Charles II tended to prefer old Presbyterians at the expense of old Cavaliers: Goldie, "Danby, the Bishops and the Whigs."

131. SCB D, fols. 64ʳ, 89ᵛ, 90ᵛ–91ʳ.

132. Compare comments in Rose, *Authors and Owners*, 23–4.

of the Laws, either by the designs of Authors, or mistake of Printers." It was only when the previous patents régime collapsed in 1642 that "Sedition and Treason came to be printed openly, and continued so to be till his Majesties Restauration." And the law patent was inseparable from all patents—they stood or fell together. To the extent that it could be classed a monopoly, it was a necessary one, similar to patents for mechanical devices. Such protection was essential "for the encouragement of Industry and Invention." The "communicating" of an invention, whether literary or technological, "to publick use, is a publick and general benefit, though the making the Invention should be perpetually appropriated to the Inventor." Powerful protection of the originator might be necessary to establish Streater's ideal of widely distributed knowledge. Examples of such privileges being allowed because their benefit outweighed their disadvantages could be cited from ancient Rome, "the pattern of Governments." His opponents had further alleged that adjudicating issues of similarity and identity with respect to patented titles was impossible, since "every Book more or less compriseth something of the Common-Law." Streater bluntly responded that this was an "*unreasonable construction*." Besides, the king was proprietor of the laws themselves and so could arbitrate their reproduction.[133] This was a characteristic argument of absolutists. It had been made before, and William Prynne had found it particularly objectionable. He had responded indignantly that the authorship of laws was "not [in] the king alone, but the king and Parliamᵗ."[134]

This was not the limit of Streater's engagement. Indeed, the centrality of his role in the whole exchange must be stressed. Without his involvement there would have been no argument. It was Streater who printed Atkyns's attacks on the Stationers' Company, and it was Streater who actually operated the patent, taking a more active role than either of his major partners. As a Stationer, moreover, Streater represented Atkyns and other patentees in the Stationers' court, attending throughout long years of acrimonious conflict. When the Company tried to seize Atkyns's law books, it was to Streater's printing house that its wardens went. They routinely referred to the resulting legal case as "Streaters Bill."[135]

133. [Atkyns and/or Streater], *Kings Grant of Privilege*, 2, 4, 6–7, 10–15; [Atkyns], *Original and Growth of Printing* (1660).

134. Inn. Temp. Ms. Petyt 511, vol. 23, fol. 20ᵛ; compare Filmer, *Patriarcha*, 45–52, and [Atkyns and/or Streater], *Kings Grant of Privilege*, 10–11.

135. SCA, Wardens' Accounts 1663–9, passim; SCB D, fols. 69ᵛ, 74ʳ, 75ʳ⁻ᵛ, 97ʳ⁻ᵛ, 102ᵛ, 113ᵛ–114ʳ, 134ʳ–140ᵛ, 167ᵛ. Streater also seems to have acted in the Company's other great struggle over patents, with Seymour: fols. 119ʳ–120ᵛ. Significantly, it seems that Atkyns himself never entered the court throughout the conflict. Most scandalous of Streater's allegations was that Warden Crooke had tried to secure the patent for himself under cover of acting for the Company—just the sort of unprincipled action Atkyns would have expected. Streater

The relation of these Restoration arguments to Streater's opinions during the Interregnum is debatable. However, that relation was almost certainly not one of simple betrayal, despite their new fulcrum of monarchy. For one thing, the high value placed on a practice worthy of the title of an "Art" had remained. During the Interregnum Streater had already emphasized a concern to increase commerce and manufactures. In this context he had demarcated proper from injurious collectives on grounds of interest. Thus "*Pyrates*" and "Companies" were both kinds of community, but the former were to be shunned because they looked to a "private good," not a public one. "And indeed," he had continued, "when those that are in *Government* mind but their private good only, they are no better then Thieves." A degree of continuity thus existed between trading and political collectives. A wise central authority should consequently oversee such lesser communities, since, for the sake of eliminating the division that caused political change, lesser groups must not conceive of themselves as independent and therefore piratical.[136] And the allegation that Stationers might alter the laws themselves may be seen as a developed version of his complaint from jail against Cromwell. Indeed, Streater himself demonstrated privately to the attorney general that Samuel Speed was doing just that. He was printing legal texts from the Protectorate that enshrined Cromwellian principles. Streater cited them by page and line to show how Speed's text tended "to the unloosinge the frame of his Ma^{tyes} Government." [137]

This tactic had the immediate effect of making Streater himself a focus in the debate. When the booksellers denied Atkyns's moral distinction between gentlemen and mechanicks, they at the same time insisted upon the essential value of craft knowledge for regulating the press.[138] They then built on this insistence by pointing out that, according to the Press Act, all *non-*patented law books must be licensed by judges. Patented texts being exempt from this requirement, a patentee's printer (that is, Streater) would gain unlimited power to print what he liked, including, in this case, "*Errors*" in the

---

was suspended, but Crooke was subsequently defeated in election for the mastership, and he pressed for his allegations to be reconsidered: fols. 105^v, 131^v, 133^r, 134^v–136^r, 137^r–140^v.

136. Streater, *Glympse*, 15; [Streater], *Observations*, 6–7, 18–20, 37–8. It was in the early 1670s, as part of the closely related struggle between Oxford University and the Stationers' Company, that Bishop John Fell seems to have coined the term "pirates" to refer to printers and booksellers who invaded others' literary propriety: see below, p. 344. It may be that the connotations were similar to those earlier implied by Streater.

137. PRO SP 44/23, p. 84; PRO SP 29/156, no. 105. The main object of Streater's attention was *Power and Practice of Court-Leets* (1666). Speed seems to have been imprisoned for debt, whence he issued his collection of homilies, *Prison-Pietie*.

138. "There is no Magick in this Art," Atkyns had retorted to such claims; "Jugglers they may be, but Conjurers they are not." To prove that gentlemen were not ignorant of craft skills, he cited the example of Charles I shaming artists by his superior knowledge of painting. Atkyns, *Original and Growth of Printing*, sigs. D1^{r–v}, D2^r.

law. Removing print from the civility of Stationers would thus have the consequence of systemic discredit. Moreover, the patentees themselves, being gentlemen, remained largely ignorant of the skills of the craft. They therefore had to employ printer underlings to do the actual printing—and those underlings were of lower status than the booksellers themselves. These, then, were the real mechanicks. Subject only to the oversight of the unskilled, these minions would find themselves empowered to produce unlicensed books without fear of retribution. The regulation propounded in the Press Act would become "illusory and of no effect." The booksellers decried Streater in particular as a notorious Interregnum pamphleteer, maneuvering to reprint—and even to patent—works of sedition created when he himself had been accustomed to "Write and Print Books of that nature."[139] Ironically, when Atkyns had singled out the notorious *Killing Noe Murder* as a scandalous tract marketed anew by amoral Stationers, he had chosen a piece that Streater himself had earlier published.[140]

When Stationers argued, their feuds impinged upon learned discourse through piracy and similar practices. This dispute was no exception. It rendered the printed law of the land entirely untrustworthy, to the extent that more than once the Privy Council was forced to intervene and ban the printing of legal works altogether. One notable victim was recusant Thomas Blount, author of *Glossographia* and numerous legal works. Blount himself was not averse to asking whether printers short of work would "print a smal unlicensed book" for him, "for more then ordinary pay." But he found himself the victim of such printing when engaged in his most important work, a legal dictionary entitled Νομο-λεχικον. This book came to the attention

---

139. *Case of the Booksellers and Printers Stated*; Atkyns, *Original and Growth of Printing*, sigs. D4ᵛ–E1ʳ. The Bible patentees likewise fell on Henry Hills and John Field, both notorious Interregnum activists, who had persuaded Cromwell to force entrance of the Bible to them in 1656: *London Printers Lamentation*, 4–7; Kilburne, *Dangerous Errors* (Kilburne revealed his royalism at this time in his attack on Marchamont Nedham, *New-Years-Gift*). See also *Conference Held between the Old Lord Protector and the New Lord General*, 5, in which Oliver's ghost wonders aloud what happened to "*Hils* and *Feild*." Proposing to print apologias for his rule, Cromwell continues:

> my old servants will be (I know) very officious and sedulous in this Employment. They shall not need to fear, that any one will print their Copy: I'le secure them by my Warrant against all the Stationers in his Majesties name, and by his Royal Privilege; and more then this, they shall print all our Acts and Ordinances without rendring any accompt.

The Company had objected strongly to Cromwell's grant: Birch, *Collection of the State Papers of John Thurloe*, IV, 584. Joseph Hunscot had made a similar point in the 1640s, when two rivals, neither of whom was a practicing printer, were appointed Printers to the Houses of Commons and Lords; one of them went on to comprint his copies: Hunscot, *Humble Petition*, 1–3.

140. *Case of the Booksellers and Printers Stated*.

of Streater and his allies in early 1671 because it was produced by their rivals in the Company. They forthwith employed Thomas Manley of the Middle Temple to produce a competing volume, aiming to drive Blount's off the market. Blount heard of the project in March: "my last dictionary is at the presse surreptitiously," he discovered, "being transcribd and mutilated, and disguisd with som new title, and this by a beggarly half-witted scholar hird for the purpose, by som of the Law-booksellers." They would "transcribe that in 4 or 5 moneths, which cost me twice as many years in compiling." Stationer John Martyn, who handled the printing of Νομο-λεχικον, reassured Blount that his own book "gets ground even among its enemyes." [141] Nevertheless, when Streater's "new mock Law Dictionary" came out, Blount felt "obligd to say somthing to it" because of its obvious reliance on his own. He managed to find over three hundred mistakes in it, which he detailed in an attack printed under Martyn's oversight. However, as he prepared a second edition of his dictionary it was not long before he overheard that his rival was again "ready to steal all my additions into a new Edition of his." Blount was well able to see the extent to which his name and his work were at the mercy of the Stationers and their quarrels.[142]

Legal works like Blount's Νομο-λεχικον or Croke's *Reports* were extremely expensive to produce. Stationers on both sides engaged themselves increasingly in alliances designed to generate sufficient capital for their publication and sufficient security for their distribution and sale without risk of piracy. These alliances rapidly spread out across London, to become intricate social webs linking and implicating a substantial proportion of the entire Restoration book trade. By the 1670s, there was "hardly a *Book-seller* or *Printer*" in London who was not involved in the conflict, and, depending on the outcome, a sizable proportion faced potential riches or disaster. In the pacts formed by Streater and his enemies lay the origin of one of the most distinctive social mechanisms of eighteenth-century publishing: the so-called "conger," established to defend expensive publishing projects from piracy. It is not an exaggeration to state that the conditions of Augustan publishing were established in Streater's battles.

By the time of Blount's misfortune, the struggle was approaching its climax. Parliament seemed inclined to call the law patent a monopoly, and hence to rule it illegitimate. The Stationers hurried to press home their advantage. The opportunity came with the lapse of More's grant in 1668–9,

---

141. Blount, *Correspondence*, 109–10, 114–5, 119, 122; Blount, Νομολεχικον. Robert Hooke bought "Blunts Law Dictionary" from Martyn in December 1674: Hooke, *Diary*, 136.

142. Blount, *Correspondence*, 45–50, 54–8, 120–2, 124–5, 146–7, 155–6. Ironically, Cowell's *Interpreter*—the legal dictionary on which Blount's was based—was itself pirated: SCB D, fols. 20ᵛ, 31ʳ⁻ᵛ. Streater helped print the 1667 edition of this work, edited by Blount.

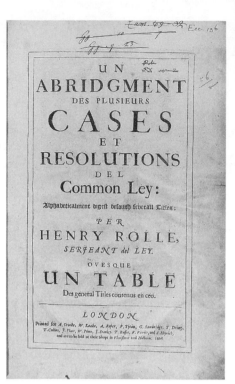

FIG. 4.5. Frontispiece and title page to Rolle's *Abridgment,* published by an alliance of Stationers to bring the struggle with Streater and Atkyns to a conclusion. (By permission of the Henry E. Huntington Library, San Marino, California.)

when it was supposed to be replaced by Edward Atkyns's reversion. The Company now determined to test the patent once and for all. It purchased and entered into the register a manuscript *Abridgment* written before the Civil War by Henry Rolle. Rolle's work was immediately licensed and prepared for the press by Sir Matthew Hale (fig. 4.5). The volume, which announced itself as a model for a future reduction of the common law to a series of printed compendia, was destined to become a central Whig resource. But an appendix designed to launch this grander project never appeared. "The obstruction of the Press diverted it," the incomplete edition explained.[143] A hundred sheets had been printed, at a total cost of over £1,000, when Atkyns and Streater managed to stop the presses.[144] Neverthe-

143. *Case of the Booksellers and Printers Stated*; PRO SP 29/178, no. 69; Weston, "England," 376–7; Williams, "Edition of the Correspondence of John Aubrey," 438; PRO SP 44/25, fol. 65ʳ⁻ᵛ. Rolle, *Abridgment* contained a substantial "Publisher's Preface" (sigs. a1ʳ–c1ᵛ) defending both the status of the common law and its own inclusion of cases from the Interregnum—exactly the kind of editorial practice that the patentees were attacking: see esp. sigs. b1ʳ, c1ʳ⁻ᵛ. The copy I used was Saint John's College, Cambridge, classmark SL.2.42.

144. SCB D, fols. 166ʳ–167ᵛ.

less, the Company began to sell these as law books. A test case was finally in the offing, capable of resolving the entire conflict between register and patent once and for all.

The resulting trial took place at King's Bench. Its verdict went in favor of the Company. Atkyns could stand no more: his finances in ruins, he was to be imprisoned for debt and die in the Marshalsea.[145] But Streater, despite himself facing financial collapse, fought on. He took the case to the House of Lords. There, in a dramatic reversal, the patent was finally adjudged lawful; gossip suggested that the first verdict had been the product of greedy judges angling to publish their own reports. At long last, Streater had won. He did so partly on the absolutist notion that the king alone was the author of laws, and partly on the strength of his new history of the press, which is the subject of the following chapter.[146] This was a severe blow to the Stationers' Company. Its register had been put to the test against royal prerogative, and had been defeated. However, even worse was at hand. The crown had finally been goaded into doing what Atkyns and Streater had always wanted, and had challenged the Company's very existence.

The Company had procrastinated until the Rolle case, continuing to defend its register and evading attempts to obtain a definitive judgment.[147] In 1670, when it again published a legal text in apparent defiance of Atkyns's patent, the Privy Council lost patience. It finally began the quo warranto proceedings for which Streater had so long argued.[148] The very survival of the Company was now at stake. The response of the assistants was correspondingly dramatic. They immediately renounced their previous stand. Acknowledging the superiority of crown prerogative over their own customs, they expressed their "hearty sorrow for haveing done any Act wch may be Interpretted a Contempt of his maj^{ties} Authority, and Prerogative Royall." [149] They agreed to a Privy Council declaration that henceforth no entrance in the Stationers' Register, "wherby a private propertie is pretended to be gained," would be valid for any legal text. Agreement on the specific issue of Coke's *Institutes*, the classic statement of custom and the ancient

---

145. *Biographia Britannica*, I, 255–6; PRO SP 44/37, p. 75, seems to suggest that Atkyns was dead rather earlier, if its subject is not another Richard Atkyns altogether, as seems to me possible.

146. *Journals of the House of Lords*, XII, 615, 642, 647, 666, 671, 704; XIII, 13. Stationers against Patentees about the Printing of Roll's Abridgment, Carter 89; *HMC, 9th Report* (1883), 38a–b, 66a–b; North, *Lives*, I, 89–90 (a reference I owe to Alan Cromartie). See also references in Stationers' Company vs. Seymour, 3 Keble 792, 1 Mod. 257, and Stationers' Company vs. Lee, 2 Chan. Cas. 66, 2 Show. K.B. 258. The defendant was Abel Roper, chosen by the Stationers' court: SCB D, fols. 171^r, 173^v, 174^r, 176^r, 176^v, 178^r, 179^r.

147. SCB D, fols. 111^r, 113^r–114^v. Prynne agreed to help the Company again against the patentees in 1666: SCB D, fol. 125^v.

148. SCB D, fols. 177^v, 179^r.

149. SCB D, fols. 111^r, 113^r–114^v, 177^v, 178^v–179^r.

constitution, came slightly later, after further dispute.[150] They also passed a bylaw establishing Atkyns's patent forever in internal Company regulations. "Coll. Atkins Byelaw" passed in mid-1675, and was included in the definitive new ordinances issued three years later.[151] At the same time, a committee was formed to reconsider all of the Company's rules, producing a series of general regulatory measures that were passed in a further attempt to preempt dissolution.[152] L'Estrange, seeing his opportunity, pressed for a substantial rewriting of all its bylaws, with the amended rules acknowledging his own authority and incorporating a clear commitment to the regulation of the press. The assistants agreed to this too, despite their earlier proud insistence on independence from the surveyor's orders. In return, they pleaded with L'Estrange to persuade the Privy Council to suspend its action. Much to their relief it agreed to do so.[153]

The patentees persisted, however, urging the Company to put its charter to a full trial against the strength of a patent.[154] Concern about whether any text was or was not a threat to the patent wracked the trade, reaching all of its members. In 1677, for example, printer William Rawlins refused to handle a work by Nathaniel Bacon, conceiving it to be a patented law book (it was called in, but not for that).[155] Embarrassingly for the Company, Warden Roper persisted in seizing sheets of another law book printed at Streater's house, despite Company guarantees that he would go unmolested. Its excuse that Roper was protecting private copies and not those claimed by the Company itself seemed, at best, lame—indeed, it reinforced the very point Atkyns and Streater had been making about the confusion of interests inherent in all Company practices.[156] So the Company's position remained weak, especially as its vital almanac patent was also under strong attack, with Streater in the van of the assailants.[157] The crown now pushed for wholesale reconstruction of the trade, urging that all book traders be forced into the

150. SCB D, fols. 194ᵛ, 195ᵛ–196ʳ, 199ᵛ, 201ᵛ, 204ʳ; Weston, "England," 376–7.

151. SCB E, fols. 6ᵛ–7ʳ, 11ʳ, 12ᵛ. Provisions for patents were included in the bylaws of 1682 (SCB E, fols. 161ᵛ–162ʳ) and 1694 (SCB F, fols. 205ʳ ff.); Stationers' Company, *Registers 1554–1640*, I, 16 (§ 32).

152. SCB D, fols. 187ʳ, 189ʳ, 195ʳ.

153. SCB D, fols. 177ʳ, 179ᵛ, 180ʳ⁻ᵛ, 189ʳ. The court at first balked at having to recognize L'Estrange, but in the end it had little choice, especially after Charles harried it for progress (fols. 195ʳ, 209ʳ⁻ᵛ). It was as part of this process that Joseph Moxon was targeted for suppression (fol. 212ʳ). The resulting declaration that the Company had no right to the law books is preserved in SCA Supplementary Documents, Series I, Box A, Envelope 1.

154. SCB D, fol. 187ʳ⁻ᵛ. Compare E. India Company vs. Sandys, 1 Vern. 127 (1682).

155. PRO SP 29/397, nos. 55–6; PRO SP 29/419, no. 85; Bacon, *Historical and Political Discourse*, I, "Advertisement" by J. Starkey.

156. SCB D, fols. 187ᵛ, 191ᵛ.

157. SCB D, fols. 193ʳ, 197ᵛ, 204ᵛ–205ʳ; Brodowski, "Literary Piracy," 56–60.

Company and that it suffer a redrafting of its charter. When Henry Twyford, Atkyns's assignee and Streater's colleague, was intruded by the king as
an assistant in 1678, he took with him a paper of "Aspersions" against the
Company.[158] The assistants could not prevent his elevation, but they took
their revenge by insisting that he supply a particularly respectful feast.

Temporarily suspended, the quo warranto issue returned in 1684 as part
of Charles II's campaign to remodel the corporations. Now the Company
at last lost its charter. For a moment, the Stationers' Company itself ceased
to exist. It was then immediately reincorporated, with new assistants and
new bylaws allowing the crown a more direct say in who got elected to the
court.[159] It was the first London company to get such a new charter, spear-
heading what soon became a sustained and systematic campaign by the
crown against all civic corporations. Again the status of the register was central to the politics of the situation. The new Stationers' Company took care
to vow to ensure strict obedience to an internal propriety now derived directly from royal "Bounty."[160] In an attempt to render its jurisdiction complete, all participants in any aspect of the book trade were to be forced once
and for all into its ranks: no more division of power would be accepted.
When James succeeded to the throne a year later, he reminded the Stationers
that the press was "a Prerogative inseparable from the Soveraignty of our
Imperiall Crowne," and for once this was true in practice.[161] The Company
got a taste of what this might mean when, to its horror, the archbishop of
Canterbury suddenly announced his intention to cease licensing all prognostications whatsoever. By outlawing almanacs, this threatened the sol-
vency of the English Stock, and thus the whole trade's continued viability.[162]
The threat passed, but in the following years prerogative involvement grew
increasingly evident as James's policy lurched toward the dissenters. Catholic
convert Henry Hills, intruded as Master to pursue this policy, led a vigorous
campaign on the king's behalf; Twyford and others were displaced from the
assistants as briskly as they had been intruded.[163] The issue of privileges
became all the more germane now, as James was likely to use his prerogative
not only to undermine the Company's copies, but to do so with explicitly
Catholic books. Hills again led the charge, with numerous titles.[164] Only in

158. SCB D, fols. 190ʳ–191ʳ, 193ʳ; SCB E, fols. 63ʳ, 65ᵛ, 69ᵛ.
159. SCB F, fols. 11ᵛ ff.
160. SCB F, fols. 13ʳ, 15ʳ.
161. SCB F, fols. 36ʳ–37ʳ.
162. SCB F, fol. 43ʳ.
163. SCB F, fols. 89ᵛ ff., 97ᵛ.
164. For an earlier example, see SCB D, fols. 165ʳ, 170ʳ. Hills's *Catholic Almanack* had
provided ample evidence of intent. Jonas Moore's *Royal Almanack* had likewise been published by royal privilege, against the opposition of the Company: SCB D, fol. 228ᵛ.

the last days of James's reign, with his desperate return to the status quo ante, did this ascendancy collapse. In his final panic James restored the pre-1684 charter.[165] The invasion of William of Orange finally removed the prospect of a comprehensive system of prerogative press regulation, and thus of an alternative to the print culture that developed in succeeding decades.

CONCLUSION

Nobody really won. The Stationers' Company never recovered its full cultural and practical authority, but, victorious though he was, Streater was broken by the expense of such a titanic duel. He expired in debtors' prison, penniless and forgotten. Yet he left three major legacies. The first was a repertoire of concepts and arguments that would continue to form the basis for debate about the nature and regulation of print for several generations. The second was the conger—a mechanism for the publication of substantial books in a piratical environment. And the third was one of the largest printing houses in London.

This printing house continued to operate, and it continued to produce works of natural knowledge. One of the last would be the greatest of them all: Isaac Newton's *Mathematical Principles of Natural Philosophy*. It was printed by Streater's son, Joseph, who had taken over the printing house from his mother, Susan. His was the name on the title page—for a while, at least. For Joseph's principles were not quite those of his parents. He was one of the foremost printing pirates in London, producing illicit almanacs by the thousand. Above all he made "lascivious" books his specialty. Now, a visitor to the Streater household would have found, juxtaposed, sheets from Newton's *Principia* and the *Philosophical Transactions* in one corner, pirated astrology in another, and in a third *The School of Venus, or . . . Ladies delight reduced into rules of practise* and *Sodom, or the Quintessence of Debauchery*. In late 1687, just as copies of Newton's work appeared in bookshops, Joseph became England's first ever victim of a state-sponsored hunt for pornographers. Before long the title page to the *Principia* had been reprinted to omit Streater's name, and he was likewise effaced from the Royal Society's *Philosophical Transactions*. After Streater, printers' names were no longer printed on the journal; a "substantial" bookseller was the most that could be tolerated.[166]

---

165. SCB F, fols. 108ʳ–109ᵛ. Blagden, *Stationers' Company*, 172, gives a summary of the chaotic changes in the Company's administration over these years. The Company settled the issue of continuity in properties during the gap by deciding that its original charter had never, in fact, really been surrendered.

166. CLRO, Guildhall Sessions, SM59, SF356, No. 67; CLRO, Mayor's Court Interrogatories, 140.12; SCB F, fol. 125ʳ; McKenzie, *Stationers' Company Apprentices 1641–1700*, 160.

Whatever Joseph Streater's principles, it is fitting that an attempt to transform the conditions for circulating public knowledge in early modern England—an attempt predicated on the centrality of such knowledge to a
sound commonwealth—should culminate in Isaac Newton's. Natural philosophy had lain at the core of John Streater's interests during the Interregnum, when he had first formulated his republicanism. His politics had been
founded in the notion of a reading commonwealth informed by the kind of
works he himself could print. His advocacy marks the genesis of a fundamental change in political culture. It is therefore appropriate that his efforts
should climax in the philosophy that, more than any other, would be touted
as epitomizing the "public reason" of the ensuing century.[167]

Meanwhile, Streater had substantially helped to make the political culture of his own time. Legal practice was in the process of being transformed
by printing. The common law that judges practiced was based on what they
called "custom," which was allegedly immemorial. Some of its defenders
even claimed that the common law *was* custom. This custom was in turn
represented as the embodiment of reason, and it had always been unwritten.[168] Now, however, the newly printed "Reports" of judges "learned in the
law" were reckoned to embody their customary reason in authoritative form,
such that any literate subject could come to understand verdicts reached
according to its axioms. By midcentury, then, Hobbes could write sarcastically of a philosopher proposing to become a judge in just two months
by using such resources. But even Hobbes insisted that such laws must be
printed and made publicly available, so that all subjects could read them and
know how to conduct themselves. "I think it were well that every man that
can read, had a Statute-book," he maintained, and Streater would have
agreed wholeheartedly.[169] Real subjects concurred: Samuel Pepys was one
who did indeed use printed books of this sort to inform himself of "law-
notions."[170] Magistrates would read charges aloud to juries composed of
men who, like Pepys, had been adequately informed "by printing the law &
most of it in the English tongue." And we know of cases resolved by reference to Croke's *Reports*.[171]

At moments of political change, such records became especially important. With the reconstruction of monarchy, printed texts were of central use

---

167. See esp. Golinski, *Science as Public Culture*; Stewart, *Rise of Public Science*. For a
claim that the "public sphere" emerged in the early Restoration, see Pincus, "'Coffee Politicians Does Create.'"

168. Burgess, *Politics of the Ancient Constitution*, 3–6, 19, 21–2, 27–8; Kelley, "Law," 84–
5; Lloyd, "Constitutionalism," 264–74; Klein, "Ancient Constitution Revisited."

169. Hobbes, "Dialogue between a Philosopher and a Student of the Common Laws of
England," 6, 27–8.

170. Pepys, *Diary*, I, 283.

171. Rosenheim, "Documenting Authority," 596–7.

in reconstituting legal and political practice. It has even been argued that
what occurred in 1660 was principally a restoration, not of monarchy, but
of law in its documentary form.[172] If that is so, then which particular texts
were to be used must have been one of the most pressing issues of the period.
The question of whether legal records, once printed, could be trusted was
in these circumstances central to political order itself. Law books were certainly printed in their hundreds. But many were falsely attributed, not a few
derived (like Hales's 1678 *Pleas of the Crown*) "from a surreptitious and very
faulty copy," and only a tiny minority are now reckoned to contain reliable
texts. The particular works central to the Streater conflict, namely Croke,
Coke, and Rolle, were perhaps the most important and influential of all.
By producing them, Streater helped to determine what the law of the land
was.[173] It is in this fundamental sense, rather than in more ephemeral questions of particular governmental form or policy, that his Restoration campaign developed from his republican experience.

Atkyns and Streater proposed a radical solution to the problem of discredit by making it an expressly political problem. They suggested direct
royal intervention in the civility of printing. Their proposal was that the
Stationers' Company, with its entire machinery for protecting "wholesome
knowledge," be replaced by a system of crown-appointed patentees, employing printers as servants. The power of the Stationer would be removed as a
threat to the power of the king. So Streater constructed powerful representations of printing and politics that intertwined. It may be argued that in
both respects his was an important stance: it was certainly of influence in
the articulation of republicanism, and, in the Restoration and beyond, it
proved a powerful threat to the Stationers' commonwealth. "Thou Soldier,
be a Merchant," cried Abraham Cowley: "Merchant, thou a Soldier be."[174]
If John Streater is a hieroglyphic of labor, then the labor he represents is in
part that needed to manage such a highly charged transit between combat
and commerce.

Yet the very cultural identity that he and Atkyns so fiercely attacked was
at the same time the character that licensed a printer like Streater to mount
such an attack at all. It underpinned his own intervention in political and
philosophical debates. The sheer range of his references was impressive
enough: a brief list would have to include classical authors like Cicero and
Suetonius, modern political writers such as Bodin and Machiavelli, natural
magic, alchemy, the Hartlibians, a full range of legal sources including both

172. Scott, "Restoration Process," 633–5.
173. McKenzie, "Speech-Manuscript-Print," 98. Coke, Croke and Rolle were also Moses
Pitt's three favorite lawyers: Pitt, *Letter*, 21.
174. "Of Avarice," in Cowley, *Works*, 756.

common and civil law, casuistry, Hermes Trismegistus, Galen, physiology, and Scripture. These were not the resources of a slavish reproducer of others' work. A remarkable participant in many of the battles of his day, Streater was a distinctive political thinker who developed a republicanism based on the construction and communication of knowledge. In particular, he made two branches of knowledge—of the law and of the natural world—central to his proposed polity. Streater demonstrated how a printer possessed of such decided views could shape the kinds of knowledge—and hence the kinds of social order—available in early modern England. He was not alone. Others followed similarly difficult paths. We need to decipher them, too.

In their arguments over print and its practitioners, Atkyns and Streater used one resource of particular authority: the past. A central element of their case was a new history of printing. In proposing a complete transformation in the cultural politics of print, Atkyns and Streater also articulated a completely new historiography of the press. They argued that with the incorporation of the Stationers' Company had been lost not only the true politics and propriety of printing, but its true history too. The next chapter shows that theirs was a historiography of some sophistication. It linked political power with dexterous skill, fostering an alliance with disenfranchised printers and challenging the very roots of print culture itself. Atkyns and Streater thereby forced a profound reconsideration of the origins and nature of the press. By looking at their arguments and the responses they provoked, we can begin to appreciate how the notion of a "printing revolution" came about.

5

FAUST AND THE PIRATES

The Cultural Construction of the Printing Revolution

If it be lawful for us . . . to invent Printing, with an infinite number
of other Arts beneficial to mankind, why have we not the same right
in matters of Government, upon which all others do almost absolutely
depend?

ALGERNON SIDNEY, *Discourses Concerning Government* (1698), 281

INTRODUCTION

What is printing, and what ought it to be? Seventeenth- and eighteenth-
century figures like John Streater strove to decide such fundamental
questions. They did so, this chapter shows, by reconstructing the historical
origins of the press itself. Such writers attempted to understand the transformations wrought by printing and its practitioners by looking back to
their first appearance and analyzing how they had developed. In knowledge
of the past they sought understanding of their present and future.

The result was not a consensus. Such writers produced radically different
accounts of the history and impact of printing, using different conventions
of evidence to arrive at radically opposed conclusions. From those divergent
verdicts they went on to generate violently conflicting recommendations for
action. So intense was their disagreement that their work was forced to address the most profound historiographical problems. Most of all, it raised
questions about the very credibility of textual evidence. An issue fundamental to the status of historical knowledge now confronted early modern writers, arising from a debate over the very craft that, one might suppose, ne-
gated the importance of the topic by rendering records trustworthy.

The immediate end of such historiographical work was not, however,
so abstruse. Representations of the past generally prove to be powerful
resources for those wishing to shape current actions. A large range of schol-

324

arship exists demonstrating that societies often—and perhaps always—possess accounts of their past that authoritatively circumscribe, in Pocock's words, "what happens, what can be known and what done." The bounds that those accounts generate, while they can, in principle, be violated, cannot routinely be broken without cost.[1] Societies therefore structure and legitimate themselves through knowledge of the past, creating present and future order out of an ordered representation of history. And this has also often been true of smaller social groups. In this chapter we shall see that practitioners of the press, at least, made creative use of their own histories to delineate cultural proprieties for themselves and their craft.

The significance of such historical perspectives in shaping cultural identities has recently been discussed extensively, not least in the history of science. Work by Jardine on Johannes Kepler, by Pumfrey on William Gilbert, and by Dear on Nicolas Cabeo and Josephus Blancanus stands out in this respect, as, for a later period, does that by Richard Yeo on William Whewell. Later in this book, indeed, John Flamsteed's articulation of his identity as astronomer royal will be seen to have been profoundly conditioned by similar labors. But all these were highly sophisticated scholars. The importance of historiographical knowledge in the relatively practical domains of a craft like printing has not been nearly so well documented. In fact, a similar approach to early modern histories of the press proves to be at least as revealing.[2] For just as Kepler or Flamsteed arrived at new accounts of what it was to act properly as an astronomer through constructive interrogation of the past, so printers and others set the bounds of proper conduct for the printer, bookseller, licenser, and reader by referring to what they believed they knew of the historical development of those identities.

Print is often hard to analyze historically since it seems to be self-explanatory—something needing only to be revealed, not created. But this appearance veils real conflict in its history. We can hypothesize that a good way to uncover the making of modern print culture may be by searching for instances when the principles that are to us most essential to print were in fact in dispute. In such cases, participants would have worked hard not only to articulate their particular, localized beliefs and actions, but to justify them

---

1. Pocock, "Time, Institutions and Action," 233; Pumfrey, "History of Science and the Renaissance Science of History," 49. Obeyesekere, *Apotheosis of Captain Cook*, is an interesting polemic partly centering on the issue of the degree to which cultures can be regarded as constrained by their representations of the past.

2. Pumfrey, "William Gilbert's Magnetic Philosophy," 14–73; Pocock, *Ancient Constitution and the Feudal Law*; Jardine, *Birth of History and Philosophy of Science*; Dear, *Discipline and Experience*, 93–123; Levine, *Humanism and History*; Yeo, *Defining Science*, 145–75; Martin, "Comment on Ecrivit l'Histoire du Livre." An example from another period is Burrow, *Liberal Descent*, 1–7.

in fundamental terms. In so doing, they would give voice to what they perceived at that moment to be the essential grounds for the particular practices and beliefs they professed.[3] In the conduct of such a debate, then, we can see through the words of the participants their creation of print itself. By looking at the historiography of printing in the early modern period, we can open a window onto long-overlooked debates about the most elementary and fundamental characteristics of communication.

Early modern writers themselves recognized the importance of such a strategy. Richard Hooker, for one, explained that he had had to publish his *Laws of Ecclesiastical Polity* because Puritans had questioned the fundamental laws structuring religious life. As a result of their challenge, he said, it was now necessary that "the very foundation and root, the highest well-spring and fountain of them" be unveiled. He therefore began his argument with God's first self-denying ordinances, made prior even to Creation itself.[4] These fundamentals, he believed, were implicit in the everyday actions of the church. But they were never normally articulated. Hooker's decision to specify them generated one of the most important books in England's religious history. Challenges to the order of print—to the "laws of bibliographical polity," as it were—necessitated analogous attempts to articulate the ultimate foundations of that order. Just as Hooker proposed, those efforts centered on analyses of the craft's "foundation and root." That is, they focused on the invention of the press itself. And the results were correspondingly influential. During two centuries of intense debate, from William Prynne and John Streater to William Blades and Samuel Smiles, print culture was constructed and constituted by such accounts. This chapter examines how and why. Its subject is the retrospective making of a printing revolution.

COSTER AND CAXTON: THE HISTORIOGRAPHY OF CUSTOM

The roots of this great debate lay in the incipient conflict between the Stationers' register and royal patents. As chapter 3 pointed out, the regulation of propriety by patents was already contentious in the reign of Elizabeth. Indeed, the origins of some of the most controversial arguments deployed by John Streater and Richard Atkyns in the Restoration may be discerned in John Wolfe's powerful attack on the system almost exactly a century earlier. This was also true of the most striking aspect of Atkyns and Streater's case: its foundation in historiography.

---

3. For the development of this approach to controversies, see Collins, *Changing Order*; Latour, *Science in Action*; Shapin and Schaffer, *Leviathan and the Air-Pump*, 6–7.
4. "Of the Laws of Ecclesiastical Polity," bk. 1, chaps. 1–2: Hooker, *Works*, I, 147–52.

Sixteenth-century campaigners already realized the power of alleging historical justification for their different concepts of press regulation. In their struggle against Wolfe, for example, the patentees told Burghley that he "would have more libertye geven to prynters and pryntinge then ever was synce the fyrst Invencon thereof," and drew on Stationers' Company records to show that privileges had been granted ever since "the saide mistery was first used in the lande."[5] The historical dimension to such claims was vital, and for a rather technical reason. It served to establish patents as objects of customary practice, identified with the craft since its original introduction. If their history simply *was* the history of printing, then the Stationers' Company could hardly argue that they were an inappropriate imposition on a craft.

This assertion was never beyond challenge. The most serious attempt at rebuttal came only after half a century, however, with the crisis of 1641. When Star Chamber fell, with it lapsed the prerogative mechanism of press regulation. Licensing ceased to be effective, and it seemed that patents were suddenly vulnerable.[6] The previous chapter traced something of the resulting conflict. With this opportunity beckoning, however, an alliance of Stationers and Puritans launched a campaign to overthrow the system altogether.

The Stationers' Company was far from alone in facing such an internal rebellion. All the London livery companies met with upheaval at this time, as disenfranchised majorities of small tradesmen confronted the power of what they called "monopolists." Their widely held perception was that this was to be the climax of a long struggle against the crown's alliance with patentees.[7] Within the Stationers' Company, in particular, the challenge was led by bookseller Michael Sparke, and by William Prynne, the notorious Presbyterian lawyer of Lincoln's Inn. The two collaborated to create a comprehensive case against patents and their holders. Sparke, enjoying a Stationer's access to Company processes and the Stationers' court, acted within the Company itself. He attacked the patentees in its court, and employed printers to produce several campaigning tracts deploying privy knowledge against them. Of these the best known was *Scintilla, or a Light Broken into Darke Warehouses*, an informed complaint against privilege holders issued in 1641.

5. Stationers' Company, *Registers 1554 –1640*, II, 71–3, 804–5.
6. For arguments at this juncture see Fletcher, *Outbreak of the English Civil War*, 30, 73–4, 79. For the struggles in the Company see Blagden, *Stationers' Company*, 131–41, and Blagden, "Stationers' Company in the Civil War Period." For similar struggles in other aspects of City government see Pearl, "London's Counter-revolution."
7. Pearl, "London's Counter-revolution," 34; Smuts, *Court Culture*, 53–5; Ashton, *City and the Court*, 202–9.

Prynne did not enjoy the same access. Nonetheless, he too had some acquaintance with the trade. Not only had he been extensively involved in opposition printing for at least a decade, almost exclusively with Sparke as his Stationer ally, but since returning from prison in triumph the previous November he had been serving as the Company's standing counsel.[8] The most accomplished common-lawyer of his age, Prynne used his legal expertise and his knowledge of publishing when he took their case to Parliament—now, with Star Chamber gone, the highest court of law in the country. For the first time, a leading Puritan lawyer was to construct a case against prerogative propriety. Given the principles by which the common law functioned, that meant constructing a historical argument.[9]

Prynne aimed to demonstrate that four particular patents were "monopolies," and as such illegal by either common law or the 1624 Monopolies Act. The first of these patents covered the English Bible, the second "the sole printing of all Law bookes whatsoever"; this was the privilege later to be championed by Streater. The remaining pair covered Greek and Hebrew Bibles, and all texts printed on only one side of a sheet of paper. Apart from the English Stock, these four grants together represented the main branches of prerogative propriety in copies. Prynne and Sparke seem to have agreed to spare the Stock itself, probably because as a corporate grant it was less evidently monopolistic, and because in any case its raison d'être was to benefit impoverished Stationers, which was also the justification for their own case. But it would inevitably prove difficult to exclude one particular privilege, since the issue of prerogative copies invariably entailed wide-ranging themes in the cultural politics of printing.

To attack his target at its source, Prynne proposed to reconstruct nothing less than the history of printing. The use of historical references in such conflicts as Wolfe's had established the form his own argument would take. He would be concerned with the same point: whether printing had once been a "common" trade, the prerogative regulation of which must be accounted illegal as infringing the preexisting livelihoods of its practitioners. Yet Prynne took care to inform himself of not only these domestic debates, but the Continental historiography of printing too. In so doing, he tapped a rich vein of resources for his own attempt.

European writers had for generations been conducting a vigorous debate over the origins, history, and impact of the press. In particular, their inves-

8. Wood, *Athenae Oxoniensis*, III, 848; Blagden, "Stationers' Company in the Civil War Period," 13. He continued to act for the Company after the Restoration (e.g., SCB D, fol. 58ᵛ), when he chaired the Commons Committee for regulating the press (SCB D, fol. 61ʳ).

9. For the principles of the common law, see Pocock, *Ancient Constitution*, Burgess, *Politics of the Ancient Constitution*, and Martin, *Francis Bacon*, 72–104, 114–22.

tigations were directed at ascertaining a place and an individual to which could be assigned credit for its invention. As Francis Bacon had put it, "inventors and authors of new arts, endowments, and commodities towards man's life were ever consecrated amongst the gods themselves," and the honor commensurate with having invented one of the classic trinity of inventions promised to be substantial. Moreover, providentialist writers had rapidly seized upon printing for its role in the Reformation. In the words of John Foxe (whom Prynne himself cited in his argument, and whose *Acts and Monuments* was just now splendidly reprinted on the Company's initiative), notwithstanding "what man soever was the instrument, without all doubt God himselfe was the ordainer and disposer thereof, no otherwise, then he was of the gift of tongues."[10] Such an opinion was of enormous influence, for since its publication Foxe's had become what contemporaries called a "book of credit" second only to Scripture in its authority. Like the Bible, it was read "thoroughly," the godly poring over its every word.[11] Provided with such emphatic testimony, no English Protestant could doubt the providential import of printing. To Foxe's millenial nation, the origin of printing was a pivotal moment in a vast, predestined scheme of doom and salvation.

What was the true history of this providential gift? Across Europe, learned opinion varied. One potential orthodoxy had it that printing had first been developed by a man named Johann Gutenberg, a goldsmith from the German town of Mainz. Helped by the capital of a local financier called Johann Fust, this Gutenberg was said to have perfected a press by 1455 at the latest. Then the two partners split up in acrimony. Their arguments generated a legal case, and with it a single document that happened to survive the centuries to testify to their collaboration. Fust and his son-in-law, Peter Schoeffer, then continued printing, but Gutenberg himself disappeared from the historical record. The art had subsequently been dispersed from Mainz with the sack of the town in 1462, and it seemed that William Caxton, a Westminster mercer, had seized the opportunity to introduce it into England nine years later. Caxton had established the first printing press in the country, setting it to work in Westminster.[12]

However, that was only one potential orthodoxy. Records corroborating this story had always been scanty. There existed no printed book bearing Gutenberg's name. Even today we know of only twenty-seven contemporary

10. Foxe, *Acts and Monuments*, I, 926–8; Bacon, *Works*, III, 301. Gabriel Naudé received a substantial pension for his story of the introduction of printing into France, published in 1630: Clark, *Gabriel Naudé*, 32–3. For the extravagant language created around another of the classic trinity, see Wolper, "Rhetoric of Gunpowder."

11. Collinson, *Birthpangs of Protestant England*, 11–12.

12. There are many accounts of this story, which is now largely accepted. A basic chronology is in Clair, *Chronology of Printing*, 8–12.

documents in which a Gutenberg was named, of which just twelve are extant, and only one mentions anything having to do with printing.[13] That one piece of evidence happens to be the legal document from 1455: it alone remains to indicate his role, and, as will become clear, it could be read in very different ways. Gutenberg's reputation was thus never likely to prove beyond challenge, especially since there had long been competitors to Mainz. Cities like Strasbourg, Avignon, Paris, Venice, Nuremberg, and Haarlem all claimed the honor of having been the first to use the press.[14] It is important to emphasize, moreover, that it was not simply a *lack* of evidence that created such ferocious controversy. On the contrary, participants found as much evidence as they needed for their attempts to support or question Gutenberg's status, in the shape of manuscripts, printed books, craft traditions, local legends, and personal expertise. They were even able to adduce documents and printed sheets claiming to verify or demolish Gutenberg's priority. It was not unknown for early modern printers to falsify colophons on old-looking books in an attempt to enhance their value, and as late as the nineteenth century respectable archivists in Mainz and Strasbourg were unveiling "Gutenberg documents" now thought to be of their own invention. Such documents convinced even the best qualified of scholars.[15] By the mid–eighteenth century, then, Haarlem, Augsburg, Paris, Lyons, Basel, Mainz, Cologne, and Venice could all display printed books, bearing what are now accepted to be false dates, that supported the claims of each respective town.[16] The credit of textual evidence in this case became controversial not just for critical reasons, but because forgery, suspicion, and error really were widespread.

Here, then, was a situation of profound uncertainty. The very knowledge that might have helped contemporaries to understand and master the problems of accreditation generated by print was itself riven by epistemological problems. Antiquarians, lawyers, and tradesmen had to tangle with a historical record riddled with ambiguity, and even imposture. Ancient manuscripts might not be ancient, and incunabula might not be incunabula. Not only was there no universally agreed core of evidence on which to construct a history; there was no consensus on what evidence itself was. No two writers agreed even on what should be counted as firm grounds on which to distinguish the genuine and significant from the spurious and immaterial.

13. McMurtie, *Gutenberg Documents.*

14. See Martin, "Comment on Ecrivit l'Histoire du Livre," 13, for the iconographic significance of different candidates.

15. For one early example see Gaskell, "Fust and Schoeffer Forgery." Later cases are documented in Fuhrmann, *Gutenberg and the Strasbourg Documents*, 35–8, and McMurtie, *Gutenberg Documents*, 225 ff.

16. Luckombe, *History and Art of Printing*, 13–14.

By the late seventeenth century, some thirty towns were competing for the honor of the press. In 1696 an anonymous scribbler (probably the printer George Larkin) resorted to doggerel verse to describe the confusion.

> Imperial Mentz herself would author prove;
> And Venice cries, she did the art improve;
> Not antient cities more for Homer strove . . .
> What man was he whom thus the gods have grac'd,
> Worthy among the stars to find a place!
> Like head of Nile unknown, thy bubbling rise
> Is hid, for ever hid, from mortal eyes.[17]

With such a shroud covering his identity, identifying the originator of printing became one of the most important problems in early modern historiography. Like the source of the Nile, the source of the press fascinated and attracted. But as early modern philosophers well knew, fascination could be a dangerous power.

Mainz aside, probably the most significant of the many claimants was the Dutch town of Haarlem. Haarlem's rival to Gutenberg was one Laurens Janssen, better known as Coster. His story seems first to have been put forward by Adrien de Jonghe, rector and teacher of natural philosophy in the town's Latin school. Jonghe told in his patriotic history *Batavia* (1588) of an old man named Cornelius, who claimed to have been servant to the inventor of printing himself. Cornelius had described to Jonghe's erstwhile teacher how Coster had casually cut some letters from the bark of a beech tree and been stimulated by the stain they made in his handkerchief to make trials with reusable wooden type. Before long, he had been able to produce letters on one side of a piece of paper. Then, pasting several sheets together, Coster had proceeded to create small books. He was in operation in this way by 1440 at the latest, and probably twenty years earlier. And one of his earliest books, Jonghe found, was actually extant in Haarlem.

The most intriguing part of Jonghe's account concerned what happened after this initial success. For Coster's prosperity had been short-lived. He had sworn his workmen to secrecy, but on Christmas Eve one of them escaped with enough knowledge and materials to set up a rival operation. Stealing through the dark streets—conveniently empty now, with the populace attending the midnight service—the workman fled Haarlem and disappeared into the country. First to Amsterdam he went, and then, fearing arrest in a town so close to Haarlem, on to Mainz. There he set up his own workshop, announcing himself as the inventor of the new art. Mainz's claim

---

17. [Larkin?], "Essay on Writing"; Dunton, *Life and Errors* (1705), 326. [Marchand], *Histoire*, 93–4, lists almost thirty towns laying some claim to the invention.

was thus the result of a notorious theft. And the name of this thief, Cornelius said, was Johann Faust.

Jonghe himself reserved judgment on this latter point, disdaining to "disturb the dead, whose consciences must have smote them sufficiently while
living." But Cornelius had no such doubts. Coster, he insisted, had died of
grief, and his old servant himself "burst into tears upon reflecting on the
loss his Master had sustained." In "a sally of passion," Cornelius "wish'd
Faust had been then alive, that he might have executed him with his own
hands."[18] His histrionics had their effect. Later writers might transform the
story's setting, and they might rename its characters, but the idea of an infamous theft having been central to the spread of printing persevered. It
became a central element in virtually all histories of the press.[19]

Jonghe's history appeared at an auspicious time for two reasons. First, it
provided important evidence for the prowess of a town of peculiar Protestant
significance. In 1573, after an eight-month siege, Calvinist Haarlem had surrendered to the duke of Alba's army only to see two thousand of its citizens
massacred.[20] The martyrdom was a turning point. The town's fate become
emblematic of Holland's desperate struggle against the Hapsburgs. Jonghe's
was thus an early example of what became a series of printed encomia appearing at a time of religious and political cataclysm, and Coster's story must
be seen as instrumental in these polemics. They revived in the Thirty Years'
War a generation later, when town preacher Samuel Ampsing appropriated
Jonghe's report.[21] Ampsing even provided illustrations of Coster's printing
house, executed by the renowned artist Pieter Saenredam (fig. 5.1). These
remarkably precise images in fact displayed the premises of Haarlem's town
printer, Adriaen Roman, who produced Ampsing's work and is known to
have identified himself strongly with Coster.[22] He, Jonghe, Saenredam, and
Ampsing all found Coster extremely useful in their struggle to construct

18. "[P]rima mali labes, quos inter Ioannes quidam, sive is (ut fert suspicio) Faustus fuerit
ominoso cognomine, hero suo infidus & infaustus, sive alius eo nomine, non magnopere
laboro, quod silentum umbras inquietare nolim, contagione co[n]scientiae quondam dum
viverent tactas . . . ut invito quoque prae rei indignitate lachrymae erumperent, quoties
de plagio inciderat mentio: tum vero ob ereptam furto gloriam sic ira exardescere solere
senem, ut etiam lictoris exemplum cum fuisse editurum in plagiarum appareret, si vita illi
superfuisset": Jonghe, *Batavia*, 253–8, esp. 256–7; translations cited from [Bowyer and Nich-
ols], *Origin of Printing*, 62–3; Palmer, *General History of Printing*, 44; Stower, *Printer's Grammar*, 11–13.

19. For example, Mentel, *De Vera Typographiae Origine*; see also Schorbach, *Der Strassburger Frühdrucker Johann Mentelin*, 244–5. Mentel claimed that Mentelin had invented the
press in Strasbourg only to have the secret stolen by a servant seduced to Mainz by Gutenberg. For a table of such theft stories, see Van der Linde, *Haarlem Legend*, 170.

20. Bonney, *European Dynastic States*, 154, 163.

21. Ampsing, *Beschryvinge ende lof der Stad Haerlem in Holland*, bound with Scriverius,
Laure-Crans voor Laurens Coster.

22. Schwartz and Bok, *Pieter Saenredam*, 35–50.

FIG. 5.1. (*left*) Laurens Coster. (*right*) Coster's printing house. Ampsing, *Beschryvinge ende lof der Stad Haerlem in Holland*. (By permission of the Bodleian Library, University of Oxford, Douce A.219.)

and defend local, national, and personal identities in a context of conflict—something that would later be used both to discredit Jonghe as partisan and to endorse him as heroic. And it was in these forms that the Coster story reached England. John Dee, for one, admired Jonghe as "a most exquisite examiner and Censurer of very many auncient historiographers," and William Camden concurred in his approbation of this new history of "John Faustus."²³

The second element favoring Jonghe's story was that its publication coincided almost exactly with the first appearance in popular culture of the legend of Dr. Faustus and his pact with the devil. The original for all later versions of this legend, the so-called *Faustbuch*, appeared only a year earlier than *Batavia*. It too claimed to recount a true story, and there is indeed evidence that it was based on the travels of a real man (fig. 5.2). It was phenomenally popular. Within five years it had been translated into virtually every European language. The English version had been published by 1592, and Marlowe's *Tragedie of Dr. Faustus* followed almost immediately. The *Faustbuch* and its immediate successors did not (as far as is known) claim

23. Sherman, *John Dee*, 198; BL Ms. Cotton Julius F. xi, fols. 306ᵛ–7ʳ, cited in Dunn, "Fragment of an Unpublished Essay."

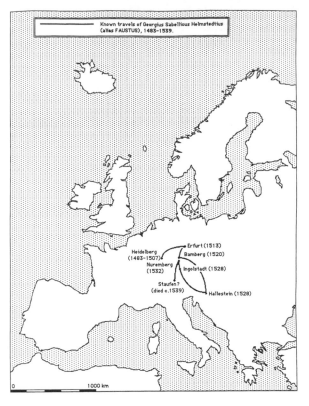

FIG. 5.2. (*left*) Known travels of Faustus, 1483–1539, as reconstructed by modern scholars. Sources: Baron, *Doctor Faustus;* Butler, *Fortunes of Faust;* Palmer and More, *Sources of the Faust Tradition.*

FIG. 5.3. (*below left*) The press descending from the heavens. Printing is shown being passed down through the mediation of Minerva and Mercury to Germany, and thence to Holland, England, Italy, and France. Gutenberg, Fust, and Coster (who is literally put in the shade) are all included, as is Caxton. Corsellis is not. Frontispiece to [Marchand], *Histoire de l'Origine et des Prémiers Progrès de l'Imprimerie.* (By permission of the Syndics of Cambridge University Library.)

FIG. 5.4. (*below right*) Frontispiece to Mallinckrodt, *De Ortu et Progressu Artis Typographicae.* (By permission of the Syndics of Cambridge University Library.)

for Faust any involvement in the invention of the press. But there was to be no shortage of writers prepared to allege some relation between two figures whose simultaneous appearance was so compelling. Perhaps Faust the printer had been the prototype for Faust the magician.[24] Such a notion was obviously attractive, not least because it offered opportunities to expand upon Foxean motifs of the press as a providential gift—a blessing handed down from heaven, as later depicted in Prosper Marchand's famous illustration (fig. 5.3).[25] However, writers eager to counter the claim of Haarlem, especially Deacon Bernard Mallinckrodt of Mainz, also referred to Faust (fig. 5.4). Mallinckrodt appropriated the figure for his home town, claiming that Jonghe's theft story had been fabricated to conceal the fact that Faust and Gutenberg were the true inventors. To such protagonists the very implausibility of Jonghe's tale was its salient feature.[26]

Few people collected and appropriated printed authorities like these as determinedly as William Prynne. The fearsomely annotated appearance of his own work was distinctive and notorious. Now, newly liberated from his island prison and exulting in the adulation of the London crowds, Prynne turned his desiccating gaze on Jonghe and his antagonists. A range of printed authorities lay before him, replete with both raw materials and, moreover, with examples of how a polemical history could best be constructed. The link between printing and providence was well established. Everything else, however, was cloaked in uncertainty. In these circumstances it had become customary to allege some treacherous theft in order to counter or explain away opposing claims. Prynne would do the same, in the service of a distinctive political vision.

Opening his assault, Prynne began with a "necessary introduction" outlining "The originall of printing." Some authors, he noted, favored the claim of Faustus, "a Goldsmith of Mentz." With Gutenberg's help, Faustus had cast metal letters and "layd inke upon y^m." But Jonghe had insisted upon Coster as the true inventor. According to him, Coster had told the secret to

24. E.g., Schelhorn, *Amoenitates Literariae*, V, 50–80. The English version of the *Faustbuch* was *Historie of the damnable Life, and deserved death of Doctor Iohn Faustus*. It is worth noting that the German *Faust* ("fist") and the Latin *Faustus* ("lucky," "auspicious," or "prosperous") had very different connotations, and the latter especially inspired mordant puns from Jonghe onward. Scholars continue to debate which is the more appropriate form. In my own text I have not tried to resolve this issue, choosing instead to reflect in turn the usage of each historical writer discussed.

25. Foxe identified the inventor as Faustus, but not as a magician: *Acts and Monuments*, I, 926 (the first edition had referred only to Gutenberg); Bechtel, *Gutenberg*, 30; [Marchand], *Histoire*, frontispiece (fig. 5.3; this was also reproduced as the frontispiece to Eisenstein, *Printing Revolution*). For an explicit association with Faust the sorcerer, see also Bagford, "History of tipography," CUL Ms. Dd.10.56, fols. 8^v–9^r.

26. Mallinckrodt, *De Ortu et Progressu Artis Typographicae*, e.g., 55, 70–1, 75. Mallinckrodt attributed the invention to F[a]ust; see also [Marchand], *Histoire*, 7n.E.

Faust, "who contrary to his oath stole away his letters, & y^n departed wth y^m to Amsterdam." Prynne gave no overt verdict on these opinions, but in concluding with Jonghe seems to have favored his account. This survey only served to support his principal aim, however, which was to describe the introduction of printing into England. Caxton, Prynne said, was the first printer "I meet w^{th}." He had set up his first press by 1478. Others had then followed his lead, the Privy Council encouraging immigrant workmen into the country to build up the trade.[27] And at this time, Prynne triumphantly announced, "I finde many Books printed here by severall Printers." Titles had therefore not been restricted to particular individuals by the monarch. The early master printers had routinely printed books "w^{th}out any speciall priviledge or patent from the king." In short, printing had originally been "common." From these "Historicall Premises" Prynne could thus announce that "this Art of Printing even in its rise & infancy was not reputed or used by the Kings of England as a thing peculiar to their disposall by virtue of their prerogative, so as none must use this art but by letters patents or gifts of priviledge." The crown's later assertion of the right to grant patents had consequently constituted an unlawful restriction on those printers who had already been practicing a common trade and to whom they had not been granted. It was an unauthorized appropriation.[28] Prerogative copies must therefore be illegal.

Prynne wanted such copies assigned to the Company, as representative of the whole Stationers' community. But in the case of one patent he went still further. The first of the four privileges he was attacking covered the English Bible. Not only could the crown not privilege the printing of the Bible, Prynne now maintained, but even entrance in the Stationers' register would be illegitimate for Scripture. Defenders of the Bible patent had argued that the king, as sponsor of the official translation, was its author. Prynne recalled "o^r learned martyr" Tyndale to counter that James's had not in fact been the first English version. In any case, he continued, "the Translation & printing of the Bible & New Testam^t in English is no new but an ancient Invention & manufacture at least 100 yeares old," and the early printing of bibles had been "not y^n in one, but in several mens hands."[29]

27. Dutch immigrants were indeed prominent in the book trade before Mary: Pettegree, *Foreign Protestant Communities*, 84–96.

28. Inn. Temp. Ms. Petyt 511, vol. 23, fols. 14^r–25^v. Prynne supported his case with Sparke's *Scintilla*: fol. 20^v. Prynne's concept of "immemorial use" is discussed in Weston and Greenberg, *Subjects and Sovereigns*, 132 ff. For an analogous argument in compass navigation, see McKeon, *Origins of the English Novel*, 201. Locke too thought that the restriction of master printers impeded "the right of the subject": Locke, *Correspondence*, V, 788–9.

29. Ms. Petyt 511, vol. 23, fols. 15^r–17^r, 19^r, 20^{r-v}, 21^v. Prynne's opposition to royal authorship is very similar to that which he voiced against absolutist arguments about the law: see above, p. 312.

Thus far the argument mirrored that against patents in general. But the word of God, Prynne insisted, "should be publike & not proper." Without specifiable human authorship, it seemed that the very concept of "propriety" collapsed. If authors were clearly identifiable for particular works, then Prynne had no objection to Parliament's assigning to them protection for their individual creations. To that extent, he was advocating the use by Parliament of powers that he disputed in the crown. And he was certainly not opposed to ordering the realm of print: Prynne was quite willing to help the Stationers' Company act against illicit importers of bibles.[30] But in the case of Scripture he was reluctant to recognize ownership of any variety.[31]

As England, Scotland, and Ireland descended into war, arguments over the early history of printing were lost in the turmoil. The committee's verdict appears to have remained unclear even to the Company. However, one patentee at least thought it likely that he would lose his privilege as a result of Prynne's arguments, and his subsequent fortunes demonstrate the power and purpose of his and Sparke's campaign. Roger Norton, resolute royalist and holder of the grant for grammars and accidences, swiftly entered his patented copies in the register in an attempt to preserve his right. But now Sparke could move against them. He told the Stationers' court that these copies had originally been "indirectly gotten," that they should belong to the Company as a whole, and that "the said Entry in the register of the Company was purposely to p'vent the disposall of them by Parliamᵗ." Sparke further testified that the Commons had determined against patents. Faced with such testimony, the assistants adjudged Norton's attempted defense "very weake and invalid," and his entrance was deleted. But Norton persevered. More than a decade of threatened legal actions later, and in a very different political world, he would finally manage to convince the assistants of his veracity. Sparke, by now old and ailing, was present as the court denounced "certaine persons," identified as "members of this Company (yet opposing the Governmᵗ thereof)," who had "misinformed" the court when they alleged Parliament to have declared Norton's copies a monopoly. Sparke stayed silent. Even so, Norton's entrances were not restored for another year

30. Ms. Petyt 511, vol. 23, fol. 19ʳ; SCB C, fol. 200ᵛ. Compare Mendle, "Ship Money," for the development of a similar account of "Parliamentary absolutism" by Henry Parker, another Stationers' Company propagandist, and Mendle, "Parliamentary Sovereignty" for its actuality. The Company also petitioned Parliament to prevent eleven Stationers, many ex-patentees, from monopolizing Bible printing, and to request the House to order that Scripture should be "Printed for the common benefit of the whole Company": Stationers' Company, *To the Honourable House of Commons*.

31. Contrast William Kilburne, a beneficiary of Parliament's order to print Scripture (and at one point an ally of John Streater), urging that it was "neither rational, nor political, that the state should be devested of the Patronage, and protection of the word of God": Kilburne, *Dangerous errors*, 14–15.

and a half, by which time Sparke was dead and Norton himself was warden. But his success did him little good. At the Restoration Norton would petition for the post of king's printer, find his request ignored, and end his days printing "his owne and other peoples copies" in the backstreets off Duck Lane.[32]

THE CONSTRUCTION OF CORSELLIS

Norton may have ended up a victim of Prynne and Sparke's timely campaign. Its most significant consequences, however, arose in the course of the dispute discussed in the previous chapter. On the basis of the patent to law books, Richard Atkyns and John Streater mounted a powerful and—for a time—strikingly successful assault on the Stationers' commonwealth.

Streater and Atkyns believed it "impossible for a Prince to rule the spirits and wills of his Subjects (since Printing came in use) without restraining the Presse." [33] To that extent they reflected widely held beliefs. But they argued that the Press Act passed in 1662 establishing licensers to this end was inadequate for the task. This was because the Act endorsed a disastrous contradiction between royal power and the Stationers' professedly autonomous conventions. As explained in chapter 4, they wanted the Act repealed. Atkyns and Streater urged that that "Petit *State*," the Stationers' Company, should be destroyed, and a new realm of printing instituted based directly in the authority of the crown.[34] Setting crown authority against Company custom in this way, they proclaimed that the future of royal prerogative itself was at stake.[35] If they had their way, they would therefore transform both the future conditions of production and reception for printed texts and the future prospects for the monarchical state. Their work accordingly became the key resource for arguments over the cultural politics of print for at least a generation.

The keystone of Atkyns and Streater's argument was a compelling and comprehensive new account of the origins and rise of printing in England.[36] They endeavored to prove not only that printing must be subjected to royal power for reasons of political safety, but that the craft was in fact the *personal property* of the monarch, belonging to him "in his Private Capacity." He therefore had the right to grant exclusive usage to chosen clients. Were the

---

32. SCB C, fols. 210ᵛ–211ʳ, 239ʳ, 274ᵛ, 276ʳ⁻ᵛ, 294ᵛ–295ʳ; Plomer, "King's Printing House," 373–4.

33. [Atkyns and/or Streater], *Kings Grant of Privilege*, 4–6, 8, 16.

34. Atkyns, *Original and Growth of Printing*, sig. E2ʳ. Unless otherwise stated, all references are to the 1664 version of this tract.

35. [Atkyns and/or Streater], *Kings Grant of Privilege*, 4–6, 8.

36. It has been claimed that at the time of their writing England was itself enduring a unique confrontation with its political past: Scott, "England's Troubles," 112, 126; Scott, "Restoration Process," 624–5.

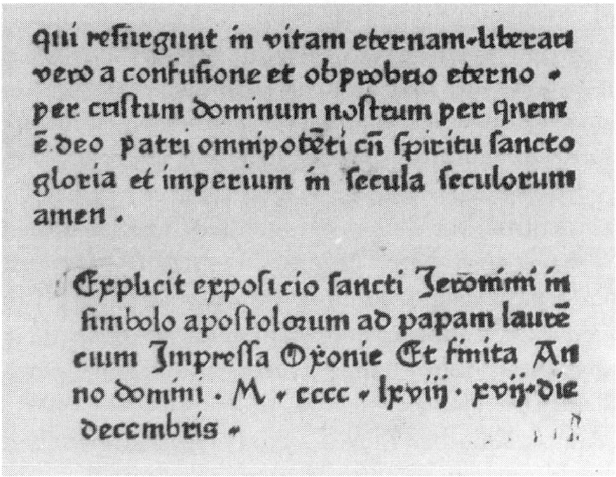

qui refurgunt in vitam eternam·liberati
vero a confufione et obprobrio eterno ·
per criftum dominum noftrum per quem
e deo patri omnipoteti cu fpiritu fancto
gloria et imperium in fecula feculorum
amen ·

Explicit expoficio fancti Jeronimi in
fimbolo apoftolorum ad papam laure
cium Impreffa Oxonie Et finita An
no domini · M · cccc · lxviij · xvij·die
decembris ·

FIG. 5.5. The printed page to which Atkyns and Streater appealed in their historiographical argument against the Stationers' Company. *Expositio in Symbolum Apostolorum*, Oxford (dated 1468, but in fact almost certainly printed in 1478). (By permission of the Syndics of Cambridge University Library.)

king to reclaim this property, they maintained, then the problems of regulation and credit so loudly trumpeted by L'Estrange and others would soon be solved as the power of Stationers would yield to that of the patentees. This property right was based on an act of investment made some two centuries earlier. Its recognition had been obliterated by a century of Company culture, two decades of republican usurpation, and the supremacy during that time of Prynne's partisan historiography. On that false account rested the Stationers' axiomatic belief that from its early history English printing had been a "common trade." The central element of Atkyns and Streater's refutation of that belief was therefore to be a history of the press in direct opposition to Prynne's. It was time to challenge the orthodoxy.[37]

Previous writers had largely followed Stow and Prynne in maintaining Caxton's press at Westminster to have been the first in Britain. But now Atkyns claimed to have encountered two pieces of evidence which proved that the traditional account was mistaken. The first of these was a book, entitled *Expositio in Symbolum Apostolorum* (fig. 5.5), printed in Oxford and explicitly dated in its colophon to 1468 — that is, to three years *before* Caxton had set up his press in Westminster. The second was a manuscript. The same "most worthy Person" who had shown Atkyns the book had now presented him with "the Copy of a Record and Manuscript" that he had discovered in Lambeth Palace.[38] This revelatory document, Atkyns claimed, provided for the first time a full and contemporary account of the real introduction of printing to England. It proved to be a story of proto–industrial espionage at the highest level.

37. Atkyns, *Original and Growth of Printing*, sigs. C1ᵛ–C2ʳ.
38. Atkyns, *Original and Growth of Printing*, sig. C2ʳ⁻ᵛ.

According to the Atkyns manuscript, Thomas Bourchier, archbishop of Canterbury, had heard of the new art shortly after its invention by "*John Cuthenberg*" in Haarlem. Bourchier had immediately urged Henry VI to facilitate its introduction into England. The king, a well-known enthusiast for such works of intellectual philanthropy, agreed to help. They resolved to bribe a workman to leave Gutenberg's workshop. Bourchier provided three hundred marks for the enterprise, the king seven hundred. They entrusted the "Management" of the plot to Robert Turnour, an official of the court, and to William Caxton, a merchant of London who was accustomed to dealing with traders in the Low Countries and who could thus travel there with ease. Turnour shaved off his beard to prevent recognition, and the two of them set sail for Holland.

They landed first at Amsterdam, then moved on to Leyden. Turnour and Caxton feared arrest should they try to enter Haarlem too brazenly—the town had already imprisoned several men arriving from other countries on the same mission. Before long the whole thousand marks had been frittered away in "Gifts and Expences," and Turnour had to write to the king requesting another five hundred. At length, however, their expenditure produced results. They struck a deal to spirit away Frederick Corsellis, "one of the Under-Workmen" in Gutenberg's printing house. Late one night, Corsellis "stole from his Fellows in Disguise, into a Vessel prepared for that purpose; and so the Wind (favouring the Design) brought him safe to *London*." From there he was taken to Oxford, where he was kept under guard until he had revealed the secret of the new technique (fig. 5.6). Hence it was that Oxford acquired the art of printing before any other city than Haarlem—with the crucial exception of Mainz. There, Atkyns alleged, it had already been introduced "by the Brother of one of the Workmen of *Harlein*, who had learnt it at Home of his Brother." This curious aside, entirely unremarked in Atkyns's own time, would a century later acquire international significance.[39] Atkyns thus claimed that printing had originally been introduced at the expense of the monarch. It had then been "Nursed up by the Nursing Father of us all," the king, with the first generation of printers being solely "the Kings sworn Servants." Even the prices of the books they printed had been regulated by the crown, through the lord chancellor's mediation. The first patents for law books had hence been granted to the queen's own servants, especially Yetsweirt. These were the patents that had descended to More—himself, like Yetsweirt, a clerk of the signet, and as such a royal servant—and thence to Atkyns himself.[40]

39. Atkyns, *Original and Growth of Printing*, sigs. C2ʳ–[C3ᵛ]; [Atkyns and/or Streater], *Kings Grant of Privilege*, 6–8.

40. Atkyns, *Original and Growth of Printing*, sig. D1ʳ.

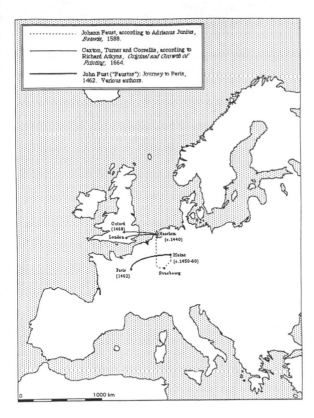

FIG. 5.6. Travels of Faust, Tournour, Caxton, and Corsellis, as recounted by early modern writers on the history of printing. Sources: Jonghe, *Batavia;* Atkyns, *Original and Growth of Printing* (1664); Palmer, *General History of Printing.*

Here, then, was a new history of the propriety of printing. If true, it implied that the press was entirely the product of royal action and investment, and that patents had been central to the development of an English book trade. Only with the incorporation of the Stationers' Company, when the printers had lost their identity as court servants in being forcibly merged with booksellers, binders, and typefounders, had this history been corrupted and forgotten. The Stationers, Atkyns declared, had "by Colour of their *Charter,* abused the Favour of the Crown, in exceeding the Authorities granted them, and assuming to themselves the whole Power of the Crown, concerning the Matter of *Printing.*" Thus "the Body forgot the Head," and they "turn'd this famous ART into a Mechanick Trade." Printing was now pursued not out of service, but "for a Livelyhood." [41] The only way to rectify this would be to return power wholly to the king's patentees, who, as the gentlemen delegates of the rightful owner, would govern a rejuvenated art with respect and diligence. Patents must be restored to superiority over entrances in the Stationers' register, which allowed any factious printer to produce laws and other supposed knowledge on the basis of entrances made

41. Atkyns, *Original and Growth of Printing,* sigs. C3^{r–v}, E3^{v}. The language of the body politic pervaded Atkyns's text; for another example, see *London Printers Lamentation,* e.g., 3–4.

during the Great Rebellion. In short, with a true history would return a true régime of the press, and, with that, a realm in which the products of print could be trusted.

The booksellers countered Atkyns's and Streater's actions by printing their own law titles, by using the Company's regulatory procedures, and by lawsuits. All of these were outlined in the previous chapter. But they also replied on the historiographical grounds pioneered by Prynne. The booksellers argued that a property existed not only in copies but in their craft itself, and that this property had once been common to its practitioners. They based this claim on their own history of "how, and when the Art of *Printing* came into this Kingdom."[42] Even by Atkyns's account, they observed, the king had not paid all of the charges for introducing Corsellis's press. Besides, although he may once have held a property in printing, he had since alienated that property by granting the Stationers a charter. That charter had recently been recognized again by the new Parliament. The first law patent had not been issued until long after the introduction of the first press, and at the point when that charter had been issued. Printing had by then become "a Common Trade and Occupation." Its techniques and procedures had been developed at the charge of its practitioners, and it now supported large numbers of apprentices, servants, and families. Practicing printers consequently held an "Interest" in their skills, restriction of which constituted an offense. The direct consequence was that Atkyns's law patent "*Must be a Monopoly.*" It was a restraint of trade, it raised prices artificially— an especially critical point in the aftermath of the Fire of London[43]—and it permitted patentees to print books in poor impressions. Therefore, they concluded, "this Freedom of Printing, is no more an Incroachment upon the *Kings Prerogative*, then the common usage of most *Trades or Arts Mechanical*, in their ordinary way of *Commerce*."

Responding to the Stationers' arguments, Streater modified his and Atkyns's earlier claim. He now conceded that although printing had indeed been introduced under Henry VI, its practice had not actually been perfected before the reign of Edward VI, and printers had by then been licensed. But in the case of the law patent this did not alter the case. No law books had been printed by the time of the first law patent, so that "the first Patent of this priviledge could *not* be pretended a *Monopoly*, or illegal, none then having the Trade, or Right of printing the Laws to be detrimented

---

42. *Case of the Booksellers and Printers Stated.*

43. The fire had destroyed all three volumes of Croke's *Reports*, for example, to which the prodigious efforts described in chapter 4 had been devoted. These now urgently needed to be reprinted. Their copies had cost hundreds of pounds each, yet were now assumed by the patentees: *Case of the Booksellers and Printers Stated.*

thereby." He steadfastly repeated the view that kings, "not onely in their publick, but private Capacity, as Proprietors," governed printing by virtue of having introduced it at their own charge.[44]

Both Atkyns and Streater were ruined by their conflict with the Stationers' Company. Yet, as chapter 4 showed, their strategy was for a time successful. The crown did indeed intervene in the Company's procedures, and it did withdraw its charter. More significant, perhaps, is the fact that their conflict saw the formulation of tactics that for decades would remain central to arguments over the production and distribution of printed works. Not the least of these was a vision of the propriety and credit of printing, based on Frederick Corsellis and the royal origins of the English press. The ramifications of their new history of the press extended to every aspect of its current use, from patents and the register to printing house conventions and even the very existence of such a person as a "Stationer." In deciding between Corsellis and Caxton, Streater's successors would face a profound choice about their own world and its future.

FAUST AND THE PIRATES:
CREDIT AND THE HISTORY OF PRINTING

Atkyns's story did not die with him in the Marshalsea; nor was it extinguished in 1688. On the contrary, it was taken up by many other writers after Atkyns and Streater themselves. The guardians of the new Oxford University Press, for example, found it invaluable for their claim that the university had enjoyed a right to print since the earliest years of the craft. Mathematician John Wallis, acting for the Oxford press against the king's printers and the Stationers' Company, began his argument by asserting that printing had first been exercised in Oxford. We have seen in chapter 2 that Moxon also adopted this argument.[45] Thomas Yates likewise deployed Atkyns's account, urging that a search for the mysterious manuscript be initiated, while Anthony à Wood approved the story in his history of the university.[46] On the other side in the Oxford dispute, King's Printer Henry Hills, too, made use of Atkyns's historiography. Hills argued that since the monarch had paid for the original introduction of printing he could legitimately appoint printers, in particular Hills himself, and that this had always

---

44. [Atkyns and/or Streater], *Kings Grant of Privilege*, 2, 4, 6–7, 10, 12, 13–15; [Atkyns], *Original and Growth of Printing* ([1660–1]).

45. Wallis, "Copy of the Account," 217.

46. PRO SP 29/292, nos. 49, 164–164(v); Wood, *Historia et Antiquitates Universitatis Oxoniensis*, 226–7. Wood was told by Thomas Blount that Coster had invented printing: Blount, *Correspondence*, 137.

prevented the university from printing more than it needed for its own internal use.[47] By 1688 such attacks had escalated into a quo warranto action against the university's printing activities, and its counsel found that the Corsellis story was still useful in this case. It would cease only with James's overthrow.[48] By that time the Oxford conflict had generated what would become a key category for describing the malpractices of the realm of print. When John Fell, bishop of Oxford and the leading proponent of Oxford printing, wanted to describe to Sir Joseph Williamson his frustration at the invulnerable community of London Stationers who violated the university's "propertie in Printing," Fell called them "land-pirats."[49] It was an evocative phrase, and one that would last.

The Atkyns history had thus become a standard resource.[50] By the end of James's reign it was a principal justification for royal patents, and could not be ignored by campaigners against them. Beyond the law, too, it proved attractive, and even for writers not engaged in defending such a specific cause. As a result, the next hundred years saw a vast controversy over the cultural, social, and economic historiography of printing, sparked by practical issues descended from Atkyns's and Streater's campaign against the Stationers' Company. On representations of its history were founded contemporaries' differing accounts of what printing was and should be. That Frederick Corsellis and Johann Faust would be central to the controversy was signaled by Moxon's insistence on supporting Corsellis in the first systematic description of the printing house. His *Mechanick Exercises* began with frontispiece portraits that instantiated models for a further century of iconography, of Coster (appropriated from Saenredam) and Gutenberg (taken from André Thevet's 1584 *Vies et Portraits des Hommes Illustres*—although others gave the same visage to Fust, or Faust) (fig. 5.7).[51]

In these circumstances of profound controversy, every aspect of historical knowledge was rendered problematic. There was very little agreement even on what sort of person a "historian of printing" ought to be. In practice the

47. Hills vs. University of Oxford, 1 Vern. 275, 24 November 1681.

48. SCA, Supplementary Documents, Series I, Box A, Envelopes 4 and 5; Box E. Johnson and Gibson, *Print and Privilege*, 167–8.

49. Fell to Williamson, 6 August 1674: PRO SP 29/361, nos. 188–188(i). This is the earliest reference given in the *OED*; similar phrases occur in several writers of the time, however, and those who concern themselves about such things may question Fell's absolute priority, especially given Streater's usages cited above, pp. 309, 313. Perhaps the earliest reference to "piracie" in the Stationers' court was in 1684: SCB F, fol. 18ʳ.

50. Stationers' Company vs. Parker, Skinner 233; Company vs. Lee, 2 Chan. Cas. 66, 2 Show. K.B. 258; Company vs. Seymour, 3 Keble 792, 1 Mod. 257. See also the Oxford quo warranto case: SCA, Supplementary Documents, Series I, Box A, Envelopes 4 and 5; Box E; Johnson and Gibson, *Print and Privilege*, 167–8.

51. Moxon, *Mechanick Exercises on the Whole Art of Printing*, lx, lxii, 1–10; [Marchand], *Histoire*, 32–3.

FIG. 5.7. Portraits of Coster, Gutenberg, and Caxton. These likenesses were first published in the sixteenth century, long after the deaths of their subjects. Historians of printing then reproduced them, with various embellishments, for the next two hundred years. Their repeated use helped readers to identify the three early printers as real, historical individuals, even though there was no evidence that any of them had in fact resembled his printed image. Moxon, *Mechanick Exercises*; Lewis, *Life of Mayster Wyllyam Caxton*. (By permission of the Syndics of Cambridge University Library.)

history of the press was being written by printers, booksellers, and hacks, by antiquarians and amateurs.[52] Whether any of these could construct a truthful history proved intensely controversial, as competing writers waxed scathing of each other's qualifications. This was not simply a matter of personal antagonisms. The best strategy for judging a printed history, contemporaries insisted, was in general to assess its writer's "character"—"his interests, his passions, the circumstances of his life, and the conjectures in which we find him."[53] For example, a tradesman might enjoy particular craft skills, enabling him to assess as evidence traces that a gentleman could not even perceive; as Samuel Speed put it, "every one is the best Actor and Discourser in his own Art." But should a reader invest trust in the historiography of a tradesman, which was necessarily subject to commercial interest? Tory licenser and cosmographer Edmund Bohun acknowledged the general doubt. "Gent. and Scholars at large are not so well qualified to Write upon this Subject [of trade] as merchants are," he admitted, "but then they ought to

52. For the status and practice of historiography see: Furet, *In the Workshop of History*, 77–98; Kelley, *Foundations of Modern Historical Scholarship*; Momigliano, "Introduction of History." For the English situation see Kenyon, *History Men*; Abbatista, "Business of Paternoster Row," 12. For writers about printing in particular, see Myers, "Stationers' Company Bibliographers."

53. Champion, *Pillars of Priestcraft Shaken*, 41.

prefer the Generall good of the Nation to that of any one particular Company or set of merchants."[54] A gentleman's judgment, being free from interest, might counterbalance the privileged skill of the necessarily compromised craftsman.[55] This was an issue of particular delicacy in constructing histories of the press, since such histories depended at all points on the mysterious knowledge of printers and booksellers. The historiography of printing accordingly became the site for some of the most profound and far-reaching of contests in the *ars historica*. What would be accounted credible evidence, and in turn how the nature of printing would be conceived, often rested on such arguments about the character of a historian.

There was an art to establishing a character of credit in historical writing. Its point of application was the question of authenticity of evidence. Historical writers increasingly adopted a probabilistic rhetoric centered on the deployment of named witnesses and their testimony. They proclaimed the historical "matter of fact," attested by such affidavits, as the foundation of their veracity. To confirm the authority of these resources they adopted a paraphernalia of footnotes, endnotes, appendices, and citations that would become characteristic of later historical scholarship. In a realm dominated by questions of personal and documentary credit, such techniques provided what Burnet called a "more effectual way to be believed." They were much needed, because attacks on the authenticity of documents were as pervasive as claims to their facticity. Allegations of forged testimony became perhaps the most common currency in historiography: terms like "falsehood," "deceit," "imposture," "sham," "fraud," and "forgery" saturated the pages of every historian, and the laborious line-by-line demolition of a writer's credit became a standard form of argument.[56] Such strategies had practical consequences, because the conclusions reached through their application were intended to direct current and future conduct.

Both historiographical strategy and, indeed, interest in the history of the press itself benefited from the burgeoning antiquarian movement.[57] It is per-

---

54. Valerius Maximus, *Romae Antiquae Descriptio*, 412; BL Ms. Add. 5540, fols. 56^v–57^r, 58^r. For representations of a Stationer's "character" see above, pp. 137–60.

55. Shapin, *Social History of Truth*, 83–4, 93–5.

56. These protocols are excellently analyzed by Champion, *Pillars of Priestcraft Shaken*, 25–52. Champion singles out for description the Convocation controversy of the 1690s, which was sparked by Humphrey Hody's publication of the so-called "Baroccian manuscript" in 1691. The manuscript provided apparent precedents in the early church for the deprivation of nonjurors. The result was some two decades of rival publications printing and contesting historical "matters of fact," including a prolonged questioning of the status of the Baroccian manuscript in terms of the credit of its transcriber. It was alleged that Hody had deliberately suppressed an appendix to the manuscript that contradicted his inferences. The controversy was remarkably similar in its structure, strategies, and outcome to that surrounding Richard Atkyns's manuscript.

57. For this movement see Levine, *Humanism and History*, 73–106.

haps no surprise that antiquaries were tempted to trace printing back to the seals and marks found on the Roman pots now being dug up all over the land.[58] But curious gentlemen also looked for evidence about fifteenth-century printing. Almost immediately they started to find more evidence for Corsellis. Some announced the rediscovery of earlier writers who had suggested priority for Oxford over London, such as the late Elizabethan polymath Brian Twynne.[59] Others found more copies of the 1468 *Expositio in Symbolum Apostolorum* which Atkyns and Streater had described. Their discoveries disposed of any contention that the first copy might have been fabricated, whether by Atkyns himself or by some opportunistic fifteenth-century forger.[60] With such powerful evidence being obtained so rapidly, attention soon turned to the manuscript Atkyns had reportedly found moldering in Lambeth Palace. This proved harder to locate. But the fact that nobody could actually find this document was neatly explained by the shoemaker and bookseller John Bagford. Bagford noted that the Cavalier polemicist John Birkenhead had borrowed it from Lambeth in 1664–65 while advising Parliament about the possibility of passing a new, stronger Press Act—probably the very bill suggested by Atkyns. He had forgotten to return the document to Lambeth Palace, Bagford explained, and it had been lost in the Fire of London.[61] It was not such an implausible suggestion. Birkenhead had indeed been involved in the construction of press legislation, Yates had heard as early as 1671 that he had indeed had the manuscript, and Aubrey knew him to have possessed "the best & choicest collections of Pamphletts of any man in England" (he urged that they be saved for a learned library in case catastrophe overtake them).[62] He was perhaps the most likely man in London to have held and lost the Atkyns record.

What matters, however, is that at this juncture nobody could assume that the document did not exist. Even the Stationers' Company, in all its long

---

58. Bagford, "Essay on the Invention of *Printing*," 2397; Mortimer, "Description of an *Antique* Metal *Stamp*."

59. Twynne, *Antiquitatis Academiae Oxoniensis Apologia*; Stower, *Printer's Grammar*, 25–6.

60. There are now some thirteen copies known to exist in various libraries: Hellinga, *Caxton in Focus*, 22. A bibliographical analysis of the book is in Hellinga and de la Mare, "First Book Printed in Oxford."

61. See Bagford's proposal for a history of printing at Oxford, cited in Stower, *Printer's Grammar*, 25. Bagford also proposed to publish a comprehensive history of the press, but to the distress of Ralph Thoresby, for one, it never appeared: Hunter, *Diary of Ralph Thoresby*, II, 37–8, 149–50; Hunter, *Letters . . . to Ralph Thoresby*, II, 133; Gatch, "John Bagford, Bookseller and Antiquary." Some of the text survives in Bagford's "History of tipography," CUL Ms. Dd.10.56, which shows that he favored Coster and Faust and thought Gutenberg was a thief. Most of his working materials ended up in Sir Hans Sloane's hands. See also Gatch, "John Bagford as a Collector."

62. *Journals of the House of Commons*, VIII, 434a; PRO SP 29/292, no. 49; Bodl. Ms. Wood F.39, fol. 331ʳ; Williams, "Edition of the Correspondence of John Aubrey," 318, 327. For Birkenhead's activities see also Thomas, *Sir John Birkenhead*, 210–11, 224–5.

battles with Atkyns and Streater, seems never to have argued that the manuscript was nonexistent—perhaps for the rather embarrassing reason that its
own charter had long since gone missing.[63] But we can see another reason if
we think about conventions of access. The Company, unlike a moderately
well-connected gentleman like Atkyns, had no patronage route into Lambeth Palace. To have bluntly accused Atkyns of lying about a nonexistent
manuscript would therefore have been an extremely risky strategy, since for
all the Company knew he might actually produce it in court. That would
clearly have been a devastating outcome. On the other hand, Atkyns, not
being a Stationer, had no access to Stationers' Hall, so he may not have
known that its own all-important charter was missing (Streater did have
such access, but had always been antagonistic to the Company's oligarchs
and was hardly likely to be taken into their confidence). The Corsellis saga
thus began with a pair of documents, neither of which actually existed, but
each of which enjoyed a kind of "virtual" being inasmuch as its nonexistence
was, for social reasons, unverifiable.[64] And Corsellis and his Oxford press
were fast becoming attested historical facts—so much so that in 1674 a Flan-
ders immigrant named Corsellis was buried under a stone lauding his illus-
trious ancestor.[65]

Caxton supporters were in retreat. The extent of their doubts was signaled in probably the most comprehensive English account "Of the first
Invention of the Art of Printing." Richard Smyth was here reduced to the
intriguing argument that even if Atkyns's account were true, Caxton should
still be regarded as the first printer in England. It had been at his instigation that this "servant & workman" had been brought across the Channel,
Smyth observed, and Corsellis had remained in this subordinate position
when in Oxford. His master had learned the art from him, and had "thereby
become the first Printer" in England, "Corsellis being employed only as the
Printers Servant to teach the Art only and not otherwise." Only Caxton had
actually published books "in his own Name as Printer."[66] It was a shrewd
argument, and it revealed an important assumption about the attribution
of responsibility for printing practices. But its very acuity served only to

63. Prynne, now keeper of records, made a hasty search for the charter in the Tower in
1662–3 in response to Atkyns's proposal for its dissolution: Blagden, "Charter Trouble." To
Delaune, the Tower's archive represented "*a perfect continuance of all the Antient Rights of
England*": *Angliae Metropolis*, 13–14.

64. The obvious reaction of a modern reader to Atkyns's theory—that he was acting out
of self-interest and that his history was *as such* inherently untrustworthy—seems not to have
been publicly alleged by any of his opponents at the time, although eighteenth-century writers would later rely upon it to discredit Atkyns's claims. There are ancient archetypes for such
origin stories, however: Grafton, *Forgers and Critics*, 9, 58.

65. Madan, *Oxford Books*, I, 245–53, esp. 246–7.

66. BL Ms. Sl. 772, passim, esp. fols. 26^v–27^r, 31^r, 34^r–38^r.

demonstrate the success of Corsellis's protagonists in undermining accepted knowledge about English printing and its past.

As its foundations lay abroad, so the consequences of this success did not stop at the English coast. The adoption of this new history had important consequences for the origins of European printing too. Atkyns's manuscript had specifically stated that printing was invented at Haarlem. Unfortunately, the case for Haarlem was still widely doubted in favor of that for Mainz. This could not be explained away, since Atkyns had claimed to be quoting the manuscript virtually verbatim, and the circumstantial details of Turnour and Caxton's expedition discounted the possibility of any mistake. Atkyns's history had to be accepted or rejected as a whole. This meant that those prepared to accept the existence of Corsellis had also to argue for Gutenberg's having operated an early press at Haarlem, and probably for his having invented the press there.

So English travelers such as Charles Ellis now began to take trips to Haarlem, searching for traces of Coster's existence. So many visited, apparently, that the harassed owner of Coster's old house unilaterally erased the civic inscription recording the building's heritage in an attempt to escape their attentions. Once back, they reported their findings to the Royal Society. There the virtuosi spent time discoursing earnestly of the history of printing. Afterward, in Jonathan's coffeehouse, Robert Hooke would pursue the subject, along with licensing, "Dr. Faustus," and the "Stationers monopoly." He borrowed French works on the history of printing from licenser James Fraser to do so, and approached Stationer Samuel Smith to inquire about incunabula. In 1682 Moses Pitt's *English Atlas*, in which Hooke was an active participant, reported another English traveler's testimony that a statue of Coster had once stood in Haarlem.[67] Bagford trumped this by announcing in the *Philosophical Transactions* the discovery of an original sheet from Coster's first press, which was now held in the Royal Library at Saint James's. He also rediscovered the primitive Coster book that Jonghe himself had mentioned: it had ended up, significantly enough, in Oxford. Yet another soon turned up in the library of Corpus Christi, Cambridge. The fact that Coster's name appeared on none of these was readily explained. He had bound Faust to silence, after all, and had probably tried to make his books look as much like manuscripts as possible so that they might fetch a higher

---

67. Pitt, *English Atlas*, IV, 178–9; Ellis, "Extract of a Letter," 1416–18; Bagford, "Essay on the Invention of *Printing*," 2397 ff.; RS Journal Book 8, 144–7; Journal Book 10, 22–3, 49, 57, 159; Hooke, *Diary*, 250; Hooke, "Diary," 174–9, 183, 205–6. See also Blount, *Correspondence*, 137. Sprat, *History*, 74, 391, referred to printing as an art that had been invented by a soldier (presumably Gutenberg, who had carried the rank of knight, but possibly the artilleryman Waldvoghel). It had at first been "private," but then had become "*common*" by "*chance*," "*friendship*," or the "*Treachery of servants*."

price.[68] Such an explanation was accepted as convincing. Ralph Thoresby might still propose his own Mainz volume as the earliest printed book, but everywhere else the evidence for Coster seemed increasingly compelling. So great were the "pregnant proofs in behalf of *Harlem*" that "the thing seems to be left no longer disputable." [69]

The Coster-Corsellis theory was becoming an orthodoxy. But if printing had really been invented in Haarlem, then how did one account for the powerful claims of Mainz? A variant of Jonghe's theft story could do so most elegantly. Ephraim Chambers's *Cyclopaedia* suggested that it had been Coster's "Associate," Gutenberg, who "stole away his Tools while he was at Church; and carried 'em to *Mentz*, where he set up for the first Inventor." Nonetheless, Chambers admitted that many attributed the "Theft, &c." not to Gutenberg, but to "*Fust, or Faust, or Faustus*." And Faust in fact became the culprit favored by most writers. John Harris's *Lexicon Technicum*, for example, maintained that Coster had invented printing at Haarlem, whence it had been stolen by Corsellis and, independently, by Faust. "As for *John Guttenburgh*, who by many Authors is said to be the first Inventor of Printing," Harris added damningly, "we cannot find one Book with his Name and Printing." [70]

Johann Faust was suddenly back in the limelight. William Leybourn—printer, mathematician, and surveyor of Stationers' Hall—even declared that he favored Faust as the true inventor.[71] Chambers, too, conceded Naudé's point that the documentation of Faust's claim to be found in early printed books was far more impressive than that for either Gutenberg or Coster. "All that is urged on their behalf," by contrast, "is only founded on Reports, Conjectures, Probabilities, forged Authorities, and the Jealousies of Cities." It might be true that the earliest surviving printed book was made by Faustus of Mainz, countered another, anonymous writer, referring to the oldest surviving colophon, which did indeed name him; but in fact the

68. Wanley, "Some Observations concerning the Invention and Progress of Printing"; Bagford, "Essay on the Invention of *Printing*"; Bagford, "History of tipography," CUL Ms. Dd. 10.56, esp. fols. 7ʳ–9ᵛ. William King satirized Bagford and Wanley as he did the Royal Society itself, but even then his 1776 editor added a statement supporting Corsellis: King, *Original Works*, I, 262 and n.

69. Hunter, *Diary of Ralph Thoresby*, I, 335; Pitt, *English Atlas*, IV, 178–9. Chambers's *Cyclopaedia* cited the Corsellis theory as established fact: II, 873, 875. See also La Caille, *Histoire*, 5–11.

70. Chambers, *Cyclopaedia*, s.v. "Printing"; Harris, *Lexicon Technicum*, s.v. "Printing"; compare Bagford, "Essay on the Invention of *Printing*," 2398, 2400. That Bagford was thinking of Corsellis when he discussed the Haarlem claim is perhaps implied by the manuscript of this paper, entitled "An Essay of yᵉ Invention of Printing," where, beside the reference to printing being first exercised at Haarlem, is a note: "Oxford booke." RS Cl.P. XVI.37–8.

71. Leybourn, *Pleasure with Profit*, Tract XI, 13–14.

Dutch had had the art first. Adopting Atkyns's history completely, this writer argued that if it was worth preserving the knowledge of inventions for posterity against time and oblivion, those *"Pyrates* of Memory and Science," then it would be intolerable to forget the invention of typography, "whereby glorious *Atchievements*, and renowned *Arts*, ingenious *Conceptions* and sublime *Speculations* are eternally registred."[72]

After stealing Coster's invention, the story went, Faust himself had begun printing. His servant Peter Schoeffer soon perfected the use of metal type—at which Faust was "so transported with Joy, that for his Reward, he promis'd he should marry his Daughter."[73] Faust himself then went to Paris to sell his printed bibles. Believing them manuscripts, the king bought one for 750 crowns and the archbishop another for 300. Only then did they compare copies. Many authors, among them Palmer, described the consequences:

> the buyers finding a greater number upon him, than it was possible for several men to transcribe in their whole life, and the pages of each copy so exactly alike, . . . he was seiz'd, try'd and condemn'd for *Magick* and *Sorcery*, and was accordingly dragg'd to the stake to be burnt; but upon discovering his Art, the parliament at *Paris* made an act to discharge him from all prosecution, in consideration of his admirable invention.[74]

"This was the whole story of the famous Dr. *Faustus*," explained Daniel Defoe, "of which so many Books and Ballads, Tales and Harlequins have been made, and such merry doings been seen here within these Two years."[75] He was referring to a revival of the tale in raucously popular theatrical performances during the 1720s, in both London and Dublin. Their sheer exuberance must have given the Faust history a public presence that surviving textual records cannot convey. The printed texts of these harlequins did, however, explain explicitly that the origin of their character lay not in the history of magic—any notion that the historical Faust had been a sorcerer was mere "superstition"—but in that of the press. Coster had invented the rudiments of printing in Mainz as early as the mid–fourteenth century, they eccentrically continued, and Faust had stolen the art from him before his visit to Paris.[76] Chambers and Harris concurred in relating the

---

72. Panciroli, *History of Many Memorable Things Lost*, 338–49, 413.

73. Bagford, "Essay on the Invention of *Printing*," 2399.

74. Palmer, *General History of Printing*, 87–8, 31–2; compare, for example, [Marchand], *Histoire*, 26. The story perhaps originated with Walch, *Decas Fabularum*, 177–83. Lazarus Zetzner, publisher of the latter, was generally associated with alchemical publication: Blair, "Restaging Jean Bodin," 410–3.

75. [Defoe], *History of the Principal Discoveries*, 223–4.

76. [Thurmond], *Dramatick Entertainment*, iii–viii; [Thurmond], *Vocal Parts*, v–x. See also [Thurmond], *Miser*; [Thurmond], *Harlequin Doctor Faustus*; Avery, *London Stage 1660–*

Paris incident. Humfrey Wanley likewise asserted that "by Indicting him of *Diabolical Magic* (or threating him with it) they at once gave birth to the Story of *Doctor Faustus.*" [77] Himself more favorable to the stoutly English account which based Marlowe's tragic hero on Roger Bacon, John Bagford nevertheless recruited Wanley's help in an effort to get English translations of this "Story of *Faust.*" [78]

What made these debates particularly significant was the lapse of the Press Act in 1695. Parliament decided that it should go because, among other reasons, it provided for reputedly monopolistic practices. [79] John Locke provided inspiration. Citing personal testimony from Stationers Awnsham Churchill and Samuel Smith, Locke addressed exactly the kind of practical and epistemic concerns so central to the argument over printing and its regulation. He alleged that the Company's register allowed it to exercise a policy of entering "as theirs" any promising title presented for publication. By such strategies, buttressed by protection against imports and by the Company's patents in classic authors, learned readers were "subjected to the power of these dull wretches who doe not soe much as understand Latin." English printed books were generally "false," and for that reason were routinely ignored by Continental scholars. This applied especially to classical texts. Patents in authors who had died centuries before the invention of printing were, he believed, "unreasonable and injurious to learning." But Locke was also one of the earliest writers to object explicitly to the Stationers' assumption of perpetual property rights in new works. He called these "unreasonable" and "absurd," and suggested instead a limit of fifty or seventy years. After the expiration of this period, he declared, there could not be "any reason in nature why I might not print them as well as the Company of Stationers if I thought fit." [80] Others would soon take up the theme of a literary propriety existing "in nature."

1800, 257–8, 812–3; Palmer and More, *Sources of the Faust Tradition*; Butler, *Fortunes of Faust*, 59–66. There was also a puppet play, *Faustus' Trip to the Jubilee*. For *Harlequin Sorcerer* see also Backscheider, *Spectacular Politics*, 167–79.

77. [Wanley], "Some Observations concerning the Invention and Progress of Printing," 1511; Chambers, *Cyclopaedia*, II, 875.

78. Bagford, "Essay on the Invention of *Printing*," 2401, 2405. Bagford's essay, sent by Wanley to be printed in the *Philosophical Transactions*, was satirized by King as "An Essay on the Invention of Samplers; communicated by Mrs. Judith Bagford: with an Account of her Collections for the same. By Mrs. Arabella Manly, School-mistress at Hackney": King, *Original Works*, II, 59–91. Roger Bacon was a subject of special interest to the Royal Society, because, as Hooke declared, he could be deemed to have been an experimental philosopher: *Philosophical Collections* 1 (1679), 14–15. At the time of Bagford's election to the Royal Society, the virtuosi were concluding not only this, but that Bacon had been the true inventor of gunpowder and the telescope.

79. *Journals of the House of Lords*, XV, 545b–546b.

80. Locke, *Correspondence*, V, 785–91, 795–6.

With the lapse of the Act, piracy suddenly faced no legal penalties—or rather, piracy against copies in the Stationers' register had ceased to exist altogether as a legal concept. With restrictions on the number of printing houses also void, the Company's customs and bylaws—in which resided the authority of the register—threatened to prove inadequate. The Company therefore tried some fifteen times between 1695 and 1714 to persuade Parliament to provide statutory protection for what was increasingly being called "the property in the copy."[81] Eventually it got its way. Yet the so-called "Copyright Act" of 1710 was not the unambiguous solution it had envisaged.[82] It recognized property in copies for the limited term of fourteen years, with extensions if the author were still alive at the end of that period. The Act said nothing about any common-law right that might exist prior to this temporary and statutory sanction. It thus remained unclear whether the Act's fourteen-year period represented protection *in addition to* an eternal underlying right, or whether it *replaced* such a right—even making the dubious assumption that that right had ever existed in the first place.[83] Moreover, the very idea of a temporary right, and one not created by a definitive act of registration, was a departure for the trade. It seemed paradoxical, even oxymoronic. Where did the right come from, and at what moment did it spring into existence? Where did it go after fourteen years?

These were very different concepts and arguments than had been applicable in the Stationers' court. They were deployed now in the realm of the law, not of the Stationers' Company. But they also played to the new judicature of public opinion. The subject of much historiographical attention in recent years, this new judicature transformed the conditions under which printed materials might come to be accounted knowledge. Would-be authors increasingly needed to appeal to a dispersed tribunal composed of the rational reading public. As Benjamin Motte, a Stationer competing to produce abridgments of the *Philosophical Transactions* for this public, put it, "The World has an absolute and indisputable power over all that appear in print." Anyone wishing to be accounted an author "must pass in review before this great Judge of them all, like the Creatures before *Adam* in *Milton*." Nobody escaped this obligation—not even "those Wonders of Nature, the *Newtons* and the *Halleys*."[84] Yet this immediately presented a paradox. The arena of public opinion, if it were to operate successfully, required printed materials to be reliable. Such reliability depended on a stable civil

81. Feather, "Book Trade in Politics"; Feather, *Publishing, Piracy and Politics*, 51–63.

82. "An Act for the Encouragement of Learning by vesting the Copies of printed Books in the Authors or Purchasors of such Copies during the Times therein mentioned": 8 Ann., c. 21.

83. See Feather, "English Book Trade and the Law," and "From Censorship to Copyright," for the legal situation, and also Feather, *Publishing, Piracy and Politics*, chap. 3.

84. [Motte], *Reply to the Preface Publish'd by Mr. Henry Jones*, 23–4.

régime of printing and bookselling, such as was advocated by the Stationers' Company or, increasingly, by advocates of authorship. But the construction of a stable and reliable régime for the press would in turn depend on historical knowledge, which must be ratified by public opinion. In this circularity originated some of the most profound problems of the public sphere in practice, as its participants wrestled with the lack of any firm foundation for credit, authorship, and knowledge.

Was there a way to break the circle? Perhaps. It was sought most keenly in the concept of property. In chapter 3 we saw how "propriety" cemented the possibility of trusting printed materials in the Stationers' commonwealth. Now, with the rule of that commonwealth contested, the fixing of what came to be called "literary" property might offer a way to do the same in the wider, public world. Arguments over the historical development of printing should therefore be seen as participating in the much wider regard for property in all its forms. Such arguments placed concerns for the state of printed expression at the center of political and philosophical attention.[85] When the first copies emerged from the Act's protection in the 1720s, controversy flared once more. Stationers undertaking such profitable works as *Paradise Lost*, Newton's *Chronology of Ancient Kingdoms Amended*, and Burnet's *Sacred Theory of the Earth* found their books being reprinted cheaply in Scotland and Ireland and imported to be sold under their noses in London. Scottish and Irish booksellers claimed that this was legal and proper. According to them, all property in these works had expired. They defended their efforts not just as legal, but as morally necessary, maintaining that they freed the public from restrictions of choice and price imposed by monopolists and from the corrupted and discreditable texts they peddled. In such circumstances one man's "piracy" was another's rightful defiance of monopoly on behalf of an exploited public. In response, London's copy-owning Stationers developed a practical strategy pioneered by John Streater in the 1670s.[86] They formed themselves into congers to protect their copies—alliances designed to share the costs and risks involved in the publishing of substantial books. Their blacklisting of offending Stationers led Dunton to call them "pyrat-congers."[87] These alliances, or their descendants, persisted for generations. John Churchill would later recall that

85. For contrasting portrayals of the "public sphere" and its emergence, see Chartier, *Cultural Origins of the French Revolution*; Habermas, *Structural Transformation of the Public Sphere*; Koselleck, *Critique and Crisis*; Goldgar, *Impolite Learning*; Landes, *Women and the Public Sphere*; Warner, *Letters of the Republic*. For the preoccupation with property, see: Hay, "Property, Authority and the Criminal Law," 18, 21, 59–60; Dickinson, *Liberty and Property*; Langford, *Public Life and the Propertied Englishman*, 1–70.

86. Cole, *Irish Booksellers and English Writers*; Hodgson and Blagden, *Notebook of Thomas Bennet and Henry Clements*, 91; Blagden, *Stationers' Company*, 174–5.

87. Hodgson and Blagden, *Notebook of Thomas Bennet and Henry Clements*, 91.

throughout the eighteenth century most standard "general and medical" titles were issued by up to twenty collaborators, providing "a sort of publishing with limited liability."[88]

Long though they lasted, congers and similar practical mechanisms were never wholly effective. When they failed, copy-owners' only legal recourse was to appeal either to letters patents, to the fourteen-year protection of the 1710 Act, or to a perpetual property they reckoned to lie in common law. The argument for the latter derived from Prynne's case for printing as a common trade. Copy holders argued that from its earliest days the book trade had recognized and commonly maintained a permanent right in literary property as recorded in the register, which therefore constituted part of custom. Patentees of legal texts and almanacs likewise resorted to the past. They alleged that the exercise of patents back to the time of Henry VIII proved that they had a legitimacy superior to, and independent of, the 1710 Act. Competitors then had to respond that this had never been the case. Maintaining either an alternative right or, more radically, that there could be no legitimate property at all in anything so immaterial as an idea, they argued that copies had originally been common and had been unjustly seized by powerful booksellers. Conflicts over the historiography of printing were indistinguishable from these struggles: they took place on the same grounds, with the same evidence, at the same time, and with largely the same combatants.[89]

The amount of writing devoted to the subject was so prodigious that no attempt at an exhaustive treatment can be made here. There is space to mention only a few of the more influential works. A profusion of such treatments announced and acclaimed the third century of printing in the years around 1730. Foremost among them was Michel Maittaire's *Annales Typographici ab Artis Inventae Origine ad Annum* MD (Annals of typography from the art's first invention to the year 1500), published in three volumes from 1719 to 1725 (fig. 5.8). Maittaire (or Mattaire) was a French émigré. A veteran of the Tory bastion of Christ Church, Oxford, and himself a nonjuror, he worked under the patronage of the elderly Tory Thomas Herbert, earl of Pembroke. He rejected both Coster and Corsellis in favor of Gutenberg.

Maittaire decided that the real question was that of the essence of printing. Coster might have developed some form of impressing using wooden characters, he admitted, but to "Gutemberg, Faust & Schoeffer" belonged

88. *Medical Times and Gazette*, 14 August 1875, 198.

89. Rose, "Author as Proprietor." Analogous arguments were being made in different situations in Germany and France, as Woodmansee and Hesse have demonstrated. Roche, "Censorship and the Publishing Industry," 5–6; Hesse, "Economic Upheavals in Publishing"; Hesse, *Publishing and Cultural Politics*, chaps. 3–4; Woodmansee, "Genius and the Copyright."

FIG. 5.8. Frontispiece to Maittaire, *Annales Typographici*. (By permission of the Syndics of Cambridge University Library.)

the credit of having developed the first true press.[90] As for Atkyns's account, Pembroke had employed an underling who had systematically searched the archiepiscopal archives, and the manuscript had not come to light. Atkyns had been arguing from private interest, Maittaire pointed out, and that made his testimony suspect. He had probably forged the whole thing, and his account should be rejected forthwith. How, then, did one account for the several printed books dated in 1468, which everyone knew to exist? Simple: they were misprints, or else forgeries by unscrupulous booksellers hoping to sell them as antiquities. Such tricks were extremely common in the piratical culture portrayed by Maittaire. He complained to another writer likewise engaged in the history of printing, Prosper Marchand, of "the Despotique Tyranny of Booksellers" which generated such a realm of distrust.[91] That "interested" writers—both booksellers and would-be paten-

90. Maittaire, *Annales*, I, 31–2.
91. Goldgar, *Impolite Learning*, 49–50.

tees like Atkyns—could not be trusted to produce true historical knowledge
was another artifact of that same world. A concrete example was soon manifested, when a bookseller announced evidence apparently confirming Corsellis's existence. Printers William Bowyer and John Nichols encountered
two previously unknown books advertised by this bookseller as having been
printed by Corsellis in 1469 and 1470. When they examined them, it was
clear "to those who are at all conversant in early printing" that their dates
were "a bungling forgery." Thus informed, the virtuosi who had flocked to
see them "looked on the whole as a lye." [92]

Marchand's own *Histoire de l'Origine et des Prémiers Progrès de l'Imprimerie* (1740), informed by its author's acquaintance with Maittaire, likewise
capitalized upon the tricentenary. Comparing the struggle to that between
seven ancient cities for Homer, and remarking that some even attributed
knowledge of printing to Adam, Marchand too eventually opted for a man
named Gutenberg. He had been born in Strasbourg, but lived in Mainz.
This man "devised a printing house at Strasbourg, and at length perfected
it at Mainz." [93] There he had built a press, before moving on to Haarlem,
whence Corsellis had been lured to England. [94]

As significant as his conclusion was the idiom Marchand employed to
convey it. He directed his claims to an adjudicating public. "The reader of
a new book becomes its judge," he insisted. And "Judges should believe only
what they see proved." Readers should form their opinions according to the
evidence adduced by quasi-legal "procedures," producing "proofs." Virtually reproducing the motto of the Royal Society, Marchand maintained that
"In a scholarly age like our own, which abounds in books, we do not need
to take people solely on their word." He therefore invented a citation system
designed to bolster the credit of his assertions at the same time as facilitating
the kind of reading pursued by such an audience. It resulted in some pages
containing only one line of text above a full page of notes to support it. His
own impartiality also came into play. Never had a subject been treated so
often as the history of printing, Marchand remarked, yet the result had been
confusion and obscurity. This was because it had been discussed hitherto
only in "fragments," each composed by a participant with an interest at
stake. Marchand claimed to be the first to provide "a full account." He
labored by such means to establish the credit of that account. [95]

92. [Bowyer and Nichols], *Origin of Printing*, 171–2.

93. "[Il] imagina l'Imprimerie à Strasbourg, & la perfectionna enfin à Maïence": [Mar-
chand], *Histoire*, 5; see also v–viii, 1–7. For Adam see also Evelyn, *Sculptura*, 11–12.

94. [Marchand], *Histoire*, 27–31. Marchand believed, however, that the *Expositio* should
properly be dated to 1478: 56; "seconde partie" (separately paginated), 126–30.

95. "Le Lecteur d'un Livre nouveau en devient le Juge. Les Juges ne doivent rien croire,
que ce qu'ils voïent prouvé dans les Procédures: & ils forment leurs Idées plus fortes, ou plus
foibles, à proportion de la Force des Preuves. Dans un Siécle d'Erudition, comme celui où

Novel mechanisms of this sort reflected the fact that in this world, print might not guarantee textual stability any more than had manuscript production. Marchand himself, to whom Maittaire had directed his complaint about booksellers, had found that when investigating printing and printed books, "everything is necessarily doubtful and uncertain." Even contemporary texts were often corrupt.[96] Marchand needed his footnoting techniques—all the more so as he was accused of perpetrating the same frauds himself. "One must not be surprised if before the Invention of Printing, when Original Manuscripts were either lost, or in the hands of a few people, there were Impostors who corrupted the copies that were made of them," admitted one writer. But "in our Century there are people capable of truncating and falsifying the Works published by the Authors themselves, and distributed everywhere," and "That is what the person called *Prosper Marchand* has done." Marchand was typically identified as possessing the qualities of the bookseller: he was notorious for venality, inaccuracy, and interest.[97] Those who promulgated such descriptions had a point. Marchand was indeed a master of illicit printing practices. He even composed an *extrait* of his own history of printing for a journal, writing it as a letter from Germany at a time when in fact he was in The Hague, and having it copied so that the bookseller would not recognize his hand.[98] Determining the degree to which he was really a fraud is far less important, however, than noting how much his tactics both epitomized and responded to the culture of discredit in which he lived and made his name.

The third, and perhaps most interesting, historian of printing was a major London printer, Samuel Palmer. He is intriguing because he, like Maittaire and Marchand, exemplified in his own work the epistemic problems of print. But he did so to such an extent that even his own identity was thrown into doubt. Palmer had originally intended to write an account of the practices of the book trade as it stood in the late 1720s. He was apparently prevented from completing this project by threats from typefounders and printers, on an "apprehension, that the discovery of the mystery of those arts . . . would render them cheap and contemptible."[99] So he turned instead

---

nous sommes, & qui a l'Abondance des Livres, Personne ne doit être crû sur sa simple Parole": [Marchand], *Histoire*, viii.

96. "Impressions, dont on ignore absolument les Tems, les Lieux, & les Fabricateurs; où tout est nécessairement douteux & incertain": [Marchand], *Histoire*, 15; see also 97–106.

97. "Friends of M. Bayle," quoted in Goldgar, *Impolite Learning*, 138, 142–3, 173. For reactions to Marchand's historiography see Berkvens-Stevelinck, *Prosper Marchand*, 39–64, esp. 40–43, 46–53.

98. Goldgar, *Impolite Learning*, 110. Even so, Marchand's *libraire* was suspected of "pruning" (*élaguer*) his *Histoire*, especially where the book reproduced textual evidence.

99. Psalmanazar, *Memoirs*, 284–5.

to the history of the trade, which he too undertook with the support of Pembroke. His *General History of Printing* (1732) asserted his credentials as historian forcefully, declaring that only a practicing printer could "form a right judgment" of the craft's history. The same skills that Stationers so jealously protected also qualified them uniquely as their own chroniclers. Amateurs and antiquarians, "for want of a sufficient acquaintance with the business of Printing," would inevitably "overlook some things of moment, which a printer would easily discover at first sight." Bowyer and Nichols's experience with the bookseller's forgery supported this argument. But what if Palmer were not, in fact, the author of his history at all?

Palmer himself had died while preparing a list of patents to complete his text. The work had then been completed by an assistant—the remarkable George Psalmanazar. Psalmanazar was a man who epitomized the complex issues of identity and credit cultivated in the world of print. He had arrived in London some thirty years earlier, claiming to have come from Formosa. At the Royal Society and elsewhere he made a series of spectacular claims for his homeland—claims that could not be assessed except on his own word, especially since the only man then in England who could pronounce on the real character of Formosan society was a Jesuit. Edmond Halley used astronomy to reject his testimony. Yet to many Psalmanazar's credibility remained undetermined.[100] He later became a great friend to Samuel Johnson, who declared that he would "as soon think of contradicting a bishop" as consider disbelieving Psalmanazar's word. Now, decades after his performance at the Royal Society, Psalmanazar claimed that he himself had written the entire text of the *General History of Printing*.[101]

Whether Psalmanazar really did compose the *General History* cannot now be determined, as it could not be determined in his own day. The claim may have been true. True or not, however, his involvement did little for the credibility of the book. Many must have noted with Bowyer and Nichols that Psalmanazar was an "impostor." Meerman would further charge that Palmer, too, routinely faked the dates on title pages in pursuit of profit, observing that "this imposter frequently deceives his readers by his craft."

100. Newton, *Correspondence*, IV, 412–3; Adams, *Travelers and Travel Liars*, 95–6. For continuing uncertainty about him see Byrom, *Private Journal and Literary Remains*, II, i, 52. John Flamsteed was able to use his correspondence network to conclude Psalmanazar's fraudulence: RGO Ms. 1.37, fols. 102^r–103^v.

101. He also alleged that Palmer had forced him into cooperation by piracy, surreptitiously encouraging the Bowyer printing house to issue a rival to Psalmanazar's edition of the psalms "with such privacy, that I never heard or dreamed of it, though I had been long acquainted with Mr. Bowyer." Palmer, *General History of Printing*, iii–v, 36; Boswell, *Life of Johnson*, 1277; Psalmanazar, *Memoirs*, 282–9. For Psalmanazar see also Abbatista, "Business of Paternoster Row"; Adams, *Travelers and Travel Liars*, 93–7, 101.

And the *General History* reproduced historical documents "after his manner indeed, that is, with little credit." This was a history in which nothing, not even its author's identity, could prudently be believed. He must be thought of, not as Palmer, but as "Palmer."

The book's problem of credit was hardly eased by the radical reinterpretation that it presented. Its great discovery, which Palmer had wanted to unveil at a "grand meeting of learned men, of which Dr. Mead was president," was that the inventor of printing had been Faust. He had devised the first press in Mainz some time after 1440. The story of the theft had been invented by partisan writers to support the claims of Haarlem, and "to deprive this *Great Man* of the honour, which he had so long incontestably enjoy'd." Attempts to maintain this libel by alleging that Coster had invented a woodblock technique failed, "Palmer" continued, because that was not true printing. His insistence that only a printer could write a true history of the press was confirmed. Antiquarians had not been able to tell whether an early book were printed by wooden or metal type—that is, by "Palmer's" criterion, whether they were dealing with *real* printing or not.

To the extent that he rejected Coster on the grounds that he had used only wooden characters, "Palmer" supported Maittaire.[102] But if Coster got short shrift, then Gutenberg fared little better. "Palmer" decided that Gutenberg had been a mere financier who had enabled the real originator, Faust, to achieve his project. Early writers had mistaken him for Faust, and the legal document in Mainz proved the latter to have been the inventor. Faust himself had attempted to maintain secrecy to protect his invention, and so the workmen who left him with the sack of Mainz in 1462, and dispersed the art to other cities, named only Gutenberg. After all, Gutenberg had been the gentleman of the partnership and the partner less devoted to secrecy.[103] Proof of Faust's claim lay in early printing patents, which named him as inventor. It was also evident in the story of his going to Paris and there suffering trial for sorcery—a story "Palmer" regarded as pure "matter of fact." He gave a suitably dramatic account of this event, claiming that Faust had been betrayed by the French king himself and had actually been "drag'd to the stake to be burnt" before agreeing to reveal his secret.[104]

"Palmer" found the story of Faust's theft from Coster incredible. As a printer himself, familiar not only with craft skills but with Stationers' conventions of security and access, he knew that the Dutchman would not have left his house unoccupied. Moreover, Coster's failure to set up another press

102. [Bowyer and Nichols], *Origin of Printing*, vii, 3–4, 200, 229, 232 n; Psalmanazar, *Memoirs*, 285–6; Palmer, *General History of Printing*, 3–7, 37–41.
103. Palmer, *General History of Printing*, 23–4.
104. Palmer, *General History of Printing*, 31–2, 87–9.

and reveal the impostor by means of his own invention showed what a ridiculous affectation the whole legend was. No master printer could ever be
so unprotective of his credit. However, "Palmer" reversed the theft story
rather than abandoning it altogether. Now Gutenberg became the thief.
"Palmer" maintained that he had stolen Faust's art after the lawsuit in 1455,
and that it was only then, having been left "in the lurch," that Faust had
traveled to Paris to recoup some capital. This had led directly to the famous
trial, and almost to his execution.[105] At the root of printing lay theft and
misrepresentation, as Gutenberg's duplicity led directly to his transfiguration. It made "Palmer" indignant that opponents had made "use of *Faust's*
noble discovery to publish and perpetuate this shame, whose honour and
memory ought rather to have been celebrated by it."[106] His name destroyed
by the very instrument of its fame, Faust's fate was emblematic of authorship
as a whole.

There was another crucial flaw in the Coster theory. This lay in his supporters' claim that he had invented printing two decades before Gutenberg.
"Palmer" regarded this claim as fatal, for imprints of such early date were all
suspect because of the tendency of printers to forge them in the hope of
selling the counterfeits. So prevalent was this practice that it led "Palmer"
to posit a simple and startling theorem, which he called his "general rule"
of historiography: "that all dates before the year 1450 are false."[107]

This "general rule" betrayed another purpose behind "Palmer's" text. He
noted approvingly that Faust had not sought to obtain "*privileges* and *patents*
for the sole printing of any particular volume." He had been forced to seek
them only later, toward the end of his life, to protect himself against the
workmen who had left him and, setting up rival operations, begun to comprint his books.[108] "Palmer" climaxed his history with a long account of
such misuse of the press. The rise of printing, he maintained, had been a
phenomenon of "pyracies" and "counterfeits," of "shameful and incorrect"
reprints of profitable texts, of "enemies to learning" and abusers of power.
These "vile . . . plagiaries" had all but destroyed the world of literature and
learning. For every Plantin or Elzevir there were "many more" who "made
a trade of reprinting some of the best editions in a slovenly incorrect man-

---

105. Palmer, *General History of Printing*, 79–80.

106. Palmer, *General History of Printing*, 41–3, 85–9. "Palmer" also denigrated the alternative legend, that Faust had stolen the technique from Mentel of Strasbourg, who had originally invented it. This was an account that existed throughout the period, in tandem with
those of Faust, Gutenberg, and Coster. It was comparatively unimportant to the debate discussed here, though, and I have therefore not accorded it such prominence.

107. Palmer, *General History of Printing*, 84. Compare [Marchand], *Histoire*, 108–9, 109–
118, listing "fake or suppositious dates" ("des Dates fausses ou supposées").

108. Palmer, *General History of Printing*, 95.

ner." His culminating chapter thus provided a long account of "the Abuses of the *Art* of *Printing*," illustrating how privileges had arisen in response to their piracy. "Palmer" held that the press had been invented in the first place only out of a need to circumvent the corrupt practices of mercenary scribes, and it was solely because of its subsequent usurpation that the patents system had become necessary. Faust's misfortune again stood for the general disintegration consequent upon the use of the press in contemporary Europe.[109]

It was in this context that "Palmer" introduced the subject of how printing had been brought to England. Atkyns's account, he decided, was substantially correct.[110] It needed only to be amended to take account of the fact that Faust, not Gutenberg, had invented the press. "Palmer" now deployed his own theft theory to do just that. According to this theory, after Gutenberg had left Mainz with Faust's secret, he had first gone to Strasbourg. There he had revealed it to one Mentel, thus creating the local legend that printing had been invented there. Then, finding himself under threat of arrest, he fled further. At length he arrived in Haarlem. It was there that he told "*Coster*, or some others" about the new technique, and together they set up a printing house in the town. It was from this workshop that Corsellis was subsequently lured to England.[111]

It was an ingenious piece of reconstruction. To support it, moreover, "Palmer" could now announce his conclusive triumph. He had found another manuscript, older than Atkyns's struggle, that confirmed independently the story of Corsellis—except that he was now called Theodore Rood, and that Bourchier alone had paid for the defection.[112] Installed in Oxford, "Palmer" recounted, Corsellis/Rood and his successors had "sworn fidelity to the king" and become crown servants. Thus it was that royal privileges had been established in common law, in a way consistent with Streater's developed version of the Corsellis history. They must therefore still enjoy validity. The whole story was conclusively proved by the fact—once again, invisible to nonprinters—that Atkyns's 1468 book had been "printed on the same shap'd letters as the *Rationale* and *Catholicon* by *Faust* (vulgarly doctor *Faustus*)." Atkyns's point about privileges—which "Palmer" had transformed into one about the contemporary rampancy of "pirates"—was triumphantly vindicated.

"Palmer's" work gained wide currency. Journals spread its interpretation widely, sometimes silently synthesizing it with other accounts. The *Weekly*

109. Palmer, *General History of Printing*, 106–7, 141, 162, 165, 241, 285–98.
110. Palmer, *General History of Printing*, 313–6.
111. Palmer, *General History of Printing*, [314–27 (marked as 122–35)]. "Palmer" adapted this account from [Marchand], *Histoire*, 28–31.
112. Palmer, *General History of Printing*, [318–27 (marked as 126–35)].

Register, for example, summarized his findings and recounted a typically confused reading. "The general voice is for *Mentz*," it declared, and "one *John Guttenberg* (or *Fust*, or *Faustenberg*)." This curiously composite individual had become "the Inventor of this Art about 1440. by Means of his having cut the Letters of his Name out of the Bark of a Tree."[113] The press had then been introduced into England by Corsellis, "Whence Printing was counted the King's Prerogative as much as Coining, but in Time it became a free Trade." The *Grub-Street Journal* also took up the story, alleging sardonically that printers' devils had been named for their allegiance to Faustus, inventor of the press—"for which he was call'd a Conjuror and his Art the *Black Art*."[114]

Opponents of the Faust account struck back in the shape of Conyers Middleton, librarian and one-time Woodwardian Professor at Cambridge. Middleton rejected Atkyns's credibility with renewed force. To him, Atkyns had been a straightforward forger—his "manner of writing" alone revealed him to have been "a bold and vain Man," and hence an unreliable informant. He had invented his history in order to support his claim to the law patent, pursuing the reprehensibly non-Newtonian method of forming his hypothesis before finding the fact. Psalmanazar was likewise "an impostor by his own confession." Nothing in his text was credible. His creation had been a history by and for tradesmen, entirely the product of "interest." The Lambeth document had never been discovered because it had never existed, and the Corsellis story—endorsed, Middleton admitted, by "all our later Writers"—must be abandoned.

So convinced was Middleton that he affected to find it bizarre that "a Piece so fabulous, and carrying such evident marks of forgery" could "impose upon Men so knowing and inquisitive." The most conclusive of those marks, and "the most direct and internal Proof of its Forgery," was the fact that Atkyns's manuscript insisted on Haarlem as the place where printing had been invented. To Middleton, this was certainly false. The 1468 Oxford book was difficult to explain away, since under normal circumstances the "Fact" of the colophon would stand as strong evidence. But Middleton maintained that it was the product of the printing house: "I take the Date in question to have been falsified originally by the Printer." This was not hard to believe. "Examples of this kind are common in the History of Printing," Middleton pointed out, false dates commonly appearing, by either fraud, contrivance, or error. He himself claimed to have seen several books thus falsified "to give them the credit of greater Antiquity," including one

113. *Weekly Register*, 126 (9 September 1732), 948.
114. *Grub-Street Journal*, 147 (26 October 1732), 1020. See also "Letter to the Publisher, in favour of Authors."

proclaiming itself to have been printed at Haarlem in 1435. And for erroneous dates he could even cite the recent inaugural speech by his own successor
as Woodwardian Professor, the date of which had been printed as 1724 instead of 1734—precisely the same mistake as must have happened in the
fifteenth century. In addition, the appearance of the book made such an
early date improbable: it was too neatly printed, and displayed signatures. In
Cambridge there existed a Venetian book of 1473 that began to use signatures midway through, thus showing the precise moment of their invention.
Middleton's distrust, then, even while it enabled him to reject Corsellis and
Coster, encouraged the glad acceptance of "Palmer's" maxim that all early
dates should be "pronounced FORGERIES." [115]

Middleton's has often been regarded as the definitive demolition of Corsellis. It is true that Philip Luckombe's *History and Art of Printing* (1771) did
maintain his view, arguing against "the notion which Palmer takes up, that
the first Printers . . . were sworn Servants and Printers to the Crown." [116] So,
rather more influentially, did Joseph Ames FRS, in his authoritative *Typographical Antiquities* (1749). [117] John Lewis, a minister from Margate, also
supported Middleton by writing a biography of Caxton. [118] Yet Middleton's
argument was by no means as conclusive as these may imply. It received
several forceful replies. [119] The most striking of all came from Gerard Meerman, who supported Coster and Corsellis with yet another remarkable extension of historiographical procedure. [120] Meerman's first assumption was
that since the press had originally been kept secret, *lack of overt evidence could
not be taken as a disqualification of any claim whatsoever.* Repeating Jonghe's
assertions, he then asserted another premise: that a theft had definitely occurred, and the thief's name had been Johann. This Johann had been a
native of Mainz, and had taken the art there having learned it from Coster
in Haarlem. Who was this man? Popular belief apparently held that he was
Faust, but this seemed unlikely. The 1455 trial documents (which "Palmer"
had read in precisely the wrong sense) showed clearly that he had been nothing more than an opportunistic financier. To establish his real identity,

115. Middleton, *Dissertation*, 2–9; [Bowyer and Nichols], *Origin of Printing*, 22.

116. Luckombe, *History and Art of Printing*, 27.

117. Ames, *Typographical Antiquities*. Interestingly, Ames complained that when writers
tried to gain access to Stationers' Hall to research the history of printing, its members would
"treat folks as if they came as spies into their affairs": Myers, "Stationers' Company Bibliographers," 40.

118. Lewis, *Life of Mayster Wyllyam Caxton*, vii–viii. See also the anonymous mid-
eighteenth-century "General History of Printing wherein is shewn The Origin of that noble
Art," written after Middleton, which endorsed Caxton but nominated Faust as the original
inventor: Regenstein Ms. Crerar 218, pp. 1–18, 35–42.

119. E.g., the anonymous "Oxonides": *Weekly Miscellany*, 26 April 1735.

120. Meerman, *Origines Typographicae*.

Meerman now drew on an aspect of the Atkyns manuscript that had not been noticed since its first publication by Atkyns himself: its claim, which Atkyns had revealed in an aside, that printing had been taken to Mainz by the brother of a Haarlem workman. This workman, he decided, had to be Gutenberg. Meerman now claimed to have found other, independent evidence that the real Gutenberg had indeed had a brother.[121] He proclaimed this as proof that Atkyns's manuscript must have existed, since this brother had been unknown in the 1660s.

Meerman's account was repeated in both law cases and periodicals. Along with the antiquarian Ames's *Typographical Antiquities*, it soon became a major resource. Luckombe began to appear a solitary figure in maintaining Middleton's view. Even William Herbert's later revisions of Ames accepted Meerman's status, suggesting that Coster and Corsellis alike be accounted inventors of wooden types. Typically, a contributor to legal arguments over the Oxford press was still relying on Corsellis in 1774.[122] Such a use was highly significant, because legal struggles over literary property were now reaching their climax. As they did so, writers puzzled anew over the invention and introduction of printing, and they also returned to the previous conflicts of the 1640s–70s. Francis Hargrave tracked down the manuscript of Prynne's original argument against privileges.[123] And Ducarel declared it "remarkable" that no verdict or details of the opposition to Atkyns's and Streater's legal arguments had been printed at the time. "Perhaps the anxiety or prudence of some former law-patentee made them unwilling to publish it," he speculated.[124] He dismissed the Corsellis theory out of hand, asserting Atkyns' evident "interest" as sufficient to disqualify the writer "upon whose sole credit it rests."[125]

Meerman's theory was reprinted in 1776, in the aftermath of its being cited in the definitive legal judgment on copyright—a term that emerged into common use for the first time in the course of these debates. Through three crucial trials the issue of literary property was decided for a generation.[126] Hargrave argued in the midst of the crisis that the absence of

121. [Bowyer and Nichols], *Origin of Printing*, 56 ff., 74–80.

122. Ames, *Typographical Antiquities* (1785–90), III, i–ii, 1386–94; White to Kettle, 2 June 1774, in SCA, Supplementary Documents, Series I, Box E, Envelope 23; compare Hargrave, *Argument in Defence of Literary Property*, 46–7, citing Prynne's case. Prynne's manuscript was also cited by Ducarel in response to Meerman, in 1760: [Bowyer and Nichols], *Origin of Printing*, 193–5.

123. Hargrave, *Argument in Defence of Literary Property*, 44–7.

124. [Bowyer and Nichols], *Origin of Printing*, 196.

125. [Bowyer and Nichols], *Origin of Printing*, 196.

126. [Bowyer and Nichols], *Origin of Printing*, 164; 4 Burr. 2417. "Copy right" (definitely two words) was sometimes used in the Stationers' records before 1720 (e.g., SCB G, fol. 70ᵛ, in 1702). Under Charles II, I know of three occurrences: a reference to a "proprietor of the

perpetual copies would mean that "pirating would then become *general*." In such an environment the pirates themselves would be wiped out.[127] And this was effectively what happened. In 1766–69, Andrew Millar gained a verdict that perpetual copyright could indeed be vested in an individual. In a long and complex judgment, the judges confirmed that "Printing was introduced in the Reign of *Edw.* 4th, or *H.* 6th." Since then, they proclaimed, literary property had never been common.[128] But within a decade this ruling was resoundingly overturned. The House of Lords resolved that there was no historical or philosophical validity to the perpetual ownership of copies.[129] Almost simultaneously, the Stationers' Company lost its patent to the sole production of almanacs, when it too was ruled to violate common law.[130] Claims to perpetual property in copies had been defeated. Copy-owners did try to get a new bill through Parliament, but with no success. In future they would have to settle for the more limited protection provided by the 1710 Act. The "pirates" had won, and their actions had ceased to be piracies.

With the end of this struggle, the need for new interpretations of the history of the press receded somewhat. The Meerman account was reinforced by Caleb Stower's *Printer's Grammar* of 1808, which took his theory into the next century.[131] Stower, like Meerman, Bowyer, Herbert, and others, saved the phenomena by distinguishing wooden from metal characters, Coster and Corsellis using the former, and argued that printing had been invented as a method of counterfeiting handwriting.[132] Controversy over Coster flared again a century after Marchand and Maittaire, with lavish four-hundredth-anniversary celebrations of the press. Mainz's ceremonies, for example, saw Gutenberg commemorated with a three-day festival incorporating masses, a new statue, an artillery salute, orations, dinners, balls, oratorios, boat races, toasts, and torchlight processions.[133] Coster and Gutenberg thus fought still, in the streets and halls of rival cities as well as

---

copy-right of the *English Bibles*" (Company of Stationers vs. Lee, 2 Chan. Cas. 66, 2 Show. K.B. 258, where it is quite possibly a later insertion); a Company bylaw of 1678 referring to Stationers' arguments over "Copy Right" (cited in Feather, *Publishing, Piracy and Politics*, 46); and a court decision of the same year over an individual "Coppy Right" (SCB D, fol. 60ᵛ). But even if this was a term in use, it remained extremely rare compared to such terms as "propriety," "title," and "copy." The *Oxford English Dictionary* traces it to the 1730s.

127. Hargrave, *Argument in Defence of Literary Property*, 32–3.

128. Burrow, *Question Concerning Literary Property*, 115.

129. 2 Black. W. 1004. The standard treatment is Walters, "Booksellers in 1759 and 1774."

130. Blagden, "Thomas Carnan."

131. Stower observed that "for a time printing was as much the *counterfeit* as the *substitute* of writing": *Printer's Grammar*, 2.

132. [Bowyer and Nichols], *Origin of Printing*, 56; Stower, *Printer's Grammar*, 19–33.

133. E.g., Van der Linde, *Haarlem Legend* (published, it should be noted, by Blades); Fuhrmann, *Gutenberg*, 35–7. For a vivid account of the celebrations in Mainz in 1837, see Knight, *William Caxton*, 80–84.

in the pages of historians. But at length the French bibliographer and book-seller Antoine Augustin Renouard made a discovery that, for us at least, could be said to bring that part of the story to an appropriate close. Not doubting that historical records confirmed the existence of a real Laurens Coster, Renouard was fascinated to hear rumors that the original manu-script of Jonghe's *Batavia*—the work that had begun the entire saga so long before—had been preserved, and could be found in The Hague. In 1824 he made the pilgrimage to see the document. With bated breath he turned straight to the page containing the Coster story. There he saw a long, clear, emphatic line drawn through the entire episode. Centuries earlier, in a gesture that his printer had chosen to ignore, Jonghe himself had crossed it out.[134]

Corsellis lasted only a short while longer. He finally suffered extinction amid celebrations of Caxton in London that rivaled those for Gutenberg in Mainz. They were orchestrated by the virulently pro-Caxton printer Wil-liam Blades. Blades's biography of his hero deployed all the technological resources of nineteenth-century publishing to buttress the credit of its case. Supported by such evidence, by 1918 Madan could pronounce Corsellis's nonexistence "a closed question."[135] As for Faust, he had retreated into si-lence rather earlier. One of his last appearances was in the work of Samuel Smiles, the champion of self-help, who used the story of the Paris trial as anti-Catholic polemic. But by 1854 Paul Dupont's authoritative history could decline even to recite the story, acknowledging only that he might have died in Paris of the plague.[136]

If Faust dropped out of highbrow historical studies, however, he did not disappear altogether (fig. 5.9). Throughout the eighteenth century he had been more than anything else a creature of popular culture. The Faust legend was kept alive by puppet plays, masques, and pantomimes performed across Europe—we have seen something of their impact in Georgian London. Very little evidence survives as to the content of these entertainments. Their scripts were never published, and when early nineteenth-century folklorists

134. Renouard, *Annales*, separately paginated "Note sur Laurent Coster," 8–9.
135. Blades, *Life and Typography of William Caxton*, esp. I, 80 n; Knight, *Old Printer and the Modern Press*, 88–96; Madan, "Two Lost Causes," 90. For the significance of celebrations such as those Blades organized to commemorate Caxton, see Martin, "Comment on Ecrivit l'Histoire du Livre."
136. Smiles, *Huguenots*, 7–8; Dupont, *Histoire de l'Imprimerie*, II, 558. Faust was briefly revived in a Smilesian hagiography of Brunel's father, but was never again authoritative among bibliographers: Beamish, *Memoir of the Life of Sir Mark Isambard Brunel*, 149–50. I owe the latter reference to Ben Marsden. See also Smiles, *Men of Invention*, 156–219, esp. 166, for the hagiography of inventors of the steam press and a remarkably similar story of workers breaking their oaths of secrecy.

FIG. 5.9. *John Faustus discovering the Art of Printing.* Engraving by Henry Fisher, 1824. (In the possession of the author.)

tried to study them, they found itinerant showmen intensely reluctant to reveal their secrets. But there is evidence that Faust as the inventor of printing did appear. Certainly he turned up in a Strasbourg puppet play, and Heinrich Heine reported that similar entertainments in his day told that Faust had invented the press.[137] Moreover, when Faust reappeared in German romantic literature toward the end of the century, this was his first incarnation. Friedrich Maximilian von Klinger's *Faustus* (1791), the novel that propelled the character straight to the center of German cultural attention, opened thus:

> FAUSTUS, having long struggled with the shadows of theology, the bubbles of metaphysics, and the *ignes-fatui* of morality, without being able to bring his mind to a firm conviction, at length cast himself into the dark fields of magic, in the hope of forcing from Nature, what she had so obstinately withheld from him. His first attainment was the remarkable invention of printing; but his second was more horrible. He discovered, almost fortuitously, the dreadful for-

137. Butler, *Fortunes of Faust*, 161 ff.; Heine, *Doktor Faust*, 16–17.

mula by which devils are called out of Hell, and made subservient to the will of man.

In Klinger's novel Faust was thus clearly identified as the inventor of the press. Indeed, he turned to necromancy only when he found his invention spurned even by Frankfurt, "the asylum of science."[138] Satan announced a festival in hell, reminiscent of those commemorating Gutenberg, to celebrate Faust's invention. The future would witness chaos and war, he proclaimed, as God retreated before its new sociology of knowledge. "Bookwriting" would become "a universal employment, by which fools and men of genius will alike seek fame and emolument." Humanity would hubristically seek to invent systems to account for the heavens and the earth, aspiring to reveal "the secret strength of nature, the dark causes of her phenomena, the power which rules the stars and bowls the comets through the void." But the result would be "doubt," which "like the fen-fire, will only shine to allure the wanderer into the morass."[139]

But the most striking moment appeared at the end of Klinger's work. Damned, abandoned by God, and cast into hell, Faust is confronted by Satan and the soul of Pope Alexander VI—the notorious Borgia Pope. Satan expresses his gratitude to him for having invented printing, "that art which is so singularly useful to hell." At this Alexander explodes. "What, a printer!" he exclaims; "and he gave himself out at my court for a gentleman, and slept with my daughter Lucretia!" Faust's reply is proud and defiant, clinging to his invention's reputation as the supreme propagator of enlightenment. But then Satan pronounces his final, devastating defeat:

FAUSTUS. My noble invention will sow more good, and will be more profitable to the human race, than all the popes from St. Peter down to thyself.

SATAN. Thou art mistaken, Faustus. In the first place, men will rob thee of the honour of having invented this art.

FAUSTUS. That is worse than damnation!

And with that truth ringing in his ears, Faust is led off to the Pool of the Damned.[140]

CONCLUSION

The discussion presented here has admittedly been far from exhaustive. Yet it has been sufficient to suggest how radical was the diversity of representations of printing and its consequences available to early modern readers.

138. Klinger, *Faustus*, 1–9.
139. Klinger, *Faustus*, 12–23.
140. Klinger, *Faustus*, 248–9. Another literary work to play on the identity of Faust/Fust was Browning's "Fust and his Friends," in Browning, *Poems*, II, 851–72. George Soane's *Faustus*, performed in 1825, wearily attributed the confusion to monkery: sig. A2ʳ.

With such a range of opinions current, the appropriate degree of authority to vest in printed materials remained far from evident. In struggling to create historical accounts of printing, seventeenth- and eighteenth-century writers were debating just this issue. The spectrum of possibilities extended all the way from absolute faith in the virtues and reliability of print (typically qualified by a denunciation of those pirates who abused the noble art) to almost equally absolute disgust and distrust (generally qualified by muted praise for the few brave souls who did produce creditable records in spite of the press's degradations). In their arguments, the very essence of print—art, craft, or mechanic trade, guarantor of knowledge or accessory to piracy—was at stake.

Constructing histories helped people to understand the nature of printing and its role in their world. Richard Atkyns's espousal of Frederick Corsellis, designed to help him win a lucrative patent right, retained its importance in the succeeding century as the stimulus for fundamental reconsiderations of printing as a cultural agent. The specific problems of the subject, however, also forced the exploitation of new historiographical resources. In arguing over Corsellis, Laurens Coster, and Johann Faust, writers concerned themselves not just with texts and records, but with the practices, skills, customs, and civility that made printing what it was. This unprecedented diversity of resources helped make Corsellis, Coster, and Faust meaningful vehicles for articulating a proper politics of print. And they were needed because writing the history of printing was a profoundly reflexive enterprise. Writers such as Marchand and Maittaire argued for the contestable credit of printed materials by constructing the history of the press—but the credit of their own historical knowledge rested on, and was embodied in, documents produced and reproduced by print itself. The result was a sustained confrontation with some of the most fundamental historiographical issues to face any writer. They compelled investigators to look elsewhere than texts alone for their evidence.

"Palmer" and his competitors wrote interpretations in which their perception of a piratical reality loomed as large as the providentialist, optimistic view of a Marchand—or, for that matter, of an Eisenstein. That is not to say that optimistic views did not exist. They did, and were expressed in learned tomes, pamphlets, and popular processions alike.[141] But Marchand's view was far from universal, and far from uncontested. Look closely at any proclamation of print as guarantor of knowledge, in fact, from Milton and Marvell onwards, and one finds that it was always a *claim* rather than an

141. For one example of an optimistic view see Barry, "Press and the Politics of Culture," 71.

observation. It was always polemical, responding to some explicit or implicit assertion to the contrary. That printing necessarily led to stabilized texts, the assurance of trustworthy records, and a progression toward ever greater enlightenment was not yet resolved. It seemed just as likely to lead to a corrosion of credit, a multiplication of error, and a degeneration toward heresy and immorality. That was precisely why some writers insisted as stridently as they did on the fact and value of fixity.

But their insistence ultimately had its effects. When Stationers, writers, and readers decided how to print, and how to approach the products of printing, the resources they drew upon to reach their decisions bore a much closer resemblance to those presented in this chapter than to any of our own cherished notions of print culture. People who attended to "Palmer" *knew* that printing bred piracy, in the way that we now know that if we jump out of a high window we fall. It was obvious and irrefutable. Contemporary evidence for it was everywhere visible, and historical evidence showed how it had become so (fig. 5.10). One of the aims of this chapter has been to

FIG. 5.10. "Works of Darkness." Daniel Chodowiecki's print (published in Berlin in 1781) graphically conveys the horror of piracy for an age of Enlightenment. It portrays the noble author losing his shirt to rapacious press-pirates, while the figure of Justice lies prostrate and despairing alongside. Ironically, the commissioner of this image was himself a keen pirate. C. F. Himburg was notorious for his unauthorized editions of, among others, Goethe. Reproduced from Tauber, *Bibliopola*, II. (By permission of the Syndics of Cambridge University Library.)

recover that very self-evidence, which now seems so alien to us. In conclusion, however, it is worth pausing over its sheer foreignness. If one believed that Faust invented the press, that the king had personally owned printing and had been robbed of it, or that Oxford had been founded by Alfred the Great and Cambridge by King Arthur, then the degree of difference between one's intuitive beliefs and what a late twentieth-century reader would regard as common sense would be, to say the least, substantial.[142] Without appreciating this we cannot properly understand the decisions contemporaries made: to publish or not to publish, how to publish and when, and how to approach printed texts. In short, without appreciating this we cannot understand print itself in their period. But we must also understand how it could be redefined to become much closer to the print we now recognize. Book trade conflicts conditioned the making and content of histories of printing; and historical knowledge in turn conditioned the outcome of book trade conflicts. The results extended into virtually every aspect of modern life. The best known was the invention of new conventions of authorship, signaled legally by the neologism of copyright. The establishment of limited copyright was not inevitable—in France, privileges and perpetual property remained at the core of the printing trade until the revolution—and concepts of the nature and history of printing played an important role in constructing such a régime.[143] In this context, the legal issue was just one aspect of a much more fundamental development. Overall, histories of the press were engaged with the problem of maintaining a realm for published knowledge within which printed books could be attributed the vital quality of credit. This problem of credit permeated their struggle, from Jonghe's first mention of Coster to Satan's speech proclaiming the hubris of printed science. "The author" emerged at this juncture as one principle on which to solve it.[144]

If "the" author emerged in this period, however, then so did one particular author: Johann Gutenberg. The two were intimately related. Anthropologists and historians of art have observed that societies often create

142. The latter two assumptions were widely held, not least by the universities themselves. Both used manuscript evidence from the Dark Ages—evidence now regarded as "forged"—to certify their claims. See Gabriel, "*Translatio Studii*"; Grafton, *Forgers and Critics*, 109. For contemporary opinion see Blount, *Correspondence*, 118–9, 152–3; Bohun, *Geographical Dictionary*, sig. Mm2^{r-v}, s.v. "Oxford." Jeremy Black remarks that in the 1730s to mention Alfred was to make a political point about national integrity and honor: Black, "Ideology, History, Xenophobia," 187.

143. Woodmansee, "Genius and the Copyright"; Hesse, "Enlightenment Epistemology"; Tinkler, "Splitting of Humanism"; Furet, *In the Workshop of History*, 99–124, esp. 101.

144. Foucault, "What Is an Author?" See also the works cited above, note 89. Feather tracks "authors' rights" (as he calls them) from the early seventeenth century, in his "From Rights in Copies to Copyright."

such "culture heroes," in terms of whom normative histories may be con-structed.[145] Early modern Europe was no exception. In creating a represen-tation of the press, writers like Michel Maittaire, Prosper Marchand, Rich-ard Atkyns, Samuel Palmer, and George Psalmanazar created figures of the caliber of Apelles.[146] Through their heroes they strove to delimit the roles printers, their trade, and even books themselves should and did play.[147]

It is perhaps unsurprising, then, that the earliest clear manifestations of a print culture identifiable with Eisenstein's appeared in the mid–eighteenth century, at the height of these arguments—and that even then they were highly controversial. Their articulation coincided with the proclamation of progress as the historical destiny of Europe. In 1750 the *philosophe* Turgot developed a crude concept of this kind after reading historians of printing such as Marchand, and used it to proclaim the advance of natural science and the consequent enlightenment of humanity. The press, and especially its use in creating learned journals, had, Turgot claimed, "increased the de-gree of certainty" about Creation until "today it is only the details which remain in doubt." As though hobbled by the discordance of this claim with the reality of printing in his own day, Turgot then stumbled and could pro-ceed no further.[148] But his point was resumed in 1793 by the fugitive Mar-quis de Condorcet, whose *Equisse d'un Tableau Historique des Progrès de l'Esprit Humain* declared the pivotal role of printing in hurling Western Europe from monkish barbarity into Enlightenment, progress, and, by now, outright revolution.

Condorcet's *Equisse* became an official manifesto of the French Revolu-tion, despite its author's own proscription. It presented the first full mani-festation of the press as a unique force for historical transformation. The "Eighth Stage" of the work was thus devoted to the "revolution that the discovery of printing must bring about," as Condorcet called it. He detailed the manifestation of its effects, first in natural science and then in every sphere of human activity. Every positive element later to be included in Eisenstein's print culture was here corralled together for the first time, all improprieties being resolutely excluded. Together they were then deployed

145. Pocock, *Politics, Language and Time*, 243; Kris and Kurz, *Legend, Myth and Magic*. See Anderson, *Biographical Truth*, for a discussion of "life-writing" in the earlier part of the period. Compare also Obeyesekere's discussion of such "myth models" in *Apotheosis of Cap-tain Cook*, 10 –1, 177–86.

146. A fascinating comparison may be made with the construction of Shakespeare at the same juncture, which rested on very similar considerations of credit, forgery, cultural identity, and authenticity. See de Grazia, *Shakespeare Verbatim*, 71–83, 132–76.

147. This was a commonplace: see Wheare, *Method and Order of Reading*, 297–300, 303–4, 316.

148. Turgot, *Progress, Sociology and Economics*, 57, 102–3, 118.

in the cause of advancing a coherent account of historical change. The press, Condorcet pronounced, had allowed copies of texts to be "multiplied indefinitely at little cost." It had therefore enabled readers to obtain any book they wanted, and hence revolutionized education. As "knowledge became the subject of a brisk and universal trade," so it had achieved a new certainty, and the foundations of continued progress had been laid. The beneficiaries, the reading public, became "a new sort of tribunal": a virtual polity, without boundaries of rank or nation, "which no longer allowed the same tyrannical empire to be exercised over men's passions but ensured a more certain and more durable power over their minds." Replacing the princely court as arbiter, this tribunal could legitimately take even politics to be its province. Its power was essential to the political "revolution" that Condorcet so trumpeted. The invention of the press had thus been the crucial anticlerical turning point in modern history, the existence of which meant that humanity could never again relapse into barbarism. "Those who dared to insist that [the public] should be kept in its old chains or to try to impose new ones upon it, were forced to show why it should submit to them; and from that day onwards it was certain that they would soon be broken." [149]

The "printing revolution" as we now know it is thus the product of a later, political revolution. It was a retrospective creation, forged with tools selectively chosen from the arguments created by eighteenth-century historians of the press for other purposes. It was designed to serve as the indispensable cusp separating Descartes, Bacon, Newton, and modernity from corruption, superstition, ignorance, and despotism. The ideology (as we may call it) of a printing revolution was thus not only a result of the French Revolution; it was perceived as a necessary one in order to render that revolution both permanent and universal. But the propositions of a Turgot or a Condorcet could not of themselves force assent. The notion achieved something like universal acceptance only in the succeeding century, at the same time as Gutenberg finally supplanted his rivals. In England, William Blades's confirmation of Caxton may be seen as representing the same moment of resolution. Both were ratified, significantly, not by the early modern craft of printing, but by the new technologies of lithography and the steam press, deployed in tandem with the minute critical techniques of nineteenth-century historical scholarship. Printers were soon learning the new skills demanded by these technologies by typographical recitation of Gutenberg's prowess (fig. 5.11).

There is irony in this. Blades insisted that the historian must rely on "the internal structure of books." There alone could be found "the only unim-

---

149. Condorcet, *Sketch*, 98, 99–123, 167–9, 175–6; Chartier, *Cultural Origins*, 32–3, 65–6; Chartier, *Forms and Meanings*, 8–13.

peachable evidence—evidence which cannot be falsified." That was why his lithographic plates were of such critical importance. He was arguing that Caxton had been the first English printer, and that he had learned his craft from Colard Mansion—an unorthodox candidate. Blades did so on the basis of their type. His representations of Caxton's and Mansion's typographical characters were therefore intended to be compared exactly, in precisely the same way as handwriting would be compared by a paleographer (fig. 5.12). Readers were encouraged to examine their facsimiles "through a magnifying glass." The irony was that no printing technique practiced in early modern Europe itself could ever have permitted such minute comparison. In its very "accuracy of Form," Blades admitted, the lithographic art falsified its subject. In its very fixity it misrepresented the impressions being reproduced, which had themselves *not* been uniform. It seemed that Caxton could be secured only by a new, different technique.

In a sense, the invention of printing was not complete until the cultural identity of its inventor had crystallized. Its reputation as guaranteeing reliable and accurate texts had never been secured by early modern printing itself, which produced massive problems of accreditation. Only a later combination of literary and material technologies could achieve such a feat.[150] This is not to suggest that a nineteenth-century printing revolution of the same form should straightforwardly replace in our interpretations the fifteenth-century revolution now in question. The steam press and the practice of lithography were as culturally conditioned, and as open to appropriation, as any hand press. If they eventually came to be accepted as creating uniform products capable of producing uniform responses in their mass readership, then that too was largely because of sustained campaigns on their behalf to establish as much. Organizations such as the Society for the Diffusion of Useful Knowledge worked hard to render the production and reception of their products regular and unvarying. But historians of Victorian Britain have shown how difficult they found their work. Real readers remained indomitably resistant to the simple models of diffusion propagated by such authorities. It is thus plausible to speculate that those models, generated largely from Enlightenment historiographies of progress such as Condorcet's, were promulgated so forcefully precisely because they were so hard

150. Blades, *Life and Typography of William Caxton*, I, vii–x, 45–61, esp. 54. Vol. II was largely devoted to substantiating this point with a thorough reconstruction of Caxton's different founts and a bibliographical and typographical analysis of his publications. It is worth identifying the persevering importance of craft skill even here, however. Blades himself rested his credit on his "practical experience" in "all branches of the Art." Moreover, the reliability of his vital facsimiles themselves was attributable to the skill of a named craftsman, Mr. A. C. Tupper of Barge Yard, Bucklersbury. On the crystallization of the inventor, see also remarks in Pinch and Bijker, "Social Construction of Facts and Artifacts," 39.

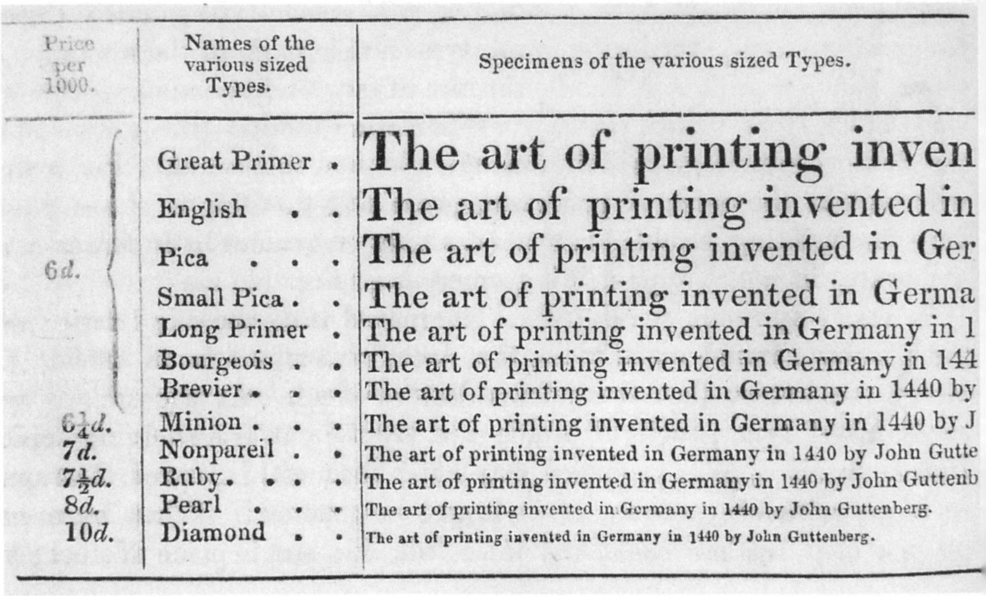

Price per 1000.	Names of the various sized Types.	Specimens of the various sized Types.
6d.	Great Primer .	The art of printing inven
	English . .	The art of printing invented in
	Pica . . .	The art of printing invented in Ger
	Small Pica . .	The art of printing invented in Germa
	Long Primer .	The art of printing invented in Germany in 1
	Bourgeois . .	The art of printing invented in Germany in 144
	Brevier . . .	The art of printing invented in Germany in 1440 by
6¼d.	Minion . . .	The art of printing invented in Germany in 1440 by J
7d.	Nonpareil . .	The art of printing invented in Germany in 1440 by John Gutte
7½d.	Ruby	The art of printing invented in Germany in 1440 by John Guttenb
8d.	Pearl . . .	The art of printing invented in Germany in 1440 by John Guttenberg.
10d.	Diamond . .	The art of printing invented in Germany in 1440 by John Guttenberg.

FIG. 5.11. Typographical training in the mid–nineteenth century. Dodd, *Days at the Factories*. (By permission of the Syndics of Cambridge University Library.)

FIG. 5.12. William Blades's reproductions of fifteenth-century characters. (*right*) *Boece de la Consolation de Philosophie*, 1477, from the Colard Mansion press. (*opposite top*) A manuscript written at Bruges for Edward IV. According to Blades, "The Writing shows the same design as the types used by Colard Mansion and William Caxton." (*opposite bottom*) *Propositio clarissimi Johannis Russell* (Caxton, Type No. 2); *Speculum Animae Henrici de Hassia* (Ulrich Zell's type). Blades argued that Caxton's "Type 2" was the same as Mansion's "large bâtarde Type" (*right*) and different from the type of Ulrich Zell of Cologne, the other candidate. Blades also compared these types to the contemporary manuscript writing from Bruges (*opposite top*). Blades, *The Life and Typography of William Caxton*. (By permission of the Syndics of Cambridge University Library.)

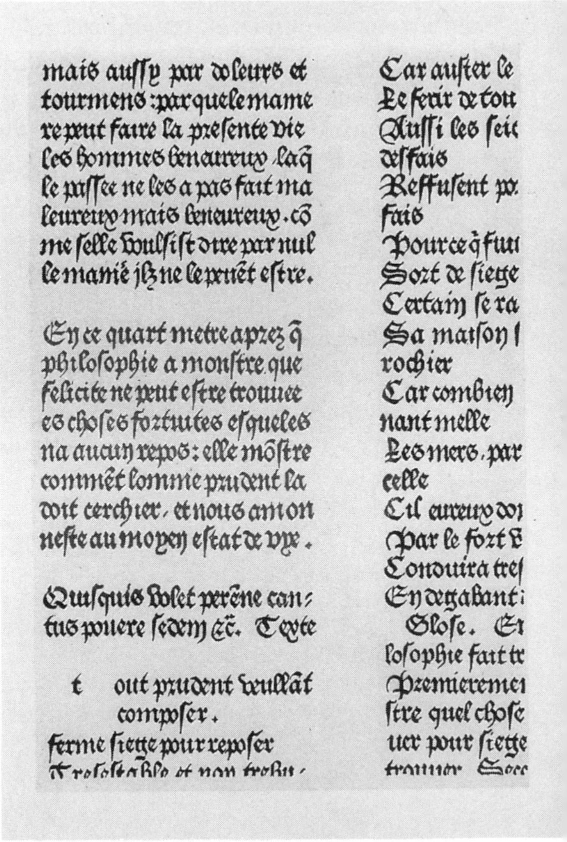

mais aussy par doleurs et
tourmens : par quele maniere
re peut faire la presente vie
les hommes beneureux laq
le passee ne les a pas fait ma
leureux mais beneureux . co
me selle voulsist dire par nul
le manie il ne le peuet estre.

En ce quart metre aprez q
philosophie a monstre que
felicite ne peut estre trouuee
es choses fortunes esquelles
na aucun repos : elle mostre
commet lomme prudent la
doit cerchier . et nous amon
neste au moyen estat de vye .

Quisquis volet perene can-
tus ponere sedem &c. Texte

t out prudent veullat
composer .
ferme siege pour reposer

Car auster le
Le ferir de tou
Aussi les sei
deffais
Reffusent p
fais
Pource q fu
Sort de siege
Certain se ra
Sa maison
rochier
Car combien
nant melle
Les mers . par
celle
Cil aureux do
Par le fort
Conduira tre
En degabant
Glose . En
losophie fait
Premieremen
stre quel chose
uer pour siege

Cy commence le liure de lordre de
cheuallerie . Prologue .

La loenge et gloire de
la pourueance diuine
dieu qui est sire et roy
souuerain par dessus
toutes choses celestes et
terrestes nous commencons ce liure de
lordre de cheuallerie pour demonstrer q̃
a la signifiance de dieu le prince tout
puissant qui seignourist sur les vii
planettes qui sont cours celestiaulz
et ont pouoir et seignourie en gouuer/
ner et ordonner les corps terrestres / pa
reillement doiuent les roix et princes
auoir puissance et seignourie sur les
cheualliers Et les cheualliers par sim̃
litude doiuent auoir dominacion et
pouoir sur le menu peuple / et contiet
ce liure viii . chapitres / Le premier
desquelz dist comment le cheuallier
hermite deuisa a lescuyer la regle et o⁊/

Propositio Clarissimi Oratoris . Magistri Jo
hannis Russell decretorum doctoris ac adtunc
Ambassiatoris xpianissimi Regis Edwardi
dei gracia regis Anglie et Francie ad illustris
simum principem , Karolum ducem Burgundie
super susceptione ordinis garterij q̃c .

d   Estimauit nos Illustrissie princeps Sa
cra regia magestas vt tue celsitudini pre
lebria sui ordinis garterij insignia ad quem per
collegas illius gloriose societatis tam spectabile
xpiani orbis fastigium vti pulcherrimum futuro
illius ordinis ornamentum dignissimi deletum
est debitis honoribus offeramus . Optantes igi
tur in primis ab immortali deo tanti primordij pros
peros in euum successus delectat paululum huius
nouelli federis deus . Vtilitatem prestanciam q̃
rimari , quatenus nec manis aut supuacua mi
litariu collegiorum reputatur inuecio . Habeant q̃
fideles amborum principum vnde peculiarius delectant
gratulati , Nam si res ab nostra memoria propter
uetustatem remotas , ex litteraz monimentis

saluauit . s̃ excecauit . Non edificauit s̃ superbia ista
uit . Ergo si sapiens ee cupis . ee q̃re scito las illi q̃ di
xit beatus homo quem tu erudieris dñe q̃ de lege tua doc
eis eum . In q̃b⁹ scola apponet tibi sacra scriptura . i q̃
uti in speculo cognosces si facies tua pulchra an feda
ibi disces vias vite a vere sapiē vias salutis a bea
tudis etne . ibi disces in tris ea quoz scia tecu pse
ueabit i ceelo . Vbi studebs qlie ad ipm pueias que
semel vidisse e oia didicisse . Infelix homo si scit alia
oia . illum aut nescit beat⁹ aut si illum scit ee si alia ne
scit . Procede anima mea a meditare huius temporis Buita
tem huius meredo preositate . Sub hoc tempe mortis
ineuitabilitate qd in tebz huanis cercus morte . qd
incercus hora mortis . Mors semibz e foribz . Juua
nibz in insidijs nullius miseret . nemini . venturo . o homo
qd e sti tuu vine diu hic . qd diuernis erupnis a te
dijs i morte abie . qd de hac vita quam itrasti cum do
lore . continuasti cu labore . exibis cu tremore . in q̃ es de
bil ad opandum facil ad seducendum fragil ad existend
pigr ad eatedum tardus ad effurgendum . Quid ee t̃ ania
mea cum delicijs corpie cu tu incorpea sis qd e cele
sti cu gaudijs mundi . vtiq̃ vil asolaco q̃ ve delea
cois e impeditiua q̃ puitate hz i sbiedo Buitate i te
pe e sticiam i fine miseiaz i affim pdicoez i exitu . Et q̃
le seds i cum corpalibz mebris quoz tam woluptati
bus ardes ut proprias non sentias delectacoes intelle
actuales . Ecce modicum a cadauer erit horridum

to realize in practice. But this is another story, which must remain to be told in a future work. Here it is sufficient to emphasize that a process of creative forgetting—about this present reality, as well as about the past—was essential to the hailing of fixity as the achievement of early printers. Gutenberg and Caxton were now remembered and celebrated, their images reproduced in paper and stone; Corsellis, Coster, and Faust suffered eclipse. With the crystallization of certainty in its inventors came a simultaneous crystallization of certainty in early print itself. And with that came the printing revolution.

Interestingly, this is not the only "revolution" to have such a history. The printing revolution and the scientific revolution have remarkably similar pedigrees. Both are creations characteristic of the modern age, retrospectively identifying moments of transformation into modernity in the Renaissance and early modern periods. Both may be traced back to the Enlightenment, but both solidified only in the mid–nineteenth century.[151] Their connection, moreover, has been of peculiar interest since the beginning. Turgot and Condorcet (and before them, of course, their inspiration, Francis Bacon) insisted on the special significance of the press for natural knowledge. It was through the advancement of the sciences, they claimed, that the progress facilitated by printing would extend to affect all humanity. Their legacy has been forcefully reasserted in our own generation. The claim that the scientific revolution rested upon the printing revolution is again prominent. A reappraisal of this claim is thus imperative, since it has been so central to images of print and its consequences throughout three epochs: the early modern era itself, the period when the concepts of printing revolution and scientific revolution crystallized into their lasting forms, and, above all, today.

With fixed and trustworthy printed texts being made available in large quantities by mechanical presses, it is said, a cumulative increase in knowledge became possible. If this account is now implausible, what replacement can be constructed to accord more faithfully to early modern representations of natural knowledge and the realm of print? Those representations, as this chapter has explained, recognized the contestable status of even the most solidly attested printed texts. Living in a world where printed materials could not necessarily be trusted, contemporaries developed a wide range of techniques, social, material, and literary, to affirm and defend what they claimed to be knowledge. In particular, they were well aware of the insup-

151. On the scientific revolution, compare Lindberg, "Conceptions of the Scientific Revolution"; Cunningham and Williams, "De-centring the 'Big Picture'"; Cunningham, "How the *Principia* Got Its Name"; Schaffer, "Scientific Discoveries"; Yeo, *Defining Science*; Jardine, "Writing Off the Scientific Revolution."

erable independence of readers. Very similar priorities engaged the practitioners of a particularly important new practice in early modern natural knowledge: the practice of experiment. Developed in England in the mid–seventeenth century, the "experimental philosophy" has always been recognized as central to the dramatic developments in natural knowledge on a European scale. Experiment, it may be claimed, depended on strategies of accreditation and communication identical in significant respects to those needed in the culture of print. Their close relation is explored in chapter 7.

Before analyzing that relation, however, it is necessary to attend more closely to the history of reading itself. The following chapter examines this practice, by reconstructing the terms in which early modern writers themselves sought to comprehend it. If books were to be made into useful tools for creating and sustaining knowledge, they realized, then the act of reading would itself need to be understood. Men and women worked to achieve this understanding by putting to use widely accepted knowledge about the human frame and its passions. Such knowledge enabled them to represent even the most intimate aspects of reading and to account for its emotional and cognitive effects. It thereby underwrote their growing acceptance that print could become a powerful instrument for enlightenment. But the passions were notoriously prone to generate pathological responses as well as healthy ones. Their analyses thus also reinforced fears that print could prove an influence for harm as well as good. Reading might indeed facilitate the creation of a new philosophy, they concluded, but only if conducted appropriately. Otherwise it was at least as likely to generate error and injury, both to the reader's own body and, by extension, to the body politic of the state. Such injury might even prove fatal.

6

THE PHYSIOLOGY OF READING

Print and the Passions

I read in a book that the objectivity of thought can be expressed using the verb "to think" in the impersonal third person: saying not "I think" but "it thinks" as we say "it rains." There is thought in the universe— this is the constant from which we must set out every time. . . .

And for the verb "to read"? Will we be able to say, "Today it reads" as we say "Today it rains"? If you think about it, reading is a necessarily individual act, far more than writing. If we assume that writing manages to go beyond the limitations of the author, it will continue to have a meaning only when it is read by a single person and passes through his mental circuits. Only the ability to be read by a given individual proves that what is written shares in the power of writing, a power based on something that goes beyond the individual. The universe will express itself as long as somebody will be able to say, "I read, therefore *it* writes."

ITALO CALVINO, *If on a Winter's Night a Traveller*, 139

INTRODUCTION

While he was still at school, the natural philosopher Robert Boyle later recalled, he had once contracted a tertian ague. All physic failed. Reduced to a melancholic state, the young Boyle returned from London to Eton in the hope that the change of air and diet might help ease his condition. But his mentors also had other remedies in mind. To "divert his Melancholy," they made their charge "read the stale Adventures [of] Amadis de Gaule; & other ~~Raving Bookes~~ Fabulous & wandring Storys." Their treatment was by no means a success. Far from curing Boyle, he later testified, the stories "prejudic'd him by unsettling his Thoughts." They thereby exacerbated his complaint, and produced an effect more lasting than any remedy might have been. Meeting in him with "a restlesse Fancy, then made more susceptible of any Impressions by an unemploy'd Pensivenesse," his

380

reading "accustom'd his Thoughts to such a Habitude of Raving, that he has scarce ever been their quiet Master since."[1]

Boyle's advisers should have read their Burton. *The Anatomy of Melancholy* had endorsed the reading of learned books, not that of romances, to counter melancholy. But then, even such a well-attested remedy was prone to be counterproductive. The unhappy patient might all too easily "make a *Skeleton* of himselfe," Burton attested, eventually coming to resemble those "inamoratoes" who read nothing but "play-bookes, Idle Poems, Jests"— and, to be specific, *Amadis de Gaule* itself. Far from being cured, Boyle risked ending up "as mad as *Don Quixot*."[2]

Luckily for him, in the end no such traumatic outcome came to pass. As Boyle later acknowledged, after much effort he did largely manage to "fixe his Volatile Fancy." He achieved this by subjecting himself to a rigorous intellectual régime. In particular, he found that mathematics provided the best tool "to fetter (or at least, to curbe) the roving wildness of his wandring Thoughts." The most effective way to restrain his meandering mind was to concentrate on the "more laborious Operations of Algebra." These, he found, "both accustome & necessitate the Mind to attention, by so entirely exacting the whole Man; that the least Distraction, or heedlessnesse, constraines us to renew our (Taske &) Trouble, & rebegin the Operation." They thus disciplined the mind out of the lax habits formed by romances. Nevertheless, the harmful effects of his earlier experience could never be eradicated entirely. Years later Boyle would still find himself leaving his manor at Stalbridge to wander alone in the fields, there to "thinke at Random; making his delighted Imagination the busy Scene, where some Romance or other was dayly acted." This odd behavior was regularly imputed to his melancholic complexion; but Boyle himself knew better. It was in reality nothing but "his yet untam'd Habitude of Raving; a custome (as his owne Experience often & sadly taught him) much more easily contracted, then Depos'd."[3] The effects of reading those romances had proved permanent, and Boyle simply had to live with them.

---

1. Boyle, "Account of Philaretus in his Minority," in Hunter, *Robert Boyle by Himself and His Friends*, 8–9. This differs significantly from Birch's version, in Boyle, *Works*, I, xvi–xvii. It was composed in around 1647–8, when Boyle was about twenty-two. See below, p. 504 note 124, for controversy about the construal of such biographical statements.

2. Burton, *Anatomy of Melancholy*, II, 90. See also Bacon, "History of Life and Death," in *Works*, V, 262–3, for the harm done by various kinds of learning.

3. Hunter, *Robert Boyle by Himself and His Friends*, 11–2; Boyle, *Works*, I, xix–xx. For the link between romances and such habits, see Markley, *Fallen Languages*, 43–4. For the effects on Boyle of reading romances, see also Harwood, "Science Writing and Writing Science," 43–4. But Boyle also expressed positive views on romances: Principe, "Virtuous Romance and Romantic Virtuoso."

Reading was clearly a powerful force. True, it could be a positive one. What originally made Boyle so "passionate a Friend to Reading," he was wont to say, "was the accidentall Perusall of Quintus Curtius." This ancient romance of Alexander the Great had "conjur'd up in [him] that unsatisfy'd Curiosity of Knowledge, that is yet as greedy, as when it first was rays'd." Here was a benefit to outweigh his "raving." In Geneva on the grand tour, moreover, Boyle would continue to pursue "above all the Reading of Romances," and would become fluent in French from doing so.[4] But it was equally evident that if one wished to retain reliability and independence of mind, then one must be careful what, and how, one read. Back in Oxford in the 1650s, then, at the time when he, Wren, Wilkins, and others were pursuing the discussions of experimental philosophy that would eventually lead to the creation of the Royal Society, Boyle applied this hard-earned knowledge well. This was the time when "the *Cartesian* philosophy began to make a noise in the world," and he could hardly avoid hearing about it. But he resolved to "acquiesce in no single man's hypothesis." Accordingly, by a publicly declared self-denying ordinance (and in defiance of the strict rules for reading his work that Descartes himself had tried to impose), "for many years he would not read over *Des Cartes's Principles*." Boyle had even refused to read Bacon's *Novum Organum*, he claimed, "that I might not be prepossessed with any theory or principles."[5]

True or not, to the historian these declarations are remarkable. A typical account of the intellectual history of Boyle's period would make Descartes and Bacon the most influential of all the disciples of "the new philosophy," yet here one sees the "acknowledged leader"[6] of experimentalism denying having read either. At the same time, Boyle claimed that the reading of romances had had a permanent unhealthy effect on him. Clearly, he must have thought that reading exercised a remarkable power over body and mind alike. And Boyle was by no means unusual in his appreciation of the power of reading. Many of his contemporaries testified to similarly impressive

4. Hunter, *Robert Boyle by Himself and His Friends*, 7, 15; compare Boyle's separate remark reproduced on p. 24, relating how, much later, Boyle had found himself suffering "violent pains" in an inn; reading an opportunely found copy of Curtius took his mind off his condition until it had cured itself.

5. Boyle, *Works*, I, 299–318, esp. 301–2. Compare similar passages in, for example: I, 317, 355–6; II, 289, 327; III, 8–9, 11; and see also Boyle, *Early Essays and Ethics*, 192–7. For Descartes's own instructions for reading his *Principles of Philosophy*, see his *Philosophical Writings*, I, 185.

6. So called in *Dictionary of National Biography*, s.v. "Boyle, Robert." Edward Davis has appraised Boyle's claim, and found no evidence to refute it. It was Hooke who, during his employ with Boyle, conducted him through most of Descartes's works; before that Boyle had indeed read only the *Passions*: Davis, "'Parcere Nominibus.'" But contrast Feingold, "Mathematical Sciences and New Philosophies," 411–2, for a dissenting view.

encounters with books at an early age. The natural historian Francis Willughby, like Boyle, was thought to have weakened his body during childhood by too much reading. Again like Boyle, he fought to become a model gentleman by struggling to regulate his "motions and desires," but never fully recovered. Still more disquieting was the experience of Abraham Cowley, who found that reading Spenser in his mother's parlor "made [him] a Poet as immediately as a Child is made an Eunuch." Even Queen Mary was thought to have been permanently damaged by her childhood reading.

Such experiences extended into adulthood too. Laudian scholar Peter Heylyn was one victim, his excessive reading engendering blindness as the "*Laboratory*" of his brain overheated and destroyed the crystalline humor of his eyes. Henry More advised Anne Conway not to read Descartes "with too much curiosity and solicitude," since it might exacerbate her persistent headaches. Rather later, the crypto-Jacobite virtuoso John Byrom used laudanum to treat his sister, Ellen, after noting that she had been "disturbed" by reading Clarendon. The treatment proved unsuccessful, and Ellen died. Many other examples could be cited, extending from the sixteenth through to the eighteenth centuries—and quite possibly beyond. From Boyle to Byrom, these diverse experiences were widely credited. They transcended place, time, sex, and social rank.[7] The message was as clear as it was disturbing. As much as it could facilitate learning and the communication of knowledge, reading had the power to determine one's future fate. It could blind, derange, and even kill.

Yet there were countermeasures. As much as Boyle's distemper was widely recognized, so too was his successful treatment well warranted. Francis Bacon himself had said that there was no "impediment in the wit" that could not be "wrought out by fit studies: like as diseases of the body may have appropriate exercises." "So if a man's wit be wandering," he had advised, "let him study the mathematics."[8] Such advice was commonly available in the seventeenth century, and there is no reason to suppose that it was not just as commonly followed. Boyle knew what he was talking about. Both his condition and its cure were widely accredited. Similar concerns affected both the concept and practice of reading for many men and women of his

---

7. Cowley, *Works*, 143–4; Willughby, *Ornithology*, sig. A2^{r-v}; Maccubbin and Hamilton-Phillips, *Age of William III and Mary II*, 4; Byrom, *Private Journal and Literary Remains*, I, 46–8; Barnard, *Theologo-Historicus*, 258–64; Vernon, *Life of . . . Peter Heylyn*, 6–7; Conway, *Letters*, 145. For Byrom's pietist reading practices see Schaffer, "Consuming Flame." The most famous reader to suffer blindness as a result was, of course, Samuel Pepys. Other examples are provided in Condren, "Casuistry to Newcastle." Such illnesses should be compared to those described in Porter, "Consumption."

8. "Of Studies," in Bacon, *Works*, VI, 497–8. Thomas Willis, too, suggested mathematics as a remedy: Willis, *Two Discourses concerning the Soul of Brutes*, 194.

age, first during their upbringing and later in mature life. The historian would therefore be unwise to disregard his testimony too hastily as simply naïve or erroneous. Such testimony was put to use in his own time, and it can now be put to use again.

This chapter does so. It examines the grounds and consequences of experiences like Boyle's. It argues that the powerful effects of reading to which he fell victim were not only widely attested, but supported by contemporary knowledge about human beings and the physical world they inhabited. In consequence, accounts of the practical experience of reading came to play a central role in arguments about the status of claims to knowledge, especially when such claims came to be controverted. In a Protestant nation, defining itself substantially through the collective and individual experiences of reading Scripture, such a conclusion was of particular importance. As this chapter shows, argument centering on professed religious knowledge became a peculiarly intense site for discussions of the nature, role, and consequences of reading. This was one reason why the representation of reading was of profound concern to pedagogic writers, who addressed the problems involved in creating good Protestant subjects—and therefore devoted considerable effort to explaining experiences like those of the young Boyle. It also helps to explain why concepts of reading became essential to the conventions adopted by the newest claimant to knowledge, the experimental philosophy.

Reading is a deceptively simple practice. It can seem so obvious and self-evident an activity that the idea of its having a history appears bizarre. But it is becoming increasingly clear that people in the past and of other cultures do not read in anything that might unproblematically be called the same way as us. Reading shares this characteristic with other, more manual skills the historical dimensions of which have also recently been identified.[9] The historicizing of reading has particularly important implications, however, for the simple reason that it is through reading that documents of all kinds are put to use and thereby produce historical effects. The history of reading is devoted to exploring this theme. It is now a flourishing field.[10] A wealth of work exists showing that if reading is considered as a practice that, like such other practices, changes across time and space, then useful insights may follow about the character of personal, political, and social knowledge. This chapter argues that the same holds true for natural knowledge.[11]

9. Sibum, "Reworking the Mechanical Value of Heat."

10. I shall not attempt a full bibliographical survey here. A survey of approaches is provided in Darnton, "History of Reading"; this should be supplemented by Sherman, *John Dee*, chap. 3.

11. Two examples are Chartier, *Cultural Origins of the French Revolution*, chaps. 2–4, and Chartier and Martin, *Histoire de l'Edition Française, II: Le Livre Triomphant, 1660–1830*, 521–58, 657–73, 801–21.

The experience of reading is extremely difficult to describe in words. If Collins's and Polanyi's arguments about the ineffable character of skill are correct, then capturing it may even be impossible.[12] The place of a reading practice, and its consequences as expressed in subsequent writings, are often traceable, being preserved in textual, pictorial, and material archives; but the immediacy of reading itself is not. Nevertheless, we may still hope to arrive at a useful understanding of how particular appropriations of books could come to be articulated in particular circumstances (and why others could not), why they had an impact, and why that impact was as it was.[13] The conventions adopted in the Stationers' court, which were investigated in chapter 3, and those developed at the Royal Society, which are the subject of chapter 7, are examples. Both could be assessed in terms of conventions of reading pursued in particular social spaces. The history of reading aims to trace and account for such dynamic processes, by appreciating the different practices by which readers in various times and places attribute meanings to the objects of their reading. It explains the global by rigorous attention to the local.

One approach to the subject lies through what Roger Chartier calls "object studies." This involves tracing the different appropriations accorded a single book as it traverses a number of distinct social spaces. Such studies combine attention to the book itself, with its format, layout, and typography—the cluster of characteristics connoted by the term *mise en page*—with research into the diverse conventions of reading in operation in its places of use.[14] An alternative is to concentrate not on one object, but on one reader. The opportunity to do this arises when such a reader has left traces of his or her reading, generally in the form of annotations on, or about, a set of books. The most impressive claims for the history of reading in Anglophonic historiography have probably been those based on the study of such annotations.[15] These traces are not necessarily rare. In the seventeenth century, especially, printed sheets bought at a bookshop would often be

---

12. Collins, *Changing Order*, chap. 3; Polanyi, *Personal Knowledge*.

13. Chartier, *Cultural History*, 6; Chartier, *Pratiques de la Lecture*, 8, 62; Martin, "Pour une Histoire de la Lecture"; Chartier, *Order of Books*, 16–17; Bourdieu and Chartier, "La Lecture."

14. Chartier, *Culture of Print*, 3; Chartier, *Cultural Uses of Print in Early Modern France*, 6–7; Chartier, "Texts, Printings, Readings"; Chartier, "Postface," 624–5; Chartier, *Culture of Print*, 4–5; Chartier, *Cultural History*, 11–12; Martin and Vezin, *Mise en Page et Mise en Texte du Livre Manuscrit*.

15. Sherman, *John Dee*, is the most sustained example of this work. Other important examples include Jardine and Grafton, "'Studied for Action,'" adapted as Grafton, "*Discitur ut Agatur*," and Grafton, *Commerce with the Classics*, esp. 185–224. A thoughtful defense of the approach is presented in Grafton, "Is the History of Reading a Marginal Enterprise?" esp. 155–6. The possibilities for the history of science are suggested by Gingerich, "Copernicus's *De Revolutionibus*."

regarded not as complete, but as remaining to be individualized by readers'
additions.[16] The study of the resulting hybrids, half printed book and half
unique manuscript, shows convincingly that "scholarly" reading, at least,
was, as Grafton and Jardine put it, a "goal-orientated" enterprise. It aimed
at immediate, active purposes, the "interpretation" of a given work varying
according to what those purposes were. The efforts of several historians have
provided us with an incipient taxonomy of annotation strategies that may
eventually revolutionize our understanding of how such interpretations were
constructed.

This chapter employs an approach rather different from these, but at the
same time one complementary to both object studies and the analysis of
annotations. It begins from experiences like Boyle's. In describing such powerful effects, Boyle's cautionary statements directed attention to what he
thought actually occurred at the decisive moment of face-to-face confrontation between reader and read. Historians have remained remarkably reti-
cent about this moment of confrontation, perhaps because it seems to embody so self-evident, so natural an act that there appears little they could
usefully say about it. Even historians of reading have largely left it alone. Yet
it ought to be central to an account of the history of reading, if only because,
as a matter of fact, descriptions of it have varied widely in different periods.
What is it that passes from page to mind when someone reads, and how
does it have an effect? This is the fundamental question with which the
analysis presented here begins. It is properly answered, however, not in our
own terms, but in those of early modern England.[17] The following account
does not propose that all individuals theorized the act of reading in the same
way—nor even that most theorized it at all. But it does identify the most
important anatomical, physiological, philosophical, and moral resources
available to them when they did need to understand it. And it shows that
when they wished to propose radical new kinds of knowledge, the need to
deploy those resources could become extremely urgent.

The most important resources available to early modern readers for describing their experiences derived from what contemporaries called the *passions*. Human beings perceived letters on a page through the mediation of
their bodies; the passions were the emotional, physiological, and moral responses of the human body to its surroundings, and thus played an unavoidable part in the reading process. This chapter provides an account of these
composite entities. They were discussed and analyzed by all branches of
society, providing an extensive array of knowledge usable in understanding
one's own and one's neighbors' conduct. The chapter argues that accounts

16. McKitterick, *History of Cambridge University Press*, xiii.
17. Robert Darnton calls in passing for such an approach in his "History of Reading,"
152. See also his "Readers Respond to Rousseau."

of reading generated with the aid of such knowledge became central to the attempted discrimination of true insight from dangerous error. Individuals who failed to control their passionate reading practices, and thereby fell prey to them, could then be diagnosed by a series of symptoms that were likewise understood in terms of the passions. And remedies could be proposed for them, disciplining the passions into conformity. By recovering this extensive and influential repertoire, the chapter provides a fresh perspective on the most personal aspects of reading. It also helps to bring the histories of reading and knowledge together.

SEEING PHYSIOLOGY

There is a fundamental problem with which to start. In early modern England, what was it to "see"? When one exercised vision, what actually passed through the air and into the eye, and how did it have an effect when it got there? Patrick Collinson has suggested that this question is really "where an account of protestant culture ought to begin." What follows will largely confirm his suggestion.[18] Once this problem has been addressed, we shall then be able to move on to the more specific question of how one saw letters on a page. These two issues are the subject of this section.

As an initial strategy, one can try interpreting Boyle's words at face value. "Prejudice," "fancy," "impressions," "habitude," "thoughts"—to an informed early modern reader these were readily recognizable terms. They were in regular use both in lay contexts and, more formally, in a variety of sciences relating to the mechanisms of perception and the workings of the mind. They should perhaps be read literally, then, to refer to processes of the mind and body. Knowledge of such processes was widely available in early modern England. It was staple to any number of discourses, ranging from everyday medicine, through casuistry and the moral advice of ministers, to highly specialized anatomical practice. Contemporaries felt able to use such resources to describe their experiences of perception and reasoning, including those involved in reading, and invested enough faith in them to act on those descriptions. The following discussion attempts to recover their knowledge and its uses.

Discussions of vision began with the eye. They typically represented it as the natural equivalent of a camera obscura (fig. 6.1).[19] This was a well-known

18. Collinson, *Birthpangs of Protestant England*, 122. An interesting examination of the physiology of viewing for a slightly earlier period is Summers's *Judgment of Sense*. Saenger, "Physiologie de la Lecture," "Silent Reading," and *Space between Words*, 1–17, use the perspective of modern physiology.

19. Kepler, *Ad Vitellionem Paralipomena*, 176–7; Molyneux, *Dioptrica Nova*, 103–4; Newton, *Opticks*, 9–11. Compare Locke, *Essay Concerning Human Understanding*, 162–3. See also Malet, "Keplerian Illusions," and Alpers, *Art of Describing*, 50–51 and passim.

FIG. 6.1. The eye represented as a camera obscura. (*left*) Beverwyck, *Werken*. (By permission of the British Library, 773.k.6.) (*below*) Scheiner, *Rosa Ursina*. (By permission of the Syndics of Cambridge University Library.)

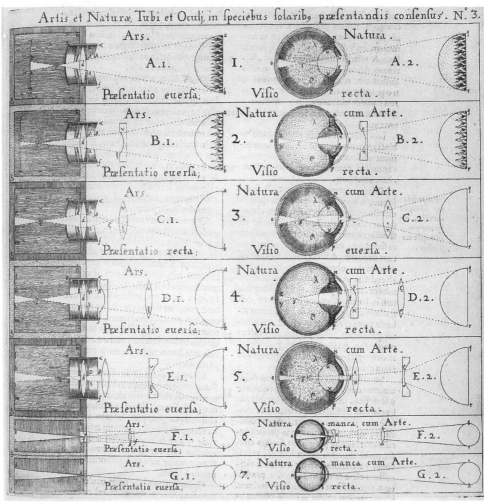

Artis et Naturæ, Tubi et Oculi, in speciebus solarib, præsentandis consensus. N.º 3.

device, familiar to a vast range of readers from Giambattista della Porta's *Natural Magick* and countless books of secrets. It could be made easily and bought cheaply. By 1655, Meric Casaubon could assume that most people "that have any curiosity" would have seen one, and the apparatus remained popular throughout the succeeding century, not least as an aid for drawing.[20]

A camera obscura consisted of a darkened chamber of any size, ranging from a small box to a room large enough to contain a human being, with a pinhole in one wall. Light admitted through this hole formed an inverted image of the scene outside on the opposite surface.[21] In the eye, correspondingly, an image was thought to be "imprinted" or "painted" (both words were used) on the retina. The process could be reconstructed using specimen eyes from cadavers or, human bodies being scarce commodities, from animals (fig. 6.2). William Briggs used sheep's eyes to demonstrate his own theory before the Royal Society. Based on such studies, artificial eyes could be constructed on the camera obscura model, Wren suggesting that one would represent a suitable gift for Charles II should he ever deign to visit the Society.[22] Such gadgets served to demonstrate the casting of an inverted image onto the retinal surface. From thence, it was assumed, "spirits" channeled in the optic nerves transmitted this image instantly to the brain. There it was again "impressed" onto something called the *sensus communis*, and thus perceived by the mind.[23] In what was by the Restoration probably the most influential general treatment of the subject, René Descartes famously placed this *sensus communis* at the pineal gland. Whether or not this was accepted, contemporaries universally believed that the *sensus communis* was imprinted at the same instant as the retina and in a manner mediated by the structure of the human body.[24]

Such a camera obscura model provided a convincing account of correct perception. But impressions incident upon the *sensus communis* need not come from the eyes. They could equally have originated from any of the senses of smell, taste, hearing, or touch. Or, more interestingly, they might not have derived from outside the body at all. For images produced by the imagination were apprehended by the same process of imprinting as those generated by the senses from exterior phenomena. Whenever the mind

20. Eamon, *Science and the Secrets of Nature*, 308; [Hoofnail], *Art of Drawing*, 7–9. Robert Boyle's operator gave an interesting account of the camera obscura and imaginative imprinting: G[regg], *Curiosities in Chymistry*, 72–82.

21. Porta, *Natural Magick*, 363–5; Casaubon, *Treatise Concerning Enthusiasme*, 43.

22. Briggs, *Ophthalmo-graphia*, 73–4; Briggs, *Nova Visionis Theoria*; Birch, *History*, I, 288–91, 391; IV, 136, 137, 203. A model eye was indeed stored in the Society's repository: Grew, *Musaeum Regalis Societatis*, 359. For Robert Boyle's experiments supporting the principle, see Royal Society Ms. Boyle P. 38, fols. 68ʳ–70ᵛ, 141ʳ–142ʳ.

23. Descartes, *Philosophical Writings*, I, 41–2, 166–7; Kepler, *Dioptrice*, 23–5.

24. Descartes, *Philosophical Writings*, I, 39–40, 152–6.

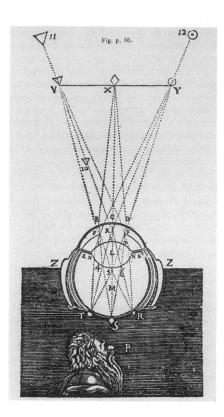

Fig. p. 36.

FIG. 6.2. René Descartes tests the camera obscura theory by peering through the eye of a bull. Descartes, *La Dioptrique*, in *Oeuvres*, VI. (By permission of the Syndics of Cambridge University Library.)

FIG. 6.3. (*above right, below*) The physiological mechanisms permitting perception and response. Descartes, *L'Homme*, in *Oeuvres*, XI. (By permission of the Syndics of Cambridge University Library.)

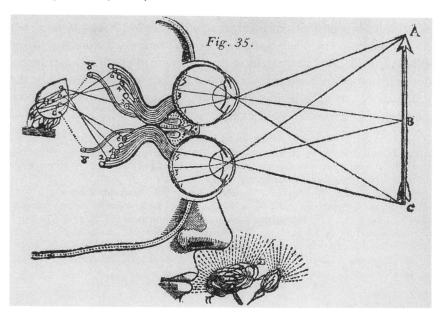

Fig. 35.

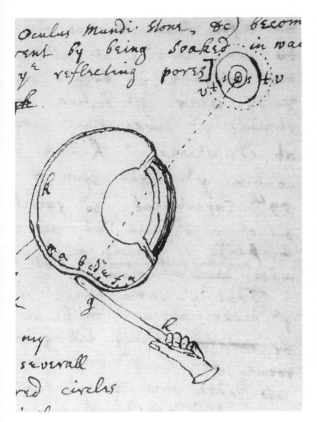

FIG. 6.4. Isaac Newton's description of experimenting on his own eye. This was one of an intermittent series of trials that Newton undertook privately over a period of at least a year in the mid-1660s. He had already concluded that his "fantasie" could excite the spirits in his optic nerve sufficiently to generate apparent images; now he "tooke a bodkin & put it betwixt my eye & yᵉ bone as neare to yᵉ backside of my eye as I could." Pressing the surface of his eye with this bodkin, he found that he could generate "white darke & coloured circles." Together the experiments illuminated the reliance of vision on physical and imaginative capacities. CUL Ms. Add. 3975, p. 15. (By permission of the Syndics of Cambridge University Library.)

either imagined or perceived an object, then, it was really considering an image traced on the surface of the *sensus communis*—and it could not always be sure which it was doing. Descartes himself therefore insisted that the term *idea* must be applied rigorously to any such "impressions," whether imaginative or perceptive in origin. Ideas of either source then acted as the spur to physical actions, the impulses inducing such actions being transmitted through the body by the same nervous system that mediated perception (fig. 6.3).[25]

This intimate and continuous interaction of body, imagination, and perception had at least one important consequence. It meant that camera obscura models of vision could never be as straightforward as their proponents had perhaps hoped. Far from having been rendered regular, and even mechanical, vision remained liable to corruption and counterfeiting, either by the imagination or by physiological conditions. Qualifications to camera obscura models accordingly became as routine as the models themselves. In

25. Descartes, *Philosophical Writings*, I, 42, 105–6.

fact, even Della Porta had noted the problem. Describing the camera obscura, he had remarked that observers had to be conditioned in order for it to function properly, because of the role of "affection" in conditioning perception.[26] Descartes, too, observed that his anatomical demonstration of the eye as a camera worked only as long as it kept its "natural" shape—"for if you squeeze it just a little more or less than you ought, the picture becomes less distinct."[27] Just what constituted proper squeezing he left unclear. And Isaac Newton endorsed such qualifications in his *Opticks*, which came to be recognized as the most authoritative of all discussions. Newton warned that vision could be corrupted if the eye were either colored, too "plump," or not plump enough. Only in the proper circumstances, and only if the perceived phenomena were not "produced or altered by the power of imagination," could knowledge of colors be considered a Newtonian science. This he had actually verified on himself, managing solely through the exercise of his "fantasie" to create an illusory perception of the Sun in his rooms at Trinity College, Cambridge (fig. 6.4).[28]

The structure of the brain and nervous system thus played an essential part in the reception, manipulation, and effects of ideas. Even with a camera obscura model of the eye, this part could not be gainsaid, since it was built into the human frame. On the contrary, it must be confronted and understood. Although mechanical philosophers might call in principle for explanations to be couched in reductionist terms, in practice this further understanding had to be physiological (and, as we shall see, even moral) in character. To account for the construction of knowledge from perceptions, one needed an appreciation of the "affections" attendant upon the human constitution.

The most significant contemporary account of this subject was to be found in the work of Oxford's Sedleian Professor of Natural Philosophy, Thomas Willis. In the early 1660s Willis undertook a series of detailed dissections of the brain and nervous system, accompanied by Richard Lower, who probably did much of the more grisly work, and by Christopher Wren, who drew the results.[29] Theirs was an epic enterprise. "Hecatombs" of cadavers were dissected—not only humans, but horses, sheep, calves, goats, hogs, dogs, cats, foxes, hares, geese, turkeys, fish, and even a monkey. In

26. Porta, *Natural Magick*, 363.

27. Descartes, *Philosophical Writings*, I, 167.

28. Newton, *Opticks*, 9–11, 48, 135–7; Westfall, *Never at Rest*, 93–5. For similar cases see Schaffer, "Self Evidence."

29. Willis, "The Anatomy of the Brain" and "The Description of the Nerves," in *Remaining Medical Works*, 55–136 and 137–92. For the circumstances surrounding this work see Willis, *Thomas Willis's Oxford Lectures*, 37–49, 52 ff.; Frank, "Thomas Willis and His Circle"; and Bynum, "Anatomical Method." The main source for anatomical work in the period is Frank, *Harvey and the Oxford Physiologists*.

London, Robert Boyle was kept informed of their labors, Walter Charleton repeated them, and Henry Oldenburg spread news of their findings across Europe.[30] Together these men created the most important work on neurology to be produced before the nineteenth century. And technical though it was, it proved extraordinarily influential in a range of contexts. Aspiring gentlemen were even exhorted to study it as a central part of their education. It was thereby also to prove of prime importance to representations of reading.[31]

It is important to convey some impression of the motivations driving Willis's enterprise, since that enterprise was a specific and unusual one. Willis was a convinced Church of England man, to the extent of having orchestrated clandestine Common Prayer services during the Interregnum. His project reflected this. Its printed representation, dedicated to his patron, the archbishop of Canterbury, revealed that Willis was not engaged in routinely didactic morbid anatomy. His true subject was what he called "Psycheology," or the "Discourse of the Soul."

Willis began from a widely shared belief that the soul was divisible into two parts: a rational component, which was immaterial, immortal, and intellectual, and a sensitive one, which was corporeal and mortal. The former could not be subjected to physiological study, but the latter could, and on this he focused. This "sensitive soul" conducted all the physical processes of perception and movement, acting through the vehicle of "animal spirits" sublimed from the blood and channeled through the nervous system. These were the same spirits as those that transmitted perceptions to the *sensus communis*. They were like internal, corporeal "Rays of Light," Willis declared: "For as light figures the Impressions of all visible things, and the Air of all audible things; so the Animal Spirits, receive the impressed Images of those, and also of Odors, and tangible Qualities." Their essence was the conveyance of perceptions. Imagination and perception were thus difficult to distinguish precisely because they depended on this same vehicle. It was a vehicle not confined to any particular organ, let alone to the mind, but "Coextended to the whole Body." Willis wanted his anatomy to elucidate its workings to the full.[32]

Believing that the sensitive soul functioned by the flow of animal spirits through material channels, Willis thought it possible to reveal those channels by anatomical practice. He especially hoped to identify in the brain

30. Birch, *History*, I, 416, 421–2, 436, 444; Oldenburg, *Correspondence*, II, 141–5, 300–9, 631–3.

31. Rousseau, "Nerves, Spirits, and Fibres"; Rousseau, "Science and the Discovery of the Imagination"; Mullan, "Hypochondria and Hysteria"; Lawrence, "Nervous System and Society in the Scottish Enlightenment."

32. Willis, *Two Discourses*, sigs. [A3^{v}]–[A4^{v}], 5, 18, 38 ff.

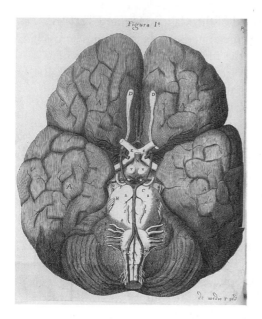
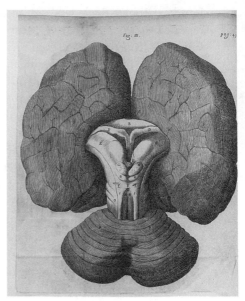

FIG. 6.5. Thomas Willis's anatomy of the human brain. These engravings show the brain
from the base (*left*) and the top (*right*). In (*left*), B is the cerebellum, C the "oblong
marrow," E the optic nerve, and F and G the motive and "pathetick" nerves of the eyes.
In (*right*), the halves of the brain have been pulled up and apart to reveal inner structures.
Here, P is the cerebellum, B the callous body (which in an intact brain would touch the
pineal gland, F), and E the oblong marrow. Willis, *Remaining Medical Works*. (By
permission of the Syndics of Cambridge University Library.)

physical features associated specifically with such functions as memory,
imagination, and the appetites. This required a novel method of dissection.
He advocated "a new way of opening yᵉ Brains," observers reported. Rather
than slicing horizontal sections through the head, he uncovered the brain
layer by concentric layer, thereby revealing "the order of Nature" (fig. 6.5).[33]
It was their embodiment in practice that lent such legitimacy to Willis's
views. His anatomical works were not just texts: they were representations
of practical procedure, performed before authoritative audiences, and this
afforded them their unique prestige.

Briefly, Willis's technique revealed two membranes enveloping the brain.
The first of these membranes was loose, and in four places it formed cavities
called "bosoms." Blood flowing into the brain collected in these bosoms,
before fine vessels carried it down into the interior of the head. Beneath lay

33. Willis, "Anatomy of the Brain," 55–62, 91, 95–7; Willis, *Two Discourses*, 23–5; Isler,
Thomas Willis, 25. For Willis's treatment of vision as analogous to the camera obscura, see
Two Discourses, 33, 75–86.

the second membrane, tightly fitting the three inner structures of cerebrum, "oblong marrow," and, to the rear, cerebellum. Its purpose was to distinguish these parts of the brain one from another, and thereby to act as a "fence" restraining the animal spirits in their proper "orbs."[34]

All physicians and anatomists knew that the animal spirits had their origin in the blood. But Willis could now discern exactly where, and hence how, they were generated. He could see within each of the bosoms a matrix of strong "Fibres" that, like "flood-gates," must control the flow of blood into the brain. Additional ligaments traversing the bosoms controlled their expansion and contraction.[35] Together these fibers regulated the flow of blood through the bosoms. When full, the bosoms acted as heat sources, gradually warming the blood flowing onward in tiny vessels beneath. Eventually, "as if it were a certain Chymical operation," this blood underwent a distillation. Its subtle extracts were then channeled toward the brain by vessels in the inner membrane, which, when injected with an ink solution, could be displayed to an audience as resembling "little serpentine chanels hanging to an alembic." Like this alchemical apparatus, they served as extra "distillatory Organs," rendering the refined blood still more "subtil and elaborated" as it proceeded. At length, they admitted only the finest "Chymical Elixir" into the inner brain, in the form of animal spirits. There they circulated "as in a publick *Emporium* or Mart" in a "free and open space" at the base of the brain. This was the "common Sensory"—the *sensus communis*. Here the brain registered the "Strokes of all sensible things." It was here that impressions from the senses and the imagination were combined, and remembered ideas received. This was also the center from which the animal spirits were "directed into appropriate Nerves" for all responsive actions. A "fountain" of animal spirits continuously flowed out from the *sensus communis*, through the spinal cord, to all parts of the body, there to "irradiate" it and spark such actions (fig. 6.6).[36]

The *sensus communis* was a space of open exchange, where the animal spirits mingled freely. But some differentiation of the motions they stimulated nevertheless remained. Most important, while the cerebrum was the site of imaginative and rationative actions, the cerebellum directed all those functions that did not rely on imagination, memory, or reason: that is, all the regular motions necessary for life. The nerves controlling respiration, nutrition, and similar functions derived their spirits from here. It seemed essential, indeed, that this distinction be maintained, for otherwise the most

34. Willis, "Anatomy of the Brain," 56–9, 81–4.
35. Willis, "Anatomy of the Brain," 80.
36. Willis, "Anatomy of the Brain," 79, 80, 82–3, 87–8, 93, 95, 96; Willis, *Thomas Willis's Oxford Lectures*, 54–6, 65–7.

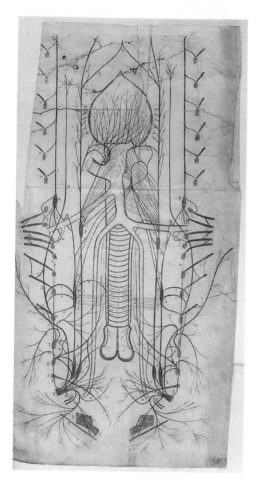

FIG. 6.6. The human nervous system.
Extending to all parts of the body,
this network of channels for the
animal spirits transmitted perceptions
to the brain and responses from it.
Willis, *Remaining Medical Works*.
(By permission of the Syndics of
Cambridge University Library.)

basic life-preserving activities of the body would have lain vulnerable to "the
winds of Passions and Cogitations." Yet even separated in this way they were
not immune, for a mechanically transmitted "sympathy" linked the spirits
in the cerebellum and those in the cerebrum, so that any passion excited in
the latter could still produce physical symptoms. In fact, whenever "a violent passion, as Joy, Sadness, Anger, [or] Fear" arose, its "impression" would
produce "notable mutations in the Organs." Hence someone subject to a fit
of rage, say, experienced changes in body temperature, heart rate, and stom-
ach functions.[37]

This, then, was the dynamic system in which vision and imagination
participated. Willis went on to describe how. He began by accepting the

37. Willis, "Anatomy of the Brain," 96, 108, 110–6; Willis, *Thomas Willis's Oxford Lectures*, 145–50.

camera obscura theory of the eye. On seeing an object, the "Optick Species" generated by the eye at the retina was transmitted through the optic nerves and into the brain. There a variety of things might happen. It might simply be reflected from the callous body back through the nervous system, yielding the sort of reflex action maintained even in sleep. But if it disturbed the spirits circulating in the *sensus communis*, then it gave rise to a passion. It could also pass still further into the cortex, when "it impresse[d] on it the image or character of the sensible Object." This generated a memory. Perception, imagination, and memory were therefore part of a single, continuous process. Seeing an object, imagining one, and reasoning with the resulting ideas and memories could never be separated from the circulation of the blood and the movements of the body.[38]

Willis showed how much a skilled anatomist could do to elucidate the nature, routes, and purposes of the animal spirits, despite the impossibility of actually seeing them in action. His work was exemplary of the efforts of anatomists and natural philosophers to understand and account for such processes. More than any other, however, it was Willis's description that became influential. The fundamentals of his account came to be widely known in succeeding years, and were put to use in an extensive range of debates. The notion that vision, imagination, and the body were intimately linked, long a commonplace, had been given a newly authoritative explanation. The proper way to approach that special instance of vision that was reading would therefore need to embrace both physiology and the faculties of the mind. Fortunately, Willis's anatomical investigations had led him to a readily available set of resources to aid such an approach: those developed in the extensive literature devoted to the passions.

A DISCOURSE OF THE PASSIONS

In order to appreciate the significance of that literature, it is necessary to grasp the meaning of the term *passion* in early modern England. Passions were "Apprehensions, resentments, or emotions of the Soul," caused by "some motion of the spirits." That is, they were the responses excited by the senses and other stimuli, such as the imagination, when they impressed the *sensus communis*: *passiones* correspondent to the *actiones* of motions impinging on the brain. They included and affected both reasoned and corporeal responses.[39]

38. Willis, *Two Discourses*, 33, 35–6, 55–60, 77–8; Willis, "Anatomy of the Brain," 63–4, 96; Willis, "Description of the Nerves," 139–40; Willis, *Thomas Willis's Oxford Lectures*, 54–6, 100; Frank, "Thomas Willis," 134.

39. Descartes, *Passions*, 23. One of the few modern writers to stress this relation of *passio* to *actio* was Collingwood: see his *Autobiography*, 128 n. 1, and *Principles of Art*, 219.

The wide scope of this definition meant that the range of early modern passions embraced some that we would not now recognize as passions at all, the desire for knowledge being a significant example. Their study, accordingly, was reckoned to be extremely important. The philosophy of the passions, wrote Catholic priest Jean Senault, might be less formally prestigious than other branches of learning, but in reality it was fundamental to them all. "For it is she that makes *Philosophers*, and which purifying their *understanding*, makes them capable of *considering* the wonders of *Nature*." In short, all knowledge rested on a foundation of knowledge of the passions. Such learning was "to *Philosophy*, the same as *Foundations* are to *Buildings*." Someone possessing adequate knowledge of—and thereby control over—the passions was in a good position to become "an *honest man*, . . . a good *Father* of a *Family*, a wise *Politician*, and an understanding *Philosopher*." Those without such knowledge would soon be forced to confess that "our Passions are chains, which make us slaves to all such as know how to manage them well" (fig. 6.7).[40]

In accordance with this principle, a large and popular literature had grown up—as extensive, probably, as that dealing with civility—describing the passions and drawing moral and practical conclusions from them. One of its contributing authors, René Descartes, had anticipated that by its title alone his own account of the passions would sell better than any of his other books; and the only one of his works that the young Boyle *would* admit to reading was this one.[41] Willis, Descartes, royal physician Walter Charleton, and others created a market for such discussions that was still flourishing in the mid–eighteenth century.[42] Willis's anatomical work, which demonstrated that every "passion of the sensitive Soul" affected both the physical body and its perceptions "whether we will or no," became one of their central foundations (fig. 6.8).

Chapter 2 argued that Stationers were amphibious creatures. They traversed what could be seen as essentially separate realms of commerce and civility. But there was a more profound sense, expressed by Sir Thomas Browne and others, in which every human being was a "great and true *Amphibium*." Each person was a soul forced to live in the alien environment of the body. It was therefore reasonable to consider the experiences, achievements, and anxieties of such a creature in terms of this disjunction. The

40. Senault, *Use of Passions*, sig. ci^v, 163. See also Kroll, *Material Word*, 219–23.
41. Descartes, *Passions*, sig. B3^v.
42. See, for example: Wright, *Passions of the Minde*; Reynolds, *Treatise of the Passions*; Descartes, *Passions*; Senault, *Use of Passions*; [Charleton], *Natural History of the Passions*; Mandeville, *Treatise of the Hypochondriack and Hysterick Passions*; Hutcheson, *Essay on the Nature and Conduct of the Passions and Affections*.

FIG. 6.7. Reason, enthroned, enchains the passions: an ideal sought by almost all readers but, it seemed, attained by few. Frontispiece to Senault, *Use of Passions*. (By permission of the Syndics of Cambridge University Library.)

discourse of the passions did just that.[43] Physicians and ministers, in particular, felt themselves qualified to use this branch of knowledge, which, traversing the gulf separating body from soul, embraced *embodied* morality—the morality of amphibians. As Bishop Edward Reynolds expressed it when introducing his own treatise on the subject, "whereas the principall acts of mans Soule are either of Reason and Discourse, proceeding from his Understanding; or of Action and Moralitie, from his Will; both these, in the present condition of mans estate, have their dependance on the Organs and faculties of the Body." With respect to the understanding, the body was "an Eye, through which it seeth"; with respect to the will, the body was "a

43. Browne, *Works*, I, 45, 66.

CREDULITY, SUPERSTITION, and FANATICISM.
A MEDLEY.

Believe not every Spirit, but try the Spirits whether they are of God: because many false Prophets are gone out into the World

Design'd and Engrav'd by W.ᵐ Hogarth.

1 John. C.iv.V.
Publish'd as the Act directs March.ʸ 15.ᵗʰ 1762.

FIG. 6.8. Superstition and the Passions. Hogarth's engraving, originally entitled "Enthusiasm Delineated," was intended to ridicule what its artist called "the Idolatrous Tendency of Pictures in Churches and prints in Religious books." At first designed to attack Catholics, in this state the engraving substitutes Methodists as its target. Various examples of "credulity" and "superstition" are prominent, including Mary Toft, the Surrey woman who had claimed to give birth to rabbits in 1726. On the right-hand side, a thermometer of passionate states appears, its summit being that of "raving" (the same state, perhaps, as that induced in the young Boyle by reading romances). The fount of the passions is a brain recognizably descended from the illustrated dissections of Thomas Willis. (By permission of Dr. K. C. Knox.)

Hand, by which it worketh." This being so, the body, while it did not possess an absolute dominion over reasoning, could exercise a "disturbing power." Its conditions and distempers affected the impressions perceived at the *sensus communis*, and could therefore distort the conclusions derived from them.[44] This was why the interaction between body, reason, and action that was summed up in the passions was so crucial to practical morality.

What made the passions especially problematic to such writers was the postlapsarian state of humanity. Before the Fall, everyone agreed, human apprehensions had been in perfect accord with nature. The senses had "made no false reports," and, being "uninterressed," had remained in conformity with Reason. The expulsion from Eden had destroyed this harmony, throwing distortive passions between the human mind and the rest of Creation. The corrupted senses of a representative early modern reader were therefore thought to be "subject to a thousand illusions." Guided by their passions, the mind was almost certain to go wrong.[45] Charleton, for one, declared that "most commonly *false Opinions* are occasioned . . . by our *Passions*."[46] The serious problem of knowledge that this implied was the reason why understanding the passions was so important. At stake were the discrimination of truth from falsity and the moral propriety of all actions resultant upon such discrimination.

Contemporary understanding of the passions was complex and highly developed and can only be summarized here. In any case, it was impossible to enumerate all the passions that could affect one's knowledge. The variety of impressions constantly arriving at the brain from the senses, memory, and imagination made their number simply too great. But writers nevertheless did frame a standard taxonomy in terms of which they and their effects could be discussed. First, they recognized a division between *metaphysical* and *physical* passions. These were relatively simple: the former were restricted to the rational soul, and were familiar to divines as the affections appropriate to religious contemplation, while the latter affected the sensitive soul through material, effluvial mechanisms. As well as these two relatively straightforward types, however, there also existed what writers called *moral* passions. These were much more complex, since they engaged the body and the soul in concert. It was in relation to these that writers articulated the full physiology of the passions.

The first stage in generating a moral passion occurred when the senses presented a *"new* and *strange* object" to the soul, thus "giv[ing] her hope

44. Reynolds, *Treatise of the Passions*, 3–5.
45. Senault, *Use of Passions*, sigs. c2ʳ–c4ʳ, 61, 105.
46. [Charleton], *Natural History of the Passions*, sig. A3ʳ; a similar point about the Fall is made in Reynolds, *Treatise of the Passions*, 5–6, 27–8.

of knowing somewhat that she knew not before." Instantly the soul "*ad-mire*[d]" this image. This admiration was the primary of all passions. It then entertained an "appetite" to know the object better, "which is called *Curiosity* or desire of Knowledge." Curiosity was thus the second passion. This passion was nothing less than "the mother of knowledge." On it depended all further intellectual inquiry; in particular, "all natural *Philosophy*, and *Astronomy* owe themselves to this passion." Typical genealogies then went on to recognize five more simple varieties of passion: love and hatred, desire, and joy and grief. All others were best regarded as compounds or species of these.[47]

There were ways of diagnosing such passions. Their concomitant motions of spirits, as Charleton reported, "change the very countenance, gestures, [and] walking." Writers thus linked a wide variety of visible symptoms, through the physiology of the passions, to processes of perception and imagination. For example, the primary passion, admiration, caused the animal spirits to be called into the brain to hold the image in place for consideration. Simultaneously they were also directed into the muscles holding the body in position and the eyes focused, so as to keep the organs in contact with the object. By such symptoms could it be recognized.[48] Such a repertoire of diagnostic signs permitted laypeople to become skilled interpreters of their neighbors' bodies. There is evidence that such knowledge was routinely used in the realm of face-to-face trust and suspicion described above in chapter 2. "Men judg of meanings by actions," observed Senault, "and read in the eyes, and face, the most secret motions of the soul." The benevolent use of such insight to temper one's own and others' social interactions was in large part what contemporaries meant when they spoke of prudence. By the same token, however, early modern citizens also became accustomed to concealing and "counterfeiting" their own passions. Governing the passions was essential if one were not to be left vulnerable to observers able to deploy skilled observation, and then employ what was called "craft" to put their knowledge to evil ends. Craft, to be precise, was the perversion of prudence: it was knowledge of the passions dedicated to immoral ends. Servants, with privileged access to the "upstairs" of one's premises and to one's less guarded moments, were among its more noted exponents. For those lacking such access, alcohol was a good way to circumvent dissembling

---

47. [Charleton], *Natural History of the Passions*, 75–89, 164. See also the similar genealogies in Descartes, *Passions*, 47–55, and [Ramesay], *Gentlemans Companion*, 139–82. For Willis on taxonomies of the passions, see Willis, *Two Discourses*, 45–55.

48. Willis had provided a detailed physiology for such phenomena, showing how, for example, contraction of the ligaments in the bosoms in conditions of "fear and great sadness" caused the blood to accelerate noticeably to the heart: Willis, "Anatomy of the Brain," 80.

strategies: a drunk, John Earle said, was "an *uncover'd man*," since "all his passions come out."[49]

In extreme cases, however, passions might prove not only revealing, but physically dangerous. The passion of admiration, for example, while harmless enough in normal circumstances, could produce "*Stupor*, or *Astonishment*"—perhaps even catalepsy—if suffered in excess. Such "immoderate" admiration could not but be harmful to the health. This was a pattern common to all the passions. Their physical symptoms merely revealed one's passionate state in normal circumstances, but became actively harmful in extreme ones. Physicians, above all, became familiar with the complaints accompanying such intense states. The symptoms they encountered included leanness, defects of nutrition, melancholy, scurvy, consumption, rheumatism, lameness, bloated faces, swollen limbs, amenorrhea, green sickness, fevers, and death. As Charleton warned, excessive passions could result in "the whole *Oeconomy* of nature" being "perverted."[50]

The problem of knowledge that the passions posed had not only personal implications, but also a much wider and even more serious political significance. The conflicts wracking seventeenth-century Europe were so violent, it was argued, because central to the human condition itself was a constant civil war. Human beings contained two distinct "faculties of *Knowing*": the understanding, which was seated in the rational soul, and the imagination, which was seated in the sensitive. Ideally, the faculty producing knowledge should have been the understanding.[51] However, the sensitive soul mediated between this faculty and the body that provided its raw materials, and was the main seat of both the imagination and the passions. By consequence a highly unstable entity, it was subject to both diseases of the body and "impressions of sensible *Objects*."[52] All reasoning was thus liable to be subjugated to a strife between the two candidates for knowledge. Neither could be dispensed with. Only the understanding could perform the essentially

49. [Charleton], *Natural History of the Passions*, 113–4, 159 ff.; Descartes, *Passions*, 88–90; Senault, *Use of Passions*, 159–62; [Earle], *Micro-cosmographie*, s.v. "A Drunkard"; [Charleton], *Brief Discourse concerning the Different Wits of Men*, 31–2, following Hobbes, *Leviathan*, 53. Anger was the other state in which passions were revealed. See also Charleton, *Brief Discourse*, 40–46, for citation of Willis on the site of the soul and the mechanisms of perception. For the practices of prudence see Shapin, *Social History of Truth*, 238–42. Images of faces in various passionate states were provided by Le Brun as what Revel calls "an alphabet of the passions that everyone had to learn to read": Le Brun, *Method to Learn to Design the Passions;* Revel, "Uses of Civility," 170.

50. [Charleton], *Natural History of the Passions*, 89–92, 109–10, 141–3; Wright, *Passions of the Minde*, 61–3.

51. [Charleton], *Natural History of the Passions*, sigs. A3ᵛ–A4ʳ, 2–3. For the divisions of the soul, see Park, "Organic Soul."

52. [Charleton], *Natural History of the Passions*, 9–10, 22–5.

judicial processes of constructing "trains of notions convenient either to Speculation, or to practice." These "royal prerogatives" meant that only the rational soul was properly entitled to "the whole *Encyclopaedia* or Zodiac of *Arts* and *Sciences*; *Theology, Logic, Physic, Metaphysics, Mathematics, Algebra, Geometry, Astronomy, Mechanics*." All these sciences were properly regarded as "the products or creatures of Mans *Mind*" (with the possible exception of theology, which was of a higher order). Nonetheless, that mind still relied on the sensitive soul for the ideas with which it worked. The imagination alone was sufficient to compound and divide sensations, thus forming ideas. A constant "*intestin war*" raged between the two, as Willis himself testified. The "twofold Knowing Power" in every subject, he declared, led necessarily to "wicked Combinations, troublesom Contests, and more than Civil Wars." It was a vital struggle, on the outcome of which rested the fate of every individual human being, and hence that of the polity as a whole. If the sensitive soul won, then the "divine *Politie*" of the rational soul would be lost forever to "the brutish lusts of the insolent usurper," and hence to its appetite for "triumphs of libidinous carnality." Moralists might with justification say that the devil "mingles himself with our most intimate corruptions, and the Seate of his warfare is the inward man." In Willis's terms, the sensitive appetite "seduces in us the Mind or Chief Soul, and snatches it away with it self, to role in the Mud of Sensual Pleasures." Charleton for one considered this the more likely outcome, "for, it is from the *Imagination* alone that [the soul] takes all the representations of things, and the fundamental *ideas*, upon which she afterward builds up all her *Science*."[53]

Proposals to tackle this problem of knowledge consequently lay at the heart of attempts to reconstruct some degree of social and moral order out of the chaos of the Civil War—and, more widely, of the Thirty Years' War. In their various ways, such diverse figures as Charles I, Thomas Hobbes, and even the notorious republican Algernon Sidney all aimed at producing polities that could successfully discipline the inescapably passionate nature of humanity and channel it to correct ends.[54] As we have seen in chapter 4, John Streater's republicanism also partook of this aim. Their answers depended on proper forms of self-discipline, social organization, literary representation, and communication. As that implies, reading and writing were profoundly implicated. Reading consequently became an important ele-

53. [Charleton], *Natural History of the Passions*, sig. A4ᵛ ff., 48–50, 54–9, 64; Browne, *Works*, I, 29–30; Lawrence, *History of Angells*, 1, 35–40; Willis, *Two Discourses*, sig. A2ᵛ, 42–3. Compare Sawday, *Body Emblazoned*, 16–22, 36, for a different account of this microcosmic conflict.

54. Sharpe, *Personal Rule*, 189–91, 227–30; Hobbes, *Leviathan*, 37–59, 483–91; Scott, *Algernon Sidney and the English Republic*, 35–8.

ment—perhaps *the* important element—in these civil wars of both microcosm and macrocosm. The immediate reason for this lay in the very fundamentals of the practice, beginning, again, with vision.

In many instances the exercise of visual perception seemed fairly straightforward, as when one simply "saw" a block of wood. The camera obscura
model accounted for these cases perfectly well. But even in such straightforward perceptions, as everyone acknowledged and Willis explained, vision was necessarily refracted through the natural economy of the passions.
There were other cases in which this became extremely clear, because some
active conditioning of that economy must be involved in them. Speaking,
listening, writing, and reading were examples. In each of these cases, simple
camera obscura–like perception must necessarily be abetted by a degree
of unconscious conditioning. An agreed account of this conditioning was
widely available, according to which "habits" had grown up in each individual facilitating the practice in question. The motions of the animal spirits, and thence the passions and imagination, in response to certain particular sensations had been regularized over long periods of repetition. A habit
of this sort was in effect a tamed, artificial passion. In learning to speak, for
example, one "habituated" the motions of the spirits so that one had only
to imagine what one wished to say, rather than specifying the countless individual movements of the body that together produced audible speech. The
"habit" acquired in developing speech, said Descartes, had "taught us to
joyn the action of the Soul, . . . the tongue, and the lipps, with the signification of the words which follow out of these motions, rather than with the
motions themselves." Similar habituation allowed a subject to understand
speech immediately, without having to undergo a conscious parsing of heard
sounds into intelligible syllables. And it was again habituation that permitted one to read words "by the figure of their letters, when they are written."
Accustomed responses rendered the translation of seen images into legible
characters virtually instantaneous and entirely indiscernible. Reading itself
depended upon a habituated passion.[55]

The concept of habits was also central to the essential task of disciplining
and pacifying the passions themselves. Habits were held to be the best hope
an individual had of countering immoral, unhealthy, excessive, or erroneous
passions. Habituation provided the key to exerting some practical "Regulation" or "mitigation" of them and their effects. Such action was regarded as
essential for English gentlemen. Without effective control of their passions,
human beings remained slaves to their own corporeality, denied the freedom

---

55. Descartes, "Règles pour la Direction de l'Esprit," in *Oeuvres*, X, 412; Descartes, *Passions*, 35–6, 43–4; Lawrence, *History of Angells*, 1.

of action definitive of the gentle state.[56] Although the rational soul could not simply remove such passions, it could perhaps habituate the individual to physiological responses taming them. There were two principal means by which this might be effected, both of which could be seen to depend on the labyrinthine matrices of vessels in the brain that Willis had revealed. First, one could imagine objects producing a passion contrary to that being experienced. Pursued intensely and at length, this could eventually produce a habit separating the motions of the blood and spirits from the impressions to which they would naturally be consequent, by accustoming them to passing through alternative channels. And second, one could learn to delay judgment of an impression, perhaps by doggedly reciting the letters of the alphabet or the Lord's Prayer. This would allow the turbulence of the spirits to recede, permitting the rational soul a more detached interpretation.[57] Contrariety and hesitation: these were the routes to virtue. Senault in fact proposed that the history of the arts and sciences constituted a series of "documents" of such efforts, urging that "the government of Passions is of such importance, and so difficult, as the better part of sciences seem only to have been invented to regulate them."[58]

The habituation process reckoned so fundamental to reading was thus the same as that proposed as the solution to the political problem of the passions. This was one reason why both Hobbes and Locke reckoned habituation "the great Thing to be minded in Education." "Education, and Discipline" were conceived to be vital for channeling and restraining the passions. Prudence should be cultivated; its depraved counterpart, "craft" or "cunning," must be shunned.[59] Locke believed that "the great Principle and Foundation of all Vertue and Worth" was "that a Man is able to *deny himself* his own Desires, cross his own Inclinations, and purely follow what Reason directs as best, tho' the appetite lean the other way," and insisted that education was the key to "imprinting" such prudence. He envisaged education in terms of the instilling of "Habits" into the minds of children by "little, and almost insensible Impressions." His recipe for bringing up young gentlemen was therefore strongly reminiscent of many recommended remedies for excessive or inappropriate passions. "By repeating the same Action till it be grown habitual in them, the Performance will not depend on Memory,

56. [Ramesay], *Gentlemans Companion*, 183–214, esp. 183.

57. Descartes, *Passions*, 36–7, 171; [Charleton], *Natural History of the Passions*, 182–5; [Ramesay], *Gentlemans Companion*, 184–5.

58. Senault, *Use of Passions*, 105, 165–73. For Hobbes on the possibility of "imprinting" passions on the mind of an audience, see *Leviathan*, 56.

59. [Locke], *Some Thoughts Concerning Education*, 18; Hobbes, *Leviathan*, 483–4; [Charleton], *Brief Discourse concerning the Different Wits of Men*, 31–2, following Hobbes, *Leviathan*, 52–4.

or Reflection," he insisted, "but will be natural." By following this strategy to eradicate every unwanted habituation, the tutor could eventually "weed them out all, and plant what Habits you please." Bowing to a gentleman, for example, would become "as natural . . . as breathing."

According to Locke, only one appetite was carefully to be fostered by the pedagogue: the passion of "*Curiosity*." This was because his aim should be to inculcate "a love of Credit." The inescapable role of curiosity in the pursuit and acquisition of knowledge made it a central element in the formation of a gentleman. Its importance applied especially in the process of learning to read, which must be encouraged by manipulating a child's curiosity through its desire for enjoyment. The early development of reading skills demanded delicacy and care. Choosing the right materials, and ensuring that children approached them in the right ways, would rarely be straightforward, and mistakes at this stage could result in danger later. The provision of cautionary advice started early. Parents were urged "above all" to keep their offspring from pamphlets, "the *Primers* of all Vice." One manual of childbirth opened by showing that printing had done more harm than guns, by at least a factor of ten. And even Locke himself seemed unsure what to recommend from the many titles competing for parents' favor. But in the end he insisted that early reading experiences must be in the form of games, not chores. By such means, he claimed, "Children may play themselves into what others are whipp'd for." When they graduated to reading their first books, works such as Aesop would be most suitable, since they combined moral lessons with "entertainment." Editions with pictures were best of all, since the images would provide a Lockean child with the necessary "Idea's" to comprehend the text. To disregard this advice and set formal tasks was to risk permanently damaging the children in one's care. "Neither their Minds nor Bodies will bear it," Locke warned. "It injures their Healths." [60]

Locke believed that education made his contemporaries "*Well fashion'd*" and able to display an "internal Civility of the Mind." And there is evidence that English subjects were indeed fashioned in this way. Throughout the early modern period, and on into the Victorian era, practicing tutors put just such notions of the nature of the child into effect, especially during the most elementary stages of education. Their catechizing and similar techniques were not (or not just) the mindless rote-learning drudgery familiar from later caricature. In fact, they rested explicitly on the assumption that correct habits must be imprinted on children while they were still malleable, and improper appetites drained of all potency through constant drilling.

---

60. [Locke], *Some Thoughts Concerning Education*, 33–4, 64, 175–89; Quarles, *Enchiridion*, century 4, no. XCIX; Oliver, *Present to be Given to Teeming Women*, "To the Christian Reader."

The resulting pedagogic practices, and the genres of literature they employed, helped form generations of men and women. Representations of the physiology of reading were thus perhaps instrumental in creating an entire British population notoriously ready to rein in its passions.[61]

But improper education could be correspondingly harmful. Bemoaning his own wandering mind, Boyle himself remarked on the misery attending "Persons that are borne with such Busy Thoughts, not to have congruent Objects propos'd to them at First."[62] Citing Willis, John Webster likewise argued that an "evil education" could cause "a most deep impression of the verity of the most gross and impossible things" to be "instamped in [pupils'] fancies, hardly ever after in their whole life time to be obliterated or washt out." He thought this true especially of pupils of melancholic disposition. It was a conventional opinion—and it meshed perfectly with Boyle's diagnosis of his own reading of romances. A poor education could instill inappropriate habits into the human frame, and thereby condition the subject for the rest of his or her life to experience improper, and perhaps even harmful, responses while reading. Unfortunately, not all pupils were appropriately trained. Physicians, Willis among them, became as accustomed to treating the symptoms of improper or excessive reading as those of the passions. They found that excessive reading could bring on a vast range of conditions. Many of them were experienced disproportionately by women, as could be explained readily enough in terms of the heightened sensitivity regularly attributed to the female body. One seventeenth-century physician thus noted that his patients complained to him that their reading brought on insomnia, breathlessness, trembling, upset stomachs, vertigo, headaches, ringing ears, "rising" sensations, and swooning. Such complaints persisted in the face of even the most fearsome seventeenth-century remedies.[63] For women in particular they were to prove highly consequential.

PASSIONATE VISIONS:
READING, CREDIT AND EXPERIMENTAL FAITH

Protestantism rested on Scripture. In reading lay its definition, practice, power, and propaganda. Accounts of what constituted creditable Scripture

61. Green, *Christian's ABC*, 233–43; Spufford, "First Steps in Literacy."

62. Boyle, "Account of Philaretus in his Minority," in Hunter, *Robert Boyle by Himself and His Friends*, 8–9.

63. Macdonald, *Mystical Bedlam*, 174, 181–3, 185–92, 288 n. 59; compare Willis, *Oxford Casebook*, 145–6 for a case involving Willis himself as physician. For women's experiences of such illnesses and remedies see also Beier, *Sufferers and Healers*, chap. 8. For the construction of passions and sensibility in the eighteenth century, see Barker-Benfield, *Culture of Sensibility*, 1–36. In the late eighteenth century, Benjamin Rush recorded the rumor that booksellers sometimes became deranged as a result of their sudden movements from one book to another: *Medical Inquiries*, 37 (a reference I owe to Steven Shapin).

and what idolatrous forgery, of how Scripture should be represented and read, and of what effects it should have on which readers consequently stood at the heart of its identity.[64] The making of authoritative, recognized texts of Scripture—the Authorized Version being by far the most important—structured its history. But Protestants felt themselves under threat. The dangers posed by popery, superstition, enthusiasm, and atheism appeared both all too real and all too united.[65] In these circumstances, the credit of books professing religious knowledge became a key battleground. And arguments connecting the reading of Scripture to the human frame and the soul became central to the discrimination of true faith from error, and even from heresy.

This was most prominently displayed in the combats, well known to historians, over what antagonists called "enthusiasm." As defined by two of its major opponents, Henry More and Meric Casaubon, enthusiasm was "nothing else but a mis-conceit of being *inspired*." It was the conviction, held especially by some of the Interregnum's more notorious religious radicals, that at certain moments God would enter into direct communication with them, and that at such moments he would grant them privileged knowledge by immediate personal revelation.[66] Such a belief clearly warranted drastic action on the part of its holder. It threatened social upheaval of unlimited extent and duration. Whether or not it actually incited violent rebellion, this led to its increasing stigmatization as a leading cause of the Civil War. More and Casaubon in the 1650s, and the Latitudinarians thereafter, were in the front line of the assault. Their campaign against enthusiasm has long been identified as an element in the articulation of "modest" schemes for experimental learning, although again the true extent of its importance remains controversial. This section presents a new account of enthusiasm and its repudiation. It argues that concepts of the passionate character of reading, and of the proper self-management that they demanded, were central to the experiences and arguments of both "enthusiasts" and their enemies. The debate over enthusiasm was a debate over the political and personal ramifications of reading.

It is appropriate to begin with the experiences recorded by an enthusiast himself. John Rogers, born in 1627, is an excellent candidate. He was among the most notorious of all enthusiasts, and, for reasons shortly to become clear, we can trace the role of reading in Rogers's development with

64. This is adumbrated in Kroll, *Material Word*, 239–74.
65. E.g., Hickes, *Spirit of Enthusiasm Exorcised*, sig. A2ᵛ, 37–9; Baxter, *Holy Commonwealth*, 31; [Ramesay], *Gentlemans Companion*, 19, 21.
66. [More], *Enthusiasmus Triumphatus*, 1–2; Casaubon, *Treatise Concerning Enthusiasme*, title page, 3, 17. For the origins and scope of the term, see Heyd, *"Be Sober and Reasonable,"* 15–23. These characterizations, of course, were polemical and contested: Smith, *Perfection Proclaimed*, is the best attempt to recover "enthusiasts'" own perspectives.

exemplary clarity. Rogers's life was repeatedly punctuated by two kinds of confrontation with God: reading and visions. Hellfire sermons heard in his boyhood had filled him with terror, and, propelled by his fear, he had scoured the Scriptures. The young Rogers had "*read* every day," he recalled: "I knew not what I *read*, but only thought the *bare reading* was enough." He learned his catechism by heart, reciting it as a talisman against the demons he knew were lurking under every bush; he wrote down the sermons he heard, and learned those too; he memorized morning and evening prayers, "out of a *book*, for I knew no better yet." All this reading threw Rogers into despair over his prospects for salvation, and he descended into suicidal despondency. Distraught, he "took the *Bible*," turned to the relevant pages, and "read them over and over and over again." It did little good: "the more I *read* the more I *roar'd* in the *black gulf* of *despair*." He would "*read*, and weep, and . . . fall flat (all along) with my face on the *ground*, and cry, and *call*, and sigh, and *weep*, and *call* for help." At length Rogers gave up reading altogether, feeling tempted to conclude that "there was no *God*" and that "all things come by *Nature*." It was a classic symptom of the despair leading to atheism and damnation.[67] He began to see demons not just under the bushes but in them, and to sit up all night in a turret in his father's orchard, wailing and drawing strange figures. Finally, as he was about to commit suicide, he was seized and tied to a bed until his fits subsided.

From this point Rogers's condition had improved somewhat, stabilizing at an "inward *malady*" of "*melancholy*." He dreamed about Scripture itself—"the *letter which killed me*"—and that the righteousness of Christ would be sufficient for his salvation. He awoke from this dream transformed. Rogers had long acknowledged that his dreams "*seised* much upon my *spirits*." But he had regarded them as products of his own "*fancy*" (that is, his imagination). This dream was different: far from emerging out of his body, it had transformed it. "I was so much changed that I was *amazed* at my self," he recalled. Now it was his previous reality that seemed imaginary. He leaped up, exclaiming, "Why, I am not *damned*! what's the *matter*? am I so filled with a *fancy*?" Again his response was to turn to the Bible. He pored over its pages with new attention until, "*divine infusions* . . . *writing* it within me," he achieved "*assurance* of *salvation*." It was only now that Rogers could begin "plainly to see *my self* (and by my self others)."

Expelled from his family's home, Rogers wandered to Cambridge. There he called the devil's attempts to lure him into necromancy a "*passion*." He would "fall to prayer [or] reading" in an attempt to ward it off. At his lowest

---

67. Pantheism was a stereotypical "atheistic" opinion: e.g., Hill, *World Turned Upside Down*, 139–40.

ebb, reduced to near-starvation in a Cambridge garret, Rogers had another dream. He dreamed that he was walking, staff in hand, to his father's house. At first he could hardly see the path, and even began to question its existence; but at length he noticed footprints from others who had passed the same way before. He followed them, and as he did so the path became clearer. Before long a fine mansion appeared to his left, from which emerged a beam of light that partially blocked Rogers's way. He walked around it. But as he did so he happened to touch the beam, and the house immediately burst into flame. He was soon overtaken by an angry posse violently accusing Rogers himself of having started the conflagration. The furious mob dragged him off to prison, at which, terrified, he awoke.

Finding himself safe in his Cambridge garret, Rogers chided himself for being scared at "a foolish *fancy*." He fell asleep again. But immediately he sank back into the same dream, which repeated itself from beginning to end—except that this time Rogers the pilgrim found himself accompanied by an old, bearded man, who provided reassurance that God had selected him to preach his Word. This "*grave ancient man*" proceeded to interpret the whole of Rogers's dream from within the dream itself. The house represented heaven, his father, God, and his staff, God's Word. Rogers would be troubled by the various ways of men, he but would follow the example (the footprints) of the saints and would find his path becoming clearer. The magnificent house represented the "*great* ones of the world." They were at present proud and ostentatious, and Rogers was to preach against them— the beam represented the cluster of powers and opinions he must circumvent in order to do so. The worldly powers would soon fall, but they would pursue Rogers and blame him for their catastrophe. With that, Rogers awoke again and found that it was finally dawn. The Cambridge "*dream* and *vision*," as he now called it, changed Rogers to the extent that his entire identity was transmuted. As he himself succinctly put it, "*I am not I.*" Assured of salvation, and with his self freshly refashioned, Rogers set forth on a pilgrimage that would lead to both Fifth Monarchism and, eventually, medicine.[68]

Preaching in Dublin in the early 1650s, Rogers collected from his listeners a long series of what he called "experiences," which he later caused to be printed. The origin of these testimonies lay in the procedure for admitting new members to his church. Before joining, he explained, every would-be congregant must attest to "some EXPERMENTAL [*sic*] Evidences of the *work* of GRACE upon his SOUL . . . whereby he (or she) is *convinced*, that he is *regenerate*." That is, everyone was expected to provide a record (often an oral

68. Rogers, *Ohel*, 419–38.

record, since the subject was unlikely to be an accomplished writer) of a transformation such as Rogers himself had enjoyed—a transformation, that is, into a new and "assured" self. This was summed up in a simple formula: "Experience, we say, *proves principles*."[69] Rogers's own Cambridge "experience"—indeed, his entire self-fashioning as constructed in this extensive testimony—constituted his personal contribution to this effort. The history presented here was an artifact of his experimental faith.

Rogers's own experience was innocuous compared to some of his congregants', which reflected in full the disease, murder, and war destroying Irish life in the 1640s. Yet the resulting accounts do betray certain common characteristics, showing the extent to which Rogers's experience was typical of so-called enthusiasts. Like Rogers himself, his subjects had often been brought up in families they described as godly. But they had at first practiced merely what they called "book" (or "legal") religion. They had then passed through a critical period, characterized as a death and rebirth, and emerged transformed, assured of their salvation. The conversions themselves generally came about by one or more of a relatively small number of possible mechanisms that, it was said, "wrought upon" and thereby "affected" the individual concerned. Hearing sermons, reading books, and having visions were the three main ones. Each was described in intimate terms. In each case success was then ascribed to the holy spirit's having "wrought" within the subject: their accounts of reading Scripture, for example, often displayed a sense of helplessness before the Word. Thus one Raphael Swinfield described how he was first "*affected*" by hearing Puritan preachers, becoming "*disconsolate*" and "*diseased*." Then, he related, a "place in *Isa*. 50.10. came into me" and "*fasten*[ed] upon me," insisting that Swinfield should trust in God. To reinforce the point, he had a dream that convinced him of his assurance. John Cooper was also converted by a dream, as were a number of others. Francis Bishop, condemned to be shot, "turned open the *Bible*" and read a passage enjoining him to trust in God; when he resolved to do so, he was freed. Hugh Leeson was first "wrought upon" by his wife, "whom *God* made the *first Instrument* of my *good*; by her often *reading* of the *Scriptures* to me . . . and by the *Spirits working* within me, with it." Adrian Strong testified that "by the word preached, and read out of *good Books* and the *Bible*, I was brought in to *God*." Finally, Mary Barker was converted by all means short of visions: by "*preaching*, and *praying*, and *reading*, in *private* and *publique*."[70]

69. Rogers, *Ohel*, 354–5, 362.
70. Rogers, *Ohel*, 396–8, 398–402, 407, 409, 411–12, [2, 9–10 (new pagination)], 413–4. Margaret Aston describes the articulation of death and resurrection as a motif in iconoclasm: *England's Iconoclasts*. I, 460.

These people, whose testimony was either written down by themselves or taken down from their own words, claimed that visions—and inspiration in general—occurred in definite cultural and practical conditions. They particularly stressed their experiences of reading Scripture, and how those experiences changed in the course of their descent into "disease" and transforming ascent into "assurance." In fact, one could characterize their personal experiences as transformations in reading practices.[71] The torpid routines of "book religion" were swept aside as God "irradiated" them directly during their exposure to Scripture. Radicals even referred to themselves as possessing an internal "Book of Conscience," "imprinted" by God's spirit to produce their visions. Appropriating mystical, alchemical, and Paracelsian sources, they spoke of the imagination, or "fancy," representing such images to the reason, which could then elaborate them into knowledge.[72] Analyzing their "experiences" of reading thus meant representing states of mind and of the body simultaneously. Rogers and his like clearly thought about the body as well as the soul. Some actually pursued medicine: William Walwyn, Laurence Clarkson, and Abiezer Coppe practiced physic, while Rogers himself eventually gained medical degrees from both Utrecht and Oxford. Medical practitioners or not, however, radicals commonly described their religious transformations by reference to the passions.[73]

This being so, it should not be surprising that women in particular found their experiences transforming. As Mack remarks, "seventeenth-century men and women *felt* certain kinds of knowledge"—and women felt them more strongly than men. Their bodies, conventionally represented as far more sensitive than those of men, purportedly rendered them all the more prone to the passions. That was why they were deemed particularly susceptible to the pathologies of reading, such as the violent headaches experienced by Anne Conway and Queen Mary. But it also had more ambivalent consequences in a society that denied advanced educational opportunities to almost all women. On the one hand, female creativity of all kinds was liable to denigration and distrust as a mere product of the passions. It was thus readily identifiable, as chapter 2 showed, with other supposedly female traits such as gossip, inconstancy, and even infidelity. To hostile eyes, the women prophets of the 1640s and beyond therefore merely displayed with unusual

71. Compare also the transformation of Jane Turner "by reading": Turner, *Choice Experiences*, 11–13, 49–58, 64, 82–3, 86, 198.

72. Smith, *Perfection Proclaimed*, 73–8; Rogers, *Ohel*, 375–6, 449–50.

73. Smith, *Perfection Proclaimed*, 5, 11, 13–17; Smith, "Charge of Atheism," 157–8. Some radicals even displayed themselves as contracting "divinely instituted madness": Smith, *Perfection Proclaimed*, 26–9, 32–5, 38–9, 50, 56, 57 n. 117. For other examples see Turner, *Choice Experiences*, 36–8; Henry, "Matter of Souls," 89, 95.

vividness a physiological difference that existing medical and ethical authorities insisted to be universal between the sexes. On the other hand, however,
male scholars could also choose to see this sensitivity as liberating. Themselves irredeemably reliant on the tortuous mechanisms of reason, they
might envy the untutored immediacy with which women prophets could
seem to experience their "conversations with God." John Rogers himself
remarked that women were often quicker to perceive spiritual truths than
men, since they were "more readily wrought upon."

This had immediate consequences extending beyond the epistemic value
attached to women's readings. Through their claims to privileged knowledge, it affected the development of women's authorship itself. As noted
in chapter 2, women authors began to appear on an appreciable scale only
in the 1640s. When they did, most were prophets newly transformed by
the kinds of experience just described. About three hundred women are
known to have become vociferously active in the radical religious movements thrown up by the disorder of the Civil War. Inspired, as Rebeckah
Travers put it, not by "ink and paper" but by "spirit, life, and power,"
many either published their experiences or saw them published by others.
The contrast was qualitative as well as quantitative. The most prolific
woman writer of the sixteenth century had probably been Queen Elizabeth
I; the most prolific of the entire seventeenth was Lady Eleanor Davies, the
extraordinary prophet who emerged at Charles I's court and remained active into the 1650s.

This unprecedented development sprang directly from arguments exploiting the physiology of reading. For once, the peculiar predicament in
which contemporary representations of female nature placed them allowed
women to venture into print while averting conventional charges of immod-
esty and insubordination. Some actually attempted to transcend a realm of
epistemic authority that was so consistently gendered by denying their wom-
anhood altogether. Several explicitly claimed to have *become* men — not just
by adopting male pseudonyms, but by announcing themselves as possessing
male souls in their female bodies. These were surely the most amphibious
of amphibians. Even more radical was the strategy of suppressing one's human nature altogether. Some could infer such suppression even while preserving the unique female sensitivity to visions generated through the passions. Appropriating traditional forms dating from the Middle Ages, women
thus testified while struck dumb, while in a trance, or while emaciated and
bedridden in the grip of a harrowing fast. What more legitimate authority
for publication could there be than a direct message from the Holy Spirit,
apprehended with vivid intensity and unshackled from the corrupt forms
of human learning? The possibilities opened up by this unanswerable ques-

tion survived the Restoration and changed the conditions of authorship for good.[74]

Such possibilities were always likely to raise terrors in many minds. John Rogers, Rebeckah Travers, Mary Cary, Elizabeth Poole—these were precisely the people whom Samuel Parker, Henry More, Meric Casaubon, and others had in mind when they condemned "enthusiasts." Medical knowledge could be of value on their side of the conflict too. Antienthusiast polemics generally charged that talk of inspiration was either deliberate imposture or evidence of madness. Credit and the human frame were brought into collision in such polemics. The imagination was well known to be unstable and capricious, the seat of "distempers" affecting the mind. "Without better evidence then their bare word," Joseph Sedgwick argued in 1653, "we may modestly suspect that [enthusiasts' visions] are nothing but the distempers of a disaffected brain." Others simply manifested "counterfeit inspiration." George Hickes agreed, defining enthusiasm as "Spiritual drunkenness, or Lunacy." It "distemper[ed] the minds of men," he elaborated, "with extravagant phancies." William Ramesay likewise opined that those who "in their *Enthusiasm*" aspired to prophesy typically went mad.[75]

A major problem with such arguments, however, was that they threatened to outlaw much that their proponents themselves wanted to defend. Sedgwick, for instance, acknowledged the importance of "experience" in much the same sense as Rogers's, and Ralph Cudworth accepted that of "irradiation." Quite as much as Rogers's congregants, Cudworth went out of his way to reject the idea that religion was simply "*Book-craft.*" Only when a spiritual truth was found "within our selves," he maintained, could we be said to be "experimentally acquainted with it." "All the Books and Writings which we converse with," Cudworth told Parliament, "can but represent Spiritual Objects to our understandings; which yet we can never see in their own true Figure, Colour and Proportion, until we have a *Divine Light* within, to irradiate and shine upon them." Such irradiated representation could happen only in the imagination. Cudworth also defined holiness as "nothing else but *God stamped* and *printed* upon the Soul." Such language was strikingly similar to that of the very enthusiasts whom

74. See especially Mack's excellent *Visionary Women*, 1, 7–10, 23–33, 57–8, 84–5 and passim (quoted from 23, italics in original); and also Hannay, *Silent but for the Word*, 1–14; Crawford, *Women and Religion*, 163; Crawford, "Women's Published Writings," 211–7, 224–6; Hobby, *Virtue of Necessity*, 26–53; Keeble, *Cultural Identity of Seventeenth-Century Woman*, 264–79. The medieval precedents for such claims are described in Bynum, *Holy Feast and Holy Fast*, 208–18, 251–9, 261–76. For a related discussion of the implications of adducing natural characteristics for the sexes, see Daston, "Naturalized Female Intellect."

75. Sedgwick, *Sermon*, 1, 5–6, 31; Hickes, *Spirit of Enthusiasm*, 2; [Ramesay], *Gentlemans Companion*, 40–41.

Cudworth, along with More, Sedgwick, Smith, and Casaubon, wished to proscribe. The crux of the conflict would therefore lie in the practical application of these arguments: the actual discrimination of proper "irradiation" from improper, and of true reading from false.[76]

Sir Thomas Browne provided one clue as to how to exercise such judgment. He reckoned that grounds for discrimination lay in the apparent mode of conveyance of candidate visions, alleging that the "the revelations of heaven are conveied by new impressions, and the immediate illumination of the soul; whereas the deceiving spirit, by concitation of humors, produceth his conceited phantasmes."[77] That is, true visions partook of the immaterial soul. False visions, like ordinary perceptions of the outside world, relied on corporeal mediation and therefore always arose in the body. They could never engage directly and exclusively with the rational soul. Henry More likewise alleged that "Enthusiasts for the most part are intoxicated with vapours from the lowest region of their Body." His fellow Platonist John Smith agreed, describing false visions as "seated only in the imaginative power," and ascribing the "many enthusiastical impostors of our age" to this phenomenon. This was no mere academic distinction: it suggested ways to discriminate in practice between true prophecy and self-idolatry. A false vision was one that could not "rise up above this low and dark region of sense or matter." Aristotelian reasoning straightforwardly implied that since it originated in the realm of change, it must always manifest instability and conflict. The "prophetical spirit" could therefore be discerned from the "pseudo-prophetical," Hales affirmed, because the latter could "rise no higher than the middle region of man, which is his fancy, there dwells as in storms and tempests, and . . . is also conjoined with alienations and abruptions of mind." Such symptoms, he added, were "commonly observed by physicians."[78]

Hales was not the only person to reckon that physicians were well acquainted with the corporeal signs accompanying false inspiration. Reference to commonly held beliefs about the structure of the body and a physician's role in interpreting its signs recurred widely. By the end of the seventeenth century, and probably before, such criteria constituted the main resource for defining enthusiasm and visions. Antagonists therefore alleged that an ex-

76. Sedgwick, Ἐπίσκοπος Διδακτικός, 51; Cudworth, Discourse, 39–41, 52, 55. Hickes was an exception, since he repudiated the need for any sort of inspiration at all: Hickes, Spirit of Enthusiasm, 34–5.

77. Browne, Pseudodoxia Epidemica, 30.

78. [More], Enthusiasmus Triumphatus, 17; Smith, Select Discourses, 194–6, 200–1; Henry, "Matter of Souls," 92–5, 98–100. The Bakhtinian resonances of "high" and "low" are particularly clear in such sentiments: Stallybrass and White, Politics and Poetics of Transgression, 2–5, 43.

perience of apparent inspiration was in fact a "distemper." It was a physiological condition, needing to be cured rather than exorcized or idolized.[79] In
short, it had natural causes.

Analysis of visions was therefore a diagnostic exercise, the chief tool for
which was knowledge of the passions. Henry More exemplified the approach. More knew Cartesian philosophy better than anyone else in the
country at this time—he it was who introduced it into English intellectual
culture, in the context of this very struggle against enthusiasm—and he
singled out Descartes's *Passions of the Soule* as an influential work. So it is
unsurprising that, like Descartes, More placed the passions at the center of
his analysis.[80] According to his treatment, enthusiasm was nothing more
than the consequence of an excess of "ecstatical passion," reinforcing an
"illusion of the imagination." This was the consequence of a broader account of the human perceptions and reasoning. Although his own proffered
physiology did not agree with Willis's, which he regarded as materialist,
More concurred with the Sedleian Professor that in practice reasoning could
never be separated from corporeal perceptions. It therefore must always be
prey to "Phantasmes." "Thoughts," he believed, "offer or force themselves
upon the mind, . . . according to the nature or strength of the complexion
of our Bodies."[81] In certain individuals (especially women), and in certain
circumstances, the images thus presented in the imagination became as
strong as those sensed in the outside world—and in such a case the party
concerned could scarcely fail to confuse the two. The dreams experienced
while sleeping were a canonical instance. Here was the real source for alleged
experiences of inspiration. In their dreams, enthusiasts attained a state of
"*Extasie*," in which the imagination was able to dominate the *sensus communis* to such an extent that the memory was "as thoroughly sealed there-
with, as from the sense of any external Object."[82] Thomas Hobbes reputedly
died with this explanation on his lips: "Dreams are the Reverse of our waking Imaginations; the motion when we are awake, beginning at one end,
and when we dream, at the other."[83]

The most systematic analysis of the political implications was to be found

79. Casaubon, *Treatise*, 28–9; [More], *Enthusiasmus Triumphatus*, sigs. [A5ᵛ]–[A6ᵛ], 2–
20; Casaubon, *Of Credulity and Incredulity*, 29–30; Schwartz, *Knaves, Fools, Madmen, and
That Subtile Effluvium*, 31–70, esp. 50–1; Heyd, *"Be Sober and Reasonable,"* 191–210.

80. More, "The Immortality of the Soul," in *Collection*, sig. [Ll4ᵛ]. For More's fight
against enthusiasm see Heyd, *"Be Sober and Reasonable,"* 92–108; for his appropriation of
Descartes see Gabbey, *"Philosophia Cartesiana Triumphata."*

81. [More], *Enthusiasmus Triumphatus*, 2–4; Casaubon, *Treatise Concerning Enthusiasme*,
211. For conflicts between More and Willis see Henry, "Matter of Souls."

82. [More], *Enthusiasmus Triumphatus*, 4–5, 27.

83. This is the final aphorism in *Last sayings, or Dying Legacy of Mr. Thomas Hobbs*.

in the greatest of all discourses on the passions, Hobbes's *Leviathan*. His most perceptive critic, Seth Ward, told Hobbes that his reasoning had "never risen beyond imagination, or the first apprehension of bodies performed in the brain." [84] He had a point. The passions played a central part in Hobbes's work. Since they stimulated all human actions, and no polity could ever reach such a state of perfection that their disruptive consequences could be eradicated, the passions lay at the root of both social order and social disorder. Hobbes analyzed the processes of reasoning, will, and memory as dependent on them—understanding, for example, was achieved as the result of that passion, the "desire of Knowledge." [85] Appropriating the common interpretation of passions writers, Hobbes maintained that the experience of a dream, along with false apparitions and spurious claims to prophecy, derived from the difficulty of distinguishing perceptions received from the outside world from imagined ones generated internally. He thus maintained that those who worshiped such nonexistent spiritual beings were in effect idolaters, "in awe of their own imaginations," and that the observable variety of such religions in the world was but a simple consequence of "the different Fancies, Judgements, and Passions." [86] Madness, similarly, was "nothing else, but too much appearing Passion," which could appear in certain circumstances as "inspiration." Enthusiasts and madmen alike were liable to be "cast out of Society" altogether, whence they existed in a state of "perpetuall war, of every man against his neighbour." That is, they occupied a position that was as close as Hobbes's contemporaries ever came to the state of nature—"that miserable condition of Warre, which is necessarily consequent . . . to the naturall Passions of men." If unrestrained, such "singular Passions" became "the Seditious roaring of a troubled Nation." This was why Hobbes pursued with such dedication the advocates of priestcraft and scholasticism. Their philosophy was merely "a description of their own Passions," and therefore "rather a Dream than Science." It warranted claims to inspiration, whether by priests or sectaries, and therefore led inexorably to civil war. [87]

In an enthusiast, then, the sensitive soul was well on the way to winning the microcosmic civil war: the "*Imaginative* facultie has the preheminence above the *Rationall*." [88] As writers on the passions declared, at the height of that war the subject "acted little less than like a Daemoniack possess'd with

84. [Ward], *Philosophicall Essay*, sig. A3ᵛ–[A4ʳ]. For *Leviathan* and the passions see also Smith, *Literature and Revolution*, 159–62.

85. Hobbes, *Leviathan*, 13–17, 19, 24–5, 30–31, 37–49, 53–4, 59–60, 69–70, 172–3.

86. Hobbes, *Leviathan*, 17–19, 75–6, 78–9.

87. Hobbes, *Leviathan*, 50–56, 62, 106, 109–11, 117–8, 130–1, 148–9, 153–4, 187, 461.

88. [More], *Enthusiasmus Triumphatus*, 40–1, 43–6, 50–1, 294–5.

a Legion."[89] Since enthusiasts effectively surrendered their reason to their passions, far from being emancipated by their "visions," as they themselves claimed, they were in fact delivering themselves up to merely mechanical reflexes. More and his friend Ralph Cudworth had a name for such individuals. They called them "*Neurospasts*." Enthusiasts were marionettes, "meer Puppets" subjugated to the mechanisms of their bodies. Since they had let the sensitive soul dominate completely, they had reverted to the status of mere beasts. The body of such a person became "perfectly *Cartesius his Machina*."[90]

But More now faced the same problem of practical demarcation encountered by Cudworth and others. In the 1640s, he himself had published Platonic poems that had expressed what looked very like ecstasies. Was he then, as his opponent Thomas Vaughan claimed, "sick of that Disease I would pretend to cure others of"? More could see the point. He himself confessed that he had "a natural touch of Enthusiasm in my complexion."[91] To illustrate the difference between his own experiences and the professed inspirations of the enthusiast, however, he now recounted a dream he himself claimed to have had at around the time of the outbreak of the Civil War. More had experienced this remarkable dream at much the same time as Rogers, on the other side of Cambridge, was falling asleep to dream of God. A comparison between the two is highly instructive.

More had dreamed that he was at a friend's house on the road between England and Scotland. Leaving this house on a bright moonlit night, he saw a series of huge figures in the sky, most prominent among them that of an old man with a long beard. Lying on his side in the heavens, this figure made a number of gestures with his arm; and finally, as More reentered the house, he intoned, "*There is indeed love amongst you, but onely according to the flesh*." Back indoors, More was able to tell his companions the import of the vision, "expounding the generall meaning of my dream in my dream." He interpreted the movements of the old man's arm as "an Embleme of the proceedings of God when he chastises a nation," adducing "reasons out of *Aristotles* Mechanicks, which I had very lately read," for the precise nature of the movements. It appeared to have been a true vision, with a valid and substantial message. But then More revealed that "the *Vision* (as I may so

89. [Charleton], *Natural History of the Passions*, 62–4, 86–7; Descartes, *Passions*, 25–9, 33–5; Willis, *Two Discourses concerning the Soul of Brutes*, 43.

90. More, *Collection*, 132–3; Cudworth, *Discourse Concerning the True Notion of the Lord's Supper*, 64; Ingelo, *Bentivoglio and Urania*, 91; [More], *Enthusiasmus Triumphatus*, 315–6. See also Gabbey, "Cudworth, More, and the Mechanical Analogy."

91. More, *Collection*, x; [More], *Enthusiasmus Triumphatus*, 309. Sir Thomas Browne made a similar admission: Browne, *Works*, I, 12.

FIG. 6.9. Frontispiece to Ptolemy's *Geographia*, printed in 1618. It was such an image that generated Henry More's supposed vision. Hondius, *Theatri Geographiae Veteris Tomus Prior.* (By permission of the Canon Librarian of Peterborough Cathedral.)

call it) in this dream" had a terrestrial origin after all. He had been reading Ptolemy's *Geographia* the evening before, and seeing a particular iconographic figure on the engraved frontispiece, "my fancy it seems having laid
hold on his venerable beard, drew in thereby the whole scene of things that
presented themselves to me in my sleep" (fig. 6.9).

Both More and Rogers described remarkable dreams springing from impressive reading experiences. Both identified their dreams as moments of
personal transformation. But they were important to them in directly contradictory ways. Rogers had moved from dismissing his dreams as artifacts
of "fancy" to respecting them as genuine visions, and simultaneously from
despair at the impossibility of his salvation to assurance that that was itself
mere "fancy." More had pursued the opposite trajectory. From a belief that
he had experienced a real vision, he had convinced himself that his striking
dream was the product of his own "Fancy." One's imagination could evidently be imprinted entirely naturally by an image on the frontispiece of
Ptolemy, without one's being aware of any unusual effects.[92] It could happen
to anybody, and could produce a seeming vision of utterly convincing reality. More went on to mention an even more convincing "*Vision* or *Enthusiasme*" that he had again experienced after reading Aristotle's *Mechanicks*. A
description he had read there of a lever-based machine for timber moving
had raised such a "Temper and frame of spirit" in him, he recalled, that "I
should be prone to suspect something more then naturall in what preceded
it, did I not consider that sometimes there may be of it self such a Terrour
and Disposition of body, that may either suggest or imitate what is most
holy or divine."[93]

Such an awareness of the power of reading to create visions through the
mechanisms of the body was far from unique to More. The effects of representing images seen in print in the imagination were well known. For
example, natural magic books and books of secrets often suggested that
would-be parents concerned to produce handsome children should place in
their bedchambers "images of *Cupid, Adonis*, and *Ganymedes*, . . . that they
may always have them in their eyes." The imagination also raised difficult
problems of idolatry, especially when, as here, the mental images involved
were of bearded old men. Puritans had long wanted to discipline such imaginative constructs out of existence, replacing them with schemes of words

92. [More], *Enthusiasmus Triumphatus*, 309–12. More's dream should be compared to
the remarkably similar experience of interpretation while still asleep that was recorded by
Descartes (*Oeuvres*, X, 181–8) and to the dream of George Starkey described in Newman,
Gehennical Fire, 64–5.

93. Tryon, *Treatise of Dreams & Visions*, 9, 20, 44, 48–51, 203–4; [More], *Enthusiasmus
Triumphatus*, 2–5, 27, 40–1, 43–6, 50–1, 294–5, 309, 312–6; More, *Collection*, x, 132–3.
Compare [Trenchard], *Natural History of Superstition*, 12–14.

able to act as their own mnemonics: that is, by printed Ramist diagrams. As Aston puts it, every Protestant was obliged to "act the iconoclast on the idol-processes of his mind."[94]

As this strategy itself implied, however, words themselves could have similar effects. Who could wonder that Chrysostom had dreamed of Saint Paul, Sir Thomas Browne asked, since he read Paul's Epistles "dayly"? These were "butt animal visions." In his own attack on enthusiasm, Meric Casaubon likewise concentrated on what he called "the strange, but natural effects" produced by words. Metaphors, for example, worked by the "representation of shapes and images" to the imagination—that is, they worked "*by a kind of Enthusiasme*." Casaubon himself could testify that when he read a passage from a classical poet, "I do not only phansy to my self, that I see those things that they describe; but also find in my self (as I phansy) the very same content and pleasure, that I should, if my eyes beheld them in some whether coloured, or carved representation of some excellent Artist." The error of the enthusiast lay in attributing to such experiences the status of certain, even divine, truth.[95]

Casaubon agreed that enthusiasts were suffering from a medical condition: they should go to a "Physician of the body." But he did not want such a strategy to be too widely applied. In particular, Casaubon did not wish to deny the reality of demons altogether. Those who had done so, he noted, had attempted to attribute *all* spirits to "a depraved fancy, or imagination." He had in mind men like John Webster, who applied his account of the power of educating the passions to explain away spirits entirely, alleging that they were "effects of the imaginative function depraved by the fumes of the melancholick humor." Angelologists, on the contrary, reckoned that angels could manipulate images already present in the imagination in order to produce apparent visions, although they could not generate new ones ex nihilo. According to Webster, reading could either cause such "effects" or, indeed, eliminate them. Webster even cited the case of a student who, by the careful reading of sacred books, had been able to expel a devil from his posterior.[96] Such writers, like Casaubon, had pointed out "how easily [the imagination] may represent to it self Devils, and Spirits," which "may make great im-

94. Aston, *England's Iconoclasts. I*, 452–66, esp. 460. For details of the production, origin, and use of images in frontispieces and broadsheets, see Watt, *Cheap Print and Popular Piety*, esp. 131–253.

95. Browne, *Works*, III, 230–1; Casaubon, *Treatise*, 135 ff., 150–1, 170 ff., 175–6, 182–4. Compare Tryon, *Treatise of Dreams and Visions*, 9, for the restriction of dreams to the sensitive soul. For Casaubon's antienthusiast campaign, see Heyd, *"Be Sober and Reasonable,"* 72–92.

96. Reynolds, *Treatise*, 8–10; Hobbes, *Leviathan*, 483–4; Webster, *Displaying of Supposed Witchcraft*, 32–4, 313, 321–2, 343–5; Lawrence, *History of Angells*, 35–6, 40, 72.

pressions in the brain, and offer themselves in sleep, or when the brain is sick." But Casaubon insisted that demons *did* exist. Moreover, they operated, like angels, precisely by casting "false *species*" into the imagination. Denying spirits meant also denying angels. In this too Casaubon agreed with Willis, Glanvill, and More. But he now found himself facing an extraordinarily delicate problem. Casaubon believed that those denying the existence of spirits were "Atheists." Yet such "atheists" relied on almost exactly the same arguments from imagination and the passions that he himself employed to crush enthusiasts. The difference was that the atheist relegated *every* spirit phenomenon to the imagination. But if there were absolutely no such phenomena not reducible to the passions, Casaubon demanded, then "What hath he left to us, that we can call *truth*"?[97] This question—the question of what could still be trusted as truth, if experience were entirely subjected to the imagination—was fundamental.

It was especially fundamental when related to reading. Such an error was at its most dangerous, needless to say, when what was being read was Scripture itself. A Protestant reading the Bible was using the eyes provided by God to "satisfie himself and others" in matters of "trust and consequence." It was this that made the correct habituation of reading so important. But enthusiasts' reading practices were dangerous. Casaubon illustrated this by the example of an ancient bishop, Synesius. Synesius used to begin reading a text, then close his eyes and extrapolate from what he had read a passage so harmonious with the work that nobody listening could tell that he was no longer reading. "It is likely that he often practised it by himself, before he adventured to do it before others," Casaubon admitted, and the applauding audience probably did not know any more of the work being read than what they had just heard. Nonetheless, "what he so supplied by his extemporary wit, did sometimes prove to be the very same that he found afterwards in the book." Such performative reading captured the fundamentals of delusive inspiration: deceit, prodigy, and display. That was why it should "very properly be referred to some kind of *enthusiasme*."[98]

A fundamental reason for this lay in the culture of discredit surrounding printed books. Enthusiasts, pursuing their professed inspirations to the exclusion of all prudence, credited the imaginative passions generated in their reading far too readily. That was why they fell foul of the sort of strong

97. Casaubon, *Of Credulity and Incredulity*, 29–30, 38, 44; Reynolds, *Treatise*, 27; Willis, "An Essay of the Pathology of the Brain and Nervous Stock," in *Dr. Willis's Practice of Physick*, separately paginated, 43–4; Browne, *Works*, I, 40–1; Casaubon, *Letter*, 30 (for the experimental philosophy and spirits). For insistence on the reality of witchcraft, compare Glanvill, *Saducismus Triumphatus*, 25–6.

98. Casaubon, *Treatise*, 160–1. For the use of books to create atheism and the attribution of miracles to the imagination, see Hunter, "'Aikenhead the Atheist.'"

impressions that had caused More's dream (and Rogers's). At the same time, this also meant that they credited printed books in general far too readily. By contrast, in Casaubon's eyes books were *not* necessarily trustworthy. Writers and printers were prone to produce "lyes, or frauds," especially if convinced that the end justified doing so. "What a world of lyes and counterfeit books" had "the conceit of *piae fraudes*" produced, for example, and "how many have been gulled and deceived by them, who doth not know, or hath not heard?" Casaubon insisted that reading must therefore be not a passive imprinting on the mind—the writing of a supposedly divine spirit—but an active and critical *labor*. Given the culture that he perceived around him, the production of safe (and true) knowledge depended utterly on this.

He had a point. Even the Bible itself could be corrupted, his contemporaries feared, and small variations in such a text could have momentous consequences. The entire Arian schism could be explained by the misconstrual of a single Greek letter. And the "errors" could indeed be deliberate. As early as 1538, Thomas Elyot had found it necessary to list heresies so that they could be "the sooner espyed and abhorred in suche bokes, where they be craftily enterlaced with holsom doctrine." William Bentley claimed that a notorious 1653 misprint of 1 Corinthians 6:9—"Know ye not that the unrighteous shall inherit the Kingdom of God?"—had generated sectarian enthusiasm in Casaubon's own time, since "many *Libertines* and licentious people did produce, and urge this Text from the authority of this corrupt Bible . . . , in justification of their vicious and inordinate Conversations." Proposals for a polyglot bible therefore stressed its purity from errors generated "by the wilful corruption of Sectaries, and Hereticks, which (as was foretold) abound in these latter times." Isaac Newton too endorsed the likelihood of intentional corruption, warning of an elaborate Catholic plot to obliterate sound Scripture by printing debased Trinitarian copies in vast numbers at presses in Spain and Italy. In Newton's eyes, the Trinitarians were powerful not because they were right, but because they possessed the most sophisticated of printing houses and distribution networks. All modern editions of the Bible were therefore suspect to him, whatever critical apparatus they might display—or, more precisely, the more elaborate the apparatus, the more suspect the edition. Others made a theological point of the concern. Before the Fall, Hales argued, just as the senses had apprehended Creation faithfully, so God had communicated his laws directly into the mind. With such communication there had been no possible doubt about "who the author was, and how far his intent and meaning reacht." But this certainty had ceased as soon as the Word was written down. It was "a great argument of our shame and imperfection," then, "that the holy things are written in books." The press had not obviated the problem. Edmond Halley might assert that "since the Invention of Printing" the survival of "exactly the same" texts had been virtually assured, but the veracity of those texts and the validity of their applications depended on their printers and readers. Yet, Ward cautioned, the literal variations encountered in different bibles ought not to lead readers "to conclude the books not to be credited." Otherwise, he pointed out, "upon the same reason it will be concluded that no Book in the world is to be credited." On the contrary, God himself had preserved such variations deliberately. He had done so to prove a point: that comparison by appropriately laborious readers could reveal "both the true sence and the true reading" of Scripture. Errata were matters of providence.[99]

Such writers argued that there was no labor more noble and more necessary than that devoted to revealing false books. It required enormous skill in obscure languages, customs, and fashions. This was one major reason why Casaubon questioned the faith placed by some of his contemporaries in experimental philosophy. Casaubon—the son of perhaps the greatest of all detectors of printed fraud, Isaac Casaubon—believed that those who, he claimed, reduced all knowledge to that produced through "natural experiments" ran the risk of losing the skills needed to ward off enthusiastic reading habits. In a learned world inhabited solely by experimental philosophers, there would be no techniques left to discriminate between true "Oracles" and "abominable forgeries," and to ward off the imaginative effects of the latter. Casaubon defended the legitimacy of the scholar in the face of such a threat. The classical learning that suggested Homer's debt to Scripture, for example, thereby confirmed the truth of the Old Testament—something profoundly necessary "in this visible sad increase of Atheism every where." In contrast, Casaubon charged that in their naïveté experimental philosophers even questioned "whether those works, generally ascribed to *Aristotle*, were, or are his indeed?" Should this perilous blend of credulity and skepticism hold sway, and people be "made incapable to uphold their faith" by an erosion of the scholarly skills needed to establish or contest

99. BL classmark 675.a.1; Starnes, *Renaissance Dictionaries*, 55; Kilburne, *Dangerous Errors*, 4–7, 10; *Brief Description of an Edition of the Bible; Propositions concerning the Printing of the Bible*; Newton, *Correspondence*, III, 83–146; Hales, "Abuses of Hard Places of Scripture," 1–3; [Halley], *Miscellanea Curiosa*, II, 1–8; [Ward], *Philosophicall Essay*, 1–2, 147–8. Compare also Bacon, *Works*, III, 287; Galileo's "Letter to the Grand Duchess Christina," in Finocchiaro, *Galileo Affair*, 87–118; Redondi, *Galileo: Heretic*, 104–5; and the comment of the greatest classical scholar of the time, Richard Bentley, that Scripture had "been under a hard fate since the invention of printing." Bentley identified printer Robert Estienne as a "Protestant Pope" whose ownership of the copy of the Bible had led to two thousand corruptions in the editions "set out and regulated by himself alone": Kroll, *"Mise-en-Page,"* 37–8 n.

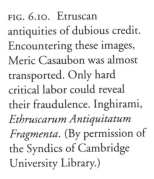

FIG. 6.10. Etruscan antiquities of dubious credit. Encountering these images, Meric Casaubon was almost transported. Only hard critical labor could reveal their fraudulence. Inghirami, *Ethruscarum Antiquitatum Fragmenta*. (By permission of the Syndics of Cambridge University Library.)

textual credit, then a "new Religion" would be the inevitable consequence. Instead of their present damaging labors, then, Casaubon suggested that the Royal Society appoint a committee to try the techniques in a book such as Porta's *Natural Magick*, "that so we might know what men may certainly trust to."[100]

Casaubon, like More, exploited his own vivid experiences of reading books to expose enthusiasm. Unlike More, however, Casaubon recalled, not a dream derived *from* a book, but a direct and industrious confrontation *with* a book. He described an encounter with a work on Etruscan antiquities which he had come across in a Stationer's shop in London (fig. 6.10). Helped, no doubt, by the bookseller, Casaubon had found its engravings so impressive that he had all but lost control of his body: "the first sight of the book did so ravish me," he affirmed, "that I scarce knew where I was, or what I did." Had he left things at that, the result might have been similar to

100. Casaubon, *Letter*, 7, 15–16, 17–18, 27.

the experiences of More and Rogers. Instead, buying the volume, Casaubon began to read it as he embarked on a boat for Gravesend. Before long he had realized his mistake. "The truth is, when once the heat or violence of my expectation (which did almost transport me) was once over," he recalled, "I began to wonder at my self." Every line of the work was fraudulent. But the point was that many other readers *did* credit it—even to the extent of voyaging to Italy to see the monuments it purported to represent. This convincingly demonstrated how "prone" readers were not only to "entertain an imposture," but to resist its overthrow thereafter. The question this raised was enormously consequential. "What wonder then," Casaubon asked, "if *Christianism* was so soon turned into *Mahometism*," when so limited was the dedication of readers "to discover the impostures of pretended *Enthusiasts*?" The implication of his experience when confronting this forgery was, then, both clear and immense. "Had these *Antiquities* been received generally, as a true piece," Casaubon warned, "half the world would have been Conjurers, and *Enthusiasts* by this time." [101]

Casaubon, More, and others thus used accounts of the effects of reading—accounts based in knowledge of the passions—to characterize and attack false claims to knowledge under the label of enthusiasm. Enthusiasts, they charged, were those who did not properly habituate their reading and their passions. Knowledge, civility, and the physiology of reading intersected here, as they put ideas of the nature and effects of reading to work in the most controversial of circumstances, to discriminate true knowledge from error, and safe veneration from rebellious sectarianism. In general terms, the view was widely shared. As the greatest of all anatomists, William Harvey, had put it, those who read a book and did not "by the aid of their own Senses, abstract true representations of the things themselves (comprehended in the authors expressions)" would apprehend not "true *Ideas*" but "deceitful *Idols*, & *Phantasms*." As a result, Harvey concluded, "they frame

---

101. Casaubon, *Treatise*, 160; Casaubon, *Of Credulity and Incredulity*, 294–300; Shapin, *Social History of Truth*. The work in question was Inghirami, *Ethruscarum Antiquitatum Fragmenta*; it was exposed in Allacci, *Animadversiones*. Casaubon also identified as an important example Annius of Viterbo, who has recently been studied by Grafton as a key figure in the history of both forgery and criticism: Grafton, *Defenders of the Text*, 76–103; Grafton and Blair, *Transmission of Culture*, 8–38. Compare Sedgwick, *Sermon*, 13–14, for his stress on the need for "industry" in reading Scripture. For a slightly later example, compare also [Trenchard], *Natural History of Superstition*, 8–9, 28, on the effects of the "Forgeries of the Papists, and the Frauds and Follies of some who call themselves Protestants." Such falsities could not have enjoyed so great a success, Trenchard felt, "unless something in our Constitutions made us easily to be susceptible of wrong Impressions." So he felt that "it is incumbent upon us, first of all to examine into the frame and constitution of our own Bodies." Trenchard described from this how "a poor Enthusiast with his Brains intoxicated with reading the Revelations" could seem to make "a lucky discovery that the last Day is at hand."

to themselves certaine *shadows* and *Chimaera*'s, and all their *theory* and contemplation (which they count *Science*) represents nothing but *waking mens
dreams*, and *sick mens phrensies*." [102]

DISPASSIONATE KNOWLEDGE: IMAGES, CREDIT,
AND EXPERIMENTAL PHILOSOPHY

Harvey was by this time revered by a certain group of men as providing
something that they, at least, "counted science." The life of the early Royal
Society will be introduced in chapter 7. Its "experimental" philosophy was
designed partly to overcome the problem of knowledge that was thought to
have fostered the turmoil of the Great Rebellion. At the forefront of this
effort stood the victim of passionate reading already introduced, Robert
Boyle. [103] Many sources could be used to illustrate the Society's involvement
with issues of knowledge and the passions, not least Boyle's own writings. However, by common consent the most impressive single document
produced during the first decade of its existence was Robert Hooke's *Micrographia*. It is therefore appropriate to concentrate on this work. Moreover,
while the spectacular engravings for which it has been remembered were
indeed unprecedented, contemporaries also recognized in the volume a pre-
scriptive model for the practice of natural philosophy itself, and therefore
for the safe and reliable attainment of knowledge. [104] If the Royal Society had
an answer to Casaubon's arguments, it was to be found here.

Hooke began by expressing concerns similar to those of Casaubon and
More. He pronounced it no wonder that existing knowledge was imperfect,
since "the *forces of our own minds* conspire to betray us." His book was dedicated to circumventing this problem, "by rectifying the operations of the
Sense, the *Memory*, and *Reason*." Hooke was thus proposing nothing less
than a "universal cure of the Mind." He aimed to achieve this cure by using
instruments (fig. 6.11). He believed that the senses could give false information for two reasons. They might be disproportionate to the objects of interest and thus unable to perceive them at all (as was the case, for example,
with atoms); or they might err in their perception of those things that they
could perceive. As a result, even the most "solid" notions of philosophers
were "rather expressions of our own misguided apprehensions then of the
true nature of the things themselves." The remedy had to reach to the essential cause of the problem. For Hooke this meant "the adding of *artificial
Organs* to the *natural*." If the operation of perception could thereby be regu-

---

102. Harvey, *Anatomical Exercitations*, sig. [¶ 5^r].
103. Schaffer, "Godly Men and Mechanical Philosophers."
104. Harwood, "Rhetoric and Graphics in *Micrographia*"; Dennis, "Graphic Understanding."

FIG. 6.11. Robert Hooke's principal instrument to discipline the passions. Hooke, *Micrographia.* (By permission of the Syndics of Cambridge University Library.)

lated, then the reformation of knowledge at which he professed to aim might be achieved. Reliance on the "strength of *Imagination*" would be replaced simply by "a *sincere Hand*, and a *faithful Eye*." The "Science of Nature" had been too long "only a work of the *Brain* and *Fancy*," Hooke proclaimed, and it was time for his artificial organs to rectify them. If his approach proved fruitful, it might even be possible to recapture the original "*unpassionate*" knowledge that had existed before the Fall.

Meric Casaubon found such aspirations incredible. Indeed, so determined was he to repudiate them that he risked breaking the prime convention of civil conversation by flatly denying the truth of a recounted incident. He questioned the power of experimental philosophy to "*moralize* men" by recalling a story given by Gassendi in his biography of Peiresc. According to Gassendi's version, Peiresc had enclosed a louse and a fly together under a microscope and observed the deleterious physical effects of the consequent passions excited in the louse. By seeing how damaging excess passions could be, the story went, Peiresc had "profited more to rule his passions in the rest of his life, then he had done by anything he had heard, or read before." Casaubon flatly refused to believe it. Peiresc could not possibly have been influenced more by two insects than by the countless writings of philosophers on the passions, which had included extensive accounts of their physiological effects. Reading, not experiment, had the potential to calm one's passions. Casaubon referred in particular to the reading of histories, which

FIG. 6.12. Hooke's representation of a period seen through the microscope. Hooke, *Micrographia*. (By permission of the Syndics of Cambridge University Library.)

could even cure physical diseases: at least two monarchs had been cured after all medical advice had proved fruitless by reading Livy and Quintus Curtius (Boyle's own favorite). He remained flatly unconvinced "what use can be made, . . . in point of life and manners, of a *microscope*." And in the meantime, Casaubon insisted, "I have not faith enough to beleeve *Gassendus* in this." [105]

Hooke preempted such denials. Imitating classical conventions, *Micrographia* began as if it were a work of geometry. Instead of a mathematical point, though—the classic starting element of that science—Hooke began with its physical equivalent, the tip of a pin. Under his microscope this sharpest of material points was revealed to be blunt and pitted. Natural points such as an insect's sting displayed no such imperfections, and Hooke took this to be powerful evidence of a Creator. The argument proved persuasive, and was frequently repeated.[106] But Hooke then turned the microscope onto "a *point* commonly so call'd": "that is, the mark of a *full stop*, or *period*" (fig. 6.12). Through the microscope, any such character, printed

105. Casaubon, *Letter*, 24–5, 31–3.
106. Hooke, *Micrographia*, 1–4; Wilkins, *Of the Principles and Duties of Natural Religion*, 80; *Memoirs for the Ingenious*, I, 208–11. The point was also stressed in the review in the *Journal des Sçavans*: Morgan, *Histoire du Journal des Sçavans*, 162–3.

or written—and Hooke examined "multitudes" of each—appeared "like *smutty daubings* on a matt or uneven floor [made] with a blunt extinguisht brand or stick's end." Thanks to a combination of irregularity of type, uneven cloth-based paper, and rough use of ink, the result resembled nothing so much as "a great splatch of *London* dirt." All letters, Hooke reported, were like this, so that seeing them *as* letters was not simple. The microscope revealed some much-vaunted tiny writing as barely readable without "a good *fantsy* well *preposest* to help one through," and in fact a good fancy was needed for all reading. Since the "Imaginations" we had of objects were not decided by "the Nature of the things themselves" so much as by "the peculiar Organs, by which they are made sensible to the Understanding," different organs would have produced different perceptions. Hooke had himself been able to read letters in what would otherwise be reckoned darkness, thanks to one of his artificial organs contrived from "an ordinary double Convex Spherical Lens." The postlapsarian disproportion of the senses to nature, and their alliance with the passions and imagination, were both necessary and precisely sufficient to allow human beings to read.[107]

The variations of perception obviously had serious consequences for knowledge: in the brain, the understanding was "apt to be sway'd to this or that hand, according as it is more affected or prest by this or that Instance." Hooke now pointed out a still greater implication of the corporeality of human beings. There existed fundamental causes of prejudice particular to individuals, he maintained, by virtue of "every Man's own peculiar Structure." Every philosopher was born to "a Constitution of Body and Mind, that does more or less dispose him to this or that kind of Imagination or Phant'sy of things." This affected the sort of philosophy he produced: "some kind of Constitutions of Body does more incline a Man to Contemplation, and Speculation, another to Operation, Examination, and making Experiments."[108] The history of natural philosophy demonstrated as much. Previous philosophers, Hooke indicated, had become "habituated" against "any thing that offered it self as a Novelty or New Discovery," and as a result they had embraced dogmatism—the Royal Society's professed antithesis, and to many a sure sign of enthusiasm. Hooke could even provide real examples to

107. Hooke, *Micrographia*, 1–4; Hooke, *Posthumous Works*, 8–9, 13. Compare Porta, *Natural Magick*, 363. It should be noted that reading letters through telescopes was being suggested at this juncture as a way of calibrating the quality of lenses when too far apart for direct comparison: Bonelli and Van Helden, "Divini and Campani," 13. Thus Molyneux (after Flamsteed) suggested that the best way to test an object glass was to put it in a telescope tube, fit an eyepiece, and look through it at the distant title page of a large book, "wherein there are generally Letters printed of divers Magnitudes." Cassini apparently used this method in the French royal observatory, fixing his title page a quarter of a mile away on a steeple window. Molyneux, *Dioptrica Nova*, 223.

108. Hooke, *Posthumous Works*, 5–6, 9, 47. Compare Reynolds, *Treatise of the Passions*, 6–7.

prove the point, relating some of the most eminent schools of philosophy to the passions and physiology of their founders:

> Just as a Man that is troubled with the Jaundice, supposes all things to be Yellow, and all things he eats, till otherwise prevented, serve to augment his Choler, by being chang'd into it: Or a melancholy Person, that thinks he meets with nothing but frightful Apparitions, does convert all things he either sees or hears into dreadful Representations, and makes use of them to strengthen his Phant'sy, and fill it fuller of such uneasy Apprehensions, so is it in Constitutions of Mind as to Philosophy. Thus *Aristotle*'s Physick is very much influenced by his Logick: *Des Cartes* Philosophy savours much of his Opticks: *Van Helmonts*, and the rest of the Chymists of their Chimical Operations: *Gilberts* of the Loadstone: *Pythagoras*'s and *Jordanus Brunus*'s, *Kepler*'s, &c. of Arithmetick and Harmony of Numbers. The Philosophy, of some Divines, is intermingled with Divinity; of others with Spirits and immaterial Agents: Astrologers endeavour to bring all things under the Power and Influence of Cælestial Bodies, and would have them the chief Efficients of the World, and indeed every one according to the things he most fancies naturally, . . . endeavours to make all things he meets with, agreeable or subservient thereto.[109]

If Hooke was right, then there was no way, even in principle, to produce true knowledge on one's own. The history of natural philosophy was a catalogue of demonstrations of that fact.[110]

Hooke did maintain, however, that the best "Remedy" for this was self-study. The philosopher must "find out of what Constitution ones self is, and to what one is either naturally or accidentally most inclin'd to believe." Then one must "accustom ones self" to "a quite contrary Supposal or Practice." It was the standard tactic, as we have seen, for remedying the passions. According to Hooke, education, breeding, and social background likewise served to "sway" the affections of the individual. He especially stressed the importance of education, which, being imbibed while young, could exercise "a kind of Soveraignty" over the understanding.[111] During schooling, Hooke opined, "the Reason of a Man is very easily impos'd on by Discourse," whether that of a tutor or that of a persuasive book. The best remedy, again, was to concentrate on imagining a directly contrary idea to the one proposed, or, if the tutor were particularly liked, to imagine a speaker against whom one held a grudge. Alternatively, one could "accustom

---

109. Hooke, *Posthumous Works*, 3–4, 9–10. Compare Descartes, *Philosophical Writings*, I, 47.

110. John Wilkins, for one, probably agreed, if his strictures against "singularity" are to be read in this sense: Johns, "Prudence and Pedantry."

111. Hooke, *Posthumous Works*, 9–11.

the Mind to an Equilibrium or Indifferency." Yet again, this is familiar as a major tactic for counteracting the passions.

But such countermeasures could only mitigate the effects of the passions; they could not eliminate them altogether. Since humans were intrinsically passionate, knowledge must be produced collectively. This was, of course, exemplified by the practice of the Royal Society. To a substantial degree, the Society's great virtue was that in creating a disciplined, polite, and above all *collective* judgment it went as far as humanly possible to eliminate passionate error. Its reading, writing, and printing practices were a core element in this scheme. Hooke's recommendation, since it valued social processes of legitimation so highly, thus necessarily brought him back to the issue of the proper recording and transmission of knowledge.

During his four decades at the Society, Hooke returned repeatedly to the problems associated with reading and writing experimental knowledge. Experiments must be "registered" as soon as they had been conducted, he insisted, in as much incidental detail as possible. They should be written down on "a very fine piece of Paper" and entered in a large book called a "Repository." Just as the quality of the lens in a microscope was all-important, moreover, so was the visual layout of this register. Its contents must be "ranged in the best and most Natural Order" so as to be "manifest to the Eye." Throughout, everything must be expressed in as few words as possible, perhaps even in shorthand, so as to be "the more obvious, and . . . thereby the less disturb the Mind in its Inquiry." It was best to write in different inks, with consistent color coding to aid immediate perception. For it was not the mere fact of registration that Hooke thought so important, but the precise manner in which information was traced out on the page. This involved constructing a visual convention of typography contiguous with the conventions of engraved images that were so prominent a part of his *Micrographia*. Only if recorded in a correct manner, pictorially and typographically, could experimental matters of fact help in his project to "rectify the Mind." [112]

The pictorial aspect of this enterprise deserves particular emphasis. *Micrographia* itself was justly renowned for its innovative use of images, of course. But in Hooke's broader schemes, typography effectively fused into illustration, as the layout and impression (in both senses) of the page conditioned the knowledge a reader took from it. Printed letters were, after all,

112. Hooke, *Posthumous Works*, 18–19, 24, 34, 36, 42, 63–5, 138–48 (esp. 139–40); Mulligan, "Robert Hooke's 'Memoranda,'" 50–3. A possible inspiration for Hooke's scheme lay in the diverse systems still being proposed for commonplacing: see esp. Moss, *Printed Commonplace-Books*, 153, 226–30; Blair, "Humanist Methods in natural Philosophy"; Blair, *Theater of Nature*, 49–81, 166–79.

images of a sort, and this was how the imagination recognized them. His friend Joseph Moxon realized this. He exemplified it in his call for characters to be crafted along Vitruvian lines.[113] Exactly analogous problems of credit therefore attended engravings and woodcuts as were created by the printing of texts. And this was a conclusion applicable in general, not just in Hooke's own context. Corporeality, credit, and commerce were all implicated in the proper use of images.

Were images to be trusted as truthful representations of the world? On what basis?[114] The issue was perhaps especially pertinent in a Protestant realm avowing emancipation from the imaginative manipulation allegedly facilitated by Catholic iconography and emblems.[115] Similar interpretative strategies to those deployed around texts were therefore called for in approaching images, including the investigation of personnel, places, and technologies associated with their production and distribution. Willughby's *Historia Piscium*, the natural history of fish that almost proved the Royal Society's undoing in the 1680s, was one example; the *Atlas Cœlestis* of John Flamsteed, treated in chapter 8, was another. Both testified to the problems of funding, making, and believing engraved images of natural bodies.[116] Evelyn's *Sculptura* was partly intended as an answer to such questions. By enabling virtuosi to understand the engraving process, it aspired to help them rid pictorial representations of "Envy, and imposture." When even this book was challenged by a commercial engraver, as chapter 7 shows, the Society responded by moving to develop its own machineries of publication. A sizable community of practitioners existed that could be called upon to generate reproducible images of all kinds. As with the Stationers—but with less formality—this community had developed its own conventions of commerce and civility. Like the Stationers, too, these conventions repeatedly clashed with the concerns of men and women wishing to become authors. The engravers had their own patentees, monopolists, and, of course, pirates.

113. Above, p. 89. See also Evelyn, *Sculptura*, 11–23, for a history of pictorial representation that described letters and images as enjoying a common origin and early history.

114. For the accreditation and counterfeiting of images, see Evelyn, *Sculptura*, 54, 62, 63–4, 75, 93–4, 96, 101–3, 117, 128–9. Evelyn cited Hevelius as a model of the gentleman knowledgeable enough to overcome the problem: 82–3.

115. E.g., Stafford, *Artful Science*.

116. Willughby's book is a particularly interesting case, remarkable for its participants' extensive reflections on the processes of collection, recording, negotiation, and imprinting involved in making trustworthy images. Those processes may be followed by the modern historian, since Willughby's collections of pictures drawn from his European travels, along with comments by Ray (the editor) and others, and proof sheets in various stages of correction, are stored at NUL Ms. MiLM25. These provide what is perhaps a unique opportunity to trace in detail the construction of standard images of creatures from a variety of sources. I hope to examine them in detail in future work.

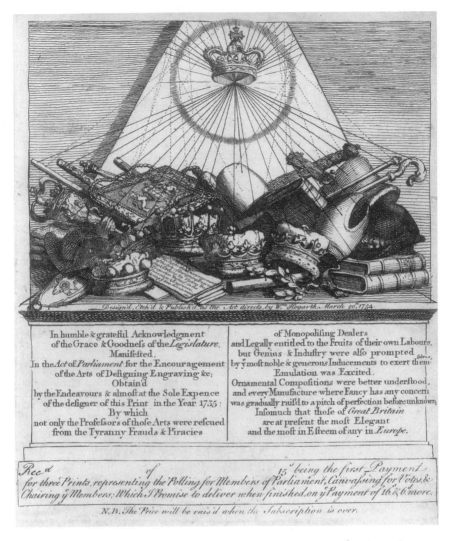

In humble & gratefull Acknowledgment of the Grace & Goodness of the *Legislature*, Manifested, In the *Act of Parliament* for the Encouragement of the Arts of Designing Engraving &c; Obtain'd by the Endeavours & almost at the Sole Expence of the designer of this Print in the Year 1735 ; By which not only the Professors of those Arts were rescued from the Tyranny Frauds & Piracies of Monopolising Dealers and Legally entitled to the Fruits of their own Labours, but Genius & Industry were also prompted by y most noble & generous Inducements to exert themselves, Emulation was Excited. Ornamental Compositions were better understood, and every Manufacture where Fancy has any concern was gradually rais'd to a pitch of perfection before unknown; Insomuch that those of *Great Britain* are at present the most Elegant and the most in Esteem of any in *Europe*.

Rec'd of 15 being the first Payment for three Prints, representing the Polling for Members of Parliament, Canvassing for Votes, & Chairing y Members; Which I Promise to deliver when finished, on y Payment of 16 & 6 more.

N.B. The Price will be rais'd when the Subscription is over.

FIG. 6.13. William Hogarth's engraving celebrating the passage in 1735 of an Act against "the Tyranny Frauds & Piracies of Monopolising Dealers," 1754. (In the possession of the author.)

They had their own notions of propriety, just as flexible and controversial as those of the Stationers' "copy." Exasperated complainants discovered that plates could be amended to an indeterminate degree by such workers, so that in a realm of unauthorized reproduction the artist bade "farewel to Accuracy, Expression, [and] Invention." The unlucky ones ended up yoked to the piracy mill themselves, becoming "no better than the Lowest of Robbers." Thus the whole enterprise seemed dominated by "the Tyranny Frauds & Piracies of Monopolising Dealers" (fig. 6.13). It was a situation replete with disturbing implications—for modern historians as well as contemporary readers, both being forced to rely on images the very creation of which cast doubt on their credit.[117]

As with texts, the credibility of pictorial reproductions could best be secured by manifesting clear control over every aspect of the reproductive process. Alexander Pitfield implied as much when he remarked that the images of dissections performed at the Académie des Sciences that he reproduced in 1688 "were not graved, till all those which were present at the Dissections found that they were wholly conformable to what they had seen." Novel techniques had to be developed for such a strategy to succeed, for, as Pitfield said, "in this the importance is not so much to represent well what is seen, as to see well what should be represented." Every author who saw an intricately designed draft for a frontispiece subjected to the caprice of an unlearned engraver knew as much. In the Royal Society, Pitfield and others drew upon the talented yet unsung Richard Waller. A protégé of Hooke, Waller uniquely combined craft skill with the civility of a Society fellow.

The most spectacular instance, however, was that of the Danzig astronomer Johannes Hevelius. Van Helden and Winkler show how Hevelius worked to create a "visual language" for his astronomy. An essential part of his enterprise was the establishment of credit in his engravings for users who might reside half a continent away. Hevelius tried to achieve this end by providing a complete, circumstantial account of their making. He covered the entire transit of an observation from telescope to printed page, including such arcane subjects as lens grinding and the different rates of shrinkage in breadth and height of damp paper as it dried. Hevelius himself may not actually have done any engraving or printing, although it is quite possible that he did (his printer certainly observed the stars with him). But he did pay for and control these processes, and the credit of the engraver and

117. Or, worse, the images might not exist at all. Pictorial representations of labor, retailing, and similar activities (and of printing and bookselling in particular) were far more likely to be made in Continental Europe than in London; that is why those used in chapter 2 often display French, Dutch, or German scenes. It is hard to say exactly why, although an explanation will clearly rest on the different criteria by which the engraving and publishing communities of these different regions reached their creative decisions—criteria involving representations of skill, economy, credibility, and audience. In fact, the images used above were generally meant to be normative as well as representative. They have been used for this reason, as well as because they are the most accurate images of printing houses and bookshops available to us. Pictures of experiments being done are another, even more striking, example: these do not seem to have been published anywhere. See *Case of Designers, Engravers, Etchers* for a polemic against the London print trade and its corruption by monopolists and pirates, and below, pp. 615–6, for the consequences of alleged piracy in the case of John Flamsteed's star charts. Schulze, *Leselust*, beautifully reproduces a wide range of Continental images related to the reading and symbolic value of books, but not to their manufacture or commerce.

printer was therefore to be "included in" his own. His images of the stars were stamped with the certificates "Observator sculpsit" (in *Cometographia*) or "Autor sculpsit" (in *Selenographia*).[118] These signaled that he was staking his reputation on a quite extraordinary claim to veracity. In Hevelius's books, the page was to be accounted a direct representation of the heavens.

It was, however, possible to question Hevelius's images. Flamsteed referred to one instance. In his *Mercurius in Sole Visus*, Hevelius had displayed an engraving of the transit of Mercury across the Sun in 1661 that, he claimed, was of just this order of veracity. He had produced the seven recorded positions by marking them with a pin on a single sheet of paper onto which he had projected the face of the Sun (fig. 6.14). But Oldenburg communicated to him doubts about this image raised by Thomas Streete, who had observed the same transit in London with Huygens. Streete pointed out that the angle of Mercury's path displayed by Hevelius seemed to contradict Streete's own calculations based on accepted observations of the planet's angle to the ecliptic (fig. 6.15). Perhaps Hevelius had in fact constructed the printed picture not directly from observation, but by combining other sheets on which observed positions had been marked. Hevelius's first response was to insist again upon the observational veracity of the figure and to remark that the angle of Mercury's orbit could be obtained "mechanically" by constructions from his engraving (fig. 6.16). This failed to satisfy Streete, who now proposed further doubts about the viability of Hevelius's technique for obtaining truthful numbers. The necessary movement of the sheet of paper between each observation, he argued, meant that important angles must vary between each of the seven traces. Hevelius now saw that Streete was in effect directly questioning the truth of his account of the marking of these positions. He reaffirmed that he had noted them on the same sheet. He had appointed the vertical point of the Sun's limb, then referred the paper to that vertical in making each observation. This, he maintained, was a more direct and truthful method that any based on calculated figures. Since it relied on no prior information, it was an instantiation of the principle of *nullius in verba*. Yet, in true Royal Society tradition, he also cited witnesses to confirm that he had indeed acted as he said, and that the recorded observations accorded to those engraved in the book. This effectively ended the mild controversy, since the stakes of continued questioning were too high. As Flamsteed remarked, Streete's insinuation of a

118. Evelyn, *Sculptura*, esp. sigs. A2ʳ–A4ᵛ; Pitfield, *Memoirs*, sig. [b3ʳ]; Ezell, "Richard Waller," 214–22; Hevelius, *Selenographia*, 210–15; Hevelius, *Machina Cælestis*, 446–7; Winkler and Van Helden, "Johannes Hevelius and the Visual Language of Astronomy"; Winkler and Van Helden, "Representing the Heavens." For the need for authors to oversee engravers' work, see Corbett and Lightblown, *The Comely Frontispiece*, I, 34–5, 45.

FIG. 6.14. Hevelius's projection technique for observing solar transits. Hevelius, *Machina Cœlestis*. (By permission of the Syndics of Cambridge University Library.)

FIG. 6.15. Huygens's portrayal of Mercury's transit across the face of the Sun, observed in London with Thomas Streete on 23 April / 3 May 1661. Huygens, *Oeuvres*, III. (By permission of the Syndics of Cambridge University Library.)

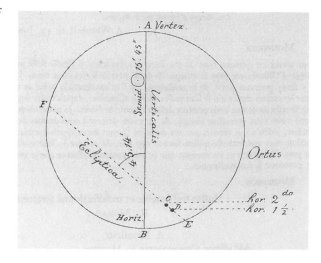

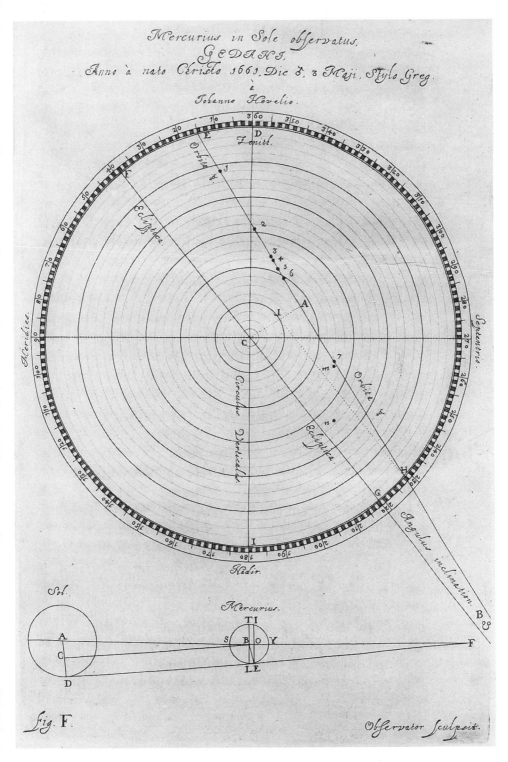

FIG. 6.16. Hevelius's use of his technique for the direct representation of the heavens to show the transit of Mercury across the face of the Sun. Hevelius, *Mercurius in Sole Visus*. (By permission of the Syndics of Cambridge University Library.)

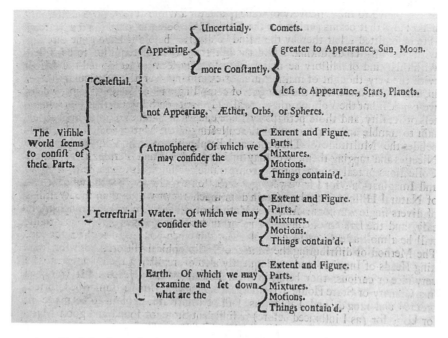

FIG. 6.17. Hooke's schema for the representation of knowledge, designed for ready apprehension by the imagination and retention in the memory. Applied in practice, the result would be pages coded by color as well as layout. Hooke, *Posthumous Works*. (By permission of the Syndics of Cambridge University Library.)

composite image must be reckoned "wide and different from the practise of that Judicious Observer."[119]

Typography and engraving alike had to be seen in the context of the credit of their producers. Flamsteed himself found this to his cost, as chapter 8 shows. Meanwhile, Hooke took the provisions of his own recipe very seriously (fig. 6.17). He emphasized just these factors, for example, in championing projects for publication. Moses Pitt's *English Atlas*, which he strongly supported, was thus designed to present "a plaine simple cleer and uncompounded Representation of the Object to the Sense," to "more easily imprint that idea the Deeper in the memory, which is the Principall use of such a work."[120] That he maintained this view so strongly should hardly be surprising, since Hooke based it on principles of mind and body that he felt to be of universal applicability. His efforts may be compared to those dedi-

119. Oldenburg, *Correspondence*, II, 182–9, 214–21, 300–309, 392–9; RGO Ms. 1.43, fols. 45ᵛ–49ᵛ; Flamsteed, *Correspondence*, I, 633–8. For another questioning of Hevelius's images, see Shapin, *Social History of Truth*, 272–91.

120. BL Ms. Sl. 1039. fols. 1ʳ–2ʳ.

cated to the production of polyglot bibles, in which "the several *Languages* shall be printed in several Columns, whereby they may all be presented to the Readers view *at once*," to synoptic bibliographical guides from Gesner's onward, and to the affinity tables and similar devices deployed by chemical writers of the next century. All involved prolonged, dedicated, and active reflection on the importance of *mise en page* for the communication, reception, and practice of knowledge.[121] As Hooke himself declared in a lecture on geometry, given these principles it was essential to follow his mechanisms for "furnishing the Mind with the true grounds of Knowledge." They were not necessary just for experimental philosophy, however. All knowledge must be communicated in such a fashion, or else it could not truly be accounted knowledge. "We see it necessary, and practised in many other things where a good habit is to be acquired." As such, it was clearly essential in "Reading . . . , and most other Manual Operations."[122]

CONCLUSION

This chapter has utilized contemporary accounts of anatomy, the passions, philosophical method, and perception, in order to encourage a widening of the terms in which we view the practices and representations of reading in early modern England. The fact that uses of this material were remarkably diverse in the period, so that the treatment offered here has at times pursued them away from a narrow concentration on reading itself and into issues of education, knowledge, gender, religious faith, and politics, only reinforces its salience.

Such a diversity of application underscores the importance that historians should attach to the history of reading as both skill and representation. John Dryden suggested another use that underscores the point. Dryden insisted upon the importance of historiography because "it informs the understanding by the memory." Since mankind was "the same in all ages," and "agitated by the same passions," nothing could come to pass unless "some Presedent of the like nature has already been produc'd." It was an entirely conventional view, shared by many in Dryden's society.[123] The argument rested on assumptions about the natural economy of the passions—an economy that contemporaries assumed to be universal and sempiternal. In

---

121. *Brief Description of an Edition of the Bible; Propositions concerning the Printing of the Bible*; Chartier, *Order of Books*, 61–88; Golinski, *Science as Public Culture*; Roberts, "Setting the Table"; Anderson, *Between the Library and the Laboratory*. For *mise en page*, see also Laufer, "Espaces du Livre," and Kroll, "*Mise-en-Page*."

122. Hooke, *Posthumous Works*, 70.

123. Levine, *Battle of the Books*, 274. Many other examples are listed in Champion, *Pillars of Priestcraft Shaken*, 25, 35–40.

perhaps the most influential introduction to the reading of history, Degory Wheare thus urged that historical literature imprinted images of characters on the mind, and thereby encouraged their emulation. "By a kind of Wax-Images," Wheare told students, the rhetorical presentation of past characters could "help, excite and irritate our cold and languishing Memories."[124] Wheare thus defined history itself as a "Register and Explication of particular affairs, undertaken to the end that the memory of them may be preserved, and so Universals may be the more evidently confirm'd, by which we may be instructed how to live well and Happily."[125] This was very much the same kind of representation as that which informed Hooke's deployment of his own "register" at the Royal Society.

This chapter began by asking what early modern men and women thought actually happened when they read. They saw letters on a page through eyes that resembled the device known as the camera obscura, which conveyed images, through the body's animal spirits, onto the brain's *sensus communis*. There imaginative and perceptual images combined, and animal spirits mingled and departed to drive the body's responses to both. The chapter traced the paths of these spirits along the channels increasingly discerned by anatomists, and demonstrated that their role was such that reading necessarily took place through a complex of what contemporaries called "passions." They knew a great deal about these entities, and were able to account for a wide variety of beliefs and actions in terms of their passionate states. Passions could be generated either by sensations or by internal bodily events. The latter was certainly the case during diseases, and physicians possessed recognized remedies for such conditions. More, Sedgwick, Hickes, and Smith capitalized on their experiences when they juxtaposed enthusiastic "visions" with passionate "vapours."

This meant that reading partook of a problem of knowledge that was one of the most intractable to face early modern society. The discussion showed the necessity for an English subject of restraining his or her passions. On success in this effort depended the status of the individual as a reliable investigator and relater of truth. This applied in all spheres, but the chapter particularly stressed the importance of the passions in accounting for what hostile contemporaries called "enthusiasm." In the 1640s, especially, radical nonconformists, convinced of what they called their experimental faith, claimed direct insights from God. For the women among them, this conviction facilitated their pioneering of forms of authorship not seen before in England. But most authorities were antagonistic. What distinguished sec-

124. Wheare, *Method and Order*, 323–4; *Universal Historical Bibliotheque*, 2 (February 1686/7), 129.
125. Wheare, *Method and Order*, 15.

tarian "schism" from "necessary separation" (such as that of Canterbury from Rome), John Hales thought, was that the former rested on "passion or distemper." [126] This was a very widely held view indeed. Religious "enthusiasts" were thus classifiable in terms of their inability or unwillingness to restrain their passions in the context of their reading. Henry More and Meric Casaubon took great pains to specify the precise nature of their opponents' errors, and did so by recounting their own most striking reading experiences. Both elided typography and images in their tales. More stressed the importance of the imagination in creating apparent visions from visually striking pages. Casaubon agreed, but went further in urging the profound danger of abandoning the labor of critical, skeptical reading in a world of forgeries. Its neglect of the skills needed for this effort was why Casaubon opposed the program of the Royal Society.[127] That program—the establishment and promotion of experimental natural philosophy—is the subject of the following chapter.

126. Hales, *Works*, I, 116.

127. George Sinclair went further still. A Cartesian, he maintained, forced experiments into "compliance with his own *fancies*, [and] was not this to study *Natural History*, as *Hereticks* do the *Scripture*[?]": S[inclair], *Hydrostaticks*, 316. Such complaints should, however, be compared to the conduct of people such as Flamsteed, who refused to send a list of errata in his *Doctrine of the Sphere* to Molyneux because the presence of unknown errors would force the reader to work through—and hence properly understand—the mathematical argument of the book. Molyneux responded by declaring that his weakness in mathematics was such that unless Flamsteed became more forthcoming, he would cease to read it altogether: he "should read with fear and distrust, and that is to read in Pain and not in Pleasure." Southampton CRO Ms. D/M 1/1, fols. 57^r–59^r.

7

PIRACY AND USURPATION

Natural Philosophy in the Restoration

Books and experiments do well together, but separately they betray an imperfection, for the illiterate is anticipated unwittingly by the labours of the ancients, and the man of authors deceived by story instead of science. The happy Royal Society adjusts both together.

EDWARD BERNARD TO JOHN COLLINS, 3 April 1671: Rigaud,
Correspondence of Scientific Men, I, 158

Know ye not that the unrighteous shall inherit the Kingdom of God?

I CORINTHIANS 6:9, as printed by John Field in 1653

INTRODUCTION

Previous chapters have argued that early modern readers faced profound problems in making use of printed books. This chapter examines how some of them overcame those problems to create new and authoritative knowledge. In particular, it takes for its subject knowledge of the natural world. Contemporaries realized that their representations of nature were changing at an unprecedented rate and in unpredictable ways. Both the promise and the perils of print became starkly evident to them as they strove to articulate agreed understandings of the universe in which they lived. The chapter asks why such people should wish to embroil themselves in print at all, and describes the difficulties they faced when they did. It then investigates how they worked to ensure that natural knowledge could be printed, published, and read while successfully preserving the integrity of both the knowledge itself and its proponents. In sum, it explains how readers put printed materials to use in order to make, contest, and sustain claims about Creation.

In principle, there is nothing unique to natural knowledge about the themes of this chapter. The problems and solutions described here were

444

relevant to a wide range of activities, devoted to the making and promulgation of arguments of many kinds. Marchand, Meerman, Palmer, and the other authors discussed in chapter 5 had to deal with them just as urgently as any of the figures discussed below. But few modern readers, perhaps, would be surprised or disturbed to find that antiquarian or critical learning could be affected by any conditions of distrust surrounding print. That the mathematics of a John Wallis, the experiments of a Robert Boyle, and even, perhaps, the natural philosophy of an Isaac Newton should be so affected is both harder to accept and more unsettling in its implications. The historical excavation of their experiences is therefore peculiarly interesting. Moreover, natural philosophers themselves identified, articulated, and proposed solutions to the problems of credit attendant upon print. In examining their efforts we are thus presented with unusually self-aware participant observers, keen to understand and even transform their situation.

They showed such interest because they had to. Philosophers who tried to become authors needed to traverse the cultural domains outlined in the preceding parts of this book. They immediately became vulnerable to all the forms of appropriation traced there. But those appropriative practices were likely to prove particularly consequential for their concerns. For one thing, as will shortly be argued at length, the economic justification of learned publishing was always fragile. An uncongenial book trade might result simply and brutally in the nonappearance of potentially valuable works. But economic decisions rested on cultural practices and representations, at even the most elementary of levels: the price of Newton's *Principia* was fixed, as Bentley said, "for ye honour of ye Book."[1] And their cultural connotations were at least as important. Philosophical writers vested much of their identities and reputations in their printed works, so that counterfeiting, abridgment, translation, and piracy threatened them with far more than merely economic damage. The repute of the individual concerned—and of the knowledge he or she professed—rested on the successful negotiation of such hazards. Writers developed certain strategies to overcome these dangers. They might coalesce and cooperate as a group, for example, combining resources to protect themselves. Such a body might even become a corporate licenser, utilizing the conventions described in chapter 3 to distinguish its books as creditable. Another possible course was to invent new techniques of communication, such as the learned periodical, the protocols of which might limit the practical powers of printers and booksellers. Still another was to police not just publication but reading, in the hope of stimulating debate while limiting conflict. The Royal Society tried all of these. In

---

1. Newton, *Correspondence*, V, 413–4.

the Society, arguments and attributions of discredit could, it was hoped, be constrained and resolved peacefully by such means. Each of its strategies is discussed below. By adopting these measures, the Society pioneered conventions that would eventually survive to underpin a reliable order of print.

Natural knowledge could be developed in a variety of ways and by a variety of practitioners. The mathematical sciences (which included astronomy) differed significantly from natural philosophy and natural history in both approach and objectives.[2] The chapter addresses themes common to each of these disciplines. But it concentrates in detail on one of them, natural philosophy, and on one kind of natural philosophy in particular. Deferring consideration of the mathematical science of astronomy to chapter 8, this chapter devotes the bulk of its substantive examination to the practice named *experimental philosophy*. This was a new enterprise, developed in mid-seventeenth-century England and identified with Robert Boyle and others in the nascent Royal Society of London. In experimental philosophy, the issues of credit associated with the printed realm became acute. Experimental knowledge rested substantially on the accreditation of communiqués about experience. These documents, whether printed or handwritten, had to be read and trusted across wide distances and in very different cultural settings. If they were subjected to systematic distrust, the experimental community could not cohere and the experimental philosophy could not succeed. The story of their establishment is thus a central element in the history of experimental science.

PROFESSING KNOWLEDGE IN A PIRATICAL CULTURE

An account of the problems and opportunities faced by gentlemen intending to profess natural knowledge must begin with the arguments presented in chapter 2. Those arguments imply an acknowledgment that once such figures took the decision to venture into print, the propriety of their words was no longer theirs. Power over the copy of any printed book would generally be held by a bookseller, or, increasingly, a partnership of booksellers. This applied in both senses of the word "copy": the Stationers possessed proprietary rights, according to their community, over the text, and in their printing houses they also exercised interpretative autonomy over the actual sheets being reproduced. They were now free to produce as many editions as they thought fit, along with the epitomes, abridgments, and translations prohibited to others by Stationers' Company protocol. Writers could at-

---

2. For the mathematical sciences, see Dear, *Discipline and Experience*, and Westman, "Astronomer's Role"; for natural history, see Jardine, Secord, and Spary, *Cultures of Natural History*.

tempt to intervene in this domain, but doing so was fraught with difficulty. The situation created peculiar problems for someone wishing to create and communicate natural knowledge through print, and demanded peculiar solutions. This section delineates some of the most obvious problems. It also outlines the simplest responses—and why they often failed. In short, it explains why the intervention of the Royal Society was necessary at all.

Writers of learned works faced all the problems associated with print that have been identified hitherto. But their effects were perhaps even greater for such works than for others. A simple reason for this was economic. Natural-philosophical books might require unusual production facilities. For such fields as mathematics, astronomy, and natural history, special typefaces were often needed. These were certain to be costly and might even prove unobtainable. Any book incorporating elaborate images was likewise certain to prove expensive to produce, apart from being vulnerable to the peculiar problems described in the previous chapter. Small and dispersed markets provided scant hope of recovering these costs—and the security even of those markets was threatened by piracy, as will be shown shortly. As a result, no London printing house could afford to specialize exclusively in learned publishing of this kind. The Oxford and Cambridge houses, which were established partly for this type of work, testified by their incessant and almost terminal difficulties to the intense problems involved.

It is important to realize the scale of the economic concerns underlying such difficulties. According to Shapin and Schaffer, at a cost of some £25 an early Restoration air-pump was "seventeenth-century 'Big Science.'" Few people could afford one, and even fewer were disposed to forfeit the time and resources needed to keep such a temperamental machine working. But publishing was liable to prove costly, too, especially given the illustrations, special typography, and expert proofing often needed. Since they were often made as presentation volumes, or at least as products for a discerning clientele, natural-philosophy books were also likely to require paper of high quality, printed with particular care. For example, Moses Pitt claimed to have spent £1,000 in buying materials for his *English Atlas*, including machinery, an old set of map plates, and a new set of type.[3] Coupled with the additional charges entailed by labor, an investment of this order generally demanded powerful patronage. Pitt himself directed his appeals to the king and the duke of York (fig. 7.1). But such ventures could prove perilous even so, as Pitt's own failure was to prove. Given the high costs of English printing, Continental competition was one threat. Dutch houses could reprint

---

3. BL Ms. Sloane 1039, fol. 4ʳ; Shapin and Schaffer, *Leviathan and the Air-Pump*, 38. Such costs may be compared with the sums invested by Cornelius Bee in learned scriptural commentaries, and by Peter Cole in purchasing medical copies: above, p. 218.

FIG. 7.1. Moses Pitt,
The English Atlas.
Frontispiece to vol. 1.
(By permission of the
Henry E. Huntington
Library, San Marino,
California.)

London books for less than it cost to import them, and they were not slow to do so.[4] The number of natural philosophers experiencing such treatment was substantial and included Newton, Boyle, Hobbes, and Flamsteed. But even enterprises like Pitt's, which had no such direct competition, often foundered.

Expensive to produce, these books were also not cheap to buy, especially in the aftermath of the Fire of London. At that moment John Collins found part of the second volume of an English translation of Galileo on sale for a stiff fifty shillings.[5] Pitt's atlas is again worth noting here, since it tells us

4. Hodgson and Blagden, *Notebook of Thomas Bennet*, 14.
5. Rigaud, *Correspondence of Scientific Men*, I, 119; Hooke later found Galileo's *Dialogue* for 6s 4d: Hooke, "Diary," 122. For John Wallis on the book trade after the fire, see Rigaud, *Correspondence of Scientific Men*, II, 474–6.

probably the upper limit on prices for books of natural knowledge. Before binding, Pitt's first volume was to be sold for forty shillings to subscribers and fifty-five to nonsubscribers. Complete, unbound, and uncolored, the subscription cost for the entire set was fixed at £18.15.00. Extrapolating from this a retail price for the bound set is not straightforward, since prices for binding varied; one near-contemporary quoted a shilling for quartos and as much as eleven shillings for folios. Evidence suggests that binding Pitt's first volume, which was inconveniently large, cost an impressive twenty-two shillings.[6] At that rate, the whole multivolume publication might have cost as much as £30 to its readers, had it ever been completed. This was as much "big science" as Boyle's air-pump—and it was every bit as fragile.

The first, and perhaps most profound, difficulty consequently lay in persuading a Stationer that such a work of natural knowledge should appear in print at all. Expensive production costs, long printing schedules (with the attendant risks of interruption), and limited markets meant that Stationers were notoriously reluctant to undertake learned titles unless they could be guaranteed to sell. In 1671 John Collins reckoned that a likely market of eighty to a hundred copies was the minimum. It does not sound like much, but mathematical titles in particular were liable to fall short of this target. Even Robert Scott, "the chief trader into France" for such books, found that he could never sell more than twenty or thirty copies of an imported mathematical work.[7] Nothing of this kind could be brought forth without a dowry, Collins sighed, so that the mathematical culture of his time was severely distorted. He even composed a discourse outlining "the ill consequences that ensue the not encouraging good books to be printed," in which he stressed "instances of many good treasures, that are by this means either quite lost, or never come to be public." Ironically enough, this discourse now seems itself to be lost. Nonetheless, it is possible to construct a long list of mathematical books that remained unpublished. Isaac Newton's proposed edition of Kinckhuysen's *Algebra* is perhaps an especially noteworthy example, given the roots of its failure in a complex combination of bookseller's caution and authorial reluctance to appear "ambitious." Now and again, it is true, transient conditions might modify this situation. Isaac Barrow's volume of *Lectiones Opticae* was one beneficiary, becoming available at a time when several booksellers had concluded that there was a market for such a piece. The London trade even competed for it, while the secretary of the Royal Society, Henry Oldenburg, helped by assiduously spreading word of Barrow's work. The Dutch *libraires* could also sometimes help as well as

6. BL Ms. Add. 4421, fol. 361^{r-v}; *Generall Note of the prises*; Browne, *Works*, IV, 171–2.
7. Rigaud, *Correspondence of Scientific Men*, I, 195–204, esp. 200. Compare Hunter, "Science and Astrology," 271, 278–9.

compete. As well as reprinting English books, they could provide an opportunity for would-be authors facing refusal by London Stationers reluctant to risk their credit on arcane titles. When John Wallis wanted to publish his algebra, he was thus forced to approach Dutch printers. But such was the doubt surrounding undertakings of this sort that approaches like Wallis's did not always succeed. Despite his relative prominence, he discovered that even the Dutch were loath to undertake his book. And in fact Barrow's *Lectiones*, too, eventually proved unprofitable. Its disenchanted booksellers returned to their caricatured refusal to undertake "any thing but toys." [8]

Economically insecure, books of natural knowledge teetered on the verge of unviability. Still, there were ways in which the publication even of lavish books could be achieved, provided that sufficient capital or credit could be secured. John Ogilby managed it by selling lottery tickets in Garraway's coffeehouse, at £2 each; Pepys was one of the winners. Others struck individual deals with Stationers. In pre–Civil War Oxford, Nathaniel Carpenter paid for the production of his *Geography Delineated* himself (at a cost of some £92, almost half of which was for paper), before selling on copies to a local bookseller. A generation later, Henry More would agree to buy a hundred copies out of an impression of five hundred, at 50 percent above their cost to print—in effect, providing the bookseller with a self-subscription. [9] This seems to have been a relatively common type of arrangement. It was also one that, as we shall see, the Royal Society itself was tempted to use, drawing upon its fellowship to guarantee a certain number of buyers.

Extending such strategies beyond individuals and corporate fellowships, another option, of increasing importance after 1660, was to publish by subscription. This was a practice peculiarly suited to the English trade. It involved persuading a number of prosperous individuals to invest enough money in a proposed publication that the project would be sufficiently capitalized to proceed to completion. Direct royal patronage aside, it was the most effective—and often the only—way to finance the printing of a truly substantial publication. If they were to succeed, however, subscription projects had to overcome formidable problems. Their main obstacle was one of credibility. Proposals issued by undertakers were in effect promissory notes, offering future benefits in return for current investment. They consequently depended more than ever on the major participants, and in particu-

8. Rigaud, *Correspondence of Scientific Men*, I, 122, 147–56, 178; II, 14–16; Westfall, *Never at Rest*, 222–32; Oldenburg, *Correspondence*, V, 468–72. For Barrow's optical work see Shapiro, "*Optical Lectures*." Fell planned to use the Oxford University press to produce a complete corpus of ancient mathematical works: Feingold, "Mathematical Sciences and New Philosophies," 435–6.

9. Van Eerde, *John Ogilby*, 85–6; Ellis, *Penny Universities*, 110–12; McKitterick, *Cambridge University Press*, 252, 327–8; Conway, *Letters*, 372–3.

lar the Stationers among them, retaining reputations for personal and financial probity. Subscription undertakers were Defoe's merchants of credit par
excellence.

Such agents developed a number of strategies to support their good
names and buttress their commercial prospects. The day-to-day progress of
a subscription enterprise would typically be managed by a Stationer, the
"undertaker," who might well be the originator of the enterprise. But the
conduct of this undertaker would be overseen publicly by a number of gentlemen "directors." The good names of the latter would then extend over
the project itself, becoming the immediate basis for an image of integrity
displayed to prospective subscribers. The identities of its directors were thus
crucial to a project's viability. In subscription proposals, the credibility of
the proposed text, the credit of the directors as knowledgeable gentlemen
prepared to vest their faith in it, and the financial credit of the undertaker
all became mutually dependent.[10] To this tripod could then be added a
fourth leg. Once sufficient subscribers had been persuaded to invest in a
project, the list of their names immediately became a further asset, generally
being printed before the work itself. Such a list was a key element in the
campaign of accreditation on which any subscription publication depended.
It represented a survey of the reservoir of social credit underpinning the
project. Its ordering by rank served to advertise the patronage of noble and
even royal figures, and it proclaimed their endorsement of the knowledge
being purveyed in the book itself.

Pitt's atlas project is again a good early example of these strategies—not
least because it was to prove unsuccessful. It was originally Pitt's own idea.
He discussed his initial plans with Robert Hooke, who introduced him and
his proposals to the Royal Society in March 1678.[11] In the absence of the
Philosophical Transactions after Oldenburg's death, Hooke, Oldenburg's replacement as secretary, saw an opportunity to create an exhaustive work of
natural history. He proposed that the Society's correspondence networks be
mobilized to provide substantial local information. Envisaging a still more
elaborate and original work than Pitt had planned, Hooke projected up to
"six hundred copperplates or maps, and about nine hundred printed sheets,"

10. Abbatista, "Business of Paternoster Row," 11–12. Proposals for printing the polyglot
Bible had stated that the "Draught" sheets had been approved by Selden, Armachanus, and
the Council of State: *Brief Description of an Edition of the Bible; Propositions concerning the
Printing of the Bible.* For a comparison with the relative rarity of Dutch subscription projects,
see Van Rooden and Wesselius, "Two Early Cases."

11. Birch, *History,* III, 397, 480; IV, 4, 21; Hooke, *Diary,* 349–53; BL Ms. Add. 4421, fols.
327^r, 359^v. Hooke's presence in this list is interesting, since by normal criteria he was scarcely
a gentleman. His qualification was presumably by virtue of his attributed skill, the corps of
directors representing a conjunction of techniques, knowledge, and personal probity.

spread across eleven volumes. The first volume alone would need the coordinated work of five skilled men, "each of them doing one fifth part of the
number or more to wit 5 or 6 mapps," while another prepared indexes, a
seventh composed descriptions in Latin, and an eighth translated them into
English. "As fast as any of these are ready they may be printed off," Pitt
optimistically forecast. They would be produced in two sites, "the tables
and Descriptions at Oxford" and "the plates & mapps at London." In order
to maintain the credit of the operation throughout, Pitt would act under
a group of "Gentlemen Directors" from the Royal Society, comprising
Wren, Pell, Gale, Vossius, Lloyd, and Hooke. A ledger would be maintained, "wherein every thing [would] be entred & signed by each agreeing," with all "Dissents to be entred & signed likewise." Draft subscription
proposals further stressed that Pitt had given security to secretary of state
and president of the Royal Society Joseph Williamson to guarantee the realization of the ambitious project, and suggested compensation by way of
alternative books for any dissatisfied subscriber. It should not be needed.
The list of subscribers already committed, Pitt maintained, would itself
"recommend so Noble and Useful a Design to the rest of the Nobility and
Gentry." [12]

Despite the endorsement of the king, his brother the duke of York, the
Royal Society, and both universities—and notwithstanding the help afforded by the Oxford press—the *English Atlas* faltered after only four volumes. It failed for a number of reasons. Given the Society's (and especially
Hooke's) other weekly concerns, the plan was probably unrealizable in the
time permitted by the subscription proposals. Their credit therefore could
not survive the attempt to create a work of such prodigious scope, and few
further subscribers came forward. But there were also more prosaic difficulties. Hooke found that the old Dutch plates that Pitt had purchased needed
expensive emendation: a figure of their original author must be replaced by
"some other Person"; a planisphere was old, worn, "full of errors," and projected to a false meridian; and many of the maps were far too erroneous
to be incorporated. He enticed Pitt to give him £200 bond in return for
Hooke's own invented "contrivance for the making mapps," which proved
impracticable. Printing had to be shifted to the cheaper site of Amsterdam,
finished sheets being shipped to London to be viewed at Pitt's "house." [13]
Gradually work slipped behind schedule. Eventually it ceased altogether,

---

12. BL Ms. Sloane 1039, fols. 3ʳ, 17ʳ, 19ʳ⁻ᵛ; BL Ms. Add. 4421, fols. 326ʳ⁻327ᵛ.

13. BL Ms. Sloane 1039, fol. 13ʳ⁻ᵛ; BL Ms. Add. 4421, fol. 361ʳ⁻ᵛ. The story of Pitt's presenting one of his unimpressive specimens to a dismayed duke of York, who blurted
out that they were unusable, is well known: Pitt responded that the margins at least were
nicely done.

although there were occasional calls to revive it even into the 1690s. Pitt himself sank into bankruptcy, arrest, and debtors' prison.

Since it depended on credit, the viability of subscription publishing was inevitably attenuated by the high proportion of proposals that, like Pitt's, never gave rise to finished books. In the eighteenth century the Abbé Prévost, who believed that the practice had been invented in late-seventeenth-century London, was one of many to observe that "greed has been seen a hundred times to abuse the credulity of the public and betray its trust through bad uses of subscriptions." Venturing one's credit on such a proposal was thus risky, and in more than an economic sense. Involvement in failures could be a mark of poor judgment. It came to be associated with the spirit of "projecting" so abominated in Augustan England. Astrologer John Partridge thus sought to discredit his rival Thomas Streete, author of *Astronomia Carolina*—the most reliable set of astronomical tables then available—by charging that he "was famous for wheedling a number of Gentlemen, by persuading them to subscribe for a Book he pretended to print, got about 150 or 200 pound of them, and then cheated them of their money."[14] In this case, as in others, what can appear to modern eyes to be economic problems were to those involved profoundly personal, and even epistemic.

At the center of these struggles stood the Stationers. Whether by subscription or otherwise, the publication of natural knowledge had to be channeled through the agency of these men and women. But individuals like Giles Calvert, Peter Cole, Joseph Moxon, and John Streater—not to mention Moses Pitt—were known to their contemporaries as active participants in the appropriation and reappropriation of images, texts, and ideas. They understood their own conduct in terms of an extensive and complex web of customary conventions, infringers of which they stood ready to identify and assail. The accreditation techniques developed in subscription publishing were designed partly to answer concern about the Stationer's identity: that was why the undertaker would be publicly subordinated to a committee of gentlemen. It was unavoidable, however, that in the domains of the Stationers theirs was the régime which threatened to prevail. And when applied to works professing natural knowledge, what the Stationers saw as infringements of their craft order became strategies of discredit, with real consequences for authors.

Those perils began at the most local of levels. In the printing house itself, the demands of learning could not be respected without qualification. Works of natural knowledge had to be integrated as well as possible into a

---

14. Hunter, *Science and Society*, 69; Robinson and Wallis, *Book Subscription Lists*; Abbatista, "Business of Paternoster Row," 9–11; [Partridge], *Flagitiosus Mercurius Flagellatus*, 9. For "projectors" see Stewart, *Rise of Public Science*, 166–211, 285–310.

prevailing domain of labor and representation. The practice of concurrent printing in particular meant that the books intellectual historians now selectively notice were seldom produced or distributed in such isolation. At its most benign, the practice resulted in these works merely being delayed while the printers concentrated on more immediately profitable material. They had to, since printing houses relied on pamphlets and ephemera, not folio volumes, for their economic sustenance. Addison maintained that "not a Tenth part of the Printer's work is done for Fame, and by Persons of Quality," and many writers found this all too true. Astronomer Royal John Flamsteed, whose experiences are the subject of the following chapter, was thus discovering a routine reality when he found that his own printers would work on "any newspapers or pamphlet" sooner than a massive, prestigious and authoritative *Historia Cœlestis,* "because news and pamphlets bring them ready money." The bookseller undertaking the publication would pay these printers only on completion of the whole project, Flamsteed discovered, or once a year if, like his own, it were planned to last longer than that. Printers were therefore forced to take on short-term work even in the midst of such large projects. In chapter 4 we saw one dramatic example of the kind of juxtaposition that could result from such practices. Joseph Streater's house produced Newton's *Principia,* pirated almanacs, and pornography at the same time. Such juxtapositions were probably the rule, not the exception.[15]

Most spectacular of all the dangers arising in the domains of print was that of outright reprinting. This was an international enterprise. The proficiency of Dutch printing houses in reproducing English works has already been noted. Far from declining as the book trade increased in sophistication, the practice flourished into the eighteenth century and remained an issue well into the nineteenth. Robert Darnton has shown in a Continental context how immensely profitable reprinting such a large work as the *Encyclopédie* could be: a small state might regard such a "piracy" as a prestigious national project. Darnton has also outlined how such unauthorized reprints could affect the text and its construal in consequential ways. But this was just the grandest international tip of an iceberg crystallized out of everyday practices in all European countries. In Britain too such practices thrived, even after the 1710 Act. Booksellers in Edinburgh and Dublin persisted in importing reprints into London, extending their scope to multivolume publications. London Stationers reacted with horror. Printer William Strahan warned that the trade "must soon be destroyed if every body is permitted to print every Thing," and Thomas Birch's bookseller, Andrew Millar, was apparently worried to death by such reprinting. Piracy of this kind affected

15. [Addison], *Thoughts of a Tory Author,* 5; Baily, *Flamsteed,* 262.

every aspect of printing, publishing, and reading. Daniel Defoe even proposed the reintroduction of licensing, so seriously did he take practices robbing authors and readers of "the Prize of Learning." [16]

Such outright reprinting hardly exhausted the possibilities. As chapter 3 made clear, questions of identity and difference between books were not so simply resolved. Printers and booksellers developed conventional mechanisms for determining such issues over the course of decades. According to these, "Epitomes" or "Abridgments" could be more controversial even than direct reproductions. [17] Defoe himself characterized abridgment as "the first Sort of Press-Piracy." It was practiced on large books of "Philosophy, History, or any Subject," he attested, and invariably generated a "false idea" of the original. So common did the practice become that Dunton reckoned "*Original* and *Abridgement*" to be "as necessary as Man and Wife." Defoe provided an account of its practical origins:

> An Author prints a Book, whether on a Civil or Religious Subject, Philosophy, History, or any Subject, if it be a large Volume, it shall be immediately *abridg'd* by some mercenary Book-seller, employing a Hackney-writer, who shall give such a contrary Turn to the Sense, such a false idea of the Design, and so huddle Matters of the greatest Consequence together on abrupt Generals, that no greater Wrong can be done to the Subject. [18]

"A Bookseller of Character and moral Honesty" would "scorn" such practices, said Campbell, restating the link between piracy and the character of the Stationer that was demonstrated in chapter 2. Since an original text could not hope to sell against its abridgment, it would soon disappear. Mathematicians like John Wallis felt that this type of "epitome" might therefore "endanger the loss of the author himself." John Streater perhaps hoped as much when he applied exactly this practice to Thomas Blount in his law-patent campaign. As Blount then found, there was little a mere

16. Darnton, *Business of Enlightenment*, 33 ff., 131 ff.; Coover, *Music Publishing*; Desmond, *Politics of Evolution*, 15, 44, 74, 120–1, 163, 204, 230–33, 237–9, 246–8, 338–9, 412–4; Bonnell, "Bookselling and Canon-Making," 55–6; Burrow, *Question Concerning Literary Property*, 2; [Defoe], *Essay on the Regulation of the Press*, 19 ff. See also [Defoe], *Attempt towards a Coalition of English Protestants*, and [Defoe], *Letter to a Member of Parliament*.

17. By the Press Act of 1662, for which the Company had lobbied in the hope of protecting copy owners, it was forbidden to reprint or import not just copies owned by another agent, but parts of copies: 14 Car. II, c. 33, § 5.

18. [Defoe], *Essay on the Regulation of the Press*, 20; Rigaud, *Correspondence of Scientific Men*, II, 552–4; Dunton, *Life and Errors* (1705), 56. For a positive theory of epitomes see Ross, *Marrow of History*, sigs. A3^r–A4^v. Perhaps the most economically significant use of the idea of epitomes, as described above (p. 260), was the Stationers' Company's when it argued that the "substance" of any almanac was the calendar prefixed to the Book of Common Prayer.

gentleman could do. Even Samuel Johnson, the most consummate of authors, could only suggest abridging the abridgments. It was hardly a virtuous solution, and any profits, Johnson suggested, should be donated to penitent prostitutes.[19]

Imitation—which, like abridgment, shaded into reprinting through the myriad qualifications negotiated by the Stationers—could also be accounted a violation of propriety. Thus a newspaper mockingly resembling the government's gazette, for example, might be condemned, although no part of the original text itself was reproduced. In 1718 the publisher of the *Oxford Post* complained of a "Grand Pirate Printer" who "designs to invade my Right, by Printing and Publishing a Paper by the Name of the Oxford Post, as also that he'l put at least the two First Letters of my Name to it, and get the same Figure at the Frontispiece." This art of imitation was deployed in all fields, including learned ones. It developed to such an extent that by the early eighteenth century it had become a very sophisticated game indeed, with the Scriblerians creating their fake virtuoso Martinus Scriblerus, and bookseller Edmund Curll inventing characters such as "Joseph Gay" to write topical texts for him. Swift's lampoon predicting the death of astrologer John Partridge, when followed by another confirming the prediction, spurred all of Grub Street to the chase; soon a riotous multiplicity of "Partridges" had utterly drowned out the unfortunate (but still living) original. In such circumstances it became virtually impossible to tell who was imitating whom, and where lay the truth. The Stationers' Company in fact removed Partridge from its ranks of almanac writers as "deceased." "Sometimes I was Mr. John Gay, at other Burnet or Addison," recalled one of Curll's hacks. "I abridged histories and travels, translated from the French what they never wrote, and was expert in finding new titles for old books." Such creative individuals were not always as impoverished as literary legend insists, nor as slavishly unoriginal. One of the most successful, the notorious "Sir" John Hill, was making some £1,500 a year in the 1750s for his botanical works.[20]

It is striking how often such "counterfeiting" pastiched the virtuoso form of life. Indeed, this was perhaps the dominant mode of satire directed against followers of the experimental philosophy. Shadwell's use of passages cited almost verbatim from the *Philosophical Transactions* is well known. Fellows of the Royal Society took a dim view of the practice when William King applied it to them again in the form of his own imitative satires on the *Transactions*. Fielding himself used an imitation of the *Transactions* to criti-

19. Campbell, *London Tradesman*, 132–3; Rigaud, *Correspondence of Scientific Men*, II, 552; Collins, *Authorship in the Days of Johnson*, 59.

20. Harris, *London Newspapers*, 142; Pope et al., *Memoirs of . . . Martinus Scriblerus*, 166–70; Nokes, *Jonathan Swift*, 79–83; Collins, *Authorship in the Days of Johnson*, 26–7.

cize the Society—one good enough to fool many readers into believing it genuine. In 1731 the Society even considered offering a reward to anyone naming the author of printed reports that recited proceedings at its meetings that never in fact occurred, and thereby endangered the reputation of "personages of the first Rank & Character."[21]

The most brazen of all Stationers' interventions took this form. This was the Athenian Society, brainchild of bookseller John Dunton. Dunton claimed that the Society held regular meetings and that it maintained "a Correspondence beyond Sea." He professed to insert material from the *Journal des Sçavans* and the *Acta Eruditorum* into its regular journal, the *Athenian Mercury*. Like the Royal Society, moreover, Dunton's Athenian Society advertised itself as a place where citizens' arguments over matters of knowledge could be brought for peaceful solution—and as the pages of the *Athenian Mercury* regularly testified, it was rather more successful at this than its more prestigious prototype. Before long, it had its own apologetic *History* to laud its achievements. Elkanah Settle even published a dialogue satire, *The New Athenian Comedy*, ridiculing a meeting of the Society in a London coffeehouse; it ended, as had Shadwell's *Virtuoso*, in a riot against the virtuosi. But Dunton's artificial "Society," as Elkanah Settle revealed, was a Stationer's Royal Society. It existed only in print, but appeared more real than the real thing. Jonathan Swift was one of the first taken in, and he bore a grudge against Dunton for years.[22]

The implication of all this for the credit of printed books was widely appreciated. Swift himself told bookseller Benjamin Tooke to investigate the law about false authorial names, "For, at this rate, there is no book, however so vile, which may not be fastened on me." "The Chief Rule in buying Books is the Author's name," agreed a journal, "which is now no Rule at all; since the Booksellers have usurp'd the making Names as well as Titles." It identified physicians John Freind and Hermann Boerhaave as notable victims. And Thomas Carnan denounced such false authorship as a product of the society that had produced not only Curll but Jonathan Wild, the infamous "Thief-Taker General of Great Britain and Ireland" hanged in 1725 and later resurrected by Fielding.[23] No citizen of the republic of letters could be guaranteed immunity from such practices, and no truth was so

21. Levine, *Dr Woodward's Shield*, 247 ff.; BL Ms. Add. 4441, fols. 120^r–121^v; McEwen, *Oracle of the Coffee House*, 33–4; Eales, "Satire on the Royal Society"; Dunton, *Life and Errors* (1705), 248–57; Shadwell, *Virtuoso*, II.ii.96–100; Schwartz, *French Prophets*, 48–9; Black, "Press, Party and Foreign Policy," 25; RS Ms. Dom. 5, no. 23.

22. [Gildon], *History of the Athenian Society*, 11; [Settle], *New Athenian Comedy*; McEwen, *Oracle of the Coffee House.*

23. Swift, *Correspondence*, I, 165–6; Stewart, "Smart, Kerrick, Carnan and Newbery," 39–40; Pope et al., *Memoirs of . . . Martinus Scriblerus; Gentleman's Magazine* 2 (1732), 1099–1100.

transcendent that it could survive immersion in them untarnished. So prevalent were they, indeed, that they threatened the very pillars of Augustan political society: liberty and property. Joseph Addison made this point in the most famous of all attacks on piracy, delivered in a moment of anger after he had discovered unauthorized copies of *The Tatler*. Piracy, Addison declared, was "an Injustice against which there is no Remedy, even in a Kingdom more happy in the Care taken of the Liberty and Property of the Subject, than any other Nation upon Earth."

> This Iniquity is committed by a most impregnable Set of Mortals, Men who are Rogues within the Law. . . . These Miscreants are a Set of Wretches we Authors call Pirates, who print any Book, Poem, or Sermon, as soon as it appears in the World, in a smaller Volume, and sell it (as all other Thieves do stolen Goods) at a cheaper Rate. I was in my Rage calling them Rascals, Plunderers, Robbers, Highwaymen; but they acknowledge all that, and are pleased with those, as well as any other Titles; nay, will print them themselves to turn the Penny.

He found himself powerless against such actions. For an author hoping to live by his wits, their effects could be calamitous. His own authorial identity was that of an astrologer, and Addison claimed that he himself could always survive by plying that trade; but more scholarly individuals would be less fortunate. Such writers would be "exposed to robbery and want." Even the greatest would be destroyed. Readers too would suffer. A bookseller who "holds his Property at the Curtesy of the designing Pirate," as Campbell warned, could not afford the risk of investing in expensive learned works. If such practices continued "we must never expect to see again a beautiful edition of a book in Great Britain."[24]

One way to avoid the troubles presented by print might be to embrace such warnings as positive recommendations, and vest faith in manuscript circulation. Certainly, as later sections of this chapter describe in detail, manuscript documents could be used both as widely distributed "publications" and as devices to help safeguard the integrity of printed materials. Isaac Newton's extensive links with networks engaged in their exchange warrant comparison with the better-known involvement of poets, antiquarians, and dramatists. They were also central to the practices of Samuel Hartlib, and of course to those of Henry Oldenburg. But ultimately it was

---

24. *Tatler* 101 (1 December 1709); Campbell, *London Tradesman*, 133–4. See also *Tatler* 102 for an advertisement against "a spurious and very incorrect Edition of these Papers printed in a small Volume." Bookseller Richard Sare was actually skeptical of the extent to which a book could be shortened by using smaller letter: Gunther, *Early Science in Oxford*, XII, 381.

difficult to believe that manuscripts could reach and unite a dispersed readership. This skepticism, as much as any practical impediment, made them inappropriate candidates to act as the sole vehicles for a brand of knowledge that distinguished itself by its openness and accessibility. And in any case, they proved scarcely less vulnerable to appropriation than printed books. If nothing else, as Francis Osborne put it, booksellers' unscrupulous ways of getting copy made *"Publication* to the world unavoidably *Necessary"* since this was the only way of "preventing a *false Impression."* [25] There was consequently no way of ensuring safety. One had to publish in order to avoid unauthorized revelation, yet publishing immediately entailed submission to the Stationers' culture.

Correspondence was particularly problematic. Neither private nor entirely public, the legal status of letters remained uncertain until at least the 1720s, when Alexander Pope brought his duel with Edmund Curll to a head to force the issue. Not even Pope, however, with all his scheming and disguises, could emerge victorious: Curll escaped clutching the rights to his correspondence and in celebration renamed his shop The Pope's Head. Recently deceased gentlemen offered particularly rich opportunities for such appropriation. The cautionary tale of Bishop Thomas Barlow—himself no mean hand at anonymous publishing, as he had confessed to Robert Boyle—demonstrated the threat to authorship. Soon after Barlow's death, a printed version of his manuscript writings appeared that suggested a sympathy for Socinianism. There was little his horrified executors could do about this "foul play." The culprit was John Dunton (again). The executors suspected him of deliberately adulterating the text, acting the "Epitomizer" and attempting to "Palm [it] for Genuine upon the World." Dunton's example should encourage everyone to take care even of what they wrote privately, they warned, lest it be exposed by some such "Relick-Monger." As John Arbuthnot said, such practices added a new terror to death. [26]

The proprieties of print thus appeared to affect both authors and the knowledge they avowed. Since their reach could extend into the realm of private papers, they also impinged upon the intimate daily conduct of philosophers. They conditioned decisions (typically made by Stationers) about whether, when, and in what form particular books would appear. They, or their violation, then threatened the uses that could prudently be made of

25. Love, *Scribal Publication*, 33, 182, 186; Osborne, *Miscellany*, sig. A2ʳ.

26. Rose, "Author in Court"; Rose, *Authors and Owners*, 49–91; McLaverty, "First Printing and Publication of Pope's Letters"; Rogers, "Case of Pope v. Curll"; Ransom, "Personal Letter"; Boyle, *Works*, VI, 306–7; Hunter, *Robert Boyle by Himself and His Friends*, 73–4; [Brougham], *Reflections to a Late Book*, esp. 7, 10–11, 19–21; Huygens, *Oeuvres Complètes*, IX, 354–6; Aitken, *Life and Works of John Arbuthnot*, 142–4. Arbuthnot was speaking of Edmund Curll.

whatever knowledge was printed. Piracy, in particular, challenged the credibility of such knowledge, casting the integrity of all printed books and the identity of all printed authors into doubt. It could be imprudent to invest one's trust in *any* printed text without good grounds. Exactly what might constitute "good grounds" in this context will be examined later. But here it should be noted that claims of piracy were seldom *just* claims of piracy. There was always some accompanying allegation of textual corruption, misrepresentation or illicit appropriation. If a given book were described as illegitimate, then its reading must be qualified accordingly. Its contents need not necessarily be dismissed altogether, although this was often the intended implication. In certain circumstances, the uncertainty attendant upon apparently unauthorized publication might actually result in *enhanced* credibility, especially if the "unauthorized" work contained scandalous or secret information. An aura of penetrated secrecy could lend authority to the most lascivious of tales. Arthur Bury's *Naked Gospel*, printed in "a stolen Impression" that restored passages Bury himself had suppressed, was thus believed more authentic than his own edition, and led to his expulsion from Oxford for Socinianism. Some writers took advantage of this tendency to spread unorthodox views, or to achieve authorship without appearing to aspire to it. Isaac Newton was one: he repeatedly considered promoting his deeply felt heterodoxy by using distant intermediaries to publish texts that could question conventional shibboleths by virtue of appearing to be unauthorized. In alchemy, similarly, an apparently unauthorized revelation might be more likely to find acceptance than one of self-proclaimed authorship, because of alchemists' views on the proper character of the practitioner as the silent beneficiary of grace.[27] In each case, the very doubt generated by charges of unauthorized publication created an opportunity for increased influence. For natural philosophers, however—and in particular for experimental natural philosophers—this was unlikely to prove a consistently successful practice. Publicly, at least, experimental philosophy set great store on honesty and openness of utterance. Nothing should be concluded by cabal. In this field, allegations of piracy were therefore almost always charges of transgression, serious enough to threaten the accused's place in the philosophical community. As such, they took one form above all others: plagiarism.

Accusations of plagiarism were rife in early modern natural philosophy. Many remarked openly upon the impossibility of becoming a philosophical

---

27. [Parkinson], *Fire's Continued at Oxford*, 1–2, 12–13; [Harrington], *Account of the Proceedings*, 22–3, 35–6, 55; [Harrington], *Defence of the Proceedings*, 46–7. See Hannaway, *Chemists and the Word*, and Moran, "Privilege, Communication, and Chemiatry," for patterns of alchemical communication.

author without "passing for a Plagiary."[28] Indeed, it is difficult to think of any prominent philosopher or investigator of the natural world who was not accused of violating propriety in this way. Among those who were, we may list William Harvey (who was accused by Walter Warner), Isaac Newton (by Robert Hooke), Robert Hooke (by John Flamsteed), Robert Boyle (by George Sinclair and John Aubrey), Edmond Halley (by Flamsteed and, before the Royal Society itself, by Hooke), James Harrington (by anonymous antagonists), Thomas Hobbes (by John Wilkins), John Woodward (by John Arbuthnot), and John Wallis (by almost everyone).[29] As participants in an enterprise strongly assertive—in the face of widespread incredulity—of its polite and useful character, such figures found accusations that they had breached these cardinal virtues both powerful and damaging. And beyond such individual cases lay the sheer ubiquity of concern that intellectual "propriety" in general was under siege. Sorbière's allegation was representative: that English writers as a whole "never cite the Books from whence they Borrow, and so their Copies are taken for Originals." Sprat may have responded indignantly that far from being *"generally stoln out of other Authors*," English works were models of original eloquence—and that in any case Sorbière himself had probably appropriated his charge from the Italians— but the allegation was uncomfortably familiar, and it touched a nerve.[30]

In the context of natural philosophy the most common term used to describe an offense against literary propriety seems to have been not "piracy," nor even "plagiary," but "usurpation."[31] As such, usurpation appeared as a theme in some surprising and significant ways. According to Evelyn, "the only reproch of men of *Letters*" was that by declining public exposure they "leave occasion for so many insipid and empty fopps to usurp their

28. [Daniel], *Voyage to the World of Cartesius*, sig. [A5^{r-v}].

29. Shirley, "Scientific Experiments of Sir Walter Raleigh," 55; Aubrey, *Brief Lives*, 320; Stubbe, *Plus Ultra Reduced*, 112 (for Harvey); Westfall, *Never at Rest*, 446–53 (for Newton); Sinclair, *Vindication*, and Hooke, "Diary," 89 (for Boyle); Hooke, "Diary," 103, 107, 109, and 111, and chapter 8 below (for Halley); Harrington (ed. Toland), *Oceana*, xviii (for Harrington); [Wilkins and Ward], *Vindiciae Academiarum*, 7 (for Hobbes); Eyles, "John Woodward," 406 (for Woodward); Aubrey, *Brief Lives*, 315 (for Wallis). Henry Stubbe also accused the entire Royal Society of plagiarism: *Plus Ultra Reduced*, 115 and passim.

30. Sorbière, *Voyage into England*, 70; Birch, *History*, II, 456–9; Sprat, *Observations on Monsieur de Sorbier's Voyage*, 248, 260–72. Sprat probably had in mind a common conception that excessive citation (on the scale of a William Prynne, say) could be evidence of pedantry. He himself cited *Eikon Basilike* as the supreme example of native English eloquence—a work that Milton famously accused of theft by inadequate acknowledgment. For Boyle's own repeated reflection on citation practices, see RS Boyle P. 9, pp. 24–6; Ms. 185, fols. 62^{v}–63^{r}.

31. E.g., Oldenburg, *Correspondence*, IV, 83, 193, and many other cases in the correspondence. Blount, *Glossographia*, defined *plagiary* as, first, a kidnapper of natives for the slave trade, and, second, "a book Stealer or book theef, one that fathers other mens works upon himself." French terms used included *larcin*: Oldenburg, *Correspondence*, IV, 399.

rights, and dash them out of Countenance." Robert Boyle decried the keeping of recipes as valued secrets, not only because it was a form of ostenta-
tion that allowed "counterfeit" recipes to circulate, but because it permitted
"fals usurpations" to cheat true discoverers. And Joseph Glanvill even found
room to include the theme in his defenses of experimental philosophy.
Glanvill argued that Aristotle had gained a *"usurp'd authority"* by having
"borrowed almost all he writ from the more *antient Philosophers.*" His own
philosophy had then been "usurp't" in turn by the Peripatetics, so that the
modern schoolmen were the unfortunate heirs to a double theft. In such
hands, the history of usurpation became central to the deployment of allegations of plagiarism and politeness alike. Sir Thomas Browne, for one, explicitly linked the issues to printing. "Thus may we perceive the Ancients
were but men," he concluded. "The practice of transcription in our daies
was no monster in theirs: Plagiarie had not its nativity with printing; but
began in times when thefts were difficult, and the paucity of books scarce
wanted that invention." [32] The remark was significant not so much for denying that plagiarism was derivative of the press, but for assuming that contemporaries supposed otherwise.

The prevalence of piracy and usurpation meant that whether printed professions of knowledge could be trusted must always be contestable. Not only
that: it must always be contestable *to an indeterminate degree.* Its very indeterminacy meant that there could be no hard-and-fast rules for overcoming
the problem. How much one should credit printed testimony would always
be a matter of ad hoc prudence, not of formulas, let alone of a general and
principled faith in the preserving powers of print. Ways of dealing with this
problem would be central to the prospects of experimental philosophy. One
hint of this is provided by the fact that many natural philosophers concerned
themselves with the technology of printing itself. It was a subject of recurring interest. Inventions relating to printing, engraving, or multiple writing
were claimed for figures like William Petty, Christiaan Huygens, Robert
Hooke, John Evelyn, Joseph Moxon FRS, Prince Rupert, and, archetypally,
Tycho Brahe.[33] Typical was Christopher Wren, whose inventions included

32. [Boyle], "Epistolical Discourse," 142–3; Hunter, "Reluctant Phillanthropist"; E[ve-
lyn], *Publick Employment,* 85–6; Glanvill, *Scire/i tuum nihil est,* 84–91; Sprat, *History,*
94; Browne, *Pseudodoxia Epidemica,* 16. For examples from literature see Lindey, *Plagiarism
and Originality,* 52, 72–9, 229–30. Ironically, Browne's book was itself the subject of piracy:
SCB D, fol. 20ʳ.

33. Boyle, *Works,* VI, 112–3; Oldenburg, *Correspondence,* I, 171; Birch, *History,* II, 376,
387–8, 396–7; Huygens, *Oeuvres Complètes,* VI, 439–81; *Philosophical Collections* 1 (1679),
39; Rostenberg, *Library of Robert Hooke,* xvii, 10 (though some of the references to a "press"
cited by Rostenberg are more likely to refer to a device for storing books than printing
them—or even to a cider press: Stubbs, "John Beale, II," 345); Birch, *History,* II, 413; Williams, "Edition of the Correspondence of John Aubrey," I, 413; Evelyn, *Sculptura*; Birch,

not only a "way of printing," but a *"Diplographical Instrument"* designed to prevent "the mischievous Craft of Corruption, Forgery and Counterfeiting" by duplicating documents with mechanical accuracy. His "instrument" offered such great potential that before long it was itself stolen.[34]

Attempts to develop printing technologies, however, were really secondary to those that concentrated on the proper place and social management of printing, publication, distribution, and reading. Subscription projects, with their gentlemen referees, offered one means of ensuring the safe production of substantial learned texts. As already seen, it was of limited success. Astronomer Royal John Flamsteed suggested another, more radical response. Flamsteed wanted to avoid dealing with booksellers altogether, and employ printers directly. Like John Streater and Richard Atkyns, he envisaged taking his work out of the hands of trade "management" (a word with very dubious connotations) and placing it under the direct oversight of the genteel, the reverend, and the learned. His plan was also analogous to the approach employed previously by his own hero, Tycho Brahe. Where Tycho had aspired to produce books in geographical isolation on his island of Hven, Flamsteed would cut production off from the commercial interests of booksellers, generating a cultural isolation even within the teeming streets of the city.

Flamsteed found this solution impossible to implement. Booksellers did not appreciate being bypassed, and, thanks to their power and connections within the Stationers' community, could severely curtail the sales of any book the owners of which tried to circumvent them. As Thomas Blount found, "they make it a Rule, not to prefer any thing, printed for private persons." ("The Booksellers term of not *preferring* a book, signifies not commending or advancing the sale of it," he explained.) Even speaking with printers directly could prove difficult. Although L'Estrange, Atkyns, and Flamsteed sometimes saw printers as potential allies, in practice they were dependent on booksellers' continued patronage for their livelihoods, and thus proved reluctant to cooperate. As late as 1739 Johnson declared that the booksellers still "threatened printers with their highest displeasure, for

---

History, I, 83; Hooke, *Philosophical Experiments and Observations*, 88–90; Moxon, *Mechanick Exercises on the Whole Art of Printing*; Raeder, Stromgren, and Stromgren, *Tycho Brahe's Description*, 139.

34. Wren, *Parentalia*, 198–9, 214–6; see also Birch, *History*, II, 396–7, 409–11. "Dr Wrens way of printing" was preserved by Oldenburg in RS Ms. 1, fol. 173ᵛ; it is a method for using a rolling press. Edward Somerset, marquis of Worcester, is now remembered, if at all, for his supposed steam engine; but over a quarter of his *Century of the Names and Scantlings of such Inventions, as at present I can call to mind* were devices for secret writing, communication at a distance, seals, and drawing aids—including ways to write "By the smell. By the Taste. By the Touch . . . as perfectly, distinctly, and unconfusedly, yea as readily as by the sight" (29).

having dared to print books for those who wrote them." And if Flamsteed found his efforts in this direction stymied, so did his great enemy. When Edmond Halley shepherded Newton's *Principia* into print, he at first planned to deal directly with a printer and distribute copies himself. The plan had consequences for the very identity of the book, Newton negotiating with Halley its contents and even its title in order to protect sales, "wch I ought not to diminish now tis yo^rs." But in the event Halley discovered that a bookseller, Samuel Smith, had to be employed. "I am contented to lett them go halves with me," he told Newton, "rather than have your excellent work smothered by their combinations."[35] That this—the supreme example of a successful publication in natural philosophy—was so threatened is a salutary reminder that no learned work was immune.

One reason why Halley and Flamsteed both encountered such problems was that they were acting as lone individuals in a city full of collectives. In succeeding years alliances therefore began to be drawn up among writers who, as Belanger picturesquely puts it, "saw no reason why the booksellers should drink champagne out of authors' skulls." Eventually this culminated in a "Society for the Encouragement of Learning," created to protect learned works. Although spurned by Bentley when it offered to undertake his edition of Manilius (at which it announced that he deserved a "fleecing from booksellers"), the society proved fairly successful in publishing medical works, only to collapse soon after attempting Newton's mathematics. Ralph opined that its members had forgotten "that the Booksellers were Masters of all Avenues to every Market."[36] Clearly, even collective action to govern the Stationers' domains was perilous. Those attempting to contain the problems of credit raised by print had to adopt strategies extending beyond the management of the Stationers' crafts themselves. They must begin with the most elementary components of communication.

Restoration natural philosophers created both new forms of sociability and new genres of writing. The experimental paper, the philosophical journal, the book review, the editor, and the experimental author were all original creations. They may plausibly be seen as mechanisms for making and protecting the credit of documentary evidence when that credit was otherwise insecure.[37] As such, their implications extended far beyond the

35. Blount, *Correspondence*, 151–2; Collins, *Authorship in the Days of Johnson*, 42–4; Cohen, *Introduction to Newton's "Principia,"* 132–3, 136–7; Munby, "Distribution of the First Edition of Newton's *Principia*," 29. For Flamsteed's problems, see below, pp. 582–5, 592. For Smith's Continental distribution network at this time, see his correspondence with Wetstein and others in Bodl. Ms. Rawl. Letters 114.

36. Belanger, "Booksellers' Sales of Copyright," 135; Collins, *Authorship in the Days of Johnson*, 16–21; Atto, "Society for the Encouragement of Learning."

37. Hannaway, *Chemists and the Word*; Golinski, "Chemistry in the Scientific Revolution," 372; Golinski, "Robert Boyle"; Golinski and Christie, "Spreading of the Word";

realm of natural philosophy itself, affecting new literary forms such as novels, travel literature, and newspapers.[38] These were much more than merely rhetorical concepts. They need to be appreciated in terms of practical responses to problems permeating the very character and use of printed reports. Above all, however, solutions to those problems envisaged that a place must be found in which authorship and reading could become safeguarded activities and where these new conventions could be formulated and applied. This meant providing a location where the accepted conventions of polite society would be visibly and reliably observed at all times. In 1660 such a place was invented. Two years later it received its charter as the Royal Society.

The Royal Society, like Isaac Newton's Trinitarians, could be seen as an authoritative center for natural knowledge because it mastered the use of the press. It came to maintain its own printers, its own journal, its own correspondence networks and its own right to license books. One may speculate that its innovative use of these mechanisms was one reason why the Society was such a tempting target for satirists—it certainly provided them with fuel. For all that its activities provided a rich seam of the ridiculous, however, they also represented pioneering attempts to contain, and even redefine, the powers of print. Its publication policy should thus be seen in the light not only of discussions of experimentalism, but also of contemporary bids like Atkyns's to regulate the domains of print. The construction and use of these mechanisms are the subject of the following sections. The most devastating demonstration of their power would be made by Newton himself. He was able to use these resources to publish manuscript letters from decades earlier, and brand his great rival Leibniz as a thief.[39]

The Royal Society's meetings at Gresham College, close to the Royal Exchange and its clusters of coffeehouses and bookshops, became the main venue at which the experimental philosophy was articulated and practiced

---

Westman, "Proof, Poetics and Patronage"; Schaffer, "Daniel Defoe and the Worlds of Credit"; Dear, "Narratives, Anecdotes, and Experiments"; Bazerman, *Shaping Written Knowledge*, 59–127; Gross, "Rhetorical Invention of Scientific Invention"; Gross, *Rhetoric of Science*, chaps. 6–8; Kroll, *Material Word*. See also Iliffe, "'Idols of the Temple,'" and Warwick, "Electrodynamics of Moving Bodies," for an important extension of the principle. I do not treat specifically here the invention of medical journals, but a similar approach could certainly be used to do so: Porter, "Rise of Medical Journalism." Compare Davis, *Fiction in the Archives*, which describes the craft dedicated to creating facticity in written documents. The first book reviews in newspapers were also of Society publications, particularly *Micrographia*: Sutherland, *Restoration Newspaper*, 84.

38. McKeon, *Origins of the English Novel*; Markley, *Fallen Languages*; Kroll, *Material Word*; Schaffer, "Daniel Defoe and the Worlds of Credit" (which makes the link with piracy explicitly).

39. Hall, *Philosophers at War*; Shapin, "Of Gods and Kings." See also Hobbes's comments on licensing, in *Behemoth*, 96, 148.

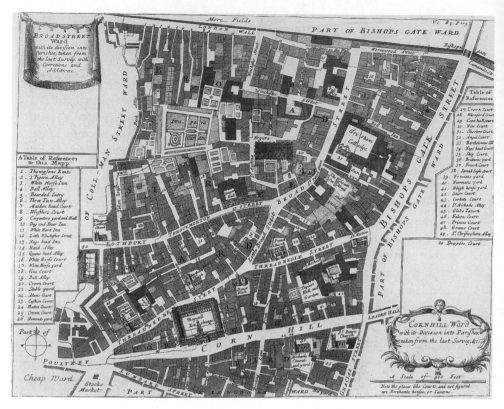

FIG. 7.2. Gresham College and Cornhill. Strype, *Survey of London*. (By permission of the Syndics of Cambridge University Library.)

(figs. 7.2, 7.3).[40] It has long been recognized that central to the Society's success (such as it was) was its publishing record—a record encompassing not just the first "scientific" journal, the *Philosophical Transactions*, but the invention of the experimental paper, and above all the successful production of Newton's *Principia*. Whatever their specific methodological approaches, histories of science dealing with this period always cite these achievements as occurring against an assumed background of an ordered, epistemologically neutral print culture, which provided no serious resistance to the virtuosi's efforts. Such an environment, needless to say, did not exist. The Society had to work to create it. Moreover, the problems attendant upon the print culture that *did* obtain meant that within the Society, too, virtuosi needed to be very careful of the criteria by which they assessed incoming works, be they printed or manuscript. This section discusses the conventions

40. The Society met at Arundel House from 1667 to 1674, then returned to Gresham until 1710, when Newton masterminded its move to Fleet Street. The literature on the early Society is substantial: Hunter's *Science and Society* and *Establishing the New Science* contain bibliographical essays.

of propriety developed within the Society for dealing with these issues. Before it does so, however, it must first address the question of why communication was so important to the Society in the first place.

The Society portrayed its diversity of interests and investigations as together embodying a new and safe pursuit of natural knowledge. It called this activity the experimental philosophy. At the same time, its fellows represented themselves as exemplifying the kind of people who should be trusted to produce and convey truth about Creation. But if experimental philosophy was a novel activity, then the "experimental philosopher" was necessarily a strange beast to early modern society. How he should conduct himself was not yet obvious. As Steven Shapin has extensively argued, the virtuosi consequently drew upon familiar resources when they articulated what the characteristics of a good natural philosopher were to be. They had an obvious example to emulate, in the figure of the English gentleman. In Restoration society, the gentleman was reckoned to be a reliable purveyor of truth.

FIG. 7.3. Gresham College. The Royal Society met here in various rooms from 1660. In 1666 the fire of London compelled it to move to Arundel House on the Strand; it returned in 1674 and stayed until 1710. Robert Hooke, as professor of geometry, had lodgings in the far right corner, where the turret he built for his astronomical observing can be seen. The Society's repository was in the upper floor of the building facing the viewer. Ward, *Lives of the Professors*. (By permission of the Syndics of Cambridge University Library.)

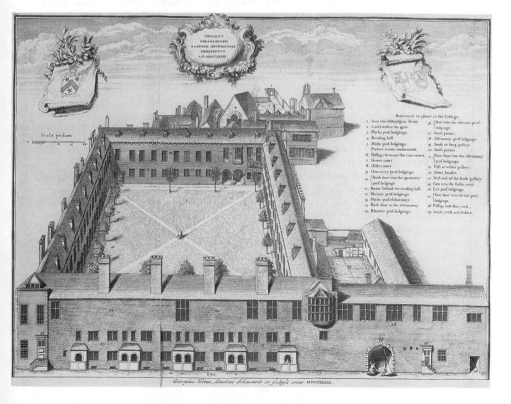

Ideally, he had an independent income. He did not have to work for others in order to subsist. He was therefore literally his own man ("free, and un-confin'd," as Sprat put it), and could be expected to proffer verdicts free from the influence of any "interest."[41] This much was taken as self-evidently true of conventional gentility in the abstract, whatever the venality of par-ticular individuals claiming the title. Indeed, we have recently seen the power of the representation in Atkyns's campaign to transform the culture of print. It was thus reasonable to model correct etiquette in experimental philosophy, too, on the proper conduct and attributes of such a figure: broad experience, modesty, moderation, freedom of action, and disinterest. Just as printing was properly done in houses, moreover, so experimental work was to be done in gentlemen's homes. Each activity sought legitimacy from the values of its setting.[42]

Such a representation also served a political end. The Society was not instituted explicitly to serve any one political interest; indeed, it repudiated such factionalism repeatedly. But its very repudiation had a point. The at-tributes it endorsed distinguished its participants from the "enthusiasts" and "dogmatists" associated with the defeated Interregnum sects and with mili-tant Catholicism. These twin threats legitimated conforming episcopalian-ism as a "middle way," and most fellows endorsed this stance. Their best response to the challenges of sectarianism and papism alike thus seemed to be to undermine the dangerous claims to exclusive certainty that both seemed to exhibit. The Royal Society professed to do that, alleging that such claims were inherently uncivil and "pedantic." As ornament, as a tool for statecraft, or simply for its own sake, learning was commendable; but if pursued dogmatically and privately—"closetwise," as Ruth Kelso puts it— it was incompatible with gentility. The exclusion of the impolite and the rejection of the impolitic were to be indistinguishable. Evelyn thus proudly told Clarendon (successor, as lord chancellor, to Bacon himself) that the

41. Shapin, "Who Was Robert Hooke?" 253 (compare Goffman, *Presentation of Self,* 63); Sprat, *History,* 67; Shapin, "Closure and Credibility"; Golinski, "Noble Spectacle." This was a standard trope of seventeenth-century social and political debates: Macpherson, *Political Theory of Possessive Individualism,* 107–59; Thomas, "Levellers and the Franchise"; Ashcraft, *Revolutionary Politics,* chaps. 2, 5–6; Diamond, "Natural Philosophy," 392. Expressing ex-perimental findings in complex mathematical terms was therefore frowned upon, since most gentlemen were not highly qualified mathematicians, and in any case mathematics was com-monly held to compel assent rather than allowing it to be volunteered. As Jeremiah Shakerley declared, mathematical language left "no hole to creep out at, no quirk for dissent." Shapin, "Robert Boyle and Mathematics"; Shakerley, *Anatomy of Urania Practica,* sig. A3^r. Such con-ventions of attestation were, of course, well known to booksellers and printers, who needed them in their struggle to accredit their own products. Bookseller Samuel Lowndes, for ex-ample, proclaimed that Henry More would "earnestly avouch" the worth of Glanvill's *Sadu-cismus Triumphatus*: sigs. A1^r–A2^v; see also 1–2 for More's account of his conversation with Glanvill's bookseller, and pp. 125–6 above for more examples.
42. Conway, *Letters,* 86–8; Shapin, "House of Experiment."

Society stood to realize Solomon's House "because it does not consist of a Company of *Pedants*, and superficial persons; but of *Gentlemen*, and Refined Spirits that are universally *Learn'd*, that are *Read, Travell'd, Experienc'd* and *Stout.*" [43]

To some, what "experiments" were remained as unclear as the character of their proponents. The Scottish philosopher George Sinclair thought that they could include "productions of Reason" even if these were "never actually tried, nor haply can be." He maintained that "supposing they were," reason could "make it evident, that such and such *Phenomena* would follow." Boyle ascribed a similar view to an altogether more sophisticated interlocutor, Blaise Pascal. But in each case this was the opinion of a distant correspondent. In the Society itself, experiment necessarily involved actual practice. The very point of an experiment was that it was *not* just a product of reasoning. It actually happened, and it had to be *shown*. In the Society, displaying an experiment before its fellows should result in their agreement upon a clearly visible "matter of fact" that would become that experiment's result. Those present invested what Wilkins called "moral" certainty in their attestation of the fact, implying that any reasonable man free from prejudice would yield his assent, as they had, to its having been displayed. Certainty about any explanation of the fact was not then demanded. [44] Matters of fact attested in this way seemed to Boyle, Wilkins, and their allies to provide good foundations for building an agreed-upon account of nature.

The Society's procedures for experimental practice placed responsibility on the audience. As witnesses, its fellows were to guarantee the veracity of experimental outcomes to those disposed to doubt them. On their personal reliability thus depended the success of the whole enterprise. This was why their perceived probity, and their representation as genteel, mattered. Their credibility could be assessed by any number of criteria, including both "*Integrity* or Fidelity" and "*Ability.*" [45] In matters of craft, especially in the mathematical sciences, skill was a recognized qualification. In the nonmathematical subjects traditionally subsumed in natural history or natural philosophy, however, personal "quality" often counted far more. Facts in these

43. Hunter, *Establishing the New Science*, 1–43; Hill, *World Turned Upside Down*, 222; Harris, *London Crowds*, 32–4; Ashcraft, "Latitudinarianism and Toleration"; Scott, "England's Troubles"; Shapin and Schaffer, *Leviathan and the Air-Pump*, chap. 7; Jacob, *Robert Boyle and the English Revolution*; Kelso, *Doctrine of the English Gentleman*, 55–6, 114–5; Naudé, *Instructions concerning Erecting of a Library*, sigs. A3ʳ–A4ᵛ; Johns, "Ideal of Scientific Collaboration." On pedantry, see also Shapin, "'A Scholar and a Gentleman.'"

44. S[inclair], *Hydrostaticks*, sig. [¶¶ 3ʳ]; Dear, *Discipline and Experience*, 208; Wilkins, *Of the Principles and Duties of Natural Religion*, 7–9. This has been seen as an important step in a transition to conditional, legalistic conventions of evidence in the period: Dear, "From Truth to Disinterestedness"; Shapiro, *Probability and Certainty*; Daston, "Baconian Facts," 338–50.

45. Compare [Ward], *Philosophicall Essay*, 89–96, 147–8.

subjects had to be visible to all reasonable men, not just to those possessed of special skills. Gentlemen were reckoned to be just such reasonable viewers.[46] In practice, then, experimental witnesses would be apportioned credit according to their place in the social hierarchy, and in particular according to their received status as gentry. They were ideally to be named in reports of the trials they witnessed. This meant that the "laborants" who actually performed the experimental work, like the "horses" and "flies" of printing houses, were not customarily mentioned in accounts of experiments and the matters of fact they generated. They were "included in their masters." Their superiors spoke for them. It all suited Robert Boyle, son of the earl of Cork, very well. His erstwhile servant, Robert Hooke, on the other hand, continued to be paid as an employee of the Society, and therefore found himself in a much more ambiguous position. In fact, contemporaries did not usually describe Hooke as an experimental philosopher at all, but as a "mechanick."[47] The connotations of such a description were made clear in chapters 4 and 5. Here, they meant that regard for his views depended on the relatively insecure foundation of his apparent technical skill. He must therefore continue without fail to display crafted devices both theoretical and mechanical.

As important as the personal quality of each witness, however, was the fact of collectivity. As one of the gentlemen collaborating to create experimental philosophy in Oxford and London during the Interregnum, John Wilkins had pronounced what he called "Society" to be central to the safe production of natural knowledge. The key was "mutual converse," he maintained. A man possessed of the "quality of sociableness" could be relied upon to labor to "mutual benefit," as opposed to the "Bookish man" who spent his time reading alone. The Royal Society concurred. Experimental philosophy was to be a conversational practice. That is, an experiment succeeded not just if its procedures and results were agreed upon—itself a collective decision—but if it led interestingly to further conversation, and thence to further experiments. Nehemiah Grew thus observed that "the generation of Experiments [was] like that of Discourse, where one thing

46. Samuel Parker thus opposed the 1678 Test Act since it obliged noblemen to take oaths about abstruse propositions such as transubstantiation, "which they neither *do* nor *can*, nor indeed *ought* to understand." These were matters "chiefly handled by the *Schoolmen* and *Metaphysicians* Skill, in whose writing is the least part of a Gentlemans education": Schochet, "Between Lambeth and Leviathan," 207.

47. Shapin, "Who Was Robert Hooke?"; Pumfrey, "Ideas above His Station"; Woodhouse, *Puritanism and Liberty*, 83. Stubbe, however, pointed out that in fact the *Philosophical Transactions* rarely listed witnesses, so that readers concerned to evaluate experimental reports could not truly "judge what *repute* they *deserve*": Stubbe, *Plus Ultra Reduced*, sig. [b3ᵛ]. The Society made its laborants sign a document enjoining secrecy about their work: RS Ms. 89, fol. 13ʳ; Shapin, *Social History of Truth*, 403–4.

introduceth an hundred more which otherwise would never have been thought of." [48] Politeness in the face-to-face exchanges at the Society itself was essential to maintain this activity, as attested by the notoriety of the relatively few incidents in which such politeness disintegrated. The "grimaces" issued during the exchange between Sloane and Woodward in 1710 are probably the best-known example. Notorious for his rudeness to visitors—and for fighting a duel at the gates of Gresham College itself—Woodward was expelled from the Society's council for his incivilities. Newton took the occasion to remark that a useful fellow must be as good a moral philosopher as a natural. [49]

Those who entered the Society and attested to experiments were thus participants. Their mere presence carried responsibilities. They were the judges and guarantors of the conclusions reached at Gresham. No one individual or interest could be allowed to sway their collective decisions. In order to recommend its knowledge as free from the dictates of any faction, the virtuosi therefore claimed prominently that the Society was open. In principle, all Charles II's subjects were free to attend and participate. Its members even proclaimed it a "Parliament," maintaining that it was representative of the political nation and modeling its conversational protocols on those of the House of Commons. [50] But the House of Commons was not, in fact, accessible to all, and in practice neither was this experimental arena, as the Society's most profound critic, Thomas Hobbes, pointedly observed. The Society really was a community largely of gentlemen. Foreigners and tradesmen were excluded unless they obtained special dispensation. So were women. Others worried about the connotations of entry under such terms: Lorenzo Magalotti, stopped at the door, declined to be admitted in the capacity of a scholar because "if I were I should not consider it the most advantageous character for getting into courts." [51] Hobbes himself claimed that

48. Wilkins, *Sermons Preached upon Several Occasions*, 252–3; Grew, *Idea of a Phytological History*, sig. [A6ᵛ]. For the idea of "conversation" see Tribby, "Cooking (with) Clio and Cleo," and Shapin, *Social History of Truth*, 114–25.

49. Halley, *Correspondence and Papers*, 127; Eyles, "John Woodward," 401, 412–14.

50. Shapin, "Pump and Circumstance"; Shapin and Schaffer, *Leviathan and the Air-Pump*, chaps. 2, 5; Hunter and Wood, "Towards Solomon's House," 68, 83. Hunter, *Establishing the New Science*, 8–9, suggests that the Society's protocols may have been based on those of Harrington's Rota (which sits oddly with his insistence on the Society's apolitical character).

51. Shapin and Schaffer, *Leviathan and the Air-Pump*, 112–5. Perhaps the only woman to be admitted was the duchess of Newcastle: Birch, *History*, II, 175 ff.; Magalotti, *Lorenzo Magalotti at the Court of Charles II*, 8. Only a few tradesmen were elected. As far as I know, for example, only two individuals from the book trade were proposed for fellowships in the seventeenth century. One, a very obscure Stationer named Marmaduke Foster, was proposed in 1678 in order to compose a library catalogue for the Society. He was turned down. The other, Joseph Moxon, was elected, but against a substantial negative vote. Hunter, *Royal Society and Its Fellows*, 28, 59, 198–9.

this selectivity skewed the Society's verdicts, and hence fatally undermined its claim to veracity. Far from unquestioned, the commitment to openness thus stood at the center both of experimental philosophy and of challenges to its authority.

This was not the only respect in which the walls of the Society's meeting place proved consequential. The problems of experiment did not end at the door of Gresham College or Arundel House. Few people could actually be present at a Society meeting, and the assent of those who could was in any case hardly the end of the matter. That assent then had to be reproduced and accepted further afield; otherwise the whole effort would be for naught. The validity of the matters of fact produced in the Society had to be recognized by much wider and more diverse audiences—including both rival academies, in cities like Paris, and philosophers accustomed to very different methods and conventions, such as the Jesuits and the court philosophers scattered across Europe. Yet even in London itself, let alone further afield, the claims of the Society were far from uncontested. The clientele of a coffeehouse could be as critical an audience as any to be found at a court or university. The need to communicate successfully was therefore as important a part of the experimental philosophy as the experimenting itself. And what had to be communicated was not just a simple fact itself, but the entire adjudicatory and legitimating framework in which it had come into existence.

Here too the conventions of gentility had a part to play. A representative gentleman displayed a certain openness and "candour."[52] The virtuosi themselves repeatedly professed their communicative openness as well as freedom of access, for this reason (and to distinguish themselves again from pedants, projectors, fraudulent alchemists, and mechanicks). *"A readiness to communicate"* was the first condition cited by Wilkins for a philosopher, before even humility, prudence, and ingenuity. Any denial of this readiness could be taken to signify antagonism to the common good, as was argued in many vernacular medical works. "You are not a good Commonwealthsman, if you do not give me leave to Print this," Andrew Yarranton told the projector of a new type of mill. Accounts of individual mathematicians and natural philosophers thus repeatedly stressed their instantiation of this virtue. Christopher Wren was a particularly noted example—more, perhaps, than any other member of the Royal Society, Wren was "beloved by all his

---

52. This was consciously contrasted with two common caricatures: of the scholar as withdrawn and antisocial, and of the alchemist as dangerously secretive: e.g., Shapin, "'Scholar and a Gentleman'" and "'Mind Is Its Own Place.'"

Acquaintances for his communicative Disposition." But other seventeenth-century figures were likewise noted to exhibit "diffusive goodness and candor" in "free converse with the lovers of mathematical studies" (Samuel Foster and Henry Gellibrand), or to be "very communicative of what he knew" (Wren again, and Isaac Barrow). Even Robert Hooke was supposedly at first "very communicative of his discoveries and inventions."[53]

Historians have often addressed these proclamations in terms of a nascent appreciation of the virtues of scientific openness. Yet experimental philosophers such as Boyle and Newton, as well as less honored figures such as Hooke, were not communicative of everything, and recommendations of candor were often qualified. Simple discussion of their positions in terms of "openness" and "secrecy" is too crude. *What* they had to communicate affected *how* and *to whom* they communicated it. In matters of alchemical knowledge, especially, both Boyle and Newton were prepared to respect a noble silence, or else to use codes and ciphers to inform only select audiences. Boyle also concealed recipes in order to barter them for those of other secretists. And Hooke respected the need for reticence about still-uncompleted mechanical inventions.[54] Moreover, the ideal of gentlemanly candor collided head-on with the real domains of print. Faced with this culture and its pitfalls, virtuosi engaged in printing and publishing underwent what soon became a conventional conversion experience. Hooke, most notoriously, was indeed cooperative—until repeated plagiarism rendered him "close and reserved." His enemy Isaac Newton's own vacillations in this respect are, of course, very well known. Wren, too, despite his reputation, was said to have clammed up after being denied recognition for solving a French mathematical challenge: "His communicative Temper in lending out Papers, never recovered." Boyle himself had always extolled open communication, but he likewise suffered its effects, and he became increasingly reclusive as time went on. And successive professors at Gresham College found that their openness, however polite, created problems. Their ideas would be lost (Barrow, whose papers were lent out and never returned), published in mangled form by others (Edmund Gunther, whose tracts were edited by William Leybourn), or directly plagiarized "under a disguised

53. Wren, *Parentalia*, ix; Wilkins, *Sermons Preached upon Several Occasions*, 259–61; Yarranton, *England's Improvement*, I, 106–8; Ward, *Lives of the Professors of Gresham College*, 83, 85–6, 93–4, 164, 187–8. There are many other examples of this ideal: for instance, the tribute to Dryden that he "was not more possess'd of Knowledge than he was comunicative of it": Hodges, *William Congreve: Letters and Documents*, 127.

54. Hunter, "Introduction," in *Robert Boyle Reconsidered*, 1–18, esp. 14–15. For Boyle's communication strategies in alchemy, see Principe, "Robert Boyle's Alchemical Secrecy"; for Newton's see Dobbs, *Janus Faces of Genius*, 170–5, and Golinski, "Secret Life of an Alchemist," 150–5.

face" (Foster and Hooke). Most frustrating of all, they might be used as "hints" from which others would then perfect their own "inventions" (the locus classicus here being that of Napier's logarithms, said to have been developed shortly after a conversation about Longomontanus's similar efforts in Denmark).[55] Candor in practice proved intensely problematic.

The virtuosi knew that the environment in which their claims would have to survive could be a harsh one. The best-known figures of the new philosophy could not escape its rigors. This is why a nuanced account of their communicative strategies is needed: the creation of experimental knowledge would depend implicitly on them. What it was that the virtuosi actually recorded in experimental descriptions, how they recorded it, through what channels they distributed it, and to which audiences, all require specification. True, there has been prolonged analysis already of the rhetorical and literary construction of experimental writing in the early Royal Society. But the rhetoric needs to be situated specifically in social practices of writing, reading, appraisal, conversation, correspondence, accreditation, and printing. A start has been made by Shapin and Schaffer, who have famously argued that Robert Boyle, in particular, developed a technique of what they call "virtual witnessing." That is, Boyle advocated recording incidental details with such minuteness that readers might submit to the illusion of having effectively witnessed an experiment themselves. Experimental replication could then become a matter of reading and believing, not of skilled dexterity. But Shapin and Schaffer further argue that there was much that an experimental report, however prolix, could not capture. Within the Society's walls, the "manner" of personal discourse told. Face-to-face interaction carried more trust, more "bond," than any printed or manuscript representation. Practice also embodied skills that no such representation could describe exhaustively. Little of this could be evidenced in reports circulated beyond the Society, and much of the interest of *Leviathan and the Air-Pump* derives from the arguments thereby made possible.

An interesting facet of Boylean rhetoric was that it was literary. Despite the objective of reproducing the experimental scene in such minute detail, no pictorial representation of the Society in action seems to have been made. Boyle and others did produce detailed engravings of particular instruments, but scarcely ever of those instruments being used. The Society certainly produced no equivalent to Tycho Brahe's prints of Uraniborg, Hevelius's of Stellaeburg, Kircher's of his Musaeum (Grew's *Musaeum Regalis Societatis*

55. Ward, *Lives of the Professors of Gresham College*, 81, 85–6, 120–1, 164, 185–8; Wren, *Parentalia*, 247; [Boyle], "Epistolical Discourse"; Boyle, *Works*, I, cxxv; VI, 37–8; Oldenburg, *Correspondence*, IV, 98–9; RS Ms. Boyle P. 35, fol. 194ʳ. See Shapin, *Social History of Truth*, chap. 4 for the problematic nature of Boyle's authorship.

did not show the place itself), or even Flamsteed's of the Royal Observatory. The frontispiece of Sprat's apologetic *History* was not a representation of a real, physical space. This may have been simply because the Society lacked a building of its own to exhibit. Had its plans to put Chelsea College to use been realized, there might indeed have been a commemorative publication. At any rate, images of the Society at work never entered the fractious community of engravers and print sellers. The absence is inevitably frustrating to historians of science accustomed to utilizing such resources. In the succeeding sections, as the discussion proceeds to trace the mutual dependencies among conversation, skill, correspondence, and print in the enterprise of experimental philosophy, it may be appropriate to recall from time to time the nonexistence of such an obviously helpful artifact. It will remind us that representations, printed or otherwise, were invariably the result of toil and expense, and as such cannot be taken for granted. Their production always requires explanation and was often determined by reasoning of which we can know little.[56]

PRESENTATION, PERUSAL, AND REGISTRATION

The Royal Society found itself faced with constructing safe conventions for the production, manipulation, and reception of printed and written objects containing claims to natural knowledge. Outside its walls, accusations of usurpation were common. They could not be permitted to become endemically disruptive within the Society. Otherwise its function as an appropriate arena for the settlement of matters of knowledge would be threatened. This section addresses the protocols developed by the virtuosi to regulate such debates. In determining what credit to accord a given work, it will show, attention came to center on the processes through which the manuscript was transformed into a published text. This means that not just publication must be considered—that is, books departing from the Society—but a range of dynamic processes involving books coming into the Society from elsewhere and even those circulating within it. A distinctive and comprehensive social mechanism arose to govern such processes. Without understanding it we cannot properly appreciate the importance of printed texts for early experimental philosophy.

56. Raeder, Strömgren, and Strömgren, *Tycho Brahe's Description*; Hevelius, *Machina Cœlestis*, 439–48; Findlen, *Possessing Nature*, 46, 82–93; Howse, *Francis Place*. Compare McKenzie, "Speech-Manuscript-Print," 87. No image was constructed of a Congreve play in performance, either: Peters, *Congreve, the Drama, and the Printed Word*, 122. For the methodological difficulties of recovering oral interactions from their printed representations, see also Fox, "Aspects of Oral Culture," 3–4, 13.

The Society set itself up as a place distinct from those in which books and manuscripts had hitherto been routinely made, published, and assessed. The proclamations of openness and gentility described above were of central importance in this respect. Authorship and the propriety of intellectual achievement would be guarded here. Unlike that of previously dominant institutions (such as the Stationers' court), the conduct of the virtuosi in dealing with written materials would be guaranteed by recognized conventions of civility, openly observed. Fellows and foreigners alike were encouraged to submit their written texts to the Society. Here all the procedures hitherto conducted by Stationers (or their lackeys, men like Alexander Ross) would be carried out in securely polite circumstances. Translation, epitomizing, reprinting, multiplication of copies, distribution to readers—all of these were now to fall under the control of the leading virtuosi. The Society would thus be a place where members could be trusted to "extract" experiments from a book in order to test the conclusions of the writer, without threatening his authorship. Translations would be made there, too, and they, rather than the originals, could be assessed without fear of corrupting the author's claims. Natural-philosophical disputes could be conducted on the basis of papers the reading, distribution, and subsequent appraisal of which were protected within a civil community.[57]

How did the Society obtain such trust? It would be extraordinary if experimental philosophers had been able to conjure an agreed-upon protocol of such central importance out of nothing. To trace its development is to reconstruct a central element in the experience of experimental philosophy, and one with its own history. There were certainly precedents. One in particular has already been addressed. The main comprehensive model for literary propriety was that of the Stationers' Company, and in fact the Society adopted a strikingly congruent solution. It embodied its propriety in a book called a "register," in which a matter of fact, experimental technique, theory, or paper could be "entered" to record the name of its discoverer and the moment of its first discovery (fig. 7.4). This similarity may not have been entirely coincidental. John Collins, an early coordinator of philosophical correspondence and publishing, had been apprenticed as a Stationer and continued to act as the Company's auditor. Moreover, John Wilkins, John Wallis, and Seth Ward had gained expert knowledge of the Stationers' procedures through representing Oxford University in negotiations with the Company over printing privileges, and Wilkins in particular played a key role in establishing the Society's register and printing policy. Wallis was to

---

57. Birch, *History*, I, 368; II, 5, 93, 97, 429, 431; compare II, 1. For keeping debates private see Birch, *History*, I, 436, 444.

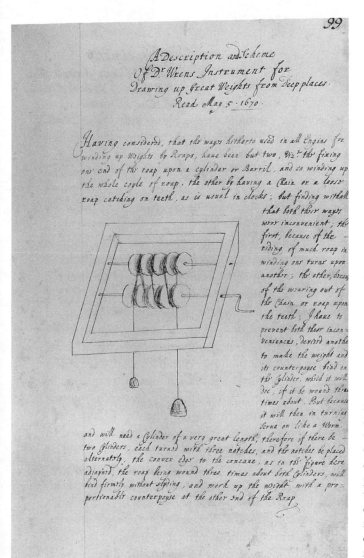

A Description and Scheme
Of Dr Wrens Instrument for
Drawing up Great Weights from Deep places.
Read May 5 · 1670.

Having considered, that the wayes hitherto used in all Engins for
winding up Weights by Roaps, haue been but two, viz: the fixing
one end of the roap upon a cylinder or Barrill, and so winding up
the whole coyle of roap, the other by having a Chain or a loose
roap catching on teeth, as is usual in clocks; but finding withall
that both their wayes
were inconvenient; the
first, because of the
riding of much roap in
winding one turn upon
another; the other, because
of the wearing out of
the Chain or roap upon
the teeth; I haue to
prevent both their incon-
veniences, devised anothe
to make the weight and
its counterpoise bind on
the Cylinder, which it will
doe, if it be wound three
times about. But because
it will then in turning
turn on like a Worm,
and will need a Cylinder of a very great length, therefore if there be
two Cylinders, each turned with three notches, and the notches be placed
alternately, the convex edge to the concave, as in the figure here
adjoyned, the roap being wound three times about both Cylinders, will
bind firmly without slyding, and work up the weight with a pro-
portionable counterpoise at the other end of the Roap

FIG. 7.4. The Royal Society's Register. A typical entry, recording Christopher Wren's contribution of a new pulley device. Note that the date on which the contribution was "read" is recorded, and the inclusion of a clear picture of the mechanism. (By permission of the Royal Society.)

continue to represent the university press in the Restoration; in his correspondence with Oldenburg he displayed a proficiency regarding the trade, and a world-weary suspicion of its practitioners, that was second to none.[58] While the new register was not explicitly a replica of that at Stationers' Hall, it is thus conceivable that a relation existed between the two. Yet the social conventions surrounding the use of this new register were to be very different.

58. SCB D, fols. 6ᵛ, 40ᵛ; Wallis, "Copy of the Account"; Scriba, "Autobiography of John Wallis," 42; Hearne, *Peter Langtoft's Chronicle*, I, CLXVIII–CLXIX; Johnson and Gibson, *Print and Privilege*, 33, 38–40, 46–8.

There may have been sources for those conventions too. The very notion
of a register was of strikingly wide currency in the Interregnum years. In
1657, proposals for an "Office of Publick Advice" had suggested that it provide "Register Books" in which citizens could "Enter" goods of their devis-
ing that they wished to sell. The contents of these would be printed in a
"Book of Intelligence" every week. More specific are the links between the
Society and a number of schemes printed in the years approaching its formation. Proposals for registration and controlled publication were present
in most such plans. That Hartlib, for example, espoused the registration and
publication of "singular industrious Attempts or experiments of profit" is
well known. John Evelyn, too, used the occasion of his 1661 translation of
Gabriel Naudé's "little Discourse of *Books* and *Libraries*" to urge the cause
of regulating flows of books with a register. "*Nullius addictus jurare in verba
Magistri*" (I am not bound to swear as any [philosophical] master dictates),
he declared, coining what would become the Society's Horatian motto. He
was referring, significantly enough, not to experimental knowledge but to
the need felt by all natural philosophers for a diverse range of printed books.[59]

The subject received more sustained attention in two specific schemes
published at the Restoration. The first of these, Abraham Cowley's project
for a "Philosophical College," went into some detail about the regulation of
knowledge and its publication. Cowley envisaged the professors in his institution having to communicate all their findings to the assembly for approval. One third of the property in such results would then be vested in
the inventor, two thirds in the college. After every trial a record would be
signed by the witnesses, then locked away and kept secret to all except the
professors. Every three years the college would then print an account in
strictly controlled Latin of the discoveries thus acknowledged.[60]

More dramatic was the continuation of Bacon's *New Atlantis* published
by one "R. H." in 1660. R. H. has conventionally been identified as Robert
Hooke, and if there is no conclusive evidence to confirm this identification,
neither is there much to overturn it. Certainly, the author of this long and
complex tract was well acquainted with the activities of the Oxford group
of philosophers including Boyle and Wren, at which Hooke (as Boyle's servant) had been a key attendant. His subsequent involvement in a series of
furious disputes over priority makes the possibility of Hooke's authorship all

---

59. *Prohibition to all persons; Office of Publick Advice*; Webster, *Great Instauration*, 67–77;
Hartlib, *Reformed Virginian Silk-Worm*, sig. A2ʳ⁻ᵛ; Johns, "History, Science and the History
of the Book"; Naudé, *Instructions concerning Erecting of a Library*, sigs. A3ʳ–[A5ʳ], 28–9. The
Latin line derives from Horace, *Epistles*, I.i.14; for Evelyn's instrumental role in establishing
it as the Society's motto, see Hunter, *Establishing the New Science*, 17, 41–2.

60. Cowley, *Works*, II, 611, 616–17.

the more appealing, because the centerpiece of the tract was a detailed portrayal of ceremonials celebrating invention and the figure of the inventor.[61]

R. H. expressed a high royalism befitting the moment. During the previous two decades, he alleged, England had reverted to a situation in which "every one had been left his own lawmaker," and "no mans person or propriety had been safe." The renewal of monarchy thus represented a return to "one more wise and expert Champion" whose laws regulated *meum* and *tuum*. In this vision, as in Atkyns's, property was dependent on a single monarch. From this central principle emerged the entire polity of Bensalem. It was a very regulated place, befitting what we know of Bacon's own centralizing aspirations.[62] In trade, the state banned fairs and peddlers to protect its citizens' livelihoods; it also compelled every citizen to follow one, and no more than one, profession. Even nobles were made to learn their one manual trade. This regulation also extended into learned activities. State-funded universities forced students to "apply themselves particularly unto that study and art they first undertake, and none other," to the end that "all experiments may be sooner reduced unto perfection." Public knowledge was to be monitored, and where necessary corrected: each university maintained a *Historiographus Regius*, who oversaw "all history that shall be put out" to prevent "sinister practices, or false glosses" distorting knowledge of events. Similarly, an academy of selected "wits" was to "reform all errors in books, and then to licence them." They alone were authorized to translate foreign works and to make "Dictionaries" in which "the proper termes of art for every notion and thing in every trade, manufacture and science" were authoritatively rendered. The admiralty funded lectures in navigation, while in physick no "*Apothecaries, Chirurgians, Women* or *Empiricks*" were permitted to practice without the oversight of a licensed physician.[63]

The clearest manifestation of this royal regulation appeared in attitudes to invention and discovery. The state offered "great encouragements" to would-be inventors. All authors of "new and good Treatises, whether Divine or humane," all inventors of "artificial inventions," and all "discoverers of new Countreys, Minerals, Earths, Waters, or Whatsoever else is useful

61. See, for example, H[ooke?], *New Atlantis . . . Continued*, 43–4, where R. H. describes the double-writing device claimed by both Wren and Petty. For the Oxford group, see Frank, *Harvey and the Oxford Physiologists*. For analyses of the book, see Davis, *Utopia and the Ideal Society*, 279–92, and Freeman, "Proposal for an English Academy." R. H.'s argument deserves to be compared to Joseph Glanvill's "Bensalem" (Regenstein Ms. 913), another continuation of the *New Atlantis* that concentrated on Latitudinarianism but stressed the need for "Modesty in Opinions" (p. 16) in order to avoid civil conflict.

62. H[ooke?], *New Atlantis . . . Continued*, preface; Martin, *Francis Bacon*, 105–71; Martin, "Natural Philosophy and Its Public Concerns."

63. H[ooke?], *New Atlantis . . . Continued*, 28, 35, 42–3, 50–53, 92; compare Sprat, *History*, 43–4.

to mankind" were accorded "Great honour and reverence as well as large rewards." The greatest were commemorated in a hall of statues, where a strangely misnamed Dr. John Harvey was among those represented. But these rewards and memorials only materialized for inventors who communicated their notions to the state. Those who concealed their inventions, far from gaining by doing so, were punished as "debtors" to the commonwealth.[64]

Cowley, too, had envisaged a gallery of inventors, singling out for statues those responsible for "Printing, Guns, [and] *America*." But R. H. took the theme much further when he described the dramatic reception in the Great Hall of Solomon's House accorded to one Verdugo, successful inventor of a new kind of paper—a significant choice of invention. The full sequence of events deserves to be noted. Verdugo is feted, before being ceremonially admitted into the learned society. Then he is asked openly to "declare his invention, with the true manner of effecting it." The intention is not, R. H. specifies, to prevent "Monopolizing," but for the good of the commonwealth: "to instruct others also in it, that the Invention should not perish with the Author; and he rather meliorated and augmented by the aemulous wits of Ingenious imitatours." Later his achievement is recorded by the "father" of the society in a great book made of the very paper Verdugo has invented, along with a note of his name and birthplace and a full account of his method, "the inventour himself being by, to attest it his invention under his own hand." This "book of Register" will then be preserved forever in Solomon's House. Among other things, Verdugo is subsequently given a ceremonial sword to wear at his side. Only "triumphant inventours" are given such a weapon, and it serves a vital purpose: "to maintain and vindicate themselves the sole Authors of that their invention against all counterfeit pretenders or gainsaying opposers."[65]

As these two descriptions imply, social mechanisms for the proper administration and recognition of intellectual achievement were an important issue to those who set up the Royal Society. Both Cowley and Hooke realized, moreover, that the issue was inseparable from that of publication. Any solution to the problem of maintaining intellectual propriety within a circle of philosophers would depend on the successful construction of a civil domain of print. Notoriously, no such domain existed in the London of the mid–seventeenth century, and it was out of the consequent frequency of

64. H[ooke?], *New Atlantis . . . Continued*, 53, 61–70. It is worth noting that when the visitor is shown some especially prized inventions, they embody not the mechanical philosophy, but the magnetic philosophy and that of sympathies and antipathies.

65. Cowley, *Works*, II, 611; H[ooke?], *New Atlantis . . . Continued*, 53–72. Such a gift makes explicit the link between priority disputes and other arguments over honor in early modern polite society.

claims about plagiarism that Hooke's and Cowley's concerns had arisen. Soon after its inauguration, the Society therefore had to consider instituting procedures akin to those advanced by Cowley and Hooke. These procedures would be in no sense peripheral to its core work of experimental philosophy. That this was so derived in part from another aspect of genteel civility—its combined proclivity and sensitivity to discord. The intimate, face-to-face practice of experimentalists' discourse was permeated by concern for honor. But this could imply a stress on competitive assertiveness as much as on personal veracity. It was increasingly seen as something won by success in challenges, Richard Allestry complaining that "a *man of Honour* is now understood only to be one that can start and maintain a Quarrel." Such challenges were more or less veiled and mitigated by the intricate conventions of courtesy created in the Society, and indeed in wider society too. But they existed nonetheless, and even proved a powerful force for new contributions. Trials of new "carriages" were thus driven by competing claims from the likes of Hooke, Moray (who sponsored a French design), and Blount; and initial efforts at blood transfusion were similarly motivated by desires to vindicate personal and national honor.[66]

In such cases, challenges often took a particular form: that of the priority dispute. The conventions described below explain why, as historians have increasingly noticed, this kind of dispute was the major form of debate in early experimentalism. The criteria for victory were decreed by these procedures of presentation and registration. As the system matured, moreover, so disputes became more complex, leading to elaborate competitions to amass archival support for the various contenders. Such contenders soon had to argue not just about the *existence* of registered records, but the *identity* of concepts recorded in them. This need could drive further practical experimentation, which in turn led to more publications, more reading, and more debates. Here, then, lay the significance within the experimental community of the prevalence of plagiarism allegations in early modern philosophy. It is difficult to overestimate their extent and importance in the work of the Royal Society. And such contests were begun, mediated, concluded, and sometimes even rewarded by books.[67]

66. Iliffe, "'Idols of the Temple,'" 161–266; Iliffe, "'In the Warehouse'"; James, *English Politics and the Concept of Honour*; Neuschel, *Word of Honor*, chap. 4; McKeon, *Origins of the English Novel*, 155–6; Birch, *History*, I, 330, 333, 463; II, 7, 24, 30–1, 67, 361.

67. In an early and famous example of a prize being offered at the Society, Wren challenged Halley and Hooke to produce the laws of planetary motion, and offered a book as incentive. Hooke claimed to possess the solution, but reserved it to himself so that "others . . . failing, might know how to value it, when he should make it publick." Newton then supplied the answer—and much more—in the form of his *Principia*. Cohen, *Introduction to Newton's "Principia,"* 54.

Where contests began was often with the presentation to the Society of a book (or a manuscript, of which more in a moment). This was a regular occurrence, well understood by participants. The habit of presenting books to the Society began early, and rapidly became essential to its continued vitality. From May 1661 any member publishing a work was supposed to contribute a copy. The first to do so, typically, was Boyle himself. But the convention plausibly derived from an older practice, the giving and dedication of books to courtly patrons, which had already established a reciprocal relation between presentation and legitimation. Hooke's first publication was thus displayed as a "Present" or "Oblation" to his master, Boyle, and Magalotti asked Sir Bernard Gascoigne to delay presenting the *Saggi di Naturali Esperienze* to the Society so that he could "have this extra introduction to the king." The link to patronage was not infrequently made still more explicit, since presentation to the Society could coincide with the distribution of gift copies to selected virtuosi present at the meeting—a performance that Robert Hooke is seen putting to good effect later in this chapter. At least once, Boyle presented a book anonymously; but, as displays like Hooke's perhaps imply, anonymity was comparatively unusual. (It was also, of course, a statement in itself.) [68] More typically, presentation was a visible, "public" act, often mediated by the Society's secretary, Henry Oldenburg. As such it would then become the starting point for a sequence of further actions. Those further actions could be taken as manifesting the Society's practice of reason. [69]

Most fundamentally, a gift so presented required a response. This would at least take the form of a correspondence. If so, the correspondence would be conceived as a polite "commerce," in which "discoveries" would be exchanged reciprocally as marks of mutual esteem. [70] But reciprocation alone is really too crude a concept to capture the range of possible responses, which displayed all the nuanced variety of contemporary civility. More substantially, for instance, a presentation might get the contributor elected to a

68. Birch, *History*, I, 25, 42, 265; II, 188; H[ooke], *Attempt for the Explication of the Phaenomena*, sigs. A2^r–A3^v; Magalotti, *Lorenzo Magalotti at the Court of Charles II*, 5–6. There is now an extensive historiography of such gift-giving in early modern Europe, into which this should be placed. See Goldgar, *Impolite Learning*, 19–21; Biagioli, "Galileo the Emblem Maker"; Davis, "Beyond the Market." A general introduction to the anthropology such works use is provided in Douglas, "No Free Gifts."

69. They were first specified explicitly in 1664: Birch, *History*, I, 488, 504.

70. Birch, *History*, I, 23–4, 26–8; for another example see II, 42. When the secretary commenced a correspondence without a previous gift of a book, he was to do so "in his own name," and extol the opinion the Society had of such printed books as the correspondent might have produced: I, 194. For the linked importance of polite correspondence and civility in publishing see the exchange over Sorbière, in I, 317. For the conventions of learned correspondence, see Neuschel, *Word of Honor*, chap. 3, and, especially, Goldgar, *Impolite Learning*, 12–53.

fellowship: when Graunt sent fifty copies of his *Natural and Political Observations upon the Bills of Mortality*, he was elected with the special approbation of the king. In many cases the Society went further still, and instituted a corporate assessment of the gift. This too was an act of politeness, signaling its regard for the author and his knowledge.

The term for such an assessment was "perusal." Typically, one or more selected fellows would "peruse" the book, abstract or translate it, and report back to a subsequent meeting.[71] For example, when the Florentine Accademia del Cimento's *Saggi di Naturali Esperienze* was finally presented, as from Prince Leopold himself, the prince was returned solemn thanks by Oldenburg, and Merret and Balle were assigned to peruse the book. Some reassignment must then have occurred, since at the next meeting it was Hooke and Pope who reported. Their comments concentrated on the propriety of the Accademia's work. The Italian experiments, they said, "had also been considered and tried in England, and even improved beyond the contents of that book," but were described "with much accuracy and politeness, and *some of them* with an acknowledgment of the origin, whence they were derived."[72] Boyle now prosecuted the experiments of doubted authorship. Pope made remarks on the book's account of sound, which gave rise to conversation about Italian and English measures of distance. And Richard Waller embarked on a translation, which would eventually be printed. Such an example illustrates not only the practice of perusal itself, but what the perusers were often looking for in that practice, and the generation from it of further experiments, conversation, and publication.

One of the distinctive features of a perusal was the fact that it was delegated. When the Society "read" a book or manuscript, its reading was often in reality the reported appraisal of selected referees. Henry Stubbe claimed that the fellows had not even read Sprat's *History*, "but, as in other cases, gave their *assent* and *applauds* upon *trust*." The identity of the perusers was therefore of prime importance. Hooke was a frequent choice; others volunteered or were requested to come forward depending on their perceived skills, acquaintances, and possible interest in the outcome. Their conclusions were expressly not to be publicized: fearing embarrassment and entanglement in dubious projects to garner subscriptions, the Society ordered that perusals be kept private. No text should receive a "public approbation" from fellows, and reports must be communicated only to the author.

71. Birch, *History*, I, 75–7; Sprat, *History*, 67. A clear example of perusal with the selective distribution of extracts involved Hevelius: II, 103, 107, 114, 127, 138, 140, 147, 301, 313, 338–9. The Society reciprocated Hevelius's offerings by forwarding books printed in England to him: II, 112; for such reciprocity see also Sprat, *History*, 310.

72. Birch, *History*, II, 256–7, 259–60, 286, 308 (italics mine).

If the work presented were in manuscript form, its perusal and subsequent handling took on slightly different significance. The presentation itself was still likely to be a passport into the Society, or an acknowledgment for prior admission.[73] But the procedure then departed from that for printed books. The offering might simply be noted and submitted for perusal. But if it were short enough, the paper might be read aloud at the meeting. Exceptionally, a long contribution could be read in parts over several weeks. The Society would often ask to keep the original manuscript, and it might even recommend it to be printed. Again, such responses served both as necessary reciprocation and as spurs to the Society's own continuing activities. John Beale's suggestions for the systematizing of cider production, for example, produced an official thanks, his election as honorary FRS, and a committee to consider his proposals. The Society then decided to further his efforts by dispersing both standardized printed exhortations (overseen by Evelyn) and grafts and seedlings.[74] Later, the virtuosi would take all papers returned on the subject and "reduce them into one compleat history," adding new "observations and experience" as they did so. The resulting report would then itself be read, recorded, and perhaps printed. In any case, it would act as the stimulus for yet another round of experimental, conversational, and corresponding activity. When pursued by trustworthy gentlemen, such tinkering with texts was, it seems, acceptable. To a large extent, it was how the Society itself maintained its vitality.

Consequent upon perusal there began the process of registration. By formally recording the contribution, this further signaled the Society's recognition of its worth. At the same time it testified to the contributor's regard for the community of virtuosi, not least by recognizing its legitimacy as arbiter of priority disputes. Boyle thus specified that its purpose was to "secure [authors] against the usurpations, not the industry or out-doings of others." The importance of the register lay in its usefulness in attempts to discriminate between these. The mechanism thus diversified over time as it grew to meet divergent challenges. In the earliest meetings, it had been envisaged that the "register" be a person. But soon it became a book, into which details of candidate discoveries could be transcribed; and then several such books.[75] At first, letters, for example, were to be registered in the same volume as regular papers. Then it was decided to provide a special "book . . . for the registering of letters only." Correspondence such as Huy-

73. Birch, *History*, I, 106; II, 394; [Stubbe], *Reply unto the Letter*, 19; Hunter, *Establishing the New Science*, 65.

74. Birch, *History*, I, 25, 33, 172, 176–7, 179; Stubbs, "John Beale, I"; Stubbs, "John Beale, II."

75. Birch, *History*, I, 6–8, 272, 280; Sprat, *History*, 94, 148; Oldenburg, *Correspondence*, IV, 193–4. On the civility of registration, see Shapin, *Social History of Truth*, 302–9.

gens's claiming priority for observing Saturn's rings was to be "entered" into this volume, which is now known as the Letter Book. This was followed by yet another register, a "book of theories" in which only hypotheses (and not, for example, matters of fact) would be entered. This in turn soon became a "book of histories and theories." Before long, these register books provided a supposedly secure mechanism for recording claims of all kinds. Along with the protocols surrounding them, they therefore became the foundation of the propriety adopted by the Society and its members. Access to them was accordingly restricted: fellows could in principle see their contents, but they must keep those contents secret from outsiders. And the practice of registration became customary to the point of obligation. In theory, only contributions specifically exempted from being entered were to be omitted, and any that seemed likely to prove particularly agonistic might be explicitly ordered to be registered.[76] Whether actual practice lived up to this principle, however, remained subject to debate—and sometimes angry accusations arose as a result.

Theories were not the only offerings to be entered. So too might be observations on contributed objects, such as Boyle's on a diamond. These were soon accompanied by proposals and queries for foreign travelers, serial observations taken over the course of years, and suggestions for future experiments. Moreover, since registration was supposed to attest to the veracity of a report, experiments that were reckoned to have failed would also sometimes be entered, in order to record the matter of fact. Given the importance of the registers, it is significant that the Society held itself qualified to extract or modify contributed papers before entering them. It could decree the inclusion of "animadversions" to a document, for example, or enter a diagram it had itself made of a candidate invention. Papers could also be entered with cross-references to other relevant entries. Theories might be entered along with the objections of an anonymous antagonist.[77] Or registration need not be of a text at all. Artifacts and inventions could also be registered, by being sealed in a box kept by the secretary until their inventors were prepared to reveal them. In this case—as, sometimes, with mathematical theories—the purpose was to protect inventors during the inevitable delay separating their initial inspiration from its finished manifestation. Fellows utilizing the mechanism were expected to try to complete their inventions within a year.

76. Birch, *History*, I, 18, 33–4, 43–4, 47, 49, 83, 102, 111, 370; II, 199, 213, 223–4. In late 1686 Halley, consumed with "private business," sent Wallis the original Royal Society minutes—"I have no Copy of the Inclosed minutes, which are as they were read before the Society, therefore I pray you to conceal any thing you shall think not proper to be publickly read, and to send me them again in your next": Halley, *Correspondence and Papers*, 74–5.

77. Birch, *History*, I, 29–30, 80, 180, 207, 260, 263, 287, 301, 306–7, 323, 425, 480; II, 89, 134, 143, 204, 261, 361, 381; III, 362–3.

This procedure was suggested by Oldenburg himself, in the name of "some member of the society." The anonymous proponent was probably Robert Boyle. Almost certainly, Boyle himself was the first to employ it, submitting a sealed paper containing "some notion or invention . . . not yet perfected." Again, the Society stressed, the measure was designed for "the better securing inventions to their authors," and to prevent their "usurpation."[78]

In the case of such devices, the system could be used even if the inventor were not a fellow of the Society at all. London craftsmen were invited to lodge their new devices with the Society's president, who would vet them for viability and register those deemed worthwhile under the seals of the Royal Society and the craftsman involved. Indeed, the Society persistently expressed hopes that outsiders would use its auspices to protect their inventions from commercial competitors and that it would thereby become a guarantor of such valuable rights in the wider commercial world. It foresaw exchanging its security of recorded authorship for the secret knowledge of artisans. At first this seemed a realistic prospect. Moray was soon able to report that Charles II had declared that "no patent should pass for any philosophical or mechanical invention, but what was first put to the examination of the society," and he himself passed on at least one such application from Whitehall. A workman approaching the Society through Boyle for help in getting a patent for his wood-softening technique was told that it would indeed offer assistance, "upon condition that he should acquaint them with the secret."[79] Others too, came forward, in the hope that a certificate of approval from the Society would constitute at least a recommendation to potential customers. Much the same hope was apparent in the number of proposals it was asked to accredit for subscription publications.[80] But in the end, these aspirations to extend Society conventions into the commercial world were never realized. The Society failed to achieve its objective of becoming a patent authority, and its power as an arbiter of propriety in the wider world was never better than fragile.[81] Its own professed openness,

78. Iliffe, "'In the Warehouse'"; Oldenburg, *Correspondence*, II, 319, 329; Birch, *History*, II, 24–5, 212, 247. The ambivalence of such concerns for a gentleman is suggested by the fact that the proposals were made anonymously.

79. Birch, *History*, I, 116, 219, 232, 252, 391, 397; for another example see II, 252, 255, 259.

80. E.g., RS JB X, 32, 44. See also Coxe's proposal, in Birch, *History*, II, 288, 292, 295, which well indicates the perceived safety of the Society, along with Blome's (388–9, 394). Compare Pitt's complaint in 1670 (II, 446–7), and his advertisement, in BL Ms. Add. 4421, fols. 326ʳ–327ᵛ.

81. The Society had to remind the king of his declaration in 1664: Birch, *History*, I, 391, 397. However, in 1713 Arbuthnot was again able to announce that Queen Anne had ordered her Privy Council to refer all applications for patents to the Society for evaluation: RS JB X, 444. For commercial conventions of intellectual property, see MacLeod, *Inventing the Industrial Revolution*, 10–143.

however qualified in reality, thwarted its aim. Tradesmen often refused to register their secrets because they believed the Society's confidentiality too insecure. As one self-proclaimed inventor put it, his discoveries were "pretty secrets, but known, they are nothing." The price for registration was exactly that an invention become "known" at a Society meeting. A few informed regulars—Hooke and Wallis among them—even voiced a feeling that registration assigned ownership not to the author, but to the Society itself. Some fellows did recommend strengthening confidentiality in order to encourage tradesmen to be more forthcoming, but with such representations current this could have little effect.[82] The register may indeed have become an authoritative archive of achievement and intellectual propriety, but its authority extended no further than the community of virtuosi themselves.

Beyond these register books and sealed boxes, there were two eventual resting places for submitted objects. The first was the Society's repository. If the register represented an archive of the members' and others' texts, the repository to an extent was an archive of their material contributions.[83] These were generally natural curiosities rather than inventions, but their provenance was still reckoned important. Hooke was thus ordered to fix a note to every artifact, "by which it might be known what they are, and by whom they were presented."[84] From 1664, he was forbidden to allow any artifact to leave the repository without written authority. The status of the repository as an archive of presented objects was fixed in public by Grew's printed catalogue, published in 1681 as an aid to a languishing Society's "Resurrection." Much of the original collection having been donated by Daniel Colwall, Colwall now financed the engravings that recorded it and was in turn rewarded by the dedication of Grew's *Musaeum Regalis Societatis* to him. The second such archive, into which this catalogue now moved, was the library. Despite Sprat's indignant denials, the Society began to think of having a library as a receptacle of printed and manuscript evidences of achievement from its early days. In a sense the Fire of London forced its hand. With Gresham College commandeered to serve as the Exchange, the Society was grateful to be provided with space in Henry Howard's property on the Strand, Arundel House. Shortly after, Howard presented the virtuosi

---

82. Oldenburg, *Correspondence*, IV, 525–6; Birch, *History*, II, 231; Hunter and Wood, "Towards Solomon's House," 75, 86. See also Wallis's suggestion that Nicholas Mercator's *Logarithmo-technia* be "entered in their Register-Book, the more effectually to declare the invention their's": Birch, *History*, II, 306.

83. Hooke was once ordered to "register" an apparatus, which probably meant installing it in the repository: Birch, *History*, II, 140. The register also constituted a "store" of experiments that could be exploited when the king visited: I, 288–9, 341.

84. Birch, *History*, I, 322. Hooke took over full responsibility for the repository in November 1663: 331–2. See also Birch, *History*, II, 306, for the parallel.

with the Arundel collection of manuscripts and books.[85] Thenceforth, it seemed, cultures of experiment, of the book, and of collecting would have to coincide here. The experimental philosopher, as Evelyn had called the proprietor of such a library, could now "name himself *Cosmopolitan*, or Habitant of the *Universe*." A rather reluctant Society was forced to develop extensive conventions for access and borrowing rights. And, again, a catalogue was printed and published in 1681.[86]

Registration was thus a central nexus of propriety at the Royal Society. The register helped to condition how conversations there proceeded, and to decide what form disputes would take. Even the Society's notorious conflict with Hobbes was sparked by his claims that it had used the register to discredit him. But as a number of historians of science have noted, such disputes were often conducted as contests for priority; this explains why. The criteria for successful intervention in this arena were decreed by the conventions of presentation, perusal, and registration. For example, Wilkins could propose that Malpighi be granted the "honour" of a discovery about eggs, since his English rival "had never brought into the Society an account, or a figure of this discovery." Malpighi, on the other hand, had allowed the Society to register "an accurate description of this discovery, acompanied with many very neat, and laborious schemes." As the register system matured, so such disputes became more complex, leading to elaborate competitions to amass archival support for the various contenders.[87] Those contenders, like the contestants described in chapter 3, soon had to argue not just for the existence of such records; they also had to engage in increasingly sophisticated and arcane arguments for and against the identity of concepts recorded therein.

That said, it is important to note that entrance *could* be declined. But doing so bore connotations. For example, Ward referred to the fact that Hooke rarely registered accounts after 1683–84 as evidence for his increasing "reserve." Tradesmen who refused to register their secrets because they conceived the Society itself to be too public were also remarked upon as exemplifying artisanal contumacy. There was, however, one excuse for declining registration that was virtually always accepted as legitimate. The registration

85. Birch, *History*, I, 23, 435; II, 136, 138, 149, 205, 212, 273, 284, 343, 345–6, 351, 355, 371–2, 410, 413–5, 433; III, 129, 311; Grew, *Musaeum Regalis Societatis*, sig. A3ʳ⁻ᵛ; Sprat, *Observations on Monsieur de Sorbier's Voyage*, 242.

86. *Bibliotheca Norfolciana*; Naudé, *Instructions concerning Erecting of a Library*, 10–11. When Wren designed a purpose-built premises for the Society, he suggested having the library and the repository in one room. Birch, *History*, II, 290; Findlen, *Possessing Nature*, 146–50.

87. Birch, *History*, I, 402; II, 164, 187–8, 197–8, 204, 210, 235, 237, 240, 242, 248, 394, 400, 409; III, 17; Shapin and Schaffer, *Leviathan and the Air-Pump*, 348.

process could politely be refused in favor of publication. Even Boyle, when asked to register an experiment, sometimes replied that he intended instead to print it. This tended to be Hooke's own response too, even in the period identified by Ward. One foreign fellow declared his intention to print a work on trees as reason for his not sending it to the Society at all.

This reflected the fact that no register could finally insulate virtuosi from the concerns of printing. There could be no substitute for publication if one wished to establish knowledge, and ways of securing knowledge, in a wider world.[88] Indeed, even in the Society itself, date of publication could override date of registration. Walter Needham made this explicit in reporting his perusal of a book by Reginald de Graaf that had provoked Swammerdam to contest de Graaf's authorship of discoveries. "Readers must be referred to the times, when the several claimants to that discovery published their books about it," Needham concluded, "and thence left to judge of the priority contended for."[89] "Surely," Wren agreed, "the *certain* Way of deciding such Controversies as these, is a publick Record, either written or printed, declaring the Time and Place of an *Invention*, first proposed, the Contrivance of the Method to practice it, and the Instances of the Success in the Execution." As manifestation of a propriety pursued in an avowedly open assembly, the register might be "public" in one sense. A printed book was "public" in another.

The Society realized this, and did not restrict itself to faith in its registers. It therefore regularly recommended that certain submitted papers be printed as books. It was particularly ready to take this step for works that it could foresee acting as material ambassadors for itself and its aims: Grew's catalogue of its repository, for example, or Perry's of its library. Yet the most the Society would generally do would be to recommend such a project to wealthy patrons, or to urge its fellows to join in a subscription. It would not normally act as undertaker itself. On the only occasion when it tried to do so, typically, it chose a richly illustrated and therefore costly project in natural history. This was the deceased Francis Willughby's *Historia Piscium*, an ambitious composite of what had originally been envisaged as two separate works of ichthyology (fig. 7.5). The venture has a notorious place in the Society's history. Although many individual fellows—and above all the president, Samuel Pepys—sponsored the production of its plates, and although, like Pitt's *English Atlas*, it had the advantage of printers in Oxford as well as London, the book's commercial failure was so absolute that the Society itself almost became its financial victim. Fellows suspected that the

88. Ward, *Lives of the Professors of Gresham College*, 185; Birch, *History*, I, 233–4, 378. Merret too declined to register what he felt to be a provisional piece: 350.

89. Birch, *History*, III, 88–9. For another example see Oldenburg, *Correspondence*, XI, 253.

FIG. 7.5. Frontispiece to Francis Willughby, *Historia Piscium*, vol. 2. (By permission of the Syndics of Cambridge University Library.)

printers had committed the "fraud" of producing supernumerary copies, thereby eliminating its own legitimate sales.[90] The experience left the Society virtually bankrupt. Its decision not to finance the production of Newton's *Principia* a year later, although more representative in any case, may well have been influenced by the debacle.

Internally, the protocols of the Royal Society might have been manifesting some success. Beyond the boundaries of its fellowship, however, work

90. Gunther, *Early Science in Oxford*, XII, 85–90, 95, 97–8, 100–8; Willughby, *De Historia Piscium*, sigs. b1ʳ–[b2ʳ] (Tab. G2 was sponsored by John Flamsteed); Birch, *History*, IV, 127, 140, 371, 380–82, 388–90, 393, 405, 437, 444, 457, 464, 466, 475, 524. For piracy by supernumerary copies, see above, pp. 99, 152, 164, 166, 173.

clearly remained to be done. Intervention in the Stationers' commonwealth could be risked only with caution—a message that, when forgotten, led to accusations of piracy, a decision not to underwrite what would become the greatest of all works of natural philosophy, and the near-demise of the Society itself. Such a situation could not be permitted to persevere. Some accommodation would have to be reached if experimental philosophy were to survive and prosper.

"PLAYING THE STATIONER": PRINT AND PRIORITY

In the search for a civility of communication, the Royal Society could not avoid meeting and negotiating with the Stationers. But on what basis could Stationer and naturalist meet? John Collins, who pioneered natural-philosophical correspondence and publication, had his own suggestion. Collins summed up his strategy by remarking before venturing into publication that "I am about to turn stationer myself." He knew the need, having originally been apprenticed to one. And it was probably the most promising strategy available. Following Tycho Brahe, it could be said that the best option for natural philosophers was to involve themselves as closely as possible in the procedures of printing—in other words, to take on the role of "Stationer" themselves. This offered the best prospect of extending the bounds of polite society into the domains of print.[91] In chapter 2 we saw one aspect of this in the common desire to attend the printing house in person. The strategy was of wider application and consequence than that, however, and was far more controversial. As Atkyns's example suggested, it involved not just the piecemeal monitoring of practices, but an effort to transform them.

Collins was not the only virtuoso to play the Stationer. Others were just as prominently involved in publishing. The experiences of Wilkins, Wallis, Ward, and Williamson have already been mentioned.[92] As secretary of state, Williamson also coordinated the government's licensing policy, and in 1676 he proposed to the Society a way of "encouraging the press of Oxford" by choosing books to be printed there for subscribers provided by the Society itself. Nor should it be forgotten that Robert Boyle played a leading part in attempts to produce bibles for America, Turkey, Ireland, Wales, and Scotland, monitoring competing projects in Holland while he oversaw the

---

91. Rigaud, *Correspondence of Scientific Men*, I, 200–1; Birch, *History*, III, 310. Halley discovered that the French Académie Royale des Sciences, by contrast, did not publish its books through booksellers at all: Halley, *Correspondence and Papers*, 48–52.

92. SCB D, fols. 6ᵛ, 40ᵛ; Wallis, "Copy of the Account"; Scriba, "Autobiography of John Wallis." Williamson was also involved in providing capital for Moses Pitt's atlas project: BL Ms. Add. 4421, fol. 326ᵛ.

English work. The story of these enterprises remains largely untold. The printing of experimental philosophy, too, may at first have been substantially financed by Boyle, who was by far its wealthiest consistent proponent.[93]

The virtuosi did not lack for experience. What was needed was the application of that experience in aid of experimental philosophy. If fellows' contributions were to be safeguarded within their community by the conventions around the register, only the right to publish books, and to defend those they did publish, could give them some hope of doing the same in the wider culture. The need was evidenced as early as January 1660/1, when Evelyn reported discussing his work on engraving with a print seller only to be told that a very similar work was about to be published. William Faithorne, who was printing the rival piece, moved to annex Evelyn's work to it. Evelyn resisted, saying that his own "additions" to the text that had been the original for both books "may be thought fit to be registered." His plight was, of course, not unusual, and the confrontation between genteel authorship and commercial appropriation would be replayed many times over the succeeding decades. But Evelyn now appealed to his colleagues for help. They were unable to assist at such an early stage. Soon, however, the prospect became brighter. In its charter, the new Royal Society gained the power to intervene and restrain men like Faithorne.

The Society gained the right to appoint its own "Typographers or Printers, and Chalcographers or Engravers," to rank between the clerk and the operator. In practice, this was immediately qualified by recognition of the emergent distribution of power in the Stationers' community. Brouncker announced that "because the Stationers and printers are of one and the same company, and may, by the confession of both sides, practise both trades promiscuously," the Society could choose booksellers as its "printers." It would be wise to do so. This resolved, John Martyn and James Allestry were chosen by ballot, having been recommended by fellows. Their commission was approved a few days later.[94] Martyn and Allestry were to be given a monopoly of printing and selling Society work, including ephemera. Their

93. For Boyle's financing of Sprat's *History*, see Boyle, *Works*, I, cxx; and for his efforts in bible publishing see ibid., I, lxviii–lxix, cviii, cxx–cxxi, cxxxix; VI, 43, 56–7, 131–3; RS Mss. Boyle L. 1, fols. 105ʳ–106ʳ, 148ʳ, 158ʳ–159ᵛ; Boyle L. 3, fols. 118ʳ–120ʳ; Boyle L. 5, fols. 119ʳ–121ʳ; Boyle L. 6, fols. 58ʳ–59ᵛ; Oldenburg, *Correspondence*, VI, 613–4; Birch, *History*, III, 310. Boyle's recognized persona was largely made by print, in some 180 editions published in 1659–1700, plus catalogues of works that stressed their chronological order: Harwood, "Science Writing and Writing Science." Harwood's is an excellent paper, but perhaps too sanguine about Boyle's (or his editors') ability to control the reception of this persona. For the continued production and effect of Boyle "epitomes" after his death, see Markley, *Fallen Languages*, 216–56.

94. Birch, *History*, I, 15, 321, 323, 366, 370, 479, 484, 488, 510; II, 18, 68, 77, 120, 122, 127, 138, 152, 153, 156, 157, 211, 240, 244, 476–7; III, 142, 155; Rivington, "Early Printers," 1–4.

work would thus include not just books and, eventually, the *Philosophical Transactions*, but lists of fellows, announcements summoning them to meetings, standardized forms listing inquiries for seamen and foreigners, sheets to be affixed to the faces of sundials, and copies of papers for internal distribution among fellows. It was anticipated that with this monopoly, and with the accreditation of the Society, they could safely agree to undertake the publication of natural-philosophical works otherwise unlikely to appear appetizing to any Stationer. And the prospect of losing the privilege on being found unsatisfactory should bind them to the proprieties of the virtuosi.

Wilkins and Jonathan Goddard drew up a set of rules for Martyn and Allestry, both rendering some of these proprieties explicit and barring them from pursuing certain Stationers' practices. They had to swear an oath not to "reprint" the Society's books, for example, nor to "print them in any translation or epitome." Tying them more positively to polite conventions, the Society ordered that they must also present two "extraordinarily well bound" copies of every Society book they printed to the king, and one each to the lord chancellor and the Society's own president. Each of the two secretaries must be given a copy too.[95] The Society thus became, in effect, a corporate "patentee," along the lines advocated by Atkyns and Streater. Like them, it derived its right from royal gift. It wished to make the normally autonomous Stationers into servants, "included in" its own genteel culture. It was trying to transform its "Printers'" domain into a space polite enough that the experimental philosophy could survive there, yet commercial enough that that philosophy could be successfully distributed.

The Society's right to license books confirmed this effort. This was an important power, not least because traversing the normal licensing process at Lambeth Palace could be an uncertain and convoluted process. While consistent ecclesiastical disapprobation of experimental philosophy was unlikely to arise, it remained unclear that the Society could rely on the support of particular members of the episcopal hierarchy at particular moments. We do know, in fact, that licensing by the Society was considered as an option when a Lambeth chaplain seemed likely to refuse a book.[96] The Society's council thus acted quickly once its right was confirmed. It ruled that no

---

95. Royal Society, *Record of the Royal Society*, 234–5, 260–1, 280–3. On the construction of the charter, see Hunter, *Establishing the New Science*, 1 ff. See also Rivington, "Early Printers to the Royal Society." Contracts still exist appointing printers according to this formula: e.g., Royal Society Ms. Dom. 5, no. 42; Birch, *History*, I, 323. There was perhaps an allusion to these rules in Newton's dismissal of Leibniz's review of his *Principia* as an "epitome": Cohen, *Introduction to Newton's "Principia,"* 153–4.

96. Williams, "Edition of the Correspondence of John Aubrey," 320. See Hobbes's suppressed comment: Hobbes, *Behemoth*, 96. For Parker's own position see Parker, *Free and Impartial Censure*.

book be granted a license unless vetted by at least two of the council members, to ensure that "such book contains nothing but what is suitable to the design and work of the Society." The form of the license was also decreed. And Evelyn rapidly obtained permission to put the right to use by printing the papers submitted to the Society concerning cider-making. Goddard and Merret were appointed to ratify what eventually became Evelyn's *Sylva*.[97]

The Society thus became a corporate licenser, taking up a role as part of the machinery for the regulation of the press. It may therefore seem ironic that to Milton, Blount, Locke, and others, freedom to propose new natural knowledge represented a major argument *against* licensing.[98] But the Society wished to announce and safeguard the credit of its own publications in a usurpatory environment, not to suppress rival works. It had no power to do the latter, and it never sought such power. In fact, it took care to state that the granting of its own imprimatur did not even imply that the Society itself unanimously endorsed the views of any book thus licensed. The important point was that its licensing power allowed it to announce its own credit in print. Its imprimatur was really to be a positive mark of distinction and authenticity, guaranteeing that a publication had been produced under conditions of propriety. Hence its concern that an issue of the *Philosophical Transactions* inadvertently printed with "neither Imprimatur to it, nor yᵉ place, where printed, nor yᵉ printer," might "appear suspicious."[99] But it was emphatically not setting itself up as a corporate author beyond offering that guarantee. Although it might order experiments to be made to appraise the veracity of theoretical claims made in a text submitted to it for licensing, it would not directly and explicitly endorse such claims.[100] This was because its greater aim was not to support a single philosophical viewpoint—or, in the shibboleth of the time, a "system"—but to extend the bounds within which its own moral culture prevailed into the markedly different domains of the printed book. It was concerned to spread a mode of conduct.

That said, licensing procedure itself seems at first to have been loosely based on that of the chaplains at Lambeth. (As seen in chapter 3, the Soci-

97. Birch, *History*, I, 344, 346–7; Evelyn, *Diary*, III, 340, 353. The next work to be considered was Charleton's investigation of muscles, which he was urged to forward to the council for examination: Birch, *History*, I, 385.

98. Milton, *Areopagitica*; [Blount], *Just Vindication of Learning*; [Blount], *Reasons Humbly offered for the Liberty of Unlicens'd Printing*; Locke, *Correspondence*, V, 785–96.

99. Oldenburg, *Correspondence*, II, 591. Compare the remark of Tycho Brahe against Ursus, mentioned above, p. 34 note 56.

100. E.g., James Young's: Birch, *History*, III, 414, 417. For the protocols of perusal mobilized when an outsider submitted a work of natural knowledge for licensing, see also the case of Moses Rusden, in Birch, *History*, III, 473–4. The Society expressed particular concern that Sprat should get right in his apologetic *History* "what is meant by their council, when they grant an *imprimatur*."

ety's omnicompetent secretary, Henry Oldenburg, was himself a government licenser for a time.) [101] Early imprimaturs thus tended to be exhaustive,
specifying even the number of sheets on which a work would be printed and
the number of plates to be included. This reproduced a licenser's tactic designed to stop extra sheets being added after appraisal. And there were in
fact instances when the Society's licensing régime seems to have been used
for suppression. The mechanism was employed to stop the publication of
reports on Petty's ship in the *Transactions*, for example. But punctiliousness
did not last for long, and even Petty was never prevented from publishing
elsewhere. Far more significant was the relation between imprimatur and
civility. The device was used to block "all, that might be offensive" from
other polemics, the most spectacular such case being the dispute over spring
watches to be discussed below. This was a function evidently essential to the
Society's wider aim of bolstering experimental conduct. It was therefore
worrying that, just as in the wider licensing system, so here the procedure
was allegedly vulnerable to practitioners pursuing their own interests. The
Society was understandably anxious to avoid charges of impropriety in the
very régime designed to manifest its probity. But opponents like Henry
Stubbe—and, in the watch dispute, supporters like Robert Hooke too—
did level such charges. They even claimed that Lord Brouncker himself
abused his authority in this respect. [102]

Equipped with this resource, meanwhile, the Society moved to exploit
it. One possible use was the publication of original manuscripts that had
never had the opportunity of appearing under such guarantees. There was a
vast potential archive of English achievement waiting to be uncovered and
printed, which would secure national pride and philosophical identity at the
same time as establishing the worth of the Society itself. So fellows enthusi-
astically sought out such materials. Thomas Harriot, Lawrence Rooke, and
William Harvey were principal targets. So, from an earlier age, was Roger
Bacon. They aspired to locate as many Bacon manuscripts as possible, have
Hooke peruse them, and then print them together. Gale explicitly moved
that in his perusals Hooke note any inventions that were now reputed to
have been made much later by other figures. Typically, the idea led to further
conversation, including much discussion of experiments purportedly made
by Bacon. Aubrey further proposed that a catalogue be made of all writings
published by fellows themselves, perhaps with a similar aim of establishing

101. Birch, *History*, II, 40, 42, 343; III, 51, 58, 60, 223–4; Oldenburg, *Correspondence*, XII,
254–5, 263–5; SCB E, fol. 17^r; PRO SP 44/43, p. 72; PRO SP 30/F, no. 73.

102. Birch, *History*, I, 212, 442, 463, 490–1, 507; II, 18, 27, 60. From 1667 the president
could license books on his own: Birch, *History*, II, 168. Stubbe's complaints are in Boyle,
Works, I, xc–xcii, xcii–xciv, xcvii; Hunter, *Science and Society*, 137–8; Wood, *Athenae Oxoniensis*, IV, 122–4.

priority. And Plot trumped this with an extraordinarily ambitious plan to create a catalogue of all manuscripts in all English libraries. None of it happened. But such exhilarating proposals did illustrate the possibilities opened up once the licensing and printing régime was in place.

They also quickly revealed the limits of the Society's power. For a start, even obtaining access to such materials could be a delicate matter, given how they were often treated in the book trade. Moreover, although Martyn and Allestry had been given exclusive rights to Society publications, that did not mean that they were compelled to undertake everything the virtuosi wished to see printed. This became very clear with respect to a project sparked by Hevelius, when he requested a translation of "eastern prince and astronomer" Ulugh Beg's catalogue of fixed stars. A manuscript of this catalogue existed in Oxford, which John Greaves had wanted to publish as long ago as 1636.[103] Here was a work that offered real international prestige. So having sent Hevelius a transcript, the Society now decided to secure the printing of the manuscript itself. Oldenburg hastily pointed out that the catalogue had been "sent him for his own private satisfaction," and that he should not, "by printing that catalogue, anticipate the Society's purpose of printing the whole book." Meanwhile, Wilkins approached Martyn to undertake the project. The Society could offer certain incentives. The overseeing of the press could be done gratis at Oxford, for example, since the translator lived there. (Wallis nonetheless urged the Society to pay him "twenty or thirty pounds," so laborious would it be to "attend and correct the press all the while.")[104] Yet, faced with the prospect of having to obtain a set of Persian type, Martyn declined the project. The Society now found itself confronting an unexpected constitutional problem. Given the monopoly it had itself vested in this Stationer, could it now circumvent him and employ a different printer? The question became all the more pressing when Martyn proved similarly reluctant to print Jeremiah Horrocks's papers.[105] It seemed that the bookseller still reigned: perhaps he would not misrepresent Society publications, but he could still thwart them. Oldenburg sheepishly wrote offering Hevelius the printing of the original after all. Eventually the Society did decide that it could nominate alternative printers, but not before Thomas Hyde had produced an elegant Persian and Latin edition from the Oxford

103. Birch, *History*, I, 120, 126, 219–20, 309; II, 51, 116 (see also 145, 410, 447); III, 316, 470–3; Ward, *Lives of the Professors of Gresham College*, 137–8. Ulugh Beg (1394–1449) was the grandson of Tamerlane. His catalogue was one of the greatest works of observational astronomy.

104. Birch, *History*, I, 390, 394, 403–4, 412–13, 415.

105. Birch, *History*, I, 410; II, 168–9; Oldenburg, *Correspondence*, V, 499–500. Eventually Spencer Hickman was employed as printer for the Horrocks project: Birch, *History*, II, 480, 488, 498.

FIG. 7.6. Henry Oldenburg. Oldenburg is holding Christiaan Huygens's spring watch, the object of the dispute described below. (By permission of the Royal Society.)

press, at his own expense. Only on Martyn's death in 1681 could the Printer's position be redefined to eliminate such powers. By then some virtuosi wanted it abolished altogether, so "prejudicial" and "disadvantageous" had it proved to their activities.[106]

The crucial agent in all these efforts was Henry Oldenburg (fig. 7.6). Oldenburg was Boyle's "publisher," and master of the Society's correspondence. He was also guardian of the registers. Both the internal propriety of the virtuosi and its external representation depended on his actions. Virtually all the Society's communications with the Continent were channeled through him. It was Oldenburg who first developed an extensive network of correspondents across Europe and beyond, making him the essential intermediary between the Society's meetings and the learned world. This was a remarkable achievement. The Society had gained a royal privilege to share "mutual intelligence and knowledge" with foreign individuals and bodies, not least because it agreed that Oldenburg's mail would be routed through the secretary of state's office to be filtered for intelligence of a rather different sort.[107] Nonetheless, maintaining relations between such a range of different interlocutors required both enormous labor and considerable diplomatic

106. Birch, *History*, I, 415, 417, 419; IV, 75, 79, 81–2; Hyde, *Tabulae*.
107. Royal Society, *Record of the Royal Society*, 235, 261; Birch, *History*, II, 260; Iliffe, "Author-Mongering," 17.

skill.[108] It also necessitated compromises. On Oldenburg's perceived neutrality and conventional invisibility depended the success of the Society itself. He therefore created an ambiguous role for himself, alternating between gentleman, employee, and "undertaker" of publications. He often portrayed himself as a private correspondent rather than a representative of the Royal Society, so that the Society could seem not to dictate subjects or conduct. But the very possibility of such autonomy also made him controversial, especially within the Society itself, because the register was in his immediate charge. He certainly made sure to tell new correspondents about this facility, reassuring them that whatever they communicated would be "well preserved as y^{rs}."[109] Papers from non-fellows would be admitted, he reassured them, provided they were first vetted by the president "for fear of lodging unknownly Ballets and Boufonries."[110] But some virtuosi expected him, as guardian of the registers, to remain more partial in his correspondence than a private gentleman might otherwise be. Oldenburg thus frequently found himself the subject of unfavorable comment, most remarkably from Hooke. As philosophers routinely accused each other of mercenary conduct—William Holder and John Wallis, for example, trading accusations that they were "Merchant[s] of Glory" who made the *Philosophical Transactions* their "common Market"—Oldenburg, as the one obligatory intermediary, suffered particularly from such associations.[111] Indeed, this reputation survived him. Years after his death, he was still recalled as one who had customarily acted "with Disingenuity, and Breach of Trust."[112]

Such controversies came to center on the greatest of all Oldenburg's achievements. Probably the most important of the Society's publishing ac-

108. It is worth remembering, then, that Oldenburg had originally been a diplomat. For the attributes of a good correspondent and the protocols of correspondence, see Browne, *Works*, IV, 40–3, and *Propositions for the Carrying on a Philosophical Correspondence*. It should be noted that correspondence may not have involved printing, but that did not mean that it escaped the world of the Stationers. Printers and booksellers were routinely recommended as channels of correspondence, both in England and abroad. The first need of any provincial virtuoso or group of virtuosi was to connect to such an agent: for example, Pitt was the London end of the Dublin Society (Hoppen, *Common Scientist*, 90), and James Collins acted for the Somerset group. Oldenburg's correspondence often used such channels.

109. Birch, *History*, II, 250, 286; Oldenburg, *Correspondence*, IV, 3–4. For other examples, see 419–24, 451–2; III, 535–8; V, 103–4, 117–8, 134–5; X, 184–6. Sprat too emphasized its role: *History*, e.g., 64–5, 72–6, 115 ff.

110. Oldenburg, *Correspondence*, IV, 120–3, esp. 121. For this process in action, see also 185–7.

111. [Holder], *Supplement to the Philosophical Transactions*, 3; Wallis, *Defence of the Royal Society, and the Philosophical Transactions*, 23, 29–30. Wallis also alleged that William Holder had attempted to have "a Paper of his own penning, but in Mr. *Oldenburg's* name" licensed by the Society's council.

112. Evelyn, *Diary*, III, 491. Wren, apparently, was wont to declare this opinion: Wren, *Parentalia*, 199, 246–7; see also 218–9, 228–9, 233, 238.

tivities was not technically the Society's at all. This was the *Philosophical Transactions*, which the secretary launched in early 1665. The virtuosi were experiencing continuing difficulties in creating a realm of print that could be used conveniently and reliably to build an experimental community. Oldenburg was always in the forefront of these efforts, whether negotiating on Boyle's behalf with the Stationers or acting to distribute books into Europe. In 1665 his new journal offered a regular vehicle for the publication of perused papers and the preservation of authorship. Papers selected for printing in the *Transactions*, such as Newton's on light, would therefore be chosen both for the "convenience" of philosophers and to secure "the considerable notions of the authors against the pretensions of others." [113] In these senses, Oldenburg's periodical was an attempt to extend the Society's register into the rather different "public" realm of print.

Oldenburg acted as both "editor" and "undertaker" of the new journal. It was formally his enterprise, despite the licensing authority the council exercised over it. In both financial and editorial terms it was supposedly independent, although few readers seem to have believed that this was really the case. [114] Nonetheless, Oldenburg did manage its finances alone (he obtained his first annual salary as secretary only in 1669), and he protested its independence with some vigor. He also edited with an admirable combination of prudence and gusto. Texts printed in the *Transactions* were rarely simple verbatim reproductions, whether of reports read at the Society, letters, or registered manuscripts. Oldenburg would routinely ensure that they honored the civility of the republic of letters, for example by eliminating explicit references to named individuals or by printing the names of contributors who themselves preferred anonymity. [115] This was the most consistent use of the Society's licensing and printing privileges to regulate philosophical civility. Invisible and essential, his labors made the venture a model of polite and learned publishing.

113. Ward, *Lives of the Professors of Gresham College*, 228–31; Birch, *History*, III, 9. Occasionally contributions never seem to have been registered, some because Oldenburg printed them in the *Transactions*, others for no known reason. This became an important issue in Hooke's dispute with Oldenburg.

114. The first issue was licensed by the council on 1 March 1664/5: it was to be "composed" monthly by Oldenburg and reviewed by council members before printing: Birch, *History*, II, 18; Andrade, "Birth and Early Days of the *Philosophical Transactions*." For a workmanlike account of the publishing history of the *Transactions*, see Kronick, "Notes on the Printing History of the Early *Philosophical Transactions*." The Society took over the journal formally only in 1752: see papers in BL Ms. Add. 6180, fols. 87^r ff., 239^r, 241^{r-v}, 243^r–244^r, 245^{r-v}; Ms. Add. 4441, fols. 20^r–24^r; Royal Society, *Record of the Royal Society*, 92–3. In France the *Journal des Sçavans* was likewise a private venture until the early eighteenth century: Morgan, *Histoire du Journal des Sçavans*, 46.

115. Hunter and Wood, "Towards Solomon's House," 52; Jones, "Literary Problems"; Oldenburg, *Correspondence*, VI, 131–6 and n.

Yet the existence of the *Transactions* was always precarious. Costing perhaps 12d per issue, the journal was intended to provide Oldenburg with an income. As he complained to Boyle, however, "I never receaved above 40. lb a year upon their account (and that is litle more, than my house-rent)."[116] The major reason was that the *Transactions* as it actually appeared represented rather less than half the publication Oldenburg had always intended it to be. He had meant to issue a Latin version that would extend its readership across Europe. But Oldenburg's Latin edition was never successfully printed—which would soon give Continental competitors the opportunity to supplant it—and its absence helped to cast the English version into economic jeopardy. The doubts about its viability became explicit when, shortly after its appearance, the plague forced production out of London. Selling about three hundred copies of the first issue he printed, Oxford bookseller Richard Davis expressed his own concern about continuing the *Transactions*. The plague had interrupted the "Trade & correspondency" through London on which such publications depended. Diurnals were now "ye only printed things y^t have anything near as quick & generall a Vent as formerly," Davis complained. Now he was reluctant to print more issues until the old one could be sold off, unless on a new arrangement that could only be unfavorable to Oldenburg once conditions improved. Oldenburg appreciated the point. He knew that a Stationer needed to possess a correspondency if he were to make the *Transactions* a success. Even in London itself, he must know to send copies to key sites such as the Exchange, and to Westminster, whence the mercury women could "disperse y^m to ye chief parts of ye Citty." Moreover, any Stationer for the *Transactions* would need contacts in such places as Cambridge, Exeter, and Bristol, and also, farther afield, in Scotland and Ireland. "If he not be a man of an active and large correspondence," Oldenburg conceded, "I had done much better, never to have committed it to him." But he also suspected that a prosperous Stationer like Davis could not truly be as insular as he claimed. Oldenburg came to believe that Davis was privy to "a kind of conjuration, and a very mysticall one, among Sta-

116. Gunther, *Early Science in Oxford*, XII, 26–7; Oldenburg, *Correspondence*, IV, 58–61. See also Oldenburg, *Correspondence*, V, xxv; VI, xxviii; X, 552–3 and n, 570. For public notices, see [Oldenburg], "Advertisement," *Philosophical Transactions* 12 (May 1666), 213–4; preface, *Philosophical Transactions* 196 (January 1692/3), 581–2; *Philosophical Transactions* 26 (1708–9), 292. For the mechanisms by which secretaries published the *Transactions* before 1752 see BL Ms. Add. 6180, fol. 241^r–244^r. On Oldenburg's importance see: Hunter, "Promoting the New Science"; Henry, "Origins of Modern Science"; Shapin, "O Henry"; Hall, "Oldenburg and the Art of Scientific Communication"; Hall, "Oldenburg, the *Philosophical Transactions*, and Technology"; Bazerman, *Shaping Written Knowledge*, 59–79. Birch recorded that in September 1666, disappointing profits from the plague- and fire-hit *Transactions* led Oldenburg to appeal for the Latin secretary's position in the government: Birch, *History*, III, 355–6.

tioners." An offended Allestry might be colluding with him to "bring downe ye price to their lure" by artificially restricting sales. It was a serious threat to his enterprise, and Oldenburg feared "collusion among ye Stationers" more than any other danger. For his part too, Davis resented the virtuosi trying to intervene in alliances within the Stationers' community, for example by stipulating which printer he should employ.[117] With antagonisms and suspicions mounting, the danger to the *Transactions* was real.

The journal survived, for the moment. But Oldenburg had been seriously worried that it might not. And he had further feared that its lapse would immediately give rise to "jealousy about the first authors of experiments." For its pages already represented a public archive of the intellectual propriety of the Society's fellows and correspondents. He offered himself as guarantor of the continued reliability of the registration system should the journal expire, vowing to act "with that fidelity, which both the honour of my relation to the Royal Society (which is highly concerned in such experiments) and my own inclinations do strongly oblige me to."[118] His concern reflected the fact that in controversies of all kinds the *Transactions* was an increasingly powerful ally. Even in the Society itself, the journal could be elevated in authority over the register and cited as proof of priority. In the wider world, it stood to become a register in its own right. That was why Oldenburg promised Boyle prompt inclusion so as to prevent "the usurpation of others," and told Huygens that English virtuosi routinely fixed their priority in discoveries "by means of my *Transactions*." Flamsteed too remarked that he had "found it frequently the subject of the Transactions, to vindicate good inventions to their proper Authors." It was also why at least one projector wrote hoping to use an issue as a de facto patent of invention, and why in quiet times the *Transactions* could reproduce material from the Society's registers themselves.[119] Hobbes might dislike having to learn

117. Oldenburg, *Correspondence*, II, 591, 643, 646–7, 649–50, 652–3.

118. Birch, *History*, II, 61–2; Rivington, "Early Printers." This was important because of persistent claims that the Society had achieved very little. Fellows were also enjoined to profess their fellowship on the title pages of any books they published, much to the bemusement of those unacquainted with this aspect of the London scene: Birch, *History*, I, 444; Oldenburg, *Correspondence*, II, 392–9.

119. Birch, *History*, III, 30, 47; Oldenburg, *Correspondence*, III, 610–5, esp. 610; X, 58–69, 463–6; XI, 419–21; Flamsteed, "Mr. *Flamsteeds* Letter of July 24. 1675." Flamsteed was referring here to the lunar theory of Jeremiah Horrocks. Streete, he claimed, had printed a diagram of this theory "without acknowledging the proper Author." Had Flamsteed not reacted, he would have been "unjust to the dead, whose papers passed through my hands to the Publick." When Halley's paper on the causes of the Noachian deluge was finally printed in the *Philosophical Transactions* some thirty years after being read at the Society, it was accompanied by a pointed note remarking that Whiston's own *New Theory* had not been published until eighteen months after Halley's had been read. See Halley, "Some Considerations about the Cause of the Universal Deluge," 125.

natural philosophy from such "gazettes," but even he acknowledged that
they were fast becoming the public representatives of experimental etiquette.
As Martin Lister said, the journal was the Society's real "saving register." [120]

The secretary's role as producer of the *Transactions* therefore meshed with
that as keeper of the register. Exercising influence over every aspect of experimental propriety, Oldenburg (and, to a lesser extent, his successors)
created a comprehensive approach to securing authorship in a natural
philosophical community. They did so in the course of a series of disputes
centering on registration and publishing.[121] But even Oldenburg was not
fully in control, as he discovered again when Williamson called him up as a
licenser. His *Philosophical Transactions* was long insecure, and he feared ca-
bals of booksellers as well as of natural philosophers. Register and periodical
made him particularly sensitive to charges of interest. This may be exemplified by Glaswegian philosophy professor George Sinclair, whose challenge
addressed fundamental elements in the Society's enterprise.

Sinclair accused the Society, and Oldenburg in particular, of perfidiously
declining to print his own contributions, which he claimed to have submitted as manuscripts in 1662. He maintained that the Society had violated
all its principles. First, he had waited in vain for a response to their presentation, which had been handled in his presence by Sir Robert Moray. Then
he had been shocked to find "in diverse books printed in English, many
things taken out of his Manuscript." The implication was that Oldenburg
was manipulating Society protocols against outsiders. Oldenburg responded
in kind, calling upon readers of the *Transactions* to compare the date printed
on the title page of Boyle's *New Experiments Physico-Mechanical, touching the
Spring of the Air* (1660), a work that he implied contained much of what
Sinclair claimed to be new in his own book, with that of Sinclair's visit to
the Society. This being done, he asserted, "it will easily appear, which party
hath the priority." Sinclair had conversed extensively with Boyle about these
very subjects during his visit, Oldenburg pointed out, and had "received
much light from him, concerning the same." Besides, he summoned Moray
himself to confirm that that he had judged Sinclair's papers unfit to be
shown in the Society, "because they seemed to him to contain no thing new
or extraordinarie." And, conclusively, Oldenburg found that it was "not so
much as mentioned any where in their Register book, that such papers came

---

120. Hobbes, *Behemoth*, 148; Lister, "Extracts of Four Letters," 668. Compare Plot's
remarks in Gunther, *Early Science in Oxford*, XII, 11–12, and [Plot], preface, *Philosophical
Transactions* 143 (January 1682/3), 2.

121. Tellingly, two of these involved inauthentic issues of the *Transactions*: the priority
disputes over transfusion (produced while Oldenburg was in the Tower) and the tuition of
deaf children: [Holder], *Supplement to the Philosophical Transactions*; Wallis, *Defence of the
Royal Society, and the Philosophical Transactions*; Birch, *History*, I, 83–4; II, 272, 352, 372.

ever before them (which yet is their constant and careful practice to do of all things of that nature)."

Sinclair responded that he had been present himself in 1662 when the paper was delivered by Moray "and received by them." It had then been submitted to the "perusal and consideration" of Brouncker, Moray, Boyle, and Goddard. It had also been Moray who had recommended that he print it. There was perhaps truth to this, in fact, since, unknown to Sinclair, his paper had actually prompted the Society's declaration that all perusals should remain secret and not be accounted corporate declarations in favor of publication. The lack of an entrance in the register could then be explained only too readily. It was obviously in the "interest" of those who had appropriated its contents and "*termes of art*" to ensure that his work "should not be recorded in the Register." Clearly, "this very pretext of not recording it, might be brought for denying, that ever they saw it." Sinclair suggested to Oldenburg that if "one of his own number" had written the paper, then he would have reported it extensively in the *Philosophical Transactions*.[122]

Sinclair's distant voice identified some insurmountable issues that attended the propriety of register and *Transactions*. That propriety *did* depend on an archive in the hands of the very men who gained by it. Room thus still remained for critics willing to question the Society's procedures for securing authorship. The Society's adoption of conventions of "perusal," registration, and publication had been intended to guarantee its civility to outsiders. Sinclair challenged every one of these. But mounting such major objections carried a correspondingly heavy cost. Sinclair's own credit was destroyed. He could not match the resources of the Society. He had no licensing privilege, and no patented printers. Sinclair could never be published in the *Philosophical Transactions* now, as he realized. Furthermore, he had laid himself open to the very charge of plagiarism which he himself had leveled, with all the archival resourcefulness of Oldenburg and the Royal Society available for the counterattack. This was the most powerful consequence of the combined practice of perusal, registration, and publication by now available to Oldenburg and his colleagues. It provided a corpus of texts and artifacts, the authority of which was founded on the self-evident virtues of a collective of gentlemen. Challenges could now be resolved into matters of historical record, and accredited to the world by a licensed, patented printing mechanism. As with the Stationers' community, the credit of printed books would rest on an unprintable manuscript—and on the oral negotiations surrounding it.

Since the Royal Society's perceived identity to a large extent rested on

122. Sinclair, *Vindication of the Preface*, 1–8; Birch, *History*, I, 105–6. When referring to Oldenburg, Sinclair used the terms "publisher" and "author" interchangeably.

these protocols, it is worth noting that even the accounts of its own origins that have come down to us were first constructed out of such resources and in response to such disputes. Sprat's *History* presented itself as a narrative "out of their *Registers*" of the fellows' meetings, aspirations, and achievements, proving that Charles II had inaugurated a "perpetual Succession of *Inventors*." Later, when John Wallis and William Holder clashed over the tuition of deaf children, their argument referred to events in the 1650s, before the advent of the Society and its register. Wallis therefore had to create a prehistory on which to base his claim. His account of men meeting at Oxford and London in the Interregnum has ever since been the main alternative to Sprat for origin stories about the Society. One of the major consequences of the Society's invention of propriety was thus the creation of its own history.[123]

USURPATION AND THE EXPERIMENTAL LIFE

The effects of usurpation were pervasive. They may be seen even on the early Society's best-known figure, Robert Boyle (fig. 7.7). To an extraordinary degree, Boyle became emblematic of the experimental philosopher. Not all philosophers were Boylean, it is true; but, to outsiders both friendly and hostile, Boyle came to stand for most of the virtuosi. In his very person, the "Christian virtuoso" represented all the characteristics of modesty, piety, veracity, and civility that such a figure supposedly possessed. Abroad, he was referred to simply as *"the English Philosopher."*[124] Yet Boyle's practical life was affected to its core by his experience of the practices surrounding printed and written books. This section examines the consequences of a culture of usurpation on the person and practice of the archetypal experimental philosopher.

Boyle complained bitterly of the effect of "usurpation" on his work. His papers were repeatedly stolen—Lister was just one acquaintance to report that "Mr Boyl, has been ill us'd by a Forreigner, that made him a Visit, lately, & (as I am told) did most dis-ingenuously, & knavishly, convey away

---

123. Sprat, *History*, sig. ¶ 3^v, 4; Wallis, *Defence of the Royal Society, and the Philosophical Transactions*. When Thomas Birch published his *History of the Royal Society* in the 1750s, he justified the act "as most proper for ascertaining the origin and improvements of the several discoveries in nature and inventions of art, and for doing justice to the claims of their respective authors." Birch, *History*, I, preface.

124. Harwood, "Science Writing and Writing Science," 37; Evelyn, *Sculptura*, sig. A3^v. The controversy over Boyle's identity has revived recently, as it has been made the vehicle for a number of historiographical clashes. See especially: Hunter, introduction to *Robert Boyle Reconsidered*; Oster, "Biography, Culture, and Science"; Principe, "Virtuous Romance and Romantic Virtuoso"; Shapin, *Social History of Truth*, chap. 4.

FIG. 7.7. Robert Boyle. (By permission of the Royal Society.)

divers manuscripts, prepar'd for the Press." Whether by this means or others, he found his discoveries published by others before he could produce them himself. These unauthorized publications, coupled with equally unauthorized reprints of texts which he *had* published, either robbed him of the credit for his works or reduced them to gibberish; sometimes they achieved both. Boyle had lost so much material by theft and accidents, he eventually decided, that in future he would "secure the remaining part of my writings, especially those that contain most matters of fact, by sending them maim'd and unfinish'd, as they come to hand, to the Press." [125] Previously he had kept notes systematically in bound volumes, but so many of these had been "surreptitiously conveyed away" that he had lost over "six centuries of matters of fact." He decided only to keep isolated sheets in

125. Bodl. Ms. Lister 3, fols. 51ʳ–52ʳ; RS Ms. Boyle P. 36, fol. 17ʳ; RS Ms. Boyle P. 10, fol. 98ʳ⁻ᵛ; Boyle, *Works*, I, cxxv–cxxviii; cf. also ccxxii–ccxxiv. See also Oldenburg, *Correspondence*, IV, 98–9, Boyle, *Works*, VI, 37–8, and Harwood, "Science Writing and Writing Science," 47. There is another account of Boyle's writing practices in Sargent, *The Diffident Naturalist*, chap. 8.

future, so that "ignorance of the[ir] coherence might keep men from thinking them worth stealing." This way, although separate sheets might disappear, whole treatises would not. And he would publish piecemeal, unfinished, prolix fragments—not just as a matter of rhetoric, but for concrete social reasons. Furthermore, the practices of usurpation affected not just the manner in which his discoveries were to be communicated, but the most intimate aspects of his everyday life. Boyle increasingly chose to be alone, although earlier his laboratory had been renowned for its openness: he even took to posting a sign on his door to the effect that "Mr. Boyle cannot be spoken with to-day." [126] His life and labor as a natural philosopher were conditioned through and through by the actuality of usurpation.

This should have great consequences for our understanding of the early fortunes of experimental philosophy. Historians of science have described how Boyle and his acolytes developed a characteristic literary form in their printed works, describing experiments in minute detail in an attempt to create the impression that their reader was an absent witness to the event recorded.[127] But Boyle was exasperated to find that his own minute scrupulosity in transcribing "matters of fact" rendered him all the more vulnerable to rivals prepared to employ piratical methods. Thanks to his punctiliousness, such individuals felt confident enough in his reliability that they did not fear the presence in his reports of any observational inaccuracy that might subsequently serve to reveal their fraud. As a consequence of his own prolix precision, then, Boyle found many writers prepared to "usurp" his work.

> For whereas when Experiments & observations are related by men whose faithfulnes is dubious, the more cautious sort of Plagiarys Think themselves oblig'd to mention the names of their Authors, least an Experiment not proving true, its falsity should be (as it justly may be) imputed unto Them, they think they may so safely relye on the truth of what our Author relates that the[ir] reputation runs no venture in making any Experiment that he delivers pass for their own.

Sometimes single experiments were transcribed, sometimes "whole Sets of Experiments if not reasonings too." Chymical recipes especially had been dispersed across Europe in this way, their veracity sometimes attested by the "Pastport" of Boyle's own name appended to them by their expropriators. Alternatively, experiments would be "abridg'd" or otherwise adapted to disguise their origin. Some of the culprits had even named Boyle "reflectingly"

126. Shapin, "House of Experiment," 386–7.
127. Shapin, "Pump and Circumstance"; Shapin, *Social History of Truth*, chap. 4; Shapin and Schaffer, *Leviathan and the Air-Pump*, 60–69; Dear, "*Totius in Verba*."

in the course of their plagiarism. *Virtual* witnesses, it seemed, were *actual* pirates.[128]

The sheer economics of piracy were daunting. As major Dutch booksellers told Samuel Smith in 1685 after they had found works by Boyle in a shipment from him,

> Since these books are very expensive, it is to be feared that they will not sell, and at the same time that they will be counterfeited and imprinted here; for a book of nine pages priced at 10 sols net [i.e., approximately 9d] is impossible to sell here, and nobody will take it at such a high price . . . A book printed here for 2½ sols will not be bought for 7, and their high prices are for the most part the reason why we can scarcely sell books printed in England.

Smith then tried to engage Dutch printers to produce Boyle texts in his name under their own, cheaper, conditions. But in the case of one book, at least, they declined, saying that it would immediately be counterfeited in Geneva, and that the counterfeiters would obtain imperial privileges forbidding the sale of the authorized version throughout the Holy Roman Empire.[129]

There was thus little Boyle could do, beyond following Oldenburg and urging his readers to note the dates of the first editions of the respective texts. Even this might be ineffective, however, so little could printed texts be believed. It was "the subtil practice of several Plagiarys," Boyle cautioned, "to assigne to the second or other subsequent Editions of their Books, the same date wth the first Impression." They would then slip into these impressions "many passages both of other Authors and divers other Experimental writers, and particularly divers members of the Royal Society, as if they were as ancient as the first Edition of their Books, wherein a due collation will discover them not to be extant."[130] Here again practices developed in (commercial) piracy shaded into (intellectual) plagiarism.

128. RS Ms. Boyle P. 36, fol. 9^{r-v}. See also Boyle, *Works*, I, cxxv–cxxvi; Oldenburg, *Correspondence*, IV, 93–9; RS Mss. Boyle L. 6, fols. 56^r–57^r, 97^{r-v}; Boyle P. 10, fol. 98^{r-v}; Boyle P. 35, fol. 195^{r-v}; Boyle P. 36, fols. 6^r, 15^r, 17^r; RS Ms. 186, fol. 145^v; RS Ms. 187, fols. 104^v–106^r.

129. "[C]omme ces Livres se trouvent fort cheres il est a craindre qu'ils ne se debiteront et au foi[s] qu'ils seront contrefait et imprimés icy car un livre de 9 feuilles petit papier mettre a 10 sols netto est impossible de le vendre icy et personne ne le prendra a un si haut prix, et si vous considerez votre avantage vous trouverez juste qu'un livre qu'on imprimeroit icy pour 2½ sols personne ne payera pour sept sols, et ces hauts prix sont pour la pluspart les Causes qu'on peut a peine debiter les Livres imprimés en Angleterre": Bodl. Ms. Rawl. Letters 114, fols. 158^{r-v}, 159^r. The prices mentioned are indeed very low by London standards.

130. RS Ms. Boyle P. 36, fol. 9^v. The example Boyle cited was Claude Bérigard (ca. 1578–1664), whose version of Heereboord's *Philosophia Naturalis* was reprinted in England in 1676 and 1684. Compare Harby, *What is Truth?* "Reader," for a writer warning that "The *Reader*,

Such conduct threatened the very roots of the experimental program. Boyle stressed "ye prejudice, such Plagiarys must naturally do to ye Comonwealth of Learning." At the very least, they encouraged the offense of "Lazines" in writers, who "find it far easier to Usurp Experim^{ts}, then to make them: & think they may securely, by turning Plagiarys, passe for Philosophers." Plagiarism was a moral offense, enough to disqualify one from the experimental community.[131] Invisible authorship vitiated the credit both of the perpetrator and of those prepared to attach their names to the suggestions later misappropriated. Moreover, by rendering all authorial claims uncertain, it threatened the possibility of that community's cohering at all. On that possibility rested the potential for virtual witnessing, and thus the authority of experiment itself.

Registration was part of the answer. As we have seen, Boyle was instrumental in erecting this mechanism. He recommended that his letters always be dated on receipt, "because frequent experience shows us how much our *English* have lost, for want of being so." But such measures could have only limited authority beyond the existing community of Royal Society fellows. Meanwhile, then, Boyle hastened the translation of his works into Latin, so that they might be published "wth less danger of being usurped by Forraigners." He published an "advertisement" warning of his misfortunes (by spilled acid as well as theft), and had it translated into French for Continental readers (fig. 7.8). And he wanted a comprehensive list of plagiarisms drawn up and printed—though, as befitted the Christian virtuoso, "wthout any severe reflections upon ye writers."

Oldenburg clearly concurred with Boyle in appreciating the dangers of unauthorized printing. He used the *Philosophical Transactions* to further Boyle's effort. The *Transactions* thus warned its readers against unauthorized Latin editions of Boyle's works, which were then being printed in Geneva and distributed even into England itself. There were two principal elements in these editions which must be noticed, Oldenburg announced, "for they may empair his Credit much." The first was that they were translations from works originally issued in English—a fact not advertised by the Geneva texts themselves. Their gross stylistic faults, the responsibility of some piratical bookseller's tame hack, should therefore not be attributed to Boyle.

---

may perhaps, find some parcels of this Treatise in Books lately, or not long, Extant. . . . I only, therefore request the *Reader*, not to impute to me, That I take any Notions (by them abused, by [sc. but] at first my own) out of the Works of those Pilfering Writers."

131. RS Ms. Boyle P. 36, fol. 15^r; Shapin and Schaffer, *Leviathan and the Air-Pump*, chap. 2 and 290 ff. Compare also Pope's comment that "a mutual commerce makes poetry flourish; but then Poets like Merchants shou'd repay with something of their own what they take from others; not like Pyrates, make prize of all they meet": Pope, *Correspondence*, I, 19–20.

The second, more serious, flaw was that all the experiments contained in the unauthorized text were dated to 1677, as if they had all originally been printed together. In fact, some had first been "made publick" up to eighteen years before. Boyle himself feared that this would result in his being accused of having "taken divers things from others, which indeed borrowed of me." Oldenburg therefore told his readers not only that the Geneva translation in question was unauthorized, but that "the Enumeration of the several Treatises, made in the Catalogue of the Lat. Edition, is not according to the time, wherein they were first printed." Thus "preposterously" misdated,

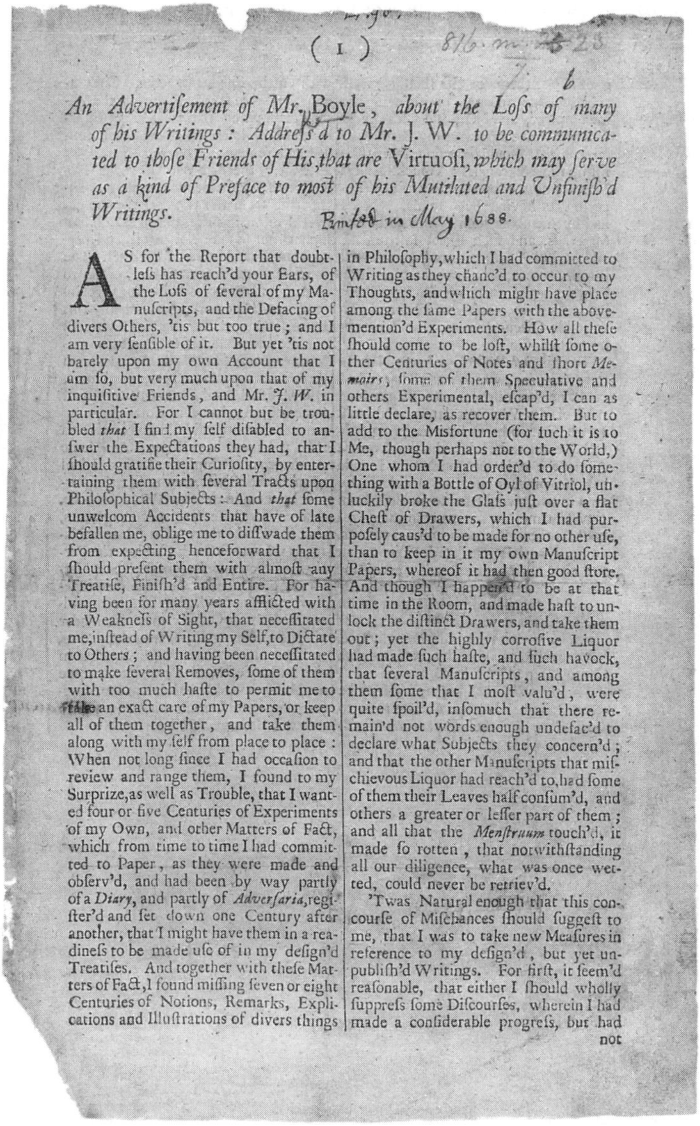

FIG. 7.8. Robert Boyle's *Advertisement about the Loss of his Writings.* (By permission of the British Library, 816.m.23[7].)

they had to be read cautiously so that "the priority of the Experiments . . . may be truly stated." He also provided a complete chronological catalogue of all Boyle's publications to help in this process. It was a powerful response—but as is shown later in this chapter, it was not necessarily definitive. So Oldenburg also went beyond the pages of the *Transactions* themselves, and used his influence with agents such as Stationer John Crooke to continue the combat against "philosophicall robbers."[132]

Boyle's iconic status lends his misfortunes peculiar resonance. Yet he was far from alone in such experiences. Robert Hooke, in particular, has long had a reputation for being disproportionately obsessed with such issues of priority. This is what makes his authorship of the continuation of Bacon's *New Atlantis* so appealingly plausible. When seen in this light, however, his concern becomes by no means so unusual—let alone, as has sometimes been hinted, paranoid. In fact, Hooke was highly knowledgeable in all practical issues surrounding the procedures of invention and the customs of commerce. He probably knew more of the guild customs governing metropolitan trades and crafts than any other active fellow of the Royal Society. When tradesmen approached the Society asking for ratification of a patent it was usually Hooke who was called upon to advise. His concerns originated in experience.

Like Boyle—and other virtuosi, such as Fairfax—Hooke feared the ability of Continental writers to plagiarize Englishmen's works. But unlike Boyle, Hooke named important names. Specifically, he accused the French Académie Royale des Sciences of stealing his ideas and publishing them in their own "memoires." He conceded that the "bashfulnesse" of English philosophers was occasionally to blame for such opportunism, as Evelyn had also admitted. But he further maintained that it was only natural for a prudent man to hesitate before publishing new opinions, and that others took advantage of such proper reticence. Hooke believed that the French would deliberately criticize an English inventor so as to dissuade him from publication and hence gain the opportunity to "defraud him of his Discovery."[133]

Hooke, again like Boyle, placed great stress on the importance of regis-

---

132. RS Ms. Boyle P. 36, fol. 57[r-v]; Oldenburg, *Correspondence*, III, 539–41; "An Advertisement of the Publisher to the Reader, Before the Latine Edition," in Boyle, *Continuation of New Experiments . . . The Second Part*, sigs. [a3[r]]–[a4[r]]; Oldenburg, *Correspondence*, II, 283, 485–9, esp. 486; IV, 93–5; Boyle, *Works*, I, cx–cxi, cxxv–cxxviii; VI, 71–2; [Oldenburg], "*An Account of some Books*." For Boyle's reluctance to name opponents—he feared making mere dissenters into enemies—see Davis, "'Parcere Nominibus,'" 165–6.

133. Oldenburg, *Correspondence*, IV, 17–18; Hooke, *Posthumous Works*, 446–9; Hooke, *Philosophical Experiments and Observations*, 388; Gunther, *Early Science in Oxford*, VII, 789–92. Compare Wallis in Oldenburg, *Correspondence*, III, 372–4.

tration as a response to such enemies. Writing a proposal for the Society on "The Method of making Experiments," he devoted more space to this than to any other topic. We saw in chapter 6 how important he conceived appropriate registration techniques to be, not just to protect authorship but in the creation of knowledge itself. Hooke thus wanted to register not simply the results of an experiment, but "the whole Process of the Proposal, Design, Experiment, Success, or Failure; the Objections and Objectors, the Explanation and Explainers, the Proposals and Propounders of new and farther Trials; the Theories and Axioms, and their Authors; and, in a Word, the History of every Thing and Person, that is material and circumstantial in the whole Entertainment of the said Society." All this must be "fairly written in a bound Book, to be read at the Beginning of the Sitting of the said Society: The next Day of their meeting, then to be read over, and further discoursed, augmented or diminished, as the Matter shall require, and then to be sign'd by a certain Number of the Persons present, who, by Subscribing their Names, will prove undoubted Testimony to Posterity of the whole History." [134] Such exhaustive accreditation procedures stipulated not just the existence of a register book, but an entire practical régime to ensure its reliability and proper use. Above all, it must be manifested orally before the whole company at every meeting. There was good reason for this: Hooke had come to be convinced that Oldenburg was manipulating his access to the register to aid his foreign competitors.

Hooke's view was predicated on the actual omnipresence of potential plagiarists, whereas Boyle, at least in his public statements, stressed their ideal absence. For their part, more genteel figures sometimes regarded Hooke as keener on personal fame than was commensurate with decency. But he had his supporters, Wallis and Aubrey prominent among them. And their notions of propriety were sometimes starkly different from those publicly espoused by the Society. Hooke it was who inaugurated the first "Clubb" of fellows, to meet so secretly that members were expected to deny its very existence. Fellows tending toward Hooke's point of view sometimes criticized Boyle himself for being too open with information in informal settings. [135] They also made it their business to urge colleagues to publish as early as possible so as to safeguard the credit of their discoveries. Wallis went on urging this as long as he lived.

The maneuvering over printed books thus became in itself a central and complex part of philosophical debate, reaching beyond the mere "commu-

---

134. Hooke, *Philosophical Experiments and Observations*, 26–8; Hunter and Wood, "Towards Solomon's House."

135. Newton too once complained of finding Boyle too open with matters of alchemical knowledge: Golinski, "Private Life of an Alchemist," 154–5.

nication" of knowledge and into its very creation. This was certainly not limited to the Royal Society: the French transfusionist Denis, too, found that the press tactics of "Enemies of New Discovery's" forced authors into print.[136] But its effects were most concentrated in the Society, and the Society developed the most systematic responses. Philosophers with access to its mechanisms, and who took the trouble to become skilled in manipulating them, could deploy that skill to win their arguments.

The supreme exponent of this strategy, as the historian might expect, was Isaac Newton. He himself suffered from unauthorized publication, as when Whiston's publication of his algebraical lectures forced him to produce an authorized text. When he died, pirate bookseller and conger member Francis Fayram produced an unauthorized English translation of his *System of the World*, again forcing his executors to publish an official version of the text.[137] But the management of printing and reading was also central to Newton's own success, from Edmond Halley's negotiations to produce the first edition of the *Principia*, though the secret editing of the *Commercium Epistolicum* to demolish Leibniz's claims to the calculus, to his and Halley's publication of Flamsteed's *Historia Cœlestis* that is the subject of the following chapter. So expert was he that even those cases in which Newton himself seemed the victim cannot necessarily be interpreted at face value. In the 1720s, for example, he was apparently incensed to find one of his manuscripts on ancient chronology being printed in France. The manuscript had fallen into the hands of Nicolas Fréret, a notorious freethinker whose views on chronology were heterodox enough to have landed him in the Bastille. In alliance with bookseller Guillaume Cavelier, Fréret published Newton's tract in the most damaging possible form: attached to a massive and authoritative chronology that starkly contradicted Newton's findings. Newton printed an angry response, linking the incident to Leibniz's alleged theft of the calculus. But this was disingenuous. As Figala has shown, Newton himself had manipu-

136. *Philosophical Transactions* 36 (June 1668), 710–15; Oldenburg, *Correspondence*, IV, 372–88, esp. 381.

137. Hall, "Newton and His Editors," 29–32; CUL Ms. Add. 4005, par. 4, fol. 9; Cohen, *Introduction to Newton's "Principia,"* 327–35. Fayram, a member of the "New" conger in this period, was spokesman for a confederacy of booksellers who in 1722 printed an "Abstract or Abridgement" in two volumes of Bingham's *Ecclesiastical Antiquities*, and "a great part of" Echard's *History of England*, thereby violating the copies of Robert Knaplock and Jacob Tonson respectively. Under Knaplock as Master, the Stationers' Company inspected the rival books, found them to be close in content, and declared that those now confirmed as reprints "tend to the overthro of the property of Copyes." Fayram's attempted reply was dismissed as "wholly evasive," and the partners were fined: SCB H, pp. 115–6, 126–35. This was the last major case of such piracy to be handled by the Stationers' court, and the assistants were already rather unsure how to respond to it; henceforth plaintiffs employed the common law.

lated the practices of piratical printing to get the manuscript published without overtly seeking authorship.[138]

Newton illustrates that the techniques of unauthorized printing could be highly useful to a philosophical writer. Reconstruction of those techniques obviously cannot explain everything in his success—they cannot, for example, account for his mathematical achievements—but they can help us to understand his development into national and international prominence. They played an important part in forging the transition between Newton and Newtonianism. But most virtuosi and philosophers, including Newton himself, generally portrayed such practices as straightforwardly damaging. In a word, they portrayed them as usurpation. For all their successes, measures against such usurpation like the register and the *Philosophical Transactions* were always less than wholly effective. So proposals were repeatedly made for their replacement. Ideas included restricting the readership for the Society's journal, and (at the other extreme) producing single-sheet "philosophical gazettes" to sell at 2d each to a wide public. As well as his exhaustive registration régime, Robert Hooke advocated a summary of the registers printed and circulated monthly among fellows, who were not to reveal the contents for at least a year. Petty proposed a weekly, monthly, quarterly, and yearly "Mercurius Londiniensis," with the weekly version incorporating "Gresham College Lectures, Experiments, [and] Transactions," along with notices of books newly published; the yearly issue would include an almanac and a map of London in color. Perhaps the most striking advice of all, however, came from John Beale. Beale outlined what he called "conduct, by which the froth of false literature, and spawn of the printing-press, may be enforced to give way to true light, and sound information." He proposed that "the Mercuryes" be used for philosophical "Communications." He then proceeded to propose enlisting the entire Stationers' community as allies in a grand project for the creation of a learned populace. Beale noted that the Stationers had established an unrivaled nationwide and international network of distribution; this should now be put to use in the reverse direction too. Provincial booksellers must start to act as conduits of knowledge. That knowledge would be channeled into London, vetted by the Royal Society, and then, if approved, printed under the Society's aegis and redistributed back through the same network.[139] It was a utopian scheme.

138. Newton, *Correspondence*, VII, 279–80, 311–2, 322–3; Newton, "Remarks upon the Observations"; Manuel, *Isaac Newton, Historian*, 21–36; Westfall, *Never at Rest*, 808 ff.; Figala, "Pierre Des Maizeaux's View of Newton's Character."

139. Oldenburg, *Correspondence*, I, 481; Boyle, *Works*, VI, 343–74, esp. 355; Hunter and Wood, "Towards Solomon's House"; Lansdowne, *Petty Papers*, 198–202, 260. Compare the adjudicatory and publicizing functions of Solomon's House, in Bacon's *New Atlantis: Works*, III, 160–4.

Ironically, it would have made the Society more dependent than ever on the culture that it spent so much effort trying to tame.

THE INTERNATIONAL MANAGEMENT OF PROPRIETY:
THE *PHILOSOPHICAL TRANSACTIONS* ABROAD

The Royal Society attempted to extend conventions of propriety beyond its walls and into the printing houses, bookshops, and drawing rooms of London. But it also relied on both correspondence and printing to establish and maintain links with a range of informants further abroad. Envoys and merchants, as well as regular carriers, transported books and papers to and from Continental Europe. Such materials were often also channeled through major European booksellers to their destinations.[140] Oldenburg was the crucial creator of both these channels of communication.

It was the *Philosophical Transactions* in particular that came to represent the Society and its practices to the world beyond Arundel House and Gresham College. The best way that world had of judging the Society was by Oldenburg's printed journal. Indeed, reading a journal like this soon came to constitute a token of one's citizenship in the republic of letters itself. That was largely why the *Transactions* was so important for establishing the Society as a guardian of credit and propriety. Although the *Transactions* was Oldenburg's enterprise, it remained clear that "The world every where looks on them as a kind of Journal of the Royal Society." [141]

It is worth noting that the *Transactions* sometimes encountered problems with its identity. What was a reader to make of Denis's *Letter Concerning a new way of curing sundry diseases* (1667), for example, or Acton's *Physical Reflections upon a Letter written by J. Denis* (a strangely Hermetic work printed for Martyn in 1668)? Both were the same size as issues of the *Transactions*, and displayed contiguous pagination and signatures with the current issue. Evelyn, for one, bound them with his copies of the journal. Similarly, William Holder issued a paper designed to resemble the *Transactions* but in fact printed autonomously.[142] For virtuosi depending so absolutely on the veracity of the *Transactions*, the implication was rather terrifying. This journal was the guardian of credit; but who would—who *could*—guard the guardian?

The full impact would be felt, however, only when the *Philosophical*

---

140. Hall, "Royal Society and Italy"; Goldgar, *Impolite Learning*, 17.

141. Ultee, "Republic of Letters"; Goldgar, *Impolite Learning*, 54–114; Martin, *History and Power of Writing*, 299–301; King, *Original Works*, II, 3–6, 8.

142. Denis, *Letter concerning a new way of curing sundry diseases*; Acton, *Physical Reflections*; [Holder], *Supplement to the Philosophical Transactions*, 9.

Transactions ventured into Europe. Foreign printings and translations of Society works were both essential for the experimental enterprise and, for this very reason, a continual problem. The Society needed to spread its word if it were to succeed, yet doing that simultaneously meant losing control of its texts. Books were the first major subject of concern. Oldenburg was besieged by requests for Latin editions of such items as Sprat's *History* and Boyle's works. But publishing such material in London was not easy, and despite his promises he often failed to produce them. This did not stop European entrepreneurs from making the attempt. Questions of national prestige as well as individual honor arose when their unauthorized reprintings appeared. Boyle himself urged both speed and secrecy on English printers, as we have seen, since "if we make not ye more hast some or other will publish some of the Chiefe particulars of it, to my Disadvantage, ye Booke being already as I find taken notice off." [143] Yet Boyle also hesitated before publishing such works as his *Origin of Formes and Qualities*, lest an English text become available before the Latin, and "Divers of ye Exp^{ts} wch possibly will appear new & somew^t Curious, may be wth or wthout a litle variation, adopted & divulged by others." [144] Meanwhile Oldenburg used his correspondence networks to warn off these rival printers (through agents including Spinoza), and threatened to add new matter to the text in an effort to discourage them. But a Dutch partnership nonetheless did attempt the *History of Colours*, much to Boyle's concern, and Spinoza himself expressed fury that these agents persisted "in spight of our teeth." Similarly, the Society attempted to hasten du Moulin's Latin version of Sprat's *History*, "for fear it should be done in Holland, to the prejudice of the author." Oldenburg's correspondence network was again a key resource in this case: when a Parisian translator proposed to translate Sprat, Oldenburg heard of it before he had even begun work and was able to mobilize allies to prevent his proceeding. [145]

Ultimately, however, such books were of less concern than the *Philosophical Transactions*. Given its function as a printed register and exemplar of propriety, it was particularly important that a bona fide Latin translation of the *Transactions* be produced. Oldenburg himself always encouraged such a translation, and indeed his initial plans had depended on it. The need was

143. Oldenburg, *Correspondence*, II, 408–10; IV, 446–7, 473–4; V, 187; XI, 63, 125–7. See also Palm, "Leeuwenhoek and Other Dutch Correspondents." For Molyneux on the international importance of the *Transactions*, and the journal's role in facilitating modest authorship, see Southampton CRO Ms. D/M 1/1, fols. 58^r–59^r.

144. Oldenburg, *Correspondence*, II, 283, 453–4. He wanted the *Hydrostatical Paradoxes* printed simultaneously in English and Latin, sheet by sheet: 613. Cf. also III, 58–9.

145. Oldenburg, *Correspondence*, II, 497–501, 509–13, 557; Birch, *History*, II, 241, 271, 344, 426.

certainly appreciated in the Society itself. Boyle suggested one by at least March 1666. Foreign readers too repeatedly asked for a Latin impression. Their requests gained added force whenever a rival periodical such as the *Miscellanea Curiosa* was introduced in the Society as an "imitation" of the *Transactions*. And Martyn for once expressed some interest. Oldenburg immediately urged haste upon him, so that "ye Dutch may not be able to print upon him with advantage."[146] By the end of 1667 he hoped that a translation would soon be complete, "there being several particulars in it, communicated by able persons, and new, wch ought to be kept from usurpation, by this way."

It was therefore a shock when Colepresse wrote from Leiden to tell Oldenburg that "a Professor here . . . is now translateing *your* Transactions in to Latine"—especially as he intended to "alter ye Method somewhat by reduceing ye severall Accounts belonging to ye same subject in to one place." Such a project threatened to ruin the *Transactions'* role as a "register" by subverting its chronological sequence. By December the project had transferred to Amsterdam. It then apparently lapsed, since no publication seems to have followed.[147] But the warning was clear. Wallis and Denis, at least, had assumed that Oldenburg both knew of and was cooperating with this Dutch project. For two more years the secretary continued to plan his own edition. In November 1670, he reported to the Hamburg professor of logic and metaphysics, Martin Vogel, that his translation was finally under way. But these plans, too, suddenly went awry. By 8 December, he had heard that an independent version was definitely being printed. This was to become a much more serious problem than the earlier attempt.

The project involved personnel spread across Northern Europe. The inspiration seemed to come from Hamburg. The translator was a cosmopolitan Frenchman, John Sterpin, resident in Copenhagen. The engravings were being produced in Frankfurt, and the printing would be done there by Daniel Pauli. Vogel, Oldenburg's agent throughout, reported that Sterpin seemed to him "ill suited" to his task, and even heard rumors that he had decided to give up in despair at his own inadequacy. But printing went ahead, and Vogel sent Oldenburg the first four sheets to emerge from the press. The partners planned to avoid competing with any authorized edi-

146. Oldenburg, *Correspondence*, III, 66; IV, 4–8, 137; Birch, *History*, II, 437, 466, 469; Hall, "Royal Society's Role"; Kronick, "Notes on the Printing History." See also Oldenburg, *Correspondence*, V, 119–21: "I should very much like to see *Micrographia* printed in Latin. If your booksellers do not want to do it it will be done in Holland."

147. Oldenburg, *Correspondence*, IV, 82–4; V, 140–2, 247–9. In addition, Justel planned a French edition: IV, 147–50. This may have been the text sold in 1965: V, 413–6, n. 2. The original *Transactions* were, however, occasionally antedated: Gunther, *Early Science in Oxford*, XII, 22.

tion by starting with the text for 1669, he said. Meanwhile, the partnership itself, its plans rumbled, ordered Sterpin to endeavor to win Oldenburg's approval. Sterpin therefore wrote to Oldenburg, telling him that his translation would appear soon and that a copy would be sent to London for his appraisal. He reassured him that the partnership would not presume to ascribe the *Transactions* to the Royal Society. However, he confessed himself "ill satisfied" with the correctors employed to vet the text, and feared that Oldenburg would find his translation badly printed.[148] This was to prove an understatement.

Oldenburg's response was an extremely effective manifestation of the usefulness of his network of correspondents. He replied first to Vogel.[149] He was to order Pauli to cease printing at once. As soon as Vogel got the letter, he rushed to the printing house and stopped production. But he was too late to prevent the appearance of the first volume, and the partners would not withdraw it from sale. Gottfried Schulz, a well-known Hamburg bookseller specializing in the international trade, seems to have been the prime mover. Schulz was already talking of employing another translator, less incompetent than Sterpin.[150] The most he would do was promise to submit any further volumes to Oldenburg's approval before publication. Oldenburg then wrote to Sterpin personally forbidding him to continue work, and told Vogel of this.

Unfortunately the Danish booksellers were not quite the "blockheads" that Sterpin's patron, Thomas Henshaw, took them for. The first volume rapidly reached the main centers of Europe, via Schulz's extensive network of distributors. Sluse expressed himself "delighted" with the copy he found in Liège. Vernon reported finding others in Paris, and Oldenburg promptly wrote again to warn potential readers there of how "falsely" it had been translated. And, most important, he now printed in the *Transactions* itself a Latin notice to his "Forrain Readers" against Sterpin's text. Nevertheless, despite these measures readers continued to rely on it in the absence of any authorized translation. The only way permanently to combat interlopers like Sterpin was to produce such a text.

This Oldenburg continued to try to do. He made his attempt, intriguingly, by moving to engage Schulz himself. By November 1671 Schulz had decided to take on the project. Vogel told Oldenburg that Schulz would send him a long letter on the subject. But it seems that he never contacted

---

148. Oldenburg, *Correspondence*, V, 203–5, 272–6, 413–6; VII, 264, 308–14, 456, 468–9.

149. Oldenburg, *Correspondence*, VII, 495. Meanwhile another correspondent had asked permission to include translated material from the *Philosophical Transactions* in his German journal: 528.

150. For Schulz, see also Oldenburg, *Correspondence*, VII, 528.

Oldenburg directly, and the deal fell through. Nonetheless, the potential market remained too large to be ignored. Two Amsterdam printers, Henry and Theodor Boom, now took up the challenge. They employed one Christoph Sand as translator. It was an ominous choice. Sand, an exiled German Socinian, had already published several scandalous religious tracts.[151] He had been working as a press corrector in Holland, and was now secretary to the English resident at Hamburg, Sir William Swan. It was there that the Booms had found him. From Hamburg he wrote a series of letters to Oldenburg, pestering him on detailed points of interpretation and informing him after the fact that he had long been making unauthorized translations of Boyle's works for the Dutch booksellers.[152] He did not ask permission for his new project; indeed, he was quite brusque when Oldenburg was slow to reply.

When Oldenburg questioned his propriety, Sand responded with his own view of the status of the author in a world of scribblers. He himself was far from unlearned, and he expected his testimony to be treated as valid by the virtuosi.[153] Yet Sand's portrayal of himself was far from that of a traditional gentleman. "I sell my services to anyone for money," he declared; the Booms paid him a ducat per sheet. Errors were not his responsibility. "I am as it were a bookseller's hack [*mercenarius*]; what I do, I do for him. If he wishes to spoil it, he may spoil what is his own." Sand's own name was not to be printed on the edition, though, "lest I should lose my good name, not being able to publish the work as I should like." He insisted on this matter of his honor. Sand was no slave. "Only the freeborn can hire their labour out for money," he pointed out. Moreover, his status as a hack remained separate from that as an independent agent:

> The bookseller did not allow himself the same freedom with regard to my own writings, and if he had so indulged himself I would not have patiently borne with him. But if an employer wishes to spoil his own property, he may. If I had refused him my labour, another person more compliant to the bookseller in his work would, by taking his pay, have made fun of my folly.

To what errors had Oldenburg especially objected? Lists crossed back and forth across the North Sea. First, he maintained his strong aversion to as-

---

151. Oldenburg, *Correspondence*, VII, 546–8, 573–4; VIII, 145–51, 330–4, 385, 392, 512–7, 629–34; IX, 197, 216–7, 352–6; [Oldenburg], "Advertisement necessary to be given to the Readers of the *Latin* Version, made by Mr. *Sterpin*." Locke was one reader to pore over these: Marshall, *John Locke*, 138–9, 392.

152. Oldenburg, *Correspondence*, IX, 424–7 and notes. Samuel Smith had been involved in importing Sand's Socinian works: Bodl. Ms. Rawl. Letters 114, fol. 2ᵛ.

153. Oldenburg, *Correspondence*, X, 409–10, 471–2, 487–9, 527–31; XI, 85–6; Birch, *History*, III, 122, 131; Sand, "Extracts of two Letters." It is, of course, significant that Sand attempted to establish himself by submitting natural knowledge to the Society.

cribing the *Transactions* to the Royal Society. Sand explained that the bookseller had insisted on the attribution, partly because Sterpin's edition had
used it, but mainly because "the work will be more readily saleable with a
grander title."[154] Even after Sand had submitted his draft preface to Oldenburg for approval, the bookseller changed it in press by adding "a new sentence ascribing the *Transactions* to the Royal Society." Moreover, the bookseller's "haste" had also led his text to substitute "invent" for "promote" at
an important passage—"for on the same day my translation was conceived
and printed[;] from the pen it went straight to the press, so that I was not
allowed to reread it even once." Oldenburg also objected to the misdating
of items in the translation, although he remarked that one case was not too
important "because this date denotes the date of writing the letter, not the
making of the observation." Perhaps most serious of all, however, was the
fact that Sand had grievously misunderstood English social titles. Oldenburg was horrified to see that important correspondents such as Huygens
had been addressed as if, in Sand's words, they were "cobblers and tailors."
This, he feared, might lead Huygens to suspect Oldenburg himself of "taking sides" in his debates.[155]

Faced with such enormities, Oldenburg became ever more convinced
that an unsupervised translation by *any* writer would be dangerous. Anyone
attempting to translate "philosophical authors" could only come up against
difficulties insurmountable "not so much from the fault of the author, as
from the nature of the matters of which he treats." Eventually he came to
the conclusion that it was "in vain" for any foreigner to attempt the task,
"since it is very difficult for anyone to manage it properly unless the author
himself first reviews everything before it is committed to the printer." One
could not hope to succeed from the printed page alone, and the danger in
trying was too great to be risked.

Sand declared himself unable to see why his edition should "begin a dispute." Indeed, he claimed to have corrected more errors than he had created.
But given the importance of the *Transactions* in such contemporary debates
as have been suggested here, this could only be a futile hope. His edition
was widely distributed, and became a talking point. Hooke went to Martyn's
shop to "discourse" of Sand's work. Oldenburg responded by printing a

154. Oldenburg, *Correspondence*, IX, 511–8, 546–8. The Booms in fact reprinted Sterpin's
text as part of their own edition. They refused to change the attribution.

155. Oldenburg, *Correspondence*, IX, 511–8, esp. 514; X, 527–31; XI, 85–6; see also XI,
114–6. Oldenburg had originally denoted Huygens by "master," which, Sand pointed out,
could be applied to tradesmen. Sand felt that classical precedents warranted his using the
titles he did. Oldenburg refused to accept this, telling Sand that "your ancient classical Latin"
had no "force to change the custom that rules among us."

long list of complaints against Sand's text, recounting dozens of miscon-
ceived readings.[156] The point was not lost on Sand himself, however, and he
had already served Oldenburg with notice that the English could not expect
to have it all their own way. He realized what the most important issue was.
"I have been led to give a warning," he declared, "that the English, when
they demand the discoveries of nations beyond the sea, and [do] not [reveal]
the discoveries of their own nation, particularly lucrative ones, ought to hide
themselves from other peoples." [157] Sand and his superiors were beginning
to resent what they saw as a practice of demanding exact details of foreigners'
inventions in order to concede their priority—and publish them in the
Transactions—but not extending the same stringency to Englishmen, whose
claims were given favored status and whose privacy was maintained.

The issue came to a head in October 1674. Oldenburg's struggle to maintain the pristinity of the *Transactions* in the face of European translation and
reprinting now collided with the violent dispute involving Wallis, Huygens,
and Hooke that is the subject of the next section. Faced with the incipient
internal and external breakdown of its régime of propriety, the Society acted
precipitately. It suddenly revoked a central part of its statutes. No longer
were its meetings to be open. Only fellows were to be admitted, and they
were to be forbidden to divulge anything of any new invention or theory
that they might have seen there. This fundamental shift was designed to
protect the virtuosi from foreigners thought to be eagerly seeking ways of
plagiarizing their findings. It was a dramatic reversal. Shortly thereafter, the
Society also reinforced its rules for keeping under lock and key "all the
books, discourses, letters, and accounts, brought into the Society; together
with the names of the authors." And Oldenburg immediately moved against
the unauthorized Latin *Philosophical Transactions*, with its dubious translations, its misdatings, and its wrongful attributions. He wrote to Sand a fierce
letter demanding that if he wished to proceed he must travel to London
and pass every page before Oldenburg himself. "There are various reasons
(which it is not possible to detail here, nor have I leisure for it) which wholly
require this," he maintained: "Nor would I predict that a translation of this
kind could ever be produced which would agree with the original, unless
undertaken in this way." He refused to explain why, saying that it was not
in his power—a coded reference to the new regulations. But in particular
he again singled out Sand's habit of referring to distinguished philosophers
and theologians by titles which "all of our people" would attribute to "contempt." This and a blistering review of the errors in Sand's text printed in

156. Oldenburg, *Correspondence*, IX, 515–6, 575; X, 527–31; XI, 114–6; Hooke, *Diary*, 12;
[Oldenburg], "Some Animadversions."

157. Oldenburg, *Correspondence*, X, 340–3. My translation differs slightly from that in
the *Correspondence*.

the current *Transactions* finally persuaded Sand that he could not hope to retain Oldenburg's neutrality.[158] The Latin *Transactions* expired.

Oldenburg's experience should serve as a cautionary reminder that what contemporaries often represented as a harmonious "republic of letters" was far from tranquil in practice. Oldenburg, and the Royal Society itself, could not succeed without powerful individuals like Schulz. It is telling to realize that by 1677, at the very latest, Schulz was again acting as distributor of Oldenburg's own *Philosophical Transactions*. Martyn would send them to Hamburg every month, whence Schulz would forward them into a Continental network of markets. Leibniz, for one, received copies through his mediation.[159] If he had been so instrumental in the near-destruction of the journal's credit by unauthorized reprinting, how could the "real" *Transactions* be guaranteed in his hands? The cases of Sand's and Sterpin's texts together also suggest some of the reasons such productions were regarded as peculiarly dangerous. Authors and "editors" like Oldenburg feared the effects loss of control over their texts could bring: arguments over priority, allegations of religious or moral impropriety, incompetent or downright malicious misrepresentations of their ideas. Continental readers would have to be extraordinarily skillful to interpret unauthorized copies safely. Matters of fact might seem incontestable in Gresham College or Arundel House, but they could soon lose their patina of facticity in such forums. Usurpation of papers, be they manuscript or printed, private or public, must be quashed.

ROBERT HOOKE, HENRY OLDENBURG, AND THE CONSEQUENCES OF IMPROPRIETY

The Continental reprinting of the *Philosophical Transactions* threatened the credit of the Royal Society's conventions abroad. But domestically too they were in danger. If there is a single episode that illustrates best all that has been said about the importance of intellectual and practical propriety in the early Society, it is the dispute over spring watches that peaked in 1675–6. The dispute epitomized concerns over the proper management of printed and written materials.[160]

---

158. Birch, *History*, III, 137–9, 159; Iliffe, "'Idols of the Temple,'" 166 ff.; Oldenburg, *Correspondence*, XI, 114–6; [Oldenburg], "Some Animadversions."

159. Oldenburg, *Correspondence*, XIII, 322. There were other unauthorized editions of the *Philosophical Transactions*. To cover all of them would be impossible. See Andrade, "Birth and Early Days of the *Philosophical Transactions*," 18. These should be compared to piracies of the *Journal des Sçavans*, which were also undertaken, Boom and Waesberge being prominent in their production: Vittu, "Contrefaçons du *Journal des savants*," esp. 311–3.

160. There is not space here to rehearse this affair in exhaustive detail; nor is such an account needed. Iliffe, "'In the Warehouse,'" provides a detailed and definitive treatment.

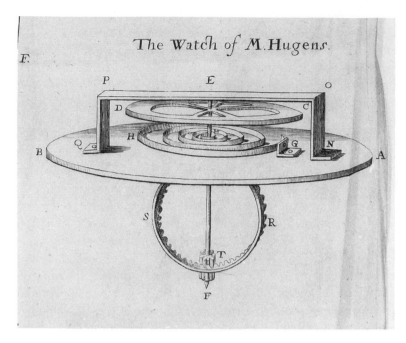

The Watch of M.Hugens.

FIG. 7.9. Huygens's design for a spring watch mechanism, as published in Oldenburg's *Philosophical Transactions*. *Philosophical Transactions*, 112 (25 March 1674/5). (By permission of the Syndics of Cambridge University Library.)

Its prime motivation was very clear. For decades, governments and individuals had been searching for a reliable way to calculate the longitude at any point on the earth, and an accurate, reliable, and portable clock offered one means to achieve this end. Huge rewards beckoned any inventor able to produce a clock of sufficient quality and reliability. Such an inventor would be both rich and honored.[161] Oldenburg was thus intrigued in early 1675 when Christiaan Huygens sent word of a new watch design that might achieve success (fig. 7.9). Huygens was a prized correspondent, who had already contributed to the Society's propriety mechanisms by suggesting the additional use of a "cypher or anagram" to safeguard inventions lodged in the register. He had contributed a cipher of his own, which was duly entered, and Oldenburg had declared himself proud of this prompt recognition of the register's worth. Indeed, Huygens continued to believe in the Society as a safe place for his papers, even considering sending his manuscripts there should he die from his serious illness of 1670.[162] Now, though,

161. Bennett, "Longitude and the New Science"; Howse, *Greenwich Time*.
162. Birch, *History*, I, 495 and n; II, 344–5, 424; Oldenburg, *Correspondence*, XII, 23. At his death Boyle left sealed papers with the Society: Maddison, *Life*, 202; Hunter, *Robert Boyle by Himself and His Friends*, 63 n. a.

five years later, Oldenburg's publication in the *Transactions* of Huygens's design for a spring watch would spark off a long and bitter dispute with Robert Hooke, which would call into question every aspect of the Society's protocols.

Huygens had again forwarded his design to the Society in the form of an anagram, "as you know I have done before for new discoveries, and for the same reason." He had subsequently provided its "explication" in a second letter, fearing that the English might already have heard it anyway through "the bad faith of the clockmaker whom I employed to construct it." He had also printed an illustration of his device in the French *Journal des Sçavans*, which Oldenburg awaited before printing his own report in the *Transactions*. Huygens now offered the Society, through Oldenburg, the possibility of taking out an English patent on his design, the benefit of which, according to Oldenburg, would go to the secretary himself. Oldenburg subsequently applied for such a patent.

It was Sir Jonas Moore who told Hooke of this application. Hooke forthwith denounced it as "treachery."[163] He claimed to have invented the same device some seventeen years before, citing as evidence a rather obscure reference in Sprat's *History*.[164] There were indeed scattered notices in the Society's records to show that he had been intermittently working on some sort of watch.[165] But there was no unambiguous register entry. Even in the early years, Hooke had insisted on showing his "secret concerning the longitude" only to the president. A complex struggle now began. Hooke accused Oldenburg, and with him Brouncker, of betraying his secret to the foreigner—an unforgivable offense for one in so important a post. He persuaded Oldenburg to let him transcribe Huygens's diagram, checked in the register for evidence of his priority (where he found "the watch with springs was made 1666 before the Society"), and dredged the journal book similarly. Meanwhile he "discoursd much" of watch mechanisms with Wren and urgently pressed Thomas Tompion to make a working specimen to his own design. These efforts only redoubled when, meeting Oldenburg at Martyn's

163. [Oldenburg], "Extract of the French *Journal des Scavans*"; Birch, *History*, III, 179, 190; Oldenburg, *Correspondence*, XI, 162–4, 176–8, 184–8, 220–3, 224–6.

164. Sprat, *History*, 247. Hooke was to do this again in dispute with Newton in 1699: RS JB IX, 170–1.

165. Birch, *History*, I, 417; II, 108, 110, 112, 134, 137, 355–6, 359–60, 372, 374, 451 (not all of these were spring watches, some of them being powered by other mechanisms); Hooke, *Diary*, 148; Sprat, *History*, 247. The Society was aware of aspirations to secrecy when Mercator implied he had a design in 1666: Birch, *History*, II, 110, 112. Sprat's work included extracts from the register made under Wilkins's supervision: Birch, *History*, II, 3, 6–7, 138, 161. The papers were referred back to their authors before printing, "seeing they were to be published with their names prefixed thereunto," and the president did his accustomed examination before passing them.

bookshop, Hooke learned that he faced the possibility of Leibniz too becoming involved.

Faced with the apparent opposition of both Brouncker and Oldenburg,
Hooke seems to have decided to abandon the Society's mechanisms for
channeling such debates. Alleging that the "raskall" secretary had long pursued a deliberate policy of neglecting to register his discoveries, he took his
case to the king himself. Hooke began presenting him with working specimens of his own watch. Oldenburg responded by encouraging Huygens to
send his own specimen watches to the Society for comparison, and recommending that he submit an attestation to Brouncker that he had known
nothing of Hooke's designs before he had sent his anagram. He urged him
not to mention Oldenburg himself in his affidavit, "for reasons which it is
not convenient to declare here." Huygens acted on the secretary's advice,
dispatching samples to Brouncker. In doing so he alleged that he himself
had let slip hints of his invention in conversation with Wren in 1661, but
declined overtly to claim that Hooke himself had acted dishonorably.

Hooke "discovered their designe" in the tavern after a Society meeting
on 8 April 1675. Outraged, he "vented some of mind" against Brouncker
and Oldenburg, and "Told them of Defrauding." [166] Williamson, however,
advised Hooke to join the secretary. But Hooke had been able to impress
the king with his design sufficiently to stall Oldenburg's patent application,
and he now widened his campaign. He spoke to Wren of Oldenburg and
his policy of "Fals information." All the while, as Oldenburg complained to
Huygens, Hooke kept his mechanism secret from the Society. This move
polarized the Society's supposedly neutral umpires. Before long Brouncker
was allowing Oldenburg to portray him as favoring Huygens, and he apparently used his own access to Charles to act for Huygens. In return Hooke
denounced him as a "Dog" and refused to attend the Society. Brouncker
sided with Oldenburg again when Hooke continued to attack the secretary
for perverting the register system. Huygens now added that Hooke had
acted improperly in not reciprocating his contribution of the anagram with
a statement of his own invention, if he had truly had it at that time. [167]

There followed a violent exchange of views in print. Hooke had demonstrated his helioscope (an instrument for observing the Sun) at the Society
on 20 May and perfected it during the following weeks. He wrote up an

166. Birch, *History*, II, 24; Hooke, *Diary*, 148, 150, 153, 155–61, 163, 171; Oldenburg, *Correspondence*, XI, 235–6, 281–3, 299–301, 307–8, 326–9, 334–6, 341–3, 378–81; XII, 18–19.
    167. Oldenburg, *Correspondence*, XI, 359–60, 375–6, 405–7, 440–3; Hooke, *Diary*, 159,
164, 247. Compare the propriety of replying to challenges as recounted in Biagioli, "Galileo's
System of Patronage." As Biagioli suggests, submissions necessitated reciprocation. Compare
the response to Prince Rupert's instrument "for casting any platform into perspective": Birch,
History, I, 329, 333, 337, 346, 348.

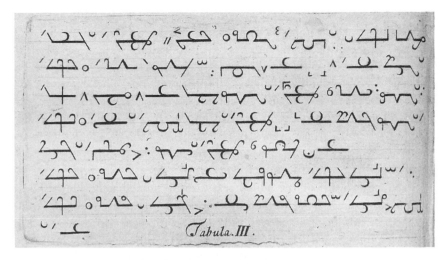

FIG. 7.10. Hooke's cryptic announcement of the principle underlying his own watch design. The translation reads: "The contriving of portable watches is comprehended as far as their regulation is concerned by two objects. The first is the causing of a countereffect to all gravity and motion, so that neither the pulling power of the earth nor position nor irregular external motion of the watch can cause any irregularity. The second is the contriving of internal regulators of the watch so that neither the irregular functioning power of the spring of the bows nor other part of the watch can disturb its motion. The first is effected by balances moving continually and oppositely, the first balance to the other. The second is effected by springs or other agents acting independently of the balances or regulators of the motion." Hooke, *Description of Helioscopes;* translation adapted from 'Espinasse, *Robert Hooke*, plate XI. (By permission of the Syndics of Cambridge University Library.)

account and gave the copy to Martyn on 21 July. He sat correcting proofs as the watch dispute continued to dominate his thoughts. Finally, he decided to add an extra section to the work devoted specifically to the dispute, in which he would condemn Oldenburg.[168] This section would have to remain outside the licensing authority of the Society. He therefore absented himself from Garraway's to stay at home in Gresham and write "against Oldenburg." Before issuing it to Martyn, he went to Wren again and discussed the piece; Wren was probably the only person apart from Martyn to see it before printing began. With his approval, Hooke gave the section one last revision, then took it to Martyn on Monday 27 September. Four days later he corrected the last printed sheet. In this last-minute addition Hooke described the "general ground of my Invention for *Pocket-Watches*" in Wilkins's universal character (fig. 7.10). As well as this brief and cryptic reference, "to fill the vacancy of the ensuing page" and thus satisfy Martyn's printer Hooke added

168. Hooke, *Diary*, 161, 170–1, 177; Birch, *History*, III, 219–20. On 10 August Hooke dined with Boyle and "Raild against Oldenburg": *Diary*, 174.

"a *decimate* of a *centesme* of my invention": ten ciphers recording other new inventions to which he laid claim. He also assaulted Oldenburg violently and at length.[169] Then, on the verge of publication, he had an attack of nerves. He suggested to Martyn that he suppress the attack. Martyn, remarkably, disagreed, and persuaded Hooke to retain it. The Stationer's role in its appearance was thus central. Indeed, in general the degree and consistency of cooperation between the two had been remarkable. Martyn was visited by Hooke almost every day, and they got on well. He was even accustomed to granting Hooke access to sheets he was printing of other fellows' books before the full works were completed.

Brouncker heard of the added text almost immediately. He rushed a "Prohibition" to Martyn forbidding its printing. There Hooke saw it. He stormed to Brouncker's quarters, only to find the peer "abroad." His first action the following day was to return, and this time he was more fortunate. Brouncker agreed to receive Hooke. Apparently the latter suggested mitigating changes, which included removing explicit references to Oldenburg as a corrupt spy; Brouncker "seemed well pleasd." The most heinous accusations may indeed have been omitted. But printing had already begun, and the postscript as it stood was scandalous enough. Moreover, Oldenburg too had heard of the attack. He rushed straight to Martyn's premises. There he found Hooke, supervising the correction of this last sheet. They confronted each other. Oldenburg told Hooke that he should have submitted his argument first to the council of the Society.[170] But Hooke had already circumvented that authority, and defied the secretary. Two days later he had complete copies of the work in his hands.

Hooke made haste to distribute copies of his *Description of Helioscopes* as a good client should: first to Boyle and Wren, then to Haak, Pope, Flamsteed, Moore, and a network of further patrons and friends. When they glanced at their copies, what they read hinted that Oldenburg had acted in concert with Huygens to suppress Hooke's priority. The author claimed to have invented the principle on which to build a watch some seventeen years earlier, and to have described it in his Cutlerian lectures in 1664. Oldenburg

169. Hooke, *Description of Helioscopes*, sigs. E1^v–E4^v, Tab. III; Hooke, *Diary*, 178, 180–2. Wren was Hooke's superior as crown surveyor, but he seems to have been regarded by many of the virtuosi as a uniquely impartial judge of matters of priority and authorship. Sprat's *History* singled him out as an honorable man who had been badly served by the register system: 311–8. Wren himself remarked that "I have often had the pusillanimity rather to neglect that right I might in justice have vindicated, than by challenging it too late, incure the jealousy of being a plagiary": Birch, *History*, I, 47. Flamsteed, who followed the watch dispute keenly and tried many times to discover the working of Hooke's watch, was reduced to asking Towneley to decipher the message in Wilkins's character for him: RS Ms. 243.1, no. 10; Flamsteed, *Correspondence*, I, 379–80.

170. Hooke, *Diary*, 183–6; Oldenburg, *Correspondence*, XII, 16–18, 39–41.

had known of this, and Huygens too would have read of it in Sprat's *History*. Hooke contrasted his own "Publick meetings" and "open" lectures at the Royal Society and Gresham College, in which he claimed to have "*published to the World*" his own invention, with the reticence and partiality shown in "the *French Journal*, or in the *English Transactions*." He was effectively implying that his spoken performance had represented truly open publication, whereas printing, if under the control of Oldenburg's private interest, was not actually publication at all.[171]

Hooke was testing the limits of the Society's tolerance. Oldenburg seized the opportunity offered by his antagonist's transgression. He told Huygens of the attack issued in the *Helioscopes* text, saying that Hooke's accusation threatened the reputation for integrity on which his own role depended. Oldenburg was concerned enough to request that his letter be burnt as soon as Huygens had read it. He then asked him to write to Brouncker to vindicate Oldenburg's honor, but begged that the prohibition aimed at stifling Hooke's attack be left unmentioned, since his testimony would undoubtedly be made public. The same day he waited on Brouncker. At Arundel House they held a "Grubendolian Caball," as Hooke disgustedly called it. There Oldenburg complained of Hooke's unlicensed printing. He pointed out that Hooke had tried to have his papers printed "unknown to Lord Brouncker," and in bypassing the Society's licensing mechanism had "underhandedly obtained a permission of someone who did not understand these matters." For his part, Martyn claimed to have printed the postscript without reading it—a standard Stationer's claim, and something Oldenburg was reluctant overtly to challenge.[172] The secretary therefore wrote to Paris attributing the blame directly to Hooke, rather than to Brouncker and the printer— the two men whom he thought Huygens would otherwise have been inclined to hold responsible.[173] Huygens replied that he was indeed surprised at Hooke's "malicious and insolent" behavior, and proceeded to vindicate Oldenburg to Brouncker.

171. Hooke, *Diary*, 173, 176, 186–7, 189; Hooke, *Description of Helioscopes*, sigs. [E3ʳ]– [E4ʳ].

172. Oldenburg, *Correspondence*, XII, 11–14; XIII, 148–51; 'Espinasse, *Robert Hooke*, 63– 9; Hooke, *Diary*, 187–8. Oldenburg's letter to Huygens, in Oldenburg, *Correspondence*, XII, 16–18, was written the same day. The unwitting "permission" was perhaps Wren's (above, note 169): although one of the most senior virtuosi, at this time he was not on the council of the Society. It is just possible that Hooke was appealing to a privilege of Wren's office as crown surveyor; Moxon certainly interpreted his as hydrographer royal as allowing him to print. Oldenburg was to be appointed a licenser a few months later. Neither *Helioscopes* nor *Lampas* displayed any imprimatur on the copies I used.

173. Oldenburg, *Correspondence*, XII, 17. In mounting this defense, Oldenburg was perhaps relying on the fact that part of Hooke's text was in Wilkins's character. But since the relevant attack was not, it must have seemed an implausible argument.

Oldenburg also used the *Philosophical Transactions* to reply to Hooke. He declared that the latter had indeed made a watch years before, but "without publishing to the world a Description of it *in print*." In any case, the design had never actually worked. Huygens, on the other hand, had been open with his own contributions, both sending his news by anagram and printing a description in the *Journal des Sçavans*. Hooke had rudely insisted on copying this figure at the Royal Society, compromising the Society's propriety and refusing to let Oldenburg leave until he had done so. Huygens's text had then been printed with the president's approval in the *Transactions*. Hooke's would have been printed at the same time, and thereby "vindicated from the Usurpation of others," if he had been civil enough so to ask. Oldenburg emphasized the civility of Huygens, of himself, and of the reader whom he asked to judge. He stressed the primacy of print for establishing priority, and he displayed Hooke's impropriety by showing both his inappropriate use of written material and his perversion of the publication process.

Now Hooke's friendship with Martyn again took a hand. Martyn revealed sheets of the *Transactions* to Hooke as they were printed. On 8 November he came to the review of *Helioscopes*. Hooke was livid. "Saw the Lying Dog Oldenburg's *Transactions*," he wrote in his diary: "Resolved to quit all employments and to seek my health." As he read his Cutlerian lectures at Gresham, he noticed with further disquiet that Oldenburg "viewd and took notes," and at the Society he found more evidence that the secretary had not "enterd" his experiments. Hooke now planned to respond by adding another postscript to the next of these lectures, which would eventually appear as *Lampas* in 1676. Meanwhile, Brouncker was reelected president amid what Hooke thought were "base doings." Despairing of the Society as "too much enslaved to a forreine spye," Hooke began to organize his own "select clubb" instead. He had "many things which I watch for an opportunity of publishing," he explained to his allies, "but not by the R.S. . . . Oldenb. his snares I will avoid if I can." At the first secret meeting of his club, Hooke discussed Newton's theft of his theory of light—another plagiarism he now blamed on Oldenburg.[174] To evade his antagonist's "snares," he and Martyn now resolved to get *Lampas* licensed outside the Society. Hooke absented himself from committees as he worked on it, and sought the approval only of Wren before proceeding with his plan.[175] The

174. Oldenburg, *Correspondence*, XII, 19–24; [Oldenburg], "[Review of] *A Description of* HELIOSCOPES"; Hooke, *Diary*, 191–3, 196–7, 199–202, 205–6, 213; Birch, *History*, III, 242–4; Gunther, *Early Science in Oxford*, VII, 434–6. Apparently this club was to have its own "Journall" (*Diary*, 207–8). It is likely that this would have had a rigorously limited circulation, and it may not have been intended to be printed.

175. Hooke, *Diary*, 245: "Told Sir Chr. Wren my Invention of flying, air pump, and my anagram. He approvd it."

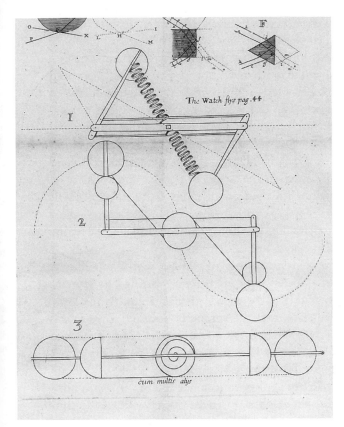

The Watch flys pag.44

cum multis alijs

FIG. 7.11. Robert Hooke's watch mechanism. This sparc portrayal was the most that Hooke was prepared to divulge in print of his claim to have invented a new spring balance watch mechanism, and he refused to let all but the most trusted or powerful viewers see the workings of the actual specimens made for him by clockmaker Thomas Tompion. The aim (as also in Huygens's design, fig. 7.9) was to use springs not to power the watch, but to regulate the motions of its balance. Whether this device was in essence the same as Huygens's design—or, almost equally important, whether it was similar enough that a patent covering Huygens's would prevent the commercial sale of Hooke's—was a central issue in Hooke's campaign against Oldenburg. Hooke, *Lampas*. (By permission of the Syndics of Cambridge University Library.)

book was granted an imprimatur by George Hooper at Lambeth Palace on 21 August 1676; that night Hooke, Hoskyns, and Wren enjoyed "Much good discourse" together until nine. It was finally published on 22 September. Hooke once more distributed copies to Hill, Hoskyns, Ent, Brouncker, Moore, and others. He gave a specially decorated one to Boyle (fig. 7.11).[176]

Lampas contained a scathing attack on Oldenburg, portraying him as an independent agent driven by personal "passion." It was a new and effective charge, exploiting the widespread caution concerning the passions described in chapter 6. Oldenburg's role as the Society's communicator made his dispassionate neutrality essential. But Hooke claimed that Oldenburg had obtained a patent on Huygens's design and that he was pursuing his own interest at the expense of English virtuosi. The secretary of the Royal Society had descended into the realm of interest, and had "made a trade of Intelligence." That was why, Hooke insisted, he had always concealed from

176. Hooke, *Diary*, 221, 246, 250–1. Intriguingly, the Sunday before collecting copies from Martyn Hooke had spent with Hoskyns in "Discourse of Martins, History of printing, &c."

Oldenburg his earlier successes with watches; Oldenburg's reports that his designs had never succeeded were based not on fact, but on an ignorance caused by his own untrustworthiness. Oldenburg seemed to assume that no report issued in another forum than his own *Philosophical Transactions* could count as evidence of authorship. Hooke thus reiterated the contrast between his own "publishing" of discoveries in his spoken lectures and the "usurpation" manifested by Oldenburg's corrupting production of the *Transactions*. Indeed, Hooke now even implied that Oldenburg had indulged in unauthorized printing of Hooke's own material. Concerned in this context to defend his brand of civility with respect to the Society's perusal and registration processes, Hooke also justified his own conduct in scrutinizing materials sent to the Royal Society. He was entitled to peruse such material thoroughly, he claimed, because "intelligence" brought to Arundel house by the secretary was properly the Society's, not Oldenburg's.

Again Oldenburg protested. He angrily responded that it was Hooke who, by departing from the Society's propriety, was returning its "Intelligence" to the status of a "trade" at the mercy of mechanics. At the same time he reinforced his own claim that the (properly licensed) *Transactions* were "secure" and hence reliably free from "Forgeries." And if he had printed Hooke's materials without his written permission, it was only so that "such particulars might be timely secured by publishing y^m in ye Transactions, since at y^t time he had not yet begun to make use of the presse himself for printing his discoveries." He had engaged Society publishing conventions only in Hooke's own interest. Oldenburg insisted that "if he had put his Invention timely enough in print, these contentions might have been prevented, or at least, more easily determined." Above all, he denied the charge of "passion"—"unless a plain Narrative of the matter of Fact be passion." [177]

Now the council of the Society moved against Hooke and Martyn in earnest. Oldenburg must be supported. At first, as Hooke noted, "They decreed nothing against me, but against Mr. Martin." The bookseller came very close to losing his official position. [178] Martyn was ordered to print in

177. Hooke, *Lampas*, sigs. G2^{r–v}, [H3^{r–v}]; BL Ms. Add. 4441, fols. 58^r–59^v. This is a draft of Oldenburg's reply to Hooke, containing significant deleted information not reproduced in the *Correspondence*. Fol. 100^{r–v} contains the draft actually transcribed in Oldenburg, *Correspondence*, XIII, 148–51. For the significance of the charge of "passion," see above, pp. 397–408.

178. Hooke, *Diary*, 253; Birch, *History*, III, 319–21. Oldenburg had served notice that he would reply to *Lampas* in [Oldenburg], "Advertisement," *Philosophical Transactions* 128 (25 September 1676), 710. A document signed by Brouncker referring the drafting of Oldenburg's vindication to Croune and Hill asks them for "what they conceive may be fit for ye Council to publish ~~by ye new Printer~~ in the next Phil. Transact. in ye behalf of Mr Olden-

the *Transactions* a notice that Hooke's second postscript had been printed without the Society's knowledge, and to declare that he himself had been unaware of its contents. Hooke "Resolved to leave Royal Society" in the face of this attack on his ally. A week later the "Grubendolian Councell" went further, delegating Hill and Croune to compose a vindication of Oldenburg to be printed in the *Transactions*. The secretary's "integrity and faithfulness" were to be vindicated, and Hooke's *Lampas* disowned as a product of the Society. With this testament Oldenburg was encouraged to print Huygens's letter granting the Society patent rights. Both duly appeared in late November, over Brouncker's prominent imprimatur.[179]

For the present, at least, Oldenburg, Huygens, and Brouncker had won. The dispute did not end with a clear moment of victory, but Huygens's debilitating illness meant that its intensity lessened markedly. Oldenburg achieved an important success by proving that his rival had indulged in improper printing. This, and the implications attendant upon Hooke's charge that Oldenburg himself was governed by "passion," caused the council to intervene on his side. What would have happened, then, if Martyn had refused either Hooke or Oldenburg access? Hooke's own conduct of the dispute deserves notice too, both for the importance of his alliance with Martyn and for the tactics of his attack on Oldenburg. The usefulness of having a privileged bookseller had also been confirmed, albeit narrowly: faced with losing his privilege, the reluctant Martyn had been persuaded to cease his aid for Hooke. It seemed that the Society's propriety had survived its sternest test. Yet the fragility of this impression was soon starkly revealed. Oldenburg died suddenly in early September 1677. His achievements fragmented with terrifying speed. Most spectacular of all was the demise of the *Philosophical Transactions* itself.

SERIAL KILLERS: THE FRAGMENTATION OF CREDIT

Modern readers are likely to be surprised that the *Transactions* failed, since the modern successor to Oldenburg's journal has a reputation as the oldest learned periodical with a continuous publishing history. The reason for such

---

burgs integrity and faithfulness to the R. Society": BL Ms. Add. 4441, fol. 61ʳ. Another draft advertisement (fol. 60ʳ) starts to claim that Martyn had "seen nothing" not just of the postscript, but of the whole text of *Lampas*. This too was deleted. The Printer had learned his lesson; he refused to touch Hooke's next book until certain that the text had been legitimately licensed: Hooke, *Diary*, 288–9.

179. Hooke, *Diary*, 255; Birch, *History*, III, 321–2, 324; "Declaration of the Council of the *Royal Society*." It may be significant that in this revised notice Martyn's denial of involvement was omitted. Hooke picked up the journal in December and called the notice "absurd": *Diary*, 261.

surprise is interesting. Perhaps the only story of triumph still flourishing in the history of science—a discipline that has otherwise been ruthlessly purged of whiggism—is that of scientific journals. The advent of the *Transactions* is everywhere seen as a transitional moment in the history of natural knowledge, signaling the advent of such icons of objectivity as experimental research, replication, openness, transnational cooperation, and peer review. It retains this aura in the historical sociology of knowledge, which, with its emphasis on "virtual witnessing" to explain the successes of experimental philosophy, again lays great stress on the credit of the *Transactions*. But in the absence of Oldenburg that credit collapsed and fragmented. And with that every element of periodical publication was thrown into doubt: periodicity, proper degrees and extents of circulation, costs, editorial control, and above all content.[180]

The immediate problem on Oldenburg's death was to replace him. Both Aubrey and Ray considered standing, but in the end Hooke himself was temporarily appointed secretary. As soon as he could gain access, the unforgiving Hooke rifled his predecessor's papers for evidence that he had been selling "intelligence." He finally claimed success in late December. It was too late to affect the outcome of the watch conflict, but other issues had now come to the fore. Since his accession, Hooke had been forcefully pressing general questions of "Secretary and method." In Boyle's garden, for example, he "had much discourse with him as about vindicating the Inventions of Authors." Hooke also pursued long and intense discussions on these subjects with such fellows as Hill, Hoskins, Wren, Aubrey, Colwall, Moore, and Evelyn, as well as with Papin and the Stationer Martyn. At Jonathan's coffeehouse, too, he pressed for reform of "experiments, intelligence, printing, the minutes of meetings &c." It was becoming a campaign. And Hooke's concerns centered on two matters that had emerged from his quarrel with Oldenburg: the register, and a proper form for periodical publication.[181]

In some ways the council concurred, but its priorities were slightly different. Concerned at the autonomy which Oldenburg had been exercising, it immediately acted to limit the secretary's role. It regulated his conduct by a series of decisions explicitly subordinating him to the oversight of the council, the president, and the Society as a whole. Correspondence was a prime concern. Oldenburg's successor was ordered to maintain his extensive

180. Existing accounts do sometimes acknowledge a "dormancy" in the *Transactions* between 1676 and 1683, but such a term itself betrays their assumption that this was no more than a brief and accidental interruption: e.g., Manten, "Growth of European Scientific Journal Publishing," 7. The argument of this section is developed at greater length in Johns, "Miscellaneous Methods."

181. Birch, *History*, III, 344; Hooke, *Diary*, 311–16, 321, 323, 326, 328, 336–8; 'Espinasse, *Robert Hooke*, 68.

network of informants—an order that had to be repeated as Hooke, for whatever reason, failed to do so. But further rules were soon instituted to prevent others from replicating Oldenburg's independence with respect to whatever correspondence did take place. Outgoing letters must be approved by the council, and incoming must be read at the Society immediately upon their receipt. They must then be physically pasted into a book before being transcribed into the letter book. The notes taken by the secretary at each meeting must be read aloud "to see, that they be rightly taken," and entered completely by the next meeting. And the registers must not leave the building. These initiatives then became part of a greater revolution. Determined to rid the Society of Brouncker, Hooke and his allies—Aubrey, Hoskyns, and others—"spread the Designe" of electing a new president. The possibility existed: immediately after Oldenburg's death, they had decreed the use of a ballot box for future votes. Wren was Hooke's first favored candidate, followed by Williamson. Weeks of politicking ensued. Brouncker stormed out of the Society's council "in Great Passion," as the various factions maneuvered to garner votes. Some declared for Wren; Croune earned Hooke's derision for seeming a "Bronkerian." Meanwhile Hooke angled for the secretary's position should Williamson succeed, writing a proposal for his own election against murmurs for Nehemiah Grew.

When Saint Andrew's Day came, Williamson was indeed elected president. Hooke found himself maintained as secretary alongside Grew, and elected to the council for the first time. "I doubt not but you have heard of the changes," he told Lister: "It hath Ile assure you very much revived us and put a new spirit in all our proceeding." He was convinced that the transformation would "not only be beneficial and delightful to the members of the Society, but to the whole learned world."[182] But Hooke's elation was short-lived. It soon seemed that Grew was to be his superior. Hooke confronted his new rival at Martyn's, accusing him of trying "slyly" to achieve seniority. He now became convinced that a "plott" had been hatched to this effect, with Hill in particular "a dog for Grew." "It seemd as if they would have me still curator, Grew Secretary," he grumbled, storming out of one postmeeting conversation at Jonathan's.

Their struggle now came to center on the other of Hooke's prime concerns, namely periodical publication. Hooke had earlier declared for sealed discourses accessible only to fellows. Now he opposed his own plan for

---

182. Birch, *History*, III, 342–3, 352–3, 366, 369, 468, 491; Hooke, *Diary*, 319, 321, 323, 328–9, 331; Gunther, *Early Science in Oxford*, VII, 463–4. Croune was "in a great Huff" at the result. For Flamsteed's contrasting reaction, see Bodl. Ms. Smith, 45, p. 31: "the President is changed, Mr Hooke fills all with discourse and mighty projects of inventions and discoverys but they are seldom seene"; Flamsteed, *Correspondence*, I, 599–602.

monthly "Journalls" to Grew's proposal to continue the *Transactions*. Boyle at first seemed to argue for Grew.[183] Hill, Lowther, and Henshaw likewise appeared to side with the *Transactions*, but Williamson was more sympathetic to Hooke. Both sides assiduously lobbied Boyle for his support, while Hooke spoke with the wealthy patron Colwall in Garraway's "about printing monthly Journalls." In January 1677/8 Hooke again "moved against *Transactions*" with fresh vigor and seemed finally to convince Williamson. The details remain unclear, but the result was that Hooke won out. His *Philosophical Collections* superseded Oldenburg's loathed journal, and the *Transactions* ceased production.

Hooke was subject to the weekly demands of the virtuosi, however, and seems to have had none of Oldenburg's diplomatic skills. The first issue of the *Collections* did not appear until 1679. "Some are only good at Hints and the first conceptions of Inventions," announced Hooke in this first number, "others at the diligent promoting and reducing to Practice." His journal would publish both.[184] It proved a difficult task, not least because Martyn died after undertaking only one issue. The second Stationer engaged, Moses Pitt, was a friend of Hooke; but he was consumed by his *English Atlas* project, and would end up bankrupt. Only with the third, Richard Chiswell, did Hooke encounter a consistently reliable operator. By this time only three issues had been published in two years. From issue 3 through issue 7, published in April 1682, Hooke and Chiswell did succeed in publishing monthly. After that, however, no further issue appeared.

From the first, Hooke's *Philosophical Collections* was ill received. Yet if the *Collections* appear (and appeared at the time) a poor substitute for Oldenburg's *Transactions*, that may have been partly because Hooke's project was intended to be something else. In fact, he was at this time engaged in an extraordinary array of publishing proposals, ranging from the impossibly huge to the infeasibly small. Many of these were experiments designed to find the best successor to the *Transactions*, rid of what Hooke saw as its predecessor's associations with impropriety. At the end of 1678, for example, he gained permission to draw up a specimen of "a small Journal of some particulars read in the Society," which he designed to send to his dwindling group of correspondents. "The said Journals shall not be sent or sold to any person but members of the Society, and to such as correspond with Mr. Hooke by the Society's directions," the Society cautioned, and even

183. Hunter and Wood, "Towards Solomon's House," 60; Hooke, *Diary*, 311–6. In late 1674 Hooke had already been discussing "proposalls about Secresy and Secretary": *Diary*, 131. Ray refused the post.

184. Hooke, *Diary*, 333, 335–8; Birch, *History*, III, 328, 366, 369–70, 396–7, 444, 450–1, 453, 460, 491, 501, 504, 514, 518; *Philosophical Collections* 1 (1679), 2.

then only to such correspondents who could "make considerable returns to him for the Society's use." Such reciprocations were to be submitted by Hooke to the Society as soon as received. Arguments continued about which Society events should be printed, and in what form. In July, Hooke found himself again urged to publish "a sheet or two every fortnight" of philosophical material from correspondents. He could not, however, print "any thing contained in the Register-books of the Society without the leave of the council and author." A month later, he was ordered "as soon as may be" to print "a relation" of all the experiments, observations, and reports that he himself had ever brought into the Society. He meanwhile "designed to publish, either once a month or once a fortnight, or oftener" a version of the *Transactions*. But then it emerged that Martyn would simply refuse to undertake the journal under the old terms. So fresh negotiations proved necessary. In December, efforts were again renewed. Amid a general restatement of the mechanisms of perusal and registration, the Society once more urged Hooke to "have a small account of philosophical matters, such as were the *Transactions* of Mr. Oldenburg, and under the same title, published once a quarter at least." Monthly issues would be even better. Gale helped by taking on all foreign correspondence, but still Hooke could not guarantee such frequency.

Amid all this urging and planning, not to mention demands for weekly experimental contributions, Hooke found it hard actually to publish. And we should not forget that these months also saw diverse proposals for other publishing projects characterized by some degree of periodicity. Hooke undertook to edit entries in the register so that they could be printed (a committee for which had included Oldenburg in late 1676). In early 1678, the Society also proposed creating an annual selection of completed projects to be printed in its name before each election day. In addition, it was now that Pitt's multivolume *English Atlas* project came up for the Society's support— which, at Hooke's urging, it received. Hooke also supervised Martyn's production of Malpighi's work on plants. For his part, Grew published his own *Anatomy of Plants* from readings before the Society; it began with a full account of the Society's perusal and registration protocols. Grew also produced the *Musaeum Regalis Societatis*, funded largely by Colwall, as a spur to revive the Society; Perry followed suit with his catalogue of the Society's library. In all, the period after the last *Transactions* saw an unprecedented consideration of different forms of publication. It should not be surprising that any new periodical lagged behind schedule, nor that its very nature remained unclear and inconsistent.

This was not the only effect of the end of the *Transactions*. To see its other consequences, however, we need to remove the blinkers customarily

TABLE 7.1 Periodicals Concerned with Philosophical, Medical, or Technical Knowledge, 1665–1700

STC	Title	Chronology, Periodicity, and Remarks
539	*Philosophical Transactions*	Ed. by H. Oldenburg, then R. Plot, E. Halley. Launched March 1665. Monthly, but irregular. Lapsed 1679–83, 1687–91. Regular from 1693.
537	*Philosophical Collections*	Ed. by R. Hooke. 1 issue in 1679, 2 in 1681, 4 in 1682. Intended to be monthly.
252A	*Mechanick Exercises*	By J. Moxon. January 1678 to mid-1680; relaunched in 1683. A book written in parts.
50	*Collection of Letters for the Improvement of Husbandry and Trade*	Ed. J. Houghton. September 1681 to June 1684. Monthly but erratic.
692	*Weekly Memorials for the Ingenious*	Published by H. Faithorne and J. Kersey. Handwritten note in Bodleian copy has "by Mr. Beaumont." January to March 1682, followed by divergent issues in competition with R. Chiswell. Lapsed January 1683.
253	*Medicina Curiosa*	June to October 1684. 2 issues only.
643	*Universal Historical Bibliotheque*	Ed. J. Cornand de la Crose and/or E. Bohun. 3 issues. January to March 1687. Modeled on *Philosophical Transactions*.
25	*Bibliotheca Universalis*	1 issue. January 1688. Published in Edinburgh.
21	*Athenian Mercury*	Ed. J. Dunton. Weekly. March 1691 to June 1697. Entitled *Athenian Mercury* after issue 1: but issue 1 and annual vols. were called *The Athenian Gazette: or Casuistical Mercury*.
189	*History of Learning/ Works of the Learned*	Ed. J. Cornand de la Crose. July 1691–April 1692. Bought up by J. Dunton.
319	*Mercurius Eruditorum*	2 issues. August 1691. Published by R. Taylor, the trade publisher.
541	*Physical and Mathematical Memoirs, extracted from the registers of the Royal Academy of Sciences at Paris*	1 issue. January 1692.
203	*Introduction to the London Mercury/London Mercury/ Lacedemonian Mercury*	Ed. T. Brown. Fortnightly. February to May 1692. An attempt at a competitor to Dunton's *Athenian Mercury*.
49	*Collection for Improvement of Husbandry and Trade*	Ed. J. Houghton. Weekly. March 1692 to past 1700. Launched with support of Royal Society fellows.

TABLE 7.1 *Continued*

STC	Title	Chronology, Periodicity, and Remarks
53	Compleat Library, or News for the Ingenious	Ed. J. Dunton, R. Woolley. Monthly. May 1692–April 1694.
254	Memoirs for the Ingenious	Ed. J. Cornand de la Crose. Monthly. January to December 1693.
188	History of Learning	1 issue. May 1694. Published by R. Taylor.
409	Miscellaneous Letters giving an Account of the Works of the Learned	Weekly, then monthly. October 1694 to March 1696.
139	An essay concerning nutrition in animals	By P. Guide. 1 issue. 1699.
191-2	History of the Works of the Learned	Eds. S. Parker, G. Ridpath, et al. January 1699 to past 1700. Published in London and Edinburgh.

All published in London unless otherwise specified.

Source: C. Nelson and M. Seccombe, *British Newspapers and Periodicals 1641–1700: A Short-Title Catalogue of Serials* (New York, 1987). STC numbers refer to this catalogue.

worn by historians of Restoration natural philosophy and look beyond the Royal Society. London boasted a competitive and vital community of printers, booksellers, and hacks. If nothing else, Oldenburg and Martyn had revealed to this community how to render a learned periodical viable. They now seized the opportunity to supplant the archetype. A cluster of new periodicals appeared, beginning with the demise of the *Transactions* and receding only temporarily with its resurrection. Table 7.1 lists their titles, personnel, and dates. Only one was a great success: John Dunton's *Athenian Mercury*, which, as mentioned above, was based in a fictive society of virtuosi. Dunton succeeded by reversing the mechanism of his original and having real witnesses contribute to a virtual Society. The others suffered any number of setbacks, from the death of the Stationer (as happened to the *Universal Historical Bibliotheque*) to piracy of such baroque complexity that those involved seem simply to have given up in despair.

The *Philosophical Transactions* was undeniably, and often explicitly, a model for all these journals. Bohun's *Universal Historical Bibliotheque*, for example, was "published by Months in the same manner as the Philosophical Transactions," and proposed to print papers not published in the Society's periodical. Bohun later proposed to produce a separate journal of such papers.[185] The *Transactions* was also the model for John Houghton's

185. *Universal Historical Bibliotheque* [1], 1687, sigs. A3ᵛ, [A4ʳ]; II (1686/7), sig.[A4ᵛ]. Bayle's *Nouvelles de la République des Lettres* became the model for periodicals on the continent: Goldgar, *Impolite Learning*, 55.

Collection of Letters for the Improvement of Husbandry and Trade, launched
in September 1681, which portrayed itself as part of the Royal Society's
own project to improve agriculture. Houghton struggled to produce two
volumes; the journal then lapsed until 1692, when a further series began.
But he again found it hard to sell, despite the public approbation and financial support of twenty-eight fellows. Even though "every hard word
was explain'd," it seemed that "*Philosophical*" weeklies had little market.
Only the introduction of advertisements and news, and a tempting offer
of cheap wholesale prices to coffee-men and hawkers, helped the *Collection*
continue.[186]

These journals ailed for want of contributions or customers. Serial piracy,
however, was the fate of the *Weekly Memorials for the Ingenious*, established
during an intermission in Hooke's *Collections* by Martyn's erstwhile apprentices, John Kersey and Henry Faithorne. The journal had an ambitious periodicity, and was dedicated to Boyle. It is probably not unrealistic to see it
as angling for Royal Society endorsement on one of the many different models for periodical production being voiced within the council at this juncture. The journal printed accounts of new books, and "transcribe[d]" essays
from such Continental periodicals as the *Journal des Sçavans*. Included in
the first issue was a summary of a book bemoaning the mass of books produced and attacking "*Plagiaries*." For ten issues it succeeded. John Flamsteed, eager to promote a competitor to Hooke, forwarded issues to his
correspondents with warm recommendations, remarking that their editor
wished to remain anonymous.[187] When the proprietors attempted to change
printers, however, disaster struck. The original printers continued to produce issues that they claimed were genuine. As a result, no copy of the journal could be definitively distinguished as genuine by any reader. Textual
content diverged, reconverged, and diverged again. Each version made ever
more hyperbolic claims for its own veracity and its opponent's duplicity.
Altogether, the unfortunate *Weekly Memorials* came to represent probably
the most complex and profound example of periodical piracy of the entire
century.[188]

Less extraordinary, but nonetheless still terminal, problems were encoun-

186. *Collection of Letters for the Improvement of Husbandry and Trade*, I, 1–4; III, 1; III, 52
et seq.; Houghton, "Whereas Mr. *John Houghton*."

187. We still do not know for certain who the editor was, although a reader suggested the
maverick naturalist John Beaumont in the margin of the Bodleian copy. Flamsteed's recommendation should be contrasted to his condemnation of Hooke, editor of the rival *Philosophical Collections*, as boastful and self-aggrandizing, as related in chapter 8. Note also that Flamsteed himself contributed an essay on malting to Houghton's journal.

188. *Weekly Memorials for the Ingenious*, 1 (16 January 1681/2), 1–5; RS Ms. 243.56; Southampton CRO, Ms. D/M 1/1, fols. 14ʳ–15ᵛ; Flamsteed, *Correspondence*, I, 855–6, 883–90.

tered by *Memoirs for the Ingenious*, begun in 1693 with an invitation for contributors to deposit material for publication at a coffeehouse. The periodical was the work of Jean Cornand de la Crose, who had previously been Le Clerc's partner in Europe and now produced a sequence of such periodicals in London. Emphasizing the fragile sales of such periodicals, he announced that "the perfect establishing of a Journal" could not be "the performance of private men." Court patronage or collective efforts alone enabled learned journals to survive. His own journal "ought to be compos'd by a numerous Society," he complained. Nevertheless, like a one-man academy, he asked that "Gentlemen" would "propose to me difficult Questions in all sorts of Sciences, as tho' I were a living Library, or had an *Encyclopaedia* in my head." Being an editor may not have made him "an Interpreter of all the secrets of Nature," he insisted, but it had certainly qualified him as a filter of credit—"a faithful Historian, who endeavours to distinguish between credible Relations, and groundless Reports." This was his title to readers' credence. In the cutthroat world of print that he knew so well, Cornand de la Crose advised that "Incredulity in matters of fact is a piece of Prudence." Unfortunately, his printers' habit of changing his words made it hard to trust even such a practiced protagonist:

> instead of *the happy constitution of this Realm*, the Printer, or Corrector have put *the unhappy constitution of this Realm*. I may justly charge it upon them, since there is neither blot, nor reference, nor anything else in my copy, that may have given occasion to that mistake, as any one may see at Mr. *Rhodes*'s one of the Booksellers of these Memoirs, in whose hands *I* have left it.[189]

With this complaint, Cornand de la Crose's ambitious journal quietly expired.

These short-lived enterprises epitomized the problems and possibilities for maintaining credible claims in print. They also helped to establish an environment for learned periodicals in general, and natural-philosophical periodicals in particular. A major participant was the Royal Society itself. In November 1682, Hooke was replaced as secretary by Robert Plot. Plot was based in Oxford, and he had determined to revive the *Philosophical Transactions* from there. Although not itself the "business" of the Society, he professed, such a "Register" for preserving experiments would be essential, and Plot, with none of Hooke's commitments, anticipated publishing monthly. But maintaining the journal again proved problematic. It found itself in unprecedented competition with Stationers for copy, fighting to publish papers in the *Transactions* because "it would be credit for ye Society to have

---

189. *Memoirs for the Ingenious* I, 263, 332, 349–50. For Cornand de la Crose, see also Goldgar, *Impolite Learning*, 62, 102, 112, 184–5.

it come out that way." Plot moved the printing of the journal to Oxford, "because printing and graving both are much cheaper and better here than at London." But still the revived work proved "wonderfully false printed"— especially the Latin sections, which virtually traduced Hevelius (who had complained of such misrepresentation before). By 1687, with its new editor, Edmond Halley, consumed by the labor of producing Newton's *Principia*, the *Transactions* was again languishing.

Soon Hooke was agitating for the chance to prove his own abilities again, by replacing the *Transactions* once more with his *Collections*. "Hally deserted *Transactions*," he noted excitedly at one point. Hooke "propounded *Collections*" again at the council in November 1689, but was defeated by "tricks." At Jonathan's, he thought it agreed that the *Collections* would indeed revive, with the Society to guarantee the same sales of sixty copies that it had warranted for Plot's *Transactions*. Yet it never happened. The problem lay in the combination of the Stationers' commonwealth with the onerous civilities expected of the secretary. In late 1685 the passions aroused by this collision burst into plain view, when Aston dramatically resigned from the post complaining bitterly of the impossibility of performing his duties. Responsibilities were now divided. The secretarial position became largely honorary. Its practical labors were to be delegated to a paid subordinate. Halley was disenfranchised from the fellowship and appointed as clerk. He thus took on much of the more thankless work of the old office, including oversight of the *Philosophical Transactions*, with no real pretense at the freedom of action of a gentleman.[190] The immediate outcome of the secretary's engagement with the Stationers was thus the destruction of the secretarial identity.

This story of a fragmentation of credit is hardly a familiar one. It deserves to be much better known. Although the *Philosophical Transactions* survived, and the *Collection of Letters*, for example, did not, that outcome was by no means clearly ordained to contemporaries. We should recognize the extent to which the world of printed journals of the late seventeenth century was one of dubious credit and risked fortunes. We should also recognize the differences between these objects: if Hooke's *Collections* or Kersey and Faithorne's *Weekly Memorials* seem inferior to the *Transactions*, that is partly because we have judged their qualities by the light of the one journal that happened to survive. It is quite possible that these other publications represented different proprieties, perhaps even different polities, of printed knowledge.

190. Gunther, *Early Science in Oxford*, XII, 13–17, 368; Birch, *History*, IV, 449–55; Hooke, "Diary," 91–2, 146, 151–2; Halley, *Correspondence and Papers*, 56–7; *London Gazette* [2870 (incorrectly numbered 1870)], 15 May 1693.

CONCLUSION

Experimental natural philosophy relied on the successful maintenance of credit through processes of correspondence and publication. Tracing the paths of printed and manuscript materials through the Royal Society and beyond gives us an account of this new philosophy in the making. The nature, fellowship, and aims of the Society had important implications for the role played in it by textual materials. Books were here elements in a culture to which patronage and norms of "politeness" were central. The Society's publications were accordingly intended to be diplomatic gifts, instruments of patronage, and status symbols as much as neutral conveyors of knowledge.[191] Those coming into the Society were treated accordingly. As has been sketched out here, an intricate array of conventions developed about how to treat books: who had access to them, what could be said about them, and how they were made and dispersed. Beyond the bounds of the Society, too, the virtuosi had firm ideas on how others should receive the learned words they sent out. In such senses, books were not just instruments of learned civility; they helped define what that civility was.

It is well known that the "experimental life" depended on the use of written and printed materials. Without them it would be severely crippled in its attempt to create consensus on matters of natural knowledge. But these very materials threatened to undermine its success, since the ways in which they were made and used were often in conflict with representations of the Society as honorable and neutral. Theirs was a world of plagiarism, of usurpation, and the ramifications penetrated every aspect of the experimental life. An unauthorized impression might be corrupt, even libelous; but as L'Estrange warned, a *"Libell* in the next Age, will be *history."* In the Royal Society, this age of piracy created a fierce reaction in favor of truth.[192] The Society, and men like Hooke in particular, became ferociously protective of records, testaments, statements, and reports. The register mechanism became the defining symbol of experimental propriety in the Society itself, and the *Philosophical Transactions* its emblem abroad. Together, the protocols established around these twin records came to constitute the channels of dialogue in the experimental community. In the Royal Society, the very character of philosophical debate emerged out of these conventions.

191. The best-known example has always been that of Sprat's *History*: Wood, "Methodology and Apologetics"; Hunter, *Establishing the New Science*, 45–71. As the preceding chapter showed more extensively, Hooke's *Micrographia* was also important in this sense—which made the distorting review printed in Sand's translation of the *Transactions* especially galling for Oldenburg. See S[and], *Acta Philosophica Societatis Regiae*, 29 (1674), 44–52, and [Oldenburg], "Some Animadversions upon the *Latin* Version, made by *C. S.* of the *Phil. Transactions*," 144.

192. *Observator in Dialogue*, I, 359; compare Eco, *Faith in Fakes*, 177.

The attempt to regulate discord almost worked. But under the strain of successive conflicts, and powerless in the face of print domains in the city and abroad, the Society's protocols faltered. Its secretary—the figure on whom, as guardian of both register and *Transactions*, its reputation for probity depended—found himself tarnished as the dupe of "interest" who bartered discoveries to foreigners. After his death, the *Philosophical Transactions* itself declined and expired. Within ten years, Oldenburg's own position had been dismantled. A succession of different models for periodical publication and social identity then attempted to inherit his mantle, each perhaps standing for a distinct kind of enterprise. Almost all expired rather quickly. By the early eighteenth century, it was feared, so profoundly had attempts to establish a civility of perusal and publication failed that new discoveries were routinely kept secret and "only communicated to friends." [193]

Yet in the end this is not a story of failure. The Society did survive; experimental philosophy eventually won out (if not in quite the form Boyle had intended); and the *Philosophical Transactions* revived to become the longest-lived "scientific" journal of them all. What science *is* has partly been decided by their endurance. It is therefore worth stating that the *Transactions* and the Society did not endure because their virtues were obvious. None of these achievements could have been realized without the strenuous efforts to discipline the processes of printing and reading traced in this chapter. Boyle, Newton, and their counterparts arguably spent as much time negotiating these processes as they did experimenting. An answer to historians' questions about the construction of early modern experimentalism might therefore come from devoting as much attention to the former activity as has traditionally been given to the latter.

193. King, *Original Works*, II, 7.

8

HISTORIES OF THE HEAVENS

John Flamsteed, Isaac Newton, and the

Historia Cœlestis Britannica

INTRODUCTION

As the new year approached, the auguries for 1717 were disturbingly inauspicious. Mars would be in Scorpio, almanacs warned. "Much fraud and dissimulation" would therefore be committed. "Tricking, Lying, and other like Knavish Inventions" would be "more than ordinary rife." As the year wore on, the Sun would move into the ascendant, and the consequences would grow more specific. "Many scandalous Pamphlets will be spread about," predicted Gadbury, producing "unhappy jealousies and fears." [1] The prospect was to be anticipated only with trepidation. And Gadbury's prophecy proved accurate. In itself, this was perhaps hardly cause for astonishment: in an age notorious for pamphleteering, it was not a very daring prediction. Nor was it remarkable that one of the most scandalous of all the many pamphlets to circulate at this time was actually the work of a fellow astrologer. Much of George Parker's new almanac consisted of mundane material, such as a year's tables of astronomical appearances, the dates for coming fairs and markets, and a healthy dose of verse homily (fig. 8.1). A substantial part, however, was dedicated to an attack on one of his rival almanac makers, and this was anything but mundane. The scurrility itself of Parker's assault was nothing unusual among the riven community of London astrologers.[2] It was the identity of his antagonist which made it extraordinary.

Parker complained that his adversary had been endeavoring to render him "Obnoctious to the World," by spreading dark rumors in the coffeehouses of London. He insisted that such "*Backbiters* and *Slanderers*" must

---

1. Gadbury, *'Εφημερις*.
2. Curry, *Prophecy and Power*, 45–91.

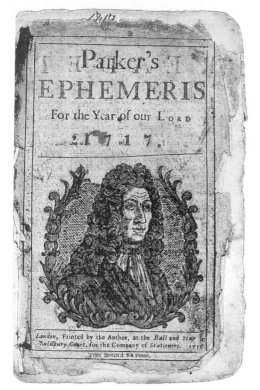

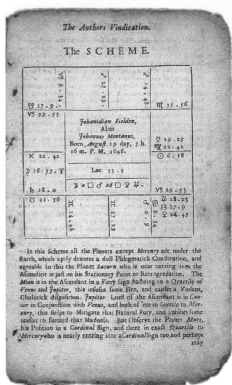

FIG. 8.1. (*left*) George Parker's *Ephemeris for the Year of our Lord 1717*. (By permission of the Henry E. Huntington Library, San Marino, California, RB337721.)

FIG. 8.2. (*right*) Parker's nativity for "Johannidian Fielden." Parker, *Ephemeris*. (By permission of the Henry E. Huntington Library, San Marino, California, RB337721.)

be ostracized. But the story being peddled against him was a peculiarly damaging one, liable to result in Parker himself suffering this ignominy. His antagonist was claiming that Parker had converted to Roman Catholicism. So soon after the Pretender's rising of 1715, this remained a dangerous allegation—and Parker had in fact long had to evade charges that he was not only Catholic, but Jacobite too. Moreover, not only did Parker's foe retail this story; he actively strove to prove it. He even claimed to know the "Instruments" responsible for "perverting me to Popery," reported the astrologer. Sensationally, he alleged that these "instruments" were none other than the president of the Royal Society and greatest living philosopher, Sir Isaac Newton, and Newton's ally at the Society, Dr. Edmond Halley.

Who was this scurrilous opponent? Parker gave a number of clues. To begin with, he supplied him with a name: Johannidian Fielden. He described this Fielden as "an Author, who (some Years since) presented the Copy of an *Almanack* to the Company of *Stationers*." He further revealed that Fielden was a clergyman, who as such ought not to indulge in "Lying" and "inventing Monstrous false Tales, and then report[ing] them for Truth." And he testified that he had met Fielden personally. The last time the two had conversed had been in 1695, when they had fallen out over Parker's inclusion in his almanac of a tide table compiled by Fielden. They had not spoken since, but it seemed that Fielden's anger still burned. Finally, Parker revealed one other significant item of information. Fielden received a state salary. In total this had amounted to some £4,000 in government funding. Yet he had produced nothing more substantial than his tide tables to show for it. Surely, Parker insinuated, "some more Polite and Greater Undertaking for the benefit of Posterity" should have been forthcoming "from a Person of his Station." £4,000 was "a Price never heard of before in any Nation whatever for such a Service," and after Fielden's demise it should never be laid out again "for the same performances."

These were substantial hints, but for proof the reader needed to turn to the details of Parker's defense. He denied the allegation of popery absolutely. Indeed, he affected to find it so absurd that he could only assume Fielden's real targets to have been Newton and Halley themselves. But these, he maintained, were men of "Excellent Conceptions" and—unlike Fielden— "Laudable performances." Newton, in particular, was well known as a sound Church of England man. Besides, Parker had only met him once, some twenty years before. On the other hand, he admitted that he did know Halley well, having "several times had the Favour of being admitted to his Conversation." Indeed, Parker publicly thanked "my Honoured and Generous Friend *Dr. Halley*" for continuing to provide him with accounts of heavenly eclipses for his ephemerides, adding pointedly that since 1695, "a like Favour and Performance is not to be Obtain'd from another Hand." [3] But he had always found Halley, too, to be a staunch defender of Protestantism. Such deep and ill-concealed malice against two upstanding gentlemen therefore required explanation. Parker resorted to his own trade to answer this need, employing what had become a standard polemical device among feuding astrologers. He constructed an astrological nativity for his opponent—a nativity based, he claimed, on one drawn up by Fielden himself. Parker reckoned that this nativity proved Fielden to possess "a dull Phlegmatick Constitution, [and] a Violent, Cholorick disposition" (fig. 8.2). It demonstrated that Parker's antagonist was "Naturally tainted with Malice" and had a "propensity to Lying and Backbiting."

---

3. Parker, *Parker's Ephemeris for . . . 1717*, "To the Reader." This almanac has not been noted before by historians of science, although several have looked for it. The copy I used is in the Huntington Library, San Marino, California (classmark 337721, item 3). Halley had publicly approved of Parker's ephemerides since their beginning: Parker, *Mercurius Anglicanus* (1690), sig. $\pi 2^v$.

Given modern attitudes to astrology, there is perhaps irony in the fact that it is this astrological scheme that establishes beyond doubt the identity of Parker's antagonist. A nativity was a portrayal of the positions of the stars at the time of its subject's birth, the principle being that those positions did much to condition his or her character. Fixing the moment of birth as precisely as possible was therefore crucial to its construction. Here, Parker gave the date of Fielden's nativity as 19 August 1646. This was the birthday, not of some bookseller's hack living from hand to mouth in a Grub Street garret, but of the greatest British astronomer of the day. Parker had presented the nativity of the first astronomer royal, the Reverend John Flamsteed.

In all other respects, too, Flamsteed fits the description Parker accorded his foe. He was an ordained clergyman, with a parish in Burstow, Surrey. Earlier in his life he had indeed attempted to produce almanacs, and he had provided Parker with tide and other data until 1695, when the two had parted company acrimoniously.[4] And above all, since shortly after its foundation in 1675 Flamsteed had been residing in the Royal Observatory at Greenwich. His time there had been plagued by rumors and insinuations that he had not produced sufficient published results to justify his state stipend of £100 a year, small and irregularly paid though that stipend was. Forty years of this salary, from Flamsteed's arrival at the observatory in 1676 to Parker's attack written in late 1716, made a total of exactly £4,000. And Parker displayed a remarkably intimate knowledge of his antagonist's past, for in the one surviving manuscript copy of Flamsteed's abortive almanac, the astronomer had concealed his identity by using a pseudonym. The name he had coined for himself was Thomas Fielden.[5] The details are decisive. Parker had launched an unprecedented assault on the very personification of British astronomical endeavor.

Flamsteed came to hear of Parker's attack even before it was published. His ally, Whig theologian White Kennett, approached the archbishop of Canterbury to get the piece suppressed, and it is possible that Flamsteed or Kennett encouraged the Stationers' Company in a lawsuit it launched against Parker over the almanac in November 1716.[6] But in public Flamsteed seems to have kept a sullen silence, despite Kennett's advice to send an anonymous rebuttal to "some creditable publick Paper."[7] The truth was that to the aged and ill astronomer Parker's was a relatively trivial offense, weari-

---

4. Parker, *Ephemeris of the Cœlestial Motions and Aspects* (1695), sigs. [A1ᵛ]–A3ʳ; Parker, *Mercurius Anglicanus* (1695), sigs. A1ᵛ–A2ᵛ, C1ʳ⁻ᵛ. For Flamsteed's views on astrology and his attempts to produce almanacs, see Hunter, "Science and Astrology."

5. Hunter, "Science and Astrology," 260, 287.

6. Brodowski, "Literary Piracy," 153.

7. RGO Ms. 1.37, fol. 68ʳ.

some but unworthy. Flamsteed was consumed by a far more serious and profound transgression of which he believed himself to have been the victim. Yet here again Isaac Newton and Edmond Halley were the central protagonists, and in this greater outrage lay the real significance of Parker's attack.

The specific charge that Parker attributed to Flamsteed was dubious. Far from being a Catholic proselytizer, Newton was in fact an extreme antipapist. But both Newton (privately) and Halley (rather more publicly) *were* heterodox in their religious opinions, and the latter, like Parker himself, reputedly harbored Jacobite sympathies.[8] So the allegation was not simply and uninterestingly false. In fact, as this chapter will show, the antagonisms among Parker, Flamsteed, Newton, and Halley reflected tellingly on important connections between moral and religious conduct, and between individual veracity and authoritative natural knowledge. Parker's polemic successfully isolated many of their central elements. Flamsteed's failure to "perform" sufficiently to justify his royal position—especially in contrast to the Newton who had authored the *Principia*—was here a fundamental issue. Moreover, it was one readily understood in terms of the personal characteristics of communicability and conversation deemed essential for a civil philosopher and a gentleman. Such adjudications were the stuff of coffeehouse ridicule. And that Parker crystallized the contrast in terms of Flamsteed's incivility versus Halley's openness was particularly wounding. Flamsteed too regarded himself and Halley as representative of opposed moral identities, but in precisely the opposite sense. To the astronomer royal, he himself represented morality in action and truth in reporting; Halley stood for atheism, indolence, theft, and untruth.

The conflicts coalesced in a printed book. By 1716, when Parker launched his attack, Flamsteed was publicly identified as the author of a large folio *Historia Cœlestis*, which catalogued the fixed stars with unprecedented accuracy and thoroughness. Both his own reputation and that of his office—in short, his very identity as astronomer royal—rested on this book, which had been printed in 1712 for distribution to the great courts of Europe. But the book had been produced against his own vociferous opposition. In fact, Flamsteed believed himself to have been the victim of the most outrageous piece of intellectual hijacking in a hundred years. For the *Historia Cœlestis* had been produced against his dogged opposition. It was the achievement of a powerful alliance, constructed and led by Newton and Halley, that embraced a range of parties from lowly printers right up to the queen herself.

8. Iliffe, "'Idols of the Temple'"; Westfall, *Never at Rest*, 312–29; Schaffer, "Halley's Atheism."

Flamsteed regarded this book as a shameful misrepresentation of both himself and his astronomical enterprise. To discover why, we shall need to go back to the themes of chapter 7 and to the character of natural knowledge in the Restoration. We shall also need to return to the foundation of the Royal Observatory in 1675. The story that this chapter reconstructs from these bases is a complex and detailed one. But it is this very complexity that makes it such an excellent vehicle to demonstrate how the phenomena discussed in *The Nature of the Book* affected even the most empirical and technical of the mathematical sciences.

An early modern astronomer needed many skills. Some of them are perhaps obvious: acquaintance with contemporary astronomical theory, for instance. But when Edmond Halley, to choose one particular astronomer, was not sitting in his observatory in Islington, he was sailing the oceans in the HMS Paramour Pink, poring over ancient manuscripts, puzzling about the semantics of Arabic, trying to retrace the itineraries of Roman surveyors, managing the mint at Chester, or expertly managing the press for his mentor, Isaac Newton.[9] Halley was not unique in the breadth of his activities, all of which were necessary to his creation of astronomical knowledge.[10] The scope of early modern astronomy required that its practitioners be capable of such polymathic activities. To be an astronomer thus meant mastering practices that to us seem only distantly related to the content of the discipline. On the other hand, some of the skills that would now be regarded as absolutely fundamental to astronomical work—in a sense that paleography, say, would not—did not always enjoy such privileged status; Flamsteed was given to referring disdainfully to self-professed astronomers who could not even use instruments. Astronomy was thus far from coextensive with what we now take it to be. One consequence is that the historian cannot justifiably isolate those aspects that seem to us the most recognizably "scientific," and ascribe a success or failure solely to them. What follows illustrates the extent to which one of those necessary skills in particular—the management of the press—was an essential prerequisite for a successful astronomer.

According to library catalogues, Flamsteed's *Historia Cœlestis* was published twice. The first version, as we have seen, appeared in 1712; a second followed in 1725. Title aside, however, these were vastly different books. The first presented a bare record of Flamsteed's star catalogue, followed by a summary of the observations on which it was based. A preface by Halley

9. Halley, *Correspondence and Papers*, 109 and passim. As clerk and secretary of the Royal Society, Halley oversaw the *Philosophical Transactions* from 1685 to 1692 and from 1713 to 1719. On the Paramour Pink he suffered a mutiny, finding that his rebellious lieutenant was angry because of "the character I gave their Lo^PPs of his Book, about 4 years since."

10. See, for example, Schaffer, "Newton's Comets."

described in frugal outline Flamsteed's role as an observer and his deficiencies as a state servant. Flamsteed, it explained, had hitherto published nothing, despite his royal patronage, public position, and state funding. He had in effect "worked [only] for himself, or at any rate for a few of his friends." But Prince George of Denmark, Queen Anne's consort, had at length intervened and charged a committee of Royal Society fellows to assess, select, and publish the fit results of his labors. Interrupted by George's death, publication had since been completed at the queen's command. To produce this text, Halley himself had had to labor extensively to "correct and amend" Flamsteed's figures. Now, however, with the publication of this material in much-corrected form, the purpose of such work would be achieved: the natural-philosophical community could build their cosmological theories on reputable observations.[11] With this "truly royal treasury of observations" available, the philosophical reader could finally "weigh all the hypotheses of celestial motions" and confirm that "that theory alone should be embraced which is proved from the supposed mutual gravitation of all bodies towards each other." All others must be rejected. The notion of astronomy presented here was one of a practice subservient to philosophy—and to Newtonian philosophy in particular. By placing the star catalogue before the observations, that notion was inscribed in the very structure of the book.

The second publication, although of similar title, was entirely different in character. In three weighty tomes it presented an entire history of observational astronomy. A long preface to the third volume placed Flamsteed's work, and the Royal Observatory itself, at the head of this grand tradition. It reproduced the tables of the greatest of all observers, from the ancients, through Ulugh Beg, to Tycho Brahe and Hevelius. These it completed with a new and authoritative catalogue of the fixed stars, compiled by Flamsteed from observations that were painstakingly recorded *before* the catalogue itself. The work thereby reflected the order of construction of the knowledge that it embodied. This was an astronomical "history" of a different sort: a complete survey of heavenly bodies. The new catalogue was twice as large as anything that had been compiled before, and with the aid of telescopic sights and micrometer gauges Flamsteed had achieved unmatched standards of accuracy.[12] Here practical astronomy was not simply a constituent of natural philosophy, its practitioners being restricted to the unreflective provision of observations for philosophers' use. It was an end in itself. Astronomy was now lauded as a religious vocation of the highest order, providing for its royal sponsor knowledge of the very structure of Creation.

11. Flamsteed, *Historiae Cœlestis Libri Duo* (1712), preface; Flamsteed, *Preface*, 189–94.
12. Flamsteed, "Estimate."

As this chapter demonstrates, the different histories in the work were designed to establish this enterprise. They were effective. This *Historia Cœlestis* was to became one of the most important publications in the history of astronomy.[13]

The story of the clash that produced these two opposed works is not an unknown one. In 1835–37 astronomer Francis Baily published much of the manuscript material relating to the feud, in an attempt to rehabilitate Flamsteed's reputation. Baily's work was of contemporary significance inasmuch as it was seen as supporting the newly formed Royal Astronomical Society against the hegemony of the Royal Society. His defense of Flamsteed against what he portrayed as the dishonorable conduct of Newton therefore drew swift ripostes from an equally partial academic élite, for whom Newton represented a moral as well as an intellectual ideal.[14] The resulting exchange gave the episode a central place in Newton studies that it has never really lost. In our own generation, Frank Manuel has drawn on the episode to illuminate his psychological profile of Newton, and it has also been treated in Richard Westfall's authoritative biography. It has otherwise appeared as an episode in the history of the Royal Observatory, while Lesley Murdin has used the conflict to help in her attempt to describe the role of the typical early modern astronomer.[15] Yet no existing account attaches much significance to the dispute itself, beyond portraying it as an unfortunate and uncharacteristic lapse from generally commendable standards of "scientific" conduct. This is strange—and it is strange for reasons central to our understanding of learned culture in the early modern period. For Flamsteed and Newton fought a battle that any contemporary participant in the production of printed works would have recognized, and one central to the constitution of knowledge. The story outlined here is best seen with the contemporary duel between Pope and Curll in mind, or the printing of Congreve's plays, rather than idealized and anachronistic representations of scientific collaboration.[16] The authorial identities of figures like Pope and Congreve

13. Flamsteed, *Preface*, 25–185. This use of multiple histories (including those of nature) each of which served to legitimate the others had become an accepted strategy in astronomical writing since Kepler pioneered it at the turn of the century: see Jardine, *Birth of History and Philosophy of Science*, and Grafton, "Kepler as a Reader," 569–71.

14. Baily, *Flamsteed*, 74 n; Yeo, "Genius, Method, and Morality," 277–8; Dreyer and Turner, *History of the Royal Astronomical Society*, 77–8 and n; Whewell, *Newton and Flamsteed*. Baily's transcriptions were replete with errors and omissions, and have here been checked where possible against originals. I have also given references where possible to the edition of Flamsteed's *Correspondence* that Frances Willmoth is currently completing; only the first volume of this edition has been published at the time of writing.

15. Manuel, *Portrait of Isaac Newton*, 292–320; Westfall, *Never at Rest*, 655–67; Forbes, *Greenwich Observatory I*, 47–62; Murdin, *Under Newton's Shadow*, 53–68.

16. McLaverty, "First Printing and Publication of Pope's Letters"; Rogers, "Case of Pope v. Curll"; McKenzie, "Typography and Meaning."

depended on their skills in negotiating with printers and booksellers, on the creative use of typography, and on the conventions of reading current in their time. So did that of the astronomer royal.

FLAMSTEED, HOOKE, AND HALLEY: CONDUCT, MORALITY, AND NATURAL KNOWLEDGE IN THE ROYAL OBSERVATORY AND THE ROYAL SOCIETY

Chapter 7 introduced and discussed conventions of propriety in the early Royal Society. As shown there, the Society developed elaborate mechanisms for the perusal, registration, and publication of new knowledge. But the Royal Society was not to be the only site for the creation of natural knowledge in Restoration England. In 1675, at the urging of Jonas Moore's Office of Ordnance, Charles II instituted a Royal Observatory on Greenwich Hill. The ordnance was concerned because, apart from any more esoteric aims, the new institution was established mainly to solve the outstanding problem besetting early modern navigation: that of finding terrestrial longitudes accurately. It was envisaged that an authoritative record of the stars and the lunar motions would facilitate such a solution. Moore provided the instruments, and his protégé, the young Derby astronomer John Flamsteed, was appointed "astronomicall observator." His annual stipend of £100 was to be paid by the ordnance. On 10 July 1676 Flamsteed moved into the building on Greenwich Hill that had been designed by Wren for the observatory (fig. 8.3). He began systematic observations from the Great Room of the building that September.[17]

This represented the only significant investment by the English crown in astronomical research during the whole of the seventeenth century—and it signally did not go to the Royal Society.[18] The implications in a world of patronage were substantial. Two institutions, two sites, and two practical régimes were to vie for the honor of producing knowledge identified as royal. The mathematical sciences would be partitioned from philosophy, as had traditionally been the case. Flamsteed was thus understandably wary of the Society's interests. And he was especially concerned about the Society's curator of experiments, Robert Hooke, who, as a creator of instruments and occasional celestial observer, was the Society's natural counterpart to the new royal astronomer. From the start they clashed. Hooke himself had noted

17. Willmoth, *Sir Jonas Moore*, 158–95; Willmoth, "Mathematical Sciences and Military Technology," 127–30; Forbes, *Greenwich Observatory I*, 8–22, 77–80; RGO Ms. 1.35, fols. 80ʳ, 81ʳ⁻ᵛ; Ms. 1.36, fol. 29ʳ⁻ᵛ; Ms. 1.37, fol. 77ʳ; Baily, *Flamsteed*, 111–2; Flamsteed, *Correspondence*, I, 307–11. For the importance of the longitude see also Howse, *Greenwich Time*, 19–67.

18. In 1674 Moore had proposed an observatory under the control of the Royal Society, to be housed in its much-regretted property of Chelsea College: Baily, *Flamsteed*, 36.

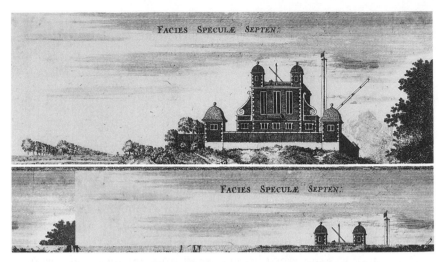

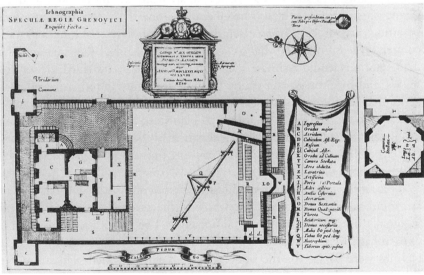

FIG. 8.3. Engravings of the Royal Observatory, by Francis Place. These engravings were among a set commissioned in the hope of creating a prestigious record of the new observatory's fabric and capabilities similar to Tycho Brahe's *Astronomiae Instauratae Mechanica*. In the event, the book never materialized, and only one of the images was used in Flamsteed's *Historia Cælestis*. (By permission of the Syndics of Cambridge University Library.)

bitterly that Oldenburg had "procured patent for Flamstead of £100 per annum and an observatory in Greenwich park" at the same time as recording the secretary's "treachery" over the patent for Huygens's spring watch. On Flamsteed's part, too, dislike began even before the foundations of the observatory were laid. It was confirmed during the watch dispute, when, despite "several promises," Hooke refused to let him see the workings of his device. Such a refusal implied a denial of Flamsteed's status as trusted and honorable—a conclusion reinforced when Hooke did show his secret to Flamsteed's patron, Moore. Hooke was placing the astronomer in the position of competitor, and Flamsteed soon came to find him intolerable.[19]

Later, in an effort to escape claims that his disputes with the Society were ascribable to defects in his character, Flamsteed was to allege that he had "kept a free & Ingenious correspondence" with its secretaries ever since Oldenburg, "& never had any differ wth them. nor with Mr Hook more y^n others have."[20] It is highly significant that he tried to establish his character in this way, and in a sense it was true enough: many people found Hooke difficult, not least of them Newton. But the awkward separation between Royal Observatory and Royal Society made such antagonism more consequential, not least because Hooke was a vital intermediary between the two. However, the incident that focused Flamsteed's outrage took place neither in the observatory, nor in the Society, but in a third site for philosophical conversation: the coffeehouse.

As we have seen, coffeehouses were important places for the production, exchange, and assessment of printed materials, as well as for the pursuit of conversations of all kinds. They were linked to experimentalism from the beginning: both the Royal Society itself and the Dublin Society may be traced to earlier "clubs" meeting in coffeehouses. Yet they could also be threatening to experimental enterprises. In the 1660s, transfusion trials were thus imperiled because, as Skippon reported, "the Coffee houses [had] endeavoured to debauch [their subject, Arthur Coga], and so consequently discredit the Royal Society, and make the Experiment ridiculous."[21]

---

19. Hooke, *Diary*, 151; RS Ms. Fl. 1, nos. 1–16; Howse and Finch, "Flamsteed and the Balance Spring." Flamsteed told Moore in October 1674 that he had written "very Freely but too suspiciously" of Hooke, and had sent him a firkin of Derby ale by way of apology: RGO Ms. 1.36, fols. 29^{r-v}; Flamsteed, *Correspondence*, I, 309–10. Frances Willmoth has suggested to me that one cause of their antagonism may have been an implicit competition between the two for Moore's patronage. As early as 1663 the Society had thought to undertake its own systematic survey of the fixed stars, in which Hooke was to have played a leading role: Birch, *History*, I, 219–20, 233.

20. RGO Ms. 1.35, no. 97: possibly a draft for Baily, *Flamsteed*, 170–1.

21. Derham, *Philosophical Letters*, 27–8; Ellis, *Penny Universities*, 21–2; Hoppen, *Common Scientist*, 23. For a coffeehouse dispute over the Society's transfusion experiments, see also St. Serfe, *Tarugo's Wiles*, 19–20.

Throughout the events recounted in this chapter, accordingly, the coffee-house was to play a pivotal role. Flamsteed's conduct was frequently swayed by his belief that the capital's coffeehouses were incorrigible sites of vigilance, adjudication, and ridicule. The contrast with Hooke, and later Halley, was striking and consequential. Both men wiled away hours in coffeehouses virtually every day. They were to prove immensely effective sites for Halley, in particular, to display his knowledge and skill during his campaign against Flamsteed. Referring to Halley's coterie, William Molyneux told the astronomer royal that "it is impossible to be at Child's Coffee house and not meet them, for there some do lead their lives almost," and we shall see that the astronomer royal came to regard Halley's conduct in such situations as particularly outrageous.[22] But at the time of the observatory's foundation it was Hooke who held the field in the coffeehouse, and who made it a particularly unwelcoming site for Flamsteed.

In coffeehouses the boundaries between mathematical science and social gossip could become remarkably permeable. By 1750, *A Dissertation on Royal Societies* could list three varieties of such an institution: the Académie Royale des Sciences in Paris, the Royal Society in London, and "a Coffee house Conversation." Earlier, Ned Ward had described that conversation as "infected with an itch of Curiosity." He characterized it as a competitive round of challenges: "if a Man funk'd a Pipe, and could not give a Reason for the Blewness of the Smoak," Ward related, "he that ask'd the question would think him an unworthy Member of so Philosophical a Club."[23] This was witty exaggeration, but it had a basis in truth, as can immediately be confirmed by scanning Hooke's diaries. Moreover, both Halley and Wren posed mathematical problems to Flamsteed on comparable social occasions.[24] But it was in Garraway's coffeehouse, near both to the Exchange and to the Royal Society, that Flamsteed encountered a more damaging challenge (fig. 8.4).

Garraway's was a favorite haunt of the virtuosi and would remain so for decades; we shall meet Flamsteed there again later, at the climax of his struggles over the *Historia Cælestis*. Here the floor would be occupied by the experimental philosophers of the nearby Royal Society, reconvening for refreshment and conversation after their weekly meeting. On one such occasion, in late 1681, Hooke suddenly turned to Flamsteed and demanded "somewhat captiously" that he solve a problem in the optics of long telescopes. When making celestial observations, he asked, was it better to set a

22. Bayle, *General Dictionary*, VII, 608–9 n. For Halley's continuing presence at Child's see also Lillywhite, *London Coffee Houses*, 157.
23. [Hill?], *Dissertation on Royal Societies*; Rogers, *Grub Street*, 227; [Ward], *Secret History of Clubs*, 18–20. Swift had earlier twinned the Royal Society with Will's coffeehouse: *Tale of a Tub*, 29. Ward, wishing to denigrate the virtuosi, actually placed them in a tavern.
24. For Wren, see RS Ms. 243.58; for Halley, see RS Ms. Fl. 1, nos. 22–3; RGO Ms. 1.41, fols. 10ᵛ–11ʳ; [Flamsteed], *Doctrine*, preface; Flamsteed, *Correspondence*, I, 716.

FIG. 8.4. Garraway's coffeehouse portrayed as the center of discredit. The coffeehouse is here made the backdrop for a nineteenth-century visual satire on the speculations of the South Sea Bubble. (In the possession of the author.)

plano-convex objective with the plane side toward the object, or the convex? Flamsteed stammered a reply: there was negligible difference, he said, but if anything it was better to put the plane side toward the object, since the less oblique angle of incidence reduced aberration. Hooke dismissed this response as ignorant, and the coffee-swilling audience took his side. Flamsteed departed in humiliation.

Challenges of this sort had long been a marked feature of the mathematical sciences; even when the Mathematics Tripos was developed in Cambridge in the 1730s, a candidate retained the right to challenge a higher student to a "mathematical duel" in a bid to raise his ranking. But Garraway's was not gownland, and Hooke, brilliant though he was in the coffeehouse, was not an academician. An ex-servant made good, his standing among the gentlemen of the Society remained precarious, and he was rarely accorded the title of "philosopher." Hooke was hardly a proper victor over an astronomer of royal credentials. Arriving back at Greenwich, Flamsteed therefore composed an "Opticall Essay" in his own vindication.[25] This

25. RGO Ms. 1.50.K, fols. 251ʳ–255ᵛ; Ore, *Cardano*, 53–107; Gascoigne, "Mathematics and Meritocracy," 550–1. For Hooke's status see Shapin, "Who Was Robert Hooke?" and Pumfrey, "Ideas above His Station." For the notion of philosophical or mathematical "duels" see Kelso, *Doctrine*, 103–4, and Shapin, *Social History of Truth*, 107–14. This incident and its consequences are discussed much more fully in Johns, "Flamsteed's Optics."

remarkable piece presented a valuable portrait of Hooke in one of the
Restoration's prime sites for presenting, debating, and deciding matters of
"intelligence."

Much was at stake. Flamsteed relied on his perceived skill as an astronomical "observator." He was now demonstrating this proficiency by lecturing on optics in Hooke's own institution, Gresham College—and he
was just reiterating his views on plano-convex telescope lenses when Hooke
launched his challenge.[26] If that skill were denied, Flamsteed's continuance
as royal astronomer, and perhaps the position itself, might be put at risk.
Hooke's argument, which implied that Flamsteed did not even know how
to set up his own telescopes properly, clearly threatened such a denial. Moreover, crucial instruments in Flamsteed's observatory were either designed by
Hooke or else were part of the Royal Society's collection, of which Hooke
was curator. On Hooke's deference thus depended both Flamsteed's personal reputation and that of his observatory. For these reasons his rejoinder
needed to vindicate not only his own conduct, but nothing less than "y^e
truth & accuracy of Coelestiall observations made with longe telescopes."

Flamsteed therefore combined optical calculations with allegations of incivility. It was Hooke's "nature," he observed, "to make contradictions at
randome, . . . & to defend y^m with unproved assertions." This was the conduct of a "mechanick," characterized by pugnacity and the tendency to propose overambitious technological devices as decisive solutions to conversational arguments. Indeed, Flamsteed alleged, Hooke's professed competence
with long telescopes itself derived from acquaintance with only a small lens
that he carried about in his pocket to flourish in the coffeehouse. He had
never retreated to the seclusion of a place like Greenwich to "meditate . . .
ye nature of refractions" in general, nor had he "calculated" angles of refraction instead of projecting machines to construct them for him. Only his
proclaiming of mechanical contrivances to replace such theoretical labors
permitted Hooke the "confidence" to insist on false assertions. His was "the
impudence of [a] solely Mechanick Artist," prepared to substitute confidence for calculation. When Flamsteed produced pertinent counterargu-
ments based in experience or theoretical optics, Hooke's response was therefore to "magnifie or assert some stupendious invention of his owne," which
he claimed would reveal the fact of the matter for all to see. But had he this
device to hand? It seemed not. "Wee must expect [it] an age or two [yet],"
Flamsteed remarked, "for hee has onely the conceite not the experiment,
which hee dares talke of not put to triall." It was not the device itself which
Hooke displayed, then, but only his own talk of it. At once both boastful
and secretive, he doubly violated the requirements of civil discourse.

26. Flamsteed, *Gresham Lectures*, 161–73.

Hooke's ability to exploit his movements back and forth between coffee-house and Royal Society made this particularly galling. While pretending to skill in the coffeehouse, Flamsteed complained, "hee makes questions to those hee knows are skilfull in them, & theire answers serve him for asser-tions on the next occasion." That "next occasion" proved to be the Society's subsequent weekly meeting, on 2 November—a day on which Flamsteed himself was to lecture at Gresham on the subject. Here, the Society's role as a space for the "showing" of experiments gave Hooke an important advan-tage. Triumphantly, he "shewed a mechanical way" of proving his claims. That his mechanism did not actually work seemed of little consequence. Flamsteed, with nothing of his own to "show," failed to convince anyone with his repeated dismissal of Hooke's argument as "false and impossible." A week later, in his absence, Hooke announced that the astronomer had "confessed" himself mistaken, and that he had now "found the demonstra-tion" of Hooke's claim—though not before "the way of demonstrating it was shewn by Mr. Hooke." [27]

According to Flamsteed, then, Hooke's "deepe Knowledge" was properly attributable to others less vainglorious than himself, and his extravagant claims for it derived from his own "Mechanick" impudence. He told Mo-lyneux that "Mr. Hookes vast promises of Inventions" were really designed "to Magnifie him selfe." And Flamsteed singled out Hooke's manipulation of the Society's perusal and registration procedures as evidence for this: "If any shall happen upon such desireable inventions," he noted, "hee has en-tred it and can produce the Minutes of the Society to prove hee knew it before them." Flamsteed described the Society itself as wilting under this appropriation of its conventions, since the prodigious production of talk was ruining the experimental setting. "Mr Hooke fills all with discourse and mighty projects and discoverys but they are seldome seene." Concluding that Hooke's "starcht humor" meant that he would refuse to accept even the possibility of his being mistaken, Flamsteed resolved to "excerpe a Cata-logue of his errors from his works" and present them to him, "to bring him to a freindlyer behavior." [28]

Flamsteed described to Towneley the most significant of Hooke's "con-triv'd devices." This was a quadrant, claimed by Hooke to be of astonishing accuracy, "of 36 foot radius y^t weighs not a pound & which hee can put in his pocket." Only those ignorant of mathematical instruments could possi-bly credit such boasts. Hooke alone could make them freely, since unlike Flamsteed he never actually had to put instruments to use on a regular basis.

27. Birch, *History*, IV, 100 –1.

28. Southampton CRO, Ms. D/M 1/1, fols. 14^r–15^v; Bodl. Ms. Smith 45, fol. 31^{r-v}; RS Ms. Fl. 1, no. 8; Dreyer, "Flamsteed's Letters to Richard Towneley," 291; Flamsteed, *Corre-spondence*, I, 883–90.

This was perhaps the point. Hooke's impractical instruments instantiated moral insufficiency, Flamsteed felt, since they were incompatible with the work of an astronomer's vocation. But unlike most of his other inventions, Hooke's proclaimed quadrant directly impinged upon Flamsteed himself. He promised to make a new instrument, "much more accurate than any yet used," for installation at the observatory.[29] He did indeed make such a quadrant, but according to Flamsteed's frequent complaints it did not live up to his "boasts." Shortly after Moore's death, the Society recalled it to its repository. Flamsteed believed that Hooke had engineered even this move, by hinting that Moore's executors were about to include it in the inventory of his possessions.[30] After it had gone, Flamsteed eventually used an inheritance from his own deceased father to fund the construction of more successful instruments, including a mural arc. The transition between these instruments became a major divide in the structure of his *Historia Cœlestis*.[31]

Flamsteed's quarrels with Hooke are worth describing for a number of reasons. They confirm the centrality at the Royal Society of "performance" in both contemporary senses of the word—display, and the realization of a promise—and show how this could affect the outcome of disputes. They also highlight Flamsteed's regard for invisible, laborious calculation above challenge and posturing. This regard, he increasingly felt, was poorly served by the conventions of the Society. And they illustrate Flamsteed's concerns about the manners and practices of "mechanicks," from the imputation of which he was always eager to absolve himself. In the case of the quadrant, moreover, they further show that when the Society's conventions were imposed on the observatory they could produce failure.

But the quadrant was not the most important example of the Society's involvement with the observatory's activity. The Society expected privileged notice of Flamsteed's work, in the same way as it solicited submissions of experiments, devices, and arguments by other fellows. Its supplying of the quadrant perhaps added weight to this expectation. However, the attempt to incorporate the observatory's results into its established perusal and publication mechanisms could easily be construed as an effort to exert hegem-

29. Birch, *History*, IV, 100–1. Flamsteed also corresponded with Hevelius about Hooke's claims, contrasting his unproved inventions to Hevelius's tried and tested instruments: Flamsteed, *Correspondence*, I, 442–9, 458–73, 487–96. For Hooke's "small new quadrant" "which being but of seventeen inches would perform the same as a quadrant of twenty four feet," see Birch, *History*, II, 69, 491–2; III, 121, 127, 135, 159. Flamsteed repeated many times his criticisms of Hooke's quadrant, but also made more ambiguous statements suggesting that it may not have been so disastrous.

30. RS Ms. 243.42; Flamsteed, *Correspondence*, I, 704–6.

31. There were actually two arcs. The first proved a failure, and was abandoned by late 1686. The second was built by Abraham Sharp, completed in 1689, and served until Flamsteed's death.

ony. Flamsteed soon found himself facing criticism from the virtuosi for not following the Society's conventions. Its president wondered aloud "why the Society did not receive some account from Mr. Flamstead."[32] Even his patron, Moore, could not long maintain his parry that "a quantity of them were ready for the press; but the booksellers were unwilling to undertake the printing of them," since the Society would immediately send Hooke to "speak with Mr. Martyn about it." Faced with such responses, Moore thought it politic that Flamsteed print his observations as they were made, rather than wait until a substantial body of them had been completed. He needed to "satisfy some p'sons that enquire oft what wee are doeing, that wee are not Idle." Molyneux more bluntly advised the astronomer to ease the pressure by printing "curiosities," and doing so "in a pompous manner fit to please and take upon a Prince."[33]

Flamsteed repudiated such suggestions as "needlesse." But they never ceased. By 1677, scarcely a year after taking up residence, he was already contemplating resignation in the face of "ye impertinences of a croud of visitants" who wanted "immature papers and writeings forced forth of my hands & detained as if I had no interest in them." He yearned to move "to some more private place where I might be Master of my selfe." Moore's suggestion that he deposit copies in the Royal Library at Saint James's was equally impalatable. But in 1678 Flamsteed conceded to this, telling Moore that he was "glad you chuse to put them into the Kings library rather then to have them printed." When he was told by a privy councilor that his post was in danger, he likewise had hastily to adopt Molyneux's suggestion, constructing a tide table and presenting it to Charles in return for an undertaking of his continuance. He also consented to publish some observations in Hooke's *Philosophical Collections*, and in 1682 deposited a copy of his book of observations at the ordnance for safekeeping.[34] These concessions to the conventions of presentation observed at court and at the Royal Society were the smallest that he could make and still remain relatively secure in his position.

This was only the beginning of a ferocious debate that would rage for the next forty years. The stakes were high. They concerned the kinds of places that the Society and the observatory were to be, the kinds of project pursued

32. Birch, *History*, III, 454–5, 458; Newton, *Correspondence*, IV, 450.
33. Bayle, *General Dictionary*, VII, 607–8 n.
34. RGO Ms. 1.36, fol. 59^{r–v}; RGO Ms. 1.42, fols. 12^v–17^r; Baily, *Flamsteed*, 118–23, 125–8; RS Ms. Fl. 1, Nos. 11, 28; Dreyer, "Flamsteed's Letters to Richard Towneley," 291–2; Flamsteed, *Correspondence*, I, 654–7; Willmoth, *Sir Jonas Moore*, 193; *Philosophical Collections* 3 (10 December 1681), 67; *Philosophical Collections* 4 (10 January 1681/2), 99–101. Flamsteed defended his work to Moore in RGO Ms. 1.36, fols. 54^r–55^r, and RGO Ms. 1.40, fols. 41^r–42^v; Flamsteed, *Correspondence*, I, 610–14.

there, and the kinds of knowledge they were thereby to produce. Was Flamsteed's a place dedicated to producing "performances" in the forms recognized by the court and the Royal Society? Was the observatory's validity to be gauged by its short-term fecundity of visible actions and printed representations? The Royal Society *was* such a place, as chapter 7 showed. It defined itself by its hosting of experimental actions, by its "perusal" and "registration" protocols, and by their representation to outsiders in the *Philosophical Transactions*. Coffeehouses, likewise, were sites for philosophical conversations, and increasingly for lecturers' displays of active powers—not to mention the reading of their descriptions in print. Should the Royal Observatory cleave to these conventions, or strive to be different in kind? This question arguably lay at the heart of Hooke's duel with Flamsteed. It was shortly to play a central part in the latter's conflict with Newton. And it implied an equally fundamental distinction between kinds of practitioner. Flamsteed regarded the "performance" a royal astronomer should produce as inconsistent with that demanded by the Society of its virtuosi. To him, to perform was nothing less than to honor one's word. With Molyneux, he felt that it was "absolutely intollerable in any man" to do as Hooke did on a weekly basis, namely to "Promise so much and performe so little." He had undertaken to the king to produce a star catalogue of revolutionary accuracy and scope. To perform this would require years of observing, cross-referencing, calculating, and, finally, printing.[35]

First raised in Flamsteed's confrontations with Hooke, these issues were to mature in what became a war against Edmond Halley. The royal astronomer first encountered Halley as a young Oxford undergraduate in March 1674/5. At first the two got on well, cooperating freely in astronomical work. But in 1677 Halley left Flamsteed's fledgling patronage and, sponsored by Moore, undertook an astronomical expedition to Saint Helena in the South Atlantic. On his return the two fell out. The immediate causes are unclear. Flamsteed himself gave at least five accounts on different occasions. Sometimes he attributed it to his accusing Halley of plagiarizing the theory of geomagnetism developed by Flamsteed's client, Christ's Hospital schoolmaster Peter Perkins.[36] Another version had it that one of Halley's friends

35. Southampton CRO, Ms. D/M 1/1, fols. 20ʳ–21ʳ; compare also 73ʳ–74ᵛ. Flamsteed was just as willing to take issue with his curate at Burstow over matters of personal morality: e.g., RGO Ms. 1.33, fols. 104ᵛ–105ʳ, 107ᵛ–108ᵛ; Ms. 1.36, fols. 94ʳ⁻ᵛ, 97ʳ. Perhaps unsurprisingly, his parishioners were apt to "murmur and grumble" at the prospect of his annual visit: Ms. 1.37, fol. 107ʳ. In 1700 Flamsteed preached a sermon against atheism that Smith wanted to see published: Bodl. Ms. Smith 60, pp. 171–2.

36. Halley, *Correspondence and Papers*, 37–41; RS Ms. Fl. 1, nos. 5–7; RS Ms. 243.68; Baily, *Flamsteed*, 193–4; RGO Ms. 1.33, fol. 111ʳ; Dreyer, "Flamsteed's Letters to Richard Towneley," 293–4. Flamsteed hinted at the allegation again later: RGO Ms. 1.33, fols. 111ᵛ–113ᵛ.

undiplomatically suggested to Flamsteed that he resign his position to Halley. Flamsteed also certainly felt that, as clerk of the Royal Society, Halley had manipulated the publication of his figures in the *Philosophical Transactions* so as to make him look foolish.[37] To others, he said that Halley harbored feelings of revenge because Flamsteed had not recommended him for the Savilian Chair of Astronomy at Oxford ("he might have debaucht ye youth of the university with his profane & lewd discourses," he helpfully explained).[38] Finally, Flamsteed also referred to the rude "enterteinment" he had received at Halley's home, and to the latter's spreading rumors in the London coffeehouses about Flamsteed's own lack of hospitality at Greenwich. From scientific error to providing an inedible dinner, any or all of these may in fact have taken primacy at various times. But it is perhaps the conjunction of all the charges that is significant, conveying as it does the intimate links between civility and accreditation insisted upon by Flamsteed. Halley's failing was thus not simply that he was unmannerly, nor just that he was untrustworthy, nor even that he perpetrated errors in astronomy, but that he exemplified the inseparability of all three characteristics (fig. 8.5).[39]

By 1686, then, when Halley had become the custodian of Newton's *Principia*, Flamsteed had made up his mind that his erstwhile protégé was untrustworthy. He had also determined him to be a plagiarist, since he spurned the labor needed to produce new knowledge himself. The most notable thing about Halley, Flamsteed now affirmed, was "his art of filching from other people, and making their works his own." This, he thought, was a

---

37. Forbes, *Greenwich Observatory I*, 75–6. Flamsteed had only given Halley the Jovian observations concerned here, he claimed, as an act of civility to erase previous conflicts. He also believed that Halley had used his (anonymous) position as "publisher" of the *Transactions* to insert mistaken conclusions into a paper of tide figures that included contributions by Molyneux, such that they would be attributed to Molyneux himself: Southampton CRO Ms. D/M 1/1, fols. 108^r–109^r, 111^r, 112^r–116^v. Flamsteed recommended Molyneux to send papers directly to the president of the Society, so as to circumvent such manipulation. Compare also Flamsteed's comment that Halley had "out of malice slansder[ed] [*sic*] me in his Tr." (RGO Ms. 1.35, no. 97), and Hevelius's suggestion that Hooke had deliberately corrupted Flamsteed's work in his own *Philosophical Collections* (RS Ms. EL. H.2.56).

38. RGO Ms. 1.35, fol. 10^v.

39. Newton, *Correspondence*, IV, 14 n. 8; Dreyer, "Flamsteed's Letters to Richard Towneley," 293–4. Flamsteed was also unimpressed by Halley's refusal to reveal to him a new method of calculating eclipses: [Flamsteed], *Doctrine of the Sphere*, preface (the copy classmarked BL c.122.e.32 seems to have been presented by Flamsteed to Hooke). For Flamsteed's account of his own openness and hospitality to Halley, and its poor reciprocation, see Southampton CRO Ms. D/M 1/1, fols. 99^r–100^r. For the rumors spread by Halley's allies in the coffeehouses of London, see also fols. 102^r–103^r. Judging by his proposal when visited by Lister's wife to prepare no greater fare than what he alone would consume, Flamsteed's idea of a "philosophicall meale" was indeed spartan: Bodl. Ms. Lister 3, fol. 101^r.

EDMVND. HALLEIVS LL.D.
GEOM. PROF. SAVIL. & R.S SECRET.

FIG. 8.5. Edmond Halley. As clerk and later secretary to the Royal Society, and as a leading ally of Newton, Halley played an important part in ensuring that philosophical, mathematical, and astronomical work would be printed and circulated. As such, his editorial practices were unusually influential. Flamsteed came to see them as the consummation of a long tradition linking illegitimate conduct to erroneous claims about Creation. (By permission of the Royal Society.)

trick learned from Hooke, into whose "designs and society" he had unfortunately fallen. Halley certainly possessed "a clear head," Flamsteed conceded, and was a good geometrician; but his indolence ruined all. "If he did but love labour as well as he covets applause, if he were but as ingenuous as he is skilful, no man could think any praises too great for him." This indolence was thus fundamental to Flamsteed's disgust. He maintained a religious regard for the correct exercise and representation of labor. This was most clearly manifested in his relations with workmen. Flamsteed encountered a very wide range of such individuals, including miners, binders (for the church bible at Burstow), brewers, mathematical-instrument makers, sailors, booksellers, schoolmasters, longitudinarians, and engravers (from whom plates and pictures must be concealed).[40] This was the com-

40. E.g., RGO Ms. 1.33, fols. 99^r–100^r, 101^r–103^v, 225^r–236^v (for miners); RGO Ms. 1.33, fol. 105^r (for binders); RS Ms. Fl. 1, nos. 1, 67; F[lamsteed], "History of *Malting*" (for brewers); RGO Ms. 1.33, fols. 107^v–108^v (for instrument-makers); RGO Ms. 1.33, fol. 111^v (for sailors); RGO Ms. 1.37, fol. 126^r (for engravers).

pany of "Knavish" "mechanicks" in which he placed Hooke. Eager to secure the "glory" of "inventions" for themselves, they yearned to "defraud"
him. They acted with secrecy, impudence, confidence, vanity, avarice,
scorn, and dishonesty, and professed to adjudicate matters in which they
had no competence. Replication of such impropriety also lay at the root of
Flamsteed's developing distaste for "philosophers." And Halley was their
representative.

Given this assessment, what made Halley a particularly galling presence
was the catalogue of southern stars that he published soon after returning
from Saint Helena. This book almost immediately became the favorite example for those, especially at the Royal Society, who believed Flamsteed
could and should publish his own observations. Halley, like Flamsteed, had
received public funds, and the contrast between their visible achievements
was made increasingly obvious. It became still more pointed when Hooke
displayed before the Royal Society a planisphere made from Halley's observations. The virtuosi quickly realized that such imprints "would be very
acceptable presents to such correspondents abroad, as were lovers of astronomical matters, if the book and planisphere were sent to some of them
from the Society." It seemed that Halley's printed results were to become
ambassadors for the Royal Society.[41] Flamsteed's contrasting failure to provide such ambassadors thus became even more pertinent.

At first Flamsteed could acknowledge Halley's achievement. He hailed
him as "our Southern *Tycho*," and ascribed to him the credit for a new
method of calculating eclipses. But as he examined the catalogue more thoroughly, and as its significance for the criticisms of the virtuosi became
clearer, Flamsteed came to see it as representing a hasty, superficial class of
work unbefitting the Christian astronomer. Here the inseparability of moral
conduct from astronomical veracity became explicit. Writing "in my defence" to Moore, he explained that Halley had had "neither opportunity
nor time" to observe for himself the motions of the Sun, its distances from
the fixed stars, and the stars' latitudes. To do all this would have been "a
worke rather of yeares then moneths." He had instead succumbed to the
pressure to produce results, being "afraid it would be said hee had done
nothing if hee make not something imediately appeare."[42] To "shun this imputation," he had taken for granted many of Tycho's observations. His catalogue derived its stellar positions by reference to these. But Tycho's positions
could "*p'haps be erroneous*." So all their errors were simply "transmitted" in

41. Birch, *History*, III, 434.
42. RGO Ms. 1.36, fols. 61ʳ–62ʳ; Baily, *Flamsteed*, 116–8; Flamsteed, *Correspondence*, I,
643–6; Halley, *Catalogus Stellarum Australium* (esp. sig. C1ᵛ, for a constellation named by
Halley after Charles II); [Flamsteed], *Doctrine of the Sphere*, preface.

Halley's text, rendering all his stellar positions untrustworthy.[43] It could still be a useful work, to those acquainted with its shortcomings, and had Flamsteed thought it "sutable" to his position he could have completed a similar catalogue. To have done so would certainly have "made a noyse and lookt a little glorious at the p'sent." But its defects would soon be uncovered. Then the royal astronomer would incur "odium"—and, he added to Moore, "you would gaine but little credit for haveing afforded y^r patronage to so ill an Astronomer."[44]

Developing a strategy that he would use many times in the coming years, Flamsteed recounted the labors of a true astronomer. His own properly ambitious project must take time. There could be no shortcuts to a new survey of the heavens. A similar task to his had employed Tycho, with six to eight assistants, for more than twenty years, and Hevelius for almost thirty. So it was evidently unreasonable to expect his to be completed in less than five. Flamsteed thus resented the assumption that he was of "that Carterlike temper that I cannot move without a goad," since its attribution of mechanic mulishness rested on a profound misapprehension of his astronomical endeavor. His critics were "the busy and least intelligent of the world," he affirmed, but at the same time "the most inquisitive and that too where they are least concerned." It was surely not fitting for the king's astronomer to bow to those who did not understand "the trouble of makeing astronomicall observations, & the labor of calculations necessary in applying them."[45] Foremost among these critics was still Hooke, whose *Cometa* Flamsteed read with disdain. "What hee has borrowed from others to make up his Volume is very ingenious," he told his friends, before going on to suggest that Hooke's prescriptions for astronomical practice rested on false grounds. "Hee professes himselfe to be a Philosopher not an Astronomer," Flamsteed remarked significantly, "& therefore I have no more to say to him but that Astronomy is ill handled when it must be ordered by ye whimsyes of Philosophy." But now Halley's work had offered a new opportunity for such criticisms, and Halley himself was rapidly replacing Hooke as the chief critic of Flamsteed's public silence. Flamsteed therefore linked the two, insisting

43. Tycho had generally referred stars' positions to one reference point, the star α-Arietis: Thoren, *Lord of Uraniborg*, 288. Flamsteed further believed that Halley had lapsed in the calculating of places from his observations, since he had done them all himself, and had not repeated them: RGO Ms. 1.33, fol. 108^{r-v}.

44. Flamsteed gave the example of Philip van Lansberg (1561–1632) as an astronomer whose reputation was thus discredited. The work referred to is probably Lansberg, *Tabulae Motuum Cælestium Perpetuae*. Flamsteed regarded him as a betrayer of the ideals of practical astronomy, e.g., in RGO Ms. 1.41, fol. 166^r; Ms. 1.33, fols. 136^v–137^v: "you must not give overmuch Credit to Langsberg Mr Horrex has prooved him to be a very wrestler of observations."

45. RGO Ms. 1.42, fols. 12^v–17^r; Baily, *Flamsteed*, 118–23; Flamsteed, *Correspondence*, I, 726–31.

that both Hooke and Halley repudiated the properly laborious character of astronomy.[46]

Almost immediately after taking up his post, then, Flamsteed found himself having to take a stand on the complex issues so often debated at the Royal Society of propriety, secrecy, the provision of private time to complete work, and publishing. To an extent, he implicitly accepted the compromises the Society had instituted.[47] He did condescend to publish material in the *Philosophical Transactions*. However, his position was complicated both by the sheer scale of the project he was envisaging and by the awkward relation between the Society itself and his new institution. The very conventions developed at the Society to preserve honorable discourse now seemed to him to embody dishonor itself, since they required him to betray both his own vocation and his royal sponsor. In 1691 the tension increased markedly when another voice joined the ranks of those urging the royal astronomer to produce evidence of his work. This voice belonged to Isaac Newton.

Newton had gained international renown following the publication of his *Principia* in 1687. The book had caused an immediate sensation. Its author attained something of the reputation of a demigod. "Does he eat and sleep? Is he like other men?" an awed nobleman had asked John Arbuthnot after scanning the work. Arbuthnot was able to reassure him that Newton "conversed chearfully with his friends, assumed nothing, & put himself upon a level with all mankind."[48] But this last was somewhat wide of the mark. Newton now acquired a devoted circle of acolytes whose access to him was much envied: Halley, Gregory, Fatio, Arbuthnot himself. To be an apostle meant immediate elevation to the first rank of European intellectuals; to fall from grace was a correspondingly devastating experience. Nicolas Fatio de Duillier and William Whiston suffered the ignominy for their public association with radical religious causes. When it befell physician George Cheyne, he retreated into the country convinced that he was about to die of grief.[49]

46. RGO Ms. 1.36, fol. 56ʳ; Flamsteed, *Correspondence*, I, 618–20; Flamsteed's comment is a late reflection of the categorical division explored by Westman, "Astronomer's Role."

47. Two important examples of Flamsteed's accepting the conventions of the virtuosi concern reciprocation and accreditation. First, Flamsteed told Towneley that an ephemeris maker recommended by Cassini was concerned primarily to "learne & arrogate oʳ ~~inventions~~ discoveries to himselfe." He would not send this individual anything more "but upon termes of commutation" (RS Ms. Fl. 1, no. 2). Flamsteed also believed that Cassini himself had appropriated Horrocks's lunar theory, altering its formulae "that hee might call it his owne" (RS Ms. Fl. 1, no. 27). Compare also RS Ms. Fl. 1, no. 122, where Flamsteed also objected to Oldenburg's "Epitomising that paper without my knowledge." Second, Flamsteed sometimes accredited testimony according to social rank: "I heard some Report of yᵉ comets appeareing in Easter weeke," he once remarked, "but being it came but from ordinary laborers I gave little thought to it." It transpired that the laborers had been right. RS Ms. Fl. 1, no. 26.

48. Westfall, *Never at Rest*, 473; Iliffe, "'Idols of the Temple,'" 253–66.

49. Rousseau, "Mysticism and Millenarianism," 200–1. For Fatio's association with the "French Prophets," see Schwartz, *French Prophets*, 72, 77–8, 93–4.

Newton now sent one of his most faithful disciples to Greenwich with a letter of introduction. This was the mathematician David Gregory, who was then a candidate for the Savilian Chair of Astronomy at Oxford. Newton expressed hope that Flamsteed would soon start publishing, if necessary piecemeal as his observing continued. His suggestion was similar to those Flamsteed had always repelled: that "it will be better to publish those [stars] of the first six magnitudes observed by others & afterwards by way of an appendix to publish the new ones observed by your self alone then to let ye former stay too long for ye latter." Gregory reported back soon after his visit.[50] It took Flamsteed himself six months to reply, however, and when he did so it was in a tone of determined self-justification. He composed at least four drafts of what became a detailed defense of his work against "a person who is allwayes puting ye Question to my freinds why I doe not print my Observations."[51] This person was Halley, whom Flamsteed had by now come to see as the leader of his critics. Flamsteed was convinced that it must have been on Halley's "suggestions & Misrepresentations" that Newton had advised him to publish so precipitately.

Flamsteed responded to Newton's suggestion by explaining at length the laborious practices involved in making astronomical observations and converting them into accurate stellar and planetary positions. He asserted that observational practice itself made Newton's suggestion unreasonable. He might as well include the stars omitted by Tycho, since "if I omitted them I must sitt still from ye time y^t one of ye stars in ye Charts had passed till the next came in sometimes 10. 12. or 14 minutes." By incorporating them, he pointed out, "I kept my self imployed"; and "my scribes paines in writeing down ye notes was not to be valewed." Moreover, this had not meant sacrificing feasibility, since his servant had recorded all the observations in an orderly enough manner that "any faithfull & diligent person" (a category to which "ye St Helena Observer" did not belong) could complete the calculations even if Flamsteed himself were incapacitated. From the tables Flamsteed constructed an "Epitome," and enclosed it with his letter to prove there was no danger of the data being lost "if it should please god to call me hence suddenly." Then he asked whether he should really be advised to stop observing just in order to "transcribe what I have done for the presse & to attend it for a twelve months to gaine a little present reputation?" To publish now would be both futile and unforgivably vain—especially if the observations not in Tycho were separated out. That would "looke more ambitiously than I can beare," he said, since it would appear to emphasize his own su-

50. Newton, *Correspondence*, III, 164–6; Baily, *Flamsteed*, 129.
51. Newton, *Correspondence*, III, 199–205; Baily, *Flamsteed*, 129–33; drafts in RGO Ms. 1.35, fols. 6^r–10^v.

periority. Besides, he refused to accept that he should be subject to the "Instructions" of such as Halley, especially as Halley's own catalogue of the southern stars was so "incompleat" (the French astronomer de la Hire had already shown how unsatisfactory Halley's observations were). Nor was Halley deficient only in his own work. He had "more of [my observations] in his hands allready than he will either owne or restore," Flamsteed complained, and by his "foolish prate" had lost all repute of being an honorable man outside the coffeehouse arena of "his Associates ye Muss's." [52] "I value not all or any of the shams of him and his Infidel companions," he concluded, "being very well satisfied that if Xt and his Appostles were to walk againe upon earth, they should not scape free from ye calumnies of their venomous tongues."

This last statement was not simply indiscriminate invective, although invective it certainly was. Halley by now had a reputation as one of the more licentious and heretical men in England. He was denied the Savilian Professorship after the archbishop of Canterbury heard of his heterodox religious views (it went to Gregory, himself hardly known for his upstanding Anglicanism). [53] Flamsteed himself called Halley and his friends "an odde sort of people that care not to be esteemed Christians." Since Protestant orthodoxy and correct moral behavior in general were conventionally deemed interdependent, it is scarcely surprising that Halley was also reputed to be an adulterer. Flamsteed's accusations of debauchery and intellectual theft were thus by no means isolated ones. But if moderation and reliability in intellectual life came only with orthodoxy in religion, then a heretic could not, even in principle, become a good astronomer. His conclusions would neither be generated by appropriately hard labor, nor bound by discrimination, sincerity, and sobriety. And they would be rushed into public view prematurely, in an indecent lust for authorship. Flamsteed came to view the inadequacy of Halley's southern catalogue as proving the point. Its observations were poor, he charged, "by reason (as I am apt to think) of his Impiety & profaneness." Unconstrained by principle, he had "sought his own reputation more then any thing else." [54]

It was thus especially galling that Halley, of all people, professed to regard

52. Newton, *Correspondence*, III, 202; RGO Ms. 1.35, fols. 11^r–12^v. I share Baily's bafflement at the term "Muss's"; the interpretation advanced by the editor of Newton's correspondence—that it was a coffeehouse club—seems to rest on a very literal reading of Flamsteed's draft reference to "his clubb of Muss's." Baily (132) suggests that it is intended for the word "must." In the eighteenth century, however, it was a slang term for a pedant. Flamsteed also called Halley's friends "people of more front y^n braine."

53. Schaffer, "Halley's Atheism." For Gregory's politics and religion see Guerrini, "Tory Newtonians."

54. RGO Ms. 1.33, fols. 107^v–108^v; Southampton CRO Ms. D/M 1/1, fols. 102^r–103^r.

Flamsteed as a subordinate.[55] In the face of such ambition, he defended his status as a theorist in his own right. Flamsteed had already noted with dismay Newton's failure adequately to acknowledge in the *Principia* his letters about comets.[56] Now he continued to assume himself qualified to comment on such topics as the physics of earthquakes, Newton's optics (in which he thought he had found a fatal flaw), the phenomena of atmospheric refraction, lunar theory, and other issues relatively divorced from the straightforward collection of data to which Halley and others urged him to restrict himself.[57] Whether Flamsteed should be accredited in such activities remained indeterminate; he lacked a university education, and had found his legitimacy in the realm of the mathematical sciences rather than philosophy.[58] But as an astronomer with a correct respect for laborious observation, he insisted on his prerogative to contribute to such enterprises. However, this prerogative was not to be accorded symmetrically. Flamsteed denied to Newton, Halley, Hooke, and other "philosophers" the competence to judge his own technical work. This extended even to its publication. Insisting on frequent and fast authorship ignored the technical requirements of the discipline, which were different from those of the experimental, medical, and natural-historical enterprises of the virtuosi. "A physitian or a Botanist would not heed me much, if I should urge him to publish a book of Plants," he protested; "nor ought I to heed those, who urge me about what they have much less skill in, then I have in Botanicks or physick." The implications of his "skill" thus extended to determining the structure, timing, and processes of publishing. In particular, printing must be done in the correct order. "The Observations of the fixed Stars, on which the Catalogue is grounded, should be publisht first," he insisted; "Next, the Catalogue of the fixed Stars, & lastly ye planets places derived from both." Publishing in any other sequence—as, he remarked, "a courtier" had recommended him to do— would be "praeposterous & Meane."[59] This revealed the proper range of his

55. In a draft for a letter to Newton, Flamsteed declared that "I will not allow him of all mankind to be a judge of what I have to doe till he shall have recovered his lost reputation both for Candor Sincerity & Gratitude"; the passage was deleted before the letter was sent. RGO Ms. 1.35, fols. 11^r–12^v.

56. Baily, *Flamsteed*, 50–1, 60; RGO Ms. 1.35, fol. 87^r.

57. Willmoth, "John Flamsteed's Letter"; Johns, "Flamsteed's Optics"; Baily, *Flamsteed*, 214; RGO Ms. 1.33, fols. 188^r–192^r, 194^{r-v}; Ms. 1.36, fols. 73^r–74^v; Ms. 1.44, fols. 21^v–44^r, 55^r–61^r; Newton, *Correspondence*, IV, 424–8; Flamsteed, *Gresham Lectures*, e.g., 161 ff., 153 ff. Flamsteed also seems to have had an air-pump: RS Ms. Fl. 1, no. 20.

58. A similar charge was made by Partridge against Parker, whose "principal Skill" was "only of an Astronomical Nature": that is, it concerned calculation only, "a work only fit for those that have nothing else to do, or rather fitter for a *Porter* than a *Philosopher*, which he imagines himself to be." [Partridge], *Flagitiosus Mercurius Flagellatus*, 15.

59. Bodl. Ms. Smith 49, pp. 261–3, 265–7. It is tempting to read this as directed against Sloane, then editor of the *Philosophical Transactions*.

authority. Flamsteed was busy creating an identity for the royal astronomer. He had to defend his province in its fullest extent.

HISTORIA CŒLESTIS

Newton, meanwhile, had been turning his attention to the last achievement needed to complete the triumph of his *Principia*. He wished to master the most difficult problem in astronomy: the theory of the Moon. By September 1694 he finally believed he was on the verge of the breakthrough. That month, Newton visited Flamsteed at Greenwich to ask for crucial data on the lunar positions. It was this meeting that set in play the final break between him and the astronomer royal.

It was at about this time, too, that Flamsteed began keeping extensive records of his relations with Newton and Halley. From now on he retained their correspondence diligently, and he would later arrange it with a view to constructing a historical account vindicating his own conduct. It is largely because of this interest in self-vindication that we are able to follow events to such an unusual extent. There are, of course, perils to using an archive constructed by a participant, especially one as impassioned as the later Flamsteed. These dangers should not be underestimated. Nonetheless, Flamsteed's prodigious collection of records and opinions, when duly reconciled with other available records, permits the detailed reconstruction of events in the observatory, the Royal Society, and the printing houses and coffeehouses of London. Together, hard work in these disparate sites achieved a major work of astronomy. It is possible that no other early modern publishing project in natural knowledge can be reconstructed so thoroughly.

It began with Flamsteed's articulating conventions of propriety and reciprocation. When Newton arrived at Greenwich in September 1694, the astronomer showed him 157 lunar positions calculated at the observatory. These were divided into three "synopses" of 52, 50, and 55 figures respectively.[60] Newton asked permission to take copies of them. Flamsteed consented, but invoked his own version of the sort of protective rule that had been developed in the Royal Society. In particular, he insisted that Newton not impart the numbers to anyone else, saying that they were not yet perfected. There was good reason for this. The Moon's position was best measured not directly but by reference to certain fixed stars. Before the completion of tables for those stars, fully accurate lunar places could not possibly be obtained.[61] Moreover, Flamsteed was also well aware that these were

---

60. RGO Ms. 1.35, fols. 76ʳ, 78ᵛ, 82ᵛ–83ʳ; Baily, *Flamsteed*, 61. Newton also received refraction tables.

61. A detailed discussion of Flamsteed's observational and calculational procedures is beyond the scope of this study. Suffice it to say that astronomical tables could not be con-

crucial materials for Newton's work. He thus imposed a further term: that "what ever emendations of ye Theory be derived from them should be imparted to me before any other." Remarkably, he was claiming precedence not only in the observations, but in cosmological conclusions generated with their assistance. This reflected his general conviction that astronomical work preceded cosmological theorizing. His governing condition, though, which in effect included all these, was that Newton be as any gentleman should be: Christian and "candid." On that basis Flamsteed agreed to share data with him—as, he admitted, he refused to do with "Mr. H." [62]

Within a week, however, Flamsteed had heard that Halley was working on lunar theory. He soon came upon further rumors that Newton had not kept the figures to himself (and certainly we know that he had discussed the meeting with Gregory). The suspicion that Newton had violated his conditions took hold. It would remain stubbornly resident in Flamsteed's memory, to revive powerfully in very different circumstances more than fifteen years later. Shortly afterward, Halley himself asked Flamsteed for the figures, which he clearly knew Newton to have seen. The royal astronomer again proposed a deal. He would reveal them provided Halley reciprocate by explaining his suggested modifications to the theory of the Moon, of which he had dropped hints at the Royal Society. Halley did so, and ran straight into Flamsteed's trap. "This I perceived was your aequation & told him so," Flamsteed informed Newton; "He was silent." Unsatisfied, Halley then came to Greenwich itself. It was only after berating him again for his behavior that Flamsteed would suffer Halley to take "a very few notes" of his observations. [63]

Newton, meanwhile, continued to write requesting lunar and other data, reciprocating with tables of refraction calculations. Responding to Flamsteed's anxious queries, he acknowledged meeting Halley, and confessed that Halley had raised with him the subject of the Moon. [64] Newton had apparently told him two of the formulas required for a comprehensive theory, which he had acknowledged that he had found with the help of Flamsteed's figures. Newton described this limited openness in terms of the same polite reciprocity. "He told me some years ago his correction of ye Moons excentricity," he explained, "& this made me free in communicating my things

structed simply by taking observations and publishing the raw numbers: they had to be corrected for time and atmospheric refraction and collated against each other to minimize errors. See Forbes, *Greenwich Observatory I*, 25–46, and Howse, *Greenwich Observatory, III*. The most detailed account of Flamsteed's calculational procedures is in Baily, *Flamsteed*, 367–410 (not reproduced in the modern facsimile).

62. Newton, *Correspondence*, IV, 12–5.

63. Newton, *Correspondence*, IV, 7, 26–33; Baily, *Flamsteed*, 134–6.

64. Newton, *Correspondence*, IV, 24–6, 34–6, 46–50, 93–7; Baily, *Flamsteed*, 133, 137–8.

with him." Halley had then asked to see the figures themselves. This Newton had refused, however, saying that he "stood engaged to communicate them to no body" unless with Flamsteed's consent. Armed with this information, Flamsteed himself again confronted Halley. He demanded that he reveal his ideas on lunar theory before receiving Flamsteed's observations. Halley explained his notion that the motion of the Moon was accelerating as the earth's bulk gradually increased due to accretion of the interplanetary ether. "I gave him the heareing," Flamsteed told Newton, "and at last told him that this Notion was yours; he answered: in truth you helpt him wth y^t." Halley's other ideas of the Moon also "smell[ed]" of Newton's.[65] By reporting these meetings Flamsteed clearly hoped to convince Newton both of Halley's impropriety and of his own trustworthiness. But they also had the effect of confirming his own distrust. By September 1695 Halley was having to ask Newton to approach Flamsteed for observations of a 1682 comet, since "he will not deny it you, though I know he will me."[66]

Despite his suspicions, Flamsteed continued to supply Newton with figures. All the while, he reminded him that the data could properly be relied upon only after the completion of his full star catalogue. Newton in return sent details of a theory of atmospheric refraction (denying he had intended to keep it secret, as Flamsteed had assumed), and reassured the astronomer that he had not spread any "insinuations" against him. Like Flamsteed himself, Newton now invoked the convention that a writer should be allowed time to perfect work in secret. He reassured Flamsteed that "if you can have but a little patience wth me till I have satisfied my self about these things & made the Theory fit to be communicated wthout danger of error I do intend that you shall be the first man to whom I will communicate it."[67] Later, after their relations had deteriorated beyond repair, Flamsteed would return to this passage, underline it, and comment, "as much [time] as he pleases[;] I have waited 5 years for y^m."

Flamsteed's anger, as well as his information, was increasingly reciprocated. Newton's patience had eroded as interminable illnesses slowed Flamsteed's work, and eventually it evaporated altogether. He became convinced that the astronomer had been "stuck" on his own work, and, confronting his calculational competence directly, ordered him to send only "naked

65. Newton, *Correspondence*, IV, 36–8. Nonetheless Halley did cite Flamsteed as providing observations for Newton's theory of the Moon, in *Miscellanea Curiosa*, I, 270–81.

66. Receiving them, Halley decided that where they differed from Newton's calculations, it was Flamsteed who was in error: Halley, *Correspondence and Papers*, 91–4.

67. Newton, *Correspondence*, IV, 38–42, 46–50, 61–3; Baily, *Flamsteed*, 139–42, 145–6. The nature and extent of atmospheric refraction were consistently of interest to Flamsteed, since virtually all astronomical observations needed to be adjusted for it. For early discussions see RS Ms. Fl. 1, nos. 2, 5.

Observations," from which Newton himself would employ a servant to calculate celestial positions. The day he received this exasperated demand, as evidence of its injustice Flamsteed scribbled on the back of the letter a list of
all the data he had imparted to Newton. But still he grudgingly complied,
complaining all the while of murmurings among Newton's circle that he had
delayed a second edition of the *Principia* by his intransigence. An abashed
Newton apparently did act to counter reports that he was being needlessly
obstructive. But Flamsteed continued to allude to a "Sparke" who "com-
plaines much I have lived here 20 yeares & printed nothing." "I doe not
intend to print a St. Helena Catalogue," he elaborated, "& for that reason I
defer the printing of any thing thus long that when I doe print it may be
perfect."[68] His dislike was only confirmed by a developing suspicion that
Halley had redirected to Newton, if not to himself, books sent from the
Continent as gifts to Flamsteed.[69]

In 1695, some six months after his confrontations with Halley, news
broke that Flamsteed seemed to have been able to observe stellar parallax. If
true, this would mean that for the first time direct evidence of the annual
motion of the earth had been obtained. The achievement was dramatic, and
it was also self-contained. Its publication need not be delayed for the general
star catalogue. Here, then, was an opportunity to prove Halley's criticisms
wrong, and to display a genuine accomplishment. John Wallis wrote from
Oxford to advise Flamsteed, typically, "not to talk too freely of it (unless to
trusty friends) till you have a considerable number of observations to justify
it." As soon as he had, he should "print them; least others perhaps supplant
you."[70] Flamsteed agreed, seeing an opportunity "to silence some busy
people y^t are allwayes askeing, *why I did not print*," and Wallis then handled
its printing himself.[71] But Flamsteed's paper referred in passing to the observations he had imparted to Newton. Wallis showed this to Gregory, who
mentioned it to Newton himself. Newton objected strongly, demanding
that his name be suppressed. An infuriated Flamsteed had to comply and
alter the "offensive innocent" paragraph. The incident rankled, since Newton seemed intent not only on remaining silent himself about any debt he

68. Newton, *Correspondence*, IV, 58–64, 67–70, 133–9, 151–6, 191–3, 284–5; RGO Ms.
1.33, fol. 104^{r-v}; Baily, *Flamsteed*, 142, 157, 158–9, 162–3. One of the few to understand and
endorse this plan was Hevelius: Flamsteed, *Correspondence*, I, 508–26.

69. Newton, *Correspondence*, IV, 65–6, 83.

70. Newton, *Correspondence*, IV, 124–5, 128–9; Baily, *Flamsteed*, 160–1. It is perhaps
worth noting that Flamsteed had not, in fact, recorded stellar parallax, which was to remain
indiscernible until the nineteenth century.

71. Wallis cautioned Flamsteed against using London printers, since their correctors were
"apt to mis-take in things Mathematical." Newton, *Correspondence*, IV, 287–8; Baily, *Flamsteed*, 163–4.

owed to the observatory, but also on silencing Flamsteed. Flamsteed found this especially unjust since he was convinced that Newton had privately passed on his figures to both Halley and Gregory. His fury now focused on the latter. Gregory, he explained to Wallis, was one of a notorious group of nonjurors habitually found at the premises of bookseller Joseph Hindmarsh, the trade's leading crypto-Jacobite. Flamsteed was appalled when Gregory advised him to use Hindmarsh as his agent, and for a time identified his persecutors with his and Gregory's "party." [72]

Newton himself had come to feel that his correspondent was meddling in peripheral activities at the expense of essential ones. Moreover, Flamsteed had not adequately reciprocated his efforts in solving such problems as atmospheric refraction. He had undertaken such work, Newton declared, only "that I might have something to return you for the Observations you then gave me hopes of"—a kind of prospective reciprocity. But, contrary to the implication of his letter to Wallis, Flamsteed had never supplied those crucial data. Instead he had been sending token figures, merely so as to receive back "what was perfect . . . & of more value then many Observations." Flamsteed glossed this opinion as "hasty artificiall unkind arrogant." Newton's statement was true, he replied, only in the sense that "Wire is of more worth then ye gould from which twas drawne." He himself had gathered, melted, and refined the "gold," and would not accept that his labors be undervalued by "ye Calumnies of disingenuous & impudent people." The only reward he expected was "that I may now & then see some of your workmanship." [73] To his friends Flamsteed went further and characterized the work Newton had done as mere tinkering with Horrocks's existing lunar theory. [74]

With each party suspecting the other of reserve, intrigue, and injustice, the very notion of a polite conversation or correspondence now seemed

72. Newton, *Correspondence*, IV, 288, 292–6, 304–5; Baily, *Flamsteed*, 164 (note by Flamsteed), 168. *"Blaspheming Hindmarsh"* had long been an opponent to Whig politics, republishing Strafford's trial in 1679 with a eulogy of the executed peer's character, and had been linked to licenser and Tory writer Edmund Bohun; after 1688 he refused to declare allegiance to the new monarchs, and later exploded with rage when the Stationers' Company told him that they were expected to contribute to William's war effort: [Blount], *Reasons Humbly offered*, 22, 28; SCB F, fol. 140^r; *Impartial Account of . . . Strafford*. Flamsteed's own allegiance was to the Whigs—Tory Thomas Hearne regarded him as a "republican"—and he was careful not to employ a High Church curate at Burstow (Baily, *Flamsteed*, 315). Around 1700, gossip flared that Flamsteed was given to justifying the regicide of Charles I. He defended himself by attributing Charles's downfall to "French contrivances" at court as much as to rebellious subjects. Thomas Smith was unimpressed: Bodl. Ms. Smith 49, pp. 265–7.

73. Newton, *Correspondence*, IV, 143–4, 150–1; Baily, *Flamsteed*, 157–8. Newton always resented this reference to Flamsteed's gold, and Machin was still regaling people with it years later: Westfall, *Never at Rest*, 541.

74. RGO Ms. 1.33, fols. 199^v–200^r.

threatened with disintegration. Flamsteed gave a revealing assessment of Newton's character to John Lowthorp that confirmed as much. Newton, he said, had been "possest with Prejudices" against him by Halley, such that Flamsteed "could have no free discourse with him." He had found his imparting his developed theories to Gregory and Halley "a Greater Breach of Promise yⁿ if he had imparted yᵉ Observations themselves." His work, he explained, was like the building of Saint Paul's. "I had hew'd the Materials out of yᵉ Rock, brought yᵐ together & formed yᵐ but yᵗ hands & Time were to be allowed to perfect yᵉ building & Cover it." He demanded that before he would give him any more data, Newton not only act to stop Halley's "reflecting discourses," but "own before Sir Chris: [Wren] wᵗ he has already receiv'd."[75] Without such repair work their reciprocal correspondence could not continue.

Given Halley's central role, however, it was perhaps not Newton's fault that his conduct had become so reprehensible. Esteeming it "the duty of all Christians . . . to have peace with all men," the royal astronomer accordingly resolved to "cure" Newton. Finding a bible in a room in Newton's house one morning while he was waiting to meet him, the Reverend Flamsteed seized his opportunity to do good. He grabbed a piece of paper and scribbled down a couplet he remembered from "a late satire":

> A Bantring Spirit has our Men possest
> And Wisdom is become a standing Jest.

Beneath, he added, "Read Jeremiah Ch.ix to the 10ᵗʰ verse." Then he went in and related to Newton the current state of the star catalogue he was so laboriously compiling, asking him and Wren to come to Greenwich and see for themselves how it must be printed. The passage he recommended warned of the prevalence of false rumors:

> they bend their tongues like their bow for lies; but they are not valiant for the truth upon the Earth: for they proceed from evil to evil, and they know not me . . . every neighbour will walk with slanders. And they will deceive every one his neighbour, and will not speak the truth. . . . Thine habitation is in the midst of deceit.

Flamsteed was sure this would work. "I do not know whether he has seen it," he told Lowthorp, "but I think he cannot take it amiss if he has; and if

75. Newton, *Correspondence*, IV, 331–2; Baily, *Flamsteed*, 174–6 (a fuller copy); RGO Ms. 1.33, fols. 185ʳ–187ʳ. The analogy with Saint Paul's was a recurring one that Flamsteed even used, rather tactlessly, to Wren himself. Typical was his scrawled comment, "Tis as impossible for Mr N. to hide wᵗ he has receav[ed] from yᵉ Observatory as to cover St Pauls with a Scotch bonnet": RGO Ms. 1.35, fol. 77ᵛ. Interestingly, Pumfrey has suggested that Lowthorp was later to be involved in an anti-Newtonian faction at the Society: "Who Did the Work," 146. See below, note 83, for the relation between his abridgment of the *Philosophical Transactions* and Flamsteed's *Historia*.

he reflects a little on it, he will find I have given him a seasonable caution against his credulity, and showed the way of the world much better than his politics or a play could do."[76] We too do not know if Newton saw the message, nor what his reaction was if he did. But the passage Flamsteed chose is significant, since it again demonstrates his consciousness of living amid a welter of falsity and rumor.

In this "habitation," he therefore decided to mount a campaign in his own defense. The message to Newton was one aspect of this offensive. Inviting Wren to come to Greenwich with Newton, Flamsteed also took care to tell him that he now had substantial results, "which you may please to take notice of whenever you fall into company where my labors are mentioned." And he sent to Oxford a very full account of his endeavors since the foundation of the observatory, to counter damaging gossip there. His correspondent in Oxford suggested that he go further still. He urged Flamsteed to compose a statement of his case, phrased "as you are a Philosopher and a Mathematician, and above all, as you are a Clergyman." This he should send to the "great men" who complained of his inactivity.[77] As far as we know, Flamsteed demurred. But he redoubled his efforts to compile evidence for what he hoped would be a final, unanswerable vindication.

During the succeeding years Flamsteed and his assistants worked to construct his full catalogue of the stars. At the same time he moved to gather the further materials needed for his grand project, including the recovery of Arabic astronomical observations from Oxford and Tychonic manuscripts from across Europe (we shall return to the latter in a moment).[78] Newton meanwhile moved to London and became master of the royal mint. In November 1703, after the death of Robert Hooke, he became president of the Royal Society (fig. 8.6). Such a man would have ready access to powerful patrons. As he ascended, Newton met Flamsteed several times to discuss possible printing. When he did, Flamsteed described something of the extent of his project. It embraced observations, the star catalogue, and a comprehensive set of engraved charts of the heavens, effectively reproducing the entire astronomical enterprise in printed form. Flamsteed told Newton that the observations must be printed first, as the foundation of the more important star catalogue, and that the charts must be engraved to accompany the catalogue. Newton urged him to delay the charts, however, raising the

---

76. Baily, *Flamsteed*, 174–6. The source for his quotation was Sir Richard Blackmore's anonymous *Satyr against Wit* (on p. 5). Blackmore's poem condemned the rise of wit as corrosive to learning, "Mechanick Arts," and a sound commonwealth, and bewailed its ascendancy in a London where "Honour fails and Honesty decays." Flamsteed had also professed his desire to see Halley "reclaimed" for Christianity: Southampton CRO Ms. D/M 1/ 1, fols. 102ʳ–103ʳ.

77. Cudworth, *Sharp*, 42; Bodl. Ms. Smith 49, pp. 261–3; Ms. Smith 60, pp. 171–2.

78. Bodl. Ms. Smith 49, pp. 257, 261–3; Bodl. Ms. Smith 60, pp. 169–70.

FIG. 8.6. Isaac Newton, ca. 1703. Charles Jervas's portrait, painted to commemorate Newton's election as president of the Royal Society. (By permission of the Royal Society.)

serious objection that they would merely serve mapmakers "to steal and transcribe into their globes." But Flamsteed was adamant, declaring that he would obtain the protection of royal privileges to obviate this risk. Neither the concern nor the response was unprecedented. Flamsteed himself was well aware of the danger, having earlier been urged to help prevent another valuable series of copperplates from falling into the hands of piratical engravers. And we have seen in chapters 3 and 4 the legitimacy and power of patents in combating piracy. Nonetheless, he was already concerned that others might intervene to change the nature of any publication he might persuade a patron to sponsor, and his insistence derived equally from this fear.[79] The fate of the charts was to become central to Flamsteed's perception of a grand transgression being perpetrated around his work.

In 1704, Newton finally published his long-anticipated *Opticks*. As with his earlier debate with Hooke, Flamsteed took Newton's new book as a chal-

79. RGO Ms. 1.33, fols. 185^r–187^r; RGO Ms. 1.37, fol. 162^{r-v}; Baily, *Flamsteed*, 174–6; Newton, *Correspondence*, IV, 331–2; Bodl. Ms. Lister 3, fol. 74^r.

lenge to the legitimacy of his own statements about the experience of telescopic observation. In particular, he believed that he could show "an easy
experiment" to disprove Newton's pronouncement that telescopic images of
stars must possess considerable diameters. Flamsteed ordered his friend and
former servant, James Hodgson, now a London lecturer in mechanical philosophy, to "discourse of this publickly." Word quickly reached Newton. On
around 12 April, only days after finishing the preface to the new book, he
came to Greenwich to investigate. Newton watched and listened in glum
silence as Flamsteed recounted his errors, adding for good measure that his
prized lunar theory was similarly divergent from astronomical observations.
Then they had dinner. At length, Newton asked to see the state of the observatory's work. Flamsteed was able to show him ranks of bound papers,
along with charts of the constellations. Newton then implied that he wanted
to see them printed and that he would recommend them "privately" to
Prince George of Denmark to be published. George was the queen's consort
and, as lord high admiral, the most appropriate patron. Flamsteed declined,
fearing that without a public commitment Newton, Halley, and Gregory
would contrive to vitiate his work to secure a rapid, economical, and impressive publication. Such a piece would suit them, since it would be adequate for the role they accorded practical astronomy; but it would misrepresent the character, practice, and purposes of Flamsteed's enterprise.[80]

Although Newton left unsatisfied, Flamsteed himself did not relinquish
hope that Prince George might be persuaded to sponsor his preferred work.
That November, he decided to see how great a project its printing would
be. He produced an estimate of the number of pages the work would require. For the first time its extent became clear. His magnum opus was to
include not only his own tables, but those of Ptolemy, Tycho, and others: it
would be a complete history of observational astronomy. In all it came to
some 1450 pages, not including sixty engraved maps and a long preface.
Work could start on printing immediately while the later sections were
readied for the press. The costs of printing "such a *Work*, as has never before passed under the Press in *England*," would be great, Flamsteed admitted, "and therefore not fit for a private Undertaker." But if Prince
George were indeed to sponsor it, his memory would be celebrated "so long
as Ships sail on the Seas, or Ingenious Men contemplate the Heavens on
Land" (fig. 8.7).[81]

80. In different accounts, Flamsteed dated the meeting to 10, 11, and 12 April. Baily,
Flamsteed, 66, 69; Newton, *Correspondence*, IV, 424–8, 465–6; Flamsteed, *Preface*, 161. For
Flamsteed's experimental attack on Newton's *Opticks*, and its possible relation to the approach
to Prince George, see Johns, "Flamsteed's Optics." Halley had dedicated a map of the magnetic variation to George: *Atlas Maritimus Novus* (1702).

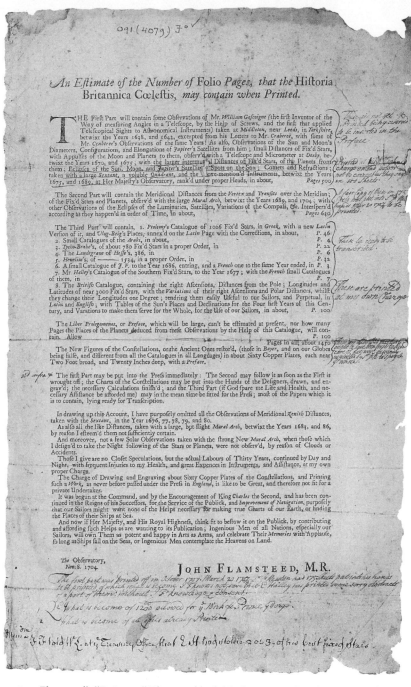

FIG. 8.7. Flamsteed's "Estimate." Flamsteed had this sheet printed to demonstrate the ambition of his plan and his readiness to realize it. Carried by his erstwhile assistant James Hodgson, it was revealed at the Royal Society at a meeting that set in train the subsequent struggles over the star catalogue. In this copy, notes have been added recording Flamsteed's eventual resentment at the outcome of each clause. At the foot, another hand has appended: "J. F[lamsteed] told W. L. at yᵉ Treasury Office that E. H[alley] had stolen 2 or 3 of his best fixed Stars." (By permission of the Royal Society.)

The intermediary Flamsteed chose to carry this message was again Hodgson. By his own account, Flamsteed gave a copy of the paper to his ex-colleague, then newly elected FRS, who revealed it at a meeting of the Royal Society.[82] The fellows present immediately pounced on the project, even though it was not formally under their aegis. After its experience with Willughby's *Historia Piscium*, however, the Society was not about to attempt financing an altogether more ambitious *Historia Cœlestis*. It therefore determined to recommend publication to the prince. Newton, Flamsteed wrote acidly, "closed in with this." The astronomer would later insist that Hodgson had revealed the document inadvertently and that Newton's Royal Society was being opportunistic in its recommendation. He was certainly unimpressed by the Society, telling James Pound that it desperately needed a new "constitution"—which, he implied, meant a new president.[83] But it seems likely that his acquiescence at the time was more willing than such retrospective insistence suggested. As we have seen, it was quite usual for the undertaker of an ambitious specialist work to submit a "proposal" or "specimen" like Flamsteed's to the Society, and almost equally standard for it to react by moving to encourage the work's publication under the wing of an eminent patron. This was one of its accepted roles. Moreover, Flamsteed's "Estimate" was clearly aimed at the prince, who could conveniently be approached through the Society's mediation. And at the time Flamsteed hailed the outcome of Hodgson's presentation as positively providential. For, intended or not, the prince agreed forthwith to finance publication.[84]

Almost immediately Flamsteed realized that sheer geography was going to play a crucial part in the fortunes of his enterprise. Living in London, Newton had daily access to a number of key sites, not least Saint James's

81. Baily, *Flamsteed*, 219; Flamsteed, "Estimate." This is reprinted in Newton, *Correspondence*, IV, 420–3. RGO Ms. 1.35, fols. 13ʳ–14bᵛ, is probably a very early sketch for such an estimate, written before the death of William III.

82. Hodgson was elected on Saint Andrew's Day, 1703—the same day as the election of Newton to the presidency. Flamsteed regarded him as his agent within the Society: e.g., Baily, *Flamsteed*, 215–6. He would become a coffeehouse lecturer after leaving Flamsteed's charge, and Flamsteed wanted the Society to contribute to the costs of his lecturing: Stewart, "Selling of Newton"; Cudworth, *Sharp*, 81–2.

83. RGO Ms. 1.36, fols. 73ʳ–74ᵛ; Newton, *Correspondence*, IV, 424–8. John Lowthorp also produced his abridgment of the *Philosophical Transactions* at this time. The first volume opened with an epistle to Prince George, defining him as almost a second founder of the Society, as evidenced by "The Commands Your *Royal Highness* has given, for Publishing, at Your own Expence, a most Magnificent *Uranography*." Lowthorp, *Philosophical Transactions and Collections . . . Abridg'd*, I, "Epistle Dedicatory."

84. RS JB IX, 85–7, 89, 90; Baily, *Flamsteed*, 70; RGO Ms. 1.36, fols. 73ʳ–74ᵛ, 102ʳ; Newton, *Correspondence*, IV, 424–8. The prince was elected FRS forthwith. It should be stressed that Flamsteed's was not the only large work sponsored by Anne or George. A brief list (in which Flamsteed's, for one, is mistitled) is in Bucholz, *Augustan Court*, 238. For the general importance of such "brokerage" in patronage systems, see Findlen, *Possessing Nature*, 362–92, and Biagioli, *Galileo, Courtier*, 19–30.

FIG. 8.8. Engraving by Francis Place,
showing the view from the observatory
toward London. Place's engraving implies
the distance of the observatory from the
city. For the aging Flamsteed, a visit to
London was increasingly an ordeal. (By
permission of the Syndics of Cambridge
University Library.)

Palace. He therefore enjoyed an unrivaled ability to decide the detailed fate
of the publication. "The distance of this place from London," Flamsteed
cautioned from distant Greenwich, "was a great impediment in yᵉ building
of it, & will prove no less to the publication of my work here done if you
doe not cordially & freindly assist me" (fig. 8.8). He belatedly drafted a
petition to the prince claiming that the engraving of the charts, in particular,
"cannot be done but at the Observatory." [85] However, as president of the
Royal Society, Newton had already acted to take such control out of his
hands. After he had waited on the prince himself to obtain his agreement to
the endeavor, George had appointed a committee of Society referees to oversee the project, comprising Wren, Francis Robartes, John Arbuthnot, and,
at their head, Isaac Newton himself. Newton added Gregory and Aston to
their number. [86] This committee was to examine all Flamsteed's papers, and
decide which of them were "fit" to be printed. This power was to result in
a radical redefinition of the project.

Flamsteed met the committee twice in London, on 19 and 27 December. [87] For a while he was even grudgingly impressed by Newton's concern, and supplied him with specimens of his tables, translations, and
charts. [88] The committee then submitted its report to the prince the follow-

85. RGO Ms. 1.35, fol. 18ʳ; RGO Ms. 1.36, fols. 77ʳ–78ʳ; Baily, *Flamsteed*, 230–1; Newton,
Correspondence, IV, 449–51.

86. RGO Ms. 1.33, fol. 121ᵛ; Baily, *Flamsteed*, 231; Newton, *Correspondence*, IV, 430–1; V,
102, n. 3; RS JB IX, 91. Arbuthnot had been elected FRS with the prince: 89.

87. Newton, *Correspondence*, IV, 431–2; Baily, *Flamsteed*, 231–2; RGO Ms. 1.35, fols. 21ʳ⁻ᵛ,
23ʳ; Cudworth, *Sharp*, 48.

88. RGO Ms. 1.33, fols. 122ᵛ–123ʳ; Newton, *Correspondence*, IV, 433–5; Baily, *Flamsteed*,
232–4. Flamsteed had (he claimed) translated the catalogue in Ptolemy's *Almagest* anew from
Greek: Newton, *Correspondence*, IV, 426–7, 433; Bodl. Ms. Smith 49, p. 271.

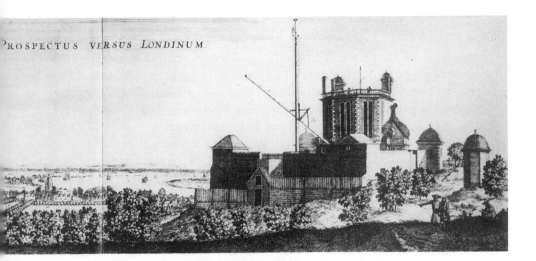

PROSPECTUS VERSUS LONDINUM.

ing January. Enough material was now ready to make up 1200 printed pages, and the expense for 400 copies could be calculated:

	p	s	d
for 283 Rea[m]s of Demy paper of 16½ inches by 22 att the Rate of 20s a Ream	283	00	00
for Composing & press work of 300 Sheets att yᵉ Rate of 20s a Sheett	300	00	00
for the Charges of an Emanuensis to Copy & Correct the pr[e]sse & to Compare & examin yᵉ papers.[89]	100	00	00
Totall	683	00	00 [90]

The committee also recommended printing the places of the Moon, planets, and comets derived from Flamsteed's observations. Some six hundred of these were already computed, with fourteen hundred remaining to be calculated. Employing two calculators to do this work,[91] and including charges for paper and printing, this would cost another £180. The total cost was thus estimated at £863.

But this was to be a very different publication from that envisaged by Flamsteed. The order of the text was to be transformed, the lengthy historical apparatus omitted, and the charts left in limbo. The loss of the charts, in particular, was devastating to the astronomer. "These were altogether necessary & ought to have been first taken care of," he later affirmed, "but were

89. The referees seem to have appointed John Machin to this position.

90. Newton, *Correspondence*, IV, 436–7; Baily, *Flamsteed*, 234; RGO Ms. 1.35, no. 19; RGO Ms. 1.33, fol. 122ʳ. Newton's draft is CUL Ms. Add. 4006, no. 7.

91. Thomas Weston (until May 1706) and John Witty (until September 1706). Other calculators and assistants were employed throughout Flamsteed's tenure.

designdly neglected by S' I. N. to spoyle y' whole." [92] Newton had already urged him to delay them for fear of piracy, as we have seen. But Flamsteed's vision of the future *use* of his book by practicing astronomers rested on their being printed. They were to be accurate visual representations of the star catalogue, amenable of rapid reference by inspection—even during the actual practice of nighttime observing, when time would be of the essence. Indeed, he wanted them begun first, as the most expensive and time-consuming part of the work. In his view it was only the prohibitive cost of the plates that had made royal assistance necessary at all.[93] Moreover, by the end of 1704 Flamsteed had drawings for the charts ready, with Orion engraved as a specimen, and the prince himself had viewed them. All this labor was now to be ignored. The referees were interested only in the numbers.

However, at least work could progress immediately on the printing of the material that had been recommended by the referees. Funds were rapidly forthcoming for this, if not for the £2,000 that Flamsteed immediately suggested should be given to him as reimbursement for expenses. Encountering Newton "accidentally" at Garraway's, the astronomer pressed him about this compensation for all his years of labor, but to no immediate effect. Soon after, the referees met Flamsteed at the Castle Tavern in Paternoster Row, right in the heart of the bookselling quarter of London. There they examined printers' specimen sheets and negotiated the administration of the project.[94] But it was now that one of the most controversial aspects of the entire project arose. The referees had resolved that an "undertaker" would be employed. This was bookseller Awnsham Churchill.

Awnsham Churchill lived and worked at the Black Swan, Paternoster Row—within a few yards of the Castle tavern. The leader of a Whig family, he was the eldest of four brothers all of whom had benefited greatly from the Revolution of 1688. Three of the four became MPs, Awnsham enjoying the patronage of the duke of Newcastle and the earl of Shaftesbury, and all four eventually gained country estates.[95] Awnsham himself had been closely associated with the political events leading to this success. He had supplied paper for the propagandists of the Monmouth rising back in 1685, and, exiled under James II, had helped to establish an important safe house for

92. Marginal note on Flamsteed's 1704 "Estimate," Royal Society. The added comment about stealing fixed stars confirms the story that Flamsteed complained of just this offense to a giggling Princess Caroline: Westfall, *Never at Rest*, 696; Leibniz, *Werke*, XI, 115.

93. Baily, *Flamsteed*, 74–6; RGO Ms. 1.36, fol. 132ʳ.

94. RS JB X, 97; Cudworth, *Sharp*, 87–9; Newton, *Correspondence*, IV, 437–8; Baily, *Flamsteed*, 219, 235; RGO Ms. 1.35, fol. 25ʳ; RGO Ms. 1.33, fol. 123ʳ⁻ᵛ.

95. Treadwell, "English Book Trade," 360–1. Family details are given in R. D., "Obituary: John Churchill"—a reference for which I am indebted to Jim Secord. Churchill's premises were later to become the home of Longman.

radicals such as John Locke in the premises of an Amsterdam bookseller.[96] Back in England in time to endorse William's accession, from then on Churchill maintained strong Continental links. Often working with his brother, John, he made a specialty of producing travel literature, and booksellers in the Netherlands even urged him to revive Moses Pitt's defunct atlas project. Churchill also became the main producer of Locke's works throughout the 1690s. The reputation of the *Essay Concerning Human Understanding* "receiv'd no small Advantage" by his association with it, reported Dunton. Dunton described Churchill as ranking second among London Stationers, after Richard Chiswell, with "an universal Wholesale Trade." He would "never starve an Undertaking to save Charges" and could be relied upon to honor subscription proposals. In all, Churchill was "well furnish'd for any GREAT UNDERTAKING."[97] His influence and his knowledge of the trade were both extensive and powerful. Locke recommended him as an expert on the practices of licensing and patents, to be consulted when the Licensing Act became due for renewal. And he was also a pioneer of new techniques for protecting the power of the Stationer, being one of the inventors of the conger system in the first decade of the eighteenth century, and perhaps the first of all to use the term "copyright."[98] Such concerns did not always support the author's interests, as remarked in chapter 2 with respect to his handling of Camden's *Britannia*. And although Locke himself might acquiesce in the printing of translations of his philosophical works, Collins told Desmaizeaux that "Mr Churchil would have no body to print any of Mr Lockes works but himself." Worse than that, even, he "would have them for nothing." Churchill thus personified the power of the bookseller: he was creditable, original, autonomous, and creative. Yet Collins's final assessment was damning: "I beleive he is not to be dealt with."[99]

The virtuosi had first dealt with this Janus-faced individual in the late 1680s. Since then he had undertaken work for both the Royal Society and the Dublin Philosophical Society, which used him as its London agent. He was known by these groups and the court Whigs (of whom Newton was a client) to be a reliable agent. Flamsteed, however, was far less approving. Churchill had not turned up to the tavern, and the specimens he had supplied seemed distinctly unimpressive. Flamsteed feared that he would swallow up the financial benefit of the publication, leaving him with nothing to

96. Ashcraft, *Revolutionary Politics*, 462–3, 486.

97. Bodl. Ms. Rawl. Letters 114, fols. 175^{r-v}, 180^r–190^r; Beddard, "Unexpected Whig Revolution," 27–8; Locke, *Correspondence*, IV, 615; Dunton, *Life and Errors* (1705), 280.

98. Hodgson and Blagden, *Notebook of Thomas Bennet and Henry Clements*, 81; Rose, *Authors and Owners*, 58 n.

99. Walters and Emery, "Edward Lhuyd, Edmund Gibson, and the Printing of Camden's *Britannia*"; Goldgar, *Impolite Learning*, 286 n. 55.

pay for assistants, and that without a dedicated astronomer overseeing the press in person unforgivable errors would be perpetrated. The men wielding power over his observations, he declared, either "know nothing of them, but how to bargain wth a bookseller," or else simply wanted the "honor" for themselves. Flamsteed foresaw himself being deprived of both profit and merit. Already he could only hope to get his charts printed by doing them himself.[100] He left the tavern determined to exert his own control.

Two days later Flamsteed had decided what to do. Without consulting Newton, he resolved to employ another printer to produce rival samples so as to discredit Churchill and prove his own competence to handle the management of the press. Yet even here his efforts were compromised by the workings of the trade. He had chosen to submit his work to John Barber, later to become the leading Tory printer in London. But "Mr. Barber is in league with Mr. Churchill," he discovered, "and acquainted with their management."[101] Such an alliance would surely stymie his plans, as Barber would not only omit to send specimens to Flamsteed, but make sure that Newton saw them first. "Mr. Churchill will convey them, and accompany him, and he shall be Mr. Churchill's servant."

Barber was not quite Churchill's creature, though, and he did eventually complete the specimens for Flamsteed. Nevertheless, Flamsteed had now realized some of the ways the trade could operate given the chance, and had decided to research further into its more obscure alliances. "I have got some further information concerning ye booksellers & Printer's Practices," he told Newton when delivering the trial sheets: "I find ye latter dare not disoblige ye former, & y^t ye Paper Stationers are so in wth y^m that I can't now learn ye Prices of Paper from y^m[:] wch before I had to do wth a Printer, was no difficulty." As suggested in chapter 2, booksellers could compel printers to frustrate a would-be author keen to circumvent their control. Churchill thus threatened to become a crucially authoritative figure. Flamsteed urged Newton not to enter into an agreement with him too readily, since it would be "a terrible Reflection on us, if we suffer a bookseller to devour that as his gaines, wch ye Prince design'd to employ for ye Honor of ye Nation & ye Queen." His suspicions were all but confirmed when Aston later revealed to him that Churchill had, after all, been at the Castle meeting. He had arrived after Flamsteed's departure, and during the subsequent discussions "all things, as he thought, were agreed but paper." Again it seemed that the bookseller—privy to agreements of which Flamsteed himself was un-

100. Hooke, "Diary," 145; RS JB IX, e.g., 5; Bodl. Ms. Smith 49, pp. 275–8.

101. Baily, *Flamsteed*, 219, 235–6, 237–8; RGO Ms. 1.33, fols. 123^v–124^r, 124^v, 126^v. For Barber and his attempts to appear politically neutral at this time, see Rivington, *"Tyrant,"* 9–10.

aware—had been raised above the astronomer. Henceforward printers and booksellers were constantly to be objects of his suspicion. "My Copy is my own," Flamsteed insisted; "I am ready to deliver it to the Press on just and reasonable conditions." But it was Newton and Churchill who were now to set those conditions.[102]

One of the most important aspects in which Churchill affected the conduct of the enterprise concerned the place where it would be pursued. Flamsteed had already tried unsuccessfully to secure the engraving work for Greenwich. Responding to Churchill's appointment as undertaker, he now urged that the printing too must take place there. He feared that in London the printing house could become a site for alteration of his work, by both printers and others with greater freedom of access than he would enjoy. Already he believed that errors had been inserted into his previous most important publication, the *Doctrine of the Sphere*, by "a spitefull p'son y^t got to the press," and the same must not be permitted to occur again.[103] But yet again Flamsteed was unsuccessful. It was not the printers who objected, but the bookseller. "The reason is plain," he told Hodgson. "At London they can print what copies they please more than they agree for, and they will be sure to sell all theirs off, before I can sell one of those the Prince allows me."[104] Printing at Greenwich would have prevented both this fraud—the manufacture of supernumerary copies, which Kirkman and others identified as the most routine form of piracy—and the high risk of textual corruption associated with unsupervised printing. Instead, Flamsteed would have to rely largely on Hodgson himself to monitor events.

After some two months, during which Flamsteed and his assistants copied figures and Newton went to Cambridge to be knighted, the referees, Flamsteed, and Churchill met again at Newton's home. They suggested that Churchill be paid at the rate of thirty-four shillings per sheet. Flamsteed initially refused to consent, but seems finally to have acquiesced in the hope that the press would finally be put to work. Newton soon brought Churchill and his printer, Bowyer, to Greenwich to view the papers. However, Flamsteed did not give up on his central concern for the propriety of the printing process. Two days after their meeting he again accosted Newton at Garraway's. He thrust on him a paper demanding that Churchill be granted no

102. Newton, *Correspondence*, IV, 441–2, 448; Baily, *Flamsteed*, 219, 220, 238–9; RGO Ms. 1.33, fols. 125^r, 126^v–127^r, 127^{r-v}; RGO Ms. 1.35, fol. 55^r. Flamsteed later learned that it had been Aston who had recommended Churchill, "who is such an one as will divide the gains with him, and leave me with nothing but the bare honor": Baily, *Flamsteed*, 247–8; RGO Ms. 1.33, fol. 129^{r-v}; Cudworth, *Sharp*, 86–7.

103. RGO Ms. 1.36, fol. 83^r; the reply is RGO Ms. 1.37, fol. 137^r; see also RGO Ms. 1.33, fols. 199^v–200^r, 136^v–137^v.

104. RGO Ms. 1.33, fol. 126^v; Baily, *Flamsteed*, 237–8.

"interest in the copy, nor any printed copies," and that he must give £1,000 bond not to print supernumerary copies or resort to inferior paper. Flamsteed also reiterated his demand for "recompense for 30 years' pains," which he believed the committee must provide for by ensuring such equitable conditions of publication. Despite Churchill's visit with Bowyer, Flamsteed also continued to send Newton samples of paper, along with warnings of the inferior imitations a commercial undertaker might substitute. He remained acutely concerned, too, that no more than four hundred copies be produced, and that Churchill not be allowed to sell any at all himself. This was not to be run as a primarily commercial affair: all the copies must be handed over to the prince for distribution, and only after the dispersal of copies to courtly recipients might some be sold. The income from those that *were* sold must then accrue to Flamsteed himself, in recognition of his labors. For Churchill to print supernumerary sheets would thus represent a serious violation of his "copy." Its economic significance would be matched by its figurative.[105] So Flamsteed again pressed that Churchill be forced to enter into a substantial bond—now of around £2,000—for adherence to the articles. Above all, he still wanted the presses physically removed to Greenwich to be under his constant supervision.

These demands resting unmet, work still could not commence. Something of an impasse now developed. The problem arose because no clear distinction could be agreed upon between technical, astronomical labor and that of producing a printed book. Newton was unwilling to draw on the prince's funds unless and until it was for the printing itself, but Flamsteed needed money to do his calculating and for the preparation of tables. His calculational work required the employment of several assistants. These must be sited not only at Greenwich but in geographically separate areas, so as to minimize the possibility either of collusion or of errors being repeated because of shared techniques. The very mathematical procedures of these calculators now came to be intimately linked to concerns over publishing. Typically, Flamsteed told Sharp not to reveal his calculations to anyone, "since both the observations and numbers are mine." To keep his figures secret, Flamsteed did not divulge the date to which they had all been calcu-

---

105. Newton, *Correspondence*, IV, 446; RGO Ms. 1.33, fol. 128^r; RGO Ms. 1.35, fols. 28^r, 30^r; Baily, *Flamsteed*, 220, 239, 241, 242, 246. "Bowyer" was probably William Bowyer the elder, born in 1663 and apprenticed to Miles Flesher Jr. Bowyer's printing house in Whitefriars burned to the ground in a calamitous fire in early 1713, but he recovered to become one of the best printers in London. Records from this later printing house survive, and are available on microfiche: see Maslen and Lancaster, *Bowyer Ledgers*. But the main ledgers begin only in 1710 and do not contain references to Flamsteed's book. The 1712 volume was in fact printed by John Matthews. Perhaps Bowyer had been disqualified for not matching up to Flamsteed and Barber's specimens.

lated. Luke Leigh was one of very few workers lucky enough to be told that they were all reduced to the beginning of 1690—"but this I desire you to keep to y^r self," Flamsteed cautioned, "for my serv^{ts} scarce know it & I purposly conceal it y^t if any one has a mind to steal it they may not know to what time they are done." Not only Flamsteed's negotiations with Stationers, then, but the practical and arithmetical details of his astronomical calculations, were premised on his anxiety to carve out and protect his authorship. But with funds exhausted, Flamsteed risked having to forgo such procedures. For a year he fruitlessly pressed Newton to draw money from the prince's account to pay for workers to calculate his tables. Finally he had to dismiss his amanuensis and calculators.[106] Meanwhile no printing was done.

Flamsteed blamed Newton for the deadlock; but more than that he blamed Halley. Appealing to Wren—"perhaps the only honest person I have to deal with"—he repeated his belief that it must be Halley's "false suggestions" that were responsible for Newton's un-Christian behavior.[107] Moreover, the royal astronomer now assigned Halley a sinister new identity. Flamsteed had always identified Tycho Brahe as the model for his own role. It is no exaggeration to say that his whole career was intended to emulate Tycho's. Early on, the Royal Observatory had commissioned a series of engravings of its site, buildings, and apparatus, in imitation of Tycho's *Astronomiae Instauratae Mechanica*; now, Flamsteed planned a *Historia Cœlestis Britannica* modeled on his hero's *Historia Cœlestis Danica*.[108] Indeed, he proposed to incorporate an edition of Tycho's work into his *Historia*, and wrote to Copenhagen to find his portrait and manuscripts.[109] But the identification ran deeper still. Flamsteed came to represent his own cultural identity

106. Baily, *Flamsteed*, 242–3, 261; Newton, *Correspondence*, IV, 476–8; RGO Ms. 1.33, fols. 101^r–102^r, 131^r.

107. Baily, *Flamsteed*, 244–6; RGO Ms. 1.35, no. 70; Ward, *Lives of the Professors of Gresham College*, 247–53. Already remarked above, p. 526 note 169, the role of Wren as a widely recognized umpire is again notable here. Flamsteed had also referred his paper on Cassini to Wren's judgment in 1702.

108. Actually a work based on corrupted copies of Tycho's manuscripts, by "Lucius Barrettus": Curtius, *Historia Cœlestis Danica* (itself named after Longomontanus's *Astronomia Danica*); see Dreyer, *Tycho Brahe*, 371–4. For Flamsteed's view of this work, see RGO Ms. 1.36, fol. 77^v; Newton, *Correspondence*, IV, 449–51; Forbes, "Library of the Rev. John Flamsteed," 124. In the draft preface to his own *Historia* Flamsteed accused Curtz of having changed Tycho's data, and labeled him a "fraud": Flamsteed, *Preface*, 99–100. The engravings of the observatory are reproduced in Howse, *Francis Place*. Only one eventually appeared in the *Historia Cœlestis*.

109. Newton, *Correspondence*, IV, 475–8, 480–4; Baily, *Flamsteed*, 261; RGO Ms. 1.33, fol. 131^r; CUL Ms. Add. 4006, nos. 3, 6; RS JB X, 147–8. In 1666 the Society had heard that Tycho's library was in Vienna in the imperial library: Birch, *History*, II, 87. This was presumably the corrupted archive previously used by Curtz.

not just as modeled on Tycho's, but as its virtual duplicate. For example, Tycho's providential patronage by the king of Denmark paralleled Flamsteed's own by the prince of Denmark. In 1703 he summarized the case thus, to a captain who had promised him an old portrait of Tycho: "I was born 100 years after him, The English Observatory was built 100 years after his, my father was averse to my Studying Mathematicks as his was[, and like Tycho] I was Designing to settel in another place when ye providence of God fixed me here." Admittedly, these "parallels" could not precisely be maintained, since by now Flamsteed had lived two years longer than Tycho, and, despite its earlier debilitating recurrences, he had not suffered from the stone—"his mortall Destemper if I mistake not"—for eight years. However, Tycho's fate nevertheless revealed grim prospects if he were ever to yield to his critics. Through "ye envy of some Disingenuous Spitfull p'sons & ye designes of avaritious favorites," he had been forced to leave Uraniborg before finishing his labors. His manuscripts had consequently languished unprinted until the 1660s, when they had been published in mutilated form by an unskilled Jesuit.[110]

Tycho's persecutors, like Flamsteed's, "had not Knowledge enough to understand how Usefull his Labors & expenses whold be." They "could not then apprehend how far reall Knowledge would be advanced by them nor of what use they would be to o^r Navigators in ye next Age." The chief "detractor" had been the imperial mathematician at Prague, Nicolai Reymers Baer, otherwise known as Ursus.[111] Henceforth, then, Halley was to be "Raymer"—the reincarnation of this insolent adversary. Ursus, Flamsteed explained, had "made it his business to depreciate Tycho Brahe, after he had been courteously entertained by him, and assured him of his inviolable friendship." Halley recapitulated the incivility. Henceforth, Flamsteed's perception of the entire conflict was informed by this identification. Yet it remained a secret. Abraham Sharp was perhaps the only correspondent to whom it was revealed, when Flamsteed complained to him of "Raymer's" attempts at subverting the registration and publication rules of the Royal

---

110. RGO Ms. 1.33, fol. 119^{r-v}; also Ms. 1.36, fol. 68^{r-v}. Before Flamsteed, Gassendi had noted how various astronomical factions had "corruptly" printed supposedly Tychonic figures, making it all but impossible to determine Tycho's true textual legacy, and Joseph Moxon, while praising the press, agreed with this: Moxon, *Tutor to Astronomy & Geography* (4th ed.), 233–71, esp. 266–71.

111. Jardine, *Birth of History and Philosophy of Science*; Gingerich and Westman, *Wittich Connection*; Rosen, *Three Imperial Mathematicians*; Thoren, *Lord of Uraniborg*, 432 ff. Flamsteed's concern for the placing and management of "calculators" also derived in part from Tycho's "computers," who, he believed, "spoyled all by Frequent miscalculating": RS Ms. Fl. 1, no. 27. The identification extended to the structure of the *Historia Cœlestis* itself. For example, Flamsteed modeled his idea for a prolegomenon of early observations—opposed vehemently by Newton—on Curtz's edition of Tycho: Newton, *Correspondence*, IV, 450, 476–8.

Society.[112] In private, however, Flamsteed's opinions were explicit and adamant. If history were to be prevented from repeating itself further, and if his observations were to be spared the fate of decay, neglect, and corruption that had befallen Tycho's, then "Raymer" must be defeated.

Against this unknown determination, Newton continued to press Flamsteed to deliver copy. Flamsteed delayed, bemoaning his subordination to the bookseller and the lack of money to fund his involved calculational régime. In October, as the first sheet of observations finally approached readiness for the press, he presented to the referees at Wren's lodgings another paper of suggested articles for restricting Churchill. Newton again disapproved. He was no more enthusiastic about an alternative Flamsteed delivered ten days later.[113] Finally, though, at two meetings in November 1705 an agreement between Flamsteed, the referees, and Churchill was drawn up, debated, and at length signed.[114] This treaty set the terms for the remainder of the enterprise.

At the first of these meetings, Flamsteed had stood by his central concern for his "Right title Interest or property" in the work and reiterated his demand that Churchill be required to give £2,000 bond to honor his word. Were this conceded, he promised that he would immediately deliver the first volume in a fit state to be printed. But the latter demand, at least, was ignored. Churchill was not required to provide any security and was allowed the thirty-four shillings per sheet previously agreed. He would receive £250 after two months of printing (one early draft had proposed £300), and the remainder on completion.[115] In return, provided that Flamsteed provide copy regularly and not delay the proofreading, he must ensure that twenty sheets a month were produced, less a sheet for every holiday. Flamsteed, on the other hand, would be paid only £250 in total, to cover assistants for correction. Half would be forthcoming as soon as the manuscript of the first volume was handed over, the rest when the second had been printed.

112. Baily, *Flamsteed*, 244, 751. See also 246–7 for a partial retraction. Newton, *Correspondence*, V, 210 n. 4. He was still referring to the issue years later: RGO Ms. 1.33, fols. 211ᵛ–212ʳ. Sharp showed at least some of Flamsteed's letters to Ralph Thoresby, reckoned to be on Halley's side: Hunter, *Diary of Ralph Thoresby*, I, 436. Newton and Arbuthnot concealed from Flamsteed the fact that they consulted Halley over getting Tycho's manuscripts for the *Historia Cœlestis*: Newton, *Correspondence*, IV, 475.

113. Newton, *Correspondence*, IV, 447–8 and n. 2; Baily, *Flamsteed*, 221, 246, 247, 250–1; RGO Ms. 1.33, fol. 125ʳ; RGO Ms. 1.35, fol. 27ʳ; Cudworth, *Sharp*, 48–9. Flamsteed asked Newton for approval of his suggested titles on 25 October: Newton, *Correspondence*, IV, 449–51 (there is a draft in RGO Ms. 1.36, fols. 77ʳ–78ʳ, with different suggestions, and another—perhaps the first—in CUL Ms. Add. 4006, 12–13).

114. Flamsteed's draft for this agreement is printed in Newton, *Correspondence*, IV, 452–3, and the articles themselves are at 454–60. Another draft is in Baily, *Flamsteed*, 253–4. See also RGO Ms. 1.35, fols. 34ʳ⁻ᵛ, 36ʳ⁻ᵛ, 39ʳ; CUL Ms. Add. 4006, nos. 8, 10; Baily, *Flamsteed*, 81.

115. Newton, *Correspondence*, IV, 452–3, 538; CUL Ms. Add. 4006, no. 8. Churchill was paid his £250 on 17 April.

Nonetheless, Flamsteed did gain certain rights over the "undertaker," in exchange for which he undertook to deliver fair copies to the referees as quickly as possible. He could correct the sheets, provided he did so reliably and quickly. He could enter the printing house and "stand by the Press" in order to prevent supernumerary copies; to make certain, he could break the forme after four hundred impressions of any sheet had been printed. Flamsteed could also employ his own engraver. Churchill and his printers had to swear not to produce more than four hundred copies, and not to deviate from the paper and typography of the approved specimens. They also had to agree never to claim any right to the property of the work, which would remain Flamsteed's. One each of the last two copies made of every sheet would go to Flamsteed and the referees for checking and collation, with any subsequent reprinting to be done at Churchill's expense. Flamsteed would be given all the sheets as they were printed and would then retain them until the whole text had been worked off. He would then present the whole to the prince. Last, and significantly, the articles gave the referees the right to demand Flamsteed's original manuscripts in order to "collate" the printed sheets with the original observations.

The book would be produced in two parts. The first, against Flamsteed's stiff opposition, would contain the catalogue of fixed stars. It would also include observations taken at Derby and Greenwich up to the advent of the second mural arc in 1689, along with general preface material. Flamsteed undertook to deliver as soon as possible a correct copy of the catalogue, containing the longitudes, latitudes, right ascensions, declinations, magnitudes, and motions of some three thousand stars, together with schemes of the layout of the printed page and figures of the eclipses and observations to be engraved. The second volume would then comprise the observations taken by the mural arc from 1689 until the printing of the book itself, with the places of planets and comets calculated from them. Needless to say, to Flamsteed this order represented a betrayal. His star catalogue still lacked observations, and moreover must not appear first. Were it to do so the book would misrepresent the observational enterprise and, in placing results before evidence, reproduce in print the techniques of a philosopher rather than those of an honest astronomer. In addition, the order ignored half of the material that Flamsteed wanted to publish. This was no longer the work that Flamsteed had projected.

Once more, however, Flamsteed had to acquiesce.[116] In early December he delivered to Newton the first hundred manuscript sheets to be printed, containing the Greenwich observations of 1676–89. Seventy manuscript

---

116. "Sir Isaac Newton has, at last, forced me to enter into Articles for printing my works with a bookseller, very disadvantageous to myself," he told Sharp: Baily, *Flamsteed*, 256.

sheets for the second volume were almost ready too. But Churchill was slow in agreeing his own terms with a printer, and it was mid-February before Flamsteed could express the hope of seeing some printed sheets. Meanwhile Newton insisted that Flamsteed also deliver to him his original books of notes—those used to record figures during nighttime vigils, from which fair copies would be transcribed during the day. He wished them "collated" with these observations. Flamsteed sent the first of the notebooks, only to find himself summoned to attend Newton in person. He took the faithful Hodgson along as a witness. Gregory, it transpired, had "collected" some five folio pages of "differences" between the originals and the copies, which he and Newton construed as "errors." Newton now demanded "that himselfe & the Dr might be informed of my ways of observeing" in order to diagnose these "errors," declaring that they were the "proper judges" of such things. But far from revealing negligence on his own part, Flamsteed retorted, the apparent errors were "all of yᵉ Drs Makeing." Gregory had assumed the distances between successive threads on the alignment screws in Flamsteed's instruments to be regular, thus revealing once more his ignorance of practical astronomical instruments. Flamsteed painstakingly erased the "emendations," expressing his "wonder" that Gregory should have presumed to make such an assumption. He then retreated, fearing only that Newton would find new ways to stymie his work since "he finds I doe not court him." The incident confirmed once more Flamsteed's opinion of Newton, not least because it took him two months to dispose completely of Gregory's contributions. Procedures of "correction" thus manifested the interdependence of observation and calculation, and the centrality of civility to both.[117]

Himself frustrated at the lack of progress, Newton now demanded that Flamsteed provide him with a token to demonstrate his continuing good faith. He asked the astronomer to deposit with him a copy of as much of the full star catalogue as had yet been completed, to serve as testimony to his intent to deliver the remainder later. Flamsteed responded by giving Wren an incomplete copy of the catalogue for onward delivery. But he again insisted on adopting a variant of the protective measures developed at the Royal Society over the preceding decades. Wren was to pass the catalogue to Hodgson, who would seal it up. Hodgson would then deliver the sealed package to Newton only once ten sheets of the observations had been

117. Newton, *Correspondence*, IV, 461–3, 467–9, 473–4; Baily, *Flamsteed*, 257–9; RGO Ms. 1.33, fol. 130ᵛ. Flamsteed delivered a further two notebooks to Newton immediately after this, on 28 February. For the limb-screw mechanism misinterpreted by Gregory, see Flamsteed, *Preface*, 120–2, 165. A decade and a half earlier, when Flamsteed came across sheets of Molyneux's *Dioptrica* being printed and saw insufficient acknowledgment of Gascoigne in Molyneux's text, he had protested to the writer, but had also remarked that the misdemeanor might be attributable to the "Corrector"—who was Halley: RGO Ms. 1.42, fols. 66ʳ–67ᵛ.

printed, and when the £125 had been paid to Flamsteed for his calculators. Newton was then to keep it sealed and confidential. Newton "seemed ne-tled" when he heard of this convoluted procedure; but he suffered it. On 15 March Flamsteed thus instructed Hodgson to hand over the packet to Newton. But still Newton maintained that the prince could not release the full sum he required and that priority must in any case be given to Churchill. Flamsteed protested that he had supplied the catalogue as agreed, but unavailingly. Newton replied "sleightingly" that it was "imperfect," and re-fused even to return Flamsteed's notebooks, which the astronomer would need if he were to correct printed sheets. The subsequent fate of this sealed package—the "pledge," as Flamsteed called it—was to become for Flam-steed perhaps the most scandalous aspect of the whole conflict.[118]

Printing began very slowly, under the everyday oversight of Hodgson as Flamsteed's London deputy. The first sheet was not finished until 16 May 1706. Flamsteed was not slow to attribute blame. "This was one of the fruits of our having an undertaker," he believed, "and leaving the printer to be paid by him." Concerned primarily for the working life of the printing house, they printed concurrently, and thus "neglected the *Historia Cœlestis* if they had but a sorry pamphlet to print." Newton himself encouraged their sloppiness—in the hearing of the more slovenly workmen, he was given to peering at printing errors nearsightedly and declaring, "Methinks they are well enough."[119] After a week of this, Flamsteed wrote directly to Churchill objecting to the sluggishness of the workers at Matthews's printing house. And the next day he went there in person and exercised his right to enter. There he directed the spacing of the tables and the use of italics for notes. After such a display of determination, the press finally began to work rather faster. Sheets B and C were done by 7 June, and by the end of the month he was correcting sheet K. But now other aspects of the agreement started to be likewise neglected. As early as the second sheet, he found that the impression was not being sent to him as the articles had directed. Again he wrote to Churchill to protest. His suspicions raised, he received another shock when Newton suddenly suggested printing an extra 100 to 150 copies. Flamsteed refused indignantly. Convinced that he now knew the reason he had not been sent the printed sheets, he "suggested that it was probable Mr C had caused more to be printed y^n he ought by 200." The prospect of supernumerary copies—the simplest form of piracy—loomed. Newton re-treated from his proposal, however, reiterating his promise that only Flam-steed would be given any copies to sell.

118. Newton, *Correspondence*, IV, 468–9; RGO Ms. 1.33, fol. 151^r.
119. Baily, *Flamsteed*, 83; Newton, *Correspondence*, IV, 464, 469, 525. Compare Williams, "Edition of the Correspondence of John Aubrey," 620, on Churchill's slowness.

Newton also repeated his pledge that Flamsteed would soon be paid. But this too proved problematic. By the time of his annual visit to his parish at Burstow in summer 1706, Flamsteed had been forced to lay off his assistants for want of funds. He again demanded his £125. Not until the end of November did the referees finally request the prince to disburse this money—and even then the sum to be given to Flamsteed proved to be only £50. As his ability to produce copy and correct proofs decayed, so the printing slowed still more. At length, Newton called another meeting with Churchill in Paternoster Row.[120] They resolved that Newton and Gregory would visit Greenwich to view the manuscripts for the catalogue and volume two. They arrived on 15 April.

At Greenwich, Flamsteed found himself presented with an ultimatum. Newton and Gregory proffered him a paper to sign, promising delivery by 1 June of the observations to be printed in the second volume, covering the period 1689–1705. This amounted to 174 sheets. He must also deliver a copy of his most correct star catalogue in order to complete the one given to Newton a year earlier in the sealed package, or else agree to perfect the sealed catalogue himself. This would complete his contributions as required by the publishing agreement, and the referees would then inspect the result. Only when these conditions had been met would Flamsteed be paid, and even then costs would be deducted if work had to be done to bring the papers to a fit state for publication. Meanwhile, Newton threatened to prevent the printing of any material more than was already in hand. Flamsteed declined to sign, and they parted on bad terms. But he promised "on the word of an honest man" that he would make haste, implying that the observations should be delivered by June and the catalogue by November.[121]

By this time about seventy sheets had been printed. Hodgson continued to oversee the printing, leaving Flamsteed in an increasingly dilapidated Greenwich to pursue his observing and calculations. At length the end came into sight. In October 1707, Flamsteed was able to start correcting the final sheets of the first volume of observations. By the end of the year, its 97 sheets had all been printed.[122] He found that a whole sheet had been omitted, and wanted to add some six more of additional data—to no avail, since Newton refused to persuade the printer to do this work—but nonetheless, the section finally existed. However, Newton's threat to delay further progress until Flamsteed delivered his remaining data was now triggered. The press came to a stop. Blame was attributed variously. Newton pointed to Flamsteed's

120. Newton, *Correspondence*, IV, 469–71, 476–8, 480, 484; Baily, *Flamsteed*, 224–5, 261, 263–4; RGO Ms. 1.33, fols. 210ᵛ–211ʳ, 131ʳ; RGO Ms. 1.35, fol. 40ʳ.

121. Baily, *Flamsteed*, 226; RGO Ms. 1.33, fol. 142ʳ⁻ᵛ; Newton, *Correspondence*, IV, 471, 487–8.

122. Baily, *Flamsteed*, 83, 264, 265; Nicolson, *London Diaries*, 409–10.

lack of "dispatch." Tancred Robinson heard that Flamsteed was charging Newton with obstructing progress because his observations contradicted the *Principia*—and it is quite plausible that he was indeed making this charge. In private, however, Flamsteed himself intimated that the halt might even be for the best, "till God remove the envious, and send us more sincere and honest persons to deal with, and manage it." Awnsham Churchill had his own view: in Flamsteed, he told Molyneux, the bookseller was dealing with "a very particular man." [123]

On 20 March 1707/8, after three months of this stalemate, there was yet another meeting at the Castle.[124] Flamsteed arrived clutching the 175 sheets of observations for the second volume, along with a corrected copy of part of the star catalogue, comprising the constellations on the ecliptic. By now he was more convinced than ever that Churchill was "useless to the business"—and, moreover, that he and his printer had broken every one of the original conditions. He believed that the meeting had been called as a result of this and to address his own lack of reimbursement. But this was not in fact its purpose. Instead Newton presented a paper for Flamsteed to sign. This paper guaranteed delivery of the second volume of observations and the completion of the sealed catalogue of fixed stars by the insertion of magnitudes within sixteen days. He must also agree to appoint a proofreader, not in Greenwich, but in London itself—a condition insisted upon by Churchill. In return for these, Newton would pay him the promised £125, and printing could proceed. Flamsteed was despondent. He found these conditions "very hard and unjust." After all, he had already shown Newton an account for expenses some £48 more than Newton was now offering to pay him.[125] But faced with the alternative of indefinite inactivity, he agreed. Taking the sealed package, he handed over the papers he had brought along, on condition that the second volume be returned to him to be revised and delivered to the printers as they proceeded, and that the ecliptic constellations be restored to him as soon as he had returned the sealed catalogue with the magnitudes inserted. Two months later he was finally paid the £125.[126]

123. Bodl. Ms. Lister 3, fol. 128ʳ; Baily, *Flamsteed*, 266–7; Cudworth, *Sharp*, 93–4; Newton, *Correspondence*, IV, 525; Southampton CRO, Ms. D/M 1/1, p. 48.

124. Baily, *Flamsteed*, 84–5. It seems likely that Flamsteed had been complaining to Arbuthnot, who was the prince's personal physician.

125. Newton, *Correspondence*, IV, 513–4, 525–8; CUL Ms. Add. 4006, 20–1; RGO Ms. 1.35, fols. 85ʳ–88ᵛ; RGO Ms. 1.33, fols. 131ᵛ–132ʳ; RGO Ms. 1.35, fol. 43ʳ⁻ᵛ; Baily, *Flamsteed*, 85–6. The "memorandum" printed in Newton, *Correspondence*, as part of item 5 is in the original clearly separate, and the last line is a later addition, referring to RGO Ms. 1.33, fol. 128ᵛ (the accounts in Baily, *Flamsteed*, 220–2).

126. He immediately paid the full sum to Hodgson. The two-month delay is according to Flamsteed's testimony (Baily, *Flamsteed*, 86 and elsewhere); but Hodgson received the money for Flamsteed from Newton on 12 April, some three weeks after the meeting at the Castle: Newton, *Correspondence*, IV, 514, 515.

The attempt to impose a London corrector on Flamsteed went against one of his most important concerns. He believed that without personal supervision, or at least that of a deputy such as Hodgson, his tables could not but be corrupted in the press, and his experience of Gregory's "correction" had only confirmed his view that astronomical truth could not survive such oversight. For a while it seemed he had evaded the possibility. But in July 1708 he sustained a new blow. Meeting without his knowledge, the referees issued a direct threat that if he did not "go on wth dispatch," they would take correction out of his hands altogether. Sent word of this "malicious" threat, Flamsteed immediately appealed to Wren—the only referee who he conceived might be sympathetic.[127] Recounting his continued willingness to facilitate the printing process, Flamsteed reminded Wren of the letters he had written to Churchill and the printers complaining of their slowness. Even at their best, he charged, they had never managed to produce sheets at anything like the covenanted rate, and when they had worked quickly the quality had deteriorated intolerably. He denied outright Churchill's charge that the delays had been caused by his not returning corrected sheets quickly enough: "if the post brought them in the Evening, I returned them next Morning, if in the Morning, they were sent back that evening after, without fayle." Flamsteed attributed the delays squarely to Newton. He reminded Wren that the omitted sheet and the six new sheets for the first volume, and 175 sheets for the second, could all be printed while he completed the all-important catalogue. Newton, however, wanted to print the catalogue *before* the second volume of observations. It was this insistence that he regarded as causing the stalemate. Flamsteed balked at it for the principled reason already outlined. It would be "altogether improper to print it before the Observations of the 2d Volume," he maintained, "because t'is almost wholly derived from them." The same fundamental cause—the identity and integrity of his enterprise—led Flamsteed to resist the removing of correction from his control.

Then, on 28 October 1708, Prince George died after a long and painful illness. With him, according to most historians, departed the authority of the referees.[128] In practice, however, they continued to disburse money to John Machin, another of Newton's circle who had been employed by him to examine Flamsteed's figures, and they proceeded to order illustrations engraved for the book.[129] Newton considered the delays to be partly the fault

127. Newton, *Correspondence*, IV, 524–8; Baily, *Flamsteed*, 87–9; RGO Ms. 1.35, fols. 44^r, 45^r–46^r. In the draft Flamsteed asks that the press be stopped while he is away at Burstow and "cannot possably look after it."

128. This assumption seems to derive from Baily, *Flamsteed*, 89–90.

129. Newton, *Correspondence*, IV, 538–9; CUL Ms. Add. 4006, 23–4; Baily, *Flamsteed*, 269, 275. Machin was paid £30 for checking Flamsteed's calculations. In 1713 Newton made

of the Ordnance Office, originator of the Greenwich Observatory and now once again its main patron.[130] Presumably he expected the ordnance to pay for the everyday running of the observatory, and reckoned this to include the provision of assistants to calculate tables. The prince's disbursement, on the other hand, was strictly to be reserved for printing and correction costs. The master of the ordnance, the duke of Marlborough, was currently campaigning on the Continent, so a settlement would have to wait. Only with a peace could something be done to provide the needed resources. Moreover, Newton also faced time-consuming troubles at the Royal Society. Flamsteed himself had not paid his dues, and, his fellowship having consequently lapsed, he had done nothing to renew it. But with the disputes surrounding the antagonism between Sloane and Woodward and the move to Crane Court now becoming painfully obvious, he felt no qualms about inferring that Newton was to blame. His politicking was destroying the Society. Sloane's *Transactions*, Flamsteed remarked, had not been published for four months, and had been "twice burlesqt publickly."[131] It was in these circumstances, just days after the most acrimonious of the Society's meetings, that Newton composed a financial account of the publication (see table opposite). The total expended came to less than half of Flamsteed's original estimate.[132]

The fall of the Whig ministry in 1710 brought a further dramatic change. The new Tory administration suddenly gave the Royal Society the power to appoint "Visitors" to the Royal Observatory.[133] They were to demand "a true and fair Copy" of all the observations made by the astronomer royal every year, which must be delivered in less than six months; they could also "Order and Direct" him to make whatever observations they deemed appropriate. In addition, the visitors were to buy from Flamsteed any instruments not already owned by the state, and then to inspect the observatory periodically and direct the Ordnance Office to carry out any necessary maintenance. This was a decisive stroke. The formerly independent observatory at

---

Machin's role in the edition a key part of his recommendation that Machin be appointed to a Gresham professorship: Newton, *Correspondence*, V, 408.

130. Newton, *Correspondence*, V, 8–9; Baily, *Flamsteed*, 270–2.

131. Hunter, *Royal Society and its Fellows*, 195; Newton, *Correspondence*, V, 8–9. Westfall, *Never at Rest*, 667, suggests that Newton effectively had Flamsteed expelled from the Society. This is quite possible. For the importance of ridicule against the *Transactions* compare also the anonymous report to Newton, in Newton, *Correspondence*, V, 17: "Twill not easily be imagin'd how greatly the Reputation of the Society, without doors, suffers upon that Account."

132. Clark Ms. N563Z.1710.Apr.8.

133. RS JB X, 252–3; RS Ms. Dom. 5, no. 46; Baily, *Flamsteed* 91; RGO Ms. 1.33, fol. 133ᵛ; Newton, *Correspondence*, V, 79–81.

	li	s	d
Charge			
Received of the Treasurer of his Royall Highness	375	oo.	oo.
Discharge			
Paid to Awnsham Churchill Bookseller for printing 98 sheets at 1^{li} 14^{s} per sheet	166	12	oo
Paid to Mr John Flamsteed 26 March 1708 in part for his charge & trouble in preparing papers for the first & second volume of his Observations & correcting the Press	125	oo	oo
Paid to Mr Machin for examining Mr Flamsteeds copy by his minute-books & also for repeating & correcting his calculations	30	oo	oo
Paid to Mr Churchill for his extraordinary charge in printing marginal notes in 60 of the above 98 sheets	6	oo	oo
Paid Mr Churchill for his charge in altering two of sheets of specimens of the worke in the beginning	2	o5	oo
Paid Mr Churchill for his loss in providing certain sorts of stamps & rules for the whole work, wch will be of no further use to him	20	oo	oo
Ballance due to his R. Highness the Princes Administrators	25	o3	oo
	375	oo	oo

once became an adjunct of the Royal Society—and hence of the man whom at least one fellow wanted to see made its "Perpetual Dictator": its president, Sir Isaac Newton. Flamsteed, horrified, called it "an accident that threatens not only to stop all his endeavours but even ruin the observatory itself." In vain he rushed to Secretary of State Henry St. John, who had issued the warrant to Newton, and protested. That having failed, he then petitioned the queen herself. Again his words went unheeded. Once more he was reduced to the fate of Tycho Brahe, who, when visitors had been appointed to oversee him, had found them "very unfit" and had abandoned his observatory altogether as a result.[134]

His attempt to appropriate its findings having stalled, Newton had succeeded in appropriating the Royal Observatory itself. And it was not long before Flamsteed began to hear rumors that his book was in danger again too. His works were once more being printed. The Royal Society had interpreted its new authority as extending to the *Historia Cœlestis*, and restarted

134. Baily, *Flamsteed*, 68, 92–3, 278–9; Newton, *Correspondence*, V, 91–2; VI, 43; Manuel, *Portrait of Isaac Newton*, 265; Westfall, *Never at Rest*, 679. Flamsteed also saw Lords Rochester and (probably) Pembroke, plus two other officials: RGO Ms. 1.33, fols. 133^v–134^r, 140^v.

the press.[135] Newton himself still held the imperfect catalogue delivered to him sealed years before, and this was to form the basis for the text. But Newton himself was now set on a second edition of the *Principia*, and was pursuing his own fraught publishing enterprise with the aid of Roger Cotes. So the project, along with the sealed pages, had been delegated to John Arbuthnot and—to Flamsteed's horror—Edmond Halley.

The Society spent three weeks agonizing over the delicate question of how to ask Flamsteed to supply the missing data. Eventually it was Arbuthnot who wrote, declaring that the queen herself had commanded that publication proceed and demanding fully updated copies of his tables.[136] Flamsteed received this message on the morning of 19 March. He spent a few days drafting notes of his work to show Arbuthnot and having quiet inquiries made in London. Then he asked to meet him at Greenwich. Flamsteed wanted to discuss what he still hoped would be his grand project. He envisaged incorporating the full catalogue, which he had substantially completed while the press had remained inactive, and new planetary tables, for which he would need further calculating assistance. Hearing of this "indirect & delatory" response, Newton brushed Arbuthnot aside peremptorily. He himself at least drafted, and quite likely sent, a vitriolic letter demanding that the data be surrendered forthwith. He pointedly reminded Flamsteed that the referees' task had been "only to print what they judged proper for the Princes honour" in making this "book of observations," and that Flamsteed had undertaken to cooperate in their decisions. This being so, he refused to consider printing anything beyond the specific catalogue and observations seen by the referees before Prince George's death, whatever Flamsteed's complaints about missed sheets or new material. Should Flamsteed hesitate any longer before sending the completion of the star catalogue, or at least sufficient raw observations such that its completion could be undertaken by others, he would be construed to be disobeying a royal command. The most that even the relatively conciliatory Arbuthnot could offer was to suggest that the new material might appear as an "Appendix," confirming that his own commission was simply to complete the referees' work.[137] At present he too wanted only the material lacking from the cata-

135. Both Arbuthnot and the Society implied that a direct command from the crown had been received to resume publication, but no such order has ever been found.

136. RS JB X, 260–3; Newton, *Correspondence*, V, 99–100; Baily, *Flamsteed*, 280; RGO Ms. 1.35, fol. 47^{r-v}; RGO Ms. 1.33, fol. 140^v (a copy, with Flamsteed's comment on the Society's hesitation).

137. Newton, *Correspondence*, V, 100–2, 105; Baily, *Flamsteed*, 280, 281; RGO Ms. 1.35, fol. 51^{r-v}; RGO Ms. 1.33, fol. 141^v (a copy); RGO Ms. 1.33, fol. 141^r. Westfall affirms that Newton's letter was indeed sent: *Never at Rest*, 689–90. Arbuthnot was busily learning of the peculiarities of academic civility at this time, which he later mocked in the figure of Martinus

logue delivered years before. Diplomacy aside, such a position did not differ materially from Newton's. Indeed, Arbuthnot's suggestion was effectively no better than that made by Newton twenty years earlier.

Flamsteed did meet Arbuthnot, at Garraway's coffeehouse on 29 March 1711.[138] He demanded that Newton return one of the two incomplete manuscript copies of the catalogue that had earlier been delivered to him, so that he could complete it. To reinforce his claim to have been poorly treated, Flamsteed also handed Arbuthnot copies of both the 1704 "Estimate" and his letter to Wren written after Newton had threatened to remove correction from his control. Most imperatively, he demanded to know if any more printing had yet been done.[139] Arbuthnot assured him it had not, and tried to soothe his anger as best he could. He refused to allow Flamsteed the correction of sheets, however, offering him £10 for every erroneous deviation from his manuscript in the printed text. A week later Flamsteed received part of the incomplete catalogue (the one Newton took him to mean was that incorporating the ecliptic constellations only, handed over along with the second volume of observations on 20 March 1707/8). Newton claimed that most had "long since" been given to Hodgson for forwarding to Flamsteed.[140]

Whatever Arbuthnot's reassurances, by the time he spoke the secret was out. A "friend," perhaps in the printing house itself, had passed on to Flamsteed two printed sheets. They were sheets 1 and 3 of his star catalogue. They proved beyond all doubt that his catalogue was indeed in the press. And Flamsteed was horrified by what he saw when he examined these sheets. Halley had been unleashed on the catalogue of fixed stars; Newton estimated that by calculating their places from Flamsteed's observational notes, he had added some five hundred stars to the hitherto sealed copy.[141] In these two pieces of paper alone, Flamsteed counted more than eighty changes from his manuscript. Moreover, Halley had not just added stars. He had also drastically altered the constellations' nomenclature, so that ancient observations no longer matched modern. All great astronomers had followed Ptolemy's names, Flamsteed complained: Ulugh Beg, Copernicus, Clavius,

---

Scriblerus. "All that relates to the sciences" came from him, Swift affirmed: Pope et al., *Memoirs of . . . Martinus Scriblerus*, 57. The last recorded meeting of the Scriblerus group took place on 12 June 1714: Sherburn, *Early Career*, 77.

138. Hodgson was also present. Newton, *Correspondence*, V, 106; Baily, *Flamsteed*, 281–2; RGO Ms. 1.35, fol. 51ᵛ; Ms. 1.33, fol. 141ᵛ (a copy).

139. It is possible that this is the copy now deposited in the Royal Society.

140. Newton, *Correspondence*, IV, 513; V, 118; Baily, *Flamsteed*, 282, 291–2; RGO Ms. 1.35, fol. 52aʳ; Ms. 1.33, fol. 143ᵛ (a copy).

141. Newton, *Correspondence*, IV, 529. This piece should clearly be dated after the publication of the 1712 edition.

Tycho, Kepler, and Hevelius. Now the new catalogue would depart from this system. Arbuthnot protested that he could find any of Ptolemy's stars immediately in the new catalogue, but to no avail: as far as Flamsteed was concerned, his grand historical project was being reduced to incoherence.[142]

This allegation—hitherto a suspicion, now a confirmed reality—rapidly took on prime importance. When Hodgson could not recall having received the part of the manuscript that Newton said had been delivered to him, then, it was simple to suggest a reason.[143] In the missing section, Flamsteed had entered Ptolemy's nomenclature alongside his own. Had Arbuthnot seen this juxtaposition, he would immediately have perceived the "outrageous fault" committed by Halley in altering the Ptolemaic names. Significantly, Newton also still held Flamsteed's copy of Ptolemy itself, lent to him back in 1705 when the referees had first been deliberating over which of Flamsteed's papers to print. Flamsteed now recommended Arbuthnot to "send for it & Collate my Translation: & Dr Hs with it for your own satisfaction." Arbuthnot responded indignantly that that was precisely what he had just done in order to make his assurance about finding Ptolemy's stars in the newly printed pages. But Flamsteed was irreconcilable, and as the book took shape, so his complaints multiplied. He demanded that all the sheets be sent to him so that he could mark Halley's "faults." Stars were not only wrongly named, he asserted, but inserted in the wrong place, or even omitted altogether. Some of their positions were wrongly recorded, by up to 15′. Many constellations were described back to front, ludicrously emulating an earlier catalogue by Johann Bayer that had visited the same outrage on Tycho Brahe.[144] Worst of all, perhaps, Halley had taken to "correcting" the copy in Child's coffeehouse, and pointing out to his "impious friends" there all of Flamsteed's purported errors.[145]

This again implied that Halley's "impudence" was inseparable from his atheism. However, Flamsteed also suspected that the effects of the latter extended to his emendations of celestial observations. Halley had long based physical arguments against the eternity of the earth on critical assessments of the observations in Ptolemy's astronomy and geography; he also suggested

142. Newton, *Correspondence*, V, 119–22. The manuscript of the first part of the work (the catalogue of fixed stars) used by Halley is now RGO Ms. 1.74; it was unknown to Baily, and was the imperfect catalogue given sealed up to Newton in 1706. This is what became pp. 1–60 of Flamsteed, *Historiae Cœlestis Libri Duo* (1712)—the part of the publication most detested by Flamsteed, and the first on the fire. A glance at this manuscript (fig. 8.9) reveals the substantial extent of Halley's emendations.

143. RGO Ms. 1.74.

144. Newton, *Correspondence*, IV, 426–7, 433, 449; V, 120–3, 129–30; Bayer, *Uranometria omnium Asterismorum*. See also Dreyer, *Tycho Brahe*, 371–4, for similar complaints made against Curtz. The point was explained in the preface to Flamsteed's *Atlas Cœlestis* (1729), 3–4.

145. Baily, *Flamsteed*, 297–8; Flamsteed, *Preface*, 175.

that some of the brightest stars had moved since Hipparchus's time. Such arguments required him to appraise the records of the stars' positions produced in the ancient world. Halley had thus been engaged since at least the early 1690s in work dedicated to confirming, rejecting, or rendering credible the observations of the ancients, in successive attempts to provide physical explications of the history and destiny of the earth. His manipulation of Ptolemaic figures now could therefore potentially affect the reading of Scripture too. Halley agreed with the more overt heretic William Whiston that there was "more Credit to be given to this one Astronomical Criterion, than to the longest Tradition."[146] Although any specific aims in this regard remained obscure, the implications of attaining certainty in stellar astronomy could clearly extend far beyond the abstruse details of natural science. The credibility of Scripture could be calibrated against such figures. Halley's editing promised to establish, or threatened to undermine, the most profound bases of religious and historical faith (fig. 8.9).

Flamsteed regarded it as a particularly gross breach of propriety that Halley's copy came from the sealed text. In fact, the package had probably been opened once already, shortly after the 20 March 1707/8 meeting. Flamsteed himself had added and amended its figures at that juncture, and we do not know if it was sealed up again after that.[147] But he nevertheless maintained that one of the most fundamental tenets of an honorable gentleman was that such undertakings be adhered to. If a discovery was delivered sealed up, did the imperative to secrecy still hold when it had been changed later? Flamsteed thought that it did, and held Newton's use of this material to be his greatest sin.[148] Moreover, Flamsteed had seen from mysteriously obtained proof sheets that Newton was also inserting into the text lunar data from the three synopses provided to him in 1694. At that time they had been communicated in confidence, precisely because their calculation had rested upon a provisional star catalogue that would later be replaced by the definitive tables. But, Flamsteed remarked, "S^r I:N: is to[o] great a person to be a slave to his word." Incensed, he told Arbuthnot that this latest Tychonic ordeal was the most infuriating of all.

I have now spent 35 years in [the] composeing & Work of my Catalogue . . .
I have endured long and painfull distempers . . . I have spent a large sum of
Money . . . Do not tease me with banter by telling me y^t these alterations are
made to please me when you are sensible nothing can be more displeasing nor
injurious. . . . would you like to have *your* Labours surreptitiously forced out

146. Schaffer, "Halley's Atheism," 24–5; Halley, "Considerations"; Whiston, *Astronomical Lectures*, 190–1.
147. Baily, *Flamsteed*, 267; Newton, *Correspondence*, IV, 459–60, n. 4, 513–4; V, 130.
148. See also Flamsteed's appeal to Queen Anne, in RGO Ms. 1.33, fol. 151^r.

Historiæ Cœlestis

Pars prior

sive

Stellarum Fixarum Catalogus

Britannicus

ex Observationibus

in Observatorio Regio Grenovici habitis

~~habitis constructis~~

☉ ad annum ~~1689~~ inchoatum 1690

constructus.

Ptol. Bayer.	Nomina Stellarum	Asc Rect	Dist a vert	Asc Rect	Dist a Pol	Longitud	Latitud	Var Var
		h ʼ ʼʼ	° ʼ ʼʼ	° ʼ ʼʼ	° ʼ ʼʼ	s ° ʼ ʼʼ	° ʼ ʼʼ	
	378	1. 23. 04. 70	45. 45	20. 46. 00	69. 17. 15	♈ 26. 50. 25	11. 01. 50 ♌	38. 10. 21
		25. 43	32. 41. 55	21. 25. 45	71. 15. 25	26. 58. 15	9. 01. 26	58. 04. 21
		21. 25. 76. 07	27	22. 51. 15	74. 36. 55	20. 49. 01	5. 23. 59	57. 78. 52. 00
1	1 In cornu 2ᵈ præcedens Bayero	36. 74. 33. 43. 17	24. 08. 30	72. 14. 45	28. 54. 00	6. 80. 30	58. 16. 21
2	2 Sequens in Cornu Boreā	37. 74. 72. 11. 25	24. 23. 30	70. 43. 55	29. 37. 59	6. 28. 16	58. 35
5	5 In Cervice	40. 10. 77. 11. 45	24. 25. 00	73. 43. 15	♉ 0. 54. 30	10. 57. 12	57. 10. 21. 39
16	16 In vertice, Bayero ☓	40. 44. 29. 24. 55	25. 11. 00	6. 56. 25	8. 1. 27. 15	10. 47. 47	59. 17. 21. 18
		46. 10. 27. 03. 37	26. 32. 30	65. 33. 05	7. 26. 14	12. 31. 52	59. 70. 21. 17
17	17 Infra supra caput ♓	49. 18. 27. 16. 15	27. 19. 30	65. 48. 15	4. 02. 12	12. 01. 02	60. 05. 21. 00
	17. 106. 183	49. 18. 30. 14. 15	27. 19. 30	68. 51. 05	2. 55. 00	9. 13. 29	59. 21. 21. 00
		49. 46. 29. 70. 15	27. 20. 30	68. 01. 45	3. 19. 18	9. 57. 12	59. 29. 21. 02
		51. 70. 27. 01. 45	27. 57. 30	65. 33. 15	4. 40. 16	12. 05. 72	60. 18. 21. 31
		53. 30. 37. 27. 13	28. 12. 30	71. 30. 45	2. 43. 49	9. 55. 76	58. 49. 20. 56
	2 17, 106, 101	53. 45. 27. 01. 35	28. 28. 15	65. 33. 05	5. 04. 41	11. 57. 20	60. 21. 20. 55
3	4 In dorso duarum Bor ♓	55. 30. 31. 44. 55	28. 52. 30	70. 16. 25	3. 46. 50	22. 45	59. 12. 20. 42
		55. 55. 33. 01. 45	28. 58. 45	71. 33. 15	3. 25. 14	6. 08. 45	59. 00. 20. 49
		56. 06. 77. 40. 45	29. 01. 30	76. 12. 15	1. 44. 58	1. 46. 25	57. 60. 14. 56
		58. 00. 27. 09. 35	29. 31. 30	65. 41. 05	5. 59. 47	11. 27. 44	60. 70. 20. 47
		58. 00. 27. 53. 50	29. 31. 30	66. 25. 70	5. 43. 28	10. 46. 00	60. 18. 20. 42
4	5 Quæ in Latus Australe ♓	2. 00. 40. 33. 02. 00	30. 14. 00	71. 33. 30	4. 32. 25	5. 37. 39	59. 18. 20. 24
		1. 50. 33. 13. 55	30. 20. 30	71. 15. 25	4. 46. 59	5. 28. 23	59. 00. 20. 30
	secunda 2ᵈ ♓	8. 04. 42. 16. 45	31. 01. 00	80. 48. 15	7. 01. 19	5. 33. 31	57. 11. 20. 10
		10. 50. 42. 40. 55	32. 42. 30	81. 12. 25	7. 30. 53	4. 09. 43	57. 42. 20. 00
		12. 20. 33. 01. 30	33. 20. 00	71. 33. 00	7. 19. 13	4. 44. 01	58. 10. 10. 52
		13. 44. 35. 10. 25	33. 26. 00	73. 11. 55	6. 41. 33	2. 49. 12	58. 50. 19. 50
5	p formis Trianguli 10ᵃ	15. 57. 37. 50. 45	33. 59. 15	76. 22. 15	6. 18. 40	0. 01. 15	59. 21. 19. 42
		14. 12. 12. 00	34. 18. 00	66. 47. 30	10. 14. 15	3. 49. 49	57. 47. 19. 29
6	7 In Renibus ♈	21. 10. 70. 53. 15	35. 19. 30	69. 24. 15	9. 10. 35	6. 07. 50	60. 18. 12. 24
18	18 Trianguli	22. 78. 25. 16. 35	35. 39. 30	71. 18. 45	11. 48. 01	10. 54. 52	58. 01. 50. 19. 10
10	10 In dorso duarum in alta	24. 57. 32. 48. 45	36. 11. 15	71. 20. 15	9. 59. 55	4. 41. 46	59. 57. 19. 10
19	19 Trianguli 18ᵃ	25. 18. 27. 06. 55	36. 19. 30	67. 38. 25	12. 35. 47	11. 17. 13	62. 11. 19. 07
	562.	1	2. 22. 91. 42. 11. 00	35. 77. 45. 80. 42. 30				

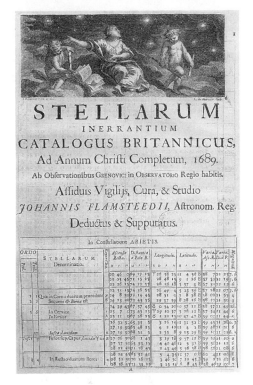

FIG. 8.9. These illustrations display the changes made by Halley to Flamsteed's tables, their appearance in the 1712 *Historiae Cœlestis Libri Duo*, and the printed form adopted in the 1725 *Historia Cœlestis*. Halley has regrouped the stars, numbered them, moved many from one constellation to another, and altered the positions of several. Note that there is no sense in which these changes can simply be said to be right or wrong (although modern astronomers in fact tend to favor Halley's emendations). The decisions here are for the most part dependent on cultural criteria, in particular regard for a tradition of classification in positional astronomy extending back to Ptolemy and Hipparchus. (*opposite*) Flamsteed's manuscript star catalogue, with corrections by Halley; this is the catalogue originally sealed for deposit with Newton. (By permission of the Royal Greenwich Observatory and the Syndics of Cambridge University Library.) (*above left*) The 1712 *Historiae Cœlestis Libri Duo*. (By permission of the Syndics of Cambridge University Library.) (*above right*) The 1725 *Historia Cœlestis*. (By permission of the Royal Greenwich Observatory and the Syndics of Cambridge University Library.)

of your hands, convey'd into the hands of your declared profligate Enemys, printed without your consent, and spoyled as mine are in ye impression? would you suffer your Enemies to make themselves Judges, of what they understand not? would you not withdraw your Copy out of their hands, trust no more in theirs and publish your own Works rather at your own expence, then see them spoyled and your self Laught at for suffering it[?] [149]

If Halley were allowed to proceed, the result would be "a ref[l]ection on ye Pr. of ye R. So." Arbuthnot, too, would "suffer in your reputation, for encourageing one, of whome ye wisest of his Companions used to say: y^t ye only way to have any buiseness spoyled effectualy was to trust it to his management."

Arbuthnot was exasperated. Since the royal astronomer would not co-operate, he warned, he himself would employ calculators to complete the catalogue from the observations in his notebooks—"and why we should not succeed as well [as you] in this piece of Journey Work I cannot imagine." [150] If Flamsteed were still dissatisfied by their "performance," he would then be welcome to print his own copy. Flamsteed responded that Arbuthnot must allow him to nominate the printer, and let him oversee a last proof at Greenwich before each sheet was allowed to be printed off. Once the material so "spoyled" by Halley had been reprinted under these conditions, he could print the rest of the catalogue. If Arbuthnot would not permit this, however, then Flamsteed would indeed have to "print it alone, at my own Charge." He would copy the catalogue afresh and reprint it with better paper and type than Halley's, making sure to "take care of ye correction of ye press my Self." Halley had forced this ultimatum from him, he told Sharp—and so had Newton, when he had "perfidiously" handed over material that had been given him in confidence. [151]

Flamsteed had another opportunity to complain when Newton convened the committee from the Royal Society to consider the instruments at Greenwich. [152] He first told the committee that all the instruments in the observatory belonged to him, not to the institution, and that they therefore lay outside the committee's remit. "As good have no Observatory as no In-

149. Newton, *Correspondence*, V, 120–2, 194; Baily, *Flamsteed*, 283–5; RGO Ms. 1.33, fol. 144$^{r–v}$; RGO MS. 1.35, fol. 54$^{r–v}$.

150. Newton, *Correspondence*, V, 119–20, 122–3; Baily, *Flamsteed*, 282–3; RGO Ms. 1.35, fol. 52$^{r–v}$; Ms. 1.33, fol. 143^v (a copy).

151. Newton, *Correspondence*, V, 120, 122–3 (Arbuthnot's copy), 194; Baily, *Flamsteed*, 285; RGO MS. 1.35, fol. 54$^{r–v}$. In private Flamsteed seems to have decided that Halley's involvement meant that the remainder of his catalogue must not be handed over to Arbuthnot: Newton, *Correspondence*, V, 129–30.

152. RS JB X, 511–2, 535. It seems that some repairs were actually undertaken at about this time: RGO Ms. 1.33, fols. 97^v–98^r.

struments," Newton grumbled. "I complained then of my Catalogue being printed by Raymer without my knowledg," Flamsteed told Sharp, "& that I was Robd of the fruits of my Labours." At this Newton erupted. He "cald me all the ill names, Puppy, &c., that he could think of." Flamsteed recalled that he had "put him in mind of his passion [and] desired him to govern it"—at which point Newton apparently almost "burst." The president of the Royal Society then pointedly reminded Flamsteed of the funds he had received from the state over thirty-six years; Flamsteed equally pointedly replied that Newton too had received a substantial income from the nation since settling in London at the mint. And when he went on to raise the subject of the sealed catalogue, Newton alleged that Arbuthnot had had an order from the queen herself to open the sealed package containing Flamsteed's papers.[153] Flamsteed flatly refused to believe this, but refrained from transgressing the bounds of civility irredeemably by telling Newton so to his face. Instead he took his leave, confident that his point had been made. On the stairs after the meeting, Flamsteed met his Raymer again. They drank a dish of coffee together while Flamsteed told Halley, "still calmly," of "the Villainy of his conduct." Then he retreated back to Greenwich. In his wake he left rumor as well as anger. The confrontation with Newton was soon the talk of London. Significantly enough, it was commonly represented as a priority dispute "about the first invention of some rarities in astronomy."[154]

Printing of Halley's edited catalogue was complete by 23 June 1711, when Halley himself sent the sheets to Flamsteed. The Arbuthnot-Hallcy-Newton *Historia Cœlestis* was then finished by early 1712 (fig. 8.10). Newton approved the accounts for the project in February. Churchill was owed £98.11.00 for paper and printing. Engraver Louis du Guernier was owed £51.10.00, and George Vertue £30 for engraving the frontispiece. One Catenaro, a painter, deserved £20 for designing the images to be engraved. Altogether the outstanding costs of printing and engraving (not including Catenaro's reward) came to £194.15.00. And Newton recommended that Halley be paid £150 for "reducing the Second Volume of Mr. Flamsteed's observations into the same Form and Method with the First Volume, and Correcting his Catalogue of the Fix'd Stars by the Observations and Computing the places of 500 Stars more from the observations, for compleating the Catalogue, and for Correcting the press and supervising the whole Work." This had been hard labor for a year. The sums requested by Newton were paid forthwith by the Treasury.[155]

153. Newton was probably referring to the claimed order mentioned at the Royal Society (RS JB X, 260).

154. Newton, *Correspondence*, V, 209–10; Cudworth, *Sharp*, 51.

155. Newton, *Correspondence*, V, 165–6, 212, 224–5.

FIG. 8.10. Frontispiece to the 1712 *Historiae Cœlestis Libri Duo*. (By permission of the Syndics of Cambridge University Library.)

When Flamsteed received the completed catalogue from Halley in mid-1711, meanwhile, he found that its "faults" were greater even than he had imagined. He forged a resolve to carry out his threat to Arbuthnot and reprint the entire catalogue himself. By April 1712 he had a complete text, and could petition the queen to permit its publication in the face of the edition derived, "in his name," from Halley's "surreptitious and imperfect Copy." Printing then began. As work got under way, Flamsteed maintained a taciturn reticence in front of his adversaries. In June, Halley turned up at the observatory with his wife and his entire family—even his local vicar. He offered to burn his edition should Flamsteed find serious flaws in it. Newton himself followed in August with a small band of virtuosi, in pursuit of the Royal Society's new powers to oversee the instruments. "I gave them a glass of wine," Flamsteed noted fastidiously. Newton promised once again to return the notebooks he had held now for some six years. Every year, the Royal Society demanded Flamsteed's observations; every year he delayed sending them until the last possible moment.[156] Sending them sealed was no use, even when they were accompanied by a stiff note enjoining secrecy. The Society would immediately open them and hand them over to Halley. Flamsteed would then find them printed in the *Transactions*, both "abridged and so spoiled by the editor of my catalogue, that I would no longer own them for mine." Such abridgment, he lamented, "robbed them of all their certainty."[157] When the queen died in 1714, Flamsteed regarded the Society's authority as terminated, and simply refused to acknowledge its demands for such material any longer.

He could afford to do this because the succession of George I in 1714 saw a change of ministry, and one that finally worked to Flamsteed's benefit. Newton had been closely associated with the régime of Oxford, now discredited, and St. John (now Viscount Bolingbroke), who fled to the Continent to become a Jacobite. The death of his greatest patron, Halifax, lessened still further his influence.[158] Flamsteed, however, gained friends in high places. At the Treasury, Newport was especially likely to prove sympathetic. So was the lord chamberlain, the duke of Bolton, who by office had control over the legacy of Prince George's library. On his petition, Flamsteed was accordingly awarded a warrant ordering that of the 340 copies of the 1712 *Historia Cœlestis* still in the hands of Awnsham Churchill, 300 should be handed over to him "as a present from his Maj[ty]."[159] After a long delay, the copies were delivered. Flamsteed immediately took them to Greenwich. There he separated out the section printed when he had still been able to correct the press, setting aside "Halley's corrupted edition of my catalogue, and [his] abridgment of my observations, no less spoiled by him." He kept

156. Newton, *Correspondence*, V, 165–6, 194, 313, 385; VI, 24, 33, 69–71; Baily, *Flamsteed*, 98–9, 304–5; RS JB X, 290, 456, 458, 503, 510, 545, 549–50; JB XI, 45; RGO Ms. 1.33, fol. 151ʳ.

157. RS JB X, 503, 510; Baily, *Flamsteed*, 99, 312.

158. Newton, *Correspondence*, VI, 232; Baily, *Flamsteed*, 314–5; Cudworth, *Sharp*, 114–5. There are parallels here with the development of Newton's dispute with Leibniz: Shapin, "Of Gods and Kings."

159. Newton, *Correspondence*, VI, 255–6. The other forty copies were to be sent to Lord Bolton, along with a statement of accounts by the referees. In fact the issue was complicated, and the Treasury had to be invoked. There Robert Walpole stepped in to facilitate the warrant: *Calendar of Treasury Books* 30.ii, 146; Forbes, *Greenwich Observatory I*, 59.

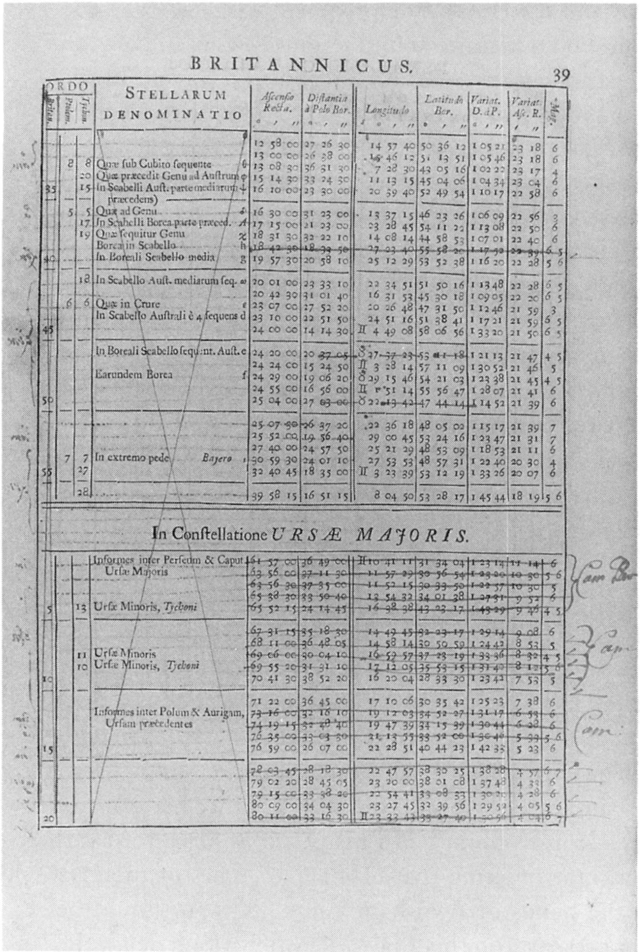

FIG. 8.11. A page from Halley's edition of the star catalogue, excerpted from the *Historiae Cœlestis Libri Duo* (1712) by Flamsteed and sent to a friend (probably Abraham Sharp). Flamsteed has here indicated the elements in Halley's version of the catalogue to which he particularly objects. He has crossed out the numeration— entirely Halley's innovation— and the system of nomenclature, which he felt departed from a long history of classifications. He has also indicated where stars should be restored to what he believes their proper constellations. Long thought to be lost, the set of sheets of which this forms a part has only recently come to light again. (From the collection of Professor Owen Gingerich.)

the former to be inserted into the edition he himself still hoped to complete.[160] A few copies of the latter he annotated and sent to friends, as cautionary "Evidence of yᵉ malice of Godlesse persons" (fig. 8.11). But in spring 1716 Flamsteed built a pyre on Greenwich Hill, and burned the sheets containing the catalogue and abridged observations. As he himself put it, they

160. This comprised the observations from 1676 to 1689. In Flamsteed, *Historiae Cœlestis Libri Duo* (1712) they are pp. 1–387 of the second pagination of Bk. I; in Flamsteed, *Historia Cœlestis Britannica* (1725) they are inserted into Bk. I after p. 40.

made a good "sacrifice to TRUTH." He would do the same to "all the rest of my editor's pains of the like nature," he declared, "if the Author of Truth should hereafter put them into my power."[161]

If 340 copies remained, some 60 had been distributed. Along with the remaining books, the government also demanded a full account of the dispersal of these copies.[162] The account made clear that, as had always been intended, the first copies of the *Historia Cœlestis* were not published in a commercial sense. Instead they had been envisaged as royal "presents," to be given to a selective list of recipients now rehearsed by Newton:

1. Publick Libraries at home and abroad,

2. Professors and other eminent Mathematicians at home and abroad,

3. The Nobility of great Britain, who have Libraries of Note,

4. Those about the late Prince who had been instrumental in promoting the work (viz. the Rt Honble mr. Compton now Speaker of the House of Commons, Mr Nicolas Treasurer, and Mr. Clark Secretary to the Said Prince) for themselves and their Friends.

5. The Referees for themselves and their Friends.

And tho Mr Flamsteed had a Gratuity paid him of £125, and by the imperfect and uncorrect Copies which he delivered, and other breach of Articles, had given us a great deal of Trouble, yet we designed to have begged of her Majestie the Remainder of the Copies for him.[163]

More than fifty of the copies no longer in Churchill's warehouse had been dispersed. Ten had gone to courtiers, thirty to the Treasury (richly bound for use as diplomatic gifts), and ten more to the observatory and Royal Academy in Paris. Newton and Halley had got one each, Flamsteed two.[164] The edition was not advertised in the *London Gazette*, and there was no

161. Newton, *Correspondence*, VI, 315; Flamsteed, *Preface*, 178; Baily, *Flamsteed*, 101, 321. One of these unburned bundles of sheets has survived, in fact, with Flamsteed's annotations: see fig. 8.11. Gingerich, "Unique Copy," details Flamsteed's notes. Halley had stressed his efforts in calculating the six constellations nearest the north pole; Flamsteed deleted much of this material. He also canceled the numeration and verbal denominations of stars, plus many of their positions (often putting them in different constellations, in which case he indicated in the margin their "correct" locations). Many individual figures also required correction. In addition, Flamsteed had by now decided to accept Hevelius's new constellations (advanced in his *Uranographia*, 1687). Halley had not, so this too required changes.

162. The account showed that £364.15.00 had been disbursed after George's death, to Halley (£150.00.00), Churchill (£98.11.00), and the engravers (£116.04.00): Newton, *Correspondence*, VI, 269. Halley received his share for "examining & correcting the catalogue of the fixt stars, adding about 500 new starrs to the Catalogue, drawing up the second book in due form from the Minute book & correcting yᵉ Press." He received £25 more than Flamsteed, who concluded that this funding must have come from the public purse: ibid., 274.

163. Newton, *Correspondence*, VI, 267–8; RGO Ms. 1.35, no. 67; Baily, *Flamsteed*, 318–9.

164. Baily, *Flamsteed*, 318–9, 321; Cudworth, *Sharp*, 122–3.

notice of its publication in the *Philosophical Transactions*. It is not known whether any copies were actually sold, but it seems highly unlikely that any were. Nor was it at first presented to the Royal Society, a copy being given by Newton only in 1717.

Flamsteed complained bitterly of the misuse of his work. "When these are served Sir Is thinks he has made so many fast friends, but at whose cost does he do it?" he asked Lowthorp, who had shown him Newton's "representation." "Yᵉ paines were mine, yᵉ expense yᵉ Prince's or yᵉ Publick, Yet I must look upon it as a favour if he voucsafe to beg yᵉ rest for me, when all persons were furnished yᵗ would buy them." Any potential market would be exhausted by Newton's gifts. This was, he maintained, "a spiteful & malitious contrivance." Newton had "contrived to dispose of yᵉ printed Volumes of my Observations in such manne[r] yᵗ they should have been spread all over Europe as *his gift* to librarys & ingenious p'sons," he told Sharp, "with Halleys Copy of my spoyled Catalogue of the fixed stars & a malitious preface preface [*sic*] of Hallys yᵗ was wrote without my knowledge." Three at least had gone into Italy—"some say to yᵉ Pope." Churchill, in league with Newton, had surely printed supernumerary copies, so ruining still more emphatically any public market Flamsteed might have exploited. At the very least, Newton himself should be made to pay the fees of Machin and Halley for "*spoyling*" the catalogue.[165]

While expressing such outrage and maneuvering to recover the undistributed copies of the 1712 edition, Flamsteed quietly proceeded with his own printing. Determined to assert his authorship, as work continued he commissioned a protrait of himself to grace the finished volumes (fig. 8.12). The catalogue itself was completed by the end of 1712. Work on the observations not already printed under his control could then begin. He repeatedly approached Newton to get back his manuscripts, even threatening legal proceedings against him to return the 175 pages of observations. Eventually they had to be calculated anew. Meanwhile, Flamsteed had to experience all over again the labor of negotiating with and monitoring printers. He found that "no printer in town has figure enough to print a whole sheet" of such tables. To make matters even more difficult, all must be done in conditions of secrecy. Flamsteed believed that Halley had threatened to pirate anything he printed. He took a house in Saint Paul's Churchyard, traveled frequently back and forth from Greenwich, and would not entrust copies of the catalogue even to Hodgson, "for fear that Raymer should wheedle him out of it." At last, in September 1716, six months after the embers of the sacrifice

---

165. Newton, *Correspondence*, VI, 273–4, 315 (italics mine); Baily, *Flamsteed*, 319–20, 321; RGO Ms. 1.35, fol. 68ʳ; Cudworth, *Sharp*, 122–3; Westfall, *Never at Rest*, 696. Flamsteed was to point out that in 1704 he had been promised all the copies other than those given by the prince to the universities: Baily, *Flamsteed*, 66.

FIG. 8.12. John Flamsteed. Engraving by G. Vertue after portrait by T. Gibson, 1712. Flamsteed, *Historia Cælestis Britannica*, 1725, I. (By permission of the Syndics of Cambridge University Library.)

had stopped glowing, Flamsteed began the final draft for his preface. This was to be a very different text from Halley's. It would trace three histories. The first would be that of observational astronomy itself, from its first beginnings to its culmination in Flamsteed's great opus. This history would introduce the local story of the observational techniques and practices from which his own achievement had been constructed. Finally, and most controversially, Flamsteed undertook to recite the true narrative of his titanic struggles with Newton, Halley, the Royal Society, and the coffeehouse tattlers—forces that had "used me worse than ever the noble Tycho was used in Denmark." This was what his painstaking preservation of so many letters, tables, drafts, warrants, and certificates had all been for.[166]

166. Newton, *Correspondence*, VI, 228, 333–4; Baily, *Flamsteed*, 98–100, 298–300, 310, 313, 314, 322, 324–5, 331; RGO Ms. 1.33, fol. 150ʳ⁻ᵛ; RGO Ms. 1.36, fol. 85ʳ⁻ᵛ; Flamsteed, *Preface*, 178.

Flamsteed never lived to see it published. Printing of the observations was all but finished when he died, on New Year's Eve 1719, but the prefatory material was still in manuscript. After his death, Margaret Flamsteed dedicated herself to completing her husband's work. She had already lived with the conflict for virtually all of her married life; now she would devote almost the rest of her natural term to achieving a fitting conclusion. Born Margaret Cooke, a granddaughter of Flamsteed's predecessor as rector of Burstow, she had married Flamsteed in 1693. She was certainly knowledgeable in mathematics and astronomy, but had always maintained a conventionally subordinate face to the outside world. She now put that knowledge to more visible use. She recruited Joseph Crosthwait in Greenwich and Abraham Sharp in Lancashire, and determined to pursue and draw her husband's enterprise to a close.[167]

Their first important task was to have the prefatory material translated into Latin. The first translator they engaged was James Pound, whom Flamsteed himself had trained to be his "candid" replacement for Halley as mapper of the southern skies. When he relinquished the task, two other translators were successively engaged, their work being checked by another of Newton's apostates, William Whiston.[168] At length, the Latin text began to take shape. Now a second difficult task could be faced. This was the engraving of the charts, which Flamsteed had always regarded as perhaps the most important—and almost certainly the most useful—part of his work. Producing these charts proved highly problematic. The project was at first undertaken by workmen in London, who were hired on the recommendation of Sir James Thornhill. These workmen proved too expensive, however, and eventually Crosthwait actually sailed to Holland to hire engravers there. These in turn proved unable to produce work of sufficient quality. At length, Margaret Flamsteed terminated their labors and returned the work to London for completion.

When it finally appeared, five years after Flamsteed's death, the new *Historia Cœlestis Britannica* was much more recognizably a *publication* than the 1712 edition had been. The three volumes issued in 1725 were sold for eight guineas in sheets (Crosthwait had suggested six, but this was thought de-

167. RGO Ms. 1.37, fols. 114ʳ, 118ʳ–119ᵛ, 120ʳ. Margaret Flamsteed's efforts should be compared to those of a number of other widows left in similar situations, such as those of Hevelius and Francis Willughby (who financed the engravings for her husband's posthumous *Ornithologiae Libri Tres*). Indeed, there is a recurrent pattern of such unsung collaboration in the history of science: see Pycior, Slack, and Abir-Am, *Creative Couples*, and Ogilvie, "Marital Collaboration," 104–5.

168. Bodl. Ms. Lister 3, fol. 75ʳ; RGO Ms. 1.33, fols. 107ᵛ–108ᵛ; Forbes, *Greenwich Observatory I*, 60; Baily, *Flamsteed*, 341. Crosthwait worked to have the translator move to Greenwich to prevent sheets being distributed before being published.

meaningly low); booksellers were allowed one set in seven. They were advertised in the general press, reviewed in the *Philosophical Transactions*, and presented to the Royal Society. Four years later, after much work, the charts of the constellations were published too (fig. 8.13). The *Atlas Cœlestis* in which they appeared was again a commercial object, produced by subscription through the agency of Stationers William and John Innys (fig. 8.14). The Innyses specialized in natural and experimental philosophy, and had just published the third edition of the *Principia* under a royal patent. Margaret Flamsteed, Crosthwait, and Sharp, having achieved a remarkable success wrought of devotion and dedication, deserve recognition in their own right. At last, Flamsteed's vision had been realized: with one qualification. At some stage, the third of his three histories—that of his duel with Newton—had slipped from the text. In the last years of Newton's life, it had become too controversial, in all probability, to be published. Flamsteed's own history was never incorporated into his *Historia*, and it remained unread for the next century.[169]

Meanwhile Halley was appointed the next astronomer royal. He immediately tried to take over the instruments at the observatory. Margaret fought to retain them, however, claiming that those not built by Flamsteed himself had been left to him by Sir Jonas Moore.[170] She won. Halley was left to begin work at the observatory with few instruments and scarce funds. Ironically, his own astronomical tables—some of them printed off as early as 1717–19, when, as Flamsteed had noted in his final letter, Halley had not been slow to exhibit them in the Temple coffeehouse—would not be published, despite criticism at the delay, for another three decades. By the time of their appearance in 1749, their author had been dead seven years. Their editor drew what he believed to be the appropriate conclusion.

> We wish our Author had printed his Observations, for the publication of astronomical Observations is of very great importance . . . It were therefore much to be wished that the Observations made at the Royal Observatory, were printed off from time to time at the public expence; for the more diligent the Observer is, the more is the Public concerned in the preservation of his Labours.[171]

169. Flamsteed, *Historia Cœlestis Britannica* (1725); Flamsteed, *Atlas Cœlestis* (1729); Baily, *Flamsteed*, 349–51, 359, 360, 363; RS JB XII, 599; "Account of a book, entitled, *Historia Cœlestis Britannica*"; Cudworth, *Sharp*, 145–6; printed prospectus in RGO Ms. 1.36, fol. 100^r. Neither Crosthwait nor Sharp received any recompense for his labors.

170. According to Crosthwait (Baily, *Flamsteed*, 342–3) this legal case advanced at least to the stage of Mrs. Flamsteed delivering an answer to a bill of the Ordnance Office. It would be interesting to know whether these arguments survive; a search at the Public Record Office failed to turn them up.

171. Halley, *Correspondence and Papers*, 11–12; Baily, *Flamsteed*, 332; Halley, *Astronomical Tables*, sigs. A1^v–A2^r.

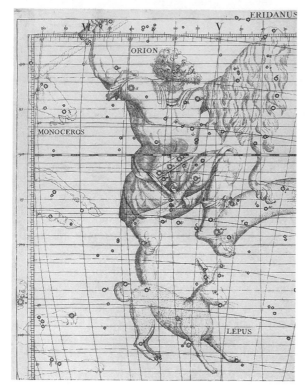

FIG. 8.13. Constellation of Orion. Orion was the constellation that Flamsteed himself chose to have engraved as a specimen before revealing his plans to the Royal Society. This is its final form as published in Flamsteed's *Atlas Cœlestis*. (By permission of the Syndics of Cambridge University Library.)

October 25, 1725. 100

PROPOSALS

For PRINTING by

SUBSCRIPTION,

THE

ATLAS COELESTIS

OF THE

Late Rev[d] Mr. FLAMSTEED, *Ast. Prof. Reg.*

In Twenty Five CHARTS;

CONTAINING,

All the CONSTELLATIONS visible in our Hemisphere. Each Chart being Twenty five Inches in Length, and Twenty in Breadth, and Constructed after a new Method of his own, wherein the *Antient Figures* are restored, and the Stars laid down from his own *correct Catalogue*. Together with two large Planispheres of the Northern and Southern Constellations.

The Designs being all ready for the Graver, and Eight of them finished, the Undertakers propose to have them all done by *Lady-Day* next.

But the Work being large, and requiring a great Disbursement of Money to carry it on, it cannot be compleated without the previous Assurance of a sufficient Number of Buyers, and without the Aid of those, who are willing to promote so very Useful a Design.

It is therefore PROPOSED,

First, That it shall be Printed on the best Imperial Paper.

Secondly, That the Price to each Subscriber shall be Two Guineas and a Half, One Guinea to be paid down at the Time of Subscription, and the Remainder on the Delivery of a compleat Set.

Thirdly, That they who Subscribe for Six, shall have a Seventh *gratis*, which will reduce the Price of each Set to Two Pounds Five Shillings, and One Shilling and Eight Pence for each Chart; and that after the Subscription is closed, none shall be sold under Three Guineas the Set.

SPECIMENS of some already finished may be seen, and SUBSCRIPTIONS taken in by the UNDERTAKERS,
Mrs. FLAMSTEED, at her House in *Greenwich*, and
Mr. JAMES HODGSON, Master of the Royal Mathematical School in *Christ's* Hospital.
And by WILLIAM and JOHN INNYS, Booksellers, at the West-End of St. *Paul's*

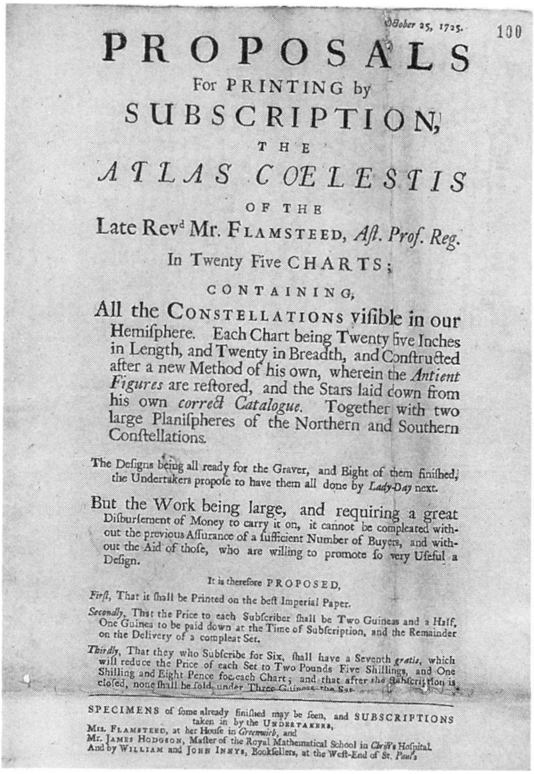

FIG. 8.14. Proposals for printing the *Atlas Cœlestis* by subscription. (By permission of the Royal Greenwich Observatory and the Syndics of Cambridge University Library.)

In the end, it seemed, Halley's plight had inspired the same moral reflection in his own critics as Flamsteed's had in Halley himself.

The modern historian may also draw a moral from this story, although hardly the same one. To become a successful philosophical or astronomical author required skillful interaction with a world of printers, journeymen, and undertakers of which we have until now been largely ignorant. The achievement of even the most apparently asocial forms of knowledge could depend on this. Halley's connections with the coffeehouse wits, and with an urban underworld altogether less visible, thus made him a powerful opponent. Two examples may serve to confirm the point. The first is that of Stationer John Senex. Flamsteed had long suspected that Senex—who became a very senior member of Desaguliers's lodge of Freemasons—was collaborating secretly with Halley to discredit his work, principally by piracy. He believed that he was illicitly incorporating his data into globes and planispheres published under Halley's name. This partly reflected the great importance attached by Flamsteed to his charts. But as has been noted already, concerns about their piracy surfaced immediately when their designs began to be drawn. As early as 1703, when he had tried to persuade a draftsman to go to Greenwich to work on these charts, Flamsteed had found that "oʳ Globe makers in London being told by him that I desired such a thing have dissuaded him, to force me to send my Charts to London *where they might copy them* & I doubt not but they would *in spite of any engagemᵗ of yᵉ draughtsman.*" He came to fear that Halley's alliance with Senex would provide a conduit for precisely this kind of appropriation, the prevalence of which was noted in chapter 6. And Senex did indeed advertise globes and hemispheres displaying all the stars of "Mr. *Flamsteed*'s Catalogue, as publish'd by Dr. *Halley*." [172] Confronted with Halley's supposed corrections to his star catalogue, Flamsteed therefore suspected that this was the motivation. The piracy came first, and Halley had altered the figures "to make them agree with his own faulty hemisphere." After Flamsteed's own death, Crosthwait too found the Stationer a continuing danger. "Senex is so much a tool of Dr. Halley's, and affronted Mr. Flamsteed so much in his life-time, by engraving the *Zodiacus Stellatus*, and putting his own name to it, in order to screen Dr. Halley from the law, that I am afraid he is not to be trusted," he warned. "Besides, he is reputed the very worst engraver in London." The

172. Bodl. Ms. Lister 3, fol. 75ʳ; [Senex], *Treatise of the Description and Use of both Globes*, sig. [A6ᵛ], final "Catalogue"; advertisement for a new map of the zodiac by Halley containing stars from the Britannic Catalogue, attached to 'sGravesande, *Mathematical Elements of Natural Philosophy*, I, in CUL White.d.80; Songhurst, *Minutes of the Grand Lodge of Freemasons*, 3, 196–7; Jacob, *Radical Enlightenment*, 125–7; Desaguliers, *Course of Experimental Philosophy*, I, sig. [Ppp3ʳ⁻ᵛ]; *Atlas Maritimus & Commercialis*, i–iii. Halley also supported applications for patents by Senex: Woodcroft, *Patents for Inventions*, 85.

relegation of this remark to a final aside is revealing of Crosthwait's scale of priorities. By September 1721, again, Crosthwait had heard that "Senex is engraving of Planispheres, and intends to publish it as done from the British Catalogue." [173] Such improprieties persisted despite all that Crosthwait could do.

A second example is provided by the astrologer with whom this chapter began, George Parker. Parker, his enemies charged, personified illegitimate claims to authorship. He used tables of eclipses from Edmond Halley (and, at first, tide tables from Flamsteed) that he himself lacked the skill to produce. He even "stole" material from the *Philosophical Transactions*. Flamsteed withdrew cooperation with Parker as he started to plan the publication of his own *Historia Cœlestis*, probably because he repudiated this mode of publication for all the reasons described in this chapter. Like Senex, however, Parker remained a continuing collaborator with Halley. In 1714–16, then, as Flamsteed's *Historia Cœlestis* neared completion, and as he moved to seize and then burn the available copies of Halley's, the astrologer offered the astronomer a good opportunity to impugn his rival's astronomical principles. Those principles were most regularly published in Parker's ephemerides. Flamsteed therefore began concentratedly to attack Parker's almanacs, taking them to be printed manifestations of Halley's incompetence. His star catalogue itself being printed, he was now occupied with calculating planetary and lunar tables for the *Historia*; he took particular care as he did so to identify egregious errors in Parker's tables for Jupiter and Saturn. The unspoken assumption, of course, was that these were more properly attributed to Halley. In the sheets of the 1712 edition that he saved from the pyre and sent to Sharp, Flamsteed further indicated that Halley had "thrust in the moon's places from the ephemerides"—or, more likely, that "the lazy and malicious thief" had copied those places from Flamsteed's own earlier notes. By mid-1716, when Parker must have been beginning work on his ephemerides for the following year, Flamsteed was also telling friends that "some say" that Newton had sent copies of the 1712 *Historia Cœlestis* to the pope. This insinuation of "odious" toadying perhaps recorded a persistent coffeehouse rumor, which may well also have reached the ears of Parker. And it was as Flamsteed began his vindicatory preface that Parker started to write his scathing response. Given his existing assumptions, Flamsteed almost certainly saw the resulting diatribe as emanating from Halley's party. His perspective was understandable. It is probable that Parker's fusillade in late 1716 was a rare open manifestation of an extensive—and usually invisible—network of people, practices, and conventions over which figures like Halley

---

173. Baily, *Flamsteed*, 95, 340, 345.

sought to exert mastery. Flamsteed and Halley committed themselves to a duel fought largely by proxies—just as Tycho and Ursus had a century before. Both Halley's and Flamsteed's authorship depended on their success. So, perhaps, did Isaac Newton's.[174]

CONCLUSION

The history of Flamsteed's book does not end with its publication. A comprehensive account of its use of such a work would be a fascinating document, but much further research remains to be undertaken before it can be realized. What can be said here, however, is that Flamsteed's books certainly were used by practicing astronomers, and used extensively. Both the *Historia Cœlestis Britannica* and the *Atlas* were immediately recognized as the best such resources available. Whiston proclaimed that Flamsteed's eclipse observations, for example, ranked "more than a thousand Arguments for confirming and establishing the Credit of Astronomical Calculations with the Unlearned as well as the Learned."[175] Both books were reprinted several times—by various agents, for various reasons, in various forms and sizes, with various alterations, and for various audiences. They were especially important, perhaps, in France, the country that dominated astronomy during the Enlightenment. But even in their original impressions, and even in Britain, they still held sway at the end of the century.

As Flamsteed had always intended, the charts in particular became essential to astronomers' work. Margaret Flamsteed and James Hodgson's dedication of the *Atlas Cœlestis* to George II articulated something of this importance, constructing a historical tradition of mapping the heavens that extended from the ancients to the Royal Observatory, and stressing the importance and utility of the new projection used in the work. The essential feature of this projection was that it generated maps that represented the heavens directly as seen by an observer. This meant that no unusual skill was needed to identify locations on the page with those in the sky; and the mutual distances between stars could be ascertained by simple inspection from the maps themselves. Moreover, the charts of the *Atlas* were fully cross-referenced to the tables in the *Historia Cœlestis Britannica*. For a working

174. [Partridge], *Flagitiosus Mercurius Flagellatus*, 15; Baily, *Flamsteed*, 311–3, 317, 323, 328, 332. It is also possible that Halley was the source for Parker's personally wounding use of the Fielden pseudonym. Halley was one of very few remaining individuals to have been active in the mid-1670s, when Flamsteed wrote his "Hecker."

175. Whiston, *Astronomical Lectures*, 190–1. Of Newton's lunar theory, on the other hand, Whiston declared himself suspicious that it "was rather deduc'd from Mr. *Flamsteed*'s Observations, than from Sir *Isaac Newton*'s own Argumentation": ibid., 360–1; see also 95–115, 180–2.

astronomer, peering through a telescope in the dark and trying to observe faint stars while obeying the strict discipline of a precise clock, such factors were all-important. As late as 1782, for example, the charts proved invaluable for Caroline Herschel's training as "an assistant-Astronomer."

Herschel testified to the extraordinary utility of Flamsteed's books in observational practices. She would employ a telescope to "sweep" the sky for comets, with her brother William seated beside her. William helped her attain the vital skill of correlating in an instant what she observed in the sky with its representation in the *Atlas* lying open beside her. "By looking at Flamsteed's Atlas I find no small star there," she might decide of an observed object, and the inconsistency would encourage her to consider the possibility of a new comet. Comets discovered in this way would then be registered and communicated to other observers, by drawing their appearances "upon the scale of Flamsteed's *Atlas Cœlestis*."[176] The procedure depended utterly on the credit of Flamsteed's charts and (subsequently) tables. The Herschels therefore appropriated and adapted Flamsteed's printed volumes. They added an index, for example, for which the original catalogue had been "not at all adapted." In such ways they made the *Historia* and the *Atlas* into objects of continued astronomical use, replete with additions, qualifications, annotations, and cross-references. Caroline continued to develop these well into the nineteenth century, using Flamsteed's work to suggest directions for future research. In 1826, for example, she proposed a new register of sweeps for comets and nebulae, all reduced to Flamsteed's time so as to match his catalogue.[177] In effect , the Herschels redefined what astronomy *was* in terms of the practices facilitated by the book.

It was at about this time that Francis Baily became Caroline Herschel's valued correspondent. Herschel thus provides a link between the creation of Flamsteed's work, its continued use in the eighteenth century, and Baily's revelation of his conflict with Newton. For Baily too was a practicing astronomer, and one interested in publishing a new revision of Flamsteed's catalogue. It would serve to reinforce the disciplinary and administrative autonomy advanced by Baily's new Royal Astronomical Society. The aged Caroline contributed material for his projected work. It would, he revealed, include "a biography by Flamsteed's own hands." His *Account of the Reverend John Flamsteed* appeared in 1835, annexed to an updated version of Flamsteed's star catalogue. It caused immediate controversy. For what Baily

176. Herschel, *Memoir and Correspondence*, 45, 51–2, 69–71, 87–8.

177. Herschel, *Memoir and Correspondence*, 60–64, 96–8, 103–4, 186–7, 197–9, 219–20; Herschel, *Catalogue of Stars*, 3–5, 23, 29–30. In 1825 she presented her copy of the 1725 volumes to Göttingen, concerned that her marginal memoranda should remain useful to astronomers: *Memoir and Correspondence*, 191, 195.

reprinted was Flamsteed's projected third history—that of his conflict with Newton. And Baily reproduced not only the omitted material from Flamsteed's preface to his *Historia Cœlestis Britannica*, but much of the collection of letters and other documents that Flamsteed had collected as evidence for its accusations. As those accusations impugned Newton, canonized as the patron saint of British science, they drew forth loud criticisms, not least from the formidable master of Trinity College, Cambridge, William Whewell. Few could readily bring themselves to credit Flamsteed's portrait. Even Caroline Herschel, for all her admiration for his catalogue, refused to endorse his criticisms. She declared for Whewell. Whatever Flamsteed's charges, she pronounced, "Newton remains Newton!"[178]

But did Flamsteed remain Flamsteed? The question of his identity had been a real one in his own time. Before him there had been no royal astronomical observer in England, and there is evidence that Flamsteed himself was represented by various contemporaries as a virtuoso, an astrologer, a rote pedagogue, and a pamphleteer.[179] He fought to establish the character of a royal astronomer against all of these, using a variety of resources. He likewise experienced a range of authorial practices in attempts to secure his position, from tide tables, predictions, ephemerides, and almanacs to his great *Historia Cœlestis*. In his conflict with Newton and Halley, all these possibilities were to collapse into the character of a man whose obstinacy and taciturnity were apparently innate. By its conclusion, even Tory Thomas Hearne— no friend to Newton—entertained no doubt that the struggle had proved Flamsteed's "snivelling, covetous Temper." That character took time to create, however, and was perhaps not completely secure until Newton's own apotheosis. The historian is entitled to recover its development.[180]

By presuming to control the correction of his catalogue while it was being secretly printed, Flamsteed declared, Halley had "made himself in some sort (but a very bad one) a proprietor in that Catalogue." To Flamsteed, Halley was straightforwardly a "thief." We do not need to endorse that perspective to see how competing conventions of honorable conduct caused it to arise. It is suggestive in this context that the main battles between Flam-

178. Herschel, *Memoir and Correspondence*, 215–6, 272–80, 285.
179. E.g., *Original Works of William King*, II, 263: "I am no Conjurer . . . and therefore I desire that Flamsteed and Partridge would neither love me as a Brother, nor hate me as a Rival." The BL has a pamphlet purporting to be by Flamsteed: *Flemstadts most Strange and Wonderful Prophecy*. Arbuthnot made Flamsteed the solicitor to a group of spoof "*virtuosi* disaffected to the government" petitioning for monopoly rights to methods of cooking with sunbeams: Aitken, *Life and Works of John Arbuthnot*, 375–8. And James Yonge met Flamsteed the "Vertuoso": Yonge, *Journal*, 24, 168.
180. RS Ms. 243.41; Willmoth, "Sir Jonas Moore," 183. Peter Ackroyd even refers to this opinion in *Hawksmoor* (p. 186).

steed and Newton took place in the period 1695–1712—that is, during almost precisely the years between the lapse of licensing and the first legal endorsement of what was to become copyright. In these years Flamsteed and his allies could no longer rely on the Stationers' register; which makes it all the more interesting, then, that they did try to do so. Flamsteed went to Stationers' Hall in person to register the copy of his *Historia Cœlestis* in 1717, and his supporters insinuated that when Halley constructed lunar tables he omitted minor equations "purely to evade an Act of Parliament, because Mr. Flamsteed's are entered in the Hall Book of the Company of Stationers." It was too late to rely on such resources, however impressive their residual aura of authority. Yet neither could they yet rest their hopes on the sanctity of scientific authorship. It was Flamsteed's misfortune (and Halley's, for that matter) that different representations of propriety and authorship were equally tenable at this juncture, with none dominating. Any and all strategies could be attempted in order to establish and protect authorship, from Flamsteed's secret reprinting of his own work to Halley's provision of data for George Parker. In this environment, even licensing had its defenders. Among them was John Wallis, who advised Flamsteed (and anyone else who would listen) on issues of secrecy and printing. Wallis specifically feared that on Flamsteed's death his manuscripts would be auctioned and thereby "fall into the French King's hands." Then, he warned, "the French astronomers would maim your observations, they would suppress some, and print others of yours in their own names." This never came to pass. For Flamsteed, Halley, and Newton, however, such possibilities were real and had drastic implications for the conduct of learning.[181]

In every respect except self-identification the *Historia Cœlestis* of 1712 was vastly different from the *Historia Cœlestis* of 1725. But that exception is highly significant. In effect, they fought for the one identity. The 1712 edition might be characterized as the Royal Society's *Historia Cœlestis*, and the 1725 as the Royal Observatory's. But books—even such expensive and would-be authoritative books as these—could not carry their own authentication with them. In an environment where unauthorized printing was seen as a real possibility, the identity of the author, the authenticity of the text, and the credibility of the knowledge contained *in* the text were all therefore destabilized. Margaret Flamsteed, in one of her last remaining letters, signaled as much when she sent a copy of the 1725 *Historia Cœlestis Britannica* to Oxford's Bodleian Library and demanded that the library dispose of its one-volume "false impression . . . which passes as the genuine

181. Baily, *Flamsteed*, 95, 240, 335; SCA, Register of Copies 1710–1746, 249; RGO Ms. 1.35, fol. 41^r; Schaffer, "Daniel Defoe"; Goldsmith, "Public Virtue and Private Vices."

work of Mr. Flamsteed." Even the 1725 *Historia* was not guaranteed safety: Senex posed one danger, and Dutch booksellers also quickly threatened to reprint it and undersell the English.[182]

Daniel Defoe represented natural knowledge as the prime example of the benefits of writing and printing, and portrayed Flamsteed and Newton as the greatest proofs of those benefits.[183] This chapter has also identified these two figures as exemplary, but for rather different reasons. Their duel demonstrated how crucial it could be for aspirant providers of authoritative natural knowledge to master the domains of print, but also how difficult this was to achieve. Flamsteed's *Historia Cœlestis* comprised perhaps the most apparently objective and socially disjunct species of such knowledge: besides the calculated figures of the star catalogue itself, the core of the work was a long series of simple, raw, empirical observations. Yet even in such a case as this, manifold problems came to the fore—the problems identified in *The Nature of the Book*, concerning the uses of books as gifts and in markets, the importance of reading, the cultural practices of printing houses, the powers and civilities of Stationers, the possibilities of authorship, and the construction of credit. The issues encountered here were those faced by any number of learned writers. Without an appreciation of them our accounts of natural philosophy and astronomy at this key juncture are unsatisfactory. The whole conflict between Newton and Flamsteed was not only *about* a book; it was also mediated by books. At every stage, books acted as the vehicles, triggers, occasions, weapons, propaganda, and result of the battle. For examples, recall Flamsteed's accusation against Halley that he perfidiously appropriated intended gifts; or his note left in Newton's household bible; or Parker's almanac, which not only Flamsteed but the Stationers' Company itself tried to suppress. These should be signposts to an exciting range of subjects, of immediate importance to the cultural historian or the historian of science. We may begin to imagine some of them by posing the admittedly unhistorical, but gratifyingly simple, question: what would the history of modern science have been if positions had been reversed, and if Flamsteed and the Royal Observatory had been entrusted with publishing Newton's *Principia*?

182. Baily, *Flamsteed*, 363–4; Cudworth, *Sharp*, 143–4.
183. [Defoe], *Vindication of the Press*, 11.

9

CONCLUSION

We like to talk about the machines which we create and which enslave us. But machines are not only made of steel. Any intellectual category we may forge in the workshops of the mind is able to impose itself with the same force and the same tyranny—and holds even more stubbornly to its existence than the machines . . . History is a strongbox that is too well guarded, too firmly locked and bolted. Once something has been put in it for safe keeping it never gets back out.

LUCIEN FEBVRE, "How Jules Michelet Invented the Renaissance," 258

Be not deceived: evil communications corrupt good manners.

SAINT PAUL, 1 Corinthians 15:33 (after Menander,
Principal Fragments, 357)

Pick up a modern book, and there are certain features about it of which you can be immediately confident. Pick up an early modern book, however, and those features become less certain. An early modern reader could not necessarily take it for granted that something calling itself John Flamsteed's *Historia Cœlestis* would be owned by Flamsteed himself as the product of his authorship. It might not have been produced with his consent, and in his view it might not be what it claimed to be. Such an object might have been made by a bookseller or printer like Awnsham Churchill—or even one like John Streater—and under conditions very different from those obtaining today. A printed book might not have been published commercially, and it might well have been made with a specific, individual reader in mind. It could have been printed in anything from a few dozen to a few thousand copies, and a copy of the "same" book encountered in Paris, say, might differ significantly from one seen in London, Frankfurt, or Rome. Trusting in such an object meant vesting valuable faith in something very unlike the printed book familiar to readers at the end of the twentieth century.

Yet it is surely undeniable that such objects, fragile, insecure, and suspect though they were, became central to the subsequent course of Western history. Knowledge, politics, social life, and cultural practices were all transformed by the possibilities they offered. Today, accordingly, there can be few historians who do not rely substantially on printed sources, whether for their raw materials or to decide upon questions worth addressing in the first place. In an uncertain world, printed materials can be put to use in ways that make them powerful. *The Nature of the Book* has tried to explain how. It has attempted to reveal the historical roots of both their uncertainty and their authority.

Those who made and used books in early modern Europe labored as they did so to produce strategies for resolving their problems of credit. Much of the present work has been dedicated to a painstaking excavation of their efforts. Hitherto, historians have rather taken at face value the persuasive power of printed materials to affect the perceptions and actions of their readers; *The Nature of the Book* has conceded that this power came to exist, but has seen it as a hard-won and brittle achievement. It has therefore proposed that a richly detailed historical approach to the printed book, identifying it as a tool for the making of context and content alike, is the right one to adopt. This concluding chapter briefly recapitulates some of its major components, making explicit some points that may have remained implicit heretofore, before speculating as to some implications for our own experience of communications.

What is the history of the book for? A plausible answer lies in the role played by written and printed materials in the constitution of knowledge. The history of the book is consequential because it addresses the conditions in which knowledge has been made and utilized. All of its further implications may be derived from this. Hence the centrality in this work, and especially in its later sections, of the natural sciences. By concentrating on natural knowledge, we can hope to demonstrate how the making and use of printed materials could affect human comprehension at the most fundamental of levels. This book has thus aspired to display the centrality of practices surrounding print in the making, maintenance, and reception of representations of Creation, not because there is anything essentially unique about science, but for the very opposite reason. Conclusions demonstrated about science should be acknowledged as credible a fortiori for less authoritative fields.

The early sections of this book argued that the "domains" of print to be found in an early modern metropolis affected the ways in which knowledge of all kinds came into being and circulated. Debates had increasingly to be conducted through the mediation of these domains, where a community of "Stationers"—printers, booksellers, binders, and others—facilitated agreement and disagreement alike. Their skills conditioned whether and how contests surrounding controversial claims could proceed to resolution. Printed pages were not intrinsically trustworthy, not least because a certain creativity was essential to the Stationer's craft. Contemporary readers could, however, assess printed books according to the places, personnel, and practices of their production and distribution. The recognition of printed books as reliable thus depended substantially on prior representations of the Stationers' community as well ordered. Fixity depended on civility.

In the seventeenth century, questions of literary "propriety" were customarily decided out of writers' and readers' reach, in the citadel of Stationers' Hall. There a surprisingly rich social protocol developed, capable of dealing with an impressive range of issues ranging from illicit printing to seditious publishing and piracy. Its solidity was further cemented by a secure coordination with the government's licensing system. The resulting combination grew into a powerful and wide-ranging system to bolster the economic and epistemological standing of all printed books. It would scarcely be an exaggeration to claim that the reliability of every published page, whether licensed or not, rested on this bilateral régime.

To some, however, the régime seemed ineffectual, if not actively iniquitous. These opponents identified an alternative source of virtue not in the autonomy of a company, but in the all-embracing powers of the monarchy. The Stuarts found themselves exhorted to replace the Stationers' conventions with a system founded in royal patents. If realized, such a proposal would represent a revolutionary change in the cultural politics of print. No longer could printing be a communal craft; it would instead become an element of court service. The security of printed knowledge would rest on the civility of such service, not on the honesty and skill encapsulated in craft customs. John Streater, who was instrumental in creating this argument, had long advocated a republicanism based in the publication of laws, his aim being to produce an informed civic populace able to recognize and fight for its own "preserving liberty." Now he and Richard Atkyns argued that the Stationers' register illegitimately challenged the power of the crown to protect *meum* and *tuum* in general. In two respects their intervention proved momentous. The strategies Streater devised for publishing substantial and authoritative books in a hostile and piratical environment established practices that endured well into the succeeding century. Their arguments, moreover, set the terms for a debate on the nature of print that would persist even longer. The future of print would now be decided in a realm of congers, pirates, and dunces—to be joined, eventually, by authors.

With this new future came a new past. Atkyns and Streater had built their case against the existing order by rewriting the history of the press. The consequences of their story resonated for the next 150 years. Questions of authenticity and credit were central to what became a sophisticated argument over the origins, character, and implications of printing. The contributors to this debate, who included some of the Enlightenment's most influential and unusual figures, helped to reconstitute contemporary representations of the press. Tracing their controversies thus serves to demonstrate that alternatives were always available for contemporaries dissatisfied with descriptions numbly proclaiming the intrinsic "fixity" of print. Their existence matters, since early modern individuals and societies made far-reaching decisions about publishing and reading by reference to just this sort of knowledge. Only toward the end of the period did a representation of print culture begin to be articulated that is identifiable with modern equivalents, and even then it was unconventional. Moreover, analyzing these disputes also helps us to understand why, when it did finally arrive, the historiography of "fixity" was eventually to become so dominant. That modern writers have been able to refer to the press's ability to impose a "logic" of cultural behavior is, in fact, a consequence of its very inability to do so: proponents had to propagandize extensively in such terms to establish fixity as plausible. By ignoring the reasons for their statements, we risk taking for a technological fact what was really a hard-won cultural artifact. Men like Streater and Atkyns worked hard to rewrite the history of printing. We need to do the same.

The scope of this effort must extend from the continental to the microscopic. This is particularly true of the history of reading. In seventeenth-century Europe, human beings were typically seen as creatures of body and soul. Their knowledge was necessarily mediated through physiological mechanisms of perception and the passions, and that included the knowledge developed through reading. Readers needed to discipline their passions if they were to avoid erroneous or even dangerous results. This had three major consequences. First, texts could not easily transcend locale. Even the most raw and direct engagement with a page would be represented and understood in terms appropriated from resources to hand, especially items of knowledge of the human frame. The process of arriving at natural knowledge by the use of texts was thus often reflexive. As is today well known, the human body has a history and a geography of its own; reconciling these with the history of reading will be a fascinating and highly consequential enterprise. Second, if, as Paul Veyne has asserted, "history is knowledge through documents," then the consequences for historians themselves may be rather disconcerting.[1] They will need to be more aware than hitherto of the historical specificity of their own reading practices. And, third, to identify the

---

1. Veyne, *Writing History*, 5.

importance of the history of reading need not imply that the use of a book or periodical was ever *arbitrary*. In fact, particular uses of a book were always more or less costly or beneficial in particular circumstances. Ideal, asocial readers could perhaps have pursued any reading at all; real, historical ones could not prudently do so, since the social costs of most readings rendered them unlikely choices. No reader was an island. The achievement of the Royal Society was partly that it established a setting in which definitions of illegitimate reading would be set by the agreed and unspoken standards of genteel civility.

The consequences of this reassessment extend into the history of knowledge, and in particular into that of what is now the most authoritative knowledge of all: science. *The Nature of the Book* has argued that the epistemological implications of the Stationers' commonwealth became central issues of concern for early modern natural philosophers. Although recorded well before 1660, their fears became acute with the development of experimental philosophy in the Restoration. The practice of experiment instituted at the newly chartered Royal Society depended substantially on the making, distribution, and use of records. The Society had to become an arena dedicated to the polite management of philosophical disputes mediated by written and printed texts. That is, it had to work to establish and protect authorship itself. It attempted to do so by means of protocols involving disciplined reading, registration, and publication. The virtuosi put into practice principles of polite reading that were just as creative, practical, and performative as the experiments that are so much better known to historians of science. Some of these pioneering practices have since become fundamental to the scientific community. It has even been claimed that they *define* science.[2] Yet at first the Society was by no means unambiguously successful. Its eventual accomplishment was thus all the more impressive. It would provide an exemplar for eighteenth-century proponents of literary and other modes of authorship. The story of how it prospered by putting print to use is therefore a central component not only in the history of science, but in that of the book too.

That experimental philosophy, which depended on witnesses' testimony, should be acutely vulnerable to conventions of communication is perhaps not too uncomfortable a conclusion. But Boylean experimentalism was certainly not the only new approach to Creation developed in the late seventeenth century, and perhaps it should not even be regarded as the most important one.[3] It could still be argued that there was (and is) a core disci-

2. See remarks in Johns, "Ideal of Scientific Collaboration."
3. Dear, for example, characterizes Boylean practice as a "detour" on the route to modern experiment: *Discipline and Experience*, 3.

pline in the natural sciences to which these concerns could be considered peripheral. The mathematics of Isaac Newton's *Principia*, say, or the raw data garnered by a practical astronomer like John Flamsteed, surely rested on secure epistemological foundations in their own right. The geometrical rigor of the former, and the sheer empirical immediacy of the latter, would render both immune from the problems of credit permeating print. Even if problems obscured their value for a while, eventually that value must be recognized. It might even seem that such a notion enjoyed contemporary support, since it was conventional to observe that mathematical language compelled assent. Yet such confidence would be unmerited, as the story of Flamsteed's *Historia Cœlestis* confirms. The implications of Flamsteed's encounter with the Royal Society and the Stationers' commonwealth extended all the way to what modern academic philosophers, in their own canting speech, call "observation statements."[4] The credibility even of raw data was rendered contestable. And Newton made his own success partly by exploiting this situation—by becoming the press practitioner par excellence. Many of his most controversial victories relied on his mastering the practices of editing, printing, publishing, and reading. Newton knew how to "play the Stationer" and win, as Flamsteed discovered to his cost. By the time he was president of the Royal Society, he was therefore in a position to use its rules of propriety and printing to ruthless effect. In so doing, he may reasonably be seen as creating—rather than simply revealing—his own supremacy as the author of his age.

In the story of the *Historia Cœlestis*, the central issues of *The Nature of the Book* became visible and compelling. That story properly extends until at least the 1830s, when Francis Baily made the struggle between Flamsteed and Newton emblematic of a new quarrel pending between his own Royal Astronomical Society and the Royal Society.[5] This, along with the earlier pursuit of Coster and Corsellis into the nineteenth century, poses questions of the chronological focus applied in the rest of this book, and of what has transpired since the end of its chosen period. They are among a number of

4. I have myself heard a philosopher of science insist on this status for Flamsteed's figures, during the course of a paper he was delivering in Cambridge. The general claim remains, I think, a common one, although now very dated; for remarks, see Barnes, Bloor, and Henry, *Scientific Knowledge*, 1–17.

5. Interestingly, when he (and all other readers) had failed to decipher the shorthand of Flamsteed's most informed correspondent, Abraham Sharp, Baily turned to Charles Babbage for help. Babbage agreed to assist, and eventually succeeded in decoding Sharp's text: Baily, *Account of the Revd. John Flamsteed* (1835), 390–1 (not reprinted in the modern facsimile). Babbage's involvement at the end point of my story suggests an appealing metaphor for the trajectory of the current book, which might be summarized as leading from an "identity engine" (the now prevalent notion of the printing press) to a "difference engine" (the printing press as reconsidered here).

more general issues raised by the approach and conclusions of *The Nature of the Book*. It is appropriate to address them now.

To begin with, it is worth pausing to correct explicitly two interpretations of my work that I have occasionally heard voiced. The first is that I mean to reattribute the "scientific revolution" to printers. This is emphatically not so. Although Newton may (very debatably) have been a pirate, most pirates were not Newton. Besides, as remarked in chapter 4, a key point has in any case been to identify the collective and practical realization of authorship, and not simply to reassign to new individuals a concept of authorship that has itself remained unchanged and unquestioned. Second, *The Nature of the Book* is not simply the negative component of a dialectic. It does, I hope, effectively challenge the validity of current interpretations of print culture. But it has not been developed solely as a critique of those interpretations, and it does not simply advocate their obverse. Its roots and claims are fundamentally different. Moreover, its argument not only questions current assumptions about print; it also explains how they came into being, and why we have found them so plausible.

More seriously, it may be thought that *The Nature of the Book* has told only half a story. If the advent of fixity merely came later than has generally been supposed, then the close focus on the early modern period maintained here has simply amounted to looking in the wrong place. For the familiar story to reappear, according to this proposal, one would just have to extend the empirical treatment forward in time to the transformation in printing that undeniably occurred in the early to mid–nineteenth century. When that change came, first to iron presses and then to mechanized, steam-powered ones, it was as much a revolution in working practices as in technology. In the eyes of William Blades, for one, it was steam printing, not the hand press, that introduced the characteristics of modern print culture. As described at the end of chapter 5, Blades emphasized that it was only with lithography and industrial printing that one could finally become certain about the identity of the first English printer of all, William Caxton. If fixity came about at this juncture, then perhaps here is the change that should really be labeled as revolutionary. If so, then the further question arises of whether this transition was implicit in the craft of printing and merely took a long time to appear, or whether, on the other hand, it was specific to the industrial processes of Blades's and later times.

If it really amounted only to a claim that the familiar "printing revolution" happened four centuries later than anyone has hitherto thought, then the argument of *The Nature of the Book* would in the end not be all that disquieting. Such a claim would imply no more than a reconsideration of the chronology of what would, in essence, remain the existing story. Our understanding of our own situation would not have been seriously challenged. In fact, I would not wish to reject the point entirely: extremely important changes did take place with industrial printing. But I nonetheless hope and think that the implications of this book will not prove so easy to assimilate. Even Blades found that the most faithful technology available to him could not guarantee accreditation unless accompanied by testimony as to the probity and skill of its practitioner, whom he named. In practice, I suspect, much the same incapacity to enforce credit was experienced by other practitioners of the steam press, and it may even persist today. So why do modern readers assert the existence of fixity? If it does not inhere in printed objects simply by virtue of their being printed, where has it come from, and how is it maintained? These are the real questions underlying the chronological contention.

In contrast to the concrete empirical detail of earlier chapters, a speculative answer is the most that can here be advanced to such general questions. Their implications, however, are certainly extensive. It has been widely claimed that the deployment of identical texts and images on a very large scale is central to the experience of modern life. How we understand their advent and nature is therefore a subject of uncommon importance. The development of truly mechanized printing with the steam press is certainly one element. The new technology increased production rates vastly, and the relative concentration of capital needed to invest in such machinery did militate against a diversity of printing operations. Place is another factor. Industrialized printing and publishing moved from the home to the factory. In doing so, it may not quite have reduced human workers to the mechanical automata called, in Dickens's evocative term, "hands," but the new location's relatively rigorous discipline did condition people and their practices, exerting a conventional pressure to uniformity. Weber's argument that the separation of workplace from living space was a key moment of transition in the historical development of modern capitalism rings true in this context.[6] Yet new technologies and new places, while essential components of a satisfactory answer, cannot provide one alone. The experiences of groups such as the Society for the Diffusion of Useful Knowledge suggest why.

The Society for the Diffusion of Useful Knowledge has already been encountered in chapter 5. It was not the only body dedicated to employing the press to create uniformity among popular readers. But it was the most ambitious, and, as the first to make full use of the steam press, the most successful. As such, it is particularly revealing of the possibilities and limitations of industrial printing. The society aimed at "diffusing" safe knowledge mechanically to the new readership of the industrial working class, by means

6. Weber, *Protestant Ethic*, 21–2; Dickens, *Hard Times*, esp. 102–3.

of its *Penny Magazine* and *Penny Cyclopaedia*. It was founded out of a long-standing fear that even books innocuous enough in restricted settings could take on dangerous, even seditious, meanings in the hands of a mass proletarian audience. So it resolved to swamp the country with cheap periodicals containing "nothing to excite the passions." Lawrence, Paine, and the writings of materialist philosophers like La Mettrie must be overwhelmed by steam-printed "useful" knowledge. Geometry would be a chosen theme, not materialism; Paleyite natural history would supplant Lamarckian evolution. By 1832 its magazine was, as Brougham crowed, "by far the most extensively circulated of any periodical works that issue from the press." It estimated its readership at the unprecedented figure of one million.

But the effects of this enterprise were not necessarily those hoped for. Critics of all political persuasions understood and attacked the project. Peacock's negligent cook, who fell asleep while reading by candlelight a tract on hydraulics published by the "Steam Intellect Society" and almost burned Crotchet Castle to the ground, stood for a Tory conviction that the project dispersed unnecessary ideas that nonetheless might still prove dangerous. Radicals, on the other hand, complained of the anemic character of the *Penny Magazine*. They clamored for "really useful knowledge," yet found that the society wanted nothing more than to "stuff our mouths with Kangaroos." Moreover, the society itself was rather conflicted in its relation to the steam press. On the one hand, it clung to a belief that the *Penny Magazine* and *Penny Cyclopaedia*, produced in vast quantities and sold at a correspondingly low price, could "diffuse" safe knowledge safely. It argued that uniform texts would produce uniform docility in their proletarian readers, the press being (in Carlyle's words) "a machine for converting the Heathen." Yet on the other, its very existence was inspired by a contradictory concern that existing books might acquire newly dangerous applications in the hands of undisciplined readers. The paradox was expressed succinctly in a contemporary satirical print pastiching the *Penny Magazine* itself. The caricature displayed both Brougham's ideal (the "broom" being used to ram copies down a captive worker's throat was a common visual pun on the name of the society's leading advocate) and the variety of readings to which steam literature could be subjected. Each resulted in its own little social disaster, from traffic accidents to falling masonry (fig. 9.1).[7]

7. [Brougham], "Progress of the People," 234–41; Peacock, "Crotchet Castle," 13–14 (13–26 is a dialogic summary of arguments over knowledge in this period); Kelly, *Adult Education,* 112–80; Laqueur, *Religion and Respectability,* 113–19, 203–27; Johnson, "'Really Useful Knowledge'"; Gilmartin, *Print Politics,* 25–6, 83–4; Shapin and Barnes, "Head and Hand." For the social and epistemological controversies fomented by other groups' efforts to distribute cheap religious works, see Knox's excellent discussion in "Dephlogisticating the Bible." I am most grateful to Alison Winter for showing me the caricature of the *Penny Magazine*.

FIG. 9.1. A radical satire on steam intellect: ways of reading the *Penny Magazine*. (By permission of the British Museum, Department of Prints and Drawings.)

Like most successful jokes, the caricature on the *Penny Magazine* encapsulated a significant truth. Organizations such as the society found that their aspirations to "diffuse" modes of conduct through uniform texts fell victim to readers no less creatively appropriative than those who had stymied comparable projects during earlier eras. Indeed, it represents one among a succession of such attempts, the best known being those of the Counter-Reformation, all of which found their prospects for success qualified by the same factors; it is interesting to observe that the historiography of popular culture until recently built its conventional chronology around such programs. A more likely candidate than technological innovation for the advent of fixity is thus the practice and representation of reading itself. As urged throughout *The Nature of the Book*, reading is a complex skill with a complex history. It is not easily disciplined by texts. But that does not mean that it is free from all discipline whatsoever. Readings need to be defended in social settings if they are to be made consequential, and social settings generate maxims of conduct that one may not breach without cost. Successful readers are those who understand and exploit such maxims most effectively. They rest on a wide variety of foundations, including representations of society, gender, and Creation itself. One possible characterization of the present book, indeed, is that it constitutes a primer of the kinds of knowledge a person needed in early modern Europe in order to succeed in his or her reading: knowledge of the circumstances and personnel involved in making and distributing books, of the history and nature of printing itself, and of the shifting bounds of civility guiding distinctions between valid and illegitimate interpretation. In those shifting bounds, perhaps, lies the true history of fixity.

Between 1500 and 1900 this knowledge changed. Nothing made radical skepticism about printed objects impossible in principle. Indeed, it remains theoretically possible today. But it became increasingly costly to propose such radical skepticism in practice. In particular, the conventions of reading as well as those of publishing were transformed by the development of authorship. Around that concept was forged a civility—a congeries of practices and representations used to discriminate propriety from impropriety in everyday life. Radical skepticism about printed books became too costly, it may be argued, because it violated that civility. Its fee might well be exclusion from an authoritative group such as the Royal Society. And as the recognition of authorship blossomed, so, in a mutually reinforcing process, arguments demonstrating a resolved identity for printing began to win the upper hand, and the credit of its products became more widespread. By the end of the nineteenth century, print and fixity were as firmly conjoined by culture as ever could have been achieved by machinery. The appropriate mode in which to analyze their alliance, accordingly, was suddenly that of quantification. Steam printing now lent itself to the new science of statistics as hand printing never had. So it was that at the 1900 Paris Universal Exposition, the German Empire estimated itself to have published more than 700,000 new books in half a century, and to be producing 24,000 new publications yearly—"one printed composition of literary worth to every 2,000 persons . . . to every three Germans one copy of a book, and to every 2 Germans a literary printed composition." Nothing, its brochure remarked, "reveals the development of the intellectual life of Germany more significantly." The quantification is as striking as the quantities themselves. No *Annaliste* would ever match such literary metrology.[8]

The emergence of fixity was a matter of convention and trust, of culture and practice. As such, fixity may appropriately be compared to the kind of impersonal trust that is now customarily vested in modern organizations on the basis of their systems of expertise, without personal contact. Such credit is very difficult to challenge successfully. But Shapin and others have suggested that this routine and almost implicit faith may be resolved into more personal interactions if the focus of analysis is close enough. The same may be true of fixity.[9] If so, it may not really be justifiable to think of a clear and distinct division between modernity and its print culture, on the one hand, and the early modern world, with its realm of piracy and propriety, on the other. When we probe beyond commonplace representations, this suggestion seems increasingly probable.

Consider the following account of the making of an author, and ask yourself whether he was living in 1620 or 1920. The man concerned was an aspirant philosopher recently returned from military service in a cataclysmic war. Clutching the manuscript of a treatise that he was convinced would transform the enterprise of philosophy itself, he traversed the world of print looking for a publisher. One entrepreneur offered to produce the book if the writer himself would pay for the paper and printing. He refused, saying that such a process would be "indecent" and would signal disrespect for the work and its would-be author. "The writing was *my* affair," he maintained, "but the world must accept it in the normal manner." He further became aware that, at sixty pages, the manuscript seemed to occupy an unpromising genre. It was not specialized enough to be respected for its erudition, and not long enough to be read as an authoritative general treatise. Only "totally hopeless hacks" published such short books on such major themes, he averred, and he would not confirm his own membership of such a group by agreeing to what we today would call vanity publishing.

Further dispiriting experiences followed. A leading philosopher of the

8. Von Halle, "German Empire," 51–2 (a reference for which I am grateful to Richard Staley).

9. Giddens, *Consequences of Modernity*, 26–36; Shapin, *Social History of Truth*, 409–17.

time suggested that he split the work into fragments and publish them as papers in one of the philosophical journals then struggling to unite a republic of letters. This too the writer declined, saying that such division would "mutilate it from beginning to end and, in a word, make another work out of it." He then approached a literary journal, sending a series of letters to the editor that even now constitute his most extensive surviving exegesis of the work. Nonetheless, the editor declined the text, citing the economic problems facing the publishing craft. At this point the writer began to contemplate suicide. The shocked editor promptly offered to print his piece out of sympathy, but even now would do so only if he could obliterate the forbidding numeration of paragraphs that made the text look like a piece of mathematics. Its writer again refused, saying that such an edition would be "incomprehensible." Who were these men to insist on such changes? he demanded to know. "Is there a *Krampus* who collects evil publishers?" At this point, during a visit to The Hague, he met another leading philosopher, himself a proven author. This new patron offered to contribute a preface to the work, and, since he was already known to printers, his endorsement would of itself render the writer's text no "risk" for any undertaker. Yet still nobody would take it up, even in the publishing center of Leipzig. The writer gave up hope and went to work in a monastery as a gardener.

By now, though, the manuscript was out of the writer's hands once and for all. The great philosopher whose patronage he had gained at The Hague had passed it on to a friend. At length, the editor of a journal of natural philosophy agreed to print this text—an editor, however, whom the writer himself believed to be "an utter charlatan" who would "tamper" with the text. Hearing of the intended printing, he tried to secure at least the reliability of the content. Would his patron personally oversee the proofs? the writer anxiously inquired. His fear proved justified, since in the event nobody did. Far from meddling with the text, however, the printers exercised too little creativity. The edition they produced was full of incomprehensible peculiarities reproduced directly from personal codes in the manuscript, which should have been translated into logical and mathematical symbols for publication. Their literal transcription was not prevented since the writer himself was never consulted, and indeed never received even the final publication. When he did at length encounter a copy—printed in Germany, but sent from England—he denounced it as a "pirated edition" (*Raubdruck*). And as his modern biographer says, this printing indeed resembled "a Shakespeare quarto—and [would be] of as little use for establishing a better text." Horrified, the writer himself then redoubled his efforts to produce a correct version. He believed his real work to have been published only when an English text at length appeared that he had overseen himself, and that included substantial changes (not the least of which was a new title). Its translator had visited him in person, and they had read through the text together while he explained its more difficult passages. With this disciplining exerted, the book finally emerged in a form satisfactory to its creator. But even now, the publishers paid nothing for their reproduction rights.[10]

This writer had undergone a grand tour of the world of print before finally succeeding in his ambition to become a published author. He had experienced rejection, the need for patronage, the essential value of face-to-face conversations, the willingness of publishers creatively to amend his work (and the incomprehensibility of the resulting text when they did *not* do so), the vicissitudes of journal editors, the difficulties of manuscript circulation, and the humiliation of piracy. He had also realized the need to discipline readers in person. But who, and when, was he? The experience could well have been Descartes's, Galileo's, Spinoza's, or Flamsteed's, and it could have befallen any would-be learned author of the sixteenth, seventeenth, or eighteenth century. In fact, however, it was the young Ludwig Wittgenstein who encountered these problems. He did so between 1919 and 1923, after returning to Austria at the end of World War I. The philosopher who suggested fragmenting his work was Frege. The patron at The Hague was Bertrand Russell. The "pirate" was the chemist Wilhelm Ostwald, who edited a journal named *Annalen der Naturphilosophie*. The English translator was Frank Ramsey, and the work that he finally helped save from these perils was published in 1922 as Wittgenstein's *Tractatus Logico-Philosophicus*. It is, of course, a founding tract of modern philosophy.

If such an important publication was produced and circulated in such circumstances, what are we to make of the assumption that fixity is central to modern life and may be taken for granted? We may reasonably doubt that modern published communication really operates in a world of unquestioning trust in such a quality. Anyone who has had to negotiate in the arena of publishing houses, agents, subcontracted printers, proofreaders, referees, and editors will need no telling that a published work is at least as much a collective product, and its content is at least as dependent on the caprice of countless collaborators, as any seventeenth-century treatise—or Wittgenstein's *Tractatus*. On an individual level, writers are very likely to testify to the compromises this necessarily involves. Collectively, modern authorship itself in practice rests on them. Moreover, it remains the case that books, periodicals, newspapers, and the other manifold products of the press are

10. Monk, *Wittgenstein*, 173–84, 191, 203–7, 216; McGuinness, *Wittgenstein*, 296–7; Janik and Toulmin, *Wittgenstein's Vienna*, 192–3; Engelmann, *Letters from Ludwig Wittgenstein*, 48–9.

put to use in a vast range of different ways, and that their consequences are as dependent on the practices of their users as on any putatively objective content they may possess. For what it is worth, my own impression is that academic readers certainly do draw upon knowledge of such elements as the character of the publisher and the institution of the author in determining their response to a given work, and that such factors play an important part in conditioning such a work's influence.

At the risk of sounding unacceptably gnomic, one may conclude from stories like Wittgenstein's that the experiences of people in modern print culture are neither the same as nor different from those discussed in the body of this book. No such simple, constant, and unambiguous relation can be identified. The complex printing and reading practices developed in specific local settings in the interim would in any case be ill served by any attempt to telescope the intervening period into one brief epilogue. But past and present may, perhaps, be *approachable* in similar ways. Needless to say, the political and moral economies of publishing and reading are enormously different now from their state in Newton's day. Nevertheless, a close examination will almost certainly reveal not an elimination of sociability and civility in the constitution of reliable communication, but a transformation of the kinds of sociability and civility involved. *The Nature of the Book* points to the importance of these changes, in the various agencies involved with the book: publishers, booksellers, editors, authors, and readers. It exemplifies the understanding of communication in such terms.[11] In this respect the current work represents a necessary and replicable unification of the historiographies of civility and print.

If the changes that have taken place are indeed changes of sociability, this will have implications for the kind of history we compose. It will need to be fine-grained social history, with a different focus and perhaps a changed chronology. *The Nature of the Book* has concentrated largely on England; it has not dealt at length with Venice, Antwerp, Frankfurt, or Paris. But it is significant that print in these different cultural settings should be appreciated as just that: *different*. Moreover, similar approaches, to which the current work is indebted, are already being applied to these other regions. It is becoming increasingly difficult to characterize a single "revolution" associated with print that maintained the same nature across them all. Instead we shall perceive a multiplicity of less immediately evident, but equally pro-

11. This relation of fixity to civility should be compared to the arguments in Daston, "Baconian Facts," 348–58, and Porter, *Trust in Numbers*, 217–31, that concepts of objectivity came about in parallel circumstances, partly as efforts to unify fractious communities of scientists. Porter's argument should be compared closely to that of Shapin in *Social History of Truth*. See Porter et al., "Gently Boyle," 1–6, 19–23, for a direct confrontation between the two perspectives.

found and consequential, dynamic processes. I myself doubt that even the invention of authorial copyright—which is probably the current candidate to replace fixity as the centerpiece of a historiography of printing revolution—can really stand muster as the focus of a single transforming change. And the contention that the cultural significance of print can properly be understood only in fully contextual terms should hold good a fortiori for modern communications technologies. In this age of worldwide networks, e-mail, fax, photocopiers, word processors, desktop publishing, and satellite communications (all of which, incidentally, played their part in the production of this book), it is especially important that we attain a judicious understanding of the role we accord such devices in our own society. Such an understanding will need to include not just the results of these technologies, but the social and cultural foundations of their authority.[12] It is interesting to note, for example, that in these spheres credibility seems again to be at a premium. Financial institutions and other corporations are laboring to establish a means of rendering electronic communication secure enough to supplant more traditional media. It is not too fanciful to compare these efforts to the Royal Society's endeavors to secure the credit of printed communications in the seventeenth century. The implications may well prove just as far-reaching.

It is consequently reasonable to question the rather hyperbolic descriptions that so often appear on television and in the press, forecasting extraordinary trends in communications technologies and warning of massive future consequences. Such accounts typically combine a sophisticated account of the technology involved with rudimentary misunderstandings of the history and sociology. Suppose for a moment that we really lived in the new age of global uniformity that is so frequently heralded. The implications for our approach to history, at least, would be radically different. In such a world, it would no longer make sense to say that the past is a different country, since countries would have become indistinguishable. Regional and national cultures would have been rendered uniform by their common subjection to News Corporation, Microsoft, and Disney, so that such an aphorism would be meaningless. The eradication of such differences would be seen as the progressive realization of communicative objectivity, in much the same way as the advent of "fixity" does today. The past would no longer be a different country—just a different channel.

The study of history in our own realm tells us that such an outcome is

---

12. A comparison is appropriate in this respect with current initiatives in the "Public Understanding of Science," which face a similar issue: should they aim to convey a simplified version of scientific knowledge, or an understanding of how science itself attains its conclusions and invests them with such substantial authority? Scientists tend to favor the former.

unlikely. Monolithic hegemony of this order is fortunately not yet achieved, and if the approach of this book is valid then its achievement may even be impossible. At least, it will not be attainable by the mechanisms now typically proposed. That is a substantial conclusion to draw. The implications of communications technologies will, of course, be wide ranging and significant, but they are unlikely to be monolithic or hegemonic. They can best be understood and mastered with an appropriate knowledge of the cultural dynamics involved, and an appreciation of their appropriations by users as well as their impositions on them. History can make a contribution to this debate. If communications technologies were intrinsically authenticating, then there would be little the historian could usefully say about that fact. *The Nature of the Book*, on the contrary, asserts our capability not just to document the link between print and veracity, but to explain it. The final assertion of this book is, then, that we can address major current issues of communication, and perhaps even explain them, by using the historian's craft. It is, I think, an optimistic conclusion.

ON THE WORLD

The World's a *Booke*, writ by th'eternall *Art*

Of the great Maker, *printed* in Mans heart;

Tis falsely *printed*, though divinely *pend*,

And all th'*Errata* will appeare at th'*end*.

FRANCIS QUARLES, *Divine Fancies* (London, 1641), 173

BIBLIOGRAPHY

ABBREVIATIONS FOR MANUSCRIPT REFERENCES

BL	British Library, London
Bodl.	Bodleian Library, University of Oxford
Clark	William Andrews Clark Library, Los Angeles
CLRO	Corporation of London Record Office
CUL	University Library, Cambridge
GL	Guildhall Library, London
Hartlib Papers	Hartlib Papers, University Library, Sheffield
Huntington	Henry E. Huntington Library, San Marino, California
Inn. Temp.	Inner Temple Library, London
NUL	University Library, Nottingham
PRO	Public Record Office, London
Regenstein	Regenstein Library, University of Chicago
RGO	Royal Greenwich Observatory Archive (stored in CUL)
RS	Royal Society, London
SCA	Archive of the Worshipful Company of Stationers and Newspaper-makers, Stationers' Hall, London; supplementary documents are listed by box (A–G, K–Q, X–Z) and item (see Myers, *Stationers' Company Archive*, 85–130, 146–80, 191–4, 203–4)
SCA, Leybourn, "Survey"	William Leybourn, "A Survey, both General & Particular; of all the Lands & Tenements Belonging to the Wpf. Company of Stationers London" (Myers, *Stationers' Company Archive*, 57, § 74)
SCB C–H	Stationers' Company Archive, Court Books C–H (1602–1733)
Southampton CRO	Southampton Civic Record Office

PRIMARY SOURCES

Absalom Senior: or, Achitophel Transpos'd. London: printed for S. E. and sold by L. Curtis, 1682.

"An Account of a book, entitled, *Historia Cœlestis Britannica, tribus Voluminibus Contenta, Authore* Joanne Flamsteedio *Astronomo Regio.*" *Philosophical Transactions* 389 (1725): 350–2.

Acton, G. *Physical Reflections upon a Letter written by J. Denis.* London: printed by T. R. for J. Martyn, 1668 [represented as part of the *Philosophical Transactions*].

[Addison, J.] *The Thoughts of a Tory Author, Concerning the Press.* London: printed for A. Baldwin, 1712.

Akerman, J. Y., ed. *Moneys Received and Paid for Secret Services of Charles II and James II from 30th March, 1679, to 25th December, 1688.* London: Camden Society, 1851.

Albemarle, Duke of. *Observations upon Military and Political Affairs.* London: printed by A. C. for H. Mortlocke and J. Collins, 1671.

Allacci, L. *Animadversiones in Antiquitatem Etruscarum Fragmenta ab Inghiramio Edita.* Paris: S. Cramoissy, 1640.

Allamand, J. N. S., ed. *Oeuvres Philosophiques et Mathématiques de M. G. J. 'sGravesande.* 2 vols. Amsterdam: M. M. Rey, 1774.

Ames, J. *Typographical Antiquities: Being an Historical Account of Printing in England.* London: printed by W. Faden, sold by J. Robinson, 1749.

Ames, J. (augmented by W. Herbert). *Typographical Antiquities.* 3 vols. London: printed for the editor [i.e., W. Herbert], 1785–90.

Ampsing, S. *Beschryvinge ende lof der Stad Haerlem in Holland.* Haarlem: printed by A. Rooman, 1628 (bound with Scriverius, *Laure-Crans*).

Arguments Relating to a Restraint upon the Press. London: printed for R. and J. Bonwicke, 1712.

Aristotle. *The Politics.* Harmondsworth: Penguin, 1981.

[Asgill, J.] *An Essay for the Press.* London: printed for A. Baldwin, 1712.

Ash, S. *A Support for the sinking Heart in times of Distresse.* London: printed by G. M. and sold by T. Underhill, 1642.

[Atkyns, R.] *The Original and Growth of Printing.* [London: n.p., 1660–1].

Atkyns, R. *The Original and Growth of Printing: Collected out of History, and the Records of this Kingdome. Wherein is also Demonstrated, that Printing appertaineth to the Prerogative Royal, and is a Flower of the Crown of England.* London: printed by John Streater for the author, 1664.

Atkyns, R. *The Vindication of Richard Atkyns Esquire. As also a Relation of several Passages in the Western-War, wherein he was concern'd. Together, with certain sighs or Ejaculations at the end of every Chapter. Dedicated to his particular friends: and intended to no other.* London: n.p., 1669.

[Atkyns, R. and/or Streater, J.] *The Kings Grant of Privilege for Sole Printing Common-Law-Books, defended; and the Legality thereof Asserted.* London: printed by John Streater, 1669.

Atlas Maritimus & Commercialis; Or, a General View of the World, so far as relates to Trade and Navigation. London: printed for J. and J. Knapton, W. and J. Innys, J. Darby, A. Bettesworth, J. Osborn, T. Longman, J. Senex, E. Symon, A. Johnston, and the executors of W. Taylor, 1728.

Atlas Maritimus Novus, or the New Sea-Atlas. London: printed for R. Mount and T. Page, 1702.

Atterbury, F. *Fourteen Sermons Preach'd on Several Occasions.* London: printed by E. P. for J. Bowyer, 1708.

Atterbury, F. *A Large Vindication of the Doctrine Contained in the Sermon preach'd at the Funeral of Mr. Thomas Bennet.* London: printed and sold by Henry Hills, 1707.

Atterbury, F. *A Sermon Preached in the Cathedral Church of St. Paul; at the Funeral of Mr. Tho. Bennet.* London: printed by E. P. for J. Bowyer, 1706.

Atterbury, F. *A Sermon Preach'd in the Cathedral Church of St. Paul; at the Funeral of Mr. Tho. Bennet.* London: printed and sold by H. Hills "For the Benefit of the Poor," 1707.

Aubrey, J. *Brief Lives.* Edited by R. Barber. Woodbridge: Boydell Press, 1982.

Bacon, F. *The Works of Francis Bacon.* 14 vols. Edited by J. Spedding, R. Ellis, and D. D. Heath. London: Longman et al., 1857–74.

Bacon, N. *An Historical and Political Discourse of the Laws & Government of England.* 2 vols. London: printed for J. Starkey, to be sold by J. Robinson, R. Bentley, J. Tonson, T. Goodwin, and T. Fox, 1689.

Bagford, J. "An Essay on the Invention of *Printing,* by Mr. *John Bagford*; with an Account of his Collections for the same, by Mr. *Humfrey Wanley,* F.R.S. Communicated in two Letters to Dr. *Hans Sloane,* R.S. Secr." *Philosophical Transactions* 310 (1707): 2397–2410.

Baily, F. *An Account of the Reverend John Flamsteed, the first Astronomer-Royal . . . To which is added, his British Catalogue of Stars, Corrected and Enlarged.* London: for the Admiralty, 1835. Facsimile reprint of *Account* only, London: Dawson, 1966.

Balzac, Honoré de. *Lost Illusions.* Translated by H. J. Hunt. Harmondsworth: Penguin, 1971.

Ball, W. *Stationars and Printers, a Privilegial, not Municipal Companie or Corporation.* [London: n.p.], 1652.

Barnard, J. *Theologo-Historicus: Or, the True Life of the Most Reverend Divine, and Excellent Historian Peter Heylyn.* London: printed for J. S., to be sold by E. Eckelston, 1683.

Barozzi da Vignola, G. *Vignola: Or the Compleat Architect.* Translated by J. Moxon. London: printed and sold by J. Moxon, 1655.

Baxter, R. *A Holy Commonwealth.* 1659. Reprint, edited by W. Lamont, Cambridge: Cambridge University Press, 1994.

Bayer, J. *Uranometria.* Augsburg: printed by C. Mangus, 1603.

Bayle, P. *A General Dictionary, Historical and Critical.* 10 vols. Edited by J. P. Bernard et al. London: printed by J. Bettenham, 1734–41.

[Bee, C.] *The Case of Cornelius Bee and his Partners, Richard Royston, William Wells, Samuel Thompson, Thomas Robinson, and William Morden, Booksellers.* [London]: n.p., [1668?] (item C900 in Wing, *Short-Title Catalogue*).

Bentley, R. *A Dissertation upon the Epistles of Phalaris. With an Answer to the Objections of the Honourable Charles Boyle, Esquire.* London: printed by J. H. for H. Mortlock and J. Hartley, 1699.

Beverwyck, J. van. *Wercken.* Amsterdam: printed by J. J. Schipper, 1667.

Bibliotheca Militum: or the Souldiers Publick Library. London: n.p., 1659.

Bibliotheca Norfolciana: sive Catalogus Libb. Manuscriptorum & Impressorum In Omni Arte & Lingua. London: printed by R. Chiswel, 1681.

Billingsley, H. *The Elements of Geometrie of the most Auncient Philosopher Euclide of Megara.* London: printed by J. Day, 1570.

Biographia Britannica. 6 vols. in 7. London: printed for W. Innys et al., 1747–66.

Birch, T., ed. *A Collection of the State Papers of John Thurloe, Esq.* 7 vols. London: for the executors of F. Gyles, for T. Woodward, and for C. Davis, 1742.

Birch, T., ed. *The History of the Royal Society of London for Improving of Natural Knowledge, from its First Rise.* 4 vols. London: printed for A. Millar, 1756–7.

[Blackmore, Sir Richard]. *A Satyr against Wit.* London: printed for S. Crouch, 1700.

Blades, W. *The Life and Typography of William Caxton, England's First Printer.* 2 vols. London: J. Lilly, 1861–3.

Blaeu, W. J. *A Tutor to Astronomy and Geography.* Edited by J. Moxon. London: printed for J. Moxon, 1654.

Blount, C. *Anima Mundi: or, an Historical Narration of the Opinions of the Ancients Concerning Man's Soul after this Life: According to Unenlightened Nature* (London, "Printed in the

Year, 1679"). Bound with other tracts as *The Miscellaneous Works of Charles Blount, Esq.* [London]: n.p., 1695.

[Blount, C.] *A Just Vindication of Learning: or, An Humble Address to the High Court of Parliament in behalf of the Liberty of the Press.* London: n.p., 1679.

[Blount, C.] *Reasons Humbly offered for the Liberty of Unlicens'd Printing . . . In a Letter from a Gentleman in the Country, to a Member of Parliament.* London: n.p., 1693.

Blount, T. *The Correspondence of Thomas Blount (1618–1679): A Recusant Antiquary.* Edited by T. Bongaerts. Amsterdam: APA-Holland University Press, 1978.

Blount, T. *Glossographia: or a Dictionary, Interpreting all such Hard Words, . . . as are now used in our refined English Tongue.* London: printed by T. Newcomb for H. Moseley and G. Sawbridge, 1656.

Blount, T. *Νομο-Λεχικον: A Law Dictionary.* London: printed by T. Newcomb for J. Martyn and H. Herringman, 1670.

Bohun, E. *The Diary and Autobiography of Edmund Bohun Esq.* Edited by S. W. Rix. Beccles: Read Crisp, 1853. Facsimile reprint, New York: Garland, 1975.

Bohun, E. *A Geographical Dictionary.* London: printed for C. Brome, 1688.

Böhme, J. *Aurora.* London: printed by J. Streater for G. Calvert, 1656.

Böhme, J. *Concerning the election of Grace.* London: printed by J. Streater for G. Calvert and J. Allen, 1655.

Bond, M. F., ed. *The Manuscripts of the House of Lords. XI (new series): Addenda 1514–1714.* London: HMSO, 1962.

Bossuet, J.-B. *Politics Drawn from the Very Words of Holy Scripture.* Edited by P. Riley. Cambridge: Cambridge University Press, 1990.

Boswell, J. *Life of Johnson.* Edited by R. W. Chapman. Oxford: Oxford University Press, 1980.

[Bowyer, W. and Nichols, J.] *The Origin of Printing: In two Essays: I. The substance of Dr. MIDDLETON's Dissertation on the Origin of Printing in England. II. Mr. MEERMAN's Account of the Invention of the Art at HARLEIM, and its Progress to MENTZ.* 2d ed. London: printed for W. Bowyer and J. Nichols, 1776.

Boyle, C. *Dr. Bentley's Dissertations on the Epistles of Phalaris, and the Fables of Aesop, Examin'd.* London: printed for T. Bennet, 1698.

Boyle, R. *A Continuation of New Experiments Physico-Mechanical Touching the Spring and Weight of the Air . . . The Second Part.* London: printed by M. Flesher for R. Davis, Oxford, 1682.

Boyle, R. *The Early Essays and Ethics of Robert Boyle.* Edited by J. T. Harwood. Carbondale: Southern Illinois University Press, 1991.

[Boyle, R.] "An Epistolical Discourse . . . Inviting All True Lovers of Vertue and Mankind, to a Free and Generous Communication of Their Secrets and Receits in Physick." In Hartlib, *Chymical, Medicinal, and Chyrurgical Addresses,* 113–50.

Boyle, R. *Works.* 6 vols. Edited by T. Birch. London: printed for J. and F. Rivington et al., 1772.

Brahe, Tycho. *Astronomiae Instauratae Mechanica.* Wandesbek: n.p., 1598.

Brahe, Tycho. *Astronomiae Instauratae Mechanica.* Nuremburg: Levinus Hulsius, 1602.

Brahe, Tycho. *Epistolarum Astronomicarum Libri.* Vol. 1. Uraniborg: from the author's printing house, 1596.

Brahe, Tycho. *Learned Tico Brahae his Astronomicall Conjectur of the new and much Admired* ✴. London: printed by B. A. and T. F. for Michael Sparke and Samuel Nealand, 1632.

Brahe, Tycho. *Opera Omnia.* 15 vols. Edited by J. L. E. Dreyer. Copenhagen: Gyldendal.

Bray, T. *An Essay towards promoting all Necessary and Useful Knowledge.* London: printed by E. Holt for R. Clavel, 1697.

Brewster, D. *Memoirs of the Life, Writings and Discoveries of Sir Isaac Newton.* 2 vols. Edinburgh: T. Constable, 1855.

A Brief Description of an Edition of the Bible. [London, 1652].

A Brief Discourse Concerning Printing and Printers. London: "Printed for a Society of Printers," 1663.

Briggs, W. *Nova Visionis Theoria.* London: printed by J. P., for S. Simpson; sold by S. Smith, 1685.

Briggs, W. *Ophthalmo-graphia, sive Oculi ejusque partium descriptio Anatomica.* Cambridge: printed by J. Hayes for J. Hart, 1676.

Bromhall, T. *An History of Apparitions.* London: printed by J. Streater, 1658.

[Brougham, H.] "Progress of the People—The Periodical Press." *Edinburgh Review* 57 (1833): 239–48.

[Brougham, H.] *Reflections to a Late Book, Entituled, The Genuine Remains of Dr. Tho. Barlow, late Bishop of Lincoln. Falsly pretended to be Published from His Lordships Original Papers.* London: printed for R. Clavell, 1694.

Browne, T. *Pseudodoxia Epidemica.* 2d ed. London: printed by A. Miller for E. Dod and N. Ekins, 1650.

Browne, T. *The Works of Sir Thomas Browne.* 4 vols. Edited by G. Keynes. Chicago: University of Chicago Press, 1964.

Browning, R. *The Poems.* 2 vols. Edited by J. Pettigrew. New Haven: Yale University Press, 1981.

Buckley, S. *A Short State of the Publick Encouragement given to Printing and Bookselling in France, Holland, Germany, and at London.* [London]: n.p., n.d.

Burrow, J. *The Question Concerning Literary Property, determined by the Court of King's Bench on 20th April 1769.* London: printed by W. Strahan and M. Woodfall, Law Printers to the King's Most Excellent Majesty, for B. Tovey, 1773.

Burton, R. *The Anatomy of Melancholy.* 2 vols. Edited by T. C. Faulkner, N. K. Kiessling, R. L. Blair, and J. B. Bamborough. Oxford: Oxford University Press, 1989–90.

Butler, C. *The Feminine Monarchie: Or The Historie of Bees.* London: printed by J. Haviland for R. Jackson, 1623.

Butler, S. *Characters.* Edited by C. W. Daves. Cleveland: Case Western Reserve University Press, 1970.

[Butler, S.] *Hudibras. The First Part.* London: printed by J. G. for R. Marriot, 1663.

[Butler, S.] *Hudibras. The Second Part.* London: printed by T. R. for J. Martyn and J. Allestry, 1664.

Butler, S. *Hudibras Parts I and II and Selected Other Writings.* 1663–4. Reprint, edited by J. Wilders and H. de Quehen, Oxford: Oxford University Press, 1973.

Byrom, J. *The Private Journal and Literary Remains of John Byrom.* 2 vols. in 4. Edited by R. Parkinson. Manchester: Chetham Society, 1854–7.

Byrom, J. *Selections from the Journals and Papers of John Byrom.* Edited by H. Talon. London: Rockliff, 1950.

"A Calculation of the Credibility of Humane Testimony." In Halley, *Miscellanea Curiosa,* II, 1–8.

Calendar of Treasury Books. 32 vols. London: HMSO, 1904–57.

Campbell, R. *The London Tradesman.* London: printed by T. Gardner, 1747.

Casaubon, M. *A Letter of Meric Casaubon D.D. &c. . . . Concerning Natural experimental Philosophie, and some books lately set out about it.* Cambridge: printed for W. Morden, 1669.

Casaubon, M. *Of Credulity and Incredulity, in things Natural, Civil, and Divine.* London: printed for T. Garthwait, 1668.

Casaubon, M. *A Treatise Concerning Enthusiasme, as it is an Effect of Nature.* London: printed by R. D., sold by T. Johnson, 1655.

The Case of Designers, Engravers, Etchers, &c. Stated. In a Letter to a Member of Parliament. London: n.p., [ca. 1735].

The Case of the Booksellers and Printers Stated; with Answers to the Objections of the Patentee. [London]: n.p., [ca. 1666].

The Case of the Inhabitants of the Town and Parish of Croydon, in the County of Surrey: concerning the Great Oppressions they ly under, by reason of the Unparallel'd Extortions, and violent illegal and unwarrantable Prosecutions of Doctor William Clewer, Vicar of the said Parish. London: n.p., 1673.

Castiglione, B. *The Book of the Courtier.* Translated by T. Hoby. 1561. Reprint, London: Everyman, 1928.

Catalogus Librorum Reverendi Doctiq; Viri Matth. Smallwood, STP. London: n.p., 1684.

The Catholick Almanack. London: printed by H. Hills, 1687.

Chambers, E. *Cyclopaedia: or, an Universal Dictionary of Arts and Sciences.* 2 vols. London: printed for J. and J. Knapton, J. Darby, et al., 1728.

The Character of a Coffee-House. London: printed for J. Edwin, 1673.

The Character or Ear-Mark of Mr. William Prinne Bencher of Lincolnes-Inne. London: n.p., 1659.

[Charleton, W.] *A Brief Discourse concerning the Different Wits of Men.* London: printed by R. W. for W. Whitwood, 1669.

[Charleton, W.] *Natural History of the Passions.* London: printed by T. N. for James Magnes, 1674.

Charleton, W. *Physiologia Epicuro-Gassendo-Charltoniana.* London: printed by T. Newcomb for T. Heath, 1654.

The Charter and Grants of the Company of Stationers. With Observations and Remarks thereon. London: n.p., n.d. (In SCA, Suppl. Doc. F, Env. 24).

The Charter and Grants of the Company of Stationers of the City of London. London: printed by R. Nutt, 1761.

Clarendon, Earl of. *History of the Rebellion and Civil Wars in England.* 3 vols. Oxford: printed at the Sheldonian Theatre, 1702–4.

Clarke, J. F. *Autobiographical Recollections of the Medical Profession.* London: J. and A. Churchill, 1874.

C[leveland], J. *The Character of a Diurnal-Maker.* London: n.p., 1654.

C[leveland], J. *Poems.* London: n.p., 1654.

Collier, J. [Tim Bobbin, pseud.] *Human Passions Delineated.* Manchester: J. Heywood, 1773.

Comenius, J. A. *A Reformation of Schooles.* London: printed for M. Sparke, 1642.

Condorcet, J. A. Nicolas de Caritat, Marquis de. *Sketch for a Historical Picture of the Progress of the Human Mind.* Translated by J. Barraclough, edited by S. Hampshire. New York: Noonday Press, 1955.

A Conference Held between the Old Lord Protector and the New Lord General, Truly Reported by Hugh Peters. London: n.p., 1660.

Contat, N. *Anecdotes Typographiques, . . . by Nicolas Contat dit Le Brun.* Edited by G. Barber. Oxford: Oxford Bibliographical Society, 1980.

Conway, A. *The Conway Letters: The Correspondence of Anne, Viscountess Conway, Henry More, and Their Friends 1642–1684.* Edited by M. H. Nicolson; revised ed. by S. Hutton. Oxford: Clarendon Press, 1992.

C[ooper], W. *A Philosophicall Epitaph in Hieroglyphicall Figures.* London: printed for W. Cooper, 1673.

Cowley, A. *The Works of Mr. Abraham Cowley.* 11th ed. 3 vols. London: printed for J. Tonson, 1710.

Craig, J. "Rules of Historical Evidence." 1699. Reprinted in *History and Theory* 4 (1964): 1–31.

Cranford, J. *Haereseo-machia: or, The mischiefe which Heresies doe, and the means to prevent it.* London: printed by J. Young for C. Green, 1646.

Croke, G. *An Abridgement of the three volumes of Reports.* Edited by W. Hughes. London: printed for J. Starkey, T. Basset and S. Speed, 1665.

Croke, G. *The First Part (Though last Publish't) of the Reports.* London: printed for A. Roper, T. Collins, F. Tyton, J. Place, J. Starkey and T. Basset, 1659.

Croke, G. *The First Part (though last publish't) of the Reports.* London: printed by and for J. Field and G. Bedell, and sold at their shops; also for W. Lee, D. Pakeman, and G. Bedell, and sold at their shops, 1661.

Croke, G. *The Reports.* London: printed by J. S., to be sold by the Stationers of London, 1657.

Croke, G. *The Second Part of the Reports.* London: printed by T. Newcomb and W. Godbid, sold by W. Lee, D. Pakeman, A. Roper, H. Twyford, G. Bedell, and T. Dring, G. Sawbridge, and J. Place, 1658.

Croke, G. *The Second Part of the Reports.* London: printed by T. Newcomb and W. Godbid, to be sold by J. Field, 1659.

Cromwell, O. *Writings and Speeches.* 4 vols. Edited by W. C. Abbott. Cambridge: Harvard University Press, 1937–47.

Cudworth, R. *A Discourse Concerning the True Notion of the Lord's Supper. To which are added Two Sermons.* 3d ed. London: printed for R. Royston, 1676.

Curtius, A. [Lucius Barettus, pseud.]. *Historia Cælestis.* Augsburg: S. Utzschneider, 1666; reissue Ratisbon: J. C. Emmrich, 1672.

[Daniel, G.] *A Voyage to the World of Cartesius.* London: printed; and sold by T. Bennet, 1692.

"A Declaration of the Council of the *Royal Society*, passed *Novemb.* 20. 1676; relating to some Passages in a late Book of Mr. *Hooke* entituled *Lampas, &c.*" *Philosophical Transactions* 129 (Oct.–Nov. 1676): 749–50.

A Declaration of the Officers of the Army. London: printed by H. Hills, for H. Hills and W. Mountfort, 1659.

Dee, J. "John Dee his Mathematicall Praeface." In Billingsley, *Elements*, sigs. [☞4ʳ]–A4ᵛ.

[Defoe, D.] *An Attempt towards a Coalition of English Protestants . . . To which is added, Reasons for Restraining the Licentiousness of the Pulpit and Press.* London: printed and sold by J. Roberts, 1715.

[Defoe, D.] *The Complete English Tradesman.* London: printed for C. Rivington, 1726.

[Defoe, D.] *An Essay on the Regulation of the Press.* London: n.p., 1704.

[Defoe, D.?] *Faction Display'd.* London: n.p., 1704.

[Defoe, D.] *The History of the Principal Discoveries and Improvements, in the Several Arts and Sciences: Particularly the great Branches of Commerce, Navigation, and Plantation, In all Parts of the known World.* London: printed for W. Mears, F. Clay, D. Browne, 1727.

[Defoe, D.] *A Letter to a Member of Parliament, Shewing the Necessity of Regulating the Press.* London: printed for G. West and H. Clements, 1699.

[Defoe, D.] *A Plan of the English Commerce.* London: C. Rivington, 1728. Reprint, Oxford: Blackwell, 1928.

[Defoe, D.] *Vindication of the Press: or, an Essay on the Usefulness of Writing, on Criticism, and the Qualification of Authors.* London: printed for T. Warner, 1718.

Dekker, T. *Lanthorne and Candle-Light. Or The Bell-mans second Nights walke*. London: printed for J. Busbie, 1608.

Delaune, T. *Angliae Metropolis: Or, The Present State of London*. London: printed by G. L. for J. Harris and T. Hawkins, 1690.

Democritus turned States-man. London: n.p., 1659.

Denis, J. *A Letter concerning a new way of curing sundry diseases by Transfusion of Blood*. London: printed for J. Martyn, 1667 [represented as part of the *Philosophical Transactions*].

Derham, W., ed. *Philosophical Letters between the Late Learned Mr. Ray and several of his Ingenious Correspondents*. London: printed by W. and J. Innys, 1718.

Desaguliers, J. T. *A Course of Experimental Philosophy*. 2 vols. London: printed for J. Senex, W. Innys and R. Manby, and J. Osborn and T. Longman, 1734–44.

Desaguliers, J. T. *Lectures of Experimental Philosophy*. London: printed for W. Mears, B. Creake, and J. Sackfield, 1719.

Desaguliers, J. T. *A System of Experimental Philosophy, Prov'd by Mechanicks*. London: printed for B. Creake, and J. Sackfield; and sold by W. Mears, 1719.

Descartes, R. *Oeuvres*. 13 vols. Edited by C. Adam and P. Tannery. Paris: Ministère de l'Instruction Publique, 1897–1913.

Descartes, R. *The Passions of the Soule in three Books*. London: printed for A. C. and sold by J. Martin and J. Ridley, 1650.

Descartes, R. *The Philosophical Writings of Descartes*. 3 vols. Edited by J. Cottingham, R. Stoothoff, and D. Murdoch. Cambridge: Cambridge University Press, 1985–91.

A Description of the Passage of Thomas late Earl of Strafford, over the River of Styx, with the conference betwixt him, Charon, and William Noy. [London]: n.p., 1641.

Des Perriers, B. *Cymbalum Mundi*. London: printed for A. Baldwin, 1712.

Dickens, C. *Hard Times*. 1854. Reprint, Harmondsworth: Penguin, 1985.

Digby, K. *Two Treatises*. Paris: G. Blaizot, 1644.

Dingley, R. *Vox Cœli; or, Philosophical, Historicall, and Theological Observations, of Thunder*. London: printed by M. S. for H. Cripps, and sold by H. Cripps, 1658.

Dodd, G. *Days at the Factories*. London: C. Knight, 1843.

Donne, J. *Essays in Divinity*. Edited by E. M. Simpson. Oxford: Oxford University Press, 1952.

Dunton, J. *Letters Written from New-England AD 1686 by John Dunton*. Edited by W. H. Whitmore. New York: Franklin, 1867.

Dunton, J. *The Life and Errors of John Dunton, Citizen of London*. 2 vols. London: J. Nichols, Son, and Bentley, 1818.

Dunton, J. *The Life and Errors of John Dunton late Citizen of London; written by Himself in Solitude*. London: printed for S. Malthus, 1705.

Dunton, J. *Religio Bibliopolae. The Religion of a Bookseller*. London: printed for P. Smart, 1694; first published with an attribution to B. Bridgewater, 1691.

Dupont, P. *Histoire de l'Imprimerie*. 2 vols. Paris: Chez tous les Libraires, 1854.

[Earle, J.] *Micro-cosmographie, or, A Peece of the World Discovered*. 5th ed. London: printed for R. Allot, 1629.

Edwards, T. *Gangraena: Or A Catalogue and Discovery of many of the Errours, Heresies, Blasphemies and pernicious Practices of the Sectaries of this time*. London: printed for R. Smith, 1646.

Edwards, T. *The Second Part of Gangraena*. London: printed by T. R. and E. M. for R. Smith, 1646.

Edwards, T. *The Third Part of Gangraena*. London: printed for R. Smith, 1646.

Ellis, C. "An Extract of a Letter to Dr *Edward Tyson* from the Reverend Mr *Charles Ellis*, . . .

That *Costerus* first invented Printing, *Anno. 1430.*" *Philosophical Transactions* 286 (1703): 1416–18.

Engelmann, P. *Letters from Ludwig Wittgenstein, with a Memoir.* New York: Horizon, 1967.

Evelyn, J. *The Diary of John Evelyn, now first Printed in full from the Manuscripts belonging to Mr. John Evelyn.* 6 vols. Edited by E. S. De Beer. Oxford: Oxford University Press, 1955.

Evelyn, J. *Memoirs, Illustrative of the Life and Writings of John Evelyn.* 2 vols. Edited by W. Bray. London: H. Colburn, 1818.

E[velyn], J. *Publick Employment and an Active Life Prefer'd to Solitude, and all its Appanages.* London: printed by J. M. for H. Herringman, 1667. Facsimile reprint in Vickers, *Public and Private Life.*

Evelyn, J. *Sculptura: or the History, and Art of Chalcography and Engraving in Copper.* London: printed by J. C. for G. Beedle, T. Collins, and J. Crook, 1662.

Every Mans Case: or, A brotherly Support to Mr. Larner. [London]: n.p., 1646.

An Exact Narrative of the Trial and Condemnation of John Twyn. London: printed by T. Mabb for H. Brome, 1664.

Expresse Commands from both the Honourable Houses of Parliament. London: printed for R. Cotton, 1642 (BL E.141.3).

Fawne, L., S. Gellibrand, J. Kirton, J. Rothwell, T. Underhill, and N. Webb. *A Beacon set on Fire.* London: printed for Fawne, Gellibrand, Kirton, Rothwell, Underhill, and Webb, 1652.

Fawne, L., S. Gellibrand, J. Kirton, J. Rothwell, T. Underhill, and N. Webb. *A Second Beacon Fired.* London: printed for the subscribers, 1654.

Filmer, R. *Patriarcha and other Writings.* Edited by J. P. Sommerville. Cambridge: Cambridge University Press, 1991.

Finch, Heneage, Sir William Scroggs, and Sir Francis North. *To all men to whom these Presents shall come.* London: n.p., 1679.

Firth, C. H., and R. S. Rait, eds. *Acts and Ordinances of the Interregnum, 1642–1660.* 3 vols. London: HMSO, 1911.

[Fisher, E.] *The Feast of Feasts.* Oxford: printed by Leonard Lichfield, 1644.

Flamsteed, J. *Atlas Cœlestis.* London: n.p., 1729.

Flamsteed, J. *The Correspondence of John Flamsteed.* Edited by E. G. Forbes, L. Murdin, and F. Willmoth. 1 vol. to date. Bristol: Institute of Physics Publishing, 1995.

[Flamsteed, J.] *The Doctrine of the Sphere, Grounded on the Motion of the Earth, and the Antient Pythagorean or Copernican System of the World.* London: printed by A. Godbid and J. Playford, 1680.

Flamsteed, J. "Estimate of the Number of *Folio* Pages, that the *Historia Britannica Cœlestis*, may contain when Printed." London: n.p., 1704 (bound with the Royal Society Library's copy of the 1712 *Historia Cœlestis*).

Flamsteed, J. *The Gresham Lectures of John Flamsteed.* Edited by E. G. Forbes. London: Mansell, 1975.

Flamsteed, J. *Historia Cœlestis Britannica.* 3 vols. London: printed by H. Meere, 1725.

Flamsteed, J. *Historiae Cœlestis Libri Duo.* London: printed by J. Matthews, 1712.

F[lamsteed], J. "The History of *Malting*, or the Method of making *Malt*, Practised at *Derby.*" *Collection of Letters for the Improvement of Husbandry and trade* nos. 7 and 8 (15 June and 20 July 1682): 63–74.

Flamsteed, J. "Mr. *Flamsteeds* Letter of July 24. 1675 to the Publisher, relating to another, printed in Num. *110* of these Tracts, concerning M. *Horroxes* Lunar Systeme." *Philosophical Transactions* 116 (July 1675): 368–70.

Flamsteed, J. *The Preface to John Flamsteed's "Historia Cœlestis Britannica" (1725).* Translated and edited by A. D. Johnson and A. Chapman. London: National Maritime Museum, 1982.

Flecknoe, R. *Miscellania.* London: printed by T. R. for the author, 1653.

Flemstadts most Strange and Wonderful Prophecy. London: printed for E. Golding, 1695.

Fludd, R. *Doctor Fludds Answer unto M. Foster, or The Squesing of Parson Fosters Sponge, ordained by him for the wiping away of the Weapon-salve.* London: printed for N. Butter, 1631.

Fludd, R. *Mosaicall Philosophy, Grounded upon the Essentiall Truth or Eternall Sapience.* London: printed for Humphrey Moseley, 1659. Originally published in Latin as *Philosophia Moysaica,* Gouda, 1638.

[Fontenelle, B. de]. *A Discovery of New Worlds.* Translated by A. Behn. London: printed for William Canning, 1688.

[Fontenelle, B. de]. *A Plurality of Worlds.* Translated by J. Glanvill. London: printed for R. Bentley and S. Magnes, 1687.

Foxe, J. *Acts and Monuments of Matters most speciall and Memorable, happening in the Church, with an Universall Historie of the same.* 3 vols. London: printed for the Company of Stationers, 1641.

Franklin, B. *Autobiography.* Edited by J. A. L. Lemay and P. M. Zall. New York: Norton, 1986.

French, J. M., ed. *The Life Records of John Milton.* 5 vols. New Brunswick, N.J.: Rutgers University Press, 1949–58.

Gadbury, J. Ἐφημερίς: *or, a Diary Astronomical, Astrological, Meterological, for the Year of our Lord, 1717.* London: printed by T. W. for Company of Stationers, 1717.

Galilei, Galileo. *Dialogue Concering the Two Chief World Systems.* Translated by S. Drake. Foreword by A. Einstein. 2d ed. Berkeley and Los Angeles: University of California Press, 1967.

Galilei, Galileo. *Le Opere di Galileo Galilei.* 20 vols. Firenze: G. Barbèra, 1964–8.

Galilei, Galileo. *Sidereus Nuncius: or, The Sidereal Messenger.* Translated and edited by A. Van Helden. Chicago: University of Chicago Press, 1989.

Galilei, Galileo. *Sidereus Nuncius.* Venice: T. Baglionus, 1610.

Galilei, Galileo. *Sidereus, Nuncius* [sic]. Frankfurt: printed at the Palthenius printing house, 1610.

Galilei, Galileo. *Sidereus Nuncius.* London: printed by J. Flesher, to be sold by C. Bee, 1653. (Bound with P. Gassendi, *Institutio Astronomica,* 2d ed.)

Galilei, Galileo. *Sidereus Nuncius.* London: printed for H. Dickenson, 1683. (Bound with P. Gassendi, *Institutio Astronomica,* 3d ed.)

Gardiner, S. R., ed. *Documents Relating to the Proceedings against William Prynne, in 1634 and 1637.* London: Camden Society, 1877.

Garret, J. *At a Court held at Stationers-Hall, On Friday the 22th day of May, 1685.* London: n.p., 1685 (broadside, subscribed "*John Garret,* Clerk to the said Company." SCA, suppl. docs., series I, Box A, env. 2, iii).

A Generall Note of the prises for binding all sortes of bookes. London: n.p., 1646.

Gilbert, J. T., ed. *A Contemporary History of Affairs in Ireland from 1641 to 1652.* 3 vols. in 6. Dublin: Irish Archaeological and Celtic Society, 1879–80.

Gilbert, W. *De Magnete.* London: printed by P. Short, 1600.

[Gildon, C.] *The History of the Athenian Society.* London: printed for J. Dowley, sold by the booksellers of London and Westminster, [1691?].

Glanvill, J. *Saducismus Triumphatus: or, Full and Plain Evidence Concerning Witches and Apparitions.* 2nd edition. London: printed by T. Newcomb for S. Lownds, 1682.

Glanvill, J. *Scire/i tuum nihil est: The Authors Defence of The Vanity of Dogmatizing, against the Exceptions of the Learned Tho. Albius in his late Sciri.* London: printed by E. C. for H. Eversden, 1665.

Glenn, J. R. *A Critical Edition of Alexander Ross's 1647 "Mystagogus Poeticus, or the Muses Interpreter."* New York: Garland, 1987.

Goodwin, J. *A Fresh Discovery of the High-Presbyterian Spirit.* London: printed for the Author, and sold by H. Cripps, and L. Ll., 1654.

Gough, R. *The History of Myddle.* Edited by D. Hey. Harmondsworth: Penguin, 1981.

Green, M. A. E., ed. *Calendar of the Proceedings of the Committee for Advance of Money, 1642–1656.* 3 vols. London: HMSO, 1888.

G[regg], H. *Curiosities in Chymistry.* London: printed by H. C. for S. Anson, 1691.

Gregory, F. *A Modest Plea for the Due Regulation of the Press.* London: printed for R. Sare, 1698.

Grew, N. *The Anatomy of Vegetables Begun.* London: printed for S. Hickman, Printer to the Royal Society, 1672.

Grew, N. *An Idea of a Phytological History Propounded.* London: printed by J. M. for R. Chiswell, 1673.

Grew, N. *Musaeum Regalis Societatis. Or A Catalogue & Description of the Natural and Artificial Rarities Belonging to the Royal Society.* London: printed by W. Rawlins, for the author [N. Grew], 1681.

Hale, Sir Matthew. *The Prerogatives of the King.* Edited by D. E. C. Yale. London: Selden Society, 1976.

Hales, J. "Abuses of Hard Places of Scripture." In *Works,* II, 1–46.

Hales, J. *The Works of the Ever Memorable Mr. John Hales of Eaton.* 3 vols. Glasgow: printed by R. and A. Foulis; sold by J. Tonson, A. Millar, and D. Wilson, London; J. Balfour, Edinburgh; and R. and A. Foulis, Glasgow, 1765.

[Hall, J.] *A Stop to the mad Multitude.* London: printed by H. Hills for T. Brewster, 1653.

Halley, E. *Astronomical Tables with Precepts both in English and Latin.* London: printed for W. Innys, 1752.

Halley, E. *Catalogus Stellarum Australium, sive Supplementum Catalogi Tychonici exhibens longitudines et latitudines stellarum fixarum . . .* London: printed by T. James for R. Harford, 1679.

Halley, E. "Considerations on the Change of the Latitudes of some of the principal fixt Stars." *Philosophical Transactions* 355 (1718): 736–8.

Halley, E. *Correspondence and Papers of Edmond Halley.* Edited by E. F. MacPike. Oxford: Oxford University Press, 1932.

[Halley, E.], ed. *Miscellanea Curiosa.* 3 vols. London: printed by J. B. for J. Wale and J. Senex, 1705–7.

Halley, E. "Some Considerations about the Cause of the Universal Deluge, Laid before the Royal Society, on the 12th of December 1694." *Philosophical Transactions* 383 (1724): 118–25.

Harby, T. *What is Truth? Or, the Patern in the Mount.* London: revised by and reprinted for the author, 1678.

Hargrave, F. *An Argument in Defence of Literary Property.* London: printed for the author, and sold by W. Otridge, 1774.

[Harrington, J.] *An Account of the Proceedings of the Right Reverend Father in God Jonathan Lord Bishop of Exeter in his late Visitation of Exeter College in Oxford.* 2d ed. Oxford: printed at the theatre, 1690.

[Harrington, J.] *A Defence of the Proceedings of the Right Reverend the Visitor and Fellows of Exeter College.* London: printed for T. Bennet, 1691.

Harrington, J. *The Common-Wealth of Oceana.* London: printed by J. Streater for L. Chapman; variant printed for D. Pakeman, 1656.

Harrington, J. *James Harrington's Oceana.* Edited by S. B. Liljegren. Heidelberg: New Society of Letters at Lund, 1924.

Harrington, J. *The Oceana of James Harrington, and his other Works.* Edited by J. Toland. London: n.p., 1700.

Harrington, J. *The Political Works of James Harrington.* Edited by J. G. A. Pocock. Cambridge: Cambridge University Press, 1977.

Harris, J. *Lexicon Technicum: or, an Universal English Dictionary of Arts and Sciences.* 2d ed. 2 vols. London: printed for D. Brown, J. Walthoe, J. Knapton, et al., 1723.

Hartlib, S. *Chymical, Medicinal, and Chyrurgical Addresses made to Samuel Hartlib, Esq.* London: printed by G. Dawson for G. Calvert, 1655.

Hartlib, S. *The Reformed Common-Wealth of Bees.* London: printed for G. Calvert, 1655.

Hartlib, S. *The Reformed Virginian Silk-Worm.* London: printed by J. Streater, for G. Calvert, 1655.

Harvey, W. *Anatomical Exercitations Concerning the Generation Of Living Creatures.* London: printed by J. Young for O. Pulleyn, 1653.

[Head, R.] *The Canting Academy, or, The Devils Cabinet Opened.* London: printed by F. Leach for M. Drew, 1673.

Hearne, T., ed. *Peter Langtoft's Chronicle.* 2 vols. 1725. Reprint, London: printed for S. Bagster, 1810.

Heereboord, A. *Philosophia Naturalis.* Edited by C. G. de Bérigard. Oxford: printed by W. Hall, sold by J. Crosley, 1663; plus at least 7 more editions to 1684.

Heine, H. *Doktor Faust: A Dance Poem, Together with Some Rare Accounts of Witches, Devils and the Ancient Art of Sorcery.* Translated by B. Ashmore. London: P. Nevill, 1952.

Herschel, C. *Catalogue of Stars, taken from Mr. Flamsteed's Observations contained in the Second Volume of the Historia Cælestis, and not inserted in the British Catalogue.* London: Sold by P. Elmsly, 1798.

Herschel, J. *Memoir and Correspondence of Caroline Herschel.* 2d ed. London: J. Murray, 1879.

Hevelius, J. *Machina Cælestis.* Danzig: printed by the author and S. Reiniger, for the author, 1673.

Hevelius, J. *Mercurius in Sole Visus.* Gdansk: printed by the author and S. Reiniger for the author, 1662.

Hevelius, J. *Selenographia, sive, Lunae Descriptio.* Gdansk: printed by A. Hunefeld for the author, 1647.

Heylyn, P. *Cosmographie in foure Bookes Contayning the Chorographie & Historie of the Whole World, and all the Principall Kingdomes, Provinces, Seas, and Isles, thereof.* "Second edition." London: printed for H. Seile, 1657.

[Heylyn, P.] *Observations on the Historie of the Reign of King Charles: Published by H. L. Esq.* London: printed by J. Clarke, 1656.

Hickeringill, E. *A Speech Without-Doors.* London: printed by G. Larkin, 1689.

Hickes, G. *The Spirit of Enthusiasm Exorcised.* London: printed for W. Kettilby, 1680.

[Hill, J.?] *A Dissertation on Royal Societies.* London: printed for J. Doughty, 1750.

Historical Manuscripts Commission. 9th Report. London: HMSO, 1883.

Historical Manuscripts Commission. *Report on the Manuscripts of F. W. Leybourne-Popham.* Norwich: HMSO, 1899.

The Historie of the damnable Life, and deserved death of Doctor Iohn Faustus. Translated by P. F. London: printed by T. Orwin, sold by E. White, 1592.

[Hoadly, B.] *A Letter to the Reverend Dr. Francis Atterbury: Occasion'd by the Doctrine lately deliver'd by him in a Funeral-Sermon.* London: printed for A. Baldwin, 1706.

[Hoadly, B.] *A Second Letter to the Reverend Dr. Francis Atterbury*. London: printed for A. Baldwin, 1708.

Hobbes, T. *Behemoth, or the Long Parliament*. 1682. Reprint, edited by F. Tönnies, Chicago: University of Chicago Press, 1990.

Hobbes, T. "A Dialogue between a Philosopher and a Student of the Common Laws of England." 1681. In *English Works*, VI, 1–160.

Hobbes, T. *The English Works of Thomas Hobbes*. 11 vols. in 12. Edited by W. Molesworth. London: John Bohn, 1839–45.

Hobbes, T. *The Last sayings, or Dying Legacy of Mr. Thomas Hobbs of Malmesbury*. London: printed for the author's executors, 1680.

Hobbes, T. *Leviathan*. Edited by R. Tuck. Cambridge: Cambridge University Press, 1991.

Hodges, J. C., ed. *William Congreve: Letters and Documents*. London: Macmillan, 1964.

[Holder, W.] *Supplement to the Philosophical Transactions of July, 1670. With some Reflexions on Dr. John Wallis, his Letter there inserted*. London: printed for H. Brome, 1678.

Hondius, J., ed. *Theatri Geographiae Veteris Tomus Prior in quo Cl. Ptol. Alexandrini Geographiae Libri VIII*. Amsterdam: J. Hondius, 1618.

[Hoofnail, J.] *The Art of Drawing and Painting in Water-Colours*. London: printed for J. Peele, 1731.

H[ooke], R. *An Attempt for the Explication of the Phaenomena, Observable in an Experiment Published by the Honourable Robert Boyle, Esq. . . . In Confirmation of a former Conjecture made by R. H.* London: printed by J. H. for S. Thomson, 1661.

Hooke, R. *A Description of Helioscopes*. London: printed by T. R. for J. Martyn, Printer to the Royal Society, 1676.

Hooke, R. *The Diary of Robert Hooke MA, MD, FRS 1672–1680*. Edited by H. W. Robinson and W. Adams. London: Taylor and Francis, 1935.

Hooke, R. "The Diary of Robert Hooke, Nov. 1688–Mar. 1690 and Dec. 1692–Aug. 1693." In Gunther, *Early Science in Oxford*, X (1935), 69–265.

Hooke, R. *Lampas: or, Descriptions of some Mechanical Improvements of Lamps and Water-poises*. London: printed for J. Martyn, Printer to the Royal Society, 1677.

H[ooke?], R. *New Atlantis. Begun by the Lord Verulam, Viscount St. Albans: and Continued by R. H. Esquire. Wherein is set forth A Platform of Monarchical Government. With a Pleasant Intermixture of divers rare Inventions, and wholsom Customs, fit to be introduced into all Kingdoms, States, and Common-wealths*. London: printed for J. Crooke, 1660.

Hooke, R. *Philosophical Experiments and Observations*. Edited by W. Derham. London: printed by W. and J. Innys, Printers to the Royal Society, 1726.

Hooke, R. *The Posthumous Works of Robert Hooke*. Edited by R. Waller. London: printed by S. Smith and B. Walford, 1705.

Hooker, R. *The Works of that Learned and Judicious Divine, Mr. Richard Hooker: with an Account of his Life and Death, by Isaac Walton*. 2 vols. Oxford: Oxford University Press, 1841.

Houghton, J. "Whereas Mr. *John Houghton*, Citizen and Fellow of the ROYAL SOCIETY of *London*." [London]: n.p., 1691; single sheet, not in Wing: CUL Sel.3.238[325].

How, J. *Some Thoughts on the Present State of Printing and Bookselling*. London: n.p., 1709.

Howell, J. *Londinopolis; an Historicall Discourse or Perlustration of the City of London, the Imperial Chamber, and Chief Emporium of Great Britain*. London: printed by J. Streater for H. Twyford, G. Sawbridge, T. Dring, and J. Place, 1657.

Howell, T. B., ed. *State Trials*. 33 vols. London: T. C. Hansard for R. Bagshaw et al., 1809–26.

Howgil[l], F. *The Fiery Darts of the Divel Quenched*. London: printed for G. Calvert, 1654.

The Humble Petition and Addresse of the Officers of the Army. London: printed by H. Hills, for Hills and F. Tyton, 1659.

Hunscot, J. *The Humble Petition and Information of Joseph Hunscot Stationer.* [London]: n.p., 1646.

Hunter, J., ed. *The Diary of Ralph Thoresby, FRS.* 2 vols. London: Colburn and Bentley, 1830.

Hunter, J., ed. *Letters of Eminent Men, Addressed to Ralph Thoresby, FRS.* 2 vols. London: Colburn and Bentley, 1832.

Hutcheson, F. *An Essay on the Nature and Conduct of the Passions and Affections.* 3d ed. London: printed for A. Ward et al., 1742.

Huygens, C. *Oeuvres Complètes de Christiaan Huygens.* 22 vols. The Hague: M. Nijhoff, 1888–1951.

Hyde, T., ed. *Tabulae Long. ac Lat. Stellarum Fixarum, ex Observatione Ulugh Beighi.* Oxford: printed by H. Hall, for the author [Hyde]; sold by R. Davis, 1665.

An Impartial Account of the Arraignment, Trial & Condemnation of Thomas late Earl of Strafford. London: printed for J. Hindmarsh, 1679.

An Impartial History of the Life, Character, Amours, Travels, and Transactions of Mr. John Barber, City-Printer. London: printed for E. Curll, 1741.

Imperato, F. *Historia Naturale.* Venice: S. Combi and G. La Nou, 1672.

Ingelo, N. *Bentivoglio and Urania, in Six Books.* 4th ed. London: printed by A. M. and R. R. for D. Newman, 1682.

Inghirami, C. *Ethruscarum Antiquitatum Fragmenta.* Frankfurt: n.p., 1637.

James I. *The Political Works of James I.* Edited by C. H. McIlwain. Cambridge: Harvard University Press, 1918.

Jonghe, A. de (Hadrianus Junius). *Batavia.* Leyden: printed by F. Raphelengien at the Plantin printing house, 1588.

Journals of the House of Commons, 1547–1714. 17 vols. London: HMSO.

Journals of the House of Lords, 1509–1714. 19 vols. London: HMSO.

Kepler, J. *Ad Vitellionem Paralipomena: Quibus Astronomiae Pars Optica Traditur.* Frankfurt: printed for C. de Marne and J. Aubry, 1604.

Kepler, J. *Dioptrice, seu, Demonstratio eorum qua Visui & Visibilibus propter Conspicilla non ita Pridem inventa Accidunt.* Augsburg: printed by D. Frank, 1611.

Kilburne, W. *Dangerous Errors in Several late Printed Bibles to the great scandal, and corruption of sound and true Religion. Discovered by William Kilburne Gent.* Finsbury: n.p., 1659.

Kilburne, W. *A New-Years-Gift for Mercurius Politicus.* London: printed for Thomas Milbourn, 1659.

King, W. *The Original Works of William King.* 3 vols. Edited by J. Nichols. London: printed for the editor, and sold by N. Conant, 1776.

King William and Queen Mary Conquerors: Or, A Discourse Endeavouring to prove that Their Majesties have on Their Side, against the Late King, the Principal Reasons that make Conquest a Good Title. London: printed for R. Baldwin, 1693.

[Kirkman, F.] *The English Rogue Continued, in the Life of Meriton Latroon.* London: printed for F. Kirkman, 1668.

K[irkman], F. *The Unlucky Citizen Experimentally Described.* London: printed by A. Johnson for F. Kirkman, 1673.

[Klinger, F. M. von] *Faustus: His Life, Death, and Descent into Hell. Translated from the German.* London: W. Simpkin and R. Marshall, 1825.

Knavery in all Trades: Or, The Coffee-House. London: printed by J. B. for W. Gilbertson and H. Marsh, 1664.

Knight, C. *The Old Printer and the Modern Press.* London: J. Murray, 1854.

Knight, C. *William Caxton.* London: C. Knight, 1844.

La Caille, J. de. *Histoire de l'Imprimerie et de la Librairie.* Paris: printed by J. de La Caille, 1689.

Lansberg, P. van. *Tabulae Motuum Cœlestium Perpetuae.* Middelburg: Z. Romanus, 1632.

Lansdowne, Marquis of, ed. *The Petty Papers: Some Unpublished Writings of Sir William Petty.* London: Constable, 1927.

[Larkin, G.?] "An Essay on Writing, and the Art and Mystery of Printing." 1696. Reprinted in *Harleian Miscellany,* 10 vols., London: printed for J. White and J. Murray, and J. Harding, 1808–13, I, 527–9.

[Larner, W.] *A True Relation of all the Remarkable Passages, and Illegall Proceedings of some Sathanicall or Doeg-like Accusers of their Brethren, againt William Larner, a Free-man of England.* London: n.p., [1646].

Lawrence, H. *An History of Angells.* London: printed by M. S., sold by W. Nealand, 1649.

Lawson, G. *Politica Sacra et Civilis.* Edited by C. Condren. Cambridge: Cambridge University Press, 1992.

Lawson, J. *Two Letters from Vice-Admiral John Lawson.* London: printed by J. Streater, 1659.

Le Brun, C. *A Method to Learn to Design the Passions.* Translated by J. Williams. London: printed for J. Williams. 1734.

Leibniz, G. W. *Die Werke von Leibniz.* 11 vols. Edited by O. Klopp. Hanover: Klindworth, 1864–84.

Lemnius, L. *Secret Miracles of Nature.* London: printed by J. Streater, sold by H. Moseley, J. Sweeting, J. Clark, and G. Sawbridge, 1658.

L'Estrange, R. *Considerations and Proposals in order to the Regulation of the Press: together with diverse instances of treasonous, and seditious pamphlets, proving the necessity thereof.* London: printed by A. C., 1663.

"A Letter to the Publisher, in favour of Authors, with a Bull of Pope *Leo X.* against Piratical Booksellers, &c." *Gentleman's Magazine* 5 (1735): 203–4.

A Letter to the Society of Booksellers, on the Method of forming a true Judgment of the Manuscripts of Authors. London: printed for J. Millan, 1738.

Levett, J. *The Ordering of Bees.* London: printed by T. Harper, for J. Hanson, 1634.

Lewis, J. *The Life of Mayster Wyllyam Caxton.* London: n.p., 1737.

Leybourn, W. *Pleasure with Profit.* London: printed for R. Baldwin and J. Dunton, 1694.

The Life and Character of J. Barber, Esq; late Lord-Mayor of London, Deceased. London: printed for T. Cooper, 1741.

The Life of H. H. With the Relation at large of what passed betwixt him and the Taylors Wife in Black-friars, according to the Original. London: printed for T. S., 1688.

Lister, M. "The Extracts of Four Letters from Mr. *John Banister* to Dr. *Lister,* communicated by him to the Publisher." *Philosophical Transactions* 198 (March 1693): 667–72.

Locke, J. *The Correspondence of John Locke.* 8 vols. Edited by E. S. De Beer. Oxford: Oxford University Press, 1976–89.

Locke, J. *An Essay Concerning Human Understanding.* 1700. Reprint, edited by P. Nidditch, Oxford: Clarendon Press, 1975.

[Locke, J.] *Some Thoughts Concerning Education.* London: printed for A. and J. Churchill, 1693.

Locke, J. *Two Treatises of Government.* Edited by P. Laslett. Cambridge: Cambridge University Press, 1963.

The London Printers Lamentation, or, the Press opprest, and overprest. [London]: n.p., 1660.

London's Lamentation for the Loss of their Charter. London: printed for A. Banks, 1683.

Longomontanus, C. S. *Astronomia Danica.* Amsterdam: printed by G. I. Caesius, 1622.

Lowthorp, J., ed. *The Philosophical Transactions and Collections, to the end of the Year 1700. Abridg'd and Dispos'd under General Heads*. 2d ed. 3 vols. London: printed by M. Matthews for R. Knaplock, R. Wilkin, and H. Clements, 1716.

Luckombe, P. *The History and Art of Printing*. London: printed by W. Adlard and J. Browne for J. Johnson, 1771.

Ludlow, E. *Edmund Ludlow: A Voyce from the Watch Tower*. Edited by A. B. Worden. London: Royal Historical Society, 1978.

Magalotti, L. *Lorenzo Magalotti at the Court of Charles II: His "Relazione d'Inghilterra" of 1668*. Edited by W. E. K. Middleton. Waterloo, Ontario: Wilfred Laurier University Press, 1980.

Maittaire, M. *Annales Typographici ab Artis Inventae Origine ad Annum* MD. 3 vols. The Hague: I. Vaillant and N. Prevost, 1719–25.

Mallinckrodt, B. *De Ortu et Progressu Artis Typographicae*. Cologne: J. Kinchius, 1639.

Mandeville, B. *A Treatise of the Hypochondriack and Hysterick Passions*. London: printed and sold by D. Leach and W. Taylor, 1711.

[Marchand, P.] *Histoire de l'Origine et des Prémiers Progrès de l'Imprimerie*. La Haye: printed by the widow Le Vier, and P. Paupie, 1740.

Maslen, K., and J. Lancaster, eds. *The Bowyer Ledgers*. London: Bibliographical Society, 1991.

Meerman, G. *Origines Typographicae*. 2 vols. The Hague: N. van Daalen; Paris: F. de Bure; London: T. Wilcox, 1765.

Menander. *The Principal Fragments*. With English translation by F. G. Allinson. London: W. Heinemann, 1921.

Mentel, J. *De Vera Typographiae Origine Paraenesis*. Paris: R. Ballard, 1650.

Merlinus Verax: or, an Almanack for the Year of Our Lord, 1687. London: printed for the Company of Stationers, 1687.

Mersenne, M. *Correspondance du Père Marin Mersenne*. 17 vols. Edited by P. Tannery, C. de Waard, and R. Pintard. Paris: Presses Universitaires, 1932–70.

Middleton, C. *A Dissertation concerning the Origin of Printing in England. Shewing, That it was first Introduced and Practised by our Countryman William Caxton, at Westminster: And not, as is commonly believed, by a Foreign Printer at Oxford*. Cambridge: printed for W. Thurlbourn, 1735.

Milton, J. *Areopagitica; a Speech of Mr. John Milton For the Liberty of Unlicenc'd Printing, To the Parlament of England*. London: n.p., 1644.

Milton, J. *Complete Prose Works of John Milton*. 8 vols. Edited by D. M. Wolfe et al. New Haven: Yale University Press, 1953–82.

Molyneux, W. *Dioptrica Nova*. London: printed for B. Tooke, 1692.

Monk, J. H. *The Life of Richard Bentley*. 2 vols. London: J. G. and F. Rivington; Cambridge: J. and J. J. Deighton, 1833.

More, H. *A Collection of several Philosophical Writings*. 4th ed. London: printed by J. Downing, 1712.

[More, H.] *Enthusiasmus Triumphatus, or, A Discourse of the Nature, Causes, Kinds, and Cure of Enthusiasme*. London: printed by J. Flesher, to be sold by W. Morden, Cambridge, 1656.

Mortimer, C. "The Description of an *Antique* Metal *Stamp*, in the Collection of his Grace CHARLES Duke of *Richmond, Lenox* and *Aubigny, F.R.S.* &c. being one of the Instances, how near the *Romans* had arrived to the *Art* of *Printing*." *Philosophical Transactions* 450 (1738): 388–93.

[Motte, B.] *A Reply to the Preface Publish'd by Mr. Henry Jones; with his Abridgment of the Philosophical Transactions*. London: printed and sold by J. Roberts, 1722.

Moxon, J. *Mechanick Exercises on the Whole Art of Printing*. London: printed for J. Moxon, 1683–4. Facsimile reprint, edited by H. Davis and H. Carter, 2d ed., London: Oxford University Press, 1962.

Moxon, J. *Mechanick Exercises: or The Doctrine of Handy-Works*. 3d ed. London, 1703. Facsimile reprint, edited by C. F. Montgomery, New York: Praeger, 1970.

Moxon, J. *Proves of Several sorts of letters.* Westminster: printed by J. Moxon, 1669.

Moxon, J. *Regulae Trium Ordinum Literarum Typographicarum: or the Rules of the Three Orders of Print Letters*. London: printed for J. Moxon, 1676.

Moxon, J. *A Tutor to Astronomie and Geographie: Or an Easie and speedy way to know the Use of both the Globes*. London: printed and sold by J. Moxon, 1659.

Moxon, J. *A Tutor to Astronomy & Geography*. 4th ed. London: printed by S. Roycroft for J. Moxon, 1686.

Moxon, J. *A Tutor to Astronomy & Geography, Or, The Use of the Copernican Spheres*. London: printed for and to be sold by J. Moxon, 1665.

N., N. *The Hue and Cry: or, a Relation of the Travels of the Devil and Towzer*. London: "Printed for *Roger Catflogger*," n.d.

Nashe, T. *The Works of Thomas Nashe*. 5 vols. Edited by R. B. McKerrow. Oxford: Oxford University Press, 1958.

Naudé, G. *Instructions concerning Erecting of a Library*. Translated by J. Evelyn. London: printed for G. Beadle, T. Collins, and J. Crook, 1661.

[Neville, H.] *Shufling, Cutting and Dealing, in a Game at Pickquet*. [London]: n.p., 1659.

Newton, I. *The Correspondence of Isaac Newton*. 7 vols. Edited by H. W. Turnbull, J. F. Scott, A. R. Hall, and L. Tilling. Cambridge: Cambridge University Press, 1959–77.

Newton, I. *Opticks*. London: printed for S. Smith and B. Walford, 1704.

Newton, I. *Philosophiae Naturalis Principia Mathematica*. London: printed by J. Streater, 1687.

Newton, I. "Remarks upon the Observations made upon a Chronological Index of Sir *Isaac Newton*, translated into *French* by the Observator, and Publish'd at *Paris*." *Philosophical Transactions* 389 (1725): 315–21.

Nicholas of Cusa. Ὀφθαλμος ἁπλους or *The Single Eye*. Translated by G. Randall. London: printed for J. Streater, 1646.

Nicholas, E. *The Nicholas Papers: Correspondence of Sir Edward Nicholas, Secretary of State*. 4 vols. Edited by G. F. Warner. London: Camden Society, 1886–1920.

Nichols, J. *Literary Anecdotes of the Eighteenth Century*. 9 vols. London: printed for the author, 1812–15.

Nicolson, W. *The London Diaries of William Nicolson, Bishop of Carlisle, 1702–1718*. Edited by C. Jones and G. Holmes. Oxford: Oxford University Press, 1985.

North, R. *The Lives of the Right Hon. Francis North, Baron Guilford; the Hon. Sir Dudley North; and the Hon. and Rev. Dr. John North . . . Together with the Autobiography of the Author*. 3 vols. Edited by A. Jessopp. London: Bell, 1890.

Nullius Nominis [pseud.] *An Apologie for the Six Book-Sellers, Subscribers of the Second Beacon Fired*. London: printed by S. G. for M. Keinton, 1655.

The Office of Publick Advice. London: printed by T. Newcomb, 1657.

Ogle, O., W. H. Bliss, W. D. Macray, and F. J. Routledge, eds. *Calendar of the Clarendon State Papers preserved in the Bodleian Library*. 5 vols. Oxford: Oxford University Press, 1869–1970.

Olaus Magnus. *A Compendious History of the Goths, Swedes & Vandals*. London: printed by J. Streater, sold by H. Moseley, G. Sawbridge, H. Twiford, T. Dring, J. Place, and H. Herringman, 1658.

[Oldenburg, H.] "*An Account of some Books: Roberti Boyle, Nobilissimi Angli & Soc. Regiae dignissimi Socii,* OPERA VARIA; Genevae, *in* 4°. *1667.*" *Philosophical Transactions* 130 (1676): 766–7.

[Oldenburg, H.] "Advertisement." *Philosophical Transactions* 12 (May 1666): 213–14.

[Oldenburg, H.] "Advertisement." *Philosophical Transactions* 128 (1676): 710.

[Oldenburg, H.] "An Advertisment necessary to be given to the Readers of the *Latin* Version, made by Mr. *Sterpin* at *Copenhagen,* of the *Philosophical Transactions* of A.*1669;* printed at *Franckfurt* on the *Main* by *Dan. Pauli,* A.*1671.*" *Philosophical Transactions* 75 (1671): 2269–70.

Oldenburg, H. *The Correspondence of Henry Oldenburg.* 13 vols. Edited by A. R. Hall and M. B. Hall. Madison: University of Wisconsin Press; London: Mansell; London: Taylor and Francis, 1965–86.

[Oldenburg, H.] "An Extract of the French *Journal des Scavans,* concerning a New Invention of Monsieur *Christian Hugens de Zulichem,* of very exact and portative Watches." *Philosophical Transactions* 112 (March 1675): 272–3.

[Oldenburg, H.] "[Review of] *A Description of* HELIOSCOPES *and some other Instruments, made by* Robert Hook, *Fellow of the R. Society*: London, *printed for* John Martyn *at the Bell in* St. Pauls *Churchyard,* 1675. *in* 4°." *Philosophical Transactions* 118 (October 1675): 440–2.

[Oldenburg, H.] "Some Animadversions upon the *Latin* Version, made by *C. S.* of the *Phil. Transactions* of A.1665.1666.1667.1668, printed at *Amsterdam* by *Henry* and *Theodore Boom.*" *Philosophical Transactions* 106 (1674): 141–4.

Old Poor Robin. London: printed for the Company of Stationers and sold by R. Horsfield at Stationers' Hall, 1791.

Oliver, J. *A Present to be Given to Teeming Women, by their Husbands or Friends.* London: printed by A. Maxwell, for T. Parkhurst, 1669.

Osborne, F. *A Miscellany of Sundry Essayes, Paradoxes, and Problematicall Discourses, Letters and Characters; Together with Politicall Deductions from the History of the Earl of Essex, Executed under Queen Elizabeth.* London: printed by J. Grismond, 1659.

[Overton, R.] *The Arraignement of Mr. Persecution.* "Europe: printed by Martin Claw-Clergie . . . ," 1645.

Oxford, University of. *Statutes of the University of Oxford codified in the year 1636.* Edited by J. Griffiths. Oxford: Clarendon, 1888.

Palmer, S. *The General History of Printing, from its first Invention in the City of Mentz, . . . Particularly, its Introduction, Rise and Progress here in England.* London: printed by the author and sold by his widow and by J. Roberts, 1732.

Panciroli, G. *The History of Many Memorable Things Lost.* 2 vols. in 1. London: printed for J. Nicholson and sold by J. Morphew, 1715.

Parker, G. *An Ephemeris of the Cœlestial Motions and Aspects.* London: printed for the author and sold at his house, 1695 (bound with Parker's *Mercurius Anglicanus*).

Parker, G. *Mercurius Anglicanus.* London: printed by J. M. for the Company of Stationers, 1690.

Parker, G. *Mercurius Anglicanus.* London: printed by M. C. for the Company of Stationers, 1695 (bound with Parker's *Ephemeris*).

Parker, G. *Parker's Ephemeris for the Year of Our Lord 1717.* London: printed by the author for the Company of Stationers, 1716.

[Parker, H.] *The humble Remonstrance of the Company of Stationers, London.* London: n.p., 1643.

Parker, S. *Bishop Parker's History of his Own Time.* Translated by T. Newlin. London: printed for C. Rivington, 1727.

Parker, S. *A Free and Impartial Censure of the Platonick Philosophie*. Oxford: printed by W. Hall, for R. Davis, 1666.

[Parkinson, J.] *The Fire's Continued at Oxford*. London: n.p., 1690.

[Partridge, J.] *Flagitiosus Mercurius Flagellatus*. London: n.p., 1697.

Peacham, H. *The Complete Gentleman, The Truth of Our Times, and The Art of Living in London*. 1638. Reprint, edited by V. B. Heltzel, Ithaca: Cornell University Press, 1962.

Peacock, T. L. "Crotchet Castle." In H. F. B. Brett-Smith and C. E. Jones, eds., *The Works of Thomas Love Peacock* (10 vols. London: Constable, 1924–34), IV, 1–212.

Pepys, S. *The Diary of Samuel Pepys*. 11 vols. Edited by R. Latham and W. Matthews. London: G. Bell, 1970–83.

A Perfect Diurnall or the Daily Proceedings in The Conventicle of the Phanatiques. [London]: n.p., [19 March 1659/60].

Phalaris [pseud.] *Phalaridis Agrigentinorum Tyranni Epistolae*. Edited by C. Boyle. Oxford: printed by J. Crooke, 1695.

Phoonsen, J. *Les Loix et les Coutumes du Change des Principales Places de l'Europe*. Translated by J. P. Ricard. Amsterdam: printed for E. Roger, 1715.

Pitfield, A., trans. *Memoirs for a Natural History of Animals*. London: printed by Joseph Streater, to be sold by T. Basset, J. Robinson, B. Aylmer, J. Southby, and W. Canning, 1688.

Pitt, M. *An Account of one Ann Jeffries, . . . who was fed for six Months by a small sort of Airy People called Fairies*. London: printed for R. Cumberland, 1696.

Pitt, M. *The Cry of the Oppressed*. London: printed for M. Pitt, 1691.

Pitt, M., ed. *The English Atlas*. 4 vols. Oxford: printed at the Theater for M. Pitt, 1680–3.

Pitt, M. *A Letter from Moses Pitt, to the Authour of a Book, Intituled, Some Discourses upon Dr. Burnet*. London: printed for M. Pitt, 1695.

Plattes, G. "A Caveat for Alchymists." In Hartlib, *Chymical, Medicinal, and Chyrurgical Addresses*, 49–88.

[Plattes, G.] *A Description of the famous Kingdome of Macaria*. London: printed for F. Constable, 1641.

[Plot, R.] "Preface." *Philosophical Transactions* 143 (January 1682/3): 2.

Poor Robin's Almanack. London: printed for the Company of Stationers, 1687.

Pope, A. *The Correspondence of Alexander Pope*. 5 vols. Edited by G. Sherburn. Oxford: Oxford University Press, 1956.

Pope, A. *The Works of Alexander Pope Esq*. 10 vols. London: printed for J. and P. Knapton, H. Lintot, J. and R. Tonson, S. Draper, and C. Bathurst, 1754.

Pope, A., et al. *Memoirs of the Extraordinary Life, Works and Discoveries of Martinus Scriblerus. Written in Collaboration by Members of the Scriblerus Club*. Edited by C. Kerby-Miller. New Haven: Yale University Press, 1950.

Porta, G. della. *Natural Magick*. London: printed for T. Young and S. Speed, 1658.

A Presse Full of Pamphlets. London: printed for R. W., 1642.

Pride, T., W. Gough, T. Bridge, R. Merest, W. Kiffen, I. Gray, G. Gosfright, and S. Richardson. *The Beacons Quenched*. London: printed by H. Hills, to be sold by G. Calvert and W. Larner, 1652.

Prideaux, H. *The True Nature of Imposture fully Display'd in the Life of Mahomet*. 5th ed. London: printed for T. Caldecott, 1712.

A Prohibition to all persons who have set up any Offices called by the names of Addresses, Publique Advice, or Intelligence. London: printed for the author, 1657.

Propositions concerning the Printing of the Bible in the Original and other Learned Languages. London: printed by R. Norton for T. Garthwait, 1653.

Propositions for the Carrying on a Philosophical Correspondence, already begun in the County of

Sommerset, upon incouragement given from the Royal Society. London: printed for J. Collins, 1670.

Prynne, W. *A Breviate of the Life of William Laud Arch-bishop of Canterbury: Extracted (for the most part) verbatim, out of his owne Diary*. London: printed by F. L. for M. Sparke, 1644.

Prynne, W. *Canterburies Doome: or the First Part of a Compleat History of the Commitment, Charge, Tryall, Condemnation, Execution of William Laud late Arch-bishop of Canterbury*. London: printed by J. Macock for M. Sparke, 1646.

Prynne, W. *Hidden Workes of Darkenes Brought to Publike Light*. London: printed by T. Brudenell for M. Sparke, 1645.

Prynne, W. *Lame Giles his Haultings*. London: "Imprinted for *Giles Widdowes*," 1630.

Prynne, W. *A New Discovery of the Prelates Tyranny, in their late Prosecutions of Mr. William Pryn, an eminent Lawyer; Dr. Iohn Bastwick, a learned Physitian; and Mr. Henry Burton, a reverent Divine*. London: printed for M. S[parke], 1641.

Prynne, W. *The Unbishopping of Timothy and Titus. Or, A Briefe elaborate Discourse, prooving Timothy to be no Bishop*. London: [for M. Sparke?], 1636.

Psalmanazar, G. *Memoirs of ****. Commonly known by the Name of George Psalmanazar; a Reputed Native of Formosa*. London: printed for the executrix; sold by R. Davis, J. Newbery, L. Davis, and C. Reymers, 1764.

Purchas, S. *A Theatre of Politicall Flying-Insects*. London: printed by R. I. for T. Parkhurst, 1657.

Quarles, F. *Enchiridion*. London: printed for H. Moseley, 1658.

Raeder, H., E. Stromgren, and B. Stromgren, trans. and eds. *Tycho Brahe's Description of His Instruments and Scientific Work, as Given in "Astronomiae Instauratae Mechanica" (Wandesburgi, 1598)*. Copenhagen: Kommission hos Ejnar Munksgaard, 1946.

[Ramesay, W.] *The Gentlemans Companion*. London: printed by E. Okes for R. Reynolds, 1672.

Renouard, A. A. *Annales de l'Imprimerie des Estienne*. 2d ed. Paris: J. Renouard, 1843.

Reynolds, E. *A Treatise of the Passions and Faculties of the Soule of Man*. London: printed by R. H. for R. Bostock, 1640.

Rigaud, S. J., ed. *Correspondence of Scientific Men of the Seventeenth Century*. 2 vols. Oxford: Oxford University Press, 1841. Facsimile reprint, Hildesheim: G. Olms, 1965.

Roberts, J., and A. G. Watson, eds. *John Dee's Library Catalogue*. London: Bibliographical Society, 1990.

Rochester, John Wilmot, Earl of. *The Letters of John Wilmot, Earl of Rochester*. Edited by J. Treglown. Oxford: Blackwell, 1980.

Rogers, J. *Ohel or Beth-shemesh*. London: printed for R. I. and G. and H. Eversden, 1653.

Rolle, H. *Un Abridgment des plusieurs Cases et Resolutions del Common Ley*. London: printed for A. Crooke, W. Leake, A. Roper, F. Tyton, G. Sawbridge, T. Dring, T. Collins, J. Place, W. Place, J. Starkey, T. Basset, R. Pawlet, and S. Heyrick, 1668.

Ross, A. *Commentum de Terrae Motu Circulari: duobus libris refutatum*. London: printed by Thomas Harper, 1634.

Ross, A. *The Marrow of History, or an Epitome of all Historical Passages from the Creation, to the end of the last Macedonian War. First set out at large by Sir Walter Raleigh, And now Abreviated by A. R.* London: printed by W. Dugard for J. Stephenson, 1650.

Ross, A. *The New Planet no Planet: or, the Earth no Wandring Star: Except in the wandring Heads of Galileans*. London: printed by J. Young, sold by M. Meighen and G. Bedell, 1646.

Ross, A. *The Picture of the Conscience drawne to the Life, by the Pencell of Divine Truth*. London: printed by T. Badger, for M. M. and G. Bedell, 1646.

Rugg, T. *The Diurnal of Thomas Rugg, 1659–61.* Edited by W. L. Sachse. London: Royal Historical Society, 1961.

Rusden, M. *A Further Discovery of Bees.* London: printed for the author, 1679.

Rush, B. *Medical Inquiries and Observations upon the Diseases of the Mind.* Philadelphia: Kimber and Richardson, 1812.

Rushworth, J. *Historical Collections of Private Passages of State.* 8 vols. London: printed by J. A. for R. Boulter et al., 1680–1701.

S., I. *The Perfect Politician: Or, A Full View of the Life and Actions (Military and Civil) of O. Cromwell.* London: printed by J. Cottrel, for W. Roybould and H. Fletcher, 1660.

S., I. *The Picture of a New Courtier Drawn in a Conference, between Mr. Timeserver and Mr. Plain-heart.* London: n.p., 1656.

S., I. Συλλογολογια: *or, An Historical Discourse of Parliaments.* London: printed for T. Firby, 1656.

St. Serfe, T. *Tarugo's Wiles: Or, The Coffee-House.* London: printed for H. Herringman, 1668.

Saldenus, W. *De Libris Varioque Eorum Usu et Abusu Libri Duo.* Amsterdam: H. Boom and the widow of T. Boom, 1688.

S[and], C. *Acta Philosophica Societatis Regiae in Anglia, Anni M.DC.LXV. Auctore Henrico Oldenburgio.* Amsterdam: H. and T. Boom, 1674.

Sand, C. "Extracts of two Letters, written to the Publisher from *Hamborough* by the Learned *Christophorus Sandius,* concerning the Origin of *Pearls.*" *Philosophical Transactions* 101 (March 1674): 11–12.

Sanderson, R. *De Obligatione Conscientiae Praelectiones Decem.* London: printed by R. N. for J. Martyn, 1660.

Sanderson, R. *Several Cases of Conscience Discussed in ten lectures.* Translated by R. Codrington. London: printed by T. Leach, 1660.

Saunders, T., J. Okey, and M. Alured. *To his Highness the Lord Protector, . . . the humble Petition of several Colonels of the Army.* [London]: n.p., 1654.

Scheiner, C. *Rosa Ursina.* Bracciano: A. Phaeus, 1630.

Schelhorn, J. G. *Amoenitates Literariae, quibus variae Observationes, scripta item quaedam anecdota & rariora opuscula exhibentur.* 14 vols. in 7. Frankfurt and Leipzig: D. Bartholomew and Son, 1725–30.

Scriba, C. J. "The Autobiography of John Wallis, FRS." *Notes and Records of the Royal Society* 25 (1970): 17–46.

Scriverius, P. *Laure-Crans voor Laurens Coster van Haerlem, Eerster Vinder vande Boeckedruckery.* Haarlem: printed by A. Rooman, 1628 (bound with Ampsing, *Beschryvinge*).

Sedgwick, J. Ἐπισκοπος Διδακτικός. *Learning's Necessity to an able Minister.* London: printed by R. D. for E. Story, Cambridge, 1653 (bound and paginated concurrently with Sedgwick, *Sermon*).

Sedgwick, J. *A Sermon, Preached at St. Marie's in the University of Cambridge May 1st, 1653. Or, An Essay to the Discovery of the Spirit of Enthusiasme.* London: printed by R. D. for E. Story, Cambridge, 1653 (bound and paginated concurrently with Sedgwick, Ἐπισκοπος Διδακτικός).

Senault, J. F. *The Use of Passions.* Translated by Henry, earl of Monmouth. London: printed for J. L. and H. Moseley, 1649.

Senex, J. *A Treatise of the Description and Use of Both Globes.* London: printed for J. Senex and W. Taylor, 1718.

[Settle, E.] *The New Athenian Comedy.* London: "Printed for Campanella Restio, next door to the Apollo, near the Temple," 1693.

Sexby, E. [Allen, W., pseud.]. *Killing Noe Murder.* [London]: n.p., n.d. [1657].

Sexby, E. [Allen, W., pseud.]. *Killing, No Murder: with some Additions.* [Edited by J. Streater?] London: n.p., 1659.

'sGravesande, W. T. *Mathematical Elements of Natural Philosophy Confirmed by Experiments, or an Introduction to Sir Isaac Newton's Philosophy.* 2d ed. 2 vols. Translated by J. T. Desaguliers. London: printed for J. Senex and W. Taylor, 1721.

Shadwell, T. *The Virtuoso.* London: printed by T. N. for H. Herringman, 1676.

Shakerley, J. *The Anatomy of Urania Practica.* London: printed by T. Brudenell, 1649.

Shakespeare, W. *William Shakespeare: The Complete Works.* Edited by S. Wells and G. Taylor. Oxford: Oxford University Press, 1986.

Sheppard, W. *An Epitome of all the Common and Statute Laws of this Nation now in force.* London: printed for W. Lee, D. Pakeman, J. Wright, H. Twyford, G. Bedell, T. Brewster, E. Dod, and J. Place, 1656.

A Short Account of Dr. Bentley's Humanity and Justice, to those Authors who have written before him . . . To which is added an Appendix by the Bookseller. London: printed for T. Bennet, 1699.

Sidney, A. *Discourses Concerning Government.* London: n.p.; sold by the Booksellers of London and Westminster, 1698.

S[inclair], G. *The Hydrostaticks.* Edinburgh: printed by G. Swintoun, J. Glen, and T. Brown, 1672 (bound with *Vindication,* but separately paginated).

Sinclair, G. *A Vindication of the Preface of the book intituled, . . . Ars Nova & Magna Gravitatis & Levitatis, from the challenges and reflections of the Publisher of the Philosophical Transactions.* Edinburgh: printed by G. Swintoun, J. Glen, and T. Brown, 1672 (bound with *Hydrostaticks,* but separately paginated).

Six Important Quaeres, Propounded to the Re-Sitting Rump. [London]: n.p., 1659.

Smet, H. *Prosodia . . . promptissima, quae syllabarum positione & diphthongis carentium quantitates, exemplis demonstrat.* London: printed [by R. Field] for Stationers' Company, 1615.

Smiles, S. *The Huguenots.* 6th ed. London: John Murray, 1889.

Smiles, S. *Men of Invention and Industry.* London: John Murray, 1884.

Smiles, S. *Self-Help.* 1859. Reprint, London: John Murray, 1958.

Smith, A. *An Inquiry into the Nature and Causes of the Wealth of Nations.* 2 vols. Edited by R. H. Campbell, A. S. Skinner, and W. B. Todd. Oxford: Oxford University Press, 1976.

Smith, A. *Lectures on Jurisprudence.* Edited by R. L. Meek, D. D. Raphael, and P. G. Stein. Oxford: Oxford University Press, 1978.

Smith, F. *An Account of the Injurious Proceedings of Sir George Jeffreys Knt. Late Recorder of London, against Francis Smith, Bookseller.* London: printed for F. Smith, 1680.

Smith, F. "The Case of *Francis Smith,* Bookseller." Appended to *The Speech of a Noble Peer of this Realm, made in the Reign of King Charles II. An, 1681.* London: printed for F. Smith, 1689 (Huntington Library, 72907).

Smith, F. [pseud.] *Vox Lachrymae. A Sermon Newly Held Forth at Weavers-Hall, Upon the Funeral of the Famous T. O. Doctor of Salamancha. By Elephant-Smith.* London: printed for T. Davies, 1682.

Smith, J. *A Compleat Practise of Physick.* London: printed by J. Streater, for S. Miller, 1656.

Smith, J. *Select Discourses.* 4th ed. Edited by H. G. Williams. Cambridge: Cambridge University Press, 1859.

Soane, G. *Faustus. A Romantic Drama.* London: John Cumberland, [ca. 1830].

Songhurst, W. J., ed. *The Minutes of the Grand Lodge of Freemasons of England, 1723–1739.* London: Quatuor Coronati Lodge, 1913.

Sorbière, S. *A Voyage into England, Containing Many Things Relating to the State of Learning, Religion and other Curiosities of that Kingdom.* London: n.p.; sold by J. Woodward, 1709.

Sparke, M. *The Crums of Comfort; with godly Prayers*. 6th ed. London: printed for M. Sparke, 1628.

S[parke], M. *The Dimension of the Hollow Tree of Hampsted*. London: printed by F. Coles for M. S., 1653 (BL 669f17[46]).

[Sparke, M.] *Scintilla, or A Light Broken into Darke Warehouses*. London: "Printed, not for *profit,* but for the Common Weles good: and no where to be *sold,* but some where to be given," 1641.

Sparke, M. *A Second Beacon Fired by Scintilla*. London: printed for the author, 1652.

[Sparke, M.] *The Second Part of Crums of Comfort*. London: printed for M. Sparke, 1652.

[Sparke, M.] *Truth Brought to Light and Discovered by Time or A Discourse and Historicall Narration of the first XIIII yeares of King Iames Reigne*. London: printed by R. Cotes for M. Sparke, 1651.

Speeches or Arguments of the Judges of the Court of King's Bench. Leith: printed for W. Coke, 1771.

Speed, S. *Prison-Pietie: Or, Meditations Divine and Moral*. London: printed by J. C. for S. S. and sold by the booksellers of London and Westminster, 1677.

Sprat, T. *The History of the Royal Society of London, for the Improving of Natural Knowledge*. London: printed by T. R. for J. Martyn and J. Allestry, Printers to the Royal Society, 1667.

Sprat, T. *Observations on Monsieur de Sorbier's Voyage into England*. London: printed for J. Martyn and J. Allestry, 1665.

State Law: or, the Doctrine of Libels, Discussed and Examined. 2d ed. London: printed by E. and R. Nutt and R. Gosling, assigns of E. Sayer, for T. Wotton and J. Shuckburgh, [1730].

Stationers' Company. *Records of the Court of the Stationers' Company, 1602 to 1640*. Edited by W. A. Jackson. London: Bibliographical Society, 1957.

Stationers' Company. *To the Honourable House of Commons . . . The Humble Petition of the Company of Stationers of the City of London*. [London, 1643].

Stationers' Company. *A Transcript of the Registers of the Company of Stationers of London; 1554–1640 A.D.* 5 vols. Edited by E. Arber. Birmingham: privately printed, 1875–94.

Stationers' Company. *A Transcript of the Registers of the Worshipful Company of Stationers; from 1640–1708 AD*. 3 vols. Edited by G. E. Briscoe Eyre. London: privately printed, 1913–14.

Stephenson, N. *The Royal Almanack*. London: printed for the Company of Stationers, 1675.

Stow, J. *The Survay of London*. London: printed by G. Purslowe, 1618.

Stower, C. *The Printer's Grammar*. London: printed by C. Stower for B. Crosby, 1808.

S[treater], A. *A Letter sent to my Lord Maior*. London: n.p., 1642.

[Streater, J.?] *The Character of a True and False Shepherd*. London: n.p., 1670.

[Streater, J.?] *Clavis ad Aperiendum Carceris Ostia. Or, The High Point of the Writ of Habeas Corpus Discussed . . . being the Case of Mr. John Streater*. London: printed by J. Cottrel, sold by Cottrel and R. Moon, 1654.

S[treater], J. *The Continuation of this Session of Parliament, Justified*. London: n.p., 1659.

[Streater, J.] *A Further Continuance of the Grand Politick Informer*. [London]: n.p., 1653.

Streater, J. *A Glympse of that Jewel, Judicial, Just, Preserving Libertie*. London: printed for G. Calvert, 1653.

S[treater], J. *Government Described . . . Together with a Brief Model of the Government of the Common-wealth, or Free-State of Ragouse*. London: n.p., 1659.

S[treater], J. *The Jesuite Discovered: Or, A Brief Discourse of the Policies of the Church of Rome, in Preserving it Self, and Dividing of Protestant States and Kingdomes*. London: n.p., 1659.

Streater, J. *A Letter sent to His Excellency the Lord Fleetwood*. London: n.p., 1659.

[Streater, J.] *Observations Historical, Political, and Philosophical, upon Aristotles first Book of Political Government.* London: printed for R. Moon, 1654 (published in eleven weekly numbers, 4 April–4 July).

[Streater, J.] *A Politick Commentary on the Life of Caius Julius Caesar, written by Caius Suetonius Tranquilius.* London: n.p.; sold by R. Moon, 1654 (issued in weekly numbers from 23 May, converting into *Perfect and Impartial Intelligence*).

Streater, J. *Secret Reasons of State in Reference to the Affairs of these Nations . . . Discovered.* London: n.p., 1659.

S[treater], J. *A Shield against the Parthian Dart.* [London]: n.p., 1659.

Strype, J. *A Survey of the Cities of London and Westminster . . . by John Stow, Citizen and Native of London. Since Reprinted.* 2 vols. London: printed for A. Churchill, J. Knapton, R. Knaplock, et al., 1720.

Stubbe, H. *The Plus Ultra Reduced to a Non Plus.* London: n.p., 1670.

[Stubbe, H.] *A Reply unto the Letter written to Mr. Henry Stubbe in Defense of the History of the Royal Society.* Oxford: printed for R. Davis, 1671.

Suckling, J. *Fragmenta Aurea.* 3d ed. London: printed for H. Moseley, 1658.

Swift, J. *The Correspondence of Jonathan Swift.* 5 vols. Edited by H. Williams. Oxford: Oxford University Press, 1963–5.

Swift, J. *A Tale of a Tub and Other Works.* Edited by A. Ross and D. Woolley. Oxford: Oxford University Press, 1986.

Theophilus Rationalis [pseud.] *New News from Bedlam: or More Work for Towzer and his Brother Ravenscroft.* London: printed for the author and published by L. Curtis, 1682.

Thomson, T. *History of the Royal Society, from its Institution to the end of the Eighteenth Century.* London: R. Baldwin, 1812.

Thoresby, R. *Ducatus Leodiensis: Or, The Topography of the Ancient and Populous Town and Parish of Leedes.* London: printed for Maurice Atkins and sold by Henry Clements, 1715 (bound and concurrently paginated with Thoresby, *Musaeum Thoresbyanum*).

Thoresby, R. *Musaeum Thoresbyanum.* London: printed for Maurice Atkins and sold by Henry Clements, 1713 (bound and concurrently paginated with Thoresby, *Ducatus Leodiensis*).

[Thurmond, J.] *A Dramatick Entertainment, call'd the Necromancer. Or, Harlequin, Doctor Faustus.* 4th ed. London: printed and sold by T. Wood, 1724.

[Thurmond, J.] *A Dramatick Entertainment, call'd the Necromancer: Or, Harlequin, Doctor Faustus.* 7th ed. Dublin: printed and sold by P. Rider and T. Harbin, 1725.

[Thurmond, J.] *Harlequin Doctor Faustus.* London: printed for W. Chetwood, 1724.

[Thurmond, J.] *The Miser: or, Wagner and Abericock.* London: printed for W. Trott, 1727.

[Thurmond, J.] *The Vocal Parts of an Entertainment, call'd, The Necromancer: or, Harlequin Doctor Faustus.* London: n.p., sold by A. Dodd, 1723.

[Tindal, M.] *A Letter to a Member of Parliament, Shewing, that a Restraint* [on the] *Press is Inconsistent with the Protestant Religion, and Dangerous to the Liberties of the Nation.* London: printed by J. Darby, sold by A. Bell, 1698.

[Tindal, M.] *Reasons against Restraining the Press.* London: n.p., 1704.

To All Printers, Booke-sellers, Booke-binders, Free-men of the Company of Stationers. [London]: n.p., [1645] (BL E288[9, 44]).

T[okefield], G. *A Catalogue of such Books as have been Entered in the Register of the Company of Stationers.* London: printed and sold by S. Speed; "Published by G. T. Clerk to the Company of Stationers," 1664.

Toryrorydammeeplotshammee Younkercrape [pseud.] *A Sermon Prepared to be Preach'd at the Interment of the Renowned Observator.* London: n.p.; sold by L. Curtis, 1682.

[Trenchard, J.] *The Natural History of Superstition*. [London]: n.p.; sold by A. Baldwin, 1709.

Tryon, T. *A Treatise of Dreams & Visions*. 2d ed. London: printed and sold by T. Sowle, 1695.

Turgot, A.-R.-J., Baron de Laulne. *Turgot on Progress, Sociology and Economics*. Translated and edited by R. L. Meek. Cambridge: Cambridge University Press, 1973.

Turner, J. *Choice Experiences of the kind dealings of God before, in, and after Conversions*. London: printed by H. Hills, 1653.

Twynne, B. *Antiquitatis Academiae Oxoniensis Apologia*. Oxford: J. Barnes, 1608.

Valerius Maximus, Q. *Romae Antiquae Descriptio*. [Translated by S. Speed?] London: printed by J. C. for S. Speed, 1678.

Van der Linde, A. *The Haarlem Legend of the Invention of Printing by Lourens Janszoon Coster, Critically Examined*. Translated by J. H. Hessels. London: Blades, East and Blades, 1871.

Vaughan, H. *Olor Iscanus*. London: printed by T. W. for H. Moseley, 1651.

Vernon, G. *The Life of the Learned and Reverend Dr. Peter Heylyn*. London: printed for C. Harper, 1682.

A View of the many Traiterous, Disloyal, and Turn-about Actions of H. H. Senior. London: "Printed for the Use of all those who do any ways believe the Real Conversion of *H. H.*," 1684.

Vitruvius Pollio, M. *De Architectura Libri Decem*. Edited by C. Fensterbusch. Darmstadt: Wissenschaftliche Buchgesellschaft, 1964.

Von Halle, E. "The German Empire and Its Inhabitants at the End of the XIXth Century." In *International Exposition Paris 1900: Official Catalogue; Exhibition of the German Empire*, edited by O. N. Witt, 1–58. Berlin: Imperial Commission, 1900.

Walch, J. *Decas Fabularum Humani Generis sortem, Mores, Ingenium, varia studia, inventa atq. opera, cum ad vivum, tum mythologice adumbrantium*. Strasburg: printed for L. Zetzner, 1609.

Waller, R. "The Preface." *Philosophical Transactions* 196 (January 1692/3): 581–2.

Wallis, J. "A Copy of the Account, which Dr. WALLIS gave to Dr. BERNARD, one of the Delegates for Printing, by a Messenger sent from *Oxford* for that Purpose, . . . *Jan. 23. 1691*." In Hooke, *Philosophical Experiments and Observations*, 217–24.

Wallis, J. *A Defence of the Royal Society, and the Philosophical Transactions, Particularly those of July, 1670. In Answer to the Cavils of Dr. William Holder*. London: printed by T. S. for T. Moore, 1678.

[Wanley, H.] "Some Observations concerning the Invention and Progress of Printing, to the Year 1465." *Philosophical Transactions* 288 (1703): 1507–16.

[Ward, E.] *The Secret History of Clubs*. London: n.p.; sold by the booksellers, 1709.

Ward, G. R. M. *Oxford University Statutes*. 2 vols. London: W. Pickering, 1845–51.

Ward, J. *The Lives of the Professors of Gresham College*. London: printed by J. Moore for the author, and sold by W. Innys, J. and R. Knapton, et al., 1740.

[Ward, S.] *A Philosophicall Essay Towards an Eviction of the Being and Attributes of God*. Oxford: printed by L. Lichfield, to be sold by J. Adams and E. Forest, 1652.

[Watson, J.] *The History of the Art of Printing*. Edinburgh: printed and sold by J. Watson, 1713.

Webster, J. *The White Devil*. London: printed by I. N. for H. Perry, 1631.

Webster, J. *The Displaying of Supposed Witchcraft*. London: printed by J. M., 1677.

[Whately, S.] *An Answer to a late Book written against the Learned and Reverend Dr. Bentley*. London: n.p., 1699.

Wheare, D. *The Method and Order of Reading Both Civil and Ecclesiastical Histories*. Translated and edited by E. Bohun. London: printed by M. Flesher for C. Brome, 1685.

Whewell, W. *Newton and Flamsteed*. Cambridge: J. and J. J. Deighton, 1836.

[Whewell, W.] Review of M. Sommerville, *On the Connexion of the Physical Sciences. Quarterly Review*, 51 (1834): 54–68.

Whiston, W. *Astronomical Lectures Read in the Publick Schools at Cambridge.* 2d ed. London: printed for J. Senex, W. and J. Innys, J. Osborne, and T. Longman, 1728.

Whitfield, W. *A Sermon on the death of the late Lord Bishop of London . . . Before the Worshipful Company of Stationers.* London: printed by J. Leake for R. Knaplock, 1713.

[Wilkins, J.] *A Discourse Concerning a New Planet. Tending to Prove, that 'tis Probable our Earth is one of the Planets.* London: printed [with the 3d impression of the *Discovery*] by R. H. for J. Maynard, 1640.

[Wilkins, J.] *The Discovery of a World in the Moone: Or, A Discourse Tending to Prove, that 'tis Probable there may be another Habitable World in that Planet.* London: printed by E. G. for M. Sparke and E. Forrest, 1638.

Wilkins, J. *The Mathematical and Philosophical Works of the Right Rev. John Wilkins.* 2 vols. London: printed by C. Whittingham for Vernor and Wood et al., 1802.

Wilkins, J. *Of the Principles and Duties of Natural Religion.* Edited by J. Tillotson. London: printed for T. Basset, H. Brome, and R. Chiswell, 1678.

Wilkins, J. *Sermons Preached upon Several Occasions.* Edited by J. Tillotson. London: printed for T. Basset, R. Chiswell, and W. Rogers, 1682.

[Wilkins, J., and S. Ward.] *Vindiciae Academiarum.* Oxford: printed by L. Lichfield for T. Robinson, 1654.

Williams, J. "An Edition of the Correspondence of John Aubrey with Anthony à Wood and Edward Lhuyd 1667–1696, with Introduction and Notes." Ph.D. thesis. London University, 1969.

Willis, T. "The Anatomy of the Brain." In *Remaining Medical Works*, 55–136.

Willis, T. "The Description and Use of the Nerves." In *Remaining Medical Works*, 137–92.

Willis, T. *Dr. Willis's Practice of Physick.* London: printed for T. Dring, C. Harper, and J. Leigh, 1684.

Willis, T. *The Remaining Medical Works of that Famous and Renowned Physician Dr. Thomas Willis.* Translated by S. Pordage. London: printed for T. Dring, C. Harper, J. Leigh, and S. Martyn, 1681.

Willis, T. *Thomas Willis's Oxford Lectures.* Edited by K. Dewhurst. Oxford: Sandford Publications, 1980.

Willis, T. *Two Discourses concerning the Soul of Brutes, which is that of the Vital and Sensitive of Man.* Translated by S. Pordage. London: printed for T. Dring, C. Harper, and J. Leigh, 1683.

Willis, T. *Willis's Oxford Casebook (1650–52).* Edited by K. Dewhurst. Oxford: Sandford Publications, 1981.

Willughby, F. *De Historia Piscium Libri Quatuor.* Edited by J. Ray. Oxford: printed at the Sheldonian Theatre, 1686.

Willughby, F. *The Ornithology of Francis Willughby.* Translated and edited by J. Ray. London: printed by A. C. for J. Martyn, 1678.

Wither, G. *The Schollers Purgatory.* [London?]: n.p., [1624].

Wood, A. à. *Athenae Oxoniensis.* New ed. 4 vols. London: Rivington et al., 1813–20.

Wood, A. à. *Historia et Antiquitates Universitatis Oxoniensis.* Oxford: printed at the Sheldonian Theatre, 1674.

Woodcroft, B. *Patents for Inventions: Abridgments of Specifications Relating to Printing.* London: Great Seal Patent Office, 1859.

Worcester, Edward Somerset, marquis of. *A Century of the Names and Scantlings of such Inventions, as at present I can call to mind.* London: printed by J. Grismond, 1663.

A Word to Purpose: Or, A Parthian Dart, shot back to 1642, and from thence shot back again to 1659. [London]: n.p., 1659.

Worster, B. *A Compendious Account of the Principles of Natural Philosophy.* 2d ed. London: printed for S. Austen, 1730.

Worster, B. *A Compendious and Methodical Account of the Principles of Natural Philosophy.* London: printed for the author and sold by W. and J. Innys, 1722.

Wren, C. *Parentalia: or, Memoirs of the Family of the Wrens.* Edited by S. Wren. London: printed for T. Osborn and R. Dodsley, 1750.

[Wren, M.] *Considerations on Mr. Harrington's Common-wealth of Oceana.* London: printed for S. Gellibrand, 1657.

Wright, T. *The Passions of the Minde.* London: printed by V. S. for W. B., 1601.

Yarranton, A. *England's Improvement by Sea and Land.* 2 vols. London: n.p.; sold by T. Parkhurst, 1698.

Yonge, J. *The Journal of James Yonge (1647–1721), Plymouth Surgeon.* Edited by F. N. L. Poynter. London: Longman, 1963.

SECONDARY SOURCES

Abbatista, G. "The Business of Paternoster Row: Towards a Publishing History of the *Universal History* (1736–65)." *Publishing History* 17 (1985): 5–50.

Abir-Am, P. G., and D. Outram, eds. *Uneasy Careers and Intimate Lives: Women in Science, 1789–1979.* New Brunswick: Rutgers University Press, 1989.

Ackroyd, P. *Hawksmoor.* London: Sphere, 1986.

Adams, P. G. *Travelers and Travel Liars 1660–1800.* Berkeley and Los Angeles: University of California Press, 1962.

Agnew, J.-C. *Worlds Apart: The Market and the Theater in Anglo-American Thought, 1550–1750.* Cambridge: Cambridge University Press, 1986.

Aitken, G. A. *The Life and Works of John Arbuthnot.* Oxford: Oxford University Press, 1892.

Alexander, J. "The Economic Structure of the City of London at the End of the Seventeenth Century." *Urban History Yearbook* 16 (1989): 47–62.

Alpers, S. *The Art of Describing: Dutch Art in the Seventeenth Century.* Chicago: University of Chicago Press, 1983.

Alpers, S. *Rembrandt's Enterprise: The Studio and the Market.* Chicago: University of Chicago Press, 1988.

Alston, R. "The British Book Trade, 1701 to 1800." *Publishing History* 16 (1984): 43–86.

Altick, R. D. *The English Common Reader: A Social History of the Mass Reading Public 1800–1900.* Chicago: University of Chicago Press, 1957.

Altick, R. D. *The Shows of London.* Cambridge: Harvard University Press, 1978.

Amussen, S. D. *An Ordered Society: Gender and Class in Early Modern England.* Oxford: Blackwell, 1988.

Anderson, B. *Imagined Communities: Reflections on the Origin and Spread of Nationalism.* Rev. ed. London: Verso, 1983.

Anderson, J. H. *Biographical Truth: The Representation of Historical Persons in Tudor-Stuart Writing.* New Haven: Yale University Press, 1984.

Anderson, W. C. *Between the Library and the Laboratory: The Language of Chemistry in Eighteenth-Century France.* Baltimore: Johns Hopkins University Press, 1984.

Andrade, E. N. da C. "The Birth and Early Days of the *Philosophical Transactions.*" *Notes and Records of the Royal Society* 20 (1965): 9–22.

Appignanesi, L. and S. Maitland, eds. *The Rushdie File.* London: Fourth Estate, 1989.

Archer, I. W. *The Pursuit of Stability: Social Relations in Elizabethan London.* Cambridge: Cambridge University Press, 1991.

Armitage, D., A. Himy, and Q. Skinner, eds. *Milton and Republicanism.* Cambridge: Cambridge University Press, 1995.

Armstrong, E. *Before Copyright: The French Book-Privilege System, 1498–1526.* Cambridge: Cambridge University Press, 1990.

Armstrong, E. "English Purchases of Printed Books from the Continent 1465–1526." *English Historical Review* 94 (1979): 268–90.

Asch, R. G. "The Revival of Monopolies: Court and Patronage during the Personal Rule of Charles I, 1629–1640." In Asch and Birke, *Princes, Patronage, and the Nobility,* 357–92.

Asch, R. G., and A. M. Birke, eds. *Princes, Patronage, and the Nobility: The Court at the Beginning of the Modern Age, c. 1450–1650.* Oxford: Oxford University Press; London: German Historical Institute, 1991.

Ashcraft, R. "Latitudinarianism and Toleration: Historical Myth versus Political History." In Kroll, Ashcraft, and Zagorin, *Philosophy, Science and Religion,* 151–77.

Ashcraft, R. *Revolutionary Politics and Locke's "Two Treatises of Government."* Princeton: Princeton University Press, 1986.

Ashton, R. *The City and the Court 1603–1649.* Cambridge: Cambridge University Press, 1979.

Ashton, R. *The English Civil War: Conservatism and Revolution 1603–1649.* 2d ed. London: Weidenfeld and Nicolson, 1989.

Ashworth, W. B., Jr. "The Habsburg Circle." In Moran, *Patronage and Institutions,* 137–67.

Astbury, R. "The Renewal of the Licensing Act in 1693 and its Lapse in 1695." *The Library,* 5th ser., 33 (1978): 296–322.

Aston, M. *England's Iconoclasts. I: Laws against Images.* Oxford: Clarendon Press, 1988.

Atto, C. "The Society for the Encouragement of Learning." *The Library,* 4th ser., 19 (1938): 263–88.

Avery, E. L. *The London Stage 1660–1800, II: 1700–1729.* Carbondale: Southern Illinois University Press, 1960.

Avis, F. C. *The Sixteenth-Century Long Shop Printing Office in the Poultry.* London: Glenview, 1982.

Aylmer, G. E., ed. *The Interregnum: The Quest for Settlement 1646–1660.* Corrected ed. London: Macmillan, 1974.

Aymard, M. "Friends and Neighbours." In Chartier, *Passions of the Renaissance,* 447–91.

Backscheider, P. R. *Spectacular Politics: Theatrical Power and Mass Culture in Early Modern England.* Baltimore: Johns Hopkins University Press, 1993.

Baillie, W. M. "Printing Bibles in the Interregnum: *The Case of William Bentley* and *A Short Answer.*" *Papers of the Bibliographical Society of America* 91 (1997): 65–91.

Barber, G. "Martin-Dominique Fertel and His *Science Pratique de l'Imprimerie,* 1723." *The Library,* 6th ser., 8 (1986): 1–17.

Barber, G., and B. Fabian, eds. *Buch und Buchhandel in Europa im Achtzehnten Jahrhundert.* Hamburg: Hauswedell, 1981.

Barker-Benfield, G. J. *The Culture of Sensibility: Sex and Society in Eighteenth-Century Britain.* Chicago: University of Chicago Press, 1992.

Barnes, B., D. Bloor, and J. Henry. *Scientific Knowledge: A Sociological Analysis.* Chicago: University of Chicago Press, 1996.

Barnes, B., and S. Shapin, eds. *Natural Order: Historical Studies of Scientific Culture.* Beverly Hills: Sage, 1979.

Barney, S. A., ed. *Annotation and Its Texts.* New York: Oxford University Press, 1991.

Baron, F. *Doctor Faustus: From History to Legend.* Munich: Wilhelm Fink, 1978.

Barry, J. "The Politics of Religion in Restoration Bristol." In Harris, Seaward, and Goldie, *The Politics of Religion in Restoration England*, 163–89.

Barry, J. "The Press and the Politics of Culture in Bristol, 1660–1775." In Black and Gregory, *Culture, Politics and Society*, 49–81.

Barry, J., and C. Brooks, eds. *The Middling Sort of People: Culture, Society and Politics in England, 1550–1800*. Basingstoke: Macmillan, 1994.

Bazerman, C. *Shaping Written Knowledge: the Genre and Activity of the Experimental Article in Science*. Madison: University of Wisconsin Press, 1988.

Beamish, R. *Memoir of the Life of Sir Mark Isambard Brunel*. London: Longman, Green, Longman and Roberts, 1862.

Bechtel, G. *Gutenberg et l'Invention de l'Imprimerie: Une Enquête*. Paris: Fayard, 1992.

Becker, H. S. *Art Worlds*. Berkeley and Los Angeles: University of California Press, 1982.

Beddard, R. "The Unexpected Whig Revolution of 1688." In Beddard, *The Revolutions of 1688*, 11–101.

Beddard, R., ed. *The Revolutions of 1688*. Oxford: Oxford University Press, 1991.

Beier, A. L., and R. Finlay, eds. *London 1500–1700: The Making of the Metropolis*. London: Longman, 1986.

Beier, L. M. *Sufferers and Healers: the Experience of Illness in Seventeenth-Century England*. London: Routledge and Kegan Paul, 1987.

Belanger, T. "Booksellers' Sales of Copyright: Aspects of the London Book Trade 1718–1768." Ph.D. thesis, Columbia University, 1970.

Belanger, T. "Booksellers' Trade Sales 1718–1768." *The Library*, 5th ser., 30 (1975): 281–302.

Belanger, T. "Publishers and Writers in Eighteenth-Century England." In Rivers, *Books and Their Readers*, 5–25.

Bell, M. "Elizabeth Calvert and the 'Confederates.'" *Publishing History* 32 (1992): 5–49.

Benjamin, A. E., G. N. Cantor, and J. R. R. Christie, eds. *The Figural and the Literal: Problems of Language in the History of Science and Philosophy, 1630–1800*. Manchester: Manchester University Press, 1987.

Bennett, G. V. *The Tory Crisis in Church and State, 1688–1730: The Career of Francis Atterbury, Bishop of Rochester*. Oxford: Oxford University Press, 1975.

Bennett, J. A. "The Challenge of Practical Mathematics." In Pumfrey, Rossi, and Slawinski, *Science, Culture and Popular Belief*, 176–90.

Bennett, J. A. "The Longitude and the New Science." *Vistas in Astronomy* 28 (1985): 219–25.

Bennett, J. A. *The Mathematical Science of Christopher Wren*. Cambridge: Cambridge University Press, 1982.

Bennett, J. A. "The Mechanics' Philosophy and the Mechanical Philosophy." *History of Science* 24 (1986): 1–28.

Berkvens-Stevelinck, C. *Prosper Marchand: La Vie et l'Oeuvre (1678–1756)*. Leiden: E. J. Brill, 1987.

Bermingham, A., and J. Brewer, eds. *The Consumption of Culture, 1600–1800: Image, Object, Text*. London: Routledge, 1995.

Biagioli, M. *Galileo, Courtier: The Practice of Science in the Culture of Absolutism*. Chicago: University of Chicago Press, 1993.

Biagioli, M. "Galileo the Emblem Maker." *Isis* 81 (1990): 230–58.

Biagioli, M. "Galileo's System of Patronage." *History of Science* 28 (1990): 1–62.

Biagioli, M. "Playing with the Evidence." *Early Science and Medicine* 1 (1996): 70–105.

Bijker, W. E., T. P. Hughes, and T. J. Pinch, eds. *The Social Construction of Technological Systems: New Directions in the Sociology and History of Technology*. Cambridge: MIT Press, 1987.

Bijker, W. E., and J. Law, eds. *Shaping Technology/Building Society: Studies in Sociotechnical Change.* Cambridge: MIT Press, 1992.

Binns, J. W. "Four Latin Poems on Printing." *The Library,* 6th ser., 4 (1982): 38–41.

Binns, J. W. *Intellectual Culture in Elizabethan and Jacobean England: The Latin Writings of the Age.* Leeds: Francis Cairns, 1990.

Binns, J. W. "STC Latin Books: Further Evidence for Printing-House Practice." *The Library,* 6th ser., 1 (1979): 347–54.

Black, A. *Guilds and Civil Society in European Political Thought from the Twelfth Century to the Present.* London: Methuen, 1984.

Black, J. *The English Press in the Eighteenth Century.* London: Croom Helm, 1987.

Black, J. "Ideology, History, Xenophobia and the World of Print in Eighteenth-Century England." In Black and Gregory, *Culture, Politics and Society,* 184–216.

Black, J. "The Press, Party and Foreign Policy in the Reign of George I." *Publishing History* 13 (1983): 23–40.

Black, J., and J. Gregory, eds. *Culture, Politics and Society in Britain, 1660–1800.* Manchester: Manchester University Press, 1991.

Black, M. H. "The Printed Bible." In Greenslade, *Cambridge History of the Bible,* 408–75.

Blackwell, R. J. *Galileo, Bellarmine and the Bible.* Notre Dame, Ind.: University of Notre Dame Press, 1991.

Blades, W. *An Account of the German Morality-Play, Entitled "Depositio Cornuti Typographicae": As Performed in the 17th and 18th Centuries.* London: Trübner, 1885.

Blagden, C. "The Accounts of the Wardens of the Stationers' Company." *Studies in Bibliography* 9 (1957): 69–93.

Blagden, C. "Booksellers' Trade Sales 1718–1768." *The Library,* 5th ser., 5 (1951): 243–57.

Blagden, C. "Charter Trouble." *The Book Collector* 6 (1957): 369–77.

Blagden, C. "The 'Company' of Printers." *Studies in Bibliography* 13 (1960): 3–17.

Blagden, C. "The Distribution of Almanacks in the Second Half of the Seventeenth Century." *Studies in Bibliography* 11 (1958): 107–16.

Blagden, C. "The English Stock of the Stationers' Company." *The Library,* 5th ser., 10 (1955): 163–85.

Blagden, C. "The Memorandum Book of Henry Rhodes, 1695–1720." *The Book Collector* 3 (1954): 28–38, 103–16.

Blagden, C. *The Stationers' Company: A History 1403–1959.* London: Allen and Unwin, 1960.

Blagden, C. "The Stationers' Company in the Civil War Period." *The Library,* 5th ser., 13 (1958): 1–17.

Blagden, C. "Thomas Carnan and the Almanack Monopoly." *Studies in Bibliography* 14 (1961): 23–43.

Blair, A. "Humanist Methods in Natural Philosophy: The Commonplace Book." *Journal for the History of Ideas* 53 (1992): 541–51.

Blair, A. "Restaging Jean Bodin: The *Universae Naturae Theatrum* (1596) in Its Cultural Context." Ph.D. thesis, Princeton University, 1990.

Blair, A. *The Theater of Nature: Jean Bodin and Renaissance Science.* Princeton: Princeton University Press, 1997.

Blayney, P. W. M. *The Bookshops in Paul's Cross Churchyard.* London: Bibliographical Society, 1990.

Blayney, P. W. M. "The Prevalence of Shared Printing in the Early Seventeenth Century." *Papers of the Bibliographical Society of America* 67 (1973): 437–42.

Blayney, P. W. M. *The Texts of "King Lear" and Their Origins.* Vol. 1, *Nicholas Okes and the First Quarto.* Cambridge: Cambridge University Press, 1982.

Bloch, M. *The Historian's Craft*. Translated by P. Putnam. Manchester: Manchester University Press, 1954.

Bluhm, R. K. "Remarks on the Royal Society's Finances, 1660–1768." *Notes and Records of the Royal Society* 13 (1958): 82–103.

Blum, A. "The Author's Authority: *Areopagitica* and the Labour of Licensing." In Nyquist and Ferguson, *Re-Membering Milton*, 74–96.

Blumenberg, H. *Die Lesbarkeit der Welt*. Frankfurt: Suhrkamp, 1981.

Bonelli, M. L. R., and A. Van Helden. "Divini and Campani: A Forgotten Chapter in the History of the Accademia del Cimento." *Annali dell'Istituto e Museo di Storia della Scienza di Firenze* 6 (1981): 3–176.

Bonnell, T. F. "Bookselling and Canon-Making: The Trade Rivalry over the English Poets, 1776–1783." *Studies in Eighteenth-Century Culture* 19 (1989): 53–70.

Bonney, R. *The European Dynastic States 1494–1660*. Oxford: Oxford University Press, 1991.

Bots, H., and F. Waquet, eds. *Commercium Litterarium: La Communication dans la République des Lettres, 1600–1750*. Amsterdam: APA-Holland University Press, 1994.

Boulton, J. *Neighbourhood and Society: A London Suburb in the Seventeenth Century*. Cambridge: Cambridge University Press, 1987.

Boulton, J. "Residential Mobility in Seventeenth-Century Southwark." *Urban History Yearbook* 13 (1986): 1–14.

Bourdieu, P. *Distinction: A Social Critique of the Judgement of Taste*. Translated by R. Nice. London: Routledge, 1986.

Bourdieu, P., and R. Chartier. "La Lecture: Une Pratique Culturelle." In Chartier, *Pratiques de la Lecture*, 218–39.

Braudel, F. *Civilization and Capitalism, 15th–18th Century. II: The Wheels of Commerce*. Translated by S. Reynolds. London: Collins, 1982.

Brewer, J., and R. Porter, eds. *Consumption and the World of Goods*. London: Routledge, 1992.

Brewer, J., and S. Staves, eds. *Early Modern Conceptions of Property*. London: Routledge, 1995.

Brewer, J., and J. Styles, eds. *An Ungovernable People: The English and Their Law in the Seventeenth and Eighteenth Centuries*. London: Hutchinson, 1980.

Brodowski, J. H. "Literary Piracy in England from the Restoration to the Early Eighteenth Century." D.L.S. thesis, Columbia University, 1973.

Brown, E. A. R. "*Falsitas pia sive Reprehensibilis*: Medieval Forgers and their Intentions." In *Fälschungen in Mittelalter: Internationaler Kongress der Monumenta Germaniae Historica München, 16–19 September 1986. Teil I: Kongressdaten und Festvorträge Literatur und Fälschung*, 101–19. Hanover: Hahnsche Buchhandlung, 1988.

Bucholz, R. O. *The Augustan Court: Queen Anne and the Decline of Court Culture*. Stanford: Stanford University Press, 1993.

Buck, L. P., and J. W. Zophy, eds. *The Social History of the Reformation*. Columbus: Ohio State University Press, 1972.

Burgess, G. *The Politics of the Ancient Constitution: An Introduction to English Political Thought, 1603–1642*. Basingstoke: Macmillan, 1992.

Burke, J. G., ed. *The Uses of Science in the Age of Newton*. Berkeley and Los Angeles: University of California, 1983.

Burke, P. *The Fabrication of Louis XIV*. New Haven: Yale University Press, 1992.

Burke, P. *The Historical Anthropology of Early Modern Italy: Essays on Perception and Communication*. Cambridge: Cambridge University Press, 1987.

Burke, P. *Popular Culture in Early Modern Europe*. London: Temple Smith, 1978.

Burke, P. "Popular Culture in Seventeenth-Century London." In Reay, *Popular Culture*, 31–58.

Burke, P. *Sociology and History*. London: Allen and Unwin, 1980.

Burke, P., ed. *New Perspectives on Historical Writing*. Cambridge: Polity, 1991.

Burns, J. H. "The Idea of Absolutism." In Miller, *Absolutism*, 21–42.

Burns, J. H., and M. Goldie, eds. *The Cambridge History of Political Thought, 1450–1700*. Cambridge: Cambridge University Press, 1991.

Burrow, J. W. *A Liberal Descent: Victorian Historians and the English Past*. Cambridge: Cambridge University Press, 1981.

Butler, E. M. *The Fortunes of Faust*. 1952. Reprint, Cambridge: Cambridge University Press, 1979.

Butler, M. *Theatre and Crisis 1632–1642*. Cambridge: Cambridge University Press, 1984.

Bynum, C. W. *Holy Feast and Holy Fast: The Religious Significance of Food to Medieval Women*. Berkeley and Los Angeles: University of California Press, 1987.

Bynum, W. F. "The Anatomical Method, Natural Theology, and the Functions of the Brain." *Isis* 64 (1973): 444–68.

Bynum, W. F., S. Lock, and R. Porter, eds. *Medical Journals and Medical Knowledge: Historical Essays*. London: Routledge, 1992.

Callon, M., J. Law, and A. Rip. "Putting Texts in Their Place." In Callon, Law, and Rip, *Mapping the Dynamics of Science and Technology*, 221–30.

Callon, M., J. Law, and A. Rip, eds. *Mapping the Dynamics of Science and Technology: Sociology of Science in the Real World*. Basingstoke: Macmillan, 1986.

Calvino, I. *If on a Winter's Night a Traveller*. Translated by W. Weaver. London: Pan, 1982.

Capp, B. *Astrology and the Popular Press: English Almanacks 1500–1800*. London: Faber and Faber, 1979.

Capp, B. *Cromwell's Navy: The Fleet and the English Revolution, 1648–1660*. Oxford: Oxford University Press, 1989.

Capp, B. *The Fifth Monarchy Men: A Study in Seventeenth-Century English Millenarianism*. London: Faber and Faber, 1972.

Carlson, N. E. "Wither and the Stationers." *Studies in Bibliography* 19 (1966): 210–5.

Carpenter, K. E., ed. *Books and Society in History*. New York: Bowker, 1983.

Carré, J., ed. *The Crisis of Courtesy: Studies in the Conduct Book in Britain, 1600–1900*. Leiden: E. J. Brill, 1994.

Cauchi, S. "The 'Setting Foorth' of Harington's Ariosto." *Studies in Bibliography* 36 (1983): 137–68.

Cavaciocchi, S., ed. *Produzione e Commercio della Carta e del Libro Secc. XIII–XVIII*. Prato: Le Monnier, 1991.

Champion, J. A. *The Pillars of Priestcraft Shaken: The Church of England and its Enemies, 1660–1730*. Cambridge: Cambridge University Press, 1992.

Chandler, J., A. I. Davidson, and H. Harootunian, eds. *Questions of Evidence: Proof, Practice, and Persuasion across the Disciplines*. Chicago: University of Chicago Press, 1994.

Chandler, R. *The Chandler Collection*. 3 vols. London: Picador, 1983–4.

Charles, L., and L. Duffin, eds. *Women and Work in Pre-industrial England*. London: Croom Helm, 1985.

Chartier, R. *Cultural History: Between Practices and Representations*. Translated by L. G. Cochrane. Cambridge: Polity, 1988.

Chartier, R. *The Cultural Origins of the French Revolution*. Translated by L. G. Cochrane. Durham: Duke University Press, 1991.

Chartier, R. *The Cultural Uses of Print in Early Modern France*. Translated by L. G. Cochrane. Princeton: Princeton University Press, 1987.

Chartier, R. "Culture as Appropriation: Popular Cultural Uses in Early Modern France." In Kaplan, *Understanding Popular Culture*, 229–53.

Chartier, R. "Du Livre au Lire." In Chartier, *Pratiques de la Lecture*, 62–88.

Chartier, R. *Forms and Meanings: Texts, Performances, and Audiences from Codex to Computer*. Philadelphia: University of Pennsylvania Press, 1995.

Chartier, R. "General Introduction: Print Culture." In Chartier, *Culture of Print*, 1–10.

Chartier, R. *Lectures et Lecteurs dans la France d'Ancien Régime*. Paris: Editions du Seuil, 1987.

Chartier, R. *The Order of Books: Readers, Authors, and Libraries in Europe between the Fourteenth and Eighteenth Centuries*. Translated by L. G. Cochrane. Cambridge: Polity Press, 1994.

Chartier, R., ed. *Passions of the Renaissance*. Vol. III of *A History of Private Life*, edited by P. Ariès and G. Duby. Translated by A. Goldhammer. Cambridge, Mass.: Belknap, 1989.

Chartier, R. "Postface." In Chartier and Martin, *Histoire de l'Edition Française*, IV, 621–41.

Chartier, R. "The Practical Impact of Writing." In Chartier, *Passions of the Renaissance*, 111–59.

Chartier, R. "Publishing Strategies and What the People Read, 1530–1660." In Chartier, *Cultural Uses of Print in Early Modern France*, 145–82.

Chartier, R. "Texts, Printings, Readings." In Hunt, *The New Cultural History*, 154–75.

Chartier, R., ed. *The Culture of Print: Power and the Uses of Print in Early Modern Europe*. Translated by L. G. Cochrane. Cambridge: Polity Press, 1989.

Chartier, R., ed. *Pratiques de la Lecture*. Marseille: Editions Rivages, 1985.

Chartier, R., and H.-J. Martin, eds. *Histoire de l'Edition Française*. 2d ed. 4 vols. Paris: Fayard, 1989–91.

Chartres, J. A. "The Capital's Provincial Eyes: London's Inns in the Early Eighteenth Century." *London Journal* 3 (1977): 24–39.

Christie, J., and S. Shuttleworth, eds. *Nature Transfigured: Science and Literature 1700–1900*. Manchester: Manchester University Press, 1989.

Churchill, E. F. "Dispensing Power and the Defence of the Realm." *Law Quarterly Review* 37 (1921): 412–41.

Clair, C. *Christopher Plantin*. 1960. Reprint, London: Plantin, 1987.

Clair, C. *A Chronology of Printing*. London: Cassell, 1969.

Clanchy, M. T. *From Memory to Written Record: England 1066–1307*. London: Edward Arnold, 1979.

Clanchy, M. T. "Looking Back from the Invention of Printing." In Resnick, *Literacy in Historical Perspective*, 7–22.

Clark, A. *The Struggle for the Breeches: Gender and the Making of the British Working Class*. Berkeley and Los Angeles: University of California Press, 1995.

Clark, J. A. *Gabriel Naudé, 1600–1653*. Hamden, Conn.: Archon, 1970.

Clark, P., ed. *The Early Modern Town*. London: Longman, 1976.

Clark, W. "The Scientific Revolution in the German Nations." In Porter and Teich, *Scientific Revolution in National Context*, 90–114.

Clarke, J., C. Critcher, and R. Johnson, eds. *Working Class Culture*. London: Hutchinson, 1979.

Clulee, N. H. *John Dee's Natural Philosophy: Between Science and Religion*. London: Routledge, 1988.

Cohen, H. F. *The Scientific Revolution: A Historiographical Inquiry*. Chicago: University of Chicago Press, 1994.

Cohen, I. B. "Harrington and Harvey: A Theory of the State based on the New Physiology." *Journal of the History of Ideas* 55 (1994): 187–210.

Cohen, I. B. *Introduction to Newton's "Principia."* Cambridge: Cambridge University Press, 1971.

Cole, R. C. *Irish Booksellers and English Writers 1740–1800*. London: Mansell, 1986.

Cole, R. G. "The Dynamics of Printing in the Sixteenth Century." In Buck and Zophy, *The Social History of the Reformation*, 93–105.

Coleman, D. C. *The British Paper Industry 1495–1860: A Study in Industrial Growth.* Oxford: Clarendon Press, 1958.

Colley, L. *Britons: Forging the Nation, 1707–1837.* New Haven: Yale University Press, 1992.

Collingwood, R. G. *An Autobiography.* 1939. Reprint, Oxford: Clarendon Press, 1978.

Collingwood, R. G. *The Principles of Art.* Oxford: Clarendon Press, 1938.

Collins, A. S. *Authorship in the Days of Johnson: Being a Study of the Relation between Author, Patron, Publisher and Public, 1726–1780.* London: Robert Holden, 1927.

Collins, H. *Artificial Experts: Social Knowledge and Intelligent Machines.* Cambridge: MIT Press, 1990.

Collins, H. *Changing Order: Replication and Induction in Scientific Practice.* London: Sage, 1985.

Collinson, P. *The Birthpangs of Protestant England: Religious and Cultural Change in the Sixteenth and Seventeenth Centuries.* Basingstoke: Macmillan, 1988.

Collinson, P. "The Sense of Sacred Writ." *Times Literary Supplement,* 9 April 1993, 3–4.

Condren, C. "Casuistry to Newcastle: 'The Prince' in the World of the Book." In Phillipson and Skinner, *Political Discourse in Early Modern Britain*, 164–86.

Constable, G. "Forgery and Plagiarism in the Middle Ages." *Archiv für Diplomatik* 29 (1983): 1–41.

Cook, E. "The First Edition of *Religio Medici*." *Harvard Library Bulletin* 2 (1948): 22–31.

Cook, H. J. *The Decline of the Old Medical Régime in Stuart London.* Ithaca: Cornell University Press, 1986.

Cook, H. J. "Physicians and the New Philosophy: Henry Stubbe and the Virtuosi-Physicians." In French and Wear, *Medical Revolution*, 246–71.

Coover, J., ed. *Music Publishing: Copyright and Piracy in Victorian England.* London: Mansell, 1985.

Copenhaver, B. P. "Did Science Have a Renaissance?" *Isis* 83 (1992): 387–407.

Corbett, M., and R. Lightblown. *The Comely Frontispiece: The Emblematic Title-Page in England, 1550–1660.* London: Routledge and Kegan Paul, 1979.

Cormack, L. B. "Twisting the Lion's Tail: Practice and Theory at the Court of Henry Prince of Wales." In Moran, *Patronage and Institutions*, 67–83.

Crawford, P. *Women and Religion in England 1500–1720.* London: Routledge, 1993.

Crawford, P. "Women's Published Writings 1600–1700." In Prior, *Women in English Society*, 211–82.

Cressy, D. "Books as Totems in Seventeenth-Century England and New England." *Journal of Library History* 21 (1986): 92–106.

Cressy, D. *Literacy and the Social Order: Reading and Writing in Tudor and Stuart England.* Cambridge: Cambridge University Press, 1980.

Crist, T. J. "Francis Smith and the Opposition Press in England, 1660–1688." Ph.D. thesis, Cambridge University, 1977.

Crist, T. J. "Government Control of the Press after the Expiration of the Printing Act in 1679." *Publishing History* 5 (1979): 49–78.

Cudworth, W. *Life and Correspondence of Abraham Sharp.* London: Sampson, Low, Marston, Searle and Rivington, 1889.

Cunningham, A. "How the *Principia* Got Its Name: or, Taking Natural Philosophy Seriously." *History of Science* 29 (1991): 377–92.

Cunningham, A., and P. Williams. "De-centring the 'Big Picture': *The Origins of Modern Science* and the Modern Origins of Science." *British Journal for the History of Science* 26 (1993): 407–32.

Curry, P. *Prophecy and Power: Astrology in Early Modern England*. Cambridge: Polity, 1989.

Curry, P., ed. *Astrology, Science and Society: Historical Essays*. Woodbridge: Boydell, 1987.

D., R. "Obituary: John Churchill." *Medical Times and Gazette*, 14 August 1875, 197–200.

Daly, J. "The Idea of Absolute Monarchy in Seventeenth-Century England." *Historical Journal* 21 (1978): 227–50.

Daly, J. *Sir Robert Filmer and English Political Thought*. Toronto: University of Toronto, 1979.

Darnton, R. *The Business of Enlightenment: A Publishing History of the* Encyclopédie, *1775–1800*. Cambridge: Harvard University Press, 1979.

Darnton, R. *The Great Cat Massacre, and Other Episodes in French Cultural History*. London: Allen Lane, 1984.

Darnton, R. "History of Reading." In Burke, *New Perspectives*, 140–67.

Darnton, R. *The Literary Underground of the Old Regime*. Cambridge: Harvard University Press, 1982.

Darnton, R. "Readers Respond to Rousseau: The Fabrication of Romantic Sensibility." In Darnton, *Great Cat Massacre*, 209–49.

Darnton, R., and D. Roche, eds. *Revolution in Print: The Press in France 1775–1800*. Berkeley and Los Angeles: University of California Press, 1989.

Daston, L. "Baconian Facts, Academic Civility, and the Prehistory of Objectivity." *Annals of Scholarship* 8 (1991): 337–63.

Daston, L. "The Factual Sensibility." *Isis* 79 (1988): 452–70.

Daston, L. "The Naturalized Female Intellect." *Science in Context* 5 (1992): 209–35.

Davenport, N. *The United Kingdom Patent System: A Brief History*. Havant, England: K. Mason, 1979.

Davies, G. *The Early Stuarts, 1603–60*. Oxford: Oxford University Press, 1937.

Davies, G. *The Restoration of Charles II, 1658–1660*. San Marino: Huntington Library, 1955.

Davies, H. W. *Devices of the Early Printers, 1457–1560: Their History and Development*. London: Grafton and Co., 1935.

Davies, J. D. *Gentlemen and Tarpaulins: The Officers and Men of the Restoration Navy*. Oxford: Oxford University Press, 1991.

Davis, E. B. "'Parcere Nominibus': Boyle, Hooke and the Rhetorical Interpretation of Descartes." In Hunter, *Robert Boyle Reconsidered*, 157–75.

Davis, J. C. *Fear, Myth and History: The Ranters and the Historians*. Cambridge: Cambridge University Press, 1986.

Davis, J. C. "Religion and the Struggle for Freedom in the English Revolution." *Historical Journal* 35 (1992): 507–30.

Davis, J. C. *Utopia and the Ideal Society: A Study of English Utopian Writing 1516–1700*. Cambridge: Cambridge University Press, 1981.

Davis, N. Z. "Beyond the Market: Books as Gifts in Sixteenth-Century France." *Transactions of the Royal Historical Society*, 5th ser., 33 (1983): 69–88.

Davis, N. Z. *Fiction in the Archives: Pardon Tales and Their Tellers in Sixteenth-Century France*. Cambridge: Polity Press, 1987.

Davis, N. Z. *Society and Culture in Early Modern France*. 1965. Reprint, Cambridge: Polity, 1987.

Dear, P. *Discipline and Experience: The Mathematical Way in the Scientific Revolution*. Chicago: University of Chicago Press, 1995.

Dear, P. "From Truth to Disinterestedness in the Seventeenth Century." *Social Studies of Science* 22 (1992): 619–31.

Dear, P. "Jesuit Mathematical Science and the Reconstitution of Experience in the Early Seventeenth Century." *Studies in the History and Philosophy of Science* 18 (1987): 133–75.

Dear, P. "Narratives, Anecdotes, and Experiments: Turning Experience into Science in the Seventeenth Century." In Dear, *Literary Structure of Scientific Argument*, 135–63.

Dear, P. "*Totius in Verba*: Rhetoric and Authority in the Early Royal Society." *Isis* 76 (1985): 145–61.

Dear, P., ed. *The Literary Structure of Scientific Argument: Historical Studies*. Philadelphia: University of Pennsylvania Press, 1991.

Debus, A. G., ed. *Science, Medicine and Society in the Renaissance*. 2 vols. London: Heineman, 1972.

De Certeau, M. *The Practice of Everyday Life*. Translated by S. Rendall. Berkeley and Los Angeles: University of California Press, 1984.

De Certeau, M. "Reading as Poaching." In de Certeau, *Practice of Everyday Life*, 165–76.

De Grazia, M. *Shakespeare Verbatim: The Reproduction of Authenticity and the 1790 Apparatus*. Oxford: Oxford University Press, 1991.

De Krey, G. S. "The First Restoration Crisis: Conscience and Coercion in London, 1667–73." *Albion* 25 (1993): 565–80.

De Krey, G. S. *A Fractured Society: The Politics of London in the First Age of Party, 1688–1715*. Oxford: Oxford University Press, 1985.

De Krey, G. S. "London Radicals and Revolutionary Politics, 1675–1683." In Harris, Seaward, and Goldie, *The Politics of Religion*, 133–62.

Dennis, M. A. "Graphic Understanding: Instruments and Interpretation in Robert Hooke's *Micrographia*." *Science in Context* 3 (1989): 309–64.

Desmond, A. *The Politics of Evolution: Morphology, Medicine, and Reform in Radical London*. Chicago: University of Chicago Press, 1990.

Dewald, J. "The Ruling Class in the Marketplace: Nobles and Money in Early Modern France." In Haskell and Teichgraeber, *Culture of the Market*, 43–65.

Diamond, W. C. "Natural Philosophy in Harrington's Political Thought." *Journal of the History of Philosophy* 16 (1978): 387–98.

Dickinson, H. T. *Liberty and Property: Political Ideology in Eighteenth-Century Britain*. London: Weidenfeld and Nicolson, 1977.

Dickinson, H. W. *Sir Samuel Morland, Diplomat and Inventor: 1625–1695*. Cambridge: Newcomen Society, 1970.

Diefendorfer, B. B., and C. Hesse, eds. *Culture and Identity in Early Modern Europe (1500–1800): Essays in Honor of Natalie Zemon Davis*. Ann Arbor: University of Michigan Press, 1993.

Dobbs, B. J. T. *The Foundations of Newton's Alchemy: or, The Hunting of the Greene Lyon*. Cambridge: Cambridge University Press, 1975.

Dobbs, B. J. T. *The Janus Faces of Genius: The Role of Alchemy in Newton's Thought*. Cambridge: Cambridge University Press, 1991.

Donaldson, P. S. *Machiavelli and Mystery of State*. Cambridge: Cambridge University Press, 1988.

Douglas, M. "No Free Gifts: Introduction to Mauss's Essay on *The Gift*." In Douglas, *Risk and Blame*, 155–66.

Douglas, M. *Risk and Blame: Essays in Cultural Theory*. London: Routledge, 1992.

Downie, A. *Robert Harley and the Press: Propaganda and Public Opinion in the Age of Swift and Defoe*. Cambridge: Cambridge University Press, 1979.

Drake, S. *Galileo at Work: His Scientific Biography*. Chicago: University of Chicago Press, 1978.

Drake, S. *Galileo Studies: Personality, Tradition, and Revolution*. Ann Arbor: University of Michigan Press, 1970.

Dreyer, J. L. E. "Flamsteed's Letters to Richard Towneley." *The Observatory* 45 (1922): 280–94.

Dreyer, J. L. E. *Tycho Brahe: A Picture of Scientific Life and Work in the Sixteenth Century*. Edinburgh: A. and C. Black, 1890.

Dreyer, J. L. E., and H. H. Turner, eds. *History of the Royal Astronomical Society 1820–1920*. London: Royal Astronomical Society, 1923.

Duke, A. C., and C. A. Tamse, eds. *Too Mighty to Be Free: Censorship and the Press in Britain and the Netherlands*. Zutphen, Netherlands: de Walburg Pers, 1987.

Dunn, K. "Milton among the Monopolists: *Areopagitica*, Intellectual Property and the Hartlib Circle." In Greengrass, Leslie, and Raylor, *Samuel Hartlib and Universal Reformation*, 177–92.

Dunn, R. D. "Fragment of an Unpublished Essay on Printing by William Camden." *British Library Journal* 12 (1986): 145–9.

Eales, N. B. "A Satire on the Royal Society, Dated 1753, Attributed to Henry Fielding." *Notes and Records of the Royal Society* 23 (1968): 65–7.

Eamon, W. "Arcana Disclosed: The Advent of Printing, the Books of Secrets Tradition and the Development of Experimental Science in the Sixteenth Century." *History of Science* 22 (1984): 111–50.

Eamon, W. "Books of Secrets in Medieval and Early Modern Science." *Sudhoffs Archiv* 69 (1985): 26–49.

Eamon, W. "Court, Academy and Printing House: Patronage and Scientific Careers in Late Renaissance Italy." In Moran, *Patronage and Institutions*, 25–50.

Eamon, W. "From the Secrets of Nature to Public Knowledge." In Lindberg and Westman, *Reappraisals of the Scientific Revolution*, 333–65.

Eamon, W. *Science and the Secrets of Nature: Books of Secrets in Medieval and Early Modern Culture*. Princeton: Princeton University Press, 1994.

Earle, P. *A City Full of People: Men and Women of London, 1650–1750*. London: Methuen, 1994.

Earle, P. *The Making of the English Middle Class: Business, Society, and Family Life in London, 1660–1730*. London: Methuen, 1989.

Eco, U. *Faith in Fakes: Essays*. Translated by W. Weaver. London: Secker and Warburg, 1986.

Eerde, K. S. van. *John Ogilby and the Taste of His Times*. Folkestone: Dawson, 1976.

Einstein, A. Foreword. In Galileo, *Dialogue*, vi–xx (written in 1952).

Eisenstein, E. L. "On the Printing Press as an Agent of Change." In Olson, Torrance, and Hildyard, *Literacy, Language and Learning*, 19–33.

Eisenstein, E. L. *The Printing Press as an Agent of Change: Communications and Cultural Transformations in Early-Modern Europe*. 2 vols. Cambridge: Cambridge University Press, 1979.

Eisenstein, E. L. *The Printing Revolution in Early Modern Europe*. Cambridge: Cambridge University Press, 1983.

Elias, N. *The Court Society*. Translated by E. Jephcott. Oxford: Blackwell, 1983.

Ellis, E. *The Penny Universities: A History of the Coffee Houses*. London: Secker and Warburg, 1956.

Elmen, P. "Richard Allestree and *The Whole Duty of Man*." *The Library*, 5th ser., 5 (1951): 19–27.

Elsky, M. *Authorizing Words: Speech, Writing and Print in the English Renaissance*. Ithaca: Cornell University Press, 1989.

Elton, G. R. *Policy and Police: The Enforcement of the Reformation in the Age of Thomas Cromwell*. Cambridge: Cambridge University Press, 1972.

Erickson, A. L. *Women and Property in Early Modern England*. London: Routledge, 1993.

'Espinasse, M. *Robert Hooke*. London: Heinemann, 1956.

Evans, R. J. W. *The Making of the Habsburg Monarchy, 1550–1700: An Interpretation*. Oxford: Oxford University Press, 1979.

Eyles, V. A. "John Woodward, FRS, FRCP, MD (1665–1728): A Bio-Bibliographical Account of His Life and Work." *Journal of the Society for the Bibliography of Natural History* 5 (1971): 399–427.

Ezell, M. J. M. "Richard Waller, S.R.S.: 'In the Pursuit of Nature.'" *Notes and Records of the Royal Society* 38 (1984): 215–33.

Faison, S. "Copyright Pirates Prosper in China Despite Promises." *New York Times*, 20 February 1996, 1, 4.

Farge, A. "The Honor and Secrecy of Families." In Chartier, *Passions of the Renaissance*, 570–607.

Fauvel, J., R. Flood, M. Shortland, and R. Wilson, eds. *Let Newton Be!: A New Perspective on His Life and Works*. Oxford: Oxford University Press, 1988.

Feather, J. "The Book Trade in Politics: The Making of the Copyright Act of 1710." *Publishing History* 8 (1980): 19–44.

Feather, J. "The Commerce of Letters: The Study of the Eighteenth-Century Book Trade." *Eighteenth-Century Studies* 17 (1984): 405–24.

Feather, J. *A Dictionary of Book History*. London: Croom Helm, 1986.

Feather, J. "The English Book Trade and the Law 1695–1799." *Publishing History* 12 (1982): 51–76.

Feather, J. "From Censorship to Copyright: Aspects of the Government's Role in the English Book Trade 1695–1775." In Carpenter, *Books and Society in History*, 173–98.

Feather, J. "From Rights in Copies to Copyright: The Recognition of Authors' Rights in English Law and Practice in the Sixteenth and Seventeenth Centuries." In Woodmansee and Jaszi, *Construction of Authorship*, 191–209.

Feather, J. *A History of British Publishing*. London: Routledge, 1988.

Feather, J. *The Provincial Book Trade in Eighteenth-Century England*. Cambridge: Cambridge University Press, 1985.

Feather, J. "The Publication of James Harrington's *Commonwealth of Oceana*." *The Library*, 5th ser., 32 (1977): 262–8.

Feather, J. *Publishing, Piracy and Politics: An Historical Study of Copyright in Britain*. London: Mansell, 1994.

Febvre, L. "How Jules Michelet Invented the Renaissance." In *A New Kind of History*, 258–67.

Febvre, L. *A New Kind of History*. Edited by P. Burke. London: Routledge and Kegan Paul, 1973.

Febvre, L., and H.-J. Martin. *The Coming of the Book: The Impact of Printing 1450–1800*. Translated by D. Gerard. London: Verso, 1984. Originally published as *L'Apparition du Livre* (Paris: Albin Michel, 1958).

Feingold, M. "The Mathematical Sciences and New Philosophies." In Tyacke, *History of the University of Oxford*, 359–448.

Feingold, M. *The Mathematician's Apprenticeship: Science, the Universities and Society in England, 1560–1640*. Cambridge: Cambridge University Press, 1984.

Feingold, M. "The Occult Tradition in the English Universities of the Renaissance: A Reassessment." In Vickers, *Occult and Scientific Mentalities*, 73–94.

Feingold, M., ed. *Before Newton: The Life and Times of Isaac Barrow*. Cambridge: Cambridge University Press, 1990.

Feldhay, R. "Knowledge and Salvation in Jesuit Culture." *Science in Context* 1 (1987): 195–213.

Feldhay, R., and Y. Elkana, eds. *After Merton: Protestant and Catholic Science in Seventeenth-Century Europe*. Vol. 3, no. 1 (spring 1989) of *Science in Context*.

Feyerabend, P. K. *Against Method: Outline of an Anarchistic Theory of Knowledge.* 1975. Reprint, London: Verso, 1978.

Field, J. V., and F. A. J. L. James, eds. *Renaissance and Revolution: Humanists, Scholars, Craftsmen, and Natural Philosophers in Early Modern Europe.* Cambridge: Cambridge University Press, 1993.

Figala, K. "Pierre Des Maizeaux's View of Newton's Character." *Vistas in Astronomy* 22 (1978): 477–81.

Figgis, J. N. *The Divine Right of Kings.* 1896. Reprint, New York: Harper and Row, 1965.

Findlen, P. "Courting Nature." In Jardine, Secord, and Spary, *Cultures of Natural History*, 57–74.

Findlen, P. "The Economy of Exchange in Early Modern Italy." In Moran, *Patronage and Institutions*, 5–24.

Findlen, P. *Possessing Nature: Museums, Collecting and Scientific Culture in Early Modern Italy.* Berkeley and Los Angeles: University of California Press, 1994.

Findlen, P., and T. Nummedal. "Scientific Books in the Seventeenth Century." In *Scientific Books, Libraries, and Collectors.* London: Bernard Quaritch, forthcoming.

Finlay, R., and B. Shearer. "Population Growth and Suburban Expansion." In Beier and Finlay, *London*, 37–59.

Finocchiaro, M. A. *The Galileo Affair: A Documentary History.* Berkeley and Los Angeles: University of California Press, 1989.

Firth, C. H., and G. Davies. *The Regimental History of Cromwell's Army.* 2 vols. Oxford: Oxford University Press, 1940.

Fish, S. *Is There a Text in This Class? The Authority of Interpretive Communities.* Cambridge: Harvard University Press, 1980.

Fisher, F. J. *London and the English Economy, 1500–1700.* London: Hambledon, 1990.

Fletcher, A. *A County Community in Peace and War: Sussex 1600–1660.* London: Longman, 1975.

Fletcher, A. *The Outbreak of the English Civil War.* London: Edward Arnold, 1981.

Fletcher, A., and J. Stevenson, eds. *Order and Disorder in Early Modern England.* Cambridge: Cambridge University Press, 1985.

Forbes, E. G. *Greenwich Observatory I.* London: Taylor and Francis, 1975.

Forbes, E. G. "The Library of the Rev. John Flamsteed, FRS, First Astronomer Royal." *Notes and Records of the Royal Society* 28 (1973): 119–43.

Foster, S. *Notes from the Caroline Underground: Alexander Leighton, the Puritan Triumvirate, and the Laudian Reaction to Nonconformity.* Hamden, Conn.: Archon, 1978.

Foucault, M. *The Foucault Reader.* Edited by P. Rabinow. Harmondsworth: Penguin, 1984.

Foucault, M. "Of Other Spaces." *Diacritics* 16 (1986): 22–7.

Foucault, M. "Qu'est-ce qu'un Auteur?" *Bulletin de la Société Française de Philosophie* 14 (1969): 73–104.

Foucault, M. "Space, Knowledge, and Power." In *Foucault Reader*, 239–56.

Foucault, M. "What Is an Author?" In *Foucault Reader*, 101–20. (Translation of "Qu'est-ce qu'un Auteur?" It should be noted that there are several French and English versions of this text, with significant differences among them. The versions listed here have been used throughout.)

Fox, A. "Aspects of Oral Culture and its Development in Early Modern England." Ph.D. thesis, Cambridge University, 1993.

Foxon, D. *Pope and the Early Eighteenth Century Book Trade.* Edited by J. McLaverty. Oxford: Oxford University Press, 1991.

Frank, J. *The Beginnings of the English Newspaper, 1620–1660.* Cambridge: Harvard University Press, 1961.

Frank, R. G. *Harvey and the Oxford Physiologists: A Study of Scientific Ideas.* Berkeley and Los Angeles: University of California Press, 1980.

Frank, R. G. "Thomas Willis and His Circle: Brain and Mind in Seventeenth-Century Medicine." In Rousseau, *Languages of Psyche,* 107–46.

Freeman, E. "A Proposal for an English Academy in 1660." *Modern Language Review* 19 (1924): 291–300.

Freist, D. *Governed by Opinion: Politics, Religion and the Dynamics of Communication in Stuart London 1637–1645.* London: Tauris, 1997.

French, R., and A. Wear, eds. *The Medical Revolution of the Seventeenth Century.* Cambridge: Cambridge University Press, 1989.

Fuhrmann, O. W. *Gutenberg and the Strasbourg Documents of 1439.* New York: Woolly Whale, 1940.

Furet, F. *In the Workshop of History.* Translated by J. Mandelbaum. Chicago: University of Chicago Press, 1984.

Furet, F., and J. Ozouf. *Reading and Writing: Literacy in France from Calvin to Jules Ferry.* Cambridge: Cambridge University Press, 1982.

Gabbey, A. "Cudworth, More, and the Mechanical Analogy." In Kroll, Ashcraft, and Zagorin, *Philosophy, Science and Religion,* 109–27.

Gabbey, A. "*Philosophia Cartesiana Triumphata*: Henry More (1646–1671)." In Lennon, Nicholas, and Davis, *Problems of Cartesianism,* 171–250.

Gabriel, A. "*Translatio Studii*: Spurious Dates of Foundation of Some Early Universities." In *Fälschungen in Mittelalter: Internationaler Kongress der Monumenta Germaniae Historica München, 16–19 September 1986. Teil I: Kongressdaten und Festvorträge Literatur und Fälschung,* 601–26. Hanover: Hahnsche Buchhandlung, 1988.

Galluzzi, P., ed. *Novità Celesti e Crisi del Sapere: Atti del Convegno Internazionale di Studi Galileiani.* Florence: G. Barbera, 1984.

Gascoigne, J. "Mathematics and Meritocracy: The Emergence of the Cambridge Mathematical Tripos." *Social Studies of Science* 14 (1984): 547–84.

Gascoigne, J. "A Reappraisal of the Role of the Universities in the Scientific Revolution." In Lindberg and Westman, *Reappraisals of the Scientific Revolution,* 207–60.

Gascoigne, J. "The Universities and the Scientific Revolution: The Case of Newton and Restoration Cambridge." *History of Science* 23 (1985): 391–434.

Gaskell, P. "A Census of Wooden Presses." *Journal of the Printing Historical Society* 6 (1970): 1–32.

Gaskell, P. "A Fust and Schoeffer Forgery." *The Library,* 5th ser., 19 (1964): 200–1.

Gaskell, P. *A New Introduction to Bibliography.* Oxford: Oxford University Press, 1972.

Gatch, M. McC. "John Bagford as a Collector and Disseminator of Manuscript Fragments." *The Library,* 6th ser., 7 (1985): 95–114.

Gatch, M. McC. "John Bagford, Bookseller and Antiquary." *British Library Journal* 12 (1986): 150–71.

Geduld, H. M. *Prince of Publishers: A Study of the Work and Career of Jacob Tonson.* Bloomington: Indiana University Press, 1969.

Gentles, I. *The New Model Army in England, Ireland and Scotland, 1645–1653.* Oxford: Blackwell, 1992.

George, M. D. *London Life in the Eighteenth Century.* 1925. Reprint, Harmondsworth: Penguin, 1965.

Gibson, S. "A Bibliography of Francis Kirkman, with his Prefaces, Dedications and Commendations (1652–80)." *Oxford Bibliographical Soc. Publications,* n.s., 1 (1947): 51–152.

Giddens, A. *The Consequences of Modernity.* Stanford: Stanford University Press, 1989.

Gilmartin, K. *Print Politics: The Press and Radical Opposition in Early Nineteenth-Century England*. Cambridge: Cambridge University Press, 1996.

Gilmont, J.-F. "Printers by the Rules." *The Library*, 6th ser., 2 (1980): 129–55.

Gingerich, O. "The Censorship of Copernicus' *De Revolutionibus*." *Annali dell'Istituto e Museo di Storia della Scienza di Firenze* 6 (1981): 2, 45–61.

Gingerich, O. "Copernicus's *De Revolutionibus*: An Example of Renaissance Scientific Printing." In Tyson and Wagonheim, *Print and Culture in the Renaissance*, 55–73.

Gingerich, O. "A Unique Copy of Flamsteed's *Historia Cœlestis* (1712)." In Willmoth, *Flamsteed's Stars*, 189–97.

Gingerich, O., and R. S. Westman. *The Wittich Connection: Conflict and Priority in late Sixteenth-Century Cosmology*. Philadelphia: American Philosophical Society, 1988. Vol. 78, no. 7 of *Transactions of the American Philosophical Society*.

Ginzburg, C. "High and Low: The Theme of Forbidden Knowledge in the Sixteenth and Seventeenth Centuries." *Past and Present* 73 (1976): 28–41.

Glass, D. V. "Socio-economic Status and Occupations in the City of London at the End of the Seventeenth Century." In Clark, *The Early Modern Town*, 216–32.

Goffman, E. *The Presentation of Self in Everyday Life*. London: Allen Lane, 1969.

Gold, J. J. "The Battle of the Shorthand Books, 1635–1800." *Publishing History* 15 (1984): 5–30.

Goldberg, J. *James I and the Politics of Literature: Jonson, Shakespeare, Donne and Their Contemporaries*. Baltimore: Johns Hopkins University Press, 1983.

Goldgar, A. *Impolite Learning: Conduct and Community in the Republic of Letters, 1680–1750*. New Haven: Yale University Press, 1995.

Goldie, M. "The Civil Religion of James Harrington." In Pagden, *Languages of Political Theory*, 197–222.

Goldie, M. "Danby, the Bishops and the Whigs." In Harris, Seaward, and Goldie, *The Politics of Religion*, 75–105.

Goldie, M. "Edmund Bohun and *Jus Gentium* in the Revolution Debate, 1689–1693." *Historical Journal* 20 (1977): 569–86.

Goldie, M. "John Locke and Anglican Royalism." *Political Studies* 31 (1983): 105–19.

Goldie, M. "John Locke's Circle and James II." *Historical Journal* 35 (1992): 557–86.

Goldsmith, M. M. "Public Virtue and Private Vices: Bernard Mandeville and English Political Ideologies in the Early Eighteenth Century." *Eighteenth Century Studies* 9 (1975–6): 477–510.

Golinski, J. V. "Chemistry in the Scientific Revolution: Problems of Language and Communication." In Lindberg and Westman, *Reappraisals of the Scientific Revolution*, 367–96.

Golinski, J. V. "A Noble Spectacle: Phosphorus and the Public Culture of Science in the Early Royal Society." *Isis* 80 (1989): 11–39.

Golinski, J. V. "Peter Shaw: Chemistry and Communication in Augustan England." *Ambix* 30 (1983): 19–29.

Golinski, J. V. "The Secret Life of an Alchemist." In Fauvel et al., *Let Newton Be!* 147–68.

Golinski, J. V. "Robert Boyle: Scepticism and Authority in Seventeenth Century Chemical Discourse." In Benjamin, Cantor, and Christie, *The Figural and the Literal*, 58–82.

Golinski, J. V. *Science as Public Culture: Chemistry and Enlightenment in Britain, 1760–1820*. Cambridge: Cambridge University Press, 1992.

Golinski, J. V., and J. R. R. Christie. "The Spreading of the Word: New Directions in the Historiography of Chemistry, 1600–1800." *History of Science* 20 (1982): 235–66.

Gooding, D., T. Pinch, and S. J. Schaffer, eds. *The Uses of Experiment: Studies in the Natural Sciences*. Cambridge: Cambridge University Press, 1989.

Goody, J. *The Logic of Writing and the Organization of Society*. Cambridge: Cambridge University Press, 1986.

Gordan, P. W. G., ed. and trans. *Two Renaissance Book Hunters: The Letters of Poggius Bracciolini to Nicolaus de Niccolis.* New York: Columbia University Press, 1974.

Grafton, A. *Commerce with the Classics: Ancient Books and Renaissance Readers.* Ann Arbor: University of Michigan Press, 1997.

Grafton, A. *Defenders of the Text: The Traditions of Scholarship in an Age of Science, 1450–1800.* Cambridge: Harvard University Press, 1991.

Grafton, A. "*Discitur ut Agatur*: How Gabriel Harvey Read His Livy." In Barney, *Annotation and Its Texts*, 108–29.

Grafton, A. *Forgers and Critics: Creativity and Duplicity in Western Scholarship.* London: Collins and Brown, 1990.

Grafton, A. "The Importance of Being Printed." *Journal of Interdisciplinary History* 11 (1980): 265–86.

Grafton, A. "Is the History of Reading a Marginal Enterprise? Guillaume Budé and His Books." *Papers of the Bibliographical Society of America* 91 (1997): 139–57.

Grafton, A. "Kepler as a Reader." *Journal of the History of Ideas* 53 (1992): 561–72.

Grafton, A., and A. Blair, eds. *The Transmission of Culture in Early Modern Europe.* Philadelphia: University of Pennsylvania Press, 1990.

Greaves, R. L. *Deliver Us from Evil: The Radical Underground in Britain, 1660–1663.* Oxford: Oxford University Press, 1986.

Greaves, R. L., and R. Zaller, eds. *A Biographical Dictionary of British Radicals in the Seventeenth Century.* 3 vols. Brighton: Harvester, 1982–4.

Green, I. *The Christian's ABC: Catechisms and Catechizing in England c. 1530–1740.* Oxford: Clarendon Press, 1996.

Greenblatt, S. *Renaissance Self-Fashioning: From More to Shakespeare.* Chicago: University of Chicago Press, 1980.

Greenblatt, S., ed. *Representing the English Renaissance.* Berkeley and Los Angeles: University of California Press, 1988.

Greengrass, M., M. Leslie, and T. Raylor, eds. *Samuel Hartlib and Universal Reformation: Studies in Intellectual Communication.* Cambridge: Cambridge University Press, 1994.

Greenslade, S. L., ed. *The Cambridge History of the Bible*, vol. 3. Cambridge: Cambridge University Press, 1963.

Greg, W. W. "*Ad Imprimendum Solum.*" *The Library*, 5th ser., 9 (1954): 242–7.

Greg, W. W. *A Companion to Arber.* Oxford: Oxford University Press, 1967.

Greg, W. W. "Entrance, Licence and Publication." *The Library*, 4th ser., 25–6 (1944–6): 1–22.

Greg, W. W. *Licensers for the Press, &c. to 1640.* Oxford: Oxford Bibliographical Society, 1962.

Greg, W. W. *The Shakespeare First Folio: Its Bibliographical and Textual History.* Oxford: Oxford University Press, 1955.

Greg, W. W. *Some Aspects and Problems of London Publishing between 1550 and 1650.* Oxford: Clarendon Press, 1956.

Gregg, P. *Free-Born John: A Biography of John Lilburne.* London: Dent, 1986.

Grell, O., and A. Cunningham, eds. *Religio Medici: Religion and Medicine in Seventeenth Century England.* Aldershot, England: Scolar Press, 1996.

Gross, A. *The Rhetoric of Science.* Cambridge: Harvard University Press, 1990.

Gross, A. "The Rhetorical Invention of Scientific Invention: The Emergence and Transformation of a Social Norm." In Simons, *Rhetoric in the Human Sciences*, 89–107.

Guerrini, A. "The Tory Newtonians: Gregory, Pitcairne and Their Circle." *Journal of British Studies* 25 (1986): 288–311.

Gunther, R. T. *Early Science in Oxford.* 15 vols. Oxford: printed for the subscribers, 1923–67.

Habermas, J. *The Structural Transformation of the Public Sphere*. Translated by T. Burger and F. Lawrence. Cambridge: Polity, 1989 (orig. 1962).

Haig, R. L. "'The Unspeakable Curll': Prolegomena." *Studies in Bibliography* 13 (1960): 220–3.

Hall, A. R. "Newton and His Editors." *Notes and Records of the Royal Society* 29 (1974): 29–52.

Hall, A. R. *Philosophers at War: The Quarrel Bewteen Newton and Leibniz*. Cambridge: Cambridge University Press, 1980.

Hall, M. B. "Oldenburg and the Art of Scientific Communication." *British Journal for the History of Science* 2 (1965): 277–90.

Hall, M. B. "Oldenburg, the *Philosophical Transactions*, and Technology." In Burke, *The Uses of Science in the Age of Newton*, 21–47.

Hall, M. B. "The Royal Society's Role in the Diffusion of Information in the Seventeenth Century." *Notes and Records of the Royal Society* 29 (1975): 173–92.

Hall, M. B. "The Royal Society and Italy, 1667–1795." *Notes and Records of the Royal Society* 37 (1983): 63–81.

Haller, W. *Foxe's "Book of Martyrs" and the Elect Nation*. New York: Columbia University Press, 1963.

Haller, W. *Liberty and Reformation in the Puritan Revolution*. 1955. Reprint, New York: Columbia University Press, 1963.

Hammond, P. "Censorship in the Manuscript Transmission of Restoration Poetry." In Smith, *Literature and Censorship*, 39–62.

Hammond, P. "The King's Two Bodies: Representations of Charles II." In Black and Gregory, *Culture, Politics and Society*, 13–48.

Hancox, J. *The Byrom Collection*. London: Jonathan Cape, 1992.

Hannaway, O. *The Chemists and the Word: The Didactic Origins of Chemistry*. Baltimore: Johns Hopkins University Press, 1975.

Hannaway, O. "Laboratory Design and the Aim of Science: Andreas Libavius versus Tycho Brahe." *Isis* 77 (1986): 585–610.

Hannay, M. P., ed. *Silent but for the Word: Tudor Women as Patrons, Translators, and Writers of Religious Works*. Kent, Ohio: Kent State University Press, 1985.

Hans, N. A. *New Trends in Education in the Eighteenth Century*. London: Routledge and Kegan Paul, 1951.

Hanson, L. *Government and the Press 1695–1763*. London: Oxford University Press, 1936.

Harris, M. *London Newspapers in the Age of Walpole: A Study of the Origins of the Modern English Press*. London: Associated University Presses, 1987.

Harris, M. "The Management of the London Newspaper Press during the Eighteenth Century." *Publishing History* 4 (1978): 95–112.

Harris, M. "Moses Pitt and Insolvency in the London Book Trade in the Late Seventeenth Century." In Myers and Harris, *Economics of the British Book Trade*, 176–208.

Harris, M. "Trials and Criminal Biographies: A Case Study in Distribution." In Myers and Harris, *Sale and Distribution of Books*, 1–36.

Harris, M., and A. Lee, eds. *The Press in English Society from the Seventeenth to the Nineteenth Centuries*. Rutherford: Fairleigh Dickinson University Press, 1986.

Harris, T. "The Bawdy House Riots of 1668." *Historical Journal* 29 (1986): 537–56.

Harris, T. "'Lives, Liberties and Estates': Rhetorics of Liberty in the Reign of Charles II." In Harris, Seaward, and Goldie, *The Politics of Religion*, 217–41.

Harris, T. *London Crowds in the Reign of Charles II: Propaganda and Politics from the Restoration until the Exclusion Crisis*. Cambridge: Cambridge University Press, 1987.

Harris, T. "Tories and the Rule of Law in the Reign of Charles II." *The Seventeenth Century* 8 (1993): 9–27.

Harris, T., P. Seaward, and M. Goldie, eds. *The Politics of Religion in Restoration England.* Oxford: Oxford University Press, 1990.

Harwood, J. T. "Rhetoric and Graphics in *Micrographia.*" In Hunter and Schaffer, *Robert Hooke,* 119–47.

Harwood, J. T. "Science Writing and Writing Science: Boyle and Rhetorical Theory." In Hunter, *Robert Boyle Reconsidered,* 37–56.

Haskell, T. L., and R. F. Teichgraeber, eds. *The Culture of the Market: Historical Essays.* Cambridge: Cambridge University Press, 1993.

Hay, D. "Property, Authority and the Criminal Law." In Hay et al., *Albion's Fatal Tree,* 17–64.

Hay, D., P. Linebaugh, J. G. Rule, E. P. Thompson, and C. Winslow. *Albion's Fatal Tree: Crime and Society in Eighteenth-Century England.* Harmondsworth: Penguin, 1975.

Heal, F. *Hospitality in Early Modern England.* Oxford: Oxford University Press, 1990.

Hellinga, L. *Caxton in Focus: The Beginning of Printing in England.* London: British Library, 1982.

Hellinga, L., and A. C. de la Mare. "The First Book Printed in Oxford: The *Expositio Symboli* of Rufinus." *Transactions of the Cambridge Bibliographical Society* 7 (1977–80): 184–244.

Henry, J. "Atomism and Eschatology: Catholicism and Natural Philosophy in the Interregnum." *British Journal of the History of Science* 15 (1982): 211–39.

Henry, J. "The Matter of Souls: Medical Theory and Theology in Seventeenth-Century England." In French and Wear, *Medical Revolution,* 87–113.

Henry, J. "The Origins of Modern Science: Henry Oldenburg's Contribution." *British Journal for the History of Science* 21 (1988): 103–10.

Henry, J. "Thomas Harriot and Atomism: A Reappraisal." *History of Science* 20 (1982): 267–96.

Henry, J., and S. Hutton, eds. *New Perspectives on Renaissance Thought: Essays in the History of Science, Education and Philosophy in Memory of Charles B. Schmitt.* London: Duckworth, 1990.

Hesse, C. "Economic Upheavals in Publishing." In Darnton and Roche, *Revolution in Print,* 69–97.

Hesse, C. "Enlightenment Epistemology and the Laws of Authorship in Revolutionary France, 1777–1793." *Representations* 30 (1990): 109–37.

Hesse, C. *Publishing and Cultural Politics in Revolutionary Paris, 1789–1810.* Berkeley and Los Angeles: University of California Press, 1991.

Hetet, J. "A Literary Underground in Restoration England: Printers and Dissenters in the Context of Constraints 1660–1689." Ph.D. thesis, Cambridge University, 1987.

Hetet, J. "The Wardens' Accounts of the Stationers' Company, 1663–79." In Myers and Harris, *Economics of the British Book Trade,* 32–59.

Heyd, M. *"Be Sober and Reasonable": The Critique of Enthusiasm in the Seventeenth and Early Eighteenth Centuries.* Leiden: E. J. Brill, 1995.

Hill, B. *Women, Work, and Sexual Politics in Eighteenth-Century England.* Oxford: Blackwell, 1989.

Hill, C. "Censorship and English Literature." In Hill, *Collected Essays,* I, 32–72.

Hill, C. *Collected Essays.* 3 vols. Brighton: Harvester Press, 1985–6.

Hill, C. "From Oaths to Interest." In Hill, *Society and Puritanism,* 370–406.

Hill, C. *Intellectual Origins of the English Revolution.* Oxford: Oxford University Press, 1965.

Hill, C. *Society and Puritanism in Pre-revolutionary England.* 1964. Reprint, Harmondsworth: Penguin, 1986.

Hill, C. *A Turbulent, Seditious and Factious People: John Bunyan and His Church.* Oxford: Oxford University Press, 1988.

Hill, C. *The World Turned Upside Down: Radical Ideas during the English Revolution.* 1972. Reprint, Harmondsworth: Penguin, 1985.

Hillier, B., and J. Hanson. *The Social Logic of Space.* Cambridge: Cambridge University Press, 1984.

Hirsch, R. *Printing, Selling and Reading 1450–1550.* Wiesbaden: Harrassowitz, 1967.

Hiscock, W. G., ed. *David Gregory, Isaac Newton and Their Circle: Extracts from David Gregory's Memoranda, 1677–1708.* Oxford: printed for W. G. Hiscock, 1937.

Hobby, E. *Virtue of Necessity: English Women's Writing 1649–88.* London: Virago, 1988.

Hobman, D. L. *Cromwell's Master Spy: A Study of John Thurloe.* London: Chapman and Hall, 1961.

Hodgson, N., and C. Blagden. *The Notebook of Thomas Bennet and Henry Clements (1686–1719), with Some Aspects of Book Trade Practice.* Oxford: Bibliographical Society, 1953 (printed 1956).

Holt, J. C. *Magna Carta.* Cambridge: Cambridge University Press, 1965.

Holt, T. G. "A Jesuit School in the City in 1688." *Transactions of the London and Middlesex Archaeological Society* 32 (1981): 153–8.

Hoppen, K. T. *The Common Scientist in the Seventeenth Century: A Study of the Dublin Philosophical Society 1683–1708.* London: Routledge and Kegan Paul, 1970.

Hoppit, J. "The Use and Abuse of Credit in Eighteenth-Century England." In McKendrick and Outhwaite, *Business Life and Public Policy*, 64–78.

Howse, D. *Francis Place and the Early History of the Greenwich Observatory.* New York: Science History Publications, 1975.

Howse, D. *Greenwich Observatory, III.* London: Taylor and Francis, 1975.

Howse, D. *Greenwich Time, and the Discovery of the Longitude.* Oxford: Oxford University Press, 1980.

Howse, D., and V. Finch. "John Flamsteed and the Balance Spring." *Antiquarian Horology* 9 (1976): 664–73.

Huffman, C. C. *Elizabethan Impressions: John Wolfe and His Press.* AMS Studies in the Renaissance, no. 21. New York: AMS Press, 1988.

Hufton, O. *The Prospect before Her: A History of Women in Western Europe.* Vol. 1, *500–1800.* New York: A. A. Knopf, 1996.

Hunt, L., ed. *The New Cultural History.* Berkeley and Los Angeles: University of California Press, 1989.

Hunt, M. R. *The Middling Sort: Commerce, Gender, and the Family in England, 1680–1780.* Berkeley and Los Angeles: University of California Press, 1996.

Hunter, D. "Copyright Protection for Engravings and Maps in Eighteenth-Century Britain." *The Library*, 6th ser., 9 (1987): 128–47.

Hunter, I., and D. Saunders. "Lessons from the 'Literary': How to Historicise Authorship." *Critical Inquiry* 17 (1991): 479–509.

Hunter, M. "'Aikenhead the Atheist': The Context and Consequences of Articulate Irreligion in the Late Seventeenth Century." In Hunter and Wootton, *Atheism*, 221–54.

Hunter, M. "Alchemy, Magic and Moralism in the Thought of Robert Boyle." *British Journal for the History of Science* 23 (1990): 387–410.

Hunter, M. *Establishing the New Science: The Experience of the Early Royal Society.* Woodbridge: Boydell, 1989.

Hunter, M. "The Impact of Print." *The Book Collector* 28 (1979): 335–52.

Hunter, M. "Promoting the New Science: Henry Oldenburg and the Early Royal Society." *History of Science* 26 (1988): 165–81.

Hunter, M. "The Reluctant Philanthropist: Robert Boyle and the 'Communication of Secrets and Receits in Physick.'" In Grell and Cunningham, *Religio Medici*, 247–72.

Hunter, M. *The Royal Society and Its Fellows 1660–1700: The Morphology of an Early Scientific Institution.* 2d ed. Chalfont St. Giles: British Society for the History of Science, 1994.

Hunter, M. "Science and Astrology in Seventeenth-Century England: An Unpublished Polemic by John Flamsteed." In Curry, *Astrology, Science and Society*, 261–98.

Hunter, M. *Science and Society in Restoration England.* Cambridge: Cambridge University Press, 1981.

Hunter, M., ed. *Robert Boyle by Himself and His Friends.* London: William Pickering, 1994.

Hunter, M., ed. *Robert Boyle Reconsidered.* Cambridge: Cambridge University Press, 1994.

Hunter, M., and S. J. Schaffer, eds. *Robert Hooke: New Studies.* Woodbridge: Boydell, 1989.

Hunter, M., and P. B. Wood. "Towards Solomon's House: Rival Strategies for Reforming the Early Royal Society." *History of Science* 24 (1986): 49–108.

Hunter, M., and D. Wootton, eds. *Atheism from the Reformation to the Enlightenment.* Oxford: Clarendon Press, 1992.

Huntley, F. L. "The Publication and Immediate Reception of *Religio Medici*." *Library Quarterly* 25 (1955): 203–18.

Hutton, R. *The Restoration: A Political and Religious History of England and Wales 1658–1667.* Oxford: Oxford University Press, 1985.

Iliffe, R. C. "Author-Mongering: The 'Editor' between Producer and Consumer." In Bermingham and Brewer, *Consumption of Culture*, 166–92.

Iliffe, R. C. "'The Idols of the Temple': Isaac Newton and the Private Life of Anti-idolatry." Ph.D. thesis, Cambridge University, 1989.

Iliffe, R. C. "'In the Warehouse': Privacy, Property and Priority in the Early Royal Society." *History of Science* 30 (1992): 29–68.

Iliffe, R. C. "'Is He like Other Men?' The Meaning of the *Principia Mathematica*, and the Author as Idol." In MacLean, *Culture and Society*, 159–76.

Iliffe, R. C. "Putting Bodies to Work: Protestantism and the Productive Individual in Early Modern England." Unpublished paper, Centre for Metropolitan History, London, 1992.

Isler, H. *Thomas Willis, 1621–1675.* New York: Hafner, 1968.

Jacob, J. R. *Henry Stubbe, Radical Protestantism and the Early Enlightenment.* Cambridge: Cambridge University Press, 1983.

Jacob, J. R. *Robert Boyle and the English Revolution: A Study in Social and Intellectual Change.* New York: Franklin, 1977.

Jacob, M. C. *The Radical Enlightenment: Pantheists, Freemasons and Republicans.* London: Allen and Unwin, 1981.

Jacquot, J. "Thomas Harriot's Reputation for Impiety." *Notes and Records of the Royal Society* 9 (1952): 164–87.

Jagger, G. "Joseph Moxon, F.R.S., and the Royal Society." *Notes and Records of the Royal Society* 49 (1995): 193–208.

James, M. *English Politics and the Concept of Honour 1485–1642.* Oxford: Past and Present Society, 1978.

Janik, A., and S. Toulmin. *Wittgenstein's Vienna.* New York: Simon and Schuster, 1973.

Jardine, L., and A. Grafton. "'Studied for Action': How Gabriel Harvey Read His Livy." *Past and Present* 129 (1990): 30–78.

Jardine, N. *The Birth of History and Philosophy of Science: Kepler's "A Defence of Tycho Against Ursus" with Essays on Its Provenance and Significance.* Cambridge: Cambridge University Press, 1984.

Jardine, N. *The Scenes of Inquiry: On the Reality of Questions in the Sciences.* Oxford: Clarendon Press, 1991.

Jardine, N. "Writing Off the Scientific Revolution." *Journal of the History of Astronomy* 22 (1991): 311–18.

Jardine, N., J. A. Secord, and E. C. Spary, eds. *Cultures of Natural History*. Cambridge: Cambridge University Press, 1996.

Johns, A. "Flamsteed's Optics and the Identity of the Astronomical Observer." In Willmoth, *Flamsteed's Stars*, 77–106.

Johns, A. "History, Science and the History of the Book: The Making of Natural Philosophy in Early Modern England." *Publishing History* 30 (1991): 5–30.

Johns, A. "The Ideal of Scientific Collaboration: The 'Man of Science' and the Diffusion of Knowledge." In Bots and Waquet, *Commercium Litterarium*, 3–22.

Johns, A. "Miscellaneous Methods: Authors, Societies and Journals in Early Modern England." *British Journal for the History of Science*, forthcoming.

Johns, A. "Natural History as Print Culture." In Jardine, Secord, and Spary, *Cultures of Natural History*, 106–24.

Johns, A. "The Physiology of Reading and the Anatomy of Enthusiasm." In Grell and Cunningham, *Religio Medici*, 136–70.

Johns, A. "The Physiology of Reading in Restoration England." In Raven, Small, and Tadmor, *Practice and Representation of Reading*, 138–61.

Johns, A. "Prudence and Pedantry in Early Modern Cosmology: The Trade of Al Ross." *History of Science* 35 (1997): 23–59.

Johns, A. "Science and the Book in Modern Cultural Historiography." *Studies in History and Philosophy of Science* 35 (1997): 23–59.

Johnson, F. R. "Printers' 'Copy Books' and the Black Market in the Elizabethan Book Trade." *The Library*, 5th ser., 1 (1947): 97–105.

Johnson, G. D. "John Trundle and the Book Trade, 1603–1626." *Studies in Bibliography* 39 (1986): 177–98.

Johnson, G. D. "Nicholas Ling, Publisher: 1580–1607." *Studies in Bibliography* 38 (1985): 203–13.

Johnson, J. and Gibson, S. *Print and Privilege at Oxford to the Year 1700*. London: Oxford University Press, 1946.

Johnson, R. "'Really Useful Knowledge': Radical Education and Working-Class Culture, 1790–1848." In Clarke, Critcher, and Johnson, *Working Class Culture*, 75–112.

Johnston, S. "Mathematical Practitioners and Instruments in Elizabethan England." *Annals of Science* 48 (1991): 319–44.

Jones, H. W. "Literary Problems in Seventeenth-Century Scientific Manuscripts." *Studies in Bibliography* 14 (1961): 69–80.

Jones, J. R. *The Revolution of 1688 in England*. London: Weidenfeld and Nicolson, 1972.

Jose, N. *Ideas of the Restoration in English Literature, 1660–71*. London: Macmillan, 1984.

Judges, A. V., ed. *The Elizabethan Underworld*. London: Routledge and Kegan Paul, 1930.

Kaplan, S. L., ed. *Understanding Popular Culture: Europe from the Middle Ages to the Nineteenth Century*. Berlin: Mouton, 1984.

Katz, D. S. *Sabbath and Sectarianism in Seventeenth-Century England*. Leiden: E. J. Brill, 1988.

Kaufmann, T. D. *The Mastery of Nature: Aspects of Art, Science, and Humanism in the Renaissance*. Princeton: Princeton University Press, 1993.

Keeble, N. H. *The Literary Culture of Nonconformity in Later Seventeenth-Century England*. Leicester: Leicester University Press, 1987.

Keeble, N. H., ed. *The Cultural Identity of Seventeenth-Century Woman*. London: Routledge, 1994.

Kellett, J. R. "The Breakdown of Gild and Corporation Control over the Handicraft and Retail Trade in London." *Economic History Review*, 2d ser., 10 (1957–8): 381–94.

Kelley, D. R. *Foundations of Modern Historical Scholarship: Language, Law and History in the French Renaissance*. New York: Columbia University Press, 1970.

Kelley, D. R. "Law." In Burns and Goldie, *Cambridge History of Political Thought*, 66–94.

Kelly, T. *A History of Adult Education in Great Britain*. 2d ed. Liverpool: Liverpool University Press, 1970.

Kelso, R. *The Doctrine of the English Gentleman in the Sixteenth Century*. Urbana: University of Illinois Press, 1929.

Kenney, C. E. "William Leybourn, 1626–1716." *The Library*, 5th ser., 3 (1950): 159–71.

Kenyon, J. *The History Men: The Historical Profession in England since the Renaissance*. London: Weidenfeld and Nicolson, 1983.

Kernan, A. *Printing Technology, Letters and Samuel Johnson*. Princeton: Princeton University Press, 1987.

Kirschbaum, L. *Shakespeare and the Stationers*. Columbus: Ohio State University Press, 1955.

Kirsop, W. "Les Mécanismes Editoriaux." In Chartier and Martin, *Histoire de l'Edition Française*, II, 15–34.

Kitchin, G. *Sir Roger L'Estrange: A Contribution to the History of the Press in the Seventeenth Century*. London: Kegan Paul, 1913.

Klein, W. "The Ancient Constitution Revisited." In Phillipson and Skinner, *Political Discourse in Early Modern Britain*, 23–44.

Knafla, L. A. *Law and Politics in Jacobean England: The Tracts of Lord Chancellor Ellesmere*. Cambridge: Cambridge University Press, 1977.

Knights, M. *Politics and Public Opinion in Crisis, 1678–81*. Cambridge: Cambridge University Press, 1994.

Knorr-Cetina, K. D., and M. Mulkay, eds. *Science Observed: Perspectives on the Social Study of Science*. London: Sage, 1983.

Knox, K. C. "Dephlogisticating the Bible: Natural Philosophy and Religious Controversy in Late Georgian Cambridge." *History of Science* 24 (1996): 167–200.

Koselleck, R. *Critique and Crisis: Enlightenment and the Pathogenesis of Modern Society*. Cambridge: MIT Press, 1988.

Korshin, P. J. *Typologies in England 1650–1820*. Princeton: Princeton University Press, 1982.

Krieger, L. *Ideas and Events: Professing History*. Edited by M. L. Brick. Chicago: University of Chicago Press, 1992.

Kris, E., and O. Kurz. *Legend, Myth, and Magic in the Image of the Artist: A Historical Experiment*. Translated by A. Laing and L. M. Newman. New Haven: Yale University Press, 1979. Originally published as *Die Legende vom Künstler* (Vienna: Krystall, 1934).

Kroll, R. W. F. *The Material Word: Literate Culture in the Restoration and Early Eighteenth Century*. Baltimore: Johns Hopkins University Press, 1991.

Kroll, R. W. F. "*Mise-en-Page*, Biblical Criticism, and Inference during the Restoration." *Studies in Eighteenth-Century Culture* 16 (1986): 3–40.

Kroll, R. W. F., R. Ashcraft, and P. Zagorin, eds. *Philosophy, Science and Religion in England, 1640–1700*. Cambridge: Cambridge University Press, 1992.

Kronick, D. A. *A History of Scientific and Technical Periodicals: The Origins and Development of the Scientific and Technical Press 1665–1790*. New York: Scarecrow Press, 1962.

Kronick, D. A. "Notes on the Printing History of the Early *Philosophical Transactions*." *Libraries and Culture* 25 (1990): 243–68.

Kropf, C. R. "Libel and Satire in the Eighteenth Century." *Eighteenth Century Studies* 8 (1974–5): 153–68.

Kuhn, T. S. *The Essential Tension: Selected Studies in Scientific Tradition and Change*. Chicago: University of Chicago Press, 1977.

Kuhn, T. S. "Mathematical versus Experimental Traditions in the Development of Physical Science." In Kuhn, *Essential Tension*, 31–65.

Lamb, M. E. "The Cooke Sisters: Attitudes toward Learned Women in the Renaissance." In Hannay, *Silent but for the Word*, 107–25.

Lambert, S. "The Beginning of Printing for the House of Commons." *The Library*, 6th ser., 3 (1981): 43–61.

Lambert, S. "The Printers and the Government, 1604–37." In Myers and Harris, *Aspects of Printing*, 1–29.

Lambert, S. "Richard Montagu, Arminianism and Censorship." *Past and Present* 124 (1989): 36–68.

Landes, J. B. *Women and the Public Sphere in the Age of the French Revolution*. Ithaca: Cornell University Press, 1988.

Langford, P. *Public Life and the Propertied Englishman 1689–1798*. Oxford: Oxford University Press, 1991.

Laqueur, T. W. *Religion and Respectability: Sunday Schools and Working-Class Culture 1780–1850*. New Haven: Yale University Press, 1976.

Larkin, P. *Collected Poems*. Edited by A. Thwaite. New York: Noonday Press, 1989.

Laslett, P. *The World We Have Lost, Further Explored*. London: Methuen, 1983.

Latour, B. *Aramis, ou l'Amour des Techniques*. Paris: Découverte, 1992.

Latour, B. "Drawing Things Together." In Lynch and Woolgar, *Representation in Scientific Practice*, 19–68.

Latour, B. "Give Me a Laboratory and I Will Raise the World." In Knorr-Cetina and Mulkay, *Science Observed*, 141–70.

Latour, B. "On the Powers of Association." In Law, *Power, Action and Belief*, 264–80.

Latour, B. "The Politics of Explanation: An Alternative." In Woolgar, *Knowledge and Reflexivity*, 155–76.

Latour, B. *Science in Action: How to Follow Scientists and Engineers through Society*. Milton Keynes: Open University Press, 1987.

Latour, B. "Technology Is Society Made Durable." In Law, *Sociology of Monsters*, 103–31.

Latour, B. "Visualization and Cognition: Thinking with Eyes and Hands." *Knowledge and Society* 6 (1986): 1–40.

Latour, B. *We Have Never Been Modern*. Translated by C. Porter. New York: Harvester Wheatsheaf, 1993.

Latour, B. "Where Are the Missing Masses? The Sociology of a Few Mundane Artifacts." In Bijker and Law, *Shaping Technology/Building Society*, 225–58.

Latour, B., and S. Woolgar. *Laboratory Life: The Social Construction of Scientific Facts*. London: Sage, 1979.

Laufer, R. "Les Espaces du Livre." In Chartier and Martin, *Histoire de l'Edition Française*, II, 156–72.

Laufer, R. "L'Espace Visuel du Livre Ancien." In Chartier and Martin, *Histoire de l'Edition Française*, I, 579–601.

Law, J., ed. *Power, Action and Belief: A New Sociology of Knowledge?* London: Routledge and Kegan Paul, 1986.

Law, J., ed. *A Sociology of Monsters: Essays on Power, Technology and Domination*. London: Routledge, 1991.

Lawler, J. *Book Auctions in England in the Seventeenth Century (1676–1700)*. London: Elliot Stock, 1898.

Lawrence, C. "Incommunicable Knowledge: Science, Technology and the Clinical Art in Britain 1850–1914." *Journal of Contemporary History* 20 (1985): 503–20.

Lawrence, C. "The Nervous System and Society in the Scottish Enlightenment." In Barnes and Shapin, *Natural Order*, 19–40.

Leed, E. J. "Elizabeth Eisenstein's *The Printing Press as an Agent of Change* and the Structure of Communications Revolutions." *American Journal of Sociology* 88 (1982): 413–29.

Lennon, T. M., J. M. Nicholas, and J. W. Davis, eds. *Problems of Cartesianism*. Kingston, Ont.: McGill-Queen's University Press, 1982.

Leslie, M., and T. Raylor, eds. *Culture and Cultivation in Early Modern England: Writing and the Land*. Leicester: Leicester University Press, 1992.

Levin, J. *The Charter Controversy in the City of London, 1660–1688, and Its Consequences*. London: London University Press, 1969.

Levine, D., and K. Wrightson. *The Making of an Industrial Society: Whickham 1560–1765*. Oxford: Oxford University Press, 1991.

Levine, J. M. *The Battle of the Books: History and Literature in the Augustan Age*. Ithaca: Cornell University Press, 1991.

Levine, J. M. *Dr Woodward's Shield: History, Science and Satire in Augustan England*. Berkeley and Los Angeles: University of California Press, 1977.

Levine, J. M. *Humanism and History: Origins of Modern English Historiography*. Ithaca: Cornell University Press, 1987.

Lewalski, B. K. *Writing Women in Jacobean England*. Cambridge: Harvard University Press, 1993.

Lillywhite, B. *London Coffee Houses: A Reference Book of Coffee Houses of the Seventeenth, Eighteenth and Nineteenth Centuries*. London: Allen and Unwin, 1963.

Lindberg, D. C. "Conceptions of the Scientific Revolution from Bacon to Butterfield: A Preliminary Sketch." In Lindberg and Westman, *Reappraisals of the Scientific Revolution*, 1–26.

Lindberg, D. C., and R. S. Westman, eds. *Reappraisals of the Scientific Revolution*. Cambridge: Cambridge University Press, 1990.

Lindey, A. *Plagiarism and Originality*. New York: Harper, 1952.

Lindley, K. *Popular Politics and Religion in Civil War London*. Aldershot: Scolar Press, 1997.

Liu, T. *Puritan London: A Study of Religion and Society in the City Parishes*. Newark: University of Delaware Press, 1986.

Lloyd, H. A. "Constitutionalism." In Burns and Goldie, *Cambridge History of Political Thought*, 254–97.

Loades, D. *Politics, Censorship and the English Reformation*. London: Pinter, 1991.

Loades, D. "The Theory and Practice of Censorship in Sixteenth-Century England." *Transactions of the Royal Historical Society*, 5th ser., 24 (1974): 141–50 (reprinted in Loades, *Politics, Censorship and the English Reformation*, 96–108).

Lockyer, R. *The Early Stuarts: A Political History of England 1603–1642*. London: Longman, 1989.

Loewenstein, J. "The Script in the Marketplace." In Greenblatt, *Representing the English Renaissance*, 265–78.

Long, P. O. "Invention, Authorship, 'Intellectual Property' and the Origin of Patents: Notes toward a Conceptual History." *Technology and Culture* 32 (1991): 846–84.

Long, P. O. "The Openness of Knowledge: An Ideal and Its Context in Sixteenth-Century Writings on Mining and Metallurgy." *Technology and Culture* 32 (1991): 318–55.

Love, H. *Scribal Publication in Seventeenth-Century England*. Oxford: Oxford University Press, 1993.

Lowood, H. E., and R. E. Rider. "Literary Technology and Typographic Culture: The Instrument of Print in Early Modern Science." *Perspectives on Science* 2 (1994): 1–37.

Lowry, M. *The world of Aldus Manutius: Business and Scholarship in Renaissance Venice*. Oxford: Blackwell, 1979.

Lynch, M. *Scientific Practice and Ordinary Action: Ethnomethodology and Social Studies of Science*. Cambridge: Cambridge University Press, 1993.

Lynch, M., and S. Woolgar, eds. *Representation in Scientific Practice*. Cambridge: MIT Press, 1990.

Maccubbin, R. P., and M. Hamilton-Phillips, eds. *The Age of William III and Mary II: Power, Politics and Patronage 1688–1702*. Williamsburg: College of William and Mary, 1989.

Macdonald, M. *Mystical Bedlam: Madness, Anxiety, and Healing in Seventeenth-Century England*. Cambridge: Cambridge University Press, 1981.

Mack, P. *Visionary Women: Ecstatic Prophecy in Seventeenth-Century England*. Berkeley and Los Angeles: University of California Press, 1992.

MacLean, G., ed. *Culture and Society in the Stuart Restoration: Literature, Drama, History*. Cambridge: Cambridge University Press, 1995.

MacLeod, C. "Accident or Design?: George Ravenscroft's Patent and the Invention of Lead-Crystal Glass." *Technology and Culture* 28 (1987): 776–803.

MacLeod, C. *Inventing the Industrial Revolution: The English Patent System, 1660–1800*. Cambridge: Cambridge University Press, 1988.

Macpherson, C. B. *The Political Theory of Possessive Individualism: Hobbes to Locke*. Oxford: Oxford University Press, 1962.

MacPike, E. F. *Hevelius, Flamsteed and Halley: Three Contemporary Astronomers and Their Mutual Relations*. London: Taylor and Francis, 1937.

Madan, F. *Oxford Books: A Bibliography of Printed Works Relating to the University and City of Oxford, or Printed or Published There*. 3 vols. Oxford: Clarendon, 1895–1931.

Madan, F. "The Oxford Press, 1650–75: The Struggle for a Place in the Sun." *The Library*, 4th ser., 6 (1925): 113–47.

Madan, F. "Two Lost Causes, and What May Be Said in Defence of Them." *The Library*, 3d ser., 9 (1918): 89–105.

Maddison, R. E. W. *The Life of the Honourable Robert Boyle*. London: Taylor and Francis, 1969.

Malet, A. "Keplerian Illusions: Geometrical Pictures vs. Optical Images in Kepler's Visual Theory." *Studies in History and Philosophy of Science* 21 (1990): 1–40.

Manley, L. *Literature and Culture in Early Modern London*. Cambridge: Cambridge University Press, 1995.

Manten, A. A. "The Growth of European Scientific Journal Publishing before 1850." In Meadows, *Development of Science Publishing*, 1–22.

Manuel, F. E. *Isaac Newton, Historian*. Cambridge: Cambridge University Press, 1963.

Manuel, F. E. *A Portrait of Isaac Newton*. Cambridge: Harvard University Press, 1968.

Marin, L. *Portrait of the King*. Translated by M. H. Houle. Minneapolis: University of Minnesota Press, 1988.

Markley, R. *Fallen Languages: Crises of Representation in Newtonian England, 1660–1740*. Ithaca: Cornell University Press, 1993.

Marshall, A. *Intelligence and Espionage in the Reign of Charles II, 1660–1685*. Cambridge: Cambridge University Press, 1994.

Marshall, J. *John Locke: Resistance, Religion and Responsibility*. Cambridge: Cambridge University Press, 1994.

Martin, H.-J. "Comment on Ecrivit l'Histoire du Livre." In Martin, *Le Livre Français*, 11–28.

Martin, H.-J. "Les Espaces de la Vente à Paris à l'Epoque Artisanale." In Martin, *Le Livre Français*, 89–111.

Martin, H.-J. *The History and Power of Writing*. Translated by L. G. Cochrane. Chicago: University of Chicago Press, 1994.

Martin, H.-J. *Le Livre Français sous l'Ancien Régime*. Paris: Promodis, 1987.

Martin, H.-J. "Pour une Histoire de la Lecture." In Martin, *Le Livre Français*, 227–46.

Martin, H.-J. "La Prééminence de la Librairie Parisienne." In Chartier and Martin, *Histoire de l'Edition Française*, II, 331–57.

Martin, H-J., and J. Vezin, eds. *Mise en Page et Mise en Texte du Livre Manuscrit*. Paris: Promodis, 1990.

Martin, J. *Francis Bacon, the State and the Reform of Natural Philosophy*. Cambridge: Cambridge University Press, 1992.

Martin, J. "'Knowledge Is Power': Francis Bacon, the State, and the Reform of Natural Philosophy." Ph.D. Thesis, Cambridge University, 1988.

Martin, J. "Natural Philosophy and Its Public Concerns." In Pumfrey, Rossi, and Slawinski, *Science, Culture and Popular Belief*, 100–18.

Materné, J. "Social Emancipation in European Printing Workshops before the Industrial Revolution." In Safley and Rosenband, *Workplace before the Factory*, 204–24.

Matthews, N. L. *William Sheppard, Cromwell's Law Reformer*. Cambridge: Cambridge University Press, 1984.

McColley, G. "The Ross-Wilkins Controversy." *Annals of Science* 3 (1938): 153–89.

McDonald, W. C. "Maximilian I of Habsburg and the Veneration of Hercules: On the Revival of Myth and the German Renaissance." *Journal of Medieval and Renaissance Studies* 6 (1976): 139–54.

McEwen, G. D. *The Oracle of the Coffee House: John Dunton's "Athenian Mercury."* San Marino: Huntington Library, 1972.

McGuinness, B. *Wittgenstein, A Life: Young Ludwig, 1889–1921*. Berkeley and Los Angeles: University of California Press, 1988.

McKendrick, N., and R. B. Outhwaite, eds. *Business Life and Public Policy: Essays in Honour of D. C. Coleman*. Cambridge: Cambridge University Press, 1986.

McKenzie, D. F. *Bibliography and the Sociology of Texts*. London: British Library, 1985.

McKenzie, D. F. *The Cambridge University Press 1696–1712: A Bibliographical Study*. 2 vols. Cambridge: Cambridge University Press, 1966.

McKenzie, D. F. *An Early Printing House at Work: Some Notes for Bibliographers*. Wellington: Wai-te-ata Press, 1965.

McKenzie, D. F. "The Economies of Print, 1550–1750: Scales of Production and Conditions of Constraint." In Cavaciocchi, *Produzione e Commercio della Carta e del Libro*, 389–425.

McKenzie, D. F. "The London Book Trade in the later Seventeenth Century." Unpublished Sandars Lectures, Cambridge, 1976.

McKenzie, D. F. "Printers' Perks: Paper Windows and Copy Money." *The Library*, 5th ser., 15 (1960): 288–91.

McKenzie, D. F. "Printers of the Mind: Some Notes on Bibliographical Theories and Printing-House Practices." *Studies in Bibliography* 22 (1969): 1–76.

McKenzie, D. F. "Speech-Manuscript-Print." In Oliphant and Bradford, *New Directions in Textual Studies*, 87–109.

McKenzie, D. F. *Stationers' Company Apprentices 1605–1640*. Charlottesville: Bibliographical Society of the University of Virginia, 1961.

McKenzie, D. F. *Stationers' Company Apprentices 1641–1700*. Oxford: Oxford Bibliographical Society, 1974.

McKenzie, D. F. "Typography and Meaning: The Case of William Congreve." In Barber and Fabian, *Buch und Buchhandel*, 81–123.

McKeon, M. *The Origins of the English Novel, 1600–1740*. London: Radius, 1988.

McKeon, M. *Politics and Poetry in Restoration England: The Case of Dryden's "Annus Mirabilis."* Cambridge: Harvard University Press, 1975.

McKerrow, R. B. *Printers' and Publishers' Devices in England and Scotland 1485–1640*. London: Bibliographical Society, 1913.

McKerrow, R. B., ed. *An Introduction to Bibliography for Literary Students*. Corrected ed. Oxford: Oxford University Press, 1928.

McKitterick, D. J. *A History of Cambridge University Press*. Vol. 1, *Printing and the Book Trade in Cambridge 1534–1698*. Cambridge: Cambridge University Press, 1992.

McLaverty, J. "The First Printing and Publication of Pope's Letters." *The Library*, 6th ser., 2 (1980): 264–80.

McLuhan, M. *The Gutenberg Galaxy*. London: Routledge and Kegan Paul, 1962.

McLuhan, M. *Understanding Media: The Extensions of Man*. 1964. Reprint, London: Ark, 1987.

McLynn, F. *Crime and Punishment in Eighteenth-Century England*. London: Routledge, 1989.

McMurtie, D. C. *The Gutenberg Documents*. New York: Oxford University Press, 1941.

Meadows, A. J., ed. *Development of Science Publishing in Europe*. Amsterdam: Elsevier, 1980.

Meli, D. B. "Leibniz on the Censorship of the Copernican System." *Studia Leibnitiana* 20 (1988): 19–42.

Mendle, M. *Henry Parker and the English Civil War: The Political Thought of the Public's "Privado."* Cambridge: Cambridge University Press, 1995.

Mendle, M. "Parliamentary Sovereignty: A Very English Absolutism." In Phillipson and Skinner, *Political Discourse in Early Modern Britain*, 97–119.

Mendle, M. "The Ship Money Case, *The Case of Shipmony*, and the Development of Henry Parker's Parliamentary Absolutism." *Historical Journal* 32 (1989): 513–36.

Merkel, I., and A. G. Debus, eds. *Hermeticism and the Renaissance: Intellectual History and the Occult in Early Modern Europe*. London: Associated University Presses, 1988.

Miller, J. "The Crown and the Borough Charters in the Reign of Charles II." *English Historical Review* 100 (1985): 53–84.

Miller, J. "The Potential for 'Absolutism' in Later Stuart England." *History* 69 (1984): 187–207.

Miller, J., ed. *Absolutism in Seventeenth-Century Europe*. Basingstoke: Macmillan, 1990.

Miller, L. "The Shattered *Violl*: Print and Textuality in the 1640s." In Smith, *Literature and Censorship*, 25–38.

Minard, P. "Agitation in the Work Force." In Darnton and Roche, *Revolution in Print*, 107–23.

Mintz, S. I. *The Hunting of Leviathan: Seventeenth-Century Reactions to the Materialism and Moral Philosophy of Thomas Hobbes*. Cambridge: Cambridge University Press, 1962.

Momigliano, A. "The Introduction of History as an Academic Subject, and Its Implications." In Wallace, *The Golden and the Brazen World*, 187–204.

Monk, R. *Wittgenstein: The Duty of Genius*. New York: Free Press, 1990.

Moran, B. T. *The Alchemical World of the German Court: Occult Philosophy and Chemical Medicine in the Circle of Moritz of Hessen (1572–1632)*. Stuttgart: F. Steiner, 1991.

Moran, B. T. "Privilege, Communication, and Chemiatry: The Hermetic-Alchemical Circle of Moritz of Hessen-Kassel." *Ambix* 32 (1985): 110–26.

Moran, B. T., ed. *Patronage and Institutions: Science, Technology and Medicine at the European Court 1500–1700*. Woodbridge: Boydell, 1991.

Morgan, B. T. *Histoire du Journal des Sçavans depuis 1665 jusqu'en 1701*. Paris: Presses Universitaires de France, 1928.

Morgan, V. "Whose Prerogative in Late Sixteenth and Early Seventeenth Century England?" *Journal of Legal History* 5 (1984): 39–64.

Morrill, J. *The Nature of the English Revolution: Essays*. London: Longman, 1993.

Morrill, J., ed. *Revolution and Restoration: England in the 1650s.* London: Collins and Brown, 1992.

Morrison, J. J. "Strype's Stow: The 1720 Edition of *A Survey of London.*" *The London Journal* 3 (1977): 40–54.

Moss, A. *Printed Commonplace-Books and the Structuring of Renaissance Thought.* Oxford: Clarendon Press, 1996.

Moss, J. D. *Novelties in the Heavens: Rhetoric and Science in the Copernican Controversy.* Chicago: University of Chicago Press, 1993.

Moureau, F., ed. *Les Presses Grises: La Contrefaçon du Livre (XVIe–XIXe siècles).* Paris: Aux Amateurs de Livres, 1988.

Mullan, J. "Hypochondria and Hysteria: Sensibility and the Physicians." *The Eighteenth Century: Theory and Interpretation* 25 (1984): 141–74.

Mulligan, L. "Robert Hooke's 'Memoranda': Memory and Natural History." *Annals of Science* 49 (1992): 47–61.

Munby, A. N. L. "The Distribution of the First Edition of Newton's *Principia.*" *Notes and Records of the Royal Society* 10 (1952): 28–39.

Munby, A. N. L. "A Fragment of a Bookseller's Day-Book of 1622." *The Book Collector* 3 (1954): 302–6.

Murdin, L. *Under Newton's Shadow: Astronomical Practices in the Seventeenth Century.* Bristol: Adam Hilger, 1985.

Murray, T. *Theatrical Legitimation: Allegories of Genius in Seventeenth-Century England and France.* New York: Oxford University Press, 1987.

Myers, R. "The Financial Records of the Stationers' Company, 1605–1811." In Myers and Harris, *Economics of the British Book Trade,* 1–31.

Myers, R. *The Stationers' Company Archive: An Account of the Records 1554–1984.* Winchester: Saint Paul's Bibliographies; Detroit: Omnigraphics, 1990.

Myers, R. "Stationers' Company Bibliographers: The First 150 Years, Ames to Arber." In Myers and Harris, *Pioneers in Bibliography,* 40–57.

Myers, R., and M. Harris, eds. *Aspects of Printing from 1600.* Oxford: Oxford Polytechnic Press, 1987.

Myers, R., and M. Harris, eds. *Economics of the British Book Trade 1605–1939.* Cambridge: Chadwyck-Healey, 1985.

Myers, R., and M. Harris, eds. *Pioneers in Bibliography.* Winchester: St. Paul's Bibliographies, 1988.

Myers, R., and M. Harris, eds. *Sale and Distribution of Books from 1700.* Oxford: Oxford Polytechnic Press, 1982.

Myers, R., and M. Harris, eds. *Spreading the Word: The Distribution Networks of Print, 1550–1850.* Winchester: St. Paul's Bibliographies, 1990.

Nash, M. F. "English Licences to Print and Grants of Copyright in the 1640s." *The Library,* 6th ser., 4 (1982): 174–84.

Nelson, C., and M. Seccombe. *British Newspapers and Periodicals 1641–1700: A Short-Title Catalogue of Serials.* New York: Modern Language Association of America, 1987.

Nelson, C., and M. Seccombe. *Periodical Publications 1641–1700.* London: Bibliographical Society, 1986.

Neuschel, K. B. *Word of Honor: Interpreting Noble Culture in Sixteenth-Century France.* Ithaca: Cornell University Press, 1989.

Newman, J. O. "The Word Made Print: Luther's 1522 *New Testament* in an Age of Mechanical Reproduction." *Representations* 11 (1985): 95–133.

Newman, W. R. *Gehennical Fire: The Lives of George Starkey, an American Alchemist in the Scientific Revolution.* Cambridge: Harvard University Press, 1994.

Nicholl, C. *A Cup of News: The Life of Thomas Nashe*. London: Routledge and Kegan Paul, 1984.

Nokes, D. *Jonathan Swift: A Hypocrite Reversed*. Oxford: Oxford University Press, 1987.

Norlind, W. *Tycho Brahe: En levnadsteckning med nya bidrag belysande hans liv och verk*. Lund, Sweden: C. W. K. Gleerup, 1970.

Nussbaum, F. *The Autobiographical Subject: Gender and Ideology in Eighteenth-Century England*. Baltimore: Johns Hopkins University Press, 1989.

Nussdorfer, L. "Writing and the Power of Speech: Notaries and Artisans in Baroque Rome." In Diefendorfer and Hesse, *Culture and Identity in Early Modern Europe*, 103–18.

Nyquist, M., and M. W. Ferguson, eds. *Re-Membering Milton: Essays on the Texts and Traditions*. New York: Methuen, 1987.

Obeyesekere, G. *The Apotheosis of Captain Cook: European Mythmaking in the Pacific*. Princeton: Princeton University Press, 1992.

Ogg, D. *England in the Reigns of James II and William III*. 1955. Reprint, Oxford: Oxford University Press, 1984.

Ogilvie, M. B. "Marital Collaboration: An Approach to Science." In Abir-Am and Outram, *Uneasy Careers and Intimate Lives*, 104–25.

Olby, R. C., G. N. Cantor, J. R. R. Christie, and M. J. S. Hodge, eds. *Companion to the History of Modern Science*. London: Routledge, 1990.

Oliphant, D., and R. Bradford, eds. *New Directions in Textual Studies*. Austin: Harry Ransom Humanities Research Center, 1990.

Olson, D. R. *The World on Paper: The Conceptual and Cognitive Implications of Writing and Reading*. Cambridge: Cambridge University Press, 1994.

Olson, D. R., N. Torrance, and A. Hildyard, eds. *Literacy, Language and Learning: The Nature and Consequences of Reading and Writing*. Cambridge: Cambridge University Press, 1985.

O'Malley, T. "'Defying the Powers and Tempering the Spirit': A Review of Quaker Control over Their Publications 1672–1689." *Journal of Ecclesiastical History* 33 (1982): 72–88.

O'Malley, T. "Religion and the Newspaper Press, 1660–1685: A Study of the *London Gazette*." In Harris and Lee, *The Press in English Society*, 25–46.

Ophir, A., and S. Shapin. "The Place of Knowledge: A Methodological Survey." *Science in Context* 4 (1991): 3–21.

Ophir, A., S. Shapin, and S. J. Schaffer, eds. *The Place of Knowledge: The Spatial Setting and Its Relation to the Production of Knowledge*. Vol. 4, no. 1 (spring 1991) of *Science in Context*.

Ore, O. *Cardano: The Gambling Scholar*. Princeton: Princeton University Press, 1953.

Orgel, S. "The Authentic Shakespeare." *Representations* 21 (1988): 1–26.

Pagden, A., ed. *The Languages of Political Theory in Early Modern Europe*. Cambridge: Cambridge University Press, 1987.

Oster, M. "Biography, Culture, and Science: The Formative Years of Robert Boyle." *History of Science* 31 (1993): 177–226.

Outram, D. "New Spaces in Natural History." In Jardine, Secord, and Spary, *Cultures of Natural History*, 249–65.

Palm, L. C. "Leeuwenhoek and Other Dutch Correspondents of the Royal Society." *Notes and Records of the Royal Society* 43 (1989): 191–208.

Palmer, P. M., and R. P. More. *The Sources of the Faust Tradition from Simon Magus to Lessing*. New York: Oxford University Press, 1936.

Pantzer, K. F. "Printing the English Statutes, 1484–1640: Some Historical Implications." In Carpenter, *Books and Society in History*, 69–114.

Park, K. "The Organic Soul." In Schmitt and Skinner, *Cambridge History of Renaissance Philosophy*, 464–84.

Parker, D. *Familiar to All: William Lilly and Astrology in the Seventeenth Century*. London: Jonathan Cape, 1975.

Parks, S. *John Dunton and the English Book Trade*. New York: Garland, 1976.

Parry, G. "John Evelyn as Hortulan Saint." In Leslie and Raylor, *Culture and Cultivation*, 130–50.

Partridge, E. *The Penguin Dictionary of Historical Slang*. Edited by J. Simpson. Harmondsworth: Penguin, 1972.

Partridge, R. C. B. *The History of the Legal Deposit of Books*. London: Library Association, 1938.

Pastoureau, M. "L'Illustration du Livre: Comprendre ou Rêver?" In Chartier and Martin, *Histoire de l'Edition Française*, I, 602–28.

Patterson, A. *Censorship and Interpretation: The Conditions of Writing and Reading in Early Modern England*. Madison: University of Wisconsin Press, 1984.

Pearl, V. *London and the Outbreak of the Puritan Revolution: City Government and National Politics, 1625–43*. London: Oxford University Press, 1961.

Pearl, V. "London's Counter-revolution." In Aylmer, *The Interregnum*, 29–56.

Pennington, D., and K. Thomas, eds. *Puritans and Revolutionaries*. Oxford: Oxford University Press, 1978.

Peters, J. S. *Congreve, the Drama, and the Printed Word*. Stanford: Stanford University Press, 1990.

Peters, J. S. "Print-World Ideology and the Double-Natured Stage: Towards an Alliance 1660–1700." *Publishing History* 19 (1988): 5–32.

Pettegree, A. *Foreign Protestant Communities in Sixteenth-Century London*. Oxford: Oxford University Press, 1986.

Phillipson, N., and Q. Skinner, eds. *Political Discourse in Early Modern Britain*. Cambridge: Cambridge University Press, 1993.

Pickstone, J. V. "Past and Present Knowledges in the Practice of the History of Science." *History of Science* 33 (1995): 203–24.

Pinch, T. J., and W. E. Bijker. "The Social Construction of Facts and Artifacts: Or How the Sociology of Science and the Sociology of Technology Might Benefit Each Other." In Bijker, Hughes, and Pinch, *Social Construction of Technological Systems*, 17–50.

Pincus, S. "'Coffee Politicians Does Create': Coffeehouses and Restoration Political Culture." *Journal of Modern History* 67 (1995): 807–34.

Pipes, D. *The Rushdie Affair: The Novel, the Ayatollah, and the West*. London: Carol Publishing, 1990.

Plant, M. *The English Book Trade: An Economic History of the Making and Sale of Books*. 3d ed. London: George Allen and Unwin, 1974.

Plomer, H. R. *A Dictionary of the Booksellers and Printers Who Were at Work in England, Scotland and Ireland from 1641 to 1667*. London: Bibliographical Society, 1907.

Plomer, H. R. *A Dictionary of the Printers and Booksellers Who Were at Work in England, Scotland and Ireland from 1668 to 1725*. Oxford: Bibliographical Society, 1922.

Plomer, H. R. "The King's Printing House under the Stuarts." *The Library*, 2d ser., 2 (1901): 353–75.

Plomer, H. R. "Michael Sparke, Puritan Bookseller." *The Bibliographer* 1 (1902): 409–19.

Pocock, J. G. A. *The Ancient Constitution and the Feudal Law: A Study of English Historical Thought in the Seventeenth Century*. 1957. Reprint, Cambridge: Cambridge University Press, 1987.

Pocock, J. G. A. "James Harrington and the Good Old Cause: A Study of the Ideological Context of his Writings." *Journal of British Studies* 10 (1970): 30–48.

Pocock, J. G. A. *Politics, Language and Time: Essays on Political Thought and History*. London: Methuen, 1972.

Pocock, J. G. A. "Time, Institutions and Action: An Essay on Traditions and Their Understanding." In Pocock, *Politics, Language and Time*, 233–73.

Polanyi, M. *Personal Knowledge: Towards a Post-critical Philosophy*. Chicago: University of Chicago Press, 1958.

Pollard, A. W. *Shakespeare's Fight with the Pirates and the Problems of the Transmission of His Text*. 2d ed. Cambridge: Cambridge University Press, 1967.

Pollard, A. W., and G. R. Redgrave. *A Short-Title Catalogue of Books Printed in England, Scotland and Ireland, and of English Books Printed Abroad, 1475–1640*. 3 vols. 2d ed. Revised by W. A. Jackson, F. S. Ferguson, and K. F. Pantzer. London: Bibliographical Society, 1976–91.

Pollard, G. "The English Market for Printed Books." *Publishing History* 4 (1978): 7–48.

Pollock, L. A. "Living on the Stage of the World: The Concept of Privacy among the Elite of Early Modern England." In Wilson, *Rethinking Social History*, 78–96.

Poovey, M. *Making a Social Body: British Cultural Formation, 1830–1864*. Chicago: University of Chicago Press, 1995.

Porter, R. "Consumption: Disease of the Consumer Society?" In Brewer and Porter, *Consumption and the World of Goods*, 58–81.

Porter, R. *London: A Social History*. London: Hamish Hamilton, 1994.

Porter, R. "The Rise of Medical Journalism in Britain to 1800." In Bynum, Lock, and Porter, *Medical Journals and Medical Knowledge*, 6–28.

Porter, R., and M. Teich, eds. *The Scientific Revolution in National Context*. Cambridge: Cambridge University Press, 1992.

Porter, T. M. *Trust in Numbers: The Pursuit of Objectivity in Science and Public Life*. Princeton: Princeton University Press, 1995.

Porter, T. M., M. Jackson, A. Johns, B. Shapiro, and S. Shapin. "Gently Boyle [a discussion of Shapin's *Social History of Truth*]." *Metascience* 6 (1994): 1–23.

Potter, L. *Secret Rites and Secret Writing: Royalist Literature 1641–1660*. Cambridge: Cambridge University Press, 1989.

Pounds, N. J. G. *The Medieval Castle in England and Wales: A Social and Political History*. Cambridge: Cambridge University Press, 1990.

Power, M. J. "The Social Topography of Restoration London." In Beier and Finlay, *London*, 199–223.

Poynter, F. N. L. "Nicholas Culpeper and the Paracelsians." In Debus, *Science, Medicine and Society*, I, 201–20.

Price, D. C. *Patrons and Musicians of the English Renaissance*. Cambridge: Cambridge University Press, 1981.

Principe, L. "Robert Boyle's Alchemical Secrecy: Codes, Ciphers and Concealments." *Ambix* 39 (1992): 63–74.

Principe, L. "Virtuous Romance and Romantic Virtuoso: The Shaping of Robert Boyle's Literary Style." *Journal of the History of Ideas* 56 (1995): 377–97.

Prior, M., ed. *Women in English Society 1500–1800*. London: Methuen, 1985.

Pritchard, A. "George Wither's Quarrel with the Stationers: An Anonymous Reply to *The Schollers Purgatory*." *Studies in Bibliography* 16 (1963): 27–42.

Pumfrey, S. "The History of Science and the Renaissance Science of History." In Pumfrey, Rossi, and Slawinski, *Science, Culture and Popular Belief*, 48–70.

Pumfrey, S. "Ideas above His Station: A Social Study of Hooke's Curatorship of Experiments." *History of Science* 29 (1991): 1–44.

Pumfrey, S. "'O Tempora, O Magnes!' A Sociological Analysis of the Discovery of Secular Magnetic Variation in 1634." *British Journal for the History of Science* 46 (1989): 181–214.

Pumfrey, S. "Who Did the Work? Experimental Philosophers and Public Demonstrators in Augustan England." *British Journal for the History of Science* 28 (1995): 131–56.

Pumfrey, S. "William Gilbert's Magnetic Philosophy, 1580–1684: The Creation and Dissolution of a Discipline." Ph.D. thesis, Warburg Institute, University of London, 1987.

Pumfrey, S., P. L. Rossi, and M. Slawinski, eds. *Science, Culture and Popular Belief in Renaissance Europe*. Manchester: Manchester University Press, 1991.

Pycior, H. M., N. G. Slack, and P. G. Abir-Am, eds. *Creative Couples in the Sciences*. New Brunswick: Rutgers University Press, 1996.

Ransom, H. *The First Copyright Statute: An Essay on "An Act for the Encouragement of Learning," 1710*. Austin: University of Texas Press, 1956.

Ransom, H. "The Personal Letter as Literary Property." *Studies in English* 30 (1951): 116–31.

Rappaport, R. "Hooke on Earthquakes: Lectures, Strategy and Audience." *British Journal for the History of Science* 19 (1986): 129–46.

Rappaport, S. *Worlds within Worlds: Structures of Life in Sixteenth-Century London*. Cambridge: Cambridge University Press, 1989.

Raven, J. "Mapping the London Book Trade, c. 1695–1820." Paper read at Munby Seminar, Darwin College, Cambridge, 9 July 1994.

Raven, J., H. Small, and N. Tadmor, eds. *The Practice and Representation of Reading in England*. Cambridge: Cambridge University Press, 1996.

Raylor, T. "Samuel Hartlib and the Commonwealth of Bees." In Leslie and Raylor, *Culture and Cultivation*, 91–129.

Raymond, J. *The Invention of the Newspaper: English Newsbooks 1641–1649*. Oxford: Clarendon Press, 1996.

Reay, B., ed. *Popular Culture in Seventeenth-Century England*. London: Croom Helm, 1985.

Redondi, P. *Galileo: Heretic*. Translated by R. Rosenthal. Harmondsworth: Penguin, 1987.

Resnick, D. P., ed. *Literacy in Historical Perspective*. Washington: Library of Congress, 1983.

Revel, J. "The Uses of Civility." In Chartier, *Passions of the Renaissance*, 167–205.

Rivers, I., ed. *Books and Their Readers in Eighteenth-Century England*. New York: St. Martin's Press, 1982.

Rivington, C. A. "Early Printers to the Royal Society, 1663–1708." *Notes and Records of the Royal Society* 39 (1984): 1–28.

Rivington, C. "Sir Thomas Davies: The First Bookseller Lord Mayor of London." *The Library*, 3 (1981): 187–201.

Rivington, C. A. *"Tyrant": The Story of John Barber, 1675 to 1741*. York: William Sessions, 1989.

Roberts, L. "Setting the Table: The Disciplinary Development of Eighteenth-Century Chemistry as Read through the Changing Structure of Its Tables." In Dear, *Literary Structure*, 99–132.

Roberts, M. "'Words They Are Women, and Deeds They Are Men': Images of Work and Gender in Early Modern England." In Charles and Duffin, *Women and Work*, 122–80.

Robinson, F. J. G., and P. J. Wallis. *Book Subscription Lists: A Revised Guide*. Newcastle: Book Subscription Lists Project, 1975.

Roche, D. "Censorship and the Publishing Industry." In Darnton and Roche, *Revolution in Print*, 3–26.

Roche, D. *The People of Paris: An Essay in Popular Culture in the Eighteenth Century*. Translated by M. Evans and G. Lewis. Leamington Spa: Berg, 1987.

Rogers, D. D. *Bookseller as Rogue: John Almon and the Politics of Eighteenth-Century Publishing*. New York: P. Lang, 1986.

Rogers, N. "Clubs and Politics in Eighteenth-Century London: the Centenary Club of Cheapside." *London Journal* 11 (1986): 51–8.

Rogers, N. *Whigs and Citizens: Popular Politics in the Age of Walpole and Pitt*. Oxford: Oxford University Press, 1989.

Rogers, P. "The Case of Pope v. Curll." *The Library*, 5th ser., 27 (1972): 326–31.

Rogers, P. "Classics and Chapbooks." In Rivers, *Books and Their Readers*, 27–45.

Rogers, P. *Grub Street: Studies in a Subculture*. London: Methuen, 1972.

Rose, M. "The Author as Proprietor: *Donaldson v. Becket* and the Genealogy of Modern Authorship." *Representations* 23 (1988): 51–85.

Rose, M. "The Author in Court: Pope v. Curll (1741)." In Woodmansee and Jaszi, *Construction of Authorship*, 211–29.

Rose, M. *Authors and Owners: The Invention of Copyright*. Cambridge: Harvard University Press, 1993.

Rosen, E. *Three Imperial Mathematicians: Kepler Trapped between Tycho Brahe and Ursus*. New York: Abaris, 1986.

Rosenheim, J. M. "Documenting Authority: Texts and Magistracy in Restoration Society." *Albion* 25 (1993): 591–604.

Ross, S. "*Scientist*: The Story of a Word." *Annals of Science* 18 (1962): 65–85.

Rostenberg, L. *English Publishers in the Graphic Arts, 1599–1700: A Study of the Printsellers and Publishers of Engravings, Art and Architectural Manuals, Maps and Copy-Books*. New York: B. Franklin, 1963.

Rostenberg, L. *The Library of Robert Hooke: The Scientific Book Trade of Restoration England*. Santa Monica: Modoc Press, 1989.

Rostenberg, L. *Literary, Political, Scientific, Religious and Legal Publishing, Printing and Book-selling in England 1551–1700*. 2 vols. New York: B. Franklin, 1965.

Rostenberg, L. "Robert Stephens, Messenger of the Press: An Episode in Seventeenth-Century Censorship." *Papers of the Bibliographical Society of America* 49 (1955): 131–52.

Rouse, M. A., and R. H. Rouse. *Authentic Witnesses: Approaches to Medieval Texts and Manuscripts*. Notre Dame, Ind.: University of Notre Dame Press, 1991.

Rousseau, G. S. "Mysticism and Millenarianism: 'Immortal Dr. Cheyne.'" In Merkel and Debus, *Hermeticism and the Renaissance*, 192–230.

Rousseau, G. S. "Nerves, Spirits, and Fibres: Towards Defining the Origins of Sensibility." *Studies in the Eighteenth Century* 3 (1976): 137–57.

Rousseau, G. S. "Science and the Discovery of the Imagination in Enlightened England." *Eighteenth-Century Studies* 3 (1969): 108–35.

Rousseau, G. S. "Science Books and Their Readers in the Eighteenth Century." In Rivers, *Books and Their Readers*, 197–255.

Rousseau, G. S., ed. *The Languages of Psyche: Mind and Body in Enlightenment Thought*. Berkeley and Los Angeles: University of California Press, 1990.

Royal Society. *The Record of the Royal Society of London, for the Promotion of Natural Knowledge*. 4th ed. London: Royal Society, 1940.

Russell, C. *The Fall of the British Monarchies, 1637–1642*. Oxford: Clarendon Press, 1991.

Rychner, J. "Le Travail de l'Atelier." In Chartier and Martin, *Histoire de l'Edition Française*, II, 46–70.

Sabean, D. W. *Power in the Blood: Popular Culture and Village Discourse in Early Modern Germany*. Cambridge: Cambridge University Press, 1984.

Sacret, J. H. "The Restoration Government and Municipal Corporations." *English Historical Review* 45 (1930): 232–59.

Saenger, P. "Physiologie de la Lecture et Séparation des Mots." *Annales* 44 (1989): 939–52.

Saenger, P. "Silent Reading: Its Impact on Late Medieval Script and Society." *Viator*, 13 (1982): 367–414.

Saenger, P. *Space between Words: The Origins of Silent Reading.* Stanford: Stanford University Press, 1997.

Safley, T. M., and L. N. Rosenband, eds. *The Workplace before the Factory: Artisans and Proletarians, 1500–1800.* Ithaca: Cornell University Press, 1993.

Sargent, R.-M. *The Diffident Naturalist: Robert Boyle and the Philosophy of Experiment.* Chicago: University of Chicago Press, 1995.

Saunders, D. *Authorship and Copyright.* London: Routledge, 1992.

Saunders, J. W. "The Stigma of Print: A Note on the Social Bases of Tudor Poetry." *Essays in Criticism* 1 (1951): 139–64.

Sawday, J. *The Body Emblazoned: Dissection and the Human Body in Renaissance Culture.* London: Routledge, 1995.

Schaffer, S. J. "The Consuming Flame: Electrical Showmen and Tory Mystics in the World of Goods." In Brewer and Porter, *Consumption and the World of Goods,* 489–526.

Schaffer, S. J. (1989). "Daniel Defoe and the Worlds of Credit." In Christie and Shuttleworth, *Nature Transfigured.*

Schaffer, S. J. "The Eighteenth Brumaire of Bruno Latour." *Studies in History and Philosophy of Science* 22 (1991): 174–92.

Schaffer, S. J. "Glass Works: Newton's Prisms and the Uses of Experiment." In Gooding, Pinch, and Schaffer, *The Uses of Experiment,* 67–104.

Schaffer, S. J. "Godly Men and Mechanical Philosophers: Souls and Spirits in Restoration Natural Philosophy." *Science in Context* 1 (1987): 55–85.

Schaffer, S. J. "Halley's Atheism and the End of the World." *Notes and Records of the Royal Society* 32 (1977): 17–40.

Schaffer, S. J. "Newtonianism." In Olby, Cantor, Christie, and Hodge, *Companion to the History of Modern Science,* 610–26.

Schaffer, S. J. "Newton's Comets and the Transformation of Astrology." In Curry, *Astrology, Science and Society,* 219–44.

Schaffer, S. J. "Scientific Discoveries and the End of Natural Philosophy." *Social Studies of Science* 16 (1986): 387–420.

Schaffer, S. J. "Self Evidence." *Critical Inquiry* 18 (1992): 327–62.

Schaffer, S. J. "A Social History of Plausibility: Country, City and Calculation in Augustan Britain." In Wilson, *Rethinking Social History,* 128–57.

Schmitt, C. B., and Q. Skinner, eds. *The Cambridge History of Renaissance Philosophy.* Cambridge: Cambridge University Press, 1988.

Schochet, G. J. "Between Lambeth and Leviathan: Samuel Parker on the Church of England and Political Order." In Phillipson and Skinner, *Political Discourse in Early Modern Britain,* 189–208.

Schorbach, K. *Der Strassburger Frühdrucker Johann Mentelin (1458–1478): Studien zu seinem Leben und Werke.* Mainz: Verlag der Gutenberg-Gesellschaft, 1932.

Schulze, S., ed. *Leselust: Niederländische Malerei von Rembrandt bis Vermeer.* Frankfurt: G. Hatje, 1993.

Schuster, J. A. "The Scientific Revolution." In Olby et al., *Companion to the History of Modern Science,* 217–42.

Schwartz, G., and M. J. Bok, eds. *Pieter Saenredam: The Painter and His Time.* London: Thames and Hudson, 1990.

Schwartz, H. *The French Prophets: The History of a Millenarian Group in Eighteenth-Century England.* Berkeley and Los Angeles: University of California Press, 1980.

Schwartz, H. *Knaves, Fools, Madmen, and That Subtile Effluvium: A Study of the Opposition* to the French Prophets in England, 1706–1710. Gainesville: University Presses of Florida, 1978.

Scott, J. H. Algernon Sidney and the English Republic, 1623–1677. Cambridge: Cambridge University Press, 1988.

Scott, J. H. "England's Troubles: Exhuming the Popish Plot." In Harris, Seaward, and Goldie, Politics of Religion, 107–31.

Scott, J. H. "The English Republican Imagination." In Morrill, Revolution and Restoration, 35–54.

Scott, J. H. "The Rapture of Motion: James Harrington's Republicanism." In Phillipson and Skinner, Political Discourse in Early Modern Britain, 139–63.

Scott, J. H. "Restoration Process: Or, If This Isn't a Party, We're Not Having a Good Time." Albion 25 (1993): 619–37.

Seaver, P. S. Wallington's World: A Puritan Artisan in Seventeenth-Century London. London: Methuen, 1985.

Seaward, P. The Cavalier Parliament and the Reconstruction of the Old Regime, 1661–1667. Cambridge: Cambridge University Press, 1989.

Secord, A. "Science in the Pub: Artisan Botanists in Early Nineteenth-Century Lancashire." History of Science 32 (1994): 269–315.

Sennett, R. The Fall of Public Man: On the Social Psychology of Capitalism. New York: Vintage Books, 1976.

Shackelford, J. "Tycho Brahe, Laboratory Design, and the Aim of Science." Isis 84 (1993): 211–30.

Shank, M. H. "How Shall We Practice History? The Case of Mario Biagioli's Galileo, Courtier." Early Science and Medicine 1 (1996): 106–50.

Shapin, S. "Following Scientists Around." Social Studies of Science 18 (1988): 533–50.

Shapin, S. "The House of Experiment in Seventeenth-Century England." Isis 79 (1988): 373–404.

Shapin, S. "'The Mind Is Its Own Place': Science and Solitude in Seventeenth-Century England." Science in Context 4 (1991): 191–218.

Shapin, S. "O Henry." Isis 78 (1987): 417–24.

Shapin, S. "Of Gods and Kings: Natural Philosophy and Politics in the Leibniz-Clarke Disputes." Isis 72 (1981): 187–215.

Shapin, S. "Pump and Circumstance: Robert Boyle's Literary Technology." Social Studies of Science 14 (1984): 481–520.

Shapin, S. "Robert Boyle and Mathematics: Reality, Representation, and Experimental Practice." Science in Context 2 (1988): 23–58.

Shapin, S. "'A Scholar and a Gentleman': The Problematic Identity of the Scientific Practitioner in Early Modern England." History of Science 29 (1991): 279–327.

Shapin, S. A Social History of Truth: Civility and Science in Seventeenth-Century England. Chicago: University of Chicago Press, 1994.

Shapin, S. "Who Was Robert Hooke?" In Hunter and Schaffer, Robert Hooke, 253–85.

Shapin, S., and B. Barnes. "Head and Hand: Rhetorical Resources in British Pedagogical Writing, 1770–1850." Oxford Review of Education, 2 (1976): 231–54.

Shapin, S., and S. J. Schaffer. Leviathan and the Air-Pump: Hobbes, Boyle, and the Experimental Life. Princeton: Princeton University Press, 1985.

Shapiro, A. E. "The Optical Lectures and the Foundations of the Theory of Optical Imagery." In Feingold, Before Newton, 105–78.

Shapiro, B. J. John Wilkins 1614–1672: An Intellectual Biography. Berkeley and Los Angeles: University of California Press, 1969.

Shapiro, B. J. Probability and Certainty in Seventeenth-Century England: A Study of the Re-

lationships between Natural Science, Religion, History, Law, and Literature. Princeton: Princeton University Press, 1983.

Sharpe, K. *The Personal Rule of Charles I.* New Haven: Yale University Press, 1992.

Sharpe, K. *Politics and Ideas in Early Stuart England: Essays and Studies.* London: Pinter, 1989.

Sharpe, K., and S. N. Zwicker, eds. *Politics of Discourse: The Literature and History of Seventeenth-Century England.* Berkeley and Los Angeles: University of California Press, 1987.

Shaw, D. "'Ars Formularia': Neo-Latin Synonyms for Printing." *The Library,* 6th ser., 11 (1989): 220–30.

Sherburn, G. *The Early Career of Alexander Pope.* Oxford: Oxford University Press, 1934.

Sherman, W. H. *John Dee: The Politics of Reading and Writing in the English Renaissance.* Amherst: University of Massachusetts Press, 1995.

Shirley, J. W. "The Scientific Experiments of Sir Walter Raleigh, the Wizard Earl, and the Three Magi in the Tower 1603–1617." *Ambix* 4 (1949–51): 52–66.

Sibum, O. "Reworking the Mechanical Value of Heat: Instruments of Precision and Gestures of Accuracy in Early Victorian England." *Studies in History and Philosophy of Science* 26 (1995): 73–106.

Siebert, F. S. *Freedom of the Press in England 1476–1776: The Rise and Decline of Government Controls.* Urbana: University of Illinois Press, 1952.

Simons, H. W., ed. *Rhetoric in the Human Sciences.* London: Sage, 1989.

Simpson, P. "Literary Piracy in the Elizabethan Age." *Oxford Bibliographical Society Publications* n.s., 1 (1947): 1–24.

Simpson, P. *Proof-reading in the Sixteenth, Seventeenth and Eighteenth Centuries.* Oxford: Oxford University Press; orig. 1935, 1970.

Sisson, C. J. "The Laws of Elizabethan Copyright: The Stationers' View." *The Library,* 5th ser., 15 (1960): 8–20.

Smith, C. W., and J. Agar, eds. *Making Space for Science: Territorial Themes in the Shaping of Knowledge.* Basingstoke: Macmillan, 1998.

Smith, N. "The Charge of Atheism and the Language of Radical Speculation, 1640–1660." In Hunter and Wootton, *Atheism,* 131–58.

Smith, N. *Literature and Revolution in England 1640–1660.* New Haven: Yale University Press, 1994.

Smith, N. *Perfection Proclaimed: Language and Literature in English Radical Religion 1640–1660.* Oxford: Clarendon Press, 1989.

Smith, N. "Popular Republicanism in the 1650s: John Streater's 'Heroick Mechanicks.'" In Armitage, Himy, and Skinner, *Milton and Republicanism,* 137–55.

Smith, N., ed. *Literature and Censorship.* Cambridge: The English Association, 1993.

Smith, P. H. *The Business of Alchemy: Science and Culture in the Holy Roman Empire.* Princeton: Princeton University Press, 1994.

Smuts, R. M. *Court Culture and the Origins of a Royalist Tradition in Early Stuart England.* Philadelphia: University of Pennsylvania Press, 1987.

Soman, A. "Press, Pulpit and Censorship in France Before Richelieu." *Proceedings of the American Philosophical Society* 120 (1976):6, 439–63.

Sommerville, C. J. *The Secularization of Early Modern England: From Religious Culture to Religious Faith.* New York: Oxford University Press, 1992.

Sommerville, J. P. *Politics and Ideology in England 1603–1640.* London: Longman, 1986.

Speck, W. A. *Reluctant Revolutionaries: Englishmen and the Revolution of 1688.* Oxford: Oxford University Press, 1988.

Spencer, L. "The Politics of George Thomason." *The Library,* 5th ser., 14 (1959): 11–27.

Spencer, L. "The Printing of Sir George Croke's Reports." *Studies in Bibliography* 11 (1958): 231–46.

Spencer, L. "The Professional and Literary Connexions of George Thomason." *The Library*, 5th ser., 13 (1958): 102–18.

Spufford, M. "First Steps in Literacy: The Reading and Writing Experiences of the Humblest Seventeenth-Century Spiritual Autobiographers." *Social History* 4 (1979): 407–35.

Spufford, M. *The Great Reclothing of Rural England: Petty Chapmen and Their Wares in the Seventeenth Century*. London: Hambledon, 1984.

Spufford, M. *Small Books and Pleasant Histories: Popular Fiction and Its Readership in Seventeenth-Century England*. Cambridge: Cambridge University Press, 1981.

Stafford, B. *Artful Science: Enlightenment Education and the Eclipse of Visual Education*. Cambridge: MIT Press, 1994.

Stallybrass, P., and A. White. *The Politics and Poetics of Transgression*. London: Methuen, 1986.

Starnes, D. T. *Renaissance Dictionaries: English-Latin and Latin-English*. Edinburgh: T. Nelson and sons, 1954.

Stewart, L. *The Rise of Public Science: Rhetoric, Technology, and Natural Philosophy in Newtonian Britain, 1660–1750*. Cambridge: Cambridge University Press, 1992.

Stewart, L. "The Selling of Newton: Science and Technology in Early Eighteenth-Century England." *Journal of British Studies* 25 (1986): 178–92.

Stewart, M. M. "Smart, Kerrick, Carnan and Newbery: New Evidence on the Paper War, 1750–57." *The Library*, 6th ser., 5 (1983): 32–43.

Stock, B. *The Implications of Literacy: Written Language and Models of Interpretation in the Eleventh and Twelfth Centuries*. Princeton: Princeton University Press, 1983.

Stoye, J. W. *English Travellers Abroad 1604–1667: Their Influence in English Society and Politics*. London: Cape, 1952.

Straus, R. *The Unspeakable Curll: Being Some Account of Edmund Curll, Bookseller*. London: Chapman and Hall, 1927.

Stubbs, M. "John Beale, Philosophical Gardener of Herefordshire. Part I: Prelude to the Royal Society (1608–1663)." *Annals of Science* 39 (1982): 463–89.

Stubbs, M. "John Beale, Philosophical Gardener of Herefordshire. Part II: The Improvement of Agriculture and Trade in the Royal Society (1663–1683)." *Annals of Science* 46 (1989): 323–63.

Summers, D. *The Judgment of Sense: Renaissance Naturalism and the Rise of Aesthetics*. Cambridge: Cambridge University Press, 1987.

Sutherland, J. *The Restoration Newspaper and its Development*. Cambridge: Cambridge University Press, 1986.

Taubert, S. *Bibliopola*. 2 vols. Hamburg: E. Hauswedell, 1966.

Taylor, E. G. R. *The Mathematical Practitioners of Tudor and Stuart England*. Cambridge: Cambridge University Press, 1954.

Thirsk, J. *Economic Policy and Projects: The Development of a Consumer Society in Early Modern England*. 1978. Reprint, Oxford: Oxford University Press, 1988.

Thomas, D. *A Long Time Burning: The History of Literary Censorship in England*. New York: Praeger, 1969.

Thomas, K. "The Levellers and the Franchise." In Aylmer, *The Interregnum*, 57–78.

Thomas, K. *Man and the Natural World: Changing Attitudes in England 1500–1800*. Harmondsworth: Penguin, 1984.

Thomas, P. W. *Sir John Birkenhead, 1617–1679: A Royalist Career in Politics and Polemics*. Oxford: Oxford University Press, 1979.

Thomas-Stanford, C. *Sussex in the Great Civil War and the Interregnum 1642–1660*. London: Chiswick Press, 1910.

Thompson, E. P. *Customs in Common*. London: Merlin, 1991.

Thompson, F. *Magna Carta: Its Role in the Making of the English Constitution*. 1948. Reprint, New York: Octagon, 1972.

Thoren, V. E. *The Lord of Uraniborg: A Biography of Tycho Brahe*. Cambridge: Cambridge University Press, 1990.

Thulesius, O. *Nicholas Culpeper: English Physician and Astrologer*. London: St. Martin's Press, 1992.

Tinkler, J. F. "The Splitting of Humanism: Bentley, Swift, and the Battle of the Books." *Journal for the History of Ideas* 49 (1988): 453–72.

Tittler, R. *Architecture and Power: The Town Hall and the English Urban Community c. 1500–1640*. Oxford: Oxford University Press, 1991.

Traweek, S. *Beamtimes and Lifetimes: The World of High Energy Physics*. Cambridge: Harvard University Press, 1988.

Treadwell, M. "The English Book Trade." In Maccubbin and Hamilton-Phillips, *Age of William III and Mary II*, 358–65.

Treadwell, M. "London Printers and Printing Houses in 1705." *Publishing History* 7 (1980): 5–44.

Treadwell, M. "London Trade Publishers 1675–1750." *The Library*, 6th ser., 4 (1982): 99–134.

Tribble, E. B. *Margins and Marginality: The Printed Page in Early Modern England*. Charlottesville: University Press of Virginia, 1993.

Tribby, J. "Cooking (with) Clio and Cleo: Eloquence and Experiment in Seventeenth-Century Florence." *Journal of the History of Ideas* 52 (1991): 417–39.

Tyacke, N. *Anti-Calvinists: The Rise of English Arminianism c. 1590–1640*. Oxford: Clarendon Press, 1990.

Tyacke, N. "Science and Religion at Oxford before the Civil War." In Pennington and Thomas, *Puritans and Revolutionaries*, 73–93.

Tyacke, N., ed. *The History of the University of Oxford*. Vol. 4, *Seventeenth-Century Oxford*. Oxford: Clarendon Press, 1997.

Tyson, G. P., and S. S. Wagonheim, eds. *Print and Culture in the Renaissance: Essays on the Advent of Printing in Europe*. Newark: University of Delaware Press, 1986.

Ultee, M. "The Republic of Letters: Learned Correspondence, 1680–1720." *The Seventeenth Century* 2 (1987): 95–112.

Underdown, D. *Revel, Riot and Rebellion: Popular Politics and Culture in England 1603–1660*. Oxford: Oxford University Press, 1985.

Underdown, D. *Royalist Conspiracy in England 1649–1660*. New Haven: Yale University Press, 1960.

Underdown, D. "The Taming of the Scold: The Enforcement of Patriarchal Authority in Early Modern England." In Fletcher and Stevenson, *Order and Disorder*, 116–36.

Vance, J. E. *This Scene of Man: The Role and Structure of the City in the Geography of Western Civilization*. New York: Harper's College Press, 1977.

Van Doren, C. *Benjamin Franklin*. London: Putnam, 1939.

Van Eerde, K. S. *John Ogilby and the Taste of His Times*. Folkestone: Dawson, 1976.

Van Rooden, P. T., and J. W. Wesselius. "Two Early Cases of Publication by Subscription in Holland and Germany: Jacob Abendana's *Mikhael Yophi* (1661) and David Cohen de Lara's *Keter Kehunna* (1668)." *Quaerendo* 16 (1986): 110–30.

Veyne, P. *Writing History: Essay on Epistemology*. Translated by M. Moore-Rinvoluci. Middletown, Conn.: Wesleyan University Press, 1984.

Vickers, B., ed. *Occult and Scientific Mentalities in the Renaissance*. Cambridge: Cambridge University Press, 1984.

Vickers, B., ed. *Public and Private Life in the Seventeenth Century: The Mackenzie-Evelyn Debate*. New York: Delmar, 1986.

Vincent, D. *Literacy and Popular Culture: England 1750–1914*. Cambridge: Cambridge University Press, 1989.

Vittu, J.-P. "Les Contrefaçons du *Journal des savants* de 1665 à 1714." In Moureau, *Presses Grises*, 303–31.

Voet, L. "The Printers' Chapel in the Plantinian House." *The Library*, 5th ser., 16 (1961): 1–14.

Walker, J. "The Censorship of the Press during the Reign of Charles II." *History* 35 (1950): 219–38.

Wallace, J. M. "'Examples Are Best Precepts': Readers and Meanings in Seventeenth-Century Poetry." *Critical Inquiry* 1 (1974): 273–90.

Wallace, J. M., ed. *The Golden and the Brazen World: Papers in Literature and History, 1650–1800*. Berkeley and Los Angeles: University of California Press, 1985.

Wallace, W. *Galileo's Logic of Discovery and Proof: The Background, Content, and Use of his Appropriated Treatises on Aristotle's Posterior Analytics*. Dordrecht: Kluwer, 1992.

Walters, G. "The Booksellers in 1759 and 1774: the Battle for Literary Property." *The Library*, 5th ser., 29 (1974): 287–311.

Walters, G., and F. Emery. "Edward Lhuyd, Edmund Gibson, and the Printing of Camden's *Britannia*, 1695." *The Library*, 5th ser., 32 (1977): 109–37.

Warrender, H. "The Early Latin Versions of Thomas Hobbes' *De Cive*." *The Library*, 6th ser., 2 (1980): 40–52.

Warner, M. *The Letters of the Republic: Publication and the Public Sphere in Eighteenth-Century America*. Cambridge, Mass.: Harvard University Press, 1990.

Warwick, A. C. "The Electrodynamics of Moving Bodies and the Principle of Relativity in British Physics, 1894–1919." Ph.D. thesis, Cambridge University, 1989.

Watt, I. *The Rise of the Novel: Studies in Defoe, Richardson and Fielding*. 1957. Reprint, Harmondsworth: Penguin, 1983.

Watt, T. *Cheap Print and Popular Piety, 1550–1640*. Cambridge: Cambridge University Press, 1991.

Weatherill, L. *Consumer Behaviour and Material Culture in Britain, 1660–1760*. London: Methuen, 1988.

Weber, H. M. *Paper Bullets: Print and Kingship under Charles II*. Lexington: University Press of Kentucky, 1996.

Weber, M. *The Protestant Ethic and the Spirit of Capitalism*. Translated by T. Parsons. London: Unwin, 1930.

Webster, C. *From Paracelsus to Newton: Magic and the Making of Modern Science*. Cambridge: Cambridge University Press, 1982.

Webster, C. *The Great Instauration: Science, Medicine and Reform 1626–1660*. London: Duckworth, 1975.

Western, J. R. *Monarchy and Revolution: The English State in the 1680s*. 1972. Reprint, London: Macmillan, 1985.

Westfall, R. S. *Essays on the Trial of Galileo*. Notre Dame, Ind.: Vatican Observatory Publications, 1989.

Westfall, R. S. *Never at Rest: A Biography of Isaac Newton*. Cambridge: Cambridge University Press, 1980.

Westfall, R. S. "Patronage and the Publication of Galileo's *Dialogue*." *History and Technology* 4 (1987): 385–99.

Westfall, R. S. "Science and Patronage: Galileo and the Telescope." *Isis* 76 (1985): 11–30.

Westman, R. S. "The Astronomer's Role in the Sixteenth Century: A Preliminary Study." *History of Science* 18 (1980): 105–47.

Westman, R. S. "Proof, Poetics, and Patronage: Copernicus's Preface to *De Revolutionibus*." In Lindberg and Westman, *Reappraisals of the Scientific Revolution*, 167–205.

Westman, R. S. "The Reception of Galileo's *Dialogue*: A Partial World Census of Extant Copies." In Galluzzi, *Novità Celesti e Crisi del Sapere*, 329–72.

Weston, C. C. "England: Ancient Constitution and Common Law." In Burns and Goldie, *Cambridge History of Political Thought*, 374–411.

Weston, C. C., and J. R. Greenberg. *Subjects and Sovereigns: The Grand Controversy over Legal Sovereignty in Stuart England*. Cambridge: Cambridge University Press, 1981.

Whitaker, K. "The Culture of Curiosity." In Jardine, Secord, and Spary, *Cultures of Natural History*, 75–90.

Wiener, P. P., and A. Norland, eds. *Roots of Scientific Thought: A Cultural Perspective*. New York: Basic Books, 1957.

Williams, G. W. *The Craft of Printing and the Publication of Shakespeare's Works*. Washington: Folger Shakespeare Library, 1985.

Williams, W. P. "The First Edition of *Holy Living*: An Episode in the Seventeenth-Century Book Trade." *The Library*, 5th ser., 28 (1973): 99–107.

Willmoth, F. "John Flamsteed's Letter Concerning the Natural Causes of Earthquakes." *Annals of Science* 44 (1987): 23–70.

Willmoth, F. "Mathematical Sciences and Military Technology: The Ordnance Office in the Reign of Charles II." In Field and James, *Renaissance and Revolution*, 117–31.

Willmoth, F. "Sir Jonas Moore (1617–79): Practical Mathematician and Patron of Science." Ph. D. thesis, Cambridge University, 1990.

Willmoth, F. *Sir Jonas Moore: Practical Mathematics and Restoration Science*. Woodbridge: Boydell, 1993.

Willmoth, F., ed. *Flamsteed's Stars: New Perspectives on the Life and Work of the First Astronomer Royal, 1646–1719*. Woodbridge: Boydell and Brewer, 1997.

Wilson, A., ed. *Rethinking Social History: English Society 1570–1920 and Its Interpretation*. Manchester: Manchester University Press, 1993.

Wilson, C. *The Invisible World: Early Modern Philosophy and the Invention of the Microscope*. Princeton: Princeton University Press, 1995.

Wing, D. *A Short-Title Catalogue of Books Printed in England, Scotland, Ireland, Wales, and British America and of English Books Printed in Other Countries, 1641–1700*. 2d ed. Revised by T. J. Crist, J. J. Morison, C. W. Nelson, and M. Seccombe. 3 vols. New York: Modern Language Association of America, 1982–94.

Winger, H. W. "Regulations Relating to the Book Trade in London from 1357 to 1586." Ph.D. thesis, University of Illinois, 1953.

Winkler, K. T. *Handwerk und Markt: Druckerhandwerk, Vertriebswesen und Tagesschrifttum in London 1695–1750*. Stuttgart: F. Steiner, 1993.

Winkler, M. G., and A. Van Helden. "Johannes Hevelius and the Visual Language of Astronomy." In Field and James, *Renaissance and Revolution*, 97–116.

Winkler, M. G., and A. Van Helden. "Representing the Heavens: Galileo and Visual Astronomy." *Isis* 83 (1992): 195–217.

Wolper, R. S. "The Rhetoric of Gunpowder and the Idea of Progress." *Journal for the History of Ideas* 31 (1970): 589–98.

Wood, P. B. "Methodology and Apologetics: Thomas Sprat's *History of the Royal Society*." *British Journal for the History of Science* 13 (1980): 1–26.

Woodfield, D. B. *Surreptitious Printing in England, 1550–1640*. New York: Bibliographical Society of America, 1973.

Woodhouse, A. S. P., ed. *Puritanism and Liberty: Being the Army Debates (1647–9) from the Clarke Manuscripts*. 1938. Reprint, London: Everyman, 1986.

Woodhouse, J. R. "The Tradition of Della Casa's *Galateo* in English." In Carré, *Crisis of Courtesy*, 11–26.

Woodmansee, M. *The Author, Art, and the Market: Rereading the History of Aesthetics*. New York: Columbia University Press, 1994.

Woodmansee, M. "The Genius and the Copyright: Economic and Legal Considerations of the Emergence of the Author." *Eighteenth-Century Studies* 17 (1984): 425–48.

Woodmansee, M. "On the Author Effect: Recovering Collectivity." In Woodmansee and Jaszi, *Construction of Authorship*, 15–28.

Woodmansee, M., and P. Jaszi, eds. *The Construction of Authorship: Textual Appropriation in Law and Literature*. Durham, N.C.: Duke University Press, 1994.

Woodward, D. H. "Thomas Fuller, the Protestant Divines, and Plagiary Yet Speaking." *Transactions of the Cambridge Bibliographical Society* 4 (1964–8): 201–24.

Woolgar, S., ed. *Knowledge and Reflexivity: New Frontiers in the Sociology of Knowledge*. London: Sage, 1988.

Woolrych, A. *Commonwealth to Protectorate*. Oxford: Oxford University Press, 1982.

Woolrych, A. *Soldiers and Statesmen: The General Council of the Army and Its Debates, 1647–1648*. Oxford: Oxford University Press, 1987.

Worden, A. B. "Literature and Political Censorship in Early Modern England." In Duke and Tamse, *Too Mighty to Be Free*, 45–62.

Worden, A. B. *The Rump Parliament, 1648–1653*. Cambridge: Cambridge University Press, 1974.

Wormuth, F. D. *The Royal Prerogative, 1603–1649: A Study in English Political and Constitutional Ideas*. Cornell University Press, 1939. Reprint, New York: Kennikat Press, 1967.

Woudhuysen, H. R. *Sir Philip Sidney and the Circulation of Manuscripts, 1558–1640*. Oxford: Clarendon Press, 1996.

Wrightson, K. *English Society 1580–1680*. London: Hutchinson, 1982.

Wrightson, K. "'Sorts of People' in Tudor and Stuart England." In Barry and Brooks, *Middling Sort*, 28–51.

Wrightson, K. "Two Concepts of Order: Justices, Constables and Jurymen in Seventeenth-Century England." In Brewer and Styles, *An Ungovernable People*, 21–46.

Yates, F. A. *The Art of Memory*. Chicago: University of Chicago Press, 1966.

Yates, F. A. *Theatre of the World*. London: Routledge and Kegan Paul, 1969.

Yeo, R. *Defining Science: William Whewell, Natural Knowledge, and Public Debate in Early Victorian Britain*. Cambridge: Cambridge University Press, 1993.

Yeo, R. "Genius, Method, and Morality: Images of Newton in Britain, 1760–1860." *Science in Context* 2 (1988): 257–84.

Zilsel, E. "The Genesis of the Concept of Scientific Progress." In Wiener and Norland, *Roots of Scientific Thought*, 251–75.

Zwicker, S. N. *Politics and Language in Dryden's Poetry: The Arts of Disguise*. Princeton: Princeton University Press, 1984.

INDEX